BLOOMSBURY GOOD HEALTH GUIDE

Foreword

Dr PATRICK PIETRONI

FOUNDER AND CHAIRMAN OF THE

BRITISH HOLISTIC MEDICAL ASSOCIATION

BLOOMSBURY

NOTICE

This book is intended as a reference volume only, not as a medical manual or guide to self-treatment. If you suspect that you have a medical problem, we urge you to seek competent medical help. Keep in mind that nutritional and health needs vary from person to person, depending on age, sex, health status and total diet. The information here is intended to help you make informed decisions about your health, not as a substitute for any treatment that may have been prescribed by your doctor.

First published 1984
This paperback edition published in 1989

Bloomsbury Publishing Limited, 2 Soho Square,
London W1V 5DE

British Library Cataloguing in Publication Data

Bloomsbury good health guide: common health problems
    and how to solve them. – (Bloomsbury health).
    1.   Health
    613   RA776

ISBN 0 7475 0367 2

Designed by Fielding Rowinski
Typeset by Rapidset
Printed by Richard Clay Ltd, Bungay, Suffolk

Contents

Foreword

by Dr Patrick Pietroni

Fortunately for the medical profession and the public the majority of people who develop a symptom do not visit their General Practitioner. Indeed over 60 per cent cope with their symptoms without recourse to the established health care services. The notion of self-care encompasses – *self-diagnosis, self-treatment, disease-prevention* and *health maintenance*. The explosion of interest in self-care is evidenced by the growing number of health journals, popular 'how-to' books, Yoga classes and keep-fit clubs. The health food industry has begun to influence supermarkets and advertising campaigns. The need for an up-to-date and well-informed guide to both the minor and common conditions we will all experience from time to time and more serious illnesses such as cancer, diabetes and heart disease is well served by the authors of the *Bloomsbury Good Health Guide*. The focus taken in many of the conditions described include a detailed dietary, vitamin and mineral description of the factors involved. The ability to literally shape our lives is nowhere more evident than in the food we choose to eat. Over 90 per cent of our total body mass is replaced every six months and the new cells are made from the nutrients obtained from our diet. We are indeed what we eat and as Hippocrates himself said, we should 'learn how to make food our medicine and not medicine our food'.

However, a word of caution is important for food faddism is an increasing symptom of our health-conscious culture. Most of the conditions described are self-limiting, i.e. they will go away on their own. Most of us will be prone to disease and distress however 'well' we practise our preventive programme. Being human entails becoming ill, being in pain, experiencing sadness, grief and anxiety, and a few sleepless nights should not send you immediately to your tryptophan or Vitamin C bottle.

Balance and common-sense are probably the most important ingredients in any self-care programme and together with the information provided in this Guide, the reader should be well prepared.

Dr Patrick C. Pietroni, MBBS, MRCP, MRCGP, DCH
Senior Lecturer in General Practice, St Mary's Hospital Medical School and founder and chairman of the British Holistic Medical Association.

Introduction

All of us come down with illnesses at some time in our lives – some of us more often than others. We either treat ourselves – say, by taking two aspirins and tucking ourselves into a nice warm bed – or we go to see our family doctor, who will often prescribe the same thing. However, what we often want is not the usual prescription and instruction to 'come and see me again if you don't get better', but a way of *preventing* ourselves from becoming ill in the first place.

The *Bloomsbury Good Health Guide* presents some of the most recent research into ways of ensuring that your body avoids falling prey to some of the most common conditions – and some that are not so common.

Nutrition is the watchword here – are you sure that you are taking in enough nutrients so that your body has the ammunition to fight disease? And if you do develop an illness, this book can suggest treatments – often less invasive than orthodox practice or involving the taking of vitamins and minerals that have far fewer side-effects than most drugs.

This book is not a medical encyclopaedia – for instance, it does not go into great detail about the causes and progress of most diseases – and illnesses such as measles and chicken pox, for which time itself is the great healer, are not included. However, the book is encyclopaedic in the vast range of topics discussed – from acne and back problems to heart disease, impotence and sexual dysfunction, traveller's diarrhoea and many, many more.

The aim of the *Bloomsbury Good Health Guide* is to give everyone the tools to understand and enhance the mechanisms that will ensure good health – both physical and emotional. Diet – and especially vitamins, minerals and other vital nutrients – relaxation and complementary therapies all play positive roles, while advice is given on what sorts of things we should all avoid so that we can grow properly and then live fully and healthily as we become older.

Recommended Dietary Allowances (RDAs) and supplement dosages

Throughout this book, reference is made to dosages of vitamin and mineral supplements, as recommended by doctors or as used by researchers in scientific studies. The following chart shows recommended nutrient dosages from three sources: *(1)* the UK Recommended Dietary Allowances (UK RDA) set by the Department of Health and Social Security, amended by the 1983 NACNE report; *(2)* the US Recommended Dietary Allowances (US RDA) set by the Food and Nutrition Board of the National Academy of Sciences–National Research Council in 1980; *(3)* the recommendations for basic supplementation and maximum daily dosage of the authors, based on their research. There are no UK and/or US RDAs in some cases.

The authors strongly suggest that you first consult your doctor if you intend to take supplements exceeding the amounts listed. Do not give children supplements except under a doctor's supervision.

Abbreviations: g=gram; mg=milligram; μg=microgram; IU=International unit

	CHILDREN				WOMEN			MEN	
	1–6	7–12	13–18	19–54	Pregnant	Breast-feeding	55+	19–64	65+
vitamin A									
UK RDA	300 μg	487 μg	737 μg	750 μg	750 μg	1200 μg	750 μg	750 μg	750 μg
US RDA	450 μg	850 μg	900 μg	800 μg	1000 μg	1200 μg	800 μg	1000 μg	1000 μg
Basic supplementation: 5000 IU*									
Maximum daily dosage; 25.000 IU*									
vitamin B$_1$ (thiamin)									
UK RDA	0.5 mg	0.85 mg	1.02 mg	0.9 mg	1 mg	1.1 mg	0.85 mg	1 mg	0.99 mg
US RDA	0.8 mg	1.3 mg	1.25 mg	1.05 mg	1.45 mg	1.55 mg	1 mg	1.45 mg	1.2 mg
Basic supplementation: 5 mg									
Maximum daily dosage: 25 mg									
vitamin B$_2$, (riboflavin)									
UK RDA	0.75 mg	1.1 mg	1.55 mg	1.3 mg	1.6 mg	1.8 mg	1.45 mg	1.6 mg	1.6 mg
US RDA	0.9 mg	1.5 mg	1.3–1.7 mg	1.25 mg	1.55 mg	1.75 mg	1.2 mg	1.65 mg	1.4 mg
Basic supplementation: 5 mg									
Maximum daily dosage: 25 mg									
Nicotinic acid (niacin)									
UK RDA	8.5 mg	12.5 mg	17.5 mg	15 mg	18 mg	21 mg	15 mg	18 mg	18 mg
US RDA	10 mg	17 mg	16.2 mg	13.5 mg	15.5 mg	18.5 mg	13 mg	18.5 mg	16 mg
Basic supplementation: 10 mg									
Maximum daily dosage: 50 mg									
vitamin B$_6$ (pyridoxine)									
US RDA	1.1 mg	1.7 mg	1.9 mg	2 mg	2.6 mg	2.5 mg	2 mg	2.2 mg	2.2 mg
Basic supplementation: 5 mg									
Maximum daily dosage: 50 mg									
vitamin B$_{12}$									
US RDA	2.25 μg	3 μg	3 μg	3 μg	4 μg	4 μg	3 μg	3 μg	3 μg
Basic supplementation: 5 μg									
Maximum daily dosage: 25 μg									
Folic acid									
US RDA	150 μg	350 μg	400 μg	400 μg	800 μg	500 μg	400 μg	400 μg	400 μg
Basic supplementation: 400 μg									
Maximum daily dosage: 1200 μg									

vitamin C
(ascorbic acid)

UK RDA	20 mg	22.5 mg	27 mg	30 mg	60 mg	60 mg	30 mg	30 mg	30 mg
US RDA	45 mg	47.5 mg	55 mg	60 mg	80 mg	1000 mg	60 mg	60 mg	60 mg

Basic supplementation: 200 mg
Maximum daily dosage: 1000 mg

vitamin D**

UK RDA	10 μg	10 μg	10 μg	10 μg	10 μg	10 μg	10 μg	10 μg	10 μg
US RDA	10 μg	10 μg	10 μg	6.25 μg	11.25 μg	11.25 μg	5 μg	6.25 μg	5 μg

Basic supplementation: 0–500 IU*
Maximum daily dosage: 0–500 IU*

vitamin E

US RDA	5.5 mg	7.5 mg	8.5 mg	8 mg	10 mg	11 mg	8 mg	10 mg	10 mg

Basic supplementation: 100 IU
Maximum daily dosage: 600 IU

Calcium

UK RDA	600 mg	650 mg	650 mg	500 mg	1200 mg	1200 mg	500 mg	500 mg	500 mg
US RDA	800 mg	100 mg	1200 mg	800 mg	1200 mg	1200 mg	800 mg	800 mg	800 mg

Basic supplementation: 800 mg
Maximum daily dosage: 1200 mg

Chromium

Basic supplementation: 50 μg
Maximum daily dosage: 200 μg

Iron

UK RDA	8 mg	11 mg	12 mg	12 mg	13 mg	15 mg	10 mg	10 mg	10 mg
US RDA	12.5 mg	10–18 mg	18 mg	18 mg	63 mg	63 mg	10 mg	10 mg	10 mg

Basic supplementation: 10 mg
Maximum daily dosage: 30 mg

Magnesium

US RDA	175 mg	300 mg	337 mg	300 mg	450 mg	450 mg	300 mg	350 mg	350 mg

Basic supplementation: 300 mg
Maximum daily dosage: 400 mg

Phosphorus

US RDA	800 mg	1000 mg	1200 mg	800 mg	1200 mg	1200 mg	800 mg	800 mg	800 mg

Selenium

Basic supplementation: 50 μg
Maximum daily dosage: 200 μg

Sodium

UK RDA				3496 mg (9 g salt)	3496 mg (9 g salt)	3496 mg (9 g salt)	3496 mg (9 g salt)	3496 mg (9 g salt)	3496 mg (9 g salt)
US RDA				1942 mg (5 g salt)	1942 mg (5 g salt)	1942 mg (5 g salt)	1942 mg (5 g salt)	1942 mg (5 g salt)	1942 mg (5 g salt)

Zinc

US RDA	10 mg	12.5 mg	15 mg	15 mg	20 mg	25 mg	10 mg	15 mg	15 mg

Basic supplementation: 15 mg
Maximum daily dosage: 35 mg

---

*The DHSS now prefers measurements of vitamins A and D to be expressed in micrograms (μg). To calculate this, multiply the number of international units (IUs) by 0.3.

**If you drink at least a pint of vitamin D-enriched milk each day or you bask in the sun year-round, you may need no vitamin D supplement. Otherwise, some extra is in order: 200 IU (60 μg) per day in most circumstances; 400 IU (120 μg) per day for the elderly in winter; 500 IU (150 μg) per day for the women who are pregnant or nursing. One international unit (IU) of vitamin E is equal to 1 mg of dl alpha-tocopherol acetate, the synthetic, stable form of vitamin E commonly added to food and found in vitamin E tablets.

• Accidents

Ivan Ivanovitch is a taxi driver in Leningrad who's been given the day off so he won't have an accident. It's not that Ivan guzzled too much vodka last night, or that his taxi's brakes are bad. No, a computer – using the fledgling science of biorhythms – identified today as a 'critical' point for Ivan, a day when he would be more accident-prone. Five thousand of Ivan's buddies were put on the same system when Soviet scientists found that most of the cabbies' traffic accidents happened on their critical days.

Well, it's debatable whether biorhythms really predict accidents. A team of researchers in the United States conducted a study that found 'no evidence for a relationship between purported biorhythm cycles and accident likelihood' (*Archives of General Psychiatry*). However, what's not debatable is that certain factors do increase the chance of your having an accident. And that you can prevent those factors (or at least be aware of them) and so prevent accidents – the fourth biggest cause of death. Only heart disease, cancer and strokes kill more people than accidents. But accidents don't only kill. They bruise, sprain, break, cut and burn. And they happen mostly at home, not on the motorway or at work.

To understand why people have accidents, safety researchers used to try to define the 'accident-prone' personality – someone who not only gets out on the wrong side of bed, but *falls* out. Lately, however, researchers have realized that everyone can go through a period in their life when they are more likely to have accidents. And they've found the reason – stress.

The odds stacked against you

'During stressful periods in life, your odds of being in an accident increase,' says Dr Abraham Bergman, a researcher at the University of Washington in Seattle.

Dr Bergman came to this conclusion after conducting a study of 103 boys aged between 12 and 15. For five months, the boys reported their accidents and also reported any 'life changes', such as moving to a new school or a serious illness in the family. After the five months were up, Dr Bergman and his two colleagues tallied the life changes and the number of accidents. The boys under little stress from change had a total of 395 accidents; the boys under high levels of stress had 946.

In a similar study, two researchers from the University of Michigan gave a questionnaire to over 500 men, asking about the stress in their lives over the previous year and also about the number of car accidents they had had. The researchers then compared the amount of stress to the number of accidents to see if they matched. They did.

Life changes and stress, they wrote, 'are significantly related to traffic accidents.' The events most likely to 'predict' accidents were 'physical stress responses' (smoking, insomnia, headaches, ulcers), problems with parents or in-laws, problems or pressure in education or on the job and financial troubles (*American Journal of Psychiatry*).

In another study to see if excess stress had something to do with everyday accidents and errors, researchers tested 31 nurses by tallying all their positive and negative 'challenging events' (ranging from illness or injury to the birth of a grandchild). From the data collected, they were able to predict successfully which nurses were most likely to suffer from a rash of physical accidents (dropping things, car mishaps) and job-related errors (mistakes in judgment) in the following weeks (*Science News*, 22 August 1981).

Stress causes accidents. But why?

'People who are under a lot of stress are likely candidates for accidents – big and small – because they can't think, act and react in a normal, relaxed manner,' says William Simons, supervisor of safety management programmes for Pennsylvania State University's Institute of Public Safety.

Instead of having their attention on the task at hand, stressed people are *preoccupied*, Simons told us. 'Stress is very significant, because should a person be having problems at home, with his marriage, his children his finances or whatever, he definitely won't be able to pay 100 per cent attention to what he's doing. When the individual is preoccupied with problems, when he's tense and worried, that's when accidents often occur.'

Another way that stress sets you up for an accident is by wearing you out until you hardly know if you're coming or going. Fatigue, said a report in the *New York State Journal of Medicine* (July 1980), is a 'reaction to stress'. And even when fatigue isn't from unusual stress but from the wear-and-tear of a typical day, it still lays you wide open for a mishap. 'Law-enforcement officers have statistics to prove that casualties increase as the day grows older' stated a report in *California Highway Patrolman*. 'The climax is reached in the late afternoon and evening hours. Drivers are tired. Their reflexes are dull.'

But people might be less dull in the late afternoon – and less likely to have accidents – if they were more fit. Those who exercise regularly don't tire as easily – and aren't easy marks for an accident. 'The degree of fitness many times determines whether there will be an accident or whether an accident may be avoided,' says Charles Peter Yost, professor and dean emeritus at West Virginia University.

Dr Yost told us that fitness prevents accidents not only by keeping you mentally sharp but by preparing you *physically* to stop an accident before it starts – for instance, by being strong enough to regain your footing after stumbling on the stairs or slipping on a newly waxed floor.

'In skiing, for example, the most important single prevention of ski injury lies in proper conditioning,' he says. He described a skiing school in Lake Placid, New York, in which 50 children put in 5000 hours of skiing and had seven fractures and five sprains among them. But the next year's class although they skied as much, had no accidents – because of a pre-ski conditioning programme.

And there's a third reason why fitness and accidents don't mix. When you're fit, you're not fat.

Weight is a risk factor

'Significantly overweight people – those who are more than 30 per cent above their ideal weight – have an increase in accident-proneness,' says Willard

Krehl, professor emeritus of Jefferson Medical College in Philadelphia, and 'the tendency toward accidents increases as the person gets heavier.'

Overweight people may be even more accident-prone if they take diet pills – or or other medications that fog the brain. For example, a British study showed that drivers who use Valium or other so-called 'minor tranquillizers' are five times more likely to have car accidents than people not taking tranquillizers (*British Medical Journal*, 7 April 1979).

There are plenty of other drugs besides tranquillizers that can make you groggy. Over-the-counter cough or cold medicines may contain antihistamines or codeine – two stupefying drugs. And, as everyone knows, alcohol and safety don't mix. Having one too many the night before was one cause of accidents among male British forge workers, researchers found. But they also discovered that they could reduce the number of accidents – whether caused by alcohol or not – if they improved the workers' diets.

Make breakfast count

The researchers divided the workers – who normally ate little breakfast – into into three groups. At mid-morning, one group received a high-energy drink, rich in carbohydrate. A second group received the same quantity of liquid, but their drink was much lower in carbohydrate. A third group didn't get anything. After four months, the researchers tabulated the number of accidents among the three groups: the men who received the high-carbohydrate drink had the fewest accidents; those who didn't get anything had the most. The researchers believe that the carbohydrate-deprived workers were suffering from 'transient malnutrition', which caused fatigue and accidents (*Scandinavian Journal of Work Environment and Health*, January 1980).

The moral of the study is: To avoid accidents, eat a good breakfast (and a healthy lunch and dinner, too). And, as we pointed out, get regular exercise. But what can you do about stress? That's a trickier problem, since it isn't always possible to avoid stress. Obviously, you shouldn't take a tranquillizer. But you're not helpless, either.

The first thing you can do is to be aware when you're under stress and becoming more accident-prone. 'A sure sign of increasing stress is a series of minor accidents,' says Simons, who advises people to 'be on guard' if they begin having too many minor mishaps. That's a must, he warns, because 'increased frequency will soon lead to increased severity.'

Second, give yourself a change of pace. In one study that compared a high-accident to a low-accident group, the low-accident people took more holidays. And a psychiatrist who investigated people who suffered disabling accidents found that, during the year before their accidents, they experienced fewer 'socially desirable events'. A break in your routine could avert a break in your leg.

Most of all, develop a healthy lifestyle. Accidents are right up there with the killer diseases – heart attacks, cancer and strokes. And like these, accidents are preventable if you eat regular, wholesome meals, stay fit, don't take drugs unless you have to and minimize stress. Health is no accident. For information on nutrients that heal the body, see HEALING PROBLEMS.

• Acne

Most people suffer from acne during adolescence. In the United States, for instance, the National Center for Health Statistics reported that only 27.7 per cent of US youths between the ages of 12 and 17 'have essentially normal skin, without significant lesions or scars,' and by age 17, a depressing 86.4 per cent have acne.

Most acne sufferers are healed by the passage of time, but for a few unlucky people, acne persists, covering their faces, necks and shoulders with welt-like sores and inflamed spots that can leave permanent scars. Dermatologists have tried helping them with X-rays, antibiotics, female hormones, anti-inflammatory corticosteroids and even steel brushes for scouring off the scars. Unfortunately, serious side-effects often accompany the long-term use of those treatments.

There are promising new alternatives, however. In experimental trials, a synthetic cousin of vitamin A – *13-cis retinoic acid* (Isotretinoin) – has cured even the most stubborn acne in many cases. Zinc supplements may work almost as well. And there is evidence that an emphasis on polyunsaturated oils in the diet can prevent or help clear acne.

In a study on 13-cis retinoic acid ('13-cis' identifies its molecular structure), doctors in Leeds used it to treat eight patients between the ages of 18 and 32 who all suffered from severe acne – ranging from small spots to deeply inflamed cysts – that therapy with antibiotics hadn't helped. They took 13-cis retinoic acid daily by mouth for four months. After one month, the amount of sebum (the skin oil that causes pimples when trapped under the skin by a clogged duct) produced by their sebaceous glands declined by 75 per cent. After four months, the patients' skin improved considerably.

The researchers described the improvement as 'dramatic'.

> By 16 weeks, there was an 80 per cent improvement in the overall grade and 80 per cent reduction in non-inflamed lesions, 90 per cent reduction in small inflamed lesions, and 90 per cent reduction in deep inflamed lesions.

According to the researchers, this synthetic form of vitamin A does what the natural vitamin does – normalizes all the epithelial tissues, including the skin – but does it much more efficiently.

Side-effects from the therapy included dryness of the eyes and inflamed lips but they weren't severe enough to make any of the patients drop out of the programme.

In fact, by cutting down the dosage the researchers were able to minimize the side-effects without sacrificing the therapeutic effect.

Most important, 13-cis retinoic acid seems to keep on working after the patients stop taking it. In experiments at the National Cancer Institute in the United States, in which 13 of 14 previously untreatable acne patients were totally cleared of acne and the remaining one improved by 75 per cent, after the treatment ended, they were acne-free for between 12 and 20 months (*New England Journal of Medicine*, 15 February 1979).

Natural vitamin A and zinc

This 13-cis retinoic acid should not be confused with vitamin A or vitamin A acid. Natural vitamin A is necessary for healthy skin, and some dermatologists prescribe it for their acne patients. But many doctors feel that, in the doses required for long-term acne therapy – as much as 300,000 IU (90,000 g) a day – vitamin A isn't safe (*see* p. 114).

Vitamin A acid (also called *retinoic acid*) is commonly applied as an ointment for acne. It dissolves the comedo – better known as a 'plug' or 'blackhead' – so that the acne sores can drain. Some doctors avoid retinoic acid because it can irritate the skin, making it more vulnerable to sunburn and to sunlight-induced skin cancer (*New England Journal of Medicine* 28 February 1980).

Vitamin A levels in the body are dependent on a good supply of zinc, and some researchers have studied the combined effect of zinc and vitamin A on acne. Dr Gerd Michaelsson, of Uppsala, Sweden has found that 'boys with severe, but not mild, acne have significantly lower serum zinc levels than healthy controls,' and that 'both boys and girls with severe acne have significantly lower levels of retinol-binding protein [an indicator of the amount of vitamin A in the blood] than healthy controls. A low-zinc diet may worsen or activate acne, especially the pustular reactions. This is seen after 10 to 14 days in acne-prone patients' (*Nutrition Reviews*, February 1981).

Dr Michaelsson first linked zinc deficiency and acne while treating a patient who suffered from a disease called *acrodermatitis enteropathica* and also from acne: he prescribed zinc for the acrodermatitis, and unexpectedly, his patient's acne cleared up. He then began experimenting with zinc and acne. In one trial, he compared the effectiveness of zinc with that of the antibiotic *tetracycline*, and found them to be virtually the same. He gave 135 mg of zinc per day to a group of 19 acne patients, and then started a second group of 18 patients on 750 mg per day of tetracycline, gradually reducing the dosage of tetracycline over the course of the experiment. After 12 weeks the skin of both groups averaged a 70 per cent improvement.

'One good thing with zinc,' Dr Michaelsson reported 'is that no serious side-effects have been found in the doses used. Oral zinc therapy is well worth considering as an alternative to tetracyclines in the treatment of patients with acne' (*British Journal of Dermatology*).

In another experiment, Dr Michaelsson compared the effectiveness of zinc with that of large doses of vitamin A. He divided 64 acne patients into four groups. He gave 135 mg of zinc per day to one group and gave 300,000 IU of vitamin A per day to a second group. A third group took both zinc and vitamin A, and a fourth group received a placebo. After four weeks, the two groups taking zinc experienced a 65 per cent improvement in their complexions, while those taking the vitamin A alone or the placebo improved by 30 and 25 per cent respectively. After 12 weeks, the zinc groups averaged an 85 per cent improvement (*Archives of Dermatology*).

Another Swedish researcher, Dr Lars Hillstrom, repeated Dr Michaelson's experiment and got similar results. He gave 48 patients 90 mg of zinc daily and gave 43 patients a placebo. After 12 weeks, 75 per cent of those receiving zinc 'were content with the therapeutic results'. 'The treatment seems to be safe, easily administered and with very few side-effects,' Dr Hillstrom and his colleagues stated. 'It can also be used in combination with different kinds of topical treatment – for instance, retinoic acid' (*British Journal of Dermatology*).

None of the researchers knows exactly how zinc works. Dr Michaelsson found that acne recurred when the zinc treatment was discontinued. He theorized that zinc may induce the release of vitamin A in the body, that it may have an anti-inflammatory effect, and that a deficiency of zinc causes enlargement of the sebaceous glands. He also thinks that a widespread zinc deficiency may contribute to acne:

> Zinc deficiency seems to be more common than previously known, and a daily intake below the recommended 15 to 20 mg is probably not uncommon. Some diets in hospitals, as well as in the average households in the United States and Europe, have been found to contain only 4 to 7 mg of zinc. [Meat, liver eggs and seafood are good sources of zinc].

The US National Academy of Sciences agreed with him.

> A recent study measuring the zinc content . . . of self-chosen food of 20 free-living adults over a period of six days detected an average of only 8.6 mg per day, ranging from 6 to 12.4 mg. These findings emphasize the need for careful dietary planning if the RDA of 15 mg per day is to be met [*Recommended Dietary Allowances*, National Academy of Sciences 1980].

A dermatologist in Los Angeles, Samuel Ayres, Jr, has combined vitamin A not with zinc, but with vitamin E to combat acne. He and his colleagues, Drs Richard Mihan and Morton D. Scribner, give their acne patients an average daily dose of 100,000 IU of vitamin A and 800 IU of vitamin E. 'We've had very good results with this treatment,' says Dr Ayres. And the doses of vitamins can usually be reduced after a few months.

The patients also are told what foods to avoid. 'Extra iodine can aggravate acne, so we advise our patients to avoid iodized salt. Excess milk, fats and sweets also can cause acne to flare up. Many commercial soft drinks contain brominated vegetable oils as stabilizers, which may irritate acne conditions too. We tell our patients to drink fresh fruit juices.'

Effects of fats on the skin

Like Dr Ayres, Dr Michaelsson is also interested in the relationship between acne and food, particularly dietary fats. Animal fats may make acne worse he says, since a switch to a vegetarian diet is sometimes followed by improvement in the skin. A low-fat diet has no effect on acne, he has found but a diet rich in polyunsaturated fats may help the skin.

Several doctors we interviewed share some of Dr Michaelsson's beliefs. One of them is dermatologist Gustave Hoehn, who has written a book optimistically entitled *Acne Can be Cured*. He believes that a diet high in polyunsaturated fats and very low in animal fat and butterfat will cure acne.

'It is not fat *per se* that is bad for acne,' Dr Hoehn says. 'It is only the thick, hard, solid fats that cause a stasis, or the inability of the sebum to flow out freely. The liquid oils – fish oils, peanut oils and vegetable oils – as well as mayonnaise and oily salad dressings do not cause acne.' He believes that butterfat and animal fat pass from the blood to the skin, clogging the oil ducts, causing irritation and turning them into spots. 'Whole milk is the biggest problem,' Dr Hoehn told us. 'The pimples will disappear when you put people on skim milk and eliminate hard fats.'

(In his book, Dr Hoehn suggests that any random survey of secondary school students will show that severe acne sufferers are heavy consumers of cheese butter, mince and, especially, whole milk. In a poll of 215 students, of the 34 students with severe or 'persistent' acne, 85 per cent said they drank whole milk often; 60 per cent of the 109 'mild' acne sufferers and 58 per cent of the 72 students who said they had no acne problem drank milk regularly. Consumption of cheese and cheeseburgers was slightly higher among the severe and persistent cases).

Stress can be a factor

Two more practising dermatologists, Milton Saunders, Jr and Irwin I. Lubowe, share some of Drs Michaelsson and Hoehn's beliefs about acne therapy. Dr Saunders is the president of the Optimum Health Foundation in Virginia Beach, Virginia. Like Dr Hoehn, he advises against an excess of whole milk and fried foods. He also discourages the use of coffee, tea or very hot and spicy foods because they may dilate blood vessels of the face and aggravate acne.

About 20 per cent of his patients are adults, Dr Saunders told us, and their therapy differs from that for adolescents. 'In many teenagers, diet is the key to acne, but among adults, stress is the key factor.' Women schoolteachers he has found, often come to him with stress-related acne. He finds that when they spend time away from the classroom, their acne begins to clear. Sales representatives are another high-risk group. Their regimen of travel, restaurant food and social drinking tends to give them pimples. Athletic stress, if it triggers the release of male hormones (in men or women), is also suspected of making acne worse.

Dr Saunders uses antibiotics, retinoic acid ointment, zinc supplements and water-soluble vitamin A (since fat-soluble vitamin A may be harmful in large doses) in an effort to heal the skin as soon as possible. 'There's no point in fooling around,' he told us. 'These people want results yesterday.'

Dr Lubowe, who practises in New York City, also prescribes water-soluble vitamin A. In addition, he advises his patients to take 400 IU of vitamin E and 50 mg of zinc daily. And, in his book, *A Teenage Guide to Healthy Skin and Hair* (1979), he expresses his own opinions on diet and acne:

> Too many fats in your diet are a common cause of acne. Since the sebaceous glands need food to function, they draw upon the daily intake of food that is transported to the skin by the blood. The worst villains

are fatty meats, carbohydrates, chocolate, cocoa, spices, iodized salt and shellfish.

The outlook for acne treatment has never been better. In the past, acne sufferers faced difficult and confusing choices between treatments of questionable value. But now there are promising alternatives, including options as simple as switching from saturated to unsaturated fats and eating foods rich in vitamin A and zinc.

• Ageing

When you've reached that point in your life when some of your friends are starting to pack to move to sheltered accommodation (if not the nursing home) it's time to do some serious thinking about how you're taking care of yourself. If you plan it right, you can be packing for a camping trip in the mountains, a summer abroad or a seaside holiday full of evening barbecues on the beach and early-morning cycling.

But it's got to be you who takes care of yourself. You can't depend on your doctor to be much help in keeping you really alive – healthy, energetic and clear-minded. Doctors are trained to prescribe drugs and perform surgery. The problems of ageing require a different approach. To make the years after middle age the best years of your life, you have to take charge of the underlying factors that determine your health. And one of the most important of these is your diet.

For example, a British study found that, of 93 geriatric patients with acute problems, none had a normal nutritional profile. Dr A.G. Morgan, consultant physician at Airedale General Hospital in Yorkshire, and five colleagues tested patients for vitamin A, thiamin (B_1), riboflavin (B_2), niacin (B_3) vitamins C, D, E and K and protein. Twenty-two of the 93 actually had less than normal levels of most of the nutrients. The most common deficiencies were in protein, niacin, and vitamins C, E and A.

Dr Morgan at first suspected 'that an inadequate dietary intake, due to disease or to physical and mental deterioration, was the most likely cause of these multiple nutritional abnormalities.' By the end of his study he concluded that 'their present illness could not have significantly contributed to their nutritional status' (*International Journal for Vitamin and Nutrition Research*).

In other words, the dietary deficiencies came before the health problems and not the other way round. That is a key point. Were these people in the hospital because their diets weren't providing them with enough of the right nutrients?

Increasing the intake of nutrients

Olaf Mickelsen, a former professor in the department of food science and human nutrition at Michigan State University, is in a good position to comment on that question, since he has participated in a number of scientific studies designed to answer that very question. He is also the author of a review of the subject, 'The Possible Role of Vitamins in the Aging Process', which appears as a chapter in *Nutrition, Longevity, and Aging.*

During a recent interview, Dr Mickelsen told us that he was 'impressed by the effects a reasonable intake of vitamin C seems to have. People who have been taking more vitamin C seem to have fewer problems when they enter the hospital.' And, as he writes in the book, 'The results of a number of studies imply that a higher than normal intake of vitamin C appears to reduce the aches and pains to which older persons are prone, to lower mortality when the aged are ill, and to increase their longevity.'

Dr Mickelsen went on to discuss a study led by a colleague of his, Dr Eleanor D. Schlenker, in which the average protein and vitamin C intakes were measured in a group of 100 women over the course of almost 25 years. The women who had higher intakes of vitamin C and protein lived longer, so the beneficial effect of increased intake is undeniable in this case.

A follow-up study two years later by Drs Schlenker, Mickelsen and two colleagues revealed:

a striking relationship between nutrient intake and physical health. Those women who on the basis of medical examinations appeared younger than their years consumed fewer calories and substantially less total fat saturated fat and fat as a per cent of total calories.

In contrast, 'lower intakes of thiamine, vitamin A, and ascorbic acid were noted among women who appeared older' (*Federation of American Societies for Experimental Biology*).

In simpler terms: Eat better, feel younger.

Another study mentioned by Dr Mickelsen is probably the classic study in the field of nutrition and ageing: the San Mateo County, California survey of health and nutrition of 577 people over the age of 50. The study was begun in 1948, with very sensitive measurements of dietary intake of various nutrients biochemical tests that are associated with health and disease (such as blood levels of cholesterol, vitamin C and sugar), and recording of diseases. Six years later, Dr Harold D. Chope re-examined 306 of the original 577 people and went to the record books to look for evidence that nutrition had played a part in their ageing process.

He found it: people with higher-than-average intake of vitamins A and C and niacin tended to live longer than those with a lower intake.

And the differences were quite remarkable. Among the people whose intake of vitamin A was less than 5000 IU (or 1500 μg [micrograms], the measurement now preferred by the DHSS) per day, the death rate was 13.9 per cent. For those whose daily intake of vitamin A was 5000 to 7999 IU (1500 – 2400 μg) the death rate was 6.9 per cent. But among the people whose daily intake was 8000 IU (2400 μg) or more, the death rate was only 4.3 per cent, less than a third that of the group getting under 5000 IU.

The data on vitamin C (also called *ascorbic acid*) was even more remarkable. Among those whose intake was less than 50 mg per day, the death rate was 18.5 per cent. For those whose daily intake was over 50 mg, the death rate was 4.5 per cent, less than a quarter of the rate for those whose diet provided less than 50 mg!

The difference that adequate nutrition seems to have had on delaying death is impressive. But what about what doctors call 'morbidity' – illness suffering and general ill health? Did nutrition affect these important factors in the lives of the people in the study?

Again, the answer was yes. As Dr Chope wrote in the report of his study:

> In subjects with low intake of vitamin A (less than 5000 IU), the incidence of nervous system, circulatory system, and respiratory system disease was high . . . Low thiamin [vitamin B_1] intake (less than 0.80 mg a day) seemed to be associated with nervous system disease and circulatory disease; the higher the intake of thiamin, the lower the incidence of diseases of these two systems. Diseases of the circulatory system and the digestive system were associated with low intake of ascorbic acid (less than 50 mg per day). Among persons with a high intake of ascorbic acid (110 mg and over) there was a low incidence of nervous system and circulatory system disease [*California Medicine*].

Looking at Dr Chope's results, you might be led to wonder how many of the people took nutritional supplements. Unfortunately, Dr Chope did not determine which people did or didn't. But there have been some studies in which the effects of vitamin supplements on health in the later years of life have been documented.

The value of supplements

A British doctor G.F. Taylor, took part in one study in which 40 geriatric patients were given supplements containing 15 mg of thiamin, 15 mg of riboflavin, 50 mg of nicotinamide (niacin), 10 mg of pyridoxine (B_6) and 200 mg of vitamin C. Another group of 40 received dummy tablets. After a year, Dr Taylor, who did not know which patients were getting supplements, was, none the less, able to determine who was or wasn't receiving supplements merely by examining them for the signs of nutritional deficiencies and other illnesses.

Dr Taylor described his experience:

> At the start of the trial I recorded 13 of the 80 patients as having no marked signs of nutritional deficiencies . . . After six months of the trial, I could not decide with certainty in more than half the cases whether they had had treatment or not . . . But at the end of the year's trial, it was obvious which patients had received active tablets and [which ones received] dummy tablets . . .
>
> In the treated group, the classical signs of malnutrition improved slowly. After 12 months' treatment, many signs had disappeared with a return to normal appearances. In some cases, improvement was still continuing after 12 months' treatment. At the end of one year's treatment, there was a striking improvement in the general physical and mental condition. In the untreated group, clinical signs did not improve and in many cases deteriorated. Deterioration during infections, and when antibiotics, steroids or diuretics were given, was especially marked . . .

One of the most dramatic and significant findings in this study arose after the trial had officially finished. All cases were observed clinically for six to nine months after stopping treatment, and signs of nutritional deficiencies reappeared in many previously treated cases [*Vitamins in the Elderly*].

This classic study not only underscores the importance of supplemental vitamins but reveals that the good they do often takes time – close to a year of regular supplementation. Further, the good they do is not some kind of 'cure'. Vitamins are concentrated foodstuffs. They nourish your body's innate desire to be healthy. As Dr Taylor noted, when the added nourishment ceased the benefits faded.

Do vitamins like A, the B complex and C extend life?

Maybe – but maybe not. A more scientific view is that rather than extending life, superior nutrition merely keeps life from being unnecessarily shortened as is so often the case. But when you've worked hard all your life and you've finally reached the point where you can pack your case and go anywhere you want, without worrying about job responsibilities or who will take care of the children, that's really quite a bit.

A diet for the best years of your life

What is it about these vitamins that keeps people healthy? Why did all those people with high vitamin intakes live longer? Why were they less often ill?

To answer these questions, let's take a look at some of these important vitamins and minerals and see what happens when they're not supplied in adequate quantities.

Vitamin A

This is the first line of defence against many illnesses. Deficiency in vitamin A leaves the body more susceptible to infection by hampering the immune system and drying out the mucous membranes. This is important for anyone, but for an older person, it can be a matter of life and death. Infections can take advantage of the body's generally less vigorous condition or complicate existing illnesses to the point where recovery is agonizingly drawn out or even impossible.

Vitamin A deficiency can also contribute to other deficiences, in an indirect way. By causing the tissues around the taste buds to dry out, vitamin A deficiency can rob you of your sense of taste. Once that is gone, you may instinctively turn to heavily sweetened foods, which don't supply anywhere near the amounts of other nutrients that you need.

It's not hard to see why vitamin A intake made such a significant difference in the results of the San Mateo study – lowering the death rate by two-thirds.

B vitamins

The same is true of the B vitamins. From one day to the next, they play a vital role in keeping our health on a straight track. Without them, our digestion can't function the way it should. Nutrients are lost. Health suffers.

But B vitamins are also important to another body system – the nervous system.

Deficiencies of B vitamins often produce symptoms that, when they occur in older people, are referred to as 'senility'. Vitamin B_{12} is so important to the nervous system that even a slight deficiency can cause fatigue, irritability and numbness. If the deficiency worsens, so do the symptoms: dementia, depression, confusion and paranoia. Other B vitamins are equally important to the proper functioning of the nervous system. Folic acid, for example, is present in the central nervous system and in the fluid of the spinal column. The whole range of 'senility' symptoms can be a result of a deficiency in folic acid. Thiamin deficiency often shows up as irritability and depression.

These symptoms can be the first step down a spiral leading from depression and anxiety to doctor-prescribed 'dope', to poorer nutrition and to further calamities of ill health. In light of the findings of Dr Morgan's study and the studies mentioned by Dr Mickelsen, the importance of the B vitamins in avoiding this spiral becomes very clear. And it's tragic that advertisements in medical journals tell doctors that the answer to these problems is the latest tranquillizer.

Vitamin C

Vitamin C is another vitamin that figures prominently in the studies on nutrition and the problems of ageing. You know how people often think of ageing as a kind of 'falling apart'. Well, vitamin C is the nutrient that helps you 'keep it all together!'

For one thing, there is now little doubt that extra amounts of vitamin C strengthen your defences against infections. And the older you get, the more you're going to depend on those defences to keep minor infections such as colds and the flu from turning into big infections like pneumonia. Recent evidence has also shown that vitamin C plays a major role in protecting the health of the arteries. Since diseases of the circulatory system kill more people than anything else, a little extra vitamin C seems like a good investment, one which could enable you to collect your pension a lot longer.

And like the other vitamins, vitamin C indirectly contributes to your supply of other nutrients. Tooth loss probably drives older people to junk food more than any other single factor. When you can't chew real food, you turn to food that has already been chewed by a machine. And machine-chewed food – processed food – won't supply anywhere near the nutritional value that fresh chewy food will.

Vitamin C comes in at the most important point in the battle to keep your teeth – your gums. Marginal deficiencies of vitamin C cause the gums to swell and bleed more than they should – that is, *gingivitis*. Allowed to proceed, gingivitis eventually leads to destruction of the periodontal ligaments and bone – the structure in which the teeth are rooted. You may have the most filling-free teeth in town, but when the periodontal bone starts to go, so do your teeth.

Looking back again, is it any wonder that the women in Dr Schlenker's study who increased their vitamin C intake over the years lived so much longer than the women who allowed their intake of this vitamin to falter?

Vitamin D

This goes hand in hand with calcium in keeping some of the most serious problems of ageing at bay. Usually, vitamin D is thought of as a young person's vitamin, one that is important for people whose bones are still growing. Well, your bones may have stopped growing 40 or 50 years ago, but you still need them every bit as much as you did back then, maybe more. As you get older, your bones invariably start to demineralize and weaken (*see* BONE DISEASE) – unless adequate calcium is supplied in your diet. But unless you are also getting enough vitamin D, which regulates utilization of calcium the mineral will not end up in your bones, where it belongs. Most of it may simply be lost in the urine.

Vitamin E

As you might expect, this vitamin is also very important to people getting past middle age. In fact, some research suggests that we may soon be calling vitamin E the 'anti-ageing' vitamin. Studies have shown that it keeps the red blood cells from ageing under stressful conditions. Whether this anti-ageing effect extends to the whole body is not known, but the fact that vitamin E protects the red blood cells is important because the red blood cells are what all the rest of the cells in the body depend upon for their supply of life-giving oxygen and nutrients.

Minerals

Besides calcium, *iron* seems to be very important. In Dr Chope's San Mateo study, low levels of haemoglobin in the blood were associated with a high incidence of chest and throat infections. The haemoglobin in red blood cells has two parts – a protein (*globin*) and an iron compound (*haem*) – and is responsible for transporting oxygen around the body. Iron makes it possible for the red blood cells to do their job, by keeping haemoglobin levels high. Without haemoglobin, the blood cannot do its job of distributing oxygen. And when the blood doesn't do this job, your whole body suffers the consequences. Loss of energy and a lack of resistance to infections are the first symptoms to appear in an iron deficiency.

Another vitally important mineral is *zinc*. If you want to maintain resistance to infections and keep your wound-healing system in good shape, zinc is one mineral you can't do without. Zinc deficiency results in loss of the sense of taste, one sense you need if you care about your diet. Zinc also apparently helps protect the prostate gland, which so often becomes inflamed sending men to the doctor with low back pain, bloody urine, impotence and decreased control over urination.

Finally, zinc appears to be important to the proper functioning of the brain and may be a factor in senility. One thing is certain: in the studies of the future that attempt to define the relationship between nutrients and ageing zinc will be right up there among the most important.

Supplements and a good diet

At this point, making sure your body is supplied with all these vital nutrients might seem pretty complicated. Actually, it's quite simple. You don't have to seek out super-high quantities of these vitamins and minerals. A good multivitamin and mineral supplement will supply adequate quantities and will be a simple, convenient way to get into the habit of providing your body with enough of what it needs. Remember, the people in these studies were not taking megavitamins. Some of them weren't even taking supplements.

Supplementing your diet is a good place to start, but it's not the whole job. You have to watch the food you eat, too. Your diet will have to be more efficient, because you'll be eating less. As Dr Mickelsen told us, 'My primary impression is that too many people are obese. As people get older, they have more time. Food becomes the only pastime they look forward to. This leads to obesity, which leads to a lot of other problems. Diabetes, for instance. People can reduce their risk of developing diabetes merely by changing their diet. Some recent research has shown that the amount of insulin that diabetics require can be reduced or even eliminated if they just increase the amount of fibre in the diet. Fibre seems to help people control body weight. Cancer is also much less prominent among lean people. There are other benefits as well.

'My advice is to eat a varied diet. Include as much fibre as possible. We're indoctrinated to think that meat is the most important item in the diet. Other things are just as important.'

Eat simple foods, fresh foods. Fish, liver, lean meat, poultry and vegetable proteins such as soyabeans and wheat germ will all supply protein and other necessary nutrients as well. Whole grains, nuts and seeds are far better sources of carbohydrates and fats than processed baked goods. Fresh fruits and vegetables are crucial to a healthy life. As a rule, the fresher and less cooked, the better. Taking a cue from this rule, fresh salads brimming with lettuce, onions, cucumbers, radishes, celery, broccoli and tomatoes, or apples pears, bananas, peaches and melon chunks, should play a starring role in your daily diet.

All of those fruits and vegetables will no doubt help you in the fibre department, but adding a little bran to one of your meals will ensure your system's getting enough bulk to keep intestinal muscles well-enough exercised to keep constipation from settling in. When you add bran to your diet, do so a little at a time, starting out with a teaspoon or less per day and gradually working up to one or more tablespoons. For every tablespoon of bran you eat drink *at least* one extra glass of water. Take it at one meal preferably not at the meal when you usually take your mineral supplements because some tests have shown that bran sometimes interferes with the absorption of minerals.

As you begin taking better and better care of yourself through your diet don't expect exciting results to occur overnight. Remember, in Dr Taylor's study the results of supplementation didn't begin to show until the study had been in progress for six months. Also keep in mind, however, that after a year the results were unmistakably apparent. So stay with it.

The secret of making the years past middle age the best years of your life is the word *active*. Take an active interest in your health and your diet.

A new pathway to a longer life

Few people die of old age. We don't just wither away into nothing at the end of our lives. Instead, the end generally comes when the ability of the body to withstand stress is overcome by a specific challenge. Old age wears people down to a point where they can no longer make it through diseases they once weathered easily.

That may sound like splitting hairs. If we've all got to go, what difference does it make exactly how it happens?

In terms of *prevention*, it makes a big difference. The older we get the less effective are our bodies' defences against disease. Researchers may never find a way to slow down the general deterioration of the body with time but preventing the breakdown of the body's defences is a very real possibility.

Preventing the breakdown of cells
The key to that breakthrough may be a group of substances called anti-oxidants. These are not some exotic new chemicals just cooked up in a million-pound research facility. They are ordinary substances, including vitamins E and C, which prevent oxidation, a common chemical reaction in the body. Oxidation is necessary for the normal working of the body, but the reaction can cause problems, too, particularly when it occurs in the fats found in cell membranes. Oxidation of those fats disrupts the delicate functioning of the cell membrane and can break it completely open, killing the cell.

The physical conditions of the body – a warm environment, exposure to light constant motion – are perfect for oxidation reactions, but the cells of the body remain intact because anti-oxidants protect them from oxidation. Some scientists have theorized that ageing occurs mainly through a failure of the anti-oxidant protective system over the years.

Studies have been done which back up that theory. Jeffrey Bland, a chemist at the University of Puget Sound in Washington State, has found that vitamin E, a common anti-oxidant in the body, prevents changes in red blood cells that ordinarily occur with old age. As red blood cells age, they often take a popcorn-like shape called a 'budded' cell. Dr Bland believed that budded red blood cells are the result of oxidative damage to the cell membrane. Oxidation, he suspected, weakens the membrane to the point where the cell pops out of shape like a weak bicycle tyre under pressure.

Sure enough, when Dr Bland exposed red blood cells to light and oxygen, the optimum conditions for oxidation, he found he could produce budded cells in the laboratory. More important, he found that when blood donors were given 600 IU of vitamin E a day for the ten days before they donated blood, their red blood cells seemed to be protected from the deformity: when the cells were exposed to light and oxygen for 16 hours, only a small number lost their normal shape. Cells from people who were not taking vitamin E were totally transformed into budded cells.

Dr Bland pointed out that the 600 IU dosage of vitamin E was chosen arbitrarily. His research has since shown that the optimal dose for each individual varies greatly, from 100 to 1200 IU daily.

Other changes at the cellular level that occur with age have been blocked in laboratories through the use of anti-oxidants. For example, a particular colouring material called *lipofuscin*, or 'age pigment', builds up in all species – from fungi to humans – as they grow older. In studies with fungi anti-oxidants have not only inhibited the formation of age pigment but also prolonged the fungi's life spans (*Mechanisms of Aging and Development*).

Denham Harman of the University of Nebraska has been working with anti-oxidants for over 20 years, and has discovered that a number of them, including vitamin E, can prolong the lives of mice. There have even been reports linking vitamin E to longevity of human cells. One study found that the life span of human cells in the laboratory was increased 100 per cent if the cells were grown in a culture with vitamin E added. Unfortunately, no one, not even the scientists who did the original study, were able to repeat that experiment successfully. The issue of whether vitamin E and other anti-oxidants modify the ageing process itself, in every individual cell in the body, remains clouded.

Anti-oxidants and the immune system

That does not mean that anti-oxidants do not promote a longer life, or prevent the ailments that make old age so difficult to bear. Anti-oxidants may still increase longevity in ways that have nothing to do with the fundamental process of ageing.

Dr Harman has been looking at the effects of anti-oxidants on the body's defences against disease. A number of years ago, he demonstrated that a number of anti-oxidants, including vitamin E and a synthetic anti-oxidant sig-nificantly enhanced the immune responses of mice (*Journal of the American Geriatrics Society*). The evidence suggested that oxidation reactions might disrupt the cells involved in mobilizing the body's defences. In another report, again demonstrating the positive effects of anti-oxidants on the life spans of mice, Dr Harman stressed the possibility that they acted by protecting the animals' immune systems (*American Federation for Clinical Research*, April 1979).

Other researchers have turned their attention to the possible links between anti-oxidants, immunity and ageing. Ronald R. Watson, has been examining the problem at Purdue University in the United States. 'The immune systems in young children and in older people are less effective than in mature adults,' he told us. 'The longer you live, the more severely infections hit you. That's why when flu vaccines come around, complications to the vaccine usually develop in young people and older people.'

Dr Watson has been testing the effects of diet on the immune systems of people in nursing homes and on laboratory animals. 'Our animal studies are going on continuously,' he told us. 'We've looked at diets high in vitamin E high- and low-fat diets and high- and low-protein diets, to see what changes they produced in the immune system.'

Dr Watson's tests of vitamin E produced the same kind of results as Dr Harman's: 'We found that vitamin E boosted one aspect of the immune response important in the body's anti-cancer defences, within a week of giving it to the mice.' Dr Watson says it remains to be seen whether that effect is the result of vitamin E's anti-oxidant action.

J. Terrell Hoffeld is another researcher looking into connections between anti-oxidants and immunity. A scientist at the [US] National Institute of Dental Research, Dr Hoffeld's work is ultimately directed towards finding a way to combat periodontal disease, an infectious disease of the gums, and to this end, he examined the action of different anti-oxidants in protecting lymphocytes from oxidation.

Lymphocytes are white blood cells that play a central role in the immune system. Dr Hoffeld found that when the anti-oxidant agents block damage to the lymphocytes of mice, the immune response of the cells goes up (*Federation Proceedings*, 1 March 1980). 'We found that agents which acted at multiple sites were more effective,' Dr Hoffeld told us. 'A whole series of biochemical reactions is involved in the initiation of oxidative damage to a cell. If you can block those reactions in the early steps, then you can block the final result more efficiently. The most effective agent we found was vitamin E. Vitamin E acts everywhere along the chain of steps, and therefore was very effective.'

Other anti-oxidants

Nutrients other than vitamin E have also been found to act as anti-oxidants. Scientists in India have discovered that vitamin A fed to rats can block the oxidation that normally occurs when tissue taken from the animals is exposed to air. When the scientists fed vitamin E along with vitamin A, the anti-oxidant effect was even stronger (*International Journal of Vitamin and Nutrition Research*).

An enzyme in the body called *glutathione peroxidase* also protects cell membranes from oxidation. The activity of glutathione peroxidase in animals has been shown to be directly related to the amount of the mineral selenium in the diet. Zinc and manganese might be needed for the proper functioning of another anti-oxidant enzyme, *superoxide dimutase*. Researchers have found that vitamin C boosts the anti-oxidant action of vitamin E and selenium, though other studies suggest that the action of vitamin C may be unreliable.

In any case, these natural preservatives are obviously among the most crucially important substances in the body. We have to have them, even at the peak of the body's vigour, and the older we get, the more important they become. Anti-oxidants may prolong life. They almost certainly help prevent the aches and ailments common to old age. And later years free of aches and ailments can hardly be called 'old age' at all.

The role of the B vitamins

To a certain group of senior citizens in the United States, it must have seemed the stuff of magic. Not that their wrinkles uncreased their snowy hair regained its colour or their bodies reverted to supple specimens of youth. No their transformation from ailing oldsters to revitalized men and women was less dramatic but none the less striking. The signs of rejuvenation and vigour were unmistakable: renewed health, diminished aches and pains, fewer nervous disorders, improved coordination, softer skin and more attractive appearance.

The man who prompted these changes is no wizard but Herman Baker who holds a doctorate in metabolism and nutrition and teaches at the New Jersey Medical School. In fact, it didn't require any sorcery at all for him and three colleagues to reverse what seemed to be the inevitable infirmities of the elderly. The secret to many so-called problems of old age, he discovered, was no more than a vitamin B deficiency that can impair one's health if left untreated.

As it happens, Dr Baker, a professor of medicine and preventive medicine, is no stranger to the field. He first launched his studies on the effects of nutrient deficits 25 years ago as an important tool in diagnosing maladies of the aged. Apparently, his interest hasn't waned. His most recent project focused on 473 elderly people – ranging from 60 to 102 years old – in New Jersey and Maryland. Of this sample, 327 lived in nursing homes and the rest resided at home. At the study's onset in 1978, blood tests and physical examinations revealed that 7 to 8 per cent of them had signs of anaemia, skin dermatitis, cracked lips, nerve disorders, muscular aches and pains and poor visual coordination. However, evaluations also showed that as many as 39 per cent suffered from 'subclinical' vitamin deficiencies that hadn't yet blossomed into noticeable symptoms or ailments.

What were the culprits responsible for this charade of 'old age' in otherwise healthy, non-bedridden people? The critical ingredients turned out to be none other than absentee members of the vitamin B family – nutrients that not only affect the central nervous system and coordination but are also crucial to mental and emotional well-being. According to Dr Baker, the elderly people he studied exhibited strikingly depressed levels of vitamins B_6 (pyridoxine), B_3 (niacin) and B_{12}, as well as inadequate amounts of folic acid and thiamin, other components of the B complex.

To remedy those deficits, the group received an injection of the entire B complex once every three months during the year's experiment. After the first jab, Dr Baker told us, symptoms began to disappear. In another 12 weeks following the second injection, the investigators noted an increased level of circulating nutrients in the subjects' blood. At the study's conclusion, the elderly's physical woes had vanished along with their vitamin deficiencies. 'They're all in good health now,' says Dr Baker.

'Vitamin deprivation may affect the young far less because they retain adequate reserves, thanks to sufficient vitamin-binding sites in the liver,' he contends. Perhaps then, increased nutrient needs in the elderly reflect, at least in part, decreased vitamin storage sites, Dr Baker speculates. In addition, metabolism difficulties and medication may interfere with vitamin absorption in later life.

Besides taking supplements, it's important to spike your diet with generous helpings of food rich in B vitamins, such as liver, whole grain cereals, nuts yeast, dark-green leafy vegetables, poultry and fish for that extra ounce of protection. After all, there's no need to grow old before your time. Remember it doesn't require any magic to hold back the clock, especially if the signs of 'ageing' are sometimes as preventable as a vitamin deficiency.

Exercise keeps you young and quick

As laboratory flasks bubble sinisterly, the aged scientist with wild flashing eyes raises the elixir of youth to his lips. He bolts it down clutches at his throat and sinks beneath the table. A few miraculous minutes later, he arises a new man, in the flush of youth. But unfortunately for the mad doctor, anybody who has watched enough old films knows that he'll finally run out of potion and, in the last scene, shockingly revert to his real age.

There's one advantage that exercise has over fuming potions: it's an elixir of youth that you need never run out of.

Most of us think – mistakenly – that getting older means slowing down taking smaller and fewer steps, avoiding hills and letting the youngsters do all the work. Our whole culture subtly teaches us to expect to slow down and degenerate as we grow older. One study of older people's attitudes found that many actually feel embarrassed to exercise in public. Social pressures often discourage even those with a positive attitude toward exercise from going out to jog or cycle.

'Doctors, too, are prejudiced against older people,' Michael B. Mock of the cardiac disease branch of the National Heart, Lung and Blood Institute in the US, told a conference on exercise and the elderly held at the National Institutes of Health, near Washington D.C. 'They think older people should be relegated to the rocking chair. They just say, 'Take it easy' and 'No going up steps.' This leads to an overmedicated, vegetative person. And it sometimes results in a person ending up in a nursing home instead of taking care of himself – if he had been given some encouragement to be active.'

Giving in to this notion of ageing is a dangerous mistake because evidence is piling up to show that getting older shouldn't mean putting away the running shoes, the hiking boots, the sweat suit or the bicycle.

Slowing the ageing process

One very good reason older people should exercise is that it can slow and even reverse ageing. According to Walter M. Bortz II of the Palo Alto Medical Clinic in California, ageing people show the same metabolic breakdown as people subjected to forced inactivity, and it is logical that exercise can slow this process down.

Maximal oxygen volume, Dr Bortz told the annual meeting of the American Geriatrics Society in April 1979, decreases by about 1 per cent every year with age and lack of exercise. This means that every part of the body of an inactive older person is getting less and less cell-nourishing oxygen the older he or she grows. However, if such people refuse to take that sitting down, they can reap the same astonishing results that mad scientists achieve in old movies, and without having to worry about running out of potion. According to Dr Bortz, with moderate exercise an older person can achieve the maximal oxygen volume of a person 15 years younger. A very active person can achieve the maximal oxygen volume of a person 40 years younger.

The reason is that exercise can compensate for bodily decline by increasing heart output, lung capacity and blood volume. With exercise, you're never too old to grow young.

Exercise may also keep ageing people's reflexes quick. Slowed reaction time (the time between a stimulus and the resulting reaction) is a problem for older people, as when in traffic it takes too long to hit the brakes.

In a study of reaction time and ageing, researchers at the department of physical education at San Diego State University tested 64 male and female volunteers ranging from 23 to 59 years of age. Half of the volunteers were runners; the other half were sedentary people. Both groups were asked to respond to a lighting stimulus by lifting their fingers from the appropriate light switch.

The results supported the view that reaction time does indeed decline with age – but with one exception. Those older people who exercised regularly didn't suffer the usual slowing down. And the researchers also noted that there appeared to be a relationship between good reaction time and good cardiovascular health (*Medicine and Science in Sports*, vol. 11, no. 2 1979).

Exercise could also help people who suffer from bone-weakening demineralization called *osteoporosis*. It is estimated that hundreds of thousands of people in the United Kingdom (most of them women) have osteoporosis, which among women over 45, causes thousands of fractures annually because of bone weakening. A study by the Nassau County (New York) Medical Center and the Medical Research Center, Brookhaven National Laboratory, shows that exercise can help fight such bone loss. In a group of sedentary women, researchers observed a decrease of body calcium in every member of the group. By contrast, among a group of women who exercised, they found that body calcium increased enough to modify bone loss (*Annals of Internal Medicine*).

Helping maintain a good sense of balance is yet another way exercise can keep people from feeling old and slow. According to C. Carson Conrad, executive director of the (US) President's Council on Physical Fitness and Sports,

> The balance mechanism of the body is commonly neglected and yet is extremely important in the fitness of older people . . . The balance mechanism is maintained through use and degenerates when not used. Many older people tend to lose their sense of balance much more quickly than nature intended. The need to use glasses and hearing aids increases the hazards for many. A well-maintained sense of balance can help make up for the problems caused by quick changes in vision from one optical focus to another. [*Geriatrics*].

Exercise can help to keep the body fit and healthy – in some cases, 15 or more years fitter and healthier than its calendar age. But getting on in years isn't only a physical matter. People feel old not only in their bodies but also in their minds.

In recent years, many doctors have come to recognize the importance of people's own evaluations of their condition and how they respond to it. The body images of some may be so positive that they think of themselves as fit and healthy despite physical complaints that would make others with negative body images feel quite ill. This self-evaluation is very important because it guides people in adopting their social roles. For example, an older person with chronic disease who considers him/herself well will continue to lead an active, unrestricted life, while one who regards her/himself as ill will lapse into feeling and acting 'sickly' (*Journal of Gerontology*).

And studies on the attitudes of elderly people show that those who exercise feel better about themselves than those who don't. On a psychological test designed to measure a person's self-image, people who exercised the least felt that they didn't live up to their ideal image of themselves. Those who exercised the most showed a good body image, close to their desired image of themselves (*Medicine and Science in Sports*).

It follows from this that taking up a programme of exercise can change a person's personality for the better. 'We know now that personality in adults is a dynamic thing, not a static thing,' says A. H. Ismail, professor of physical education at Purdue University (and former Olympic basketball player). 'There can be changes, and the changes that are produced through a fitness regimen are in a positive direction.' For 20 years, Dr Ismail has been conducting fitness programmes involving hundreds of participants and has found that those who scored low on emotional stability tests before exercising showed marked improvement afterwards.

Exercise, diet and mental alertness

Exercise has been shown to improve not only the self-image and psychological strength of older people but also their mental sharpness.

It stands to reason that good oxygen levels in the blood can boost brain power. Working with that logical hunch, Claude Fell Merzbacher of the department of natural science at San Diego State University in California gathered together a group of 31 volunteers to test the effect of diet and exercise on their mental skills. The volunteers were part of a group enrolled in a diet, exercise and education programme at the Longevity Research Institute of Santa Monica. The average age of the group was 60 years, and every member suffered from cardiovascular or some other degenerative disease such as diabetes or arthritis – diseases that, at an advanced age, are especially trying and distracting.

For 26 days, the volunteers followed the Institute's exercise programme consisting mostly of daily walks. At the same time, they ate a wholesome high-fibre diet containing no fats or oils (except those in grains, vegetables and fruits and very small amounts of meat), minimal cholesterol, no simple carbohydrates, especially refined sugar and honey, and no added salt.

Both before and after the completion of this regimen, the group were given various tests. On one test, which measured socialization, self-control tolerance, achievement and intellectual efficiency, the volunteers showed higher scores after the regimen. This meant improved verbal fluency, quick clear thinking, intellectual efficiency and perceptiveness. On another, which measured changes in mental sharpness, the group again scored higher after the combined diet and exercise regimen. And all this in the remarkably short time of less than a month (*Perceptual and Motor Skills*, vol. 48, 1979).

Exercise can rejuvenate your body and sharpen your mind. However, 'perhaps the greatest benefit of maintaining physical fitness', suggests Conrad, 'is the degree of independence it affords. This is a quality to be prized in the later years of life. There is a great psychologic and financial advantage in having the ability to plan and do things without depending on relatives, friends or other help. To drive your own car, to succeed with do-it-yourself projects rather than trying to find and to pay someone else for the service, and to go and come as you please in terms of physical ability to do so these are major assets that we believe regular physical exercise can help achieve.'

Begin gradually

Don't expect to jump into a vigorous exercise programme. Start slowly. Warm up. Old hearts especially need to be worked slowly at first. Each day do just a little more. Start with modified calisthenics, then add one more step each time you exercise. The only competition is with yourself, progressively improving strength, flexibility and endurance.

For the more strenuous programmes see your doctor first. Even when older people have been shown to have no medical symptoms, 30 per cent are found to develop problems during overly vigorous exercise.

Older people are just as trainable as younger ones, says Herbert A. de Vries director of the exercise physiology laboratory at the Andrus Gerontology Center in California. They can become active even if they have never been in good shape or previously active in their lives. 'We were all amazed at how well older men and women swam after six months of instruction in an experimental programme. Some 80-year-olds could swim 20 to 30 widths of the pool. That is better than many college kids can do.'

Swimming uses all our muscles and promotes good breathing. It is excellent for those with arthritis and paralyzed people, for they can often move more freely and do movements in the water that they cannot do elsewhere.

You needn't be a runner to grow young and quick through exercise. 'A good brisk walk will do the trick for the vast majority of people,' says Henry J. Ralston of the department of anatomy at the University of California (San Francisco) Medical Center. The important step, the 'biggest change', according to William L. Haskell, assistant professor of cardiology at Stanford University School of Medicine, 'is to get the people who are doing nothing to do something.' Brisk walks, running, stair climbing, cycling, gardening and home repairs are some activities he suggests.

Light physical exercise such as leisure-time walking, cycling or gardening is particularly good for the heart. A study by Dutch scientists involving the population of four communities concluded that those forms of exercise practised for at least half an hour a day, can have as beneficial an effect in preventing heart attacks as more vigorous and more frequent exercise. The really high-risk group were people who sat around all day, at the office or at home, moving about for no more than two hours a day.

The researchers warned, however, that interrupting a programme of regular light exercise for even a few weeks can undo its good effects. For example, the resumption of exercise in the spring after a winter break may, they suggest account for the 'spring peak' in heart attacks. 'A person's physical fitness achieved by regular exercise, is lost within a few weeks of ceasing the physical activity,' they pointed out. 'Those who find and take the opportunity to walk, cycle or work in the garden all year-round are probably far better off' (*American Journal of Epidemiology*, December 1979).

People often think it's their due to be able to slow down and have others wait on them. Sure it's fun to be pampered, but you can be pampered to death. Even many of our labour-saving devices are doing just that! With many power tools, we are losing much of our forced activity. Many flats have no gardens to dig in or repairs to be made. A steady programme of exercise is the only answer.

It has been proven that active people lead much better lives. Body rebuilding must constantly go on. The building materials are a sensible diet with regular physical and mental activity. To quote Don S. Wenger, former president of the [US] National Association for Human Development: 'Use the brain, use the body, use the life, don't lose it!'

Life gets better as we get older

Grandma Moses painted her first picture when she was 78 years old. The biblical matriarch Sarah started her family after she turned 90.

Not everyone has the talent to be an artist or the inclination to be a mother later in life, but we do all have one thing in common: in many ways the years we have to look forward to can be better than the ones we have passed. Studies have shown that IQs often go up and stress goes down; we may become more secure both emotionally and socially; we are also less susceptible to certain illnesses.

As our age goes up, so does our confidence and capacity for concentration – two reasons why we often make better students when we are long past what is traditionally considered college or university age. 'Older people make excellent students, maybe even better students than the majority of 19- and 20-year-olds,' says gerontologist Barbara Ober. 'One advantage is that they have settled a lot of the social and sexual issues that preoccupy their younger classmates. They aren't in school for a party or because their parents forced them to go. They are more serious in their studies and they cut classes less often.'

Dr Ober speaks from experience. Not only is she a college teacher, serving as assistant professor of sociology at Shippensburg State College in Pennsylvania, but not long ago, she, too, was a member of that group she calls 'non-traditional students', receiving her doctorate after she had celebrated her 50th birthday.

Increased insight and intelligence

Exploding the cliché about old dogs being unable to learn new tricks Thomas Dolgoff thinks the opposite is often true.

Although age doesn't necessarily bring wisdom, the breadth of experience that comes only with age increases a person's insight, according to Dolgoff who at age 70 is a management and organizational consultant at the Center for Applied Behavioral Science of the Menninger Foundation in Topeka, Kansas. 'When you can relate a new concept to a fact you already know, you are better equipped to grasp that concept and to retain it,' explains Dolgoff. 'There are ways in which a person's memory actually improves with age.'

Empathy is another advantage that older people have, particularly when studying the social sciences. Psychology is a tool they have honed consciously or unconsciously, through longer dealings with greater numbers of people. Related subjects such as anthropology and sociology become easier to grasp.

Sometimes, a person's actual intelligence measurably increases with age. In studies directed by Ewald W. Busse, dean of the medical school at Duke University in Durham, North Carolina, some people's IQs rose along with their years. Speaking at a regional meeting of the American College of Physicians Dr Busse noted that the people who grew cleverer all had one thing in common: a willingness to explore new worlds. Whether they did their exploring through direct participation or through reading made little difference.

Increased adaptability and sensitivity

'The truth is that people actually grow more tolerant, more open-minded and more objective in their thinking as they grow older,' comments Dolgoff. 'That makes them more adaptable.'

And, thanks to your increased adaptability, the best time to move is also when you are older, according to studies conducted at Purdue University. According to Professor Marjorie A. Inman, of Purdue's department of consumer sciences and retailing, 'In general, fewer psychological stress factors are present, and older people adapt more easily to their environment.' Her report concluded that whether they relocate or not, life improves for most people as they grow older.

Love improves, too.

'Once you've made all the mistakes, you aren't likely to repeat them,' says Harold Rosenberg, a New York family practitioner and stress therapist. Among his patients, he says, there are several octogenarian newlyweds, 'but that doesn't mean you have to get a new partner to enjoy true love. Growing together in a relationship gives a fuller, deeper sense of love. You have better understanding, of the other person and of yourself.' Even your sex life can improve because you are putting less emphasis on the superficially physical.

Relaxation and introspection are typically allied in meditation. 'Meditation is also something you do better when you are older,' says psychologist Gay Gaer Luce, noting that religious leaders are usually quite old. 'As people grow older, they become more intuitive, sensitive and psychic. This is one reason why older people are often more religious. It is also why they can be more creative.'

Dr Luce is one of the founders of SAGE, the Senior Actualization and Growth Explorations group located in San Francisco. She recalls how a heightened capacity for intuition helped one 80-year-old artist in her painting. 'Much of that has to do with an inner-directedness that comes with age, when we pay greater attention to seeking inner satisfaction. This isn't selfishness, by any means. Because they refuse to seek endorsement and approval by a youth-oriented society, older artists will finally paint what pleases them,' Dr Luce explains, 'and it is only through this kind of labour of love that we can ever produce a masterpiece.'

A better sense of health

Dr Luce also observes that this same inner-directedness gives older people a better idea of their health. 'We grow more in tune with our bodies because we filter out distractions. Earlier in life, we are so focused outward, we tend to ignore our internal body. We concentrate too much on how it looks. We don't "hear" the signs.'

'As we get older, we are more aware of the difference a change in diet makes,' says Dr Martin Feldman of New York City. 'The hydrochloric acid in our stomachs diminishes, and we have to watch what we eat, but that can be a blessing in disguise if it helps us to eat the right things.'

Other bodily changes mean we can get by with less sleep as we age, and changes in our endocrine systems free us from acne and other skin problems. Some people also enjoy fewer allergies, notes Michael E. Aronoff, an ear-nose-throat specialist in Olathe, Kansas. Older people also benefit from freer breathing, thanks to the fact that tonsils and adenoids disappear.

'There are different functions for the different ages of life,' concludes Dr Luce. 'We can look forward to a period of internal compensation and spiritual growth that can make the later years of life the most satisfying.'

• Alcoholism

Alcoholism is one of the most common chronic diseases in the United Kingdom. While its staggering financial costs – in terms of medical care, lost work days and car accidents – can be estimated, its toll in human misery is incalculable.

Traditional therapy for alcoholism generally follows a multi-stage pattern. The first stage is detoxification, when an alcoholic goes 'cold turkey', for a week, sometimes with the help of tranquillizers. The next step often includes encounter sessions and lectures. The third step, when the person goes home calls for regular attendance at Alcoholics Anonymous meetings. The treatment's customary goal is to heal the alcoholic's psyche and spirit. It's hoped that he or she will discover the emotional and psychological roots of the addiction and 'talk them out'.

Those methods have saved many alcoholics from a miserable life and a premature death, but as valuable as such techniques may be in individual cases, their overall performance record has not been outstanding. They haven't put a dent in these statistics: more than 50 per cent of all dried-out alcoholics eventually go back to drinking; 20 per cent of all traffic fatalities are linked to alcohol (approximately 2000 a year); 25 per cent of all hospital beds are filled by people with alcohol-related illnesses. In all the public pays about £2 billion a year in terms of medical care and lost productivity as a result of alcoholism.

A different approach

This rate of failure has motivated a lot of people in the alcoholism treatment field to look for more effective therapies. Although they're still very much in the minority, there are a growing number of doctors and others who say that more attention should be paid to the *physical* disease of alcoholism. They agree that emotional problems have to be faced but, they argue, the alcoholic, in order to recover, must also discover the underlying biochemical factors that created the disease, and treat them. They maintain that the alcoholic who undergoes a radical nutritional overhaul – a switch from sugar cigarettes and coffee to whole grains, fresh produce and vitamin supplements – has a much better chance of staying permanently dried out than one who doesn't.

One member of this new and vocal minority is Joan Mathews-Larson, a certified chemical-dependency practitioner and director of the Health Recovery Center, a state-licensed clinic for alcoholics in Minneapolis. Motivated by the suicide of her alcoholic son, she decided to pursue a doctorate in nutrition and to open a treatment centre where alcoholism would be treated by restoring the body's normal biochemical balance through diet and supplements as well as by psychological counselling. She knows she is a maverick, but she believes her programme works.

'Only a small percentage of the alcohol treatment centres in the United States use the nutritional approach,' she told us. Much of the field still treats alcoholism as a psychological disorder. And most members of Alcoholics Anonymous don't even know that there's a physical and nutritional approach. 'But people recover very nicely here without confessing their sins in group therapy sessions and without being made to feel ashamed of their disease. What we're doing is much more basic to their recovery. You wouldn't put a diabetic in group therapy and expect him to "talk" out his disease. Yet this is what many people expect alcoholics to do.'

Alcoholism, for Ms Mathews-Larson, is an inherited physical disorder that has severe psychological complications. She says that alcoholics have a peculiar genetic defect that causes their bodies to metabolize alcohol into a highly addictive, morphine-like substance called *tetrahydro-isoquinoline*, or THIQ, and most alcoholics also develop hypoglycaemia, or low blood sugar. They crave alcohol and sugar in any form, but both substances put them on a physical and emotional roller coaster that only more of the same can bring to a temporary halt. Certain food and chemical allergies, she says can also cause craving for alcohol.

She believes this vicious cycle can be broken. When alcoholics first enter her six-week programme, she sends them through a battery of tests. For example she has their hair analysed for nutrient deficiencies and toxic metal buildup. She orders blood-sugar tests for hypoglycaemia. She puts them on a fast to unmask potential food allergies and has a staff doctor check for hidden physical and psychiatric problems.

Then come the vitamins. Recovering alcoholics need replacement of the B vitamins, plus plenty of vitamin C and certain amino acids, she says. To stay in her programme, they must also kick their coffee, tobacco, white flour and sugar habits. While most alcoholism counsellors say that their patients need those crutches in order to cope with withdrawal, Ms Mathews-Larson believes that they just delay recovery.

James A. was one of Ms Mathews-Larson's clients. With the aid of emotional counselling, he has been sober ever since going through her programme last year. He has only good things to say about it. 'I remember the first group meeting I went to there,' he said. 'I heard people saying that alcoholism was a biochemical problem, not a mental problem. And I thought, "Maybe it's just a problem in my biochemistry. Maybe I'm not going crazy." After the programme, I felt like I was on a fairly even keel for the first time in my life. People who knew me couldn't believe it.'

Other patients at the Health Recovery Center have had similar success. Mary W., a 27-year-old mother of two boys, was one of them. 'Both of my parents were alcoholics, and I started drinking when I was 14,' she told us. 'I was always very depressed, and when I started drinking, it made me feel good. I could hold my liquor better than anybody, but I was still always tired and unhappy.'

Mary went to the Health Recovery Center when she was planning her second pregnancy. She had been drinking and using drugs during her first pregnancy and her son grew more slowly than normal. He later became hyperactive and suffered from multiple allergies. With her second child, she wanted to avoid making that mistake again. Having known Joan from a prior attempt to dry out she went to see her.

She found out that hidden food allergies may have made her depressed and added momentum to her alcohol abuse. 'I found out that I was allergic to beef wheat and dairy products,' she said. She also learned a lot about healthy food. 'In group therapy, we didn't talk about what was wrong with our marriages. We talked about good places to buy wholesome food and ways to cook it. We found out what to have for breakfast and what to snack on during the day. And one of the workers took us on a tour of natural food co-ops.'

Two years after going through the programme, Mary says she is happier than she has ever been. 'I wake up feeling good, and I feel good all day. And my second baby was much bigger and stronger than the first.'

Sugar and caffeine

Some nutritionally oriented alcoholism therapists zero in on their clients' sugar addiction. 'The sugar craving in sober alcoholics is very striking,' says Kenneth Williams of the University of Pittsburgh School of Medicine. Dr Williams has observed the sugar addiction phenomenon in his own patients who are recovering alcoholics or drug abusers. Sugar seems to hold as strong a power over them as alcohol, and he attributes this to hypoglycaemia, a disturbance of sugar metabolism that affects mood and behaviour.

'Most sober alcoholics are hypoglycaemics, which may explain their intense cravings for substances like sugar and caffeine,' says Dr Williams, who has been researching the relationship between hypoglycaemia and alcoholism. He believes that many recovering alcoholics must avoid sugar and caffeine. However, 'hypoglycaemia is one of the most controversial areas of medicine,' he says. 'Many doctors think that the hypoglycaemia theory is quackery, and frankly, if you had asked me about it a few years ago, I would have agreed with them.' His opinions changed as he began working with his patients. He saw not only how alcohol and drugs created havoc in a patients' system but how sugar and caffeine could have similar disturbing effects. Those observations eventually led him to take a more serious look at hypoglycaemia, and he now tests both sober alcoholic and drug-abuse patients using a new method to determine if they have the condition. This measures moment-to-moment changes in the patient's mood during a glucose tolerance test (GTT).

While the presence of the disorder might explain the alcoholic's intense cravings for sugar or alcohol, a lot of questions remain unanswered. For example, researchers in the field still do not know whether hypoglycaemia is a result of a person's drinking or a cause. 'Several of my sober alcoholic patients have told me that they had hypoglycaemia diagnosed before they even started drinking,' says Dr Williams. 'And mothers come in and tell me that they think they can tell which one of their children is going to be an alcoholic. They'll say that the kid is a real sugar addict and is hyperactive. We'll bring the kid in for a GTT, and sure enough, he's hypoglycaemic. It may be that one type of hypoglycaemia leads to drinking while another does not. We really don't know yet.'

One thing researchers *have* apparently determined is that a person is at a higher risk of becoming an alcoholic if the immediate members of his family are alcoholics. 'It may be a metabolic problem – an unusual way of metabolizing carbohydrates – or something that is passed on genetically,' says Dr Williams.

In addition to avoiding sugary foods, Dr Williams says, avoiding caffeine is important for recovery from alcoholism. 'A family of a recovering alcoholic will often report a "dry drunk" syndrome in which the sober alcoholic acts as if he were drinking even though he hasn't touched a drop. He may show signs of an agitated depression migraine headaches and panic attacks. He also may have very intense cravings for sugar and caffeine. One of my patients drank 70 cups of coffee a day and experienced those symptoms. He cut back on his caffeine intake, changed his eating habits and started taking supplements. It made a big difference in his symptoms.'

It may sound like a simple enough regimen to follow, but if alcohol is that closely linked to sugar and caffeine consumption, it's not going to be any picnic for an alcoholic to scratch those two substances off the menu either. 'My patients find it very difficult to stay off sugar. One woman did her best to avoid it, but finally she hopped into her car one night and drove until she found a bakery. She went inside and proceeded to eat two dozen jam doughnuts. 'Another woman who walks in her sleep told me she went into the kitchen one morning and discovered she had eaten an entire two-layer chocolate cake with mocha icing.'

Dr Williams says that the similarities between sugar and alcohol are very striking. Both are carbohydrates devoid of nutrients other than calories, and they are the only two substances absorbed directly into the bloodstream from the stomach. Both substances can cause memory blackouts and intense cravings in people addicted to them. Once people start consuming them, they also can lose control of the situation even to the point of hiding their sweets or bottles and lying about their intake. A lot of us may not personally know what an alcoholic binge is really like, but most of us at one time or another have gone on a 'sweets binge'.

One might think that the hypoglycaemia theory would be of some interest to the organization designed to help alcoholics cure their disorder. But while the theory is not all that new, interest remains cool.

Dr Williams is on the US national board of trustees of Alcoholics Anonymous: 'If you go to an AA meeting, one of the first things you notice is the fact that black coffee doughnuts, cookies and candy are on the refreshments table. 'Those are the very things my research has found to be harmful to some recovering alcoholics.'

'AA members are not really budding examples of good nutrition. Nutrition is considered an outside issue,' says one AA member in New York City who has belonged to the organization for the past 11 years. 'We're told to eat sundaes, candy, anything with sugar in it, if it will satisfy our cravings. During the first 90 days, we say deal with your alcohol problem in any way that you can. If that means drinking coffee and eating sugar, then do it. I ate ice cream every night for a whole year when I quit, but I don't have to do that now.'

Although AA has chosen to leave a physical approach to alcoholism to the medical profession, Dr Williams says that the earliest beginnings of Alcoholics Anonymous were tied to hypoglycaemia. 'Bill Wilson and Dr Bob Smith were the original founders of Alcoholics Anonymous in 1935,' he explains. 'A few years later, Mr Wilson discovered that he was hypoglycaemic. He consumed large amounts of caffeine and sugar and suffered depressions and other hypoglycaemic symptoms. He finally found help by changing his diet.'

A social approach

Perhaps the most unique approach to alcoholic treatment is the 'Unbar' in Cleveland, Ohio, a service of the West Side Community Mental Health Center. It combines an anti-hypoglycaemia diet with a social approach to the problem.

Its directors have set up a private 'bar' for recovering alcoholics and family members of alcoholics. 'The majority of alcoholics in our area have spent nearly a lifetime in a tavern setting,' says Wayne Lindstrom, the Unbar director. 'The tavern was a place to do everything from celebrate to grieve.' So the Unbar was established as a combination social centre and alcoholism treatment programme. Upstairs are the counselling offices and downstairs is the bar – complete with jukebox, colour TV, pool table and pinball machines.

'Since there is strong evidence that recovering alcoholics experience hypoglycaemia, we have served only fruit juices and decaffeinated coffee. There are no cigarette machines and no candy bars. We serve popcorn sandwiches and peanuts,' says Lindstrom. 'We don't serve any exotic concoctions because this is pretty much a blue-collar clientele. When they were drinking alcohol, they weren't drinking anything fancy, and they don't want anything fancy now. We hope to introduce milk shakes like banana or yogurt in the future, but that's about it.'

That decision will be up to the membership council, a group of Unbar members who have the final say over most of what goes on in the social centre; for example, the council decides on how the dues are spent. While Lindstrom thinks the Unbar's self-governing policy is a good idea, he has observed the drawbacks of democracy. 'The council recently voted to bring in soft drinks. I tried to state my position as best I could, but the final decision was left up to them.' While the other refreshments will stay, the decision for soft drinks needles Lindstrom. Yet he well understands how hard it is to break old habits.

'I think the members probably believe the hypoglycaemia argument, but we're really going against a whole lifetime of conditioning with them. There are probably 300 taverns in this part of Cleveland alone. Many of our members are out of work, have limited incomes and are used to diets that are high in carbohydrates and sweets. They have already had to give up drinking. When you ask them to give up sugar, coffee and smoking, it's a little too much to handle.'

Lindstrom isn't discouraged, however, and continues to lecture on the importance of following a high-protein, low-carbohydrate diet. 'A definite minority of the members have made the changes,' he says, 'and they do feel better.'

Dr Williams agrees that the sober alcoholic really has to work at overcoming his cravings for other potentially harmful habits. He urges his patients to substitute protein for sugar. 'If the person does not feel satisfied, he should wait a little bit or eat something more, but he should try to avoid reaching for sugar.' If the patient continues to avoid sugar, his craving for it will eventually diminish. His craving for alcohol should do the same.

Adding vitamins and glutamic acid

One indispensable nutritional tool in the Health Recovery treatment regimen is glutamic acid, a little-known amino acid. Twenty-five years ago nutrition pioneer Roger J. Williams, of the University of Texas began recommending this amino acid to alcoholics, which, he said, could allay the unendurable craving that causes so many alcoholics to backslide. Ms Mathews-Larson agrees: 'We've found that glutamic acid does everything that Dr Williams says it does.'

The B vitamins can also reduce the craving for alcohol, Dr Williams believes. That alcoholism can cause B vitamin deficiencies, most experts in the field agree, but Dr Williams reversed that formula and took the unorthodox position that a deficiency of the B vitamins can cause excessive drinking. He may be right. Experiments in Finland in 1977 showed that rats made deficient in B vitamins are more likely to choose alcohol than water when both are offered to them. Supplementation reversed their tastes (*British Journal of Addiction*).

Many doctors share Ms Mathews-Larson's views. One of them is Harry K. Panjwani, a New Jersey psychiatrist and former member of the advisory committee of the National (US) Council on Alcoholism. He says that, by mixing vitamins and psychotherapy, he has helped many alcoholics turn their lives around within a few months.

Dr Panjwani puts each new patient on a regimen of glutamic acid niacinamide (a B vitamin) and vitamin C – at least 500 mg of each per day. He believes that alcoholics who regain their health via good nutrition are much better at working out the problems that gave rise to their addiction. Just taking drink away and leaving a person with addictions to cigarettes, coffee and sugar isn't enough, he says: 'That's treating the disease, not the whole person.'

Nutrition is also stressed in a new programme at an alcoholism rehabilitation clinic at the Brunswick Hospital Center in Amityville, New York. Joseph Beasley, who directs rehabilitation at the 86-bed facility, told us that his patients are asked to give up sugar, cut back on refined food and begin a multivitamin programme after rigorous individualized diagnoses. They're also encouraged to use the clinic's paddleball courts and Nautilus machines. 'We feel that this, along with traditional therapies, is where alcoholism treatment is now,' Dr Beasley says.

In California, Jerzy Meduski, a professor at the University of Southern California and a member of the Task Force for Nutrition and Behavior in Los Angeles County, also believes in giving vitamins and glutamic acid to recovering alcoholics. In one study, he supplemented the diets of 100 alcoholic prison inmates for two years and achieved great results. 'The craving for alcohol seems to be the effect of an imbalance in nutrition. That is almost always the case,' Dr Meduski says. 'There is no doubt that there is a positive response to nutritional supplementation.'

Yet another nutrition-minded alcoholism counsellor is Mark Worden, former editor of *Alcoholism: The National Magazine*. 'Does a poor diet increase the chances that an alcoholic will go back to drinking?' Worden asks rhetorically. 'You can say that, if an alcoholic's body is well prepared for stress by good nutrition and a healthy lifestyle, then the likelihood for him or her going back to his or her old way of dealing with stress – alcohol – is probably less.'

Staying on the wagon

Is the nutritional approach, then, the most effective form of treatment? The only way to find out would be to compare recovery rates. The programme that kept the most alcoholics dry for the longest amount of time would emerge the winner. However, such data is hard to come by: it's just too impractical to keep tabs on a large group of people for several months or years. But the few figures that are available on this subject lend credence to the nutritional approach.

For instance, Ms Mathews-Larson claims that one year after leaving her programme, about 82 per cent of her patients are still sober. Those results are far better, she says, than the numbers published by the (US) National Institute on Alcohol Abuse and Alcoholism. The NIAAA's figures show that only 15 to 20 per cent of all treated alcoholics stay dry for as long as two years.

A nutritionist at the Elmhurst Alcoholism Program in New York City also came up with pro-nutrition figures. Lillian Yung studied a group of 64 alcoholics to see whether the ones who stayed sober the longest ate differently than those who quickly went back to the bottle. The results surprised her. She found that 45 per cent of the alcoholics who stayed sober for more than 50 days after leaving treatment were taking vitamin supplements but only 19 per cent of those who couldn't stay sober for 50 days used supplements. Those figures hinted that vitamins can indeed help.

'The failure rate for conventional alcoholism treatment is in the upper 80th or even 90th percentile,' Dr Yung told us. 'There have been reports that much of the counselling and group therapy that alcoholics get has no effect on how long they stay sober. That encouraged me to look at the problem from a nutritional standpoint.'

A study done in Texas adds more evidence to the nutrition theory. At a Veterans Hospital Medical Center in Waco, Ruth Guenther looked at the effects of nutrition on a group of hard-core alcoholics, men who had been drinking, on the average, the equivalent of 13 oz of alcohol a day for the previous 15 to 20 years. She discovered that alcoholics who ate well could stay sober longer.

The men were studied in two groups. Dr Guenther asked the first group to stay on the standard hospital diet, and asked the second group to switch to a special diet plan that she had prepared. This experimental diet included foods such as wheat germ, bran, decaffeinated coffee and unsweetened fruit in conjunction with the regular hospital diet. She also asked the second group to swear off all snacks except for the nuts, cheese, peanut butter and milk that she provided. Finally, she asked them to keep taking a multivitamin supplement for six months after their release from the clinic.

The results were gratifying. When interviewed, the alcoholics on the special diet told Dr Guenther that they felt 'calmer and more relaxed'. More important, their recovery rate was very high. Six months after they went home 81 per cent of the vitamin group were still sober; by comparison, only 38 per cent of the control group had not taken a drink (*International Journal of Biosocial Research*, January 1983).

That satisfied Dr Guenther, and her conclusion echoes the sentiments of Ms Mathews-Larson and the others: 'A combination of psychotherapy and nutritional therapy may be more successful than conventional treatment for achieving long-term recovery from alcoholism.'

The befuddling of the earth

Alcoholism is only one of a host of problems associated with the excessive use of alcohol. Some countries report that 50 per cent of their crime is alcohol-related. In addition to its massive contribution to traffic accidents, excessive drinking is a factor in many home and industrial accidents. Absenteeism and low productivity have also been shown to be related to the abuse of alcohol. Besides the public health significance of these examples of alcohol-related problems, there are the adverse health effects of heavy drinking – such as increased prevalence of cirrhosis, pancreatitis and certain forms of heart disease and cancer, and lowered resistance to infection. It has also been shown that excessive drinking by pregnant women is associated with retarded development of the unborn child, and that people with serious drinking problems have a suicide rate of up to 80 times that of the general population.

What is profoundly disturbing is the disproportionate increase in the world consumption of alcohol. World statistics of recorded production show that in the years 1960 to 1972, the quantities of wine produced increased by 20 per cent, of distilled beverages by 60 per cent, and of beer by 80 per cent. In 25 countries with fairly complete statistics, annual per capita consumption of alcohol increased by a proportion ranging from one-third to five times.

Taken together, the medical, psychiatric and social costs of drinking are a heavy economic burden in an increasing number of countries. For example, it has been calculated that the annual cost may be as much as £50 billion in Western countries (1984 data), and there is no reason to believe that such massive costs are incurred only in the developed world. On the contrary, it appears that developing countries may be particularly vulnerable to alcohol-related problems. The extent and seriousness of these are only now beginning to be realized, and there is a real danger that if appropriate action is not taken, these problems will constitute a serious obstacle to the socio-economic development of those countries and a severe burden on their available health services.

In Brazil, first admissions to hospitals with a diagnosis of alcoholism tripled between 1960 and 1970. In Chile, 30 per cent of the budget for medical and psychiatric services is spent on medical care of alcoholism and its consequences. In Yugoslavia, 50 per cent of all male admissions to psychiatric hospitals in 1973 had alcoholism as their first diagnosis. Cirrhosis death rates in Anchorage, Alaska increased by 142 per cent between 1959 and 1975. In most countries for which valid data can be obtained, cirrhosis now ranks among the five leading causes of death in the 25-to-64-years age group.

In many countries, individuals are subjected to new demands and stresses at a time when old forms of family and community support are diminishing. Drinking often becomes a symbol of prestige and success, as well as a ready tranquillizer. Young people, alienated from traditional values, are often at particular risk, as are women, who may be exposed for the first time to the possibility of drinking.

Evidence accumulated over recent years points to an established and close relationship between a country's per capita alcohol consumption and its experience of alcohol-related problems. While this might seem to be no more than the scientific substantiation of commonsense experience, it runs counter to traditional thinking that has seen alcoholism as something innate in the individual rather than as a problem related to the degree of exposure to drinking. It is also an association that indicates the possibility of prevention, since it suggests that *any reduction in per capita consumption will be attended by a significant decrease in alcohol-related problems*.

This relationship is dramatically demonstrated by mortality statistics collected in France between 1907 and 1956. These reveal a rapid decline in cirrhosis mortality rates at times of severe restriction on the availability of alcoholic beverages during the two world wars, and an equally rapid increase when alcohol again became available. For France as a whole, the decline in cirrhosis mortality among middle-aged males was of the order of 50 per cent, while in Paris, where there was less possibility of circumventing the rationing system, the decline was more than 80 per cent.

Of greatest significance, perhaps, is the evidence that simple advice, if given by a credible source, can be as effective as prolonged and intensive therapy in reducing the problems associated with drinking. The possibility of dealing with problems related to alcohol use thus comes within the province of different types of health workers.

The fact that seemingly simple interventions can be as effective as more intensive regimens means that the treatment of alcohol-related problems can be undertaken in countries lacking specialized medical services. It also suggests that it is not the exclusive province of the health services. Traditional healers and acknowledged community leaders become potential therapeutic allies if their influence is tempered by a knowledge of the ways in which alcohol-related problems manifest themselves. (*See also* NIGHT BLINDNESS)

• Allergy

Your Aunt Ethel eats strawberries and her eyes itch. Your son John gets diarrhoea from shellfish. And if your next-door neighbour even *sniffs* cooked cabbage, she breaks out in a rash.

Food allergy. Everybody is familiar with the *acute* kind, when eyes water or a rash pops out minutes after you eat the guilty food. But someone who sits down every morning to a breakfast of eggs, toast and coffee may have a *chronic* food allergy – to eggs, toast and coffee.

Sounds odd? It's not. Chronic food allergy isn't a strange medical sub-speciality whose cases turn up once a decade. Some experts estimate that *60 per cent* of the people at doctors' surgeries have symptoms either caused or complicated by chronic food allergy. One allergist even makes this bold assertion: 'Food allergy is one of the leading causes of illness in Westernized society.' So why isn't there a doctor in town who knows about it?

First, doctors aren't trained to recognize chronic food allergy. Second it's a hidden disease – hidden even from the person who has it. Say you're allergic to wheat. All you know is that you're tired most of the time. Or headachy. Or depressed. Or nervous. Or your muscles ache. You don't know that wheat is causing these problems. And you don't know that you're actually *addicted* to wheat – an addiction every bit as real as an addiction to alcohol or drugs. It's a *food* addiction that is slowly destroying your health.

Food addiction – that's what a chronic food allergy really is. And since an addiction to food is basically like an addiction to anything else, we can understand it by looking at one of the most common addictions – to cigarettes.

The first time you smoked a cigarette (if there was a first time), you didn't enjoy it. Unlike the happy smokers in ads, you felt awful – dizzy and sick. That was the first time. If you kept at it, the second time was a little easier, and the tenth time a snap. What happened was that your body *adapted* to the poisons in cigarette smoke, a reaction scientists call the 'specific adaptation response'. But adaptation leads to addiction.

The 'lift' smokers get from cigarettes is caused by the specific adaptation response, the body going into overdrive to deal with the poison. As the hours pass, the adaptation stops; however, so does the 'lift'. And smokers are dropped into nervousness, depression or headache – the withdrawal symptoms of a cigarette addict. They begin to have an instinctive, driving urge to feel good again – the craving for a cigarette. They are hooked. And food addiction can hook you the same way.

Remember that food addiction is an allergy. Your big brother may have dared you to smoke that first cigarette, but nobody really knows why some people become allergic and others don't. (Heredity is a popular theory.) In any case those who become allergic usually develop allergies to the substance they're exposed to most, such as pollen and dust. And sugar. And wheat. And eggs. The foods that, alone or as ingredients, most people eat every day, perhaps many times a day. When people are allergic to pollen, their noses clog. But when people are allergic to a food, their bodies may cope with the allergy by gearing up a specific adaptation response.

Soon, they crave the lift they get from the foods they are allergic to. If they don't eat those foods, they begin to have withdrawal symptoms. (For instance, do you wake up in the morning feeling grouchy or with a headache and do these symptoms stop with breakfast? If so, you could very well be a food addict). So they eat. And eat. And eat. Most likely, they don't even know they are addicted. They only know that they feel good after eating their 'favourite' foods. But specific adaptation can't last for ever. A panic button, it can be pushed only so often – then it breaks down. Scientists call this stage 'exhaustion', and during exhaustion, the allergy surfaces in full force.

Food allergies have a target organ (i.e. a specific part of the body that they attack), which varies from person to person. Wheat, for example, may damage the digestive tract in one person; in someone else, it might affect the heart muscles or brain. As long as adaptive responses work, you never notice the steady erosion of health, but when these wear out, you finally become aware of a problem that's been going on for months or years.

'Only when one or more of specific adaptive responses taper off and the stage of exhaustion is approached does he [the person with food addiction] start to complain – a change ordinarily regarded by all concerned as the onset of the present illness,' wrote Theron G. Randolph, a Chicago doctor and expert on food addiction, in his book *Human Ecology and Susceptibility to the Chemical Environment.*

When the target is the brain

And when the food addict starts to complain, it may be about *emotional* difficulties.

The brain, as we mentioned, is often a target organ for food allergies. 'If the part of the brain affected is one that controls certain behaviour patterns, this allergic irritation will produce recognizable mental or behaviour changes,' says British psychiatrist Richard Mackarness in his book *Not All in the Mind.* And these 'mental changes' aren't for the better.

In his book *Food Allergy*, Dr Frederic Speer includes a list of emotional problems that have been caused by food addiction:

> Increase in temper; screaming attacks; patient is mean or sulky irritable, whining, impatient, quarrelsome, sensitive, easily hurt, unhappy morbid, depressed, restless, tense, nervous, jumpy, fearful, anxious irresponsible, erratic, uncooperative, unpredictable, pugnacious, or cruel; can't be pleased; is not open to reason; cries without cause; worries, feels terrible, contemplates suicide; is nervous and high strung; chews clothes and bedclothes; has nightmares; loses pride in work, in clothing and in cleanliness; doesn't care; can't make decisions; loses interest in the opposite sex; has childish compulsions.

You'd be hard pressed to think of a negative emotional response that isn't on the list. 'Food addiction is like that,' says William Philpott, an American specialist in food allergy. 'It can cause any type of emotional problem. But usually a food addiction causes either a heightened or a lessened response. A person becomes either manic or depressed, wildly excited or totally apathetic.'

The reason for these ups and downs, Dr Philpott told us, is that a food addiction abnormally increases or decreases the amount of neuro-transmitters in the brain, the chemicals responsible for determining most behaviour. Food addiction also causes emotional upset by swelling brain tissues, which irritate sensitive nerves. (This type of swelling, says Dr Philpott, is responsible for 69 per cent of all headaches!)

Aggressive or allergic?

Dr Barbara Solomon, another American food allergy specialist, told us a case history of a young man whose severe mood swings were caused by food sensitivity.

'A 17-year-old boy came into my office with many of the signs of a chronic food allergy: blotchy skin, swollen eyes, red nose. I tested him for 200 foods, and found that he was allergic to 70. This boy had been going to a psychiatrist for six years, and had been labelled an "aggressive personality". He told me himself that he was a "Dr Jekyll and Mr Hyde type" and that he would suddenly feel violent and cruel. Well, after he stopped eating the foods he was allergic to, he simply lost that "agressive personality" and was discharged by his psychiatrist.

'One day, however, he ate squash [a type of marrow], a food he is allergic to. Well, he went right down to the police station in his town, planted himself at the front desk and irrationally began "demanding his rights". They told him to beat it. But he was back every day for the next three days. You see, it takes four days for a food to leave the system. After four days, he was back to normal.'

Not everyone with a food addiction behaves that strangely. Anxiety nervousness, apathy – common emotional problems – can be caused by a food addiction. But how can you tell if your tendency to loaf on the job is caused by a loaf of bread?

One way to tell if you have a food addiction, says Dr Philpott, is to deliberately skip a meal. If, after a few hours, you begin to feel bad – not just hungry but *very* irritable, tense, headachy or nauseated – chances are that you're addicted to a food and have begun to experience withdrawal symptoms. Another sign of food addiction, he says, is being overweight.

How can you begin to correct the problem? One step is to increase your intake of nutritional supplements.

Food addiction can lead to a deficiency of vitamin A, says Dr Philpott which causes the mucous membranes to over-react and clog the respiratory tract. It can also lead to a deficiency of the B complex vitamins, particularly B_6, and of vitamin C. A lack of these vitamins, he says, 'produces unhealthy brain function'.

Dr Philpott believes that 80 per cent of all Americans have a food addiction, and that the same number probably have sub-optimal levels of vitamins B_6 and C. He suggests that people with a food addiction should supplement their diets with 'supernutritional' levels of these vitamins. But over and above nutritional supplementation, he believes that eating a highly varied diet goes a long way towards either the cure or prevention of food addiction. And, if possible, the foods you eat should be organically grown.

Hidden chemicals

Many people aren't allergic to food. They're allergic to chemicals – one or more of the thousands that find their way into the food supply. You could, wrote Dr Randolph, be allergic to:

> foods containing insecticide spray residues, fumigant residues, certain chemical preservatives, sulfur residues, colored chemical flavoring or sweetening agents; foods stored in plastic containers or canned in lined tins; the fats of commercially available beef, lamb, some chicken and other fowl.

In addition, he condemns food that has been standing in or cooked in chlorinated water.

'After a person becomes allergic to one substance, the allergy usually spreads to other foods and to chemicals in the environment,' explains Dr Philpott. He told us a story of a woman who was addicted to her *lipstick*: 'When she became tense during the day, she would automatically put on a fresh coat of lipstick and feel relieved. She never gave the phenomenon a second thought, and until she came to our clinic, she never realized the connection.'

Chronic food and chemical allergies cause many problems besides emotional upset. Dr Solomon, who tests all her patients for food allergies, has found they often are associated with ulcerative colitis, colic, migraine headaches sinusitis, psoriasis, acne, asthma, arthritis and other conditions. Because chronic food and chemical allergies can cause serious illness and because allergic patterns are highly individual, Dr Solomon and all the other experts we talked to advise anyone who suspects a chronic food allergy to see a doctor who can competently diagnose and treat the problem.

For more information on allergy, see ASTHMA, HAY FEVER, SINUSITUS.

• Alzheimer's disease

In Alzheimer's disease – the type of senility not caused by strokes or other circulatory problems – you gradually lose your intellect and memory. As years pass, deterioration continues. Finally, you sink into a world of confusion, unaware of your surroundings, your memory almost completely gone.

Five per cent of all people over 65 have a severe memory loss because of Alzheimer's disease, and 10 per cent have a mild loss. Yet no one knows its cause. In autopsies of people who had it, however, doctors found very low brain levels of substances necessary for the formation of *acetylcholine*, the neuro-transmitter that plays a vital role in memory and intelligence. Could a lack of acetylcholine be the cause? Could choline – an essential nutrient necessary for the formation of acetylcholine – be the cure?

For a few people with Alzheimer's disease, some of them over 80 years old choline at least meant a slightly better life. After receiving choline, they became 'less irritable and more aware of their surroundings', according to the researchers who conducted the study. 'Patients who had been unable to find their way to the dining room sometimes seemed able to do this after treatment with choline,' they noted (*Lancet*). In another study, researchers gave choline to ten patients whose average age was 77. Of the ten, three 'seemed less confused after . . . choline treatment' (*Lancet*).

In a study conducted at the New York University School of Medicine researchers wanted to verify the safety, tolerance and effectiveness of choline combined with another substance that acts as a metabolic enhancer. They selected ten patients with mild to moderate memory impairment and treated them for seven days. After that time, a psychiatrist independently rated three of the patients as 'clinically improved'. Memory testing in these same three people revealed an average improvement of 70 per cent in verbal memory retrieval (*New England Journal of Medicine*, 11 June 1981).

Again, choline was a help. But not much of one, and not for many people. Why not?

Choline, it turns out, works best *before* Alzheimer's disease has taken a firm grip. When researchers gave choline to patients under 65 who were in the beginning stages of the disorder, *all* of the patients reported a 'substantial improvement in everyday memory' (*Lancet*).

Deficiency of acetylcholine as a cause for Alzheimer's disease was confirmed in formal trials in California, where patients with moderate to mild symptoms were given *tetrahydroaminoacridine*, a drug that delays the removal of acetylcholine from the brain. After a year, some have shown dramatic improvement, although this therapy only controls symptoms – it does not repair the damage already done to the brain (*New England Journal of Medicine* 13 November 1986).

Many researchers have suggested that using lecithin instead of choline might have improved their results. Lecithin is a naturally occurring substance containing choline and may be better absorbed by the body. In a study on memory loss researchers gave 17 memory-impaired students (six of whom had Alzheimer's disease) a drug that improves memory. The drug wouldn't work, however, unless it was given with a concentrated form of lecithin (University of Texas Medical Branch news release, 13 March 1979).

A team of investigators in Montreal also gave lecithin daily to patients with Alzheimer's disease (*Lancet*). While four of the seven patients showed no clear improvement, the investigators added, 'The clinical impression was that patients A, B and C responded to treatment: During the tests, they seemed to understand instructions faster and more clearly, their verbal rambling was less striking, and they were more cooperative . . .' They concluded: 'This pilot study suggests that oral doses of lecithin, the major dietary source of choline, might help a proportion of patients with Alzheimer's disease at an early stage of their illness.

In a recent report in *Science* (12 December 1986), it has been suggested that discovering the presence or absence of A68, an abnormal protein that has been found in the brains of those who have suffered from Alzheimer's disease may be the 'basis of a reliable diagnostic test for the disease'. If this proves to be the case, further therapy to relieve the symptoms of the disease could transform the futures of those afflicted with Alzheimer's disease.

(*See also* MEMORY PROBLEMS.)

Anaemia

Doctors rarely hit the nail on the head when it comes to diagnosing an iron deficiency. They'll nod knowledgeably that women – especially menstruating women – face a greater risk of depleting their iron stores than men. They readily admit that an iron deficiency is sometimes the cause of vague and misleading symptoms. And they're the first to recognize anaemia as the last deadly straw in iron deficiency.

Yet how many young women suffering from fatigue, irritability, heartburn heart palpitations, dizziness, headaches, weakness, itching all over the body and hair loss (all symptoms of iron deficiency) drag themselves to their doctors for assistance and slouch away with little more than an 'its-all-in-your-head' diagnosis and a catch-all prescription for tranquillizers?

We'd venture to say, quite a few. Not that indigestion or irritability can't be brought on by a bout with nervous tension, doctors are often eager to lay the blame on nerves when it involves a female patient – even though as one American specialist has pointed out, one-third to one-half of apparently healthy young women are, in fact, iron-depleted.

Although that worn-out, rundown feeling is the most common symptom of an iron deficiency, it's by no means the only one. And it's not the first one doctors have mistaken for an emotional disturbance.

A curious array of symptoms

Look at 62-year-old Florence Robbins (not her real name). According to doctors at Goodfellow Air Force Base Clinic in San Angelo, Texas, Mrs Robbins had an itch for six months that made her skin feel as if it was crawling with hundreds of invisible insects. And there was no letup in sight. Oddly enough however, the doctors found no rash, no skin disorder, nothing. Just a minor nervous condition ('psychogenic itching'), which they assured her would go away in time if she took the drug meprobamate, a mild tranquillizer, they prescribed.

Mrs Robbins left the clinic and diligently took her medication, but the itching didn't stop. And if there wasn't anything disturbing her when she started tranquillizer treatment, there was now. Congestive heart failure. Shortness of breath and chest pains similar to angina complicated her already trying ordeal. Now, this was clearly not neurosis!

The doctors conducted a thorough examination and, to everyone's surprise found that she had severe iron-deficiency anaemia. Mrs Robbins was immediately treated with 60 mg of iron three times a day. After a few days, she reported feeling better than she had in months. And within one week, her incessant itching was gone for good (*Journal of the American Medical Association*).

But why does an iron deficiency produce such a curious array of symptoms? And why are these symptoms frequently overlooked as a warning signal?

'The symptoms of an iron deficiency are individualized, and you don't have to be at the point of severe anaemia to feel the effects,' says James Cook professor of medicine and director of haematology at the University of Kansas Medical Center. 'I've seen patients with marked anaemia who didn't seem to have any symptoms, and others with only slightly depressed iron levels who came to my office complaining of any number of related problems.'

Many times it's not that easy to diagnose an iron deficiency, either. 'I know of cases where people suffering from appreciable fatigue responded to iron therapy even though initial blood tests did not show an abnormally low haemoglobin level,' Dr Cook told us. 'This is not, of course, to say that some people feign improvement. It's just that what is considered normal for one person may represent an iron deficiency in another. The key is individualized haemoglobin levels.'

Haemoglobin is the most essential component of our red blood cells. A pigmented protein, it's what makes red blood cells red. But most important it's what gets life-sustaining oxygen from point A in your lungs to points B to Z in every cell and tissue of your body.

Every time we take a breath, oxygen molecules are sucked through the membranes of the lung walls into the microscopic pouches of haemoglobin and whisked off by the bloodstream to nourish all the body cells.

A woman's special needs

To say that haemoglobin has an important task is putting it mildly. And that should give you a good idea of the importance of iron, since iron is necessary for the body's production of haemoglobin. Without iron, there would be no haemoglobin. And without haemoglobin, there would be no life.

But how much iron does the body need to keep haemoglobin levels up to par?

Well, according to Dr Cook, that depends on many varying factors. For example, if you're an average male, you're probably on pretty solid ground. The iron in your daily diet more than compensates for that 1 mg of iron that is lost daily via the skin and urinary and gastro-intestinal tracts, he says.

But if you're an average female, your health could be balancing precariously on a tightrope. Preliminary data from a nationwide survey by the US Department of Health and Human Services in 1974 revealed that 95 per cent of American women aged 18 to 44 are not getting enough iron – only a little more than one-half of the recommended dietary allowance set at 18 mg for menstruating women (*Ob. Gyn. News*).

Why?

To begin with, a woman generally eats less than a man – which means less iron. And if she's trimming her waistline by cutting down on iron-rich foods such as meat and cereal and substituting such poor iron sources as skimmed milk, yogurt and cottage cheese, then her iron intake is sure to fall short.

But it's not bad enough that she's eating less iron than a man. Her body requires more – almost twice as much of the mineral to make up for monthly losses during normal menstruation.

And that doesn't take into account special circumstances. Like the excessive blood loss of *menorrhagia* (heavy or prolonged menstrual bleeding) caused by physiological problems or the use of certain intra-uterine devices (i.e. the 'coil') for contraception. Or the regular use of aspirin, which tends to cause irritation and bleeding of the stomach lining. Or the drain of maternal nutrient stores during pregnancy. In addition, there are several stages of life when iron requirements increase.

The growth spurt between infancy and adolescence is one. In fact, according to home economics professors Catherine C. Johnson and Mary F. Futrell iron-deficiency anaemia is 'the most prevalent nutritional disorder among children in the United States' (*Journal of the American Dietetic Association*). For this reason, the American Academy of Pediatrics recommends that iron supplementation should be started no later than four months of age in full-term babies and two months of age in premature babies. And that brings us to an excellent reason for breastfeeding.

According to a recent study conducted by the department of pediatrics at the State University of New York Upstate Medical Center in conjunction with the Veterans Administration Hospital in Syracuse, human milk has a unique ability to promote iron absorption. Breastfed infants absorbed between 60 and 70 per cent of the iron in their diet while bottle-fed babies absorbed only 10.6 per cent (*Pediatrics*).

Teenagers, too, are sometimes victims of iron-deficiency anaemia. Dietary surveys show that 75 per cent of all American boys and girls 12 to 18 years old don't get enough iron (*Journal of the American Dietetic Association*). And it's not only their iron levels that don't make the grade: another study showed that anaemic children between the ages of 12 and 15 had poorer vocabularies, reading skills, arithmetic concepts and problem-solving abilities than their non-anaemic schoolmates (*Journal of Pediatrics*).

Anaemia knows no generation gap either. Our senior citizens are at risk as well. Of a group of 484 elderly persons in a nursing home and hospital in Toronto, 151 (31 per cent) had anaemia or were receiving therapy for anaemia of which iron-deficiency anaemia was the most common type (*Journal of the American Geriatrics Society*).

The Canadian investigators blamed faulty diet as the anaemia-causing factor but well-known nutritionist and director of the Institute of Human Nutrition at Columbia University in New York City, Myron Winick, offers another possible explanation. Since hydrochloric-acid secretions in the stomach decline with advancing years, iron absorption may no longer be what it was in younger days he wrote in the *Journal of the American Pharmaceutical Association*.

Absorption the key to preventing deficiency

And absorption is the key to preventing an iron deficiency even in younger healthy adults. After all, only about 10 per cent of the iron we eat is absorbed and used by the body. Dr Cook explained it this way: The average menstruating woman may actually need only 1.5 mg of iron a day to replace losses. But in order to insure that she'll absorb that amount she's got to eat 15 mg (or 10 times the required amount).

However, how much she eats may not be as critical as what she eats, Dr Cook adds. 'The nature of the diet is more important than the amount of iron it contains,' he told us. 'You can't look at your total iron intake and say "Wow, I'm getting 5, 10 or even 15 extra milligrams of iron a day." If it's not the right type of iron, that extra boost isn't going to do you any good.'

Dr Cook came to this conclusion a few years ago, when he and his colleagues at the University of Washington School of Medicine in Seattle observed – much to their surprise – that 15 out of 21 infants eating iron-fortified cereals were iron-deficient. Assessing just how much iron the babies were getting from the cereal, the doctors discovered that less than 1 per cent of it was actually being absorbed (*Pediatrics*).

It seems that there are different types of iron: one is readily absorbed by the body, another is partially absorbed, and a third is relatively inert and unabsorbable.

The cereal manufacturers were fortifying their product with the inert substance because it didn't discolour or reduce the shelf life of the cereal. Technically, they were meeting the letter of the law for mandatory iron fortification, but nutritionally they were shooting blanks.

You can make sure your nutritional shotgun is loaded and ready to fight off iron-deficiency. Just stock your fruit basket with such iron-rich goodies as apricots, prunes and raisins. Or keep a jar of wheat germ perched on your refrigerator shelf to strew across the morning's cereal or to sneak into your evening's meat pie.

Better yet, reinforce your iron stores with the health food favourite that's tops on the iron list – blackstrap molasses. Just one tablespoon of blackstrap molasses provides 3.2 mg of iron. To get that much from meat, you'd have to eat a McDonald's Quarter-Pounder or a Big Mac.

That's not to say, however, that meat isn't a superior source of iron. It is, says Dr Cook, and for more than one reason.

First of all, one-third of the iron found in liver, beef, fish or poultry is in an active form. In other words, a generous serving of cooked calf's liver (the iron king of meats), which contains 12 mg of iron, immediately provides you with 4 mg of available iron. And not only that, explains Dr Cook. Meat is also important because it somehow enhances the absorption of dietary iron.

But if you really want to steer away from the doldrums of iron deficiency your best bet is iron supplements, says Dr Cook.

Look for the word 'ferrous' on the label. According to Dr Cook *ferrous* compounds contain appreciably more absorbable iron than *ferric* supplements. For example, two tablets of ferrous gluconate contain 70 mg of iron, of which about 25 mg will be utilized by the body. And that, he says, amounts to more available iron than you could get from eating 14 steaks.

Folic-acid deficiency

Now, no one doubts the importance of iron. It's the critical ingredient of haemoglobin, the molecule in red blood cells that carries oxygen from the lungs to the tissues. And no one doubts that many people, particularly pre-school children, women of childbearing age and the elderly, have a diet that's inadequate in iron. But iron is only one instrument in an orchestra of nutrients that helps pour forth a steady stream of new blood cells from our bone marrow. Iron may be first violin, but vitamins are the French horns oboes and timpani.

Folic acid, for instance. Without this B complex vitamin, the body cannot manufacture some of the molecular building blocks of DNA. The DNA molecule, in turn, is the secret of cell division. Less folic acid means less DNA, which means a slowdown in the creation of new cells, including red blood cells. (Folic-acid deficiency also causes the production of abnormally large red blood cells.) Like iron, folic acid is a nutrient many people don't get enough of in their food. One doctor called folic-acid deficiency 'the most common vitamin deficiency in man.'

'Evidence is accumulating that folacin [folic acid] deficiency may be more widespread than previously suspected.' That was the conclusion of a team of University of Florida and University of Miami researchers who recently studied blood samples from 193 elderly, low-income volunteers. Knowing that they would discover a high rate of nutrition-related anaemia (an abnormally low concentration of red blood cells or haemoglobin) in this group, the researchers hoped to single out the cause of the anaemia. Surprisingly, the missing link wasn't iron. It was folic acid.

Based on the folic-acid content of their red blood cells, 60 per cent of the volunteers fell into the category of 'high risk' for folic acid deficiency and another 11 per cent were a 'medium risk'. Fourteen per cent were frankly anaemic. At the same time,

> the iron status of these elderly people was normal and indicates that the anaemia was not due to a dietary iron deficiency. These findings . . . point out the fallacy of the rather widespread assumption that anaemia always reflects dietary iron deficiency . . . It is important to reassess the true incidence of iron deficiency worldwide in view of mounting evidence of the extent of folacin deficiency. [*American Journal of Clinical Nutrition*, November 1979]

A glance at the diets of the elderly volunteers revealed an absence of foods rich in folic acid. Only 17 per cent of the group said they ate fresh vegetables, and, in spite of the abundance of fresh oranges and grapefruit in Florida, only 30 per cent reported eating citrus fruits. Some of these people also customarily boiled their vegetables for several hours, thereby destroying most of the nutrient.

Liver is the best source of folic acid. It's also, conveniently, a primary source of other nutrients that the blood thrives on, such as vitamin B_{12} iron, riboflavin and vitamin A. Folic acid can also be found in lentils, other beans of various kinds and most vegetables. Whole-grain bread, meat and eggs are moderately good sources.

The elderly, with their tea-and-toast diets, aren't the only ones who risk folic-acid deficiency. Teenagers, with their diet-cola-and-hamburger diets need extra folic acid to keep up with their accelerated growth rate, but many of them aren't getting it. In a study of 199 12-to-16-year-olds from low-income families in Miami, researchers found that approximately 50 per cent of these adolescents were deficient in folic acid and about 10 per cent deficient in iron.

Again, in a paper presented to the Federation of American Societies for Experimental Biology, the researchers stressed that folic acid shouldn't be eclipsed by an overemphasis on iron.

> The incidence of folic-acid deficiency during adolescence has not been widely studied. In fact, the potential for a folic-acid deficiency is often ignored. If anaemia is present, it is generally assumed to be due to an iron deficiency.

American researcher James Dinning calls folic-acid deficiency among teenagers a 'high-priority area' and believes that it may affect more people than, for example, high cholesterol. Of particular concern was the impact of low folic-acid levels on adolescent girls, especially in light of the high rate of teenage pregnancies in the United States. According to Dr Dinning 'a long-term folic-acid deficiency prior to pregnancy has been found . . . to adversely affect the outcome of pregnancy.'

Depending on the severity, folic-acid deficiency can trigger a wide range of symptoms. Sleeplessness, irritability, forgetfulness and depression are associated with acute deficiency. Lethargy, weakness and loss of colour are symptoms of the megaloblastic anaemia (a type characterized by oversized incompletely formed red blood cells) that can result from this deficiency.

Here's a brief list of some other nutrients that work with folic acid and iron in the process of blood formation:

Vitamin B_{12}   You can't talk about folic acid without mentioning vitamin B_{12}. Without this, the folic acid needed for DNA synthesis remains trapped in a form the body can't use. Meat, poultry, fish and eggs all supply vitamin B_{12}. Fruits, vegetables, grains and grain products do not contain it.

Riboflavin (Vitamin B_2)   The complex mechanism of blood production relies partly on this vitamin. In a study of pregnant women in Germany, supplementation with both iron and riboflavin much more effective in raising the red blood cell count than iron alone (*Nutrition and Metabolism*). Researchers in London found that even a marginal deficiency of riboflavin can shorten the life span of red blood cells (*Proceedings of the Nutrition Society*, February 1980). Foods rich in riboflavin are brewer's yeast, liver and beef heart followed by milk, cheese, eggs, green leafy vegetables and grains.

Vitamin C   How about including a savoury tomato salad with your steak? According to Dr Cook, including vitamin C with the average meal can nearly quadruple the amount of iron you absorb from it. Dr Cook cites two studies to confirm this. In the first, the addition of just 60 mg of vitamin C to a meal of rice more than tripled iron absorption. And in the other study adding papaya containing 66 mg of vitamin C to a meal of maize boosted iron absorption by more than 500 per cent.

Vitamins A and E   There's evidence that both of these vitamins play a role in moving iron from the diet to the blood. In people deficient in vitamin A, iron supplementation did not raise the haemoglobin levels unless accompanied by therapy with vitamin A (*American Journal of Clinical Nutrition*). And vitamin E, in combination with vitamin C, has been reported to enhance the uptake of iron into the process of blood formation.

So, where anaemia is concerned, don't take your cues solely from ads about iron on the TV. Good nutrition is too complex for that, and putting energy back into 'tired' blood means more than just pumping iron. It means making sure your diet provides the whole spectrum of nutrients necessary for healthy maintenance of the blood.

• Anal itching

This condition – in fancy medical lingo, *pruritis ani* – is a pain in the butt. Doctors usually can't figure out what's causing it (harsh soap poor hygiene, worms or a minor injury to the area are some possibilities), and may send you away with a prescription for cortisone and the brilliant advice not to scratch.

More useful advice might be not to *eat*. At least not coffee, tea cola, chocolate, beer and tomatoes. An article in a medical journal (*Diseases of the Colon and Rectum*) says these foods are the cause of *pruritus ani*.

To find out for sure, conduct an experiment on yourself. Eliminate these foods from your diet for a few days and see if the itching goes away. If it does, don't eat the foods for two weeks – and then eat them again. If the itching returns in a day or two, you know that it's never time for tea or any of the other foods that contain caffeine.

Lester Tavel, a proctologist in Texas, told us that the stimulants in chocolate, coffee, tea and cola may irritate the bowel, causing *pruritus ani*. But besides eliminating these foods from the diet, Dr Tavel also suggests *adding* a food: *Lactobacillus acidophilus* or *Lactobacillus bulgaricus*, the cultures that ferment milk and are found in yogurt.

Dr Tavel's claim is backed up by a study of 87 people with the problem who were given *Lactobacillus acidophilus*. For 84 per cent, the itching completely or almost completely disappeared (*Diseases of the Colon and Rectum*).

Also, says Dr Tavel, 'Most people with *pruritus ani* – or any intestinal irritation – are deficient in the B complex vitamins.'

• Angina

The pain known as angina, or *angina pectoris* is usually concentrated on the left side of the chest. It begins as a feeling of strangling tightness, heaviness or suffocation. The pain may radiate to the neck and jaw and even down the left arm.

Angina is not a disease in itself; it is merely a shrill warning signal that the heart is not getting enough oxygen. Usually its underlying cause is a narrowing or partial blockage of the coronary arteries, which carry blood to the heart muscle. That happens when the artery walls become layered with fatty deposits called *atherosclerotic plaque*.

The symptoms of angina don't represent a full-blown heart attack, but they are a warning that a heart attack could occur at some time in the future. Angina pain is triggered by any activity that puts added strain on the heart.

Physical exertion, a heavy meal, cold weather, emotional upset all can lead to angina within seconds or minutes.

Retraining your flabby heart

With pain like that lurking around every bend, it's easy to see why most angina sufferers shun any kind of exercise. For some, even a walk to the post-box or the corner shop might usher in an attack. However, people medically capable of exercising who can overcome their fears and actually exercise more stand a better chance of relieving their angina, says cardiologist Richard Stein.

'In our studies with over 60 patients either on home bicycles or in a community exercise programme, we've found reduced frequency and intensity of angina pain in the majority of patients experiencing the training response,' Dr Stein told us. What he calls 'the training response' refers to the ability to exercise or perform a task at a reduced heart rate, therefore lowering the heart's oxygen requirement. Such a response is achieved by gradually intensifying exertion, causing the heart to beat at 75 per cent of its maximum rate for brief four- to five-minute periods.

Dr Stein, director of the exercise laboratory and the coronary heart disease treatment and prevention programme and associate professor at State University of New York Downstate Medical Center in Brooklyn, explained the process to us:

'The physiological basis for these effects is well known and observable even in healthy individuals. For example, if you were to run up a flight of stairs today and then take your pulse, it might be 150. But keep doing this for several days or weeks and take your pulse again. You'll find that it is now considerably lower.'

'The same principle works with angina patients who may start with fairly light exercise and progress slowly to more demanding tasks. Doing such exercises over and over keeps lowering the pulse so that the heart doesn't have to work as hard or require as much oxygen.'

Of course, Dr Stein's patients don't begin by running up flights of stairs. After careful stress testing, each is given a personal exercise programme tailored to his or her own capabilities and limitations. 'You must constantly upgrade the exercise programme, based on the participant's improvement in fitness, or you will fail to progress,' Dr Stein points out.

Many of those enrolled in Dr Stein's programme have increased their mobility and expanded their lifestyles in significant ways. Some can once again play tennis without discomfort or danger, while others are again able to enjoy sex without experiencing angina pain.

Exercise benefits confirmed

Other researchers are reporting equally encouraging results. Writing in *Mayo Clinic Proceedings*, Dr Charles C. Kennedy and five colleagues described a one-year graduated exercise programme involving eight men, ranging in age from 44 to 50, all of whom suffered from mild angina. Four had previously had heart attacks.

The men met at a local YMCA three times a week for a 45-minute exercise session tailored to their individual needs. They walked, jogged, did some stretching exercises and then finished off with swimming or a game of volley-ball. When the 12 months were up, all eight showed remarkable gains. Three had considerably less angina pain, and five were completely symptom-free!

In addition, the authors noted, 'The psychologic improvement experienced by each patient was perhaps the most striking aspect of the exercise programme; they became much more positive in their attitude toward work, family and hobbies.'

More good results with exercise were reported even earlier on America's West Coast when Albert A. Kattus, professor of medicine, division of cardiology, at UCLA, declared in *Medical World News*:

> We have our patients walk anywhere from two to four miles a day, working toward a goal of four miles in an hour's time. We have a number of patients who at first couldn't walk more than 200 yards without having to stop in pain but who are now walking a daily four miles in an hour and don't even experience their angina anymore.

Just as exercise helps relieve angina, there's good evidence that a generous amount of physical activity in daily life helps to prevent angina symptoms from ever developing in the first place. An Israeli study of more than 10,000 middle-aged men and women in 58 kibbutzim found that heart problems were less likely to occur in gardeners, kitchen workers, industrial labourers and other active types than in their more sedentary colleagues: teachers, managers and bus drivers, for example (*Journal of Chronic Diseases*). Among men, the risk of developing angina was more than twice as great for sedentary individuals. For sedentary women, the risk was more than three times larger.

The importance of personal habits

Diet, too, is worth looking into. For one thing, angina attacks often occur immediately after a big meal, when the victim over-indulges.

What you eat may be just as important in the long run as how much you eat. At the Downstate Medical Center, for example, Dr Stein told us that the diets of exercising angina patients are individually reviewed and modified as needed. The emphasis is on a low-saturated-fat, low-cholesterol regimen with moderate amounts of carbohydrate.

There's even some evidence that a vegetarian diet, if followed long enough might be of some benefit. Two researchers at Kingston Hospital in Surrey decided to treat four patients with severe angina by removing all animal products from their diets: 'All four cases experienced complete relief of their symptoms at the fifth to sixth month and were able to engage in strenuous activities. A follow-up of five years showed no return of their symptoms' (*Lancet*).

That diet may have worked because it was high in fibre. At a meeting of the United States Section of the International College of Surgeons, an Italian physician made a startling claim for the high-fibre diet. In addition to its usefulness in relieving the symptoms of diverticulosis (*see* DIVERTICULAR

DISEASE), the diet – which included 25 to 50 g of wheat bran daily – brought a reduction in the incidence of attacks of angina.

What you *drink* can also affect your angina. A team of doctors in California found that when angina patients drank small amounts of whisky, they felt pain more quickly when they exerted themselves. Only after drinking 5 oz of whisky did they feel less pain (perhaps they were feeling no pain). That amount of alcohol isn't good for anyone.

Cultivating the fine art of relaxation is another worthwhile objective for the angina sufferer. Since emotional upsets and stresses can trigger an attack it stands to reason that learning to relax effectively is time well spent. Meditation, quiet contemplation, music and a good book are all possible approaches.

If you have angina and are a smoker, you should seriously consider giving up. 'Anginal patients who stop smoking experience fewer anginal episodes and can exercise more before developing an anginal attack,' wrote Wilbert S. Aronow in *Preventive Medicine*. He notes that smoking aggravates angina for at least two reasons: nicotine increases the heart's oxygen demand, and at the same time, carbon monoxide in the smoke gets into the blood and interferes with oxygen delivery.

Other forms of air pollution are equally dangerous. In another study by Dr Aronow, chief of cardiology at the Long Beach Veterans Administration Hospital in California, angina patients were taken for 90-minute rides in heavy freeway traffic with the windows rolled down. Even this brief exposure to airborne pollutants intensified their angina symptoms (*Annals of Internal Medicine*).

Vitamins may help

Although not nearly as firmly established as the above negative influences, there is also some indication that certain vitamins could conceivably play a positive role in angina management. For example researchers at the Oak Ridge National Laboratory in Tennessee recently found that rabbits injected with vitamin C developed 60 per cent less plaque buildup in the artery leading from the heart, even though they were on a high-cholesterol diet (*International Journal for Vitamin and Nutrition Research*). As we've seen, fatty plaque formation in major arteries is a major underlying cause of chronic angina.

There is some clinical evidence that high doses of vitamin E might also be of help. When Terence W. Anderson of the University of British Columbia compared two groups of angina patients, he found that those taking 3200 IU of vitamin E daily (an amount that should be taken only under a doctor's supervision) had a 'slightly more favourable' response than those not taking the vitamin. But the results were not dramatic enough to be 'statistically significant.'

More interesting to Dr Anderson, however, was the second part of the trial involving 15 angina patients who had already been taking vitamin E for some time. Without their knowledge, seven people in this group were given bogus pills containing no vitamin E at all. Within three weeks, three of these subjects had to drop out of the trial because their angina had become so much worse. A fourth patient stayed on, but complained of increased pain.

Meanwhile, among the eight people who continued taking their vitamin E daily there was no increased angina pain. Dr Anderson called these latter findings 'intriguing', but far from conclusive, considering the small size of the group (*Canadian Medical Association Journal*).

Another doctor, Harvey Walker, Jr. from Clayton, Missouri, told us that vitamin E can help angina. A patient of Dr Walker's in his mid-50s reported terrifying anginal pain in his left chest when he walked uphill into the wind on his way to the local hockey arena. Although he was popping glyceryl trinitrate tablets under his tongue, he still had anginal symptoms severe enough to force him to cancel his season ticket for the hockey games. After a few months of taking vitamin E, lecithin and other supplements, however, his chest pain subsided. He no longer needed drugs and was able to make it to the hockey games without pain. He achieved this result even though he was overweight and smoked heavily.

Of course, such reports are no proof that vitamin E will work for you, but considering the demonstrated safety of this supplement, it might be worth a try. A dosage range of 800 to 1000 IU seems most likely to produce results. Those with high blood pressure should not begin taking vitamin E until the condition is under control, and you should only take vitamin E in dosages of more than 600 IU daily if you are under a doctor's supervision. (*See also* HEART DISEASE).

• Appendicitis

The appendix is a mystery organ. It doesn't seem to *do* anything – except get infected, swell up, hurt and cause a lot of trouble if it splits open before it's removed. That nasty sequence of events is called *appendicitis*, and whether or not you get it seems as predictable as a game of Russian roulette. To a few doctors, however, appendicitis has a logical cause: poor eating habits.

According to an American pathologist, a weekend of stuffing yourself may cause acute appendicitis early in the week.

That's the observation of Dr Lloyd Roberts, who found that admissions for acute appendicitis cases the most common reason for emergency surgery – peaked on Sundays, Mondays and Tuesdays, and fell off during the rest of the week. He reviewed the cases of 137 patients at the Penobscot Bay Medical Center in Rockland, Maine, from mid-1976 to 1978. The first three peak days averaged 23.3 admissions versus a mean of 16.5 patients during the remaining slower days (*Journal of the Maine Medical Association*, December 1979).

Acute appendicitis has an incubation period of a few hours to several days. Thus, Dr Roberts suspects there's 'clearly something about the weekend' that increases susceptibility to or causes the malady. He cites television watching, exercising, outdoor exposure, eating, drinking, sleeping and sexual activity as the chief weekend over-indulgences. However, he singles out 'dietary excess' as the culprit most likely associated with acute appendicitis.

His conclusions may be buttressed by the findings of a leading British scientist. Denis P. Burkitt maintains that acute appendicitis was a medical curiosity and rarity until the introduction of refined, fibre-deficient food. According to

Dr Burkitt, the appendix is often first blocked by a 'small, hard lump of faecal matter, about the size of a pea . . . This exists only in the presence of the firmer faeces that are associated with fibre-depleted diets.' Once blocked, the appendix becomes infected.

'Keeping the bowel content soft seems to provide the best safeguard against the development of appendicitis,' says Dr Burkitt. 'Sufficient fibre in the diet will do this.'

• Arthritis

One summer a number of years ago, a mysterious plague struck three small towns in Connecticut on the east coast of the United States – an outbreak of arthritis. It levelled its victims with chills, fever and a painful swelling of the joints that sometimes lingered for months. Where had it come from? What was the cause? No one knew.

After a good deal of the slow, solid medical detective work that makes few headlines, doctors came up with an explanation for 'Lyme arthritis' (named after the town where it first appeared). It was caused by a virus, they suggested which was carried by a tiny tick that infested the local woodlands. Caution and protective clothing, they said, could prevent the disease.

A modestly happy ending. A really happy ending would be the announcement that doctors had found the cause of all arthritis, and a way to prevent it but that, unfortunately, is another story. To the frustration of medical science – and the pain of some 5 million people in Britain – the disease remains a mystery.

Not a simple mystery, either. 'Arthritis' isn't just one disease: the word means 'inflammation of the joints', and it includes in its painful embrace over 100 distinct disease states.

Arthritis may be a mild swelling of a single joint, which yields easily to a month of drug therapy, nutritional therapy or no therapy at all, or it can be a vicious, agonizing condition that inexorably spreads through every joint in the body. It can be caused by bacteria, by a virus (like Lyme arthritis) or by a disruption of body chemistry (like gout).

The two most common forms of arthritis osteoarthritis and rheumatoid arthritis – are real mysteries. No one knows what causes them. And no one knows why osteoarthritis – a wearing away of cartilage so common that doctors call it 'part of the normal ageing process' – remains a mere nuisance for some people but becomes a crippler for others.

Also unknown is why rheumatoid arthritis follows such an erratic course like a river that never flows the same way twice. It can appear, lie quietly for a number of years and then flare up. It can spread progressively and cause complete disability. Or it can go away – all by itself – and never return (in 10 to 20 per cent of cases, that is exactly what happens).

Arthritis, in other words, can be a harsh, unpredictable and frustrating enemy. And an enemy, it seems, against which medical science has provided highly questionable weapons: powerful drugs that, in the words of one sober conservative textbook of medicine, 'can cause greater morbidity [illness] than the underlying disease'. Not exactly encouraging, is it?

Yet the story isn't entirely discouraging, either. While no one can offer a sure cure for arthritis, there are a lot of possibilities. Remedies have brought relief to some arthritics (but not others). Nutritional factors that scientists have labelled 'deserving of further study' can play a part in the treatment of arthritis. Then there are antidotes to pain as unlikely as sex (the side-effects of this 'therapy' are said to be quite pleasant) and funny movies.

Most encouraging of all, there's the growing realization that you can do something – a lot, in fact – in your fight against arthritis. It's that intangible X-factor – your own attitude – that can very possibly decide whether arthritis is a minor annoyance, a hardship or a disability.

One thing you must wonder about doing, if you have arthritis, is testing some of the vast armoury of folk, home and traditional remedies that some people swear by. Should you try them? Why not, as long as they offer no danger and don't come with suspiciously high price tags?

Home remedies

You'll have nothing to lose, for example, by checking out the 'sleeping-bag treatment'. This totally non-toxic pain-relief formula was discovered by an 11-year-old Boy Scout who suffered from juvenile rheumatoid arthritis. Waking up in the morning, for him, invariably meant stiffness and pain – except when he went camping and slept in his sleeping bag.

Hearing of his experience, a doctor soon had hospitalized arthritis patients spending their nights in sleeping bags – and reporting marked reduction in pain. By conserving steady, uniform body heat, it seems, the sleeping bag brought natural relief.

Or there's alfalfa. We've received enthusiastic descriptions of relief gained with both alfalfa tea and alfalfa tablets. Other people report that particular foods, like watercress, parsley and cherries, have produced measurable improvement. There are foods, however, that may cause arthritis to *worsen*: the nightshade plants – peppers, potatoes, tomatoes aubergines, tobacco.

Norman F. Childers, professor of horticulture at Rutgers University, was stricken with severe arthritis many years ago. After reading that cattle grazing on plants of the nightshade family developed severe arthritic pain, he experimented by withdrawing these foods from his own diet, and he achieved complete relief from his arthritis. He then organized a group of 'cooperators' – thousands of individuals with arthritis who were willing to withdraw these foods from their diets experimentally. A large number of them are partially or totally relieved of their stiffness, aches, pains and restricted joint mobility. Moreover, when many of these people were bold enough to try eating nightshade plants again, they experienced a rapid return of their troubles.

When Dr Childers published his findings, it was predictable that his colleagues would be resistant. And they were – to the extent that they tried to prevent Dr Childers from reading his papers at conventions. The public was inclined to place more faith in Dr Childer's integrity and competence.

A few of his experimenters reported failure; the majority claimed benefits ranging from relief to total recovery, which in some instances occurred in people so badly crippled by arthritis that they were confined to bed or were using walkers or wheelchairs. Perhaps the most striking comment came from a professor who had initially been totally resistant to Dr Childer's findings. He remarked:

> It looks as if I am beginning to weaken a bit relative to the effects of nightshade plants on many people with arthritis. Last summer, I eliminated these particular vegetables from my diet. Previously, for a year, the little finger of my right hand was badly affected – I could not open it without assistance when arising in the morning. Since early last November, that trouble has entirely disappeared. Why? I don't know, but it looks as if the variations in diet, the elimination of the nightshades could well have been responsible. I hope so . . .

It must be emphasized that Dr Childers doesn't blame all the arthritis in the world on the eating of potatoes, tomatoes, peppers and aubergines. He is addressing himself to what amounts to a sensitivity in some arthritics. The average yearly consumption of potatoes in the United States, per person, is large enough to provide 9700 mg of solanine, a poison so strong that a single dose of that size would kill a horse. It isn't improbable that a gradual intake of this toxic substance, common to all white-potato products, might still be too much for some extra-sensitive people.

Dr Barbara Solomon of Baltimore, Maryland also believes that arthritis may be relieved by eliminating foods to which a person is allergic. She has had striking success relieving the pain of arthritis sufferers by eliminating citrus fruits and eggs from their diet.

'There's nothing unusual about this. Over and over again, arthritic patients would come to me and say, "When I eat oranges, my joint pains are worse." "When I eat eggs, my arthritis flares up." So I've experimented. I always eliminate these foods from the diets of those I see with arthritis. And by and large, they do better. Also, I've heard of quite a few other doctors who are doing the same. It seems obvious to me, on the basis of my experience that for some reason arthritics are hypersensitive to – this is, they have an "allergy" to – citrus fruits and eggs.'

A British study backs up Dr Solomon's theory but emphasizes different foods. While following a diet that excluded certain foods to which they might be allergic, 20 out of 22 patients suffering from rheumatoid arthritis found their symptoms relieved. On the average, it took ten days for the patients to begin feeling better.

The foods to which one or more of the patients were sensitive included grain, milk, seeds and nuts, beef, cheese, eggs, chicken, fish, potatoes onions and liver. Sensitivity to grain products led the list, affecting 14 of the patients. When they later tried eating the allergens, 19 of the patients found their arthritis worsening sometimes in as little as two hours (*Clinical Allergy*, vol. 10, no. 4, 1980).

Low-fat diets and rheumatoid arthritis

Two researchers at Wayne State University in Detroit have made an observation as exciting and unexpected as the arthritis-allergy link: that painful swelling and stiffness of rheumatoid arthritis appear to be aggravated by fatty foods and can be dramatically reduced by a low-fat diet. So far, low-fat diets have been found to produce complete remissions in six patients with rheumatoid arthritis. Although that number is small, carefully supervised clinical studies of more patients are currently under way.

Charles P. Lucas and colleague Lawrence Power first observed this remarkable side-effect in two obese patients with active rheumatoid arthritis, who were put on a low-calorie, low-fat diet for weight loss. Within days, both experienced remission of the stiffness and swelling in their joints – and they remained symptom-free for 9 to 14 months. However, within 24 to 48 hours of eating fatty foods, the stiffness returned.

Taking this intriguing cue, Drs Lucas and Power studied the effects of a low-fat diet on four other arthritic patients for seven weeks. Using 'scaled criteria' to rate precisely the amount of joint swelling and morning stiffness the patients experienced, they found that during the seventh week of the diet joint swelling had been reduced from 26 to 6 points, and morning stiffness from an average of 215 minutes to just 11. Once again, they observed that the symptoms returned within 72 hours of eating fat-containing foods.

It made no difference whether the fats were vegetable oils or animal fats they reported: chicken, cheese, safflower oil, beef and coconut oil all seemed to aggravate the condition.

Although they cautioned that the experimental group tested to date is a small one, the researchers suggested that 'dietary fats in amounts normally eaten in the American diet cause the inflammatory joint changes seen in rheumatoid arthritis' (*Clinical Research*, vol. 29, no. 4, 1981).

Relief with vitamin E

Nutritional supplements, too, may bring benefit to some arthritics. In one experiment, 29 Israeli arthritis patients – 4 men and 25 women – at Hasharon Hospital in Tel Aviv were randomly assigned to either a group taking 600 IU of vitamin E a day or a group taking an identical but inert placebo. Then, at the end of ten days, the groups were switched.

At the end of the experiment, fully 15 of the 29 'experienced marked relief in pain' while taking vitamin E, while only 1 of 29 patients had such a reaction to the placebo. That's especially significant when you consider that these patients had been living with their woes for an average of over nine years.

Now, to what may we attribute these happy findings? It sure beats the doctors. I. Machtey and L. Ouaknine, wrote in the *Journal of the American Geriatrics Society*, 'The beneficial influence of tocopherol [one type of vitamin E] on joint symptoms in osteoarthritis cannot be explained at present.' They take a stab at a possible explanation or two – tocopherol's anti-inflammatory potentials in laboratory animals, perhaps? – and wrap up with a modest proposal: 'It would seem that further studies of this subject are warranted.'

Zinc and vitamin C for rheumatoid arthritis

Zinc supplements have also been reported significantly to relieve the symptoms of rheumatoid arthritis in people who had obtained no relief from conventional treatments (*Lancet*).

Peter A. Simkin, rheumatologist from the University of Washington, Seattle based his study on the hypothesis that zinc is somehow necessary for the health of the joints. When the membranes of the joints become inflamed, local zinc levels may be depleted. And blood serum levels of zinc are known to be lower in people with rheumatoid arthritis. He reasoned that replacing the zinc in these tissues by means of diet supplementation might reverse the inflammatory process and increase a person's resistance to the disease.

For his study, Dr Simkin chose 24 people with active cases of rheumatoid arthritis. Conventional therapies such as aspirin, gold injections and a host of arthritis drugs had failed to significantly relieve their symptoms. These medications were, however, continued throughout the study. For the first 12-week period, half the people were given zinc sulphate supplements, (which provided 50 mg of zinc) three times daily, and half were given placebos – pills that appeared to be identical but contained no zinc. For the second 12 weeks, all received zinc supplements. Results of the therapy were measured by evaluating its effect on the various symptoms of rheumatoid arthritis.

Over the first 12-week period, people taking zinc 'fared better in all clinical' measurements of their symptoms. The swelling in their joints went down by 26 per cent compared to no real change in the people not taking zinc. Joint tenderness also improved, but the differences were not significant.

After 12 weeks, morning stiffness decreased significantly in the people who took zinc, whereas it didn't decrease at all in those who didn't take zinc. Further improvement in morning stiffness occurred during the second 12 weeks on zinc. Changes in grip strength were disappointing, but people who received zinc were able to improve their score when they were timed walking over a 50-foot course.

Perhaps the most impressive result of the zinc therapy was measured in how the people themselves evaluated their condition. They were asked to judge their 'overall condition' as well as any 'change since last visit' at intervals during the study. Dr Simkin wrote:

> In both overall condition and change since last visit there was a clear trend favouring zinc over placebo. Patients receiving zinc reported overall improvement at every evaluation interval during both the double-blind [first 12 weeks] and the open [second 12 weeks] phases of the trial.

Dr Simkin told us that his results were 'very encouraging' and that he is continuing the use of zinc supplements in people with rheumatoid arthritis. He said there were some exciting personal stories involving people whose lives were changed for the better by the zinc therapy. Unfortunately, Dr Simkin would not share these stories with us, explaining that he did not wish to sensationalize the experiment.

We share Dr Simkin's desire not to sensationalize the results, but we also share a sentiment he expressed in his paper when he said:

> Active rheumatoid arthritis presents a major therapeutic challenge to every clinician. The disease may be devastating, and accepted thera-

peutic agents are too often ineffective. As a result, new drugs of high potential toxicity have been introduced and used widely in attempts to arrest the progression of this disease. Safer and more effective therapy is badly needed.

In Denmark, researchers at the University of Copenhagen have also reported great success using zinc to treat patients with psoriatic arthritis, which is characterized by scaly red patches on the skin. After only six weeks on zinc supplements most of the patients were able to move their fingers and wrists more easily than before and were no longer plagued by swollen joints and morning stiffness.

The researchers thought it particularly significant that none of the arthritics, who averaged 50 years of age, had suffered from an outright zinc deficiency. 'Serum zinc values before treatment were within the normal range so the effect of treatment is not explained by the alleviation of an absolute deficiency,' they said (*British Journal of Dermatology*, October 1980).

Lack of vitamin C is another real and present danger for arthritics according to a study performed at Trinity College in Ireland. There investigators found that patients with rheumatoid arthritis had blood levels of the vitamin well below the normal range – 'compatible with a diagnosis of subclinical scurvy' was the unreassuring way they put it. 'There is an increased need for, or increased destruction of, ascorbic acid [vitamin C] in rheumatoid arthritis,' the researchers concluded. If your arthritis means large, regular doses of aspirin, you probably need even more vitamin C. Just a little bit of aspirin, according to one study, can triple the amount of vitamin C excreted by the body.

Activity is essential

Careful attention to nutrition is important, but if you really want to stave off the disability that threatens with arthritis, you'll have to take an active role. And we mean that literally. 'Active' as in 'exercise'.

'Exercise is essential in dealing with arthritis,' says George Ehrlich director of the division of rheumatology at the Hahnemann Medical School and Hospital. If you don't exercise a painful joint, 'the muscles around it start to waste away. This means the joint will function even more poorly – it's a cycle. Exercise increases the range of motion of the joint – it limbers you up. And it builds up the muscles around it.'

What kind of exercise? 'Anything that doesn't tax the joint.' Some find swimming ideal, Dr Ehrlich says, and isometrics are quite effective for many.

One type of exercise that has proven especially beneficial is yoga. Its careful, controlled movements and stretches are ideal for improving mobility maintaining muscle tone and combating the stiffness of arthritis. And when yoga exercises are done properly – that is, gradually, and *never past the point of discomfort* – there is small risk of overtaxing joints.

Sexual activity and a positive outlook

Sexual activity can also help relieve pain. When doctors at the Sexual

Dysfunction Clinic of Chicago's Cook County Hospital questioned 55 arthritics about their sexual activity, 24 – nearly half – reported that sex not only made them feel better, but actually relieved pain.

These patients ranged in age from the 20s to the late 60s, but most were in the older range. 'The reports were often striking,' Wanda Sadoughi, director of the clinic, told us. 'Not just "the pain was reduced," but "I was free of pain for several hours." '

How does sex relieve arthritic pain? 'It could be any number of things,' Dr Sadoughi says, 'something biochemical or hormonal, perhaps. And the emotional aspect is obviously important. Possibly it involves both. Stress, after all is both psychological and physiological, and sex can alleviate stress.'

Many arthritics allow their disease to slow them down sexually more than they have to, Dr Sadoughi says, and this is unfortunate. 'Sex is a wonderful source of self-esteem – the feeling 'I'm still wanted, I'm still worthwhile.' A good sexual adjustment can improve your whole outlook toward life. These patients in the study didn't allow the disease to disable them.'

Just such a positive attitude, in fact, could be the most powerful weapon you can bring to the struggle against arthritis. 'You can't give up' says John Baum, professor of medicine at the University of Rochester in New York State. 'You have to fight the disease. We have patients with severe arthritis, severe deformity, who refuse to give up, and they do as well as patients with milder cases but less determination. Your desire to keep on going is the most important thing. If you aren't determined to make the best of your illness doctors can pour in drugs, pour in everything, and it won't do any good.'

Stress as a trigger

For many years, doctors have suspected a connection between rheumatoid arthritis and emotional stress. Recently, Dr Baum examined the medical records of 88 children who had been treated for juvenile rheumatoid arthritis at a Rochester hospital. He found that 28 per cent of them – many more than in the general population – came from broken homes. And for half of these, the divorce or death of a parent had taken place within two years of the onset of the disease.

'Quite possibly, stress is a trigger for juvenile arthritis,' Dr Baum said. 'It probably doesn't cause it, but it may set it off.'

The same thing applies to adults, says Dr Ehrlich. Emotional stress can initiate rheumatoid arthritis in a susceptible person, and once the disease has established itself, stress can make it worse. 'Acute stress – losing your job, a death in the family, a divorce – can make arthritis flare up. It makes you vulnerable. When you're under stress, your body's defences can be breached.'

Small, constant irritations are less dramatic but can be just as harmful. 'There's such a thing as wholesome stress,' Dr Ehrlich says. 'A challenging job, for instance – that's exercise for the mind. It's unwholesome stress frustration, that lays you open to the disease.'

At the Arthritis Center at Philadelphia's Albert Einstein Medical Center Dr Ehrlich says, psychologists and psychiatrists work with patients, teaching them how to deal with frustration and stress. Other clinics, such as the Pain and Health Rehabilitation Clinic in LaCrosse, Wisconsin have used relaxation training to reduce pain.

Acupuncture

Acupuncture may also have an important role to play in pain relief for arthritis.

In an article that appeared in the *Bulletin of the New York Academy of Medicine*, Phillip Sechzer and a colleague, Soon Jack Leung, of the Maimonides Medical Center, revealed their figures on patients who came to the Center for treatment over a six-month period. The figures included 223 patients who received a total of 1271 acupuncture treatments for conditions ranging from arthritis to multiple sclerosis. The largest group of patients consisted of 109 individuals who suffered from different types of arthritis such as rheumatoid arthritis and osteoarthritis. Final figures showed that 81 patients classified as having arthritis of one kind or another experienced either complete or partial improvement of their conditions (4 patients experienced complete improvement, 77 exhibited only partial).

• Asthma

Imagine what it would be like to try to breathe with a 20 stone gorilla sitting on your chest. That'll give you an idea of the panic and feeling of helplessness an asthmatic experiences during an attack. If you have asthma yourself, you know just what we mean.

Fortunately, asthma isn't always that bad. Some days you just wheeze – your airways whistle and rattle as you breathe ever so cautiously. You cough – not a healthy, productive cough but a dry, nagging cough. Exercise seems to be entirely out of the question.

If you could peer inside your chest, you'd discover what's behind the struggle for air. The muscular fibres around the bronchial tubes, or airways tighten up or twitch at the least provocation – cold air, air pollution, over-exertion, perhaps. Or they act up after an encounter with something to which you're allergic – pollen, dust, mould spores, pet dander, food or a drug. At the same time, the linings of the lungs react by becoming swollen and inflamed. And the lungs produce a sticky mucus that no amount of coughing will force out. All that swelling and tightening blocks the free flow of air.

That's asthma. And if you have it, you share your frustrations with about 5 per cent of the British population. In fact, asthma is the most common chronic disease of childhood. Some asthmatics grow out of the disease, just as some teenagers grow out of acne. For others, the years of wheezing and fatigue go on and on. Either way, it's a long wait.

So what can you do to get the gorilla off your chest?

No doubt, you've already learned a few basic defensive tactics – farming out the dog, purging the house of dust and mould, and shunning whatever foods give you trouble. And for some people, such avoidance tactics alone will take care of the brunt of the problem.

'In children, particularly, I find that taking care of the environment – dust control, mould control, pet control – may be more than 50 per cent of the secret of allergy relief,' says Constantine Falliers, an allergist in Denver and editor of the *Journal of Asthma*. 'And I've seen many people who have just stayed away from food dyes and preservatives, and all their symptoms suddenly disappeared.'

One of the dyes Dr Falliers is referring to is *tartrazine* – or E102 to give it the name you will find on food labels – a common problem for asthmatics, who may also be sensitive to aspirin, a notorious asthma trigger.

Other asthma triggers, however, are ever-present but less obvious. The biggest offenders are pollen, pollution and unexpected pets in other people's homes – to say nothing of tobacco smoke, an asthma trigger in the sense that it irritates already sensitive airways. So you need to take the offensive – by stopping asthma before it starts and knowing how to thwart an attack at the earliest warning signal.

Self-help

Air filters are a basic defence against asthma. Doctors we spoke to told us that the best models are the High-Efficiency Particulate Air (HEPA) filters, which have been known to relieve asthma symptoms within 10 to 30 minutes. And a study at a summer camp for asthmatic children in West Virginia found that the use of HEPA filters in the bunkhouses significantly reduced the number and severity of asthma episodes (*West Virginia Medical Journal*).

At home, air filters are just as effective. 'I nearly always prescribe air filtration,' says Robert W. Boxer, an allergist in Chicago. 'I feel that it's helpful. I've seen patients for whom adding an air filter to their asthma therapy has helped their asthma immensely.'

Still, you can't always live in a well-filtered bubble. Some airborne asthma triggers are bound to slip through, to gum up your lungs with mucus and strangle your airways.

To unstick your breathing equipment, drink plenty of fluids. Water and other beverages act as natural expectorants, keeping mucus thin and coughable says Dr Doris Rapp, author of *Allergies and Your Family* (1981). She recommends drinking 4 – 8 fl. oz of liquid every waking hour, if at all possible. Just be sure you don't drink *cold* beverages – the chill can shock sensitive airways into spasms. And be careful to avoid drinks that contain cola or food dyes, common asthma triggers.

Taking your beverages hot helps even more. A warm drink acts as a natural bronchodilator, or airway relaxer, as it glides past respiratory passages. Drinking soup or herb tea when you feel an attack coming on will do fine. 'Sometimes a warm liquid relaxes the bronchial tubes, and you may not even need to use your bronchodilator spray,' says Dr Falliers. 'We've had kids in the hospital for treatment, and when they can't breathe, we try to get them to drink something warm, maybe just water or something with a little more flavour, like hot apple juice. They relax, control the panic and start breathing quietly again.'

Controlling panic is a big part of controlling asthma. If you know you're an asthmatic and begin to sense an attack coming on, you may tend to panic and fight for air. That tightens your chest further. For children, the anxiety is heightened if they see Mum or Dad panic, too. So if your child has asthma, you can help by simply trying to appear calm and confident, no matter how frantic you may actually feel. The sight of a reassuring adult in itself may help the youngster. 'Some children relax the minute they see their doctor enter the room, even before they're given any medication,' says Dr Rapp.

Relaxation, in fact, is such a useful shield against asthma that many doctors are teaching child and adult asthmatics alike variations of a relaxation technique described in 'How to relax away an asthma attack' (*see box*). Because it loosens tightened muscles surrounding airways relaxation is a form of protection that can be used whenever an asthmatic feels an attack coming on.

Deep breathing and exercise

In a subconcious effort not to tax temperamental lungs, asthmatics tend to take short, shallow breaths, which some doctors call 'stingy breathing'. By filling and emptying only the top portion of the lungs, however, asthmatics don't pull in enough oxygen. During an attack, they get even less. 'The average asthmatic is breathing at only 60 or 70 per cent of capacity,' Dr Falliers told us. 'And during an asthma attack, that can drop to 20 per cent.'

In the throes of an attack, you may actually turn blue for lack of oxygen. 'But if you're having an attack, you don't think about breathing physiology and oxygen metabolism,' says Dr Falliers. 'You just think of how to get your next breath.' By learning to breathe deeply and efficiently, you can increase the amount of oxygen you take in, so an attack isn't nearly as disabling.

Exercise can also help. Interestingly, school teachers who have asthmatic children in their classes often become confused about exercise. One child has

---

How to relax away an asthma attack

The following relaxation technique, practised for five minutes a day, can be turned on whenever the chest starts to feel tight or other asthma warning signals arise.

1 Stand up and hold your arms out straight. Close your eyes and hold your breath. Lift your chin toward the ceiling and grit your teeth. Make all your muscles *very* tight. Keep your arm muscles tight, your fists tightly clenched, your legs stiff and your toes stiff. Hold for a few seconds.

2 Now, let everything go limp, like a balloon that's being deflated. Completely relax all your muscles until you feel like a wet noodle. Open your eyes.

3 Gently collapse to the floor. Close your eyes again. Keep your arms legs and even your face limp and loose.

4 Imagine yourself floating down a lazy river on a soft raft. Concentrate on each of your muscles and how nice and floppy they all feel.

5 Breathe softly and easily as if you were cosily asleep in your bed. Stay quiet and droopy, enjoying the lack of tension in your chest and body.

6 Open your eyes.

Remember that wet-noodle feeling, and turn it on whenever you feel nervous short of breath or have any other sign that an asthma attack may be coming on.

Deep breathing for asthma relief

By learning to breathe correctly, asthmatics can ward off wheezing, chest tightness and shortness of breath. The following exercise can be practised lying down, standing or sitting, and should be done daily.

1 Think of your chest and stomach as a container for air. Breathe in through your nose, *slowly* filling the bottom of the container first. Continue until the stomach feels inflated, like a balloon. If you place your hand on the spot just above your navel, you can feel it rise and fall with each breath.
2 Exhale slowly through your mouth. The 'container' should feel completely empty and your stomach should feel flat before you inhale again.
3 Repeat. Inhale and exhale 12 times.

SOURCE: *American Lung Association Newsletter*, May 1981

a doctor who says, 'This child has asthma, so he can't take PE.' Another child's doctor says, 'This child has asthma and should be encouraged to exercise.'
Who's right?

'They're both right,' says Dr Falliers. 'Until the asthma has been treated a child should be excused from exercise. But as treatment progresses, the child should be encouraged to develop and improve his or her fitness.'

That's because improving overall fitness can help control asthma.

'If you're not fit – if you haven't exercised in six months – and then you start exercising, your heart will beat very fast,' explains Dr Falliers. 'But if you're physically fit, your heart will beat more slowly. And a slower heartbeat means better absorption of oxygen from the lungs. Being fit is like having your carburetor properly adjusted: you run, and breathe, more smoothly.'

Of course, exercise can also help keep your weight down, which is also beneficial for asthmatics. 'If you have two inches of excess fat around your diaphragm, it's going to make it harder for you to breathe,' says Dr Falliers. 'For a person with asthma – or any kind of breathing problem – being over-weight is like wearing a very tight garment. You don't have enough room for your muscles to expand the lungs.'

The type of exercise you choose will make quite a difference to how well you tolerate exercise. Activities that involve brief spurts of action separated by rests, are much less apt to trigger asthma than sports that call for continuous exertion. An asthmatic who goes in for golf, for example, is not as likely to start wheezing and coughing as one who runs the mile. Swimming, too, is ideal for asthmatics, provided that rest is taken at proper intervals.

'So often, it's not the exercise that triggers asthma, but fast breathing of cold air,' says Dr Falliers. 'Cold air irritates sensitive airways. If you breathe through your nose instead of your mouth, the air will be warmed, and you may not react.'

A light, cotton face mask may also help to protect against cold, dry air – or pollen and air pollution, for that matter. Scientists at the US National Asthma Center in Denver observed the effectiveness of face masks on ten boys and girls, all asthmatic. After exercising for six minutes, the youngsters experienced much less asthma than usual – or none at all. The researchers concluded that a 'simple face mask may be an inexpensive [non-drug] alternative for alleviation of exercise-induced asthma' – especially in runners and skiers (*Journal of the American Medical Association*, 14 November 1980).

Similar research at Yale University also demonstrated the protection offered by face masks against exercise-induced asthma. In both air-conditioned and refrigerated rooms, asthmatics with face masks fared better than those without masks – probably due to the rewarming of air inside the mask, said the researchers, adding, 'We have shown that under [these] circumstances . . . the use of a mask offers a simple, inexpensive and effective form of [protection],' (*Annals of Allergy*, January 1981).

Wearing a scarf pulled up over your mouth before going outdoors in winter achieves the same effect.

Vitamin C.

During the 19th century, it was noticed that sailors with scurvy stopped wheezing when they ate citrus fruits, and modern research shows that vitamin C may help to widen air passages during exercise or exertion. In one study volunteers who customarily suffered asthma after exercise were given 500 mg of vitamin C before an exercise test. Their tolerance of exercise was doubled (*Journal of the American Medical Association*, 13 February 1981).

However, vitamin C seems to help asthmatics whether they tolerate exercise or not. In another study, asthmatics who took 1000 mg of vitamin C a day had less than 25 per cent as many asthma attacks as those receiving an inactive dummy pill. When they stopped taking vitamin C, though, they once again suffered the same number of attacks as the untreated people (*Tropical and Geographical Medicine*, vol. 32, no. 2, 1980).

So breathe easier. By definition, asthma is a reversible condition, and relief depends largely on factors that you can control.

'Proper education of the public and the right health attitude – not waiting until the damage is done, but preventing it – that will be the secret of success in controlling asthma,' says Dr Falliers. 'And if that puts us allergists out of a job, that's just fine!'

• Athlete's Foot

Ringworm fungi – the most common cause of athlete's foot – just love the inside of your shoe. Steamy and warm, it's like a year-round tropical rain forest. Dermatologists agree that the basic strategy against a troublesome foot or body fungus is to make its life miserable by keeping it clean, dry and well ventilated. During the Vietnam war, when many soldiers were troubled with skin fungi, the growth was halted when they switched from heavy clothing and boots to loose airy clothing and sandals.

The same tactic is a good one in your own personal war against the stuff. Avoid tight, ill-fitting shoes and non-porous socks, wear open-toed shoes or sandals as often as possible, and dry your feet thoroughly after bathing especially between the toes and around the nails. You might also try alternating shoes each day, leaving the unoccupied pair in a well-ventilated spot.

As a topical medication, vitamin E has been used with good results on athlete's foot, according to anecdotal evidence. One reader of the American magazine *Prevention* wrote that she had been bothered for several years with a fungal infection beneath her toenails, several of which actually fell off, causing such pain that 'I was unable to stand the pressure of any closed shoes.' Though she had tried 'every known topical medication' her doctors recommended, nothing worked until she pierced a couple of vitamin E capsules and used the contents nightly for two weeks. 'The results were nothing short of miraculous!' she exulted.

Another reader reported applying honey to a long-lived fungal infection between his toes before going to bed (wearing socks to avoid a mess), and 'within a week all signs of the infection had disappeared.'

Honey as a cure for athlete's foot had suggested itself, he wrote, when he found a partly empty honey pot that had survived a long, hot summer. Though the pot had been closed, the honey was completely free of fungus – 'which suddenly made me suspect that honey has a built-in fungicide.'

Another reader reported relief from the itching after regular applications of apple cider vinegar. Still another, making use of one of her grandmother's all-purpose remedies, tried using mutton tallow. She reported that her step-father's feet, terribly infected with the fungus, had been healed with sparing applications of fat cut from around lamb kidneys, cleaned, melted down over low heat and strained into clean jars.

Don't make the mistake of thinking that athlete's foot is always a mild and benign itch. If it gets into your feet and you keep them warm and moist, you can be in for big trouble. Athlete's foot, in its serious form, is a combination of fungus and bacterial infection, and a complete cure requires careful (and sometimes difficult) treatment of both organisms. Prevention through keeping the feet cool and dry, is simpler.

• Autism

Children with autism suffer from a stubborn psychosis that leaves them withdrawn and silent, virtually cut off from the outside world.

However, Bernard Rimland, director of the Institute for Child Behavior Research in San Diego, California, has seen amazing changes occur in these youngsters when given large amounts of pyridoxine (vitamin B_6) – usually several hundred milligrams – along with other nutrients, especially magnesium.

In a study published in the *American Journal of Psychiatry*, Dr Rimland and two medical colleagues described what happened when 16 autistic children stopped taking their pyridoxine. The experiment was set up in such a way that neither the youngsters, their parents nor the doctors knew when the children were taking vitamin B_6 and when they were taking a worthless substitute. But in 11 of the cases, the children's behaviour gave the secret away. This deteriorated noticeably when they stopped taking the vitamin and improved just as sharply when they resumed.

Without the vitamin, the children refused to talk. They would whine and shake nervously, hide under blankets or retreat into their rooms. Interest and involvement in their surroundings shrank to a minimum. But with vitamin B_6, those same youngsters began to talk more, read, ask questions and play games. They became calmer and better able to socialize with their friends and family.

Best of all, there were no side-effects such as those that accompany most behaviour-altering drugs.

• Back Problems

'My problem started when a dog jumped at me, and my neck snapped,' says Dr Mervin Rhoades, a New York veterinarian. 'An orthopaedic surgeon put me in traction, but my back got even worse. Then he sent me to a neurosurgeon, who said I should have surgery. I said no and went to another orthopaedist, who treated me with acupuncture. I've had 72 treatments, and I've gotten gradual relief, although I still can't move my neck too much.'

'I felt like my back was in a vice,' explains Yvonne Lappas, a New York artist who says she's had severe back pain for five years, ever since she twisted too far backward during a yoga exercise. 'The pain radiated all the way around to the front, and it was excruciating. I went to a gynaecologist and he said I should have a hysterectomy.'

'I started having the pain about 40 years ago, when I went into my father's business,' says Frank O'Neal, a retired Philadelphia salesman. 'I never really wanted to be in his business, and I guess you'd have to say it was psychological, but that didn't make the pain any less. When I left the business after five years, the pain went away, but I've had occasional pain ever since then whenever I have a domestic problem or a serious problem at work.'

These people are by no means alone with their bad backs. In the United States alone, about 80 per cent of all adults will at some time in their lives seek medical attention for back pain, and about 35 million will experience such pain regularly. The National Center for Health Statistics reports that severe chronic back pain causes more visits to US doctors than any other ailment except respiratory infections, and new cases are appearing at the rate of at least 2 million a year.

'Silent' injuries that catch up with you

Chronic, severe back pain interferes with almost every activity. The type of pain experienced by Dr Rhoades and Ms Lappas probably causes more loss of work than all other ailments combined, according to Leon Root, an orthopaedic surgeon at the Hospital for Special Surgery in New York. The cause of all this misery, according to Dr Root, coauthor of *Oh, My Aching Back*, is 'trauma,' or injury.

This trauma can be a sudden, twisting injury to the lower back, a blow to the area, a fall from a height in which you have a sudden compression of bones and disks in the spine, a sudden strain from lifting a heavy object, or it can result from any of a number of other dramatic events.

Dr Root pointed out that less dramatic forms of injury can also be categorized as trauma.

Chronic trauma is sleeping on a poor mattress for many years. Chronic trauma is sitting slumped in a chair in a position which produces continual strain on your lower back.

Chronic trauma is any recurring strain put on your back, however mild the strain may be. Chronic trauma occurs in most of our daily lives – many times during each day, day after day. The cumulative effects of chronic trauma eventually reach a point at which the back is no longer capable of withstanding them. This is the point when pain occurs.

For instance, we've been told for years how 'sloppy' sitting hurts us. But according to Henry L. Feffer, professor of orthopaedic surgery at George Washington University Medical Center in Washington DC, sitting itself, no matter how it's done, puts a lot of stress on the back.

'If one sits poorly – say, in an overstuffed chair or a badly designed car seat – then that puts greater pressure on the discs in the lower back,' explains Dr Feffer. 'But even when one sits correctly, the pressure within the spinal discs is still twice that when standing. And the pressure when standing is twice that when lying down.'

Psychological stress may also cause back pain. 'An individual develops pain in his back as a defense mechanism in a situation in which he finds he can no longer cope with emotional difficulties,' wrote Dr Root. 'But the pain he feels is still real and must be treated.'

'[People] today are overstressed and underexercised,' adds Hans Kraus, a New York orthopaedist and author of *Backache, Stress and Tension.* 'If muscles are tense for too long, it gets painful, as in a tension headache. You can lift 10 pounds and get the same pain in your back that another person gets from lifting 200 pounds.'

Back pain can be part of ageing when the discs between the spinal vertebrae deteriorate. They act as shock absorbers between the vertebrae, but if they are not functioning properly, the ligaments surrounding them can be sprained. This causes swelling, which puts pressure on a nerve, which can produce crippling pain. The result is a 'slipped', or herniated, disc.

Surgery

Traditionally, surgery has been a common method of treating injured or diseased discs, although many orthopaedic specialists are now admitting that much of the surgery has been unnecessary.

'I have seen patients who have had up to 11 operations . . . who came to me because their backs hurt as much as ever,' says D. Keith McElroy, assistant clinical professor of orthopaedic surgery at Columbia Presbyterian Medical Center in New York, who was once consulted by the late President John F. Kennedy about a spinal fusion operation and advised against it. 'Only 5 per cent of low back pain requires surgery,' he says.

What can the chronic back sufferer do, then, to avoid the pain?

Almost all experts are now convinced that, except for the tiny number of congenital deformities or serious injuries that require surgery, the bad-back victims themselves can do a great deal to keep the pain away.

Changing your habits

The first thing the sufferer absolutely must do is get down to normal weight if he or she is overweight. If you are overweight, the spine becomes overloaded and is under constant stress.

The natural inclination of most back sufferers is to avoid as much physical movement as possible. However, this often makes matters worse, since prolonged periods of time in bed or sitting in a soft chair weaken the muscles that support the lower back and thus tend to pull the vertebrae even further out of alignment. In addition, most experts now feel that braces and corsets should be avoided.

Bend your knees when using a footstool, and avoid deep sofas. Avoid stooping bending backward or bending forward with the knees straight.

'Lift with your legs, not with your back, and carry objects close to the midline of your body,' says Homer Pheasant, a former orthopaedic surgeon and director of the Adult Back Clinic at the Los Angeles Orthopedic Hospital. Lifting the wrong way can cause a disc problem, he cautions. 'If you lift a 70-lb weight the wrong way, it can put a 1050-lb load on your lower back.' For more complete information on how to lift, see the section in this entry, 'How to lift *anything* without hurting your back.'

Avoid any sudden activity the first thing in the morning before your joints have become loose. Do not engage in any vigorous activity without warming up first, and be careful while shovelling, especially when you have a load of snow that sticks to the shovel: unloading the snow with a sudden thrust can be brutal on the back.

On long plane rides, try to get an aisle seat so you can get up frequently to stretch. On long car rides, and at work, try to stop and stretch at least once an hour. Experts say that the greatest pressure to the discs is caused by sitting in soft chairs for extended periods of time and that the pressure is least when one is flat on one's back with the knees propped up. Try to sleep on your side, though, with your knees drawn up, and use a good, firm mattress.

Diet plays a key role

Good nutrition plays a key role in maintaining a healthy back. One nutrient especially important in the prevention and treatment of back pain is vitamin C. James Greenwood, Jr., clinical professor of neurosurgery at Baylor College of Medicine in Houston, told us that 'a significant percentage of patients with early disc lesions are able to avoid surgery by the use of large doses of vitamin C.' And that of those who have surgery, 'the degree of recovery is better and the number of re-operations reduced.' He has little doubt of vitamin C's responsibility in producing and maintaining a good recovery, since 'symptoms recur usually within about three months after vitamin C is stopped, and maximum relief is experienced in three months . . .

'Vitamin C's most dramatic immediate effect,' says the Texas neurosurgeon 'is to prevent and relieve muscle soreness resulting from unusual exercise such as a hunting trip wading through marshes, or sailing.' Following his recommendation, both his patients and his colleagues find relief from muscle soreness by taking 1500 mg of vitamin C a day before an unexpected exercise schedule.

Dr Greenwood recognized the value of vitamin C more than 20 years ago, when he achieved relief from a painful back ailment he had suffered from for ten years. He realized that vitamin C is a construction material required to mobilize and build collagen – a protein substance contained in the supporting tendons, bone, cartilage, etc, that hold the body together.

It was this relationship of vitamin C to the building of collagen that prompted Dr Greenwood to try vitamin C for his own back problem. About four months after taking 100 mg three times daily, he noticed that he could exercise without difficulty, but when he stopped the vitamin C regimen, his pain returned.

He applied the benefit of his own experience to more than 500 patients with disc problems who reported gratifying relief as long as they continued vitamin C, and he reported his preliminary results to the scientific community in the *Medical Annals of the District of Columbia*. Today, Dr Greenwood starts all his patients on 1500 mg of vitamin C a day (500 mg with each meal) and recommends increasing that amount in case of infection.

Vitamin C isn't the only nutrient important in keeping a back healthy. 'A lack of calcium, protein, vitamins and other factors would not only weaken the back but cause generalized weakness,' adds William K. Ishmael, a former specialist in internal medicine and rheumatology and professor of clinical medicine at the University of Oklahoma Health Sciences Center. He told us that he frequently finds women on crash diets complaining of muscle twitching – a sign of calcium deficiency. In such cases, he usually finds that a vitamin D supplement twice a week will relieve the problem, because vitamin D aids in the absorption of calcium.

Backache is frequently a physical sign of emotional tensions – a psychological stress. So anti-stress nutrients, such as the B complex and vitamin E, in addition to vitamin C might also prove helpful.

However, diet should not stand alone in the fight against back pain. 'Adequate nutrition,' says Dr Greenwood, 'including optimum vitamin C, and daily exercise will eliminate many back pains, strains and disc ruptures.'

Your anti-pain prescription

The one indispensable item for any chronic back sufferer is a programme of regular, specially designed exercises that a person of any age can do. Dr Root, a victim of chronic back pain himself, can attest to the value of such a programme.

When I wound up in traction because of a bad disc, I realized I had to exercise. I do it every morning, and not only has it eliminated the pain, but it also gives me a good psychological set for the day. If I don't do the exercises for three days in a row, I get the pain again.

Such an exercise programme was developed by Dr Hans Kraus for bad back sufferers of all ages. The six-week programme, offered to both men and women in many YMCAs and YWCAs all over the United States, consists of two 45-minute sessions a week, plus daily homework. The programme, called 'The Y's Way to a Healthy Back', teaches 18 exercises focusing on relaxation, muscle strengthening and improving flexibility.

The six basic Y exercises that follow are designed to relax and tone you up.

1 To loosen up the muscles, lie on your back, knees bent. Wobble – one at a time – your neck, shoulders, arms, thighs, legs and feet. Raise each arm, then each leg, slowly letting them drop to the floor. Make your whole body feel heavy by saying over and over again to yourself, 'My neck feels heavy; my head feels like it weighs a ton,' etc.

Now tighten the muscles in your neck, arms, legs and abdomen. Then let go. You probably won't even realize how tense you really are until you learn what being relaxed is all about.

2 Take a deep breath as you bring your shoulders up. Let go as you exhale. Repeat three times.

3 While still on your back with knees bent, let your head roll slowly all the way to the left, let go, then return to the centre position. Now, roll your head slowly to the right, let go, and return again to the centre. Repeat three times.

4 Still on your back, pull your feet up halfway to your buttocks keeping your arms at your sides. Slowly draw one knee up as close as you comfortably can to your chest.

Now lower the leg back to the starting position, let it slide forward and drop. Return it to the original flexed position. Repeat with the other leg. Do the same thing three times with each leg.

5 Lie on your left side, head cradled in your left arm. Bend your knees until you're in a modified foetal position. Slide your right knee up toward your chest as far as you comfortably can.

Slowly slide the leg to an extended position. Do this three times. Turn and repeat with the other leg.

6 Turn over on your stomach, resting your head in your hands. Tighten the buttocks muscles, and hold them taut for two seconds. Let go, and repeat three times.

Reverse the order, starting with exercise five and going back to exercise one.

'Some students complained at first that they really weren't doing anything,' says Bob Glover, who has been an instructor – trainer of the Y's back programme. 'They weren't convinced anything was happening because it didn't hurt. But when they learned to do the exercises correctly, they discovered how much good their bodies were getting out of them.'

'By the time you finish these exercises, you're really relaxed,' says Alexander Melleby, national consultant to the YMCA's back programme.

'There's no sweating. These are therapeutic exercises. They aren't supposed to turn you into a combat-ready Marine.'

Loosen up your tight, aching shoulders

A leading osteopath gives the following advice for back problems:

Pain in the upper back and shoulders afflicts almost as many people as low back pain, which is the most common back problem. As in so many other illnesses, our backs are the victims of the city life, the sitting-down way of life. Let me explain.

The way we live and work in our modern society puts too much of the wrong kind of stress on this part of the body. For most of our daily activities, we sit over a desk, bench, typewriter, sewing machine or steering wheel. Washing dishes, cooking, typing, driving – our arms are always in pretty much the same position, straight out in front of us. If we lived a more rural life, our daily chores would guarantee plenty of twisting and very little sitting in the same tensed position.

Poor posture of this type causes a gradual buildup of tension across the shoulders, tension that affects the many nerve pathways in this area that control the hands, arms, head, heart, lungs and upper abdomen. Hour after hour of this tension builds up to a point where the tightness follows us to bed. We wake up with numb arms, a painful back or a headache.

Keep in mind that many of our daily routines are potential troublemakers and that taking early steps in strengthening the upper back will prevent attacks of severe stiffness and pain in the future.

Ask yourself if your working and playing hours put a lot of strain on this area. If you spend hours sitting in a stooped position over a desk, bench or steering wheel, you're probably giving little or no motion to the upper spine – motion it needs to stay healthy and loose. Of course, we occasionally have the natural protective reaction to this poor posture, which takes the form of restlessness or the desire to get up and stretch. Giving in to that urge is sometimes all that's needed. But it's important to do it frequently enough to make sure the effects of poor posture don't climb into bed with you. If you don't get rid of them by bedtime, you may wake up with aching shoulders and a stiff, painful upper back.

There is nothing so helpful as regularly moving these tense areas, which is what nature tries to tell us with the 'restlessness reflex'. I often tell lorry drivers, for instance, to make a habit of turning their heads to look over their shoulders once every mile and to stop every two hours for a good five-minute stretch and a short walk. And this advice is good for anyone who must be at the wheel for long periods at a time. Modern cars are made so low that the seats are more conducive to sleeping than to paying attention to the road. To overcome this, the driver has to thrust the head forward and concentrate with little or no motion given to the upper back. This builds up tension. How often have you heard people say that they must rest up after a long driving trip? You won't need that rest at the end of your trip if you follow my suggestions for stretching and relaxing during it.

Injuring your upper back

In a manner of speaking, you could call this chronic, unrelieved stress to the shoulders an injury, but the usual, sudden type of injury or sprain can also lead to lingering pain and stiffness. Usually, a shoulder joint injury causes pain and swelling immediately, but a minor strain that might be caused by a sudden twist or jerk may go unnoticed for a day or more until pain swelling and stiffness leave you virtually disabled.

First aid for an injury of this type – or for any sudden strain, sprain or bruise – is to apply cold in the form of ice or cold-water packs for the first 12 to 24 hours. Applications of cold should keep the swelling to a minimum. Heat should be applied after a day or so, when you are getting the injured area back in operation.

The most important thing to remember in treating a sprain or injury to the upper back is to get those joints moving again as soon as possible. If motion isn't restored within a few days, tension and stiffness will build up as nerve reflexes reduce circulation to these parts. This condition can get even more debilitating if the pads of fatty tissue that surround the joints, or the ligaments that connect bones to other bones, become inflamed. We call this a 'frozen shoulder', and it can take a long course of therapy to 'break the ice.'

Pain and stiffness across the back and shoulders can also be caused by an upper-respiratory infection such as a cold or flu. This is possible because the tissues in the nose, throat and chest are supplied by nerves centred in the spinal cord, which come around from the upper back and neck. Messages sent over these nerve pathways go both ways, so we have the inflammation of the nose and throat tissues sending messages of trouble back to the spinal cord. Some of these result in pain reflexes in the tissues around the spine while others stimulate the nose, throat and chest with various messages designed to heal the inflammation. But the messages to the upper back unfortunately result in aches, pain and stiffness, some of nature's warning signs.

Reflexes such as this can come from even more distant parts of the body. Stomach ulcers, gall bladder and liver disease, pancreatitis, small intestine inflammation and heart conditions can all radiate messages to the nerve pathways of the upper spine and cause pain and tenderness there. Doctors sometimes use such clues in diagnosing internal problems. The Orientals have mapped out acupuncture points for these reflexes, where the well-placed acupuncture needle can help ease the pain and stimulate healing reflexes. Since more of these points are concentrated in the area across the shoulders than any other place in the body, you can see how many possible sources of upper back pain there are.

By this time, I hope you have some idea how important this area of the body is to us, how easily it can get us into trouble. You should also recognize that the cause of irritation might be a remote part of the body. Although a doctor's opinion and treatment may be necessary in many cases, you can do quite a bit yourself to eliminate your shoulder and upper back pain. Naturally, if such pain is the result of some internal problem or the inflammation of some organ, a doctor's care will be necessary. The exercises I am about to describe will not heal an ulcer or a congested liver, if that is what is causing your upper back pain.

More likely, however, you should be able to recognize whether it's really posture or some disease that is giving your upper back a bad time. Check your posture for round shoulders or a stooped position. Does one shoulder tilt downward or more forward than the other? Do the head and neck assume an erect straight position? Do you spend much of your time at a bench or desk? If so your upper back pain is probably the result of poor posture. And the sooner you establish a routine that will prevent back and shoulder problems, the better your health will be.

Preventive exercises

Here are some simple routines that everyone can do to prevent the problems I have been discussing.

First of all, almost any exercise will do some good, by stimulating circulation and generally increasing motion in this area. Swimming, golf tennis, walking . . . all have this beneficial effect. But concentrating on the specific area can reduce the amount of time required to relieve or prevent shoulder aches.

For instance, if there is stiffness and soreness in the large shoulder joint, try this: Bend forward and support yourself with the hand of the good arm on the back of a chair. Allow the afflicted arm to drop downward. Then swing this arm back and forth, side to side and, finally, in circles both clockwise and anti-clockwise. This gives the joint a gentle-motion stretching without the added weight of the arm when you are standing erect. Bending over this way is more effective because it stretches the ligaments, where the swelling is.

Another gentle stretching act for a stiff shoulder joint is to lie down on your back with knees raised and arms out at your sides. Gently roll away from the stiff shoulder side until it feels ready to rise off the floor. Now gently rock back and forth. The weight of your arm is enough to stretch the tense ligaments of the shoulder. But you are not really using the muscles around that joint, which might cause more harm than good.

One of the most effective primary stretching motions for all upper spinal tension as well as for stiff shoulder joints is what I call the 'cat stretch'. Get down on your hands and knees, with your hands pointing forward. Keep your elbows stiff as you bend your knees and come down and back on your legs. This motion stretches the shoulders and upper back. While you're doing this, be careful not to hold your breath. Just breathe easily. If you add a slight bouncing motion at the point where you begin to feel the stress, you will help release tight tissues.

While you're down in this position, you can try what I call the 'peanut roll'. First, bring your hands back until both arms and upper legs are perpendicular to the floor, with your fingers pointing towards each other below you. Now from this first neutral position, allow your elbows and knees to bend in order to bring your chin or nose close to the floor near your knees. Now move your chin forward to your fingers, as if you were rolling a peanut forward on the floor. Then come up to the neutral position. Reverse the stretch by first getting down with your nose or chin near your fingers and then 'rolling the peanut' back towards your knees, ending in the neutral position. The entire exercise should take only three to five seconds. Repeat it three or four times, and don't hold your breath.

If these exercises are easy for you, you can add a different stretch by turning your head at the starting neutral position and rolling the peanut with one ear both forward and backward, then repeat with the opposite ear.

One of my favourite stretching positions is called the 'shoulder roll'. Frequently a sudden release of tension is felt during this stretch, as more motion is given to the upper spinal vertebrae. Lie flat on your back, legs a little apart, hands clasped in back of your neck. Keep your elbows forward while you pull your head off the floor a few inches. From this neutral position, twist your head and shoulders to the right so your elbow touches the floor. Then twist to the opposite direction and touch the floor with the other elbow. As you go from side to side, rolling across your upper back six to eight times will stretch and tone the upper spinal tissues. Again, I must emphasize: the ideal motion involves relaxed breathing and taking just one or two seconds to go from left to right.

Yoga techniques

Yoga has taught me a very effective stretch position for the entire spine, which I call the 'yoga twist'. It can be done in a chair or while you are sitting on the floor. First, lock the lower part of your spine by crossing your legs and holding the top knee with the opposite hand. Place the other hand on the floor a little behind you or clasp the back support of a chair. Rotate your head and shoulders towards this supporting arm to an extreme twist position. Hold this twist for four to eight seconds, breathing regularly. Change your hands and arms around to twist in the opposite direction. This exercise is very effective when done once in each direction, but it can be done several times.

Another good yoga position that can be adapted for stretching is the 'arch'. Lie stomach-down on the floor, but hold your head and chest up with your arms outstretched in front of you. Simply twist your head around to one side as if you were trying to look at your heel. Hold this for four to five seconds, then twist to the other side.

The more acute and painful the condition, the more gently the stretching is done.

Even if you don't have any pain or stiffness in the shoulders or upper back, these exercises can still benefit your health. Of course, they are not meant as substitutes for exercise such as running, cycling, walking, swimming and other sports. The healthy person who will best weather the effects of ageing and stress is the person who gets as much motion as possible into his or her life.

How to lift anything without hurting your back

A physics professor at Tufts University in Massachusetts has written a very practical, readable book called *My Back Doesn't Hurt Anymore* (1980). This little book explains why your back hurts and shows you how to lift and carry almost anything without triggering an excrutiating spasm in your lumbar region (the lower back and source of the word 'lumbago').

The author, Jack R. Tessman drew from his own experience with back pain to write the book. A few years ago, he leaned over a safety gate – the kind used to prevent children from tumbling down stairs – to pick up one of his young daughters. He felt a twinge at first, and the twinge led to a painful, almost disabling, muscle spasm in his lower back. Just a few days later, however, he found that he could carry heavy boxes without pain – if he carried them on his back.

Dr Tessman turned the spotlight of his scientific mind on this apparent contradiction. 'I'm constantly sensitive to why things work the way they do,' he told us, and he applied his physicist's knowledge of concepts such as vectors and foot-pounds to what he calls the 'biomechanics' of his aching back.

Over the ensuing years, he swapped notes with medical doctors. He learned from Swedish researchers that different activities such as lying down or laughing or picking up a 40-lb box put varying amounts of stress on the lumbar region. He also delivered a guest lecture at the Tufts medical school, where doctors encouraged him to put his ideas on paper.

Two reasons for pain

There are two basic reasons, Dr Tessman found, why the lumbar region is so prone to injury, and why so many millions of people suffer from back pain. These two factors demonstrate clearly why apparently harmless jobs like raising a window or taking out the rubbish bin cost us so much pain.

The first reason concerns our discs, and there's not much we can do about it. During the first 15 to 20 years of life, blood circulates through these tough, flexible shock absorbers that fit between the bones of our spine. During those 20 years, the discs, as Dr Tessman puts it, 'are in their prime'. After early adulthood, however, the blood supply to the disc gradually stops. It becomes weaker and more vulnerable and, if damaged, it heals slowly, if at all.

The second reason for back pain, Dr Tessman asserts, is bad habits of lifting and carrying. These habits are within our control, and they are the focus of his book. Using the principle of the lever, he shows how the act of reaching forward and down to pick something up – a paper clip, for example – can lay a tremendous stress on the lumbar discs. His findings matched those of the Swedish researchers, who measured the pressure inside the disc during the act of lifting.

Stress on the lower back can result in a muscle strain, a muscle spasm (the muscle's way of locking to protect itself from further injury) or what is erroneously called a 'slipped disc'. A slipped disc means one that has ruptured under pressure. A ruptured disc may touch a nerve and cause a pain so deep and sharp that, Dr Tessman says, anyone who hasn't felt it can't imagine it at all.

The right way to lift

In brief, Dr Tessman's advice is: Don't bend forward to pick up anything unless there's something there to support your weight.

The physics behind this advice is simple and straightforward. Imagine that you and a friend want to ride a seesaw at the neighbourhood playground. Your friend weighs 7 stone and sits 5 ft away from the pivot point at the centre of the plank. You sit down on the other side of the plank, but only 1 ft away from the pivot point. To balance your friend, you would have to weigh 35 stone.

Now imagine your body as a seesaw. Your arms, reaching down and forward are like your friend's half of the plank. Your hips are like the pivot point. Now your lower back muscles strain to lift that load. But since they are close to your hips, they have no leverage. It has been estimated that, in an activity such as shovelling, the back muscles must pull with a force 15 times the weight of the object lifted.

The solution to this problem is simply to lift and carry things beside or behind you, making the load work with your back muscles instead of against them.

Specific examples, illustrated and explained, are the best part of *My Back Doesn't Hurt Anymore*. In the past, you may have received vague advice about not lifting heavy objects, but Dr Tessman shows how to prevent back pain while dealing with the inevitable burdens that present themselves every day.

Imagine, for a moment, a normal day:

The alarm clock is ringing; it's 6 A.M. Getting out of bed is your back's first test of the day. Push yourself up and forward with your hands, and swing your feet around.

Next stop is the bathroom. When shaving or washing your face, take a load off your back by flexing at the knees or supporting your weight with a free hand. Then, while you're dressing, bring your foot up instead of bending forward to slip on socks or tights.

Outside, on the door mat, lies the morning newspaper. Instead of bending over, bend at the knees and keep your back as straight as possible.

At breakfast, even little exertions such as reaching into the refrigerator for a carton of milk or reaching across the table for a platter of eggs could aggravate an existing back problem. Later, before you go out for the day, you might want to give your child or grandchild a bear hug. Avoid reaching over a cot railing or a safety gate to pick him or her up. Instead, lower the railing or open the gate, and flex your knees rather than bend over.

Assuming that you have been to work and are now ready to come home (there's no room here to cover the multitude of hazards on the job), you might stop to buy groceries. Supermarkets can pose a real dilemma for someone with a bad back. Carrier bags can be heavy, and deep-well shopping trolleys create awkward lifting situations.

Instead of one big carrier bag, try carrying two smaller ones, one in each hand. When loading bags into the car, don't put them on the floor. Put them on a seat, or in the rear if you have an estate car.

As the afternoons grow longer, you may want to do some gardening after work. If you're spading compost or soil, keep the payload end of the spade at your side or behind you. Dr Tessman even suggests digging behind yourself, as if you were paddling a canoe. If you're putting in early peas or lettuce or onions, kneel rather than lean over, and if you kneel, use your forearm to prop up your weight.

Changing tyres is another chore that can be a disaster for your back. To avoid the crunch, squat or sit on a stool when you pull off the tyre. When loosening the nuts, always push down with the spanner.

Back inside the house, it might be time to open a window that's been shut all winter. If you face the window and pull up on the handles or grips, your back will think you're trying to lift the house. Instinct may tell you to do it that way, but it's far better to put your back to the window and raise it behind you.

The same principle applies to carring a trunk, a sofa or any other heavy weight. Hold your end behind you.

The day is almost done. You might want to give your child or grandchild a ride on your shoulders before he or she goes to bed. If you let the child use a sofa or chair to climb on to your shoulders, you won't hurt your back. (For women who want to take infants with them during the day, what's best for their backs is to carry the child on the back in a rucksack-like affair.)

Your last chore of the evening involves that hallowed ritual: taking out the rubbish. If you try to carry a loaded rubbish bin in front of you, by the handles, your back may never forgive you. Get your teenage son to take it down to the kerb, or drag the bin behind you, or, best of all, put the bin on a cart with wheels.

Myths worth puncturing

As well as giving advice, Dr Tessman also punctures a few myths about the back. Strong arm and back muscles, he says, can't protect your discs. On the contrary, the stronger they are, the more likely they are to bite off a load that's more than your back can chew, so to speak.

Certain traditional exercises are also taboo. Dr Tessman says that bending over to touch your toes and doing sit-ups place unnecessary strain on the discs. He prefers deep knee bends for strengthening the thigh muscles, and deep breathing exercises for developing the abdominal muscles.

Of course, sometimes Dr Tessman's schedule gets frantic, and he forgets his own rules. That's when he relies on his family to remind him of the motto of his book: 'Be kind to your discs.'

Give your back a good night's rest

Do you often wake up in the morning with a backache? How about a stiff neck? Or maybe your whole body feels kind of stiff and achy after a night's sleep – nothing you can't usually shake off in an hour or two once you get your body moving again. Maybe you've just dismissed it as old age creeping up.

Did you ever suspect that it could be your bed? You know, the one you've been sleeping on for 10 or 20 years now. Sure, it sags a bit, and you do tend to roll towards the middle. But it's kind of cosy, in a way. What's more you've grown attached to that old mattress, so it couldn't be that, could it?

It not only could be, it probably is. According to Robert G. Addison associate professor of orthopaedic surgery at Northwestern University Medical School and director of the Center for Pain Studies of the Rehabilitation Institute of Chicago, 'All night long as you sleep on a too-soft or too-hard bed, your muscles are working overtime to align your spine. It's no coincidence that many people wake up in the morning with a backache. They haven't given those muscles any time off to rest.'

'Sleep is our longest single postural activity,' adds Lionel A. Walpin clinical director of physical medicine and rehabilitation at Cedars – Sinai Medical

Center in Los Angeles, 'and we have the least control over it. We turn over rapidly dozens of times during the night and can stress tight muscles without even knowing it. Then, to make matters worse, we remain in contorted positions for long periods of time – putting additional strain on muscles tendons, ligaments, nerves and joints.'

Considering that we spend one-third of our lives in bed, it's not surprising that assorted back ailments afflict millions of people each year. What is surprising is that many of those sufferers could probably find relief simply by sleeping on the right mattress.

'There is a rapidly growing awareness among doctors and the public that natural and pain-free sleep is essential for good health,' says Dr Walpin.

Even though doctors recognize the problems that the wrong bed can create they can't agree on a solution. Probably because there isn't one – there are many. 'No bed is perfectly suited for everyone,' notes Dr Addison, who has helped design mattresses for major bedding manufacturers. 'However, the ideal mattress should cradle the spine in the same position as if you were standing with good posture.'

Usually, that takes a firm mattress. Our body weight is not evenly distributed, so we need adequate support under places that sink deepest into the mattress – the hips, chest and head in particular. A good mattress should distribute weight evenly so that one part of the body is not stressed more that another.

'In designing a mattress, we use a system called angles of deflection according to body weight,' explains Dr Addison. 'That means we measure how much the mattress dips when pressures from the head, shoulders, hips and feet are exerted on it. In a well-constructed mattress, these angles of deflection should vary less than 5 per cent. This indicates that the person's weight is very evenly distributed exactly what a good mattress should do.'

Finding the right mattress
However, not all mattresses are created equal, and consequently, some do not distribute body weight in the most desirable way.

To prove that point and to find out which beds did the job best, an experiment was conducted. 'Of course we couldn't test every bed on the market,' Steve Garfin of the University of California at San Diego wrote.

> But we did test four of them an 'orthopedic' hard bed, containing 720 coils in the mattress, plus a bed board and box spring; a standard 500-coil soft bed; a standard 10-inch-deep water bed; and a new hybrid bed composed of a central core of water surrounded by polyurethane foam.

Five volunteers (all in good health) were asked to lie on each of the beds, which had first been covered with a special pressure-measuring sheet.

What the researchers found, said Dr Garfin, was that in both the prone (on the stomach) and supine (on the back) positions, the hard bed and the water bed distributed weight more evenly over the entire body than the other beds. The soft bed and the hybrid bed, on the other hand, recorded extremely uneven pressures. In fact, all five persons studied felt the latter two beds were uncomfortable, while there were no complaints about the other two (*Archives of Physical Medicine and Rehabilitation*, September 1980).

Shortly after that study was completed, Dr Garfin decided to test the same four beds again, only this time all the volunteers chosen suffered from chronic low back pain.

> The standard 'orthopedic' bed that is hard or extra firm is generally the type of bed recommended by most physicians and textbooks dealing with chronic low back pain. 'Water beds are, in fact, discouraged by most doctors who treat this condition. But then we'll meet people with chronic low back pain and they'll tell us that water beds work for them. 'Presumably, firm mattresses are effective in relieving back pain by helping straighten the lumbar (lower) back, but if that's true, a water bed theoretically should not afford any relief. Weight distribution on a water bed is even, and the spinal contours are probably unchanged. Yet, one-half of the patients in this study felt symptomatic relief on this bed. As expected, the other half listed the hard bed as their first choice.
>
> 'Of interest was that all patients except one felt that the hybrid bed caused a deterioration in their condition, and in fact, two patients quit the study early after sleeping on the hybrid bed. [*Pain*, February 1981].

'When it comes to low back pain,' Dr Garfin told us, 'a hard bed is still the preferred support structure. However, a water bed offers an alternative to those patients not helped by the hard bed.'

Two kinds of pain

However, according to Dr Walpin, choosing a bed for comfort alone is not always a wise move, especially for patients with bad backs.

'It's important to determine what's causing the back to "misbehave" and hurt,' he told us, 'before deciding which is going to be the best bed for you. Of course, there are lots of reasons why your back may ache, and some of them are very serious ailments indeed. I'm not referring to the serious ones here but to the more common, everyday aches and pains that many people suffer at one time or another. Of those, there are two main kinds – *postural* pain and *dysfunctional* pain.

'Postural pain comes on gradually. You may notice it developing after hunching over a desk for an hour or so. It's relieved, however, when you stand up and stretch or just change your position. People with pure postural pain are the ones who wake up in the morning stiff and sore. They were probably sleeping in the wrong positions for hours, but because the pain came on slowly, it didn't cause them to wake up during the night. These people can choose a mattress for comfort alone, and that should relieve their postural distress.

'With dysfunctional pain, on the other hand, you wake up suddenly during the night with pain, but on awakening in the morning, you can feel fine,' Dr Walpin added. 'Then you stand up, bend over and – wham – instant pain again. With dysfunction (abnormal function of muscles and joints), you don't have full mobility. Also, treating only the pain, in this case, is not synonymous with recovery. You need to restore the normal strength, length and flexibility of the dysfunctioning muscles and joints, too.

'Choosing a bed for comfort alone would probably be a mistake here because it may foster the continuation of the problem. People with dysfunctional pain need a firm mattress. But I have patients who will tell me that they were sleeping on a soft bed, bought a firm one, and now their backs hurt more than ever. That's because a firm mattress tries to put you in the proper position by restoring the normal curvatures of your spine. The muscles and ligaments are being stretched and balanced (which is good), but at first, this can also hurt.

'On the other hand,' says Dr Walpin, 'if you continue to sleep on a soft bed, you wind up continuing to have unbalanced muscles that are too short on one side of the spine and too stretched on the other. At first, it may actually feel better to you than the firm mattress only because you are compensating for these abnormal, weak muscles – the very ones you are trying to correct. But, because the dysfunction continues, you remain more susceptible to physical stress and strain and a worsening of the very condition you're trying to cure.'

Naturally, we can't recommend a particular brand of bed for you, whether you suffer dysfunctional pain, postural pain or (we hope) no pain at all. We can't even say for certain that an inner-spring mattress is definitely better than a water bed, or that an air or foam mattress won't work as well. (It's probably possible to find people who would swear that theirs is best, yet that really won't help you decide what's right for you).

However, we can give you some guidelines. Dr Walpin believes that 'versatility' in all bedding products is the ideal. For instance, he helped develop a unique bed pillow that is named after him and that offers four different degrees of head and neck support simply by turning the pillow around or over.

And, before you invest in a new bed, you may want to try and improve the one you've already got. 'You can customize your own bed board,' suggests Dr Walpin. 'Instead of using a solid piece of plywood under your mattress, cut individual wood slats to fit your bed. Make each slat about 4 ft by $1^1/_4$ ft. Then you can move the slats to where you need the most support.'

If that doesn't help enough, you can start shopping. But don't be hasty. This is one purchase that deserves your time and attention. A five-second flop on a couple of beds in the local furniture shop just will not do.

'If you have to try out a mattress in the shop,' advises Dr Addison, 'lie down on it for ten minutes at least. Study what happens to the bed as you vary your position. When you lie on your back, your buttocks should be supported and you should feel that support. You should be able to lie comfortably on your stomach without unnaturally arching your back, although I don't recommend this as a primary sleeping position. On your side, your shoulders and hips should sink in slightly so that your spine settles into a horizontal, not a curved, position.'

And remember, when it comes to firmness, don't be swayed by manufacturers' labels such as 'super-firm', 'ultra-firm' or the very medical-sounding 'ortho-firm'. There are no industry-wide standards when it comes to bedding descriptions, so what you feel is what you get.

What you get, you may have to take lying down, so to speak, for years.

'Walk as though you are wearing a crown'

Do yourself a favour. Next time you're getting dressed, take a moment to check your posture in the mirror. Better still (if your ego is up to it) invite your friends and family to turn a critical eye on the way you stand and carry yourself while you walk.

Chances are you won't be pleased with the results.

However, before you shrug off those hunched shoulders or that protruding abdomen as something you should have corrected years ago – 'before it was too late' – do yourself another favour and listen to Raymond Harris, former president and director of the Center for the Study of Ageing in Albany, New York, and author of *Guide to Fitness After Fifty*.

'Bad posture,' says Dr Harris, 'can be corrected. And it's never too late to start.'

The fact is, it's not easy to face the world with poor posture. When you're slumped forward, it shifts your body weight backward from the vertebrae of the spine to the muscles and ligaments of the lower back – which leads to fatigue disfiguration such as swayback (abnormal hollowing of the spine, medically called *lordosis*) and pain.

'Swayback is a real problem,' explains Benjamin S. Golub of the back service at the Hospital for Joint Diseases and Medical Center in New York. 'The muscles and ligaments of the lower back are just not designed to support our weight.' According to Dr Golub, a strong, straight posture is no luxury. 'You need good posture for all activities,' he told us, 'including standing sitting and bending.'

So let's get back to that mirror. This time, you're going to see how you look with the right standing posture – one that will shift your weight back where it belongs, to the spine.

Stand erect, keeping your body firm yet flexible.

Relax.

Look straight ahead and distribute your weight evenly on the ball of each foot – not the toes or the heel. You should be able to raise your heels without leaning forward.

Slightly tilt your lower pelvis forward and upward. Imagine that you're holding a coin between your buttocks and you'll feel them tightening (don't bend your knees). As you shift into position, your buttocks should tuck in and the small of the back – the lumbar curve – should flatten into a slight arc.

'And flattening the lumbar curve,' says Dr Golub, 'is the name of the game.'

Hold your chest high. As you raise your chest, your shoulders naturally roll back and your stomach pulls in. (A slumping chest or sagging abdomen restricts your ability to breathe efficiently – and comfortably). But don't arch your back and suck in your stomach; this only develops the tense posture of a soldier at attention. 'The military style of posture is too rigid,' warns Dr Golub. 'Don't be a martinet.'

Your goal is good vertical alignment. That is, you should be able to drop an imaginary plumb line from just behind the ear, through the shoulder, the sacrum (the last bone of the spine and part of the pelvis), behind the hip and the knee, and through the ankle.

Although it sounds like quite a goal – connecting all those bones – there are only three manoeuvres to remember. Stand erect. Tilt your pelvis. Raise your chest. Everything else takes care of itself and falls naturally into place.

Don't be discouraged if you find yourself twisting like a go-go dancer in front of the mirror while trying to align your body. Chances are your body is accustomed to being 'out of line', and at first, good posture may seem uncomfortable or unnatural, creating tension in your lower back. But with time – and practice – you will be at ease.

Good posture, then, is a skill, just like playing a musical instrument or riding a bicycle. And like other skills, it will improve steadily with practice. No matter how bad things look in the mirror, a little determination will go a long way to straighten out your reflection. Once you make up your mind to put in the effort, you may be surprised at how easy it is to improve your posture.

Three steps to good posture

According to Dr Harris, there are three basic parts to the process.

First, he says, be aware of your posture. Monitor your posture in mirrors and shop windows – instead of fiddling with your hair or straightening your clothes. 'The idea,' he explains, 'is to mobilize your thought processes. The best way I know to do this is to walk as though you are wearing a crown.'

Second, consciously place yourself in the proper positions. Dr Harris suggests that you practise lying flat on the floor on a slantboard (a piece of wood built on a slant so that you can rest with your feet higher than your head) or on a wide, strong ironing board with the small end propped up about 6 to 10 inches. In this position, your spine will straighten and your back will flatten. Muscles are relaxed and at ease. Small pillows can be placed behind the neck and the knees to ease any strain on the spine.

The final component of the good posture process is stretching, massaging and exercising your muscles. 'Gentle massage is especially helpful for those over 50,' says Dr Harris. For some, he also recommends hanging from a chinning bar: 'It stretches muscles gently and gets them working properly . . . it brings the back into proper alignment and relieves pressure on the nerves and discs.'

Even rolling around on a padded or carpeted floor is beneficial. Dr Harris claims that it restores joint mobility by improving muscle tone and helps the muscles hold the body in proper posture.

When you think about posture, don't overlook the importance of proper breathing, he adds. Diaphragmatic – or belly – breathing is the basis for really good health.

Let's take a moment and try it.

Place your hand between your navel and ribs and take a deep breath. Your hand goes out as your diaphragm drops. Exhale, and your hand goes inward as the diaphragm rises. Again, practice makes perfect.

Good posture eases back pain

If you suffer from back pain, improving your posture is especially important, according to orthopaedist Golub. While good posture won't correct osteoporosis, fractures, disc degeneration or other back problems, it can help reduce the effects of back disease. 'And bad posture superimposed on other back disorders only compounds your problems.'

The best exercises for improving posture, he says, are those designed to strengthen the stomach muscles. 'The stomach muscles are the key to the back. When tight and strong, they automatically tilt the pelvis and diminish the lumbar curve.'

Whatever exercises you use to improve your posture, the important thing is to do them regularly, says Hyman Jampol, director of the Beverly Palm Rehabilitation Hospital in Los Angeles and author of *The Weekend Athlete's Way to a Pain-Free Monday*. 'You can't exercise only when you feel like it. You need to have a programme, just like you have one for brushing your teeth or your hair or for going to the hairdressers,' he says. 'You should strengthen your stomach muscles and stretch your back muscles for about ten minutes the first thing each day. Soon this will snowball. The more you do the better you feel, and the more you want to do.'

Good ways to round out an exercise programme include walking, cycling swimming and dancing. If you can, do them all.

(*See also* MUSCLE PROBLEMS.)

• Bad Breath

You can have bad luck or a bad name. Hear bad news or bad language. Come down with a bad cold, or just plain feel bad. But the worst of them all the one that really makes you embarrassed, insecure and panicky (and the one you'd probably most like to avoid) is *bad breath*.

Well, breathe easy. You can prevent bad breath, but not by swilling mouthwash sucking on mints or brushing with flavoured toothpaste. Those so-called remedies, which we'll deal with later, only mask the odour and may even worsen the smell of your breath in the long run. No, there are better, *natural* ways to prevent bad breath. But first you have to know its cause.

And one cause of bad breath, says Michael Lerner, a dentist from Lexington Kentucky, is 'blowing air over something that doesn't smell good.'

That 'something,' he told us, is usually an infection or an inflammation of the gums. 'Ninety-five per cent of the people in America have inflamed gums,' he says, 'and that means most Americans have some degree of bad breath.' The inflammation, he explains, develops when bacteria accumulate on the teeth and produce toxic waste products that irritate and weaken the gums. And while the areas of inflammation are too small to see, you can't miss them. 'If your gums bleed easily when you brush, your gums are inflamed,' says Mr Lerner.

But the problem is easy to correct. Two or three days of proper brushing and flossing will 'disrupt the bacteria and increase tissue resistance,' he says. He also suggests taking 'good levels' of vitamins A and C and the bioflavonoids to strengthen the gums.

The tongue needs cleaning too

Cleaning your teeth and maintaining healthy gums is a first-step in achieving fresh breath, but to complete the job – in fact, to do *most* of the job – you need to clean your tongue.

That tongue brushing works is ancient history and scientific fact. Muhammad told his followers, 'You shall clean your mouth' – including the tongue. Romans used iron tongue-scrapers, and other cultures made them from ivory tortoise-shell, whalebone and wood. For modern man, however, a soft-bristle toothbrush will do. And the modern 'command' to clean the tongue comes not from a prophet, but a scientist.

Joseph Tonzetich, a professor at the School of Dentistry of the University of British Columbia in Vancouver, conducted a study to find out the most effective way to reduce bad breath. Eight volunteers – all of whom suffered from a case of 'morning mouth' – used one of three methods to freshen their breath in the morning: brushing their teeth, brushing their tongue or the two methods combined. Before and after the volunteers cleaned their mouths, Dr Tonzetich measured the amount of sulphur-containing gases in their breath – the gases that create the odour of bad breath. He found that brushing the teeth reduced mouth odour by 25 per cent. *But brushing the tongue reduced mouth odour by 75 per cent!* When the two methods were combined, odour was reduced by 85 per cent *(Oral Surgery)*.

'Tongue brushing,' Dr Tonzetich told us, 'is the single most effective method of decreasing breath odour.'

If the thought of tongue brushing makes you gag, don't worry. Researchers who conducted a study on tongue brushing found that people who had never brushed their tongues before quickly made it a habit. 'The patients,' they wrote 'reported a feeling of cleaner mouths' and 'cleaner breath' and, since this experiment and introduction to this procedure, have continued to brush their tongues' *(Journal of Periodontology)*.

However, even tooth and tongue brushing combined don't completely eliminate bad breath. Why not?

'You can't remove all breath odour through oral cleansing because not all breath odour comes from the mouth,' says Dr Tonzetich. Fifteen per cent comes from *inside* the body. 'Chemicals produced by the metabolic activity of the body, such as digestion, are picked up in the blood and eliminated through the lungs via the mouth.'

In short, bad digestion can mean bad breath.

Bruce Pacetti, the director of nutritional research at the Florida Holistic Medical Center, believes that most digestion-related bad breath is caused by four foods: caffeine, refined sugar, white flour and cow's milk. 'These foods upset human biochemistry, which can result in either the fermentation of carbohydrates or the putrefaction of proteins in the digestive tract. In either case, noxious chemicals are produced, may enter the bloodstream and may be breathed out through the lungs.'

Michael Lerner believes that a lack of digestive enzymes in the stomach causes bad breath. 'The odour of food that has been incompletely digested in the stomach comes up through the oesophagus and the throat and out through the mouth,' he says.

Poor digestion or poor oral health (or both) account for most cases of bad breath, but there are other causes. Alcohol. Tobacco. A throat infection. Dirty dentures. Mouth ulcers. Bad breath is even a side-effect of some prescription drugs. But whatever the cause, many people with bad breath try to solve the problem with mouthwash. It's a wishy-washy solution.

Why mouthwash won't work

Most mouthwashes work by killing bacteria. But after an hour or two, the bacteria are back – with reinforcements.

'Mouthwash is terrible,' Philip Parsons, a dentist in Florida, told us. 'They lower bacteria, but more grow back than before.'

Mouthwashes are a chemical soup, with a pinch of dye and a dash of artificial flavour. They also contain enough alcohol to kill, if not a horse, then a small child. (The medical literature documents two cases of children who drank a bottle of minty mouthwash, lost consciousness and almost died.) One brand is 140 proof! (Listerine, the best-seller, is a milder vintage, containing 25 per cent alcohol.) That's good news for closet alcoholics, but bad news for everybody else. Because alcohol, swirled and gargled once, twice or even three times a day, can seriously damage the tissues in your mouth and throat – causing the very type of inflammation that results in bad breath. (See also DRUG SIDE-EFFECTS.)

Gum disease, sore tongues, burning palates, ulcers in the mucous membranes of the mouth – too much mouthwash has done it all. When students rinsed their mouths with full-strength mouthwash twice a day for two weeks, many developed inflammation, ulceration or other reactions. The reaction rates of the four different mouthwashes tested ranged from 6 to 15 per cent (Journal of Oral Medicine).

What about people who don't stop using mouthwash? Their inflammation may get worse. It might even turn into cancer.

That's not true for everybody, of course, but heavy users of mouthwash people who use it more than once a day year after year, seem to be at a high risk for head and neck cancer. For instance, when doctors studied 11 patients with head and neck cancer who had never used alcohol or tobacco (the two main risk factors for this type of cancer), they found that 10 of them were heavy users of mouthwash (Journal of Oral Surgery, April 1979).

Another person in the study developed new pre-malignant lesions in her mouth after cancerous tissue there had been surgically removed. She had been a heavy smoker but swore that she had stopped when her cancer was first diagnosed. On closer questioning, the doctors found out that she was a heavy user of mouthwash and advised her to stop. In a few months, the lesions cleared up.

Mouthwash, wrote the doctors, 'may indeed be carcinogenic for susceptible individuals.'

Mouthwash doesn't have to contain alcohol, however. You don't even have to buy it in a shop. Just put a few drops of peppermint oil in a glass of water. Or take a glass of tea (at room temperature) made with peppermint, fenugreek or parsley, three herbs said to sweeten the breath. If your breath is in a bad way, there's a way out – the natural way.

• Baldness

When Egyptologists unearthed the oldest known medical text, what do you think they discovered? What wisdom had the men who built the sphinx and the great temple of Karnak left buried in the ancient sands? The secret of eternal life? The formula for raising up a mummy? Not quite. But one thing they did find was a home remedy for baldness – consisting of the fat of a lion, a hippopotamus, a crocodile, a serpent and an ibex. Although today these ingredients are hard to come by, there are many hair products available on chemists' shelves that, though less exotic, are probably equally effective.

Throughout the ages, humans have felt a special and tender concern for the loss of their hair. The roll of purported cures and of famous personages who worried their heads over going bald is impressive. Julius Caesar, at the height of his power, when you might suppose that all his insecurities had been allayed, wore a laurel wreath to conceal his balding imperial dome. In modern times, Woodrow Wilson, often regarded as one of America's more intellectual presidents, sought out special head massages.

Eventually, some form of noticeable baldness affects 65 per cent of the total male population, and this sizable potential clientele is being offered a variety of remedies ranging from the reputable and successful to the positively fraudulent and dangerous.

Artificial fibre implants fall into the latter category; these were banned by the US Food and Drug Administration after being universally condemned by reputable doctors. (Fibre implants should not be confused with hair transplants; *see below.*) But there are other baldness remedies that lie somewhere between safe and dangerous.

Some doctors have attempted to treat baldness through the use of female hormone injections and creams. The results have been disconcerting. High dosages of oestrogen will stop progressive baldness and may cause hair to grow, but the side-effects amount to a chemical castration – loss of sexual drive, breast enlargement, and changes in the male distribution of body hair – leaving those who are willing to consider any cure for their baldness with a difficult dilemma.

Some researchers, however, are highly optimistic that the long-awaited cure for baldness will be found in chemicals that suppress the male hormones but avoid the feminizing side-effects. Such 'anti-androgens,' as they are called are not female hormones. Instead, they inhibit the male hormones by competing with them for the same enzymes and binding sites. But the problem with most known anti-androgens has so far been that they seem to produce as many side-effects as they suppress. These are so toxic that at present the use of anti-androgens for a cosmetic problem like baldness is quite unreasonable.

The importance of zinc

So far, there is no 'cure' for baldness, but new evidence suggests that premature loss of hair and perhaps balding may be linked to a shortage of zinc.

'Animals fed zinc showed a six-to-one difference in hair growth when compared with zinc-deficient animals,' Jeng M. Hsu told us. Dr Hsu, who is chief of biochemistry research projects at a Veterans Administration Center in Florida also found changes in the hair protein structure when zinc was deficient in the diet.

Rats who had the zinc taken out of their diets lost their hair in another study as well, and researchers further concluded that the deficiency was 'a possible explanation of greying of black hair.'

A bald 27-year-old diabetic reported hair growth after being placed on insulin zinc therapy (Lancet). And in another case, a 20-year-old man suffering from a severe zinc deficiency developed baldness and scalp problems that cleared up when the zinc was returned to his diet (Journal of the American Medical Association).

Hair transplants

If you are still inconsolably hair-lorn and willing to submit to minor surgery to ease your mind, then there is a remedy: a hair transplant. Hair transplants done by a qualified doctor are recognized as reasonably safe and generally successful, and have been performed on over 4 million people. (They should not be confused with the fraudulent fibre implants, with which they have nothing in common.) In hair transplants, plugs of the patient's natural hair and hair follicles, not strands of synthetic fibres, are grafted on to the bald areas of the scalp. Since the patient's own natural hair is used neither the foreign-body reactions nor bacterial infections characteristic of fibre implants are a problem. Nevertheless, hair transplants are a form of minor surgery and should not be undertaken lightly.

Hair transplants are, in fact, follicle transplants, the purpose of the operation being to transfer follicles that are genetically programmed to resist the male hormones that trigger baldness to areas whose follicles have given up. In nine months, the transplanted follicles should produce full-length hairs whose survival rate is over 90 per cent.

And the end result? Generally, it's good. But since the hair density won't be the same as a full head of hair, the transplantee will have to invest in good hair styling.

To have a transplant performed, you need two things: enough surviving hair to supply the grafts and enough money to pay the fee. Some transplants have been performed using grafts from donors other than the transplantee, but the problem with that is the same as with heart transplants: tissue rejection. Finding a doctor who is qualified to perform hair transplants is essential, as sloppy technique can result in severe scarring or disfigurement. The price of a transplant depends on the number of grafts and the cost of a full transplant can easily reach over £5000.

If the surgical cure for baldness is out of the question, is there anything else you can do? Unfortunately, for the most common form of baldness – hereditary baldness – there isn't. It is caused by a combination of hereditary predisposition, ageing and the activity of the male hormones. There is nothing to be done about it. There are other, temporary forms of hair loss caused by vitamin and protein deficiencies or unhealthy diet that can be prevented or reversed by good nutrition and general health (see HAIR PROBLEMS) but eating and living well cannot perform the miracle of bringing dead follicles back to life.

Of course, not every man who is bald finds the condition unbearable or even particularly worthy of his attention. Some scratch their noble heads and wonder what all the fuss is about. In view of the possible risks and the certain expense involved in even the safest baldness remedy, perhaps it's worth considering their attitude. 'Baldness is a natural condition,' observes skin biologist William Montagna, 'not a disease. There's no real problem.'

Except in the mind, of course. And if that's where the problem is, that's where the best 'cure' should be aimed. Learn to stop imagining that baldness is bad or abnormal. A change of attitude is perhaps the best baldness 'remedy' of all.

• Bed-wetting

Allergy can disturb bladder function and lead to bed-wetting. When the bladder is the target for an allergic reaction, its wall swells and loses elasticity. Thus, the volume of urine it can hold is reduced. The smooth muscle becomes irritated, with a tendency to spasm. The shutoff valve shares these adverse reactions and is thereby less able to perform its function. In addition, because allergic children suffer from undue fatigue, they tend to sleep more deeply and do not sense the call of nature.

A study of 500 children indicated that cow's milk was the most frequent cause of allergic reaction. Other foods indicted include eggs, chocolate, grains and citrus fruits. These observations, reported by Dr J. C. Breneman before the American College of Allergists, emphasize that children should not be punished for bed-wetting and that emotional problems in these children are the result rather than the cause of the condition.

• Bladder infection (cystitis)

It's the most uncomfortable kind of infection there is. Sometimes it comes on suddenly with such force that you wonder if you'll make it to the lavatory in time. Then it burns when you urinate, and even when you're done that full-bladder feeling is still there, only there's nothing left to come out. You pace around with a fidgety feeling like a four-year-old. Still, the ache continues, moving up into the abdomen and back. Next time you urinate you may even see a little blood. It's enough to scare you to death.

A rare disease? Hardly. Millions – mostly women – fall victim to bladder infections (cystitis) each year, and for 80 per cent of them it won't be the last time, either. In fact, so common is this ailment that it's sometimes referred to a a 'cold in the bladder.' But don't let that fool you. It's not at all as simple as a runny nose. Urinary-tract infections (UTIs) can affect the urethra (the tube which vents urine from the bladder) or kidneys as well as the bladder. They're caused by any number of treacherous bacteria, but most often by *Escherichia coli*, a normal inhabitant of the bowel and harmless when it remains in its own territory. But let those bugs wander into the normally sterile area of the urinary tract, and you could wind up with a full-blown case of UTI.

For women, the bacteria don't have to wander very far. One look at the female anatomy shows you why. A woman's urethra is only $1^1/_2$ inches long just a short walk for the bacteria to reach the bladder.

Besides that, the urethra and the rectum (the original source of the *E. coli*) are close together.

No wonder women outnumber men by more than ten to one in cases of UTI. On top of that, some women have the bad habit of wiping from back to front, making a short trip even shorter for the bugs. Add underwear in fabrics that don't breathe (nylon and other synthetics), tights and tight jeans, and you've got the warm, dark, moist environment that *E. coli* thrive in.

Which they do with zest in women of all ages. According to Calvin M. Kunin chairman of the department of medicine at Ohio State University School of Medicine, all women are susceptible to UTIs, but the prevalence increases about 1 per cent per decade of life in adult women and may be as high as 10 per cent in elderly women.

'Honeymoon cystitis'

Still, there are certain stages in a woman's life when flare-ups seem almost predictable. Like just after her first few experiences of sexual intercourse. Cystitis, the most common type of urinary-tract infection, is so common at this time that it's been dubbed 'honeymoon cystitis'.

The theory is that any bacteria in the neighbourhood of the urethra have a good chance of being pushed up into the bladder during intercourse. Once the honeymoon is over, though, cystitis may still be a lingering reminder of those more active nights. In fact, women with a history of UTI are more prone to it during pregnancy, especially during the last trimester. That's when the space inside is at a premium and the bladder gets wedged between the uterus and the pubic bone, so that it may not be able to empty itself completely. Any bacteria remaining from previous infections dive into the pool of leftover urine and start multiplying.

What's worse, says Dr Kunin, is that there appears to be some change in the urinary tract during the last part of pregnancy that makes it easier for these bladder bacteria to spread upward and invade the kidneys.

Still, giving up sex isn't the answer, according to Leo Galland, assistant clinical professor of medicine at the University of Connecticut. Along with sociologist Kiku Odatto, Dr Linda Granowetter and nurse-social worker Kitty Doebele, Dr Galland conducted a study that compared 84 women with a history of recurrent UTI with a group who were free of this problem. Their purpose was to determine if there were any notable differences in the sexual, hygiene and urinating habits of women with recurring UTI and those who had never been affected.

Contrary to popular belief, sex was not the culprit it was originally thought to be. 'The sexual habits of the patients and controls were strikingly similar,' says Dr Galland. 'Not only were both groups sexually active, but they contained about the same percentage of women having fequent intercourse (three to seven times a week). Discomfort associated with sexual encounters was also distributed evenly.'

Other factors

There was one factor related to sexual behaviour that was significant, however and that had to do with postponing urination after intercourse. The majority of the controls (68 percent) frequently voided within ten minutes of sexual intercourse while only 8 per cent of the patients did.

However, the most striking difference between patients and controls was the high frequency of 'holding it in' among the patient group.

Voluntary retention of urine for more than an hour after experiencing the urge to 'go' was present in 61 percent of the patients but in only 11 per cent of the controls. And more than two-thirds of the patients reported waiting three hours or longer before urinating. [*Journal of the American Medical Association*, 8 June 1979].

Not surprisingly, while the urine is accumulating in the bladder, so are the germs. But there's more to it than that. Jack Lapides of the University of Michigan Medical Center has spent 20 years investigating the causes of urinary-tract infections. He speculates that ignoring nature's call damages the wall of the bladder, making it more susceptible to infection.

The distended or full bladder causes a decreased blood flow through its veins. The anti-bacterial agents naturally found in the bloodstream are also decreased, and the body can't defend itself against incoming germs. 'In the female patient,' says Dr Lapides, 'it is primarily poor voiding patterns that cause overdistention of the bladder, thus accounting for most urinary-tract infections.'

Considering the consequences, it's hard to imagine anyone consciously choosing to ignore the urge for even one hour, but apparently women do consistently hold it in, and for lots longer than that. In one group of 250 women that Dr Lapides studied, 66 per cent were infrequent voiders, going only once in five to ten hours!

And it wasn't for lack of facilities, either. Dr Galland's patients most frequently cited embarrassment in social situations and unwillingness to use public toilets as their reasons for putting off what comes naturally. Others just didn't want to take time out from their activities, whether at home or at work. And those reasons were not unique to this particular study, either. Dr Lapides's group listed the very same reasons as Dr Galland's patients, adding that sometimes there were too few toilets at their place of work or in various shopping areas, or that they were afraid of contracting a venereal disease in a public toilet. Some unfortunate women ignored the inevitable as long as possible because neck-to-thigh foundation garments were such a hassle to remove.

A regimen that works

The fact is, no excuse is good enough when your health is involved. Especially when prevention of UTIs can be as easy as going to the toilet – frequently, of course.

Dr Galland's experiment proved that point. After the initial study, the patients were then given a basic preventive regimen to follow. It included regular urination (about every two hours), voiding ten minutes after intercourse, drinking eight glasses of fluid a day and wiping front to back after urinating.

After six months, the patients showed a re-infection rate of only 15 per cent – more than encouraging when you consider that cystitis usually recurs in about 80 per cent of sufferers.

It's no wonder that both Dr Galland and Dr Lapides stress the importance of frequent urination as the first step in a preventive programme. If you're prone to recurrent urinary-tract infection (and even if you're not), it makes good sense to follow the regimen that they suggest.

And take some hints from the patients they interviewed, too. That means making time for normal functioning, no matter how involved you are with activities. Wear clothes that don't stifle your ability to urinate frequently. And while you're at it, make sure that undergarments are cotton (for better air circulation), and change them every day. Keep your bottom clean and dry, and avoid chemical irritants such as scented powders, perfumed sprays or bubble baths.

If, in spite of these precautions, you feel the symptoms of UTI coming on immediately start to drink plenty of water. Eight glasses a day is recommended, and that's usually enough to flush out your urinary tract of invading bacteria. Besides, the more dilute the urine, the less painful voiding will be.

'An alternative to water,' says Dr Galland, 'is cranberry juice. But don't substitute any other fruit juices for the eight glasses of water. Cranberry juice is unique and good because it contains hippuric acid that inhibits the growth of bacteria.'

Others heartily agree. Wisconsin doctor D. V. Moen reported success with cranberry juice almost 20 years ago. In the *Wisconsin Medical Journal* he recommended two (6 oz) glasses daily for continued relief of urinary symptoms (*see also* URINARY PROBLEMS).

Meanwhile, in your effort to purge the germs from your urinary tract, don't forget old reliable vitamin C. 'Its presence in the urine may actually promote good health in the bladder and kidneys,' says Dr Alan Gaby of Baltimore Maryland. 'Vitamin C can kill some bacteria, including *E. coli*, the most common cause of urinary-tract infections. That killing power is especially strong at the uniquely high vitamin C levels that are possible in the concentrated fluid of urine. Doctors have used vitamin C for years to prevent urinary-tract infections in people likely to develop them. It's generally assumed that the vitamin works by producing an acid urine that inhibits the growth of bacteria. In fact, vitamin C does a poor job of acidifying the urine. The effectiveness of the vitamin is more likely related to a direct bactericidal [bacteria-killing] action.'

While battling an infection, it's best to stay away from coffee, tea alcohol and spicy foods, since they may irritate your already sensitive urinary tract.

It *is* possible to cure a urinary-tract infection without ever having to resort to antibiotics. Still, if the self-help remedies you try don't relieve symptoms within 24 hours, it's time to see a doctor. An infection in the bladder should not be ignored, since there's always risk of kidney involvement.

• Body odour

There's a mineral that appears to be involved in the prevention of body odour. It's called magnesium, and chances are, if you're eating a standard diet, you're not getting enough of this essential nutrient.

Which is why your armpits smell? That's right, says B. F. Hart, a doctor in Fort Lauderdale, Florida. Dr Hart has found that magnesium, when administered with zinc, para-aminobenzoic acid (PABA) and vitamin B_6, can effectively control offensive body and breath odours.

Body odours are related to the body's total health, he insists. He told us 'When I use magnesium orally with zinc, PABA and vitamin B_6, it clears up not only body odours but breath odours as well.'

But surely, you say, magnesium's deodorant powers are confined to only the most extreme cases?

'No,' says Jonathan V. Wright, a nutrition doctor from Washington State. 'I find that in just about any case magnesium can lessen the odour.'

Another doctor has used zinc on extreme cases – with equal success. 'About two years ago, I saw a patient who was being given 220 mg of oral zinc sulphate (equivalent to 50 mg of elemental zinc) three times daily by his surgeon as part of the management of recurrent leg ulcers,' reported Dr Morton D. Scribner of California in the *Archives of Dermatology*. The man was observant enough to notice that, while he was taking zinc, there was a big reduction in perspiration odour. 'This problem, which has been most distressing to him for most of his adult life, returned within days after the zinc was discontinued.' He started taking the capsules again, and the odour again diminished, as his wife was happy to confirm. 'Based on this observation,' Dr Scribner wrote 'I have given zinc sulphate to five other persons, with uniformly good results.' Most were helped by as little as 20 mg of zinc daily. 'All had tried a wide variety of deodorants and antiperspirants without success,' he added. 'This report is submitted in hope of helping other unfortunate persons who suffer from socially incapacitating perspiration odour.'

• Bone disease (osteoporosis and osteomalacia)

A, B and C scrawled on a blackboard. The white cliffs of Dover. An ostrich egg and a pearl. A mother's milk. Your skeleton and your teeth.

The cool, lovely whiteness they all share comes from calcium – the fifth most abundant element on earth, and the mineral you need more of than any other. Without it, your body would collapse because it's the primary building block of bones. In addition, a small amount of calcium circulates through your soft tissues, insuring the proper pumping of your heart, and the health of your blood, muscles and nerves. Calcium, a mineral of many talents, is a friend you can't afford to be without.

As you get older, a calcium deficiency may show up dramatically one day when you have a minor fall and shatter a hip. Or you may join the millions who each year, suffer spontaneous fracture – a break without a fall.

Most likely, that seemingly impossible accident is due to *osteoporosis* (literally, 'holey bones'). It means your skeletal structure has become demineralized, brittle and as riddled with holes as a sponge. It's far more common among elderly women than men because, at menopause, the oestrogen (female sex hormone) factories shut down, causing a downward shift in the body's ability to absorb calcium. And since even a healthy body absorbs calcium rather poorly, any further reduction can really get you into trouble.

Poor calcium absorption isn't a modern-day affliction either: 4000-year-old skeletons unearthed at an archaeological site in the United States showed roughly the same amount of age-related bone mineral loss you might expect to find underneath your own skin. What is new is the growing evidence that instead of being simply the inevitable consequence of old age, osteoporosis 'may soon come to be regarded as a bone disease of nutritional origin,' in the words of Anthony Albanese, a researcher at Burke Rehabilitation Center, White Plains, New York.

Calcium supplements

Recently, for example, a research team at Kentucky State University became concerned when a survey of elderly women showed that up to 92 per cent had varying degrees of osteoporosis. Could a calcium-enriched diet slow down stop or even reverse the steady loss of bone in osteoporotic women? The scientists decided to put the question to the test.

The regular diets of 20 elderly women were supplemented with three slices of cheese and three calcium capsules every day for six months. At the beginning and end of the study, the density of each subject's finger bones was measured using a precise X-ray technique called *quantitative radiography*.

Result? Eleven of the 20 subjects showed increased bone density, 3 hadn't changed and 6 others showed decreased density. 'The results suggested that even with a mean age of 70 years, some elderly persons can benefit from supplementary Ca [calcium] and Ca-rich foods to improve bone density,' the researchers concluded (*American Journal of Clinical Nutrition*, May 1981).

That fact wouldn't surprise Dr Albanese. For the last ten years, he has administered various calcium supplements (in doses of 750 to 1000 mg per day) for different periods of time to 526 women at two centres in New York State and charts their bone density by quantitative radiochemistry. That means that he has X-rays of people's bones read by a machine, rather than relying on a set of subjective human eyes to rate the X-rays for bone density.

His findings read like a history of election returns in a one-party town. Those given calcium supplements developed denser, stronger, more calcified bones. Those given placebos kept deteriorating. However, because osteoporosis is of sufficient complexity, no two women responded the same to supplements.

In some, only a mild increase in density resulted after more than three years. In others, density increased remarkably. One 62-year-old woman, who started out with bones more porous than six other women aged 36 to 54, ended up, three years later, with bones denser than those of the youngest.

In general, the women's bones did not respond with calcification until six to nine months of daily supplement-taking had elapsed. 'In some of those women bone loss has been going on for 20 years. You can't expect to put it back so fast,' Dr Albanese told us.

The older you are, the longer you have to wait for better bones. At a New York nursing home, women (whose average age was 84) took a year and a half to respond to supplements, but when they did, their bones grew denser by 11 per cent, while a non-supplemented control group experienced an 8 per cent decrease in bone mass during the same time period, Dr Albanese said.

Why osteoporosis develops

How and why does this slow, treacherous decline in bone strength get started? There are probably many reasons.

One is inactivity. Bones gain strength in response to stress and lose it through lack of use. In one study, bones in the playing arms of professional tennis players were shown to be some 30 per cent stronger than those in their non-playing arms. Oestrogen withdrawal, malabsorption of calcium and low calcium intake are other factors leading to decline.

While bones in a dusty museum case are dry, white, lifeless things, your bones are busily, vividly alive. They grow and change, even after you've 'stopped growing'. Among the many other things they do, your bones play a key role in maintaining blood calcium levels. When the level drops below a certain point little tides of calcium sweep out of storehouses in your bones. This is called *resorption*. When the level in blood rises, calcium is either excreted or swept back into the bones and absorbed. Those two opposing tides – resorption and absorption – stay roughly in balance until early middle age when the resorption tide becomes stronger. As a result, one study showed, bone mineral content in females over 35 declined at the average rate of 1 per cent a year. That's very important because mineral content is closely related to bone strength. In 20 or 30 years . . . well, that's trouble.

To test whether physical activity and/or supplements of calcium and vitamin D (to aid absorption of calcium) could reverse or slow that tide of bone mineral loss, researchers at the University of Wisconsin's Biogerontology Laboratory conducted a three-year study on a group of 80 elderly women. The volunteer subjects were chosen from residents of a rest home and ranged in age from 69 to 95. They were divided into four groups: one group exercised 30 minutes a day, three days a week; a second group received 750 mg of calcium and 400 IU of vitamin D each day; another group exercised and received the same amount of calcium; and a control group received placebos.

At the end of the study period, the control group had lost more than 3 per cent of the mineral content in their bones, but the calcium and the exercise-only groups registered a net increase in mineralization of roughly 2 per cent. The scientists concluded that 'the present study clearly indicates that bone loss in the aged female may be reversed and maintained at a higher level of BMC [bone mineral content] through physical activity or calcium and vitamin D supplementation' (*Medicine and Science in Sports and Exercise*, vol. 13, no. 1, 1981).

'Prevention makes better sense'

Clinical evidence of calcium's power to fight osteoporosis is exciting news, but the fact is, if you could put a halt to bone loss before it ever began, you'd be a whole lot better off.

'Calcium supplementation, once you've got it [osteoporosis], will only gain you a few percentage points,' says Robert P. Heaney, professor of medicine at Creighton University School of Medicine in Omaha, Nebraska. 'Prevention makes a lot better sense than treatment.'

Dr Heaney told us that, largely because of their decreased ability to absorb calcium, post-menopausal women – even those who are completely free of osteoporosis – should probably double their calcium intake. 'The [US] RDA (recommended dietary allowance) for adults is 800 mg but our studies indicate they should be getting a gram (1000 mg) or a gram and a half a day,' he suggests. 'The old idea that you need calcium only until you stop growing just doesn't hold water anymore.' He adds that, in general, women would also do well to choose a more vigorous lifestyle earlier in life: 'Walk more, drive less, take up tennis. . . . This may not be a guarantee that you won't get osteoporosis, but it certainly can lessen the risk of getting it.'

And getting enough calcium shouldn't be much of a problem. 8 fl. oz of skimmed milk provides over one-third of the RDA. So does an ounce of Gruyère cheese. If you're still concerned about getting enough, there's always bone meal, dolomite or other calcium-containing supplements. And rest assured that calcium supplements are better 'medicine' than what your doctor may prescribe: oestrogen.

Doctors used to prescribe oestrogen freely for osteoporosis. They knew that a woman's natural flow of this hormone helps regulate the normal metabolism of bone, and they knew that the oestrogen supply stops at menopause. Putting two and two together, they prescribed oestrogen for osteoporosis.

In this case, however, two and two equalled trouble. Oestrogen seemed to stop the advance of osteoporosis, but it wouldn't make bones stronger. Worst of all, many women's bodies didn't seem to want the new hormones and fought back by developing side-effects – serious ones like cancers of the uterus and breast, and high blood pressure. Obviously, there had to be a better way.

Calcium, as we pointed out, is the better way, and striking findings at Hammersmith Hospital in London have added confirmation to that fact. In a study that involved tracking 48 osteoporosis patients over a period of 10 years (an average 3.5 years' participation by each patient), a team of endocrinologists think they may have found the best proof yet that calcium by itself can reverse osteoporosis – and do it effectively for long periods of time.

The patients were divided into two groups. The first included 25 people who suffered from 'typical' osteoporosis – 24 post-menopausal women and 1 man over 60 – with an average age of 67. The second group included men and women suffering from osteoporosis for other, less common reasons, and their average age was 47.

The study was organized in five stages. In the initial stage, each patient was put on calcium lactate gluconate supplements according to their individual needs. They continued taking calcium supplements throughout the experiment. In the second stage, the patients were given one hormonal regimen, and in the third stage they were switched to another hormonal regimen. In stage four, all hormone therapy was stopped. At each stage, patients were tested for their 'calcium balance.' Calcium balance simply means the difference between the amount of calcium going into the body and the amount being excreted. At stage five, their calcium balances were measured for the last time.

The experiment was a success in terms of nutrition and health. It showed that each patient's calcium balance improved and that more calcium was returning to their jeopardized bones and making them stronger. The removal of the hormones at stage four lowered the calcium balance, but overall it still remained positive. For the researchers, this meant that calcium, as well as being safe is apparently effective for all but the most stubborn cases of osteoporosis. They concluded:

> We consider that the first line of treatment for most osteoporotic patients is to institute a high calcium intake and to reserve supplementary hormone treatment for those patients with continuing vertebral fractures occurring, say, after a year on high calcium alone. [*Clinical Science*, no. 62, 1982].

The researchers had good reason to look for an effective, oestrogen-free treatment. Surveys have shown a definite relationship between oestrogen use and endometrial, or uterine, cancer. As one survey revealed:

> For 30 years, from 1940, the incidence of endometrial cancer in the United States was more or less stable, but a marked rise was noted for the period 1969 to 1973 in data from a number of cancer registries. This rise exceeded 10 per cent per year in some areas and was greatest in women aged 45 to 74 years. It was suggested the increase might relate to use of oestrogens sales of which has risen fourfold in the years 1963–73. A fall in oestrogen prescriptions in early 1976 was followed by a fall, within a year, in endometrial cancer incidence . . . [*Lancet*, 20 June 1981]

Besides cancer of the uterus, oestrogen therapy has been linked to breast cancer, gall bladder disease, high blood pressure, breast tenderness and other ailments. Because of this, many doctors have stopped prescribing oestrogen. However, it should be noted that other research has shown that it was oestrogen taken on its own that caused overgrowth of the tissues of the endometrium which mimicked pre-cancerous changes. In many cases, this can be avoided by the woman taking another female hormone *progesterone* (or a synthetic variety) for a few days a month, which will cause the endometrium lining to be shed (as in a menstrual period).

Calcium and Vitamin D

Other doctors are investigating calcium in combination with vitamin D. One of these is Ashok Vaswani of the Brookhaven National [US] Laboratory.

In a recent study, Dr Vaswani, Dr John F. Aloia and others encountered problems with oestrogen side-effects. They had prescribed a combination of oestrogen, calcium and fluoride for nine osteoporosis patients suffering from back pain due to weakened, compressed vertebrae. The combination was a success: It relieved much of the pain and the disability that went with it but the patients also had 'a high frequency of estrogen-related complaints' (*Journal of the American Geriatrics Society*, January 1982).

Dr Vaswani also respects patients' objections to oestrogen. 'Everybody's becoming aware that they might face osteoporosis eventually,' he told us. 'It's a very complicated area. People have many choices, and they need to think carefully about them. It's their body, of course, and they should participate in whatever treatment they choose.'

Patrick Ober, an endocrinologist at the Bowman Gray School of Medicine, in Winston–Salem, North Carolina, also uses calcium and vitamin D instead of oestrogen. 'When there are two kinds of treatments and one, like calcium, is benign and just as effective, then I'm inclined to go with it,' he told us. 'There doesn't seem to be any hazard to taking calcium.'

James Buchanan of Pennsylvania State University has been treating osteoporosis patients with a daily combination of 1000 mg of calcium and a very small amount of a synthetic, more potent form of vitamin D. 'I feel like I've got a good thing going here, with a low risk,' he told us. 'Oestrogen works, but there's no reason to use it as long as the calcium/vitamin D combination works.' Dr Buchanan has treated about 150 patients in the past two years. Many of them were unable to walk, lie down or do something as simple as sewing without pain. He was able to relieve pain and disability in 85 per cent of the patients. He says he gets results in a few months.

There's a catch to using oestrogen, Dr Buchanan says. If the oestrogen therapy is used and then stopped, bone loss will be faster than ever eventually catching up with the losses experienced by those patients who never took oestrogen at all.

Seasonal variations

You may have noticed that most of these researchers used calcium and vitamin D. We know why calcium works, but why ask vitamin D to tag along? Vitamin D is a remarkable substance that is synthesized in your skin when it's struck by ultraviolet light, and which goes on to play a key role in your body's calcium metabolism, helping the body absorb the mineral.

During the short, dim days of winter, when you're either indoors or bundled up much of the time, lack of sunshine on your skin can result in a steady drain on your vitamin D supply, until by late winter or early spring your bones may actually begin to ache. Worse, if this shortage is allowed to continue, newly formed bone can become soft and misshapen – a condition known as *osteomalacia*, or adult rickets.

Fortunately, there's a way around this problem short of waltzing around the garden in the buff. Ordinarily, you manufacture most of the vitamin D you use through this magical meeting of skin and sun (hence its nickname, the 'sunshine vitamin'), but vitamin D is also available, though not plentiful, in the natural food supply. By making sure your diet is adequate in vitamin D – and seeking out the sun during the darkest months – you can make it through winter without the dull aches and pains of a deficiency. Unfortunately, recent studies show that many people experience a sharp decline in their vitamin D supply during the winter.

One such study was conducted by doctors at the University of Dundee, where levels of ultraviolet light in sunshine are 'very low or negligible' from November to February. Over a period of a year, the researchers studied the vitamin D status of three groups of people by measuring their serum levels of the major circulating form of vitamin D, 25-hydroxyvitamin D, or 25-OHD for short.

The groups were divided according to occupation and amount of exposure to sunlight: a group of gardeners in the local parks department worked outdoors all day, winter and summer; hospital staff got their sunshine mostly on weekends or after work; and a group of elderly people who were confined indoors, received virtually no natural or artificial sunlight at all.

The results showed that 'in each group, the seasonal changes were highly significant,' with the highest 25-OHD levels recorded during the late summer and autumn and the lowest during the late winter or early spring. And '25-OHD levels were higher in the outdoor workers than in the indoor workers, who in turn had higher values than did the elderly patients' (*American Journal of Clinical Nutrition*, August 1981).

The researchers noted something else of interest: the more sunshine the subjects got, the later in the season their 25-OHD levels peaked. While ultraviolet light was strongest in July, for example, the gardeners reached their highest levels in November; the elderly people peaked in August. Perhaps, as the researchers suggested, 'in the outdoor workers, vitamin D synthesis continues well into the autumn with continued exposure, and so vitamin D stores continue to increase.'

What all this means to your health was demonstrated in another study conducted by a trio of doctors in Leeds. The doctors examined biopsies from hip bones of 134 patients who had suffered suspicious fractures of the femur (thigh bone) over a period of five years. They concluded that 37 per cent of the patients were suffering from osteomalacia. But what was most disturbing was the fact that by far the largest number of fractures occurred in a period stretching from February to June. 'As would be expected if this seasonal variation was attributable to variation in the supply of vitamin D dependent on sunlight, the proportion of cases with osteomalacia is highest in the spring and lowest in the autumn,' they noted. *(Lancet)*

Why is there a two- to six-month time lag between the shortest days of the year (the third week in December) and the appearance of fractures caused by weakened bones? Well, vitamin D is fat-soluble and thus easily stored by the body. Your cupboards may be full to overflowing by the end of the summer and may not run out until late winter or even early summer.

The elderly at risk

This is something older people should make special note of. Because according to a study at Ichilov Hospital in Tel Aviv, the elderly may have trouble making use of vitamin D even if they live in a sunny climate and get plenty of vitamin D in the foods they eat.

The Israeli doctors compared serum 25-OHD levels of 82 elderly people and 30 young control subjects. They discovered that 15 of the elderly subjects – nearly 20 per cent – had outright vitamin D deficiencies, and 28 more had borderline levels. Even elderly farm workers who got plenty of sunshine – their vitamin D status was considerably better than those older people who were confined indoors – were still 'significantly lower' than the youthful control group (*Israeli Journal of Medical Sciences*, January 1981).

'It seems likely that impairment of vitamin D metabolism at several points in the metabolic pathway, rather than simple under-exposure to sunlight, is a major factor in vitamin D deficiency in the elderly,' the doctors concluded. They suggested that perhaps ageing impairs the body's ability to produce certain active forms of vitamin D, which in turn slows down the absorption of calcium through the intestine. Result: an increased risk of faulty bone mineralization.

There may be other factors working against vitamin D nutrition in older people, according to Michael F. Holick of the department of medicine at Harvard Medical School. 'Ageing significantly reduces the skin's capacity to produce vitamin D_3,' Dr Holick explains. 'The skin of a 70-year-old can make about half the vitamin D_3 precursor produced by a 20-year-old,'

Normally ultraviolet wavelengths in sunshine, striking your bare skin convert a lipid substance called 7-dehydrocholesterol into previtamin D_3. This is unstable when heated and slowly converts to vitamin D_3 (an active form) in the deeper layers of your skin. You don't actually make vitamin D_3 during sunlight exposure; it takes three or four days for the whole manufacturing process to run its course, so your body is busy producing vitamin D_3 long after you come in out of the sun. In the elderly, however, this marvellous machinery has begun to lose its efficiency. 'It's not too surprising, really, because age decreases all metabolic functions,' Dr Holick told us. Also, the skin actually thins with age, so there are fewer cells to synthesize the vitamin.

What's to stop your skin from producing too much vitamin D? (Being fat-soluble and thus easily stored, the nutrient can be toxic in high doses.) It's widely believed that tanning is the answer: in response to extended exposure to sunlight, the skin produces the pigment *melanin* to shield its deeper vitamin D-producing layers from ultraviolet light. However, Dr Holick contends that, while this may be a factor, it isn't the most important one. His research has shown, he says, that too much sun causes previtamin D_3 to break down into a pair of biologically inert (useless) substances, thus preventing the overproduction of vitamin D.

Too much sun, of course, can also increase your risk of skin cancer and accelerate the ageing of your skin, but Dr Holick believes it may be time to 're-evaluate the natural benefits of sunlight' for older people who may not get enough vitamin D in their diets. How much sun should you get? Well, 30 minutes of sun exposure twice a week in Southern Britain in the summer should be 'more than adequate' for lightly pigmented people over 60 years old, Dr Holick says.

Keeping your vitamin D stores in order really shouldn't be too difficult even if you rarely venture into the sun. A recent study in Norway – at latitude 70 degrees north, where the sun hangs below the horizon a full two months of the year – is a case in point. Over a period of a year, serum 25-OHD levels were examined in 17 healthy adults living in Tromso. Although the lowest concentration was found in March, blood levels overall remained 'at a constant and fairly high level' throughout the year (*Scandinavian Journal of Clinical Laboratory Investigation*, vol. 40, 1980). The researchers attributed this sunny finding to good nutrition and the widespread consumption of dairy products fortified with vitamin D.

Lack of vitamin D

Vitamin D isn't very common in the natural food supply. The foods that contain it in high amounts are all of animal origin, with the greatest amounts occurring in saltwater fish high in oil, such as salmon, sardines and herring. Fish-liver oils are highly concentrated sources of vitamin D, and egg yolks and liver also contain substantial amounts.

The fortification of milk and other milk products since World War II is one reason the childhood bone disease called rickets is today considered, in the words of one researcher, 'a medical curiosity.' In the days of the Industrial Revolution, when children were confined to sunless sweatshops in smoggy cities, it was a serious health problem, and it was still fairly common as late as the 1940s. However, by 1969, a survey of over 6000 children of low-income families in the United States showed that only 0.1 per cent had bowing of the legs (a symptom of rickets).

Yet recently, some doctors have begun to worry that rickets 'may still be a significant problem in some population groups.' Over a period of a year, for example, four children from Hartford, Connecticut were diagnosed as having rickets caused by poor diet. The youngsters exhibited 'classic' symptoms of rickets, from bowing of the legs to general weakness, delayed motor development and low weight, but because their doctors were not familiar with the condition, a correct diagnosis wasn't made for months (*Pediatrics*, July 1980).

After examining the youngsters' dietary histories, doctors concluded that

> particular groups of children, namely vegetarians, children breastfed for an unusually long time, and black children, are at risk to develop the nutritional deficiencies of vitamin D and calcium metabolism that lead to clinical rickets.

Vegetarians, because they may not get enough milk and milk products; black children, because their dark skin blocks the ultraviolet light that triggers vitamin D_3 production; and breastfed children, because human breast milk may be inadequate in vitamin D – though this is still a controversial point.

One thing all four youngsters had in common: they turned up at the hospital at the end of the winter. After months indoors, or outdoors only when they were buttoned up to the ears, they just hadn't been getting enough sunshine to kee   their vitamin D batteries charged and humming. Add to this a diet deficient in vitamin D, and by winter's end they were in serious trouble.

If their situation sounds uncomfortably like yours, you might try jetting off to the Canary Islands for a week or two . . . or just make sure you get enough vitamin D, through fish, dairy products, supplements or sunshine.

Exercise, smoking and caffeine

While you're out catching those rays, go for a long walk or a jog. No exercise means weak bones.

In one American study, 13 men and 25 women over 70 were put on an exercise programme for a year, emphasizing vigorous walking or jogging for at least one hour every day. On the average, the group did not lose any bone mass during that year *(American Journal of Clinical Nutrition)*. However, that's an average. Some of those in the study did lose bone mass. Those who exercised least lost 9 per cent of their bone.

So go out and kick up your heels. And if you've still got it, kick the habit too. 'Patients with symptomatic osteoporosis before age 65 included a striking predominance of heavy habitual smokers,' reported a study in the *Journal of the American Medical Association*. Why should smoking burn up bones?

Here's one possible answer: [Women] smokers as a group have an earlier natural menopause than non-smokers' *(Lancet)*. It all adds up: At menopause oestrogen plummets. When the oestrogen level drops, unless you take extra calcium, you lose bone. And the sooner the menopause, the more bone is lost. So, since smokers get their menopause sooner, they get osteoporosis sooner.

And, while you're giving up smoking, consider swearing off caffeine, too. Caffeine, in the form of coffee, tea or colas, seems to interfere with calcium absorption. Drs Robert Heaney and Robert R. Recker of the Creighton University School of Medicine in Omaha, Nebraska, in a long-term study of 168 women between the ages of 36 and 45, found that even a moderate amount of caffeine in the diet may be associated with a deterioration in calcium balance.

The women in their study averaged relatively small intakes of caffeine – equivalent to about two cups of coffee a day – and had already suffered from a net calcium loss of 22 mg per day. The addition of only one more cup of coffee cost them 6 more mg per day. This figure seems small, the doctors wrote, but a negative calcium balance of only 40 mg per day is 'quite sufficient to explain the 1 to 1.5 per cent loss in skeletal mass per year noted in postmenopausal women'. They add that women who consume a lot of caffeine also seem to consume fewer calcium-rich foods *(Journal of Laboratory and Clinical Medicine*, January 1982).

Don't let your bones flunk the test of time. Bone up on calcium, vitamin D and exercise.

• Breast Problems

You read a magazine here, a newspaper there. You watch TV and browse through pamphlets and brochures as you wait for appointments. When it comes to health matters, up-to-date information may come in bits and pieces, and that can be frustrating at times.

Take questions concerning breast care and breast problems, for instance. Even though you probably have read about it in lots of places, you still may be fuzzy on certain details. The first question is, where do you go to refresh your memory? How many old newspapers or magazines will you have to pore over before you find the answers you're looking for?

We've all experienced that dilemma at one time or another, which is one reason why this book includes a question and answer section on breast problems.

Q. I've noticed stretch marks appearing on my breasts lately. What causes them?
A. Stretch marks apparently are due to alterations in the elastic fibres of the skin. Oddly enough, they do not occur in everyone. 'Some women are susceptible to stretch marks with weight gain and pregnancy, while others are not,' says Alvin Krakower, a New Jersey gynaecologist.

Q. Is there anything I can do to make stretch marks go away?
A. If you mean is there anything you can personally do, we don't have any reliable advice. If you are terribly concerned about them, though, you should know that 'they can be helped considerably by tightening the skin through plastic surgery. Women with sagging breasts especially can reduce stretch marks through surgery, but it is almost impossible to eradicate the stretch marks *per se*,' says Robert M. Goldwyn, a plastic surgeon in breast reconstruction at Harvard Medical School. However, undergoing major surgery for cosmetic improvement should only be considered if the stretch marks are drastically affecting your life. Counselling should be tried first.

Q. Can anything be done to prevent breasts from sagging?
A. Christine Haycock, associate professor of surgery at the New Jersey Medical School, says that good bra support during vigorous physical exercise will help prevent the problem and eliminate soreness. Dr Haycock has tested many bras and has determined that the more rigid, well-designed sports bras prevent lateral and spiralling motions of the breast.

The bra should not bind but should limit breast motion to the body. She advises women to jump up and down when trying on the bras to make sure there is little bouncing and no pain. She also suggests that the bra's metal fasteners be covered and seams padded for comfort. The bra should have non-elastic wide straps, and the back strap should be wide and low. Bra cups should be cotton (not a synthetic), and the material should be both non-allergenic and non-abrasive. Generally, underwires in the bra also are not recommended, says Dr Haycock.

Q. I have small breasts and would like to know what I could do to enlarge them. Are there any products on the market that will help?
A. A few years ago, the US magazine *Prevention* published the results of its own research into that very question. Back then, it was learned that there were no exercisers, nutritional supplements, massagers, creams or hormone preparations that would really increase breast size. The same response seems to hold true today. A woman's breast size is determined by her genetic makeup and the amount of weight she carries. Weight gain and pregnancy are the only things that will increase actual breast size.

In some magazines, you may still see certain ads implying that their products will make you more buxom. 'Let the buyer beware,' says Tom Ziebarth, attorney for the Consumer Protection Division of the US Postal Service and prosecuting attorney on many of the cases regarding breast enlargement ads.

For instance, certain powders and other products are advertised as having the power to increase breast size, but they are actually designed to make you gain weight, he continues. If a woman gains weight, her breasts indeed may expand but so will the rest of her.

Q. I recently was in an accident and suffered a severe breast injury. Does that increase my chances of developing breast cancer in the future?
A. The verdict apparently isn't in on that one. 'I don't know if it has actually been proven one way or another,' both Drs Krakower and Goldwyn said. Dr Krakower remarked that, when he went to medical school years ago, students were taught the 'theory of chronic irritation' and told that injuries to the breasts might lead to eventual breast cancer. Elsewhere, a doctor may tell you that breast injury does *not* increase your chances for breast cancer.

Q. I've heard that obesity and breast cancer are somehow linked. Could you explain that?
A. Researchers have found that a diet high in fat makes a woman more susceptible to breast cancer. In other words, the fatter she is, the more likely she is to develop breast cancer. The fatty nature of breast tissues combined with circulating hormones makes the breasts more vulnerable to the harmful influence of cancer-causing substances (carcinogens) that enter and circulate throughout the body. Fat-soluble carcinogens are easily stored and recycled not only by breast fat but by total body fat. Consequently, it's to a woman's advantage to reduce her fat intake and to keep her weight down.

Q. My doctor says I'm in perfect health, but occasionally my breasts feel tender and sore. Why?
A. Pain and tenderness are common breast complaints in women. Those problems may occur with or without a lump.

Disease-free breasts can be enlarged, painful and tender due to water buildup in the fatty tissues just before or during your period. It may be caused by too much sodium (as from salt) in the body. In some women, the buildup is a habitual response to the natural rise in the hormone oestrogen that occurs before menstruation.

It is important to note that 80 per cent of all breast lumps are benign and *not* cancerous.

Q. My neighbour tells me that my eating habits might be partly responsible for my occasional breast discomfort. Is that true?
A. Possibly, if you like salty foods. Cutting down on salt intake is very likely to reduce water retention and pain. Some doctors also believe that supplemental doses of vitamin B_6 will bring comfort. Backed up with lesser amounts of other B complex vitamins, B_6 has a natural diuretic effect on water buildup. Vitamin B_6 also may regulate hormonal imbalance in some women.

Q. Is there any relief for occasional breast pain?
A. If the discomfort is unbearable, your doctor may prescribe a thiazide diuretic. The drug flushes excess water out of the fatty tissues and the body. Side effects are possible, however. The drugs may cause toxic reactions such as a rash, headache, fatigue or nausea. If you experience any of those problems your doctor can change your prescription to something else. Such diuretics can also cause a loss of potassium in the urine, so a supplement of this mineral should be taken at the same time.

Another approach is to take small doses of another hormone, progesterone, to counteract oestrogen's effect.

Before resorting to drugs or hormones, you might try enlisting the support of your bra for relief. Wearing a bra to bed during the problem period brings relief to many women. Even for daytime wear, especially if you are a 36C or larger, an inadequate bra can aggravate either premenstrual pain or pain due to benign disease.

Q. How do I know it's time to see a doctor about a painful breast condition?
A. If pain lasts for more than a few days of your menstrual cycle, forces you to wear a bra all of the time, wakens you at night or makes household chores, sports or office work unbearable, you need medical attention.

Dr Krakower adds that, when a woman experiences breast pain after menopause she should be examined by her doctor to rule out any sort of mass that may have developed.

Q. I do a self-examination regularly to check for any unusual lumps, but is there anything else I should look for?
A. A clear or bloody nipple discharge, pain, enderness and redness inverted or cracked nipples should be examined by your doctor. Sometimes the problems can be benign, other times they may be malignant. That is why

prompt medical attention is necessary to determine the cause and appropriate treatment.

For information on benign breast lumps, see FIBROCYSTIC DISEASE.

• Bronchitis

A study by J. Rimington, published in the *British Medical Journal*, details the smoking habits and methods of 5438 cigarette smokers. About 8 per cent smoked their cigarettes without removing them from their mouths between puffs. The doctor called these smokers 'drooping' cigarette smokers, and the rate of chronic bronchitis (a constant inflammation of the bronchi, the airways that extend into the lungs) among these people – 41 per cent – was considerably greater than among those smoking cigarettes in the normal manner – 33 per cent.

Dr Rimington concluded, 'Whatever the reason for this excess of chronic bronchitis among the "droopers" . . . there seems little doubt that it is a dangerous method of smoking cigarettes involving greater risk of developing chronic bronchitis.'

Garlic: shield against bronchitis?

Irwin Ziment, of the Los Angeles County–Olive View Medical Center notes that residents of Britain are more prone to bronchitis than those residing in areas such as the Mediterranean, where (in theory at least) the humidity should cause equal numbers of cases of the complaint. He suggests the differing levels of garlic consumption as one reason why this does not happen. Dr Ziment believes that garlic may prevent bronchitis by loosening mucus, thus stopping its buildup in the bronchi (*Journal of the American Medical Association*). (*See also* EMPHYSEMA.)

• Bruxism

Bruxism – tooth grinding – is more than an unpleasant habit. A Swiss dental scientist, Peter Schaerer of Bern, has said that people who clench their teeth during sleep or during a 'confrontation' can cause damage to the teeth gums, jaw joint and muscles (*Journal of the American Dental Association*).

According to Emanuel Cheraskin and W. Marshall Ringsdorf, Jr., bruxism is a nutritional problem that can be relieved with increased daily supplies of calcium and the B vitamin *pantothenic acid*. Drs Ringsdorf and Cheraskin carried out a nutritional survey of a group of people, some of whom were bruxists. Those without bruxism recorded higher levels of pantothenic acid and calcium intake. A year later – after dietary instruction – the entire group was surveyed again. This time the doctors found that those bruxists who had significantly increased their intake of the two relevant nutrients were no longer tooth gnashers (*Dental Survey*). (*See also* HEADACHES.)

• Cancer

Cancer is a disease marked by the uncontrolled division of cells. In most types of cancer, these cells proliferate and grow into tumours that destroy surrounding tissue. When cancer cells spread from the tumour throughout the bloodstream and into the lymphatic system – by a process called *metastasis* – new growths may form in other parts of the body. Some cancers are more easily treated than others, but one thing is certain: if cancerous cells continue to spread throughout the body unabated, healthy cells are pushed aside, and the body loses its ability to fight back.

Cancer is the most challenging of chronic diseases, and it provides an excellent example of how chronic prevention – that is, prevention over a period of time – can work effectively. Of course, many mysteries about cancer remain to be explained, and the problem of trying to cure cancer is indeed complex and difficult. In this entry, we will focus primarily on understanding what factors in our environment contribute to cancer and how prevention fits in.

Carcinogens are the agents that ignite the fire of cancer, causing a change in normal cells so that they do not repair themselves properly but continue to divide. But no fire burns without fuel. Chemicals and even foods promote the growth of cancer, and so are called *cancer promoters*. Only one exposure to a carcinogen can spark the cancer, but many repeated exposures to promoters are needed by the cancer to ensure its growth. Some cancers may not follow that exact route of development, but it is the feeling of many experts that one dose of carcinogen, followed by many exposures to promoters over time, may lead to cancer.

'If the medical profession and the public were to apply all that is currently known about cancer and its causes, a majority of human cancers would probably be prevented,' says Ernst L. Wynder, president of the American Health Foundation, a New York-based non-profit organization devoted to basic research into the cause and prevention of disease.

Chemicals in the environment – the ones that seem to get all the press – appear to be responsible for only a small percentage of human cancers, adds J.H. Weisburger, the Foundation's vice-president for research. Most cancers he says, are caused by the way we live – things, in short, that are our responsibility.

Of these, the most important single factor appears to be diet. 'Epidemiologic and laboratory data suggest that diet is an important factor in the causation of various forms of cancer, and that it is correlated to more than half of all cancers in women and at least one-third of all cancers in men,' notes Gio B. Gori, former deputy director, division of cancer cause and prevention, at the National Cancer Institute.

The fat connection

Numerous studies have indicated that diets high in fat have been linked to increased risk of colon, breast and prostate cancer. The evidence comes mainly from surveys in which comparisons were made between people with different eating habits. And the bottom line is: the higher the percentage of fat in a population group's diet, the higher the death rate from these cancers.

'There exists a worldwide correlation between bowel cancer and fat consumption,' Dr Gori has written. Where fats make up a large part of the diet, as in Scotland, Canada and the United States, bowel cancer is common. Where fats are scarce, so is the disease.

No clear association has been made between cancer and any particular kind of fat, saturated or unsaturated, animal or vegetable. Rather, it's the *total amount of fat* in your diet that appears to be the decisive factor.

In the standard British diet, nearly 50 per cent of total calories come from fat – and in Britain breast, prostate and colon cancers are all too common. In Japan, on the other hand, fat intake averages 10 to 20 per cent of total calories, and the incidence of these cancers in Japan is among the lowest in the world. Unfortunately, as Japan becomes increasingly Westernized and its people learn to love fatty foods, there has been a rise in the incidence of these cancers.

The precise mechanism at work is not known, but many researchers now believe that by-products of bile acids, which the body produces to break down fat, are *co-carcinogenic* – that is, while they may not *cause* cancer they promote its development.

A high-fat diet is also suspected of upsetting the body's hormone balance and thereby contributing to prostate and breast cancer. Women who consume a lot of high-fat milk products have a higher rate of breast cancer than women who eat less milk and more eggs (*Cancer Research*, September 1979).

G. Hems of the Department of Community Medicine in Aberdeen tabulated the breast cancer rates in 41 countries and related them to local diets. 'It was concluded that variation of breast cancer rates between countries arose predominantly from differences in diet,' he wrote in the *British Journal of Cancer*. And one place where the shadow of suspicion fell most darkly was consumption of fats. Other studies have confirmed that the disease is less common in poor and developing nations, where rich foods are rarely on the menu, than in the wealthier countries of the West. Like bowel cancer, breast cancer increases among Japanese immigrants who give up their low-fat diet for our high-fat one. And among Seventh-Day Adventists in the United States breast cancer mortality rates are only one-half to two-thirds those of Americans in general. Many members of this religious group are vegetarians whose intake of saturated fat and cholesterol is bound to be well below the average.

Two studies graphically demonstrate the sensitivity of hormone levels (and through them, quite possibly, the promotion of cancer) to the diet. In South Africa, native black women suffer very little from breast cancer, while white women fall prey to the disease much more frequently. Their diets are markedly different, too: the diet of the black women is vegetarian and very low in fat – less than 20 per cent of total calories – while the whites consume a typical Western diet in which fats provide a big 40 per cent of calories. Peter Hill formerly of the American Health Foundation, measured the hormone levels in groups of black and white women and found more significant differences: the black women had lower levels of a number of hormones, including prolactin which is intimately involved in breastfeeding and the menstrual cycle.

He put the black women on a Western diet for periods of six weeks to two months, then measured their hormones again. Now, he found, the proportions of various hormones had changed significantly – they began to resemble the hormone profile of white women. And these new hormone levels – including the rise in prolactin – are ones that have been associated with increased rates of breast cancer (*Federation Proceedings*, 1 March 1979).

Dr Hill conducted a similar study with South African and North American men. Rural, vegetarian, black South African men have a far lower rate of prostate cancer than North American men – and their diet has about half the fat of the diet consumed in America. Testing their urine, Dr Hill found that the South Africans excrete considerably fewer androgens and oestrogens than their American counterparts.

For three weeks, Dr Hill had his subjects switch diets: the Americans ate low-fat, vegetarian food, and the Africans ate rich American fare. Even in this short time, a change in diet meant a switch in hormone profiles, too. There was a marked increase in androgen and oestrogen excretion among the Africans while that of the Americans decreased to the point where it resembled the hormone levels of the low-risk group.

It is important to remember that, in these studies of diet and cancer, what is generally measured is *total* fats. While replacing saturated with polyunsaturated fats may cut down the risk of heart disease, it seems to offer no protection against cancer. In short, as Dr Weisburger told us, 'If people really made an effort to lower their fat intake – by using low-fat milk and dairy products and fewer fat-containing foods like fatty meat, butter and salad dressing – breast, bowel and prostate cancer could be significantly reduced.'

Fibre's anti-cancer action

There is good evidence that a diet rich in fibre may reduce your chances of getting colon cancer, one of the most common cancers in the United Kingdom. Why? There are several theories.

It's been suggested that fibre may work simply because it 'dilutes' those cancer-causing bile acids. Or that, by speeding up the passage of waste through the intestine, it reduces the amount of time colon carcinogens are in contact with the intestinal walls. Or that fibre binds with carcinogens, making them, in effect, harmless.

This last theory was demonstrated in one study in which a cancer-causing agent called DMH was mixed in a solution with various kinds of fibre, such as wheat bran, citrus pulp and alfalfa. It was discovered that each type of fibre, to varying degrees, bound with the DMH, leading the researchers to suggest that 'the protective effect of certain types of dietary fiber against chemically induced colon cancer may in part be attributed to enhanced carcinogen binding by dietary fiber in the colon' (*Journal of the National Cancer Institute*, August 1981).

Two important studies using laboratory animals have shown the effect of fibre on colon cancer. In one case, colon tumours were significantly reduced as fibre intake increased; in the other, colon tumours were also greatly reduced as bran intake went up and fat intake went down (*Canadian Journal of Surgery*, January 1980; *Journal of the National Cancer Institute*, April 1979).

'In the United States, large-bowel cancer ranks highest in incidence of all types of cancer, except for easily detectable and curable skin cancer,' says Bandara S. Reddy, who heads the nutrition division of the Naylor Dana Institute for Disease Prevention. (In the UK cancer of the colon is the third most common cancer in men and second most common in women.) He noted that the lowest rates of colon cancer occur in Africa, Asia and South America, where people eat cereal and vegetable-based diets high in fibre and low in fatty foods such as meat. Two exceptions are Argentina and Uruguay, where beef is more widely available and bowel cancer rates are high.

When Dr Reddy and several associates compared a low-risk population of healthy middle-aged men living in Kuopio in Finland with a high-risk group in New York City, they found some interesting differences. Although both groups ate a diet that was relatively high in fat, the men in Finland also ate large amounts of fibre, while those in New York did not (*Cancer Letters*). 'The people in Finland were consuming more than twice as much fibre as the people in New York,' Dr Reddy told us.

As it turned out, the men in Kuopio ate considerable amounts of whole rye bread and whole grain cereals – excellent sources of dietary fibre – and they tended to have bulkier stools. In fact, their daily stool output was three times greater than that of the New York group. So while total bile-acid production in both groups was the same, the tumour-promoting bile acids were more diluted in the Finnish group.

Additional evidence of fibre's protective value turned up in a study by the Kaiser – Permanente Medical Care Program and the California State Department of Health. The researchers examined the diet histories of 99 patients with colonic and/or rectal cancer and compared them with the diets of 280 people in a control group without gastro-intestinal cancer. The patients with colon cancer had tended to eat high-fibre foods less frequently than the control group (*American Journal of Epidemiology*, February 1979).

To be specific, the people who ultimately developed colon cancer had been less inclined to eat such foods as oatmeal, bran cereal, lentils, chickpeas and other pulses, turnips, potatoes and cabbage.

An even more direct link – at least in animals – between fibre and cancer protection was demonstrated by researchers at the McGill University Surgical Clinic and Montreal General Hospital in Canada. They found that, when laboratory rats were injected with a tumour-causing chemical, subsequent colon cancer was reduced in those rats with fibre in their diet. And the more fibre the animals ate, the less likely they were to develop cancer (*Lancet*).

'In the American diet,' Dr Reddy told us, 'adding a good source of cereal fibre such as wheat bran to the diet would be the best protective approach.' The same would be true for the British diet.

Pectin (the indigestible polysaccharides found in fruits and vegetables and extracted from apples to set jam) is another good source of fibre. Researchers fed rats a diet that included either alfalfa, pectin or wheat bran, and then injected them with a cancer-causing substance. Pectin and wheat bran 'greatly inhibited' tumours in the colon, say the researchers, but alfalfa (which is also very high in fibre) had no effect. 'These results,' they wrote, 'indicate that the protective effect of fibre in colon carcinogenesis [the development of cancer] depends on . . . the source of fibre' (*Journal of the National Cancer Institute*, July 1979).

The enormous value of vegetables

In a massive study of prostate cancer among 120,000 Japanese men epidemiologists searched for some pattern in the dietary habits of those who had a significantly lower cancer rate. They found one. The figures, they reported, 'revealed a significantly lower age-standardized death rate for prostate cancer in men who daily ate green and yellow vegetables. This association is consistently observed in each age group, in each socio-economic class, and in each prefecture [geographic area]' (*National Cancer Institute Monographs*, 53, 1979).

The scientists pointed out that other evidence supported this finding. Vegetarians living in the United States, such as Seventh-Day Adventists, have also been shown to have a lower risk of prostate cancer than the general population. What, precisely, was the key element involved? Perhaps vitamin A they suggested. But don't forget: vegetables are also low in fat, high in fibre, and rich in many vitamins and minerals.

A study by a team of health researchers at Western General Hospital in Edinburgh has generated a lot of interest in the carrot. It seems that, when they fed approximately seven ounces of raw carrots to five healthy people each day for breakfast for three weeks, some very interesting things happened. The carrots exerted a remarkable effect on bowel function, probably as a result of their fibre content. Stool weights increased by 25 per cent and bile-acid excretion in the stools rose by 50 per cent.

Carrots may also play a role in bladder cancer prevention, according to a study undertaken at the Roswell Park Memorial Institute in Buffalo, NY. When Curtis Mettlin, and Saxon Graham compared the dietary records of 569 bladder cancer patients and 1025 age-matched controls, they found that the cancer group ate carrots less frequently than the controls. There were differences in consumption patterns for other vegetables and milk as well, but the gap in carrot intake was the most significant. Drs Mettlin and Graham speculate that the exceptionally high vitamin A content of carrots may account for their association with a decreased risk of bladder cancer (*American Journal of Epidemiology*, September 1979).

In another study at Roswell Park, the two researchers compared the diets of 257 men with colon cancer with those of 783 non-cancer patients. They found that cancer risk decreases as vegetable intake rises. However, looking closer they noticed that the effect was most clear-cut with certain specific vegetable dishes: cabbage (including sauerkraut and coleslaw), Brussels sprouts and broccoli – all cruciferous plants. The more of those items people ate, the less likely they were to get colon cancer (*American Journal of Epidemiology*, January 1979).

One possible explanation cited by Drs Graham and Mettlin: cruciferous vegetables contain natural substances called *indoles*, which induce a cancer-blocking activity in the intestines – at least in laboratory animals.

Soyabeans are also an excellent non-meat food to focus on in a search for a special anti-cancer effect. Soyabeans are high in protein, very inexpensive and eaten widely in some parts of the world, such as in Japan. If we are going to eat less meat to improve our health, we need an alternative food, and soya beans are an excellent choice. The fact that those Japanese people who eat the most soyabeans tend to get less cancer than others is especially encouraging.

Walter Troll, professor of environmental medicine at New York University Medical Center, demonstrated that feeding soyabean foods to experimental animals reduces the severity of cancer. And he has theorized that if people ate more soyabeans, they could also reduce the severity of cancer and perhaps prevent it. Of extreme interest is the fact that Dr Troll is on the track of a specific substance in soyabeans that could very well have an anti-cancer effect.

Dr Troll had thought about the fact that people who are vegetarians or who tend toward vegetarianism have less cancer. He had also noted that a class of substances called *synthetic protease inhibitors* countered the effect of chemicals that can cause skin cancer. Dr Troll then got the idea of feeding soyabeans – which contain natural protease inhibitors – to test animals that were made susceptible to cancer by X-ray treatments or applications of cancer-causing chemicals.

In two different test situations, the soyabean diets worked. In one series of experiments, Dr Troll and his colleagues at NYU exposed rats to X-rays to induce breast cancer, then fed some of the animals a soyabean diet rich in protease inhibitors and some of the animals a diet containing no protease inhibitors. The result: 74 per cent of the rats fed a diet containing no protease inhibitors developed breast tumours, but only 44 per cent of those fed the high-protease inhibitor, soyabean diet developed tumours. The study which was printed in *Carcinogenesis* (June 1980), concluded, 'These findings suggest that proteases may play an important role in tumorigenesis [tumour promotion] and that diets rich in protease inhibitors may prevent the expression of such activity.'

In the second study, mice fed soyabeans were protected against skin cancer. The evidence for a similar effect in humans is highly suggestive. Dr Troll made this comment in a published abstract describing his work: 'Natural-occurring protease inhibitors such as those found in soyabeans may offer a novel method of preventing cancer in man.'

What's more, protease inhibitors are found in all beans – not just soyabeans.

Vitamin A: buffer against cancer

It's long been recognized that vitamin A is essential in maintaining the structural integrity of the cells that cover the body's internal and external surfaces. The cells of this tissue, called the *epithelium*, cover all the major organs of the body and line its various passageways. Scientists know that there is a significant relationship between the effects of vitamin A on the cells of the epithelium and the development of cancer in those tissues. And cancer in those tissues, which include the bronchial tubes and throat stomach, intestine, uterus, kidney, bladder, testes, prostate and skin accounts for more than half of all cancers in both men and women.

Michael B. Sporn of the (US) National Cancer Institute, a leading authority on the vitamin A–cancer connection, explained to us that an important factor in vitamin A's cancer-preventing potential may be its control of a process called *cell differentiation*: 'Differentiation is the process that makes the cell what it is, that allows it to carry out the normal functions of a cell. When a cell *de*differentiates, those functions are lost, and the cell enters a primitive state. Its behaviour becomes similar to that of a cancer cell. Proper maturation does not take place in cells that are dedifferentiated. Vitamin A is known to be involved in the maturation process, and that's why we chose vitamin A, rather than some other vitamin to study.

'Many of the body's hormones are also involved in the proper maturation of cells, and vitamin A had the same hormone-like effects, but unlike a hormone it cannot be manufactured in the body. The body must get its vitamin A from outside sources, and if it doesn't, the cells dedifferentiate, entering a state similar to that of cancerous cells.'

Animal studies have shown that vitamin A deficiency increases the risk of lung, bladder and colon cancer – all cancers of epithelial tissue. Scientists at the Massachusetts Institute of Technology (MIT) reported an increased incidence of colon cancer in vitamin A-deficient rats exposed to cancer-causing chemicals, even in those that were only marginally deficient in the vitamin and exhibiting none of the common signs of vitamin A deficiency (*Cancer*). The scientists reported:

> In our studies, the vitamin A levels have been only marginal, as opposed to acutely deficient, and the recognized clinical or histologic [microscopic] evidence for acute deficiency was not observed. Thus, with some segments of our United States population subject to marginal vitamin A deficits, we should consider the potential for tumor induction without obvious evidence for nutritional deficit.

In other words, it's possible that a slight deficiency of vitamin A, while not enough to cause symptoms like dry, bumpy skin, could be opening the door to something far more serious.

There is indirect evidence that vitamin A deficiency does indeed cause tumours in men. In a ten-year study of 122,261 men aged 40 and above, Japanese scientists found that those who reported a low intake of green and yellow vegetables suffered death rates from prostate cancer over twice as high as those who ate plenty of vegetables. The link between green and yellow vegetables and prostate cancer deaths was observed in every age group, every social class and every region studied. The scientists speculated that the mystery ingredient of the vegetables responsible for this trend might very well be vitamin A.

Another indication of a vitamin A–cancer connection is the low blood levels of vitamin A reported in victims of several kinds of cancer. In one study patients suffering from bronchial cancer had significantly lower levels of vitamin A in their blood than cancer-free subjects. In another conducted in Pakistan, lower blood levels of vitamin A were found in patients with cancer of the mouth and oropharynx (the opening of the digestive tract just below the mouth) than in healthy subjects. Over 50 per cent of the cancer patients had blood levels of vitamin A below World Health Organization standards, as compared to only 3 per cent of the healthy subjects *(Clinical Oncology)*.

The importance of vitamin A in cancer prevention is probably best demonstrated by the fact that the vitamin and some of its chemical relatives have been shown to cut back the incidence of cancer even beyond the reductions seen in the correction of vitamin A deficiency. As Dr Sporn wrote in *Nutrition Reviews*:

> It is readily apparent that many people whose diets meet all current nutritional recommendations develop invasive epithelial cancer. It is known that the normal cellular mechanisms in epithelial can repair a certain minimal level of molecular and cellular alteration caused by carcinogens and prevent the development of the malignant phenotype. If the level of carcinogenic exposure is too high and too prolonged, however, invasive malignancy will eventually result.

In the increasingly polluted environment in which we live, of course, the normal cellular defences against cancer are often overwhelmed. 'A pharmacological enhancement of these control mechanisms is an attractive approach to the problem,' Dr Sporn concluded.

Since vitamin A is the key to these cellular controls, the logical step was to feed laboratory animals vitamin A-enriched diets and test whether their resistance to cancer was increased. In 1967, the first important studies were carried out with hamsters administered doses of a cancer-causing chemical directly on to the windpipe. A test group were also fed a form of vitamin A following the treatment with the chemical. In hamsters fed the vitamin A, the development of cancer was markedly suppressed. In other studies, vitamin A was found to suppress the development of cancer in the bronchial tubes, stomach vagina and cervix of test animals.

Scientists have used derivatives of vitamin A to suppress not only the chemical generation of cancer, but the cancer-causing action of radiation as well. Vitamin A has also been shown to reduce the chance of regrowth of breast cancers in rats after surgical removal of the tumours.

Some scientists believe that vitamin A's cancer-preventing action may not be limited to just one particular kind of tissue in the body. They have found evidence that vitamin A has properties that might work against development of cancer in all the body's tissues. Malcolm B. Baird of the Masonic Medical Research Laboratory in Utica, NY, recently told us about his work in this area.

'All the work done so far has suggested that vitamin A exerts its anti-cancer activity by interfering with the proliferation of cancer derived from epithelial cells. The studies have suggested that vitamin A was effective only against carcinomas – the cancer occurring in the epithelium. The basic idea behind this research was that vitamin A exerted some kind of control over the growth and development of epithelial cells. Dr Sporn feels that the reason vitamin A shows a cancer-preventing effect in animals is its effect on the growth of the epithelially derived cancer. We wanted to find out if there might be some additional effect of vitamin A at work.'

Dr Baird and his colleague, Linda S. Birnbaum, used a test devised by Bruce Ames of the University of California at Berkeley to identify possible cancer-causers. Dr Ames found that 90 per cent of the substances that cause genetic changes in a certain strain of bacteria also have been found to cause cancer. Scientists generally believe that substances that cause cancer do so by disrupting the genetic material in cells and transforming them into a cancerous state.

Drs Baird and Birnbaum decided to see if vitamin A might interfere with this process of genetic disruption in Dr Ames's bacteria. It does, they found and in some conditions it blocks the process completely. Dr Baird told us that their findings suggested that vitamin A acted by interfering with the conversion of the cancer-causing chemical into its active form. 'Most carcinogens are non-toxic in themselves and are only converted to their toxic form once they are taken into the body. Our findings indicate that vitamin A can, in some instances, inhibit the transformation of the carcinogen to the toxic form.'

Dr Baird, incidentally, used natural forms of vitamin A in his research. 'In the course of most people's lives, it's the naturally occurring forms of vitamin A that they will come in contact with.'

Beta-carotene

Most of the latest research on vitamin A and cancer focuses on the form of the vitamin called beta-carotene, (also known as *provitamin A*). Carrots, sweet potatoes, dark leafy greens, apricots, yellow melon and watercress are excellent sources of beta-carotene. Once inside our bodies this important nutrient is converted to usable vitamin A.

The evidence is so impressive, in fact, that the conservative (US) National Research Council, convinced that there's a link between diet and cancer, has gone public with a list of dietary recommendations designed to reduce the risks of developing cancers, especially those that attack the lungs, stomach throat, skin, bowel and bladder. One of the things the council recommends is that everyone should eat plenty of foods rich in beta-carotene.

And that's not all. The news about beta-carotene is so promising that the (US) National Institutes of Health is now funding what is believed to be the biggest population study ever undertaken to test the hypothesis that beta-carotene does prevent cancer. The two-pronged study (the other half deals with aspirin and heart disease) is being conducted by Harvard Medical School and involves approximately 25,000 doctors throughout the US. They are taking either a beta-carotene supplement or a placebo (dummy pill) every other day. Questionnaires concerning their dietary intake and current health status are being tallied at six-month intervals. At the end of the five-year study, the incidence of cancer in both the placebo and the supplement-taking groups will be measured.

'We hope the Harvard study will show exactly how important beta-carotene is in preventing cancer,' Micheline Mathews-Roth of Harvard Medical School says. 'The studies to date show that there is something in beta-carotene-rich foods that has an effect on cancer. But whether it's the beta-carotene or some other component of the vegetables isn't known for sure yet.'

That doesn't mean you have to get rabid about rabbit food, either. 'The studies show that those who benefited from the beta-carotene in fighting cancer weren't eating *huge* amounts of vegetables,' says Dr Mathews-Roth, whose own studies have found a preventive link between beta-carotene and skin cancer. 'What it does show is that people aren't eating even the three ounces a day or so that they should be getting.'

So, the bottom line is that it's a good idea, in fact a *wise* idea to get your full allowance of wholesome greens and yellows each and every day. 'We think it is prudent for all apparently healthy adults to include in the daily diet one or two servings of the vegetables or fruits that are rich in beta-carotene,' says Richard B. Shekelle, an eminent researcher in diet and health at Rush–Presbyterian–St Luke's Medical Center in Chicago. 'The weight of evidence at this time suggests that people who eat these kinds of foods on a regular basis run a lower risk of getting cancer than those who don't.'

Dr Shekelle sent the cancer-research community into a spin with the results of his long-term study on beta-catotene and its effects on the deadliest of malignancies to man – lung cancer. His study actually began as a long-term investigation into coronary heart disease on 2107 workers of a Chicago-based plant of the Western Electric Company, and one aspect was to take dietary records of the participants. When it came to plotting vitamin A intake, Dr Shekelle and his colleagues decided to divide the vitamin intake into that which came from animal sources (whole milk, liver, cream, butter and cheese) and that which came from beta-carotene-rich fruits and vegetables.

Over the next 19 years, 33 of the men developed lung cancer – all positively related to cigarette smoking. However, Dr Shekelle and his colleagues noticed something else very significant in those who developed lung cancer. The rate was highest in those who ate the least amount of beta-carotene foods and lowest in those who ate the greatest amount. The result: an eight-to-one difference in risk between the lowest and highest carotene-intake groups (*Lancet*, 28 November 1981).

Also of major significance is the work of Eli Seifter, Guiseppi Rettura Jacques Padawer and Stanley Levenson of the Albert Einstein College of Medicine in New York City, who have published studies pinpointing the benefits of beta-carotene and vitamin A in fighting cancer in animals. 'Our studies show that if you inoculate mice with low doses of tumour cells, about 50 per cent of them will develop tumours. However, in those pre-treated with beta-carotene supplements, only 10 per cent develop tumours,' Dr Seifter told us. 'We also did a study in which we let the tumours grow to a certain size before we started beta-carotene supplementation. With beta-carotene, the tumours grew more slowly than normal and the animals survived longer.'

Perhaps the team's most dramatic experiment was a two-year study concerning the effects of radiation therapy, beta-carotene and vitamin A supplementation on cancer-induced mice. The mice were inoculated in the leg with cancer cells which were permitted to grow. The mice were then divided into six treatment groups. Dr Seifter explained: 'The radiation dose we used was comparable to the dose in many cancer patients. That is, it was enough to reduce the tumour but not make it disappear. The dosage needed for that is too powerful. In the case of our mice, it would have burned off the leg.

'The first group got no diet therapy and no radiation therapy. The tumours grew, and the animals died in 41 days. The second group got vitamin A but no radiation therapy and died in 60 days. The third group got beta-carotene and no radiation therapy and died in 61 days. And the fourth group got radiation therapy and no dietary supplementation and survived 83 days.'

'So far, radiation therapy proved to be the best of the single treatments but when it was *combined* with dietary supplementation, life expectancy was much greater.'

'In the group that received radiation and vitamin A therapy, the tumours got smaller to the point where you couldn't feel them any more. Only one animal regrew the tumour and died. The others lived out the first year. The same results were found in mice given radiation therapy and beta-carotene.'

The benefits of beta-carotene became even more obvious in the second year when these survivors were again divided into groups. 'Of the animals kept on vitamin A, none redeveloped its tumour, and all lived a normal mouse life of two years. However, five of the six taken off of vitamin A regrew their tumours and died.

'In the beta-carotene group, those kept on the supplements also remained tumour-free. And of those in which the beta-carotene was held back, only two redeveloped their cancers. And this is where the significance lies. The vitamin A-deprived mice got their tumours back in 66 days, but it took the beta-carotene-deprived mice 204 days to regrow their tumours.' Even after developing cancer twice, they managed to survive 654 days – the natural life span of a mouse.

'It appears that the beta-carotene-fed mice retained a sufficient supply in their bodies to protect them from cancer even after they stopped taking the supplements,' says Dr Seifter.

Treating cancer with vitamin A

What about people who have cancer? Does vitamin A have anything to do with improving the outcome of the disease? According to one study at the Wisconsin Cancer Center, cancer patients have an advantage in healing if their vitamin A status is good. The study involved 37 women with breast cancer who were scheduled to undergo chemotherapy. Of those with low vitamin A levels only 36 per cent improved with treatment, 24 per cent remained stable and a full 40 per cent worsened. But in the group of women who had normal or high vitamin A levels, 83 per cent improved, and only 17 per cent were listed as stable. What's more, none of these women grew worse (*Proceedings of American Association for Cancer Research*, 1981).

In Arizona, researchers have been investigating a derivation of vitamin A – vitamin A (or retinoic) acid – in the treatment of cancer. Drs Norman Levine and Frank L. Meyskens worked with two patients who had widespread melanoma (a particularly dread form of skin cancer) that had been unresponsive to conventional therapy (*Lancet*, August 1980). They were instructed to apply a solution of vitamin A acid to each skin cancer over two or three months, wrote Dr Levine. At the end of their treatment, skin biopsies were taken to determine how successful the vitamin A acid was. 'One patient had had about 20 metastases [distant areas of cancer to which the original tumour has spread], and the tumours regressed completely,' said Dr Levine. So far the patient remains free of tumours.

How much vitamin A?

'No human population at risk for development of cancer should be allowed to remain in a vitamin A-deficient state,' Dr Sporn has written *(Nutrition Reviews)*. Considering the relatively trivial cost of supplementation of the diet with a minimum daily requirement of vitamin A, he adds, 'this is certainly a goal which should be met for the entire population.'

And, Dr Sporn told us, 'Vitamin A deficiency is not as rare as one would think. There are groups that don't eat well, that don't get enough vegetables and milk products, which are good sources of vitamin A, and thus have marginal vitamin A intakes. For example, women trying to lose weight, living on coffee and cigarettes and junk food, are probably missing vitamin A as well as other vitamins and minerals.'

It's hard to say exactly how many people in Britain suffer from vitamin A deficiency. Statistics from the United States may give us an indication: in a survey of 10,126 Americans aged 1 to 74 conducted by the National Center for Health Statistics found that while the average intake of vitamin A was at or above the minimum acceptable standards for various segments of the population large percentages of each group were getting less than the necessary amounts of vitamin A. About 40 per cent of children aged 1 to 5, 57.4 per cent of the population aged 18 to 44, and 56.2 per cent of the people aged 60 and over had substandard intakes.

Dr Seifter suggests that we should strive to eat natural sources of beta-carotene on a daily basis. 'Daily intake should be from five to ten milligrams,' he says. That's equivalent to 8375 to 16,750 IU (or 2513–5025 microgram equivalents, the unit now preferred by the DHSS) of vitamin A a day – the amount in one or two carrots.

But you needn't stop there if you don't want to. Although beta-carotene converts into beneficial vitamin A in the body, it doesn't lead to the side-effects that taking too much vitamin A (in supplement form) can produce. You may be aware that taking too much vitamin A – more than 50,000 IU (15,000 ug) a day – can be toxic. Not so with beta-carotene. Sure, you can get too much. A warning indication would likely be a colouring of the skin, like the 50 orange-faced people who were diagnosed in 1942 as having severe carotenaemia after consuming 5 – 8 lb of carrots a day! Getting over that required getting off beta-carotene.

The other nice thing about beta-carotene is that finding the vegetablesand fruits rich in it is simple. Spinach, carrots, dandelion, beetrootgreens kale, yellow melon, broccoli and pumpkin are just a sampling ofthe edibles that are rich in beta-carotene. And, they're the very things youcan easily grow in your own garden.

Vitamin C

A good deal of work has also been done on the effect of vitamin C on cancer.

One study has suggested that vitamin C may protect some women who are at high risk of developing cervical cancer. In another, vitamin C 'completely inhibited' tumour growth in cells exposed to a chemical carcinogen called MCA even when the vitamin was added to the solution as late as 23 days after exposure. The importance of this finding, the researchers noted, was that vitamin C had never before been shown to inhibit tumour growth so late in the process of cancerous transformation (*Cancer Research*, August 1980).

An intriguing study in Hawaii has revealed a strong correlation between dietary intake of fresh fruit and vitamin C, and a lowered incidence of stomach (gastric) cancer. The authors compared the incidence of this type of cancer among four groups: Japanese who migrated to Hawaii from Japan; whites who migrated to Hawaii from the mainland; Hawaiian-born whites; and Japanese. These statistics were also compared with overall stomach cancer rates in the United States and in Japan.

'All four comparison groups showed a similar pattern of increasing cancer incidence with age,' the researchers found, 'but the rates for Japanese (whether in Japan or Hawaii) are higher than for Caucasians at all ages.' The very highest rates were found in Japan, the lowest in the United States.

Could there be some cultural factor involved, some ethnic difference between the lifestyles of Japanese and Americans? There was good reason to suspect there might be, since stomach cancer has dramatically declined in the United States over the past 40 years – except among immigrants from Japan and northern Europe. There is further evidence that the critical factor might be a dietary one, since other studies have linked certain foods common to the Japanese diet with higher stomach cancer rates.

Taking a cue from these reports, the Hawaiian researchers examined the dietary intake of these suspected foods in their study group. They discovered that high stomach-cancer rates were indeed associated with foods such as dried, salted fish, pickled vegetables and rice. They also noted that fresh fruit and vitamin C (in foods or in supplements) were associated with a decreased incidence of the disease.

Dr John Weisburger and his associates at the American Health Foundation theorize that vitamin C, when taken with foods treated with nitrite may prevent certain cancer-causing agents from forming. In their work, they conclude that taking vitamin C regularly, from childhood onward, may prevent gastric cancer (*Preventive Medicine*, May 1980).

Nitrites are a by-product of nitrates. Nitrites and nitrates themselves are not carcinogenic, Dr Weisburger explains. A natural part of the environment nitrates occur in soil and drinking water and provide essential nitrogen for plants to grow. Researchers have found that when we eat, the bacteria in our mouths form nitrites from the nitrates in our foods. Sodium nitrate and nitrite may be used as preservatives and colour fixatives in cured meats, and people who pickle foods use a high-nitrite/high-salt solution. And when some foods are not refrigerated and are left at room temperature for a while nitrites may be released then as well. So people can ingest nitrites and nitrates from a variety of sources.

The problem is that under certain conditions they can react with substances and produce carcinogens, called *nitrosamines*. Dr Weisburger and his colleagues suggest that the process may lead to stomach cancer, especially when there is a lack of vitamin C in the diet.

People living in Japan, Iceland and other countries with less temperate or even frigid climates appear to be at a high risk of developing gastric cancer. The disease seems prevalent in 'the northern parts of the world or in mountainous regions with relatively little daily access to fresh fruits vegetables and salads,' the researchers wrote. The incidence of gastric cancer has declined in the United States, they added, suggesting that a higher intake of vitamin C may be the reason.

Dr Weisburger believes people should avoid pickled foods, but if they can't, he suggests eating them with lettuce, tomatoes and other foods containing vitamin C. He also thinks that other foods that contain nitrates such as bacon, are acceptable as long as vitamin C is present to prevent any mutagenic [precancerous] activity from occuring later in digestion. 'Since there is vitamin C in lettuce and tomatoes, if you eat a BLT [bacon, lettuce and tomato sandwich] . . . you would have enough vitamin C in all of those foods to counteract the nitrite,' he says.

The vitamin C and the nitrite have to be in the stomach at the same time to prevent the mutagens from forming, he continues. 'Food stays in the stomach for two or three hours. So drinking a glass of orange juice at seven o'clock and eating nitrite-treated foods at eight may work, but the foods shouldn't be eaten too far apart. Vitamin C should either be added to the food or be a part of the meal.'

While gastric cancer has decreased in both the United States and Britain the problem of colon and rectal cancer continues to be significant. Some American researchers believe that it may be linked to different levels of vitamin C intake that exist geographically in the United States.

According to the National Cancer Institute, some 77,000 Americans develop colon cancer in a year, and 42,800 die from it. However, there is a lower incidence of colon and rectal cancer in Florida and the south-eastern United States, as well as in California and Arizona. The incidence of large-bowel cancer in those regions is one-half the national average, note Henry C. Lyko and James X. Hartmann of Florida Atlantic University. They suggest that the higher consumption of citrus fruit, which is high in vitamin C, may be the reason. Regular citrus consumption is part of the south-eastern Florida lifestyle, they report, and two-thirds of the families there have an average of three citrus trees per household. According to Lyko and Hartmann, people who consume a diet high in beef, fats and proteins are at a higher risk of developing large-bowel cancer, but

> . . . there is increasing evidence that vitamin C may prevent the development of large-bowel cancer, and the most encouraging aspect of these findings is that it may be easier to get Americans to supplement their diets with citrus or vitamin C than to persuade them to change their dietary habits appreciably.

At Children's Hospital in Los Angeles, researchers have scrutinized vitamin C from another angle. What happens when normal cells are exposed to a carcinogen, and vitamin C is added afterwards? Can vitamin C keep tumours from forming? William F. Benedict and Peter A. Jones are only at the earliest stages of working out those questions, but preliminary results are encouraging.

The researchers took mouse-embryo cells and exposed them to a carcinogen for 24 hours. Then they removed the carcinogen and immediately added vitamin C to some of the exposed cells. They found that vitamin C completely prevented cell transformation that normally occurs after exposure to cancer-causing agents. Then they took cells that had already transformed and had never before been in contact with vitamin C. They divided these cells into two groups: vitamin C was added to one group; the second group was left alone. 'The dish of transformed cells that got the vitamin C changed back into normal-appearing cells,' Dr Benedict told us.

That doesn't happen in every instance, however. If you took transformed cells and added vitamin C to them, 75 per cent of the cells would go back to normal, Dr Benedict explained. The remaining 25 per cent would still be in the transformed state. They would not change back, despite the addition of vitamin C. 'We think the transformation process of a cell is a progression,' said Dr Benedict. 'Vitamin C may revert a cell back to normal if the transformation process has only gone so far.'

Is there any difference between normal cells and the transformed cells that suddenly appear normal after getting vitamin C? 'We don't think there is,' said Dr Benedict.

The doses of vitamin C used were much smaller than those used in other studies, and once the transformed cells had reverted to normal, the researchers discovered that the vitamin was no longer needed. 'When we took the vitamin C away, the cells did not transform again,' says Dr Benedict. The vitamin C had apparently made an irreversible change in the cells, and they remained normal in appearance. 'Usually, when you take other cancer-blocking agents away, within three or four days you have transformed cells appearing in the dish again.'

He emphasizes that their research does not address the question of vitamin C's effects on cells *after* they have become a tumour. The relevance of their findings lies with blocking a tumour from forming. Vitamin C may change transformed cells back into their normal state before they grow into a tumour he says.

'I'm pretty convinced that if people maintained a reasonable . . . intake [of vitamin C], we would see a diminished incidence of cancer,' said Ewan Cameron a Scottish surgeon who has conducted much of the research on vitamin C and cancer. 'If you can alter even a little the very, very advanced cancer patients, then all logic suggests you should be able to alter the very early stages of the illness,' he told us. 'And, of course, the earliest stage of the illness is before the person has cancer at all.'

In Dr Cameron's studies on advanced cancer patients, the disease was sometimes altered more than 'a little'. 'We published a paper reporting dramatic relief of bone pain in four out of five patients with skeletal metastases,' he said. 'Bone cancer is usually a pretty painful situation . . . Vitamin C, however, relieves the pain. And this is not because vitamin C is itself, a pain reliever or a narcotic. It's because the pain is due to the steady expansion of the tumour against the inelastic bone. Vitamin C slows down the expansion and thus relieves pain.'

Dr Cameron has seen cases in which vitamin C not only slowed down tumour growth but reversed it. 'One old man, a stationmaster, came in with cancer of the pancreas. I operated on him, and he went home. He wasn't given vitamin C yet. Four or five months later, he came back with a big malignant liver. He wasn't going to die that week, but he was a very sick man. Very definitely on a downhill slope. We started him off on vitamin C and his liver shrank back in size and, contrary to many expectations, he went home.'

Over the past eight years, Dr Cameron has compared the survival time of terminal cancer patients who receive vitamin C to similar patients who don't. He has found that vitamin C increases survival time an average of 330 or more days (some of the patients are still alive) – 6.6 times longer than patients who didn't get vitamin C.

Vitamin E

In a study conducted by William R. Bruce of the University of Toronto mutagens in faeces were measured before and then three weeks after taking daily doses of vitamins C (400 mg) and E (440 IU).

'We observed a significant decrease in the levels of mutagens,' said Dr Bruce, 'so we conducted another study. Only this time, volunteers were put on a diet including brown bread (high in fibre with additional daily vitamins C [100 mg] and E [110 IU] or on a diet including white bread plus a placebo'. When the volunteers went from their usual white bread diet to the one containing vitamins C and E and fibre, the levels of mutagens dropped.

'But the reverse was also true,' said Dr Bruce. 'Switching from a diet including brown bread and vitamins C and E to one containing white bread increased the levels of mutagens in the faeces. The levels of these mutagens can differ in various populations at risk for colon cancer, but it's clear that diet is a contributing factor.'

Vitamin E has been shown to inhibit the breast-cancer-causing action of the chemical *daunorubicin* in rats and the colon-cancer-causing effects of *dimethylhydrazine* in mice. The vitamin may also protect against cancer of the colon by preventing the formation of nitrosamines and nitrosamides in the stomach.

Researchers at the Ontario Cancer Institute in Canada have shown that the wastes of people eating a normal diet contain chemicals that cause mutations in a special strain of test bacteria. Scientists know that chemicals which cause the mutations very often also cause cancer, and results of various tests led the Canadian researchers to believe that the chemicals they found in the faeces were probably nitrosamines and nitrosamides (*Environmental Aspects of N-Nitroso Compounds*).

The most interesting developments came when the researchers tested the effects of vitamin E on the levels of the suspected cancer-causing chemicals. Supplementation of people's diets with 120, 400 and 1200 IU of vitamin E a day led to significant reductions in the amounts of the chemicals in the faeces (*American Association for Cancer Research Abstracts*, March 1980).

That result clearly supports the idea that vitamin E blocks the formation of nitrosamines and nitrosamides, and the Canadian researchers are now testing vitamin E to determine if it can block the recurrence of threatening growths (called *polyps*) in patients with cancer of the colon and rectum.

Vitamin E's potential as an anti-cancer agent has just begun to be explored. Researchers at the University of Colorado Health Science Center recently found that combinations of the vitamin and anti-cancer drugs worked synergistically, meaning that their combined effect was greater than the sum of their separate abilities. In some cases, vitamin E increased the ability of chemotherapy to inhibit the growth of cancer cells, and the vitamin also promoted differentiation – i.e. the normal, healthy development of cells into their specialized roles in the various organs.

> If the present results can be applicable *in vivo* [in living bodies], the combination of vitamin E with some of the currently used therapeutic agents may help to improve the present management of metastatic NB [nerve cancer] and other neoplasms. Such an adjuvant [a substance that aids another] could reduce the dose requirements of cytotoxic [anti-cancer] drugs without reducing the cell-killing or differentiating effects. [*Proceedings of the Society for Experimental Biology and Medicine*, vol. 164, 1980].

To explain those effects, researcher Kedar Prasad theorizes that, in the nucleus of a cell, a molecule of vitamin E might be attached to the chromosomes, and the presence or absence of vitamin E in those critical places might affect cell behaviour. 'It is possible that vitamin E plays a role in normal cell development. Aberrations in vitamin E metabolism may play a part in cancer,' Dr Prasad told us. 'If this turns out to be true, it would dramatically increase the importance of vitamin E.'

Selenium

There's evidence that vitamin E works with a partner: the trace element *selenium*. The two work together on an electronmicroscopic level to protect cell membranes, cell nuclei and chromosomes from damage caused by carcinogens. Both of the nutrients are anti-oxidants, which means that they protect cell membranes and nuclei from damage by peroxides. Through the enzyme *glutathione peroxidase* (GSH-px), selenium neutralizes peroxides, while vitamin E prevents dietary fats from turning into them. Together, they lower the amounts of peroxide in our tissues.

There are several theories about what else selenium does, on the cellular level, to prevent cancer. John A. Milner of the University of Illinois speculates that selenium's effect on rapidly dividing cells might explain why his laboratory mice didn't get cancer when they received selenium supplements.

Dr Milner transplanted cancer cells into healthy mice and then injected some of them with selenium salts. After six weeks, all of the unsupplemented mice were bloated with tumours and were double their original weight, but the supplemented mice were trim, healthy and tumour-free. Selenium continued to protect the mice for three weeks after supplementation stopped. 'Complete inhibition of tumour development was observed for all selenium compounds administered at a dose of two micrograms per gram of body weight' (*Science*, August 1980).

Dr Milner told us that his results might have 'profound implications' for cancer prevention. He suspects that selenium somehow slows the growth of cancer cells wihout affecting healthy ones.

The possibility that selenium slows down cell division also interests Gerhard Schrauzer, a chemistry professor at the University of California's Revelle College and perhaps the nation's leading selenium researcher. He believes that selenium prevents cancer partly by delaying cell division long enough for a carcinogen-damaged cell to repair its chromosomes. 'If cells suffer chromosomal damage, they may become malignant unless the damage is repaired before the cell divides. Any agent which retards mitosis [cell division] but does not inhibit DNA repair could be considered as a potential anti-carcinogenic agent' (*Advances in Nutritional Research*, vol. 2 1979).

Dr Schrauzer estimates that, among people who don't smoke or otherwise expose themselves to large doses of carcinogens, an adequate supply of selenium provides effective resistance to cancers of the intestine, rectum breast, ovary, prostate, lung, pancreas, skin, kidney and bladder, as well as to certain types of leukaemia. Selenium does this, he says, not only by retarding cell division but also by promoting the production of the enzyme GSH-px which turns peroxides into harmless water. It may also aid the production of interferon, the body's natural anti-viral and anti-cancer drug.

In one experiment, Dr Schrauzer found that selenium can prevent or delay the appearance of breast tumours in mice that have been infected with a carcinogenic virus. Dividing the infected mice into four groups, he put the first group on a high-selenium diet containing 1 part per million (ppm) of selenium and a second group on a low-selenium diet with only 0.15 ppm – the same proportion found in the average American human diet. He fed a third group the 'high' diet for only the first half of the experiment and fed the fourth group the 'high' diet for only the second half of the experiment.

At the end of the experiment, the high-selenium group had the fewest tumours (27 per cent), while those mice on the average American diet had the most (77 per cent). The third group, which was on the high-selenium diet for only the first half of the experiment, showed a 69 per cent tumour rate. The fourth group, on the high-selenium diet for only the second half, had a tumour rate of 46 per cent.

The earlier selenium supplementation begins, the better, Dr Schrauzer believes.

> Dietary selenium prevents and retards tumour development only as long as it is supplied in adequate amounts . . . Maximum protection is achieved if supplementation is introduced early and maintained over the entire life span of the animals. However, a 'late' protective effect of selenium is still apparent. [*Carcinogenesis*, February 1980].

Most significantly, if selenium can prevent breast tumours in mice, Dr Schrauzer says, it may prevent them in humans. In partial confirmation of that theory, researchers elsewhere have found that breast cancer patients have 'significantly' less selenium in their blood than do healthy women (*Journal of Surgical Oncology*, vol. 15, no. 1, 1980).

At the Baylor College of Medicine in Houston, Daniel Medina is working on a way to prevent some of the 90,000 new cases of breast cancer found in American women each year. He has successfully used selenium against breast tumours in his lab animals.

'The most promising result of our research,' Dr Medina told us, 'is the fact that selenium can inhibit, in the early stages, the development of tumours that were introduced by viral or chemical carcinogens. What we're looking for now is a mechanism of how it works and what will be a safe but preventive dose.'

In one experiment, Dr Medina gave a normal diet to one group of mice and a diet with 20 times the normal level of selenium to a second group. Then he gave the animals high doses of carcinogens. After six months, 75 per cent of the unsupplemented mice exhibited 'pre-neoplastic lesions' – cellular damage that often leads to tumours – while only 25 per cent of the supplemented mice showed such changes. Six months later 80 per cent of the low-selenium animals had developed tumours, compared with only 18 per cent of the high-selenium mice. Significantly, Dr Medina told us, the supplemented animals showed no ill effects; even at the artificially high doses, their growth and reproductive abilities were normal and healthy.

Dr Medina hopes his finding will lead to the prevention, though not the treatment, of breast cancer in women. 'In the human population,' he says 'pre-neoplastic lesions in the breasts of women can be detected with mammography [X-rays of the breast].' It's possible to identify high-risk women by the distinct changes in the microscopic architecture of mammary ducts.

B complex vitamins

We've discussed some of the most important nutrients widely recognized as having anti-cancer activity vitamins A (especially beta-carotene), C and E and the trace mineral selenium. But some fascinating research also indicates that different B vitamins play varying roles in the cancer picture.

Vitamin B_{12} Over 20 years of painstaking work by Sister Mary Eymard Poydock, professor of biology and director of cancer research, and her associates at Mercyhurst College in Erie, Pennyslvania, have now produced results which indicate that a combination of vitamins C and B_{12} may have a powerful effect against cancer. While Sister Eymard's work has been confined to laboratory animals, the implications for further research are obvious.

Sister Eymard has been testing a substance that had been advanced as a possible anti-cancer agent. The first results were promising, and the name 'mercytamin' (from the Sisters of Mercy) was given to the substance. Mercytamin was actually a combination of vitamins C and B_{12} and a variety of enzymes. Through scientific testing of the solution, the enzymes and other chemical additives were eliminated as possible active agents. Finally only the vitamins remained, and the name mercytamin was dropped.

Sister Eymard held back on publishing her findings until she was certain that the results she was getting were true. 'We've done enough experiments now, testing hundreds of mice, to establish that it works,' Sister Eymard says. 'We've got it down to a point now where if you do it according to the 'recipe', it will work every time.'

Sister Eymard and her research staff implanted three common types of cancers into laboratory mice – sarcomas (cancerous growths of connective tissues), carcinomas (cancers of skin-like tissues) and leukaemias (cancers of the blood-forming organs). These cancerous tissues were implanted both in the abdomens and under the skin of the mice. The mice were then injected with the mixture of vitamins C and B_{12} (in a ratio of one part B_{12} to two parts C) near the sites of the tumour transplants.

Within four days, some of the tumours from the abdomens of the mice were removed, and the cells were examined under the microscope. There was a dramatic change in the tissue: *the cancerous cell division had stopped completely*.

The tumours growing under the skin were treated the day after the implant with the C/B_{12} combination. The results were similar – no tumours would grow. In the control animals (those mice with transplanted tumours that were not given the C/B_{12} combination), the tumours continued to grow at a rapid rate.

Inhibiting tumour growth was only part of the results of Sister Eymard's experiments. She also wanted to see if the C/B_{12} mixture would prolong the lives of animals already suffering from cancer. To find out she and her colleagues injected the mixture into the abdomens of diseased mice near the cancerous growths for seven successive days.

Treated animals lived longer than those mice not given C and B_{12}. In fact, all the treated mice outlived the control group. It appeared that the combination of C and B_{12} not only inhibits the growth of cancer cells but also prolongs the lives of animals that have cancer.

'There are few things presently on the market that will ensure a 100 per cent survival rate with cancer,' Sister Eymard says, 'but we had a 100 per cent survival rate after the controls were dead. Most of the treated mice outlived the controls by two or three weeks.'

To be sure that it was really the C/B_{12} concoction and not an unknown factor present in mice that was responsible for her results, Sister Eymard conducted experiments on free-living cancer cells growing on a culture medium. The vitamin C/B_{12} complex was used as a treatment on three types of cancer cells, and on healthy cells as well. The treated cells, an untreated control group and the healthy cells were left to incubate.

At the end of the incubation period, the untreated control group was infested with cancer cells. In the treated cancer cells however, *not one cancer cell of any of the three types was to be found*. The healthy, non-cancerous cells were unaffected by the C/B_{12} complex. It appeared that Sister Eymard had found a cancer-inhibiting agent that not only stops many kinds of cancer, but does so with absolutely no side-effects in healthy tissue.

Sister Eymard also tested each vitamin separately to determine if either was primarily responsible for the anti-cancer effects. The combination of the two vitamins, however, always performed much more effectively than either one alone.

Tests showed that the combination might be working by boosting the animals' immune systems to fight the cancer. Sister Eymard is confident that with more experimentation, especially on larger mammals and humans, the vitamin C/B_{12} combination could prove to be a useful preventive weapon in the fight to eliminate cancer.

The scientific community has taken note of Sister Eymard's findings. A spokesman for the American Cancer Society, which helps fund Sister Eymard's research, told us, 'The physicians on the committee which reviewed Sister Eymard's work were most impressed with the results she was getting. She has come forth with work of considerable promise.'

Thiamin (Vitamin B_1) That a lack of thiamin causes cancer has yet to be proved, but that an abundance of thiamin treats the disease – at least in laboratory animals – is a fact.

Tumours, transplanted in laboratory animals, were treated with an anti-cancer substance. When the animals received thiamin, the 'anti-tumour activity' of the substance increased. In other animals with cancer, the growth of their tumours slowed after they received yeast, and a researcher theorized that 'the effectiveness of the yeast could well be due to its content of thiamin' *(Oncology)*.

Folic acid Research findings have shown that birth control pills cause localized folic-acid deficiencies in the uteruses of women who take them. These localized deficiencies manifest themselves as cervical dysplasia which, left untreated, can progress into cancer. However, researchers at the University of Alabama treated cervical dysplasia by giving patients a 5 mg folic-acid supplement twice a day – more than 20 times the US recommended dietary allowance and the results have been excellent *(see* CERVICAL DYSPLASIA).

Vitamin B_6 Doctors are saying that vitamin B_6, which is also known to keep the immune system healthy, may even help prevent breast cancer from recurring. In research done at the Imperial Cancer Research Fund Laboratories in London, patients undergoing treatment for breast cancer were studied to determine the likelihood that their cancer would return. What the doctors did was analyse the patients' urine for a by-product of vitamin B_6 metabolism known as 4-PA. Low urinary amounts of 4-PA reflect a vitamin B_6 deficiency, and the results of the study showed that patients who excreted lower levels of 4-PA had a significantly greater probability of recurrence of breast cancer than those who excreted higher levels *(European Journal of Cancer,* February 1980).

Nutrient deficiencies linked to certain types of cancer

We've pointed out how aspects of the diet influence various cancers. The protective effect of vitamin A is strongly associated with epithelial cancers for example, while folic-acid is associated with cervical health. In the same vein, deficiencies of other nutrients are associated with the development of certain cancers.

Cancers of throat and liver related to low zinc

Paul M. Newberne and his colleagues at the department of nutrition and food science at MIT reported at a trace element conference that low levels of zinc could make some people susceptible to cancer of the oesophagus. They studied a group of Chinese men between the ages of 45 and 75 who were in reasonably good physical and nutritional shape, but who were diagnosed as having throat cancer. Tests were made of the zinc and copper content of their blood serum, hair and throat tissue. A control group of healthy men was given the same battery of tests.

All the cancer patients were found to have reduced zinc levels in all specimens. Was that low zinc level involved in the cause of their cancer, or was it caused by the cancer itself? To try to answer that question, the same researchers did a companion study, in which they gave rats a zinc-deficient diet and then subjected them to applications of nitrosamine, the cancer-causing substance that is thought to be involved in throat cancer. (The Chinese men ate a great deal of fish, which tests showed contained nitrosamines.) The zinc-deficient rats got cancer more rapidly than did rats given a diet containing adequate zinc.

Dr Newberne and his co-workers said in their report that 'diminished zinc reserves may sensitize the oesophagus to environmental carcinogens, such as nitrosamines.' That is a hypothesis, they said, not an established fact, but so far the experimental evidence points clearly to zinc having a protective effect against throat cancer in animals.

In a study reported at another trace element meeting held in West Germany, A. Mathur and co-workers at the Swedish universities of Malmo and Lund found a similar effect. They analysed the livers of people who had died of cancer and compared those results with tests made from liver tissue of healthy people killed in traffic accidents. In all cases, the livers of the cancer victims had less zinc than those of the controls.

Low iron and stomach cancer

At an American Chemical Society meeting, a microbiologist presented evidence that iron deficiency in the diet not only can cause gastric ulceration and the loss of stomach acid, but may be connected to stomach cancer as well.

Selwyn Broitman of Boston University School of Medicine told us, 'In the South American population studied, lack of iron coupled with a high intake of nitrates seems to lead to stomach cancer.'

Magnesium

The involvement of magnesium deficiency in the development of some types of cancer has also been well documented. 'Gastric cancer has long been associated with soil and water low in magnesium,' Dr Mildred S. Seelig noted in a paper she delivered at a meeting of the International Association of Bioinorganic Scientists. 'Cattle leukaemia has also been reported in areas with low magnesium supply or availability.'

One study of leukaemia in cattle was conducted by Julian Aleksandrowicz director of the Haematological Clinic of the Institute of Internal Medicine in Krakow, Poland. Dr Aleksandrowicz reported that the incidence of cattle leukaemia in Poland varied significantly between the northern and southern halves of the country, the difference corresponding to the occupation zones in Poland before World War I. The Prussians, who occupied the northern half of the country, farmed the land intensively, stripping it of important minerals including magnesium. In the south, the occupying Russians and Austrians practised a more natural, old-fashioned style of agriculture, which left the land in better shape for future generations.

Dr Aleksandrowicz found that cattle leukaemia occurred much more frequently in the northern, magnesium-poor section of the country. He also reported that while human leukaemia in Poland had increased sharply in certain areas since 1960, there had been no change in the areas with magnesium-rich soil and water.

Scientists in Holland in the 1950s concluded that the low magnesium content of purified river water was one cause of the higher cancer death rate observed in districts where purified water was drunk. The same researchers found a correlation between low cancer mortality and limestone soils rich in calcium and magnesium (*Soil, Grass and Cancer*).

The connection between magnesium deficiency and the development of cancer is supported by a number of laboratory studies as well. Dr Pierre Bois at the University of Montreal showed that 'deficiency in magnesium in the diet of young rats was associated with the formation of tumours in the thymus gland – lymphoma.'

A team of scientists working under George M. Hass in Chicago has produced leukaemia in rats by feeding them a diet only slightly deficient in magnesium. Dr Hass's work is particularly impressive in that he was working with a breed of rats normally resistant to the development of cancers of the lymph system including leukaemia and lymphoma.

Don't Smoke

Although many magazine advertisements like to equate smoking with adventure youth and enhanced sexuality, cigarettes are probably the greatest single contributor to cancer deaths in the United Kingdom. Lung and other respiratory cancers account for about 40,000 deaths per year, or over one-quarter of the total cancer mortality. Cigarettes probably account for 80 to 85 per cent of these deaths. The overall cancer rate has been going up mainly because of the spectacular 50-year climb of lung cancer rates, and as Dr Weisburger has written, 'It is no secret that the main cause for this important increase . . . can be traced to the smoking of manufactured cigarettes' (*Texas Reports on Biology and Medicine*).

Smoking has also been implicated as a promoting factor in some occupational cancers. Asbestos workers and Colorado uranium miners who smoke are at greater risk than their non-smoking co-workers. In uranium mines in Ontario, smoking was banned underground in 1973. According to a Canadian industrial medicine consultant, 'The most effective immediate step to reduce the incidence of occupational lung cancer would be to concentrate on reducing smoking' (*Canadian Medical Association Journal*, 8 September 1979).

Lung cancer is not the only cancer associated with cigarettes. Cancers of the throat and mouth are also linked to smoking, especially when alcohol use is involved. Smokers have higher rates of pancreas and bladder cancer, and smokers who also use a lot of artificial sweeteners increase their risk of bladder cancer still further. Male smokers are also more likely to develop kidney cancer, and female smokers are more prone to cervical cancer than non-smokers.

Although the carcinogens in cigarette smoke aren't considered very strong puffing 20 or more cigarettes a day for several years seems to have a cumulative cancer-causing effect. The smoke also apparently damages a mechanism the lungs have for clearing themselves of poisons. Another theory is that the particles in smoke are large enough to hold on to other carcinogens and carry them deeper into the structure of the lung. Cigarette smokers also suffer from a chronic deficiency of vitamin C, which is vital to the body's cancer defence system.

It's never too late to stop – even when it comes to smoking. Even, in fact, when it comes to diagnosed lung cancer: patients who stop smoking at the time of diagnosis live longer – some actually free of disease – than those who continue to smoke even after learning the bad news. At least that's the conclusion of a group of doctors and nurses from the National Cancer Institute in Washington, D.C.

In their experiment, 112 patients (all with diagnosed lung cancer) were divided into three groups. One group of 20 had stopped smoking permanently before diagnosis, another 35 stopped at the time the diagnosis was made, and the third group (57) continued smoking. All the patients were similar in regard to severity of disease, age and sex as well as numbers of cigarettes smoked per year, and all were placed on standard cancer treatments at the start of the experiment.

However, the similarities ended when it came to survival time. Not one patient who continued to smoke survived disease-free for more than 96 weeks while several patients in each of the other two groups were free of lung cancer 103 to 220 weeks after the start of the experiment.

It's known, wrote the researchers, that cigarette smoke inhalation causes rapid depression of antibody (disease fighter) production within lung tissue. They speculated that the body's defences against tumour growth may be restored when smoking is discontinued, prolonging the life of these lung cancer patients (*Journal of the American Medical Association*, 14 November 1980).

So if you don't smoke, you're already way ahead of the game. If you do, giving up is worth the effort.

Avoid excessive sunlight

'Skin cancers are the most common malignant tumours of white-skinned people,' reported a group of doctors in *Preventive Medicine* (March 1980). 'In the USA 300,000 to 400,000 new skin cancers develop per year almost all of which are preventable.' Why? Because almost all of them are caused by chronic exposure to the ultraviolet radiation (UVR) in sunlight.

The doctors pointed out that if you avoid the sun between 11 A.M. and 1 P.M., the brightest hours of the day, you also miss out on 50 per cent of the sun's UVR. It's that simple. Although only a small percentage of skin cancers prove to be fatal, they noted, fair-skinned people who sunburn easily (particularly people of Irish, Scottish or Welsh descent) should be especially careful because their lack of skin pigmentation makes them vulnerable to sunlight's damaging effects.

Mind over disease

Body and mind work together – like marriage partners – 'in sickness and in health'. And, say researchers, how a person reacts to having cancer can, to some extent, determine the outcome of his or her struggle against the disease.

In a major study of breast cancer patients in Britain researchers classified the women according to the way they responded to the diagnosis of breast cancer. They found four distinct approaches to the disease among the women they interviewed. Some reacted with complete denial that any of the signs of their disease were serious. The denial was so complete that some patients told the researchers after mastectomies that their breasts had been removed only 'as a precaution.' Other women took the attitude that they could personally fight and defeat the disease. They tried to find out everything they could about breast cancer in order to conquer it. A third group acknowledged that they had cancer, accepted the diagnosis stoically and made no effort to find out anything more about the disease. The last group reacted by simply giving up. They felt totally powerless to improve their conditions and resigned themselves to an early death.

There were dramatic differences in the survival rates of the four groups. Three-quarters of the patients who responded to their diagnosis with either denial or a firm fighting spirit were alive and well five years later. However, only 35 per cent of the other women – those who either accepted their fate stoically or gave up completely – were still alive at that time. The patients in those two groups accounted for 88 per cent of the women who had died within five years (*Lancet*, 13 October 1979).

Similar findings have been reported in studies conducted to determine who gets cancer in the first place. A classic study, begun in 1946 among students at Johns Hopkins Medical School outside Baltimore, Maryland, compared psychological tests administered then with the students' health in later years. Not only was cancer found to be associated with a particular personality type, but that type was remarkably similar to the psychological profile of those who later committed suicide.

Express your anger

'In the 1950s, two researchers looked at the life history patterns of about 400 cancer patients,' Marjorie Brooks of Jefferson Medical College in Philadelphia told us. 'They found the patients had some very interesting similarities. Many of them seemed unable to express anger or hostility in defence of themselves. The patients *could* get angry in the defence of others or in the defence of a cause. But when it came to self-defence, they didn't follow through.

'Suppressed hostility was another significant factor appearing in some of the other patients. They seemed to lack the discharge mechanism needed to allow anger to surface, so they kept all of their anger inside.'

Other research, which focused on British women undergoing breast biopsies 'indicated that women who were very, very seldom angry and women who were highly volatile were more likely to have malignant tumours than women who had an appropriate expression of anger,' said Dr Brooks.

Her own research seems to confirm previous findings. She recently surveyed 1100 women who did not have breast cancer and compared the results to those of 15 women with benign tumours and 15 women with malignancies. 'A significantly higher proportion of both benign and malignant patients stated they had experienced much more anger during the previous year than the 1100 respondents who did not have disease,' Dr Brooks told us. 'A larger percentage of women having malignancies had felt angry more often than the women having benign tumours. And a larger percentage of women with benign tumours had felt angrier the previous year than women in normal health.'

The *ways* in which the women expressed anger also were different. Women with malignant breast cancer were more likely to apologize for their anger, even when they were right, said Dr Brooks. So whenever they *did* express their hostility, they often took it back.

Women with benign tumours tended to get angry and stay angry. Their anger often became an unresolved internal conflict. Women in normal health, on the other hand, were more likely to blow up and then forget about it, said Dr Brooks. They redirected their attention and energies to more pleasant things.

Dr Brooks' research suggests ties between anger and progression of disease. 'Often, people feel angry over being dependent and helpless in a treatment situation,' she said. 'But if that angry energy can be redirected, they feel less stress, and quite likely their physical condition will be positively affected.'

'Imaging' away cancer

Findings about the importance of the mind's role in disease have led O. Carl Simonton, a Texas doctor and his wife, Stephanie Matthews-Simonton, to set up a programme for terminal cancer patients. At their Cancer Counseling and Research Center, patients practise a kind of meditation called *imagery*, in conjunction with traditional cancer treatments. They visualize the cancer cells in their bodies being overwhelmed by their treatment and flushed out of their bodies. Then they 'image' good cells – healthy cells – taking over and, in their mind's eye, picture themselves as healthy and free of disease.

In their book *Getting Well Again*, the Simontons report that over a four-year period they worked with 159 patients with diagnoses of incurable cancer. At the end of that period, 63 were still alive, having survived an average of 24.4 months after their diagnosis – more than twice the national norm for similar cancer patients. Even the patients who had died lived $1^1/_2$ times longer than ordinary patients. Of those who were alive, some 40 per cent were either improving or had no evidence of the disease whatsoever.

When you consider that 100 per cent of those patients had been told they had incurable cancer, you get some idea of the importance of the mind in healing. A study of the Simontons' patients has found that their performance on psychological tests is a better indicator of their chances for survival than even the seriousness of the disease at the time of the tests. Their state of mind seems to be more important for survival than their physical condition.

• Carpal tunnel syndrome

Carpal tunnel syndrome is a neurological disease caused by the pressure of wrist ligaments rubbing against the median nerve of the hand. Those with this syndrome often complain of a burning or tingling sensation in the hands and fingers, as well as morning pain and stiffness in the joints. They may also have a weak handgrip and night-time muscle spasms or brief paralysis.

John M. Ellis is a Texas doctor who has pioneered vitamin B_6 (pyridoxine) therapy for carpal tunnel syndrome. In a study carried out jointly with Karl Folkers and co-workers at the University of Texas, Dr Ellis treated ten people with severe pain and stiffness problems. Six were actually being considered for wrist surgery as a last resort to relieve their discomfort.

Because all of these individuals were found to have a deficiency of pyridoxine, the researchers decided to prescribe a relatively high dosage of the vitamin: 300 mg daily. The results were remarkable.

A 33-year-old woman, who did vigorous work with her hands at a furniture factory, had complained of nightly numbness and tingling in her right hand. The hand was swollen, and she was unable to grasp objects tightly. There was additional numbness and tingling in her cheek. After taking vitamin B_6 for four weeks, she reported that all symptoms were relieved. And she never missed a day of work.

Another woman, aged 35, had suffered with pain and stiffness for five years. She was continually dropping objects at work, where she assembled screen doors. Finally, the pain in her hands became so bad that she was kept awake four or five hours each night, and terrible shoulder pain prevented her from combing her hair. The researchers reported that, after four weeks of vitamin B_6 therapy, 'there was complete relief of shoulder pain, remarkable reduction in swelling of hands and feet, improved speed and range of flexion of fingers, and improved handgrip.' Other people experienced similar improvement while taking the vitamin.

In a second study with vitamin B_6 and seven carpal tunnel patients, Dr Ellis noted equally great benefits. Some of these individuals had suffered finger and hand pain for five to ten years, and a few had experienced such great nerve sensory loss in their fingertips that they couldn't feel pressure even when a sharp needle penetrated their skin and drew blood. Yet they, too, were helped by vitamin B_6 *(Research Communications in Chemical Pathology and Pharmacology)*.

• Cerebral palsy

'Perhaps 50 per cent of the misery of cerebral palsy doesn't even have to exist,' declares Marshall Mandell, an allergist and medical director of the New England Foundation for Allergic and Bio-Ecologic Diseases. he states that he has made a 'wonderful breakthrough' in our understanding of cerebral palsy [CP], a partial paralysis caused by damaged nerve tissue that is thought to affect approximately one in every 400 children born in the United Kingdom where they are commonly (and wrongly) known as 'spastics'.

Dr Mandell's claims are the result of a study of 29 cerebral palsy patients, which showed that almost all of them had allergic or allergy-like reactions to substances in food, water or air. When the offending substances were removed from their diet or environment, Dr Mandell told us, many of the symptoms the patients had come to associate with CP – from painful muscle spasms and fatigue to convulsive seizures – were 'greatly improved or eliminated.'

A number of years ago, Dr Mandell explained, a young man from Florida was referred to him for allergies that produced sinus disorders and bronchial asthma. When the young man walked into his office, the allergist was surprised to notice that he had cerebral palsy – the first CP patient he had seen in 30 years of practice.

After taking a comprehensive personal health history of the young man including his allergic reactions, and then exposing him to tiny amounts of various substances, the reaction-producing culprits were isolated. In fact, Dr Mandell discovered, by administering or withholding the allergens, 'we could aggravate or reduce symptoms he'd lived with all his life, that he just accepted as the inevitable consequence of CP. . . . We were turning his symptoms on and off!' Intrigued by these results, Dr Mandell began seeking out other CP patients. In all, 29 volunteer patients were referred to him and then tested for allergies and allergy-like sensitivities. Result: '90 to 95 per cent had allergies of various kinds. Some had 8 to 12 food allergies alone.'

Cerebral palsy, often the result of injuries suffered at or near the time of birth, is generally considered a permanent, 'non-progressive' disorder, Dr Mandell said. But many of his study patients reported marked changes in their symptoms from day to day, a fact he considered an 'outstanding clue' that allergies were at work.

Dr Mandell now believes that cerebral palsy creates 'biologic weak spots', primarily in the brain and nervous system, which make the body especially vulnerable to allergens. He thinks that all CP sufferers should be evaluated for allergies by a qualified, ecologically oriented allergist paediatrician or family doctor, especially if there is a marked variability in their symptoms.

• Cervical dysplasia

This is a condition in which abnormal cells that might be pre-cancerous are found in the cervix. In an investigation performed by C. E. Butterworth professor and chairman of the department of nutrition sciences at the University of Alabama, 47 young women who were on the Pill and who had mild-to-moderate cervical dysplasia were studied. Some of the women received oral supplements of 10 mg of the B vitamin *folic acid* daily, (20 times more than the US recommended dietary allowance), while the others received placebos.

The results of the study are impressive. The women taking therapeutic doses of folic acid improved significantly, while the unsupplemented women showed no change.

Furthermore, wrote Dr Butterworth, 'There were four cases of apparent regression to normal among subjects receiving folic acid supplementation, but none in the unsupplemented group.' There were four cases of apparent progression to cancer among the unsupplemented subjects but none in the group receiving folic acid supplementation. 'The data are interpreted as indicating that oral folic acid supplementation may prevent the progression of early cancer to a more severe form and in some cases promote reversion to normalcy' (*Contemporary Nutrition*, December 1980).

Remarking on the findings, the *Journal of the American Medical Association* said that 'folic acid supplementation may help reduce the risk of cervical cancer in women taking combination [containing both oestrogen and progesterone] oral contraceptives' (15 August 1980). (*See also* CANCER.)

• Cold sores and mouth ulcers

Two of the most common, and most annoying, diseases of the mouth – cold sores and mouth ulcers – still puzzle scientists. However, evidence is building that indicates they may be early warning signals of nutritional inadequacies.

Cold sores

Cold sores are caused by the *herpes simplex* virus, and some scientists consider them only second to the common cold in prevalence. A cold sore first appears as a tiny, painful red area, usually at the outer line of the lips or inside the mouth. Overnight, tiny blisters form. Sometimes there is just one; sometimes the infection is widespread. When they break, they leave a painful scab that lasts from 7 to 14 days. In some people, cold sores recur regularly, causing frequent discomfort and embarrassment, but they can also have worse consequences. The infection can also spread to the eyes, where it causes conjunctivitis or corneal ulcers (which can damage eyesight), and it can spread, via oral sex, to the genitals, where extremely painful genital herpes may develop which (in women) may be dangerous for any children born to them. In most people, most of the time, herpes remains latent, living peaceably among healthy tissues.

Scientists know that the herpes virus is transmitted by direct contact. Some people have thought that kissing passes on the infection. The Roman emperor Tiberius apparently accepted that explanation, because nearly 2000 years ago, he tried to halt a herpes epidemic by prohibiting public kissing.

That method probably failed, if Te-Wen Chang of the New England Medical Center Hospital's infectious disease service is right. According to Dr Chang who was the first to describe rare herpes infections of the throat, 'kissing would have to be pretty violent to activate the virus. Some trauma of the skin seems to be necessary.'

Stress, such as overwork, emotional upset or illness (hence the name 'cold sore'), appears to be another factor. The sensitive mouth registers stress early on. Nutrition, too, is a factor. A variety of nutrients have been successfully used to treat the troublesome virus.

Robert J. Peshek, a dental surgeon who practises in California, reports many successes with a therapy consisting of diet, vitamins and other nutrient supplements. Years of clinical experience and biochemical investigation persuaded Dr Peshek that attacks of cold sores are stirred up by poor absorption of calcium. He counteracts the virus by having his patients bombard it with an assortment of nutrients designed to improve calcium absorption. These include calcium fortified with magnesium, essential fatty acids (which counter the traumatizing effects of sunburn), *Lactobacillus acidophilus* (a beneficial bacterium that helps to keep the intestines in good working order), vitamin B complex (which is low in herpes sufferers) and vitamin E (applied directly to the skin).

Dr Peshek also recommends that those suffering from herpes and other mucous membrane ulcers avoid acidic foods (especially large amounts of citrus juices and fruits) and high-fat foods, and that they instead fill up on alkaline foods such as vegetables, bananas and skimmed milk.

'Because oral ulcerations appear to respond to a variety of nutrients, it's good to attack on all fronts and then progressively tailor the treatment to the individual's special needs,' Dr Peshek told us. 'I've treated several hundred patients according to my programme with a high percentage of success.'

Dental surgeon Don E. Nead has had remarkable results using vitamin E on cold sores. First he dries the sore, then he applies 20,000 IU of vitamin E in oil with a piece of gauze for 15 minutes. This technique has reduced or eliminated the sore's pain in less than eight hours and, in many cases, healed the sore itself in 12 to 24 hours.

In the case of large sores, the applications are increased. One patient suffered from a large ulcer that was so painful she was almost unable to eat or speak. Dr Nead instructed her to apply the vitamin E oil three times a day for three days. This brought immediate relief of the pain and healing of the ulcer. Dr Nead reports an almost 100 per cent success rate with this technique.

The response of the herpes virus to a variety of nutritional supplements is borne out by the work of other researchers. At the US National Naval Dental Center outside Washington, D.C. scientists found that a bioflavonoid – vitamin C combination reduced herpes blisters and hastened their healing. The complex was most effective when taken preventively before the full eruption of the blisters, as soon as patients noticed a sensation of irritation.

Herpes treatment with lysine

Cold sores have also been successfully treated with an amino acid called lysine. Dr Christopher Kagan of Cedars – Sinai Medical Center in Los Angeles observed that another amino acid that lysine counteracts promoted the reproduction of herpes virus. He reasoned that supplements of lysine might suppress the virus that the antagonistic amino acid helped to breed.

Forty-five patients with recurrent cold sores volunteered to test Dr Kagan's theory and were given 800 to 1000 mg of lysine daily. The results amazed Dr Kagan and his colleagues. They found that pain from the sores disappeared abruptly, overnight, in every instance. New sores didn't appear and the rate of healing was far speedier than the patients had experienced in the past.

However,

the most encouraging finding, other than more rapid control and limiting of infection – was the reduction in frequency of recurrences. Patients who sought help because of the persistence and frequency of infection were maintained infection-free while on lysine.

Those who had previously lost work because of severe, incapacitating herpes infection experienced rapid healing and continued suppression on a maintenance dose of 500 to 1000 mg a day.

Finally, yogurt is a time-honoured remedy still used by some doctors. 'All my patients with cold sores receive yogurt,' says Morton Malkin an oral and maxillo-facial surgeon in New York. What's the healing secret in yogurt?

Yogurt is milk that's been fermented by bacteria, but they're not viral bugs like herpes. They're good bacteria (with long names like *Lactobacillus acidophilus* and *Lactobacillus bulgaricus*). When the good bacteria in yogurt crowd out herpes, cold sores vanish. Many commercial yogurts don't contain acidophilus, however, so Dr Malkin gives it to his patients in tablet form. He also tells them to take high doses of B complex vitamins and to increase their fluid intake. The results are amazing. 'I have successfully treated hundreds of patients with this regimen,' he says.

Mouth ulcers

Mouth ulcers – or *aphthous stomatitis* , the painful red or yellow sores found inside the mouth and on the tongue – share many of the symptoms of cold sores, but laboratory tests show that the herpes virus can't induce mouth ulcers. It's estimated that anywhere from 20 to 50 per cent of the population suffer from these. Like herpes infection, mouth ulcers break out in burning blisters in the mouth, but unlike herpes, they develop only on the red part of the mouth and not on the skin near the lip. Also, scientists believe that unlike herpes, mouth ulcers cannot lead to more severe diseases. Still, these sores are painful enough. Some people suffer widespread attacks, leaving them with a mouthful of misery. Eating and drinking become difficult, and repeated outbreaks can demoralize the victim. The Greek word *aphthae*, after which mouth ulcers take their medical name, means 'to set on fire.'

No one is sure what causes mouth ulcers. Again, physical trauma seems to play a part. Slight injury while brushing the teeth or eating abrasive foods tends to produce them. Emotional stress is likewise a factor. The earliest medical reports of this type of infection, in 1889, involved women who were all having money problems and a psychologist at the National Institute of Dental Research in the United States has even suggested that there is an 'aphthous personality'. And another factor is nutrition.

An extensive six-year study by Scottish scientists, involving 330 patients shows that poor nutrition figures strongly in the occurrence of mouth ulcers. Nutritional deficiencies were discovered in 47 patients, or 14 per cent of the group, and of these 23 were deficient in iron, 7 in folic acid and 6 in vitamin B_{12}, and 11 suffered combined deficiencies.

This group was then treated with iron and vitamin supplements, with striking results. All of them had suffered recurrent bouts of mouth ulcers throughout their lives, but 23 were completely healed, meaning that they were free of mouth ulcers for at least six months after receiving the supplements. In 11 others, there was definite improvement, with the ulcers appearing only occasionally. According to the researchers, the patients' prompt response to the supplements suggests that the nutrients may directly affect the mucous lining of the mouth where mouth ulcers occur.

Like other mouth diseases, mouth ulcers and herpes may be early warning signs of bigger problems. A sore mouth may be trying to tell you that your life is too stressful or that some of your nutritional levels are low. Although the sores may hurt like the dickens, your mouth is only trying to be helpful. Listen to it: give your own mouth a hearing.

• Colds

Colds. They're nebulous little ailments, hard to pin down and subject to all sorts of factors, including stress.

The viruses that cause them are much tinier than bacteria (which can at least be seen under an ordinary microscope) – parasitic infectious agents with no real life of their own. They can thrive only by commandeering living cells of their host (that's you) and using them for their own ends – namely multiplication.

Faced with this annual challenge to health (colds strike primarily in winter), we have two possible choices. We can sit back, cross our fingers and hope that the viruses will spare us until April rolls around, or we can build up our bodies' natural defences to fight and resist winter-time 'bugs'.

The former do-nothing course is probably best typified by the reaction we recently got when we asked a distinguished professor of preventive medicine at a large American university for some advice on avoiding winter infections. 'There is absolutely *nothing* you can do,' replied the professor, a widely recognized authority on the common cold.

'But surely,' we persisted, 'you *must* have some ideas about preventing colds.'

The professor, who has spent years tracking down clues to this most common of ailments (even travelling to Antarctica, one of the coldest spots in the world), thought for a moment and then offered this: 'Well, you *could* stay away from people. That doesn't mean you'd have to worry about going to a movie for a couple hours. But within your own family, you should avoid associating at length with anyone having a bad cold. And you should avoid contact with mucus secretions. Keep your hands and face clean.'

Not exactly mind-boggling revelations, even if they do come from an expert.

Is that really the whole story when it comes to colds and flu prevention? Must we sit back, shunning human contact, and merely wait and hope? Or can we do something positive to strengthen ourselves, to bolster our inner defences? The recent findings of several scientists and doctors suggest most emphatically that we *can* do something – starting with vitamin A.

Vitamin A: infection fighter

During an infection, vitamin A levels in the body drop, a sign that the nutrient is probably being used up at a much faster rate than normal. Mothers around the world have known for generations that a daily spoonful of cod-liver oil, a rich natural source of vitamin A, helps prevent colds in their children.

More evidence of vitamin A's important infection-fighting role comes to us in a study by Sushma Palmer, a staff scientist with the National Academy of Sciences and assistant professor of paediatrics at Georgetown University in Washington, D.C. Dr Palmer has done research with children suffering from Down's syndrome (mongolism). Youngsters with Down's syndrome have physical malformations and are mentally retarded; they are also much more susceptible to respiratory and other infections than normal children.

Dr Palmer has theorized that infants with Down's syndrome may be born with a less-than-adequate supply of vitamin A, which, by reducing the formation of mucus-producing cells, could make them easy prey for colds, bronchitis and other respiratory ills. 'Frequent infections could gradually impair absorption of vitamin A, thereby reducing serum [blood] levels and depleting liver stores,' she noted '. . . Vitamin A deficiency may be precipitated by a variety of mechanisms, each feeding on itself or on each other, constituting a vicious cycle.'

To see if she could break this vicious cycle, Dr Palmer matched a group of 23 Down's children with their normal brothers and sisters as well as other children and divided them into two groups. One group received supplemental water-soluble vitamin A over the next six months; the other group did not.

Detailed health records were kept for all the children, and at the end of six months the results were tabulated. Dr Palmer reported that the Down's youngsters who took vitamin A had a significant and very substantial *decrease* in infections as the study progressed. And their normal brothers and sisters who received extra vitamin A also had fewer infections – far fewer than normal children not getting the vitamin A supplement *(International Journal for Vitamin and Nutrition Research).*

'In general, vitamin A may offer a protective effect against infection, not just in Down's syndrome, but in all segments of the population,' Dr Palmer told us.

What makes vitamin A so effective against infections, even in unusually disease-prone children? For one thing, the nutrient is a proven fighter against dangerous bacteria.

That was demonstrated by Benjamin E. Cohen and Ronald J. Elin, two National Institute of Allergy and Infectious Diseases (US) researchers. They exposed several groups of mice to lethal doses of bacteria and fungi. Some animals received supplementary vitamin A prior to their infection, but the rest didn't.

In one trial, mice inoculated with *Pseudomonas aeruginosa* – a strain of bacteria responsible for many human woes including some colds – all died within 24 hours, *except* those treated with vitamin A. Those lucky mice showed some infection in the blood for the first three hours, but by the fifth hour after inoculation with *P. aeruginosa*, their blood was virtually sterile and infection-free. They had successfully met the challenge and survived (*Journal of Infectious Diseases*).

Drs Cohen and Elin added that, interestingly enough, vitamin A was not able to kill the same bacteria directly when mixed in a test tube. Instead, vitamin A may work indirectly by boosting the body's natural network of resistance, the immune system.

As vital as vitamin A is in strengthening our bodily resistance to winter infections, it's only half of the story. The other half is vitamin C, or ascorbic acid.

Boosting immunity with vitamin C

When Stanford University biochemists Patricia R. and Carlton E. Schwerdt exposed human cell cultures to vitamin C for two days and then infected them with cold viruses, the results were impressive.

According to the Schwerdts, the vitamin produced an interferon-like activity that slowed down the cold viruses' growth. Thirty-two hours after infection, the virus yield was only 5 per cent of the growth in cultures not protected by vitamin C, and after 48 hours, the yield was just 2.5 per cent. Vitamin C had just about stopped the cold virus in its tracks.

That was in a test tube. To get a clearer picture of what actually happens inside the body of a person in the grip of the common cold, let's turn to a report by Dr C.W.M. Wilson and co-workers at Trinity College, Dublin (*Journal of Clinical Pharmacology*).

During a cold, according to the Irish investigators, concentrations of vitamin C are reduced in the inflamed mucous membrane lining the nose and throat, and elsewhere in the body as well. Supplementary vitamin C restores depleted tissues.

> Host resistance to the viral invasion is increased, and tissue repair is enhanced. This is associated with reduction in the severity of the toxic and catarrhal [mucus discharge] symptoms of the cold syndrome.'

In an Australian study, 95 pairs of identical twins – perfectly matched for age, sex and genetic makeup – were used to compare the cold-fighting power of vitamin C with that of a placebo (in this case, a pill that looked just like the vitamin, but contained only lactose, or milk sugar). For 100 days one of each pair of twins took a gram (1000 mg) of vitamin C daily, while the other took the placebo, though neither knew which was which. They were also asked to make careful note of the duration and severity of colds, should they appear.

When the results were analysed, the research team concluded that vitamin C shortened 'the average duration of cold episodes by 19 per cent' (*Medical Journal of Australia*, 17 October 1981). If you're interested in knocking one day off a five-day cold, in other words, you might try vitamin C. Interestingly, the Australians also found that 'females had significantly longer, more severe and more intense colds than males.'

In another study, scientists from the Naval Medical Research Institute outside Washington D.C. took a look at the relation between plasma vitamin C levels and the general health of 28 crewmen on a submarine before, during and after a 68-day patrol. They noted that the group with the lowest plasma vitamin C had twice as many 'symptoms of the common cold than the high group' (*Journal of Applied Nutrition,* vol. 34, no. 1, 1982).

What that means is that, by maintaining relatively high levels of vitamin C in their bodies during those long, lightless weeks under the sea, some of the submariners were able to fight off respiratory infections considerably better than their shipmates.

Cold medications

While vitamins A and C may help you feel better faster, watch out for commonly used remedies that can actually make you feel worse. Aspirin may be one of those remedies, says Joe Graedon, pharmacologist and author of *The People's Pharmacy-2* (1980). First, it actually increases the number of viruses dramatically. Second, it may lower the body's production of interferon, a natural anti-viral substance. Third, it may stop vitamin C from getting into the white blood cells, which are the cells that fight infection.

Decongestants aren't all they're cracked up to be, either. 'No clear-cut evidence exists for the efficacy of oral decongestants,' wrote a team of doctors in the US journal *Pediatrics.*

Spray decongestants, too, neither shrink the swollen mucosa (the membranes lining the nose and respiratory system) nor clear mucus out of the nose. What a spray decongestant actually does is to shrink the mucosa temporarily, but if used repeatedly, it also chemically irritates it, and the mucosa swells up again later, becoming more swollen than before. Not only that, but the decongestant also lowers the amount of natural antibiotic secreted by the mucosa and partially cripples the cilia – tiny hair-like stalks on the surface of cells – which are responsible for sweeping away germs. The end result: congestion is worse. Spray decongestants can even lead to sinusitis, a chronic sinus infection.

For more information on aspirin, decongestants and other cold remedies that may not help colds, see DRUG SIDE EFFECTS.

Heat, liquids and spices

There *are* natural treatments that work, and they may work for any upper-respiratory-tract infection.

'Heat, applied locally and in a warm, well-humidified room, promotes thinning of secretions,' advised a team of doctors writing in the *Nebraska Medical Journal.*

And another doctor, Byron Bailey of the University of Texas Medical Branch recommends applying that heat with hot towels – one to two hours four times a day *(American Family Physician).*

Drinking plenty of liquids – a time-honoured remedy – also helps clear congestion. Double the amount you normally drink, using water, fruit juice and herbal teas. (Fenugreek, anise and sage teas are traditional herbal remedies for ridding yourself of mucus.) And one liquid you shouldn't neglect is hot chicken soup.

A team of doctors at Mount Sinai Medical Center in Miami Beach, Florida asked 15 healthy volunteers to drink hot chicken soup. Before they drank it the researchers measured their nasal mucus velocity – how fast the top layer of mucus moved out of the nose – and then measured it again after they drank the soup. The researchers found that hot chicken soup increased nasal mucus velocity by 33 per cent, but when the volunteers drank cold water, nasal mucus velocity decreased by 28 per cent.

'Hot rather than cold liquids might be preferable in the recommendations for fluid intake in patients with upper-respiratory-tract infections,' they suggested *(Chest)*.

However, the 'full prescription' for chicken soup, according to California doctor Irwin Ziment, 'also calls for the addition of plenty of pepper and garlic' *(Journal of the American Medical Association)*. Dr Ziment pointed out that these spices are 'expectorants,' substances that thin mucus and clear it out of the system. And although Dr Ziment doesn't mention it, any list of expectorants should include not only garlic and cayenne pepper, but onions as well.

Humidifiers, moustaches and beards

The fact that more people suffer from colds in the winter may actually have more to do with low indoor humidity due to central heating than low outdoor temperatures. According to George Green, professor of mechanical engineering at the University of Saskatchewan in Saskatoon, nursery and infant school children's absences are more than 40 per cent higher when schools aren't humidified, and employees of two unhumidified local hospitals miss work 10 to 15 per cent more often than those at a humidified one.

Without humidifiers, schools in Saskatchewan averaged only 22 per cent humidity levels, while in January some hospitals scored a bone-dry 12 per cent. It has been shown that greater relative humidity results in lower survival time for many bacteria and viruses.

And, when all else fails, try the method of preventing colds expounded by a Florida doctor. Unfortunately, it works only if you're a man. Sinet M. Simon recommends that his patients grow moustaches and beards to ward off respiratory ailments.

'The cold virus is a filterable virus, and the hairs of the beard act as a filter,' Dr Simon told us. In 40 years of general practice, he said, 70 per cent of his male patients who have hirsute jaws usually weather the cold and flu season without a sniffle. 'It's terrific,' he said.

He himself, however, faces the world smooth-cheeked. 'I encounter too many staph germs and other micro-organisms that I could transmit from patient to patient,' he explained. 'I treat a lot of children, so I have to be careful. I'd love to have a beard – but I would have to shampoo it five or six times a day, and I don't have the time.'

See also entries that deal with various cold-related symptoms, such as COUGHING, FEVER, SORE THROAT.

• Colic

Numerous drugs are prescribed for infantile colic, or stomach pains, but none of them deserve a mother's thanks – even when the baby stops crying.

For five years, J. Crossan O'Donovan, of the paediatrics department at Baltimore City Hospital, studied 97 infants with colic. Taking his lead from a 24-year-old study which showed that atropine derivatives – medications commonly prescribed for colic – actually make the disorder worse, Dr O'Donovan compared the effects of a homatropine compound on one group of colicky infants with the effects of a non-therapeutic placebo on another. After two weeks, 70 per cent of the colicky infants in *both* groups improved.

Yet, Dr O'Donovan noted in his report, 'Combination medications containing these compounds in addition to phenobarbitone and an alcohol solution are . . . marketed and widely used to treat colic' (*American Journal of Diseases of Children*, October 1979).

Perhaps if those infants had been breastfed, they might never have suffered colic in the first place. 'Colic is less common in breastfed children,' said Robert Kaye, chairman of the department of paediatrics at Hahnemann University and Hospital in Philadelphia. 'One possible cause of colic is overfeeding. Mothers bottle-feeding their babies don't always know when they've had enough. But breastfeeding leaves it up to the baby to stop when he's had enough.'

Even so, breastfed babies *can* develop colic. And sometimes the culprit is cow's milk – that is, milk that the *mother* is drinking. A Swedish study found that when mothers of 66 colicky babies stopped drinking cow's milk, the problem cleared up in 35 cases. Apparently, the large molecules in cow's milk that cause colic were showing up in the mothers' milk as well, and so passed to the babies' sensitive bowels.

• Constipation

Constipation is a condition in which bowel movements are infrequent or incomplete. More often than not, says Victor Pellicano, a New York State doctor, chronic constipation is the accumulated effect of years of faulty diet characterized by deficiencies in vitamins and, especially, fibre.

'The best way to ward off constipation is by increasing your consumption of fibre-rich foods, including bran cereals, whole grains, raw fruits and vegetables, and by getting adequate amounts of fluids,' he says.

A Swedish study found bran to be significantly superior to laxatives in treating patients suffering from constipation. The researchers agree with Dr Pellicano's assertion that 'prevention is the best treatment' and recommend preventing constipation by taking 20 g of bran daily, mixed in with your food (*Scandinavian Journal of Gastro-enterology*, vol. 14, no. 7, 1979).

However, to some doctors who treat constipation, 'bran' seems to be a four-letter word. A study conducted by a team of researchers from the University of Maryland School of Pharmacy showed that laxatives are *the* most frequently prescribed drugs in nursing homes and that almost no constipated patients are advised to increase their intake of bran or any other kind of fibre. *(Journal of the American Geriatrics Society)*.

Of the 73 elderly patients in the study, 50 used laxatives and 16 used more than one. But, say the researchers, 'No patients were managed with dietary intervention.' And of the 50, probably none *should* have been using laxatives. 'Valid indications for the use of laxatives are limited,' the researchers point out, since the best treatment for constipation 'involves the use of naturally laxative foods such as fruits and vegetables, oatmeal cracked-wheat bread or bran.'

'You should also avoid a sedentary lifestyle, because lack of exercise may contribute to constipation,' Dr Pellicano says. 'Many of the same factors associated with varicose veins are seen in cases of constipation, and for that reason, many people have both. On the other hand, primitive people who eat a lot of high-fibre foods and aren't troubled with constipation rarely get varicose veins, either.'

• Coughing

Fever and sore throat are *private* miseries, but coughing announces to the world not only that you're sick but that you're projecting your sickness into the air around you. Coughing makes you a sort of double agent in winter's war. When you start coughing you'll find out that even your best friends will wave good-bye as they cover their noses and mouths and walk away.

Actually, that cough may be your best friend. Uncomfortable and unsociable as it may be, it's probably serving a very useful purpose, that of clearing your air passages for breathing.

Unfortunately, many people – including doctors – don't recognize this and try to get rid of the cough. According to the *British Medical Journal*,

> The fact that a patient has a cough does not indicate that he needs treatment for it. Enormous sums of money are wasted on cough medicines . . . But in most cases of acute cough, no medicine is needed. The doctor should explain that the cough serves a useful purpose in clearing the air passages, so that it is unwise to suppress it. The cough is a necessary evil . . . If any medicine is given for an acute cough it should at least be safe and cheap, for it is unlikely to achieve anything.

Herbal throat soothers

For instance, the safest way to treat a cough is not to try to eliminate it completely, but rather to soothe the throat. Many people rely on cough drops for that purpose. *The Practical Encyclopedia of Natural Healing* by Mark Bricklin (1983) says that:

> The active ingredients in many commercial cough drops, suitable for common, uncomplicated coughs, are wholly or largely herbal. One English brand [Fisherman's Friend], for instance, which is quite powerful, contains eucalyptus oil, cubeb (an extract of the berries, I

presume), tincture of capsicum (an extract of red pepper in alcohol), extract of glycyrrhiza (licorice), and menthol (the essential oil derived from peppermint). All this is put together in some kind of sugar base, although they don't specify what kind. Many cough drops use honey instead of sugar.

You can make your own herbal preparations for coughs colds and sore throats, too. Instead of gargling with some commercial mouthwash, make your own herbal gargle, starting with a strong brew of elder blossoms and sage leaves and tops. To this add some honey, a small amount of oil of sweet almonds, and five drops of oil of cloves for every 8 fl. oz of gargle. A strong tea made from honeysuckle may help soothe mucous membranes. And kidney beans when brewed and boiled (for at least 10 minutes) with garlic, may go a long way towards relieving a persistent cough.

For a post-nasal drip-related cough that might keep you from sleeping, one source advises sleeping on your stomach.

Lots of fluids, such as fruit juices and chicken soup, work better than expectorants, others say. Vaporizers and humidifiers sometimes help a cough but adding aromatic jellies to the steam may lower the body's resistance to infection, according to one doctor we consulted.

Allergy as a cause

One often-overlooked but highly treatable cause of a cough that outstays a cold is food allergy. Elmer Cranton, who specializes in preventive medicine and holistic therapies in Virginia, says he has recognized a 'post-flu milk-allergy syndrome'.

'A cough that hangs on after a cold is commonly an unsuspected food allergy,' Dr Cranton told us. 'Some people might have been eating a lot of a certain food they were sensitive to, usually milk or wheat or a combination of foods, but didn't know it. And there were no symptoms of an allergy until after they caught a cold or the flu.'

To discover the guilty food, Dr Cranton proceeds with an elimination diet – all suspect foods are removed from the diet for seven to ten days, then are re-introduced to the patient one by one until something provokes an allergic response. Dairy products, wheat products, yeast, eggs and citrus fruits are common allergens, he says. 'We've found that only six or seven days after elimination of the offender, the cough stops. Afterwards, if they stay away from that food for a month or so, they can frequently begin eating it and slowly build up their tolerance to it again.'

Other doctors have also found a link between coughing and allergy. Ernest K. Cotton, a lung expert at the University of Colorado Health Sciences Center in Denver, says that 'allergic skin testing may be important in some patients,' and a British specialist says that 'most recurrent coughs, if not due to colds, are allergic in origin' (*British Medical Journal*).

Regarding over-the-counter cough medications, Dr Cranton says, 'I tell my patients to use as little of them as they can get away with,' because they might mask a serious illness and because they contain suspicious chemicals.

'Nobody's tested them in combination,' he told us. 'Each one by itself might be harmless, but when you look at all of them together, they might do some harm.

'I think that one of the reasons we're seeing more and more allergies to good foods, like milk and wheat, is the great burden of foreign substances we're exposed to – in over-the-counter drugs, as well as food additives and pollution. The average American consumes five to six pounds of chemicals a year,' he says.

• Cramp

Modern medical science really has no clear idea what causes cramp, the painful knotting up of muscles, but scientific literature *is* full of reports by doctors who – without knowing the 'why' behind their treatment – have cured muscle cramps with nutritional therapy, especially with vitamin E and calcium.

In a letter to the *Medical Journal of Australia*, Dr L. Lotzof reported giving daily doses of about 300 mg of vitamin E to 50 patients suffering from muscular cramps. *In all 50 patients, almost all cramping stopped.* And as soon as Dr Lotzof's patients stopped taking vitamin E their cramp returned.

Two American doctors, Samuel Ayres, Jr. and Richard Mihan of Los Angeles treated 125 of their patients who were suffering from night-time leg and foot cramps with vitamin E. 'More than half of these patients had suffered from leg cramps longer than five years, and many of these had had cramps for 20 to 30 years or longer,' the doctors wrote (*Southern Medical Journal*). But vitamin E made short work of even these long-standing cramps. *Of the 125 patients, 123 found relief from their cramps after taking vitamin E*, and 103 of these had 'excellent' results: 'complete or nearly complete control' of cramp.

A daily dose of either 300 or 400 IU of vitamin E cleared up most cramp. Some patients, however, needed more. So, if you begin taking vitamin E for cramp and find that a daily dose of 400 IU has little or no effect, you may want to try a larger amount.

Also, if you find that vitamin E does work, stick with it. 'In a number of instances . . . it was learned that cramps recurred when treatment was stopped or greatly reduced, but promptly responded again when treatment was resumed,' the doctors explained.

All in all, the doctors feel confident that vitamin E will do the job.

> The response of nocturnal [night-time] leg and foot cramps to adequate doses of vitamin E is prompt, usually becoming manifest within a week, and occurs in such an overwhelming number of cases that it appears almost specific for this ailment.

However, not only nocturnal foot and leg cramps were healed by vitamin E. Nocturnal rectal cramps, cramping of abdominal muscles, and cramps from heavy exercise were also 'relieved completely' with the vitamin.

Now, walking is *not* a heavy exercise, at least not for most people but if you have intermittent claudication – a painful cramping of the calf muscle that sneaks up on you after you've walked too far and often caused by circulatory disease – a stroll around the block can have your calf muscle playing the 'heavy' in a very unpleasant muscular melodrama. Well, help is on the way. No white hats or shining armour – just our old friend, vitamin E.

Knut Haeger, a Swedish surgeon, selected 47 men with severe intermittent claudication. He gave 32 of them vitamin E; the rest received drugs to improve circulation (*American Journal of Clinical Nutrition*). After about three months, the men were tested to see how far they could walk without pain: 54 per cent of the vitamin E group walked 1 kilometre (five-eighths of a mile) the test's maximum distance, but only 23 per cent of the second group could walk that far.

How did vitamin E help these men to walk? Vitamin E may stop intermittent claudication – and all cramp – by improving circulation. After about $1^1/_2$ years of taking vitamin E, 29 out of 32 men in Dr Haeger's study had an increase in the flow of blood to their calves. That's a big contrast to those who took prescribed drugs: after $1^1/_2$ years, 10 of 14 of those men had a *diminished* flow.

However, vitamin E isn't the only nutritional supplement that can ease cramp. As far back as 1944, research indicated that calcium can go a long way in relieving this. In that year, Dr Elizabeth Martin reported a study in which 79 of 112 young children were completely relieved of 'growing pains' – the night-time cramps that can have a young child kicking and screaming – with either calcium phosphate or bone meal, a supplement containing calcium (*Canadian Medical Association Journal*).

Dr Martin also gave her pregnant patients calcium supplements. None of these women suffered the usual aching legs or nocturnal cramp that are so common in pregnancy. She noted that, while all the women were spared leg cramp and had healthy babies, the babies of the mothers who took calcium also had exceptionally long, silky hair and long, beautifully formed fingernails! Unfortunately calcium supplements do not work for all pregnant women with cramp, but it is worth a try.

Severe cramp

It nearly happened. The patient's cramp – a severe type known as *tetany* – lasted five days, in spite of constant dosing with muscle-relaxing drugs, and the complications were almost fatal. 'The cramp was impossible to break', says William Rea, head of the Environmental Control Unit at Brookhaven Hospital in Dallas. 'The patient almost died.'

And two other patients in the unit had cramp almost as bad. 'Severe spasms of the back or neck would leave those muscles so tender they couldn't be touched,' Dr Rea said. 'If the patients would lie down on the cramped area they would be in excruciating pain.'

But though these three patients suffered from unusually severe cramps, they had something in common with a few of the hundreds of other cramp patients treated by Dr Rea: 'All these patients,' he said, 'had low blood levels of calcium.'

'For muscle contraction to be normal, adequate levels of calcium must be present in the body,' said Dr Ralph Smiley, a colleague of Dr Rea. 'We make sure all our patients with cramps are getting enough calcium,' he said.

'Some patients with tetany, in particular, may need calcium to relieve their cramp,' says Dr Rea. 'Once you get them on a maintenance dose, calcium lessens the seizure-like activity of tetany and helps prevent it from occurring.'

For milder cases of cramps, the 'maintenance dose' is 900 mg of calcium a day, says Dr Smiley. But, he adds, not only cramp patients need this amount. 'The average person is low on calcium, and it would be a prudent preventive measure for most people to supplement their diet with the mineral.'

For information on the cramp that causes period pain, see MENSTRUAL PROBLEMS.

• Criminal behaviour and juvenile delinquency

Crime and violent behaviour aren't usually thought of as diseases, but the anti-social tendencies of many criminals and youthful offenders may be directly related to chemical disturbances in the body. Writing in *Offender Rehabilitation*, Leonard J. Hippchen said that about 10 per cent of the population may suffer from deficiencies and/or dependencies (meaning unusually high needs for certain nutrients) that can change perceptions of reality leading the sufferer to act upon illusions and resulting in behaviour that can be harmful to him/herself and others.

That bad nutrition and bad behaviour are closely linked is the truth, and nothing but the truth, but the people running the criminal justice systems in various Western countries are just beginning to wake up to the fact. They're being shaken awake by a small group of men and women who realize that no approach to criminal rehabilitation – social casework, psychotherapy, group therapy, psychiatry, academic and vocational training – can possibly work unless a good diet backs it up.

'Of the nearly 2 million criminals in jail [in the United States], over 70 per cent have been there before,' Alex Schauss says. 'So something has to be wrong with the way most criminals are rehabilitated.'

Schauss is a State Corrections Training Officer for the Washington State Criminal Justice Training Commission. He oversees the training of parole and probation officers, who deal with criminals out of prison. To keep them out Schauss has put together a course called 'Body Chemistry and Offender Behavior'. Its many topics include diet, vitamins, minerals, stress, food allergy and exercise – detailed information about health that the probation officer passes on to the offender. But can this approach really soften a hardened criminal?

'Not one single probation or parole officer has called me and said this approach doesn't work, and if it didn't, I would be hearing about it,' says Schauss. Studies back up that claim.

Schauss chose 102 people who had committed crimes and were on probation. He had some of them receive nutritional counselling and others traditional counselling. (Traditional counselling involves advising offenders about their job, housing, clothing, family problems and other areas of daily life – except what they eat.) Schauss found that 34 per cent of the people receiving tradi-tional counselling committed another crime, compared with only 14 per cent of those receiving nutritional counselling.

In another study, Schauss again had probationers receive nutritional coun-selling. This time, he compared the probationers' arrest records before, during and after the counselling. Eight months after the counselling had ended, not one of the probationers had been re-arrested.

Nutritional counselling works – beyond a shadow of a doubt. Schauss ex-plains why: 'Most people, criminals included, are extremely naïve about diet and how it affects their body and mind. Simply educating a criminal about nutrition, showing him that bad dietary habits ruin his mental and physical health and keep him behind bars, helps him give up those habits.' And of all bad habits, too much sugar may be the worst.

Most repeat offenders eat a glut of sweets, soft drinks and other goodies that add up to 300 – 600 lb of sugar a year, about three to six times more than the average in Britain. Eating that much sugar can cause a disorder in blood sugar metabolism called *hypoglycaemia* (low blood sugar) and studies show that almost 90 per cent of all inmates have it. Many of the symptoms of hypoglycaemia are psychological: irritability, paranoia, sudden violent behaviour – that is criminal behaviour. Educate a prison inmate about sugar (and caffeine and alcohol, which can also cause hypoglycaemia), help him cut it out of his diet, and you can end up with John Doe instead of John Dillinger II. And most prisoners, says Schauss, want that help.

'The one common denominator of inmates is to get out of jail. People don't like to be behind bars. About 70 per cent of the convicts who receive nutritional counselling change their diet for the better and keep it changed.'

And that change may include eliminating all the foods to which a prisoner is allergic.

Food allergies

These work just like hay fever, only for pollen substitute eggs chocolate, maize, citrus fruit, milk or wheat. (People may become allergic to the foods they eat most often, and these foods, being so common, account for most food allergies.) But while hay fever and similar allergies attack the nose, a food allergy may attack the brain – and can make a good person go bad.

The brain is often a target organ for food allergy. Immediately after eating the offending food, a person's behaviour may change for the worse. His brain can fog over, leaving him apathetic and sluggish, or he can go wildly hyperactive. In either case, he lacks good judgment. He doesn't see whole situations and reacts instead to fragments and details.

If he becomes apathetic, he needs a severe and heightened thrill to interest him in life – being chased by police, being wanted by the law, being in danger. If he becomes hyperactive, he works on a different time clock than the rest of society, demanding things now and using violence to satisfy his urgent needs (*see* ALLERGY).

It's not only food that can trigger violence, but also chemicals to which a person is allergic. Schauss illustrates the point with a story of 'chemical warfare.' 'A boy at school suddenly became ruthless and violent, beating up other kids and breaking furniture. Our staff investigated and found that he was allergic to fumes from the school's floor wax. 'How many convicts mired in the criminal justice system started going downhill after a few incidents like this? If someone's actions are socially unacceptable, people start to think of him as a misfit. If he repeats those actions often enough, he is labelled a misfit. Inevitably, he begins to think of himself as a misfit, and to act like one.'

To break this cycle, which Schauss has named 'biocriminogenesis', criminals must avoid the substances to which they are allergic and improve their diet. They also need psychological counselling to restore their self-esteem, but before counselling, they need nutritional supplements.

'Many delinquents and criminals do not have sufficient biochemical reserves to make positive mental changes,' says Dan MacDougal, a lawyer from Atlanta Georgia. MacDougal is a consultant to the Dougherty County Judicial Service Agency, an organization that works with juvenile delinquents. The agency, he says, 'teaches them the proper use of will and new behaviour patterns that are not based on fear or hostility, but are based on love.'

Before psychological treatment starts, however, every delinquent undergoes biochemical testing and is then given nutritional supplements to correct any chemical imbalance. (The agency must be doing something right. Dougherty County has the lowest juvenile crime rate in the United States). 'Vitamin B_6 lowers impulsivity and violent behaviour,' MacDougal says. 'Vitamins A, C and E aid in detoxifying a person whose violent behaviour is being caused by heavy metal poisoning.'

Metal poisoning

Heavy metals – lead, cadmium, mercury and arsenic (to name a few) – pollute air, water and food. Most people aren't very affected by the heavy metals in their body. Some are.

'I see lead poisoning contributing to an awful lot of criminal behaviour,' says Barbara Reed, chief probation officer of the Municipal Court in Cuyahoga Falls, Ohio. Mrs Reed treats most of her probationers with diet, suggesting a steady fare of natural, unprocessed foods and the complete elimination of refined carbohydrates and caffeine. Of the 600 people who have followed that diet, 89 per cent have never committed another crime. 'But some need more help than a better diet,' Mrs Reed said. 'They need a vitamin and mineral regimen to cleanse their bodies of heavy metals.

'One man was referred to me after he had committed two felonies: trafficking in drugs and carrying loaded firearms. He was diagnosed as having lead and aluminium poisoning. After three months of special treatment and a good nutritional diet, he was eager to return to regular work.'

Schauss also relates a case of a man with heavy metal poisoning: 'A man was being held in the county jail who had been arrested for assaulting a policeman. During his arraignment, his behaviour disrupted the court proceeding. Two psychiatrists and a mental health specialist interviewed him. One psychiatrist diagnosed him "acutely schizophrenic". The other two experts agreed he was a full-blown "paranoid schizophrenic." All three predicted that by the age of 30 he would become a vegetable.'

'Well, our staff looked at him and noticed symptoms of lead poisoning. Tests were conducted and showed that he was suffering from toxic levels of arsenic, lead, mercury and cadmium in his system. Through vitamin and mineral supplementation, chelation therapy [which removes lead from the body] and counselling, he improved rapidly.'

However, Schauss, Reed, MacDougal and many other professionals agree that nutrition is only one facet of biochemical treatment. Exercise, too, is very important, as are proper lighting, fresh air and sufficient sleep. 'These are terrific tools,' says Mrs Reed. 'By improving a criminal's health, we help him to perform better in the other rehabilitative services.'

Good health. For thousands of criminals, it's the best accomplice for a permanent jailbreak – and a break with the past.

• Cystic fibrosis

Two natural therapies – diet and exercise – have shown promise in treating the symptoms of a mysterious, incurable disease that afflicts about one in 2000 of the population – cystic fibrosis.

Cystic fibrosis (CF) is a hereditary defect that causes problems in certain glands, particularly the pancreas, the sweat glands and the glands that secrete mucus. Because many people with cystic fibrosis cannot digest or absorb food properly, they often suffer from poor nutrition. Thick mucus accumulates in their lungs and can cause progressive lung damage and an early death.

Researchers at the University of Pennsylvania School of Medicine and the Wistar Institute put a group of 13 children with cystic fibrosis on a special dietary supplement of corn oil, vitamin E (to prevent oxidation) and pancreatic enzymes.

'Kids with cystic fibrosis have difficulty absorbing fats,' says David Kritchevsky, one of the researchers. 'The corn oil supplement and enzymes help get these fats into the bloodstream.'

After a year on the supplement, all the children gained in height, and 11 of the 13 gained weight and seemed 'healthier and happier' to their parents. In individual cases, said Dr Kritchevsky, the diet helped relieve such symptoms as diarrhoea, excessive sodium loss and the problems of poor nutrition.

A role for vitamin E

The idea that CF children may be deficient in vitamin E isn't new. It's been suspected for some time, since the body's uptake of vitamin E depends largely on its ability to digest and absorb fats. Yet, until now, researchers had a hard time making that theory stick. For one thing, traditional blood tests that measure the total vitamin E levels never show much difference between CF patients and healthy controls, and even if they did, doctors would say that vitamin E deficiency isn't much to worry about.

Researchers at the National Institutes of Health outside Washington, D.C.

suggest otherwise. Singling out *alpha tocopherol* (the most important component of vitamin E) in blood samples taken from CF patients, they found that all of 52 suffering from intestinal dysfunction were deficient in the vitamin. And – more important – they discovered that this defiency has a decided effect on the red blood cells.

Red blood cells taken from vitamin E-deficient CF patients had a much shorter lifespan than those taken from healthy persons with adequate vitamin E levels. This reduced survival rate was boosted back up to normal with vitamin E supplementation in dosages ranging from 50 to 400 IU per day. (*Journal of Clinical Investigation*).

What does this mean to the CF patient? Philip M. Farrell, head of the NIH investigation, explained, 'Taking vitamin E isn't going to cure CF. But I'd say it's likely to be of some benefit. It's conceivable, for example, that the severe lung disease associated with CF puts stress on the red blood cells which are involved in transporting oxygen. Since vitamin E affords some degree of protection to these blood cells, it's likely that a vitamin E-supplemented child will have the edge in fighting CF.

'And there's another thing that we didn't mention in the report,' Dr Farrell said. 'The vitamin E content in lung tissues is normally very high. In view of the pulmonary problems in CF patients, I think that says something!'

Of course at this point Dr Farrell is just speculating on the implications of a vitamin E deficiency. However, he is sure of one thing: 'Patients with CF should be given daily doses of a water-soluble form of vitamin E.'

How much? 'We gave our patients five to ten times the [US] Recommended Dietary Allowance,' he replied. 'The RDA for children is 5 – 10 IU per day.'

Exercise

Regular running may also have a place in the treatment of cystic fibrosis, according to David Orenstein, a paediatrician now at LeBonheur Children's Hospital in Memphis, Tennessee. In a study held at Cleveland's Case Western Reserve University School of Medicine, Dr Orenstein had a small group of young cystic fibrosis patients participate in a programme of running walking and other exercises. The programme involved three hour-long sessions per week for 12 weeks.

'I'm somewhat encouraged by the results,' Dr Orenstein said. The regular exercise routine apparently helped the patients to keep their lungs clear of mucus, reducing the danger of lung damage that is a principal threat in the disease. 'Exercise may help to slow down deterioration of lung function,' he said.

Other results were less tangible but just as important, according to Dr Orenstein. 'The kids increased their ability to do exercise, to do work, and they had an increased sense of well being. There was a beneficial effect on their outlook – on their view of themselves.'

The results of his programme, Dr Orenstein stresses, are suggestive, not conclusive. But they were promising enough to prompt the National Institutes of Health to fund a larger study, involving more children and more precise instruments to document the results of exercise.

• Deafness

If you're conscientious about maintaining your health, you probably undergo periodic checkups for your teeth, eyes, heart and blood pressure. No use taking unnecessary chances.

But when was the last time you gave your ears a second thought – or even a first thought, for that matter? Maybe it's time you did.

Ear problems are hardly a rarity. More people suffer from hearing disorders than from heart disease, cancer, blindness, tuberculosis, multiple sclerosis and kidney disease combined. It's true that ear diseases are rarely fatal, but do you want to take the chance of losing the sense that allows easy communication? Are you ready to give up music, a baby's laughter, a friend's amusing story or words of love?

Fortunately, many ear problems are preventable, curable or treatable, if you know what to do. In fact, there are very few people who suffer from total deafness. Instead, hearing losses can cover the entire spectrum, from slight to severe.

The problem is, loss in hearing most often comes on so gradually that you may be unaware that it's happening – a major reason why ear care is given so little emphasis. On the other hand, the usually slow deterioration of hearing can actually work in your favour by giving you more time to act before the situation gets out of hand.

Of course, we're not implying that everyone has, or will ultimately have problems with their ears, but it's difficult to ignore the fact that, right now, about 30 per cent of adults over 65 have a hearing handicap. Our job is to help keep *you* out of the statistics.

First, it's important for you to understand a little bit about how your ears work. If you could peer deep enough into a human ear, you'd be amazed at how tiny the whole hearing mechanism is. Tiny and delicate. Within the space of a cubic inch, your ear is capable of changing the physical pressure of sound waves into distinct electrical impulses. In other words, your ears actually *feel* the sound waves in the air (which are like ripples on a lake), then amplify and transmit those sensations to your brain. Your brain translates the impulses and tells you what you're hearing.

Sounds simple? It's not. Vibrations are passed along from the eardrum to the three tiny bones (called ossicles) in the middle ear, to the inner-ear fluid, to the cochlea (a snail-shaped bone containing up to 16,000 microscopic hair cells) and finally to the auditory nerve, which carries the vibrations (now electrical impulses) to the brain where they are perceived as sound.

Damage to any of these tiny, intricate parts – whether from injury or or infection – is what triggers the beginning of hearing loss. It's the amount of damage and the specific part involved that determine the degree of impairment for each individual.

If you suspect that you may have a hearing loss, ask yourself these questions: Do you frequently have to turn up the TV? Do people seem to be mumbling more than they used to? Do people often have to repeat what they say to you? Do you miss parts of sentences or words?

If you answered 'yes' to any of the above, you may indeed have a hearing disorder. Your family doctor will probably be able to tell you for sure by performing a quick, simple and painless test, or you may be referred to an otologist (ear specialist).

Excessive noise

What's causing the loss of hearing is not as simple to determine however, but excessive noise should be the first cause doctors consider, says Aram Glorig, an otologist at the House Ear Institute in Los Angeles: 'Noise creates more hearing losses than all other causes combined.' What's worse many people, *not only industrial workers*, are exposed to potentially harmful noise levels without even knowing it.

Factories have been notorious for their excessive noise, much of which has now been regulated by the Health and Safety Executive. But while industry has been forced to protect the hearing of its employees, what about the rest of us in and out of work? Music, road traffic, stereo headphones, airports, TV, video arcades, tube trains – all are capable of producing noise levels that may be damaging to the ear with prolonged exposure.

Each time your ear is assaulted by loud noises, some of the delicate hair cells in the cochlea are torn away. Since there are thousands of hair cells there is no obvious hearing loss at first. But keep up that kind of abuse for years, and the damage becomes apparent – and permanent.

'The tendency is to lose the ability to hear the higher frequencies (or pitches) first,' says Peggy Williams, an audiologist with the American Speech – Language – Hearing Association in Rockville, Maryland. 'That means you'd have trouble hearing the consonants in human speech, but you'd still be able to hear the vowels, which normally occur at lower frequencies. For example you would have difficulty distinguishing between the words *tap, cap* and *rap, or bite, kite* and *flight*. It's easy to see why communication begins to suffer when hearing loss does.'

Although it usually takes years of exposure for the permanent effect of noise-induced hearing loss to appear, there are some early warning signs that should be heeded. You'll know if the noise is at a hazardous level if you have to talk louder in order to converse face to face. If you hear any ringing buzzing or roaring in your ears after a particular exposure to noise, it may indicate damage to hair cells. If you experience diminished hearing sensitivity following noise exposure, that's a bad sign, too, even if it goes away after resting.

Once damage has occurred, it's irreversible, so your best bet is clearly through prevention. That means protecting your ears with some kind of device when exposed to hazardous levels of noise. 'However,' according to Darrell E. Rose, head of audiology at the Mayo Clinic in Rochester, Minnesota, 'it is important to remember that if the protective unit is uncomfortable, most people will not wear it.' Earmuff-type protectors, for example, work very well, but they are uncomfortable. Cotton plugs are comfortable and commonly used, but in actuality, they offer very little protection from noise. 'We have had the best results with soft-foam plugs,' Dr Rose wrote. 'The foam is rolled between the fingers and thumb until it is small enough to insert in the ear; it conforms comfortably to the shape of the ear canal.' What's more, he added, the plugs are inexpensive, can be worn repeatedly and are very effective in reducing noise. (*Postgraduate Medicine,* August 1981).

Hearing loss and ageing

Noise isn't the only thing that causes hearing loss. 'Sometimes as we grow older, we lose a bit of our hearing capacity,' says Harry Rosenwasser, an otologist and director of medical affairs with the Deafness Research Foundation in New York City. 'That's known as *presbycusis.* It's similar to the deterioration that many people experience with their eyesight as they age.'

'Presbycusis is a normal consequence of ageing,' adds Robert J. Keim former associate professor of oto-rhino-laryngology at the University of Oklahoma Health Sciences Center. It does not lead to total deafness, but it can cause a hearing handicap that's severe enough to isolate the afflicted person from society.

In most cases, this type of hearing loss responds well to the use of hearing aids, which can easily put the person back in touch with life. Better yet, there may be a way to prevent presbycusis, or at least to delay its onset. And it may be as simple as changing your diet.

That's what doctors set out to prove in a nine-year study conducted in Finland. The researchers had good reason to believe that a low-fat diet might prevent hearing loss. Earlier they had studied the hearing ability of the primitive Mabaan tribe, who live in a noise-free environment in the Sudan and consume a diet consistently low in saturated fats. After testing, the researchers found that the tribespeople had low cholesterol levels, virtually no coronary artery disease, no high blood pressure and no atherosclerosis (clogging of the arteries). What's more, compared with other people from quiet or industrial areas, they showed *superior* hearing with ageing particularly in the higher frequencies – just where you'd expect deterioration.

The scientists reasoned that the same diet that keeps coronary arteries open may also be responsible for keeping the tiny vessels in the ear open, too. And since the inner ear depends upon a constant fresh flow of blood for the nutrients that keep it functioning, it's easy to see why clogged arteries can affect your hearing.

With that in mind, the researchers decided to test their theory using patients in two separate mental hospitals in Finland. In one hospital (called Hospital K by the doctors), the usually high-saturated-fat diet was continued while in the other (called Hospital N) unsaturated fats were substituted for the saturated ones.

After five years, the two groups were compared. Not surprisingly, patients from Hospital N (the low-saturated-fat group) had much lower cholesterol levels and significantly less coronary heart disease. But on top of that patients aged 50 to 59 had much better hearing than those ten years younger in Hospital K (the high-saturated-fat group).

To further prove their point, the researchers decided to reverse the diets of the two experimental groups. Within four years of the diet reversal, the hearing in the now low-saturated-fat group was improved, while the hearing in the now high-saturated-fat group was worse. 'Our audiological studies lead us to conclude,' said the researchers, 'that diet is an important factor in the prevention [and reversal] of hearing loss' *(Acta Otolaryng)*.

Watch for wax

On the other hand, a hearing loss may be due to something as normal and correctable as earwax. 'But forget cotton-tipped swabs,' advises Dr Williams. 'If anything, those devices push the wax in even farther, causing impaction.

'Normally, the waxy buildup in your ears works itself out in several ways. The action of your jawbone while chewing is one way. But there are also little hairs in your ear which are normally bent towards the outside. A cotton swab inserted in your ear pushes those hairs backward so they are facing the wrong direction. Then the normal cleansing action in your ears can't occur.

'What's worse, of course, is the danger of going in too far,' Dr Williams told us. 'And this happens more frequently than you'd imagine. One little slip and you may puncture the eardrum and possibly dislodge the ossicles. The result may be permanent deafness.'

If wax does build up in your ear, it can diminish your hearing, but restoring it is really simple in this case. Just let the doctor do the job. He or she uses a special syringe and warm water to flush the wax out, and knows how far he or she can safely go.

'There are several over-the-counter earwax softeners that you may have seen,' adds Dr Williams, 'but I don't recommend them. They *do* work to soften the wax, but their acidity can also eat away at the skin if used too often. What's worse is that if there is any opening at all in the eardrum, the product can gain entry to the middle ear and cause infection.'

• Depression

Mary sits slumped in a chair, her mascara smeared by an hour of crying, her thoughts as black as the circles under her eyes.

'Why did I bother putting on makeup this morning? I'm ugly and that's that. John must hate me. And what's the use of looking good, anyway? Life is so empty, so useless. If only I could run away.'

However, for Mary, and for millions of others, there's no running away – from depression. *Serious* depression. Not just a day of the blues, but weeks, perhaps months, of symptoms like these : You hate yourself and everyone else. You speak hesitantly in a dull monotone. You can't concentrate or make decisions. Sex is a chore. Headaches are frequent. Sleep is restless, and during the day you move like a sloth. You feel frustrated, trapped, hopeless. And when you think of suicide (which is often), it's with relief.

Who gets depressed? Anyone can. But twice as many women as men do. Pregnant women. Women who've just had a baby. Post-menopausal women. Women on the Pill.

However, often the cause of their depression isn't psychological; it's physical – a nutritional deficiency.

Low tryptophan levels

Two reports in the *British Medical Journal* pointed to the possible role that tryptophan (an essential amino acid found in most protein foods) may play in depression. In the week after they had given birth, 18 women were tested for severity of depression and blood levels of tryptophan. Doctors found that those with the severest depression had the lowest levels of tryptophan. Other researchers discovered that post-menopausal women with depression have a disturbance in their tryptophan metabolism very similar to that found in patients hospitalized for depression.

In addition, an American study showed that, in the days before menstruation a time of depression for many women, tryptophan metabolism is disturbed *(American Journal of Psychiatry)*. In another, 11 hospitalized depressed patients were given the nutrient. After a month, seven of the group had less anxiety, guilt, insomnia and weight loss, all common problems of depression, and the overall depression of the 11 (as measured by standard tests) dropped by 38 per cent. When the researchers who conducted the study measured the levels of tryptophan in the patients' blood, they found the highest levels among those who had improved the most *(Communications in Psycho-pharmacology)*.

Tryptophan therapy may be a good substitute for anti-depressants. Researchers compared tryptophan with a well-established anti-depressant drug called *amitriptyline* (brand names: Domical, Elavil, Lentizol, Tryptizol). The drug is very effective in relieving the symptoms of depression, but it can be toxic and leave severe side-effects (among them urinary retention, blurred vision, an irregular and overly fast heartbeat, drowsiness, fits, impotence) in its wake. Tryptophan, on the other hand, is virtually harmless. Very few users suffer even mild side-effects, and those who do report that they are transient.

The study, which took about 12 weeks, tested a group of 115 patients (aged 18 to 65) who were considered by their family doctors to be depressed enough to require anti-depressant drug treatment but not sick enough to need a psychiatrist. They were divided into four groups: One took only tryptophan another took only the drug, the third took a combination of the two, and a control group took a placebo. Throughout the experiment, the severity of depression was rated using a special five-point scale.

At the end of the study the researchers found that tryptophan and amitriptyline were equally effective in relieving depression. However, relief was greatest among the people on the combination therapy. What's more, 'fewer patients withdrew because of severe side-effects on the combined treatment than on amitriptyline alone,' said the researchers. In particular, the increase in heart rate seen with the drug was much less marked in the combined-treatment group, suggesting that tryptophan may neutralize some of the bad effects of amitriptyline.

The researchers concluded that tryptophan is a 'satisfactory alternative' to amitriptyline, and that patients diagnosed as suffering from a depressive syndrome could be given a trial of treatment with tryptophan for about four weeks.

Those showing a worsening of symptoms at any time or failing to improve within this time should receive a tricyclic anti-depressant [amitriptyline] in addition to tryptophan. This regimen would combine minimum side-effects with maximum therapeutic effects for most patients in the under-65 age group. [*Psychological Medicine*, vol. 12, no. 4, 1982].

Low vitamin B$_6$ levels

A study of 15 depressed pregnant women showed that those with the deepest depression had the lowest blood levels of vitamin B$_6$ [pyridoxine] *(Acta Obstetricia et Gynecologica Scandinavica)*, and numerous others have shown that women on the Pill who become depressed have low levels of vitamin B$_6$ *(Lancet)*.

In addition, a group of researchers at Northwick Park Hospital outside London examined a number of patients admitted to the hospital's psychiatric unit, and they observed that a lack of vitamin B$_6$ in some of them seemed linked with depression. In the study, 66 patients were examined, and 16 were found to have low levels of vitamin B$_6$ as their only deficiency. Of those 16 patients, 9 (56 per cent) suffered from depression.

In their study, the scientists cited previous research demonstrating that pyridoxine is an effective treatment for depression associated with oral contraception. 'B vitamins are cheap and readily available, and free from troublesome side-effects', they said.

The researchers concluded that 'more attention should be paid to assessing the . . . pyridoxine status of the mentally ill in the hope of detecting and correcting deficiencies' *(British Journal of Psychiatry*, September 1979).

A crucial chain reaction

Why tryptophan? Why vitamin B$_6$?

Because of *serotonin*.

Serotonin is a neuro-transmitter, one of the chemicals in your brain that helps control moods, and some scientists theorize that low levels of serotonin cause depression. However, to have enough serotonin, you need enough tryptophan, which is essential in its formation. And to have enough tryptophan, you need enough vitamin B$_6$, without which tryptophan can't be formed. Vitamin B$_6$, tryptophan, serotonin: the chemical chain reaction that forms this neuro-transmitter is more complex, but these links are crucial.

Oestrogen can break them. This female hormone can block the activity of vitamin B$_6$, forcing it out of the body. And oestrogen can speed up the metabolism of tryptophan, making less of it available to form serotonin. That doesn't happen every day, but if oestrogen levels are high – if you're pregnant, taking the Pill or about to have your period – then you can have a shortage of tryptophan or vitamin B$_6$. And a long face.

The solution? Replace the nutrients.

When 250 'depression-prone' women received oral contraceptives supplemented with vitamin B_6, 90 per cent remained free of severe depression *(Ob. Gyn. News)*. In another study, doctors measured the blood level of vitamin B_6 in 39 depressed women on the Pill and found that 19 had a severe deficiency. When they gave these women the vitamin, the mood of 16 improved *(Lancet)*. Those women probably got more than just an increase in their vitamin B_6 levels. Many women on the Pill suffer from a blood sugar disorder. When they take vitamin B_6, however, that disorder improves *(Contraception)*.

Not everyone suffering from depression is a woman, of course. But studies show that tryptophan and vitamin B_6 may help anyone who's depressed. Doctors measured the severity of depression in patients hospitalized for the problem and then gave them tryptophan and vitamin B_6 for one month. After the month they again measured their depression. It had decreased by 82 per cent *(British Medical Journal)*.

In another study lasting one month, doctors gave tryptophan and niacin (another B vitamin) to 11 depressed patients. (Ten were women, and their average age was 52. More than likely, they were in the throes of post-menopausal depression). Why niacin? The doctors knew that, in some studies depressed people took tryptophan but didn't get any better. They theorized that the tryptophan hadn't been metabolized properly and that niacin would correct this problem. They were right. After a month on tryptophan and niacin the patients' blood levels of tryptophan rose almost 300 per cent, and their depression fell by 38 per cent *(Lancet)*.

Researchers have also found they could give *too much* tryptophan. Depressed patients receiving 6 g of tryptophan and 1500 mg of niacin (as nicotinamide) a day didn't improve, but those receiving 4 g of tryptophan and 1 g of niacin did. In the opinion of the researchers, there is an 'optimum range' for blood levels of tryptophan in depressed patients and that giving too much or too little of the nutrient is useless *(British Medical Journal)*. However, even the lower levels of nutrients in this study should be taken only under a doctor's supervision.

Tryptophan, niacin and vitamin B_6 aren't the only nutrients involved in depression.

According to Dr Jose A. Yaryura-Tobias, 'A person suffering from depression may do well with tryptophan, but I like higher doses of vitamins B_1 [thiamin] and B_6, because they help activate the energy transport system in the body. At my clinic, Bio-Behavioral Psychiatry in Great Neck, New York, we also use phenylalanine. That is an amino acid which in the body is converted to phenylethylamine, an anti-depressant. At times, drugs are a necessity, but they are never used without the nutrients.

'The point is, we don't limit ourselves to one type of therapy. It wouldn't make sense to do that. Illness has many causes, so how can we expect to help all our patients with only one method of treatment? The patient must understand, too, that results will take longer with the natural therapies than with the drugs. When a drug is used, the results are very dramatic. But you can have bad side-effects, too. With the tryptophan and vitamins, results will be gradual, taking maybe ten weeks to reduce symptoms completely.

But the benefits here are obvious – no side-effects to mess you up in other ways.'

Minerals for the blues

Calcium and magnesium may also help chase the blues. In one study depressed patients had 'significantly lower' blood levels of magnesium than healthy people *(Journal of Nervous and Mental Disease)*. In a second depressed patients who took the drug *lithium* and improved had a rise in their magnesium levels, while the magnesium levels of those who took lithium and didn't improve stayed much the same *(Lancet)*.

August F. Daro, a Chicago obstetrician and gynaecologist, routinely gives all his depressed patients calcium and magnesium. 'Many depressed men and women are short on calcium and magnesium,' he told us. 'I put them on a combination of 400 mg of calcium and 200 mg of magnesium a day. These minerals sedate the nervous system, and most of the depressed patients feel much better while taking them. Calcium and magnesium especially take care of pre-menstrual depression.'

Low folic acid and emotional lows

Nowadays, more and more doctors are also looking into folic acid deficiency as a cause of depression.

Folic acid is another member of the B vitamin clan, and it's easy to see the resemblance. Like all the other B vitamins, folic acid is critical to the functioning of the central nervous system. And being particularly concentrated in the spinal column – the hub of nervous system communications – folic acid might even be considered the big brother of the B vitamin family.

A study at McGill University in Montreal examined the folic acid levels of three different groups of patients: those who were depressed; those who were psychiatrically ill but not depressed; and those who were medically ill. Six of the patients were men, 42 were women, and their ages ranged from 20 to 91 years.

The researchers discovered that 'serum folic acid levels were significantly lower in the depressed patients than in the psychiatric and medical patients . . . On the basis of our results, we believe that folic-acid deficiency depression may exist' *(Psychosomatics,* November 1980).

Would folic-acid therapy help clear up depression?

To find out, we asked A. Missagh Ghadirian, head researcher in the study who is now in the department of psychiatry at the Royal Victoria Hospital in Montreal. 'Based on my clinical observations, it seems that people whose depressions are purely due to folic-acid deficiency do get better with folic-acid therapy,' Dr Ghadirian told us. 'To make absolutely sure, we will have to wait for the results of the second phase of our study, in which folic-acid therapy is used.'

Such positive findings for folic-acid therapy may explain the remarkable case of a young woman with 'baby blues', or post-partum depression. Her pregnancy and the delivery of her baby had been uncomplicated, but several weeks after delivery, she became progressively withdrawn and emotionally unstable. Soon she became disoriented and panicky, and had hallucinations about large, ugly figures that intended harm to her and her new child.

Hospitalized in two different psychiatric facilities for a period of 19 months, she received shock treatments and various tranquillizers. She also tried to commit suicide three times. According to the doctor who saw her as a result of her third suicide attempt, 'She was an attractive but very distressed-appearing young woman who was extremely frightened, whining and literally withdrawn into the corner of her hospital room'. Three blood tests for folic acid levels were performed on her, one of which was reported as very low, and two of which were reported as 'none detectable.'

The doctor's report continued:

'She was treated for anemia with 5 mg of folic acid twice a day . . . for ten days [a large therapeutic dose]. On the seventh day of folic-acid treatment, an improvement in the mental status was noted; by the tenth day, a complete remission had occurred. The patient was discharged on 1 mg of oral folic acid daily.

[She was followed for another $2^1/_2$ years without evidence of any psychiatric disturbance. She became an active student in nursing school and did very well academically. [*American Journal of Obstetrics and Gynecology*].

An amino acid to reverse depression

The story of another woman, who responded not to a vitamin, but to an amino acid – *tyrosine* (made in the body from phenylalanine, the amino acid prescribed by Dr Yaryura-Tobias) – is also instructive.

By the age of 30, this woman had suffered from severe depression for several years. Treatment with drugs only made her worse, but when a team of doctors from Boston and Cambridge, Massachusetts gave her tyrosine supplements, her condition 'improved markedly' *after only two weeks*. 'She said she felt better than she had in years and showed striking improvement in mood, self-esteem, sleep, energy level, anxiety and somatic [physical] complaints' (*American Journal of Psychiatry*, May 1980).

A psychiatrist working with the woman also noticed the improvement – and the worsening of her condition that occurrred when a placebo (a non-therapeutic pill) was substituted for the tyrosine without the knowledge of either the woman or her psychiatrist. The researchers noted that 'within one week of placebo substitution, her depressive symptoms began to return.' After a total of 18 days, she was more depressed than she had been before she started taking tyrosine.

However, the woman's story has two happy endings: 'her depression was again completely alleviated' when she resumed taking tyrosine, and her case inspired further research into this amino acid.

In another case, studied at the New York Psychopharmacologic Institute, two patients suffered from depression that failed to respond to standard drug therapy and had to take powerful amphetamines ('speed') to remain symptom-free. Two weeks after they started taking a special form of tyrosine before breakfast, they had so improved that one of them was taken off amphetamines entirely, while the other one was able to reduce his dosage by two-thirds (*Lancet*, 16 August 1980).

'The most common cause of depression'

Before Dr Daro gives nutritional supplements, he checks to see if the patient has low blood sugar, or *hypoglycaemia*.

'The first thing I do when depressed patients come to see me,' he says, 'is have them take a glucose tolerance test, the laboratory test that measures blood sugar levels. Anyone who has depression, apprehension, anxiety, crying spells or loss of desire for sex should have this test. Low blood sugar is the most common cause of depression, though it's not commonly diagnosed.'

To treat depressed patients who have hypoglycaemia, Dr Daro recommends a diet rich in protein and free of refined carbohydrates and coffee. 'A lot of depressed people don't eat well,' he says. 'Perhaps they'll have a cup of coffee and a sweet roll for breakfast. I make sure they eat three good meals every day. A good diet has to be the foundation of the nutritional treatment of depression.'

And a poor diet can make depression worse. 'Depressed people generally don't eat well, which will make any nutritional deficiencies more severe and may aggravate their depression,' Dr Yasuo Ishida of St Louis told us.

David R. Hawkins, medical director of the North Nassau Mental Health Center, tells the story of a rabbi who brought his wife in for an examination because of her long bouts of depression. 'For 15 years she had been depressed. For 15 years they did not function normally as husband and wife. 'Occasionally she had to have outpatient shock treatments.

'We performed the five-hour glucose tolerance test. During the first three hours, she was absolutely normal. On the fourth hour she dropped down into the low 40s [a blood sugar level of near 100 mg of glucose per cubic centimetre of blood is considered normal], a precipitous drop.'

When the woman was switched over to a high-protein, low-carbohydrate diet most of her problems subsided. 'Several months after we had seen her,' says Mollie S. Schriftman, executive director of the Center, 'and prescribed a diet for her, she was leading a normal life.'

Excessive coffee and prescribed drugs

Psychiatric patients pay a heavy penalty for excessive use of coffee which is associated with severe mental and emotional disturbances. Heavy coffee drinkers score higher on tests for anxiety and depression and are more likely to have a disturbance diagnosed as psychotic.

Although 250 mg of caffeine (the dose at which symptoms may be caused) may seem like a sizable amount, it really isn't, in light of these figures: a cup of coffee may contain from 29 to 176 mg depending on the size of the cup and the method of its preparation; the average amount per cup is 60 to 80 mg. Cola beverages supply about 40 mg per serving, a small chocolate bar about 25 mg. And many headache preparations contain sizable amounts of caffeine.

So an individual consuming three cups of coffee, two headache pills, a chocolate bar and a cola drink ingests about 400 mg of caffeine – more than 50 per cent above the level that causes symptoms.

Speaking of pills, it's important to realize that certain medications are sometimes the root of depression. According to an article in the *Journal of the American Geriatrics Society*.

> Drugs, either prescribed by a physician or taken independently, often are responsible for the development of depression, the aggravation of a pre-existing depression or the production of depression-like symptoms such as sedation, apathy and lethargy.

And, the report continues, the elderly are 'particularly likely' to develop 'depressive side-effects.' Doctors who are confronted with depressed elderly patients may even diagnose a person as senile and pass over the depression altogether. (*See also* SENILITY.)

Drugs are far from being the only cause of depression in the elderly. 'There are a number of physical illnesses that appear to generate depressive symptoms in the elderly,' wrote Dr Monica D. Blumenthal. 'When recognized [depression in the elderly] is amenable to treatment; misdiagnosed, it can lead to invalidism and death' (*Geriatrics*, April 1980).

Drugs may cause depression in the young as well as in the elderly. Episodes of depression are not an uncommon complication of therapy with cortisone and ACTH [*adrenocorticotropic hormone*],' according to a group of doctors in Italy. When treating a five-year-old girl for chronic hepatitis, they noticed that, during her first week of ACTH therapy, she appeared depressed and became less sociable. By the second week of therapy, she was noticeably uncommunicative and had periods of crying (*Pediatrics*, April 1980). Fortunately, the side-effect of mental depression in that type of therapy can be successfully treated using high dosages of vitamin C.

Of course, not all drug therapy is avoidable, but it's wise to be aware that depression may be a side-effect.

Anger turned outside in

A low-grade depression may occur in people who do not face up to their anger and turn it inward instead. 'Low-grade depression is found more often in women than in men,' says Marjorie Brooks of Jefferson Medical College in Philadelphia. 'Some women may feel powerless at times, but instead of getting mad, they get depressed. As a result, they may constantly feel tired or have a chronic "headachy" feeling.'

Dr Brooks believes that people must retrain themselves to accept anger as a normal emotion and deal with it accordingly. 'Expressing anger is necessary for good health,' she says, 'but it doesn't mean a brick over the head. That action only brings retaliation and guilt. Anger is a normal emotion that is a result of our genetics, upbringing and cultural patterns. The biggest problem we face is learning how to discharge it in a manner that is both acceptable in society and healthy for the self.'

The link with cancer

Housewifery, strangely enough, may be one of the most dangerous occupations. A 15-year study in Oregon showed 'a significant excess of cancer mortality amoung housewives' compared with women working outside the home. The researchers couldn't figure out whether exposure to household chemicals overconsumption of food, coffee and cigarettes, or mental depression was the likeliest explanation (*Women & Health*, Winter 1979).

In postulating a link between depression and cancer in housewives, the Oregon researchers raised an interesting question. Can depression lead to cancer, or at least contribute to its development? Several doctors say yes.

People with a depressive response to life, who react to stress with feelings of despair and who habitually deny and repress their emotions, appear to have a greater risk of cancer, according to Claus Bahne Bahnson of the Valley Medical Center in Fresno, California. Similarly, Lawrence LeShan, in his book, *You Can Fight for Your Life* (1980), profiles the cancer patient as, typically, someone who suffered emotional isolation during childhood, only to have his or her hopes for a fulfilling relationship raised and dashed later.

'People who have a particularly depleted and unsatisfying childhood are more vulnerable later in life to developing malignancies,' Dr Bahnson told us. 'Individuals who are very rigid and use denial and repression and lack awareness of their own emotions both develop cancer more often and, when they develop cancer, have a poorer prognosis.'

Dr Bahnson believes that depression can upset the body's hormone system and this might adversely affect the immune system, which guards the body against cancer, as well as other diseases. (*See* CANCER.)

The need for exercise

The need to 'talk it out' is strong in us humans, but it appears that we also need to move our bodies in order to break out of depression. Researchers are finding that exercise of all kinds is a powerful therapy.

'Running seems a sensible treatment for many depressed people, since it's not expensive, and unlike some other treatments, it has beneficial physical side-effects,' wrote Dr John H. Greist and his associates at the University of Wisconsin in a paper entitled 'Running Out of Depression' *(Physician and Sportsmedicine)*.

Dr Robert S. Brown and his colleagues at the University of Virginia used a wide array of physical activities to get patients back on their feet. In the same journal issue, they noted 'the inertia that accompanies the depressed person's increasing tendency to withdraw, his constriction of interests and pre-occupation with unhappiness makes it tempting to hypothesize that some of the features of depression may be symptoms of a primary movement disorder.'

They discovered that breaking out of that lethargic behaviour is not easy but before too long, a more positive self-image, which is a potent reinforcement to continuing in the programme takes shape. 'Exercise is also effective in fending off the depressed and pessimistic moods that mentally healthy people have from time to time,' they added.

'Just minor, non-vigorous exercise like walking a block can produce measurable, beneficial psychological changes,' says Ronald Lawrence, a California psychiatrist – neurologist. Dr Lawrence is the founder of the American Medical Joggers Association, a nationwide group of in-shape doctors who practise what they prescribe and are rapidly running away from the traditional image of the rotund family physician.

'It's estimated that one of every ten Americans suffers from depression,' he says. 'One thing that has made running in particular and exercise in general a success is that people can use it to treat their own depression.' If you're down, it can make you feel more up – and if you're up, well, it can help your spirits soar.

To understand why, let's jog into the inner workings of the central nervous system.

Basically, the brain sends out a command in the form of electric current and the nerves are the routes these messages take to the 'doers', the muscles. However, between each nerve cell and the next is a gap – a *synapse*, to use the proper term – that can be bridged only with certain chemicals called neuro-transmitters. Of these, adrenalin is probably the most familiar, and there are others such as noradrenalin, serotonin and the mysterious endorphins – morphine-like substances recently discovered to be enhanced by both exercise and acupuncture.

When the system is functioning as planned, the messages come down the road find the right bridges and are delivered to the correct address. But nerves are sensitive to all sorts of stresses, and when overwhelmed, the 'route' quickly becomes a maze of potholes, wrong turns, floods and detours.

'In depressed people, we see decreased noradrenalin levels,' explains Dr Lawrence. 'Actually, you can't measure that directly, so we look for a substance called MHPG, a breakdown product of the neuro-transmitter. With exercise, MHPG levels rise, so we assume there is a corresponding rise in noradrenalin. The end result is a significant decrease in depression and an increase in synaptic transmission. The brain becomes more alive.'

That shows up graphically as an increase in blood flow coursing through certain regions of the brain – a direct contrast to depression, in which regional blood flow is decreased. 'Positron-emission scans [a special type of X-ray] reveal an enhanced use of the right brain, the so-called 'female', or 'artistic', brain. Rhythmic exercise allows the mind to wander, fantasize and enter a tranquil state of clarity and uncluttered thinking,' Dr Lawrence adds. The right-brain switchover during a workout might account for a good part of the peacefulness of perspiring.

So, too, might the observed rise in serotonin, a neuro-transmitter found in reduced quantities in depressed patients. The jump in serotonin levels goes hand in hand with feeling better mentally.

Sleep deprivation as therapy

If exercise can wake up the brain, so can staying up . . . for many hours at a stretch. Consider this case:

Every Saturday night for six months, a 26-year-old Greek woman stayed up all night eating, drinking, singing and dancing in nightclubs. And at the end of that time? You're probably expecting us to say she collapsed on the steps of the Acropolis with cirrhosis of the liver. Well, what happened was that she recovered from a serious depression that was destroying her health and her life.

And it was her doctors – at the Athens University department of psychiatry – who had prescribed staying up all night and most of the next day as treatment, although the patient decided *where* she was going to 'take the treatment.'

The woman, referred to as Ms A, was what her doctors call a 'rapid cycler' who suffered from severe depression once a month, with the attacks lasting about a week or more. On several occasions she tried to commit suicide. She frequently wept, was ravaged by guilt feelings, lost interest in her husband and had great difficulty sleeping. She was given the drug *imipramine* (brand name: Tofranil), but it failed to help.

The idea of sleep deprivation to bring someone *out* of certain kinds of depression is not exactly new – even though it's not widely known. However what the Greek doctors were interested in was a trial of sleep deprivation as a *preventive* measure in a person who had a history of going in and out of depressions every month.

At first, Ms A was placed on a regimen of staying awake for 36 hours at a stretch once a week, in a hospital setting. That went on for ten weeks, during which time she was completely free from depressive episodes. Upon being discharged from the hospital, she was instructed to continue the same programme, which she did, in the company of her husband.

At the time the doctors wrote their report, Ms A had been well and free from all depression for a period of eight months and two weeks, even though – on her doctors' instructions – she had quit her Saturday night escapades some two months earlier.

It's quite possible, the doctors suggested, that further studies will confirm the usefulness of sleep deprivation therapy in several kinds of depressive disorders for which drugs such as lithium and anti-depressants are ordinarily given. And except for big nightclub bills, there are no side-effects that have been noted.

Depression in the dark months

Like a thermometer, many people's spirits slide during the winter. It's not uncommon. Changing temperatures mean changing lifestyles, prodding sun worshippers to shut themselves off from civilization and seek a cosy den in which to hide – making the winter seem longer and dimmer than it really needs to be.

And it's not just the people in cold climates who are affected. Winter also means shorter days, and that affects everybody. 'There is a fear of the dark in the winter-time, especially in some cities,' says Milton N. Silva professor and deputy chairman of the department of psychiatry at the Medical College of Wisconsin in Milwaukee. 'Winter means getting up in the dark and coming home from work in the dark. People react to that.'

Even people in mild climates aren't immune to it. When the winter solstice arrived on 22 December, people in sunny California found their freedom in daylight short-lived when the sun went down at 4.48 P.M., only 9 hours and 53 minutes after it had arrived.

Generally speaking, however, the colder it is, the darker it will be. In some of the coldest parts of the inhabited world, such as Alaska and Scandinavia, there is very little daylight at all from 1 November to February. For example, the sun sets in Tromsø in northern Norway on 27 November leaving its residents in the dark until 16 January. And even then it peers through for only 1 hour and 20 minutes.

The long periods of darkness have given Scandinavians the societal stereotype of possessing dour personalities, says James E. Cathey, secretary of the Society for the Advancement of Scandinavian Study. He says the people have not successfully found a way to cope with the darkness, and they yearn for spring and sun.

Some light is being shed on the theory of daylight and how it affects the psyche, with studies done at the National Insitute of Mental Health, outside Washington D.C. A team of psychiatrists there has completed the initial stages of a long-range study of 30 people with a history of winter depression and summer elation. Although they caution that their data is preliminary they are encouraged by their first findings that some winter depressives can be treated effectively not through drugs or therapy, but using a special artificial light that can approximate the sun's spectrum to mimic the longest day of the year. The volunteers were asked to turn on the lights during the winter for three hours each morning and night. The researchers believe that some patients responded dramatically to the pretence of extended daylight.

Similar research is now being carried out in Britain, which has had the same positive results.

How to beat the winter 'blahs'

Although winter may not send most people into a debilitating depression the darkness and cold of the season do have a tendency to get a lot of people down. The trick is to keep it from happening. This compilation of ideas from psychiatrists, psychologists, sports enthusiasts and social-service directors can be the ammunition to fight it.

With the myriad of sports clubs and community-organized health programmes popping up across Britain, there is no reason why anyone should have to forgo the exercise he or she was getting under brighter skies. Being unable to afford the fancy private clubs is no excuse, either. Almost all towns and cities have at least one or more community-service organizations that offer energy-exerting programmes for little or no cost.

'There is nothing you do in the summer-time that can't be brought indoors in the winter-time,' notes William B. Zuti, national director of health-enhancement programmes for the YMCAs of the United States. 'Actually, it is in the winter-time that we see the heaviest participation in formal organized activities'. He feels that organized indoor activity is ideal. 'Not only do you get exercise, but you socialize and you get to meet a lot of people. That's not so easily done in the summer-time'.

Exercise aside, there are other things you can do to keep yourself from being homebound in the winter.

'Weekly suppers with some of your neighbours is a good way to be with others,' says Dr Silva. 'Organize book clubs or card nights and participate. Don't seclude yourself.'

Indulge yourself. 'Go to a shopping centre and shop, store to store, for something you've been wanting for a long while,' suggests Louis Leaff professor of psychiatry at the Medical College of Pennsylvania. 'Or, call a friend and meet for lunch. 'Just a weekend visiting your family a three-hour drive away could break the back of the blues,' he adds. 'Or visit the zoo, or a favourite museum or restaurant.'

'Throw a party,' suggests Dr Emery. 'Don't be down because you aren't being invited anywhere. Take the initiative and do the inviting.'

Rather than hide from nature in the winter, adapt to it. See it for its beauty – try to capture it, says Gary Emery, director of the Center for Cognitive Therapy in Los Angeles and author of the book *Own Your Own Life: Three Steps to Achieving Independence* (1982). A course in photography or just the pure enjoyment of taking pictures may help you appreciate the season more.

Idle time can be used for self-improvement too. 'People can use the winter-time to take a course in something that might save a life,' comments a spokesperson at the American Red Cross headquarters in Washington, D.C. 'We recommend CPR [cardio-pulmonary resuscitation] – it's a proven lifesaver – first aid or water safety.'

Improve your mind. Read a book. Learn a language. Take a class.

Doing volunteer work is another way to conquer the blues. Not only does it help others, but it can be personally rewarding as well. Government cutbacks have pulled the reins on a multitude of social-service agencies that must now depend more on volunteers to keep their programmes going.

Winter can be particularly frightening for the infirm and elderly in cold climates, says Dr Silva. 'The fear of physical injury and lack of access to friends and religious activities can produce anxiety, depression and guilt.' One of the most difficult aspects of winter for these people is not being able to get around for ordinary errands. 'Develop cooperative shopping arrangements with neighbours,' he recommends. 'Purchase stamps and staple items in larger quantities than usual so fewer trips are necessary. Being prepared can make you feel more secure.'

Social restriction is another problem. 'People who live in blocks of flats should make it a point to meet other people in their buildings,' Dr Silva says. 'Many estates have community centres for the residents to have social gatherings. People should be encouraged to join in.'

A hobby that is particularly good for the infirm and the blind is shortwave-radio listening. Winter is the prime time for tuning in broadcasts from remote corners of the globe because on the lower bands you need darkness both where the signal is being sent and where it is being received. It's a sedentary hobby, but it keeps you in touch with the world.

'I'm a firm believer in fantasy, as long as you don't lose track of reality,' says Dr Silva. 'If you can't take a holiday this winter, start thinking about the one you want to take next summer. Get travel brochures for the places you can afford to go to and for the South Pacific and places you always wanted to visit. This is a great way to indulge your fantasies. The positive anticipation of planning a holiday can make winter much more endurable.'

Then, of course, there are the almost-inevitable *post*-holiday blues that occur particularly after Christmas. 'The post-holiday blues is a common affliction,' says Fred Vondracek, associate professor of human development at Pennsylvania State University. 'People really mobilize themselves to enjoy their holidays, but some have exaggerated expectations. They hope the holidays will cheer them up once and for all. They soon learn that life just doesn't operate that way, and they feel a big letdown.

'Other people who get the blues see people having a good time and enjoying themselves, and they feel left out and alone. Those who are chronically depressed may drink heavily through the holidays. They may even attempt suicide. The chronically depressed individual has a medical – psychological problem and frequently winds up checking into a hospital. It's a fairly well documented fact that mental health centres have an influx of patients just after the holidays. On the other hand, a lot of well-adjusted people experience the post-holiday blues. But they know why they are feeling down and can pull themselves out of it without professional help.'

Celebrate life every day

People with the blues can take their own initiative and cheer themselves up. 'We don't need to wait for special occasions,' says Dr Vondracek. 'And we don't have to be elaborate, either. Go home after a hard day's work and enjoy a nice dinner with your spouse. If you like football, take yourself to a football match. If you'd rather be mountain climbing, go climb a mountain. Anytime you do something you enjoy, you celebrate life.'

'Every person knows in his own way what will make him happy,' says Herbert Holt, a practising psychiatrist in family and marriage counselling in New York City and author of the book *Free to Be Good or Bad*. 'If we are sitting around feeling sorry for ourselves, a little creative imagination can lift us out of that state. Make a change in tempo. One person might enjoy painting; another might prefer swimming. If you're tired of household chores, take a walk around the neighbourhood.

'There are tremendous benefits when people focus away from their routines and give themselves a little celebration,' Dr Holt told us. 'Our own bodies have magnificent mechanisms called endorphins (and encephalins), which will go into action to uplift our spirits or sooth us.' Researchers have discovered that these neuro-transmitters which are natural soothing substances released from the brain, apparently neutralize unhappy moods in people when they spend time with those they like or begin doing something they enjoy, explains

Dr Holt.

Mark Tager, an Oregon doctor, believes that people often dwell too much on the routine aspects of their lives and overlook the importance of having fun. Dr Tager says that having fun is intrinsic to our well-being, 'but when I ask my patients if they're having fun in their lives, they stare at me and say "Fun?" '

'I personally use any excuse I can to celebrate, including every Christian and Jewish holiday there is. What you do is get a big calendar that lists everybody's birthday from Shakespeare to Buddha. You'll even know when national flower day is, and you can be prepared to celebrate it. By celebrating, I don't mean goofing off or wasting time but allowing a few good thoughts on a nice subject to pass through your mind.'

However we decide to perk up our lives, we should keep a realistic perspective. 'No one goes from one joyous moment to another in life,' says Dorothy Susskind, a clinical behavioural psychologist in New York City. 'It is perfectly natural to feel unhappy with ourselves at times. Underneath it, we all know that basically we are loved, respected, understood and needed by others.'

• Dermatitis

Dermatitis is a catch-all term for inflammation of the skin. Symptoms can include itching, red blisters that ooze and get crusty, and in chronic cases the surface of the skin becomes hard and fissured. It is caused by an allergic reaction to any number of things – food, household cleaners and chemicals are common triggers. And their target is often the hands.

Cleaning up can sometimes be worse for your hands than soiling them in the first place, says Gary S. Nelson, a safety engineer with the Texas Agricultural Extension Service. 'Numerous cases of dermatitis are not caused directly by substances used in the workplace, but by materials used to wash up,' says Dr Nelson. 'Many times, the most available cleaning agent is a dermatitis-producing solvent.'

Some of the most common cleaners around the house can be the worst for your skin. Turpentine, white spirit, petrol, liquid paraffin and lacquer thinner are the ones that come to mind. Those solvents do their job only too well. Paint and grease aren't the only things they take off. 'You're actually dissolving your hands, that's what you're doing,' Dr Nelson warns.

The skin, he explains, acts as a barrier against injuries and irritants. It's also a two-way water barrier, preventing liquids from seeping into the body and keeping body fluids from leaking out. To do this job, the skin has to be flexible, and it relies on natural fats and oils to stay that way. Strong solvents 'defat' the skin and allow it to dry out and crack open. 'The solvent will both dry out the skin and then irritate it,' says Dr Nelson. 'Drying out the skin then makes it susceptible to damage by other substances.'

To avoid using solvents, people should use gloves when they use oil-base paint, Dr Nelson advises. He also recommends using the so-called waterless hand cleaners. Farmers and other agricultural workers, in particular, ought to become more alert to such problems, Dr Nelson says, since they often work alone without the benefit of the safety measures enforced in many factories. They also tend to reach for the handiest, rather than the safest, hand cleaner.

Housewives' eczema is probably the most common kind of hand dermatitis. Just dipping the hands in and out of hot, soapy water too many times a day can defat the skin, causing 'dishpan hands'. Frequent contact with such domestic items as bleaches, floor and furniture waxes, detergents, soiled nappies, or the juices of raw citrus fruits, potatoes, tomatoes and garlic can severely irritate the skin as well.

Once healthy skin becomes damaged and cracked, it is also more vulnerable to becoming 'sensitized', or allergic, to a foreign substance (*see* ALLERGY). For that reason, rubber gloves are not recommended as protection for women whose hands are already inflamed. Not only can excessive sweating under the gloves further harm the skin, but certain chemicals in the rubber might provoke an allergic reaction. And once the allergy begins dermatitis can occur whenever and wherever rubber products touch the sensitized person's body.

Norman Levine, a professor of dermatology at the University of Arizona Health Sciences Center, has offered certain precautions to anyone who is prone to hand dermatitis. Vinyl gloves, he said, are better than rubber for handling potentially irritating substances. Also, hand washing should be kept to a minimum and only lukewarm water and mild soap should be used. Gloves ought to be worn in cold, windy and/or dry weather; potentially allergy-inducing medications should be avoided; and rings should be removed.

Also, patience is the greatest virtue in curing hand dermatitis. Even when the hands become smooth again, the tender loving care must be kept up. 'After a severe episode of hand eczema,' Dr Levine has stressed, 'the skin may require up to four months after visible healing to return to its healthy state' (*Modern Medicine*, 15–30 March 1980).

In the case of the infant with nappy rash, or anyone else with inflamed skin special care must be taken in choosing which medication to apply. Certain over-the-counter creams and even some that are prescribed by a family doctor may contain 'sensitizers' that may initiate an allergy that the person will have for the rest of his or her life.

Common sensitizers

F. William Danby, a practising dermatologist in Kingston, Ontario, says that perfume reactions are common among patients who have trouble with their skin. (In his opinion, fair-skinned people are more sensitive than swarthier types.) But identifying the chemical that caused the reaction can be very difficult. The fragrance in a shampoo, for example, can give some people a rash, but the fragrance itself may be composed of several hundred ingredients and its exact formula may be a trade secret.

Fragrances and other sensitizing chemicals are widely used. One of them – *cinnamic aldehyde* – can be found in soap, toothpaste and ice cream. More than 500 tons of *hydroxycitronellal* – sometimes also used to scent bubble bath – are used each year in synthetic perfumes in the United States alone. Other chemicals that can give people trouble are *paraphenylenediamine*, an ingredient in hair dye, and *formaldehyde*, which is found in disinfectants, shampoos, foot sprays photographic chemicals, high-gloss paper and other items.

The least-suspected of the common sensitizers, Dr Danby says, is nickel. About 3 per cent of the women who have their ears pierced develop a lifelong sensitivity to any metal products containing free nickel atoms. This includes such common objects as nickel-chrome door handles, car bumpers and some coins as well as earring posts. Dr Danby recommends 'hypoallergenic' earrings (i.e. ones that are at least 14-carat gold), in which there is no free nickel.

Preventing allergies

More than ever, people are exposed to an enormous number of chemicals some of which aren't even listed on package labels. No one knows how sensitive he or she is until an allergy develops, and a person may use a product for years, Dr Danby points out, before the body decides that it has had enough and decides to react. The best idea is to prevent the problem by keeping the skin from becoming dried out and cracked open in the first place. Next, be careful with those substances that commonly cause allergic reactions.

Sometimes improving your diet can strengthen your resistance to allergens. In one case, a young woman had suffered from eczema on her hands since the age of nine and had controlled it with a standard prescription for cortisone cream. When she was 30, however, the skin condition spread to her face, and she was catching colds every couple of months. She sought medical help.

Arthur Hochberg, an herbalist – psychologist from Philadelphia, advised her to cut white flour and sugar out of her diet and recommended large amounts of brewer's yeast, vitamin C and water-soluble vitamin A. The regimen also included camomile tea, kelp, spinach and beetroot greens, cod-liver oil and the exclusive use of olive and safflower oils in cooking.

'Now my face is perfect,' the woman says. 'It used to be awful. It was swollen; it itched; it was red and scaling. Now my only problem is protecting it from the sun. I also feel energetic for the first time since my first pregnancy. I don't need naps in the afternoon anymore.' She also cut her use of cortisone. 'It amazes me that I only have to use it once or twice a week because I was one of those people who couldn't go anywhere without a tube of cortisone.'

• Diabetes

Lots of people think of diabetes as an unusual disease that mysteriously afflicts a few people in the next town. They may even know people who have it, but they never suspect that they could contract the disease themselves.

At first glance, the statistics seem to back up that attitude. Only about 1 per cent of the British population (600,000 people) have documented cases of diabetes. A similar number are estimated to have undiagnosed diabetic conditions.

However, the number of those with diabetes is growing, and complications of the disease magnify its impact. The number of known diabetics has increased in recent years, perhaps as much as 50 per cent in the last decade, for reasons no one really understands.

In 1975, the official report of the (US) National Diabetes Commission listed diabetes as the third leading cause of death in the United States, accounting for 300,000 to 350,000 lives lost each year. The toll is even higher when you consider the deadly complications of diabetes. One-half of the people who die from heart attacks and three-quarters of those who die from strokes develop their circulatory diseases as a result of diabetes. Heart disease is the major cause of death among diabetics.

Diabetes represents a failure of the body's system of carbohydrate metabolism. When we eat carbohydrates, glucose (blood sugar) is produced and either used immediately or stored for later use. Stored glucose is released into the bloodstream whenever we need an added energy boost. Insulin, a hormone produced by the pancreas, regulates the level of glucose in the blood. In diabetes, there is either not enough insulin produced or what is does not hold down glucose levels. As a result, about 30 per cent of diabetics need injections of insulin to stay alive.

There are two types of diabetes. Type 1, or 'juvenile diabetes', usually occurs in childhood and generally has more severe symptoms. The condition is often referred to as 'insulin-dependent', since the pancreas manufactures virtually no insulin, and it is almost always necessary to take insulin to replace the hormone.

The more common type of diabetes is Type 2, commonly called 'maturity-onset diabetes', and it usually occurs after age 50. Diabetics in this category do not often suffer from a lack of insulin. In fact, insulin levels may even be higher than those of healthy people. But despite this, Type 2 diabetics cannot keep down the levels of sugar in their blood.

The American Diabetes Association estimates that one out of every 20 people will be diabetic at some time in the course of their lives, and the older we get, the more susceptible we become. Some 40 to 60 per cent of people in their 80s suffer from diabetes.

Weight, like age, is an important factor determining who gets diabetes. 'Most diabetes is curable,' says Dr Kelly West, who has been involved in a worldwide study of diabetes coordinated by the World Health Organization. 'If early in diabetes, a person loses weight and keeps it off, the disease may never come back.'

A case history reported in the journal *Annals of Internal Medicine* illustrates the process. A woman in her late 20s came to Cleveland, Ohio hospital weighing over 14 stone – nearly twice her normal weight – and suffering from diabetes. After six months of intensive dieting, her weight was down to just over 9 stone – and her diabetes had disappeared.

Interestingly, research tells us that perhaps an even more important factor than weight is the *distribution* of excess weight in the body. A study of obese women found that those whose fat was primarily located on their upper body ran nearly 11 times the risk of getting diabetes as people with no weight problem. By comparison, *generalized* obesity made people only three times more likely to get diabetes (*Clinical Research*, April 1980).

While we may be able to reduce our total body weight, it's hard to tell it how to distribute itself on our frames, just as it is hard to avoid old age. And other uncontrollable factors, such as heredity, play a part in the disease. Fortunately, scientists are beginning to uncover a number of ways to manage the disease naturally, if and when it does strike.

How fibre helps

Researchers are finding that some Type 1 diabetics can decrease their need for the drug, or even eliminate it. Some of the most encouraging successes have been achieved using a high-carbohydrate, high-fibre diet. Fibre is the material in vegetables, grains, nuts and fruit that passes through the digestive system without being absorbed. Foods high in fibre include spinach prunes, jacket potatoes, almonds, wholemeal bread and bran cereals.

Dr James Anderson of the University of Kentucky has been working with high-fibre diets for a number of years. Studies of lean diabetic men showed that the diet reduces the need for insulin and also lowers the levels of fats in the blood that have been linked to heart disease.

In one study, 20 lean men who were on insulin therapy were placed on a weight-maintaining, high-fibre diet for about 16 days. Total calories for the diet comprised approximately 70 per cent carbohydrate, 21 per cent protein and 9 per cent fat. Carbohydrate foods were a natural combination of carbohydrates and fibre, and included whole grains or grain cereals and breads, starchy vegetables such as maize, beans and peas, and other vegetables and fruit.

Researchers divided the patients into three groups. The first group had been taking 15 to 20 units of insulin daily. Nine of these ten patients were able to discontinue their insulin therapy on the high-fibre diet. Most of them also developed lower glucose levels in their blood after fasting and after meals.

The second group had been taking between 22 and 34 units of insulin daily. Their insulin was reduced to an average of 12 units a day, and two of the patients were able to discontinue insulin on the high-fibre diet.

The third group consisted of patients requiring between 40 and 57 units of insulin daily. On the high-fibre diet, there was a slight reduction in their insulin doses, and their average blood sugar and urine sugar values also decreased.

'These short-term improvements have been sustained for up to five years in lean patients who follow high-fibre maintenance diets,' Dr Anderson reported (*American Journal of Clinical Nutrition*, November 1979).

Another study by Dr Anderson involved diabetic patients with weight problems. Obese patients, like the lean, were able to lower both their use of insulin and the levels of dangerous fats in their blood by eating a high-fibre diet (*Obesity and Bariatric Medicine*, July–August 1980).

Predictably, the most dramatic improvements occurred in those who lost large amounts of weight on the diet. Fibre is particularly helpful in that regard. A comparison of high- and low-fibre diets, Dr Anderson reported, showed that 'satiety [feeling of fullness] ratings were consistently higher on the high-fibre diet than on the low-fibre diet.' When their diet was richer in fibre the patients felt full sooner, ate less and thus lost more weight.

It's important to remember, though, that since a high-fibre diet can decrease insulin requirements, diabetics receiving insulin should be cautious when changing their diet.

Of the many types of fibre, pectin seems to be especially useful in diabetes. Pectin is a natural fibre usually derived from plant cell walls and citrus fruit pulp.

In a French study, scientists found that a pectin-rich apple supplement lowered the number of ketones (products of fat metabolism), which may be produced if fat is used by the body to supply energy when carbohydrates (because of a lack of insulin) cannot. This is significant because the accumulation of ketones results in *keto-acidosis*, a serious symptom of advanced diabetes in which the victims feel extremely thirsty and their skin and tongue are dry. Diabetics run the risk of developing keto-acidosis whenever they eat foods high in refined carbohydrates.

If pectin can lower the ketone count, could it also control the rise in the blood-sugar level symptomatic of diabetes? To test that, a team of British researchers fed two groups of diabetic volunteers a carbohydrate meal; some of the meals contained supplementary pectin (about ⅓ oz), and others did not. The diabetes of one group was mild enough to be controlled by dietary regulation alone (Type 2), while that of the other group was so severe as to require insulin treatment (Type 1). Both groups underwent a 14-hour overnight fast before eating.

In the Type 2 volunteers, the pectin supplement significantly lowered the rise in blood-sugar concentration after the carbohydrate meal. That amounted to a 42 to 60 per cent reduction in the rise of blood sugar, an impressive management of diabetic metabolism. However, for the Type 1 diabetics, the effect of pectin provided reason for even higher hopes. Pectin lowered the blood sugar level by 36 per cent – a decrease great enough, speculated the researchers, to reduce the diabetics' insulin requirements.

Pectin's power to lower blood sugar, without increasing insulin may hold some good news for non-diabetics, too. The researchers cited an experiment in which a pectin supplement, even in non-diabetic volunteers, lowered the amount of insulin required to maintain a healthy blood-sugar level.

An Israeli study not only supported these findings but also yielded impressive new data: pectin might be therapeutic in treating a pre-diabetic condition in obese patients. Six obese subjects showed an exaggerated insulin response to test meals similar to that occurring in early diabetes. However, after they received a dietary supplement of 10 g of pectin and 16 g of guar gum (another plant fibre) for three consecutive days, their insulin levels significantly dropped (*Israel Journal of Medical Science*, January 1980).

In Poland, 30 diabetics were monitored for three weeks as they took ⅕ oz of pectin with each meal. 'In the majority of cases, dietary pectin supplementation improved glucose tolerance . . . the pectin-fortified diet could be considered as an important therapeutic tool' (*Diabetologia* September 1981).

In the past, the conventional diabetic diet was one that *restricted* carbohydrates: if diabetics have trouble using starches and sugars, the reasoning went, they'd better not have too much of them. Instead, they were advised to steer clear of rice, cereal, fruit and sugar, and told to eat meat cheese, eggs and other foods generally low in carbohydrates but high in fat and cholesterol.

However, clinical trials such as Dr Anderson's suggest that a high *unrefined* or *complex*-carbohydrate diet actually *improves* the body's ability to use starches and sugars. Like a loss of weight, the theory goes, it makes the cells of the body more sensitive to insulin so the little that the pancreas can produce goes a lot further – sometimes far enough to make injections of the hormone unnecessary.

Other diets that reduce blood sugar

Perhaps the food factor that diabetics really need to restrict is *fat*. When fat enters the bloodstream after a fatty meal, it interferes with insulin's action, preventing it from lowering blood sugar. So blood sugar begins to rise – and then the trouble starts. On the other hand carbohydrates, especially complex ones, help insulin function normally.

J. Shirley Sweeney demonstrated this back in 1927. Dr Sweeney gave healthy volunteers a high-fat diet for two days, then tested their blood-sugar response. In all cases, blood-sugar levels were significantly elevated. When Dr Sweeney put these same volunteers on a high-carbohydrate diet, their blood-sugar levels decreased (*Archives of Internal Medicine*). Since then other studies have confirmed the same beneficial effects with high-complex-carbohydrate, low-fat nutrition for both the prevention and treatment of diabetes.

Other researchers have found that some diabetic patients – even Type 1 diabetics, can drastically reduce their need for insulin when they eat a diet mainly comprising raw food. The diabetics (who consumed from 50 to 80 per cent of their food raw) ate such foods as vegetables, seeds, nuts, berries melons and other fruit, honey, oil and goat's milk. The researchers theorized that the diet works because of the 'non-inactivated enzymes that are present in raw items' or because of 'the fast transit that is inherent in a raw diet' (*Annals of Internal Medicine*).

'Transit time' is the time it takes food to pass through the digestive tract. A diet of mostly raw foods – which is rich in fibre – passes through in 18 to 24 hours; a diet of mostly cooked food that is not particularly high in fibre takes 80 to 100 hours.

One Indonesian doctor gets right down to specifics when he 'prescribes' food for diabetics: eating large amounts of green beans and raw onions may help lower your blood-sugar, says Dr Askandar Tjokroprawiro. In separate studies 20 diabetic outpatients ate the equivalent of $1\frac{1}{2}$ lb of green beans daily for a week, while another 20 ate the equivalent of $2\frac{1}{2}$ oz of raw, chopped onions for the same length of time. At the end of seven days, the subjects' blood-sugar levels were compared with what they were prior to the diet, and the doctor found a 'statistically significant' reduction. Eating those vegetables may have therapeutic value for victims of *diabetes mellitus* (the medical name for the condition), Dr Tjokroprawiro concluded in a presentation to the 15th International Congress of Internal Medicine, reported in *Internal Medicine News* (1 December 1980).

If your mother told you to eat slowly and chew every bite, she may have known what she was talking about. In a study of 22 patients with a mild form of Type 2 diabetes, scientists rated each patient as to how quickly he or she ate a meal: less than 6 minutes was considered hasty; 6.1 minutes to 9 minutes was medium; and 9.1 minutes or more was slow.

The results showed that the blood-sugar levels of the hasty eaters fluctuated more widely than those of the medium and slow eaters. Furthermore, the hasty eaters had wider swings in their body weight during treatment. Said the scientists: 'An adequate instruction on eating behavior should be included in the management of the diabetic patient' (*Tohoku Journal of Experimental Medicine*, April 1980).

Refined sugar and diabetes

That 'adequate instruction' should include a lesson on avoiding sugar. A sweet tooth can cause a lot more damage than a few rotten teeth.

Sheldon Reiser, laboratory chief of the US Department of Agriculture's Carbohydrate Nutrition Laboratory at the Nutrition Institute in Beltsville Maryland, has completed a series of studies that seems to confirm suspicions that the white stuff we so casually stir into our morning cup of tea may just be the icing on our cake of serious health concerns, including diabetes.

'We had done rat studies and found that a whole host of health risk factors were evident in rats when they were fed table sugar as opposed to starch [i.e. unrefined carbohydrate],' Dr Reiser told us. 'For example, rats fed table sugar get fatter than animals fed starch, even though the number of calories consumed is similar.'

Dr Reiser and his team of researchers then set out to discover exactly how table sugar, given to human beings in amounts slightly higher than those consumed by the average American, affects metabolic functions. To do this they enlisted 19 volunteers (ten men and nine women) who agreed to take their meals at the Nutrition Institute. All were fed a diet similar in carbohydrate fat and protein composition to the average American diet. There was just one variable: during the first six weeks, approximately half of the group received 30 per cent of their total caloric intake as wheat starch given in the form of wafers, while the other half took an equal percentage of their intake as sugar eaten as a cake-like dessert. In the second six-week period, the groups exchanged diets (*Federation Proceedings*).

A 30 per cent chunk may sound at first like a random selection, but, Dr Reiser assured us, it was not. It's close enough to the average American sugar intake of 15 to 24 per cent to produce realistic results, and yet it's inflated just enough to compensate for the fact that the 19 volunteers would be on this sugar regimen for only six weeks as opposed to an entire lifetime of sugar consumption. The average sugar intake in Britain is 16 to 18 per cent.

In addition, Dr Reiser tried to distribute the calories over the day in such a way as to simulate the American meal pattern. 'People tend to skip breakfast eat a light lunch and then gorge themselves at dinner just before they plop in front of the TV for the night,' he told us. 'So we fed our volunteers two basic meals: one light meal consisting of only 10 per cent of their total caloric intake early in the day and a large dinner consisting of the remaining 90 per cent bulk of the calories in the evening.'

Once a week upon rising and before eating, the volunteers were asked to roll up their sleeves and give blood for analysis. One interesting finding was that blood sugar and insulin levels were significantly and consistently higher while the volunteers were on sugar than when they were on the starch diet.

What does all this mean? According to Dr Reiser, it indicates that sugar consumption – even in the daily amounts typically consumed by your average American (or British person) – could be a contributing factor in the development of Type 2 diabetes.

Refined sugar enters the bloodstream very quickly, Dr Reiser explained. If you load a person with sugar, his or her blood-sugar level increases rapidly causing a surge of insulin to be released. Keep up the same diet on a day-in day-out basis – as was the case in these six-week trials – and insulin insensitivity may result. Eventually you need more insulin to do the same job.

'This is precisely what happens in late-onset diabetes,' Dr Reiser told us. 'Hyperinsulinism [high insulin levels in the blood] precedes its onset.'

Chromium: a blood-sugar regulator

Consuming highly processed low-chromium foods and high levels of sucrose and other simple carbohydrates that stimulate chromium excretion may be leading to dietary deficiencies of chromium – an essential trace mineral. The decrease in dietary chromium may be related to the high incidence of diabetes in the Western world. Why?

'Our hypothesis is that chromium is necessary for insulin to have an effect,' explains Walter Mertz, director of the US Department of Agriculture's Human Nutrition Research Center.

However, before we look more closely at why we need chromium to keep insulin on the job – and diabetes at bay – let's see exactly why our diets ended up having so little of the health-giving mineral.

When Dr Henry A. Schroeder, pioneer trace-metal researcher, examined the chromium content of various human tissues, he found something rather unforeseen: in the bodies of Americans, the concentration of the metal dropped as they aged. Oddly, such was not the case with Africans and others from less well-developed parts of the world. Dr Schroeder traced this to the Americans' consumption of overly processed foods in which the chromium content is refined away.

Let's take ordinary table sugar as an example. Nearly all of the chromium in sugar cane vanishes in processing, so satisfying a sweet tooth with sucrose adds nothing to our 'precious metals' bank account. Worse still, it causes a hefty withdrawal, for metabolizing sugar drawn on the services of the chromium – insulin team. When the partners have finished their task, a good part of the metal fraction is excreted in urine. This story – all take and no give – appears to be the same for overly refined white flour.

'Therefore, the typical American diet, with about 60 per cent of its calories from refined sugar, refined flour and fat, most of which is saturated, was apparently designed not only to provide as little chromium as feasible, but to cause depletion of body stores of chromium by not replacing urinary losses,' wrote Dr Schreoder in *Trace Elements and Man*.

However, if we get enough chromium – and good sources include brewer's yeast liver, jacket potatoes, fresh vegetables and whole-grain bread – how does it work to keep us healthy? Well, it combines with other nutritional factors in the body to form a substance called *glucose tolerance factor* (GTF). Then, as Drs Anderson and Mertz have explained, insulin and GTF team up to direct the following processes: (1) glucose uptake; (2) oxidation of glucose to carbon dioxide; and (3) incorporation of glucose into fat (*Trends in Biochemical Sciences*). In other words, in the body's energy department insulin and its essential sidekick GTF stoke the stoves, vent the waste gases and add future fuel to the woodpile. This well-tuned efficiency keeps the system young.

What happens if GTF decides not to show up for work?

Without its partner, insulin must put in loads of 'overtime' to try to get the same job done, but it's never enough. To make matters worse, the beta cells of the pancreas, where the hormone is produced, can grow weary to the point of taking early retirement. Type 2 diabetes is often the end result, and this, of course, is one of the worst possible finales of a lifetime of lack of sufficient chromium.

However, enough chromium can have just the opposite effect. 'It may be possible to prevent, or at least delay considerably, the onset of maturity-onset diabetes in susceptible individuals,' Dr Anderson told us.

Some of us, as we get older, lose the ability to convert the chromium in our diet to GTF, Dr Anderson says. Why this happens is unknown, but 'the loss of the ability to convert chromium to a usable form that often occurs with increasing age may be reversible in the early stages. Mildly diabetic patients often respond to chromium supplementation.' In fact, Drs Anderson and Mertz have noted, 'It should be pointed out that some individuals have reduced their requirements for insulin by including brewer's yeast . . . in their daily diets.' Yeast is one of the best sources of chromium.

Unfortunately, as Dr Anderson told us, there exists no good way to assess chromium status with an eye towards who is and who will become deficient. Given this uncertainty, and the tendency of the body's supply of chromium to decrease with age, a chromium supplement looks like excellent preventive medicine.

Extra nutritional needs

Besides needing extra chromium, diabetics have higher-than-usual needs for several other nutrients.

Vitamin B6 Researchers in Australia discovered that diabetics with diabetic neuropathy (disorders of the peripheral nervous system affecting the lower extremities) had lower concentrations of vitamin B_6 (pyridoxine) in their blood than diabetics who had no symptoms of neuropathy (*Australian and New Zealand Journal of Medicine*).

At the Thordek Medical Center in Chicago, researchers gave vitamin B_6 supplements to diabetics who suffered from neuropathy and who showed signs of a vitamin B_6 deficiency. Problems such as pain, burning and numbness began to disappear. By the end of the experiment, symptoms were either greatly reduced or completely gone. In addition, the researchers noted that their patients said they had less 'eye trouble' and that their eyes 'felt better' (*Journal of the American Podiatry Association*). Symptoms recurred when some of the patients decided to stop the supplements, but these problems abated after vitamin B_6 was administered again. The researchers hypothesized that 'sensory disturbance termed diabetic neuropathy can be associated with a pyridoxine deficiency.'

And when a group of 13 women who developed diabetes in late pregnancy were given 100 mg of pyridoxine daily, their bodies regained much of the ability to safely handle blood sugar. This improvement occurred in spite of the fact that levels of insulin – which normally keeps blood-sugar levels well within bounds – were unchanged, and in some cases actually fell (*American Journal of Obstetrics and Gynecology*).

According to Dr William N. Spellacy and co-workers who conducted the trial at the University of Florida College of Medicine, these results indicated that routine blood tests to measure vitamin B_6 might be a useful way to screen women at special risk for developing diabetes during pregnancy. The authors also suggested that the current (US) Recommended Dietary Allowance of vitamin B_6 for pregnant women – 2.6 mg – may need to be boosted.

Vitamin C This is another needed nutrient. For one year, a Czecho-slovakian team gave a daily 0.5 g dose of vitamin C to patients with Type 2 diabetes. They found that the patients' blood-cholesterol levels had dropped a 'striking' 20 per cent. Triglycerides, another blood fat linked to circulatory problems, were also reduced (*International Journal for Vitamin and Nutrition Research*).

Vitamin E Research has indicated that some diabetics may benefit from taking supplements of vitamin E. The vitamin has proven fundamental in keeping platelets (tiny disc-shaped cells in the blood) from aggregating, or 'clumping', which lowers the risk of buildup on artery walls. Since diabetics are prone to circulatory problems, vitamin E is particularly important.

In addition, the ability of vitamin E to inhibit platelet aggregation seems to have a therapeutic use in diabetic retinopathy, a complication involving inflammation of the retina in the eye. In one study, vitamin E was tested on ten patients with diabetic retinopathy and ten healthy volunteers. A chemical substance was used to trigger platelet aggregation in both groups. When vitamin E was administered, the grouping of platelets was slowed down in *both* groups (*Acta Haematologica*, vol. 62, 1979).

Another study of vitamin E conducted by Margaret O. Creighton and John R. Trevithick at the University of Western Ontario indicated that the nutrient may prevent cataracts in diabetics. Cataracts involve cloudiness of the eye lens that causes partial or total blindness. Elderly diabetics are particularly susceptible to cortical cataracts, which occur in the back part of the lens.

The researchers put rats' lenses in a high-glucose solution and produced cortical opacities. The rats' lenses appeared similar to those seen in human senile and Type 2 diabetic cataracts, but when vitamin E was added to the solution, cataract development was inhibited: 'The cortical cataracts were completely gone when vitamin E was in the solution,' Dr Creighton told us. 'Vitamin E completely prevented cataracts from occurring on the lenses in the test tube.'

The researchers were continuing to investigate vitamin E. Although their new studies are incomplete, 'they look very encouraging.' If the findings of their preliminary work are confirmed, vitamin E may hold new promise for diabetics. 'If a person became diabetic, we might be able to prevent cataracts from starting with vitamin E, or at least it might take longer before they did set in,' explains Dr Creighton. 'In the meantime, diabetics might try vitamin E,' she adds. 'If you have your physician's approval, it wouldn't hurt to be taking it while we await more data.'

Zinc   Not only may a diabetic pancreas produce less insulin than a normal one, but it may also contain only about half the amount of stored zinc. In addition, zinc increases the potency of insulin and increases glucose tolerance. So it's no wonder that extra zinc may be helpful in diabetes – and helpful even if you don't have diabetes. Researchers have found that a zinc deficiency can result in a pre-diabetic condition that can lead to trouble later in life.

Fitness is a factor

Last, but not by any means *least*, is the fitness factor.

'Exercise is a very positive adjunct to diabetic therapy,' says Greg Peterson special assistant to the chairman of the board of Federal Express Corporation in charge of medical and health systems development. 'But the amount and type of exercise, as well as exercise frequency, has not yet been determined.'

Peterson served as a research assistant to Dr Peter Forsham, at the University of California, San Francisco, in experiments with exercising Type 1 diabetics. They studied the effects of exercise on six normal individuals and on six with Type 1 diabetes by measuring the amount of platelet adhesion (stickiness) in blood samples before and after exercise.

'When you cut your finger, platelet adhesion is the first line of defence against bleeding,' Peterson explains. 'But platelets clump together inside the blood vessels of diabetics even when they haven't suffered a cut. A diabetic's increased platelet adhesion can cause trouble with his blood circulation which may be the underlying cause of some of the long-term complications of diabetes.'

In the California study, the platelet adhesion of both normal subjects and Type 1 diabetics decreased after exercise. Platelet adhesion dropped down to the normal range for the diabetics, and decreased adhesion was maintained for nine hours after exercise in one subject and for 24 hours after exercise in another.

'While exercise may be good for some diabetics, we caution those who already have had retinopathy problems diagnosed. They should be *extremely careful* about exercise, since exercise can raise the blood pressure and that can cause problems. Diabetics with retinopathy should *not* do exercises that would raise their blood pressure, jog or do any physical activity without first checking with their physicians.'

Peterson, a diabetic himself, says that nutrition and exercise are valuable considerations for anyone, but diabetics should never make changes from their daily routine without their doctors' approval.

For information on diabetes-related eye disorders see VISION PROBLEMS.

• Diarrhoea

Nearly everyone suffers from diarrhoea once in a while. Stomach cramps and loose, watery stools strike some people when they are nervous or upset and others when they over-indulge in succulent summer fruit. Diarrhoea frequently adds to the miseries of winter viruses and flu, too.

Such occurrences of diarrhoea are usually self-limiting and will take care of themselves. Chronic diarrhoea, however, can indicate a serious ailment (such as colitis) and should be checked by a doctor.

Diarrhoea in babies

This can be very serious, because infants are so easily dehydrated. In treating infectious diarrhoea in infants, doctors often tell mothers to omit milk from the diet and replace it with 'clear fluids', including carbonated beverages, juices and soups such as chicken and beef broth. However, many such fluids contain so much sugar or salt that they actually may worsen and prolong the baby's illness, according to studies at the Hospital for Sick Children in Toronto (*Canadian Medical Association Journal*, 8 September 1979).

The high sugar content of many carbonated beverages, juices and other liquids may cause a sugar-induced diarrhoea. It has been recommended that beverages containing a lot of sugar be diluted to at least half strength to avoid problems.

High concentrations of salt, common in some prepared soups, pose another potential hazard. Too much salt in dehydrated children can make them vulnerable to complications such as seizures and irreversible brain damage. Because of the extraordinarily high salt content of many commercial soups, the researchers suggested that homemade soups with no added salt might be more acceptable.

Dangerously high amounts of salt or sugar also can arise when liquids are prepared from crystals or concentrate, the researchers noted. Adding extra amounts from a package or incorrect measuring can make the salt or sugar levels higher than they should be.

The (US) Center for Disease Control in Atlanta, Georgia recommend the following as one type of homemade fluid therapy to combat dehydration: combine 8 fl. oz of fruit juice (orange, apple or other), half a teaspoon of honey and a pinch of salt in a glass. In a second glass combine 8 fl. oz of boiled or carbonated water and a quarter teaspoon of baking soda. Have the baby drink alternately each mixture. Additional carbonated beverages or water should be drunk and solid foods and milk should be avoided until recovery.

Breast milk protects against diarrhoea

Breastfed babies are far less likely to develop dangerous intestinal infections than bottle-fed babies, say two California paediatricians. Over a period of two years, Spencer A. Larsen, Jr. and Daryl R. Homer studied all the infants under one year old who were admitted with severe vomiting and diarrhoea to the Kaiser – Permanente Medical Group hospital in Hayward California. Of the 107 babies, they found that only one was breastfed at the time of admission – far fewer than in the general population served by the medical group.

About one-third of the hospitalized bottle-fed infants were breastfed at birth, the doctors said, but all had gone on the bottle at least a month before they became sick. These findings suggest that 'breastfeeding plays a major role in protection against intestinal infections,' the researchers concluded, and they pointed out that similar studies in Britain and in underdeveloped countries have shown the same thing.

Natural remedies for diarrhoea

Some common food substances have proven remarkably useful against diarrhoea.

Carob powder In a Canadian study of 230 infants with diarrhoea only three were not cured by the addition of carob powder to their formula. The treatment apparently worked because carob contains high levels of fibre which, as recent research has shown, can clear up digestive problems including diarrhoea.

Yogurt This seems to be beneficial in maintaining or restoring the health of the intestinal tract. 'In many countries along the Mediterranean Sea and in the Balkans, yogurt has been used for years as a remedy for infantile diarrhoea by both laymen and physicians,' wrote Drs Molly Niv, Walter Levy and Nathan M. Greenstein in *Clinical Pediatrics*.

The three doctors fed yogurt to half of a group of children hospitalized with severe diarrhoea. Those in the yogurt group ate a little less than 4 fl. oz three times daily, while the rest of the children received an anti-diarrhoeal drug. More children in the yogurt group than in the drug group recovered within three days.

Bran The normal functioning of the intestinal tract depends upon the presence of adequate fibre – the kind that absorbs water and forms soft bulk. Fibre like bran. Bran relieves both constipation *and* diarrhoea. It is not a laxative; it is a normalizer of bowel functions. Transit times – the amount of time it takes for food to pass through the body – are lengthened in individuals with chronic diarrhoea who eat bran, but they are shortened in those with constipation. Bran thickens the loose, watery stools of diarrhoea and softens the hard, dry stools of constipation. A few tablespoons (less for a child) followed by a glass of water should do the trick in a few days. If diarrhoea persists, see your doctor.

Pectin This is a fibre found in fruit, particularly apples cherries, bananas and citrus fruit. 'Pectin allows water to be absorbed from the colon,' says Dr David Jenkins of the University of Toronto, 'and has been given to individuals with chronic diarrhoea.'

One group of people who might benefit from pectin are those who have 'dumping syndrome'. Not long after eating, they may suffer from dizziness, abdominal discomfort and diarrhoea, caused by the too-rapid movement of food and fluid through their digestive tracts. British doctors successfully used pectin to treat dumping syndrome in 11 patients recovering from abdominal surgery (*Lancet*, 16 May 1981). After drinking a glucose solution, all of these patients soon suffered characteristic gastro-intestinal distress accompanied by hypoglycaemia (low blood sugar). However, when ⅓ oz of pectin was added to the solution, their symptoms were either abolished or reduced, and blood glucose levels were kept under better control.

'Pectin added to the glucose meal slowed gastric emptying,' the researchers noted, 'and since dumping is related to rapid emptying, the abolition or reduction of symptoms in our patients was almost certainly due to slower transfer of glucose from the stomach to the small gut [intestine].'

Traditional remedies   These include eating Gruyère cheese, brown rice, barley or bananas, or drinking a tea made from mallow root or wild thyme.

'Chewing-gum' diarrhoea

A 66-year-old woman who was a patient of two doctors in Miami Beach, had a three-month history of severe chronic diarrhoea, having to go to the toilet between 12 and 50 times a day. Yet, there was no mucus, blood, cramp, fever nutritional deficiency or other signs of real illness. X-rays and probes of various kinds revealed nothing of interest. Making it all the more frustrating, every kind of anti-diarrhoea medicine in the book was tried without success.

What was the problem?

Chewing gum, her doctors say. 'When dietary history was re-examined at length,' they wrote in the *American Journal of Digestive Diseases*, 'it was revealed that the patient habitually chewed 50 to 100 sticks of sugarless chewing gum daily, to aid her in weight reduction. Upon abrupt withdrawal of chewing gum, all diarrhea ceased and gastro-intestinal complaints abated.'

The explanation for this chewing-gum effect is that most sugarless gums – as well as many foods for diabetics – contain sorbitol, and this, it turns out tends to have a laxative effect in large doses. Usually, in an adult, that effect would not be noticed unless the person was consuming 10 or more pieces of gum a day. At the rate of 50 or even 100 a day, the effect can be disastrous. Drs Lee D. Goldberg and Norman T. Ditchek dubbed the syndrome 'chewing-gum diarrhoea'.

(*See also* TRAVELLER'S DIARRHOEA.)

• Diverticular disease

In diverticular disease, numerous small pockets or sacs (*diverticula*) form along the wall of the colon (large intestine). Doctors believe these pockets form at weak spots in the bowel, where undue pressure and contraction force the intestinal lining to bulge like a rubber balloon.

Diverticular disease can cause uncomfortable feelings of distress, but, in some cases, it may produce few symptoms and go unrecognized. However, there is always the danger that one of the sacs will become inflamed or infected causing severe pain and cramping. If the condition becomes serious enough, the bowel may actually be obstructed and surgery is sometimes necessary.

'This epidemic of [diverticular] disease occurred within the briefest of historic times, within the past 70 years, or a single lifespan,' British surgeon Neil Stamford Painter has pointed out. 'Diverticula didn't become prevalent in the West – and scarcely exist today in primitive societies – till after the turn of the century.'

That's when newer milling methods further reduced the content of dietary fibre in flour. 'In the 19th century,' Painter says, 'people were adjusting apparently, to *less* fibre than provided by a primitive diet. But as fibre reduction continued, a breaking point came, beyond which the intestinal tract could no longer function normally.' As a result, diverticular disease and other problems like constipation and haemorrhoids have flourished.

'In Western countries,' says Dr Denis P. Burkitt, 'about one in ten people over the age of 40 and one in three over 60 have diverticular disease. Constipation is now recognized as the underlying cause.' And fibre as the cure.

'In almost all British clinics and in an increasing proportion of American clinics, all patients with diverticular disease of the colon, with or without symptoms, are put on high-fibre diets,' says Dr Burkitt. 'In some hospitals this approach has reduced the proportion of patients requiring surgical treatment by as much as 90 per cent.'

How can a high-fibre diet help diverticular disease?

Researchers reporting in the *British Medical Journal* set out to answer that question. According to I. Taylor and H.L. Duthie of the University Surgical Unit Sheffield Royal Infirmary, among Westerners aged 70 or over, as many as 70 per cent show some signs of diverticular disorder. Yet 'fewer than 12 cases have been observed in rural Africa in the last 20 years.' They point out that 'the most important dietary difference in these societies seems to be a considerable reduction of fibre intake and an excess of refined carbohydrate in the Western diet.' In other words, people of the Western world are not eating enough natural whole grains and other high-bulk foods to keep their bowels in good working order. Instead, they are filling up on starchy white bread, white sugar and other highly refined foods that tend to gum up the bowels.

Diet vs bran vs laxatives

To see if supplemental bran could help overcome the effects of this dietary imbalance, Drs Taylor and Duthie selected 20 people with diverticular disease. Eight had recently suffered acute attacks of painful diverticulitis and two had required surgical drainage of a diverticular abscess.

Five of the patients were placed on a high-fibre, high-residue diet including fruit, vegetables and grains. Five others were given a bulk laxative that also contained an anti-spasmodic agent. The remaining ten received bran supplements: every day they received nine tablets, each containing 2 g of bran, for a total of 18 g of bran daily. After one month, those receiving bran switched over to one of the other regimens, and vice versa.

The results were clear-cut, and dramatically in favour of bran supplementation. All the patients reported some improvement, no matter which of the three treatments they received. While eating the high-residue diet, 20 per cent experienced complete relief from pain, distension and other symptoms. Of those taking the bulk laxative, 40 per cent reported similar relief. *However, a significantly greater number of the patients – 60 per cent – were completely symptom-free while taking the bran tablets.*

Similar advantages were observed in all areas studied. Stool weight, for example, increased in all patients, but this increase was greatest among the bran group. (Because large, moist stools move through the colon more smoothly and are easier to pass, intestinal muscles don't have to strain as much. In regions of Africa where diverticular disease is almost unknown, stool weights are considerably higher than in Western countries.)

Intestinal transit time – a measure of how quickly consumed food is moved through the gut and eliminated – decreased among all 20 people, but the reduction was greatest among bran users. This is another good sign, indicating that the intestinal tract is working as it was designed to work. Transit times were reduced from 96.6 hours to 76.4 hours with the high-residue diet, to 71.7 hours with the laxative, and to 56.1 hours with bran.

Even more important, the bran tablets reduced the number of contractions that produce damaging high pressure inside the colons of diverticular victims. Some muscular contraction is necessary to move the bowel contents along and trigger regular bowel movements. But in diverticular disease, such pressure occurs too often – causing the intestinal walls to balloon out of shape. Bran brought colon pressure activity back down to within normal limits; neither of the other two treatments had any significant effect whatsoever.

As a final confirmation that bran was helping, Drs Taylor and Duthie measured low-level electrical activity inside the colon. Most diverticular patients including 80 per cent of those in the study, have an abnormally rapid electrical rhythm. Bran supplements were able to cut that figure in half which was significantly more improvement than occurred with the other regimens.

'We have found that bran compressed in the form of tablets is not only convenient and acceptable but also effective,' the doctors concluded.

Although controversy exists on how best the bulk [missing from refined diets] should be replaced, there seems to be no adequate replacement for substantial amounts of bran. Bran proved to be the most effective treatment not only in improving the symptoms in patients with diverticular disease but also in returning to normal the abnormal pathophysiological changes.

The benefits of bran

What makes bran so effective? It puts back into the modern diet one factor that is woefully lacking: fibre. 'Diverticular disease of the colon is one of several disorders characteristic of modern Western civilization. A diet deficient in cereal fibre is generally regarded as the predisposing chief factor,' said Drs Taylor and Duthie.

The importance of putting fibre back into the diet, this time in the form of bran flakes, was again demonstrated in a second *British Medical Journal* report by two doctors, A.J.M. Brodribb and Daphne M. Humphreys, at the Royal Berkshire Hospital in Reading. For at least six months, the researchers fed bran to 40 patients with diverticular disease. All improved while consuming bran: 60 per cent of all symptoms – such as flatulence, distension, pain and bloody stools – were completely eliminated, and another 28 per cent of symptoms were significantly relieved. Again, as in the study by Drs Taylor and Duthie, stool weight increased, transit times improved and episodes of high intracolonic pressure were less frequent.

Drs Brodribb and Humphreys point out that bran seemed to act as a normalizer of bowel activity. Transit times, for example, were shortened among those patients with a tendency towards constipation, but they were also *lengthened* in individuals with diarrhoea. 'Many patients initially passed either liquid motions or very hard motions,' the authors noted. 'Some alternated between the two. Bran effectively thickened liquid motions and softened hard motions. Similarly, patients with very frequent motions defecated less often after bran, and constipation was successfully relieved.' On the whole, all transit times tended to normalize towards a 48-hour mean.

There were other good signs. Straining on defecation – a cause of painful haemorrhoids – was sharply reduced. And most patients were able to give up the use of laxatives.

The authors indicated that 'most patients were initially sceptical of the idea of being treated with only bran.' But they soon were convinced.

A few patients failed to take the bran on the occasional weekend when they were away from home and noticed that their original symptoms started to return within three days. At the end of the trial, most patients were determined to continue to take bran indefinitely.

Just as bran proved an effective treatment for diverticular disease, it could also serve as a powerful deterrent in healthy individuals, Drs Brodribb and Humphreys suggested. 'A high-fibre diet might protect against the development of the condition, as well as relieving symptoms,' they concluded. With evidence like this, you'll probably want to add bran to your daily diet if you haven't already.

To get the beneficial dosage recommended by Drs Taylor, Duthie, Painter and others, you'll need to consume about six teaspoons of bran a day. You can either add it to other foods or mix it with milk, fruit juice or soups. And remember, it's imperative to take plenty of liquids along with your bran. The natural fibre in bran depends on absorbed moisture to form bulk in the bowels.

Pectin

Another friend for your intestines is pectin, another source of fibre. Thanks to its water-bonding power, pectin can moisten and help eliminate the hard, dry faeces that accumulate in the colon and cause ballooning of the intestinal wall.

The best and most practical way to perk up your diet with pectin is to eat apples – whole, sliced, grated or blended into apple sauce, but always with their skins. Other tasty sources include cherries, bananas, pineapples tomatoes, grapes, peaches, raspberries, avocados pears, raisins, carob and sunflower seeds.

• Dizziness

Vertigo – dizziness – haunts over 50 different conditions and can be a symptom of something as common as the menopause or as critical as multiple sclerosis. But to understand dizziness, we first have to get a handle on *balance*.

Balance is the flip side of dizziness, the smooth music you move to almost all of the time. That music is played by senses of sight, touch and hearing, by body position and by the inner part of your ear. The music has a conductor: the brain. It coordinates all the different parts – the senses, the inner ear – into a tune with a message: where you are, where your limbs are in relationship to each other, and the speed and direction in which you are moving.

However, if balance depends on many body systems and parts, a disorder in any one of them – an ear infection, an episode of low blood sugar, poor circulation cutting down the blood flow to the brain – could cause dizziness, and that's often just what happens. Take a look at an ear infection for instance.

The hardest bone in your body shields the inner ear, a delicate system of canals filled with watery fluid that flows from one point to another as your head moves. At the same time, the sensory hairs within the canals relay your movements to the brain. The inner ear also works with the eyes and the muscles that take care of posture to keep you balanced.

When the inner ear becomes infected, its messages are garbled. The slightest head movement sends the brain a topsy-turvy report that can make you feel that you are spinning around, or light-headed, or nauseated – you may even vomit. And not just an ear infection can do that; an inner-ear disease called Menière's syndrome, or a skull injury, or a tumour in the ear – really anything that disturbs the inner ear – can have the same effect.

Dizziness has many causes

Because dizziness can accompany over 50 conditions, it's important to have it medically evaluated.

● In a study of over 6000 people, dizziness was found to be a symptom in those who had high blood pressure.

● Doctors at the Emory University School of Medicine in Atlanta, Georgia found that spells of dizziness and fainting are sometimes caused by disturbances in heart rhythms.

● Blood-sugar problems such as hypoglycaemia can cause dizziness, according to a doctor writing in the *Laryngoscope*.

● In a letter to the *British Medical Journal*, another doctor noted that vertigo – which, he said, usually occurs in 'older age groups' – is often found in young women taking the Pill.

● Even drugs that treat dizziness can *cause* dizziness: 'Many of the preparations used indiscriminately for "dizziness" are sedatives and will only make the situation worse,' says an article in the *British Medical Journal*.

Doctors have some clues to help them track down the cause of dizziness. If your ears ring during a dizzy spell – a condition called *tinnitus* – the problem is probably in your inner ear. For example, a study done at Northwestern University Medical School in Chicago on dizzy patients found that 40 per cent had inner ear disorders. However, Dr Roger Hybels told us that the cause of dizziness in many people who come to the Lahey Clinic in Boston is obscure and that, 'except for an explanation of the problem', they often do not receive any specific treatment. If they are treated, he said, it is mostly with drugs.

Treating dizziness with diet

Dr Hybels is one doctor who recognizes that the culprit in many cases isn't the inner ear – it's poor circulation. 'Circulatory disorders in the brain or the ear can cause dizziness,' he says. An article in *Postgraduate Medicine* also pointed out that 'in a person more than 40 years old, sudden dizziness probably represents a vascular [circulation] disorder.'

Another doctor, James T. Spencer, Jr. of Charleston, West Virginia, sees dizziness sufferers 'all the time', and treats many of them with diet. And only 10 per cent of those on diets, he says, require additional drug therapy to relieve their dizziness symptoms.

'Of all the problems that could cause dizziness, poor circulation is frequently the culprit,' Dr Spencer told us. 'High levels of blood fats like cholesterol and triglycerides cut down the blood supply to the inner ear and cause almost all dizziness. A proper diet is the best form of therapy I have found for these patients, and it is a very rare case in which the dizziness does not disappear.'

He prescribes a diet that completely eliminates white sugar and white flour and emphasizes lean meat, whole grains and fresh vegetables and fruit. 'When a person comes into my office complaining of dizziness, I hand him a diet sheet that outlines what his food intake should be. When I see him next, in about two weeks, he usually tells me: "I haven't had any dizziness since I went on this diet." ' Dr Spencer has successfully treated over 1500 patients.

Another doctor, W.D. Currier of Pasadena, California, has had similar success. 'The problem of dizziness almost always comes from excessive fats and refined carbohydrates in the diet. Just eliminating these dietary errors usually corrects the problem, unblocking the blood supply to the balance centre in the ear,' he told us.

Although Dr Currier emphasized that 'no single vitamin cures any disease including dizziness,' he pointed out that vitamins C and E, the B complex and certain minerals are particularly helpful in treating dizziness. Dr Spencer too, suggests that his patients take 1000 mg of vitamin C and a vitamin E supplement along with a multivitamin and mineral supplement. 'I think it's good for everyone to take extra vitamins C and E as a preventative measure to stop dizziness from ever developing,' he says.

To cope with the dizzy spell itself, Dr Spencer tells his patients to 'stop what they're doing, sit down or lie down, and let it pass.' But, he adds 'Better advice is to prevent the dizzy spell with a good, prudent diet.'

• Drug side-effects

'Take two aspirin and call me in the morning. By the way, the aspirin may make you deaf and dizzy, destroy certain vitamins, ulcerate your stomach and harm your kidneys.'

How many doctors warn you about all the possible side-effects of a drug? Not too many. And for good reason.

'Doctors are reluctant to scare their patients,' says Joe Graedon, a pharmacologist and author. 'They want the patient's trust. And they also want to avoid creating a psychosomatic reaction. For instance, if a doctor tells a patient who is taking medication for high blood pressure that he may become impotent, impotency may develop as a result of that suggestion.'

Yet more and more people want to know about side-effects. You do. Of course you respect your doctor's reluctance to fill you in on a clutter of information that might scare you away from a treatment you need, but you also respect your body – and your health. And you realize that your doctor may clam up because he sees your questions as a challenge to his authority . . . or he isn't very good at translating medical jargon into plain English . . . or he is pressed for time . . . or he doesn't know what the side-effects are.

The truth is, you can't afford not to know. Hospitals report that 20 per cent of their patients are admitted with a drug-caused illness, and some experts claim that prescription drugs kill as many as 140,000 each year in the United States alone. Nonprescription drugs (commonly called over-the-counter, or OTC drugs) aren't any better. They can ruin your kidneys, your liver, your stomach – in fact, any organ or system – and at dosages their labels claim are safe. As Graedon says, 'There is no such thing as a completely safe drug.'

Aspirin and paracetamol

Aches and pains don't always need a quick fix from the chemist. Particularly since OTC painkillers are like any other hired killer – efficient but mean and nasty into the bargain.

Take aspirin, for instance. (And a lot of people do. Americans, for example use more aspirin than any other OTC drug – 50 billion pills each year.) Aspirin eats away at the coating of the stomach that protects it from the acids that digest food, and it also slows clotting time. In short, your stomach bleeds – and may not stop for two days. Studies have shown that, in the United States aspirin causes one out of every seven hospitalizations for bleeding of the digestive tract. And people who regularly take aspirin more than four days a week have a greater chance of developing ulcers than people who use less of it.

The buffered variety is no better than the plain stuff. Buffered aspirin offers 'little or no protection', wrote three doctors in the *New England Journal of Medicine* (17 July 1980). They reported a study in which people were given large doses of either aspirin or buffered aspirin – and those taking buffered aspirin suffered just as much (sometimes serious) stomach bleeding as those taking plain aspirin.

The bleeding may be worse if you wash down the aspirin with a cough or cold remedy that contains alcohol. (Many are higher proof than wine or beer; some are as much as 68 per cent alcohol.) Like aspirin, alcohol slashes at the stomach's lining. Together, they're very hard to stomach. 'The considerable risk of mixing aspirin and alcohol is too little known,' said an editorial in the *British Medical Journal*. And all that bleeding can put your iron levels in the red. Iron-deficiency anaemia among people who take aspirin 'is more common than realized,' wrote Dr René Meguy in *Postgraduate Medicine*.

When you take aspirin, you get burned – and not only in the stomach. The oesophagus – the digestive tube that runs from your mouth to your stomach – is also a target. A doctor discovered that almost all his patients who had oesophagitis (inflamed oesophagus), hiatus hernia (a rupture of the oesophagus) or heartburn (often caused by a faulty oesophagus) were regular users of aspirin. According to Dr Vernon M. Smith, 'The heavier the aspirin usage, the more severe the symptoms'. And he added, 'Withdrawal of aspirin without other treatment measures, frequently is followed by a relief of symptoms' (*Southern Medical Journal*).

Aspirin can make a cold worse

Still, for all aspirin's drawbacks, most people would rather be wounded by it than felled by a cold or flu. The only thing is, aspirin may make a cold worse.

'It appears that aspirin acts in three ways that are negative for cold sufferers,' Joe Graedon told us. 'First, it actually increases the number of viruses dramatically. Second, it may lower the body's production of interferon, a natural anti-viral substance. Third, it may stop vitamin C from getting into the white blood cells, which are the cells that fight infection.'

That aspirin chokes off the cells' supply of vitamin C is bad news whether you have a cold or not. Drs W. Marshall Ringsdorf, Jr. and Emanuel Cheraskin called the vitamin C-lowering effect a 'severe blow' to health. When aspirin is taken for four or five days, they pointed out, large amounts of vitamin C are lost in the urine, and the white cell and plasma vitamin C levels stabilize just in excess of scurvy (*Alabama Journal of Medical Science*, vol. 16, no. 3 1979). In addition, the two doctors reported that some scientists believe that 'supplements of vitamin C must be given several times a day to persons who take aspirin for several days or longer.'

Adults who decide not to take aspirin for a cold but still give it to their children (just to make sure) are making a big mistake. Big enough to be fatal. A study shows that children who have a cold (or other type of viral illness such as chicken pox) and take aspirin are more susceptible to Reye's syndrome a rare but sometimes deadly disease. As a result of this link between aspirin and Reye's syndrome, the governments of both Britain and the United States have forced the withdrawal of all paediatric ('junior') aspirin products.

Not only is aspirin bad for a cold, but it can also give you a particular type of cold – stuffy nose and hay fever. People allergic to aspirin may develop *rhinitis* (stuffy nose) in their 30s or 40s and, as time goes by, come down with a severe case of asthma. However, those with the problem may never even realize that they are allergic to aspirin. In one case, a doctor found out that a woman with chronic rhinitis took aspirin regularly and had her stop using the drug. One week later, her nose was almost clear (*Rhode Island Medical Journal*, March 1980).

Aspirin doesn't deliver a blow just to the nose. It can land a kidney punch too.

Other aspirin side-effects

In a study of patients with kidney failure, 20 per cent of the cases were caused by aspirin (or other painkillers such as paracetamol and phenacetin [now withdrawn in the UK]). In a few instances, people who had been kept alive by having their blood mechanically cleansed by a kidney machine could only stop using the machine if they stopped taking the OTC painkiller.

'This condition has been unrecognized and under-diagnosed by physicians,' wrote Drs Martin Goldberg and Thomas G. Murray in the *New England Journal of Medicine*. In a separate study, they noted that '85 percent of the patients are women above the age of 35 who have been taking analgesics [painkillers] for recurrent headache or backache.'

The doctors say that advice to stop taking painkillers fell on deaf ears in about 50 per cent of their patients. Perhaps the patients *were* deaf. A study of patients who took 'long-acting' aspirin tablets (which have very high dosages) showed that 28 per cent became deaf compared to less than 1 per cent of patients who took normal aspirin. All the deaf patients regained their hearing as soon as aspirin levels were reduced or discontinued (*Journal of Clinical Pharmacology*).

The people who most need to hear about the dangers of aspirin are pregnant women. Unfortunately, they often take aspirin as if it were good for them. Aspirin is the drug most frequently used during pregnancy: a study of pregnant women showed that 64 per cent used aspirin, and many took it regularly for as long as six weeks. The result of this regular use may be a highly irregular pregnancy – a longer one, with longer labour and more bleeding before and after delivery. Their babies also have a tough time of it. Children born to mothers who use aspirin during pregnancy weigh less and are more often stillborn or die shortly after birth. Perhaps worst of all, mothers who use aspirin during pregnancy may have a four times greater risk of having a baby with a certain type of birth defect.

The hazards of paracetamol

Fed up with aspirin's side-effects, many people turn to paracetamol, a pain reliever marketed under a variety of brand names and found in combination with other drugs in 200 products. However, said an editorial in the American Journal, the *Annals of Internal Medicine*, 'the increasing use and availability of acetaminophen [paracetamol] has turned up a darker side.' What's the black mark against paracetamol?

'Irreversible damage to the liver,' says Dr Harry Carloss, who works at the Scripps Clinic in La Jolla, California. Dr Carloss began studying paracetamol several years ago when a patient of his died from an overdose of an OTC painkiller that contained the drug.

'The woman had broken up with her boyfriend,' says Dr Carloss, 'and she took the drug as a suicidal gesture – not really to kill herself but to attract attention. However, she did die – of liver failure.'

In another case, a three-year old girl died when her family doctor prescribed a deadly dosage of a paracetamol syrup to treat the flu. 'The child's doctor was completely unaware of the effects of the drug on the liver,' says Dr Carloss. 'While it's not excusable for a doctor to be so totally unknowledgeable about a drug, it's understandable when you consider the number of new drugs on the market. That's why it's important to increase public awareness.'

Dr Carloss believes the lack of warnings about paracetamol could lead to more deaths. He points out that you could take a deadly amount of the drug by using recommended dosages of a combination of four OTC products containing paracetamol: cold tablets every four hours, a cough suppressant, sinus tablets and a syrup to help you fall asleep. Even if you take normal doses of one product, you could still be in trouble. A 59-year-old woman who took a paracetamol painkiller for one year developed severe liver damage. When she stopped taking the drug, her liver healed. 'The possibility that acetaminophen [paracetamol] . . . causes chronic subclinical injury ultimately ending up with clinical manifestations cannot be excluded,' wrote the doctors who reported the case (*Annals of Internal Medicine*).

In addition, a large dose of any drug containing paracetamol may be deadly if it is taken with alcohol, says a doctor at the Minneapolis Veterans Hospital. The doctor and two other researchers conducted animal studies on the drug and alcohol after a paracetamol-caused death of a chronic alcoholic who had been taking large doses of the drug to relieve pain. The study showed that the lethal dose of paracetamol for mice drinking alcohol was much lower than for mice that did not drink it. The doctor warned that phenobarbitone, a powerful drug used as a tranquilliser or sleeping aid, would have the same effect as alcohol, and that people who take phenobarbitone or drink a lot should never exceed recommended doses of any drug containing paracetamol.

Vitamin A destroyed

While paracetamol and aspirin pick on different parts of your body, they may share one side-effect – they both destroy vitamin A. Rats given daily doses of either paracetamol or aspirin for three weeks had lower levels of vitamin A in their blood than rats not given the drugs. 'Long-term effects of these drugs on vitamin A status . . . are not known,' said the researchers who conducted the study (*Federation of American Societies for Experimental Biology*). But who wants to be the guinea pig that finds out?

Alcohol and caffeine

Lurking in your bottle of medicine may be a stiff shot of alcohol. At least 500 medicinal products, including cough syrups, pain relievers and sedatives, contain up to 68 per cent alcohol. Most whisky, by way of comparison, contains only about 40 per cent. According to Dr John A. Newsom who presented these facts at an annual meeting of the California Medical Association, this creates a problem in caring for patients (*Internal Medicine News*, 15 May 1979).

People with disorders such as peptic ulcer, diabetes mellitus and obesity – and many who are pregnant – all commonly receive alcohol-containing drugs. So do alcoholics who are supposedly on the wagon or being rehabilitated. The results of the drug-alcohol cocktail include high blood-sugar levels followed by a sharp decline, central nervous system depression, and fluid and potassium loss.

Dr Newsom told us: 'Abstinent alcoholics need only small amounts of alcohol to trigger them back into an alcoholic state.' One ounce or more per day is a threat to the unborn babies of pregnant women. Drugs may rush through the system faster, become less effective or, in the case of aspirin, enhance bleeding when they interact with alcohol.

Alcohol in medication also promotes repetitive use of the product. 'Depending on how much and how frequently the medication is used, 10 per cent may become hooked on it,' says Dr Newsom.

A few organizations have requested that there be greater control over the amount of alcohol added to medications and that alcohol be identified more prominently on the label. However, even many doctors are unaware of the problem.

Why is alcohol added to medications in the first place? Drug companies find it to be a cheap and excellent solvent. Both the DHSS and the US Food and Drug Administration condone this and generally view alcohol in drugs as being inactive, meaning it has no use in treating the problem.

'Alcohol should be acknowledged as an active ingredient in medications, and labelling should warn of addictive potential and contra-indication for anyone suffering from alcoholism,' Dr Newsom says, since 'it looks like drug companies will continue to use alcohol in medications until they are pushed into developing a safe substitute.'

The danger to children

The parents of a 33-month-old girl found their daughter in a stupor outside the bathroom one morning, a partially empty bottle of mouthwash nearby. An ambulance rushed the child to the hospital, where casualty department attendants flushed saline solution into her stomach, warmed her with a heater, and continued the intravenous feeding begun by the ambulance personnel. The next day the child was well enough to go home.

This incident prompted doctors at the University of New Mexico and experts from the New Mexico Poison, Drug Information and Medical Crisis Center to take a closer look at mouthwashes. They published their findings in the journal *Pediatrics* (August 1980).

The researchers found that, during an 18-month period (January 1978 to June 1979), the National Poison Center Network in the United States had received reports of 422 cases of mouthwash ingestion in children under the age of six. The troublemaker in mouthwash is ethanol (a type of alcohol). *There is more ethanol in mouthwash than there is in wine and beer.* The New Mexico researchers found that the ethanol content of five leading mouthwashes ranged from a low of 14 per cent to a high of 26.9 per cent. However, one brand is 140 proof (*see* BAD BREATH).

Caffeine

You won't be surprised to hear that over-the-counter stimulants (as used by countless revising students) contain caffeine. After all, it is a common and generally safe pick-me-up. However, you might not expect to find it in painkillers, cold tablets, allergy pills or aids for period pain. But you will, and in amounts that approach, and sometimes surpass, a cup of coffee. Alone, that might not cause a problem, but added to the amounts of caffeine many people consume on an average day, it could make for a nervous day or a sleepless night.

Antacids

In an article in the *Journal of the American Medical Association* (5 December 1980), a group of doctors related a sad and baffling story. A female patient of theirs had developed osteomalacia – adult rickets. A bone in her leg had fractured; others were pitted with holes. Parts of her once-hard skeleton were little better than cotton wool. Blood tests also showed incredibly low levels of phosphorous – a mineral that keeps bones strong.

It turned out that she had been taking large daily doses of a non-prescription antacid for the past six months (and smaller amounts for the past 12 years). The antacid contained aluminium – and aluminium blocks the absorption of phosphorus. She was taken off antacids in the hospital and told not to take them once she went home. Her phosphorus levels quickly returned to normal, and within a month she could get out of a chair by herself and rarely used a walker. Three months later, she could walk perfectly, and her legs felt fine.

Pleased by this quick and simple cure, the doctors advised their colleagues to be aware 'of the potential complications of antacid therapy'. But not only doctors should be on the lookout for the side-effects of non-prescription antacids – those pills, liquids, powders and medicine-coated chewing gums that claim to relieve indigestion. You should, too.

Antacids whittle away your bones – even when you take the amount the label tells you to. That's what Dr Herta Spencer found out when she gave 11 people two tablespoons of an antacid three times a day and watched their mineral metabolism go haywire.

Normally, says Dr Spencer, the body uses most of the phosphorus in the diet except for 25 per cent that ends up in stool. But when 11 patients at the Veterans Administration Hospital in Hines, Illinois took the antacid – and remember, at the recommended dosage – their stools contained 75 per cent of all the phosphorus they ate. And phosphorus wasn't the only mineral the antacids detoured out of the body: the patients also absorbed up to 20 times less fluoride. Although that trace element is a poison in large quantities small amounts of it, says Dr Spencer, 'may be important for the maintenance of normal bone structure'. And, she adds, 'interference by aluminium-containing antacids with the absorption of fluoride may further contribute to the development of skeletal demineralization.' In other words, antacids are anti-bone.

And here is the straw that breaks the backbone. Antacids don't block the absorption of calcium, Dr Spencer has found, but they do shove some of the calcium already in the bones out of the body. Yet, what they leave behind may be even worse – aluminium.

The level of aluminium in the blood doubles when you take an aluminium-containing antacid. But that aluminium also parks itself in your organs including your brain – and it may snarl the chemical traffic that keeps your mind alert. Too much aluminium in the cells of the brain, some scientists believe, is a cause of senility (*Gastroenterology*, March 1979). Others claim that excessive aluminium might cause colon cancer, but even if it doesn't, there's no question that antacids mess up a normal colon, the last section of the intestines. 'Diarrhea or constipation is expected with any effective antacid,' said an article in the *Annals of Internal Medicine*. In a study of ulcer patients on antacids, 66 per cent had diarrhoea (*New England Journal of Medicine*).

Antacids may also set you up for traveller's diarrhoea. Two people travelling abroad with a group of others developed brucellosis (a type of bacterial infection) after all of them ate contaminated dairy products – and they were the only two who were taking antacids. The doctor who reported the cases said that brucellosis bacteria are usually tamed by stomach acid, but in this instance, there probably wasn't enough acid to do the trick. And, he pointed out, the low levels of stomach acid produced by antacids may also target a person for traveller's diarrhoea and other diarrhoea-causing bacterial infections that tourists sometimes pick up, such as amoebic dysentery and cholera (*Lancet*).

However, some tourists who take antacids won't have that problem. The product they use may *increase* stomach acid.

Acid rebound and kidney damage

One antacid ingredient (calcium carbonate) causes 'acid rebound'. The chemical – which does take the sting out of acid already in your stomach – also triggers the release of a hormone that tells the stomach to pump out more acid. The acid level falls at first, but bounces right back – and to a level higher than it was to start with.

(If you take calcium carbonate as a nutritional supplement, don't worry. Such supplements deliver, at the most, 1 g or so of calcium carbonate a day – and that level is completely safe. However, a day on antacids could give you 8 g or more of calcium carbonate. And it's at that high level, day after day, that trouble starts.)

And while your stomach is on a seesaw, your kidneys may be on a slide to poor health. A large dose of calcium carbonate can be rough on them too. It cuts down their blood flow, clogging delicate filters and tubes. The end result may be a very sick person: no appetite, cranky, tired, nauseated, perhaps dizzy and confused. In one case, a woman taking antacids – and no more than the label recommended – came down with those symptoms. Tests at the hospital showed that her kidneys were in bad shape, and she was taken off antacids. A week later, she was 'mentally normal', and a checkup four months later showed that her kidneys had healed (*Canadian Medical Association Journal*, 8 September 1979).

It's cases like this that make doctors say, 'In view of these hazards, we cannot recommend the use of calcium carbonate for routine antacid therapy' (*New England Journal of Medicine*). Yet plenty of antacids with this ingredient are still on the market.

. Two or three weeks on antacids containing sodium bicarbonate could also hurt your kidneys – and wreck a salt-restricted diet. Four tablets of one popular antacid with sodium bicarbonate contain over 1 g of sodium (salt) – too much for anyone on a salt-restricted diet. 'Patients on sodium-restricted diets often unwittingly ingest large quantities of sodium by taking non-prescription drugs,' said a report in *Modern Medicine* (15 February 1980). 'Because so many Americans are chronic antacid users, these drugs are a common source of sodium.'

One brand of antacid with a lot of sodium also contains aspirin – which is a cause of ulcers, the very problem that drives many people to antacids in the first place.

No help for heartburn

You might be wondering if antacids do you more harm than good. But some doctors think they don't do any good at all!

Heartburn patients who received either antacids or placebos (medically inactive pills) had no less pain when they took the antacids. In short, the antacids didn't work. In one part of this study, 18 patients were given either the antacid or the placebo for 30 consecutive episodes of pain, and their pain levels were measured every five minutes for the next 30 minutes. The difference in pain relief between the real and the fake drug? None (*Internal Medicine News*, 1 August 1979).

In another study of patients with a gastric (stomach) ulcer, 15 of whom took an antacid and 13 a placebo, doctors found that 'the rate of healing of the ulcer and the relief of pain is not influenced by treatment with a standard antacid preparation.' Again, the study showed that antacids don't work. But doctors think they do. 'All [doctors] prescribe antacids' for stomach ulcers, wrote the researchers who conducted the study (*Digestive Diseases*). Every last one of them is probably wrong.

They make the same mistake when they prescribe antacids for a duodenal ulcer (an ulcer in the first part of the intestines). 'Antacids are generally accepted as effective in the relief of pain arising from duodenal ulcer,' wrote a team of doctors who conducted a study to see if there was anything to this belief. There wasn't. Of the 30 patients with duodenal ulcer who took either an antacid or a placebo to relieve pain, four had relief from the antacid and three from the placebo, but 23 thought neither had worked (*Gastroenterology*).

In spite of all this evidence, some people might continue taking antacids. If they do, they should be very careful about what other drugs they take.

● Dr Spencer warns that antacids can worsen or even set off a bone disorder caused by corticosteroid drugs.

● Diuretic drugs (i.e. ones that increase urination) can be a problem. The woman with impaired kidney function was in particularly bad shape because she also took a diuretic.

● Antacids block the effect of tetracycline, an antibiotic.

● In addition, according to an editorial in the *British Medical Journal*, antacids change the acidity of the urine and may either increase or decrease the rate at which a drug is excreted – leaving you with either too little or too much.

Occasional use of antacids may not do you any harm, but frequent or daily use even for as little as two weeks, is chancy. Your health is the acid test – and antacids don't pass.

Cortisone

Doctors used to prescribe aspirin to relieve inflammation, but now, more often, it's cortisone. Why?

Cortisone works wonders. It can subdue inflammation in such serious ill-nesses as arthritis, hepatitis or lupus erythematosus (a degenerative disease of the connective tissues). It can knock out nettle rash or sunburn overnight. Twenty-five million prescriptions a year have been written for it in the United States alone, and now the US Food and Drug Administration *and* the British government think it's safe enough to be sold over the counter.

However, sometimes this synthetic adrenal hormone – one of a group of drugs called *corticosteroids* or, more commonly, *steroids* – does its job too well. By suppressing inflammation, it also suppresses a necessary step in the body's natural immune response. When misused, it can provoke side-effects as serious as stunted growth in children, depression or shrivelled-up adrenal glands. At its best, cortisone treats only the symptoms of a disease rarely the cause.

At some point in your life, you or a member of your family will probably be advised to use cortisone. Therefore, it's a good idea to know what side-effects to expect from cortisone use and to know a few nutritional ways to deal with them.

Impairment of wound healing is one side-effect of cortisone that has been recognized for many years. The exact mechanism isn't known, but a surgeon at the University of California School of Medicine in San Francisco, Thomas K. Hunt, has speculated that inflammation serves as a kind of physiological alarm system, which cortisone somehow 'switches off'. However, Dr Hunt has been able to switch the alarm back on with topical applications of vitamin A.

He treated an 18-year-old girl who was receiving prednisone, a cortisone-like drug, for lupus erythematosus, and a five-year-old girl who was receiving the same drug to suppress an immune reaction during a kidney transplant operation. Both developed skin ulcers that failed to heal. However, Dr Hunt found that their wounds would heal at a normal rate if he applied vitamin A ointment (200,000 IU per ounce). The vitamin A treatment worked in spite of the cortisone therapy (*Annals of Surgery*).

Other adverse effects

Researchers at the University of Louisville School of Medicine in Kentucky have shown that cortisone therapy can create other problems as well. Dr Hiram C. Polk, Jr. confirmed previous experiments which showed that some types of steroid therapy can depress the ability of certain white blood cells to rush to the scene of an infection and begin killing bacteria and swallowing up debris around a wound (*Journal of Surgical Research*).

Other researchers report that cortisone and cortisone-like drugs interfere with the body's attempts to form collagen, the fibrous protein that is a necessary building block for bones, skin and connective tissue. This can be particularly dangerous for children. According to a report from Greece, eight children, aged 9 to 14, suffered a diminished rate of collagen formation and a diminished rate of growth while receiving steroid therapy for rheumatic fever and kidney disease (*Archives of Disease in Childhood*).

In a dramatic example of this problem, a 13-year-old boy in Boston Massachusetts suffered permanent retardation of height as a result of prolonged use of steroids for relief of eczema on his entire body since the age of 18 months. 'The growth-suppressing effect of glucocorticoid ointment which led in this case to permanent short stature,' wrote Hans Bode who treated the boy at the Shriners Burns Institute in Boston, 'is an additional reason for avoiding prolonged treatment with glucocorticoid ointments' (*Journal of the American Medical Association*, 22 August 1980).

Still another serious side-effect of long-term cortisone therapy is depression. 'Episodes of depression are not an uncommon complication of therapy with cortisone and ACTH [adrenocorticotropic hormone],' according to a group of Italian doctors. In treating a five-year-old girl for chronic hepatitis, they noticed that, during her first week of ACTH therapy, she appeared depressed and became less sociable. By the second week of therapy she was noticeably uncommunicative and had periods of crying (*Pediatrics*, April 1980).

Fortunately, these side-effects – depressed immune response, impaired collagen formation, depression – have responded to high doses of vitamin C. Dr Polk in Louisville found that the vitamin reversed cortisone's effect on the immune response and restored the ability of white blood cells to kill bacteria. In Athens, vitamin C brought the rate of collagen formation back to normal in children on steroid therapy. And in Italy, vitamin C given intravenously neutralized the steroid's impact on the five-year-old's mood.

Besides the side-effects already mentioned, more problems associated with long-term use of cortisone can be found in reference texts on prescription drugs. For instance, cortisone or related drugs are not advised for pregnant or nursing women or for anyone over 60 years old. In older people, even small doses of cortisone over long periods of time 'can increase the severity of diabetes, enhance fluid retention, raise the blood pressure, weaken resistance to infection, induce stomach ulcer and accelerate the development of cataract and softening of the bones' (*The Essential Guide to Prescription Drugs*, 1980).

For reasons like these, some doctors fear that members of the public might misuse even the mild cortisone preparations that can now be sold over the counter in the United States (and is now available in Britain). 'I'm really surprised the FDA passed it,' says Dr Hunt. 'It can soften your skin so much that you wouldn't be able to shovel snow without blistering.' In Boston, Dr Bode warns that overuse of steroid ointment on the skin can cause *striae*, or stretch marks.

A California dermatologist has also spoken out against the legalization of OTC cortisone. Victor D. Newcomer fears that mothers might use the ointment on nappy rash instead of putting on clean nappies, or that someone might use it to quell the symptoms of ringworm, without killing the infection. 'Some of my patients use a tube a day,' Dr Newcomer said. 'They get the idea that if some is good, more is better' (*Medical World News*, 4 February 1980).

'We're going to regret these preparations,' says Dr Emanuel Cheraskin of the University of Alabama. 'History repeats itself for those who don't read it. There are millions of people who take aspirin for headaches, but not one of them is suffering from an aspirin deficiency,' he says, implying that cortisone merely masks a problem and never gives the body what it needs to heal itself.

That concern is echoed by Dr Hunt in California. 'The corticosteroids can make a wound feel better, but at the expense of the healing process,' he says. 'Wounds should get red, they should itch and sting a little. If they don't you may not be healing properly.'

Cold and cough medicines

It happens occasionally to even the most dedicated vitamin C-taker. Your nose gets stuffy, your head aches, your throat gets scratchy, you ache all over – a cold. What to do? Well, one drug manufacturer offers some partially good advice – rest, keep warm, drink liquids. But what you probably shouldn't do is reach for a commercial cold remedy.

When most people have a cough, they head for the nearest chemist and buy one of the many cough syrups, drops or capsules that are available without a prescription. In 1980, according to the US Food and Drug Administration, Americans coughed up more than $1 billion for over-the-counter cough medications that claim to stop a cough outright or help clear the lungs of mucus.

Was that money well spent? Probably not. Since 1972, the FDA has been studying the effectiveness of cough medications, along with other non-prescription drugs, and has found that many don't live up to their advertised promises. Doctors often agree. One told us that OTC cough medicines 'aren't worth a darn, not any of them', and others say that natural remedies are safer, cost less and work just as well.

Dr Sidney M. Wolfe runs the Public Citizen's Health Research Group (a Washington, D.C., consumer activist group that has sued the FDA to make that agency take ineffective drugs off the market faster) and he has also co-authored a book, *Pills That Don't Work* (1980). Based on research by Dr Wolfe and others, the following is a brief rundown of common cough-syrup ingredients, along with facts about their doubtful usefulness.

Expectorants Manufacturers contend that these drugs increase the watery excretions produced by cells in the upper respiratory tract. Theoretically, those secretions loosen mucus and phlegm, making them easier to cough up and out of the lungs. But they often don't work as advertised.

'Expectorants are alleged to stimulate the flow of bronchial secretions,' says one medical bulletin. 'While there is no sound evidence to support this theory, these agents [terpin hydrate, ammonium chloride, guaiphenesin, etc.] are widely used' (*Harvard Medical School Health Letter*).

The FDA decided in 1976 that guaiphenesin, which has been used in cough syrups since at least 1905 (and is an ingredient in such British OTC cough medicines as Dimotone, Linctifed and Lotussin and the *only* ingredient in Robitussin) probably doesn't work. However, so far, products containing this ingredient remain on the market in the US, pending the outcome of lawsuits and laboratory tests.

While the expectorants probably don't work, that doesn't mean they're harmless. Large doses of aluminium chloride, for example, can upset the body's acid – base balance. Syrup of ipecac may be toxic to young children and possibly adults, and terpin hydrate may cause nausea and vomiting.

Even if expectorants did work, some cough medications don't contain enough. For example, one popular bedtime cough remedy, which is 25 per cent alcohol – 50 proof – contains only about one-third the amount of expectorant said to be needed for effectiveness.

Suppressants This group of medications tranquillizes or deactivates the part of the brain that controls the cough reflex. They shouldn't be used by anyone who has a 'productive' cough – i.e. one that's doing its job in bringing up phlegm from the lungs.

'While it is tempting to interfere with Mother Nature's attempt to "raise phlegm", it is generally unwise to do so,' says the *Harvard Medical School Health Letter*. 'Such action will often prolong the siege and at worst may lead to serious breathing difficulties.'

Suppressants shouldn't be given to people with coughs due to asthma or chronic bronchitis, the *Health Letter* also points out. They rely on coughing to clear their lungs, and 'giving large amounts of cough suppressants to such persons might lead to life-threatening results.'

Antihistamines Dr Wolfe maintains that antihistamines thicken fluids in the lungs and make them more difficult to cough up – the opposite of the desired effect. He also points out that many popular cough syrups (Benafed, Benylin and Lotussin in the UK) contain the antihistamine *diphenhydramine*, despite the fact that diphenhydramine hasn't been shown to stop coughs.

People who are kept awake at night with a cough due to post-nasal drip sometimes use this kind of medication to dry their natural secretions, but that can be harmful. Dr Wolfe says that antihistamines are appropriate only for allergies. (*See also* 'Antihistamines' *below*.)

Decongestants These drugs are not useful to anyone with a cough wrote Brent Q. Hafen in his book *The Self-Health Handbook* (1980). People with high blood pressure, diabetes, and heart or thyroid disease must avoid decongestants for health reasons, according to Dr Hafen, and most everyone else should do the same.

> Unless you are suffering from severe stuffiness and inability to breathe you might be better off staying away from decongestants: they serve to dry up secretions and remove water from the system – exactly the opposite of what you need, which is to moisten and loosen the membranes. (*See also* 'Nasal sprays' *below*.)

Multi-ingredient cough medicines 'Avoid the expensive, potentially harmful and essentially ineffective "shotgun" cough-and-cold combinations,' wrote Dr Wolfe. These drugs, usually called 'cold capsules', sometimes have conflicting effects on a cough.

> The various components [of a multi-ingredient medicine] may interact with one another to enhance toxicity, inhibit effectiveness or simply expose the consumer to extra unwanted side-effects, often with no additional benefit.

Cough drops and syrups   The American Dental Association points out that sugar is a hidden ingredient in many non-prescription drugs and that 'some of the worst offenders are sugar-laden cough drops and throat lozenges.' This 'medicinal candy', dentists say, causes dental decay, especially when people carry boxes of 'fruit-flavoured cough drops, which attack their teeth all day long'. Cough syrups are damaging, too, because 'their coating action not only soothes a cough but bathes the teeth in sugar long enough to trigger dental decay' (*American Pharmacy*, October 1979).

If you're shopping for cough syrups or drops, you'll find that they aren't equally sweet. One type of American cough drop is 69 per cent sugar, while another has no sugar. One company manufactures cough drops that contain 66.2 22.0, 3.2, 2.5 and 0 per cent sugar. The sweetest cough syrup available contains 44 per cent sugar, but others contain none.

If, despite the uncertainties, you do go shopping for an OTC cough remedy, it might be a good idea to get some expert advice. Barbara Korberly of the Philadelphia College of Pharmacy and Science told us that chemists can't diagnose your problem, but they can give you valuable information about each medicine. 'People should go to their pharmacists and ask, "What can I do for my cough?" The pharmacist may ask them, "What is it that brings you here now? What is your major symptom?" '

A chemist will often be able to recommend a remedy that will minimize symptoms, will cause the fewest side-effects and will not conflict with the consumer's other medications or conditions, Dr Korberly says.

At any rate, most normal, uncomplicated coughing, as one British authority put it, is a 'necessary evil' and resolves by itself. And Dr Wolfe says 'Coughing, especially if you are coughing something up, is a healthy way to clear your respiratory tract. If a cough lasts more than a week or if you are having difficulty breathing . . . consult a doctor.'

Nasal sprays

It seems odd that you could become addicted to nasal sprays, but, sadly it's all too common. 'There's a fancy name for this,' explains James H. Heroy assistant professor of oto-laryngology at Johns Hopkins University School of Medicine in Maryland: *'rhinitis medicamentosa'*.

The pattern for contracting the habit is similar in most cases. A person comes down with a stuffy nose for one reason or another – perhaps due to a cold trauma, broken nose, sinusitis or allergy. That's when the person decides to use a decongestant.

'What we're talking about now are the nose sprays and drops,' points out Dr Heroy. 'Oral decongestants [those taken by mouth] don't have the property that would cause an addiction. Sprays and drops work beautifully for a while. However, virtually all these products, which are topical treatments, irritate the mucosa [membranes lining the nose and respiratory system]. After the spray wears off, the mucosa experiences what we call a "rebound effect" and actually gets worse than it was before. Then the person sprays again to keep the nose decongested, but there's that rebound effect to deal with. You get to the point where the spray works for shorter and shorter periods of time. Then you wind up with people who go to the drugstore, buy five sprays and use them all up in the course of a day. At this point it has become a physical addiction – they'll be spraying every 20 minutes or so!'

Jeremy H. Thompson is a professor of pharmacology at UCLA Medical Center. He explains that decongestants work by decreasing the size of blood vessels inside the nose. By thus decreasing the flow of blood, the swelling of the mucosa decreases, as does the amount of nasal secretions.

'The active ingredient that accomplishes this,' says Dr Thompson, 'is called a *sympathomimetic*. Ephedrine is one commonly used. Sometimes a spray includes two different things: a decongestant and an antihistamine. The latter is used to reduce an allergic reaction. Unlike decongestants, antihistamines are not responsible for rebound.'

How much is too much?

Just how long does it take before a person runs the risk of addiction? 'Once you get past a week of continuous use, you're tempting fate,' says William R. Wilson, associate surgeon in oto-laryngology at the Massachusetts Eye and Ear Infirmary in Boston. 'The problem we're talking about is a common one.'

The outcome of nasal spray or drop overuse is an indefinitely congested runny nose caused not by the cold or sinusitis, but by the decongestant itself. Other side-effects include soreness, irritation and – if the spray includes ingredients such as ephedrine – rapid heart rate, sweating, nervousness and tremors. In addition, Dr Heroy describes patients he's seen who eventually end up with a small hole burned through the septum, the inner wall that divides the nostrils.

'I haven't found a brand that doesn't cause a rebound effect,' says Richard Jackson, research director of ear, nose and throat diseases at Emory University School of Medicine in Atlanta, Georgia. 'The problem is in the concentration of the active ingredients. The feeling in the medical community is that the long-acting ones (such as 12-hour sprays) aren't as intense. They could cause a rebound effect but not as quickly as the shorter-acting ones that are used more often.'

The reason? The concentration of the active ingredient is spread out over longer periods of time. Dosages are not shotgunned into work as rapidly.

While the drug companies admit to an awareness of the problem, they feel there isn't much that can be done to prevent addiction other than what they're already doing. And that, basically, refers to the label directions on each bottle.

'People can overuse sprays and drops,' explains Norma Walter, assistant director of communications for Sterling Drug. 'But everything overused can harm you – even water.' Art Cooney, director of communication services at Bristol-Myers, is more direct: 'There's a presumption of absolute safety in over-the-counter drugs that there ought not to be. We've run some ads in newspapers across the country telling people this, but there is no campaign in the world that will get everyone to follow directions. The thing to do,' he concludes, 'is to always read the label.'

But a look at many decongestant labels would leave the consumer in a mist as to the length of time a product can be safely used. For example, while one brand of nose drops may inform the consumer not to use them for more than three days, other brands may make no mention on the bottle as to how long is long enough. In fact, the wording, 'May be repeated every three [or four] hours as needed,' as it appears on many labels, seems to indicate that the product can be used safely for an indefinite period of time. That, of course is not true.

Finally, what is the cure for decongestant addiction?

'The treatment is either to go cold turkey,' explains Dr Heroy, 'and stop use altogether, with all the problems of withdrawal, or to use steroids to ease inflammation during the cold-turkey period. I tell my patients not to use sprays or drops more than three or four days.'

In about two weeks the rebound effect should subside. 'But often,' points out Dr Wilson, 'people are unable to tolerate those two weeks, and revert back to using the nasal spray.'

The things to remember about nasal decongestants are that overuse causes a physical addiction, not a psychological one, and that just because they're easy to obtain doesn't mean that they're not potentially harmful.

Herbal relief for nasal congestion

If you have a stuffed-up nose, you don't have to choose between nasal-spray addiction and misery. There are natural remedies for nasal congestion, and they don't hook you on anything but health.

For instance, there's a long tradition of loosening and expelling mucus with herbs and spices that act as expectorants. Garlic is perhaps the best. In one experiment, a researcher gave a specially concocted mixture of garlic oil and water to over 70 people with a clogged or runny nose. In every case congestion cleared up within 20 minutes.

Eating garlic should have much the same effect, and the most nose-clearing way to get it into your diet may be as a spice in hot soup. Hot soup, a study has shown, speeds up the flow of mucus out of the nose. Adding other 'fiery' spices and herbs to the soup, such as cayenne pepper, horseradish and onion will probably hasten relief.

Not only hot soup, but hot liquids of all kinds help unclog the nose. Drink plenty of hot herbal expectorant tea. Among the expectorants are fenugreek anise, sage and maidenhair.

You can also use the herb eucalyptus, but not as a tea. Instead, put eucalyptus leaves in a large pot of boiling water for about five minutes. Then turn off the heat and, with a towel draped over your head, lean over the pot and breathe in the herbal vapours.

Nutritional supplements, in the form of vitamins A and C may also help.

Antihistamines

Even though antihistamines don't cause problems when they are ingredients in nasal sprays, they aren't completely innocuous.

If you've been taking antihistamines for any length of time to combat a stubborn sinus infection, you may be all too well aware of one negative side-effect – a noticeable voice change. Antihistamines, explains Frank B. Wilson dean of the faculty of rehabilitation medicine at the University of Alberta at Edmonton, are 'mucosal drying agents'. (Also included in this class of chemicals are mood-elevating anti-depressants.)

'The drugs dry out the vocal cords, which need a great deal of lubrication,' Dr Wilson told us. 'The voice then tends to become breathy, and it goes down in pitch as the vocal cords become inflamed.'

Fortunately, the inflammation of the vocal cords is not permanent, and the voice 'tends to come back within six months', after drug use is ended.

A tranquillizer-like ingredient in antihistamines may also cause a tic tremor or twitch. An article in the *New England Journal of Medicine* described a woman who used antihistamines regularly and developed twitches and tremors in her face. When she stopped using the medication, her condition improved.

Skin-care preparations

'Sometimes I think over-the-counter medications help keep me in business,' Nia Terezakis told us. Dr Terezakis is on the dermatology faculties of both Louisiana State and Tulane University Schools of Medicine and is also a busy New Orleans clinician. She is a strong advocate of 'simple, inexpensive treatments' and, sometimes, 'no treatments at all for common skin problems'. 'Bland is best' in her eyes, largely because of the possibility that OTC preparations will lead to secondary irritation and allergy. Writing in *Postgraduate Medicine* (June 1980), she said:

> Some of the most popular and most highly advertised commercial skin-care products are the greatest culprits as far as skin diseases are concerned. Products that would be perfectly safe on most normal skins can cause problems on diseased skin that are too numerous to list.

In the case of an infant with nappy rash, or anyone else with inflamed skin, special care must be taken in choosing which medication to apply. Certain OTC creams and even some that are prescribed by a family doctor may contain 'sensitizers' that may initiate an allergy the person will have for the rest of his or her life.

According to the *Monthly Index of Medical Specialities (MIMS)*, a monthly journal sent to all family doctors in the UK, which lists all prescription drugs and their ingredients, the following are the 'known sensitizing agents' (January 1987): beeswax (white and yellow), butylated hydroxyanisole, chlorocresol, clioquinol, EDTA (and salts), ethylenediamine hydroxybenzoates (parabens), lanolin and/or derivatives, neomycin (0.25 – 0.5 per cent), propylene glycol, sorbic acid.

Drugs for cardiovascular diseases

A drug prescribed by your doctor for an illness has most likely been carefully chosen to cure whatever ails you. However, many drugs do have side-effects, at least for some people, and many doctors are reluctant to warn about them in advance for fear of triggering a psychosomatic reaction. Nevertheless, drug reactions are *real*, and can range from the mildly unpleasant to the downright deadly, so it's up to you to ask about potential problems before you start taking any medication. Even if it's for heart disease, the number one killer in the United Kingdom. Today, doctors can choose between surgical or drug treatment for many kinds of cardiovascular (i.e. heart and blood vessel) problems. Unfortunately, surgery often doesn't really 'cure' the disease, while the drugs given for the various ills that usually accompany heart disease – such as high cholesterol levels, hypertension (high blood pressure) and a tendency to form blood clots – can have serious side-effects.

Cholesterol-lowering drugs

The search for substances capable of depressing cholesterol levels in the blood is one of the most pressing in ongoing medical research. Cholesterol concentration (or, to be more precise, the level of low-density-lipoprotein [LDL] cholesterol) constitutes an important risk factor for damage of blood vessel walls by atherosclerosis (clogging of the arteries by fatty deposits) which may bring about a heart attack or stroke.

Pharmaceutical companies have developed several drugs that depress blood cholesterol levels in experimental animals and also in humans. The substance most employed has been *ethylester of chlorphenoxyisobutyric acid* (clofibrate is its generic name; Atromid-S is the clofibrate product most frequently prescribed) because short-term tests revealed no serious adverse side-effects from its use. To be effective, this drug must be taken indefinitely and in rather high doses.

However, extensive surveys, lasting several years, carried out in both the United States and Europe and involving several thousand people, have shown clofibrate to be less effective in depressing blood cholesterol than had originally been claimed. In addition, when used continually, this drug has several negative side-effects, the most evident of which is the formation of gallstones. The European study even showed the overall death rate in persons on a long-term clofibrate regimen to be significantly higher than for those not taking the drug.

The chemical structure of the majority of other drugs with a cholesterol-depressing action indicates that their regular use also raises the possibility of adverse side-effects.

High-blood pressure drugs

Three drug companies manufacture it. Thousands of people in Britain take it. And, says the US government's National Cancer Institute in a report issued in 1980, it causes cancer in laboratory animals.

The drug is *reserpine*, and it's for high blood pressure. Cancer would just be another notch on its belt: reserpine has already been linked to such serious side-effects as depression, disturbed heart rhythms, angina, glaucoma – even impotence. And other drugs that treat high blood pressure (called *hypotensive* or *anti-hypertensive drugs*) have just as many potential dangers, their side-effects including arthritis, liver disease diabetes, heart failure and senility. No wonder over half the people who receive a prescription for a hypotensive drug don't take it regularly.

Hypotensive drugs were first introduced during the early 1950s, with hardly any testing as to their safety, says Dr Solk Robinson, of Michigan City Indiana.

In the early 1970s, he realized that thiazides, – diuretics used to control high blood pressure – might cause heart attacks, and he published that finding in the *Journal of American Pharmacology*. However, says Dr Robinson, most hypotensive drugs, including thiazides, are still on the market – and still doing their dirty work. He estimates that of the 15 million people in the United States who will take hypotensive drugs within the next five years, 100,000 may be killed by the drug rather than by the disease. And, he points out, many of those deaths will be improperly reported, since a death by a stroke or a heart attack is usually attributed to natural causes and seldom to the side-effects of drugs.

Digoxin

One drug often singled out by experts as a cause of reversible senility among other problems, is digoxin (brand name: Lanoxin), a drug often prescribed for heart patients. 'The danger of giving digitalis [digoxin] to the elderly has received much attention in the past 20 years,' says a report in the *Journal of Clinical Pharmacology* (November–December 1979).

The article goes on to describe four elderly people who suffered from 'digitalis intoxication'. One woman, who 'before admission lived independently without mental impairment or depression, appeared depressed and lost her capacity for self-care' after one week on digoxin. After three weeks on the drug, 'she was severely depressed, unmotivated and at times lethargic. She stated, "I have given up." '

Another woman was 'alert and cooperative' but became 'anxious and restless' after two weeks on digoxin. After doctors took her off the drug, however, 'she appeared relaxed and was resting comfortably.' In the next few days, 'her mental status' returned to normal.

Sleeping pills, tranquillizers and anti-depressants

Sleeping pills promise you sweet dreams. But they can break that promise – and your bones, too.

Two British doctors studied elderly patients with broken thigh bones at a hospital in Nottingham. They divided them into three groups according to the time the break occurred: morning, afternoon or night. It turned out that 93 per cent of those who had broken their thigh bones during the night were taking barbiturates (drugs often used as sleeping pills), but only 6 per cent of those who had broken their bones in the morning – and no one who had suffered a broken thigh bone in the afternoon – were on barbiturates. 'This striking association strongly suggests that barbiturate use is a major factor in producing nocturnal [night-time] falls resulting in femoral [thigh bone] fracture,' asserted J.B. MacDonald and E.T. MacDonald in the *British Medical Journal*.

These elderly people fell because barbiturates deliver a one–two punch to the nervous system: they loosen up muscles and slow down breathing. Waking up sluggish, dizzy and unsteady – punch-drunk on drugs – they got up out of bed and went down for a longer count than ten. But it probably wasn't their first fall. Dr MacDonald pointed out that barbiturates make the mind clumsy, too: 'Barbiturates commonly cause . . . confusion in old people, which is reversible when the drugs are withdrawn.'

Sounds like most doctors would hurry up and 'withdraw' barbiturates, right? Wrong. Despite a campaign in Britain to cut down the amount of barbiturate use, Dr MacDonald discovered that over 50 per cent of the people referred to the geriatric outpatients' service in Nottingham in the year of his study were on barbiturates – a more than 10 per cent increase from three years earlier – and an incredible 92 per cent of those outpatients were taking sleeping pills of some kind or another.

Is it the cold, damp weather that's driving Britain's elderly to drugs? Is too much tea keeping them awake? Maybe. But one thing we know that's keeping them – and millions of others – from getting a good night's sleep is sleeping pills.

In Britain, one woman in every four habitually takes either a prescribed sleeping pill or an over-the-counter preparation. But insomniacs should swear at, not by, their sleeping pills. They would only be joining the crowd: sleeping pills have already been damned by scientific researchers in study after study for, among other things, causing insomnia.

An editorial in the *Journal of the American Medical Association* summed up these studies with a sweeping condemnation of sleeping pills. Their use the editorial asserted, 'does not get the patient to sleep any faster but rather increases nightly awakenings, abolishes deep sleep and continues to affect sleep patterns for five weeks after drug withdrawal.'

One study cited in the editorial was carried out by a team of researchers at the Sleep Research and Treatment Facility of Pennsylvania State University. Over a period of three nights, the researchers compared the sleeping patterns of ten insomniacs who were long-term users of sleeping pills to insomniacs who did not take them. To their surprise, they discovered that sleeping pills were not a ticket to dreamland but a roadblock:

> A striking finding was the fact that all these patients had as great or greater difficulty in falling or staying asleep, or both, than the insomniac controls who were not using medication.

They also found that pill-taking insomniacs had less 'rapid eye movement (REM) sleep', the part of sleep associated with dreaming, when sleepers' eyes dart back and forth, up and down as if they were actually watching their dreams.

In other, longer studies, the doctors noted that, when patients who had used sleeping pills for a long time suddenly stopped taking them, they experienced a 'marked increase' in REM sleep. But not only were their dreams more frequent, they were also more intense, sometimes nightmarish. They also had severe insomnia, and when they did fall asleep, it was 'frequently fragmented and disrupted'.

Sleeping pills can 'fragment' more than your sleep. Your whole life could go to pieces, ripped apart by drug addiction.

A sleeping pill, says an editorial in the *Lancet*,

> has the effect of hampering natural sleep when the drug is stopped – indeed, anxiety may be increased. The consequent insomnia, restless-

ness and nightmares lead to a request for repetition of the prescription, and dependence is thus established.

But what makes sleeping pills really dangerous is that they do work – for about two weeks. Testing five popular prescription sleeping pills, the researchers at Penn State found that four of them were 'initially effective in inducing or maintaining sleep' but 'showed a marked decrease in effectiveness . . . by the second week . . . 'The loss of effectiveness,' reported the researchers, 'may frequently lead to the use of multiple doses' of sleeping pills.

But with sleeping pills, more is not merrier, especially if the sleeping pills your doctor prescribed were barbiturates.

Remember them? The cripplers. And killers.

'Barbiturates are the drugs most often used in suicide attempts and in successful suicides both in the United States and elsewhere,' said a *New England Journal of Medicine* editorial.

Of the 38 million prescriptions for sleeping pills given out by doctors in the United States every year, 10 million are for barbiturates. How many of those 'suicides' were people who – without consulting their doctors – had gradually increased their intake of sleeping pills until they ended up sleeping a lot more deeply than they had planned?

The demand for valium

Sleeping pills are not the only drugs that kill. A lot of people who take tranquillizers are dead – on their feet. And a lot of people do take tranquillizers.

The most widely prescribed drug in the United States and the United Kingdom is the tranquillizer Valium. In the US, doctors scribble out over 30 million prescriptions for it a year in the hope of satisfying the endless stream of people who flood their offices demanding fast, fast relief from the slow burn of daily tension. And 15 per cent of American adults – 20 million people – use, if not Valium, a sedative or tranquillizer of some kind.

Many doctors believe that tranquillizers are a safe, valid answer to emotional stress. However, most people outside the medical profession take the commonsense view that tranquillizers don't really cure anything and may even prevent people from working out their problems (*American Journal of Psychiatry*). That's our opinion, too.

Tranquillizers put a chemical cushion between you and reality, but that cushion is no guarantee of a soft life. That cushion smothers, choking you in apathy and a false sense of well-being. But there's another reason not to take tranquillizers, a physical reason.

In a letter to the *Journal of the American Medical Association*, Dr David Haskell of the Boston University School of Medicine remarked:

> I have seen several patients experiencing barbiturate-type withdrawal symptoms after four to six months of diazepam [Valium] therapy doses as low as 15 mg per day. Symptoms such as tremors, agitation, fearfulness, stomach cramps and sweating made patients extremely uncomfortable.

What Dr Haskell was talking about is not merely psychological but physical addiction to a drug used almost casually by millions of people. While the media scream about a heroin epidemic in the inner cities, tranquillizers are quietly hooking millions in the suburbs. The comparison with heroin is not farfetched. According to the US government's latest report on drug overdoses Valium is the number-one abused drug across the United States, right up there with heroin – and alcohol.

Valium's likeness to alcohol goes beyond sharing top spot on the hit-up parade. Like alcohol, Valium 'reduces alertness, judgment and physical co-ordination to the degree that could render it unsafe . . . [for the patient] to drive a car or operate dangerous physical machinery,' said an editorial in the *Canadian Medical Association Journal*.

For instance:

• Forty elderly men who took Valium had an 'increase in fatigue and decreases in memory and motor function' (*Journal of the American Geriatrics Society*).

• Another study showed that, after only one week of taking Valium, people read more slowly and were highly inattentive. But what was really frightening was that they were not aware of any change in their reading habits. A summary of the study in *New Scientist* concluded: '. . . Valium users may not be very good at assessing their ability to function efficiently when taking the drug.' Just like a drunk who thinks he's Mario Andretti but whose finishing line is a telephone pole.

• A British study showed that drivers who use Valium or other so-called 'minor' tranquillizers are five times more likely to have a car accident than people not taking a tranquillizer (*British Medical Journal*, 7 April 1979).

Valium is also widely prescribed for back problems because it is a swift and sure muscle relaxant, but some physical therapists feel it is overprescribed and can hinder therapy in some cases. 'We call it the "I don't give a damn" drug,' one says. 'It always makes patients want to do more verbally than physically. They say, "I'm going to exercise," but they lack the motivation.'

According to the *Medical Letter*, a well-respected professional publication that allows no drug-company advertising, 'there is no convincing evidence that Valium is superior to aspirin or a placebo in relieving the pain of reflex muscle spasm associated with trauma or inflammation.' The drug is also known to reduce muscle tone in patients with motor disorders. The side-effects include drowsiness, fatigue, habit formation and adverse reactions when mixed with alcohol.

But tranquillizers may have another, more serious side-effect: brain damage. Sixty-six heavy users of sedatives were subjected to in-depth tests of their brain functions after three weeks of being off drugs. Forty-five per cent of them were found to be 'mildly to moderately impaired' (*Science News*).

With these facts, how can a doctor conscientiously send away an anxious tense patient with a prescription for Valium? However, just that scene is being played out in doctors' surgeries – over and over again. One 'patient' who is almost always anxious is a woman in labour. Before delivery, it is not unknown for doctors to dose mothers-to-be with Valium or Librium, another popular tranquillizer, but the mother is taking tranquillizers for two.

Writing to the *New England Journal of Medicine*, Dr John W. Scanlon warned that giving Valium to women in labour may actually cause depression in the newborn! He also cautions that Valium may lower a newborn's body temperature and negatively affect his or her respiratory system, heart and blood. 'Caution must be observed about the questionable use of such potent and ubiquitous drugs for both routine and "high-risk" obstetric deliveries,' he asserted.

Anti-depressants

When you consider that twice as many women as men take tranquillizers and that their use has skyrocketed in the past decade, well, it's enough to make you a trifle depressed. But if you do feel depressed, think twice before telling a doctor. He might prescribe a drug that can be just as dangerous as a tranquillizer: an anti-depressant.

Millions of prescriptions are written every year for anti-depressants. Powerful drugs, many of them frequently cause side-effects such as dizziness insomnia, restlessness, nausea, constipation and drowsiness. One type, the *tricyclics*, sometimes produces a particularly dramatic side-effect: sudden death. In a letter to the *Journal of the American College of Emergency Physicians*, Lester Haddad detailed a 'marked increase' in the number of people admitted to his hospital's casualty department because they had taken an overdose of tricyclics. Of 30 such cases, six people were in comas. Tricyclics, he cautions, 'have a thin margin of safety'.

'Thin' may be an overstatement. Tricyclics may be downright unsafe.

'Although initially thought to be innocuous, tricyclic anti-depressants have earned a growing reputation for their sometimes noxious effects on the cardiovascular system,' warned a psychiatric team writing in the *Mayo Clinic Proceedings*. They measured the effects of tricyclics on 19 depressed patients. Although four of them had no problems with the drug, '5 had mild symptoms of slight dizziness on standing, 8 had moderate symptoms of being lightheaded or dizzy while walking, and 2 had severe symptoms, being unable to walk.'

The patients were dizzy because the drug made their blood pressure plummet to dangerously low levels. Warning that tricyclics are especially risky for older people with heart disease, the team added: 'The magnitude of the decreases in blood pressure in the patients observed is also alarming.'

Another drug sometimes used to combat depression (but more common in the treatment of schizophrenia) is thioridazine (brand name Melleril). Medically termed a 'major tranquillizer', thioridazine does not lower blood pressure. It lowers sex drive. According to a team of researchers writing in the *American Journal of Psychiatry*:

> Various . . . forms of sexual dysfunction, including diminished sexual interest, difficulty achieving and maintaining erection, and inability to achieve orgasm, have been associated with most if not all of the major tranquillizers, including thioridazine.

Polling 57 male patients who had taken thioridazine, the authors found 'a 60 percent incidence of difficulties in sexual function' – and this in an anti-depressant. Talk about counterproductive!

Compounding all these problems is overprescribing. A recent study by the Californian state government has revealed a widespread misuse of major tranquillizers and anti-depressants – so much so that doctors are having difficulty telling honest-to-goodness psychiatric symptoms from drug side-effects!

In some cases, researchers found that the drugs themselves were probably causing the very problem they were supposed to treat. At other times different drugs cancelled out each other's effects. Some patients were receiving several drugs that had different brand names – but were chemically identical! One patient was being treated with 21 different drugs. A 19-year-old girl was receiving 13 drugs – seven of them sedatives.

But the problem of overprescribing is worst among a group that society considers over the hill: people in nursing homes. A US governmental conference on 'Drug Use and the Elderly' reported a study of 295 nursing homes in which a substantial number of patients said that they felt 'drugged' or that they received too much medication. Many of the conference participants believed that 'overprescribing of tranquilizers, sedatives and hypnotic drugs [sleeping pills] is a common means of controlling patient behavior in these institutions.'

An advertisement for a tranquillizer in a major American medical journal goes so far as to show a nurse looming over a white-haired, pyjama-clad woman and handing her a pill: The tranquillizer, the ad tells doctors, 'helps you relieve "institutional" anxiety'.

However, all elderly people – not only those in nursing homes – can be targets of overprescription. 'Particularly stressed' at the conference on drugs and the elderly 'was the widespread and excessive use of tranquilizers and other central nervous system drugs to help the elderly control anxiety tension, insomnia, depression and agitation.'

This is the situation in the United States, but we in Britain should not sit back and say 'It can't happen here.' It can, and it does.

Oral contraceptives

The birth control pill takes its toll on various nutrients in the body including zinc, folic acid and vitamins C, B$_6$ and B$_{12}$.

An editorial in an issue of the *Journal of the American Dietetic Association* reports that half of all Pill users have low levels of vitamin B$_{12}$ in their blood. That could be making these women nervous, for vitamin B$_{12}$ – like all the B complex vitamins – helps maintain a well-functioning nervous system.

Frequently, women on the Pill are depressed, and many researchers believe this is a symptom of vitamin B$_6$ deficiency. In two studies, depression in Pill users cleared up after they took B$_6$ supplements. In addition, a B$_6$ deficiency can cause the digestion of protein to go on the blink and lower resistance to infection. High levels of the vitamin help you cope better with stress.

In a study of Pill users and vitamin C, 63 women took the Pill for at least a year and 63 did not, and during that time, both groups got the same amount of vitamin C in their diet. However, at the end of the year, the average vitamin C levels in the white blood cells of the women who took the Pill were much lower than the vitamin C levels in the women who did not (*American Journal of Clinical Nutrition*).

The typical oral contraceptive user takes one pill a day. She should however be taking two: along with her birth control pill, she should be taking a folic-acid supplement. That's because research shows that birth control pills cause localized folic-acid deficiencies in the uteruses of women who take them. These localized deficiencies manifest themselves as cervical dysplasia which, left untreated, can progress into cancer. (*See* CERVICAL DYSPLASIA.)

There's another folic-acid-linked symptom that might come as a surprise. A group of researchers at the New Jersey Dental School in Newark uncovered evidence that linked inflammation of the gums to the folic-acid-depleting side-effect of oral contraceptives (*Journal of Dental Research*).

Richard Vogel, one of the researchers involved in this study, cautioned us that this was only a 'pilot study' – meaning that only a small number of people had been tested – and at this point the results were not meant to be considered conclusive evidence. However, he said, data gathered from this investigation lean towards the implication that the depressed folic-acid levels experienced by women on the Pill might lower the resistance of their gums to bacterial infection. This could mean an uphill battle against gum inflammation.

Drug – nutrient interactions

A scientific study has shown that some of the ingredients used in common over-the-counter pain, cold and allergy remedies lower blood vitamin A levels in animals. And that could be bad news if the same holds true for humans. Vitamin A protects and strengthens the mucous membranes lining the nose, throat and lungs, and these shield you against infection. However, without enough vitamin A they can break down, providing a cosy home for germs and bacteria. The very drugs that are supposed to help you get rid of a cold may actually prolong it!

The researchers who conducted the study – Phyllis Acosta, a dietitian at Emory University in Atlanta, Georgia, and Philip Garry, a nutritionist at the University of New Mexico in Albuquerque – fed rats four common ingredients used in OTC pain, cold and allergy remedies. Dividing the animals into four groups, they fed each group a different ingredient. But not all of the rats were fed the same dose levels: some were fed one-half, some normal and some two times the normal doses suggested for children. After three weeks, the levels of vitamin A in all four of the group were tested. The result: all four ingredients at all dose levels caused a decrease in vitamin A in the blood. Some of the decreases were over 40 per cent, and the average decrease was almost 30 per cent.

Dr Acosta reported her study at the annual meeting of the Federation of American Societies for Experimental Biology. She told us that future research will show if these four OTC drug ingredients decrease vitamin A levels in the blood of people, too.

However, there's already plenty of other research to show that drugs can play nasty tricks on a person's nutrients. All of us take medicine at some time or another, and all of us know that medicines can cause side-effects. For example, antihistamines can make you drowsy, and aspirin can upset your stomach. But what few people realize (and that includes doctors), is that a side-effect found with a wide array of drugs is nutritional deficiency.

That's right, nutritional deficiency – even if you plan your diet carefully to give yourself plenty of every vitamin and mineral.

Many drugs either stop the absorption of nutrients or interfere with the cells' ability to use them. That means a drug can cause a nutritional deficiency 'even when the diet is adequate', says Dr Daphne A. Roe, author of *Drug-Induced Nutritional Deficiencies*.

How do you protect yourself? Well, the first step is to find out which drugs rob the body of nutrients and what these nutrients are. You already know that aspirin steals vitamin A, but its thievery doesn't stop there: researchers have found that the routine use of aspirin can also lead to a folic-acid deficiency. In a study of 51 patients with rheumatoid arthritis, 71 per cent had low levels of folic acid in their blood. All had been taking aspirin (*Drug Therapy*).

Drugs that drain minerals

Another class of drugs that eases the pain of arthritis is the corticosteroids (cortisone is a member). As we mentioned earlier corticosteroids are powerful medicines and are also prescribed for skin problems, eye and blood disorders and asthma. But corticosteroids are too powerful. They smash zinc.

Researchers conducted a study of 24 asthmatics: 16 had taken corticosteroids regularly for at least three months; 8 had not. The zinc levels of the corticosteroid patients were, on average, 42 per cent lower than the levels of the untreated group (*Postgraduate Medical Journal*).

Barbiturates, another type of drug we talked about earlier, can also destroy nutrients. A study compared 21 people who took barbiturates to 30 who did not. The barbiturate group had much lower calcium levels (*Postgraduate Medical Journal*).

Anti-tension drugs such as barbiturates are the most commonly prescribed drugs in the United States, but not too far down on the list are drugs used for such digestive complaints as constipation or ulcers: laxatives and antacids. But the routine use of these drugs could give your body something to really complain about.

Lubricant laxatives such as mineral oil also block the absorption of vitamins A and D. And taking too much of any kind of laxative can flush large amounts of potassium out of the body – and that could mean that your health goes down the drain. Low potassium levels can lead to heart problems and muscle weakness.

Diuretics – drugs often used to treat high blood pressure – can also flush potassium out of the body, and doctors routinely prescribe potassium supplements along with diuretics. However, a new study shows that the potassium in these supplements is practically useless – it can't get to the cells. Why not? Diuretics also deplete magnesium, a mineral that is vital in the utilization of potassium by the body (*British Medical Journal*).

Antibiotics, the bacteria fighters, also rob the body of potassium. Studies have shown that the antibiotic *neomycin* decreases the absorption of potassium – and of calcium, iron and vitamin B_{12}.

Vitamins E and C block certain drug side-effects

Not all scientific research on drugs and nutrition is aimed at finding out which nutrients a drug destroys. For example, a recent study shows that vitamin E can stop the destructive side-effects of a drug.

The drug is Adriamycin (generic name: doxorubicin hydrochloride), an antibiotic. It's also one of the most commonly used anti-cancer drugs, capable of treating at least ten forms of cancer. Trouble is, it can have a devastating side-effect: the gradual destruction of the heart muscle. However, a team of scientists at the (US) National Cancer Institute drew up a model of how the drug might damage the heart, and then theorized that vitamin E could shield the muscle.

Research already shows that vitamin C may protect people – particularly older people – against the toxic effects of drugs. A group of ten older people who were deficient in vitamin C were metabolizing the painkiller *phenazone* (sometimes used for painful ear infections) very slowly. When eight of these people were given supplements of vitamin C for two weeks, their metabolism of the drug speeded up. 'It seems clear that a vitamin C deficiency in man causes a small but demonstrable impairment in drug metabolism that can be reversed by correction of the deficiency,' wrote the study's author in the *British Medical Journal*. And another study warned that 'ascorbic acid [vitamin C] deficiency may contribute to the adverse drug reactions found in the elderly' (*Journal of Human Nutrition*).

How drugs interfere with nutrient uptake

Drug	Nutrients affected	Drug	Nutrients affected
Antacids	calcium iron phosphorus thiamin	Digoxin (Lanoxin)	potassium thiamin
Antibiotics	vitamin B_{12} folic acid vitamin K magnesium	Diuretics	vitamin B vitamin C calcium magnesium potassium zinc
Anti-coagulants	vitamin K	Glucocorticoids (e.g. hydrocortisone)	vitamin C vitamin D potassium
Aspirin	vitamin C folic acid	Hydralazine (Apresoline)	vitamin B_6
Barbiturates	vitamin C calcium vitamin D	Levodopa (L-dopa)	vitamin B_{12} folic acid
Cholestyramine (Questran)	vitamin A vitamin B_{12} vitamin D vitamin K	Metformin (for Type 2 diabetes)	vitamin B_{12}
		Mineral oil	vitamin A vitamin D vitamin K vitamin E
Colchicine (for gout)	vitamin B_{12} potassium		

Taking extra vitamin C may be one way to guard your body against the side-effects of drugs in general, but that leaves the problem of nutritional deficiency. This, of course, can be remedied.

'A drug-induced nutrient deficiency can be corrected only by giving large enough doses of the deficient nutrient to compensate for the loss caused by the drug,' wrote Dr Roe. But, she continued, 'Nutritional side-effects are preventable. Most of them occur because physicians are unaware they exist.' But you aren't.

• Emotional problems

Doctors have given names to a number of psychological disorders with recognizable clinical symptoms. Some of these are discussed elsewhere in this volume under such headings as DEPRESSION and SCHIZOPHRENIA. Under discussion here are a variety of less specific emotional problems that might simply be called 'problems of living'. They are the common difficulties we've all encountered at one time or another, involving our relationships with family and loved ones, our needs for comfort and companionship, our hopes and fears about the future. While the stresses arising from them can persist for years without apparent ill effects, they can do hidden damage, making our daily lives less satisfying than they should be and even injuring our physical health. Sometimes these problems become serious enough to require professional help. The emphasis here, however, is on how we can use many professionally approved self-help techniques of communication, motivation and relaxation to improve the state of our emotional health and become happier, more effective human beings.

Danger signs: recognizing an emotional crisis

The symptoms of a classic nervous breakdown have long since been described by psychiatrists who deal with mental emergencies at big-city hospitals and by mental health workers who sit by the phones at 24-hour hotlines in almost every town. The symptoms, roughly, come in three types.

First, the physical signs. Several of them involve the digestive tract. If you're starting to 'swim' in trousers that were tight last year, then depression might be robbing you of your appetite. Or heartburn and diarrhoea may keep you running for antacids and Kaolin and morphine. Other common physical symptoms of a nervous condition are high blood pressure, headaches, constipation, muscle tension, insomnia and rapid pulse.

Look for emotional signs, too. Do you panic over little things, like misplacing a chequebook or car keys? Or lose your temper if your son or grandson drops a glass full of milk on the floor? If you think your boss is out to get you or if you still feel guilty about sins committed years ago, you might be ripe for a crisis.

Then there are behavioural signs. Maybe you've just stopped going to the weekly games of bowls or bridge. Maybe you have stopped grooming yourself carefully. Or you have started clinging to your spouse for safety. You could be entering a danger zone.

If you or a person you love is between 40 and 60, be on the lookout for symptoms of the famed 'midlife crisis'. Brent Q. Hafen of Brigham Young University, author of a book called *The Crisis Intervention Handbook* (1982), described problems some people face in midlife, when they're suddenly afraid of ageing and of losing their financial security – especially if inflation threatens to tarnish their golden years.

> Some people in their forties and fifties reach a point where they realize they aren't going to be promoted, and they may feel depressed at finding themselves in a job they don't like. These kinds of feelings are frightening and may surface as apathy or depression or friction in the marriage. People may also feel that they've lost their youth and need to be reassured that they're still handsome or desirable.

You can tell a lot about the way your spouse feels by listening carefully to what he or she says, Dr Hafen added.

> If a person says, 'I've never felt this way before,' then they're probably bewildered by the circumstances they're in. If someone says, 'I've got to do something, but I don't know what,' then they're becoming desperate. A helpless person will say things like, 'I can't manage this myself,' and the person who feels apathetic might say, 'Nothing can help me. I'm in a zero situation.'

Menopause can be a particularly vulnerable time. 'In order to prevent a crisis during menopause,' Milton N. Silva, an American therapist, says, 'a woman's husband must give her reassurance about her femininity. To a woman, her first menstruation [may have] symbolized the beginning of her femininity, and she may interpret menopause as the end of it. She'll take it as a sign of old age, and she may feel that she's lost her appeal.'

Suicidal signals

Signs of suicidal thoughts, of course, are important to look for in people of any age. Fortunately, a suicidal person usually sends out clear signals, and if you know how to read them, you might just save someone's life – or even your own.

'Suicidal people almost always give a definite indication of their intentions,' Dr Silva says. 'They withdraw socially; they decide to make out a will. They talk about themselves as if they're going on a long trip. It doesn't happen overnight.

'One suicidal patient I know started to give away his possessions to his friends. He'd say to somebody, 'You've always admired my watch – take it and remember me by it.' A suicidal person may also stop returning your calls, and when they're invited to a party, sometimes they just don't show up.'

The workers who answer the phones at local crisis-intervention hotlines like those operated by the Samaritans are also experts at identifying potential suicides. 'If we think someone is suicidal, we try to keep them on the phone and start asking them questions,' one American hotline worker said. ' "Do you have any thoughts about harming yourself? Do you have any pills or guns in the house?" ' A lot of people are afraid to ask a person if they have suicidal thoughts because they don't want to plant the idea in their minds. But it's been widely recognized that talking about suicide won't encourage them to go through with it. Suicidal people want to talk.

'Suicidal people often have a plan,' she added. 'And the more elaborate the plan, the more serious they are about doing away with themselves. For example, if a woman tells us that she wants to die on a certain mountaintop in her favourite dress and jewellery, then we know she's serious.'

Mental health professionals are also trained to look for signs of psychosis – that is, signs that mean someone has lost contact with reality. At St Vincent's Hospital in New York, for example, there's a Psychiatric Emergency Walk-In Service where psychiatrists examine people who seem to be in psychological crisis, diagnose them and decide whether they should be hospitalized or sent home.

One of those psychiatrists is Robert Campion. 'If you're talking about psychosis,' he says, 'look for signs that a person can't deal sensibly or logically with what's going on around them. Their thinking may be disorganized, and they may say things like, "When I got up this morning, I ate a bowl of cornflakes for television," or "My landlord has made all the doorknobs in the building radioactive, and I can't get out."'

Other signs

Aside from psychosis, violent tendencies also have some identifiable symptoms. Some psychiatrists, especially those who testify at criminal trials, use a test that sometimes enables them to spot a potentially aggressive person. The doctor asks an accused person to draw, for example, a house, a tree, a man and a woman. A violent man usually draws an abnormally large or claw-like hand on the male figure.

At times, however, the symptoms of a mental crisis defy easy analysis. Indeed, to an outsider, the causes of a breakdown may seem inappropriate or trivial. Take the case of a sturdy woman executive who broke down for no apparent reason after flying from London to Edinburgh on a routine business trip, or the case of a man who became inconsolably depressed on 16 June. The outside observer doesn't know that the woman's close friend died in Edinburgh several years before, or that 16 June was the anniversary of the man's divorce. Then there's the straw-that-broke-the-camel's-back syndrome. For example, one woman who for months stoically endured the death of her child suddenly broke into tears when her washing machine overflowed.

Husbands and wives can be the best and worst evaluators and judges of each other's mental and emotional state. Only a spouse might know, for instance, whether a partner is happier or unhappier, is sleeping more or less soundly and so forth. On the other hand, some adults may have an urge to isolate or 'dump' the spouse who needs help. And that's not good.

'A breakdown can really frighten a family,' says Ann Cain, a professor of psychiatric nursing at the University of Maryland. 'When someone is severely depressed, the threat that he or she will commit suicide scares the spouse and the children. Those families are frequently eager to hospitalize the depressed person.

'But they have to see that the person with the psychiatric symptoms is really acting out the emotional issues that are going on in the whole family. It's a family problem, not just an individual problem. The family should stay in touch with the problem and recognize their part in the process.'

Sometimes a family may be fooled into thinking that a parent or grandparent has a mental problem, when what he or she really has is a physical one. This is often true of older people.

As one doctor said, 'If the person is over 35 and has no personal or family history of mental or emotional problems, then there might be some underlying, unappreciated physical problem. It could be a hormonal condition like a thyroid disturbance or even a tumour.'

What you can do
What can you do if someone you know is nearing their breaking point? Many things.

Take them to a quiet place and get them to talk about their fears or feelings. Bolster their confidence and try to patch up their broken self-image. Listen carefully to what they have to say and let them cry or shout if they need to.

What can you do if *you* are in a crisis? First, here's what not to do. 'The biggest problem,' says New York City psychiatrist Frederic Flach, 'is when people aren't aware of their own symptoms or pretend they just aren't there. That's the worst situation you can put yourself in. Those who say that nothing is wrong, or who think, "I have to be strong all the time," have the least chance of recovering from a crisis. When they deny that a problem exists, they are not only defeating themselves but also the efforts of those around them.'

It doesn't take much effort, really, to prevent most problems from getting out of hand. Take your mind off your own troubles, Dr Hafen suggests, by working in the garden or knitting a jumper. Take an evening class or join a choir. Bake biscuits for an elderly neighbour or do odd jobs for him or her. If all else fails, and the problem seems overwhelming, don't hesitate to seek professional help.

Above all, think of your crisis as a chance to improve. As one psychiatrist told us, 'The character that stands for "crisis" in Chinese writing is really two characters combined. The first one stands for "stress" or "danger", but the other one stands for "opportunity".'

Body signals: the silent language

Words are important tools for communicating our needs to others, but they are not the only ones. Yawning, sending penetrating looks, nudging and glancing at your watch – all of these acts are examples of non-verbal communication – a silent language that often speaks louder than words. Even when we aren't consciously sending, the message is often 'written all over our faces'. Sometimes we can't help it; we fidget, blush, laugh or get goose flesh – silent signals come pouring forth all the time.

It's very possible, psychologists say, that we can learn a lot about ourselves and the people around us if we become more sensitive to such non-verbal statements. They can clue us in to unconscious feelings, they can help us nip problems in the bud, and they can help prevent us from getting our 'signals crossed' with our fellow men and women.

For example, with a gesture as simple as hanging up your coat when you come home from work, you might be signalling how you'll spend a whole evening with your family. You may not be conscious of your non-verbal statement but your spouse may be.

In *The Silent Language*, the American anthropologist Edward T. Hall describes this common interaction:

> When a husband comes home from the office, takes off his hat, hangs up his coat and says 'hi' to his wife, the way in which he says 'hi', reinforced by the manner in which he shed his overcoat, summarizes his feelings about the way things went at the office. If his wife wants the details, she may have to listen for a while, yet she grasps in an instant the significant message for her; namely, what kind of evening they are going to spend and how she is going to cope with it.

Hugging, kissing and emotionally charged facial expressions are other spouse-to-spouse signals, and a knowledge of them might help you prevent family quarrels. In a similar way, awareness of the expression on your face might alert you that you're having the same old disagreement with your spouse.

Tuning in to our own facial expressions might help us understand our emotions better. One California psychologist, Paul Ekman, has made a speciality of teaching himself and others to sense the expressions on their faces. He proposes, for instance, that a tightening and narrowing of the lips is a sign of anger. 'When my lips tighten,' he says, 'I know immediately that something's making me angry.'

Sometimes you can learn a lot from your own hands, says Randall Harrison of the Langley – Porter Neuropsychiatric Institute in San Francisco. For example, you might be talking to a friend about yourself, your spouse and your children. As you speak, you may be making a short of chopping motion with your hand, which Dr Harrison calls a 'baton'. If you insert the baton between the words 'I' and 'my husband', he says, you may be revealing an emotional barrier between you. In the same way, you might indicate a barrier between yourself and your children, or between your husband and your children, and so on.

You may also find yourself fidgeting. Finding out when you fidget can show what makes you – unconsciously – anxious. In one case, according to Dr Harrison, a young husband was talking about his apparently unexplainable anxiety. He spoke at length about his love for his wife and his happiness with her, but every time he mentioned her, he nervously pulled his wedding ring on and off. Further talks uncovered repressed conflicts in the marriage, which were later resolved.

The way you sleep also tells your spouse something about your feelings. In fact, recognizing changes in sleep behaviour might help you nip marital problems in the bud. Dr Samuel Dunkell, in his book *Sleep Positions, The*

Night Language of the Body, said that 'Even in sleep, we use our bodies to communicate with or express our feelings about our partners.'

If you sleep in positions that Dr Dunkell called the 'spoon' and the 'hug', then you may be expressing your love to the fullest. In the spoon, the man and woman lie on their sides, facing in the same direction and 'nestling against one another like two spoons in a drawer'. In the hug, the sleepers lie on their sides, facing and embracing each other.

On the other hand, Dr Dunkell proposed, if you sleep with your arms spread wide, dominating the bed, you might be saying that you want to dominate the marriage. And if you sleep on your back, you might be telling your spouse – unintentionally – that you feel superior.

> Couples who have been together for some time can make use of their knowledge of sleep positions to keep their fingers on the pulse of their emotional union. Changes in the sleep position of a partner can . . . indicate what is currently happening in the partner's life space . . . Being aware of the significance of such changes can sometimes make it possible for a couple to focus and deal with a conflict before it becomes too disruptive.

What appearance tells us

Your appearance and personal grooming also have a big impact – whether or not you are aware of it – on the judgments that some people may make of you (and *their* appearance might partly colour your opinion of them). According to studies at the University of Minnesota, if you are considered physically attractive, many people will jump to the conclusion that you are outstanding in other ways. In one survey, attractive people were rated warmer, more poised, more sensitive, kinder, more sincere and more likely to succeed in marriage or career than others. Asked to predict the personalities of people depicted in head-and-shoulder photographs, students in another study assumed that the attractive people were more interesting, strong, modest, outgoing, exciting and responsive.

The clothes you wear, of course, tell people a lot about you. In *The Language of Clothes* (1981), author Alison Lurie told it like this:

> Long before I am near enough to talk to you on the street, in a meeting or at a party, you announce your sex, age and class to me through what you are wearing – and very possibly give me important information (or misinformation) as to your occupation, origin, personality, opinions, tastes, sexual desires and current mood . . . By the time we meet and converse, we have already spoken to each other in an older and more universal tongue.

Sometimes our clothes reveal more than we suspect. Ms Lurie, a professor at Cornell University, says that when we wear the popular 'layered' look, the colour and style of the inner layer may tell people what's *really* going on inside us. For instance, a woman who wears a frilly pink blouse under a sensible grey suit announces that under her business-like exterior lives a lively, female spirit. Conversely, the woman who wears a curvy silk suit over a mouse-grey sweater might be telling us that on the day she may look charming, but underneath she is preoccupied or depressed. Among men, an architect wearing a tan cord suit, but a business shirt and tie underneath, is reassuring his clients 'that their buildings will not run over the cost estimate or fall down.'

Clothes, says Dr Harrison, start by being merely functional, but later we use them to make statements about ourselves. Sometimes clothes become what he calls 'tie-signs', or signs of loyalty and allegiance. For example, football fans tend to wear a team's colours after the latter wins an important match, and couples often wear matching jackets or jumpers or rings as tie-signs.

One cautionary note on the use of non-verbal language: it can be very ambiguous. Even if you express yourself accurately, the person on the receiving end still might misunderstand you, for, as research has shown, the other person's mood and prejudices can distort the signals you send. In one study, people were asked to listen to a man reciting the alphabet and to identify the emotion expressed in his tone. One listener felt it to be sad, another thought it sounded fearful, and a third called it loving.

Ultimately, by becoming fluent in non-verbal language and using it more, you may be helping yourself physically as well as socially. One psychologist at the University of Connecticut has found that people who consistently express themselves visually – by being animated or direct or by responding to happy or sad events with appropriate facial expressions – are apparently under less physiological tension than other people and may put their bodies under less stress over the course of their entire life-times.

Groaning: drug-free tension relief

Certain patients emerging from an anaesthetic after an operation will spontaneously begin to groan. People in extreme pain often begin to groan in an attempt to relieve their pain. However, nurses and doctors generally discourage groaning in hospitals. 'Quiet, Mrs Jones. Your groaning upsets the other patients.' Groaning is often viewed as a negative and disturbing activity.

However, Louis Savary has discovered that groaning is helpful, and for more than just physical pain. It can also provide temporary relief for certain emotional pressures. Dr Savary leads workshops dealing with stress and tension, presenting groaning as a helpful technique.

'Once, at a workshop with many nurses participating, I talked about the therapeutic qualities of groaning. I explained how, despite the fact that our culture discourages groaning within anyone's range of hearing, it is a healthful process. Some participants showed signs of disbelief, so I decided to introduce them to groaning.

'I explained I would like them to lie on their backs on the carpeted floor and give out deep, full-bodied groans. I then gave a sample groan. Watching and hearing me groan, they could picture themselves doing the same thing, and they laughed in embarrassment.

'With a bit more encouragement, the participants each found a place on the floor. When I invited them to begin groaning, I heard instead giggles and laughter: a sign of embarrassment, of course, but also a sign of tension. I let them get the laughter out of their systems. After a few minutes of giggling, everyone settled down and began to groan, with jazz music playing in the background.'

After 15 minutes of deep groaning, Dr Savary asked participants to describe how they felt. Here are some of their comments: 'I feel relaxed for the first time this week;' 'Tenseness gone;' 'No more tension headache;' 'My body feels limp and relaxed, inside and out;' 'My insides have settled down;' 'I have a whole new excitement about the workshop;' 'Maybe there *is* a way to get relief from stress and pressures.'

Dr Savary reminded them that they had brought about this temporary relief of tension, exhaustion and their other emotional pain simply by groaning. They had not used any chemicals or drugs; they hadn't even needed any structured physical movements such as yoga or aerobics. 'I wanted to show that the basic formula for getting some relief from certain kinds of physical and emotional stress is very simple,' said Dr Savary. *'Lie down and groan deeply for at least 10 minutes.* If the situation doesn't permit lying down, then groan sitting or standing. That seems to work just about as well.'

Physically, groaning helps you relax. One dominant desire of people under severe pressure is to be able to relax. Groaning facilitates relaxation by involving your entire body in gently rhythmic activity. First of all, because groaning requires deep, regulated diaphragmatic breathing, maximum amounts of oxygen are supplied to all parts of your body. Groaning also produces strong vibrations within your body, which effects a kind of inner message. As you continue to groan deeply and become more and more relaxed, you can begin to feel your groaning creating vibrations, not only in your throat but also in your stomach and chest, and sometimes even in your sinuses. Usually, physical relaxation is the state in which the body can best begin to heal itself. Tension hardly ever helps healing and hardly ever relieves pain.

Psychologically, groaning is healthy, too, for when it is consciously done, it creates a focus of attention for your mind. Dr Savary usually suggests that groaners imaginatively picture their anger, hurt, fear or frustration. When they exhale, he asks them to visualize the sources of their tension being released out of their bodies and minds. In that way, their psychological systems are involved in the groaning. The destructive or exhaustive emotions are acknowledged and consciously let go.

A strong groan begins with a deep breath that distends and seems to fill the lower intestines. The pressure, felt there and then pushed out, meets momentary resistance in the throat, where the sound of the groan begins. When the throat is fully opened, the contained air rushes out and, as it passes the voice box, creates the sound we usually associate with groaning.

A groan is generally much stronger, louder and more forceful than a sigh. A groan's objective is also different from that of a sigh. Usually a sigh symbolically acknowledges relief: 'I'm glad that's over.' You sigh with relief when, for example, a difficult exam is finished, a long report is turned in, a crucial meeting is over, a critical medical report says 'non-malignant'. In each of those cases, a sigh would be an appropriate sign that the body and mind feel relief and gratitude.

In contrast, the groan is most appropriate not when the pressure is taken off but *while it is still on*. The groan acts like a valve that releases a strong overflow of pressure or pain while it is still building up. No matter how distasteful or disapproved the pressured feeling may be, let it come out of you. Otherwise, just as rubbish, when kept indoors indefinitely, develops a repulsive odour that eventually fills every part of the house, so if emotions and pains fit for disposal are kept blocked inside, they eventually overwhelm your entire self.

Moaning, a gentler form of groaning, usually begins when the strong overflow of pressure or pain lessens. Although the pressure or pain is still present, it no longer has the intensity that tends to produce a groan. Moaning signals a continuous but not quite intolerable level of pain or pressure. Moaning has a self-comforting quality and can generate the soothing effects of a continually voiced chant. Moaning also helps release anxiety.

It is a tradition at Oberlin College in Ohio that, during the week of final examinations, students gather near the social centre at scheduled times for 'primal moans'. In an effort to release almost overwhelming tension, always at a high point during final exams, students in groups use moaning, groaning, shouting, stomping and shaking to release their anxieties and fears.

Groaning may be used regularly, at set times, with great effectiveness. A supervisor in charge of a department used to build up much frustration at work each day. When he got home, he often took out his frustration on his wife, his children and their pets. Dr Savary suggested groaning on the way home from work. 'Keep your windows rolled up,' he advised, 'and no one will hear your groaning. Groan away your daily overflow of pressure.' The man discovered that, on days when he spent part of his half-an-hour drive home groaning, he arrived much more relaxed than usual and did not need to take out his frustrations from work on his family. So he decided to make groaning a regular part of his journey home every workday.

Groaning is a valuable pressure-releaser for people in jobs and relationships where they have no options or alternatives. For example, superiors, administrators, management personnel, nurses, teachers and parents usually cannot avoid situations that generate pressure, conflict and frustration daily, almost hourly. Groaning does not eradicate the source of the pressure – nothing can do that as long as the person remains in that type of job or relationship – but it can help deal with the overflow of pressure as it builds up.

One caution about groaning. It is rather noisy and should be carried out where it will not disturb others – for example, in a car with the windows closed. Or, if others must hear your groaning, give them advance warning that the groaning they are about to hear is not a call for help.

Finding the child in you

As an ancient philosopher put it: 'The great man is he who does not lose his child's heart.' Maybe we've made a mistake in allowing our childhood selves to become such strangers to our selves as adults. Because if we're concerned about total health – physical, emotional, spiritual – children have much to teach us about the good life that we may well have forgotten.

'I have a favourite verse from the Bible that refers to something called "astonishment of the heart",' says 61-year-old Marty Knowlton, founder of *Elderhostel*, a remarkable holiday/learning programme that is sending elderly people in the United States back to college. 'Now I just love that phrase. To me it means the capacity for wonder that little kids are born with, that they usually have stomped out of them by the time they reach junior high school [i.e. the age of 12 or 13]. As we get older, we learn to think about things in certain ways, so they never happen to us in any other way. But kids can be struck with wonder over the commonest thing.'

Knowlton is no stranger to the astonished heart ('I'm constantly feeling the symptoms,' he says) partly because of his exposure to youthful students who are over 60 and still excited about what they don't know. To him, the capacity to wonder is closely linked to something else: 'the ultimate excitement that comes from learning, not for some concrete goal, but just for the pure joy of it.'

Oddly enough, that's almost exactly the way Stephen Polsky, a clinical psychologist in California, described play:

> . . . One of the most important things about children that adults tend to neglect. By 'play', I mean doing things you enjoy for their own sake, without any particular goal in mind. Some adults never allow themselves that sort of non-goal-directed behavior; they're always trying to *accomplish* something. But there has to be a time when adults let up, when they're not out to achieve anything.

To Desmond Morris, British author of *The Human Zoo*, one of childhood's most precious qualities is the urge to 'seek and find and test', to explore, to invent, to discover. When those qualities are retained into adulthood, he says, we call it creativity, and its rewards can be great:

> The child asks new questions, the adult answers old ones; the child-like adult finds answers to new questions. The child is inventive; the adult is productive; the child-like adult is inventively productive.

Unabashed love of fun
The capacity for wonder, the love of learning, the ability to play, and creativity. To this list of kids' natural talents we might add an unabashed love of fun, a lack of concern about appearances, and the ability to set self-importance aside whenever a little plain old silliness is called for. (Kids also have the unsettling ability to *see through* self-importance. 'Fossils are dug up by archaeologists,' one kid told American TV personality Art Linkletter. 'If dogs dug them up, we'd call them bones.')

On the other hand, there are many facets of our childhoods that we left behind for a very good reason. For instance, without really realizing it, kids can be terribly cruel. They're self-centred. They really *aren't* as open to change as we'd like to think. Teenagers tend to take themselves deadly seriously. And so on.

'Let's distinguish between childishness, which I take to be negative, and child-likeness, which is positive,' Dr Polsky says. 'For example, it wouldn't be childish to play *when it's appropriate*; it would be childish to do so when it's not.'

Delia Ephron, in her delightful little book *How to Eat like a Child*, provides some insights into the world of children that may serve to illustrate Dr Polsky's point. In case you've forgotten, for example, here's how to eat mashed potatoes:

> Pat mashed potatoes flat on top. Dig several little depressions. Think of them as pools or ponds. Fill with gravy. With your fork, sculpt rivers between pools and watch the gravy flow between them. Decorate with peas. Do not eat.

Children's delight in creation, their fascination with colours and textures, and their steadfast refusal to do something against their will are qualities we'd admire in adults – at the right time, in the right place and for the right reason. But not at the dinner table. Real maturity may be knowing when and where certain kinds of behaviour are appropriate . . . even eating like a kid.

The value of play

'Learning to balance love, work and play is one of my frequent prescriptions to patients,' says J. Gray McAllister III, a psychiatrist in North Carolina. 'So many people have left at least one of them out of their lives, and very often it's play. There are lots of adults who never learned how to be a child.'

Why is play so important? Well, that's a question social scientists have been wrangling with for years – for the most part with a total lack of playfulness. Their sombre theorizing has answered the question in dozens of different ways, but there's still little agreement even on what play *is*. Even though it's easy to recognize playful behaviour in a dog, a dolphin or a child, it can take so many different forms that it's next to impossible to define.

Several things are known. First of all, we play because it's fun, and that's reason enough. Also, wrote Mike Ellis in his book *Why People Play*, 'research has been done showing clearly that the playful behavior indulged in by the young is critical for their development.' Adds Dr Polsky, 'Kids *need* to play. If they haven't worked out the emotional issues appropriate to that stage, if they're not allowed to "be kids", there may be problems later in life.'

What's more, Dr Ellis quotes an earlier researcher as observing,

> In general, play is more frequent, more variable and occurs during a longer portion of the lifespan in higher animals than in lower. The play of fishes appears infrequent and stereotyped when compared with that of lower mammals, while the play of dogs is less diversified and prolonged than that of monkeys and apes.

What does it all mean? Desmond Morris suggests that play is part of man's unending search for stimulation. Perhaps because our nervous systems are more advanced than those of lower animals, it takes longer and more intricate stimulation to satisfy us. And in the process, we discover and rediscover the world: 'Each bout of playing is a voyage of discovery.'

Perhaps the benefits of taking a child-like delight in life can best be described by considering what happens if we don't.

One of the most common casualties of adult life, it seems, is the emotional openness we had as children. If a five-year-old boy is unhappy, there's no mistaking it – even across a crowded room. Twenty years later, that child will have learned that a certain degree of control is a mark of maturity, and he will also have devised enough 'adult' disguises to mask his unhappiness from other people and perhaps even himself.

'If you don't let those feelings out, you're likely to pay for it somewhere,' Dr Polsky says. 'It may come out in a different form – for example, repressed anger may come out as depression or even physical disease.'

It's a condition of adult life that can be thought of as 'emotional constipation', says psychiatrist Hugh Riordan, director of the Olive W. Garvey Center for the Improvement of Human Functioning in Wichita, Kansas. 'Many organs of the body for example, the heart, bladder or bowels – are essentially fill/hold/release mechanisms,' Dr Riordan says. 'Your bladder fills and holds, but if you don't release it, it bursts. Emotions work the same way. The trouble is that, while kids have no trouble with their release mechanisms, many adults do. 'People should remember that humans are the only animals that both laugh and cry. To deny yourself either one is to be less human.'

Poetry: the latest word in healing

Poetry is one of the latest tools of the American health professions. It is used in fields as diverse as mental health and dentistry. Poetry is helping the stressed to relax, the stricken to recover and the psychotic to relate. A new breed of psychotherapist – the poetry therapist – is dispensing verses that may work better than Valium. Whether a person is mildly depressed by everyday cares, or traumatized by rape or cancer, help is available through the poetic prescription.

And in mental hospitals, drug-abuse clinics and prisons throughout the United States, poetry is helping the severely disturbed to face reality. This application seems ironic, because people have an initial tendency to look at a poem as a thing apart from reality. 'The truth is that poetry is, in fact, one of the most effective "grounding" mechanisms that exists,' according to psychiatrist and author Jack J. Leedy. Working with numerous agencies in New York City, Dr Leedy has seen 'addicts go from being hooked on heroin to being hooked on Hopkins, Herrick and Homer.' In responding to the words of a poem, the patient learns that his problems are universal; that somebody – even a long-dead English poet – understands. Fear and rage no longer loom as monsters about to engulf him but may be seen for what they are: all-too-human emotions.

'Poetry may be utilized in reflecting the inner turbulent mental state experienced by the patient. Thus, the inner becomes the outer, or the conscious, making it tangible and workable,' explains W. Douglas Hitchings, therapist and contributor to Dr Leedy's books *Poetry Therapy* and *Poetry the Healer*. When depressed patients are given poems to read, they will often 'open up' and start talking about their own emotions while they are talking about a poem.

'Something there is that doesn't love a wall,' wrote poet Robert Frost. And, says certified poetry therapist Joy Shieman, poetry is one such thing.

'Poetry tears down walls, whether they exist between people, or within ourselves.'

Ms Shieman is director of the poetry therapy programme at El Camino Hospital, 40 miles south of San Francisco. One of the most useful poems in her work is Robert Frost's classic 'The Road Not Taken'. It is a poem about indecision, an affliction that all of us have experienced at some point in our lives. One depressed woman, after reading it, was able to face the conflicting demands of her husband and job. Another poet prominent in Ms Shieman's work is the late Loren Eiseley, who was also respected as an anthropologist. One of his poems, 'The Face of the Lion', has been especially useful.

'It is a poem about a stuffed toy that Eiseley held as a child, in the dark when no help ever came,' Ms Shieman explains. 'In the poem, he confesses how he, grown to be a great man of science, is humble enough to keep the toy, is human enough to still find comfort in its "shoe-button eyes", which stare at him from the bookshelf over his desk.' Reading this poem often leads into a discussion of strength, for which the lion provides an excellent metaphor. Ms Shieman, whose list of clients has even included lorry drivers, says, 'Men respond to this poem because it builds their self-esteem and allows them to accept a part of themselves that may have made them feel embarrassed or guilty. But they learn that true strength is revealed in admitting one's weakness.'

Poetry helps foster the proverbial courage to change the things we can, strength to accept what we can't change, and wisdom to know the difference. A Kentucky social worker learned that lesson when poetry helped her to battle breast cancer. Margaret Massie Simpson discovered she had cancer in 1959. After two radical mastectomies, she was moved to chronicle her experience in a book, *Coping with Cancer*. Poetry enabled her to cope.

In the hospital for her first operation, Mrs Simpson started reading poetry to take her mind off her pain. Within two years, she was writing verses of her own, dwelling heavily on images of water and the sea. She wrote a poem called 'Devil Fish', and seemed fixated on a water-skiing trip she had taken shortly before surgery. Later, as she told Dr Leedy she understood the full meaning of her metaphor: She had been drowning in self-pity.

'A few months after surgery, I recognized that my main problem was emotional, not physical,' she wrote to Dr Leedy. 'I had thought I was running from death and fear. My problem was that I was afraid of life.'

In the meantime, she discovered that the physical benefits of poetry were also very real. 'Under cobalt, linear acceleration and during chemotherapy treatments, I have found that recitation of remembered poetry and the writing of my own poetry have been powerful anesthetizers,' she wrote.

> During each crisis or period of pain over the past 15 years, I have found the writing of poetry a trance-like anesthesia, relieving me from fear and confusion. There was no fear of the operation. There was only anticipation of removing the lump, one barrier between me and health. Without fear, I did not develop many of the side difficulties experienced by many other cancer patients, such as the nausea and the pain produced by fear.

Pain induced by the fear of pain is a factor in many types of surgery, not just mastectomies. In Brooklyn, an oral surgeon has found that 'poetry could be considered a good substitute for tranquillizing drugs, narcotics and sedatives in producing pre-operative relaxation.' Morton Malkin has an assistant read poems to the patients in his waiting room. 'My own judgment was that fear and anxiety were diminishing noticeably during the poetry sessions,' Dr Malkin said. 'Most patients felt that doctors who were concerned enough about their patients to present poetry in the waiting room would necessarily be more gentle and compassionate. This reduced apprehension even further. And poetry can also help members of the patient's family, who are often just as nervous as the patient.'

Dr Malkin's patients are partial to the poems of Emily Dickinson, Robert Frost and William Carlos Williams.

Body rhythms and rhyme

Poetry doesn't always rhyme, but it does have a rhythm structure that is sometimes unsophisticated, sometimes quite profound, according to Joost A.M. Meerloo. There is rhythm even in free verse. Verses tend to be clocked to a poet's body rhythms, Dr Meerloo says, and the poets we like best tend to be those whose body rhythms match our own. Rhythm is what gives poetry its 'balancing' effect. Poet Allen Ginsberg links poetry to measured breathing and meditation.

Among elderly people, 'everyone is a poet, didn't you know?' says Sylvia Baron, editor of *Expanding Horizons*, a literary magazine of poetry and prose that specializes in publishing the works of this age group. She calls it a forum for 'voices of the third age'. Some of the most powerful verses of our day are being written by hands so stiff they can barely hold a pen. Older people have the experience and insight that gives them a lot to say, and they have a need to say it. Poetry gives them a way to say it; *Expanding Horizons* gives them a means to be heard.

'No one gets paid for writing or putting out this bi-annual magazine,' says Ms Baron. 'It is a lot of hard work for a few people, and their interest is in improving the literary quality of older people's writing and providing an outlet for them.' Ms Baron is a retired schoolteacher living in New York City. Although *Expanding Horizons* was launched in 1977 by an *Elderhostel* programme at the University of Massachusetts, the magazine is now published out of Ms Baron's living room. It's a completely non-profit, volunteer operation.

'Writing poetry helps fulfill the will to live on, to continue engaging in worthwhile and satisfying endeavours of an artistic nature or a service nature, and these factors should not be overlooked when we want to consider preventive "medicine" as one of the goals of life,' Ms Baron says. 'Writing poetry motivates us to go on living. There is also much pleasure in being published in a worthwhile literary magazine.'

Dr Leedy agrees, adding that there is much pleasure to be gained by subscribing to one – or in keeping a collection of poetry in your medicine chest. Dr Leedy quotes literary giant Robert Graves, who said that 'a well-chosen anthology is a complete dispensary of medicine for the more common mental disorders and may be used as much for prevention as cure.'

Touching

Psychologist James J. Lynch, in studying the effects of human contact on health, has spent hours in coronary care units observing patients threatened with the possibility of sudden death. In his book *The Broken Heart*, he wrote:

> I have been struck by the way that most people finally say good-bye. They will speak to each other, if the patient is physically able, usually in subdued tones; they will try to make every effort to appear confident, and sometimes they will even joke. But when they say good-bye, it is almost as if some deep, primitive, instinctive ritual takes over . . . Just before leaving, they will stop speaking and silently hold the patient's hand or touch his body or even stand at the foot of the bed and hold the patient's foot.

Words somehow seem insufficient; everything is expressed in a touch.

At the instant when life is boiled down to its essentials, people choose the sense of touch as the best line of communication, although scientists say that touch is by no means the most sensitive of the senses. The energy required to produce an impact that the skin can feel is 100 million times greater than that needed to produce sound in the ear. The nerve receptors of the eye respond to energy outputs that are one ten-billionth the amount needed to get a reaction from the skin. The ability to pinpoint feelings of cold or warmth is much less precise than the sensations of touch or pain. And the body's sensitivity to touch varies greatly. At the worst, in the middle of the back, two pencil points held any closer than $2^1/_2$ inches from each other feel like just one stimulus.

In a way, however, it is perfectly appropriate that people fall back on the sense of touch. 'In the evolution of the senses, the sense of touch was undoubtedly the first to come into being,' anthropologist Ashley Montagu wrote in his book *Touching: The Human Significance of Skin*.

> Touch is the parent of our eyes, ears, nose and mouth. It is the sense which became differentiated into the others, a fact that seems to be recognized in the age-old evaluation of touch as 'the mother of the senses'. Touch is the earliest sensory system to become functional in all species thus far studied, human, animal and bird.

And our hands are not made of brick, after all. The sense of touch can be highly developed. An expert miller can determine a grade of flour by rubbing it between his fingers. Textile experts can tell what dye has been used on a fabric by the way it feels in their hands. The sense of touch is sensitive enough, sophisticated enough, to enable blind people to read braille. The accumulated wisdom of humanity enters the brain just as easily through the fingertips as it does through the eyes.

The missing link

John G. Bruhn, associate dean for community affairs at the University of Texas Medical Branch in Galveston, thinks that human contact is exactly what's missing in modern doctor – patient relationships. Developments in medical technology and the introduction of new kinds of health professionals trained to examine patients have seriously reduced the amount of touching that goes on between doctor and patient, he believes.

In an article in the *Southern Medical Journal*, Dr Bruhn wrote:

> The quality of health care depends not only on how well physicians and other health professionals perform their tasks and the reliability of the technologies they use, but also on their ability to be human. To touch and be touched is part of the process of staying well or getting well.
>
> In folk medicine in many cultures, there is a lot of touching involved, and it humanizes the medical process. It is possible that women doctors may feel more free to touch their patients than men. More women go into primary care, fields like pediatrics and obstetrics. It is generally more acceptable in our society for women to be open, to express their feelings.
>
> But modern medicine is a very restrictive discipline. The restrictions it places on individuals may dampen even whatever natural freedom the woman doctor might feel to touch her patients.

'Mothering' and marasmus

Modern medicine has clearly disrupted at least one important natural pattern of human contact – the ties that must be established between a mother and her infant at birth. The importance of touching to human beings is most obvious when you consider the simple fact that babies who are not touched will die.

In *Touching*, Dr Montagu wrote:

> During the 19th century, more than half the infants in their first year of life regularly died from a disease called *marasmus*, a Greek word meaning 'wasting away' . . . As late as the second decade of the 20th century, the death rate for infants under one year of age in various foundling institutions throughout the United States was nearly 100 percent.
>
> It was not until after World War II, when studies were undertaken to discover the cause of marasmus, that it was found to occur quite often among babies in the 'best' homes, hospitals and institutions, among those babies apparently receiving the best and more careful attention. It became apparent that babies in the poorest homes, with a good mother, despite the lack of hygienic physical conditions, often overcame the physical handicaps and flourished. What was wanting in the sterilized environment of the babies of the first class and was generously supplied to babies of the second class was mother love.
>
> Recognizing this in the late 1920s, several hospital pediatricians began to introduce a regular regimen of 'mothering' in their wards . . . At Bellvue Hospital in New York, following the institution of 'mothering' on the pediatric wards, the mortality rate for infants under one year fell from 30 to 35 percent to less than 10 percent by 1938.
>
> What the child requires if it is to prosper, it was found, is to be handled and carried, and caressed, and cuddled, and cooed to, even if it isn't breastfed. It is the handling, the carrying, the caressing and the

cuddling that we would here emphasize, for it would seem that even in the absence of a great deal else, these are the reassuringly basic experiences the infant must enjoy if it is to survive in some semblance of health.

Studies have shown that the more contact a mother and child have with each other after birth, the stronger the ties between them seem to be. In the recent past, hospitals routinely presented the new mother with her baby for only a short time after delivery, before the child was whisked off to the nursery. Parents were often not allowed to pick up crying infants in the nursery, fathers were barred or discouraged from being present in delivery rooms, brothers and sisters were kept from seeing their mother or the new baby. It was hygienic, mechanical birth for a hygienic, mechanical age.

However, when departures were made from this sterile routine, the results were significant. In one early study at Case Western Reserve University in Cleveland, mothers and babies who received routine treatment were compared with mothers who were given an hour of skin-to-skin contact with their babies at birth and five hours of extra contact each day. At one month after birth, the mothers who had extra contact with their babies showed much more affectionate behaviour towards their babies and were more likely to look into their eyes. At one year, the extra-contact mothers spent more time at their children's sides during visits to the doctor and more time soothing their children when they cried during the examination. At two years, these mothers used fewer commands and more questions when talking to their children. At five years, their children had higher IQs and scored better on language tests than the children who had been treated routinely at birth.

Scientists in Sweden found that even a slight increase in skin-to-skin contact between mother and child at birth can have important consequences later on. Mothers and infants who spent just 15 to 20 minutes together immediately after birth were compared with those who went through the routine procedure. Except for those 15 minutes, the two groups had identical experiences. At 36 hours after the birth, first-time mothers who had extra contact with their babies more often than first-time mothers without the extra contact, and their babies cried only half as much. After three months, the effects of those 15 minutes were still apparent. The extra-contact mothers continued to show more affection for their children, and their infants laughed or smiled more frequently. Fifteen minutes of touching had established an emotional bond so apparent that it could be scientifically measured.

Even before research proved that such things could happen, people were calling for restoration of the human touch to human birth. The French obstetrician Frederick Leboyer developed a system of birth to eliminate the gleaming-porcelain, bright-lights, slap-on-the-rump shock tactics of most hospital delivery teams. Leboyer birth takes place in a silent, darkened room. The baby rests quietly on his mother's stomach after birth, still attached to her by the umbilical cord, and is gently massaged for four or five minutes. The umbilical cord is cut only after it has stopped pulsating, and the baby is then immersed in a warm-water bath.

Again, the benefits of touching at birth are evident in later years. Leboyer babies observed in France at ages one, two and three show advanced psychomotor development. They were particularly adroit with both hands, started walking earlier and had less trouble with toilet training.

Stimulating massage

Dr Leboyer believes that touching between mother and child continues to be important after birth. In his book *Loving Hands*, he recommends to Western mothers techniques of infant massage he observed in India. 'The massage involves stimulating and touching the baby with a gentle, firm, slow stroke from the head to the toes, with special attention given to the spine,' Susannah Benson, a teacher of a Pennsylvania workshop in Leboyer massage, told us.

'I first used Leboyer's techniques on my own child. We adopted him when he was ten months old, and we were told then that he was potentially deaf, and potentially a slow learner, and potentially this and potentially that. Of course, he was none of those things – it was probably just that he had not been given enough stimulation. But when they told me he was, I decided I should take counteracting steps, which is why I read Leboyer's book. Later, I got the idea of giving the course through the local mental health organization.

'Parents in the class have discovered the pleasure of setting aside a time for being with their child on a level of intimacy not previously experienced. Mothers tend to become caretakers of their children. They may not give themselves the extreme pleasure of intimacy with their babies.'

Infants should not be massaged until after they are one month old, Ms Benson says, but there are really no limits on how long the daily routine should continue. 'Why ever stop something so pleasureable? If it's good for adults, it's good for children!'

Unfortunately, people in many Western countries are not convinced that touching really *is* good for adults. Our culture is one of the few in the world where touching between adults is uncommon, except for a few special situations. For example, Frank N. Willis, Jr., a psychologist at the University of Missouri at Kansas City, has observed the rates of touch among pre-school American children, and while they do better than American adults, they are far behind even the adult rates for other nationalities (*Psychological Record*). It is believed that, starting before the age of two, American children are conditioned to keep their distance from others.

The situation dismays Dr Willis. 'Our culture is just out of touch,' he says. 'There are other countries with the same problem, such as the Scandinavian nations, Germany, Great Britain, but in the majority of the world, touching is much more frequent. This is certainly the case in the primitive cultures. And it's universal in youngsters, no matter what the culture. Touching encourages social relations, it is reassuring, it is stress reducing.

'Touching is common in primates other than man, like chimpanzees, for example – zoologists have described them as contact animals. Grooming occupies hours of their time. All this indicates that we have gotten away from what is the sensible pattern.'

The soothing art of massage

Giving a thorough and effective massage isn't only easy – it's fun. For you don't need any familiarity with formal anatomy to give a good massage. Nor do your need the Herculean hands of a burly Swedish masseur. And all that's needed in the way of equipment is some padding to lay on the floor and some vegetable oil.

Do you and your partner have a few idle moments and a warm and private room? Then you're ready to begin learning the soothing art of massage. Read on – and enjoy.

The first instruction is: Don't use your bed for massage. A bed is too soft to provide a firm enough support. So, instead of bouncing around on yours, take two or three blankets, fold them lengthwise on the floor, and cover them with a sheet. You can also use foam as a padding; or move a single mattress on to the floor. But whatever padding you use, make sure it's at least an inch or two thick, and it should be wide and long enough so that when your partner lies down, there's still room for you to sit or kneel to one side.

Also, you might want to turn off the overhead light; both the atmosphere and your partner will be more relaxed. Bright light that falls directly on the face will cause your partner to tense his or her eye muscles.

Keep the room warm and free of draughts. George Downing, author of *The Massage Book*, cautions that 'Nothing destroys an otherwise good massage more quickly than physical coldness.' If your partner begins to feel cold, use a spare sheet to cover the body parts that you're not working on.

Now prepare the oil. Why use oil at all? Without a lubricating agent, your hands can't really apply enough pressure and still move smoothly over the skin. When applying oil, put about a half teaspoon into your palm and then spread it smoothly on your partner's skin. Keep the oil near you during the massage; a shallow bowl makes a handy container. Cover the entire surface area you're about to massage – arm, leg, hand or back – with a barely visible film. Massage experts recommend vegetable oil – but don't use peanut or corn oil. Sesame and olive oils are the easiest to wash out of sheets and clothes. You can scent the oil, mixing in a few drops of essences such as clove, cinnamon, lemon, rosemary or camomile.

'Does that feel good?'

Before you actually use specific strokes, here are a few general hints. Keep your hands relaxed. Also, apply pressure. You'll probably discover that your partner wants quite a bit more pressure than you had expected. But use the weight of your whole body to apply pressure rather than just the muscles of your hands and arms.

Experiment with all the different ways of moving your hands that you can think of. Move them in long strokes. Move them in circles. Explore the structure of the bone and muscle. Move slowly – then speed up your tempo. Or use only your fingertips, pressing them firmly against the muscles or brushing them lightly over the skin. Gently slap. Or tap. Ask your partner for feedback: *Is that enough pressure? Does that feel good?*

While you're taking care of your partner, don't forget to take care of yourself. Keep your back straight whenever possible. And don't worry about how much or how little you do. You'll be moving and positioning your body in many new ways; if you don't take care of yourself, you'll end up with sore muscles. For now, concentrate on one or two body parts at a time.

Although the massage is arranged in a particular order, you should start wherever you want and end wherever you want. If you decide to work on more than a single part, apply more oil each time you move to a new area.

Finally, try to minimize the amount of turning over that your partner has to do. (It's easiest to work on the arms, hands, feet and neck while your partner is lying face up.)

Most of the strokes described here were taken from Downing's *Massage Book* and from *Psychic Massage* by Roberta Delong Miller. These books are excellent for those who want to learn more about massage.

Be kind to your spine

Let's start with the back, for this is the most important part of a massage. The spine is the stalk of the central nervous system, and anxiety and nervous tension are often caused by nothing more than tight, sore muscles around the spine. Loosening these can, in the words of George Downing, bring a 'deep sense of release'.

First, straddle your partner's thighs. It's the easiest way to work on the back.

Now put your hands on the lower back with your fingertips pointing towards the spine. Move your hands straight up the back. When you get to the top of the back, separate your hands and bring them over the shoulder blades to the floor, and then pull them back down along the sides. Do this stroke four to six times.

Now work with your thumbs on the lower back. Use the balls of your thumbs, and make short, rapid strokes away from you towards the head. Work close to the spine just below the waistline, first on the left hand side and then on the right.

Now put both hands on one hip with your fingers pointing straight down. Pull each hand alternately straight up from the floor, working up to the armpit and then back again. With each stroke, begin pulling one hand just before the other is about to finish so that there is no break between strokes. Do both sides.

Now move to the upper back. Knead the muscles that curve from your partner's neck on to his or her shoulders. Work these muscles gently between your thumb and fingers.

Now use your thumbs on the upper back just as you did on the lower back.

Finally, take the heel of your hand and place it at the base of the spine. Gently press and release, moving little by little up the spine to the neck.

A new way to touch

Now that you've finished the back, ask your partner to turn over so that you can massage the arms. But first, we'll learn a new stroke: the *effleurage*.

Place your hands together, one hand on top of the other and thumbs interlinked. When you move your hands, make your strokes long, flowing and unbroken, and put your weight on the heels of your hands rather than on the fingertips. This is an effleurage.

First, effleurage the entire arm, from the wrist to the shoulder, taking your hands up over the shoulder and down the side of the arm.

Now massage the inside of the wrist with the balls of your thumbs, paying particular attention to the muscles on the top of the arm.

Return your partner's arm to his or her side.

Now explore and massage the shoulder joint with your fingers. And end with another effleurage of the entire arm.

Soothing strokes for the browbeaten

Now let's go on to the head. Don't apply any oil to the face before you begin; just put a few drops on your fingertips. Massage the forehead just below the hairline with the balls of your thumbs. Start from the centre of the forehead and glide both thumbs at once in either direction. Continue to the temples; now move your thumbs in a small circle. Repeat this stroke until you have covered the whole forehead – your last stroke should run just above your partner's eyebrows.

Cover the forehead with your entire left hand – heel towards one temple, fingertips towards the other. Press down. Now using the right hand, slowly and evenly add more pressure until maximum pressure is reached (your partner will tell you if it's too much). Hold for ten seconds, then release very slowly. Massage lore has it that this stroke can be used to cure a nagging headache.

Now that you've smoothed your partner's harried brow, move on to another area of tension of the face: the jaw. Lightly grasp the tip of the chin between the tips of the thumb and forefinger of each hand. Follow the edges of the jaw until you have almost reached the ears, then glide the forefingers into a small circle on the temples. Do this stroke three times.

Most of us have neck and shoulder muscles that are habitually tense – so much so that we don't even realize they're tight and bunched up. That's why loosening these muscles feels so very good.

First massage in egg-shaped circles just above the shoulder blades. Turn your palms upward as you work under the body. Start at the outer shoulders, work in towards the spine, then back along the shoulders. You might want to change the direction, speed and width of your circles as you go. Now work between the shoulder blades and the spine. Move your fingertips in small circles. Then put your hands under the back of your partner's head, gently lift it a little and turn it slightly to the left until it rests easily in your left hand. Massage the neck with your free hand. Then turn the head and work on the other side.

Just by working with these simple instructions, you'll soon begin to realize massage's many benefits. Not only does it make you feel good, it also improves circulation and can relax muscle spasms.

Russ Nichols and Sasha Brook, massage consultants with the University of California, say that massage often proves useful in relieving fatigue and tension and is a wonderful way to express affection. They caution, however, *not* to do a lot of massage right away. Rather, they suggest, do a little at a time and gradually, if you care to, work up to a whole-body massage. Begin by working on those parts that are especially sore and stiff. They also feel that massaging your children is a fine idea. Most parents touch only their child's hands, head and feet – but children, too, love to be touched all over.

Whether you make massage a daily event for all the family or reserve it for those special romantic evenings, rest assured that a tender touch is a gift that is both a joy to give and to receive.

Solace: the overlooked need

Paul C. Horton, a psychiatrist in Connecticut, believes in the power of teddy bears, security blankets, sailboats, movies and memories. Also songs, pets, prayers, heroes and babies.

What do all those things have in common, and what power do they possess?

'They're all *solacing objects*,' says Dr Horton. 'They're things that can give us comfort and peace – that can soothe us – in a world that doesn't always seem to offer much comfort or peace. They are, I think, the very essence of life itself.'

A teddy bear the very essence of life? Well, it's a little more complicated than that, true, and Dr Horton spells out all his ideas on the subject in his book *Solace: The Missing Dimension in Psychiatry* (1981). The result of five years of research, clinical observations and case studies, this is a scholarly work that's also lively and readable.

To Dr Horton, solacing objects are things that can help us recapture the deep sense of soothing comfort we felt when we were very young.

As infants, we have a very close and emotionally satisfying relationship with our mothers. Our needs are being met. We're fed and cared for by a special person who seems to belong to us alone. We learn to anticipate the voice, the look, the cuddling of our mother.

Because of this special relationship with our mother, we develop a basic trust in others and in the world around us. And this first relationship is so enormously satisfying that it actually becomes a permanent part of ourselves.

And that's where teddy bears and security blankets come in. As we get a little older – between the ages of two and six – we're forced to give up the illusion of our mother as our sole possession, and, according to Dr Horton, we often choose a colourful stuffed animal, a soft blanket or a similar object to soothe us and remind us of our all-important first relationship with her. Interestingly, sometimes we choose a 'fierce' stuffed animal, like a lion or a tiger, as our special friend, or sometimes we have an imaginary friend to whom we can talk endlessly.

'But whatever objects we choose,' said Dr Horton, 'they are thinly disguised representations of our early satisfying relationship. And they all help us make the transition from our mothers as our entire world to living in the world at large.'

Somewhat older children may choose 'superhero' dolls as their companions. And when we are between the ages of about 7 and 13, collections of such things as aeroplane models, beer cans, soldiers and dolls can be solacing objects. They may help us feel comfort when we're afraid or confused.

'The most difficult and stormy time emotionally is adolescence – the ages between 15 and 25,' Dr Horton wrote.

The main reason is that it's very hard to find dependable solacing objects. Kids can be depressed and anxious. They're trying to grow up and trying to turn away from their parents. But they're not mature enough to establish mature relationships.

In fact, adolescents are on a desperate search for solace. The objects they used when they were younger – dolls, stuffed animals – are frowned upon by themselves as just being kids' stuff. So they sometimes turn to dangerous things, such as drugs or alcohol, that can be self-destructive. They also turn to music.

One of my young patients could hardly string his words together to make sentences. He was very inarticulate. But he could tell me story after story about his favorite rock groups.

What does all this mean for adults? A lot. 'Solacing objects are important at all stages of life – adulthood as well as childhood,' said Dr Horton.

The objects can be quite different, however. A young person's means of self-soothing are often prominently visible – the teddy bear, for example – and are not hard to identify. But later in life, the solacing means are likely to be more subtle.

Let me tell you about a 55-year-old woman whom I hypnotized for pain relief. When I asked her to relate a happy event from childhood, she told a story about a train trip she took to meet her father. 'I can still smell the pungent smoke from the steam engine,' she said, 'and I can see and feel the old velvet curtains, mohair seats and clean white linen; scrambled eggs and ice cream – the latter served in a silver dish – have never tasted so good; the train swaying gently, the *clickety-clack, clickety-clack*, the sudden *clang, clang, clang,* and whistle and whoosh of a passing engine – all vividly soothing – live on in my memory.'

This patient was able to use her childhood memory of a train to provide almost complete relief from pain that narcotic analgesics only partially and unsatisfactorily alleviated. Indeed, vehicles for solace may relieve all sorts of pains – physical as well as emotional and spiritual. For example, people who are depressed have often simply forgotten, at least temporarily, their means of self-soothing. And identifying a seriously depressed person's characteristic ways of self-soothing and sense of security, and discovering how he or she did it, or tried to do it, just prior to the onset of depression, is frequently as valuable as the prescription of an anti-depressant drug.

Dr Horton's patients come to him for help with a variety of problems: loneli-ness, unremitting anxiety, panic attacks, boredom and just a general feeling that life is meaningless. He tries to help them in several different ways. First, he helps them understand that the need for solace is important. In many cases, that means showing a patient that being too reality-oriented – thinking that we have to be 'grown-up' and 'realistic' all the time, may make us think that it's somehow childish to need comfort every once in a while.

Second, Dr Horton helps his patients to see that what is solacing for each individual is a very personal matter. For one person, re-reading a favourite book may be soothing, for another a stuffed animal may do the trick, even if the person is an adult.

Dr Horton also tries to show his patients that having a 'safe harbour' in the home is crucial. That may mean simply making time at dinner for a family to talk together quietly rather than argue with each other, or finding time to read together or listen to music together. The point is to try to find an 'island of solace' in our daily routines.

'These days, new ways of finding solace are necessary,' said Dr Horton.

Some of the solutions for providing comfort during the last two decades – alcohol, drugs, tranquillizers, technological advances, promiscuous sex, upward mobility and the like – have proved ineffective.

I think we're going to see some interesting trends in seeking solace or comfort. There will be a return to greater intimacy: close and lasting love relationships, friendships and a reinforcement of family ties. The birth rate may increase because babies are a powerful potential source of solace for some people.

People will seek jobs that acknowledge family needs. High salaries, bonuses and stock-option plans will not be satisfying enough, and geographic relocation will be resisted. A return to religion will be possible. Music that's soothing and melodic, whether classical or modern, will again be in vogue, as will ballroom dancing. Pets will enjoy a resurgent popularity because they have always been a comfort. Similarly, stuffed animals, blankets, high-quality personalized pillows and other warm and cuddly objects will be in great demand.

A little help from our friends

Scientists are discovering that if you have an active social life filled with friends, relatives and even acquaintances, you'll not only feel better, but you'll actually *be* better. Although this idea is becoming more widely accepted in medical circles, most people are still relatively unaware of it.

'We have little doubt that lifestyle is as important as pills, doctors and hospitals,' says Dr Robert L. Taylor, 'but it's hard to convince the general public just how important lifestyle can be. The public has accepted the idea only to a degree. The public will agree to the idea that friends can make you feel good, but when you tell them that having friends might help them live longer, they think you're being a little flaky.'

What evidence is there for the idea that contact with others may help you stay healthy? Plenty. At a symposium of scientists called 'The Healing Brain', much of the discussion centred on that very topic.

Loneliness is stressful

In his opening remarks, David S. Sobel noted that 'we have radically under-estimated how sensitive the human organism is to environmental factors such as social networks.' Dr Sobel is acting chief of Preventive Medicine at Kaiser – Permanente Medical Center in San Jose, California.

Robert Ornstein, associate professor of medical psychology, University of California, San Francisco, pointed out that, although we cannot yet assess the effects of human contact on our own brains, animal studies have revealed some remarkable facts. 'Social contact has a demonstrable effect on brain size,' says Dr Ornstein. 'For example, young rats deprived of rat pals can lose up to 10 per cent of their brain size. And if you put old rats – the equivalent of a 65-year-old person – in with young rats, the old rats' brains grow. Ten years ago no one would have believed that the brain has this ability to keep reshaping itself.'

Perhaps the most impressive evidence on the subject was presented by Lisa F. Berkman, of the department of epidemiology and public health, Yale University. Along with her colleague, S. Leonard Syme, Dr Berkman has examined the relationship between social contact and health based on a nine-year study of 4725 men and women living in Alameda County, California.

Drs Berkman and Syme looked at four different sources of social relation-ships: marriage, contacts with close friends and relatives, church or synagogue membership, and informal and formal associations with various clubs and organizations. The results of their study showed that

in each instance, people with social ties and relationships had lower mortality rates than people without such ties. Each of the four sources [of social contact] was found to predict mortality independently of the other three; the more intimate ties of marriage and contact with friends and relatives were stronger predictors than were ties of church and group membership.

In fact, the study showed that men who were most isolated from others had a mortality rate 2.3 times greater than men with the most social connections, while women had a mortality rate that was 2.8 times higher. The figures also showed that the more isolated a person is, the more likely that person is to die of heart disease, circulatory diseases, cancer, digestive- and respiratory-system diseases and even accidents (*American Journal of Epidemiology*, February 1979).

At the 'Healing Brain' symposium, Dr Berkman elaborated on her findings. For example, she pointed out that she had found one important psychological factor that could also predict good health: how satisfied people said they were with their lives in general. Thus, if you have a good social life, and you also feel good about your life, you may be even healthier.

Dr Berkman also noted that no matter how good your health practices are, if you are socially isolated, they may not do you much good. 'Social ties predicted mortality independently of cigarette smoking, alcohol consumption, obesity, sleeping and eating patterns, and utilization of preventive health services,' said Dr Berkman.

Scientists are quick to admit that they do not know exactly why people who have a lot of social contact live longer than those who don't. All sorts of reasons have been proposed: people may tell other people about good health practices, or sociable people may feel less depressed, or social contact may help the immune system ward off diseases. In any case, Dr Berkman feels that 'loving and nurturing may be as important as *being* loved and nurtured.'

Such an idea is supported by George E. Vaillant in his book *Adaptation to Life*. Dr Vaillant is the current director of the Grant Study, which since 1939 has been following various aspects of the lives and careers of a group of Harvard University graduates. Of the men whom Dr Vaillant has worked with, he has been able to categorize 40 as either 'friendly' or 'lonely' – that is, those who have the capacity to love and those who do not.

Of all the ways he has subdivided the men of the Grant Study, Dr Vaillant says that his categories of 'friendly' and 'lonely' have 'proved the most dramatic'. Among other things, the capacity to love was associated with

> subsequent physical and mental health. Half of the lonely but only one of the friendly had developed a chronic physical illness by age 52. At some point in their adult lives, half of the lonely but only two of the friendly could have been called mentally ill.

Writing in the *American Journal of Medicine* (April, 1979), Dr Leon Eisenberg has perhaps summed up the people-who-need-people situation most eloquently.

> There are, of course, no pharmacies available to fill a prescription for 'spouses, confidants and friends, p.r.n. [as needed].' The point remains that social isolation is in itself a pathogenic factor in disease production. Mechanisms of social bonding are as ancient as the evolution of our species; their disruption has devastating impact. Good friends are an essential ingredient for good health.

Being alone without being lonely

Social psychology researchers Carin Rubenstein and Phillip Shaver of New York University have observed that loneliness does not necessarily depend on the number of people around us or on life's varied circumstances. Instead, loneliness seems to be the result of how people interpret their situations. Loneliness is a combination of individuals' personal expectations of life and their reactions to their environment.

'Young people who live with their parents after leaving school are generally lonelier than older people who live alone,' says Dr Rubenstein. 'A young person in this situation has different expectations. If there's no boyfriend or girlfriend in the picture, they face a social – psychological conflict. For young people, being alone is almost a stigma. They figure, "Oh gosh, it's Saturday night and I'm all alone. Better not let anyone know it." That may make them very unhappy and make them feel very lonely. It's just something they have to grow out of.'

Everyone may feel lonely on occasion but, apparently, the more time people spend alone, the more they get used to it. Eventually their perceptions of solitude can alter.

Discovering your 'god within'

Through their research, Drs Rubenstein and Shaver discovered that when people feel lonely, they generally react in one of two ways. The 'sad passivity' reaction means that the person is very passive when feeling lonely. Sleeping, eating and crying seem to be the three major activities in this camp. The second reaction is 'creative solitude', and many older adults fall into this bracket. When they feel lonely, they may read, listen to music, work on a hobby, study, write or play a musical instrument.

'Loneliness is often a synonym for boredom,' Dr Rubenstein continues. 'People who spend their time creatively when alone are learning to deal with solitude. They forget about their loneliness and begin feeling more calm, relaxed, creative and happy.'

The art of being alone seems to have been ignored by some and abused by others in Western society. Conflicts over how best to spend one's time can erupt as early as childhood.

'If a child sits staring at a dandelion for two minutes, some adult will come along and holler, "What in blazes are you trying to do? Can't you find something to do with yourself?"' says Alexander Reid Martin, a former head of the American Psychiatric Association's Committee on Leisure. 'What the adult fails to realize is that the child *is* doing something. But the sense of wonder, fascination and enterprise in his solitude is lost after the adult's intrusion.

'So many times we're at the mercy of those around us – our parents, foster parents – telling us what to do. So many times we are not left to our own inner resources. We're chased away from what we're doing and told to do something else.'

Dr Martin stresses 'inner resources', saying that people should turn to the 'god within' when they feel lonely. There they will find whatever they need to know in order to move forward with their lives.

'The word "enthusiasm",' he explains, 'comes from the root word *entheos*, which means "the god within". Enthusiasm for something cannot be superimposed on someone; it has to come from inside a person. I have seen some overly aggressive occupational workers in psychiatric hospitals poke, prod and push patients to try to get them enthused and involved in some new programme. The patients just get stubborn and dig in their heels. Eventually, they may give in and take part only to please the worker. The therapist winds up happy, but the patient is bored to death.'

Similar problems occur when someone is bereaved over the sudden death of a spouse. Dr Martin believes that friends and family should respect the person's right to mourn. After a while, the bereaved may be led back into the mainstream of life, but it must be done gradually and gently.

'It's difficult to rekindle enthusiasm in people who have experienced a serious loss,' he says. 'You must not push. You must let their enthusiasm light itself; you can't light it for them. That doesn't mean you should sit by and do nothing. Pay close attention to them. Be alert and listen to what they say. Their enthusiasm will not lie fallow long. See what it is that kindles their flame and sets them going.

'All of us were born with inner resources. In order to be able to use our faculties, abilities and inventiveness in some constructive, creative way, we must rely on them,' concludes Dr Martin. 'People will never feel lonely if they will turn to their god within.'

You can go to the zoo, take in a new art exhibit or enjoy an excellent restaurant and a film by yourself just as much as with a companion. But mastering the art of being alone does not mean turning into a misanthropic recluse. People are meant to be enjoyed as much as solitude. Sometimes we just can't bear being alone, and probably those are the times when we shouldn't be. Our inner resources or 'god within' occasionally may tell us it's time to hobnob with others.

'There is a delicate balance in life between enjoying the company of others and enjoying the feeling of autonomy,' says Dr Rubenstein. It often takes time and patience to achieve that balance.

David A. Chiriboga is an associate professor of psychology in residence and the director of a longitudinal study on mental health and divorce at the University of California at San Francisco. He has found that married people who have enjoyed being socially active are often devastated after a divorce.

'My own experience was typical,' says Dr Chiriboga. 'I had grown up in a large family, had had roommates [in university] and got married after I graduated. After I was divorced, I found I wasn't used to being alone. Suddenly I was coming home to an empty house. It was devastating to think that my wife wouldn't be walking through the door later in the evening. Frightening. I was afraid to be alone. For a long time, I would have the radio playing all day. I would go out and get lots of books and make sure I wouldn't run out of reading material before I fell asleep.

'Time passed, and I started getting more comfortable with it. Realizing that I could enjoy being alone was a major discovery for me. The choice was mine – I could spend time with others if I wanted to, or I could choose to be alone.

'Now I really try to set aside time for myself. I have a boat in a little town not far from where I live. On weekends, I go out in the boat and usually prefer going alone. I like to relax out on the water and to think my own thoughts.

'When you are close to others, life is a compromise. If you're suddenly left alone, you should see it as an opportunity to discover yourself. Take it as a challenge. Find out what you want to be, where you want to go and what gives you pleasure. Anyone is an interesting person if he lets himself be. All people have to do is to look inside themselves.'

Getting in touch with yourself

When we do look inward, the opportunity is there not only to understand ourselves better but to better understand those around us.

Peter Martin is a clinical professor of psychiatry at the University of Michigan Medical School and a former head of the APA's Committee on Leisure. 'Everyone has an inner and outer self. The outer self must deal with family, friends, culture and all of the other aspects of civilization. We modify and compromise the outer self in order to deal with the people around us,' Dr Martin said. 'But the inner self is the true self. People in touch with their inner selves have a true sense of identity. They have a feeling of security in knowing who they really are. By knowing their true selves, they can teach their outer selves how to interact with others.'

People who want to get better acquainted with themselves may use a variety of self-communication techniques that may put them in touch with their inner thoughts and feelings.

'Talking out loud to oneself privately is healthy and actually may be a better way of tackling problems than suffering in silence,' says Murray Halfond, a professor of speech at Temple University in Philadelphia. 'Saying things out loud when we're alone is a catharsis – a tension release. After all, we vocalize when we are under great stress. If we bang our thumb with a hammer, we may swear or say *ouch*. We do something to get the experience off our chest.'

Dreams, meditation and diaries also can be effective. 'Diaries are good methods of self-communication if you write more than "I swept the floor and made the beds today." A diary should not dwell on a subject continuously but should record our thoughts and our interactions with others.'

In one exercise, Dr Halfond instructs his students to write a dialogue depicting themselves communicating with someone out of their past. 'They don't have to read it or show it to anyone. The scripts can show the students insights about themselves. People can also use a tape recorder to sound out their problems. Or they can record their day-time fantasies. We daydream or fantasize, but we never make any use of those thoughts. Our subconscious could be more important to us than our conscious self. We should tune in to it.'

Content to be alone

People who have learned to be content both with themselves and with others just can't lose. Ruth Mills of Santa Monica, California, is one of those people. At 91 years of age, Mrs Mills hosts a radio show 'The Art of Being Your Age' every Monday afternoon. She says she interviews a lot of interesting people and really enjoys her job. She also indulges in a few other outside activities.

'I take one or two classes a semester at Santa Monica College. I just finished one on the Middle East. I enjoy playing bridge, and I have very interesting friends who enjoy talking about different things.'

Since she lives with a daughter who is frequently away, Mrs Mills has quite a bit of time to herself. 'I love being alone. It doesn't bother me in the least. I do a lot of sewing. I make some of my own clothes. I love to read biographies, and I keep up on the political events of the day. I do the housework and go for walks. And I know that, if I want to do something else, I can. If people want to sit in a chair and rock, by golly, it's their privilege. But I would deteriorate if I did it.'

Mrs Mills realizes that some people find it difficult to adjust to being alone. Her advice echoes that of the experts: 'Find something outside of yourself that is interesting. There's something inside of you that will tell you what it is. But you do have to make an effort. You just can't lie back and say, "Bring me something that's interesting." ' You have to get out and look.

'Keep your thoughts good. Find joy in life and remember that gratitude is very important. Be grateful for what you've got.

'Oh, I have times when I could start feeling sorry for myself. It goes on a bit, but then I say, "Now, listen, that's enough of *that*!" ' The command is issued in a voice suddenly reflecting all of the patience and compassion of a US Marine drill sergeant. She stops speaking for a moment, then adds, almost wistfully, 'I just push those thoughts right out of my head and think – "Isn't it wonderful that the sun is shining?" '

Are you a workaholic?

Workaholics are not extinct dinosaurs in the age of the 35-hour work-week and 'leisure counsellors'. They still walk the earth, turning such highly valued qualities as industriousness, determination, ambition and success into ends in themselves and, in the process, turning themselves into nervous wrecks.

'Workaholics are people who just don't know when to stop working,' says John M. Rhoads, professor of psychiatry at Duke University Medical Center. 'Some people seem to lack an inner monitoring device for regulating the work-rest-recreation balance. Plagued by a compulsive need to work, they deny the existence of fatigue and push themselves beyond reason. Workaholics are the sort of people who lengthen their workday to compensate for their lessened ability to produce, which only accentuates the problem. They not only become more tired, but they also eliminate exercise or recreation time, further diminishing their recuperative capacity.'

That people in high-pressure, high-powered executive jobs are often workaholics is well known. Not so well known is that many ordinary people – from school children to housewives and elderly people – can be workaholics, too.

'Everyone is susceptible,' says Dr Rhoads, who has conducted two ground-breaking studies on workaholism. 'Compulsive absorption in work may be brought on by many kinds of pressure. It may be emotional problems or it may be money problems or a tough deadline. Suddenly you have to really put your nose to the grindstone, work longer hours, work on weekends, neglect your family, friends and other activites. We all have to do that *sometimes*. It becomes a problem only when it becomes habitual.'

Once workaholic behaviour becomes habitual, the early symptoms that we mentioned become more severe. Workaholics typically suffer from a variety of psychosomatic illnesses such as anxiety reactions and heart, circulation and stomach ailments. These are not imaginary maladies, like the diseases of the hypochondriac, but very real medical problems. In many cases, they drive the workaholic to drug dependency on tranquillizers or obsessive reliance on cigarettes or alcohol.

Who can become a workaholic?

In Dr Rhoads's first study of workaholics, he presented a typical case: a 39-year-old housewife and mill worker who finally sought psychiatric help when she came down with excruciating headaches, chronic fatigue, crying spells, weight loss and constipation. When the results of physical and laboratory tests showed that she was not suffering from any disease, Dr Rhoads questioned her about her work habits.

He discovered that she was known to all her friends as a fanatical housekeeper. Rather than make her daughter iron her own clothes and clean up her own room, the mother felt compelled to do it herself. 'I know she's taking advantage of me,' Dr Rhoads's patient told him, 'but I just can't stand to pass the room and see the mess.' The woman was also unable to keep a cleaner because she couldn't tolerate tasks that weren't done perfectly. Her family insisted that the house was clean enough, but that couldn't dissuade the woman from her compulsive cleaning (*Journal of the American Medical Association*).

That woman may have been too lenient with her daughter, but in other cases, unrealistic expectations in young people can turn *them* into little workaholics. 'Students . . . frequently suffer similar difficulties as they attempt to "do their best" without having a realistic definition of just what their "best" should be,' wrote Dr James C. Sams in the same journal in response to Dr Rhoads's study. The misconception of the school child,

> and especially the college student, as one who has limitless energy and abundant rest and recreation may cause the unwary physician to fail to consider the possibility of overwork as a cause for vague symptoms in this age group and may result in a spurious [false] diagnosis of mononucleosis [glandular fever].

We might think of elderly people as even less susceptible to workaholism than housewives and students. The elderly, it seems, have paid their dues and look forward to a happy retirement when they can do all the things and (if they can afford it) visit all the places they couldn't while they were working. Often the truth is just the opposite.

Among already established workaholics, fear of retirement seems universal. 'Retirement, to me, is the most dreadful thought in the whole world,' one workaholic told Marilyn Machlowitz, a psychologist for the New York Life Insurance Company and author of the book *Workaholics* (1980). 'You will often find,' she says, 'that it is precisely the ageing workaholic – such as the late George Meany [US trade union leader], for instance – who pushes for raising the age of retirement.'

Dr Rhoads reports that some elderly people who cannot accept the physical limitations of poor health or ageing may turn to obsessive work to prove their continuing worth in the form our society most readily recognizes. 'One often finds such persons in their 60s attempting to maintain their schedule of 40 years ago,' he says. 'That would be fine if they could handle it. But that's precisely the problem with the workaholic, young or old: he doesn't know how to handle a busy schedule. He goes too hard for too long, and that takes its toll.'

Breaking the circle

When workaholism is habitual and shows the more severe symptoms, its victims need to be reoriented, to be made aware of their physical and emotional requirements and to attend to them. That involves helping them understand the origins of their work compulsion and counselling them with respect to future work patterns.

'Workaholism seems to be a character problem having various origins,' says Dr Rhoads. 'But there is some agreement that it generally stems from attitudes towards work guided by parental or cultural attitudes that the workaholic has picked up. The "work ethic" is probably the culprit here. It's striking that in my field there are few articles dealing specifically with problems of overwork, but, by contrast, a large number dealing with the inability or unwillingness to work. Apparently, we are all so agreed on the inherent sinfulness of laziness that we overlook even the obsessive causes of overwork.'

That attitude is well illustrated in remarks by some of the workaholics in Dr Rhoads's study. One man, a 55-year-old solicitor who never worked fewer than 65 hours a week and had not had a holiday for five years, felt guilty if he felt tired. If he left work early or didn't go in early, he also suffered from a guilty conscience. 'I feel sinful if I'm not working,' he told Dr Rhoads. When advised to relax and take a holiday, another workaholic said: 'Fun is something you have to learn to do by working hard at it.'

'Workaholics are commonly attempting to solve life's problems by excessive, distracting work,' explains Dr Rhoads. 'Overwork may represent an effort to maintain a clear conscience by saying to the world: "See, I am blameless. I have done all that I could, even working to the edge of total exhaustion."'

In mild cases of workaholism, a holiday and counselling may be all that is required. Dr Rhoads has sometimes even taken advantage of the compulsive nature of workaholics to set up a rigid schedule of rest and recreation. But in any event, an evaluation of the workaholic's attitudes towards work is essential. Dr Sams best sums up the general approach: 'I have found it useful to compare their overwork and decreased efficiency to a finely tuned car spinning its wheels in the snow: the need is not to burn more fuel, race the engine faster and dig in deeper, but to let up on the accelerator so that normal progress can resume.'

Letting up on the accelerator is not the same as letting the car idle. A hard worker, who enjoys his or her job and is dedicated to it, is not the same as a workaholic. 'Long hours of work are not what makes one ill,' says Dr Rhoads. 'If the work is enjoyed and provides a reasonable amount of freedom, there is no good reason for an individual to become ill. But the crucial factor is certain personality features that enable the individual to cope.'

To determine what precisely distinguished the healthy hard worker from the workaholic, Dr Rhoads conducted a follow-up study with 15 'effective, successful, physically and mentally healthy' workers who *thrive* on extremely long schedules (at least 60 hours a week). Those volunteers answered a questionnaire about lifestyle, attitude towards work and personal attributes. He compared the results with data from his study of workaholics.

'The most striking personality feature of the healthy hard workers in contrast to the workaholics is that they know when to stop. They could spot fatigue and respond to it promptly. Most respond by leaving work early or taking time off. They schedule and enjoy holidays, spend time with their families, keep up with their friendships, and exercise regularly. In short, they have other outlets for their drive besides work.'

By contrast, one psychiatrist has described workaholics as 'leisure neurotics'. 'It may sound silly, but some people don't like time away from the work routine,' explains Richard Kraus, chairman of Temple University's department of recreation and leisure. 'They can't adjust to having free time and using it properly. On weekends, they virtually break down. In very extreme cases, they may take trips, but after a day or two – even a day or two abroad – they fly back. Leisure implies a kind of personal freedom, and they can't deal with that. They can't leave the security of their job's routine. Work, for them, is a structured, organized, socially approved activity with a clear outcome.'

The prospect of unfilled, unscheduled time can be scary. 'A good instance of how scary the freedom of leisure time can be is that, in a work-obsessed society such as ours, we tend to organize even our leisure,' Dr Kraus says. 'We schedule ourselves for leisure time: we take classes and learn 'leisure skills', we compete and we gain status through our play. Obligation is an important factor – we have commitments to the community band, the bowls team and the Girl Guide troop.

'The original meaning of leisure, on the other hand, implied that it was time for freedom, contemplation, choice, and was not necessarily structured, purposeful or even constructive. Leisure is more ambiguous than work, with a wider range of choices and outcomes. It's very hard for someone who has the kind of rigid personality one observes in workaholics to accept the freedom.'

Although leisure time may be truly 'free time' only when it remains unscheduled, it is not the same as mere resting or idleness. 'That is the idea of free time that a work-ethic society develops,' says Dr Kraus. 'If you're not working, then either you're idle or resting up to work more. But leisure is something positive. It's time when you can discover yourself, when you can make your biggest commitment to life and get your greatest enjoyment and satisfaction.'

Happy families

Modern living puts a strain on family harmony, but there are things we can do to keep the home fires burning brightly. Experts point to at least five qualities that happy families have:

- love
- appreciation for each other
- open communication
- a willingness to spend time together
- strong leadership

Most specialists say that a loving family starts with a loving marriage. It's the flame that lights the fire that warms the house. 'The family is a by-product of the relationship between husband and wife,' says Daniel Araoz, president of the Academy of Psychologists in Marital Sex and Family Therapy. 'The family will stay strong only if the couple keeps the original motivation that brought them together,' he says. 'They need to feel they are happier together than they are alone, and that they accept each other as they accept themselves. If a couple has those feelings, they'll be passed along to the children.'

Love between grandparents and grandchildren can also keep a family together. Children may rebel against their parents, grow up and move away, but when grandchildren come into the world, families seem to be reunited.

In a survey at Wesleyan University in Connecticut, dozens of elderly couples told psychology professor James J. Conley that they often disagreed with their children on moral and political issues and felt a distinct 'generation gap'. But love for their grandchildren managed to bridge that gap.

Ninety per cent of the couples surveyed rated their relationships with their grandchildren as 'good to excellent'. They called this new source of love a 'solidifying factor' in their families and said it brought about substantial 'wound healing'.

Mutual admiration

One way to express love is to start a miniature 'mutual admiration society' in the home. According to Nick Stinnett, a family specialist at the University of Nebraska, families who appreciate each other fare better than those who don't. A lot of people don't express compliments because they don't want to sound insincere, Dr Stinnett says, but it's important to overcome those inhibitions.

According to Alice Honig of Syracuse University's College of Human Development in New York State, family members can either tear each other down or build each other up. Family life can proceed in a 'vicious circle' (tearing down) or in a 'virtuous circle' (building up). 'In unhappy families,' Dr Honig says, 'everyone provides constant alarms to make each other tense and upset and distressed. Each child and each adult knows the others' weak spots, and they know how to shame or embarrass each other.

'In happy families, the same principle works in reverse. Whether it's remembering to write an anniversary card or striving for good results in school, each person can figure out what they can do to make the others pleased and happy. They learn to accommodate each other and to make each other comfortable.'

Some psychologists say that a technique called 'strength bombardment' can help some families learn how to praise each other. In this game-like method, each person takes a turn to enumerate his or her own good qualities and then listens to more praise from each of the others. 'The "strength bombardment" technique is very simple, but the results have been amazing,' one therapist says.

Communication and doing things together

Open, honest lines of communication and a habit of doing things together are two more hallmarks of a happy family, and they go hand in hand. One seldom works without the other. 'Often families are so fragmented, so busy and spend so little time together,' says one therapist, 'that they communicate with each other through rumour.' It's important, however, that the family avoid a 'smothering' togetherness or a 'false' togetherness, such as being glued to the television together.

Sometimes families find themselves 'spread too thin' and short of time for each other. When this happens, Dr Stinnett recommends scheduling a family conference. During this meeting, each person should make a list of all of his or her activities. By weeding out activities that aren't rewarding or important, they might find more time for each other.

The importance of good communication can't be over-emphasized. Unexpressed anger (or even unexpressed love) may destroy a family. 'Mutual trust is basic,' says Eleanor Siegl, director of the Little School, a small private school in Bellevue, Washington. 'You've got to express whatever it is that's on your mind. If you don't talk about your doubts and fears and pleasures, they'll become a wedge between you.' Dr Stinnett adds that happy families 'get mad at each other, but they get the conflict out in the open, and they are able to talk it over . . .'

For families who have difficulty communicating over great distances, Dr Araoz recommends a frequent exchange of letters with photos, phone calls or even tape recordings. 'Those are nice ways of keeping a family close in spirit,' he says. 'With all the different holidays, there are plenty of opportunities to send greeting cards, which only take a minute to write.' When the parents are no longer living, he suggests that one of the elder children take charge and maintain a central clearinghouse for news and gossip, and organize reunions.

A clear chain of command

Someone definitely has to take charge before a family can start pulling itself up by the bootstraps. For Jody Schor, a therapist at the Philadelphia Child Guidance Center, a happy family must have an organized chain of command, from the adults down to the smallest child.

'Families work when the rules are explicit and said out loud. The role of each family member should be clear, and the children should be differentiated from each other. They shouldn't be lumped together as "the kids".'

Not that the family should be a dictatorship. Adults should be willing to apologize when they are wrong; but they should do it with dignity. And someone has to keep an eye on the light at the end of the tunnel – happy families deal with crises by managing 'even in the darkest of situations . . . to see some positive element, no matter how tiny, and to focus on it,' Dr Stinnett says.

All the experts we spoke to noticed that happy families share one quality: they make an effort to become happy.

'For relationships to survive, you have to make an effort,' Dr Araoz emphasizes. 'It's like a plant. If you don't water it and give it light, it won't grow.' Dr Honig adds, 'It's not easy. It's a real challenge to find a way to live so that none of us is being browbeaten. It takes goodwill, thinking, problem solving and ingenuity.'

Happy families are 'on the offensive', Dr Stinnett has found. The strong families he studied 'didn't just react; they made things happen. We may have talked too much about families . . . being at the mercy of their environment. In fact, there is a great deal that families can do to make life more enjoyable. These strong families exercised that ability.'

The healing power of the family

Doctors have always known that healing is a mysterious process. However, although no one has ever claimed that it's purely the result of the application of medical knowledge, many doctors and medical researchers feel uncomfortable with aspects of healing that can't be scientifically measured. As a result, the effects of such things as social and family ties on health are seldom investigated. And the healing power of the family is seriously under-estimated.

Researchers have observed in a number of studies that married people have lower death rates than those who are single, widowed or divorced. Widows, particularly in the first year after their husband's deaths, have many more symptoms of physical and mental disease, as well as higher death rates.

Scientists know that several traditional cultures characterized by close social ties, including those of Japan, Italy, Greece and Yugoslavia, enjoy low rates of heart disease. For example, Japanese-Americans living a Westernized life have a much higher rate of heart disease than Japanese living in Japan, just as Americans in general have a higher rate of heart disease than Japanese.

Usually this is explained solely in terms of diet or health habits, but a recent study of Japanese-Americans in California revealed that people who had clung to traditional Japanese culture had lower levels of heart disease than those who did not, even when factors such as diet, blood pressure and smoking were taken into account (*American Journal of Epidemiology*). Traditional Japanese culture emphasizes strong community ties and support of the individual by the people around him. That is very different from the American emphasis on achievement by the hard-working, ambitious and independent individual.

The closest researchers have come to examining directly the effects of social and family ties on health was an American study of 6928 people in Alameda County, California. Using figures derived from a nine-year follow-up study of people first surveyed in 1965, they found that 'people who lacked social and community ties were more likely to die in the follow-up period than those with more extensive contacts' (*American Journal of Epidemiology*, February 1979). They also found that the more intimate ties, such as marriage and friendship, had a more powerful effect on health.

Treating the whole family

That may be news to the scientific community at large, but to Harold Wise, a doctor practising in New York City, it's as familiar as the last patient who walked out of his office. Dr Wise has always been intrigued by the influence of the family on individual health. He believes that a great potential for healing exists in the family.

'In the regular medical examination, you ask about the presenting complaint, in a biological way – when did the symptoms begin and so on. Most people in internal medicine are psychologically aware, but they haven't integrated the psychological history into the examination. They wouldn't dwell very much on the emotional aspects of the patient's family. Just in order to get a holistic view of the patient, I always ask a few questions about family life and get a brief three-generational family history.

'So a person comes in with increasing infection over the last six months. When you get a family history, you find out that her father died six months ago. You find out that she's spent the last year nursing her dying father . . .

'Now a widow or widower is very vulnerable to disease,' says Dr Wise. 'You know the data about mortality within the first year. The problem is that the rest of the family has not been attended to. Anybody in the family can be sick, and often you're not seeing the sick one, the really sick one. The really sick one may be the one at home, and the person coming to see you may be the chief support person who needs bolstering up. So you have to treat the whole family system.

'Whenever I can, I see a family together. When patients come alone, I ask them to bring a photograph of their family, so they're not abstractions in my head. Sometimes they bring home movies, so I can see how they look, and how they work.'

There are a number of benefits to seeing families together, Dr Wise believes. 'It's important to have a couple tell their stories so the other person hears it. I ask, "Was your birth normal, what were the circumstances of your family's life before your birth, were there deaths in the family?" In a period of an hour, an hour and a half, they get to know a lot about each other. Then I examine them together, one helping as I examine the other. I enjoy it, because it's a much more human event when there's a couple there.

'After I see a family, I sit down with them, and we'll work out a health plan together for the next year. It includes their diet and activity level, but it also includes how much time they're going to spend with each other, the ways that they can nourish each other. We work it out. I write it down, and there's a copy for me and a copy for them.'

At times, Dr Wise brings his own family into his practice. 'I'll carry out what I call co-practice. After I do the workup, my wife, June Cooperstein, and I will sit down, and we'll talk through the health plan with the family. Not only are you getting the input of another pair of eyes, but often it's critical for the family to get both a man and a woman's input. Often, where people don't open up to me alone, they might open up to her a lot.'

Dr Wise's concern for the health of the whole family has naturally led him to an involvement in the problems of older people. He regularly jogs across Central Park from his office to visit older patients in their homes. In many cases, he has become the only family those people have. 'I realize the most important thing I'm providing is contact,' he says, 'allowing them to do a life review, which they ought to be doing with their own family.'

The therapy works both ways, he says. 'You get very quickly to the first stage where they open up to you. But when I begin to open up to them, their wisdom provides me with important guidance for my own life. It becomes a shared thing. Older people have tremendous wisdom.'

The tribe as healer

The most dramatic part of Dr Wise's practice is his use of the family reunion as a tool for healing. Through what he calls the 'therapeutic family reunion,' he has mobilized that power to bolster the family in times of illness. The reunions have been followed in some cases, he says, by recovery from diseases as serious as cancer.

He has organized about 25 such reunions but makes a point of emphasizing that they are exceptional occurrences in what is otherwise basically a traditional practice. Sometimes, however, circumstances dictate a departure from tradition.

'Say you have a young mother dying of cancer. You know that her life, and her child's, her husband's, her sisters' and brothers' lives are going to be devastated. That devastation will affect them for 25 years, and the next generation to come. When I have a situation like that, I suggest that the whole family come together for a whole weekend. I don't mean just the immediate family. I mean all the family, three or four generations, including cousins, uncles, aunts.'

'When I was studying the roots of the healing process in tribal medicine, for example, the clan was always involved. What I'm saying doesn't click in most people's heads in 20th-century America.

'But as I began to work more and more in this area, I realized how much we under-estimate the power of the family. For a million years, mankind has lived in families, and only in the last hundred or so years have people begun to split up. But the influence of the family is still there, the patterning is still there.

'The oldest healing form, in tribal medicine, involved bringing the whole clan together and working things through for 24 hours, or 72 hours. That was the way they did it. When anyone was ill among the old Hawaiian healers, they would regard it as a problem not only of the person but of the whole system. They would ask, "What's going on in the family that makes one of its branches sick?" They would bring everyone together, and everyone had to confess any negative feelings they had towards the person or each other, and forgive each other, before the healer would work with the sick person.

'Among the Kung Bushmen of the Kalahari Desert of Africa, families would meet weekly. When anyone was ill, they would dance all night. They would speak to their ancestors as well as to each other, and have a catharsis of whatever tensions had built up over the week.'

Reunions as therapy

'It's hard to say exactly what goes on at a reunion,' says Ross Speck, a Philadelphia psychiatrist who uses similar techniques in his work with schizophrenic patients. 'When you have that many people together, things are happening all over.' Dr Speck recently participated with Dr Wise in the reunion of a cancer patient's family. 'We met on a Friday evening and worked long into the early morning, then assembled again the next day. We were together all day Saturday and Saturday evening. Usually it's nice to meet in the home, but in this case, we met at a hotel at the seashore, with 35 members of the patient's family.

'We worked as a team, eight or nine specialists from different fields. An encounter group specialist would work to break down resistances. If the people became restless, we would do exercises. When we left, there were huge flow sheets tacked up on the wall, and the kids were sitting around while the older people made kinship maps, explaining where this uncle came from in Germany, and so on. They were retribalizing their heritage.'

'One of the useful things is to go off the usual schedule,' Dr Wise says. 'Things seem to break open when you get off the usual schedule. It doesn't happen until about 12 hours have passed, in some cases 24 hours. You go into what I call the family level. It's a level where you're so tuned in to each other, one person seems able to speak for everybody. It's a very primal feeling, a sense that you have stepped out of time. And once the family is into that level, no one will leave.' He laughs. 'You'll beg them, "Hey, come on, give me a break, let's get some sleep!"'

'It's a very moving event. And, to my astonishment, there have been some remissions of the disease in the dying person.' In fact, Dr Wise has experienced only one case in which the family reunion has not been followed by an improvement in the patient's condition.

Dr Wise generally organizes reunions around people suffering serious illnesses like cancer or heart disease, but he has worked with patients with other complaints, too. He told us of one patient suffering from Munchausen's syndrome, a psychological condition in which the patient repeatedly checks into the hospital with detailed physical complaints, all of which are false. Dr Wise's patient would make 150 visits to her doctor in one year.

'I found that this person was the negative focus of her family. She was totally isolated, by her children, her ex-husband, her sisters, her friends. No one would come near her, and when you were around her, you knew why. She emanated negativity. That's how she related to everybody, from the bus driver to the doorman. She was on many medications.

'We brought the family together for two six-hour reunions. She's now down to just one medication and has had only three visits to her doctor in the last year.'

Exactly how the reunions combat disease is a mystery to Dr Wise, but he does have some ideas about what's going on. 'When a person is cut, he heals. There's a healing force within him. There is likely a similar healing force within the family.

'I saw pictures of an elephant dying and what the elephant herd did to keep it alive. The families where the healings have happened go through a similar movement in that the sick person is taken into the centre and surrounded with a spiral. It's almost as if you take your wounded hand and hold it here,' Dr Wise says, clutching his hand protectively to his chest. 'I have a lot of notions about what's happening, but I don't have a theory that satisfies me. All I know is that the reunions are very healthy for the family. And as the ill person is a part of the family, it's also critical to that person.

'You can clear out everything that prevents families from getting together, the unresolved grief, the unexpressed anger, and get to what lies underneath – a tremendous amount of love. If people feel supported and loved, they seem to heal better. The immune system seems to work better. But whether there's a remission of the disease or not, I know that this work is important for the healing of the family itself.

'I believe families can do this on their own,' Dr Wise adds. 'And it's not a one-time thing. You don't work it out in one meeting. In my family, reunions have become part of what we do. The first one we had – in fact, the whole idea of a therapeutic reunion – was initiated by my brother David, who is a psychologist in San Francisco. Every time there's a wedding, we meet afterwards. I'm going next week to a cousin's wedding and then the following month to another cousin's engagement party, and every time I go, we feel more connected. Our baby girl connects with a huge clan now, and they're always coming to New York. In terms of her life, she knows she has family practically anywhere she goes, whether it's California or Canada.

'Not everyone is going to go around meeting as whole families like that, for a weekend, but they can meet for shorter periods. Even a five-minute change can be a big change. If I can get a couple to sit down in a relaxed way, not so they're feeling any obligation, give each other a little massage for five minutes each day, I can show them that their blood pressure drops. 'It's the little things you can do that make a difference.'

The 'budget blues': a family challenge

Family therapists have begun to find that money worries can contribute to a whole host of psychological stresses in families – anxiety, tension, insomnia and depression to name a few. And those in turn can promote physical ailments such as arthritis, high blood pressure, ulcers or heart attacks.

In a survey done by *Psychology Today* (May 1981), respondents were asked which emotions they remember associating with money: 71 per cent recalled anxiety; 52 per cent, depression; and another 52 per cent, anger. That's because there's so much tied up in our capacity to earn a living.

For many of us, money represents security – a way of being in charge of our lives. For others, money means control or power. 'There's an unspoken myth among families,' says Craig Everett, a family therapist from Tucson, Arizona, 'that whoever controls the money controls the family. In other words, the person who pays the bills has the power.' For still others, money represents prestige – the sign that they've 'made it'.

It's easy to see that, when those values (right or wrong, real or imagined) are taken away – either through inflation or, worse yet, the loss of a job – a person's self-esteem may be badly damaged. Worry and self-recrimination skyrocket, while confidence in the future and in oneself plummets. In extreme cases, hope and ambition – the characteristics that make people work harder – are destroyed.

'The important factor today,' says Herbert C. Modlin, senior psychiatrist at the Menninger Clinic in Topeka, Kansas, 'is being able to cope in order to alleviate family anxiety. We have to recognize the reality of money problems without becoming angry at each other.'

'That can be pretty difficult,' says Philip Nastasee, a clinical psychologist at the Center for Psychological Consultation in Allentown, Pennsylvania, 'especially if the couple's values surrounding money are totally divergent.'

A blueprint for teamwork

Milo Benningfield agrees. 'Each partner has his or her own style of dealing with money,' says Dr Benningfield, a practising psychologist in Dallas. 'It's kind of like a blueprint that each one has etched in his or her own mind, which stems from the way their own parents handled money. When a couple hits a financial crisis, they automatically reach back to their own blueprint to deal with the situation. What they sometimes discover is that they have very different blueprints, and hence the conflicts begin.

'First I teach them to communicate what their differences are. And we look at what they learned about finances from their parents. Then we develop a *third* blueprint: one that's all their own. Neither feels that the other is getting his or her own way, because together they have their joint blueprint. If a couple learns to negotiate, compromise and communicate (in other words, work as a team), there are very few things they can't tackle.'

That's especially important for couples hit with unemployment, the ultimate money problem. 'People going through stressful life experiences tend to draw in,' says Marion P. Willis, a psychologist at Temple University's Counseling Center in Philadelphia. 'They suppress their fears. They look around and see other people who don't appear to be sharing their nervousness and worry about being hungry and out of work. As a result, they tend to think that they are the only ones with problems. This only makes them more depressed and more stressed. In the long run, you must recognize that you are your own best agent of change.'

To begin with, you need to build strong support systems with other people, says Dr Willis. 'We need intimacy on various levels with various people to survive. Humans don't operate well alone. We need to risk trusting others in interpersonal relationships. We do that by learning to listen to others and ourselves. This is a way to find that others are in similar (although slightly different) situations, and with similar problems, and that knowledge makes us feel not so alone in being stressed.'

'Developing a sense of solidarity – perhaps by forming a democratic family council – is one way to do that,' adds Dr Modlin.

In fact, the social support of the family, particularly of the spouse, can be a major buffer against the effects of stress, according to James S. House, associate research scientist with the Institute for Social Research at the University of Michigan. 'People need to be reassured that they are still worthwhile and that the problems they have are not entirely their fault. It's important for them to recognize that they, personally, did not fail, but that they are, in many respects, victims of environmental events. Even among the long-term unemployed, we found that those who had that kind of strong emotional support had much lower levels of stress.'

'People who do the best recognize money worries as a chance to be creative,' says Dr Benningfield. 'They look at the total situation and approach it as a challenge – a chance to grow. They experiment with different ideas and then develop the ones that work best for them. There's a certain positive attitude that shines through in couples who want to work together.

Taking control

'Money limitations don't have to mean money worries,' adds Dr Modlin. 'Stop and take inventory, then do something – anything – no matter how simple or seemingly insignificant. Doing something is better than doing nothing, because any action you take makes you feel less helpless and more in control of your life.'

'Start from the premise that no income you will earn will ever be large enough to cover *all* your wants,' says Sylvia Porter, author of the US best-seller *Sylvia Porter's Money Book*. 'Accept the theory that the more income you have, the greater will be your desires. Make up your mind that if you want something bad enough, you will sacrifice other things for it.'

In the meantime, examine your yearly income and outgoings. If your income appears too small to go around, it could be that you forgot to take into account the 'nibblers' – those little items that, according to Ms Porter, nibble away at your income until there's nothing left. Or perhaps you ignored the 'bouncers', the big expenses that crop up a few times a year and make giant dents in your income – insurance premiums for house, health or car, for example. Or maybe you missed the 'sluggers' – the unexpected expenses such as major car or household repairs. It's important to plan for those a small piece at a time. A separate account that you feed monthly will ease the burden when the yearly bills come due.

Learn what's worth sweating over and what isn't. According to Harry Browne, author of *How I Found Freedom in an Unfree World*, it isn't worth worrying and fretting over small expenditures – say, under £5 or £10. 'I see people who will spend hours (if not weeks) pondering a $15 [£10] expenditure,' wrote Browne.

> They feel they have to because of their limited means. Such choices are subjective, of course. Some people love to shop. I'd much rather spend my time listening to a Puccini opera or making love than trying to choose between a $6 item and an $8 item.

However, the other extreme is no better. That is, spending indiscriminately with the use of credit cards. 'I've seen couples who were $30,000 [about £20,000] in debt,' says H. Don Morris, of the American Association of Credit Counselors. 'They'd have 16 or 17 credit cards that they were using all at once to spread out their available credit. That is a blatant over-use of the system. These people use credit cards to supplement their income and then find themselves in over their heads. It's frightening to be that much in debt.

'Our first recommendation is to cut up the credit cards.' Plastic surgery, so to speak. 'Besides,' continues Morris, 'the interest on credit cards really adds up. You could make much better use of that money. That's not to say that credit cards are necessarily the villains. Clearly, it's how you handle them that counts. As long as the item you're buying is already included in your budget, it's OK to charge it. When the bill comes, pay the whole thing in full – not just the minimum due. If you can't afford to pay the full amount, you're overspending.'

To get the full impact of your buying habits, try paying all your bills in cash. You won't be nearly so eager to part with the green stuff as you are when you're using that piece of plastic.

The most for your money

The idea, of course, is to get the most for your money. When it is limited (or even when it's not), you can lower your anxieties and worries about it if you know you've spent it wisely.

'When you spend,' says Sylvia Porter, 'you buy more than material things such as bread and shoes; you make decisions that determine your whole way of life. Your decisions bring you closer to – or perhaps send you further away from – your ambitions, your aspirations, the things and non-things that are really most worthwhile to you.

'Take the trouble to think out your own philosophy of living and your ambitions for the future. Develop a plan of control over your spending. Then you will make progress towards the kind of living that means the most to you.'

Hatching a new life in the empty nest

In the 1950s, a woman who was upset by her children's impending departure from home was said to be in the throes of the 'empty-nest' crisis. Indeed, the very phrase evokes an image of a depressed and frightened woman clinging to an outmoded identity as she languishes in her lonely house.

That woman of 30 years ago presents a sharp contrast to the mother of today, eager to be liberated from child-rearing duties to pursue a new life of her own.

According to David A. Chiriboga, a psychology professor, the 'empty nest' is probably a difficult period for no more than 5 per cent of middle-aged couples. 'It *can* be an overwhelming experience,' concedes Dr Chiriboga, who is part of the Human Development and Aging Program at the University of California in San Francisco. 'Especially,' he notes, 'for a woman whose whole identity is wrapped up in being a mother.'

Former studies may have exaggerated the severity and prevalence of the 'crisis', he says, because they were rooted in psychiatric reports of two and three decades before, of women hospitalized or receiving therapy for depression. In recent years, however, this so-called traumatic time has been re-evaluated and re-interpreted by sociologists and psychologists drawing from community data. Even so, medical journals still frequently feature advertisements trumpeting anti-depressant medication for women suffering from this 'empty-nest' syndrome.

Greeted with relief

In his own work, Dr Chiriboga has learned that most middle-aged parents pull through the transition quite smoothly. Other current studies, moreover, increasingly support this view: the children's exit isn't necessarily the wrenching ordeal it's cracked up to be.

To be sure, it may signal a critical readjustment and serve as a pointed reminder of advancing old age for some parents. Most studies conducted over the past decade, however, found that the youngest child's approaching launch into the world is generally greeted with relief, not dismay. For these parents, then, the 'empty nest' heralds a second honeymoon, a renaissance of once-abandoned dreams, freedom.

The possibility for self-growth, maintains Lillian Rubin, a Berkeley, California sociologist and psychologist, has become an exciting reality for women who told her, 'My only career has been my children.' For most, she says, motherhood had meant sacrificing their own desires and subordinating their own needs to the children's. Hence, says Dr Rubin, 'It's not surprising that when day-to-day care ends and the children leave, relief comes.'

Consider the sigh of relief expressed by a 55-year-old mother of two, married for 32 years to a salesman: 'It's time for me now. I feel like a yucca plant, finally blooming after 30 years.'

Or this 48-year-old mother of three, married to a doctor who wondered where the 'brainwashing' about the supposed midlife crisis was coming from: 'Everything just falls into a pattern when you're ready.'

'I'm ready.' That's what Dr Rubin heard again and again from 160 women she studied, aged 35 to 54, mostly eager to be released at last from child-rearing responsibilities. It is true, concedes Dr Rubin in her book, *Women of a Certain Age: The Midlife Search for Self* (1979), that some women are lonely, depressed, hesitant and mostly frightened as they face an uncertain future. However, she points out, only one mother interviewed suffered classical 'empty-nest' blues.

Donald Spence, who directs the gerontology programme at the University of Rhode Island, agrees that earlier studies overplayed the 'empty-nest' stage as a terrible upheaval. 'It's not nearly as traumatic now,' admits the sociologist, whose own reports dating from the 1960s characterized that transition as an unhappy time for women.

In part, he believes, women's new exultant attitudes reflect changing times. Not only are women more career-oriented now, he says, but their children are adopting more conventional lifestyles. In the turbulent 1960s, he notes, many young people rebelled against their parents' traditional values by dropping out of school and taking drugs.

The vulnerability of fathers

If anyone needs help these days coping with the 'empty nest', a recent study suggests that it may be the father. Robert A. Lewis, director of the Center for Family Studies at Arizona State University, discovered that nearly a quarter of the men in a sample of 118 parents in a Georgia community were distressed when their children left home.

The findings confirmed Dr Lewis's hunch that his personal experience may be more widespread than commonly thought. 'When my oldest son was ready to leave for college,' he said, 'I started realizing I missed a lot when the kids were young. I'd hit the top of my career and thought, "What now?" I felt a sadness, thinking, "When can I recoup my loss?"' Indeed, Dr Lewis learned that his emotional turmoil was by no means unique. One man was so devastated by his daughter's marriage that he developed a drinking problem.

Of course, because every family's child-rearing patterns are different, there are no simple solutions guaranteed to ease this potential crisis period. Current data reveal that women who suffer most from the break are disappointed in their children and have poor relationships with them. These women may feel that their mothering role isn't over yet and still need to control their offsprings' lives.

Researchers point out, however, that one of the best preparations for the separation is thinking about it and accepting it as inevitable before it occurs. They suggest several measures that will enable you not only to cope well with the 'empty-nest' process, but even to welcome it with an open mind.

• Develop new hobbies and interests to fill the expanded leisure hours. Now's the time to try your hand at gardening, tennis, weaving, ceramics or whatever grabs you. Exercise such as jogging, swimming and cycling will help you stay fit and relaxed.

• Donate your skills and time to a worthy cause or organization. Volunteering at schools or with youth groups can fill the void left by your own children's absence.

• If you've always yearned to study Shakespeare or learn furniture refinishing, enroll in the Open University or take adult education classes.

• Study a foreign language and then (if you can afford it) visit the country.

• Try out a part-time job or return to the full-time career you suspended during your child-rearing years.

• Plan to enjoy a second honeymoon by doing more things as a couple, such as taking long walks in the evening, travelling, dining out or just playing games together.

• Broaden your social circle by joining clubs and making new friends.

• Discuss your fears with a family counsellor or with other parents who've been through the transition already.

• Emphysema

Emphysema is a chronic, debilitating disease of the lungs that is characterized by coughing, wheezing and extreme shortness of breath. It may be caused by smoking or by long-term exposure to pollutants in the air, and it is often preceded by chronic bronchitis. Thousands of people in the United Kingdom are crippled by one or both of these diseases, and their incidence is increasing. Emphysema is one of the major diseases responsible for causing disability in working men who should be at the prime of their productive lives.

Today's medicine is certainly keeping more emphysema victims alive. But too often, although they may be alive, they are scarcely living. There is hope, though, for those who suffer from chronic obstructive lung disease. And that hope is not based on some miracle drug but on a therapy that is completely natural and depends on the activity of the patient rather than the doctor.

Pedalling back to health

For a period of five years, Dr Harry Bass conducted an experiment in rehabilitation with 12 men and women who all suffered from bronchitis and/or emphysema. These patients were in bad shape. They had all stopped smoking – not necessarily because of a desire to improve the poor state of their health, but because they were simply too short of breath to smoke! Physically, they had deteriorated to a dangerously low point. They suffered from chronic shortness of breath (*dyspnoea*) and – as measured by the amount of oxygen reaching their cells – could perform work at only about 25 per cent of the capacity of even the most unfit but 'healthy' members of society.

What made Dr Bass's problem even harder to solve was the vicious cycle of inactivity. Shortness of breath limited the patients' activity, which further shortened their breach. The only way out of the cycle, he decided, was graded exercise. For that graded exercise, he chose a stationary bicycle.

'First, the patients were given a thorough clinical evaluation, including a medical and detailed respiratory disease history, physical examination, pulmonary function tests, and chest X-rays,' said Dr Bass. The average age of the participants was approximately 60: the oldest was 75, the youngest 42.

'I instructed them to exercise at home using a stationary bicycle with an odometer (to measure distance) and variable wheel tension. After five years of graded exercise training, 8 of the 12 who remained active claimed that they could "do more" with less shortness of breath. Oxygen requirements at a resting state decreased in 11 of the 12 and remained unchanged in 1. Oxygen requirements for exercise decreased in 10 patients and remained unchanged in 2. Heart rate was the most useful index to clinically assess fitness. All patients had a decrease in resting and exercise heart rate.

'One man was 75 when the experiment was begun,' Dr Bass continued. 'Recently, he travelled to Africa on a safari. Another man who was 75 now goes out every day and puts in a full shift with his construction company.'

Significantly, during the five years of exercise training, hospital days were reduced to one-fifth of those needed by these patients during the five years preceding their exercise training. Complications associated with their lung disease were reduced to one-third of the former level.

In the past, it was commonly believed that pulmonary function deteriorates at a constant rate in patients with chronic obstructive pulmonary disease, despite therapy. Therefore, it was felt that exercise programmes for sufferers of emphysema and bronchitis were worthless. Dr Bass found, however, that lung function did *not* deteriorate in eight of the patients he studied.

The healthy-lung vitamin

No matter how useful the exercise, if you live in a city (or commute to one) or if you smoke, you're up against lung damage. Smog, cigarette smoke and car exhaust contain nitrous oxide (NO_2), a noxious gas that harms the lungs and makes us susceptible to lung problems such as emphysema. But there is a nutrient that seems to protect the sensitive tissues in our lungs against NO_2-induced damage: vitamin A.

Experiments performed at the Delta Regional Primate Research Center of Tulane University in New Orleans have shown that animals exposed to pollution suffered far less damage when they were supplemented with vitamin A. According to James C.S. Kim, that's because vitamin A is needed by the lungs to provide mucus cells, which serve to trap toxic substances. From there, cilia (hair-like projections on the cells) escort the foreign particles out of the body.

Without adequate vitamin A, however, the lung cannot produce mucus-secreting cells, and the cells become dry and hardened. Moreover, they lack the cilia necessary to sweep away toxic substances. So the lungs become susceptible to all kinds of infections and disease. Dr Kim believes that vitamin A safeguards the lungs and that supplements may help forestall emphysema and other lung problems associated with old age.

For more information on the subject, see LUNG PROBLEMS.

• Epilepsy

The most common symptoms of epilepsy – a chronic nervous-system disorder resulting from abnormal brain-wave patterns (detected by elec-tro-encephalograms, or EEG tests) – are seizures ('fits'), which can range from mild twitches to violent convulsions that leave the victim unconscious. Besides having to contend with seizures, people with epilepsy have to deal with negative public attitudes that often create a greater disability than the disorder itself.

So pervasive are these negative feelings about epilepsy that nearly half the people with it hide the fact from all but the closest of family members. That's a lot of secret-keeping, too, because epilepsy affects about five people in every 1000 – that is, approximately 275,000 in Great Britain alone.

The condition can result from a brain injury before or at the time of birth, very high fevers during early childhood and infectious diseases such as mumps or measles. Vitamin and mineral deficiences, low blood sugar, chemical imbalances in the body or even brain tumours could be at the root of the disorder. In fact, anything that harms the brain can ultimately lead to epilepsy. And then again, usually no cause can be found at all.

Whether or not a reason for the epilepsy is ever identified, treatment often involves the continual use of anti-convulsive drugs – either one or several at a time, depending on the type and severity of the seizures. In about half the sufferers, the seizures can be totally eliminated and in another 30 per cent they are greatly reduced. But that still leaves 20 per cent – about 55,000 people – who aren't helped by drugs, and even for the ones who do find relief, many must learn to live with unpleasant side-effects or other complications of long-term drug use.

Nutrition: the new weapon against epilepsy

'There's going to be a revolution in the methods of treating epilepsy over the next 20 years.' That's what J.O. McNamara believes, and he should know. He's the director of the epilepsy center at the Veterans Administration Medical Center in Durham, North Carolina, and he has been working on this problem for years.

'The importance of diet in regulating seizures is just starting to come out,' Dr McNamara said. 'And I think we are going to find out that nutrition plays a more important role in seizure control than anyone might have previously suspected. I'm very happy about the results we're getting.'

These results involve the use of choline (a chemical made by the body from protein, which is involved – as *acetylcholine* – in the transmission of nerve impulses) in the treatment of human complex partial seizures (CPS), a type of epilepsy. Dr McNamara theorized that choline may function as a natural anti-convulsant, because when substances are present that interfere with choline's action, seizures increase.

To test his theory, he selected four patients with CPS whose drug therapy was not working. During the four-month study, each patient was given choline along with his existing drug regimen. Doses started at 4 g per day and were gradually increased to 12 or 16 g per day by the third month.

'Our principal finding,' wrote Dr McNamara in *Neurology* (December 1980) 'was that a marked increase in plasma [blood] choline concentrations was associated with shorter duration of complex partial seizures and less post-seizure fatigue.' The patients, too, considered themselves much improved and expressed resentment when choline was discontinued after the study. 'Even though there was actually a slight increase in seizure frequency, the patients viewed this as an acceptable compromise,' Dr McNamara told us. 'Choline therapy is probably not the be-all and end-all for epilepsy, but it does show promise. It's even possible that choline will help other types of epilepsies, but we won't know that for sure until we have tested the effects of choline on each separate type.'

Another nutrient that has prevented epileptic convulsions in some cases is vitamin B_6, or pyridoxine, according to Japanese researchers. In theory, vitamin B_6 promotes an increase in the level of gamma-aminobutyric acid (GABA), a substance responsible for the calming of nerve activity (*Journal of Nutrition Science and Vitaminology*, vol. 25, no. 5, 1979).

Missing trace minerals

'A deficiency of manganese may play a role in some cases of epilepsy,' says Yukio Tanaka of the department of biochemistry at Montreal Children's Hospital. Dr Tanaka first suspected this connection when he observed that rats deprived of manganese were abnormally susceptible to convulsions under certain conditions. He applied this theory to a little boy who was suffering from convulsive disorders that did not respond to medication. When he checked the level of manganese in the child's blood, it was less than half the normal value for children.

Manganese was given to the boy by his neurologist to raise his blood levels to normal. When that happened, his condition was noticeably improved. He had fewer seizures, and his gait, speech and learning were all better than before treatment started (*Journal of the American Medical Association*).

Dr Tanaka then checked the manganese levels of other children at the Montreal Children's Hospital and found that about a third of those who suffered convulsions had lower levels than neurologically normal children. 'I'm optimistic,' Dr Tanaka says, 'that manganese holds some hope for certain types of epilepsy, but we still have much investigating to do to determine how effective it will be.'

That's how epilepsy researchers from the department of neurosurgery at Johns Hopkins Hospital in Baltimore feel about another mineral, magnesium. Their work has demonstrated that magnesium can suppress epileptic bursts of electricity in the brains of experimental animals. The degree of suppression increased when more magnesium was given, but the dose still remained safe.

'Further clinical study of the anti-convulsant properties of magnesium may broaden its clinical usage to include seizure disorders not well controlled by present therapeutic approaches,' said the researchers. Their study suggests that magnesium 'may have clinical applicability in treating a wider range of acute convulsions' (*Epilepsia*).

Selenium and vitamin E

When adults develop epilepsy it's often due to a severe blow to the head. Known as *post-traumatic epilepsy*, the disorder can emerge anywhere from one month to a year after the original injury. Each year, thousands of people develop this epileptic condition after car, bicycle or motorbike accidents.

L. James Willmore, a neurologist and associate professor at the University of Texas Medical School, may have found a possible solution to the problem. He explains that a blow to the head causes internal bleeding, and the ruptured red blood cells leak iron. This, in turn, leads to the formation of hydrogen peroxide, which is damaging to brain tissue. Dr Willmore theorizes that selenium and vitamin E, which are both anti-oxidant nutrients, may help prevent post-traumatic epilepsy.

Using rats, Dr Willmore duplicated the condition that may occur in people after a head injury. Injections of selenium and vitamin E prevented epilepsy from occurring in 72 per cent of the rats. In another group of rats given no treatment, only 6 per cent escaped epilepsy (*Experimental Neurology*, March 1980).

'So far, the research has been limited to experimental animals, but the results inspire new hope that this form of epilepsy may be prevented,' says Dr Willmore.

Diets for childhood epilepsy

One of the best treatments for childhood epilepsy is a diet. And it often works after medication fails.

Dr Samuel Livingston and his colleagues at the Samuel Livingston Epilepsy Diagnostic and Treatment Center in Baltimore have reported in *Developmental Medicine and Child Neurology* that the diet is the most effective therapy for children who have the involuntary muscle twitching called *myoclonic jerking*.

Most of us know what myoclonic jerking is because it sometimes occurs – quite harmlessly – as a muscle twitching that snaps us to attention just as we're drifting off to sleep. But in attacks of myoclonic epilepsy, the jerking is much more violent and may last as long as 30 seconds and recur up to 100 times a day. The seizures may be triggered by sounds, lights, hurt feelings or even a change in posture. Often, the condition fails to respond to medical treatment, and drugs that are used can cause very serious and harmful side-effects.

The diet prescribed at the Livingston Center is an extreme one. Fat contributes fully 80 per cent of total calories (from butter, cream, mayonnaise and bacon). Protein and carbohydrate needs have to be met by the rest of the diet. What's more, although unappetizing and difficult to prepare, the diet must be strictly followed – at least in the beginning. Any increase in carbohydrates – even too much fruit – can lead rapidly to more attacks. But when the diet is strictly followed, seizures are usually controlled within 10 to 21 days. Then, the amount of fat in the diet can usually be reduced to normal over a two-year period.

For children unable – or unwilling – to eat these large amounts of fat, the diet may be modified to include a tasteless oil comprising *medium chain triglycerides* (MCT), according to Dr Peter Huttenlocher of the University of Chicago. MCT oil is blended with skimmed milk and added to baked goods to make up 60 per cent of their diet. The remaining calories are varied to include some of the child's favourite foods.

These diets – technically known as 'ketogenic' – are thought to control epilepsy by increasing the body level of ketones, products of fat digestion. The large quantities of fat may temporarily cause stomach cramps or even vomiting, but the diets are free of the serious side-effects of anti-convulsant medication. And doctors at the Livingston Center, who have successfully prescribed the diet for myoclonic epilepsy for over 40 years, say there is no evidence that it increases serum cholesterol or heart disease.

Drug-free treatment for a young epileptic

At an annual workshop for families of deaf, blind and multi-handicapped children in the United States, a mother told the story of the escape of her small daugher, an epileptic, from drug treatment – thanks to a medical nutritionist.

The child was a beautiful, healthy, happy baby until the age of $2\frac{1}{2}$, when she began to have seizures after waking from her naps. An electro-encephalogram was abnormal. That led to the prescription of phenobarbitone, 75 mg daily, a sizable dose for a little girl. It didn't help the seizures, but it did drive the little girl into a private world, lying on her blanket, sucking her fingers, or rocking back and forth for hours. She became lethargic, gained too much weight and lost her coordination, with resulting falls and injuries.

That was only the beginning of a series of drugs that did nothing for her seizures. In addition, the parents were told that the child, now $5\frac{1}{2}$, was functioning at the mental level of a two-year-old. A diagnostic centre, in addition to finding the little girl retarded, suggested that she needed special education for the handicapped and that her medication be continued, despite its ineffectiveness.

At this point, the mother encountered an article – 'Something Wonderful Has Happened to Charlie,' by Lynne Rakowitz Woodward (Oklahoma Parents Association of Deaf-Blind/Multi-handicapped Children, 1980) – written by the mother of a child with difficulties of the same kind, who had been helped significantly by a special diet and vitamin therapy. The little girl's mother was astonished to find that the doctor who had prescribed the regimen described in the article practised in the city where she herself lived, and so she communicated with him. In the consultation that followed, she was told that about 50 per cent of seizures are related to maladaptive reactions to foods, chemicals or inhalants. The others have multiple sources, some identified, others unknown. The doctor thought it might be possible, by using a controlled diet (excluding foods to which the child was sensitive) and large doses of vitamins, to discontinue the drugs.

Test meals of a single food each were prescribed, with frequent taking of the pulse to detect the speedup that indicates adverse reaction. A diary was kept of the child's behaviour patterns before, during and after meals. She had adverse effects from half the foods tested, some of which triggered seizures. Maize, which the child strongly preferred, was her worst enemy.

The youngster was put on a rotation diet (eating allergenic foods only once every four days) prepared especially for her and supplemented with a number of vitamins. The mother noted that her improvement was immediate. Barring the foods that she could not normally metabolize stopped the seizures. A week later, all seizures stopped.

Controlling brain rhythms

More and more doctors are experimenting with holistic therapies to help epileptic patients. One with a unique approach is M. B. Sterman, chief of neuropsychology research at the Veterans Administration Medical Center in Sepulveda, California, who treats patients with *grand mal* epilepsy (major epilepsy) whose seizures persist despite drug therapy. He trains his patients to increase or suppress brain rhythms at different frequencies, thereby exerting control over their own conditions.

'The biofeedback method we use,' wrote Dr Sterman in the journal *Human Nature*,

> rewards the patients for producing rhythmic middle-frequency brain waves. We monitor our patients' electro-encephalograms in the laboratory, and when they produce the right rhythms, a bell rings. Telling them to relax and to think about pleasant experiences helps them to increase those rhythms.
>
> The results are encouraging. In six out of eight patients, the rate of seizures decreased an average of 74 percent, and the improvements continued after training was stopped.
>
> Studies such as these demonstrate that biological disorders are susceptible to behavioral modification. And behavioral methods must certainly be considered safer and more desirable than current treatments with drugs.

Francis M. Forster retired director of the Francis M. Forster Epilepsy Center at the Veterans Administration Hospital in Madison, Wisconsin, uses another type of behavioural approach called 'Pavlovian conditioning'. He treats patients with *reflex epilepsy*, a type of seizure disorder in which attacks are brought on by such everyday activities as eating, reading or listening to music.

'About 6 to 7 per cent of all epilepsies are of this type,' Dr Forster says.

'We condition the patient so that the thing which triggers his attacks becomes innocuous.

'For example, if a certain piece of music causes a seizure in our patient, we will reproduce that seizure in the lab. Then we keep playing that same melody over and over as the patient returns to consciousness. We will play it for one hour twice a day until it no longer evokes the negative response. It takes about two weeks to condition most patients,' Dr Forster says. 'Then each time we locate something which triggers a seizure, we repeat the conditioning programme. Often we are able to reduce the amount of drugs the patient takes.'

Ultimately, researchers hope to find a cure for epilepsy. Meanwhile, seizure control with less dependence on drugs is a promising substitute and a step in the right direction.

• Fatigue

Chronic fatigue – a feeling of tiredness or exhaustion that doesn't go away with rest – drags more people to doctors than any other problem. However, there's nothing physically wrong with 80 per cent of them (at least according to their X-rays and lab tests).

Or is there?

If you've been in and out of a doctor's surgery for chronic fatigue, and your personal weather report is still 'foggy', then there are a number of nutrients that might help. Even a slight deficiency in any one of these could put your vitality under the weather.

Nutrients for a natural lift

Magnesium and potassium The first nutrient you could consider is *magnesium*. This sparks more chemical reactions in the body than any other mineral, and in a severe deficiency, the whole body suffers. You stumble instead of walk, feel depressed, have heart spasms. Doctors are trained to recognize these and over 30 other symptoms of severe deficiency, but they aren't trained to recognize a mild deficiency of magnesium. It has only one noticeable symptom – chronic fatigue – but that fatigue can easily be cured.

In a study of magnesium and fatigue, 200 men and women who were tired during the day were given the nutrient. In all but two cases, waking tiredness disappeared (*Second International Symposium on Magnesium*).

Tiredness is hard to define. But, in many cases, it means tired muscles – muscles that feel leaden or drained of energy. A lack of magnesium, which helps muscles contract, can cause that tiredness. So can a lack of *potassium*.

Potassium deficiency is a well-known hazard among long-distance runners and professional athletes. The mineral helps cool muscles, and hours of exertion use it up. If it's not replaced, the result is chronic fatigue – even for a highly trained athlete. 'When you lack potassium,' says Dr Gabe Mirkin, runner of marathons and co-author of *The Sportsmedicine Book*, 'you feel tired, weak and irritable.'

Potassium deficiency and the weakness that goes with it aren't limited to athletes. In one study, researchers randomly selected a group of people and measured their potassium intake. Those with a deficient intake of potassium – 60 per cent of the men and 40 per cent of the women in the study – had a weaker grip than those with a normal intake. And as potassium intake decreased, muscular strength decreased (*Journal of the American Medical Association*).

You could probably put up with a few days of weakness, but after a few months, you feel terrible. 'In chronic potassium deficit,' wrote a researcher who studied the mineral, 'muscular weakness may persist for many months and be interpreted as being due to emotional instability' (*Minnesota Medicine*).

Another doctor chose 100 chronically fatigued patients – 84 women and 16 men – and put them on a supplementary regimen of potassium and magnesium. Of the 100, 87 improved.

'The change was startling,' wrote Dr Palma Formica in *Current Therapeutic Research*:

> They had become alert, cheerful, animated and energetic and walked with a lively step. They stated that sleep refreshed them as it had not done for months. Some said they could get along on six hours' sleep at night, whereas formerly they had not felt rested on 12 or more. Morning exhaustion had completely subsided.

Almost all patients have undertaken new activities, she noted.

> Six who had not worked outside the home before obtained part-time jobs. Two of the pregnant patients continued to work for a time. Several of the husbands called and expressed appreciation of the physical improvement and consequent increase in emotional well-being of their wives.

Some of these patients had had chronic fatigue for over two years, yet it took only five to six weeks of magnesium and potassium therapy to clear up their problem.

Vitamin B$_6$ 'If a person feels fatigue, then taking certain vitamins and minerals, over and above what we get from our ordinary diet, should certainly decrease that fatigue.' So says John H. Richardson, a biology professor at Old Dominion University in Norfolk, Virginia. About three years ago, Dr Richardson, partly as a doctor and partly as an avid jogger, became interested in the relationship between different nutrients and stamina, so he set up a series of experiments to test the effects of vitamins and minerals on the endurance of lab animals. One of the vitamins was B$_6$.

Dr Richardson assembled two groups of 20 rats each. He fed all of them on normal rat food and conditioned each of them on an exercise wheel for 30 days. One group was supplemented with vitamin B$_6$ and the other wasn't. At the end of one month, he attached the rats' calf muscles to a spring and measured how many seconds they could maintain a contraction. In human terms, he said, it was like timing how long you could hold yourself in the 'up' position of a chin-up

The supplemented rats were stronger.

Time to fatigue was measured for all animals. Results indicate that contraction time for B_6 animals was significantly longer than controls. This study suggests that vitamin B_6 given orally increases stamina. [*Journal of Sports Medicine and Physical Fitness*, June 1981].

Dr Richardson says he isn't sure why vitamin B_6 works. He only knows that it works consistently, and he believes it will work for people as well as for animals. 'In terms of performance or well-being,' he says, 'I think we could feel better than we do if we took this nutrient. A lot of people walk around fatigued from lack of sleep or overwork or stress. I know I do. But with B_6, we might live closer to our potential. We wouldn't get tired so quickly, we would feel better, we could function at a higher level.'

At Oregon State University, James Leklem has been intensively studying the blood of 15 male cross-country runners and trained cyclists between the ages of 14 and 18. In all of these young men, he found that the vitamin B_6 levels of their blood rose when they worked out. That extra amount of the vitamin had to come from somewhere, Dr Leklem reasoned, but there was no change in diet to explain the rise, and the body can't synthesize its own vitamin B_6. Apparently, the body met its needs by mobilizing the vitamin from tissues in the body.

'We have seen that vitamin B_6 levels in the blood go up during exercise,' Dr Leklem says. 'Unfortunately,' he adds, 'our intake of B_6 isn't as good as it might be, and this all comes down to eating better, really.'

Meanwhile, at the University of Oregon, scientists have also been investigating the link between this vitamin and exercise. 'There is always an increase in the need for B_6 during physical stress,' Frantisek Bartos says. 'People in general have a greater-than-RDA [Recommended Dietary Allowance] need for the vitamin, but in athletes, the need is even more pronounced. We know that the amount of B_6 in a normal diet is not sufficient.' Dr Bartos says that vitamin B_6 supplements have increased his own energy.

If those findings are valid, then there are many elderly people living in a state of unnecessary fatigue. In a recent survey of men and women between the ages of 60 and 95 in central Kentucky reported in the *International Journal of Vitamin and Nutrition Research* (December 1981), 'ageing was associated with a decline in . . . vitamin B_6 status.'

The survey showed that 56.6 per cent of the patients in nursing homes and 43.5 per cent of the elderly living at home were deficient in vitamin B_6. More seriously, 27.3 per cent of the institutionalized elderly and 17.9 per cent of the non-institutionalized elderly were 'severely deficient'. Decreased digestive ability, use of diuretic medication, social isolation, limited income and lack of family support were among the reasons suggested for the widespread deficiency.

Wheat germ oil This may be another powerful anti-fatigue factor. Not much has been reported about wheat germ oil recently, and there are only a handful of wheat germ oil experts around. The patriarch among them is Thomas K. Cureton, Jr., professor emeritus and director of the Physical

Fitness Institute at the University of Illinois, who spent 22 years, from 1950 to 1972, studying the energy-producing effect of the nutrient on athletes as well as older adults and boys. In 1972, he published a landmark book on the subject, *The Physiological Effects of Wheat Germ Oil on Humans in Exercise*. 'Wheat germ oil is a kind of a fuel,' Dr Cureton says. 'It aids the production of energy in the muscle cells.'

He has found that wheat germ oil stabilizes the nervous system, lowers the pulse and increases the rest interval of the heart during work or exercise. These changes indicate better resistance to stress. In his book, Dr Cureton wrote:

> We have found that in 22 years of working with people who have taken wheat germ oil (WGO), or the related substances, there are measurable benefits and, unquestionably, benefits that cannot be measured, and no harmful effects have ever been observed . . . WGO and octacosanol [the active ingredient of wheat germ oil] taken in moderate amounts will enable most human subjects to bear stress better.

'And you don't have to be an athlete to benefit from it,' Dr Cureton says today. 'In fact, we saw more improvement among people not in training, people who weren't at the top of the fitness ladder.' In one of his experiments, wheat germ oil 'helped the endurance of middle-aged men running the all-out treadmill test and produced significant gains over a matched [but unsupplemented] group that took the same course of conditioning exercises for eight weeks.'

In what might be the most dramatic demonstration of wheat germ oil's power, Dr Cureton points to the results of the swimming events at the 1956 Olympic Games in Melbourne. Four American swimmers who started taking wheat germ oil six months before the Games all did well: one won a gold medal in the 200-metre men's butterfly, another set a world record in the 1500-metre swim, and two more placed first and second in the women's 100-metre butterfly. The other Americans who didn't use the supplement did poorly.

The gold medalist in the 200-metre butterfly was Bill Yorzyk, now an anaesthetist, and, amazingly, he still attributes some of his stamina to wheat germ oil . . . and he still uses it. Dr Yorzyk says, 'I feel strongly that wheat germ oil has helped me. I notice a difference if I forget to take it for a few weeks, and I notice a difference when I start back on. But I have no scientific evidence to back that up. It's purely anecdotal.' Dr Yorzyk says that his wife and children also take wheat germ oil daily.

Dr Cureton advises that wheat germ oil doesn't work overnight. He estimates that you will feel a difference in four to five weeks. The dosage in his experiments was about a teaspoonful a day. When wheat germ oil is sold in capsules, it is often measured in 'minims', in which case, the daily dose would be 60 minims. The oil is best absorbed when taken on a relatively empty stomach directly after exercise, Dr Cureton says. Now past 80, he swims and trains with weights for two hours a day and takes the supplement while he's still warm from exertion. Wheat germ, if it is very fresh, works almost as well as the oil, he says, and suggests a half cup (4 fl. oz) of it a day.

Pantothenic acid   There also seems to be a link between pantothenic acid (a B vitamin) and fatigue. It's known that, from pantothenic acid, the body builds co-enzyme A (CoA), a catalyst necessary for the conversion of food to energy. Low levels of CoA can be dangerous. In one experiment at the University of Nebraska, Hazel Fox and colleagues compared two groups of men – one group received the vitamin and the other was totally deprived of it. After 10 weeks, the deprived men were listless and complained of fatigue (*Journal of Nutritional Science and Vitaminology*).

That was an extreme case, but Dr Fox has found that most Americans consume barely as much as the lower end of the US RDA of 4–7 mg. 'The intake of pantothenic acid by Americans is decreasing,' she says. 'In 1955, when I first measured the intake of the vitamin by college women here in Lincoln, the average was about 7 mg a day. We rarely get figures that high now. The average is 4 or 5 mg. People just don't eat three square meals the way they used to. People aren't choosing the right foods. There are too many processed foods.

'Fatigue has been described as a symptom of pantothenic-acid deficiency,' she adds, 'and I would make a guarded statement that the evidence shows a relationship between fatigue and low pantothenic acid intake. It's something we need to look into.'

Although the current US recommended allowance for the vitamin is only 4–7 mg, it wasn't always that low. In 1963, a researcher in Hungary reported that 'a healthy adult person requires about 15 mg of pantothenic acid daily,' and he went on to say that physical work, surgery, injury and gastro-intestinal infections can double the need for this nutrient. A deficiency can be caused by liver disease, allergies and sometimes as a side-effect of drugs, he noted.

To avoid a pantothenic-acid deficiency, avoid processed foods. Researchers at Utah State University studied a wide range of foods and found that products made from 'refined grains, fruit products and extended meats and fish, such as frankfurters, sausages and breaded fish fillets' are low in pantothenic acid. Also, pantothenic acid is water soluble, so part of it may be lost during cooking.

The elderly and others who eat lightly should make sure that they eat foods rich in pantothenic acid: beef, chicken, potatoes, oat cereals, tomato products and whole-grain products (*Journal of the American Dietetic Association*, February 1981).

Vitamin C and iron Two other anti-fatigue nutrients are vitamin C and iron. Since vitamin C helps the body absorb iron, the two naturally go together.

In a study of fatigue among anaemic workers on a tea plantation in Sri Lanka, researchers found that iron supplements made them more productive. The group of anaemic workers receiving iron was compared to a group of normal workers, and all were sent out to pick tea leaves on the same hills and in the same way that they had picked them all their lives. The result, significantly, was that the iron supplements enabled the anaemic workers to equal and even outpick the normal workers (*British Medical Journal*, 15 December 1979).

In a similar study of fatigue among female garment-factory workers in the Philippines, researchers discovered that iron and vitamin C supplements improved the output of workers who were moderately to severely anaemic, but didn't change the productivity of workers who were only mildly anaemic (*Journal of Occupational Medicine*, October 1981). (*See also* ANAEMIA.)

Miners in Czechoslovakia who received 1000 mg of vitamin C a day reported less fatigue and faster reaction times after taking the vitamin (*Review of Czechoslovak Medicine*). And a study of over 400 people who filled out a questionnaire that asked them to list their vitamin C intake and their 'fatigue symptoms' showed that those who took over 400 mg of vitamin C a day had less fatigue (*Journal of the American Geriatrics Society*).

Vitamin C may relieve fatigue by cleansing the body of pollutants, such as lead and cadmium. A doctor in a Swiss village found that his patients who lived close to a busy road had twice as much fatigue (and insomnia, depression and digestive disorders) as those living 50 or more yards from the road. He treated these patients with vitamin C, vitamin B complex and calcium. Over 66 per cent got relief.

Folic acid and vitamin B_{12}　The B complex vitamin *folic acid* is a must for the creation of normal red blood cells. Without enough of this nutrient, red blood cells are too large, strangely shaped and have a shortened lifespan. A lack of healthy red blood cells means less haemoglobin, which in turn means less oxygen delivered to the body. The result is lethargy, weakness, fatigue.

A psychiatrist found that four of his patients with 'easy fatigueability' and other symptoms had low levels of folic acid. He supplemented their diet with the nutrient, and as folic-acid levels rose, fatigue disappeared (*Clinical Psychiatry News*).

However, all the folic acid in the world won't do you any good unless you get enough vitamin B_{12}. Folic acid remains trapped in a metabolically useless form until B_{12} releases it. The latter, however, is more than folic acid's understudy. It plays an important role of its own: it can relieve tiredness.

Twenty-eight men and women who complained of tiredness but who had no physical problems were given vitamin B_{12} and then asked to evaluate its effect. For many of the 28, the vitamin not only made them feel less fatigued, but also improved their appetite, sleep and general well-being (*British Journal of Nutrition*).

Beating the 'three o'clock slump'

One type of fatigue that affects nearly everyone is the 'afternoon slump'.

'It strikes most people right after lunch,' says John D. Palmer of the University of Massachusetts. He sets it at one o'clock. Other people report that it strikes them at many different times – sometimes as late as four o'clock – and in many different ways.

It may make you restless or lethargic, depressed or dull-witted – or some perplexing mosaic of them all. And it isn't only a psychological phenomenon. 'We scientists call it the postprandial [after eating] dip,' says Dr Palmer. 'It is characterized by a drop in body temperature, blood sugar, work efficiency and mood.'

But it doesn't have to get you down. One good way to see that it doesn't is by taking a good look at some other things that go down – down the hatch, that is.

'If you want to stay alert in the afternoon, have a light lunch. Avoid bread, potatoes and other stodgy foods.' That's the advice of Timothy H. Monk, research psychologist with the department of neurology at Montefiore Hospital in New York City. Dr Monk began his research in Sussex after a study conducted by a colleague there had found that 'people who had eaten a heavy lunch suffered impaired judgment and were less able to detect signals. They could not differentiate as well between varying sizes and intensities of light.'

'An excellent antidote for the afternoon slump is to eat a 100 per cent raw lunch,' says Ray C. Wunderlich, a doctor in Florida. He agrees with Dr Monk, saying that 'overeating at lunch-time is one of the biggest causes of fatigue in the afternoon. A heavy meal will drag you down, making you feel tired and heavy afterward.

'Even if your lunch isn't totally raw, many people should get rid of refined foods, sugars (including honey) and high-carbohydrate fruits such as dates, figs and bananas,' Dr Wunderlich says. 'Eat a salad for lunch, one containing such things as watercress, sprouts, chick-peas, tofu, tuna, sardines, seeds and nuts. Or have a chick-pea spread (hummus) and sprout sandwich on whole-grain bread.'

For afters, he adds, you may wish to take a vitamin and mineral supplement. 'Many times, the afternoon slump occurs because the supplements people took with breakfast are all used up by mid-afternoon,' he says. 'If these vitamins and minerals are not restored at the midday meal, a person may "run out of petrol" by mid-afternoon.' The most susceptible nutrients are magnesium, calcium, zinc, chromium, copper, vitamin B complex and vitamin C.

When the slump hits you, another way to restore many of these nutrients is by enjoying a glass of orange juice with a spoonful of brewer's yeast stirred in. That's also a good way of dealing with the hunger pangs that often accompany the afternoon slump.

The worst thing you can do is probably the most common way of dealing with that snacking urge: eating bars of chocolate or drinking soft drinks.

Our biological rhythms

'Another reason we feel sleepy in the afternoon is that we naturally operate with a 12-hour cycle superimposed on a 24-hour day,' explains Dr Monk. 'It's a holdover from when we were babies, and many scientists think that our bodies actually expect to take a rest at that time of day.'

In many parts of the world, people do. 'In Mediterranean and Latin American countries, for example, the afternoon siesta is the rule rather than the exception. People go home at lunch-time and sleep up to four hours in the afternoon, then return for an evening's work. But in our culture, the thing to do is sleep at night,' Dr Monk says. People who indulge in siestas, however, can get by with less than eight hours a night, which means they can wake up earlier.

According to Dr Wunderlich, it is not a good idea to go to bed too late. 'The most important hours for sleep are between 10 P.M. and midnight,' he says. 'The way our bodies' rhythmic cycles work, those are the hours of sleep that pay off during the afternoon of the next day.' If you don't feel like sleeping then, you will surely feel it 12 to 16 hours later.

That's when you'll also feel your oats – or anything else you had for dinner the night before. 'Dietary excesses have a way of showing up after about 16 hours,' Dr Wunderlich explains. 'That's one reason why a heavy dinner with a lot of meat or other protein is not a good idea.'

Another reason is that the short-term effect of a big evening meal is to keep you alert, which is not a good idea when you want to be asleep at 10 P.M.. On the other hand, the short-term effect of a big morning meal is to keep you alert, which is a good idea for the rest of the day. So, if it's protein you want, eat it for breakfast.

A team of researchers in Morristown, New Jersey revealed that 79 per cent of their patients who complained of fatigue, fluid retention (oedema) or both had skimped on breakfast. However, after being placed on a high-protein breakfast programme, 40 out of 58 patients 'reported obvious, in some instances dramatic, reductions in fatigue and fluid retention' (*Medical Tribune*).

Eating what they ate – including such things as meat, fish, cheese, gelatine and brewer's yeast – should also sustain you through that 10 A.M. coffee-break time with nary a need for a nibble. You'll be alert and satisfied, and the feeling will hold through noon, too, when that slump-beating light lunch is all you'll probably want – or need.

Exercise fights fatigue

A light bite will also make your lunch hour seem longer. Rather than linger at the table of temptation, do something that will improve your sleep, your diet, your outlook and your body, as well as your afternoon. Go outside. 'College kids have the right idea,' Dr Palmer muses. 'I see them playing frisbee on the lawns after lunch.' You don't have to be quite so energetic, however. Any light exercise is good. Exercise undoubtedly invigorates people. At the Duke University Preventive Approach to Cardiology (DuPAC) programme in North Carolina, researchers gathered 32 people between the ages of 25 and 61 who had sedentary lifestyles. They asked 16 of them to walk or jog for 45 minutes, three times a week, for ten weeks; the other 16 were controls and remained inactive. Before and after the programme, the experimental group took tests to measure their sense of vigour. After the experiment the participants described themselves as more 'lively', 'alert', 'full of pep' and 'energetic', and less 'exhausted', 'bushed' or 'weary' than those in the control group. (The experimental group was unaware that they were being tested for vigour.)

Dr Wunderlich recommends taking a brisk ten-minute walk. 'And breathe deeply. Overlooked factors in afternoon fatigue may include being sedentary and breathing stale air all day. Get some fresh air – and sunshine. Sometimes it also helps to take a walk to clear your head when the slump hits you, but it is well within your power to beat it before it occurs.'

• Fever

Any fever over 102°F (38.9°C) is severe enough to let the doctor know about, especially when such a fever persists without apparent cause, such as flu or some other disease. (It could indicate a serious ailment.) A prolonged fever can do harm by rapidly dehydrating the sufferer, causing malnutrition, and generally weakening resistance. In cases of serious fever, general sponging of the body or wrapping the person in a wet sheet for short periods of time will help. Plenty of fluids should be given, and as much good food as can be comfortably eaten.

A mild fever is not necessarily dangerous, however. In many cases, it is actually beneficial. That's the opinion of a growing number of scientists who have been studying the healing role of fever in both animals and humans.

'Within the past decade, considerable data have appeared which support the ancient belief that moderate fever is beneficial,' says Matthew J. Kluger, professor of physiology at the University of Michigan Medical School and author of numerous papers on fever.

The healing fire

Experiments in animals have shown just how beneficial a moderate fever can be. In one study, says Dr Kluger, adult rabbits were infected with bacteria. All those that received an aspirin-like substance to lower their fever died, but more than 70 per cent of the infected rabbits who maintained a fever survived (*Pediatrics*, November 1980).

Of course, human beings aren't likely to die from a moderate infection, fever or no fever. Still, if fever is so beneficial to animals, there must be something in it for us as well. That something turns out to be *endogenous pyrogen* (EP), a substance that seems to enhance our immunity against disease – our host – defence responses, as researchers say.

When you are challenged by bacteria or viruses, the number of white cells in your blood increases, explains Charles A. Dinarello, assistant professor of medicine and paediatrics at Tufts University School of Medicine in Boston. 'As part of their role in fighting infection, these cells engulf and destroy bacteria and viruses. When this happens, it seems to stimulate the cells to produce endogenous pyrogen' (*Human Nature*, February 1979).

Once EP is produced, it leaves the cells and travels through the bloodstream to the brain. There it seems to jolt the body's internal thermostat (located in the hypothalamus), probably stimulating the production of substances called prostaglandins, which, in turn, reset body temperature to a higher level.

Now the body must generate and conserve heat until its temperature reaches the new 'set point', says Dr Dinarello. The blood vessels constrict, diverting blood away from the skin so that less heat is lost into the air. The need for more heat signals the muscles to contract rapidly, causing shivering and chills. Then you throw on another blanket and warm your bedroom, which helps raise the body temperature even more.

Fever is the sign that endogenous pyrogen has been released from the white cells and that your body is fighting the infection. In fact, says Dr Kluger, 'the release of EP might well be one of the first lines of defence against infection, triggering an array of non-specific host – defence responses.'

EP-stimulated fever is responsible for an increase in mobility of the white blood cells and for their enhanced efficiency in killing germs. What's more, EP stimulates the production of special proteins associated with the immune response. Curiously, it also dramatically reduces the level of iron circulating in the bloodstream.

During an infection, iron is bound up and stored in the liver. Apparently, bacteria need iron to thrive even more than we do. By temporarily removing iron from the bloodstream, the body in its wisdom makes the mineral unavailable to the germs and, consequently, they cannot grow.

Fever's boost to the immune system is particularly important for people whose own defences against infection have been diminished. 'We see lots of patients whose defences have been severely compromised – because of cancer or chemotherapy for cancer, for example,' says Philip Mackowiak, associate professor of internal medicine at the University of Texas Health Science Center in Dallas. 'They need every possible aid in fighting an infection. We may be doing those patients a disservice by giving them anti-fever medication at the same time we're treating the infection. Especially since, according to our own research, antibiotic-induced destruction of bacteria is enhanced at fever temperatures. It could be that if you were taking an antibiotic and you could stand the discomfort of the fever, you would get well sooner. But this is completely hypothetical at this point.'

Conversely, researchers don't know for sure if taking aspirin would lengthen the course of an illness, but they do know how aspirin works to reduce a fever. When endogenous pyrogen is released into the bloodstream, it also stimulates prostaglandin production in the brain, which turns up the body's thermostat, causing fever. Aspirin interrupts that cycle before prostaglandins are produced. Paracetamol works in the same manner, only without some of the negative side-effects associated with aspirin.

How hot is too hot?

Just how high a fever climbs depends on how much endogenous pyrogen the white cells produce, how well the blood vessels and muscles conserve and generate body heat, and the quirks of your own individual internal thermostat.

'A high fever is really overkill,' Dr Mackowiak told us. 'There is a limit to the positive effects of increased body temperatures. Studies in experimental animals show that when the temperature begins to approach the range of 104° to 105°F, [40–40.6°C], it becomes detrimental to the animal as well as to the germs. High fevers can be especially dangerous to people with heart conditions because of the rapid heart rate and increased metabolism that accompany elevated body temperature. But under normal circumstances, fever is not too heavy a load to bear.'

Dr Dinarello adds, 'Reducing fever can eliminate unpleasant side-effects, such as malaise, headache, chills, sweating, water loss and muscle and joint aches. But it can also eliminate what may be a socially adaptive effect of fever.'

Other doctors agree that it's unlikely the phenomenon called fever would have been retained for so many hundreds of millions of years of evolutionary adaptation and in so many different groups of living creatures if it had no ultimate benefits.

'Now that we know the essential elements of fever, endogenous pyrogen and prostaglandins,' says Dr Dinarello, 'we may soon know when it is best to reach for aspirin, when to let fever run its natural course and when to use fever as a weapon against disease.'

If you use aspirin to lower a fever, keep in mind that the DHSS have recommended that parents *not* give aspirin to children under the age of 12 (or 18 to be *really* safe) because it has been linked to Reye's syndrome, a serious complication of viral diseases (*see* REYE'S SYNDROME).

Exercise produces fever

While fever may be a natural consequence of infection, that's not the only time you experience an increase in body temperature. During strenuous exercise, your body temperature can go up several degrees. Of even more significance, though, is the fact that endogenous pyrogen may be at the root of this exercise-caused rise in body temperature, just as it is during an illness. That's the opinion of Joseph Cannon, a PhD candidate who works with Dr Kluger. 'Initially, besides elevated body temperature, we know that during exercise there is a mobilization of white blood cells, an increase of the proteins associated with the host – defence response and a suppressed blood iron concentration,' Cannon says. 'Since these are also the same phenomena that occur during the initial phases of infection, we suspected that endogenous pyrogen may be responsible for both.

'To test our theory, we took blood samples from volunteers both before and after one hour of exercise (at 70 per cent aerobic capacity) on a stationary bicycle. Plasma samples taken after exercise were then injected into rats. The rats responded with increased rectal temperatures and decreased plasma iron concentrations. Injections of plasma taken from the same people before exercise had no such effect on the rats.'

Although the evidence looks good, Cannon and Dr Kluger cannot say for certain that the temperature-elevating substance they found in the plasma of exercisers is indeed endogenous pyrogen. 'We know that there's something in their plasma that has that effect, but more research is necessary to confirm our theory,' Cannon says.

Even if it is endogenous pyrogen, the two researchers don't know exactly how much is produced during exercise. 'Probably much less than during an infection,' says Cannon. 'Injecting plasma from a sick person into a rat causes a larger decrease in iron levels (about 50 per cent) than does plasma from an exercising person (about 25 per cent).

'We do know that the increase in body temperature during exercise is proportional to the intensity of exercise. That's because as you exercise, your metabolism can increase up to twenty-fold. Since human activity is only 25 per cent efficient, that means 75 per cent of the energy we use during exercise goes towards producing heat. Our volunteers had temperatures of about 101.7°F [38.7°C]. On a hot day, mine has gone up to 102°F [38.9°C]. What's more, after exercise stops, body temperature remains elevated much longer than would be expected if the body were merely dissipating heat generated while exercising. It's possible that, during exercise, the body's thermostat is reset, as occurs during a fever, and EP may be involved.

'Perhaps there is some truth to the claim that regular exercise wards off infection,' Cannon suggests.

• Fibrocystic disease

Fibrocystic breast disease, also known as *benign cystic mastitis*, has certainly frightened many women who, on awakening in the morning, have found painful lumps in their breasts. The conditions strikes almost half of all women at some point in their lives, usually between the ages of 30 and 50.

Immediate relief is gained by minor surgery, either in the doctor's office by needle aspiration or in a hospital on an outpatient basis for surgical removal of the lump. You may feel better at first, but the disease tends to be chronic, so you may find yourself returning for repeated removal of lumps or fluid.

Vitamin E seems to offer a safe, effective remedy for these cysts. It seems to reverse the abnormal ratio of oestrogen and progesterone circulating in the body during the menstrual cycle. That change in hormone levels is an antidote to oestrogen's disturbing effect of cyst formation in the breast.

Robert London, director of clinical research at Sinai Hospital in Baltimore, has observed promising results from daily oral doses of 600 IU of alpha tocopherol (a type of vitamin E) in one group of women studied. 'We treated 26 women patients in the study,' says Dr London. 'The cysts cleared up in 10 of them. Twelve more had fair responses, and only four showed no response to the treatment. That's an overall positive response of 85 per cent, and no side-effects were noted. It certainly seems to be a rational therapy for this common problem if further studies bear out our preliminary observation.'

Of course, Dr London was not entirely surprised at the results. In an earlier experiment, he and his colleagues had prescribed vitamin E to a dozen women with breast lumps. In seven, the lumps vanished, three experienced fair improvement, and only two didn't improve for some reason.

Right now, Dr London is looking for the most effective dose level of vitamin E. If all goes well, it might eliminate the need for hormone-adjusting drugs, which many doctors prescribe for fibrocystic breast disease. Danol (danazol), a male-hormone-based synthetic steroid, apparently works but has been known to cause nausea, hot flushes, nervousness, depression and menstrual irregularities in some women. Although some women respond better than others, says Dr London, relief usually follows within, at most, two months of starting vitamin E.

The role of diet

Eliminating coffee, tea, chocolate and colas from your diet also may help. All of those substances contain bioactive chemicals called *methylxanthines*, which accelerate chemical activity involved in the body's cell metabolism and cause certain sensitive tissues to proliferate.

John P. Minton of the department of surgery at the Ohio State University College of Medicine found that benign breast lumps completely disappeared within two to six months in 13 out of 20 women when they completely eliminated these items from their diet. He says that the condition will return in patients who resume their former methylxanthine intake, and that the disorder is more quickly reversed in younger patients.

• Fingernail problems

Nails, those horny disposable growths at the ends of your fingers and toes, may be the next rage in the medical world. Researchers are giving them a lot of attention these days. They're discovering that nails grow more slowly in sickness and old age than in good health and youth. Nails are harder in the malnourished than in the well fed, and there's evidence that deficiencies in iron, zinc and vitamin E can affect the texture and colour of the nails.

More significantly, certain changes in the nails' appearance and chemical content may be warning flags that pop up years in advance of an actual disease. Some researchers now see the nails as a major diagnostic tool of the future, as a 'window' on the inner processes of the body. One chemist suggests that a healthy nail may very well mean a healthy body.

Brittle nails

Brittleness is one of the most common nail complaints, and there are several possible reasons why it happens. One is iron deficiency. Researchers in Sheffield found that the nails are sensitive to changes in the body's total supply of iron and that a shortage of iron in the nail seems to be a sign of iron deficiency anaemia. The researchers also found that, among five women suffering from iron-deficiency anaemia, all complained of brittle nails, but after supplementation with iron, the nails were no longer brittle. Low iron in nails apparently meant low iron in the body, and brittleness was the clue.

'All the patients . . . complained of brittle nails', the researchers noted. 'This improved with treatment and, in parallel with clinical and a haematological [blood] improvement and well-being, there was a steady increase in nail iron content' *(Journal of Clinical Pathology)*.

Impaired circulation can also cause brittle nails, according to Norman Levine, a dermatologist at the University of Arizona College of Medicine. In a roundup of several kinds of nail problems, Dr Levine noted that brittle, thin, ridged nails that are flattened can be a sign of Raynaud's phenomenon, which is characterized by poor circulation in the fingers and toes brought on by exposure to cold or by emotional upset. Dr Levine also found that hypochromic (lack of colour) anaemia, which is usually the result of an iron deficiency, can cause 'spoon nails' which are flattened or spoon-shaped and thin. But the nail returns to normal if the underlying anaemia is treated.

'A complete physical examination should always include inspection of the fingernails and toenails' because of their clues to other disorders, wrote Dr Levine in *Modern Medicine* (15 August–15 September 1979). As the farthest tissues supplied by the circulatory system, the nails would logically show the first sign of trouble.

Another common cause of brittle nails is overexposure to solvents, detergents, nail polish and nail polish remover. Kidney problems and fungal diseases of the nails have also been mentioned as causes of brittleness. There is still apparently no consensus on whether ingesting unflavoured gelatine will make nails less brittle. Nails, like the skin and hair, are made mainly of a tough protein called keratin. Gelatine also contains protein, but not the same kind. One researcher we talked to said gelatine doesn't help; another said it might help; and a third said his wife uses it, but she can't tell whether it works or not.

Fungal infections

Some people, especially those who work around the house, are plagued by fungal infections around and under the nails. These infections can be hard to treat, and they may keep coming back. Any disruption of the skin around the nail – e.g. a hangnail or skin that's been broken by too much contact with solvents or detergents – can open the door to a whole family of yeast-like fungi. Use of tetracycline antibiotics such as Terramycin or Aureomycin can sometimes cause or aggravate one of these infections.

One method for dealing with these infections comes from the Soviet Union. Dr Eugene M. Farber of Stanford University, using an idea he says he borrowed from the Soviets, placed plasters of urea, a nitrogen-rich product of protein metabolism, on the toenails of 35 people suffering from painful or unsightly fungal infections. In seven to ten days, the urea loosened the nail from its bed, so that both the nail and the dressing could be removed together. Without the nail, the underlying infection could be treated more easily.

Dr Farber says the urea treatment is a cheap, safe and practically painless alternative to surgical removal of the nail. Its only drawback is that the dressings must be kept on the toes for a week or more (*Cutis*).

Zinc and White Spots

White spots or bands on the nail or on the nail bed (the soft tissue under the nail from which the nail grows up and out) are another common problem. Zinc deficiency has been implicated as the cause of these white markings.

Carl C. Pfeiffer of the Brain Bio Center in New Jersey proposes several links between zinc and white spots. In the 1950s, Dr Pfeiffer says, the white markings were first associated with low blood levels of albumin, a protein to which 70 per cent of the zinc in the blood is attached. Kidney or liver disease can cause albumin to be excreted through urine, and when it is flushed out, Dr Pfeiffer says, it can take zinc with it. This kind of zinc loss, as well as a deficiency of zinc in the diet, can cause the white marks.

Interestingly, Dr Pfeiffer also connected the white spots with a temporary zinc deficiency that a woman may experience a week before her period or that might result from fasting. He believes that the population in general consumes less zinc that it should – an average 11 mg per day, compared with the US Recommended Dietary Allowance of 15 mg per day (*Journal of the American Medical Association*).

A doctor in Texas believes that the white markings 'occur much more often than reported after a great variety of acute stresses, in deficiency states and with toxic reactions.'

Yellow nails

If your nails turn yellow, your body may be warning you – months or years in advance – that something is rotten in the state of your lymph system (which drains excess fluid from your tissues), and possibly your respiratory system. Yellow nails may also mean a shortage of vitamin E.

In one case history, a 65-year old woman suffered from thick, yellow nails, chronic bronchitis and lymphoedema, a swelling caused by blockages in the lymph system. Her nails had been yellow and had not grown in the previous 11 months. She had had occasional numbness in her fingertips for 30 years, leg cramps for ten years, and bronchitis for eight months. All of these problems were relieved by vitamin E.

Her doctor, Samuel Ayres Jr., of Los Angeles, wrote in the *Archives of Dermatology* 'The abnormal appearance of the nails was probably dependent on the slow rate of growth, which in turn was probably due to the impaired lymph drainage.' He felt that vitamin E would help relieve her circulatory problems, and he prescribed 800 IU daily. In about six months, her leg cramps improved, and her nails were growing out normally. After two years, with a maintenance dose of 400 IU per day, she reported that all of her original symptoms had gone or were greatly improved.

There are other, rarer, connections between the nails and disease. In a few cases, a darkening of the nail can mean a vitamin B_{12} deficiency. If the nail is white near the cuticle but dark near the tip, that may be what has been called 'a flag of chronic kidney disease'. Liver or kidney problems as well as chronic anaemia may cause white nails.

Healthy nails, healthy body

The use of the nail as a diagnostic tool is really just beginning. Chemists and nutritionists are analysing the chemical makeup of the nail and trying to interpret what it means. There's a good possibility that nail samples will eventually replace the hair sample as an indicator of an individual's trace-mineral profile.

For the past few years, Carl Moore, a professor of chemistry at Loyola University in Chicago, has been collecting toenail clippings from all over the world – from Europeans, from South Africans, even from ten-year-old children in New Jersey. He dissolves the nails in nitric acid and tests each one for its copper, zinc, chromium, cadmium, calcium and lead content. This information goes into a computer, along with the age, sex, geographical location and medical history of every toenail donor. What Dr Moore hopes to prove – and what he will only tentatively assert until all the evidence is in – is expressed in this comment he made to us: 'A healthy nail is usually found on a healthy body. If the organism has a problem, it's likely to show up on the nails. If there is something unusual about the nail, then there must be something causing it to be like that'.

The implication is that, if you can match the early stages of a disease with a certain mixture of metals in the nail, you might be able to detect the first symptons of chronic diseases such as arthritis, heart disease and diabetes, and to treat them – nutritionally – before they begin. You might also be able to detect the first sign of cadmium or lead poisoning among workers who handle those metals.

The advantage of nails, Dr Moore explains, is that they're a compressed record of chemical trends that occur in the body over a period of several weeks. In contrast, urine or blood samples reveal only day-to-day or hour-to-hour changes. When a baby is born, for example, its fingernails are already 15 weeks old, making them a record of the child's ante-natal metabolism. Also, Dr Moore uses toenails because the World Health Organization, in its research, felt that toenails are less exposed to contamination than fingernails.

Along the path of his research, Dr Moore found studies showing that women, for no known reason, have more gold in their nails than men do. He also found that, apparently because of better circulation, right-handed people will have more trace metals in their right hands. The reverse is true for lefties.

Another researcher, John R. K. Robson, a professor of nutrition at the Medical University of South Carolina in Charleston, has been running tests similar to Dr Moore's. He's been assaying hundreds of fingernails for their magnesium, iron, calcium, zinc and copper content, and he hopes to link these metals to health problems.

He began studying fingernails in 1969, when he discovered that fingernails are harder among persons suffering from protein malnutrition. He told us that a deficiency of protein prevents the calcium in nails from ordering itself in the right pattern.

Eugene Kanabrocki, a chemist at the US Customs Laboratory in Chicago, has also studied the trace-metal content of the nails. He became especially interested in chromium, zinc and selenium – three trace metals believed to help protect the body from chronic diseases – after finding that his own nails contained much less of them than did the nails of his 16- and 12-year-old sons. In particular, his nails contained only about a third as much chromium as his younger son's. Some researchers heed their own findings by supplementing their diets, and Kanabrocki is one of these. He takes a brewer's yeast supplement daily, mainly for its chromium content.

• Flatulence

Although flatulence – or 'wind' as it's known – can sometimes be a sign of a serious bowel problem or a food allergy, it's usually nothing more than an embarrassment. But there are ways to deal with this 'social problem'.

A study conducted at the Loma Linda University School of Medicine in California shows that activated charcoal cuts down the amount of gas formed after eating beans and other 'gas-producing' foods.

For the study, Raymond Hall, associate professor of physiology at Loma Linda, selected 30 men and women, aged 18 to 40, who were in good health and had never had digestive problems. 'We fed them a bland, non gas-producing meal and measured intestinal gas generated over an eight-hour period', Dr Hall told us. 'The next day we fed them a meal high in gas-producing foods –

beans, wholewheat toast, peaches and fruit juice. For this meal, however, we divided them into two groups and gave one group activated charcoal capsules and the other placebos [identical-looking but medically inactive pills].'

The group receiving placebos, says Dr Hall, produced large amounts of gas, but the group receiving activated charcoal produced much less – no more, in fact, than after the bland meal. And when the two groups ate another gassy meal, this time with the placebo group receiving the activated charcoal and vice versa, the results repeated themselves: placebo group, lots of wind; activated charcoal goup, gas levels same as the bland meal.

'Activated charcoal reduces the amount of gas either by absorbing the gas itself or by absorbing the intestinal bacteria that produce the gas,' explains Dr Hall. But no matter how it works, he believes that activated charcoal is 'a good cure for wind. If a person has a gas problem, it's well worth trying.'

For the best results, Dr Hall suggests taking activated charcoal shortly after a meal, but, he emphasizes, this won't quickly clear up a case of wind that's already developed. 'It takes several hours for activated charcoal to reach the lower intestinal tract where the gas is being produced,' he says.

Beans seem to be the worst offenders when it comes to gas-producing foods. Flatulence is caused by the absence of enzymes in our systems to break down the trisaccharides (complex sugars) in beans into simple sugar. The undigested trisaccharides are acted upon in the lower intestine by the bacteria that reside there, producing carbon dioxide gas, or flatulence. However, there's no reason to avoid these tasty, versatile and nutritious pulses. Just try preparing them this way, suggested to us by Joseph Rackis of the US Department of Agriculture's Midwestern Regional Research Lab in Illinois: Soak beans in water for at least three hours. After soaking, boil the beans in water for at least 30 minutes, then discard the water. If more cooking time is required, add fresh water and start again.

• Flu (influenza)

Both the common cold and the flu are caused by viruses, so what seems like a cold at first may develop into a full-fledged attack of flu. However, while a cold may allow you to function more or less normally, the flu can make you feel like you've been marched over by a division of soldiers. And it gets even more complicated because the flu sometimes sneaks up on you and doesn't produce any symptoms at first, but if you don't take care of yourself, you could end up with viral pneumonia.

The flu and the common cold can start out pretty much the same: sore throat, congested breathing, runny nose. Coughing is a very common symptom of the flu, though. The cough is brief and dry and occurs in spasms. There may also be pain in the chest. Eyes will be red and watery, and the face will be flushed. If the fever goes up over 101°F (38.3°C) and is accompanied by chills, headache, muscle and backaches and extreme tiredness, you've been captured by the flu. Consider yourself a prisoner of war and take it easy. Wait out the fighting still taking place inside your body between the flu viruses and your body's defences by drinking lots of fluids, staying in bed, and eating the best food you can. Chances are that the flu infection will run its course in a few days and you'll feel good as new afterwards. However, don't get out and act like it just yet, because you're not quite home free.

While you're down and out with the flu and your defences have their hands full, pneumonia-causing bacteria sometimes sneak in. And flu viruses can also cause pneumonia. Either form of pneumonia can be the second half of a one-two punch that can land you in hospital, or at least at the doctor's surgery for a few weeks' supply of antibiotics.

So stay at home a number of days and nurse yourself through. Is this the time to bring out the cold pills? No. Keep focused on the principle that comfort is the best medicine, even though that comfort is going to be more difficult to achieve now than it was in the very first days of your flu.

Grandma's Comforts

Hal Z. Bennett, author of a book called *Cold Comfort – Everybody's Guide to Self-Treatment of Colds and Flu* (1979), describes some traditional, commonsense ways of dealing with the flu.

Cosying Up   Take a very hot bath, as hot as you can stand, and then snuggle up in a nice warm bed. Remain there the whole day and through that night, even if doing so means you're neglecting your family. Read a good book or write letters to special friends who are far away. Drink lots of fluids.

For a scratchy or sore throat, try:

Hot lemon tea   Cut up two whole lemons and add to a pot of boiling water. Let steep for ten minutes. Drink with a tablespoon of honey to the cup.

For a scratchy throat with nasal or sinus congestion, there is:

Hot ginger milk   Heat, but do not boil, a pan of milk. To this, add two or three slices of fresh ginger. If fresh isn't available, use $1/4$–$3/4$ teaspoon of ground ginger. Serve hot with honey to taste.

Or try this:

Vinegar and honey   Mix equal parts (one tablespoon each) of apple cider vinegar and honey in hot water to relieve nasal congestion and aches. Can also be used to gargle.

Some cures were potent indeed:

Herbs   Herbalists today base most of their remedies on age-old recipes handed down from one generation to another. Teas such as camomile, rosehip and peppermint are used by many people to relieve symptoms of the common cold and flu. Teas of cayenne (red pepper) are said to be excellent for relieving a cough.

Cod-liver oil and garlic   A remedy for a cold or flu, which most of us probably prefer to forget, is that dose of cod-liver oil two or three times a day. Or how about swallowing some garlic?

Why old remedies work

Many traditional remedies have survived from generation to generation for the simple reason that they work. Sometimes the remedies are effective because, like the doctor prescribing pills, one feels better doing something, rather than sulking around waiting for nature to take its course. However, there is often a physiological basis for the traditional remedies, and one researcher found it intriguing to attempt to trace what some of these might be.

The physiological basis for the first remedy mentioned here 'cosying up' – is in some ways the most obvious. The main ingredient here is warmth. We know that heat increases the body's production of natural substances to reduce the viruses' ability to reproduce (*see* FEVER). Moreover, it speeds up the body's metabolic rate, creating an active, rather than a sluggish, system for cleansing away dead cells and creating new ones to replace those damaged by the viruses. And by raising your body temperature, you make a less inviting environment for the viruses. In addition, the warmth relaxes you. This absence of stress, we know, is particularly therapeutic – not only because it opens tiny capillaries throughout your body, thus increasing the flow of blood to areas of infection, but also because it keeps down your production of the hormone *cortisol*, which can reduce antibody production.

Similarly, relaxation is important in that part of the remedy which suggests writing letters to friends who are far away. During such an activity, you can daydream about pleasurable times you spent with those friends in the past, and this open, relaxed mental state, similar to some meditative states, has a definite beneficial healing effect.

Finally, drinking plenty of liquids is important in maintaining a healthy fluid level in your body. With your body temperature raised, you use up a lot more moisture than usual, and it is essential to maintain that fluid level at all times. The hot lemon tea and the ginger and the vinegar and honey recipes probably help relieve a scratchy or sore throat in two ways: first, they stimulate blood flow to the mucosal tissue of your throat; and second, they may help change the alkaline environment of your throat to a healthier acid level. Of course, lemon, ginger and vinegar also have the effect of relieving congestion, probably by stimulating those cells in the mucosal tissue of both the nasal passages and throat, which produce fluids to thin thickened mucus.

Fending off the flu

There are ways to keep from falling victim to the flu. Good nutrition can help put a barrier between you and the flu come winter.

In the three winter months of November, December and January, we as a nation spend more time huddled together for warmth in the home, at pubs and on public transport than in the other nine months combined. In addition, we eat far fewer fresh vegetables and fruit and, during the holiday period, we overeat, drink too much, stay up late and go out visiting and shopping far more than at other times of the year.

Coincidentally – or maybe not so coincidentally – this is also the time of the year when cold and flu viruses decide to go on their annual rampage.

Why winter ushers in the flu season, no one really knows. Flu researchers at the Center for Disease Control in Atlanta, Georgia suspect that the holidays bring an 'increased chance of transmission'. People crowd together at parties and in shops. Students come home from college and university, possibly bringing strange viruses along with their dirty laundry and radical ideas.

Researchers know that the flu follows a fairly regular cycle, but they don't think that flu rates automatically rise as the temperature drops. One theory has it that migrating birds, such as the mallard duck and the artic tern, unwittingly carry flu bugs from continent to continent. (Flu viruses are believed to have originated among birds, which have developed an immunity to them.) Most puzzling of all, the flu virus itself constantly changes in subtle ways and constantly forces our immune system to adapt by producing new kinds of antibodies. Some say the flu will always be with us.

Faced with this dilemma, there are at least three routes you can take. You can stock up on cold capsules and cough syrup. You can wait for a new vaccine to be developed. Or you can try the nutritional approach and shore up your resistance against whatever strange new strain of flu virus that nature decides to throw at us this year. The best way to do that is to make sure you have an ample supply of the vitamins and minerals that play a necessary role in maintaining a strong immune response.

'Nutrition is important here,' wrote a Scottish bacteriologist in the *Proceedings of the Nutrition Society* (May 1980), 'because an immune response which is not supplied with the necessary building blocks, energy or catalysts will clearly be incapable of its maximum efficiency.'

Vitamin C

One nutrient that stands between you and the flu is, of course, vitamin C. Nobel prize winner Linus Pauling is the best-known advocate of this vitamin, but other researchers have also spoken out about the beneficial effect of large doses of vitamin C on the immune system.

Benjamin V. Siegel, professor of pathology at the University of Oregon Health Sciences Center, has been studying vitamin C for several years. In experiments with mice, Dr Siegel and his assistant Brian Leibovitz found that a lack of vitamin C depresses the activity of natural immunity police called T-cells (white blood cells that seek and destroy viruses and cancer cells), and that supplements of vitamin C enhance it. Vitamin C also appeared to intensify the ability of white blood cells to rush to the scene of an infection, swallow foreign particles whole and kill bacteria.

The most exciting news, Dr Siegel says, is that vitamin C seems to stimulate the production of interferon, the natural anti-viral protein produced by cells under attack. In mouse tissue cultures, he reports, the amount of interferon doubled in the presence of vitamin C. 'I take it myself, it doesn't seem to do any harm. And it seems to be doing a lot for the animals.'

The question of whether vitamin C can actually boost resistance above normal or is simply a necessary ingredient of the body's normal immune response has also been investigated. Is vitamin C the icing on the cake, so to speak, or is it part of the cake itself?

According to Richard S. Panush, a researcher at the University of Florida College of Medicine, vitamin C is the icing. Dr Panush, working with Jeffrey C. Delafuente of St Louis University, found that vitamin C 'significantly augmented' the action of one type of human white blood cell in a test-tube experiment. They achieved their best results when they added fresh vitamin

C to their cell cultures every day. The longer the cells were exposed to the vitamin, the better the immunological response (*International Journal for Vitamin and Nutrition Research*, vol. 50, no. 1, 1980).

In a previous experiment the two men found that supplements of 1–3 g of vitamin C per day 'significantly enhanced' the white blood cell response of volunteers, as compared to a group given a placebo (*Clinical Research*, April 1979).

Zinc
Another nutrient vital to the immune system is zinc. This mineral is a critical ingredient of our defences.

'When even marginal amounts of the necessary complement of dietary zinc are missing,' says Pamela J. Fraker, an immunologist at Michigan State University, 'the immune response quickly deteriorates.' The Scottish bacteriologist we quoted earlier adds, 'Nutritional deprivation of zinc in mice leads within 28 days to severe deficiencies of cell-mediated (T-cell) immunity. In man . . . zinc deficiency leads to T-cell failure and probably to a predisposition to infection.'

How exactly does zinc work for you? Zinc apparently helps in the division of white blood cells and strengthens cell membranes. There is also evidence that the body needs zinc for wound healing and for the formation of collagen, the fibrous protein that is the chief constituent of connective tissue (*Archives of Disease in Childhood*, December 1979). A group of researchers at the University of California have shown that mice whose mothers were deprived of zinc during their pregnancy have severely under-developed spleens and thymuses. Both of those organs play important roles in immunity (*Journal of Nutrition*, April 1980).

The B vitamins
There is also some evidence that the B vitamins are needed for a fully orchestrated immune response. In a paper delivered at an Amerivan Chemical Society convention in Houston, Texas, researchers from the Massachusetts Institute of Technology reported that a folic-acid deficiency hindered white blood cells from multiplying and was, in general, associated with an increased susceptibility to infection in humans and animals. Also, unborn laboratory animals that received low levels of methionine (an amino acid) and choline (a B vitamin-like nutrient) while in the womb suffered from an impaired resistance to certain kinds of infections later in life.

At the University of Pittsburgh School of Medicine, biochemist A.E. Axelrod has shown that without the B vitamins folic acid, pyridoxine (B_6) and pantothenic acid, laboratory animals cannot produce the antibodies required to defend against invading micro-organisms such as the flu virus. The B vitamins also seemed to contribute to the 'anamnestic response' – the body's ability to remember invaders and be prepared to attack them if they appear a second time. However, Dr Axelrod cautioned that he worked only with animals and only with extreme deficiencies, and he couldn't assume that the same would be true in humans.

Vitamins A and E

These may also take part in the immune response. Researchers at Colorado State University observed a great increase in the resistance to infection of mice and chickens after their diets were supplemented with vitamin E. The vitamin apparently stimulates the production of antibodies by the glands and invigorates the action of phagocytes, a type of white blood cell that engulfs foreign material in the bloodstream (*Federation Proceedings*, June 1979).

As for vitamin A, researchers in Thailand recently found that animals deficient in vitamin A have fewer antibodies in the secretions of their mucous membranes – in the nose, for example. Certain changes in these membranes, resulting from the shortage of vitamin A, allow micro-organisms to colonize or penetrate them more easily and find their way into the body. Ordinarily, the membranes would trap these organisms and expel them (*Clinical and Experimental Immunology*, April 1980).

So if you'd rather not get into cold capsules or cough syrup in a big way, and you can't wait for the vaccine, the best thing – and maybe the only thing – you can do is to make sure you're protected by all the nutrients you need for a strong immune response.

• Foot problems

You look down on them. You squeeze them, squash them, pound them into the ground, and when they start to give you trouble, you curse them. To put it bluntly, you walk all over them. Just about the only thing you don't do to your feet is what you should do – treat them with respect.

Aching feet are more likely to elicit chuckles (if they belong to someone else) or wry appeals for sympathy (if they belong to you) than serious attention. Corns, bunions, hammer toes and the lot are easier to complain about than to correct. What's worse, the disregard with which you contemplate these down-to-earth organs is likely to be shared by your doctor.

'There's a tendency to ignore the feet,' says Melvin Jahss, chief of the Orthopedic Foot Service at New York's Hospital for Joint Diseases and Medical Center, and founder and past president of the American Orthopedic Foot Society. 'Doctors pay little attention to "minor" things like aching feet, but they can cause a lot of problems. When your feet hurt, you hurt all over.'

It's a fact that foot miseries have a way of 'infecting' the whole person. Aching feet can make it hard to feel anything but tense and irritated. 'If your feet are bothering you, you're going to subliminally pull away from the source of pain,' says Elizabeth H. Roberts, New York podiatrist and author of *On Your Feet*. 'You'll throw your posture out of line. And the more out of line your body is, the greater the stress and fatigue. When you're slumped over, your digestive tract won't function well – it will be cramped for space. You're likely to develop lower back problems, knee problems.'

Most important, perhaps, is the damage that bad feet can inflict on your plans for a full, active life. 'You'll cut down on your social life,' says Dr Roberts. 'You're not going to want to play tennis, go for long walks, do the things that make for better respiration, that keep your body agile, that keep you feeling young.'

By making walking a painful obligation rather than a pleasure, a simple bunion or a verruca can turn a vigorous person into a sedentary one who sits on the sidelines watching television, as circulation, muscle tone, and *joie de vivre* simultaneously waste away.

A lot can go wrong

It seems no exaggeration, in fact, to call the feet the foundation of good health. If so, it seems a particular shame that so many foundations are in such poor repair. Some 80 per cent of us suffer from aching feet at some time or another – according to surveys in the United States, it is the third most common medical complaint. And these complaints are not always trivial: at the Hospital for Joint Diseases, says Dr Jahss, some 20 to 25 per cent of all surgical cases involve the foot.

Why is the foot so vulnerable to ache and injury? For one thing, it is a very complex organ, a structure of 26 bones (12.5 per cent of all the bones in the entire body), 56 ligaments and 38 muscles. With each step you take, the whole ensemble must shift and flex properly to carry your weight. There's a lot that can go wrong.

What's more, this complex structure takes a heavy dose of wear and tear. By the time the average person is 35, his/her feet have carried him/her some 45,000 miles.

'When you walk, each step puts your entire weight on each foot,' says Dr Jahss. 'Pushing forward, raising your heel as you step, you may concentrate a force greater than your weight on a localized area – if you weigh 11 stone, for instance, the ball of your foot may carry $14^1/_2$ stone. Do this 1000 or 2000 times a day, and you're really beating the soles of your feet on the ground. If you hit your head against a wall 2000 times, it would be sore. That's what happens to your feet – the bones, the ligaments hurt after a while.'

Being farthest from the heart, the feet generally have the poorest circulation in the body (and this diminishes with age), which means that infections and inflammations are slow to heal. (And the warm, moist climate created by shoes and socks, incidentally, provides perfect growth conditions for bacteria and fungi.)

The natural shocks that feet are heir to may sound severe enough, but if they belong to a modern man or woman, the abuse is compounded. While it's a treat to beat your feet in the mud, it's no fun to pound them on pavement, which is exactly what most of us do.

'We're the first animals to walk upright, on two feet, and it's possible that our feet are not built to bear as much weight as we give them,' says Neal Kramer, podiatrist and member of the American Academy of Podiatric Sports Medicine. 'When we walked on soft grass, there was no problem. But now we spend most of our time on hard surfaces, and our feet have to absorb a lot more shock.'

If, like many people, you stay off your feet whenever possible, they will become even more vulnerable, experts say. A sedentary way of life makes feet weak. Encased in shoes all day, your feet remain immobile, denied for the most part the exercise they would get if you went barefoot. 'Certain foot muscles are far less pronounced than they were in bygone days – they just don't get a chance to develop,' says Dr Kramer.

The wrong footwear

When you get to the bottom of many foot problems, what you'll find is a pair of shoes. Too many people give style and appearance disproportionate weight when choosing shoes – at the expense of their feet. Cinderella's stepsisters weren't the first women to try to win a prince by jamming their feet into tiny footwear, nor were they the last. The price has been high.

'If you put your hand into a glove that kept squashing it, you hand would bother you – and it doesn't have to bear the weight the foot does,' says Dr Roberts.

Under the constant pressure and friction of ill-fitting shoes, your foot defends itself by producing the dead, toughened tissue of a callus. A corn, made up of the same tissue and formed in the same way, projects downward, into the foot, concentrating pressure into a point of pain. Shoes that press down on the toes can produce ingrown toenails or a painful thickening of the nail over the big toe.

According to Dr Jahss, some shoe styles are particularly liable to cause difficulties. 'About 85 per cent of the foot problems I see are in women,' he says. 'This is because of the style of women's shoes – they don't conform to the foot. High heels make the whole foot slide forward; it jars in the front of the shoe. The higher the heel, the more weight is carried on the ball of the foot, which can cause a callus. If a woman has a wide forefoot, it will be especially jammed and will raise the danger of such deformities as corns, bunions and hammer toes.'

Other styles are associated with other problems. The platform shoes of the 1970s, according to doctors, caused painful bleeding under the big toenail. And tight boots can actually cut off circulation. By distorting the normal way in which the foot strikes the ground and carries weight, ill-designed, ill-fitting shoes can cause damage to muscles and joints. Bunions, which are inflammations of the joint where the toes meet the foot, are often due (at least in part) to shoes that force the big toe into an unnatural angle. High heels, worn habitually, can shorten the Achilles tendon, laying the wearer open to injuries.

While shoes can be blamed for many foot problems, they can't be held accountable for all. 'Many people have a hereditary imbalance,' says Dr Kramer. 'They don't bear weight evenly and properly. A difference in limb length or an injury can produce this, too. The result may be an imbalance in muscles of the foot and leg and persistent pain'. If your foot tends to jut forward while walking, for instance, you'll end up walking on its inner rim. Not only may this produce foot problems, it will put the knee, thigh, back and shoulder out of line.

Pain that starts in the head

Strange as it sounds, those pains in your feet may have started in your head. According to René Cailliet, head of physical medicine and rehabilitation at the University of Southern California, the way you walk reflects the way you feel. 'When you're depressed, you walk more sloppily, with a shuffling sort of gait. There's less spring in your step. The mechanical stress that results can cause foot problems.' A cycle can develop, Dr Cailliet points out. 'Pain depresses you further, and this seems to magnify your emotional difficulties.'

Although verrucas (medically called *plantar warts*; painful growths on the bottom of the feet) are caused by a virus, it's often an emotional crisis or state of depression that brings them forth. And, while some people get stomach pains when they're upset, others get aching feet. 'If you're uptight, your feet may reflect it,' says Dr Jahss. And the anxiety that accompanies steady pain may aggravate it. At the orthopaedic foot clinic at the Hospital for Joint Diseases, they find that psychiatric consultations are often quite helpful, according to Dr Jahss.

By the same token, the first step to healthier feet should probably take place in your head. It is essential to recognize that your feet are not mere decorations, but sensitive, vital parts of your body deserving of good care. They have enough to carry without the added burden of vanity. (This vanity can be taken to a ludicrous extreme, says Dr Jahss: 'I've had patients who needed orthopaedic shoes for deformities but wouldn't wear them because they were ugly. They wanted to be operated on instead.')

How to shop for shoes

When buying shoes, you'd do well to follow the example of podiatrist Neal Kramer: 'I use style as the last criterion – after fit and sensible design'. Whatever the style, make sure the shoe fits. And don't settle for cheap footwear: 'With shoes, you get what you pay for'.

To give your toes a chance to spread out naturally, your shoes should be about $1/4$ inch longer than your longest toe. They should be high and wide enough not to squash your toes. The shank (the part of the shoe between the ball of the foot and the heel) should be wide enough to accommodate the bottom of the foot. Ideally, there should be no more than a 2-inch difference between the height of the heel and the sole. The sole should be flexible enough to bend with your foot and thick enough to absorb some of the shock of life on concrete.

'The shoe should conform to the foot, not the foot to the shoe,' says Dr Jahss. 'Children's shoes conform to their feet, so we don't see children with the foot pains and complications that adults have. If adults wore kids' shoes, they'd be fine'.

Give an eye to material when you buy shoes. Because they retain heat and moisture, some non-porous synthetic materials are more likely to promote fungus and bacterial infections than naturally porous leather.

Everyday foot care

You should realize, though, that some people are born with a greater tendency to such deformities as corns, hammer toes and bunions. Wearing proper footwear will minimize the chances of such problems developing, Dr Roberts says, 'but there are no guarantees. I've seen Guatemalan peasants – who never wore shoes in their lives – with bunions.'

Dr Cailliet recommends exercise – regular walking – to keep the feet strong and problem-free. 'Muscles must be exercised or they waste away; bones must be used or they soften,' he says.

If feet in your family seem especially vulnerable to disorders, ask your family doctor to refer you to a podiatrist or orthopaedist. 'He or she will identify potential weaknesses and give you advice on getting the best results,' says Dr Roberts. Special shoes, inserts or exercises may delay the onset of symptons.

The same advice – *see a professional* – applies even more strongly if your feet are actively giving you trouble. And the earlier the better. Like many medical problems, disorders of the feet respond best when treated early. And many systemic diseases – diabetes, circulatory problems and rheumatoid arthritis, for example – may show up first in the feet, so they provide an early-warning system that a doctor can use to your advantage.

For obvious reasons, self-surgery is more of a temptation when a corn, rather than an inflamed appendix, is involved, but it's still a poor idea. Given the sluggish circulation of the feet, a slight slip of the razor may result in an infection that refuses to go away. Padding around a corn to take pressure off it is fine, but avoid medicated foot pads. Many are treated with salicylic acid, which, unfortunately, has a more destructive effect on healthy flesh than on the hardened tissue of the corn.

If you have diabetes, your feet are especially vulnerable to dangerous infection. Never attempt anything that might cut or damage them.

What can a doctor do for just plain aching feet? If the root of your problem is a poor walking gait or the incorrect way you hold your foot, he can prescribe exercises, special shoes or other treatments. 'It's never too late to re-educate muscle,' says Dr Roberts.

Custom-built shoes or inserts can protect your feet from aches and pains to which they are particularly subject. An arch support, for instance, distributes the weight over the entire foot, rather than in just one area. If your foot has a particularly high arch, you may suffer from pain under the metatarsal bones (in the ball of the foot). A specially made shoe with a proper support may prevent the strain and the pain.

Ironically, you may encounter foot troubles when you take Dr Cailliet's advice and start walking, especially if you've grown used to a very sedentary way of life. 'Feet can recover their proper ability to function, but they need time,' he says. To minimize the pain of transition to an active life, do it gradually, building up tolerance to greater time and distance at your own pace. Shedding excess weight will take some of the load off your feet and minimize trouble at this time, too.

For walking, make sure your shoes are well cushioned, with soles that are thick enough to deal with the increased punishment of hitting the pavement over and over. A solid lace-up shoe is well designed for walking, says Dr Kramer, and good hiking boots will also do fine. He particularly recommends well-designed running shoes. They're good for walkers for the same reason they're good for runners: a sophisticated design that includes solid cushioning and support for the foot.

If you're an active runner, jogger or tennis player, incidentally, you should expect your share of foot pains. When you run or engage in running sports, your feet receive a force equal to three or four times your body weight each time they touch down. When pain or injury does occur, it should be given time to recover (difficult as that may be to anyone devoted to a regular regimen of running) and, if necessary, medical attention. An uncorrected foot injury can lead to a small change in running gait with big (and undesirable) results.

Morton's toe and exercise

If you have what's known as Morton's Toe, exercise may pose some special problems. Just what *is* Morton's Toe?

Well, it's attached to Morton's Foot, for starters. An that's a syndrome first noted in 1935 by Dr Dudley Morton, who observed that people with notice-ably long second toe metatarsals (the bone that stretches from the base of the second toe down to the ball of the foot) may be prone to foot breakdown if they are very active. Morton's Toe owners can often (but not always) be identified because their second toes are longer than their first toes.

No one took much notice of Dr Morton's observation until the running craze hit in the 1970s. Then George Sheehan, a noted running doctor, unearthed Morton's research and coined the terms Morton's Foot, to describe a condition suffered by many long-distance runners.

In Morton's Foot sufferers, the second toe bone absorbs some of the body weight that should be absorbed by the big toe bone. That's because it hits the ground sooner than the big toe bone. The foot compensates for the big toe's delay in reaching the ground by pronating excessively. Pronation causes the foot to roll too sharply in or out – and that can mean all kinds of twisting problems, including arch strain, runner's knee and shin splints.

Besides commonly having a big second toe, Morton's Foot sufferers often have calluses under the ball of the foot or directly under the second toe bone, says John Pagliano, a podiatrist in Califonia and a well-known runner's foot specialist in the United States. They also can experience a burning sensation in the toes.

Dr Pagliano says runners who suspect they have a Morton's Foot that is causing mild pain should try wearing highly cushioned running shoes to cushion the front of the foot and relieve stresses. The shoe should also have good rear-foot control (usually a firm heel counter) to keep the foot from pronating too sharply. Severe Morton's Foot sufferers can be fitted with a specially designed shoe device to correct the problem.

Morton's Foot runners also should avoid hard surfaces such as cement, says Dr Pagliano. But overly soft surfaces, like sand, can cause further foot instability.

Foot care for special conditions

Intelligent foot care is particularly crucial for anyone with diabetes, heart disease or arthritis. In those illnesses, few things are as important as staying active – yet the aching feet those conditions often bring make activity less than tempting. The important thing is to break the cycle of inactivity (under a doctor's supervision) and start a new cycle. The more you walk, the more you'll maintain the circulation in your legs, the less pain you'll have and the more you'll feel like walking.

If you've grown resigned and accustomed to the steady throb and sharp jabs of problem feet, it may take some energy to exchange complaints for constructive action. To overcome inertia, try to visualize the difference – the big difference – that healthy, pain-free feet can make in your life.

For information on fungal infections that afflict the feet, see ATHLETE'S FOOT; for information on muscle cramping problems, see CRAMP.

• Gall bladder problems

She used to be between 40 and 50 years old, but she's getting younger. She used to have a lot of children, but they're getting fewer. She used to have blonde hair, but it's getting darker. She used to be a woman, but . . .

What's going on here?

We're describing the typical victim of gall bladder disease. The profile is changing as the disease becomes more widespread – an increase that the experts say could be prevented. This is because, for the most part, it's what you put into your mouth that causes gall bladder disease, and it's what you put into your mouth that can cause it to go away. Obviously, gall bladder disease has a lot to do with your diet.

Eating too many foods that are too high in cholesterol has been linked to a variety of disorders, including heart disease and cancer. However, cholesterol has an even more direct link to gall bladder disease.

Your gall bladder is about the size and shape of a pear. It's located just under your liver, behind your bottom right rib, and it stores some of the cholesterol produced in the liver, some of which your body needs in order to digest food. Along with lecithin and various bile acids, cholesterol is a constituent of bile, which the liver secretes during digestion. After digestion, any unused bile is stored in the gall bladder, where it remains until the next meal.

If the meal is a fatty one, rich in dietary cholesterol, the bile becomes 'saturated' with cholesterol. And as the bile awaits its next job, the excess cholesterol starts to separate out, since bile tends to stabilize at a certain ratio of cholesterol to lecithin to acid. The excluded cholesterol reacts like a bored and lonely adolescent: it plays ball by itself; then it sulks; and then the soft fatty balls calcify into rock-hard gallstones. As well as cholesterol stones, two other types of gallstones may develop: mixed stones (comprising cholesterol and bile) and pigment stones made of green bile pigment).

Later, a gallstone may go out looking for trouble – in the small bile duct leading from the liver and gall bladder into the small intestine. If it gets stuck there, the gallstone may cause gall bladder inflammation, liver damage, hot and cold flushes that mimic the menopause, jaundice, pancreatitis, nausea, vomiting and colic: in short, gall bladder disease. In the advanced stages of the disease, when the gallstone is *really* stuck and the gall bladder is badly infected, surgery may be unavoidable. But things needn't get that bad, because gallstones – and gall bladder disease – *are* avoidable.

Dissolving stones

One of the liver's own bile acids is a compound called chenodeoxycholic acid (CDCA). The latest scientific findings indicate that supplemental CDCA will dissolve most of the gallstones in about half of the patients who take the medicine every day for two years. However, there are side-effects: everything from diarrhoea to a 10 per cent increase in serum cholesterol, particularly in the low-density lipoprotein (LDL) fraction that has been implicated in heart disease. 'This side-effect,' cautions Kurt J. Isselbacher of the gastro-intestinal unit of Massachusetts General Hospital in Boston, 'cannot be taken lightly, because such an increase may pose an added risk for those patients prone to coronary artery disease' (*Annals of Internal Medicine*, vol. 95, no. 3, September 1981).

One of the best ways to lower your risk of acquiring coronary artery disease also happens to be one of the best ways to increase the efficacy of CDCA, and that's to alter your eating habits. C. Noel Williams, head of the division of gastro-enterology at Dalhousie University in Halifax, Nova Scotia, found that the gallstones of patients on CDCA, who were also placed on a diet low in fats and refined carbohydrates but high in protein, fibre and complex carbohydrates, dissolved in about one-third the time it took those on CDCA alone. Right now, Dr Williams is looking into the effects of diet alone, without CDCA. People placed on a special diet programme after treatment with CDCA have not had a return of gallstones in six months or more.

Dr Williams says that bran is a good source of the fibre he recommends, and another Canadian researcher may have the reason why. In a series of studies conducted by Dr Roderick M. McDougall at the University of Alberta, both gallstone sufferers and healthy controls who ate 50 g of bran cereal a day excreted double the usual amount of cholesterol in their stools – indicating that the cholesterol had been cleaned out of their gall bladders (*Journal of the American Medical Association*, 16 March 1979).

A good way to get the protein Dr Williams recommends is to eat soyabeans. A study done on hamsters at the Wistar Institute of the University of Pennsylvania in Philadelphia revealed that

> substitution of vegetable [soya] for animal [casein, a milk derivative] protein significantly inhibited the development of gallstones in hamsters . . . Of even greater interest is the observation that a solubilizing effect is seen when [soya] protein is administered to hamsters with pre-established gallstones [*American Journal of Clinical Nutrition*, November 1979]

Lecithin

Cholic acid (an acid occurring naturally in bile) and lecithin (a phospholipid that is the main emulsifier in the blood and comprises part of the myelin sheaths covering the nerves) have together been shown to dissolve gallstones taken from human patients. Scientists in Australia decided to see if the same effect seen in test tubes could be reproduced within the human body. They gave a group of five gallstone patients cholic acid and lecithin and monitored both the chemical composition of their bile and the size of their gallstones.

In three patients, the gallstones got smaller or disappeared completely. In all five patients of the group whose bile was tested, the chemical tendency of the bile to form stones was decreased. 'A combination of cholic acid and soyabean lecithin does lower the cholesterol saturation of bile,' the researchers concluded, 'and may promote gallstone dissolution' (*Lancet*).

A study of eight gallstone patients tested lecithin alone. The lecithin clearly reduced the patients' pain and, again, altered the chemistry of bile in a way that would help dissolve the stones. One patient had fewer and less serious attacks of pain, improved bile chemistry and an apparent decrease in the size of his gallstones (*American Journal of Gastroenterology*).

Lecithin occurs naturally in foods other than soyabeans – egg yolks and liver also contain large amounts – but to reap the benefits of lecithin's action in the bloodstream, it's probably best to stick with the relatively *unsaturated* soyabean lecithin rather than try to utilize the saturated lecithin in animal sources. In a study with Rhesus monkeys, Robert J. Nicolosi, a Harvard biochemist, found that unsaturated lecithin lowered cholesterol and triglyceride levels. (Dr Nicolosi's monkeys had been on a diet of high cholesterol and sugar for ten years prior to the study.) He told us that he believes that saturated lecithin would *not* have caused the beneficial changes in his monkeys that the unsaturated lecithin did, but, he adds, the question as to whether saturated or unsaturated lecithin is an important determinant in the response still needs to be resolved.

The effect of soyabean lecithin on cholesterol deposits *has* been compared to egg yolk lecithin in laboratory rabbits, however, and the soyabean variety proved to be a much more effective anti-cholesterol agent.

The lecithin supplements you can buy at health food shops, etc. are derived from soyabeans and come either in granule or capsule form. The granules are much more potent, one tablespoon equalling ten 1200 mg capsules in lecithin content, or about $7\frac{1}{2}$ g of lecithin.

Diet and gallstones

So, it might be a good idea to eat a bowl of bran cereal with soya milk for breakfast – sprinkled with lecithin granules (which have a nut-like flavour). At any rate, it's definitely a good idea to eat breakfast: a French study revealed that young women who either skipped breakfast or had only coffee experienced a much greater incidence of gallstones than young women who ate a morning meal. The researchers concluded that long intervals between meals 'might increase the risk of gallstone formation' (*British Medical Journal*, 28 November 1981).

With the same amount of protein and a taste that is very similar, soya milk lacks most of the cholesterol contained in regular whole milk, and it has only 74 calories per 8 fl. oz – about half the amount you get from cow's milk. That's something to keep in mind, because counting calories – or, in any case, losing weight – may have a profound effect on gall bladder disease.

It is certainly true that anybody who eats the high-fat, high-cholesterol foods that may cause gallstones is likely to be overweight, and the famous Framingham Study of 5000 Massachusetts residents revealed that being 20 per cent overweight *doubles* a person's susceptibility to gallstones. And a person who is really obese – say 22 stone – produces twice the amount of biliary cholesterol of someone who weighs half that amount.

Going on a diet worked wonders for a 42-year-old woman with a painful gallstone the size of a small apple. The woman, who was 55 lb overweight, refused to have gall bladder surgery but took her doctor's advice and followed a 1000-calories-a-day diet.

After 15 months, she had lost 41.8 lb – and her gallstone had disappeared. Four months after that, the woman had lost 55 lb and was down to her ideal weight of 10 stone; her gall bladder was functioning normally and continued to do so, according to her doctor, J. R. Thornton of the University Department of Medicine at the Bristol Royal Infirmary. Dr Thornton concluded that 'this patient's gallstone dissolved solely because she dieted and attained normal body weight' (*Lancet*, 1 September 1979).

To the extent that you may be prone to develop gallstones, exercise after dinner is an especially good idea because according to Vlado Simko, a specialist in digestive diseases, and formerly in the department of internal medicine at the University of Cincinnati College of Medicine:

> exercise performed when no food is entering the body probably improves the cholesterol solubility in bile and helps in preventing formation of cholesterol crystals, perhaps the starting point for cholesterol gallstones

Exercising after a meal, Dr Simko believes, increases the flow of bile and improves the efficiency of digestion, specifically improving the intestinal absorption of fat.

• Glaucoma

There are several kinds of glaucoma, a disease that strikes the eyes. The most common form doesn't cause pain: instead, the angle of vision is gradually reduced. It usually is detected only during a routine eye examination but can cause loss of vision if allowed to progress without treatment. Another type of glaucoma causes attacks of symptoms that come and go. There can be vision loss, halos around lights, some pain in the eye and head, and even nausea and vomiting. Anyone with these symptoms should see a doctor right away.

To have a clearer idea of the mechanics of glaucoma, think of the fluid inside an eye as being like the water in a full bathtub. Imagine that water is slowly running into the tub, and there is a slow leak through the drain. If that tub were like a normal eye, the water coming into the tub at the top would equal the water leaking out at the bottom. The tub would not overflow.

A tub representing an eye with glaucoma would not have a balanced intake and outflow. The drain of the eye, called *Schlemm's canal* , would be partially blocked. Water could not pass away fast enough, and the tub would overflow.

Of course, the human eye can't overflow like a bathtub. So when more fluid comes in than goes out, pressure builds inside the eye and that can be very destructive to the delicate structures inside the eye. Often, vision is impaired, and in extreme cases, blindness results.

Dr Ira A. Abrahamson, Jr., in his book *Know Your Eyes*, says 'Glaucoma might be compared to a rock lying on a bed of green grass.' If you let the rock stay on the grass for a long time, it will kill the turf underneath, but if the rock is moved soon after it's put there, the grass will spring back to life. With glaucoma, finding out about the problem early is very important.

Prevention of glaucoma is by far the best approach. Until recently prevention was not thought possible, because the cause of glaucoma was not known. Strictly speaking, we still don't know why the canal draining the eye becomes blocked, but thanks to observations and research in Africa, it appears clear that nutrition is an important factor. A doctor there has found that good nutrition can often cure and can prevent some cases of glaucoma. He's Stanley C. Evans, director of research of Eye Centres (Nigeria), Inc. That organization is an ophthalmic-nutritional clinic, and the research results produced there could reverberate around the world.

Eye problems in Africa

Eye disease is an extremely serious problem in West Africa. The incidence of blindness is roughly eight times what it is in industrialized countries, but that is only the tip of the eye-problem iceberg: Dr Evans estimates that eye disorders are 10 to 15 times as common in Nigeria as they are in the United Kingdom. Even more shocking is his claim that 'over 50 per cent of the population suffer from one form of eye disorder or another which lowers the visual acuity and visual efficiency.'

These eye problems have a staggering effect on health. In addition, there is great loss of income and efficiency. Traffic accidents, too, have become an extremely serious problem; but many people continue to drive, even though they have very poor vision, for fear of losing their jobs.

The traditional approach to these eye problems in Africa is to fit people with glasses, but that doesn't solve the problem and it often makes it worse. Much of the poor vision there is caused by physical disease, and the disease process continues regardless of the use of lenses to aid sight. In fact, the glaucoma problem in Africa is so widespread that loss of sight can occur within days of a person being examined and told that his or her eyes are OK. Children as young as eight years old get glaucoma in Nigeria, while in the West it is considered a disease of older people.

There are also serious nutrition problems in Nigeria. While there is not much outright starvation, the typical Nigerian diet is high in starchy foods such as maize, millet, rice and sweet potatoes and low in fruit, green vegetables and protein. In addition, widespread poverty makes it difficult for many families to buy enough to eat. The result is widespread deficiency of vitamin A and protein, as well as shortages of other important vitamins and minerals, including iron and calcium.

Dr Evans's approach to preventing and even curing eye disease is based on improving nutrition. He treated a group of 15 patients by giving them large daily doses of vitamins A, B complex, C and E and additional amounts of protein. In most cases, he claims, the pressure inside the eye – a measure of glaucoma – was reduced to within normal limits within a week, and vision improved as well. In short, he says, he has found improved nutrition to be a much better cure for glaucoma than drugs, which he has also used during his 30- year career practising ophthalmic nutrition.

These nutrition experiments are just part of Dr Evans's work. He has made nutritional counselling part of his eye practice for years and has seen many examples of eye improvement when people's vitamin intake is changed. Today, he rarely uses drugs.

Other dietary deficiencies

Glaucoma has also been linked to thiamin deficiency. Measuring the thiamin blood levels in 38 patients with glaucoma, researchers found that they had a 'significantly lower' average level than 12 healthy people (*Annals of Ophthalmology*, July 1979).

Other evidence of a diet–vision relationship is accumulating. We were told of the work of Dr Evans in Nigeria by Merrill J. Allen, professor of optometry at Indiana University. Dr Allen told us that he has seen similar effects of nutrition on glaucoma in the United States. Hopefully, more eye doctors there and elsewhere will get interested in nutrition studies.

Glaucoma is a dangerous problem. It would be a serious mistake for anyone who even thinks he has glaucoma to avoid being tested and treated conventionally. Many more older people should also have routine tests for pressure inside the eye, even if they don't have symptoms. Avoiding tests and treatment for glaucoma means running the risk of blindness.

There is no risk in trying to prevent glaucoma, though. We should all be doing that, simply by eating the best possible diet and making sure we get adequate vitamins.

• Gout

Gout is a painful, hereditary form of arthritis that appears to be caused by faulty metabolism of purines, substances found in high-protein foods. Purine metabolism produces uric acid, which is normally excreted in the urine, but with gout, it is kept in the blood, where it forms crystals that are deposited in the joints and cartilage. Seventy per cent of the time, the joint that suffers is that of the big toe. This becomes swollen, inflamed and too painful to walk on. After a few days or weeks, the symptoms subside, but they come back, and as the disease progresses, the attacks come more frequently and last longer. Gout can be treated medically, and sufferers are told to avoid high-purine foods such as organ meats, sardines and gravies. But adding something to your diet – cherries – might help clear up gout for good.

Over 30 years ago, Ludwig Blau cured his gout by eating six to eight cherries each day (*Texas Reports on Biology and Medicine*). He didn't get the idea from a herbalist, though. Looking for something to eat one evening, he snacked on a bowl of cherries. The next day, the pain in his gouty big toe – pain so intense he used a wheelchair – was gone. And it never came back as long as he ate cherries, but if he stopped even for a few days, the gout returned. In his article, Dr Blau mentioned 12 other people who cured their gout by either eating cherries or drinking cherry juice.

Since Dr Blau's story was first printed in the early 1950s, many readers have written to the US magazine *Prevention* to say that they have successfully treated their gout with cherries. A man who had suffered with gout for 15 years got almost total relief by eating cherries every day. A woman whose gouty, swollen knee ached and throbbed for two years cured herself in a week by eating cherries. Canned, frozen or fresh do the trick, readers say. And it doesn't matter whether the cherries are the sweet or sour variety.

• Gum disease

'Open wide, please.'

'The plaque between your teeth tells me that you haven't been flossing the way I asked you to. There's a lot of tartar on those molars, too, and the bleeding along the gum line shows that you haven't been brushing correctly.'

'But don't worry. We'll just peel some skin of the roof of your mouth and graft it onto your gums. And we'll replace those loose teeth with some nice bridgework. You'll be smiling again in no time, and it'll cost only a few hundred pounds.'

If you're one of the many who suffers from periodontal, or gum, disease, you may have heard this sort of spiel from your dentist. According to the Health Education Council and the Scottish Health Education Group, among adults aged 35 and over, who still have some natural teeth, over 90 per cent show evidence of peridontal disease. Tooth decay is what ruins children's teeth, but for adults, the enemy is gum disease.

The disease starts when a coating of plaque forms on the teeth. Plaque is a sticky film of food and bacteria that accumulates between teeth, along the gum line and behind poorly fitted dentures. If you don't carefully remove all of the plaque every day, the overlooked bacteria will attack your gums. The gums may start to bleed and pull away from your teeth, and when they do, you're in trouble: the infection can strike at the tooth sockets (called the alveolar bone), and the teeth may eventually loosen and fall out.

The scary part of periodontal disease is that it can sneak up on you. One doctor compares it to glaucoma and says 'You don't know you have it until your teeth get loose.' Actually, there are warning signs. Bad breath is one and so are bleeding gums, but the bleeding may stop and there may not be any pain, even when the disease is silently progressing. Antibiotics are sometimes used to halt infection, and surgery might be needed to repair the damage.

Unfortunately, treatment is painful, time-consuming and expensive. The process of stripping away the infected gums can take six to eight months and cost a packet, but that's less than half of it. Only skin grafts can replace the lost gums, and if any teeth come out, the price of fancy gold and porcelain bridgework can be astronomical.

Indeed, nature has been unfair to the gums. Not only are they continuously bathed in an infectious mixture of bacteria and food particles, but they may be the last to get their share of indispensable vitamins and minerals. Even when the rest of the body has enough vitamin C and folic acid, the gums may still be deficient, and when the blood needs more calcium, it robs the tooth sockets first. As a result, the gums need extra amounts of those three nutrients.

Vitamin C

There is evidence that vitamin C protects gums from infection, but no one knows how, exactly. Some researchers think that it makes white blood cells tougher and faster and better at killing bacteria. Others say that vitamin C promotes the formation of healthy new gum tissue. And still others think that it latches on to iron molecules, thus depriving bacteria of one of their essential foods.

However, the dentists who use vitamin C in their practice for treating or arresting periodontal disease don't wonder how it works. They just know that it does. One such dentist is Robert C. Miner, who practises in New Hampshire. 'If I see someone with periodontal disease, I recommend Vitamin C, along with calcium,' Miner told us. 'As far as results go, it's hard to document the effects. But I know that if people with trench mouth [a gum disease caused by poor nutrition and stress] start taking a gram of vitamin C a day, and take a short course of antibiotics, the condition will improve.'

Robert Miner should know. He inherited a good deal of his expertise from his father, who was also a dentist. 'He was dean of the Harvard School of Dentistry between 1919 and 1944,' Miner says, 'and he was a pioneer in the use of nutrition in dentistry. At the time, he was a maverick, but today the things he suggested have become common practice. I grew up with those ideas, and I've tried to carry them further.'

'My feeling is that if the body has adequate nutrition, it is more likely to resist disease. In well-nourished people, you don't see the kind of breakdown that you see in people who are undernourished. And I should add that 80 to 85 per cent of the people who wear dentures are undernourished, because they avoid most of the foods they have trouble chewing'.

A whole raft of experimental data verifies the importance of vitamin C in gum disease. For instance, researcher Millicent Goldschmidt of the University of Texas Health Science Center at Houston has mixed vitamin C in liquid and given it to monkeys. The vitamin reduced to very low levels the population of one of the disease-promoting types of bacteria in the monkeys' mouths. The bacteria need iron to survive, and the vitamin C may somehow keep it away from them. Similar research has been going on in both the United States and

Yugoslavia. In Seattle, Washington, Olav Alvares and a team of researchers put a group of monkeys on a vitamin C deficient diet for 25 weeks and discovered that it made their gums easy prey to inflammation. The 'pockets' – that is, undesirable pouches between teeth and gum where bacteria like to hide and flourish – were larger than normal in the vitamin C deficient animals. A diet low in Vitamin C apparently elevates the risk of gum disease, they concluded (*Journal of Periodontal Research*, November 1981).

In Yugoslavia, experiments have shown that vitamin C might be able to reverse the kind of gum breakdown seen in periodontal disease. Researchers there looked at samples of cells taken from the gums of 21 volunteers whose diets contained very little vitamin C. Under an electron microscope, the researchers saw the biological equivalent of a tumbled-down brick wall. Collagen and other structural components, which are the bricks and mortar of healthy tissue, were literally broken and dishevelled. However, after the volunteers were given 70 mg of vitamin C daily for six weeks, the cells pulled themselves together and began to look organized and vigorous. The changes 'correspond to a very early phase in tissue regeneration' wrote the researchers. They noted that vitamin C is necessary for the formation of collagen, which is a protein, and that collagen is a critical building block for the gums and a lot of other tissues. Vitamin C deficiency alone won't cause periodontal disease, the researchers said, but it can make it worse (*International Journal of Vitamin and Nutritional Research*, vol. 53, no. 3 1982).

Calcium

This is another key ingredient in the prevention or arrest of periodontal disease. A growing number of researchers say that calcium deficiency can weaken the alveolar bone, making it more vulnerable to infection and ruining its ability to grip and anchor the teeth.

'Calcium has nothing to do with the teeth, actually,' says Anthony Albanese, director of research at the Burke Rehabilitation Center in White Plains, New York. 'It has to do with the alveolar bone, which surrounds the teeth. This is the most active bone in the body; it turns over its calcium frequently, picking up calcium from the blood and giving it back.'

Women should be especially conscious of their calcium intake. Like the rest of the bones in a woman's body, the alveolar bone tends to become more fragile and calcium deficient after menopause. 'We find that women's teeth become loose after they've had two or three pregnancies,' Dr Albanese told us. 'That's because the unborn child needs 400 mg of calcium a day, and its needs take precedence over its mother's.'

During pregnancy, many women suffer from inflamed gums – estimates range from as low as 30 to as high as 100 per cent of them.

Beyond that, women frequently go on diets, which limit their calcium intake, and when they reach the menopause, they lose even more, says Dr Albanese. He recommends extra calcium, along with a vitamin D supplement to improve calcium utilization.

'We start our women patients on calcium as early as we can,' agrees John M. Cusano, a nutrition-oriented dentist in New York State. 'We tell them that even the American Medical Association recommends a gram of calcium a day for post-menopausal women. When my patients ask me why their doctor doesn't prescribe calcium for them, I just say that he probably hasn't heard about it. If he knew, he probably would.'

Cusano is something of a model among nutrition-minded dentists. 'We started using nutrition in our practice about seven years ago, and we've had excellent results,' he told us. 'We explain to our new patients what it means to eat a balanced diet. When they first come in, more than half of them are eating an inadequate amount of vegetables. We try to get them to eat more vegetables, and we try to get the big coffee drinkers and smokers to cut down.

'Then we put them on a supplement programme. At first, we 'shotgun it' by giving them a small multivitamin supplement. After the body acclimates itself to the vitamins, we start them on 1500 mg of vitamin C per day, or 500 mg with each meal. Then, if they have periodontal disease, we start them on calcium supplements. After four to five weeks, we have them on the full programme, which includes all the B vitamins, vitamin C, vitamin E and calcium.

'Some of the patients ask me why they need more than the minimum daily requirement of the vitamins. I tell them that the minimum daily requirement is fine if they're looking for minimum daily health. But we're looking for maximum daily health. A lot of it depends on whether we can motivate the patients. We have a microscope here, and we let them look at the bacteria that are damaging their teeth. When they see them, they believe it.'

Unfortunately, in the United Kingdom prevention-minded dentists are very few and far between. Rather than being paid a capitation fee as GPs are – that is, an annual payment for each name registered with them – they are paid by the DHSS on a 'piecework' basis: fees for every procedure performed (fillings, cleaning, bridges, dentures, etc.). Teaching patients preventive measures to avoid tooth decay and gum disease simply isn't paid for. In addition, paying dentists for treatment only often leads to overtreatment – particularly unnecessary fillings.

Folic acid and other helpful substances

This B vitamin also seems to play an important role in stopping the advance of periodontal disease. According to one theory, the gums themselves can be deficient in folic acid even when blood tests show that the rest of the body has enough. And a lack of this nutrient apparently weakens the gums' ability to fend off bacteria.

Under experimental conditions, folic-acid deficiency has been corrected with a mouthwash that contains the vitamin. At the New Jersey Dental School, researchers asked a group of 15 volunteers with inflamed gums to gargle twice a day – after breakfast and right before bed – with some folic-acid-rich water. After 60 days of gargling, the researchers examined the group's gums.

The gums had soaked up the folic-acid like sponges, and the volunteers' gums were much less inflamed. They were also less inflamed than the gums of a 15-member control group who had been asked to gargle with plain water for 60 days (*Journal of Oral Medicine*).

In another study of 30 women performed during their fourth and eighth months of pregnancy, those who rinsed their mouths twice daily for one minute with a folic-acid mouthwash experienced a 'highly significant improvement' in the health of their gums (*Journal of Clinical Periodontology*, October 1980).

Folic acid isn't the only balm that can be applied directly to the gums to prevent periodontal disease. Paul Keyes, a former researcher at the (US) National Institute of Dental Research, says that applying two common household products – baking soda and/or salt – can also help. If mild infection is already present, hydrogen peroxide may be added. This should be used with professional guidance and supervision, though.

'For example, you can use half- or full-strength hydrogen peroxide, depending on a professional's recommendation, to wet your toothbrush instead of using water,' Keyes, who now lectures for the non-profit International Dental Foundation, told us. 'Then dip the brush in baking soda and smear the mixture along the gum line, making sure to get in all the crevices between the teeth and gums.

'The mixture has four effects. It disorganizes bacteria and foams them away. It also selectively disinfects or kills some of the bacteria, and it detoxifies bacteria and bacterial by-products.'

• Haematuria

Haematuria – blood in the urine – isn't a disease in itself, but a symptom. It can be caused by a urinary-tract infection, a kidney stone or an injury to a kidney. It occurs in some distance runners, too. If all these are ruled out, consider what you have been drinking.

Pepsi and Coca-Cola – and probably all carbonated soft drinks – can be hard on your body. Daniel Thompson, a doctor in Wichita, Kansas, says he has discovered that soft drinks can cause haematuria. In a letter to the *Journal of the American Medical Association*, Dr Thompson detailed two cases of men with haematuria. Both men were hospitalized, and after three days their haematuria stopped.

'Both of these patients were released to return to work on the same day,' Dr Thompson wrote. 'They both returned within the week with gross hematuria. They both had identical jobs at soft-drink bottling plants checking bottles for foreign material. When they were thirsty, they would take a bottle of carbonated beverage off the line and drink it. They rarely drank water. They were both advised to drink no more soda pop, and neither had hematuria again that summer.' Dr Thompson told us that the men worked at a Coca-Cola and a Pepsi bottling plant.

And at the very moment we called, Dr Thompson told us, there was a ten-year-old girl 'in my office right now' with physical problems from drinking soda. The girl did not have blood in her urine but had burning when she urinated.

'What we see in lots of kids – the hot and heavy drinkers of soda pop – are difficulty in sleeping, belly aches, burning during urination and blood in the urine,' Dr Thompson told us.

Things may go better with Coke, but people go better without it, it seems. Especially younger people – the primary-school children and teenagers who drink more than their share of the billions of pounds worth of soft drinks sold every year.

What are the long-term effects of this habit? Dr Thompson wanted to see more facts before answering. But he knew one thing for sure: 'Certainly not good health.'

• Haemorrhoids

Haemorrhoids – commonly called 'piles' – are grape-sized swellings in the anus. Historians say that a severe case of haemorrhoids kept Napoleon off his horse at Waterloo, delaying the battle and losing him the war. Haemorrhoids have figured in another war – doctors have fought for years over exactly *what* they are and *how* they are caused.

Some doctors blame haemorrhoids on evolution: according to this theory, gravity tugs at the anus, pulling it out of shape. Others say that haemorrhoids are hereditary. Still others fault the body's basic design: years of use almost inevitably rupture the anal veins. All of these theories have one thing in common: they believe that haemorrhoids are an unpleasant but practically inevitable feature of life. In short, haemorrhoids are *natural*.

However, Denis P. Burkitt, a British surgeon, has mustered a huge army of evidence and routed all these theories. Writing in the *British Medical Journal*, Burkitt presents studies showing that haemorrhoids are 'rare' among rural Africans (so much for haemorrhoids being 'natural'), but in urban Africa, 'where Western dietary customs have been adopted over recent years,' haemorrhoids are on the increase.

What's in the Western diet that causes haemorrhoids?

It's not what's in the diet; it's what's left out. Fibre.

Fibre is the indigestible part of a food, the roughage that adds bulk to the stool. Natural foods such as vegetables, fruit and grains are high in fibre, but refined 'Western' foods such as sugar and white bread are low.

The typical diet of rural Africa relies heavily on natural foods; the natives who eat it pass large, soft stools – and almost never have haemorrhoids. The typical Western diet relies heavily on refined foods; those who eat it tend to pass small, hard stools.

However, they don't pass them easily. They push. They grunt. They strain. And straining – day after day, year after year – punishes the anus with high, unnatural pressures. Haemorrhoids are the result.

Well, that tells you what *causes* haemorrhoids. But what *are* they? 'Nothing more than a sliding downward of part of the anal canal lining.' wrote Hamish Thomson *(British Journal of Surgery)*.

In another article, Thomson explained that thick 'cushions' of tissue, veins and muscle in the anal canal allow it to be either wide open during defecation or tightly closed before and afterward. The cushions are built to stay in the anal canal, but straining and bombardment by hard faeces can push them out of the anal canal. It is these fallen cushions that doctors call haemorrhoids.

'Accepting this explanation,' wrote Thomson, 'it follows that haemorrhoids are preventable . . . by adding bran [the high-fibre husk of wheat] to the diet to ensure the regular passage, without straining, of a soft stool.'

Great – if you don't have haemorrhoids. But what if you do?

'Bran should always be added to the diet' of a person suffering from haemorrhoids, advised Thomson. By softening the stool, bran saves the irritated tissues of a haemorrhoid from more wear and tear. However, bran is only a first step. Bioflavonoids could be the second.

Bioflavonoids are a group of substances found most abundantly in the white rind of citrus fruits. A doctor in Switzerland treated over 200 haemorrhoid patients with a bioflavonoid. The results, he said, were 'extremely encouraging, especially where early stages of the disease are concerned. Pain and pruritus [itching] . . . often . . . disappeared entirely.'

But if your haemorrhoids are painful – and especially if they're bleeding – it's time to see your doctor, who may refer you to a specialist. The latter may decide that your haemorrhoids should be removed, but don't let him or her talk you into a haemorrhoidectomy, the surgical removal of haemorrhoids. This operation is very painful and doesn't always give complete relief. It's also usually unnecessary: 'Many patients are undergoing needless haemorrhoidectomies,' said an editorial in the *British Medical Journal*. The editorial favours more conservative – and less painful – methods of removing haemorrhoids.

One such method is *cryosurgery*: a doctor freezes the tissues of the haemorrhoid, killing them, and in a short while the haemorrhoid falls off. Another method is 'rubber-band ligation' in which the haemorrhoid is tied off with rubber bands, stopping circulation and, as in cryosurgery, the tissue dies and falls off. Cryosurgery is virtually painless, and the discomfort from rubber-band ligation is only slight; both methods can be performed in a doctor's surgery.

• Hair problems

In a popular American comic strip, the heroine tells her best friend, 'I know why women aren't prepared for life'. Brush in hand, standing before a mirror, she continues: 'We wasted our grade school educations worrying about our hair. We wasted our high school educations worrying about our hair. We wasted our college educations worrying about our hair.

'All things considered,' she asks in the last panel, 'shouldn't our hair look better than this?'

Considering the amount of nutrients wasted by all that worrying, the answer is no.

Stress preys on many of the vitamins and minerals needed to grow healthy hair, and researchers have found that deficiencies in B complex vitamins, zinc, protein and other nutrients can leave us looking as bad as we feel. How many times have you heard somebody say 'I only feel good when my hair looks nice'? That isn't just vanity speaking. What's growing on your head is often a good indicator of what's going on inside of it – and in the rest of your body as well.

Your hair reflects a state of lethargy by appearing dull and lifeless; when you feel tired and tense, your hair may be limp and oily. A vicious cycle starts when concern over your looks compounds the problems that fostered their decline in the first place.

Every year, we as a nation spend millions of pounds on products promising to lengthen, thicken or otherwise improve the appearance of our hair. Look at the ingredients panel on the average hair-care product, and you'll find that it contains such things as protein, vitamins, wheat germ, milk, eggs and honey. Sounds good enough to eat, doesn't it? According to some experts, that's precisely what we should be doing.

That does not mean you rush out and devour the nearest bottle of shampoo. What it does mean is that you can improve the condition of your hair and scalp by eating certain foods.

Protein is important

Protein is a basic ingredient in many shampoos, conditioners and cream rinses. It is also the major ingredient in hair itself, which is at least 90 per cent protein. While this should not necessarily be the main ingredient in your diet, its importance ought not to be ignored.

Tests on 52 human volunteers showed that supplementing their diets with protein in the form of 14 g of gelatine daily increased the diameter of individual hair strands by as much as 45 per cent in only two months (*Nutrition Reports International*). 'Diet can influence hair growth and quality,' the report concluded, and 'gelatin exhibited one of the highest specific dynamic effects of any food.'

A hairdresser and two dermatologists concurred that a strong hair is a healthy hair. The study noted that the gelatine-induced 'increase constitutes an improvement in the mechanical properties of the hair', including strength. When volunteers stopped eating the gelatine, their hair reverted to its original diameter within six months.

Unflavoured gelatine powder is available in health food shops and supermarkets. A 14 g dose is roughly equivalent to seven teaspoons. You may prefer to imbibe it as some test subjects did – dissolved in vegetable juice – but researchers found that 'gelatin exhibited its greatest effects when ingested alone and on an empty stomach.'

Vitamin E reverses greying

When Canadian psychiatrist Abram Hoffer started going grey, he was able to reverse the process by taking 800 IU of vitamin E in capsule form daily. Now, at the age of 63, ten years later, he boasts a healthy head of thick black hair, the envy of men half his age.

Vitamin E has also been shown to retard the ageing process, a startling fact in light of the finding that grey-haired people have a higher mortality rate than people the same age whose hair hasn't turned grey. After studying 480 Mexicans between 1948 and 1969, researchers concluded that 'there may be a relationship of greying hair to senescence [ageing]' (*Social Biology*).

Dr Hoffer suggests that grey hair is a symptom of body degeneration, which, in his case, was halted by vitamin E.

Improvement with zinc

If grey hair has you worried, you might also want to consider zinc. When laboratory mice lost most of their hair through induced zinc deficiencies, researchers also found a decrease in the amount of tyrosine (an amino acid) in what hair they had left. That was seen as 'a possible explanation of greying of black hair'.

Zinc can be depleted by high stress, according to researchers at Case Western Reserve University in Cleveland. For a good source of zinc, wheat germ comes to the fore. Other sources include brewer's yeast and pumpkin seeds.

Interestingly, while excessive hair loss may be a result of crash dieting, it is rarely a complaint of calorie-conscious high-fashion models. Beauties who tip the scales at $8^1/_2$ stone while standing five-foot-ten are at least as concerned with the quality as with the quantity of the food they consume.

Hairdresser Hugh Harrison, whose work takes him on assignment around the world, observes that 'most models travel with big bottles of vitamins.' Taylor Miller, a New York model whose career on American television and in mail-order catalogues was woven from the golden braids that hang well below her waist, told us she favours a high-protein diet augmented by 'lots of fresh fruits'.

Models 'don't eat junk food and very seldom indulge in alcohol,' Harrison adds. 'If they are addicted to anything, it's lots of sleep.'

Never let anyone tell you that beautiful women aren't clever. They know that alcohol destroys B vitamins and that sleep is a panacea for many ills. When your looks are your livelihood, you're bound to let them go to your head. We should all follow suit.

How to avoid hair damage

Times have changed since the days when a girl brushed her hair with 100 strokes while waiting for her beau to come by and take her out. One of the biggest changes has been in how often we wash our hair, making it more susceptible to damage. 'All that oil gave grandmother's hair a protective coating that we don't have today with frequent shampooing,' says Vera H. Price, associate clincial professor of dermatology at the University of California.

Some Australian researchers conclude that brushing can damage hair, causing split ends (*Journal of the Society of Cosmetic Chemists*). Dr Price admits that tangled hair – wet or dry – is easily damaged by rough handling. She recommends purchasing a good comb or brush (one with widely spaced and rounded bristles or teeth) and using it very gently. Although no conditioner or cream rinse can repair damage already inflicted on hair, such products will prevent further damage, she told us. They protect the hair in much the same way grandmother's natural oils did and can reduce friction by as much as 50 per cent.

Jojoba (pronounced *ho-ho-ba*) is a conditioner derived from the oil of a South American bean plant. Taylor Miller swears by it. In her native Texas, she was a natual blonde, but moving to New York caused her locks to darken. A hairdresser suggested she streak (bleach) them. Under the heat of a curling iron, the bleached parts became extremely dry. 'It was awful,' she recalls.

A different hairdresser told her that his baldness had been held at bay by jojoba. Miller doused her own head with it and her hair felt much better. The streaking is nearly grown out of her hair by now, she told us, 'and I would never have it dyed again.'

On the whole she takes a natural approach to hair care. She no longer permits hairdressers to use curlers on her, 'so they braid it instead,' and she rarely uses a hairdryer. 'Even when it's cold out, I'd rather have it freeze.'

Hair loss

Hair loss used to be pretty much solely a problem for older men. But today's stress, drugs, diets and diseases, not to mention some so-called hair-care products and techniques have made thinning hair more common among younger people. Generally, hair loss falls into four categories. *Systemic* indicates either a reaction to a medication or an internal disease or gland problem. *Infectious* refers to a bacterial or fungal condition. *Hereditary* is related to genes. And *traumatic* means actual damage to the scalp and hair by excessive waving, bleaching, drying, colouring, brushing or combing.

Men have no monopoly on the problem. Equality in the work force has taken a worrisome turn for young women who find that they are losing their hair at a rate to rival the man in the office next door. Job pressures have been added to home pressures to place today's woman under tensions her grandmother never knew. Consequently, reported cases of female baldness have increased over the past decade or so. Losing her hair leads to additional worrying, says Irwin I. Lubowe, clinical professor emeritus of dermatology at the New York City Medical College. 'And that in turn makes even more of her hair fall out.'

B vitamins and other nutrients to counter stress

One good thing you can do when under stress is to eat more (you guessed it) wheat germ. It's a good source of B vitamins (except B_{12}) for your nerves, plus protein and vitamin E. All those nutrients have proven successful in making hair healthy.

Choline is a B vitamin-like nutrient that's useful in counter-acting the effects of stress. Recently, scientists at the Albert Einstein College of Medicine in New York were able to induce toxic levels of stress in baby animals by limiting the amount of choline in their diets. For the past 25 years, Dr Lubowe has been recommending choline supplements to his patients, with what he calls 'significant' results.

Wheat germ isn't the only source of choline. Lecithin is another good choice that also supplies inositol, a B complex vitamin with a particular affinity for choline. Like old friends, inositol and choline support each other in times of stress – German scientists have published findings on their anti-hypersensitive (blood-pressure-lowering) properties. We recommend making the most of that symbiotic relationship by eating wheat germ and lecithin together (see recipe). Lecithin is available in capsules and granules, while soyabeans and liver are good food sources.

Yet another B complex component, biotin, is credited with starting hair growth and stopping nervous disorders in a ten-month-old boy *(Archives of Dermatology*, October 1980). It's another suggestion on Dr Lubowe's list of supplements and is found in egg yolks. Raw egg whites actually hinder its effectiveness, but when the albumen is cooked, the culprit – a substance called *avidin* – is destroyed by heat.

Other biotin-rich foods include liver, milk, yeast and kidney. All are also good sources of pantothenic acid, another B complex vitamin that, in one experiment, caused the greying hair of ageing rats to return to glistening black.

Pantothenic acid may be destroyed by too much heat, so it's a good idea to eat your egg yolks raw, as in our recipe. Save the whites and add them to the whole eggs used in omelettes. If you are deficient in one B complex vitamin, chances are you're also deficient in another. In people with a pantothenic-acid deficiency, vitamin B_6 (pyridoxine) is often lacking, too. That's why Dr Lubowe favours taking the entire complex rather than individual B vitamin supplements for general hair care.

Milton Saunders, Jr., a dermatologist in Virginia, has helped patients save their hair with nutrients. He says:

'Some of these cases were obviously nutritional problems, such as women on crash diets who suddenly began to lose their hair three to six months later.' There were also problems caused by nutritional deprivation due to the foetus's development in the last trimester of pregnancy. Other reasons for hair loss were less obvious, such as the women who were losing hair as a result of birth control pills and subsequent vitamin and mineral deficiencies.

Seven Wonders 'hair food' cocktail

The following drink contains protein, choline, inositol, pantothenic acid, biotin, vitamin E and zinc: the seven ingredients nutritionists most often recommend for growing healthy hair.

8 fl. oz. plain yogurt
8 fl. oz. orange juice
3 tablespoons wheat germ
3 tablespoons brewer's yeast
1 tablespoon lecithin granules
1 teaspoon vitamin C crystals
1 raw egg yolk
1 envelope (1 tablespoon) unflavoured gelatine powder
honey to taste (optional)

Combine all ingredients and blend until smooth. If you don't have a blender, use a rotary beater or put everything into a lidded jar and shake vigorously. The tonic makes a quick and nutritious breakfast or a substantial bed-time snack. Another nice feature is the high vitamin C content. The effectiveness of B vitamins in combatting stress has been shown to improve in the presence of vitamin C.

'I just sat down and said to myself, "What is needed for hair growth?" Well, I'm not a biochemist, but I had a basic idea that we needed the essential amino acids, we needed some zinc and we needed some vitamin E. I tried this regimen on some of my patients, and *blam!* They started growing hair.'

See also BALDNESS.

• Hangovers

We certainly don't recommend that you partake of the grape regularly, especially on a heavy basis. But, once in a while, almost anyone can get caught up in the joy of a happy occasion and drink too much.

Hangover remedies abound, and most of them don't seem to work very well. However, there's actually a way to prevent an over-indulgent evening from becoming a dreary morning after – edible charcoal.

Hangovers are caused by substances called *congeners* – and activated charcoal absorbs them. In an experiment conducted at Columbia University College of Pharmaceutical Sciences in New York City, researchers found that in test-tube conditions similar to a person's stomach, activated charcoal absorbed 93 per cent of one congener and 82 per cent of another.

In a second experiment, 68 volunteers – non-drinkers and moderate social drinkers – drank either 2 fl. oz of whisky, which has a high level of congeners, or 2 fl. oz of charcoal-filtered vodka, which has almost none. The researchers then measured their hangover symptoms the next day: 25 per cent of the whisky group had stomach-aches, 27 per cent had bad breath, 9 per cent had headaches, 7 per cent had dizziness and 6 per cent had fatigue. On the other hand, only 2 per cent of the vodka group had headaches or stomach upset, and there was no bad breath, dizziness or fatigue (*Southwestern Medicine*).

The time to prevent the 'morning after' is the night before. A few tablets of activated charcoal taken before going to bed after an evening of over-indulgence may do the trick.

• Hay Fever

All the symptoms of hay fever – the red, watery eyes, constantly runny nose, perpetual sneezing, intermittent congestion and even the asthma that characterizes the disease at its most severe – are caused by *histamine*. This is a potent natural compound released when the immune system responds to an allergy-provoking substance. A relatively benign piece of rye-grass pollen (or anything else) can set off an alarm in a sensitive person. Your body reacts as if you had a cold, but there are no germs present.

Happily, hay fever has something else in common with the cold: both respond to treatment with vitamin C. That's because vitamin C is a natural anti-histamine.

In a series of studies, researchers at the department of obstetrics and gynaecology at Methodist Hospital in New York found that blood levels of vitamin C bore an inverse relationship to blood levels of histamine; as one went up, the other went down, and vice versa. 'Persons with low plasma ascorbate [vitamin C] levels have high histamine levels,' the researchers noted after processing blood samples from 400 'healthy' volunteers.

Next, the researchers took 11 people with low levels of vitamin C or high levels of histamines and placed them on a programme of vitamin C supplementation. Improvement was rapid, occurring within three days.

It would seem that ascorbic-acid deficiency is one of the most common causes for an elevated blood histamine level, as all 11 of the volunteers given 1 g of ascorbic acid daily for three days showed a reduction in blood histamine. [*Journal of Nutrition*, April 1980].

'The need for vitamin C seems to be greater in some allergic patients,' agrees clinical nutritionist Lyn Dart, a registered dietitian. In her work as manager of the nutrition department at the Environmental Health Center in Dallas, Dart has found that large doses of vitamin C are sometimes quite effective. 'The average allergy sufferer with a vitamin C deficiency usually responds to 4–8 g a day when trying to stave off a reaction or clear up a reaction in progress,' she told us.

The responses of his own patients in Bennington, Vermont, have convinced Stuart Freyer of the same thing. 'The hay fever season in Vermont can be pretty severe,' says Dr Freyer, who has emphasized nutritional therapy for six of the 12 years he's been a practising oto-rhino-laryngologist (ear-nose-throat specialist). He gives his hay fever patients 'relatively high amounts of vitamin C. Five grams or more is typical.' But when advising his patients to take that much vitamin C, he cautions them to increase their calcium supplementation as well.

'High levels of vitamin C may bind with calcium and pull it out of the bones,
then flush it out in the urine when the body discards any excess vitamin C. Vitamin C may also combine with calcium in the diet to interfere with absorption.

'There really should be no problem with calcium deficiency if people either use vitamin C in its calcium ascorbate form, rather than its simple ascorbic acid form, or if they supplement the ascorbic acid with adequate amounts of calcium. I usually recommend my patients take 400 to 600 mg of calcium a day during hay fever season.'

Dr Freyer has also found that vitamin C works better when his patients take B complex vitamins, especially pantothenic acid, along with it.

'I recommend 200 to 500 mg of pantothenic acid, plus another 50 mg of B complex,' he says. 'Sometimes, when a patient has impaired absorption – and many people with allergies do – I also give them pancreatic enzymes: These help to break down the foods so vitamins can be absorbed better.'

If you really want to get the most out of your vitamin C during hay fever season, take it with citrus bioflavonoids as well. Studies done on animals have shown that citrus bioflavonoids may favourably alter the body's metabolizing of vitamin C, by raising the concentration of the nutrient in certain tissues and enhancing its bioavailability (*American Journal of Clinical Nutrition*, August 1979).

In his own practice, Brian Leibovitz, an Oregon nutritionist, has found citrus bioflavonoids are the answer to many a hay fever victim's prayers.

'More than once, I've had a hay fever patient who did not respond to vitamin C recover when given citrus bioflavonoids,' he says. Early in his career as a nutritionist, Leibovitz worked with Linus Pauling on the latter's studies with vitamin C. In his own research, done while a graduate student, Leibovitz found that large doses of vitamin C significantly reduced the mortality rate of mice with laboratory-induced anaphylaxis, a potentially fatal allergic response. In a paper delivered at a national meeting of the American Chemical Society, Leibovitz concluded that 'these results suggest the possible use of ascorbic acid in human immediate-type hypersensitivities (allergy, asthma, anaphylaxis).'

Anaphylaxis isn't the only type of allergic reaction that may be fatal; a person could die from an asthma attack, too. And 'left untreated, hay fever can develop into asthma,' says a spokesperson at the National Institute for Allergy and Infectious Diseases outside Washington, D.C.: 'Actually, "hay fever" is something of a misnomer because it isn't only caused by hay and it isn't characterized by fever. Basically, when it occurs in the nose, it's called *allergic rhinitis*.'

Asthma, Leibovitz notes, responds even better to citrus bioflavonoids than allergic rhinitis does. 'In fact, a standard treatment for asthma, a drug called *sodium cromoglycate*, is nothing more than a synthetic bioflavonoid-like molecule,' he told us. 'I have found citrus bioflavonoids work just as well for people with hay fever-induced asthma.'

Another thing that seems to help some people with hay fever is vitamin E, and findings by a Japanese researcher concur that vitamin E exhibits anti-histamine properites. After he injected 20 volunteers with histamine, Mitsuo Kamimura, of the department of dermatology at Sapporo Medical College, noted that the skin around the injection site swelled up. However, when he gave the volunteers 300 mg doses of vitamin E daily for five to seven days before injecting them with histamine, there was far less swelling than before (*Journal of Vitaminology*).

Finally, Leibovitz rounds out his programme by telling his patients to give up junk food and cigarettes. Dr Freyer does the same. 'Smoking, in particular, increases the need for vitamin C,' says the latter. 'Smoking is an irritant; it is also an allergen. Smoking is madness for anyone who suffers from hay fever'.

But if you do smoke, Dr Freyer cautions that hay fever season is, ironically, not the best time to quit. 'Any change in your routine, your daily habits, is bound to cause stress – and stress will often aggravate an allergic reaction. I always advise my patients to go easy on themselves at this time of year.'

So take it easy and breathe easy. A positive outlook, supplemented by vitamin C, bioflavonoids, pantothenic acid and vitamin E may be just what the doctor ordered. Just because there is pollen outside is no reason you can't be out there, too.

• Headaches

The body has only a limited number of ways to say '*Ouch!*' Pain is one of them. Generally, anything that produces pressure, inflammation or damage in or around the pain-sensitive areas of the head can result in headache pain. Even then, the pain can vary, depending on what's happening. Most headache pain is thought to be generated by one of three different mechanisms: irritation of sensitive nerve endings in the head and neck as a result of tense muscles (as in tension headaches); irritation of nerve endings as a result of the swelling of delicate blood vessels (as in so-called vascular headaches); or inflammation of the lining of certain tissues (as in sinus headaches).

Exactly what causes those unwelcome changes is still a mystery, though, in spite of much medical research. Most theories hold that certain trigger factors within *and* without us – stress, hormones and chemicals in food and air, to name a few – prompt the body's blood vessels and tissues to release certain noxious substances that, in turn, affect nerve endings. But since most headaches fall into a few distinct categories, keeping any headache at bay means first understanding what kind of headache you've got.

Tension headache

Few people are unfamiliar with this aching or squeezing discomfort, as if the head were wrapped with a tight band or clamped in a vice. Tension headache may last for a few hours, a few days or – rarely – even years.

Although some researchers disagree, the source of discomfort in a tension headache most probably lies in muscles of the neck or scalp that automatically knot up with tension when we're anxious, upset or worried. We're not talking about fleeting tension, the kind we feel when we recoil from a loud noise, but tension without letup, like the kind caused by brooding over a stack of bills or working in a crowded restaurant. Or tension may build up in muscles according to the way we sit, stand, crane our necks and so on. Either way, it doesn't take long before prolonged muscle contraction – and, consequently, tightening around blood vessels – results in dull, steady pain on both sides of the head. Indeed, many tension headache sufferers can actually feel the tightening in the head or neck.

What triggers a tension headache? A child who starts screaming the minute the babysitter arrives can do it. So can an argument with your spouse. Or filing your income tax return. Or trying to unsnarl your chequebook. If you are tired *and* tense, stress-generating events like these are all the more likely to land you with a tension headache.

Stress-caused tension headaches often strike when we can't vent our anxiety or anger, but they can strike even when we *anticipate* an unpleasant event. Or they can catch us totally off guard. They may be conspicuously absent during a period of actual anxiety or stress, only to hit later, when we

0think all our troubles are over. What happens in that case is that muscles accumulate tension during the period of stress but hold off with pain for a grand finale. You may even wake up with tension headache first thing in the morning.

While the tension headache isn't a 20th-century invention, it's surely one of the hallmarks of modern life. If a videotape of just one night of prime-time commercial television survives for a 1000 years, 30th-century archaeologists will probably conclude that we all ran madly about in search of headache relief and found it in little white pills and 'tiny time capsules'. However, although you wouldn't know it from the ads, there *are* other ways to relieve a tension headache than running for the nearest aspirin bottle. Essentially, all of them involve relaxing those tightened-up muscles.

One good one is to soak in a warm bath with your shoulders and neck submerged. Or stand under a warm shower. Warmth gets the blood flowing again and loosens muscle contractions.

If a bath or shower isn't handy (or convenient), you can try an Oriental technique that's related to acupuncture. It's called shiatsu (or acupressure), and it uses pressure from your fingers. For information on shiatsu and illustrations for relieving a headache, see page 567. Also, see Bonnie Prudden's technique for relieving headache pain on pages 570–71.

Progressive relaxation

Place a healthy, relaxed, secure individual in peaceful, anxiety-free surroundings, and his or her chances of becoming burdened with stress-related headaches will be very remote. Yet a sure way to make a tense person even *more* tense is to say, 'Relax'. If one could, one would. Then there's 'Avoid stress' – advice we would love to follow if we only knew how.

Who can avoid stress with a myriad of things to be done at the office, a stack of unpaid bills waiting at home, and occasional car troubles or a marital tiff? You'd have to live on the moon to *really* get away from it all.

Stress-related headaches are sometimes surprisingly easy to squelch, however. One doctor tells of a woman whose headache completely disappeared when her husband took over the family chequebook. That responsibility had always brought out the worst in her, simply because she was the type of person who took great pains to pay every bill as soon as it arrived in the post – and, like many of us, she always seemed to run out of money before she ran out of bills. Sometimes it just doesn't pay to be *that* conscientious!

Your problem may not be your chequebook. Maybe you are fastidious about housework. Or you can't stand the thought of leaving any assignment unfinished until tomorrow. Or, weary as you are, you feel you must write up your reports the minute you get in from a business trip. In fact, some doctors are convinced that there is actually a migraine personality (*see* p 315). While there is no scientific proof – i.e. no controlled experiments – years of seeing migraine sufferers come and go have led many doctors to the conclusion that people damned with migraines are generally ambitious, hard-working, hard-driving, demanding of themselves and others, eager to please and sensitive to criticism. (In short, your basic workaholic).

The same goes for cluster headache sufferers (*see* p. 317). Doctors' general impressions, psychological tests and a detailed study of patients demonstrated that cluster sufferers tend to be highly conscientious – to a fault, you might say – and share many of the traits of the migraine personality, with the addition of heavy goal orientation. That all adds up to what is sometimes known as the Type A personality – a mix of traits that, incidentally, can land you in the cardiac ward, even if you don't get headaches.

Hard-driving or not, though, you don't have to put up with tension headaches any longer. An easy-to-learn technique called progressive relaxation was developed by Dr Edmund Jacobson, author or *You Must Relax*. It can enable you to *avoid* tense muscles brought on by the little battles of daily life, thus averting the headaches that tense muscles often produce. Besides headaches, progressive relaxation (or variations of it) has been used to treat a host of other stress-related physical problems – ulcers, colitis, high blood pressure and angina – plus phobias and anxiety.

Dr Jacobson's basic principle is this: by deliberately relaxing all of our muscles, group by group, we can shed accumulated tension from our bodies. Because tension buildup in our facial, neck and head muscles is behind many headaches, the progressive relaxation principle, with special focus on those muscles, may be adapted as a useful and effective anti-headache technique for some people.

In the following section, 'How to train yourself to relax' we have provided a basic progressive relaxation technique. After practising this once or twice a day for two or three weeks, you should be able to get through hassles more calmly, with less agitation than you customarily do – and with fewer headaches. If you wish, make a tape of the instructions to help you proceed through the technique for the first week or so. After you feel you know it well enough, continue to practise every day. You can then also invoke the state whenever you feel tension beginning to mount in your face, neck and head muscles. To avert a headache after any stress-producing situation – like making a big decision at the office or 'discussing' the household finances with your spouse – first run through a minute or two of progressive relaxation. And by all means, use it when you need to avoid getting all knotted up with tension before a big sales meeting or your salary review. Then there are the ultimate tests: Try it the next time you have to chaperon a gang of unruly kids or straighten out a computer error on your phone bill. Your chances of getting a headache in all such cases will be pared down considerably.

Remember, unless tensions are systematically defused, they're likely to explode into a headache. That's not to say we don't need to get our fair share of sleep. But as a matter of fact, progressive relaxation is an excellent prelude to sleep. It gets us set for truly restful sleep.

How to train yourself to relax

Take a comfortable position, either sitting in a chair with both hands resting in your lap and feet flat on the floor, or lying down on your back with your feet aganst a wall or heavy piece of furniture. Close your eyes. Proceed through the following steps *slowly* (from a tape, if you wish, or have someone read them to you), lingering on each to concentrate as you first tighten and then relax each muscle group. The technique takes about 20 minutes to complete – but after several daily practice sessions, you'll be able to quickly invoke the state of relaxation in two or three minutes whenever you feel tension beginning to mount.

Make a tight fist with your right hand. Feel the tension in your right hand, your right wrist and forearm. Experience the tension and, now, relax. Just allow those muscles to relax, to go limp. Let the tension flow from your forearm, your wrist, your hand and your fingers. Allow the tension to drain right out of your arm, your forearm, down to your wrist, through your hand and through your fingers. Continue to relax your right arm. Now make that fist once again. Tighten up your fist, your wrist, your forearm . . . feel the tension . . . feel the difference between your tense, tight muscles and your relaxed state of a moment before. Now, let those muscles relax . . . just allow them to go limp. Let your arm relax, your wrist, your hand and your fingers. Continue to relax your arm, your wrist, your hand and your fingers. As you do, you may feel that arm seem to sink, to become more relaxed and comfortable. Focus on allowing that arm to become more relaxed.

While continuing to relax your right arm, make a fist with your left hand and left arm. Make a tight fist. Now feel the difference between your left arm and your right arm. Now, relax your left arm. Just allow those muscles to go . . . allow your forearm to relax; your wrist, your hand and your fingers. As your left arm becomes more relaxed and more comfortable, you'll experience the sensation that it seems to be sliding down or sinking into the state of relaxation you are experiencing in your right arm, your right hand, your fingers. Continue to relax both arms: your left arm, your left hand, your fingers . . . your right arm, your right hand, your fingers. As you do, you'll experience a sense of well-being, a sense of comfort, as you begin to relax and feel better. Both arms become more relaxed as the muscles seem to give up the tension that they were carrying about. Allow both arms to relax, both hands, as you let the tension drain out through your fingertips.

While you continue to relax both forearms and both hands, tense your upper arms and shoulders. Feel the tension, the tightness, and now, relax. Just allow those muscles to go, the muscles in your arms and your shoulders. Let the tension roll down your arms and out through your hands and fingertips. Allow the tension to roll off your shoulders and give away the muscle tightness as everything feels more comfortable and more relaxed. Your forearms are relaxed, your hands are relaxed, your shoulders are becoming much more relaxed, your upper arms are relaxed. Your whole upper body starts to feel more relaxed and more comfortable. Continue to relax your shoulders, your arms, your forearms, your hands, your fingers, as your whole upper body begins to feel more relaxed and more comfortable.

Now tense up your neck muscles. Feel the tension in your neck . . . it's probably the tensest part of your entire body. And now, relax those muscles. Allow those muscles to go. Concentrate on the muscles in the back of your neck. Let the tension drain down through your shoulders, your arms . . . out through your hands and your fingertips. Let the muscles in the front of your neck go. Let that tension drain. Those tight muscles are now giving up tension and stress as your entire body feels more relaxed. Your shoulders feel more relaxed, your arms, your hands, even your fingers. Just allow that tension to drain from your neck. Concentrate on allowing your neck to relax. If you're sitting and you feel as if your head wants to tip forward to take some of the weight off your neck, that's quite all right, because it may, as you allow some of the tension, stress and tightness to drain from those muscles. Allow your head to tip forward a bit as gravity seems to pull you down, as it seems to tug at you and make you feel very comfortable and very relaxed. Your neck is more relaxed, your shoulders, your arms, your hands and your fingers. Keep on relaxing. Your whole upper body feels more relaxed and more comfortable. Allow the tension to drain from your neck as you sink into a more relaxed state, a more relaxed feeling throughout your upper body. Your shoulders are more relaxed, your upper arms, your forearms, your hands and your fingers. Continue to relax . . . keep relaxing your upper body.

Now push up on your toes (or, if lying down, push against a wall or chair with your toes) and create some tension in your legs. Create the tension and tightness, and now, let it go. Allow the tension to drain from your legs, right through your feet into the floor. Allow the tension, the tightness, to roll out . . . let the muscles in your legs go. Allow the muscles in your legs to become more relaxed and more comfortable. As you do, you'll feel a sense of well-being, of comfort – a generally good feeling about your whole body as you allow your body to relax . . . your legs feel more relaxed, your feet, your neck, your shoulders, your arms, your forearms, your wrists, your hands, your fingers. Continue to relax your entire body. Relax your neck, your shoulders, your hands, your legs, your feet, as your entire body slips into a more comfortable state of relaxation.

Now make a frown with your forehead. Tighten those muscles around your forehead . . . and now, relax. Allow your forehead and facial muscles to relax. Allow your face to relax . . . it doesn't have to do any work, just relax . . . let those muscles go. Allow your forehead to relax, your eyes, your cheeks, your lips. Allow all the facial muscles to go, to relax. As they do, you'll feel a sense of well-being throughout. Your neck is more relaxed, your shoulders, your arms, your hands, your fingers, your legs, your feet. Allow your entire body to become more relaxed and more comfortable. Continue to relax your facial muscles, your eyes, your forehead, your cheeks, your lips, your entire face. Allow those muscles to relax, plus your neck, your shoulders, your arms, your hands and the rest of your body.

You may notice that your breathing has been rhythmic and pleasant. Now take a deeper breath, and hold it. Feel the tension through your chest, and now, let it all out. Continue breathing at your normal pace . . . at a comfortable rate. Breathe in, feel the tension in your chest, and now, it just rolls out and you feel more comfortable. Take another deep breath and, as you exhale, think to yourself, 'Calm . . . calm . . .' Once again, a deep breath and think to yourself 'Calm . . .' as you exhale. Each time you do this, your body becomes more relaxed and comfortable. Once again. Just continue breathing at a comfortable rate.

Continue to relax. Your face is more relaxed, your shoulders, your neck, your arms, your hands, your wrists, your fingers, your legs and your feet.

And you have a sense of extreme comfort throughout your body as you allow yourself to be placed in a more relaxed state and a more comfortable state.

Now imagine walking in a wood on a warm day – not a hot day, but a warm day. The light seems to break through the trees and you have a tremendous sense of well-being, a tremendous sense of comfort. You haven't a care in the world . . . you can just absorb the good feelings around you: the sights, the smells, the sounds. And you say to yourself, 'I'm calm, I'm relaxed' Picture yourself walking quietly through the wood, the sun breaking through the trees; you feel very much at peace with yourself . . . and the world, feeling very good throughout your entire body and telling yourself, 'I'm calm, I'm relaxed.' Continue to relax. Use whatever image conjures up feelings of tranquillity for you – perhaps a beach at sunset or a meadow at dawn.

To conclude the exercise, slowly count to four. With each number, you'll feel a bit more alert. *One*, you begin to shed some of the deeper relaxation. *Two*, you're a bit more alert . . . feeling very good and very comfortable. *Three*, you'll be alert very shortly and you'll be able to think but you will remain in a nice relaxed state. And *four*, you may open your eyes.

Migraine headache

There are two types of migraine: classical and common. Both affect only one side of the head at a time and are marked by painful irritation and swelling of the arteries of the head. However, each has its own characteristic constellation of symptoms.

Classical migraine is preceded (and, less frequently, accompanied) by a characteristic aura, described variously as a period of mild confusion, lightheadedness, flashing lights, blind spots in the field of vision, plus supersensitivity to noise, and even partial paralysis.

Common migraine is also know as the 'sick headache', for good reason. Pain is accompanied by nausea and often vomiting. Common migraine is preceded not by an aura, exactly, but most often by a general feeling of ill-being, sometimes with irritability or depression. (Less frequently, an exaggerated and unexpected sense of well-being [euphoria] precedes a migraine). Eighty per cent of all migraines are common migraines, rather than classical.

In either case, people having migraines look miserable – their faces may be pale, swollen and covered with sweat. Often they hold their heads in their hands as if desperate for comfort.

It's generally agreed that migraine headaches of either type are caused by constriction of tiny blood vessels in the head during the pre-headache phase and swelling (dilation) of those same blood vessels during the headache phase. The result: intense, debilitating pain. The constriction and swelling have something to do with changing levels of certain chemicals in the body – serotonin and prostaglandins – which act on blood vessels.

Foods and beverages containing tyramine – a substance that is believed to cause a reduction in the brain chemical *serotonin* – are known trigger factors for many migraine suffers. Tyramine is found in cheese, chocolate, yogurt, beer, red wine, gin, bourbon and vodka, among other foods and drinks. When Dr Edda Hanington, consultant to two British migraine clinics, questioned 500 migraine sufferers on which foods appeared to precipitate their attacks, the foods cited, in order of frequency, were: chocolate, cheese and other dairy products, citrus fruits, alcoholic drinks, fatty fried food, vegetables (especially onions), tea and coffee, meat (especially pork) and seafood (*Journal of Human Nutrition*, vol. 34, no. 3, 1980). For some reason, salt, nitrites (preservatives used in some meat products, such as sausages), nicotine in tobacco smoke, car exhaust, sun glare, missed meals, low blood sugar and strenuous physical exercise may also trigger migraines.

As with tension headache, migraine is more likely to attack when you are tired or under stress. And also like its less brutal cousin, migraine may not hit until Friday evening or Saturday morning, when you're about to relax. Migraine may also pounce in regular attacks, once or twice a week, or it may strike once a month, or only three or four times in a lifetime.

For some reason, many migraine sufferers were prone to car sickness as children. In many cases, migraines start up when a person is in his or her 20s or 30s, then – mercifully – decrease later in life, thanks to the general loss of elasticity of artery walls that tends to accompany the ageing process. For the same reason, older migraine sufferers may experience the aura or pre-headache phase, yet be spared the actual migraine attack.

Women are more susceptible to migraine than men, possibly due to hormone fluctuations at certain times. In women so besieged, classical migraine tends to flare up during pregnancy, then decrease with the menopause and age. In contrast, female sufferers of the common migraine may find relief from recurrent attacks during pregnancy and suffer more during the menopause. Menstrual periods and use of oral contraceptives can trigger either classical or common migraine.

For some reason, migraines tend to run in families, although the relationship has not yet been conclusively explained by genetic makeup.

How to tell if it's a migraine

Many people say they have migraine when what they really have is just a blockbuster of a tension headache. (No picnic, granted; but no migraine, either.) To officially qualify as a migraine, a headache is generally characterized by at *least* three of the following:

● It occurs again and again (attacks vary widely in intensity, duration and frequency).

● At onset, it affects only one side of the head (although the affected side may not always be the same one).

● It is accompanied by loss of appetite and sometimes nausea and vomiting.

● It is preceded by either of two pre-headache phases: an aura of flashing lights or blind spots, or a vague sense of foreboding, irritability and sense of ill-being.

● It is shared by someone else in the family. Up to 65 per cent of migraine sufferers know of at least one family member who also has migraine.

Regular exercise to reduce frequency

A regular running programme can benefit people with migraine headaches, according to Otto Appenzeller of the neurology department and headache clinics at the New Mexico School of Medicine. He's seen several patients find relief by jogging seven to nine miles daily at a speed of seven to nine minutes per mile. 'I have 18 patients who suffered from migraines. After reaching this level of activity, they are headache-free and medicine-free,' he told us.

Dr Appenzeller who is a marathon runner himself, believes that such a programme would be good for just about anyone whose health permits it. If the results of his research are any indication, you'll lose weight, feel better and, he predicts, 'you will be cured of *all* headaches.'

What makes exercise so effective in silencing headache's heavy artillery? No one is really sure, but there are plenty of theories.

Dr Appenzeller speculates that endurance training such as running, cycling and swimming may spur the body to produce an important enzyme. That enzyme might prevent blood vessels in the brain from expanding and painfully pressing against nerves.

Cluster headache

This can be a real nightmare, as anyone who's had them will tell you. It is a variant of migraine, and the pain is unbearable: a searing, stabbing, burning or steady boring pain on one side of the head, concentrated in or around one eye, leaving it bloodshot and teary. Nasal stuffiness, runny nose and sweating are also common. Sometimes the pain spreads to both sides of the head and is accompanied by deep pains in the neck.

Like a migraine, a cluster headache (also know as *migrainous neuralgia*) is caused by irritated, swollen blood vessels. It may be triggered by too much alcohol, nicotine and other substances that cause distention of the blood vessels. 'Many patients note that drinking alcohol . . . will induce an attack of pain within minutes,' says Dr Robert S. Kunkel, president of the American Association for the Study of Headache (*Modern Medicine*, 30 November–15 December 1980).

Cluster headaches get their name because they occur in groups. Each attack may last anywhere from 30 minutes to two hours but is part of a barrage of up to four or more headaches daily. Most occur over periods of anywhere from three to eight weeks, usually during spring or autumn. They may strike every day for weeks or months and then disappear – only to return several months later. Why the period or pattern, no one knows.

Cluster headaches start quickly and pass as suddenly as they begin. Among all headaches, clusters are most likely to strike during rest – two to three hours after retiring or during sleep in the early hours of the morning.

People who keep track of such things tell us that men, especially those in middle age, are more prone to cluster headaches than women. And, while cluster headaches can occur at any age, most frequently they plague the 30-to-60 age group, with no family tendency. While you may generally be prone to one, you may not necessarily suffer an attack unless certain triggers are present. It appears, for example, that men with cluster headaches tend to smoke and drink alcohol more than people without them.

Once the cluster headache strikes, it's hard to treat. Despite that dreary outlook, however, some cluster victims are finding relief, and in a very improbable manner – not with drugs or pain-numbing narcotics, but through programmes of regular, vigorous exercise. One doctor reports that some patients find that vigorous exercise helps lessen the pain – they jump out of bed and start doing calisthenics (exercises such as jumping jacks and deep knee bends).

One such case was described by Dr Appenzeller and a colleague, Dr Ruth Atkinson in the journal *Headache*. The patient, a 56-year-old senior administrator for a government agency, had suffered severe headaches for several years. Eventually, the pain became a *daily* occurrence.

'It is excruciating and feels as though a finger were pushing out my eyeball from the upper rear of the orbit,' he complained. 'At least 65 per cent start when I am asleep and awaken me when pain becomes strong enough. During an active cycle, two headaches per night are common, and I have had as many as five per night between 10.30 P.M. and 6 A.M.'

Antihistamines, painkillers and other drugs were ineffective in controlling the symptoms. Then the man stumbled upon a curious pattern:

'The headaches occur during quiescent periods an hour or two after lunch or dinner, when I am reading, watching TV or having casual conversation. They have never occurred when I am working around the house, during backpacking, skiing, or playing tennis. . .

'Because I never had headache during physical activity, I tried running one evening when I felt pressure starting to build in my head. I ran 220 yards in 25 seconds, and within three minutes all pressure had disappeared, both nostrils were clear and no pain developed. A headache awoke me later that same night, and I ran in place until my heart rate was 120 per minute.'

Within a few minutes, the pain was gone.

The patient has continued ever since to counter successfully his frequent headaches with exercise. 'Usually one running session is enough, and the pain stops within five minutes.'

There is possibly an added benefit to the therapy. As Dr Atkinson points out, the man's 'fine physical condition may in part be attributed to the exercise he gets in attempting to control his headache.'

Extra oxygen
Extra oxygen may be another key to solving the cluster headache mystery. In a letter to the *Journal of the American Medical Association*, a San Fransisco optometrist, Jerold F. Janks, described how oxygen helped him.

'I have been a victim of cluster headaches for the past 12 years . . .' he confessed.

The intensity of pain is the same regardless of sidedness, but for some reason, the left-sided clusters, in addition to involving the eye, ear and neck, also involve the left upper molars, the left side of the soft palate, and the left side of the Adam's apple.

Janks tried many medications without success. Then, five years ago, he visited a neurologist who suggested that if all else failed, he might try oxygen.

He put an oxygen tank with breathing mask next to his bed and started using it during attacks. The result? 'I am still a cluster statistic but not a victim,' he reported. Breathing oxygen 'totally aborts the headache in less than ten minutes'. With another tank in his car and one at the office, Janks said, 'I have reduced my cluster headaches from episodes of devastation to mere inconvenience.'

Physical therapy for 'mechanical' headaches

Some chronic headaches are caused by 'mechanical' problems – i.e. those caused by an abnormality of some structure in the body. Sometimes these require surgery to repair, but often physical therapy works as well, or better.

Dick Erhard, physical therapy director at the Joseph Yablonski Memorial Clinic near Pittsburgh, Pennsylvania, used a combination of active and passive techniques to relieve Blanche Galey's mysterious headaches.

'I thought I had a brain tumour,' Mrs Galey recalls. 'When I stood up straight or sat up straight, I had no pain. But when I bent over to tie my shoe or pick up something, it hurt.'

The sharp pain sent her to the hospital, where a gamut of tests left her with no firm diagnosis. Brain scans, X-rays, blood tests – all proved inconclusive. She had a cortisone injection, which helped relieve the pain temporarily. Anti-histamines 'didn't do anything for me. I was still getting the headaches.'

A local general practitioner found the key. 'She had me lie down on my stomach and very gently pressed a spot on my lower back. I immediately got an excruciating headache! This was the first time anyone had touched my back, even though I had spent a week in the hospital for tests.'

Mrs Galey was sent to Erhard, who found 'both lumbar and cranio-cervical spine involvement' – weaknesses in the neck and lower back that brought pressure on nerves, causing the pain when she bent over.

'It might have been relieved by diazepam [Valium],' Erhard explains, 'but the problem was so obviously mechanical rather than chemical that I thought drugs would just treat the symptoms.' He began a combined series of active and passive therapy.

The passive technique he used is called 'joint mobilization' – careful manipulation of affected joints to stretch spasmed muscles and allow weakened discs to heal. Joint mobilization is not new – osteopaths and chiropractors have used versions of it for years – but physical therapists have found wider applications for the technique.

To illustrate how it works, place one hand flat on a table, palm down. Now raise the index finger, keeping the rest of the hand flat, and note how far you can raise it. This is the limit of the voluntary, active range of motion of the large joint at the base of the finger. However, if you gently lift the finger with your other hand, you can raise it higher. This additional capability, called 'joint play', is present in every joint as a safeguard against traumatic dislocation.

Physical therapists have found that manipulating an ailing joint to the absolute limit of its capability can bring relief from pain and aid healing. It is a subtle and strikingly simple technique, requiring a thorough appraisal of the problem and a gentle touch, but it can have profound results.

Erhard manipulated Mrs Galey's neck, gently helping her push her chin in against her upper chest and rotate her head. He also taught her and assisted her to straighten her neck. For her lower back, he prescribed gentle press-ups that left the pelvis flat on the floor while elevating the upper trunk. This type of press-up is an extension exercise because it allows the vertebrae of the lower spine to separate slightly, thus relieving pressure on the discs. Such separation and extension also causes a weakened disc to protrude forward rather than to the side or back, thus missing the nerves that exit from the spinal column.

After a few months of such active and passive treatment, Mrs Galey's headaches had gone. The exercises continue, however, as a preventive measure.

Whilst most people don't have such severe spinal problems, physical therapists say that most people carry their heads too far down and forward, thus creating head and neck aches. To break that habit, one therapist tells her patients to practise looking up at the ceiling 30 times, twice a day.

Here are two more neck strengtheners: Lie face down across a bed with your head hanging over the edge. Lift your head as far back as possible. Do that 30 times, twice a day. Then sit in a chair and hold a towel like a strap behind your head. Push your head back into the towel and resist with your arms. Hold for a count of three.

Ten unsuspected causes of headaches

Usually, the causes of headaches are painfully obvious – your tough day at the office, your harrowing journey home, your whining four-year-old and dinner boiling over on the cooker. But sometimes headaches *can't* be traced to the 'usual' causes. The following are ten types of headaches with causes that you might have overlooked.

1 The caffeine-withdrawal headache   According to Sanford Bolton of St. John's University in New York City,

Caffeine is a potent drug, affecting the central nervous system, cardiovascular system, gastrointestinal tract, adrenaline release and muscle contraction.. . . Because of the ubiquitous use of tea, coffee and cola beverages, caffeine is probably the most widely used drug. As such, it is subject to overindulgence and abuse. [*Journal of Applied Nutrition*, vol. 33, no. 1, 1981]

The immediate effects of caffeine are 'coffee nerves'. Symptoms, such as shaky hands and an overall jittery feeling, become apparent within a hour of drinking as little as one cup of coffee (about 100 to 150 mg of caffeine). The effects last several hours. Then you crash.

Coffee initially raises blood sugar (one reason you get a lift), but soon the body's insulin over-rides that, and you're left with a letdown feeling.

For those who can't stop at one cup, the adverse effects are multiplied, too. A syndrome known as *caffeinism* occurs in people who drink five or more cups of coffee a day (about 500 mg of caffeine.) The syndrome is very much like anxiety neurosis, and the people afflicted suffer from nervousness, irritability, agitation, headache, muscle twitching and rapid heartbeat.

Unfortunately, if your headaches are due to your caffeine habit, breaking the habit is going to hurt, too. You can quit cold turkey, but look out. Caffeine is, after all, habit forming and possibly addictive. That means when your body is deprived of its usual 'fix' it may rebel. The most common sympton is a headache, that begins about 18 hours after your last cup of coffee, according to John F. Greden of the University of Michigan Medical Center writing in the *New England Journal of Medicine* (24 July 1980). It begins with a feeling of cerebral fullness (as if your brain were too big for your head) and rapidly progresses to a painful and throbbing headache. It peaks about three to six hours after onset, explained Dr Greden, but it's not unusual for the pain to last a day or more.

A person desperate for relief may reach for an aspirin, but again, beware. Many over-the-counter pain remedies contain – what else? – caffeine. Sure, your headache will go away, but then you're hooked again and have to start all over.

Besides the headache, you may also feel extreme irritability, lethargy or anxiety. In fact, the same kind of anxiety associated with heavy caffeine consumption is experienced during withdrawal as well.

Still, if you persevere, it won't be long before you see some positive results – only about three days. However, it may take two to three weeks before the full benefits are felt. Then you'll notice that you are sleeping more soundly, feel more relaxed during the day and are better able to handle everyday stresses.

Or you can try tapering off. Some people find this method less painful because they spread out the final event over several weeks. But that doesn't mean you get off scot-free. Depending on how addicted you are, your symptoms may be severe just from cutting down. One man who was accustomed to 15 cups of coffee a day had severe headaches on weekends when he drank much less. How you cut back is really up to you. Just do whatever feels most comfortable. You may choose to reduce your intake by one cup per week or one cup per day. Remember, each reduction in caffeine is a plus for you.

2 The MSG Headache If a headache strikes soon after you've eaten a pleasant Chinese dinner, you may be a victim of the 'Chinese restaurant syndrome'. Some people also complain of pressure and tightness in the face, burning over the trunk, neck and shoulders, and a pressing pain in the chest. The headache usually takes the form of pressure or throbbing over the temples and a band-like sensation around the forehead. The culprit in this case isn't the Chinese food itself, but the *monosodium glutamate* (MSG) that is sometimes used quite heavily to 'enhance' flavour.

Since MSG is used in many processed foods – especially soups, stews and luncheon meat preparations – by manufacturers who want to give the flavour of meat without actually using more than a smidgen of the real thing, you don't have to 'eat Chinese' to get the headache. Every year nearly 20,000 tons of MSG are manufactured in the United States alone. In controlled tests, reported by Frederick J. Hass and Edward F. Dolan, Jr., in their book *What You Can Do about Your Headaches*, only a very small percentage of people did not react to very large doses of MSG. The average dose that produced a response was not much higher than the amount recommended by a leading manufacturer for flavour 'enhancement'.

To avoid Chinese restaurant syndrome, you don't necessarily have to avoid Chinese restaurants, but you do have to keep off the MSG. When you order your meal, ask the waiter or waitress to tell the chef to please not add MSG to your food. If the food is prepared fresh and not received already processed – i.e. if the restaurant is worth coming back to – that should present no problem. Eating something free of MSG early in the meal may protect you against MSG in what you eat later.

3 The hot dog headache Again, the villain is an additive. This time, it's the sodium nitrate and nitrite that processors add to hog dogs and other meats such as ham, bacon, luncheon meats and sausages. The chief function of the chemical is to keep the meat bright red, but the chemical can also dilate your blood vessels and cause a headache.

To avoid hot dog headaches, you might try boiling meats containing the additives and throwing away the water. Since nitrates and nitrites are water soluble, a lot of them will dissolve out of the hot dog. But the best way to make sure that you're not getting any of these chemicals is to eat meat that is nitrate- and nitrite-free. Supermarkets seldom carry such meats, but health food shops usually do; in addition, there are increasing numbers of butchers providing 'additive-free' meat.

4 Ice cream headache If you manage to get through the main course of your dinner without some additive in the food giving you a headache, you're still not safe. Your dessert – if it's cold enough – might give you an ice cream headache. Sudden cooling of the roof of the mouth and the throat can overstimulate nerves there and cause a headache. To prevent this type of headache, cold items such as ice cream and cold beverages should be eaten or sipped slowly to allow the mouth to adjust to the drop in temperature.

5 The salt headache Another common part of the diet that can trigger headaches is salt. Dr John B. Brainard, from St Paul, Minnesota, tried restricting the salt intake of a group of 12 people who regularly suffered headaches. They were told to avoid all salted snack food such as pretzels, nuts and potato crisps between meals. Only two of the people reported no reduction in their frequency of headaches, and in three of them, headaches disappeared entirely (*Minnesota Medicine*).

So far, you might have the impression that the safest course is not to eat at all. But *that* can give you a headache, too.

6 The hunger headache This can occur whether you feel hungry or not, because low blood sugar apparently is the trigger. In fact, you don't have to be fasting to have low blood sugar. If you eat too much sugar or refined carbohydrates, the flood of insulin from your pancreas may drive your blood sugar low enough to cause a headache. And alcohol, even a small amount, can also lower your blood sugar that far.

If you get headaches between meals or just before meals, your previous meal may not have supplied you with enough protein, fats and carbohydrates to keep your blood sugar where it belongs. The simplest solution is to eat between-meal snacks consisting of high-protein foods such as peanuts, yogurt, non-sugared homemade museli, sunflower seeds or some fresh, unrefined food such as bean sprouts, fresh fruit or raw vegetables.

7 The noxious fumes headache Breathing unhealthy concentrations of carbon monoxide, a main ingredient of car and lorry exhausts, can give you a headache – or kill you, if the concentration is high enough and the exposure long enough. Improperly adjusted coal, oil or gas stoves and heaters can also give off carbon monoxide fumes.

And if 'home' is a caravan, a headache may be waiting for you there. A research team in environmental health at the University of Washington, Seattle, responding to numerous complaints of headaches by people who live in mobile homes (caravans), tested the air in these homes. The team found high levels of formaldehyde, a chemical used to manufacture the particle board that goes into the walls and floors of mobile homes. Other sources of formaldehyde are plywood, plywood finishes and urea formaldehyde, a substance used to insulate houses.

Levels of formaldehyde in some of the newer houses were higher than the permissible exposure level set by the (US) National Institute of Occupational Safety and Health. According to Peter A. Breysse, associate professor of environmental health, it takes more than four years for the formaldehyde to dissipate to a relatively safe level.

However, even if you live in a 200-year-old stone house, commute to and from work by sailboat, and manage to avoid all of the above hazards, you might still find a headache waiting for you – in bed. In fact, you might give it to yourself!

8 Headaches from bruxism and improper bite   One of the ways you might do that is by grinding or clenching your teeth, a practice called *bruxism*. According to dental surgeons, William R. Cinotti and Arthur Grieder of the College of Medicine and Dentistry of New Jersey, four out of five bruxists are women. 'Inner conflicts' are usually the cause, they say, and the problem can best be resolved if the bruxist learns to relax and reduce stress (*Dental Survey*). Some people have found that adding calcium supplements to their diet solves the problem by relaxing their nerves (*see* BRUXISM). You don't necessarily have to grind your teeth at night to get a bruxism headache. Excessive gum chewing can also tire the chewing muscles in the jaw and result in a headache.

However, jaw problems that lead to headache aren't only caused by bruxism and excessive chewing. A bad bite can cause tension in the muscles around the temporo-mandibular joints – the places just in front of the ears where the lower jaw, or mandible, joins the skull. When a person's teeth do not mesh properly, he or she is forced to chew in an unnatural manner. This can throw the temporo-mandibular joints out of place. Even if the jaw is only slightly out of place, the muscles at the joint are constantly straining to set things right. That constant tension can result in a headache that can be relieved only by correcting the way the teeth come together. Minor problems can be solved by a dentist grinding down or building up individual teeth in the mouth, while more serious cases require orthodontic treatment. (*See also* TEMPORO-MANDIBULAR JOINT [TMJ] SYNDROME.)

9 The turtle headache   You give yourself a 'turtle headache' by sleeping with the covers pulled up over your head. Actually, the headache is caused by the buildup of carbon dioxide and the reduction in the oxygen supply. The same thing can happen in a crowded, stuffy room or car. If you suffer the turtle headache and can't seem to obey your own before-sleep commands to keep the covers below your head, try 'short-sheeting' yourself. Tuck in an extra foot or so of the covers at the foot of the bed. Then, you won't be able to pull them up over your head during the night.

10 The sunstroke headache When you spend too much time in the sun unprotected by clothes, beach hat or a deep tan, your body can become dehydrated. The fluids around the brain and the spinal column become depleted, and the blood vessels rub painfully on surrounding tissue. If slowly replacing the lost body fluids by drinking small amounts of warm water over a two- or three-hour period doesn't relieve the headache, your sunstroke may be more serious. Consult a doctor.

Warning

Certain headache symptoms prompt people to seek medical help, and well they should. While the following are not meant to frighten you, they may point to conditions that go beyond simple headache – and can even be life-threatening (such as a tumour). Don't hesitate to see your doctor if you have headaches that are characterized by one or more of the following:

● They occur often enough to prevent you from carrying out your normal daily activities.

● They are constant and unrelenting.

● They cause you to take more than 16 aspirin or paracetamol tablets a week.

● They come on suddenly and severely, like a bolt out of the blue.

● They are suddenly new to you – that is, occur more frequently or with increasing severity over a short span of time.

● They are accompanied by fever or a stiff neck.

● They are associated with local pain in the eye or ear or elsewhere in your head, trouble with speech, hearing loss, neurological symptoms, such as blurred vision, seizures or loss of alertness or consciousness, or loss of body function.

● They are accompanied by disturbances of thought processes, such as confusion, loss of memory, poor concentration or inability to think clearly.

● They are associated with sleep disturbances, such as insomnia or wakefulness in the middle of the night.

When you make an appointment, insist that the doctor's receptionist set aside ample time for a thorough examination. Take along a complete list of the medication you take regularly – prescription and over-the-counter. Remember, items such as oral contraceptives and antacids count as drugs, even though they may not treat a disease *per se*. Also include on your list any trigger factors you may associate with your headaches, plus chemicals you know you are exposed to at work.

● Healing problems

You might be recovering from major surgery, a car accident, or just a bad fall. Someone or something has cut, punctured, broken, bruised or scorched your body.

The wound throbs with pain. Your body's metabolism is thrown into high gear, drawing on all its reserves to move cells to the damaged tissue, produce new cells to replace those destroyed and, finally, bind the new cells together into new tissue. Vitamins, minerals and protein, which are needed just to carry on day-to-day body maintenance, are suddenly called on to join in these emergency repairs. Your body has its work cut out for it.

You can help the work of wound healing by eating well. For example, Canadian researchers found that malnourished animals suffered twice as many complications during healing and died of those complications twice as often as normally nourished ones (*Annals of Surgery*). Nutrition is crucial to healthy wound healing, so if you have healing to do, you'll want to know which nutrients have been found to be particularly important for repairing your body.

Heroes of healing: protein and vitamin C

Absolutely essential for rebuilding body tissue is protein. Protein contains the amino acids necessary for the body's growth and maintenance. Without an adequate intake of protein, vitamins and minerals can't make their important contributions to the healing process. However, human beings, unlike plants, can't manufacture their own supply of this basic nutrient, so they must make sure to get their protein ready-made by eating a good diet. Your need for protein increases when you're recovering from a serious injury – say, an operation or a burn that has put you in hospital. Now is the time to fill up with milk, eggs, cheese, fish, turkey, liver and wheat germ – both for protein's own rebuilding powers and so that other natural healing aids will also be able to do their jobs.

Injury also steps up the body's demand for certain nutrients, particularly vitamin C – a little hero of healing power. According to researchers W. Marshall Ringsdorf, Jr. and Emanuel Cheraskin of the University of Alabama School of Dentistry 'A deficiency of vitamin C impairs wound healing in experimental lower animals and human beings and . . . an excess accelerates healing above the normal level.'

Vitamin C is a star in the cellular dramas of wound healing because it regulates the formation of collagen, a protein that's the main structural ingredient in connective tissue – the stuff your body uses to patch up its holes. As Dr Guido Majno, a professor at the University of Massachusetts Medical School, explains: If a cat scratches your hand, the wound is repaired

> not with the original tissue but with a material that is biologically simple, cheap and handy: connective tissue . . . a soft but tough kind of tissue, specialized for mechanical functions, primarily that of holding us together; it fills the spaces in and around all other tissues.

Because the creation of collagen depends on vitamin C, a deficiency can disturb the 'architecture' of that connective-tissue repair job and delay the completion of the whole healing project. In one study, vitamin C deficiency in human cells decreased collagen production by 18 per cent according to one biological measurement, and by 75 per cent according to another (*American Journal of Clinical Nutrition*, March 1981).

In another experiment, designed by dentists Cheraskin and Ringsdorf, two gallant dental students with normal ascorbic acid (vitamin C) levels allowed them to remove a tiny 'plug' of tissue from their gums. In order to precisely measure the speed of healing, the wound was painted with a blue dye and photographed each day until the blue dot (indicating unhealed tissue) disappeared. After a two-week rest, the students had another 'plug' extracted from their gums – but this time, they also took 250 mg of vitamin C with each meal and at bedtime (for a total of 1 g daily).

A comparison of the healing sequences in both cases showed that the vitamin C supplemented wounds healed 40 per cent faster than those made when the students were eating a 'normal' diet. When the experiment was repeated using a daily dosage of 2 g of vitamin C, the wounds healed 50 per cent faster (*Oral Surgery, Oral Medicine, Oral Pathology*, March 1982).

Actually, vitamin C's healing power has been recognised for decades. In the 1940s, A. H. Hunt reported that wound disruption or breakage had been reduced by 75 per cent since doctors at St Bartholomew's Hospital in London began routinely administering ascorbic acid to all patients having abdominal operations. Over a period of 30 months, Hunt observed that 'leakage from suture lines has occurred in but one of a large number of operations.'

More recently, in another British study, vitamin C's effect on the healing of bedsores was studied. Twenty surgical patients suffering from bedsores were divided into two groups: One group was given two 500 mg vitamin C supplements daily, and the other was given two placebos (or chemically inactive pills). After a month, precise measurements of the wounds showed that the bedsores in the vitamin C group had decreased in size by 84 per cent; the placebo group showed only a 42.7 per cent decrease. 'It is well established that in scurvy [vitamin C deficiency], wound healing is delayed and that the healing process may fail completely,' the scientists observed (*Lancet*).

When you're recovering from any kind of injury, it's crucial to keep your diet rich in vitamin C, because injury drains your body's supply. American researchers found that ascorbic acid levels in the white blood cells of surgical patients had dropped by 42 per cent three days after surgery (*Surgery, Gynecology and Obstetrics*). Drs Ringsdorf and Cheraskin suggest that this and other studies showing a drop in ascorbate levels may indicate that 'during post-surgical recovery, the vitamin C in the body migrates toward and concentrates in the healing site.'

Whatever the case, Duke University's Dr Sheldon V. Pollack told us 'If you're recovering from injury and you're seriously ill, elderly, don't eat properly or otherwise have low vitamin C levels, it would be wise to take one or two grams of vitamin C a day'.

Increased need for vitamin A

Vitamin A works hand in hand with vitamin C in the healing process. Once vitamin C makes the formation of collagen possible, vitamin A increases the rate at which the new collagen cross-links to form and strengthen new tissue. Animal experiments at Albert Einstein College of Medicine in New York have shown that even minor wounds increase the need for vitamin A: the wounds of laboratory animals given vitamin A supplements showed stronger healing and less risk of the wound breaking open (*Annals of Surgery*).

Injured people need more vitamin A, too. Severely injured persons, such as burn and accident victims, can need it so badly – their blood levels drop so steeply – that they can develop gastro-intestinal 'stress' ulcers. A study by Arizona doctors found that by giving burn patients injections of from 50,000 to 100,000 IU of vitamin A twice daily, stress ulcers could be decreased to less than one-third of what they were in an unsupplemented group (*Modern Medicine*).

Vitamin A is also a wound healing 'must' for people who are taking cortisone (a steroid drug) for the relief of arthritis or other kinds of inflammation. Anti-inflammatory drugs such as cortisone or even aspirin retard the healing of open wounds and increase the risk of infection. Vitamin A can restore normal healing.

That was confirmed in both animal and human studies. In a study of wounded rabbits being given cortisone, researchers found that the application of vitamin A directly onto the wounds returned healing to normal despite the continued administration of cortisone. All wounds treated with vitamin A healed within 25 days.

The researchers also reported the case of an 18-year-old girl, taking an anti-inflammatory drug for a skin disease, who banged her leg and developed a nasty ulcerated wound. Despite normal treatment, the ulcer continued to enlarge and showed no signs of healing. Vitamin A ointment was applied to the wound three times daily for three weeks. Within only three days of the first application, the wound began to heal; 28 days later, it had completely healed (*Annals of Surgery*).

Diabetics very often suffer from slow-healing wounds, a problem that can be worsened by another problem: they're also more apt to pick up infections. However, in a study conducted by researchers at the Albert Einstein College of Medicine, supplemental vitamin A was shown to increase wound strength in diabetic animals. The researchers also believe that vitamin A helps fight wound infections.

The researchers concluded that vitamin A works to strengthen wounds mainly by increasing the accumulation of collagen.

> We believe that just as supplemental vitamin A improves immune responses of traumatized animals and surgical patients, it will be especially useful in preventing wound infection and promoting wound healing in surgical diabetic patients [*Annals of Surgery*, July 1981]

The need for zinc

However, vitamin A isn't the only natural wound healer that can counter the effects of cortisone. Zinc can, too. Researchers at Cleveland Metropolitan General Hospital discovered that patients being given long-term cortisone therapy had low blood levels of zinc and they also suffered from delayed wound healing. When they were given zinc supplements of 150 mg per day, their wounds healed completley (*Lancet*).

Zinc also works as a teammate of vitamin A to support the body's response to infection and inflammation. Without zinc, vitamin A stores could not be mobilized.

In fact, zinc is a valuable co-worker at many levels of the healing process. It is essential for the production of protein and collagen, and it is necessary for normal growth and reproduction of cells. Without zinc, the new cells needed to form new tissue cannot be made. So for anyone, zinc deficiency is something to be concerned about, but for someone with an injury, adequate amounts of zinc could be crucial. For more information, see TRAUMA.

Vitamin E and the B vitamins

No list of natural wound healers would be complete without vitamin E. Dorothy Fisher, a nurse-therapist, formerly with the Pottsville Hospital and Warne Clinic in Pennsylvania, reports unusual success in treating bedsores, diabetic ulcers and ulcerated surgical incisions with both capsules and ointments of vitamin E.

Nurse Fisher describes the case of a patient suffering from extensive ulceration over his lower body. He had previously been treated in five different hospitals and clinics without success. Nurse Fisher gave him no antibiotics and no steroids. Instead, she gave him 800 IU of vitamin E twice a day and treated the sores directly with vitamin E ointment. In less than four months, the patient could be sent home where the wounds healed completely (*The Summary*).

The late Dr Wilfred E. Shute, a veteran vitamin E researcher, reported that vitamin E helps accelerate wound healing, is 'the ideal treatment for burns' because of its ability to limit cell death to those cells that have been killed by the burning agent, and can even help reduce old scar tissue when applied directly. Keloids – progressively enlarging, raised scars caused by overproduction of collagen during the healing process – can be prevented by taking vitamin E orally and also applying it directly to the fresh wound, Dr Shute said.

Not everyone agrees. Dr Pollack, while observing that 'there is some data to suggest that vitamin E can promote wound healing,' told us that 'the research is still kind of up in the air . . . we just don't know the precise role, if any, that vitamin E plays in wound healing.'

There is also growing evidence that at least some of the B vitamins are involved in human wound healing. In one recent study, experimental animals fed diets rich in thiamin (vitamin B_1) were found to have heavier, denser granulation tissue (new tissue formed during wound repair) than those on deficient diets.

Based on thiamin's known biological activities in the body, the researchers concluded that it probably aids healing by helping the body step up its energy metabolism at the healing site, where the furious breakdown and buildup of cells require tremendous amounts of usable fuel (*Journal of Surgical Research*, January 1982).

Helping your body heal itself from the inside makes good sense. But there are some good natural ways to speed the process externally, too.

Healing with charcoal

Marjorie Baldwin, a doctor at the Wildwood Sanitarium and Hospital in Georgia, uses activated charcoal to promote healing. 'Any inflammation – an area that is red, painful, swollen and hot – responds to charcoal. We apply charcoal as a poultice if the inflammation is on the outside of the body or give it by mouth if the inflammation is in the digestive tract'.

Dr Baldwin describes the case of a young Type 1 (insulin-dependent) diabetic whose foot was saved from amputation by charcoal. 'This young lady had caught pneumonia, and her feet were soaked in hot water. Because she was diabetic, her feet were damaged, and she developed severe infections. Antibiotics didn't clear them up. The doctors suggested that one foot be amputated, but she refused and came to us for treatment. We put that foot in a plastic bag filled with a mixture of charcoal and water that was about the consistency of cream. The foot was kept in the bag round the clock, and the mixture was changed four times a day. She walked out of our clinic – on both feet.'

British doctors have also used charcoal to treat infections. A letter to the *Lancet* (13 September 1980), one of the world's most prestigious medical journals, described the use of charcoal-saturated cloth for wounds that were infected and discharging and had a bad odour.

The doctors applied a single layer of this charcoal cloth to the wounds of 26 patients with chronic leg ulcers and 13 patients with unhealed surgical incisions. 'A noticeable reduction in wound odour occurred in 24 ulcer patients and 13 surgical-wound patients,' the doctors wrote. And they found that the charcoal cloth reduced odour longer than 'standard dressing material'.

The doctors noted that charcoal may have reduced the odour by adsorbing bacteria. (An *adsorbent* is a substance that attaches things to its surface rather than absorbing them into itself.') It's a possible explanation, since, says Dr Baldwin, 'Charcoal is the most powerful adsorbent known to man. Charcoal adsorbs up to thousands of times its own weight,' she explains. 'It has enormous surface area – like a football field-sized piece of tissue paper rolled up into a tiny ball – and the more surface area charcoal has, the more adsorbent it is.' (One pound of activated charcoal has a surface area equal to 125 acres!)

Many uses for aloe

Since biblical times, aloe vera has also been valued as a healer.

'The aloe vera has fantastic potential for assisting in the healing of skin injuries, such as minor burns and cuts,' says Wendell D. Winters, associate professor of microbiology, who is studying the plant in his laboratory at the University of Texas Health Science Center at San Antonio. And when he goes home, 'I, like others, occasionally use fresh aloe for external minor abrasions,' Dr Winters confides. 'Personally, I'm quite bullish on it.'

He isn't the only one. Often referred to as the 'burn plant' (and known botanically as *Aloe barbadensis*), aloe vera does a lot more than simply soothe burns. Rick Chavez, a Seattle-based dentist, uses it in his oral surgery work. 'I have pain-free patients,' he boasts. Dr Chavez uses a commerical aloe preparation to quell the discomfort of having a tooth removed; he told us that aloe also hastens healing of an extraction site.

Saliva

Some researchers say that all of us carry a potent healing promoter around with us all the time. At the Royal Children's Hospital in Melbourne, they have been studying what takes place when animals lick their wounds, and they have come up with a few surprising answers.

They believe that saliva may aid healing by making the wounds knit faster. When wounded mice were caged separately and were unable to lick their wounds, the researchers found that the wounds healed slowly. Injured mice that were caged together, however, shared communal grooming and wound-licking routines, and their wounds healed more rapidly. When the scientists removed the salivary glands from the animals' lower jaws, wounds healed slowly. When salivary glands beneath the tongue were also removed, the wounds healed even more slowly.

The researchers, reporting in *Nature* (June 1979), concluded that an active substance in the salivary glands may speed up wound contraction. This could be important in human surgery someday, they noted, since wound contraction appears similar in all mammals.

So, the next time you peel your knuckle along with the potato, give in to the instinct and pop it into your mouth. It couldn't hurt.

• Heart disease

Heart disease is still the United States' number-one killer, but the day may come when journalists have to pin that cliché on some other disease, because in recent years the mortality rates have been dropping steadily. In fact, since 1968, deaths from cardiovascular disease among American men have fallen by some 25 per cent.

What are we to make of that? The figures make one thing startlingly clear, says one researcher, who points out that advances in the treatment of heart disease account for only a small part of the decline.

Unfortunately, this decline in the incidence (and death rate) of heart disease has not occurred in Britain. In fact, Northern Ireland and Scotland hold the title for the worst record of heart disease in the Western world. What have the Americans learned about heart-attack prevention over the past few decades so that they are less likely to die of a heart attack. The following items, culled from the most recent medical research, are among the 'rightest' things we could find for narrowing your chances of a heart attack.

Food and your heart

Close your eyes and you can almost taste it. The thick, tender slab of roast beef. The baked potato overflowing with butter. The salad bathed with lucent oils. The generous chunk of butter melting on warm bread. Dessert? A fat wedge of cheese cake, of course.

Where are the feasts of yesteryear?

If your household is like that of many health-conscious families, they have fallen victim to nutritional good sense – the knowledge that a healthy diet is one that has less of what these rich, tasty foods provide in such abundance: fat.

Cut down on saturated fat and cholesterol

When the US Senate's Select Committee on Nutrition and Human Needs issued its 'Dietary Goals for the United States', three of the six principal recommendations involved reducing fats and related substances. Even the French, whose dedication to the rich delights of the table is legendary, have effected an about-face of sorts with *cuisine minceur*, which attempts to take the grease out of 'gourmet'.

Is the fear of fat exaggerated? Not to judge by the research that continues to emanate from laboratories and universities throughout the world. By now, the connection between fat and heart disease should come as a surprise to no one. Atherosclerosis – the buildup of fat and cholesterol on artery walls – is often responsible for sudden death from heart attack and the lingering disability of stroke. And six decades of evidence, as the *New England Journal of Medicine* put it, 'have provided a considerable degree of certainty' that fat in the diet can promote these fatty deposits in the arteries.

In the case of heart disease, blame does not fall equally on all fats. Chemically, the fats in food come in several varieties. Saturated fats (each atom of carbon carries all the hydrogen it can hold – i.e. it's 'saturated' with them) are most commonly found in meats. Polyunsaturated fats (the carbon atoms have room for more hydrogen) are found more abundantly in vegetables and in fish and fowl.

A large body of research indicates that saturated fats are the ones to watch in guarding against heart disease. Where the diet is rich in these animal fats, heart disease is generally a problem. Yet people like the Eskimos, whose high-fat diet consists largely of polyunsaturates, suffer very little from heart attacks.

Some studies have found that merely substituting polyunsaturated for saturated fats can lower the level of cholesterol in the blood and, presumably, the risk of heart disease. In Finland, long-term patients at one mental hospital were given the normal Finnish diet, high in such saturated fat sources as eggs and whole milk products. In another hospital, much of the saturated fat was replaced with polyunsaturated fat. After six years, the diets were switched. Researchers found that when patients received the experimental diet, their blood cholesterol dropped sharply. What's more, the rate of death from coronary heart disease in the hospital on the experimental diet fell to half the rate at the other institution (*Circulation*, January 1979).

Other studies have suggested that a reduction in saturated fats can raise the level of high-density lipoproteins – a fraction of cholesterol considered valuable because it apparently resists the buildup of fatty deposits. (HDL cholesterol is the abbreviated form). A diet high in saturated fats, on the other hand, is often associated with a high amount of low-density lipoproteins (LDL cholesterol), which is the type of cholesterol you *don't* want.

In addition, the substitution of polyunsaturated for saturated fats can reduce the tendency of the blood to form thrombi, or tiny blood clots, which may initiate heart attacks and strokes.

If you want to drop your fat intake down to a significantly low level, though, you'll have to be aggressive about it. Trimming the fat off the roast is necessary, but not sufficient, because most of the fat that finds its way into your body – some 60 per cent, according to the US Department of Agriculture – is what they call 'invisible fat' and is likely to be overlooked.

Even after the fatty edge is removed from a steak, for example, the meat itself harbours a considerable amount of fat – some 40 per cent of its calories. The same people who keep butter off the table may continue to look at cheese with a fond eye, although two-thirds of the calories in some hard cheeses derive from fat.

You may think of sweets as primarily sources of sugar, but less obvious contributions of fat may be even more significant. For example, nearly half the calories in ice cream, and more than half the calories in milk chocolate, come from fats. Lard looks like fat and baked goods don't, but remember that the latter are often full of the former: a croissant, for example, owes half its calories to fat.

Like it or not, some of the most concentrated sources of fat are to be found in fast-food restaurants. A meal at McDonald's is nearly 40 per cent fat, while a serving of Kentucky Fried Chicken is 55 per cent fat.

The trouble with 'stale' cholesterol
Some research indicates that the dangers of a high-cholesterol diet may have less to do with cholesterol itself than with oxidation products formed when stored cholesterol goes stale. The findings show that cholesterol-containing foods such as eggs, dairy products and meats might increase the risk of heart disease, but only when they are less than perfectly fresh, and are contaminated by those oxidation products.

As we've mentioned, scientists have long agreed that cholesterol is an important risk factor in the development of heart disease. It was first observed in 1912, when rabbits fed cholesterol developed atherosclerosis. This clogging of the blood vessels can eventually lead to a complete blockage of the artery by a blood clot, which, if it occurs in vessels supplying the heart or brain, can kill.

The controversy is not whether cholesterol contributes to this chain of events. The question is whether or not cholesterol actually causes the damage to the arterial wall that sets the process in motion. C. Bruce Taylor, a pathologist at the Veterans Administration Hospital in Albany, New York, believes he has proof that the most important factor is not the presence of cholesterol in the diet, but whether the cholesterol is fresh or stale.

A team of scientists led by Dr Taylor took isolated chemicals formed when cholesterol undergoes oxidation, and compared the effects those chemicals have on the arterial walls of rabbits with the effects of purified cholesterol. The researchers also compared the effects of feeding the rabbits fresh or stale cholesterol. In both cases, the finding – reported in the *American Journal of Clinical Nutrition* (January 1979) supported Dr Taylor's hypothesis.

A concentrate containing the products of the cholesterol oxidation produced damage to the walls of the rabbits' arteries both in long-term (45 days) and short-term (up to 24 hours) experiments. In both tests, the cholesterol contaminants clearly caused more damage to the artery wall than purified cholesterol did. In short-term feeding tests conducted with fresh cholesterol and cholesterol stored for five years, the stale cholesterol was significantly more damaging to the arterial wall than the fresh. The damage produced was exactly the kind that scientists believe to be the initial step in the development of atherosclerosis.

'I was surprised by the findings,' Dr Taylor told us. 'I'm an old-timer, and we've assumed for years that it was one thing – cholesterol – that was causing problems. Now we find that we were a little bit wrong.'

Some understatement, given the amout of wasted research effort that mistake may have caused. For 40 years following the first observations of cholesterol's effects on arteries, scientists did not have the sophisticated techniques necessary for the separation and identification of cholesterol's contaminants. 'Had the currently available, elegant methods for separation and identification of spontaneous oxidation products of cholesterol . . . been available 40 years earlier,' Dr Taylor wrote in his report, 'an inordinate number of cholesterol feeding experiments, which now seem to warrant re-evaluation, might have been interpreted more properly.' Many deaths from heart disease might have been avoided as well.

Dr Taylor and his colleagues then began work to identify the most harmful of the cholesterol contaminants and to determine what foods might be most susceptible to this kind of spoilage. 'Our group has isolated derivatives of cholesterol from powdered eggs and powdered whole milk,' he reported.

> One member of our group has also isolated derivatives of cholesterol from two readily available retail packaged foods that contain dried whey [whey is made from whole milk] and dried whole eggs or egg yolks. One product is a powdered custard mix; the other is a pancake mix.

Dr Taylor suspects that contaminants form easily in a number of other foods, because of the ease with which cholesterol undergoes oxidation. He told us, 'The only way to prevent oxidation, according to chemists I've talked to, is to store the cholesterol in a vacuum or under the atmosphere of pure nitrogen, and, if possible, in a very deep freeze. Room temperature and air can really make things go rapidly. We've found that brand-new cholesterol when it's opened is already 5 per cent broken down into other products. You can put cholesterol in a heating oven at a temperature of 80°C [176°F] for a period of two weeks, and 40 to 50 per cent of it will be broken down.

'It is probable,' Dr Taylor continued 'that smoked fish, smoked meat and smoked sausages may have had enhancement of breakdown of their cholesterol during their exposure to heat while being smoked. Since these smoked meat products are often stored at room temperature, the breakdown of the cholesterol molecules may be a continuing process. Some cheeses, particularly those exposed to air at room temperature for long periods during processing and later stored at room temperature, may also contain significant quantities of toxic cholesterol derivatives.'

Dr Taylor thinks there is historical evidence of the toxic effects of cholesterol derivatives. 'There was a high incidence of atherosclerosis,' he told us,
'in men who were in the military in Korea and Vietnam, and they were fed a
good deal of powdered eggs and milk. It may be that if the care and storage
of food were improved, there might be a reduction of arterial disease.'

Restricting sugar

Call us junkies. Addicts. Weak-willed people who can't get through the three
o'clock slump without a sweet fix, not to mention a year without putting away
over 90 lb (per person!) of that sandy white substance.

We're hooked on sugar. And don't fool yourself: avoiding the sugar bowl
doesn't necessarily mean you've kicked the habit. An unbelievable number
of pre-packaged food items under colourful labels are concealing some type
of sugar additive. And we're not only talking about sugary baked goods, sac-
charine desserts and pre-sweetened cereals. Check the labels on many baby
foods, commerical fruit drinks, salad dressings, soups, tomato sauce, some
canned vegetables and most tinned fruits. Nothing is sacred. Not even dog
food. Even some of that has sugar.

And the problem is, our sweet tooth is causing a lot more damage than a
few rotten teeth.

In the experiment carried out by Sheldon Reiser and a team of researchers
at the USDA's Carbohydrate Nutrition Laboratory near Washington, D.C. to
study exactly what effect sugar has on the blood (*see* DIABETES), not only did
they discover that blood sugar and levels of insulin (the hormone necessary
for sugar metabolism) were consistently higher while the volunteers were
on sugar than while they were on the starch diet, but most interesting was
this observation: 'It appears that insulin levels and triglyceride levels have a
tendency to rise simultaneously.'

Triglycerides and cholesterol are both fats found in the blood. For a
long time, triglycerides were given a backseat on the list of risk factors for
coronary artery disease. Today, however, they are considered as important
as cholesterol, according to Dr Reiser.

The link between sugar and heart disease isn't new to some. Back in
1972, John Yudkin, a prominent British doctor, biochemist and nutritionist,
insisted that sugar is the primary cause of heart disease. In his book *Sweet
and Dangerous*, Dr Yudkin noted that he first suspected that sugar might
pose a potential threat at the same time that Ancel Keys of Minneapolis was
probing correlations between fat consumption and coronary mortality rates
in various parts of the world. Dr Yudkin studied the data and found that,
although the fat and heart disease relationship was apparent, an even better
correlation existed between sugar consumption and coronary mortality
rates.

Two subsequent studies on select individuals confirmed his suspicion. The
people with coronary artery disease or peripheral vascular disease (circulation
problems in the blood vessels of the arms and legs) ate more sugar than did
healthy persons.

In the first study, the average sugar intake for coronary patients was 113
g per day (about $^1/_4$ lb); for those with peripheral vascular disease, 128 g;

and for the healthy persons who served as controls, only 58 g. The second study produced more of the same results.

The persistent Dr Yudkin didn't stop there. Working first with rats, then with chickens and finally with people, he found that a daily intake of table sugar caused a moderate increase in blood cholesterol and a substantial boost to serum triglycerides – precisely what Dr Reiser and his research team at the Carbohydrate Nutrition Laboratory have discovered.

They found that when the people ate sugar, their cholesterol, and especially their triglyceride, levels were significantly elevated after a 12-hour fast. Curiously, they also discovered that the adverse effect of sugar on triglycerides was more pronounced in men than in women – and potentially more dangerous. Men, it seems, tend to start out with higher resting triglyceride levels than the women, giving them less leeway before levels rise into the danger zone.

Dr Reiser explains how this finding seems to fit into the puzzle of heart disease: 'Sugar stimulates insulin production, which in turn increases triglycerides. But this effect is more pronounced in some people than in others. We call it "sugar sensitivity". And it may explain why one person who eats, say, 30 per cent or more of his total calories as sugar may have no overt symptoms, whereas another person who limits his sugar intake to 10 or 15 per cent of his total caloric needs falls ill to some sugar-related problem.

'Men appear to be more sugar-sensitive than women,' notes Dr Reiser, 'and, interestingly enough, men are also more prone to heart disease than women.'

Although we've discussed sugar and fat individually, it's important to realize that the *combination* of high sugar *plus* high fat in the diet equals a particularly high risk of heart disease, according to Dr Reiser. For example, if you feed a rat a diet of sugar and cholesterol, he says, you'll increase its blood cholesterol level over and above what you would have on a diet with the same amount of cholesterol but with starch. Sugar, he tells us, is not the sole villain of this story, but it does instigate the worst results when it combines with the other pitfalls of the Western diet – like saturated fats and cholesterol-rich foods.

There are foods, however, that don't have to be avoided. They actually improve heart health by lowering cholesterol.

What are those foods?

Garlic, onion, fish oils, pectin (and other types of fibre), aubergine, yogurt and lecithin-containing foods such as soyabeans. There may be others still in the laboratory, but these particular foods have already been shown to serve a cholesterol-lowering function.

Garlic

Not only are people who eat large amounts of garlic rarely plagued with respiratory complaints, but they are also less likely to acquire hardened arteries and subsequent heart disease. For centuries, garlic has been hailed as a blood purifier. In a study of the dietary habits of seven countries, researchers found that inhabitants of garlic-happy Greece, Italy and Dalmatia (now part of Yugoslavia) have fewer coronary complaints than the citizens of Britain, Finland, Holland and the United States (*Lancet*, 19 January 1980).

At the University of Benghazi in Libya, Drs R. C. Jain and D. B. Konar fed one group of rabbits a diet rich in cholesterol for 16 weeks. Three other groups of rabbits received the same diet, laced with various amounts of garlic oil. When the aorta (the main artery leading from the heart) of each animal was examined, the differences between groups were striking. Due to their high-cholesterol diet, all the rabbits' arteries showed some of the fatty plaques of atherosclerosis, but the animals who had no garlic in their diet suffered nearly twice as much arterial damage as those who were protected by the highest doses. The animals who had lesser amounts of garlic had somewhat less protection from atherosclerosis (*Atherosclerosis*).

That's good news for garlic-loving rabbits, you might say – what about people? Another study by Dr Jain suggests that garlic offers the same protection to human beings. For three weeks, he gave six young men a diet that included 5 g of crushed garlic daily (about two good-sized cloves). Each week, the doctor analysed the fat levels in their blood. One thing he found was that their cholesterol levels dropped – gradually – over that period of time. Reducing cholesterol, as we've said, reduces the risk of coronary heart disease. Garlic, it seems, is good news for people, too.

Remember, however, that some studies have suggested that the type of cholesterol in the blood is the crucial factor: low-density lipoprotein (LDL) cholesterol raises heart disease risk; high-density lipoprotein (HDL) choles-terol seems to protect against heart disease. If you follow this distinction, then garlic may be even better news. What garlic reduced, Dr Jain found, was specifically the amount of LDL cholesterol in the blood of the young men who ate it (*American Journal of Clinical Nutrition*).

People whose tastes run to garlicky salads and pungent pasta sauces can expect the same kind of benefit, according to a study conducted in India. There, a team of researchers led by Dr G. S. Sainani of the B. J. Medical College in Poona, analysed blood samples from three groups of people with different dietary habits.

All three groups ate a primarily or entirely vegetarian diet, but in the first group, they spiced their meals with a good deal of onion and heavy amounts (two or three cloves daily) of garlic. The second group never touched onion or garlic, and the third preferred only small amounts of the pungent vegetables.

Among those who shunned garlic and onion, Dr Sainani found, there were consistently higher blood levels of LDL cholesterol and triglycerides than among the garlic eaters. These people also had less HDL cholesterol than the others. And the people who ate a lot of onion and garlic had healthier levels of blood fats than those who ate just a little.

Its power to keep cholesterol levels in check is enough to recommend garlic – highly – to anyone who wants to minimize his or her risk of heart attack. However, there's a good deal of research indicating that garlic provides addi-tional protection for your heart and circulation in an entirely different way.

Blood clotting is a vital and complex process. It begins, apparently, when tiny blood cells called *platelets* aggregate, or clump together. After a certain point, a blood chemical called *fibrin* forms long strands to tie the clot up into a tight bundle. This is what happens when you cut yourself – the result is a plug that prevents excessive bleeding.

However, when the process occurs spontaneously – within arteries that have become encrusted with the fatty plaques of atherosclerosis – the result is tiny blood clots, or *thrombi*, that can lodge in a coronary artery (causing a heart attack) or in a vessel of the brain (causing a stroke). Garlic, it seems, can protect against this dangerous spontaneous clotting in two ways. It makes platelets less 'sticky', so they won't clump together too easily. And it can promote the action of natural blood chemicals that dissolve clots that have already started to form.

Dr Arun Bordia, of the R.N.T. Medical College in Udaipur, India, took blood samples from six healthy volunteers and treated them with chemicals that make platelets clump together. Then he repeated the process, adding garlic oil to the blood samples. 'Garlic significantly inhibited platelet aggregation,' Dr Bordia reported. Garlic oil in the blood, in other words, kept platelet clumps from forming. If garlic oil was added after the platelets had started to aggregate, it seemed to reverse the process.

Dr Bordia found a similar result when he put his volunteers on a diet that included 25 mg of garlic oil daily. After five days, there was a marked reduction in platelet aggregation, which suggests that eating garlic is a natural way to make platelets less sticky (*Atherosclerosis*).

According to the results of another experiment of Dr Bordia's, garlic may help to dissolve clots that have begun to form, by increasing the blood's fibrinolytic activity – its ability to dissolve the chemical fibrin, which makes clots thick and strong.

Dr Bordia gave ten healthy adults hefty doses of garlic oil for three months, testing their blood regularly. He found a gradual rise in fibrinolytic activity and after three months of garlic, this clot-dissolving ability more than doubled. When garlic was discontinued, fibrinolysis gradually dropped back to its original level.

A high level of fibrinolytic activity is especially important for people who have had heart attacks – to prevent recurrences. Dr Bordia gave garlic to one group who had suffered myocardial infarction (the medical term for heart attack) more than a year before; he started another group on garlic within 24 hours after their heart attacks. Here, too, garlic led to a swift, significant rise in fibrinolytic activity – 'within a few hours', according to Dr Bordia. For those patients in the crucial recovery period after their heart attacks (a second thrombosis, at this point, could easily be fatal), ten days of garlic therapy led to a 63 per cent increase in fibrinolysis. After 20 days, clot-dissolving activity had nearly doubled.

There are powerful drugs, of course, that can do the same thing – reduce the tendency of the blood to clot – but those must be watched closely to avoid side-effects such as excessive bleeding. 'In our own studies,' Dr Bordia noted, 'administration of as much as 60 g of crude garlic (the equivalent of some 20 cloves) daily for three months has led neither to side-effects nor to a bleeding tendency. As such, this herbal remedy seems to be clinically acceptable and safe.'

In fact, garlic's virtues should astonish no one who looks closely at diets and diseases around the world. Is it a coincidence that the countries of the Mediterranean (e.g. Greece, Spain and Italy) and Latin America, where garlic is favoured in cooking, have lower heart disease rates than those, like our own, where bland foods are preferred?

Where does garlic get the power to aid the body in so many ways? What seemed magic to healers of centuries past – magic so powerful that it could rout evil spirits as well as illnesses – may actually be a group of highly active substances, including enzymes and sulphur-containing compounds. According to the theory, they can influence a broad range of chemical processes within the body.

Those compounds, incidentally, may be the same ones that give garlic its pungent, persistent odour – announcing to all the world that this flavourful herb is stong medicine.

Onions

These, of course, need no introduction. You no doubt use onions as a garnish or a spice, to add their unique pungency to other foods. But the onion is also capable of taking the cholesterol sting out of foods.

To test the effect of onion as a cholesterol-lowering agent, K. K. Sharma and three colleagues associated with the S.N. Medical College in Agra, India, gave a group of men $3^1/_2$ oz of butter spread on four slices of bread first thing in the morning after a 13-hour fast.

On subsequent days, the men got their bread and butter with various accompaniments: once with 50 g (about $1^3/_4$ oz of raw onions and another time with boiled onions. On another occasion, raw onions were not given until two hours after the butterfat meal.

The results? When butter alone was given, cholesterol levels two hours later increased from an average of about 211 to 232. Four hours after eating the butterfat, cholesterol was all the way up to 241, for a total rise of 30.6 points. But when raw onion was eaten at the same time, the total rise was only 9.4 points (*Indian Journal of Nutrition and Dietetics*).

And boiling the onions had no effect on their ability to prevent the rise of cholesterol levels. That means, say the Indian scientists, that the active principle involved is not destroyed by heat and is not soluble in water. And that, indeed, is good news. It means that no matter how you eat your onions – raw, sautéed, boiled or stewed – the active principle of cholesterol protection is still working for you.

If you have been depriving yourself of the pleasure of egg dishes, minimize the risk and enjoy them with onions. Chopped spring onions with a soft-boiled egg are delicious. An omelette with onion and green peppers is a very satisfying meal.

Fish oil

The first clues turned up when scientists studying the health of different world populations noticed the low incidence of coronary heart disease among Eskimos and among Japanese people living in fishing villages by the sea. Although widely separated geographically, they had at least one thing in common: both groups consumed tremendous amounts of fatty fish, fish oil, whale blubber and other marine life that fed on fish.

How could that be? Hadn't decades of research shown that diets high in fat, particularly animal fat, were a major cause of heart disease? Further studies revealed that both the maritime Japanese and the Eskimos had low levels of triglycerides, high levels of HDL cholesterol and a reduced tendency for their blood to clot. All those things are the classic signs suggesting a sound, healthy cardiovascular system. What was going on?

Digging deeper, researchers found that the blood of these fish-loving people also contained high levels of two fatty acids called *eicosapentaenoic acid* (EPA), and *docosahexaenoic acid* (DHA). Where do EPA and DHA come from? From fish, fish oil and the fat of marine animals who live on fish. Could these substances be the key to the healthy hearts of the Eskimos and the Japanese? Two recent studies suggest that may very well be the case.

Over a period of a year, researchers at the Northern General Hospital in Sheffield measured the effect of fish oil (taken in capsule form) on 76 subjects. Some took enough to give a daily intake of 1.8 g of EPA, and others took twice that amount, 3.6 g a day. Meanwhile, cholesterol levels, triglycerides and bleeding times were monitored.

Elevated cholesterol and triglycerides may be warning signs of coronary trouble. Bleeding time is also an important measurement, because the platelets may also aggregate along blood vessel walls, forming a clot. 'The narrowing of blood vessels through atherosclerosis is a very dangerous situation,' William E. M. Lands, head of the department of biological chemistry at the University of Illinois, explains, 'but what really causes a coronary event is the clot; platelet aggregation plays an important role in its formation.' Apparently because their platelets are less 'sticky', and so don't clump as easily, Eskimos have long bleeding times.

Although the British volunteers receiving 1.8 g of EPA didn't show any change in bleeding time, those getting twice that amount 'showed a highly significant increase in bleeding time,' the researchers noted. Serum triglycerides also dropped 'markedly' in all subjects within a month after they began taking the oil, and after a year the change was still apparent. HDL cholesterol levels were not as responsive: They rose after a month, stayed high for six months, then returned to their original level before the year was up. 'These changes,' the scientists observed,

> are consistent with a reduction in the incidence of thrombosis [clotting] and a slowing down of the atherosclerotic process. An increased dietary intake of marine oils, particularly those rich in EPA, may reduce the risk of coronary artery disease in patients on a mixed diet. [*Lancet*, 31 July 1982]

Another group of British researchers decided to take a closer look at what was actually happening to the platelets when fish oil was added to the diet. Thirteen patients with ischaemic heart disease (reduced blood flow) were given fish oil containing 3.5 g of EPA every day for five weeks. At the end of that time, the scientists noted some interesting changes.

Anything that cuts down on the interaction between blood vessel walls and platelets, they explained, probably lessens your chances of developing an atheroma, or abnormal fatty mass that clings to a vessel wall and blocks blood flow. And five weeks of fish oil produced changes that, in effect, cut down on this dangerous interaction – for example, by reducing the total number of platelets in the heart patient's blood by 15 per cent. 'These findings suggest that a diet rich in . . . eicosapentaenoic acid (EPA) . . . will reduce platelet/vessel-wall interaction and may reduce the risk of ischaemic heart disease,' the researchers observed (*Lancet*, 5 June 1982).

Taking the cue from their British counterparts, American researchers have also been exploring the potential of this potion from the sea. One group, at the Oregon Health Sciences University, designed a study using both fish oil and salmon meat (rich in both EPA and DHA). After 28 days on the salmon diet, the researchers found that plasma cholesterol levels in apparently healthy volunteers dropped by 17 per cent and triglycerides plunged by as much as 40 per cent. Among subjects whose blood fats were already elevated, the change was even more dramatic: cholesterol levels dropped 20 per cent or more, and triglycerides went down by as much as 67 per cent (*Journal of the American Medical Association*, 12 February 1982).

'Subjects with elevated cholesterol and triglycerides seemed to show the most marked response to the fish oil,' wrote William S. Harris, one of the Oregon researchers. 'As a rule, the higher these levels at the outset, the further they dropped when the fish-oil program was started.'

And in Japan, researchers at the Chiba University School of Medicine have turned up results that seem to fit the rest of the pattern that's emerged in labs around the world. They compared the blood of a group of men and women from a Japanese fishing village with the blood of a second group from an inland farming village. The seaside dwellers, they noted, had much thinner, less viscous blood – and they also ate more than twice as much seafood as the landlubbers.

Then the researchers fed the farmers enough EPA, in capsule form, to make up the difference between their diet and that of the fishermen. After four weeks, the Japanese scientists reported that the farmers' blood had become significantly thinner and slower to form a clot. They suggested that

a seafood diet reduces blood viscosity, the effect of the diet may be attributable mainly to EPA, and the ingestion of EPA-rich seafood may be of use for the prevention and treatment of thrombotic disorders (*Lancet*, 25 July 1981).

Is there any danger that EPA might thin the blood to the point where excessive bleeding becomes a problem? 'We've never had anybody with a clinical bleeding problem, even at 70 to 120 g [of fish oil] a day,' Dr Harris told us. Adds Dr Lands, 'Fish oil only increases bleeding time from, say, three minutes up to seven minutes or so. Also, platelet function isn't the only mechanism responsible for clotting; the plasma protein *fibrinogen* serves as a "backup" system as well.'

How much would a person need to take before these celebrated effects begin to occur? 'That's the question,' Dr Harris laughs. 'We simply don't know.' In his study, volunteers consumed $1/2$–1 lb of salmon daily, plus 2–3 oz of fish oil, depending on their body size. That, he admits, is more than even most hardened fish lovers would care to eat. Yet other studies have shown beneficial effects from much smaller amounts.

One British doctor, writing in the *Lancet* (6 October 1979), suggested

that
> a realistic way of improving the EPA level of the diet is the regular consumption of an EPA-rich oil from fish, such as cod-liver oil. Two teaspoons daily (10 g) would contribute 1 g of EPA to the diet, about 10 times the present level of intake.

On the other hand, the taste of straight cod-liver oil is so awful it's legendary. But fish oil in capsule form is now commercially available.

However, perhaps the most pleasant way to take advantage of this exciting research is simply to increase your consumption of fish moderately. 'It certainly couldn't hurt, and some people may even be glad to know they don't have to avoid fatty fish,' says Dr Harris. 'Eating more fish would also tend to replace red meat in the diet, which many of us eat too much of anyway.'

Which fish are richest in EPA and DHA? Almost all fish contain some EPA, but among the richest are salmon, trout, haddock, mackerel and sardines.

Fibre

Evidence has accumulated in recent years that several naturally occurring substances in plants, designated by the general term 'dietary fibre', exert an effect similar to that of cholesterol-lowering drugs. One such natural fibre is pectin, long used in the making of jams because of its ability to form gels.

Studies on experimental animals done by Emil Ginter and colleagues at the Institute of Human Nutrition at Bratislava, Czechoslovakia have produced conclusive evidence that simultaneous administration of vitamin C and pectin significantly decreased cholesterol concentration not only in blood, but also in the liver. When taken daily, a test preparation containing 450 mg of vitamin C and 15 g of citrus pectin lowered total blood cholesterol in humans after six weeks. This decline was characterized by a decrease of the dangerous LDL cholesterol, while the concentration of the protective HDL cholesterol remained unchanged.

That an apple a day can keep the doctor away has never been proven by scientific testing, but, because of its pectin content, an apple a day might help to keep high cholesterol levels away. And pectin has also been shown to limit the amount of cholesterol you'll absorb from a meal rich in fats.

Hans Fisher, chairman of the department of nutrition at Rutgers University in New Jersey, tested college students who were eating at least two eggs daily and found that after three weeks, those who took pectin had an average cholesterol count of 157, while those who did not take the pectin had a count of 191 – more than 20 per cent higher.

'It is clear that pectin offers partial protection against the problem which may arise from cholesterol ingestion,' Dr Fisher wrote in *Nutrition, Diet and Cholesterol in Cardiovascular Disease*. 'Where there is no overload of cholesterol in the diet,' he told us, 'pectin may not be necessary to limit its absorption. But when a typically fat-rich American diet is eaten, pectin does have a definite regulatory role to play.'

P. N. Durrington and colleagues at the University of Bristol department of medicine reported in the *Lancet* that 12 g (about $1/2$ oz) of pectin taken daily with meals resulted in an average decrease of serum cholesterol of 8 per cent.

To get the most pectin out of your apple, don't peel it. Citrus fruits, too, are a good source of pectin, especially the part just under the skin. Pectins are present in the white membrane more than they are in the fruit itself. So instead of drinking orange juice, eat the whole thing.

Pectin isn't the only dietary fibre you should consider when it comes to a healthy heart. One British study followed a group of 337 men for ten years and found that those who consumed the most cereal fibre suffered far less coronary heart disease than those who ate the least: there were five cases of heart disease in the first group and 25 in the second (*British Medical Journal*).

Some types of grains may work better than others. Hard red spring wheat and maize bran, for example, were reported by a US government scientist to increase the percentage of HDL cholesterol. As a bonus, wheat caused a decrease in LDL – and a 17 per cent decrease in total cholesterol. Dr Juan Munoz, formerly with the Human Nutrition Laboratory of USDA in Grand Forks, North Dakota, also said that the wheat and maize, as well as a number of other sources of fibre, reduced triglycerides (another form of blood fats) by about 15 per cent.

One medical scientist has reported finding actual improvement in the clinical signs of heart disease in patients taking supplementary fibre. Renzo Romanelli, professor of gerontology and geriatrics at the University of Pisa in Italy, reported to a conference of the International College of Surgeons that a number of patients taking wheat bran daily enjoyed a reduction in the number of angina attacks. In five patients over 70 years of age, Dr Romanelli said, tests showed improvement in cardiac efficiency, and ECG signs of oxygen lack in the heart muscle were diminished. In 14 patients between 72 and 94 years of age, he added, there was complete disappearance of a particular type of circulatory inefficiency that commonly occurs during staining during a bowel movement. The professor explained that with a low-fibre diet, which often results in constipation and the need to strain, high pressures that built up in the area of the colon can reduce the output of the heart. Bran stops this cycle from occurring.

Fibre, this specialist in the health problems of ageing told the assembled surgeons, is so important that its inclusion in the daily diet should be considered an important part of preventive medicine.

The same feeling is apparently shared by several British doctors writing in the *British Medical Journal*. Dr J. N. Morris and colleagues suggested that lack of fibre in the diet may well be a major cause of coronary thrombosis – a blood clot that blocks the flow of oxygen to the heart. Dr A. D. Robertson argued that the reason Scotland has seven times as much coronary thrombosis as it did before World War II is because of the lack of fibre. 'Pre-war,' Dr Robertson said, 'the common Scottish breakfast included porridge made from coarse meal, soaked overnight. The main meal frequently included homemade soup, thick with a good supply of vegetables and pulses [i.e. peas and beans]. Now it is flakes (if that) and creamed tinned soup . . .'

More foods your heart will love
Aubergine Eating this will help lower the amount of cholesterol absorbed from fatty foods. That's what an Austrian scientist, G. H. A. Mitschek

of the University of Graz, discovered when he fed a high-cholesterol diet to a group of laboratory animals. If the animals were fed aubergine along with cholesterol-rich foods, they enjoyed a remarkable degree of protection from the buildup of fatty plaques in their blood vessels. What the aubergine actually does is break down in the intestine into various components that bind with excess cholesterol and carry it out of the digestive system. Dr Mitschek also noticed that aubergine does its best work when eaten at the same time as a fatty meal (*Experimentelle Pathologie*). That's convenient, because aubergine is traditionally served as an accompaniment to cholesterol-rich fatty foods such as meat and cheese.

Beans One of the pioneers of cardiovascular epidemiology is Ancel Keys, mentioned earlier in this entry. It was his study of the effect of pulses, especailly beans, on serum cholesterol that led him to team up with his wife, Margaret, to write a cookbook, *The Benevolent Bean*. This cookbook is prefaced by a treatise in praise of beans.

The Keyses compared diet and the resulting serum cholesterol levels among men in Minneapolis and Naples. Finding the serum cholesterol level lower among working-class Neapolitans than among the American men, the couple set out to see what would happen to a group of Minneapolis men who ate the Neapolitan diet, which was rich in pasta and beans. They found that, on a high-bean diet, the serum cholesterol level of the Minneapolis men dropped by 9 per cent.

'So if you happen to be interested in cholesterol control, beans or any leguminous seeds merit a prominent place in your diet,' the authors concluded.

Just how much (or many!) beans should we eat? 'Perhaps it would be overdoing it to urge that everyone eat a pound of beans a week, but half a pound a week might be a good idea,' the Keyses said. That would double our intake of pulses and something else in the diet would have to be reduced to keep total calories in line.

Yogurt Even when it's made from whole milk, yogurt actually reduces the amount of cholesterol in the blood. This paradox was observed by George V. Mann of the department of biochemistry, Vanderbilt University School of Medicine, during a study of the diet of Masai tribesmen.

These primitive African people have very low blood cholesterol levels to begin with, but when they consumed large quantities of yogurt, even though some of them gained weight, blood cholesterol levels dropped significantly. Weight gain itself is known to raise cholesterol levels, but the more weight gained (presumably because of the volume of yogurt consumed), the more cholesterol levels went down. Dr Mann suspects that the yogurt bacteria produce a substance that blocks cholesterol production in the liver (*Atherosclerosis*).

In a subsequent study of Americans, yogurt lowered cholesterol, while an equal amount of unfermented milk did not.

Nutritional supplements for your heart

Lecithin In the world of nutritional supplements, lecithin (LESS-uh-thin) is something of an enigma to many people. It's not a vitamin (although it does contain two substances – choline and inositol – that scientists usually consider essential parts of the B complex). It's not a mineral either (although it contains an essential mineral – phosphorus). Nor is it a protein food or a source of fibre.

However, lecithin is proving to be a very important substance none the less. Research is now confirming that, for the thousands of people who have discovered lecithin and include it with their meals every day, the 'less' in lecithin's first syllable may be prophetic. Evidence is rapidly accumulating that lecithin, taken regularly, holds the promise of less cholesterol, less heart disease, less angina pain, even less gallstone disease.

Before we look at all those bright prospects one by one, it might help to keep these basic facts about lecithin in mind: It's a fat-like substance (a phospholipid) found in the membrane lining of all living cells. It occurs in nature in many different forms, including one that's manufactured right inside our bodies. Lecithin plays an important role in the absorption of fats from the food we eat and an equally important role in the safe transport of those fats (lipids) through the bloodstream.

So it's not surprising that one of the most significant ways that lecithin is proving beneficial to health is in treating people with dangerously high cholesterol levels.

One clinical study about lecithin was reported by Dr L. A. Simons and two associates at the University of New South Wales Medical School and St Vincent's Hospital Lipid Clinic in Sydney. In these trials, fairly large doses of supplementary lecithin were fed to both healthy and high-cholesterol individuals with encouraging results. The lecithin used (as in all the subsequent applications to be discussed) was derived from soyabeans and is noteworthy for its particularly rich content of unsaturated oils.

Dr Simons first got the idea of trying lecithin after noting that several patients with elevated blood cholesterol levels suddenly showed dramatic and unexplained improvement. Close questioning revealed that in each case, just prior to their remarkable cholesterol plunges, they had begun taking lecithin on their own. Those were all people for whom orthodox diet management and drug therapy had failed.

So the Australian researchers started feeding approximately 3/4 oz of lecithin granules daily to seven high-cholesterol patients and three healthy volunteers. In three of the patients and one of the normal subjects, cholesterol levels fell significantly – by as much as 18 per cent (*Australia and New Zealand Journal of Medicine*).

However, the most exciting part of the trial, according to Dr Simons, was the fact that the reduction was almost totally confined to the LDL cholesterol.

With two of the patients, cholesterol was reduced still further (by up to 22 per cent) by combining lecithin therapy with clofibrate (Atromid-S), a widely used cholesterol-lowering drug. This last finding was 'extremely encouraging', according to Dr Simons and his associates. All in all, they were quite pleased by the fact that, unlike many drugs, lecithin alone produced no adverse side-effects and was convenient, palatable and relatively inexpensive.

Similar good results have been reported by Belgian doctors at the Simon Stevin Research Institute in Bruges. They gave 100 patients with serious blood fat imbalances intravenous lecithin and observed cholesterol reductions of up to 40 per cent within 14 days (*Medical World News*). Other patients took lecithin by mouth, and their cholesterol levels fell, too – although not to the same degree. Once again, it was the dangerous LDL fraction of cholesterol that was effectively lowered.

During the 1970s, studies in several countries cast a favourable light on the beneficial effects of lecithin – especailly its ability to change the proportion of HDL to LDL.

• *Sweden, 1974:* Five 50-year-old men took 1.7 g of lecithin per day for nine weeks, also abstaining from alcohol. Their HDL went up an average of 30 per cent (*Nutrition and Metabolism*).

• *Seattle, Washington, 1977:* At the University of Washington, 12 volunteers with normal cholesterol levels took 36 g of lecithin for five successive three-week periods. Their HDL increased by an average of 3.6 per cent, and their LDL decreased by 7 per cent (*Clinical Research*).

• *Italy, 1978:* Twenty-one patients with elevated cholesterol took 1.8 g per day of lecithin, drank no alcohol and cut down on their intake of saturated fats. More than 92 per cent of the patients with elevated LDL returned to normal levels. 'The present results,' noted the researchers, 'underline the therapeutic value of [lecithin] in hyperlipaemic patients [those with elevated cholesterol]' (*Current Therapeutic Research*).

• *Los Angeles, California, 1980:* Ronald K. Tompkins, of the department of surgery, UCLA School of Medicine, reported on his study of four men and one woman, 64 to 84 years old who took 48 g of lecithin per day for 24 months. In addition, they reduced their fat intake to 50 g per day and their cholesterol to 300 mg, and they ate no fried foods or foods high in saturated fats. 'The entire group showed a decrease in cholesterol values during the low-fat and lecithin combinations,' said Dr Tompkins. Indeed, the average drop in cholesterol was 22 per cent (*American Journal of Surgery*).

Actually, these findings, as significant as they are, merely serve to confirm what a Los Angeles doctor, Lester M. Morrison, discovered about lecithin many years ago. In the January 1958 issue of *Geriatrics*, Dr Morrison – who was then senior attending physician at Los Angeles County General Hospital – reported on his search for 'a lipid-reducing agent which could be incorporated in the diet as a natural food product' and 'would be valuable both in treatment and prevention of excessive blood fats associated with atherosclerosis. 'I have found such a food product in soybean lecithin . . .' he concluded.

Dr Morrison had already observed a 15 to 25 per cent fall in cholesterol levels in several patients taking lecithin, but he wanted to do better and to prove beyond a shadow of a doubt that such a happy result could in no way be explained by chance.

He selected a group of 15 people with a history of stubbornly high cholesterol, four of whom had already suffered heart attacks. All had followed low-fat diets and taken cholesterol-lowering drugs for from one to ten years. Yet only two had been helped, but this pair – the only ones in the group whose cholesterol levels had been successfully prodded into the normal range – still suffered recurring angina pains in the chest, for which they had to take glyceryl trinitrate tablets. The 15 patients – 4 men and 11 women – ranged in age from 38 to 80. One woman of 52 had an astoundingly high cholesterol reading of 1012 mg per 100 ml of blood. (Normal for her age is 160 to 330 mg!).

For each of the people, Dr Morrison prescribed a regimen of two table-spoons of granular lecithin three times daily. This amounted to 36 g, or a little more than 1 oz. The powdered lecithin was mixed with milk or fruit juice to mask its rather bland taste and was taken at the beginning of each meal.

The results were little short of miraculous. After taking lecithin for three months, 12 of the 15 individuals experienced 'striking' cholesterol reductions. 'In the 12 patients who showed a favourable cholesterol response,' Dr Morrison noted 'the average fall of serum cholesterol was 156 mg, or 41 per cent . . .'

The woman whose cholesterol had hovered immovably at 1012 saw that level dip to 322 after the first month and then all the way down to 186 after three months. Another person with an initial reading of 328 finished with a low of 192. And others gained similar benefits.

But there were other, unexpected surprises as well: the people felt a lot better. According to Dr Morrison,

> Patients frequently volunteered the information that they experienced an increase in well-being, energy and capacity for physical and mental exertion. Bowel function was frequently improved, especially in the older patients.

And the two people with angina pains reported that all symptoms disappeared after they started taking lecithin.

It's no wonder that Dr Morrison concluded that lecithin is a 'potent agent' against heart and artery disease and an 'effective cholesterol-lowering agent'.

What makes lecithin so effective? Scientists are still undecided about the exact mechanism by which this remarkable substance accomplishes its effects, but there are several plausible explanations.

Dr Morrison, for example, preferred to focus on lecithin's natural emulsifying properties. That is, lecithin has the ability to take particles of fat such as cholesterol – which are normally insoluble in the blood – and keep them suspended in clear solution while they travel through the arteries. That way they never get a chance to settle out and form dangerous deposits of fatty plaque on blood-vessel walls.

Dr Simons in Australia, on the other hand, points out that lecithin – because it is derived from soyabean oil – has a very high content of linoleic acid, an essential fatty nutrient found in safflower, sunflower and other unsaturated oils. Large doses of linoleic acid can lower cholesterol levels, and, by making the blood less 'sticky', lessen the likelihood of clots. The Australian investigators have also discovered that more cholesterol passes through the system undigested when a person consumes lecithin.

Still other scientists believe that lecithin forms a chemical middleman, or 'ester' inside the body that can actually dissolve already-formed fatty deposits on artery walls and carry them away. And it appears that soyabean lecithin, because of its higher content of such unsaturated oils as linoleic acid, would be even more effective at this scouring job than the body's own lecithin.

No matter what factor should ultimately prove responsible (they may all overlap), lecithin's value is perhaps best summed up by noted University of Texas biochemist Roger J. Williams, in his book *Nutrition Against Disease*.

It is known that lecithin has soap-like characteristics, is a powerful emulsifying agent, and its presence in the blood tends to dissolve cholesterol deposits. When there is substantially more lecithin in the blood than cholesterol – a ratio of 1.2 to 1 is said to be favorable – the actual amount of cholesterol can be high without the blood plasma getting milky . . . Lecithin is an enemy of cholesterol deposits, and consuming more lecithin is a useful preventive measure.

How much lecithin do you need to take if you're concerned about keeping your arteries as free-flowing and clear of deposits as possible?

You'll recall that Dr Morrison's patients took six tablespoons, or a bit more than 1 oz of lecithin granules daily, at least initially. But after 90 days, they were able to drop down to a maintenance dose of one or two tablespoons daily. For people who aren't facing the kind of seriously elevated cholesterol problems that his patients had at the outset, the latter dosage would probably be a good starting figure as well. (Keep in mind, too, that the higher levels did produce some stomach upset in at least a few people. But those same people were able to tolerate one or two tablespoons a day with no problem.)

The granular form of soyabean lecithin can be sprinkled on your breakfast cereal, stirred into beverages or mixed with your food. You can also greatly increase your intake of soyabean lecithin by emphasizing the original product, the soyabeans, in your diet. Sprout them, stir-fry them, use them in soups and casseroles – instead of meat or in addition to meat – or in tomato-sauce dishes like lasagna.

For a supply of soyabeans always ready for the pot, try this tip from the *Beginner's Guide for Meatless Casseroles* by Ellen Sue Spivak: Soak a batch of beans overnight. Drain and spread them on a baking sheet, then freeze. When they are frozen as hard as marbles, place them in a plastic bag and keep them in the freezer. Thus you will always have pre-soaked beans that cook faster, ready to go into innumerable dishes.

Brewer's yeast If it's a healthy image you want, you can't beat brewer's yeast. Not just because it's loaded with vitamins and minerals, and not just because it's 50 per cent protein, either. There's something about the way brewer's yeast is biologically put together that makes it more than just a simple collection of nutrients.

That's what researchers like J. Clint Elwood, a professor of biochemistry, are beginning to discover. He and his colleagues from the State University of New York Upstate Medical Center at Syracuse conducted two studies to determine the effect of brewer's yeast on serum cholesterol.

In the first trial, volunteers were instructed to take 20 g (about two tablespoons) of brewer's yeast each day for a total of eight weeks. Blood samples were taken before the experiment began and again after the fourth and eighth weeks. The blood was analysed for its cholesterol level each time.

Although all the volunteers appeared healthy, 16 of the 26 tested actually had cholesterol levels above normal (anything above 250 mg per 100 ml of blood is considered *hyperlipidaemic*). Yet, after eight weeks of brewer's yeast supplementation, the cholesterol levels of this group decreased significantly, says Dr Elwood. The average decrease for all subjects was 10 per cent, but a few of the volunteers had truly dramatic reductions in their total cholesterol levels. One dropped by approximately 110 points, while another decreased by 100, placing them both within the normal range.

'But the exciting part,' Dr Elwood told us, 'is that brewer's yeast had the same positive effect on the volunteers whose cholesterol levels were already within the normal range.'

There's more good news from this study, though. The researchers also measured the level of HDL cholesterol before and after brewer's yeast supplementation, and apparently, while total cholesterol was going down, HDL cholesterol was on the rise. In fact, every one of the hyperlipidaemic volunteers who started out with a low HDL cholesterol level responded with an increase after eight weeks on brewer's yeast. And not to be outdone, the normal group saw their HDL cholesterol improve just as much. In all, 21 out of 25 subjects (that's 84 per cent) responded with a decrease in an increasingly important measurement, the ratio of total cholesterol to HDL cholesterol. The lower that ratio, the better.

The second trial by Dr Elwood was similar to the first, except that the volunteers (all healthy and normal) were instructed to take only 10 g (or about one tablespoon) of brewer's yeast per day – half the amount of the first group. Then the same blood tests and comparisons were made as before.

Even though these volunteers took only 10 g of brewer's yeast, they still had significantly lower total cholesterol, higher HDL cholesterol and a lower ratio after the eight weeks of the experiment. Dr Elwood wrote:

> The most striking observation to us is that HDL cholesterol was changed in normolipidemic, physically active, relatively young people as well as in hyperlipidemic subjects by 20 or 10 g of . . . brewer's yeast for eight weeks. Work is now under way in our laboratory to further isolate and identify the cholesterol-lowering agent present in this yeast, which we believe may be chromium. [*Journal of the American College of Nutrition*, vol. 1, no. 3, 1982].

Chromium   The most valuable contribution of chromium may be a smooth-flowing cardiovascular system.

Atherosclerosis – clogging up of the arteries – is a plague of the Western world. No surprise really: too much smoking, cholesterol and stress, and too little exercise are the culprits, right? Only partly.

According to Dr Henry A. Schroeder, pioneer trace-metal researcher,

> Practically everybody with clinical atherosclerosis of moderate severity has a mild form of diabetes, and the long-known fact that people with moderate and severe diabetes have especially severe atherosclerosis . . . links the two disorders of fat metabolism and sugar metabolism together and demands a search for a single causal factor basic to both.

And that link seems to be chromium.

'Chromium deficiency has been implicated as an important factor in the pathogenesis [development] of atherosclerosis and coronary artery disease,' wrote Dr Abraham S. Abraham and his colleagues at the Shaare Zedek Hospital in Jerusalem (*American Journal of Clinical Nutrition*, November 1980).

As we've said, one of the hallmarks of arterial problems is deposits of fat – plaques, to use their technical name – on artery walls. Shepherding fats to their proper place in the body requires the teamwork of insulin and its trace-metal partner. When the partner's not around, the work doesn't get done and plaques increase – with unpleasant possibilities.

'There is increasing evidence that atherosclerosis is a substantially reversible process,' suggested the researchers.

Working with rabbits, Dr Abraham induced arterial disease by feeding his charges a high-cholesterol diet to the point where plaques nearly covered the inner surface of the artery leading from the heart.

Once established, these fatty deposits are usually considered to be pretty much resistant to change. But not this time.

After a relatively short treatment period of 30 weeks with chromium, there was a substantial regression of the atherosclerotic lesions . . . as compared to the group that did not receive chromium.

Does it work for people?

It's too early to tell whether the metal can totally reverse damage already done, but there's tantalizing evidence that it can prevent arterial damage.

Rebecca Riales, a West Virginia nutritional researcher, monitored a group of eight doctors for six weeks to examine the effect of chromium (in the form of brewer's yeast) on two different kinds of serum cholesterol – HDL and LDL (*Chromium in Nutrition and Metabolism*, 1979). Despite the doctor-participants' 'nonbelief in the value of the supplement', the brewer's yeast had a striking effect. HDL, Dr Riales wrote, increased by an average of 17.6 per cent. And as the protective factor went up, the 'bad guy' LDL, decreased by 17.8 per cent. This is comparable, she noted, to the LDL reduction resulting from a stringent low-fat diet, but interestingly, no one in the experiment changed his eating habits.

Which means that this versatile mineral may provide both a cleaning service for your circulation and the best kind of cardiovascular insurance on the market.

Vitamin C Vitamin C, researchers have found, is a good defence against cholesterol, clogged-up arteries and heart disease. Testimony comes from Britain, where 11 elderly hospital patients with coronary artery problems took 1 g (1000 mg) of vitamin C daily – resulting in a decrease of total blood cholesterol levels in only six weeks. That prompted researchers to assert that 'atherosclerosis and ischaemic heart disease are not inevitable features of ageing' (*Journal of Human Nutrition*, February 1981). That's not all they found.

When they started their gram-a-day supplementation, most of the heart patients had vitamin C deficiencies; the men also had correspondingly low levels of HDL cholesterol. 'After six weeks' treatment with ascorbic acid [vitamin C], the mean [average] HDL cholesterol concentration had increased,' the study noted. What's more, that benefit was not restricted to the heart patients; all 7 men in the 14-member healthy control group enjoyed it as well.

The seven women who acted as controls experienced no significant change in lipoprotein cholesterol, but that doesn't mean vitamin C is guilty of sex discrimination. Women naturally have high HDL levels, which is one reason they are less prone to heart attacks than men. All the women in the control group had healthier HDL levels.

The evidence that vitamin C can protect as well as defend, that it is as beneficial to high-risk subjects as to those already afflicted with heart disease, may be the most compelling aspect of the British investigation. The research team has entered a plea for higher recommended daily intake of vitamin C because 'latent ascorbic-acid deficiency may be one of several preventable 'risk' factors contributing to the present epidemic of ischaemic heart disease in the Western world.'

Not only has it been linked to heart disease, but a vitamin C deficiency is more common than you might think.

The heart patients in the British experiment weren't the only ones suffering vitamin C deficiencies at the outset: some of the 14 'healthy' control subjects were deficient, too. The study noted that 'low blood ascorbic acid levels are often found in elderly patients.'

Nobel Prize-winning vitamin C advocate Linus Pauling suspects that as much as 99 per cent of the world's population suffers from a deficiency of the nutrient. Dr Pauling agrees that the current US Recommended Dietary Allowance (RDA) – about 60 mg (the British RDA is only about 30 mg) – is 'much too low' and says he would like to see it raised to 'at least 150 mg'. His colleague, scientist Irwin Stone, and British doctor Geoffrey Taylor are two other vitamin C champions who go so far as to suggest that today's coronary epidemic may be but a modern version of that ancient sailors' scourge: scurvy.

Like human beings, guinea pigs are one of a handful of species unable to manufacture vitamin C in their own bodies. When the vitamin is withheld from their diets and scurvy is induced in the laboratory, they develop weak arteries with interior bruises like those that are symptoms of the beginnings of atherosclerosis. No matter how those bruises are acquired, they become a magnet for wayward LDL cholesterol, which collects there in layers of plaque – perhaps a misguided attempt to shelter the injured area. If such is plaque's intent, it succeeds all too well, eventually narrowing the blood's passageway until it becomes a dead-end road. Our body's reaction is a heart attack.

The detour signs start going up in guinea pigs' arteries when their vitamin C reserves are in the range of 15 micrograms (μg) per gram of body weight (a microgram is one-millionth of a gram, or one-thousandth of a milligram). That's about the level where we are when we have a cold – if we've been getting only the RDA. Taking greater amounts of vitamin C puts us way ahead of the game.

Vitamin C isn't just a police officer directing cholesterol traffic through the bloodstream and forcing loitering platelets to break it up and move on. After a heart attack has occurred, a high level of the vitamin can pay off like an insurance policy.

That's what Scottish doctors at Southern General Hospital in Glasgow reported several years ago, when they discovered that blood levels of vitamin C drop down to scurvy levels within 6 to 12 months after a person suffers a heart attack. They concluded that the vitamin C was diverted to the heart to help rebuild the damaged coronary tissue (*British Heart Journal*).

Their findings were borne out by another study in which Dr Jairo Ramirez and colleagues at the University of Louisville in Kentucky found that the ascorbic acid concentrations in the white blood cells of 150 patients with heart disease were 'significantly lower' than those of a control group. And they remain dangerously low for several weeks after a heart attack, before gradually increasing to a stable level. That phenomenon may occur even when there is no change in daily vitamin C supplementation (*American Journal of Clinical Nutrition*, October 1980).

Dr Ramirez also noted that cholesterol is higher in patients deprived of vitamin C and that increasing amounts of the vitamin causes an increase in the liver's production of a substance called *cytochrome P-450*, which speeds up the conversion of cholesterol into bile.

Anthony Verlangieri, now associate professor of pharmacology and toxicology at the University of Mississippi, has determined that vitamin C helps the body manufacture another chemical compound: *chondroitin sulphate A* (CSA). He was working in the biochemistry laboratory at Rutgers University when he discovered that CSA acts as a sort of mortar in healthy artery walls and that cholesterol only attaches itself to damaged artery walls that lack this compound.

While Dr Verlangieri was experimenting with CSA in his New Jersey laboratory, he was unaware that a research team 3000 miles away in California had also isolated CSA and was using it to treat heart attack victims. It worked so well that deaths due to coronary complications dropped by a whopping 80 per cent in those patients treated with CSA. Dr Morrison, the scientist who conducted the pioneering studies on lecithin, headed the research team. He suggests that CSA can also prevent 'over one million heart attacks a year'.

Vitamin E   This is a versatile vitamin, but among its most impressive feats is the ability to raise the level of HDL cholesterol, lower the level of VLDL (very-low-density lipoprotein, an equally nasty relative of LDL) cholesterol, and lower total triglycerides. Vitamin E has also been shown to lower the risk of buildup on arterial walls by keeping platelets from clumping up.

One study on vitamin E was run by a pathologist who tested his own blood cholesterol while taking daily doses of the vitamin. In the process, he stumbled on what he thinks might be an important new method for preventing atherosclerosis.

William J. Hermann, a pathologist at Memorial City General Hospital in Houston, was setting up new tests to study the distribution of cholesterol in the blood of the hospital's patients. On sampling his own blood – which happened to be handy – Dr Hermann found only 9 per cent HDL, a sign of higher-than-average risk. At about the same time, with no idea that it would eventually affect his laboratory work, he urged his father to start taking vitamin E. The elder Hermann, a man of 60 at the time, was in good health, but there was a family history of cardiovascular problems, and Dr Hermann had seen evidence that vitamin E can prevent unsaturated fats in the body from turning into bulkier, 'stickier', potentially more harmful saturated fats. His father agreed, but he also persuaded his son to start vitamin E therapy. Dr Hermann began taking 600 IU of vitamin E per day.

The 'dog days' of August passed by. Dr Hermann went on holiday where he drank almost no alcohol (which may have increased his HDL fraction) and even gained a little weight (which can decrease HDL). When he got back to his lab, he tested his blood again. He found 'with astonishment' that, after taking vitamin E for 30 days, 40 per cent of his blood cholesterol was not attached to HDL.

'I came back from vacation and the results had changed so dramatically that for two days I thought the experiment had failed,' Dr Hermann told us. Then he realized that the vitamin E had apparently shifted the cholesterol, taking him from what was considered a higher-than-average to a lower-than-average risk of atherosclerosis.

Although he is frequently sceptical of vitamin therapy claims in general, Dr Hermann was excited by his discovery. He decided to put the accidental discovery to a test. He picked five people with average amounts of HDL cholesteral and five with low HDL cholesterol and placed them all on 600 IU of vitamin E per day. The results: all five people with cholesterol problems improved radically within a few weeks, and though the experiment was small, Dr Hermann was impressed because vitamin E had a positive effect on nine of the ten volunteers.

In publishing his findings, Dr Hermann wrote, 'The results were so obviously significant and of potential value to the medical community that we wish to report them in their somewhat tentative form' (*American Journal of Clinical Pathology*, November 1979).

What does Dr Hermann's experiment mean to someone who is concerned about preventing or delaying the onset of atherosclerosis? It means that he or she may be able to use vitamin E as another defence against cholesterol buildup in the arteries. Exercise, such as long-distance running, has also been shown to decrease the risk of atherosclerosis (*New England Journal of Medicine*, 14 February 1980). Both exercise and vitamin E seem to raise the amount of cholesterol in the HDL complexes. That indicates that excess cholesterol is leaving the cells and getting dumped out of the body in a healthy way.

In Dr Hermann's experiment, the three men and two women who started out with a very low level of HDL cholesterol all raised that level by between 220 and 483 per cent. The effect of vitamin E was consistent, even though the volunteers ranged in age from 28 to 55 and had widely varied exercise and eating habits. One woman of 55, who was overweight, took longer to respond and needed 800 IU per day, but her results were ultimately the same.

All five of these high-risk subjects moved within seven weeks or less to an average or even above-average level of HDL cholesterol. They also lowered the levels of VLDL cholesterol and triglycerides in their blood by about one-quarter and one-fifth, respectively, thereby mitigating two more warning signs of impending atherosclerosis.

Of the five volunteers with initially average cholesterol distribution, four saw their HDL fraction rise to between 127 and 237 per cent of its original value. The only person who did not seem to benefit from the vitamin E therapy was a 33-year-old man with an average HDL cholesterol level. His HDL fraction stayed the same after 30 days.

The total amount of cholesterol in the blood hardly changed at all for any of the subjects, but that didn't matter. Dr Hermann stressed: 'What matters is whether the cholesterol is on the way in [bound to LDL] or on the way out [bound to HDL].'

Vitamin E, according to Dr Hermann, may help maintain a healthy LDL–HDL balance. At some point in the biochemical process, the vitamin seems to enhance the metabolism of cholesterol, but Dr Hermann wasn't sure where. His best guess was that vitamin E enables cell membranes to let cholesterol pass out of them more easily, making it available for HDL pickup.

Dr Hermann believes that his was the first experiment to show a direct relationship between the use of vitamin E and a higher level of HDL cholesterol in the blood. But he is not the first doctor to notice that vitamin E has a beneficial effect on the circulatory system. Others have pointed out that vitamin E can inhibit the formation of dangerous blood clots by cutting down on 'platelet aggregation' – a process we've talked about earlier but will reveiw here.

Normally, platelets are pretty independent characters that slip and slide through the bloodstream with no real desire to latch on to other blood cells. But when the word is out that there's been damage to a vessel wall, they stick together – literally. Within seconds, they're clinging to the crack in the vessel and sticking to each other to build up into a thickened gooey mass – just perfect for plugging the gap in the vessel wall and preventing further blood loss.

It is this clumping of platelets – the first, most crucial step of blood-clot formation – that scientists refer to as 'platelet aggregation'. Usually, it only takes a few minutes after injury for other substances to get caught up in this sticky mass and form a clot.

However, sometimes something goes amiss. Instead of clumping on a damaged vessel wall, the platelets begin to congregate on the wall of a healthy artery. If they grow into an unruly mob and are joined by other chemical agitators, a blood clot could form within the blood vessel and cause real trouble.

Deep-vein thrombosis (a blood clot in the leg) and phlebitis (another condition of the legs characterized by inflamed vessels and clot formation) are caused by spontaneous clotting. Both conditions can be painful, but the real problem arises when the clot journeys up the leg and gets caught in a major blood vessel of the heart, lungs or brain. If a blood clot gets stuck in a coronary artery that is obstructed by cholesterol deposits and blocks blood flow, a heart attack could result. Similarly, a clot may lodge in the lungs (pulmonary embolism) or brain (stroke) and again pose fatal possibilities. Any substance that might interfere with platelet aggregation could act as a protective measure against such problems.

That substance is vitamin E.

One of the studies on the vitamin and platelet aggregation was published in the *Proceedings of the Society for Experimental Biology and Medicine*. Lawrence J. Machlin and a group of researchers at the drug company Hoffman–La Roche in New Jersey compared blood samples taken from vitamin E deficient rats to those taken from animals receiving extra doses of the vitamin.

Not surprisingly, the supplemented animals had the edge against clotting. For one thing, platelet aggregation was significantly reduced in all the rats of the vitamin E group. In addition, after 15 to 16 weeks on a deficient diet, the rats began producing more and more platelets. And this, researchers speculate, may also contribute to the increased clotting: The more platelets you've got bumping into each other in the bloodstream, the greater the chance of their sticking together and setting off the series of reactions leading to a blood clot.

Paediatricians at the State University of New York Upstate Medical Center have reported a similar correlation in two children seen at the centre. Blood samples taken from both girls were found to be extremely low in vitamin E and abnormally high in platelets. To test the clotting capacity of the blood samples, the doctors added certain chemicals that cause platelet aggregation to test tubes of the blood and compared the reaction to samples taken from healthy children which were also mixed with the chemical agent.

As expected, the platelets from the deficient girls clumped more readily than those from the control group. However, both platelet count and the high clotting tendency were reduced to normal following vitamin E supplementation (*Journal of Pediatrics*).

This finding falls in line with the results of studies conducted by Manfred Steiner, a blood research specialist and associate professor of medicine at Brown University in Providence, Rhode Island. In one of Dr Steiner's earlier works, blood samples taken from several healthy volunteers were similarly exposed to chemical agents to simulate the type of platelet clumping that might occur spontaneously in a blood vessel. When vitamin E was added to the test tube, however, this clumping was kept to a minimum.

In a similar study, Dr Steiner first put the volunteers on a vitamin E regimen (1200 to 2400 IU daily) for a few weeks and then took blood samples, which he exposed to the same chemical agents used before. Again, he reported, vitamin E minimized platelet sticking (*Journal of Clinical Investigation*).

Other research on platelets and vitamin E has been conducted by R. V. Panganamala of the department of physiological chemistry at Ohio State University School of Medicine. 'Any time platelets stick together inside an intact blood vessel, it's a problem,' Dr Panganamala explained. 'But that can happen when the platelets produce too much *thromboxane*, a substance that enhances their stickiness. It can also happen if the vessel wall doesn't produce enough *prostacyclin*. This chemical has the opposite effect on platelets – that is, it keeps them free-flowing and slippery.

'In our experiment,' he continued, 'we wanted to see what effect vitamin E had on those two chemicals. We used animals that were normal and healthy to begin with and divided them into two groups. One group received a diet high in vitamin E, while the other's diet had no vitamin E at all. After 10 to 12 weeks, we tested the levels of thromboxane and prostacyclin in the animals. We found that those deficient in vitamin E had significantly higher amounts of thromboxane, while at the same time, their vessels lost the capacity to produce prostacyclin.

'It's our current understanding that the proper ratio of thromboxane to prostacyclin is imperative if platelets are to move through the blood without aggregating at the wrong time. If the ratio's out of balance, there is a far greater chance of thrombosis [blood clots] occurring. Vitamin E helps keep these substances in precise, proper balance.'

Because of the success of that experiment, Dr Panganamala wanted to try a similar experiment using diabetic animals. 'We know that people with diabetes are particularly vulnerable to circulatory problems,' he told us. 'So we decided to see if the thromboxane and prostacyclin balance was adversely affected in animals with that condition.

'First, we created diabetes in a group of experimental rats. After the diabetes was established, we tested their levels of thromboxane and prostacyclin and found that they were out of balance – too much of the first and too little of the second.

'Next, we supplemented the rats' diet with vitamin E. Within eight to ten weeks, the two chemicals were back to their normal levels.'

However, good circulation is dependent on more than smooth-flowing platelets. It's just as important to keep your blood vessels free of fatty buildup. And vitamin E can help again.

To prove this, researchers from the department of internal medicine at Kyoto University in Japan conducted a study to examine the effect of vitamin E on lipid peroxidation. (Lipid peroxides are fat-oxidation products that are toxic to human and animal tissues. It's suspected that, when they accumulate in blood vessels, they impair circulation by promoting atherosclerosis and blood clots.) The researchers found that animals fed a diet deficient in vitamin E actually produced significantly more of these peroxides than the vitamin E supplemented group.

The good news here is that the damage created by the vitamin E deficiency was reversible. The results support the possibility, cited by the researchers, that administration of vitamin E 'could prevent and ameliorate vascular [vessel] damages in some pathological states associated with the accumulation of lipid peroxides in the vessels' (*Prostaglandins*, April 1980).

J. C. Alexander would heartily agree. He's done his own experiments at the University of Guelph in Ontario, on the effects of vitamin E on oxidized fats.

'Accumulation of oxidized fats in tissues can have a toxic effect,' Dr Alexander told us. 'It certainly did with our experimental animals. We saw evidence of cellular damage to kidney, heart and liver tissues.

'In this particular experiment, we used rat heart cells to test the influence of vitamins E and C on the biological effects of oxidized fats. These vitamins (probably in their role as anti-oxidants) counteracted the adverse effects, such as excessive lipid accumulation, in the rat heart cells.

'This is especially important,' explained Dr Alexander, 'because there is evidence that oxidized lipids can accelerate symptoms of vitamin E deficiency such as lipid peroxidation and fragile red blood cells. There is no doubt in my mind that vitamin E is a potent anti-oxidant and extremely important in maintaining a healthy circulatory system. Anyone who doesn't believe that is fooling himself.'

Selenium In a study of over 45,000 Chinese – the most massive study ever done on selenium deficiency in humans – supplementation with selenium wiped out a heart disorder affecting 40 out of every 1000 children in certain areas of China.

'Keshan disease' is a form of cardiomyopathy – that is, heart muscle damage due to unknown causes. Symptoms include enlargement of the heart, galloping pulse, weak heartbeat, low blood pressure, oedema (fluid retention) and abdominal pain. Half its victims die.

What stands out as most peculiar about Keshan disease is its distinct geographical distribution in relation to selenium in soil, food and human tissues. In places where selenium is low, Keshan disease is common, but in high-selenium areas, the disease is nowhere to be found.

Low-selenium soil was noticed first. 'It was as if selenium in soil acted as a physical barrier against the disease,' said G. Q. Yang of the Chinese Academy of Medical Sciences in Peking. Because the dividing line was so uncannily well defined, the research team felt they were on to a cure – and possibly a preventive – for Keshan disease. They tested samples of blood, hair and staple foods (wheat, maize, rice and soyabeans) from affected and non-affected areas of China. The relationship was confirmed. Low soil selenium meant low dietary and body levels of the mineral – and a high rate of Keshan disease. On the other hand, soils adequate in selenium were accompanied by adequate or high dietary and body levels, and disappearance of Keshan disease.

The answer stared them in the face. In 1973, a programme of supplementation with selenium was begun for thousands of children in the affected areas, with a relatively equal number left untreated as a control group. The death rate in those treated plummeted from 50 per cent to 6 per cent, a spectacular improvement. The number of new cases per 1000 dropped from 40 to 1. The programme was expanded. In four years, selenium's protective effect was so apparent that all children in the disease-prone areas studied were given selenium. Of 12,000 children so treated, none came down with Keshan disease.

There's no question that selenium was a pivotal factor in the Chinese study. 'However, it's unlikely that selenium is the only factor in the disease,' Dr Yang pointed out. 'Other aspects of diet could be important. Protein needs to be studied. Vitamin E could be important. Both need further study.' There's also some evidence that a virus could be involved to some extent, added Dr Yang.

Even before Dr Yang's discovery, selenium was counted among the five minerals to be studied in relation to heart disease by the World Health Organization. Low selenium levels are strongly linked to high rates of cardiovascular disease in 26 countries, including the United States, especially when cadmium, a harmful heavy metal, is present. Cadmium is strongly suspected as a contributing cause of heart disease because it seems to raise blood pressure. Selenium may counteract that effect and protect against heart disease and stroke, which often accompany high blood pressure.

Finland has one of the highest coronary heart disease rates in the world. In central and eastern Finland, where rates are highest, people have the lowest blood selenium levels in the country. As with Keshan disease in China, those two factors seem to coincide geographically.

'More studies will be done, but the relationship is obvious,' said Pekko Koivistoinen, head of the department of food chemistry and technology at the University of Helsinki. Dr Koivistoinen told us, 'On taking a closer look, we see that farming families, who subsist on food grown locally, have the lowest selenium of all, as well as the highest rates of heart disease.'

Overall dietary intake of selenium is low in Finland – 30 μg a day for men and about 20 to 25 μg a day for women. That compares to 50 to 200 μg a day judged to be essential to good health by the National Academy of Sciences in the United States and generally accepted as adequate elsewhere.

What accounts for Finland's low selenium is a combination of factors. The country has very little selenium-rich sedimentary rock, plus a humid climate, heavy rainfall and acid soil, all of which reduce selenium's availability to forage and food crops and make Finland an ideal laboratory for further study, says Dr Koivistoinen.

'We have low selenium to start out with. We can look at how that affects health. Added to that, we also have low chromium. Chromium is linked not only to normalization of insulin response in diabetics but to reduction of LDL cholesterol in the blood. Finns have high cholesterol. In that respect, those two factors together – low selenium and low chromium – could explain to a certain extent why I think we have in our country an exceptionally high rate of coronary heart disease.'

While in Finland there has been nothing like the large-scale programme of selenium supplementation seen in China, many Finns have decided to make up for low selenium on their own rather than wait for formal public health action. People are eating more fish, which is the richest source of selenium, Dr Koivistoinen told us. And they're taking supplements.

In the United States, a similar correlation seems to be shaping up between selenium and heart disease. Sections of the south-eastern coastal plains of Georgia and the Carolinas have the highest stroke rate in the United States – so high that it's called the 'Stroke Belt'. Heart disease there is also very high. And it's a low-selenium area. In north-western Georgia, by contrast, heart disease is lower and blood selenium levels are higher.

High blood pressure begins early in life in the Stroke Belt. Jim Andrews, Curtis G. Hames and James C. Metts, Jr. of the Community Cardiovascular Council in Savannah, Georgia, found that of 10,000 17- and 18-year-olds screened, 8 per cent had blood pressure readings of 140/90 or above, considered high for their age. Cadmium was also high.

'That's the time to intervene,' Dr Metts told us. 'Once they leave school and get on the assembly line, we've lost them' – until they show up in their 40s and 50s with heart disease, that is. Dr Metts has treated some of his patients with selenium, on an individualized basis, and has witnessed some encouraging results.

One scientist, Kaarlo Jaakkola from the University of Jyvaskyla in Finland, has used selenium *and* vitamin E to treat a group of 30 patients with heart disease. All the patients suffered from constant, moderate to severe chest pain and needed large amounts of glyceryl trinitrate and other medications to control the symptoms.

During the experimental period, daily doses of vitamin E and selenium were given while the other medications were kept about the same. In the group treated with vitamin E and selenium, the first positive effects were usually seen two weeks after the beginning of the treatment and the maximum effects after one to two months. With the majority of the treated patients, noted the Finnish researchers, 'the average daily usage of nitroglycerin [glyceryl trinitrate] decreased significantly,' and they were able to walk farther without discomfort. They concluded that vitamin E, together with selenium, has a beneficial effect on patients with ischaemic heart disease, possibly because those nutrients play an important role in the intracellular anti-oxidant defence mechanism protecting cells from damaging lipid peroxides.

Vitamin B$_6$ Elizabeth Kornecki of the Thrombosis Center at Temple University in Philadelphia, and Harold Feinberg of the University of Illinois Medical Center in Chicago, have found that pyrodoxal phosphate, one of the active forms of vitamin B$_6$ in the body, inhibits the action of a number of the chemicals that cause platelets to stick together in the bloodstream. Once the platelets stick, they release granules containing ADP into the bloodstream.

ADP (adenosine diphosphate) is one of the platelet-aggregating chemicals that vitamin B$_6$ acts to inhibit, and is contained in grain-like particles within the platelets. 'A cloud of ADP makes the platelets in the blood adhesive to one another, and they form a plug which blocks the flow of blood out of the damaged vessel. That's a very simplified version of what happens, but it's accurate.'

Other chemicals in the body that play a role in platelet aggregation include thrombin, collagen, adrenalin and arachidonic acid. It's a complex process and, obviously, does not result in blood clots every time some slight injury occurs in a blood vessel. Problems arise only when abnormally sensitive platelets form clots that are not needed to stop bleeding. The tantalizing possibility, Dr Feinberg says, is that 'by simply altering our diets, we might end up with less reactive platelets, platelets which still form clots when necessary but don't produce all this other trouble.'

Drs Kornecki and Feinberg demonstrated that pyridoxal phosphate inhibits the action of ADP and partially interferes with platelet aggregation triggered by adrenalin and arachidonic acid (*American Journal of Physiology*, vol. 238, no. 1, 1980). In another study, they showed that vitamin B$_6$ also inhibits thrombin directly (*Biochemical and Biophysical Research Communications*, 12 October 1979). Although the studies did not involve vitamin B$_6$ taken directly by patients (it was added to blood samples taken from the patients), the implication is strong that including the vitamin in the diet might help control platelet aggregation.

'There may be a relationship,' Dr Kornecki told us, 'but how positive it is is up to speculation. The results are very interesting, though. Here is thrombin, which is a very potent inducer of platelet aggregation, plus ADP, arachidonic acid and epinephrine [adrenalin], and an essential vitamin inhibits their platelet-aggregating action to some extent.'

Even now, though, the evidence for vitamin B$_6$ is not confined to test-tube studies. Drs Kornecki and Feinberg point out that birth control pills have been associated both with low levels of pyridoxal phosphate in the blood of women taking them and with an increase in platelet aggregability. Women on the Pill, not surprisingly, have an increased risk of developing blood clots and atherosclerosis. Vitamin B$_6$ has already been used to correct depression and mood changes in women taking the Pill, symptoms that might be caused by a deficiency of that nutrient.

People suffering from an inherited disorder called *homocystinuria* are also at a higher risk of developing circulatory problems. One sympton is the increase in the tendency of the platelets to stick together, and vitamin B$_6$ has been shown to impede this action.

Most important, researchers at Northwestern University and Temple University medical schools in the United States were able to test directly the effects of vitamin B_6 on platelet aggregation. Volunteers in the study were given just one dose of 100 mg of the vitamin. As expected, platelet aggregation was significantly reduced, in some cases not returning to normal levels for over two days after the vitamin B_6 was taken (*Circulation*).

Vitamin B_6 may also protect the circulatory system by preventing the buildup of cholesterol in the blood. One study with rats found that large doses of the vitamin in a high-fat, high-cholesterol diet reduced the accumulation of cholesterol in the blood usually produced by the diet (*Australian Journal of Biological Sciences*).

If you're older, you should take particular care that you're getting enough vitamin B_6. Not only are the elderly more susceptible to heart problems, but they often suffer vitamin B_6 deficiencies as well. Of the older people tested in nursing homes for one study, over 30 per cent had abnormally low blood levels of vitamin B_6 (*Journal of the American Geriatrics Society*, October 1979).

Thiamin Few people in the West die of beriberi heart disease, but many of them have a heart problem – a problem they might solve if they upped their intake of thiamin (vitamin B_1).

When researchers measured the thiamin blood levels of over 125 elderly people, they found that 32 per cent were deficient in the nutrient – and that heart pain was more common among those with a deficiency (*Nutrition and Metabolism*).

In another study, researchers from the University of Alabama Medical Center measured the daily thiamin intake of 74 people and then had them fill out a questionnaire in which they listed their cardiovascular [heart and circulatory system] complaints. Dividing the people into 'high intake' and 'low intake' groups, they found that those with a low intake of thiamin had almost twice as many cardiovascular complaints (*Journal of the American Geriatrics Society*).

In a third study, researchers compared the levels of thiamin in the heart muscles of 12 patients who had died of open-heart disease to the levels of ten who had died of other causes. They found that the heart patients had an average thiamin level of 57 per cent lower than the other patients. (*Nutrition Reviews*).

A study from Japan provides more proof that thiamin strengthens the heart. There, in the ten days before heart surgery, a group of 25 patients received thiamin, while another group of patients did not. When their hearts were artifically stopped to perform the operation, only 10 per cent of the thiamin group had abnormal heart spasms, compared to 30 per cent of the other group. And, when their hearts were revived at the end of the operation, 30 per cent of the thiamin group had heart spasms, compared to 95 per cent of the others (*Medicine Tribune*).

Calcium Calcium is intimately involved with bones and teeth, as we all know. But it's closely associated with the health of your heart. How? By lowering cholesterol.

You may be frowning at this point, which is understandable, since you've probably heard that calcium is sometimes deposited with cholesterol in arteries that surround the heart. The truth is, calcium deposits occur when intake of this mineral is too *low*, not too high. Strange, but that's what the experts say.

In fact, researchers have shown time and again that the US Recommended Dietary Allowance (RDA) of 800 mg of calcium is too low (in Britain, the RDA is 500 mg), while even tripling it usually causes no adverse side-effects.

One study involved subjects taking more than 3000 mg of calcium per day. It was carried out several years ago by Harold Yacowitz, a researcher from Fairleigh Dickinson University in New Jersey, who had a hunch that there may be a connection between calcium and fat absorption. So he prescribed 3370 mg of calcium (710 mg from dietary sources and 2660 mg from supplements) for four men with normal cholesterol levels (less than 250 mg). After only four days, their blood cholesterol decreased by an average of 14 points. Encouraged by these results, Dr Yacowitz decided to test another group of volunteers by giving them much less calcium (a total intake of 1600 mg per day) but for a longer period of time – three weeks. What he found was that the smaller amount of calcium not only did the job of lowering cholesterol but decreased triglycerides as well. And the higher the initial cholesterol and triglyceride levels, the more dramatic were the results, with cholesterol levels dropping by as much as 48 points and triglycerides by a maximum of 115. What's more, the major decrease occurred within the first week of the study and stayed at the lower levels for the remainder of the test (*British Medical Journal*).

But how does calcium reduce serum cholesterol and triglycerides? 'It was important to answer this question,' Dr Yacowitz told us, 'since there was some concern that perhaps these lipids [fats] were being deposited in the liver, blood vessels and other tissues. Fortunately, that isn't the case. Calcium combines with fatty acids in the gut and results in the excretion of calcium soaps. Increased calcium intake resulted in increased fat excretion.'

Since that time, other researchers have conducted studies that link calcium to cholesterol and other lipids.

One in particular, Anthony A. Albanese of the Burke Rehabilitation Center in White Plains, New York, is noted for his studies of post-menopausal women and osteoporosis (bone loss). While experimenting with the use of calcium to counteract that disease, he was surprised to discover that, along with increasing bone density, calcium decreased the serum cholesterol 'in a striking and highly statistically significant manner in the supplemented group only' (*Nutrition Reports International*). And his study was done using normal, healthy elderly women, not patients with cardiovascular disease. The cholesterol-lowering effects were accomplished with only 1025 to 1200 mg of calcium per day, even less than Dr Yacowitz had used in his second experiment.

About the same time as Dr Albanese's study was being conducted, another experiment was getting underway at St Vincent's Hospital in Montclair, New Jersey. This time, however, the eight men and two women tested were known to be hyperlipidaemic (having very high blood fats). Most had cholesterol levels between 300 and 500 mg at the start of the study (remember, normal is below 250) and had maintained those high levels for the previous 12 months. Yet after taking 2000 mg of calcium a day for one year, their cholesterol levels decreased by an average of 25 per cent. 'Calcium carbonate,' says Dr

Marvin L. Bierenbaum, the researcher who conducted the study, 'should be considered as a potential agent for usage in long-term studies designed to produce hypolipidemia [low blood lipids], since it appears to be effective and without significant side-effects' (*Lipids*).

The lowest serum lipid values were achieved after the first six months of supplementation and then stayed low for the remainder of the study period. 'The cholesterol level would probably go right back up again,' Dr Bierenbaum told us, 'if the calcium supplementation were discontinued. That's because these people have a genetic tendency towards hyperlipidaemia. They must continue to take calcium to keep their cholesterol and other lipids lowered.'

Magnesium Many years ago, a lone researcher discovered that deaths due to stroke occur more frequently in areas of Japan where the water is soft (i.e. it contained few or no mineral salts). Of course, at that time it was too early even to suggest that soft water might contain a dangerous substance, or that hard water had some protective factor, or, for that matter, whether the water had anything at all to do with the statistics. It could have been coincidence.

Anyway, it wasn't easy convincing people that something capable of clogging water pipes could ward off death from clogged arteries that suddenly shut off blood and oxygen supply to the brain or heart. However, it seemed even harder to disprove.

Study after study uncovered the same correlation, at least with regard to heart attacks. In England and Wales. In Canada. In the United States. In Norway. Always the same – the harder the water in a given area, the lower the cardiovascular death rate. And conversely, the softer the water, the higher the toll of heart attack.

Not only that, but more recent studies have disclosed that the proportion of 'sudden death' is significantly higher in the soft-water areas. 'Sudden death' refers to a complication that may follow a heart attack when the heart suddenly stops beating effectively and goes into rapid, uncontrollable spasms called *fibrillation*. Since these random contractions are not capable of pumping blood, death ensues.

In England, for example, death certificates were obtained for men and women aged 30 to 59 years old in six towns with soft water and six towns with hard water. Not surprisingly, for every age group, death rates from heart disease were higher in the soft-water areas. However, it was also noted that the proportion of sudden deaths was consistently higher in the soft-water towns than the hard-water areas when subjects were classified by age or social class (*Journal of Chronic Diseases*).

Canadian researchers have likewise found a correlation between soft water and sudden deaths. After gathering statistics from various regions of Ontario, Dr Terence W. Anderson of the University of British Columbia's department of preventive medicine and biostatistics discovered that although the actual number of heart attacks did not vary too greatly from soft- to hard-water locales, the tendency for fibrillation to occur resulting in sudden death was higher in the soft-water cities.

Why? There's more than one reason to believe that the magnesium found in abundance in hard-water supplies may somehow toughen the heart against sudden disturbances in heartbeat.

First of all, the heart muscle of persons living in hard-water areas (where cardiovascular death rates are low) tends to contain more magnesium than those of persons living in soft-water locales. In heart muscle samples collected at autopsy from 83 cases of accidental death and analysed for mineral content, Dr Anderson reported, magnesium varied significantly between hard- and soft-water areas. In fact, magnesium concentrations were 7 per cent lower in the heart muscle of subjects who lived in the soft-water areas of Ontario (*Canadian Medical Association Journal*).

What's more, the heart muscle of heart attack victims contained, on the average, 22 per cent less magnesium than the muscle of healthy persons who died accidentally – a finding that echoes the results of an Israeli study published in the *New England Journal of Medicine*.

Autopsy reports from Drs Barbara and J. R. Chipperfield of the University of Hull at first appear to contradict the above. Measuring the magnesium levels in healthy persons from two distinctly hard- and soft-water towns in England who died of accidental causes, they found that the magnesium levels were occasionally higher in the soft-water regions.

However – and here they account for the seeming contradiction – the proportion between magnesium and potassium (another mineral considered extremely important to the functioning of the heart) was such that a relative deficiency in magnesium existed in these soft-water areas. Wrote the researchers:

> The relative decrease in the magnesium concentration in normal heart muscle in the soft-water area may affect the activity of magnesium-activated heart enzymes and thus increase the risk of death when a myocardial infarction [heart attack] occurs. [*Lancet*].

Magnesium has been shown over and over again to play an important role in the prevention of heart arrhythmia (abnormal heart rhythm) or fibrillation. In an editorial published in the *American Heart Journal*, the Chipperfields explained that, in heart tissues, magnesium is involved in reactions that are essential to the contraction of heart muscle.

No wonder magnesium has been used to treat cardiac arrhythmias for years. In fact, Dr Lloyd T. Iseri, James Freed and Alan R. Bures cited two cases in which magnesium proved to be life-saving medicine.

You already know this life-and-death scene from TV hospital dramas. The patient lies asleep, connected by wires to a heart-monitoring system, which transmits the pattern of the heart's rhythm to a television-like screen. Suddenly, the pattern becomes irregular and a buzzer goes off, warning the nurses that the patient is in fibrillation. Within seconds, doctors and nurses have rushed into the room, shoving a mysterious machine in front of them. Then the heart specialist zaps the patient's chest with a powerful electrical current in a desperate attempt to shock the heart back to normal.

Well, that's exactly what happened when a 54-year-old nurse was admitted to the hospital for alcoholic heart damage. As she was being wheeled to the intensive care unit, fibrillation developed. Her heart was shocked back into rhythm with one of those machines. But again, without warning, her heart lapsed into spastic contractions, and she had to be brought back with electrical shock, only to fall back out of rhythm again, and again. In fact, within three hours' time, she had to be revived eight times!

The woman was immediately started on magnesium sulphate, which was added to the fluid being given to her intravenously.

Twenty-four hours later, blood tests revealed magnesium levels above normal. No further arrhythmias occurred. She was discharged ten days later.

However, magnesium's role in heart disease doesn't stop there. A group of doctors at Georgetown University Medical Division and the District of Columbia General Hospital in Washington, D.C. report that this important mineral has a decided effect on lowering blood pressure – another serious risk factor in heart disease.

(*See* HIGH BLOOD PRESSURE.)

Habits that hurt your heart

Alcohol

For a healthy heart, you must be careful with your total diet – including what you drink. For years, doctors have been saying that drinking alcohol is good for people with coronary artery disease because alcohol increases blood flow to the heart. However, a study conducted by Howard S. Friedman, chief of cardiology at the Brooklyn Hospital and associate professor at State University of New York Downstate Medical Center, indicates that drinking alcohol actually could be harmful to heart patients (*Clinical Research*, 1979).

Dr Friedman measured the distribution of blood flow in a dog's heart before and after a coronary artery was obstructed, inhibiting blood flow to a section of the muscle. The flow was measured again after giving the animal alcohol. 'Alcohol did increase the blood flow to heart tissue that was working well and behaving in a normal fashion,' Dr Friedman told us. 'But the heart area with the narrowed vessel was receiving even less blood than it had been getting before!'

Alcohol dilates blood vessels, explains Dr Friedman. More blood can be delivered through healthy vessels that are dilated, but a narrowed or obstructed vessel already is dilated as much as possible. 'The narrowed vessel cannot take any more blood, so the blood is redistributed away from that area to the good areas of the heart. This might be considered a 'coronary steal', he says.

Four measures of spirits or four beers taken very quickly could create this same effect in people with heart failure or coronary artery disease. 'Those people should limit their use of alcohol,' says Dr Friedman. 'If used at all, alcohol should be used with moderation.'

Coffee and tea

Chain-drinking cups of coffee and tea – especially black instant coffee – may be harmful to the heart and circulatory system. The villain seems to be tannic acid.

Coffee and tea both contain tannic acid, and researchers in India have recently found that, when they fed a diet rich in tannic acid to laboratory rats, the rats experienced damage to their heart muscle, and an increase in the cholesterol levels of their blood. The rats received the human equivalent of six cups or more of black tea or black coffee per day (*Indian Journal of Nutrition and Dietetics*, vol. 16, no. 9, 1979).

Instant coffee and boiled, loose-leaf tea were both found to be rich in tannic acid. Ground, percolated coffee and tea made from tea bags contained less of the acid, according to the study.

Milk, luckily, tends to neutralize tannic acid, but only to a degree. Adding 2 fl. oz of milk to a 8 fl. oz of black coffee reduced the tannic acid content by about 30 per cent.

Smoking

Smoking does bad things to the lungs. Everyone is aware that substances in tobacco smoke can cause lung cancer and emphysema. Almost as well known is the effect of tobacco smoke on the pipes leading into the lungs – the bronchi. Chronic bronchitis is a problem that many smokers have to contend with.

The effect of smoking on the heart and the circulatory system is much more mysterious. It isn't as easy to visualize tobacco smoke getting into the heart as it is to imagine how it penetrates the lungs and their tissue. For that reason, the connection between smoking and heart health is not well understood by the average person, nor is it widely accepted as a bad result of the smoking habit. Sure, we all know that smokers are told to stop by their doctors after they show signs of heart trouble or have an attack. But why? What is happening inside the smoker's body that hurts the heart?

Actually, tobacco smoke hurts the heart more than it does the lungs. That may be hard to believe, but it's true. 'The major organ most affected by smoking is the heart,' Dr Anthony Owen Colby, wrote in an article in *Modern Medicine*. To back up that statement, he pointed to US Public Health Service figures which show that smokers have a three times greater risk of getting a heart attack than do non-smokers – and also that if they get a heart attack, smokers have a 21-times greater risk of dying from that attack. It is also known that the act of smoking combines with other bad habits that can lead to heart attack in a way that multiplies the chance of affliction or death. In other words, smoking hurts the heart on its own, and in combination with other common accompaniments such as lack of exercise, tension and bad eating habits.

What actually happens to relate a puff on a cigarette to the process of heart weakening?

Carbon monoxide is one villain in the drama. Tobacco smoke contains that odourless gas, which has a unique power to hurt the heart. Oxygen, not carbon monoxide, is the gas that the heart loves. 'The heart utilizes more oxygen than any other organ in the body,' Dr Colby points out. And he says further that the heart takes from the blood 100 per cent of the oxygen that is delivered to it, even during sleep and other periods of rest.

When carbon monoxide enters the lungs, the mechanism of oxygen delivery to the heart is drastically disrupted. Haemoglobin, the blood substance that picks up oxygen in the lungs and delivers it to the heart, goes berserk in a peculiar way. Haemoglobin, perversely, prefers carbon monoxide to oxygen –

in fact, prefers it 250 times as much. So levels of about 5 per cent of carbon monoxide in the air drastically reduce the amount of oxygen that the heart is able to get. When that happens, the heart is not able to function with its normal efficiency, and has to beat faster to avoid oxygen starvation.

Doctors know that carbon monoxide not only cuts off the flow of oxygen to the heart but also harms cells that are vital to the heart's proper functioning. Carbon monoxide causes the mitochondria (the power plants of the cells) to swell and disintegrate. The injured cells are not able to produce energy – thereby weakening the heart.

And there's more. Research reported by Poul Astrup of Copenhagen shows that carbon monoxide prevents cells that make up the lining of the coronary arteries from exchanging oxygen and other nutrients with each other – a vital process, since these cells (almost unique among all body cells) have no other way to get nourishment. The result is degeneration of the interior of the coronary arteries of a type very similar to atherosclerosis.

So much for carbon monoxide. The nicotine in tobacco smoke also has a bad effect on the heart. Nicotine is a powerful drug, and it is particularly harmful to a weakened heart because it upsets the normal electrical impulses which are the sparks that cause the heart to function. The importance of electricity to the heart becomes apparent when you remember that the electrocardiogram (ECG), which is a way of examining the heart's electrical profile, is the basic tool for assessing heart health. A nicotine-influenced heart doesn't get its electrical signals quite straight. One part of the heart tends to beat ahead of its normal time, and another tries to beat behind schedule. Not being able to beat with the proper synchronization, the nicotined heart tends (under stress) to relapse into very fast, uncontrolled ventricular beats that render the heart useless for pumping blood. 'In reality,' says Dr Colby, 'it is precisely this mechanism that leads to sudden death.'

Fortunately, the heart is tremendously receptive to help that we can give it by changing our lifestyles. However, quitting smoking means avoiding *all* cigarettes – not just the high-nicotine types. According to research by the ongoing Framingham Heart Study, 'there is no evidence that the filter cigarette of the 1960s and early 1970s conferred any protection from coronary heart disease (CHD) for men, (*Lancet*, 18 July 1981).

It's too early to tell how safe the newest generation of filters might be, but the smart money is on 'not very'. Nicotine is certainly reduced, but, wrote Dr William Castelli, senior author of the study, 'nicotine lowering does not have much effect on CHD risk.'

Exercise and your heart

It was only in the last decade, says Thomas K. Cureton, Jr., that scientists began to understand precisely how endurance exercise such as jogging, swimming or bicycling may prevent heart disease.

'Endurance exercise depends on fuel being furnished to the muscles, and liquid fat – cholesterol and triglycerides – is a far more important fuel than carbohydrates,' he explains. 'Any exercise that lasts longer than 30 minutes has got to be nourished by liquid fat. Up to a few years ago, that wasn't understood. It wasn't known that the muscles burn fat directly – scientists thought that carbohydrates were the main fuel. Well, that's only partially true. Carbohydrates are quickly exhausted. After 15 minutes of exercise, fat is burning, and after 30 minutes, the nutrition is almost wholly fat – the same fat that has been clogging the arteries of the cardiovascular system.'

Many of the experiments that helped prove this fact were conducted by Dr Cureton and his graduate students at the University of Illinois. 'In one typical experiment,' says Dr Cureton, 'the researchers divided 45 people into three groups of 15 each. All were given the same kind of training work. The first group, however, exercised for 15 minutes, the second for 30 minutes and the third for 45 minutes. The 15-minute group had no change in cholesterol. The 30-minute group had moderate but insignificant changes. But the 45-minute group had significant changes. The conclusion is that you need to exercise for more than 30 minutes at a time to make significant changes in the fat content of the body.'

What if you already have heart disease? Can exercise still help?

According to Richard Stein, director of the Cardiac Exercise Laboratory at the State University of New York Downstate Medical Center, doctors recognize that, while heart disease may require some curtailment in activity, it rarely necessitates a complete withdrawal from active life. In fact, it is that fearful, protective attitude, rather than the disease itself, that often threatens to make heart attack victims into lifelong invalids.

'Taking a patient and throwing him out of a job and putting him into a very dependent position where everybody picks up after him and talks softly in front of him – that turns him into a neurotic, sick cripple,' Dr Stein says. 'It gives him less to live for.'

The heart patients who work out under Dr Stein's direction are more likely to start businesses than sell them, to play ball with their kids than to insist on silence around the house. With the caution of a scientist, Dr Stein won't speculate on whether or not exercise prevents further heart attacks, but he will cite enthusiastically the human accomplishment of his programme.

'We certainly have created a group of patients who are robust, vigorous, back at work, living full, meaningful lives, who have in no way had their lifestyle cramped by the disease,' he says.

As little as 12 weeks after a heart attack, patients may start their return to a full life by coming to the laboratory for evaluation. Unless problems like severe heartbeat irregularities contra-indicate it, patients are given a stress test: a brisk walk or jog on a treadmill with Dr Stein and nurse Florence Frank keeping careful watch over their ECG pulse rate and blood pressure. 'We assess how much exercise the patients can safely do. On the basis of that, we devise an exercise programme for them to follow,' says Dr Stein.

Pedalling back to health

Here, an exercise programme generally means an ergometer – a stationary exercise bicycle that can be adjusted to make pedalling strenuous or easy. In two more sessions at the laboratory, patients are trained to use the ergometer, adjusting it to bring the heart rate up to the point where a positive training effect is produced (about 75 per cent of the heart's maximum capacity).

Tested and trained, they will take home an ergometer of their own and follow their 'exercise prescription' three times a week, for at least 30 minutes each session. They will come to the exercise lab every three months to have the performance of their hearts monitored while they work out. 'As patients get more fit, we up their prescription – increase the amount of exercise,' says Dr Stein.

What do patients get for all this effort? One of the first and most important benefits, says Dr Stein, is psychological – a victory over fear. 'After you've had a heart attack, it's very difficult to push it out of your mind, convince yourself that you're well, and concentrate on living. It's easy to become a 'cardiac neurotic', an individual who's constantly concerned that the next moment he or she is going to die.

'But if you work out on a bicycle three times a week, or go out and run around a track and work up a sweat, then this kind of problem is taken care of. You're proving to yourself that you can exert yourself and not die.'

The change in a patient's outlook, says Ms Frank, can be striking – and immensely rewarding. 'People are so frightened when they come in here, and they're so happy when they've got into exercise. They no longer have to fear their daily activities, since they know they can do much more strenuous things. They learn to live pretty much as they did before – prudently, but without fear.'

There was a man in his early 50s, Dr Stein recalls, who after a mild heart attack found a return to normal activity virtually impossible. Medically, he was doing quite well, but he complained of extreme fatigue. Several months after his heart attack, he had not yet resumed his sex life.

'Both he and his wife were extremely nervous about any activity, including sex,' Dr Stein recounts. 'So we had the wife watch his stress test. We pointed out, at each stage, what kind of activity demanded an equivalent exertion: "Now he is mowing the lawn," we told her. "Now he could be having sex; now he could be playing tennis. You can see that his heartbeat, his ECG are fine." And the visual impact of the demonstration was enough to dispel their anxieties, allowing them to resume their sex life, and making it possible for him to enter the exercise programme.'

In general, Dr Stein says, statistics show that participants in the Downstate programme have reaped substantial emotional and psychological benefits. Tests of life satisfaction, self-image and sense of well-being show dramatic improvement. 'And we've seen a significant reduction in the amount of sleeping pills that patients need, a decrease in their use of tranquillizers.'

With regular exercise, Dr Stein adds, heart patients don't just *think* they are capable of more activity – they generally *do* become capable of more activity.

'It's called the training response,' he explains. 'If you ran up ten flights of stairs, your pulse would be, say, 180. But after running up those stairs every day for six weeks, your pulse wouldn't go higher than, let's say, 140. Your muscles would be doing the same amount of work and requiring the same amount of oxygen, and your heart would have to pump the same amount of blood. But now your heart has been trained to eject more blood with each beat, so it doesn't have to pump as many times. And at a lower heart rate, your heart itself needs less oxygen than it did before.

'So let's say a man with coronary disease gets chest pains at a heart rate of 150. After training, he'll still get his pain at 150. But where two flights of stairs would cause him pain before, now he can go up four flights of stairs before reaching that point. He may be able to go through an entire day without that kind of physical stress. It's an improvement in efficiency – you can do more external work (like walking) for the same cardiac work. So you can tolerate more exercise.'

Such physiological improvements, Dr Stein says, mean that some 20 per cent of the patients who stay in the programme for over a year are able to cut down on the use of cardiac drugs. Many, he adds, report a decrease in symptoms.

More impressive than statistics, though, are the participants themselves. 'We have heart patients who are more fit than the average sedentary non-cardiac individual,' Dr Stein says. 'If you go over to the Y, you'll see people who have had heart attacks running vigorously for 30 minutes at a time.'

At the 92nd Street YMCA, on Manhattan's Upper East Side, cardiac patients sweat and strain alongside healthy joggers in a programme directed by the Cardiac Exercise Laboratory. The Y is no hospital, but it has its own stress-testing centre ('with equipment just as sophisticated as that in my laboratory,' says Dr Stein), and a staff that includes a cardiologist, a nurse and a nutritionist. Participants at the Y are given individually designed exercise programmes, built around their preferences and needs. It may involve running in place, skipping rope, doing sit-ups or calisthenics, or running. 'We ask, "What do you find fun? What turns you on?" ' Dr Stein says.

They also meet with the nutritionist for advice on improving their diet and with a social worker for counselling on how to reduce the stress in their lives.

'About 45 per cent of our people have had heart attacks,' says Charles Bronz, health and physical education director at the Y. 'They are treated the same as those people who enter the programme for preventive reasons. We find that bringing the two groups together has a beneficial effect for everyone.'

For heart patients, the benefits can be striking. 'We had one 51-year-old man who'd had a heart attack and double bypass surgery,' Bronz recalls. 'When he first came here, all he could do was work out, slowly, on a bicycle. Now he's running. In five months, his endurance has improved by nearly 50 per cent.'

Another man had very severe angina – chest pains that reflect insufficient blood flow through the coronary arteries. 'When he first started in the programme, four years ago, his "run" was more like a fast walk. Now he's playing singles tennis. His endurance has almost doubled.'

Training, Bronz points out, can help some heart patients perform feats that healthy people might envy. 'We have one man, a psychiatrist, who'd had two heart attacks. He's doing particularly well. He even caught a mugger! Some kid grabbed his wife's bag – he chased him for two blocks and caught him!'

One thing that makes the Y programme successful, apparently, is the friendly community setting. 'People take an interest in each other,' says Bronz. 'If somebody misses a few sessions, they ask, 'Hey, where's John?'

And at the Y, they recognize that, after a heart attack a patient's family may need as much reassurance as he or she does. 'Often, children don't know how to act,' says Dr Stein. 'Shall I take out the rubbish so Daddy won't have to?' they ask. 'Can I talk to Daddy about staying out late Saturday night, or is that going to get him upset and give him another heart attack?'

'So we have Family Day and invite the family down to watch everybody exercise. Watching Dad put on a sweat suit, jog for 30 minutes and work up a good sweat – that goes a long way towards eliminating those fears. If you just tell them, "Don't worry about your father," it won't have the same effect.'

Preventing the first attack

Healthy people who want to prevent heart attacks also find support at the Y. Motivated, often, by the illness or sudden death of a close friend or relative, they sign up for rigorous stress testing and blood tests to determine the health of their hearts and arteries and the risk of future trouble. Those who pass the tests with flying colours are sent on their way, says Bronz. 'Whatever you're doing, we tell them, keep it up!' Those with a medium to high risk of heart disease – about 10 per cent of the people tested – are invited to join the programme. Like the cardiac patients, they receive individually designed exercise schedules, advice from the nutritionist, stress counselling from the social worker and encouragement from the nurse.

'That's why the programme works so well – it doesn't just come at prevention from one aspect,' says nutritionist Gail Levely. 'It's comprehensive.'

Participants, she adds, seem uncommonly receptive to nutritional advice. 'Some come to see me periodically for counselling on weight loss or to see if their diets are OK. I encourage a low-fat, high-carbohydrate diet, lots of whole grains and fresh fruit and vegetables, less beef and more chicken and fish. They are really open to change.'

Barbara Eisenstein, whose years as a coronary care unit nurse have taught her the need for programmes like Downstate's, is particularly enthusiastic. 'Once someone gets into the physical aspect of the programme, it becomes a way of life,' she says. 'It gives him or her a wholly different outlook, and it's all to the good.'

That, in effect, is the fundamental idea of the Downstate programme – to start both patients and non-patients on the path to a healthier, more vigorous lifestyle. 'All we try to do is form a lifetime habit of exercise,' says Charles Bronz. 'We encourage people to be on their own.' More than a few of his patients have, in fact, become 'enthusiastic exercise addicts', Dr Stein says.

But what about risks? Everyone has heard tales of stress tests interrupted by fatalities, and of apparently healthy middle-aged men found dead on the side of the running track.

One study that Dr Stein likes to cite shows the likelihood of death or serious complications in the course of a stress test to be 1 in 200,000. In a good, modern centre, he speculates, the risk may be even less. 'We do very careful screening before exercise testing, we always have a doctor and a nurse trained in ECG and cardiopulmonary resuscitation, and there's always a full set of cardiac-arrest equipment. With better monitoring devices, we can pick up early warning signs of when to stop a test.'

Exercise itself, Dr Stein grants, does involve some increased risk for a heart patient. 'We minimize it by bringing your heart rate higher, when we test you on the treadmill, than it will be when you train. And overall, we lower the daily risk of the individual by putting him in a training programme. If you exercise enough to train, in other words, then running for the bus on a windy day will involve less physical stress than it would otherwise.'

In the years since the programme began, he adds, 'we've found out that people's hearts and bodies are much sturdier after a heart attack than we had thought. We're comfortable prescribing more exercise than we used to – we seem to do it safely.'

Similarly, he says, much of the anxiety about running for healthy people is exaggerated. For a vigorous, active person under 40, without symptoms or significant risk factors (such as overweight or smoking), 'a stress test may be an unnecessary precaution. If you're in your late 40s, though, a stress test would be appropriate every three or four years.' And the 'competitive nut' who pushes himself the extra two miles, or who ignores the heat of summer, may be moving into a high risk zone, Dr Stein adds. 'And if you feel an irregularity in your heartbeat or you start to have chest pains you've never had before, be prudent and see your doctor.'

Lifelong exercise protects best

A study involving thousands of men gives credence to Dr Stein's claims about heart disease and exercise. When 36,500 male alumni of Harvard University who enrolled between 1916 and 1950 were studied, researchers found that those who continued to engage in vigorous physical activity after graduation were at less risk of heart attack.

In fact, those who were not active in sports during their university days but later became physically active were better protected than the beefy fellows who charged across the goal lines at the university and later settled into sedentary lifestyles. While warning that diet and psychological factors can't be completely ruled out as elements involved in heart attack risks, the researchers stressed that the protective influence of exercise is very important (*American Journal of Epidemiology*).

A reason to live

A study of 92 heart attack and angina patients at the University of Maryland Hospital in Baltimore determined that those who owned pets had fewer cardiovascular difficulties and a significantly lower mortality rate than those who owned no pets.

And it didn't matter whether the pet was a dog or an iguana. Of the 53 pet owners, only 3 (5.6 per cent) died within a year of discharge from the hospital, compared to 11 out of the 39 (28.2 per cent) who did not own pets. That's because pets, theorizes James J. Lynch (who heads the facility where the research was carried out), give their owners a reason to live.

In other research, Dr Lynch has found that people who live alone have higher incidences of disease and premature death. And in an Australian study, researchers found that 26 people who had recently lost their spouses had a significant reduction in their bodies' immune function, a condition that was linked with an increased susceptibility to coronary artery disease and other diseases.

In his book on the medical consequences of the lack of human contact, Dr Lynch reports a number of cases in which striking changes in the heartbeats of cardiac patients were apparently caused by the simplest touch. In one instance, Dr Lynch and his colleagues observed a 54-year-old man with heart disease. The man died after 14 days of intense medical care and a period in a deep coma. As he lay dying, a nurse came to his bedside and briefly held his hand. His heart, despite the coma, reacted immediately. The heart rate decreased and the rhythm of the heartbeat stabilized, and both remained improved after the nurse left.

Stimulated by cases like this, Dr Lynch decided to examine the effects of touching on a larger scale. Because pulse taking was a simple kind of touching that all patients regularly experienced, Dr Lynch decided to observe its effects on arrhythmia (irregular heartbeat) in a group of over 300 cardiac patients.

> After examining these patients, it was clear that even the routine event of pulse palpation could alter the frequency of cardiac arrhythmia in coronary care patients. In some of the patients, indeed, pulse taking had the power to suppress completely arrhythmias that had been occurring.

More and more, social and psychological prevention of coronary heart disease is taking its place alongside 'traditional' measures such as diet and exercise. Friendship is important, for example, because social isolation has been shown to be a significant risk factor. In one study, social isolation levels – measured by marital status, church attendance and group affiliation – were used to rank over 4000 middle-aged men. And the highest incidence of CHD was found among the most isolated, the lowest among the most social. (*See* EMOTIONAL PROBLEMS.)

However, the news on families isn't all good: high blood pressure and coronary artery disease tend to run in families, studies have shown. If one or both of your parents have or had heart disease, that means you are at higher risk for developing it yourself than the general population. But even if not, you'd do well to take the suggestions in this entry to heart.

• Heartburn

Almost everyone knows the feeling – a burning sensation behind the breastbone that sometimes occurs when you're tense or nervous, or have eaten too much. It's called *heartburn*, although it has nothing to do with the heart. Usually, it's not serious, although if heartburn becomes chronic you should see your doctor because it could be a symptom of a digestive problem. Lots of people take antacids for heartburn, but they shouldn't, for the simple reason that they don't work!

In one trial, heartburn patients who received either antacids or placebos (medically inactive pills) had no less pain when they took antacids. In short, the antacids didn't work. In one part of the study, 18 patients were given either the antacid or the placebo for 30 consecutive episodes of pain, and their pain levels were measured every five minutes for the next 30 minutes. The difference in pain relief between the real and the fake drug? None (*Internal*

Medicine News, 1 August 1979).

However, there is natural relief for heartburn, and it comes from the sea. An extract of the seaweed kelp, called *algin*, has proved effective against heartburn.

Researchers selected 60 patients with complaints of heartburn and acid regurgitation and divided them into three groups: one received a placebo, another received an antacid, and a third received antacid and algin. All 60 patients took six tablets a day for two weeks.

The number and duration of heartburn episodes were significantly reduced in the group receiving algin. Neither the placebo nor the antacid alone had a significant effect (*Lancet*).

• Heat rash

During the early months of World War II, American troops battling for the islands of the South Pacific were also doing battle with an annoying rash known to doctors as *miliaria* and to the rest of us as 'heat rash' or 'prickly heat'. The intense burning and itching sensation of prickly heat is caused by a blockage of the sweat ducts. Strained by intense heat and humidity, the body's evaporative cooling system breaks down, and instead of being exuded through the pores, sweat becomes trapped beneath the skin, resulting in a rash that feels like its name.

Dr Robert L. Stern, writing in the *Journal of the American Medical Association* not long after the war, reported his attempts to alleviate the disorder among the Pacific troops with 'all the available lotions and medicaments of possible aid, changes of clothes and soaps,' multiple vitamins, and vitamins A and D, all of which had 'no noticeable effects'. But when he tried vitamin C, in doses of from 300 to 500 mg daily, it gave 'dramatic relief to most patients. The itching cleared and the rash subsided, usually within half an hour, the effects lasting 6 to 24 hours.'

The power of vitamin C against the pain of prickly heat was demonstrated in a more controlled study carried out in Singapore by dermatologist T. C. Hindson, of the British Military Hospital there. It began with one of those happy accidents that the history of science is so full of. An Australian Air Force officer, troubled by a rash in his groin that had resisted all medication for a year, told the doctor that it suddenly cleared up in the course of a week when he caught a cold and started taking 1 g of vitamin C a day.

Intrigued by this and the results of other exploratory tests, Dr Hindson set up a study using 30 children who had been plagued by prickly heat for at least eight continuous weeks prior to the test. Half the youngsters were given a placebo and the other half vitamin C. In order to ensure that he wouldn't bias the results, Dr Hindson himself did not know who was getting which. Only the hospital pharmacist knew.

After two weeks, the rash had disappeared completely on ten of the 15 children receiving vitamin C. Four others showed improvement and one remained unchanged. By contrast, nine youngsters in the placebo group showed no change and two had got worse. The rash had either cleared up or improved in the other four.

The 11 children in the placebo group whose prickly heat had either shown no improvement or had actually worsened were then given vitamin C and checked after two more weeks. The rash had cleared completely in six children and improved in the other five.

Admitting that the exact mechanism at work remained unclear, Dr Hindson concluded tht 'ascorbic acid [vitamin C], when given in high doses, is effective in the treatment and prevention of prickly heat.' He also noted one of the vitamin's greatest advantages: 'No unwanted side-effects have been recorded from such doses to date' (*Lancet*).

Air-conditioned offices and work areas in muggy climates have made heat rash almost obsolete, but for those who still suffer from this condition, beauty writer Virginia Castleton recommends tea made from raspberry leaves, which can soothe and have a calming effect when used as a light wash. Elder flowers are also soothing for heat rash. Like raspberry lotion, they produce the best effects when applied immediately after towelling dry following a cool shower. You might find additional relief by applying a dusting of cornstarch or powdered white clay following the lotion.

• Heat stroke

The afternoon sun is like a furnace. The humidity is so thick you have to make an effort to push through it. You're dripping with perspiration, and even the few pieces of clothing you have on cling like soggy dishcloths. So naturally you head for a shady hammock and reach for . . . what? A cool beer?

You'd be better off reaching for vitamin C.

As you lie in your hammock, your body moves quickly to cool itself. Blood vessels expand, the heart pumps rapidly to deliver overheated blood to the skin's surface for cooling. Sweat pours off the skin. Those reactions may be sparked by hormones from the adrenal glands, which contain a higher amount of vitamin C than any other body tissue. If the hot weather just won't quit and your vitamin C is depleted, then the body's temperature stays high and you're headed straight for heat cramps, heat exhaustion and maybe even heat stroke.

Now, it's bad enough sweltering on your hammock in your own garden, but imagine what it must be like to travel and work during a scorcher. That was the case with a salesman covering an Indiana – Illinois district reported in the *Annals of Internal Medicine* (October 1979) by Dr George A. Poda. If the temperature rose above 85°F (29.4°C) the man became sick and very weak. As a result, he missed most of his summer sales work.

'When he came to me, I remembered a World War II story about using vitamin C for heat stroke,' Dr Poda told us. 'Army personnel stationed on the Egyptian coast were then having a bad time with the heat. Some smart Army doctor thought of giving them vitamin C, and after that their problems disappeared. So I had the salesman take 100 mg of vitamin C three times daily during the summer months. Even though temperatures stayed at 90°F

(32.2°C) and higher, up to 105°F (40.6°C), he was able to drive his non air-conditioned car and function. If he forgot to take his vitamin C, he got sick again.'

Alternative to salt tablets

Dr Poda also told us about the success of vitamin C in an even harder case of heat intolerance: a tennis professional who couldn't teach or play tennis in high summer temperatures. 'By taking 500 mg of vitamin C a day, he, too, was able to go about his business,' according to Dr Poda.

Dr Poda has routinely prescribed vitamin C supplements instead of salt tablets for those who have to work outdoors in the high temperatures of South Carolina. 'Salt tablets are dangerous for people with heart disease or a disposition towards it,' he says. 'And sometimes they make even healthy people sick. On the other hand, there are no harmful side-effects from vitamin C, and it's extremely effective. Although we often have hot and humid weather, we've had no cases of heat exhaustion with workers taking vitamin C.'

South Carolina scorchers are one thing. But vitamin C has shown its ability to improve heat tolerance even with workers in hot, humid mines. For years, the South African government had been using a simple exercise called the 'stepping procedure' to acclimate new mine workers to the heat of the mines. By repeatedly going through that routine in progressively hotter and more humid air, they gradually accustomed themselves to the conditions they will encounter in the mines.

However, researchers with the Industrial Hygiene Division of the Chamber of Mines reported that, despite this preparation, mine workers had a rapid drop in blood levels of vitamin C during their first three months of work. Heat stress was burning up vitamin C in the workers' blood, even though their intake of it would normally have been adequate.

The researchers decided to test whether supplements of vitamin C would reduce heat stress and improve acclimation. They divided 60 new mine workers into three groups. To one group they gave 250 mg of vitamin C and to another 500 mg. To the third group they gave a placebo. The workers then went through the step-test acclimation.

Results (reported in the *Journal of Applied Physiology*) showed not only that the vitamin C supplemented workers acclimated to heat more quickly, but also that their heat tolerance improved. Whereas it previously took an average of eight days to acclimate a worker fully (and in some cases as long as 15 to 18 days), with vitamin C supplementation the time was cut to four or five days in over 90 per cent of those tested.

The South African mining industry found those results so impressive that it instituted a standard supplementation programme which provides each mine worker with 200 to 250 mg of vitamin C daily.

Hot spells deplete potassium

However, vitamin C isn't the only nutrient to watch during the 'dog days'. When you reach for the vitamin C, you should also grab a banana. That's because bananas, as well as other fruit and vegetables, contain potassium, an essential mineral that many people get too little of in summer.

During a two-week hot spell in Detroit, Stanley H. Schuman of the Medical University of South Carolina and George W. Williams of the University of Michigan School of Public Health measured the effects of heat stress on the body's potassium supply in 631 university hospital outpatients. They described the hot spell as 'warm but not record breaking'. During the first week, humidity was stifling, with average day-time temperatures higher than 80°F (26.7°C) and average night-time readings above 60°F (15.6°C). During the second week, day-time highs climbed above 90°F (32.2°C) for four straight days. All told, 115 'excess' deaths in the city were reported during the heat wave.

Did low potassium levels have something to do with those deaths? After running more than a dozen biochemical tests on the volunteers, the researchers compared the results with similar readings taken from 698 outpatients at the same hospital during a cool two-week period a month earlier.

Drs Schuman and Williams discovered a drop in potassium levels from June to July. Although the dip was not enough to count as an outright deficiency, they described it as 'significantly lower'.

The researchers speculate that the reason for the drop was the potassium-poor meals many people eat in summer.

> The inclination to substitute fad foods such as carbonated beverages, alcoholic drinks, low-calorie substitutes and convenient snacks instead of balanced meals is probably never stronger than during the malaise, fatigue and discomfort of sustained humid, hot weather

wrote the researchers. Unfortunately, such items are exactly the ones most likely to be lacking in potassium.

According to the Food and Nutrition Board of the (US) National Research Council, an adequate daily intake of potassium for a healthy adult is about 2–6 g. A cola drink such as Pepsi contains only 7 mg of potassium per serving. A frosty lager contains just 46 mg, and the whisky in a mixed drink just 2 mg. An ice lolly – that instant summer-time refresher – contains absolutely no measurable potassium.

That's why you should reach instead for a banana (420 mg of potassium). And for a glass of orange juice (440 mg), a large carrot (340 mg), a bowl of strawberries (270 mg), a juicy tomato (244 mg), a salad with shredded red cabbage (270 mg in every 3 oz) or some refreshing watermelon (175 mg per slice). In fact, most unprocessed fruit and vegetables are excellent sources of potassium. It's a good idea, therefore, to take advantage of the summer's bounty and eat lots of fresh salad greens, vegetables and fruit.

Drs Schuman and Williams conclude their study with this carefully worded suggestion:

> . . . improvements in dietary intake during hot weather might reduce some morbidity and mortality associated with recent urban heat waves . . . It may be prudent during prolonged hot spells to advise heat-susceptible segments of the population to watch the potassium

values of foods consumed and for their physicians to be alert for early and reversible signs of potassium depletion. [*Ecology of Food and Nutrition*]

Protecting yourself against the heat

Remember these tips next time you find yourself in the midst of a heat wave:
● Drink plenty of water *and* fruit and vegetable juices. They contain not only the liquid but also the minerals your body needs to resist the effects of heat.
● Avoid prolonged exertion in the sun. Get your exercise early in the morning.
● Dress in lightweight clothing. Natural fibres such as cotton are usually more comfortable than synthetics as they permit the cooling circulation of air. They're also very absorbent, which draws heat away from the body and keeps you cool and dry.
● Avoid sudden changes from hot to cold or cold to hot places. Go easy on air conditioning. Even healthy people accustomed to living in hot climates suffer substantial heat stress when they leave air-conditioned buildings for the summer outdoors.

Irina I. Cech of the School of Public Health at the University of Texas Health Science Center in Houston has found that daylong 'protection' from the heat in that muggy city prevents the body from adapting naturally when the need – and the temperature – come up. As Dr Cech told us, 'We live in an urban environment in which we create an artificial climate inside the buildings, cars and houses which is much cooler than any place else. So people – even though they live in a place where it is very hot outside – have no true exposure to the heat except during these very short hops between the car and the house or office building. Air conditioning has become an affordable necessity. We're dependent on it in our houses, schools, offices, shopping centres and cars. It is actually difficult to imagine living otherwise. In fact, cooling by any means other than air conditioning is not even considered in modern building design. Modern buildings do not even have windows that open!'

What this means, according to Dr Cech, is that those who rely on air conditioning to this extent never give their bodies the chance to adapt to the heat. And that can be a problem for their health. Dr Cech found out how much of a problem it was when she carried out her study, which was published in *Urban Ecology*. She took 22 sedentary office workers and exposed them to the normal summer heat of Houston for a period longer than they were accustomed to: half an hour. The first 15 minutes were spent in the shade, where the temperature ranged from 86° to 91°F (30–32.8°C). And the next 15 minutes were spent in the open, where the temperature ranged from 88° to 95°F (31.1–35°C).

Indications for the amount of stress the people experienced were measured by their oral temperature (ie by mouth), pulse rate, skin temperature and subjective reactions to the heat. As Dr Cech told us, 'The stress is very great; the whole body responds to the heat. The whole system goes to work – the sweating mechanism. And depending how well a person is adapted to the heat, the adaptation goes differently.' What Dr Cech found was that these otherwise healthy people – who had been living in sweltering Houston for at least eight years – had the same response to the real thing that you would expect of people who had never been exposed.

Both sexes reported feeling hotter, thirstier, more irritable and tired in the sunlight than in the shade. For the individuals accustomed to air conditioning, an exposure to the summer outdoor heat is a substantial thermal burden. A short exposure to an outdoor environment, even shaded, was sufficient to cause a rise in all physiological variables measured.

In her paper, Dr Cech agreed with the work of other researchers who argue that a power failure or a mechanical breakdown might cause massive heat-related illnesses and deaths at temperatures even lower than those with which increased mortality was associated before the era of air conditioning. She believes that this dependence on artificial climate control is potentially dangerous for elderly people, or people with impaired respiratory functioning who might be totally dependent on air conditioning. 'The people used in our study,' she says, 'were young and healthy – and they were stressed by the heat.' Dr Cech says that the way to combat this problem is to return to a more natural way of dealing with the heat. The idea is to give the body the chance to adapt to the heat and give nature the chance to cool off our buildings.

'A person needs approximately 100 minutes of uninterrupted exposure every day for about two weeks in order to be accustomed to outdoor heat,' says Dr Cech. 'So I suggest that people expose themselves to the heat rather than hide from it. One hour, or even a half hour, is better than nothing. The thing to do is make being outdoors part of your routine every day. Swim, walk, jog – whatever takes you outdoors and keeps you there long enough.'

And for the architects with whom Dr Cech is working, she recommends making full utilization of natural cooling techniques such as cross ventilation to help us keep our cool – and our health – when summer fires up the front burner.

• Hepatitis

A particularly troublesome viral disease, hepatitis often strikes surgical patients who have had blood transfusions. A nine-year study of Japanese hospital patients who had received blood transfusions revealed that 2 g of vitamin C given daily sharply reduced the number and severity of serum hepatitis cases. By the seventh year of the study, hospital administrators felt so strongly about the preventive properties of the nutrient that 'the decision was made, for ethical reasons, to give vitamin C in large amounts to essentially every patient. During the period 1967 to 1973,' the report continued,

there were 150 patients who were given blood transfusions and who received little or no vitamin C (less than 2 g per day). Of these patients, 11 developed hepatitis (7 per cent) . . . Among 1100 similarly transfused patients who received 2 g or more of vitamin C per day, there were no established cases of hepatitis and only a few questionable cases. *[Journal of the International Academy of Preventive Medicine]*

A number of American doctors and others, elsewhere in the world have also reported success in treating hepatitis with large doses of the vitamin, given both by mouth and by injection.

• Hiatus hernia

Hiatus hernia is the Lon Chaney of internal distresses: it's the condition of 1000 faces – all of them scarier than the real one. On any given day, a stiff, frightening chest pain could send you to the hospital labelled as a possible heart attack victim. (And that's what you might be, so don't take any chances.) But if what you really have is a suddenly apparent, kicking and screaming hiatus hernia, your doctors, at first glance, might think you are having either a coronary, biliary colic, pancreatitis, a gastric or duodenal ulcer, a disorder of the oesophagus (gullet), a digestive malfunction, angina or any one of many other good but wrong guesses.

It's really a sheep in wolf's clothing, though, and hardly a rare, exotic disease. Estimates as to the number of people who have hiatus hernias go as high as 78 per cent, and most don't even know they have them. It's a sneaky – and, usually, asymptomatic – little digestive-tract devil. And, more often than not, it is nothing much to worry about, despite the pain.

What is hiatus hernia? A normal oesophagus, in its long, narrow descent from the mouth to the stomach, must pass through a taut sheet of muscle: the diaphragm, which may be thought of as both the floor of the chest and the ceiling of the abdominal cavity. To get to the stomach, the oesophagus pokes through a teardrop-shaped opening in the diaphragm called the *hiatus*. It's at this point that the oesophagus and stomach join, and where a valve system (the *lower oesophageal sphincter*) keeps deposited food (and the acid working to digest it) from backing up into the oesophagus.

In a hiatus hernia, the *upper* part of the stomach has slid up past the diaphragmatic hiatus (weakened, perhaps, by age) and into the chest. From 75 to 95 per cent of hiatus hernias are of this 'sliding' type. These come and go, sliding back and forth, depending on body position and other factors. In another kind, the 'rolling', or para-oesophageal, hernia, the oesophagus – stomach junction stays in its normal location (as opposed to the action of the 'sliding' type), but a portion of the large *lower* curved section of the stomach rides up through the hiatus and rolls forward in the chest cavity. These 'rolling' hernias can be big problems and may require surgery, but they're relatively rare.

A hiatus hernia, in and of itself, is not a painful condition. Whereas, for example, a broken arm results in pain, a hiatus hernia results for the most part in nothing except an anatomical deviation. The major difficulty associated with 'sliding' hiatal hernias is gastro-oesophageal reflux, which is a backwash of stomach juices and which, in the case of hiatus hernias, is probably caused by the stomach's unnaturally altered position. Reflux happens when the oesophageal sphincter is weak and allows acidic gastric fluids to travel in the wrong direction.

It's important to know that reflux can happen in somebody who doesn't have a hiatus hernia. Just because you have heartburn doesn't mean you have the condition and, conversely, just because you have a hiatus hernia doesn't mean you're bound to have heartburn, chest pains, acid backup into the throat or other reflux-associated discomforts. But, then again, you might. A visit to your doctor ought to let you know what your inner story is.

How do hiatus hernias get that way? Nobody's sure, and it probably varies from case to case. It could be the result of a congenital problem, or a side-effect of being pregnant or having given birth, or an offshoot of over-eating or obesity. Any undue increase in abdominal pressure can do the deed. Some researchers believe that straining during defecation can cause the stomach to be pushed up through a weakened hiatus.

Keeping the problem at bay

The usual treatments and advice have little to do, actually, with fixing the hernia itself but rather address the issue of keeping the reflux in check. Some of these bits of wisdom are:

- Lose weight.
- Avoid bending or stooping.
- Don't wear tight belts or girdles.
- Avoid alcoholic beverages (and cola drinks, too).
- Don't smoke (it helps produce stomach acid, which is just what you don't need more of).
- As with peptic ulcers, eat several little meals every day, rather than a couple of large ones.
- Wait at least $2^{1}/_{2}$ to 3 hours after a meal before lying down.
- Sleep with your head elevated 8 to 10 inches.
- Avoid drinking coffee and eating chocolate (they weaken the oesophageal sphincter), and avoid acidic foods, such as oranges, grapefruit and tomatoes.
- Be wary of garlic, onion and peppermint, too.
- Avoid taking oestrogen drugs – they aggravate heartburn (among other things).

Studies have shown a link between hiatus hernia and gallstones – where you find one, chances are pretty good that you'll find the other – and suggest that lack of fibre in the diet is to blame for both. Lowering animal-fat consumption and increasing fibre, especially in the form of bran, prevents gallstones. At the same time, a high-fibre diet increases the size of stools and eliminates the straining that can cause hiatus hernia. Wrote British researcher Denis P. Burkitt, 'The hypothesis that fibre-depleted diets are a major factor in the causation of hiatus hernia is consistent with all that is known of the disease' (*American Journal of Clinical Nutrition*, March 1981).

The most serious physical effects related to hiatus hernia have to do with damage to the oesophagus. The acidic stomach juices wash back into it and normally cause only inflammation and irritation (and, one researcher suggests, asthma attacks). Continued reflux, however, can cause ulceration, scarring and, ultimately, blockage of the oesophagus, requiring surgery. And matters get worse if you use aspirin. The aspirin 'may become trapped for extended periods in the oesophagi of patients with oesophageal hiatus hernia,' wrote Dr Vernon M. Smith; this trapping action allows the aspirin to 'injure alkaline mucosa by direct contact . . .' *(Southern Medical Journal)*.

By cutting out acidic foods – especially citrus fruits and fruit juices – in order to avoid complications, some reflux/hiatus hernia sufferers have come down with vitamin C deficiencies bordering on scurvy. For these people, vitamin C supplements are probably just what the nutritionist ordered.

Many doctors will cavalierly prescribe frequent antacid use to patients with hiatus hernia-related heartburn problems. The antacids will cover up the hurt – but long-term consumption of antacids containing aluminium compounds could leach your body of calcium, resulting in the thinning of your bones and bone pain.

Only the most severe cases warrant surgery. If there is a potential of the herniated stomach pinching off the oesphagus, bleeding, or danger of lung or heart damage, then an operation is necessary. But only about 5 per cent or less of hiatus hernia patients require anything other than good medical advice and a change in habits. Besides its general uselessness, unwarranted hiatus hernia surgery also can be risky, and may itself produce new symptoms far worse than any associated with the original discomfort. It's best to get a second opinion.

• Hiccups

Scientists don't exactly understand what hiccups are or how to cure them. They know, roughly, that they are a spasm of the diaphragm, the flat strip of muscle wedged between the chest cavity and the abdomen. And they know that a gobbled meal, a fit of laughter or any of 70 causes can somehow irritate the nerves that lead to the diaphragm and set off the spasm. (The noise that goes with it is made when air is sucked in and then suddenly stopped by tightened vocal cords.) Beyond that – especially how the nerves are calmed down so that hiccups stop – it's still pretty much of a mystery. So, although the following cures have worked for millions of people, why they work is anybody's guess.

To stop hiccups, you could try: swallowing a teaspoon of honey or vinegar; pulling on your tongue; breathing into a paper bag; holding your breath; drinking water while covering your ears tightly; having someone pat you on the back; applying cold to the back of your neck; making yourself sneeze with pepper. Or take charcoal tablets.

'I have treated my cases of hiccups with charcoal tablets,' wrote a doctor to the *British Medical Journal*, 'and have instructed patients to continue chewing them at least once an hour and in extreme cases continuously. In most cases, I have met with success on this simple regimen.'

Another suggestion is to take a glass of water and put a knife in it, with the blade in the water. Press the handle against your head and drink the water – the whole glass.

The only thing wrong with this technique is that it does look a little strange, to put it mildly. So here's an alternative. Soak a wedge of lemon in angostura bitters. Put the wedge in your mouth and suck it. That should do the trick, according to a letter in one medical journal.

Here's another hiccup stopper, this one from the *Journal of the American Medical Association*: Take a cotton-tipped swab and massage the roof of your mouth. The exact spot you want to massage is just behind where the hard palate in the front of your mouth turns into the softer palate in the back of your mouth. Rub the tip of the swab gently on the spot for a minute or so, and the hiccups should disappear.

The good thing is that even if none of those remedies works for you, the hiccups should go away on their own. If they don't – if they last for hours or days – then you may have an illness and you should see your doctor.

• High blood pressure

'If not for yourself, then do it for your family,' goes a popular American TV ad campaign. The pitch is aimed at people with high blood pressure and its purpose is to encourage them to take their medication every day.

In the background are families working and playing, loving and caring. The implications are, of course, that if you don't take your blood pressure medicine every day, you may lose everything. And your family will lose, too – a provider, a friend, a loved one.

High blood pressure, also called *hypertension*, means that the arteries carrying blood around the body are in a state of tension, which makes it difficult for the heart to pump blood through the system. That's why high blood pressure is intimately connected to catastrophic cardiovascular diseases, including heart attacks and strokes. According to statistics, if you have high blood pressure (and millions do) and are between the ages of 45 and 74, your risk of heart attack is three times greater, and your risk of stroke seven times greater, than people with normal blood pressure. In fact, an estimated 850,000 people die each year in the United States alone from high blood pressure-related cardiovascular diseases. High blood pressure, one doctor has remarked, is

> the most prevalent and most dangerous precipitating factor in the genesis of cardiovascular diseases, the leading cause of death in the United States and other industrialized countries.

Many things are known to increase your odds of getting high blood pressure, including stress, lack of exercise and excess weight. Heredity plays a part, too. The dismal fact is that, if both your parents have it, chances are about three in four that you'll get it. If only one parent has it, your chances are a little better than one in two.

So it's heartening to see public-service messages aimed at trying to stamp it out, but the American ads lean heavily on the use of drugs to accomplish that end. Not that drugs aren't sometimes called for, but they also have some distinct drawbacks, too – namely, side-effects such as drowsiness, dizziness, dry mouth, depression, nausea, headache and heart palpitations. In fact, these side-effects are one of the main reasons why most patients do not adhere to their prescribed course of treatment with drugs.

We think there's another way. In fact, we've compiled alternatives to drug therapy – alternatives that research indicates have the potential to augment, or in some cases *replace*, standard treatments. Of course, if you're now on medication for high blood pressure, see your doctor before considering any drastic changes.

Potassium up, sodium down

Potassium and sodium are both electrolytes, meaning they each carry a tiny electrical charge, and the two substances carry on a sort of unceasing tug-of-war across the cell walls. The stakes are the delicate electrical and chemical balance of the cells, and hence the body.

When sodium is winning, cells contain more water, and potassium is dumped into the urine for excretion. When potassium is winning, cells get rid of sodium and water. Although sodium has it own role to play in the body's chemistry, it is needed only in minute amounts – and anything above that can be considered a bona fide potassium burglar, robbing the system of a vital mineral and sending it on its way . . . where it will do nobody any good.

Two recent studies of this cellular shoot-out, conducted at the London Hospital, Whitechapel medical college, have turned up intriguing new indications that potassium may somehow act as a shield against sodium-induced hypertension.

In the first study, a group of 16 people with mild hypertension and a group with normal blood pressure received two different diets, each for a period of 12 weeks. During the first 12 weeks, both groups ate their normal diet, plus sodium tablets. During the second period, their normal diets were supplemented with potassium, and they were instructed to avoid excessively salty foods and not to add salt while cooking or at the table.

The high-sodium diet produced a slow rise in blood pressure in both groups, but during the high-potassium/low sodium diet, 'both systolic and diastolic blood pressure fell sharply and significantly in the hypertensive group in contrast to small but insignificant rises in the normotensive [normal blood pressure] group.'

A month after the study ended and the subjects had returned to their regular eating habits, both groups were tested one final time. It was discovered that the hypertensives' blood pressure had shot right back up again. The researchers concluded that the key factor in the startling drop in pressure during the high-potassium/low-sodium diet had been the increased potassium, since their regular diets included only a marginal rise in sodium but a much greater decline in potassium. They added, however, that 'the mechanism of this depressor [pressure-lowering] response remains unknown' (*Lancet*, 10 January 1981).

Curious about how the sodium/potassium balance might affect those with a family history of hypertension, the British researchers set up a second experiment. They altered the two nutrients in the diets of two groups of young men, with and without family histories of high blood pressure.

It was discovered that, in both groups, sodium loading in the diet caused a 'similar and significant' increase in blood pressure, much as in the first experiment. However, when dietary potassium levels were increased at the same time sodium was reduced, the researchers noted a 'striking contrast' in the response of the two groups. Among the sons of normotensive parents, potassium had no effect or slightly raised the blood pressure, while among those with hypertension in the family, it significantly lowered the pressure.

Perhaps, the scientists suggested, it is only those who have a family history of high blood pressure who are sensitive to the pressure-lowering effects of potassium, and they may actually develop hypertension if the potassium level in their diet is inadequate (*Lancet*, 17 January 1981).

Yet other studies seem to suggest that potassium's gentle powers have an effect on nearly everybody, even those without the family curse. In one survey, 86 vegetarian Seventh-Day Adventists were compared with 86 non-vegetarian Mormons (both groups abstain from alcohol, nicotine and caffeine). It was discovered that 'both groups have lower-than-average blood pressure, but vegetarians had significantly lower blood pressure than did non-vegetarians' (*Preventive Medicine*).

Since fresh fruit and vegetables are among the best sources of potassium, could it be that increased reliance on them results in a higher potassium/sodium ratio and thereby acts as a natural high blood pressure preventive?

That conclusion is suggested by a study conducted during the 1960s in Georgia. A dietary analysis of random samples of the white and black populations revealed that, although there was no real difference in sodium intake between whites and blacks, the blacks consumed less than half the amount of potassium that whites did – and their blood pressure, as a group, was also considerably higher. (Across the United States, hypertension is almost twice as common among blacks as among whites; the reason is a matter of dispute.) The researchers concluded that

> the only way to explain the higher prevalence of hypertension among blacks appears to be their much lower potassium intake, caused by low consumption of fresh fruit, salads, vegetables, and the traditional long cooking of meats and vegetables with loss of intracellular potassium into the cooking water. [*Nutrition and Metabolism*, vol. 24, 1980]

Harold Battarbee, an associate professor of physiology at Louisiana State University School of Medicine, also points out that overly processed foods contribute to the problem. Why? Because potassium is substantially lost when foods are canned or frozen. Not only that, but the natural balance between sodium and potassium is actually reversed.

According to the US Department of Agriculture's (USDA's) *Nutritive Value of American Foods* (Handbook No. 456), for example, a cup of raw peas contains 458 mg of potassium and just 3 mg of sodium. But when those same peas are canned, salt added during the process raises the sodium level to 588 mg (nearly a 200-fold increase), while the potassium is roughly halved, down to 239 mg. 'There need to be some changes in the way foods are processed in industry and at home,' Dr Battarbee says. That seems clear, and the effort is already underway. But what is the proper sodium/potassium ratio in a healthy diet? That's not so clear.

No minimum daily requirement of potassium has been established by the National Research Council, though 2.5 g is the commonly cited figure, with the average diet containing between 2 and 6 g a day. Sodium, by contrast, is required in only tiny amounts, with 0.5 g a day or even less usually considered sufficient to fulfill its bodily role. (One teaspoon of salt contains a shade more than 2 g of sodium.)

Dr Battarbee admits he doesn't know the ideal ratio, but 'keeping it to one-to-one would be beneficial, though that doesn't mean it's optimal . . . less sodium would be better.' Author and chemist Philip S. Chen, claims the ratio should be closer to two to one.

The basic problem with our uptown civilized ways was boldly underlined by Dr George Meneely, a researcher at the Louisiana State University School of Medicine, who has spent three decades studying the effects of altered sodium/potassium levels in rats. Dr Meneely produced convincing evidence that increased potassium levels could greatly extend their lifespan. As he reported:

> In nature, there is a relatively small amount of sodium in *any* diet, and there is much more potassium than sodium in *all* natural diets. There is an extensive literature evidencing that many peoples have lived healthy lives for generations without adding sodium chloride [table salt] to their food. [*American Journal of Cardiology*]

Dr Hugh Trowell takes the point a heartbeat further. In a recent letter, he pointed out that, among primitive hunter – gatherers who add no salt at all to their food and who consume only about 2 g of naturally occurring sodium a day, 'blood pressures do not rise with age, and essential hypertension [high blood pressure not due to any specific disease] is virtually unknown' (*British Medical Journal*, 13 September 1980).

Compare that to the estimated daily intake of the average Briton, who gets about 10 g of salt naturally from his or her food and during cooking, plus 4–10 g added at the table. That comes to something like 14–24 g of salt a day (about 6 or 10 g of sodium). At the same time, we've seen that potassium is often depleted in processed foods.

That's a long way from Adam's lunch.

Luckily, by one of those strange and convenient natural laws, many foods high in potassium are also low in sodium. A big banana, for instance, packs 503 mg of potassium and only 1mg of sodium; 8 fl oz of orange juice contains only 2 mg of sodium to 496 mg of potassium. Other great sources of potassium are apricots, yellow melon, broccoli and wheat germ. Black treacle is also rich in potassium, as are chicken, salmon and halibut.

Because potassium is water soluble, large amounts may leach out of potentially nutritious vegetables and be lost in the cooking water. So it's a good idea to use as little water as possible when boiling vegetables, and to use that water in soups and gravies. Or, better yet, steam your vegetables.

There are so many good sources of potassium that there's really no need for a healthy person to take supplements, some of which tend to irritate the stomach lining. (See the table on page 386 for good sources of potassium.)

Spice up – without salt

Here are some tips for making your food tasty without touching the salt shaker:

Vegetable and meat soups   Add a little vinegar, wine or lemon juice.

Chicken soup   Use ginger, one clove, bay leaf, two peppercorns.

Cream soups   Try cinnamon and nutmeg (use a light touch).

Cucumbers   Marinate in tarragon vinegar.

Asparagus   Sprinkle tips and stalks with nutmeg before serving.

Aubergine   Season with tomatoes, bay leaf, basil, oregano.

Mashed potatoes   Perk up with garlic, parsley flakes and fresh parsley, a touch of cayenne and a bit of paprika. (Cook the potatoes with a clove of garlic and some fresh parsley. Discard garlic and parsley, Mash potatoes, add parsley flakes, cayenne and paprika. Dill is very nice, too. Experiment. Try curry for a touch of India.)

Green beans   Add nutmeg or summer savory.

Veal   Chopped fresh or dried mint goes well.

Lamb   Rosemary is excellent. Pepper and ginger rubbed on before grilling is very nice.

Roast Meat   Use a bay leaf, garlic and onion powder.

Try some do-it-yourself seasoning with herbs. Use attractive, labelled shakers containing oregano, basil, thyme, caraway, sesame, poppy seeds, dried mushroom powder (you can buy it, or make it yourself by drying a few mushrooms and pulverizing them), celery seed, marjoram, summer savory and ground sunflower seeds.

The good news about calcium

'We believe that calcium may be as important or even *more* important than sodium as a factor in high blood pressure,' says Cynthia Morris, an epidemiologist at the Oregon Health Sciences University. 'We have seen that higher amounts of calcium in the diet correlate with *lower* blood pressure levels.'

Ms Morris is referring to the studies that she and her colleagues, J. Stanton and David McCarron, carried out. In one, they used data compiled from a diet survey of 12,000 people. The volunteers were divided into groups according to their blood pressure (normal, borderline and hypertensive), age and race.

'Depending upon the subgroups,' says Ms Morris, 'the hypertensive's calcium intake was 10 to 65 per cent less' than the healthy individual's. What's more, of the 17 nutrients assessed, reduced calcium intake was the only consistent variation between the normals and the hypertensives (*Kidney International*, vol. 23, 1983).

In another study, these same researchers compared the dietary calcium intake of 44 normotensive controls and 46 people with high blood pressure. They found that the normal people consumed an average of 886 mg of calcium each day, whereas the hypertensives took in only 668 mg per day – or 25 per cent less.

'As further evidence of the difference in the amount of calcium consumed by the hypertensives,' added the researchers, 'only 8 of our 46 hypertensives reported consumption over 1 g of calcium per day, whereas 18 out of 44 normotensives reported greater than 1 g' (*Science*, 16 July 1982).

Best sources of potassium

The minimum daily requirement is estimated to be 2500 mg.

Food	Portion size	Amount (mg)
Potato	1 medium	782
Avocado pear	½	680
Black treacle	1 tablespoon	585
Sardines, drained solids	3 oz	501
Flounder	3 oz	498
Orange juice	8 fl oz	496
Tomato, raw	1 medium	444
Banana	1 medium	440
Milk, skimmed	8 fl oz	406
Cod	3 oz	345
Yellow melon	¼	341
Beef liver	3 oz	323
Apricots, dried	1½ oz	318
Peach	1 medium	308
Spinach, cooked	2½ oz	292
Carrot	1 raw	246
Tuna, drained solids	3 oz	225

Adapted from: Catherine F. Adams, *Nutritive Value of American Foods in Common Units,* Agriculture Handbook No 456 (Washington, D.C.: Agricultural Research Service, US Department of Agriculture, 1975).

Consumer and Food Economics Institute, *Composition of Foods,* Agriculture Handbook No 8–1 (Washington, D.C.: Agricultural Research Service, US Department of Agriculture, 1975).

It seems that, even though the hypertensives were within the lower limits of calcium recommended by the US government, they still were receiving inadequate amounts. 'We'd like to see people get about 1 g of calcium a day,' Ms Morris told us. 'We think that's an adequate amount, even though some researchers recommend as much as 1400 to 1600 mg per day.'

One who does is Jose Villar, assistant professor at the school of hygiene and public health, Johns Hopkins University, in Baltimore. That's because he's done experiments, with Jose M. Belizam, that lead him to believe that a total intake of about 1.5 g of calcium a day may be the optimum amount.

In one study, Dr Villar and his colleagues divided 57 normal, healthy volunteers (between the ages of 18 and 35) into two experimental groups. For 22 weeks, one group received 1 g of supplemental calcium per day and the other a placebo. Both groups already had about 0.5 g of calcium in their daily diets, bringing the total to just over 1.5 g for the supplemented group.

Periodic blood pressure readings showed that the calcium-supplemented group had a significant decrease in diastolic pressure (the second reading in blood pressure measurement taken when the heart is resting between beats). For women it was a 5.6 per cent reduction and for men a 9 per cent reduction (*Journal of the American Medical Association,* 4 March 1983).

'These findings confirm the relationship between calcium and blood pressure,' says Dr Villar, 'although we don't know for certain just why it works.

'We do know that calcium plays a central role in the tone of the arteries. That means it controls how open the arteries are. When the cells of the smooth muscle (which lines the arteries) have too much calcium inside, the arteries tend to contract, raising blood pressure. So, anything that affects how much calcium crosses into those cells also affects blood pressure.

'One of those factors is parathyroid hormone (PTH), which influences the cell membrane and enhances the entry of calcium into the cell,' Dr Villar told us. 'We think that too much PTH means too much calcium in the cell and, consequently, increased blood pressure. Yet that's just what you get with a *low* calcium diet. On the other hand, increasing the amount of calcium in the diet *decreases* the PTH levels. Less calcium moves across the cell membranes, arteries remain open and blood pressure goes down.'

In fact, that's the theory behind calcium blockers, the newest drugs on the market for high blood pressure. According to Dr Villar, calcium blockers may decrease the blood pressure levels in much the same way as increasing calcium intake does. Both work to reduce intercellular concentration of calcium and produce relaxation of the smooth muscles.

For pregnant women, developing hypertension means the difference between healthy, trouble-free childbirth and a disaster. That's why Dr Villar is so pleased with the results of a study of his that was published in the *American Journal of Obstetrics and Gynecology*.

'Blood pressure is different in pregnant women than in non-pregnant women,' Dr Villar explained to us. 'Usually blood pressure is lower than normal in the second trimester of pregnancy and higher than normal in the third trimester. We wanted to see what would happen to blood pressure readings if calcium were given.

'We divided our volunteers into three groups. One group received 1 g of calcium per day, another group got 2 g, and the third group took a placebo. At the end of the experiment, we found that blood pressure increased as usual in the third trimester for the placebo group, while the group receiving 1 g of calcium had only a small rise in theirs. But the 2 g group had *no* increase in blood pressure at all in the last third of their pregnancy.

'Normally, the [US] RDA [Recommended Dietary Allowance] for pregnant women is 1200 mg,' says Dr Villar. 'But we got the best results with 2000 mg. Our data suggest that a 2000 mg RDA would probably bring the women close to the desired intake.'

If that's the case, then most people aren't getting nearly enough. What's more, it seems that the older people are, the less calcium they ingest – just when they need it most.

In a study done in London, researchers found that increasing age was associated with a significant decrease in total serum (blood) calcium and significant increases in blood pressure. 'Our findings,' say the researchers, 'provide further evidence for the importance of serum calcium as a correlate of blood pressure' (*Lancet*, 27 November 1982).

Getting enough calcium in your diet means consuming milk, cheese and yogurt, sardines, shellfish and salmon, dark green vegetables, watercress and parsley.

'The truth is that humans can adapt to very low calcium intakes,' points out

Dr Villar. 'But we don't know yet what the ultimate consequences of these deficiencies are. This report and other calcium-restriction studies in animals seem to indicate that the adaptation to low calcium intakes could lead to increased blood pressure. Inversely, high calcium intake, which is associated with lower blood pressure, may produce a protective effect against hypertension, at least in laboratory rats.'

Cynthia Morris heartily agrees. In fact, both researchers are in the midst of new experiments that test directly calcium's effect on high blood pressure. 'Since calcium works to lower the blood pressure in normal people, we are now testing its effectiveness on known hypertensives,' Ms Morris told us.

'We are going to try calcium to treat moderate increases in blood pressure in pregnant and non-pregnant women,' adds Dr Villar. 'We don't plan to test it on chronic or really high blood pressure, though. We think that calcium is best used as a preventive rather than as a treatment. After all, if you live a lifestyle for 20 to 25 years that facilitates high blood pressure, then starting on calcium isn't going to erase all that damage. In fact, trying to prevent increased blood pressure with calcium alone won't work if the rest of your life is crazy. But if, for example, you keep your weight down and limit the stress in your life, then adding more calcium may give you that extra margin of safety.'

The benefits of magnesium

A team of doctors, headed by Robert Whang, from the Veterans Administration Medical Center in Oklahoma City, recently completed a study that examined the magnesium and potassium levels of 1000 people being treated with diuretics (pills to reduce water retention) and other common medications for high blood pressure.

The patients were divided into four groups according to their magnesium and potassium levels. Group one had low magnesium and low potassium; group two, low magnesium and normal potassium; group three, normal magnesium and low potassium; group four, normal levels of both. The researchers then observed how each of the patients in the four groups responded to anti-hypertensive drugs.

'Patients with low serum magnesium, regardless of the level of potassium, required a greater number of anti-hypertensive drugs for the same degree of control of their blood pressure than patients with normal magnesium levels,' said the researchers.

What's more, 'this study has demonstrated that hypomagnesemia [low magnesium levels] as well as hypokalemia [low potassium levels] occur with regularity in treated ambulatory hypertensive patients.' The researchers found that about 5 per cent of their patients had low magnesium levels, but they were quick to point out that this greatly understates the problem. That's because the level they used as 'normal' was actually much lower than the usual 'normal' range for their hospital. More important, however, is the finding that low magnesium levels may be caused by the diuretics given for high blood pressure and, in turn, may interfere with the effectiveness of other blood-pressure medications.

This study, said Dr Whang, suggests that magnesium as well as potassium supplementation may be important in the treatment of patients with high blood pressure (*Journal of the American College of Nutrition*, vol. 1, no. 4, 1982).

If you're beginning to wonder if you're getting enough magnesium every day, take a close look at your diet. Do you eat whole grains and wholemeal bread? They are excellent sources of magnesium. Nuts, spinach, black treacle, brown rice and soyabeans supply a hearty amount, too.

A deficiency of magnesium is not as uncommon as you might think. Dietary surveys have shown that average diets often contain only 200 to 250 mg of magnesium per day. This is far below the US RDA of 300 to 400 mg per day for adults, says Mildred S. Seelig of the New York University Medical Center. 'Until we can define, more precisely, how much magnesium is needed for health maintenance at different ages and under different physiologic, pathologic, dietary and environmental conditions, it is better to provide more than less magnesium,' says Dr Seelig.

For maintenance in adults, Dr Seelig recommends that women get at *least* 340 mg and men between 500 and 700 mg per day. That should provide 'a margin of safety that will meet needs even under conditions of increased requirements' such as heavy stress. 'Whether increasing the magnesium intake of humans might reduce the incidence and severity of diseases with characteristics like those seen in magnesium deficiency is a provocative possibility,' Dr Seelig speculates.

High fibre, low blood pressure

Few people even suspect that dietary fibre has anything to do with blood pressure, yet a series of experiments reported in the late 1970s should lead any person concerned about preventing high blood pressure to pay more attention to the fibre in his or her diet. One of the things found by the British researchers, all from the University of Southampton, was that, on the average, people who eat a lot of fibre tend to have lower blood pressure than those who eat relatively little fibre.

Interesting, but is there anything more to it? To find out, the scientists asked some of the people who were used to eating a high-fibre diet to switch to a low-fibre one. Then they asked the people who normally ate a low-fibre diet to eat more fibre, mostly in the form of wholemeal bread and bran.

The result? The blood pressure of those eating the low-fibre diet went *up*, while the blood pressure of those eating the high-fibre diet went *down* (*British Medical Journal*, 15 December 1979). Evidently, the observed relationship between fibre and blood pressure is no mere happenstance.

It's been known for some time that fat in the diet influences blood pressure, so more experiments were carried out to see how fibre would fit into this picture. What emerged was the finding that when the people eating the low-fibre diet – and developing higher blood pressure – were given polyunsaturated fat instead of the saturated fat that they normally ate, their blood pressure went down. But the protection may also work the other way around, at least in laboratory animals. Earlier work carried out at the same university showed that when rabbits were given a diet high in saturated fat (which produced high blood pressure), much of the increase could be blocked by feeding them a high-fibre diet. Inasmuch as most people in Britian eat a diet unhealthily high in saturated fat, and in view of the fact that high blood pressure is a major health problem today, this animal experiment may have important implications.

There is still more evidence that dietary fibre has an effect on blood pressure, and this time it's not from laboratory animals, but from human beings. The research was done on 12 men, aged 37 to 58, who were given either a low-fibre or a high-fibre diet to eat for 26 days. At the end of that time, each group changed over to eat the other kind of diet for another 26 days. Meanwhile, scientists from the Nutrition Institute of the USDA and from the College of Human Ecology at the University of Maryland carried out a large number of tests to determine the effect of the different diets.

One finding was that the average blood pressure of the group after eating the low-fibre diet was 117/80, while after the high-fibre diet it was 114/74. That looks like an interesting reduction, but technically, it's not what is called a 'statistically significant difference.' In other words, there's at least some possibility that it could have happened by chance alone. However, when they checked the difference on the six men out of the 12 who had diastolic pressures of 80 or more on a low-fibre diet, the scientists were intrigued to discover that the average blood pressure had dropped from 123/88 to 118/78 after just 26 days of the high-fibre diet. And that *is* a statistically significant difference. Apparently, the beneficial effect of fibre is more pronounced in people who need the reduction the most. (*American Journal of Clinical Nutrition*)

Here's another interesting fact about this study, which was carried out by June L. Kelsay and colleagues: the amount of fibre that the men ate was not unrealistically high. In fact, they ate no bran, or even any whole-wheat products at all. Nearly all the fibre came from common fruits and vegetables such as carrots, cabbage, spinach, broccoli, squash (marrow), blueberries and oranges. Except for the fibre, the diets were designed to be the same in terms of calories, fat and other aspects, so that any changes in metabolism could be attributed to the fibre alone. It's possible, of course, that there would be even more of a beneficial effect on blood pressure with more fibre. It would be relatively easy to do that, without going overboard, just by eating a single serving each day of such fibre-rich foods as beans, nuts, wheat germ or bran.

The likelihood that fibre has a beneficial effect on blood pressure fits in with several other scientific observations made in recent years. It's been reported, for instance, that people who tend to eat more fibre have a relatively low rate of coronary heart disease. Why this is so isn't known, but it could be because fibre tends to control blood pressure, which is, of course, a major contributor to heart disease.

It's also known that vegetarians have relatively less heart disease than their meat-eating counterparts, and here again, the reason could be that vegetarians eat more fibre and consequently have lower blood pressures. In fact, there already is a study of vegetarians showing that they do tend to have low pressures and that those vegetarians who eat no animal products whatsoever (i.e. vegans), not even eggs, for instance, have the lowest blood pressures of all (*American Journal of Epidemiology*). Researchers in Western Australia, in a study reported in the *British Medical Journal* (6 December 1980), found that, when 58 people with mild hypertension were persuaded to eat a vegetarian diet which also included eggs, milk and extra fruit and vegetables, their systolic blood pressure (i.e. when the heart beats) fell by 5mm of mercury. The Australian researchers reckon that this seemingly small difference could reduce the number of heart attacks in men aged 55–59 years old by about 7 per cent.

One way to interpret these findings is to suspect that meat or animal products tend to cause high blood pressure. But the other possibility is that the additional fibre that must be eaten when you avoid such fibre-free foods as meat, butter, milk and eggs is actually helping to prevent any unhealthy elevation of blood pressure.

Twelve steps to avoid high blood pressure

1 Reduce your sugar intake

The average Briton consumes over 90lb of sugar per year, and although it's yet to be proved that people who consume large quantities of sugar, soft drinks and baked goods run the risk of increasing their blood pressure, animal studies do suggest such an effect. One experiment on monkeys showed that adding sugar to a high-salt diet makes the blood pressure jump even higher than with salt alone (*American Journal of Clinical Nutrition*, March 1980).

In a study at the University of Maryland, a team of scientists headed by Richard A. Ahrens examined the effects of sugar on blood pressure in rats. They found that even moderate levels of sugar in the diet significantly raised the animals' blood pressure (*Journal of Nutrition*, April 1980).

'There has been a lot of criticism over the years of studies linking sucrose [table sugar] to hypertension, heart disease, diabetes,' Dr Ahrens told us. 'People like Fred Stare at Harvard have been defending sucrose, saying whenever a study comes out that the levels of sucrose fed were higher than the average person eats.

'So we were very careful to stay within the range of typical sugar consumption in this country [about $3^{1}/_{2}$ oz per day in the US]. The highest levels we fed were 20 per cent of the total calories in the diet. We observed striking changes in blood pressure as low as the 10 per cent level.'

In an earlier study, Dr Ahrens discovered that sugar causes problems for men as well as for rats (*Federation Proceedings*). 'We found that people fed sucrose experienced significant elevations of blood pressure. This was a five-week study. At an intake of 200g (approximately 7 oz) of sucrose a day, the blood pressure averaged 5 points higher. Those eating 200g averaged 78 points diastolic, while those who were not eating any sucrose averaged 73 points diastolic. That was a change of 5 points in five weeks.'

Again, the introduction of sugar into the diet throws the complex regulatory systems of the body out of whack. In his research with rats, Dr Ahrens found that sucrose in the diet seemed to depress the production of sucrose in the body and that in turn lowered the amount of sodium excreted from the body. Sodium, of course, has been implicated as an important cause of high blood pressure. The more sugar you eat, the more sodium is retained in the body, and the higher the blood pressure. That's the general hypothesis, but exactly how each of the steps leads to the next has not yet been determined.

2 Eliminate caffeine

That means giving up coffee, tea, chocolate and many soft drinks. But it's worth it: doctors at Vanderbilt University School of Medicine in Nashville, Tennessee, found a 14 per cent rise in blood pressure after volunteers consumed the equivalent of about two cups of coffee (250mg of caffeine). This suggests, say the researchers, that habitual coffee drinking or other caffeine consumption could elevate a marginal blood pressure level into hypertension (*New England Journal of Medicine*). So it's better to switch to decaffeinated beverages to be on the safe side.

3 Eat more onions and garlic

Some folk remedies really work. And doctors are now finding scientific reasons why they do. People have claimed for years, for example, that onions reduce high blood pressure. Now we know why. Chemical analysis of onions confirmed the presence of prostaglandin A_1 a hormone-like substance that can lower blood pressure.

Garlic has also been lauded for its ability to lower blood pressure. In one study, scientists from the Bulgarian Academy of Sciences in Sofia tested extracts of garlic on 46 hypertensive patients. Most of those tested showed a drop in blood pressure of about 20 points, as well as a pronounced decrease in physical symptoms (*American Journal of Chinese Medicine*, Autumn 1979).

(*See also* HEART DISEASE.)

4 Avoid alcohol

We all know that alcohol probably isn't the best thing for our health, but, on the other hand, a few glasses of beer or wine a week won't hurt, right? It doesn't look that way, say researchers at the University of Tasmania, in Australia. They completed a study that provides evidence suggesting 'any alcohol consumption is associated with increased blood pressure' (*Medical Journal of Australia*, 23 August 1980). The researchers interviewed 85 physically active men, asking about their age, height, weight, smoking habits, family history, salt consumption and alcohol intake. They also took the men's blood pressures. Then they analysed the information they had collected.

Their conclusions? That of all those variables considered, alcohol consumption appeared to be the main contributor to high blood pressure. Further, that up to 10 per cent of all hypertension could be the result of alcohol consumption.

5 Don't smoke

If you've kicked the smoking habit – or are still trying to – here's another good reason for staying away from that infernal weed.

A group of researchers in Dunedin, New Zealand determined that, among people with mild cases of high blood pressure, smokers are more likely than non-smokers to lapse into a more severe 'accelerated' form of the disease.

The researchers compared 58 people suffering from severe hypertension with a matched control group of 58 people with mild cases of hypertension. Thirty-eight of the severe cases smoked cigerettes regularly, while only 26 of the mild cases smoked. Ruling out the possibility that high blood pressure could make a person want to smoke, the researchers concluded that cigarettes may not cause high blood pressure but they might make it worse (*New Zealand Medical Journal*, 25 June 1980).

6 Lose weight

Sure it's difficult to lose weight, whether it's 5lb or 50lb, but when it comes to high blood pressure, you may be surprised to learn that you don't have to take it all off to get results. That's what researchers at the UCLA School of Medicine found out when they tested 25 obese patients. After a 12-week controlled reducing diet, there was a significant decrease in blood pressure to the normal range in all patients who had started out with hypertension.

Furthermore, say the researchers, these reductions do not necessitate that the patients attain ideal body weight, since only 24 per cent reached that goal. A 10 to 30 per cent reduction towards ideal body weight appeared to be sufficient to lower blood pressure, since blood pressure was significantly reduced in all the patients, whether they had started out hypertensive or not (*New England Journal of Medicine*, 16 April 1981).

7 Exercise

Aerobic exercises such as running, brisk walking and cycling can help you run away from high blood pressure. Robert Cade, professor of medicine at the University of Florida in Gainesville, has been studying the relationship between blood pressure and exercise for about ten years – ever since he cured his own hypertension by jogging every afternoon.

In the laboratory, Dr Cade studied the effect of exercise on 370 hypertensive volunteers, measuring their blood pressure before and after several fast-paced 20-minute rides on a stationary bicycle. 'About 96 per cent of the patients showed a significant drop in blood pressure after three months of exercise,' says Dr Cade. And the improvements were impressive – anywhere from 10 to 50 points down.

8 Learn to relax

Just as important as revving up your motor is winding it down. That's where relaxation techniques come in.

According to Herbert Benson, associate professor of medicine at Harvard Medical School, patients with high blood pressure should be instructed to practise relaxation techniques for 20 minutes, one or two times a day. They should sit in a comfortable position, close their eyes, concentrate on relaxing each muscle group individually, and repeat a word or phrase of their choosing each time they exhale. Patients who practise this type of meditation, which is simple to learn, may significantly decrease their blood pressure (*Lancet*). (*See also* 'How to train yourself to relax', pp 312–315.)

9 Learn to talk more slowly

It's true. People who have high blood pressure are usually very fast talkers. 'Some hypertensives don't put commas in their sentences,' says James J. Lynch. 'And they don't breathe properly, either – not while they're speaking, anyway. The result is a rapid elevation of their blood pressure.'

Dr Lynch, who is professor of psychiatry at the University of Maryland School of Medicine in Baltimore, has been able to demonstrate blood-pressure response to rapid talking through the use of new computer-controlled equipment. 'Traditionally, blood pressure has always been taken with a cuff and a stethoscope,' Dr Lynch told us. 'This method requires silence from both the patient and the doctor. The new automated blood-pressure monitor allows the doctor to record the rises in blood pressure during conversation and other routine special interactions, because a stethoscope is not used.

'For the first time, we were able to see blood pressure as a dynamic interactive system. We found that virtually everyone's blood pressure goes up (anywhere from 10 to 50 per cent) within 30 seconds after speaking begins. But hypertensives are the most reactive. The higher a person's blood pressure when quiet, the more it goes up when speaking. We examined almost 2000 people – from newborn babies, to the elderly, normotensives, hypertensives, and it happened virtually every time.

'Now we are able to use this information to treat hypertension patients without drugs. And some of those who are on drugs have been weaned off them.

'Basically, what we do is teach patients how to speak more slowly, and we teach them how to breathe while they speak. They learn to put the commas back into their speech – the "comma" being the pause for a breath of air.'

Apparently, the method works. Dr Lynch and his associates have successfully treated 30 patients so far and have followed some of them for as long as three years. 'And some of these were the so-called "last resort" patients . . . the ones whose medications were no longer doing the job and whose hypertension was out of control,' adds Dr Lynch. 'Within five months, we got them down to normotensive levels – with *no drugs*. The results have held, too, through two to three years of follow-up. It takes a good deal of work and determination from the patients, but as they start feeling better, it motivates them to continue.

'This is not a quick cure or a gimmick,' Dr Lynch points out. 'It's a gradual resetting of the body, downward. And it's a workable alternative to drugs.'

10 Shut out disturbing noises

We mean everyday noises, like alarm clocks jangling, loud work-place noises, car engines, even televisions blaring. Noises like these can cause blood pressure to soar. It did in an experiment with monkeys. Researchers had the monkeys listen to the ordinary sounds of a worker's life for nine months. During that time, blood pressure went up an average of 27 per cent. When the experiment was over and the noises stopped, the raised pressure persisted for at least a month (*Science*, 27 March 1981).

11 Get a pet

A dog, a cat, even a tankful of fish can have beneficial effects on your blood pressure, according to Aaron H. Katcher, associate professor of psychiatry at the University of Pennsylvania.

'Companion animals, in particular, provide an access to intimacy.' Dr Katcher told us. 'You talk to your pet more slowly, you smile a great deal, voice tones become gentle, the cadence of speech changes. It's a much more relaxed dialogue, characterized by a combination of touching and talking. Pets exert a calming influence throughout the day, which probably has a lot to do with the blood-pressure-lowering effects. In the patients we've studied so far, a 12 to 15 per cent drop in blood pressure has been recorded in the presence of pets.

'In fact, anything that turns your attention outward to the natural environment around you is a powerful way of controlling tension, thereby lowering blood pressure,' continued Dr Katcher. 'That's because it interrupts your pattern of silent worrying – the kind of internal dialogue that you have with yourself about everything that's wrong with your life. Just looking at a tank of tropical fish, gazing into an open fire or watching waves on a beach, all have a kind of stress-reducing effect. They have extremely hypnotic qualities because they are phenomena which are always different yet always the same.

'By considering the interactions of the non-human world around us, we can build a more complete therapeutic programme for outpatients who have high blood pressure or other illnesses.'

12 Take your own blood pressure

Doctors used to think that patients might be made anxious by knowledge of their own blood pressure, thereby causing it to increase. But it doesn't work that way. Instead, several studies found that most patients felt reassured by doing it themselves. This sense of well-being or security may account, at least in part, for the decrease in blood pressure that many of these patients experienced.

That's what happened in a study conducted at the University of Washington in Seattle. Blood-pressure readings were taken at home twice a day for one month by 60 volunteers with hypertension. At the end of the month, significant decreases in blood pressure (10 points or more) occurred in 43 per cent of those tested. If further studies support this observation, say the researchers, then 'home blood pressure readings should be used on a wider scale for treatment purposes. They are easier to administer than other behavioural treatments (such as biofeedback), and the observed decreases appear to be of the same order of magnitude' (*American Heart Journal*, November 1979). (*See also* STRESS.)

• Hospital malnutrition

Surgery is one of those things we like to think usually happens to somebody else. However, operations are becoming more frequent instead of less, so chances are pretty good there's a scalpel out there with your name on it.

If and when that time comes, is there anything you can do to better your chances of a successful, uncomplicated operation and a speedy recovery?

Yes. Figure that your surgeon, however expert he or she is with a scalpel, is a rank amateur when it comes to nutritionally preparing your body for surgery.

It's the rare surgeon who checks a patient carefully for pre-operative vitamin deficiencies. And after the operation, the surgeon expects an intravenous solution to supply all your nutritional needs. A popular handbook for American doctors reads:

> The well-nourished and reasonably healthy patient, who is subjected to a single and relatively uncomplicated major surgical procedure, or who suffers moderately severe trauma, does well in the immediate postoperative period with a relatively simple program of parenteral infusion.

What that means is that all the surgeon has to worry about is if the sugar water is plugged into your vein. What follows *this* introduction is a discussion of the finer points of intravenous cuisine.

Now, intravenous feeding may be a life-saver in cases where the patient is unconscious or otherwise unable to take food by mouth. But gadgets such as the IV feeding bag have a way of flooding over the boundaries between use and *overuse*. And that's a dangerous trend, because 'parenteral nutrition,' as doctors call it to give it the offical sound of high technology, is often *mal*nutrition.

The use of parenteral feeding regimens 'can only satisfy a small portion of the nutritional requirements of a debilitated patient,' says Michael Bresner in the *Journal of Oral Surgery*. Dr Bresner goes on to calculate how many calories a patient could be expected to receive during a day of intravenous feeding. Arriving at a total of 600, he says,

> This is about a quarter of the needs of a healthy individual and far less than the convalescing, debilitated patient requires. It, therefore, becomes apparent that an adequate or concentrated nutritional diet should be resumed as soon as possible. In light of this, the established pathway of prolonged parenteral fluids, clear-liquid diet, full-liquid diet, soft diet and regular diet may not be adequate for the increased nutritional demands.

Problems with IV feeding

Intravenous feeding can cause other problems. Worthington G. Schenk, Jr., professor of surgery at the State University of New York at Buffalo School of Medicine, warns that 'amino acid imbalances in patients with multiple injuries have been aggravated by inappropriate use of intravenous glucose.' Dr Schenk says that critically ill patients should not be maintained on intravenous feedings for long periods. (*Journal of the American Medical Association.*).

Doctors at St Joseph's Hospital, McMaster University, Hamilton, Ontario, found deficiencies in both folic acid and vitamin B_{12} in four of their patients maintained on intravenous feeding. They recommended that 'all patients receiving TPN [total parenteral nutrition] for more than three weeks should probably receive folic acid and vitamin B_{12} supplements routinely' (*Canadian Medical Association Journal*).

Although intravenous feeding may be more convenient to the nursing staff and more technologically satisfying to the surgeon, it definitely hasn't resulted in better nutrition for surgical patients. Quite the opposite – a series of recent studies has uncovered widespread serious malnutrition among surgical patients.

One report of surgeons' neglect of their patient's' nutrition comes from a group of doctors at the General Infirmary in Leeds. All 105 patients in the surgical wards were examined for protein-calorie malnutrition, anaemia and vitamin deficiencies. Abnormally low values in all these nutritional standards were found to be common. But what is even more interesting is that the worst nutritional levels were found in the patients who had undergone major surgery and were in the hospital more than a week afterwards. More than half of these people had lost too much weight and were suffering from protein – calorie malnutrition. Blood levels of vitamin C were too low in 46 per cent, riboflavin in 36 per cent, folic acid in 27 per cent, and vitamin B_6 in 18 per cent; 37 per cent were anaemic. G. L. Hill and seven other colleagues found that only 22 of the surgical patients had any mention at all of nutrition in their notes, that all but five of these comments were merely short ones, that only 17 patients had ever been weighed during their hospital stay, and that only five patients had any record of any kind of nutritional therapy at all.

So, as Dr Hill concluded, 'these abnormalities had gone almost entirely unrecognized, even in patients with sepsis [toxins in their blood or tissues] after major surgery, who would benefit from improvement in nutritional state' (*Lancet*).

In a Boston, Massachusetts municipal hospital, Dr Bruce R. Bistrian and three colleagues found that *half of the surgical patients were malnourished* in the two most basic nutrients: protein and calories. 'This report,' concluded the researchers, 'confirms recent studies suggesting that nutritional support of hospitalized patients has been neglected' (*Journal of the American Medical Association*).

Both Dr Bistrian and Dr Hill, in lamenting the sorry state of nutritional care in modern hospitals, suggest that medical schools should pay a lot more attention to nutrition. That's a good idea, but it's not going to help you if you need surgery before a new crop of doctors trained in nutrition reaches the hospitals. Until then, you're on your own. Since your doctor probably doesn't know, and may not even *care*, which nutrients you need to heal fast and free of complications, you're going to have to take some extra measures with your diet. And in case you have to explain them to your doctor, you're also going to need to know why you're taking these extra measures.

Your body needs help to heal itself

The surgeon's knife is going to make extra demands on your body's ability to heal itself, so you have to hustle some super-nutrition into your life. Since the circumstances that lead to surgery often rob you of nutrients, you might be entering the hospital with a deficiency in one or more vital food elements.

For example, pain or discomfort may keep your appetite down so you don't eat as well as you should. Vomiting, diarrhoea and bleeding can also rob your system of important nutrients. Simply *worrying* about your operation can put your nerves into overdrive and raise your requirements. Finally, just lying in bed for a few days waiting for your turn in the operating theatre speeds up the rate of protein breakdown in your tissues. If you're not replacing it in your diet, you'll go into that operation with a dangerous protein deficit.

And don't forget that surgery itself is an injury, too, as far as your body is concerned. The only difference is that the surgical wound is made under sterile conditions, which lessen the chances of infection.

However, even under ideal operating conditions, healing a wound demands an enormous effort. You may be using up nutrients *twice* as fast as normal. New tissue must be manufactured and laid down in just the right places. Infection must be kept at bay. Your nutrient requirements, as Dr Bresner says, 'should be greater than the minimum requirements to provide a ready reserve against variations in health and disease.' He says a surgeon should examine the state of a patient's nutrition and delay operating until any deficiencies can be corrected through dietary changes and supplements.

That's good advice if your surgeon knows which nutrients are especially important to healing, but as we pointed out, the chances of that happening are about as great as a plumber knowing how to take out your appendix. So you're going to have to do it yourself. And the time to start is now, because if you ever need emergency surgery, there won't be time to build yourself up nutritionally.

We're not suggesting you start *now* taking all these nutrients in the quantities needed by surgical patients. Don't do that until the time comes to prepare for surgery and to speed healing after your operation. But you will want to start right now looking at your diet and seeing whether or not you're adequately supplied with these nutrients for the everyday strains and stresses and the little bumps and bruises that might not call for anaesthesia and stitches but none the less still make for some extra effort on the part of your healing machinery.

Getting enough calories

First, you should know how to avoid the form of malnutrition that seems to be most common in surgical wards – protein – calorie malnutrition.

Calories are the most basic element of your diet. *Modern Nutrition in Health and Disease* (1964 edition) states, 'The ideal minimum requirement for a patient postoperatively or a patient with trauma [injury] or infection should be 3000 calories.' Dr Bresner says that a feverish, 'severely injured patient may use as many as 4000 calories per day.' A severely burned patient, because of the enormous amount of tissue that must be repaired, might require as many as 5000 calories a day.

If you don't get enough calories in your diet, your body will break down protein for energy. But your body also needs that protein to use as raw material for healing. So a deficiency of calories can lead to some real problems during convalescence.

Since calories are so fundamental, all food contains calories. So if calories were all you had to worry about, getting the right foods would be a simple numbers game and this entry could end here.

Naturally, there's more to it. Your body needs the fuel that calories provide, but which foods those calories come from can make the difference between a speedy recovery and a long, painful convalescence. So you should choose your calories in terms of the other nutrients you need. Of course, that's true even when you're not scheduled for surgery, but now the game is a lot faster, and the stakes are a lot higher. You will want as many odds as possible in your favour before you're wheeled into the operating theatre.

The critical need for protein

Your body is going to need all the protein it can get for ready use in healing and infection fighting. Low protein levels make infection a more likely possibility, delay healing of fractures and wounds, cause anaemia and poor tissue repair, and disturb the function of the heart and the liver.

If you're deficient in protein, the normal stresses of surgery, such as minor blood loss and anaesthesia, could put your body in a state of shock. And shock, which is a drastic, life-threatening, sudden lowering of the blood pressure to the point where blood almost stops circulating, is even more dangerous on the operating table.

How much protein do your need? Dr Bresner says that a convalescing person needs about twice as much as a normal, healthy person. That means you're going to have to eat a lot more of the foods that provide protein.

For example, a medium-size egg supplies 6 g of protein; 8 fl oz of milk, 8 g; a small piece of chicken, 8 g; a 3 oz serving of calf's liver, 25 g; and 2¹/₂ oz peanuts, 19 g. If you ate all of these in one day, you would get 66 g of protein.

Since a healthy person requires about 1 g of protein for every 2.2 lb of body weight, 66 g of protein would be enough for a person who weighed about 10 stone. However, if that person had wounds to heal, he or she would need twice as much protein, or about 132 g. So besides eating more of these particular foods, a convalescing person would have to find some other high-protein foods: 6¹/₂ oz of diced beef or mince, for example, supplies about 36 g of protein; 8 oz of cottage cheese supplies 30 g. These two foods alone would supply the additional 66 g of protein a person who weighs 10 stone would need.

Sometimes convalescing people don't have the appetite to get down high-protein foods. Eggs, non-fat dried milk and whole milk can be whipped up with a little honey and baked into a custard that even a person whose appetite isn't that strong will find palatable.

If you eat plenty of high-protein foods – e.g. milk, eggs, cottage cheese, fish, poultry, liver and wheat germ – *before* your operation, you won't need to correct a deficiency, only to maintain the high level of protein that's already in your blood, healing your injuries or surgical wounds and keeping them healed.

Vitamins in special demand

Protein and calories are not all that matter. As surgeon Harold A. Zintel says, 'The importance of vitamin therapy in seriously ill surgical patients might be emphasized in a simple analogy. It is, of course, useless to supply abundant amounts of lumber, steel and bricks for the repair of a damaged building if hammers, nails, bolts and cement are not available to fashion the former materials into a functioning part of the building. It is just as foolish to provide carbohydrate, fat, protein and potential calories in the presence of subclinical vitamin deficiencies and expect the body to restore a functioning part or parts of the body efficiently.'

Vitamin A This heads the list of vitamins essential to healing. In order for your surgical wound to heal, collagen, – the 'cement' that holds tissue together – must be laid down between new cells. Vitamin A influences the rate at which the new collagen is linked, so your vitamin A status has a lot to do with how fast and how well you heal.

The wound healing of animals given vitamin A was better than that of non- supplemented animals in experiments performed by Eli Seifter and his colleagues at the Albert Einstein College of Medicine in New York.

Apparently, the worse your wound, the more vitamin A you need. Severely injured persons, such as burn and accident victims, can actually develop stress ulcers as a result of the trauma they are going through. An Arizona study found that, by giving burn, trauma and post-operative patients injections of from 50,000 to 100,000 IU of water-soluble vitamin A twice a day, the incidence of these ulcers could be cut to *less than a third* of what it was in an unsupplemented group (*Journal of Trauma*).

If your doctor gives you the steroid drug cortisone to suppress unwanted inflammation, you'll also need more vitamin A. Cortisone also inhibits wound healing, but vitamin A, taken internally or applied directly to the wound, can counteract this effect and restore normal healing.

Thiamin (vitamin B₁) This is necessary for the utilization of carbohydrates. The more carbohydrates in your diet, the more thiamin you need. One study has shown that people on intravenous feeding can develop a thiamin deficiency in as short a time as four or five days. And long before a really severe deficiency develops, symptoms such as loss of appetite, irritability, pain and lack of interest in important matters show up – just the kind of things that can make convalescence agonizing.

Riboflavin (vitamin B₂) This is necessary for the utilization of protein. Since protein is the raw material for wound healing, a riboflavin deficiency will keep you in that hospital bed longer than you have to be.

Niacin (*nicotinic acid*) This B vitamin is necessary for the utilization of both protein *and* carbohydrates. And, apparently, the first body function to suffer when there's a deficiency of niacin is the use of protein for repair. Later on in a deficiency, nervousness, depression, loss of appetite, redness of the tongue, ulceration of the gums and diarrhoea develop.

Pantothenic acid This B vitamin is important to the storage and ultilization of protein. It also plays a role in the proper functioning of the adrenal glands, which govern the body's response to stress. An injury, burn or operation is probably the most highly concentrated stress anyone ever experiences. So you don't want your adrenal glands to become exhausted when you need them most.

Pyridoxine (Vitamin B₆) This is also necessary for efficient use of protein. Pyridoxine is vital to the body's response to foreign invaders – which can include infecting organisms. So a deficiency can lead to a greater chance of developing an infection that will slow healing and keep you laid up longer.

Folic acid This B vitamin helps maintain and restore the red blood cells, and it aids in the development of white blood cells (leucocytes) which are the mainstay of the body's defence against infection.

Vitamin B$_{12}$ This also has a vital role in the function of the red blood cells and keeps the body's ultilization of protein as efficient as possible.

Biotin Another B vitamin, this may be important to the body's use of protein. One study which shows that biotin levels are low in the blood of children with burns and scalds suggests that the vitamin may be required for tissue repair (*Journal of Clinical Pathology*).

Viatmin C This should be at the heart of your 'nutrition under the knife'. The most important link in the healing chain of events is the formation of collagen, the glue that holds cells together and makes healing possible. If there's not enough vitamin C in your system, collagen production will be inadequate. Your wounds won't heal. And there's a good chance of that happening if you're not careful, because after any serious injury – surgical wounds included – the body's metabolism of protein and water-soluble vitamins gets jolted into high gear. You can quickly start needing a lot more than you have.

The consequences of running out of vitamin C can be disastrous. A study of over 1400 surgical patients with infections confirmed that their blood levels of vitamin C were as low as those of people with scurvy (*Journal of the American Dietetic Association*). If this happens to you, though, chances are your doctors won't write it down in your notes or tell you that you have scurvy. More likely, they'll just say – when your wound starts to fall apart and gets worse instead of healing – that you're not doing quite as well as expected, that there's nothing to worry about, and that you'll have to be in the hospital a week or so longer.

A vitamin C deficiency can let you go further 'down' under the anaesthetic than either you or your surgeon is counting on. And you might end up staying 'down' longer, too. At the very least, getting enough vitamin C may help protect you from painful and persistent bedsores, the curse of long hospital stays. A British study found that by supplementing hospital patients with two 500 mg tablets of vitamin C each day, bedsores healed almost twice as fast. (*Lancet*).

We were not surprised, therefore, when surgeon Philip Thorek, medical director of Thorek Hospital and Medical Center in Chicago, wrote, 'Vitamin C is the surgeon's vitamin' (*New Dynamics of Preventive Medicine*).

Minerals for healing

Potassium Necessary for the utilization of protein.

Iron Important if there is loss of blood.

Calcium Supremely important if there are broken bones to heal.

Zinc This is so critical to healing that its importance cannot be over-emphasized. Surgery, injury, burns and broken bones all call for zinc to perform its healing work. Zinc is vital to the production of collagen and the utilization of protein. It is necessary for normal growth and reproduction of cells. So without zinc, the new cells needed to form new tissue cannot be made.

And once these cells are made, zinc increases their ability to survive. Zinc is also important to the body's response to infection and inflammation. And vitamin A, the first vitamin we talked about, is not mobilized from body stores unless zinc levels are adequate.

With all these facts in mind, it's no wonder that the medical literature is overflowing with reports of how people given supplements of zinc heal much faster than people not given them. One study found that surgical patients given a zinc-supplemented diet appear to have pinker, cleaner, healthier-looking new tissue in their rapidly healing wounds. (*Surgery, Gynecology and Obstetrics*).

The most remarkable of these reports, though, is one in which zinc supplements actually *cut in half* the number of days women had to remain in the hospital after gynaecological surgery. We're not talking about cutting a three-day stay down to a day and a half: the average post-operative stay for the women not receiving the supplements was 37 days, but those who received zinc supplements for a week before their operation were able to go home after *18 days*. The amount of zinc these women received was small: 150 mg spread out over each day.

If your doctor has you packing for the hospital, good nutrition should be the first thing you take along with you. And even if your horizon is clear of surgery right now, your diet should still be supplying adequate amounts of the important nutrients we've been talking about. There may *not* be a scalpel with your name on it. But, after all, that's what health is all about: keeping it that way. (*See also* HEALING PROBLEMS.)

• Hyperactivity and learning disabilities

Johnny doesn't wake up, he blasts off – an unguided missile.

His bath leaves the bathroom floor a swamp and the towels a soggy mess. He yanks clean clothes out of every drawer in his bedroom but rushes half-dressed into the kitchen looking for his shoes. During breakfast, he throws toast at the dog. And when he's given money for an overdue library book, he drops it on the floor and won't pick it up.

Before he falls into a restless sleep at 10.30 that night (to the relief of his tense and exhausted parents), Johnny will have started a fire in a wastebasket, knocked over a lamp, kicked his sister and accompanied this home horror movie with a soundtrack of yelling, whining and loud singing.

Johnny is hyperactive.

No one knows how many children are hyperactive (nor do doctors all agree on this diagnosis) but, for example, it is estimated that there are 10 million hyperactive children in the US alone, 90 per cent of them boys. These children literally terrorize their parents, teachers and friends (if they have any). Their behaviour, says an expert on the subject, 'is sometimes appropriate for a battlefield, not for the classroom, home or playground.'

Johnny is a typical example. Of the over 100 different symptoms of hyperactivity listed in medical journals, he has most of them. His short attention span means that he can't concentrate, and he flits from one project to another. He can't sit through a class, his homework, a meal or a TV programme. He's clumsy. He has trouble skipping, walking in a straight line or throwing a ball where he wants it to go. He reaches for things and knocks them over. His drawings and handwriting are poor, and he can't do anything that requires steadiness and precision. He has trouble even buttoning his shirt.

He's aggressive. He wants to touch – or hit – everyone and everything. And when he gets it into his mind to do something, he can't be stopped – no matter how dangerous it is. (And it's often dangerous to himself. One hyperactive child had a habit of riding his tricycle in front of moving cars). To top it all off, he has trouble sleeping (just getting him into bed is like tucking in a beehive).

Why is Johnny hyperactive?

Experts don't agree about the causes of hyperactivity and learning disabilities. Some say the problems are a matter of genes, tragic but unavoidable defects passed from parent to child. Others hold that complications in pregnancy, such as abnormal labour or maternal illness, are the cause. Still another camp believes that sickness during infancy can damage the brain, resulting in problems when the child grows older. And many theorize that a child's home life – how he interacts with his parents, brothers and sisters – is a major factor.

Well, no matter what anyone *thinks* causes hyperactivity and learning disabilities, some doctors and educators are *curing* them – without using drugs.

The Feingold diet

The late Ben F. Feingold, a paediatrician, allergist and chief emeritus of the department of allergy, Kaiser – Permanente Medical Center in San Francisco, was one of those doctors. He advanced his revolutionary theory about hyperactivity in his book *Why Your Child Is Hyperactive*. Dr Feingold contended that many cases of 'hyperkinesis', or hyperactivity, in children are caused by eating artificial colourings, flavourings and chemical additives. To cure or lessen hyperactivity, he said, was simply a matter of eliminating all additive-containing foods from the diet. He also suggested eliminating foods containing salicylates, a naturally occurring chemical that his research showed might contribute to hyperactivity in some children. (*See table on page 404.*)

Every child consumes food additives – an average of about 5 lb a year. They don't have to try hard: thousands of additives colour, flavour and preserve our food. The additives are, of course, chemicals; most of them are what scientists call low-molecular compounds. Drugs, too, are low-molecular compounds. Could the additives affect the body like a drug? A drug that drives children crazy?

Dr Feingold claimed that, in his practice, up to 50 per cent of the hyperactive children on the 'Feingold diet' improved. And scientific studies continue to back him up. For example, when Arnold Brenner, a paediatrician in Maryland, put 32 of his hyperactive patients on the diet, he didn't want them to get better.

He had a 'desire to disprove the Feingold hypothesis.' Instead, he *proved* it. Eleven of the 32 children had an 'excellent response': a dramatic decrease in hyperactivity, restlessness and distractability. Eight other children 'probably improved', as judged by their teachers, parents and Dr Brenner.

In all, 19 of 32 got better (*Clinical Pediatrics*). When Dr Brenner checked up on the 'excellent' children six months later, he found that three of them had gone off their diet – 'with marked deterioration in their school performance.'

In another study, 31 hyperactive children were given allergy tests to measure their sensitivity to salicylates and artificial colourings and flavourings. Of those who were sensitive, 15 were put on the Feingold diet. All but one of these children, wrote the author of the study, 'responded with improved behaviour in the areas of overactivity, distractability, impulsiveness and excitability. Sleep . . . problems were resolved partially or completely (*Medical Journal of Australia*).

'I have about 30 patients in my practice who are hyperactive,' says Paul Kushner, a paediatrician in a suburb of Philadelphia. 'I've urged all of them to use the Feingold diet, and at least 15 are following it actively. Some had been bad enough to be thrown out of school, but every single one on the diet has shown a significant improvement. All the parents swear by it. I think most other paediatricians would only try it if it had come out of a study from a major institution or if it was fully approved and sanctioned by the American Medical Association.'

Barry Leonard, a New Jersey paediatrician who himself has a hyperactive seven-year-old daughter, has found the Feingold diet to be successful both in his practice and in his own home. 'I've had several successful cases where I was able to take the children off drugs,' he says. 'Some have not been so successful, but that may be because the entire family was not willing to remove all the foods with artificial additives from the house. This has to be done for the diet to work, but the other children in the home may not want to go along with it. The enthusiasm of the physician is also very important.

Foods containing natural salicylates

Salicylate foods may be re-introduced to the diet following four to six weeks of avoidance, provided no history of an allergy to aspirin (which contains salicylates) exists in the individual or his or her family.

Almonds	Currants	Peaches
Apples, Cider and cider vinegar	Gooseberries	Plums and prunes
Apricots	Grapes, Raisins, wine and wine vinegar	Raspberries
Blackberries	Mint	Strawberries
Cherries	Nectarines	Tomatoes
Cloves	Oranges	Oil of wintergreen
Cucumbers and pickles		

SOURCE: Benjamin F. Feingold, *Why Your Child Is Hyperactive* (New York: Random House, 1975).

'We had a problem at first with our own daughter because we keep a kosher home. In other words, since we couldn't have butter with meat, we had always used margarine, but that has additives. We finally found a soyabean margarine in a health food store, which solved that problem,' said Dr Leonard.

Other parents readily testify to the diet's success. After Dr Feingold's book was published, an exhilarated New Jersey mother who found the diet to be successful with her own child started the first chapter of the Feingold Association, to spread the Feingold diet gospel. As more and more parents across the country achieved long-overdue success with this diet-oriented therapy, the number of chapters proliferated so that there are currently about 60.

One of the branches filled with enthusiasm is the Philadelphia-area chapter. Animated Feingolders insist passionately that almost every hyperactive child they know who has followed the diet rigidly has become a dramatic success story.

Kevin is one example.

A Miracle for Kevin

Cynthia had literally tried everything except an exorcist, but her eight-year-old son Kevin still acted more like a wild animal than a human child. She says her life was a living hell from the day she brought the infant boy home from the hospital.

'It started right after I fed him his first commercial baby food,' Cynthia recalled vividly. 'He literally never slept, and he screamed 24 hours a day. The neighbours thought we were monsters, that we were constantly beating the child.

'The first doctor we took Kevin to said the boy had colic. He gave Kevin some medication, but he turned purple and shook all over. That turned me against drugs, and my feeling got even stronger later on when I got a job with a drug company and learned about the side-effects of many drugs. We later learned he had an allergy to milk. But removing dairy products from his diet still didn't solve the problem.'

For several years, Kevin's parents shuffled their son to one doctor after another, but the boy was as intractable as ever. 'We must have taken him to every psychologist, neurologist and paediatrician in Philadelphia, but nothing worked, including two years of psychotherapy.'

The disruption that Kevin's bizarre behaviour caused to his parents' marriage was incalculable. 'My husband and I were always at each other's throats,' Cynthia admitted. 'My in-laws wouldn't come to dinner. We couldn't even go out to a movie or a restaurant because no one would babysit.

You could talk to a wall better than you could talk to my child. I thought he hated me. He could destroy a room in five minutes, and he almost destroyed me. He attacked me physically, and I still have the scars to prove it. If I hadn't walked away from him one night when he was four years old, I could have beaten him to death! On another occasion, my husband got so mad he smashed his fist against a wall in frustration and broke his hand.'

In nursery school, Kevin would throw temper tantrums on the classroom floor, run outdoors in the winter with no coat on, and attempt to strangle other children. Later they found out he had dyslexia (an impairment of the ability to comprehend written language), which they thought caused his frustration, but his disruptive behaviour continued. Finally, Kevin's parents took him to psychologist Robert Fisher ('the zillionth doctor we'd been to'), who suggested they try the Feingold diet.

Since they had tried everything else, they immediately placed Kevin on the diet, completely excluding salicylates (found in many fruits, vegetables and drugs) and foods containing artificial colourings, flavourings and chemical additives.

'After two days on the diet, Kevin actually slept soundly for the first time in his life,' Cynthia related. 'I wanted to wake him up just to tell him how happy I was. It took me a year to get over the shock. We kept him strictly on the Feingold diet, and after a few months there was an absolutely unbelievable difference. Now he's a normal child.

'It's incredible. Kevin actually hugs me now and says, "I love you, Mommy." When I tried to hug him before, he'd hit me with something. There's no possible way to express the gratitude we feel for the Feingold diet.'

The story of Leslie

'Our daughter Leslie was very, very aggressive at three years of age.' said her mother, Herma. 'She had few playmates because no children wanted to play with her. A year later, we took her to a child psychologist, who said what she needed was a speech therapist. So we took her to a speech therapist, but she got so frustrated with Leslie that she refused to let her come back.'

Leslie was sent to a special school in Philadelphia, but her behaviour got worse instead of better. 'The whole neighbourhood knew about her,' Herma recalled. 'She made all of our lives a living hell. Her older sister stopped bringing friends home, and she'd sometimes deny that Leslie was her sister.

'There were also problems with our marriage. My husband suddenly preferred attending business meetings instead of coming home. We never did anything as a family. I don't know how many babysitters we went through. We couldn't go to a restaurant because Leslie would yell. 'I'm not going in!' If she had to wait more than five minutes for food, she'd scream. Once I lost control of myself and slapped her face in a restaurant.

'I couldn't even take her into a doctor's waiting room because she'd start to scream. She'd walk up to other children in a bowling alley or beauty shop and punch them for no reason at all.

'I finally learned about the Feingold diet from a friend. I told her it sounded ridiculous. 'What could artifical colours and flavours in foods possibly have to do with uncontrollable behaviour?' I asked her. I later saw an article in a newspaper about the Feingold diet, so I figured there was something to it after all.

'So I contacted the New Jersey Feingold Association chapter, got a copy of the Feingold diet, and put the whole family on it. We didn't suddenly become the ideal family, but the results have been magnificent. Now she's a real nice kid. Our relationship is wonderful, and my husband and I are no longer complete strangers. The diet has also been more healthy for the rest of us.

'Before Leslie was on the diet, she'd wake up almost every night, walk around in a semi-sleepwalk state and scream out, 'Won't somebody please help me?' When we tried to comfort her, she'd hit us, curse us and kick us. Or I'd wake up in the middle of the night, and she'd be standing there staring at me. These things have only happened once or twice in the 18 months since we started on the diet.'

Another member of the group told us that her ten-year-old son, Eric, used to have a short attention span, no sense of humour, poor muscle coordination and dyslexia in spite of an IQ of 130. He cried very often and was compulsively aggressive.

'My paediatrician assured me that he was just a normal, bright, active child,' she related. 'Later, a psychiatrist told me he was simply 'all boy'. Then, at the age of six, his teacher said he was emotionally disturbed. Finally, a psychologist tested Eric and discovered he was hyperactive with visual perception problems and motor-coordination difficulty.

'After that came two years of drug therapy. While the drugs did calm Eric down, they had drastic side-effects. I watched him burning himself out. You can imagine my relief when I discovered the Feingold diet. I was afraid I was turning my son into a junkie, but within three months of starting the diet, Eric was off drugs, and a normal, happy child. For the first time in his life, he had friends to play with and got along with his friends in school. His dyslexia disappeared, and his only problem now is with motor coordination, which makes writing difficult for him.'

One common mistake made by parents of hyperactive children, is of course, to punish a child severely for wild behaviour. 'Both my husband and I are from families where you got spanked if you didn't behave, but spanking never worked with our son, Keith,' said another mother. 'I finally learned about the Feingold diet from a girlfriend, and it worked wonders. It even relieved the nightly leg cramps suffered by another one of our children, which doctors couldn't even cure.'

'All or nothing'

One of the most important aspects of the Feingold diet is that it is an 'all or nothing' proposition. If a child on the diet takes a single bite of an artificially flavoured or coloured food, it can trigger an almost psychotic reaction that may take two or three days to subside.

'We had one nine-year-old boy who was doing very well on the diet,' says Dr Daniel Kanofsky, who worked with Dr Feingold at the Kaiser – Permanente Clinic in San Francisco. 'His next-door neighbour thought the boy's parents were punishing him unfairly by not giving him sweets and cake, so the neighbour took the boy into her kitchen one day and fed him 10 or 12 biscuits.

'Soon afterwards he had a mini-psychotic episode. He told me he was being controlled by someone on Mars, a type of symptom that's characteristic of schizophrenia. He also said he was hearing music all the time, and his experience was similar to an LSD trip. I've heard similar stories over and over again about kids who went back off the diet. Apparently, these children on the diet lose all tolerance for the chemical additives, and they become extremely sensitive to them.'

A culprit in sugar

One institution that pays close attention to Dr Feingold's theories and other diet-related theories of behaviour is the New York Institute of Child Development in New York City, which treats hyperactive children. Researchers there suspected some time ago that sugar might complicate the problem, and to test their theory, they studied the blood sugar metabolism of 265 children enrolled at the Institute. They found that 74 per cent of the children had an inability to digest and assimilate properly sugar and other refined carbohydrates. And when they put the children on a corrective diet – a low-carbohydrate, high-protein diet that cut out all sugar and emphasized frequent feedings of such foods as cheese, fish, chicken, nuts and eggs, along with fruits and vegetables – the children were no longer hyperactive after two to three weeks.

Based upon evaluation of over 2000 children, the Institute has drawn up a checklist, which should be a useful guide for parents who are trying to track down difficulties related to their children's nutrition.

Typical questions are: Is there a history of allergy in the family? A history of diabetes? Was the child a colicky baby? Did you have feeding problems requiring changes in milk formulas? Were there difficulties in introducing strained and solid baby foods? Is his/her appetite poor? Does he/she crave sweets? Are there other, marked food cravings? Is his/her intake of fruits and vegetables infrequent? Is s/he markedly thirsty? Is s/he markedly sensitive to light, noise or touch? Is s/he subject to many colds or respiratory infections? Is s/he a bed-wetter? Does s/he have dark circles under her/his eyes? A pasty complexion? Skin problems such as eczema? A short attention span?

Staff members of the Institute say that these symptoms are the most common in children whose behavioural and educational problems are related to nutrition.

Other health professionals assert that sugar can disturb learning. 'We change a child's behaviour dramatically by lowering his intake of sugar,' says Patricia Hardman, director of the Woodland Hall Academy in Maitland, Florida, a school for children with hyperkinesis (another name for hyperactivity) and learning disability. 'At Woodland Hall,' she says, 'sugar is eliminated from the diet of every child.'

'If a child comes to school extremely depressed or complains that nothing is going right, or if he flies off the handle and can't be controlled, we ask him what he's been eating. It's almost always the case that the night before he had ice cream or a soft drink or some other food with a lot of sugar.'

'We had one child who was tested for his IQ and scored 140. Three days later, he was tested and scored 100! It turned out that Grandma had come for a visit and that morning had made the child panacakes for breakfast, and, of course, they were smothered in sugary syrup. Well, we waited another three days – three days without sugar – and tested him again. Sure enough, he scored 140. There's no doubt about it. Sugar makes children poor learners.'

Why does sugar cause hyperactivity?

When an excess amount of sugar enters the bloodstream, the body manufactures large amounts of a hormone called insulin to bring blood sugar levels back to normal. The extra insulin, however, sparks the release of other hormones from the adrenal glands that excite the brain and nervous system: a child becomes irritable, overactive and easily upset. Daily overuse of sugar can wreck the mechanisms that regulate blood sugar, leading to *chronic* overactivity, irritability and upset. In short, hyperactivity.

The story of a little girl named Kimberly is typical of a child who was hyperactive because of sugar.

'Sugar makes me mean'

Sugar and spice were what five-year-old Kimberly was supposedly made of, but her parents will tell you that there's nothing nice about a little girl with a disposition like hot pepper. Three months on Ritalin, a mental stimulant commonly prescribed in the US for hyperactive children (but discontinued some years ago in the UK), only made her sleepy and lethargic. It wasn't until the sugar was removed from her diet that Kimberly became a sweet, normal child.

The average American child consumes close to $3^1/_2$ tablespoons of sugar every day, and, according to Ronald J. Prinz of the department of psychology at the University of South Carolina, that's enough to make some hyperactive kids more so. According to Kimberly's mother, it was enough to make her 'mean': 'She had a very nasty temper, and our main concern was that she was up all night. During the day, she was very whiny and would not sit still.'

Kimberly was a participant in one of a series of Dr Prinz's experiments linking sucrose (sugar) consumption with hyperactivity in children. His first study compared sugar in the diets of 28 hyperactive children with that of 28 normal children in a control group and noted 'that sucrose in high amounts might aggravate hyperactive children.' Perhaps more significantly, his initial study concluded that 'it may well be that an association between sucrose consumption and behaviour is not limited to hyperactive children' (*Journal of Consulting and Clinical Psychology*, vol. 48, no. 6, 1980).

Kimberly's entire family has reduced its sugar intake and has switched to fruits and nuts instead of cakes and sweets, and fresh fruit juices instead of sugar-laden soft drinks. Using whole-grain bread rather than white bread has also helped Kimberly's condition.

Kimberly adapted well to the new diet, her mother says, because they implemented it as a game. After a year and a half without sugar, Kimberly feels 'special rather than deprived, especially when her teacher gives her a piece of fruit when the other kids are eating candy.'

Although her parents don't monitor everything Kimberly eats – especially at playmates' homes because 'you don't put a label on your kid' – they can tell if she's eaten sugar by an immediate change in her behaviour. 'But she's aware of it,' her mother adds. 'She even says, "Sugar makes me mean."'

Supplements to help the hyperactive child

Ray C. Wunderlich, a Florida paediatrician and author of a book on hyperactivity, believes that vitamin and mineral supplements also help the hyperactive child.

'Niacin [nicotinic acid] is a truly remarkable substance. In doses of 0.5 g three or four times a day, the behaviour of the hyperactive child is often normalized. And when another of the B vitamins, pantothenic acid, is used, a hyperactive child frequently becomes more interested in group participation.'

Patricia Hardman also uses vitamins at Woodland Hall. 'We have found that aggressive children frequently have deficiencies of vitamin B_{12} and that hyperactive children are often deficient in B_6.'

Another proponent of vitamins for hyperactive children is Allan Cott, a New York psychiatrist. 'Vitamin B_6 is vital in the production of serotonin, a chemical in the body that influences behaviour,' he says. 'Low levels of serotonin produce depression in the adult and hyperactivity in the child.'

Dr Cott's statement is supported by a research study that compared the blood serotonin levels of 11 hyperactive and 11 normal children. The hyperactive children had much lower levels of serotonin in their blood, and when the children were given vitamin B_6, their serotonin levels rose (*Pediatrics*).

'It works as a natural tranquillizer,' he says, 'and has a remarkable calming effect.' And other researchers have found that magnesium and zinc deficiencies are common among hyperactive children (*11th Annual Conference on Trace Substances in Environmental Health*).

Both Dr Cott and Dr Wunderlich prescribe large amounts of vitamin C. 'Allergic conditions frequently respond to high doses of vitamin C,' says Dr Wunderlich. 'And since hyperactivity is often caused by allergy, vitamin C is useful in reducing or eliminating hyperactive behaviour in some children.'

Allergies handicap learning

Dr Wunderlich isn't the only doctor who thinks that allergies are linked to hyperactivity.

'I'm totally convinced that a lot of learning disabilities are caused by kids' adverse reactions to multiple ecological factors – allergies – and if you reduce or neutralize their total allergic load by altering their diet and environment, most of them can be helped,' says Allan Lieberman, a South Carolina paediatrician and clinical ecologist. 'And there's no question we're witnessing an epidemic. Schools [in the United States] are geared for 2 to 4 per cent, but I feel that learning disabilities may affect as many as 20 per cent [one out of every five] of our students.'

Many orthodox allergy specialists are up in arms over this idea. According to William Crook, a Tennessee paediatrician and a long-time champion of the allergy-educational handicap concept, writing in the *Journal of Learning Disabilities* (May 1980): They say,

'This is quackery, witchcraft! You can't talk about allergies unless you can prove there's a mechanism by which they work.' Well, as yet we can't, but doctors use many therapies quite successfully without knowing how they work either.

Based on reports that have appeared in the literature during the last 60 years and my own clinical observations, I am absolutely certain that what a child eats can make him dull, stupid and hyperactive.

Ninety-four per cent of the hyperactive kids I've seen are allergic to foods or food colours of some sort. With an elimination diet, I've found there's a five- or six-to-one chance the behaviour can be controlled without drugs.

'Allergies affect different areas of the brain in different children,' says Doris Rapp, a paediatrician from Buffalo, New York. 'For example, we've seen reading ability plummet from eighth-grade [i.e. age 13 years] to fifth-grade [age 10 years] level because of an allergic challenge. And in one particularly graphic study, we noticed handwriting changes. The children's writing became large, irregular, upside down – there was letter reversal, even mirror-image writing.'

The Jekyll-and-Hyde nature of the behaviour – fine one moment and very different the next – should make parents suspect an allergy. 'Great mood swings, along with chronic headaches, shoulder and leg aches, bloating, dark circles under the eyes, tension, fatigue, red earlobes, glassy eyes . . . these are all warning signs that tell you to take a hard look at a child's diet,' Dr Rapp says.

Culprits that often cause trouble are wheat, milk, maize, eggs, citrus fruit, chocolate and peanuts. 'You can be allergic to almost any food.' Dr Crook says. 'And, curiously, you tend to be addicted to it as well.'

Sometimes dietary changes aren't enough. 'There's no such thing as a diet suitable for everyone,' says Gary Oberg, an Illinois paediatrician. 'Besides, if you concentrate only on food, you may miss the boat. When it comes to allergy-induced learning disabilities, we have to consider the entire world potentially guilty.'

Dr Leiberman agrees. 'I recently had a young woman – a first-year student at the local university – complain in my office, "I have yet to pass an exam, and I graduated top of my class at high school." She was desperate,' he recalls. 'She turned out to be allergic to mimeograph [Roneo] paper and ink. It left her absolutely confused and unable to concentrate.' Armed with 'ecological awareness', she was able to once again pass exams with flying colours.

Allergies can even affect an entire school, but uncovering the cause of one 'total disintegration' of learning required Dr Lieberman to play a medical Sherlock Holmes. 'We noticed that this epidemic of confusion, letter reversal and mirror-image writing occurred about the same time two years in a row. Well, the school is right beside a pecan [a nut] grove and gets a pretty good blast of aerial pesticide [i.e. malathion] at that time.

'Since it was a special academy for the learning disabled, we suspected that many of the children were particularly sensitive to a variety of allergens. Sure enough, when we ran a double-blind study comparing them with learning-disabled children in a non-farming community, every single child from the rural school reacted to the pesticide, while only one-quarter of the urban youngsters did. Incidentally, we used malathion in supposedly "safe" amounts.'

But there's more than Roneo paper and insecticides. 'I've seen disabling reactions to carpet sprays, paint varnishes, tobacco, perfume, formaldehyde, felt-tip pens. . . . The list goes on,' says Dr Lieberman.

For some youngsters, the learning environment itself may be hazardous to educational health, but it needn't be. Allergies, once identified, can be overcome, asserts Dr Crook, and he's accumulated enough success stories to feel confident.

'My plea to sceptics is to visit me and other doctors who feel the way I do, to hear what I hear in my office every day and become convinced of the honesty and integrity of our results,' he says. 'I was a sceptic, too, at first, but our methods work – simply and beautifully.'

And they often work where conventional treatment – based largely on drugs whose long-term effects remain unknown – offers only a chemical straitjacket.

'Most of all, listen to our patients and their families and teachers,' Dr Cook concludes. 'We're helping these children!' (*See also* ALLERGY.)

The facts about drugs

One thing all the doctors that we interviewed agree is that drugs for hyperactivity *aren't* the answer. Yet an estimated 2.5 million hyperactive children in the United States alone are treated with the mental stimulant Ritalin; in the UK, amphetamine and amphetamine-based drugs (e.g Dexedrine, Volital) are given. These all have what scientists call a 'paradoxical' effect on hyperactive children: they slow them down. For over 20 years, no one knew why, but now researchers have shown that amphetamines given to hyperactive children in fact speed them up – but in an unusual way.

'Their responses are still increasing in rate, but the variety of response is decreasing,' wrote Barbara Sahakian, a researcher at the Massachusetts Institute of Technology, in an issue of *New Scientist*. In other words, the child is able to do a few simple things over and over. Amphetamines only *appear* to calm hyperactive children. What they really do is turn them into robots.

'Amphetamines decreased responding in novel situations and on novel tasks or in learning tasks where changes in behaviour were necessary,' wrote Dr Sahakian.

And, like any drug, amphetamines can have side-effects. They can cause insomnia. They can make children lose their appetite and lose weight. And they can stunt growth.

Treating hyperactivity and learning disability naturally

When Hugh W. S. Powers, Jr, a general paediatrician in Dallas, started interviewing the parents of 'problem' children, he heard many angry complaints about the generally accepted medical treatments for children with learning disabilities and behaviour and hyperactive disorders. 'And they were dissatisfied for one very good reason: lack of results,' Dr Powers says.

'The conventional treatment for these problems [in the US] is the drug Ritalin. Now, the use of Ritalin has had considerable success with *certain* children. But the statistical breakdown is that only 50 per cent partially benefit from it, while 25 per cent don't get any benefits and another 25 per cent get worse. And the only alternatives to Ritalin that the conventional doctor will usually consider are tranquillizers or psychiatry.

'But what really galls these parents,' he continues, 'is the doctor's attitude that there isn't some other solution when his or her methods fail. Here they are with a child who's doing poorly in school or running wild all over the place at home, and the doctor is, in effect, telling them: 'My methods may not work, but I'm not going to try something else.''

Dr Powers is willing to try something else. 'You could say I've had a lifetime interest in nutrition. One of my aunts worked with E. V. McCombe of Johns Hopkins, one of the fathers of nutritional medicine in this country, and so I was getting vitamins even as a kid. Then, at medical school, I studied the physiology of nutrition. But it was about 12 years ago that I became interested in functional problems of the nervous system and learned that changes in levels of blood sugar affect behaviour. So I got interested in how to manage blood sugar, and I started educating myself further in nutrition.'

From that beginning, Dr Powers's background as a general paediatrician broadened naturally to a multi-faceted nutritional approach. He now uses nutrition to treat not only problem children with learning or behaviour difficulties but also those with allergies or those who simply get sick a lot with minor illnesses.

The first thing Dr Powers does when parents bring their children to him is to sit down with them for two hours and take a detailed case history, including family, pregnancy and past medical history, as well as a record of the family's daily diet. He does that for several reasons. 'One is to rule out any serious hidden medical problem. Then, too, I want to know whether there's a hereditary pattern to the child's problem – whether his parents and siblings have had something similar.'

'But most enlightening is to find out what sort of dietary examples the child is being given at home. Not only what *his* diet consists of, but also what kinds of food he sees his parents eating. I need to know whether I'm going to have a hard time getting a child to cut down on sugar because his father sits at the dinner table eating tubs of ice-cream.'

Following indications in the case history, Dr Powers may want to conduct a complete physical examination or laboratory studies such as blood count, urinalysis and a five-hour glucose tolerance test (used to diagnose diabetes). These will help to narrow down the child's specific problem.

'In most cases,' says Dr Powers, 'I begin treatment with a general nutritional programme. That consists of eliminating sugar, other simple carbohydrates and caffeine – including cola drinks – starting the day with a high-protein breakfast, and using appropriate vitamin supplements. I start with this because it's safe and effective for a wide variety of problems. Now, if the child's problems continue, I won't hesitate to try other treatments. But I seldom have to – the nutritional programme usually takes care of the problem. In fact, I've had parents tell me that the results are often amazing.

'Take the case of learning and behaviour difficulties – kids who are either too tired or too restless to pay attention in school and those who are either mopey or running all over the place. In their extreme forms, such symptoms often indicate hyperactivity. Kids with these problems respond remarkably well to a diet that eliminates sugar and limits other simple carbohydrates –

syrup, treacle, honey, maize sugar and so on. That's because the root problem here appears to be their blood sugar levels.'

In a study that Dr Powers conducted with 260 problem children, he found that blood sugar levels consistently correspond to behaviour and performance in school. Sugar made them irritable or listless. 'But after starting the general nutritional programme,' says Dr Powers, 'there was consistent improvement. One 15-year-old girl was a poor reader, doing badly in school, and had a history of headaches, fatigue and needing more sleep than normal. After a year on the programme, she underwent a striking change. She gained three years in reading comprehension and became bright, cheerful and outgoing.'

When you know these children's typical diet, it's not surprising that Dr Powers's sugar-control programme helps their problems. 'These kids usually eat a terrible diet. Sugared cereal, jam on sweet toast, sweet biscuits, cake and colas with almost every meal and lots of ice cream. Their consumption of whole grains, fresh vegetables and sources of protein such as pulses, fish and fowl is generally minimal. For children to think and behave well, they need to have the right food.'

Caffeine is also a problem. 'Kids are doing themselves a lot of harm by the way they down colas,' says Dr Powers. 'There's about half a cup [4 fl oz] of coffee in a 10 oz bottle of Coke – not to mention six tablespoons of sugar. Some kids drink the stuff by the quart [32 fl oz]. They're practically poisoning themselves. A quart of cola contains about 300 mg of caffeine; a toxic dose of caffeine is 500 mg.'

Children who consume large amounts of caffeine as well as sugar may be plagued by chronic irritability, inattention, poor memory, psychosomatic complaints and hyperactivity, all culminating in severe academic or even psychological problems. 'I've treated several psychotic teenagers who reported drinking two or three *quarts* of cola a day,' says Dr Powers. 'But another of my patients whom I call the 'queen of all cola addicts' outdid even them. She used to consume a variety of soft drinks straight from the dispensing machine that her well-meaning father had placed in their home. That and a heavy load of sugary food were really fouling her up. She refused to do schoolwork, was sullen and fatigued, and would often break out into unprovoked crying. 'I just yelled out loud and broke my pencil in half,' she told me about one of these incidents. When she was brought to me, she'd already been seeing a psychiatrist. I put her on the general nutritional programme, but she followed it very erratically. Still, the last word from her father was that she's definitely better without sugar and colas.'

In addition to eliminating bad foods from the child's diet, Dr Powers aims at increasing the good food. 'Good dietary management should build up the child's resistance as well as limit harmful foods,' he explains.

'I prescribe a diet of fish and chicken, organ meats like liver, fresh vegetables, unsweetened yogurt and small servings of cheese. These are resistance foods. They provide the body with its raw materials and arm it against infection. And it's no accident that they also help to stabilize blood sugar, so that the child will also *feel* better.'

Together with a group of his patients' mothers, Dr Powers has compiled the guidelines shown in the table on p 415 for a diet for children.

Diet for blood-sugar control

Foods to use	Foods to avoid
Meats: Beef, lamb, veal, pork pork, chicken, turkey, any fish	**Meats**: Any processed or cured meat.
Vegetables: All kinds, at least two at a time.	**Vegetables**: None.
Vegetable juices: All	**Vegetable juices**: Those processed with any additives.
Fruits: Fresh fruit in limited quantity (one-quarter piece per day for younger children).	**Fruits**: Excessive amounts.
Fruit juices: All natural. Dilute for small children to 1 fl oz of juice to 3 fl oz of water, one to three times a day.	**Fruit juices**: Those with added sweeteners.
Breads: Including baps, crumpets, cream crackers, biscuits all made from whole grains.	**Breads**: Those with two or more sweeteners.
Cereals: Any made from natural, whole, unrefined grains.	**Cereals**: Those with additives or preservatives.
Rice: Natural, whole grain. (e.g. brown rice).	**Rice**: Processed.
Pasta: Spaghetti, noodles, etc., all natural, whole grain, can be egg, spinach or Jerusalem artichoke enriched.	**Pasta**: Those made from white flour.
Beverages: Emphasize water. Milk, herbal teas, diluted fresh fruit juices, vegetable juices acceptable Sugarless, caffeine-free (i.e. light coloured) soft drinks infrequently.	**Beverages**: Coffee, tea, all dark-coloured soft drinks. Anything sweetened with sugar, sorbitol, mannitol, xylitol.
Sweeteners: Fructose, tupelo honey, treacle, carob syrup, rice syrup and maize syrup only in small applied amounts and only in low-sugar recipes.	**Sweeteners**: White refined sugar, brown and demarara sugar, honey, in recipes. Any sugar or syrup straight on to food. Sorbitol, mannitol, xylitol.
Desserts: Ideally all no-sugar such as nuts or popcorn. Low-sugar desserts (made with the allowable sweeteners listed above) in small portions and only on special occasions, not to exceed twice a week.	**Desserts**: All sugar-containing desserts.
Chewing gum: None.	**Chewing gum**: All gums of any kind.

Diet for blood sugar control *(Continued)*

Foods to use	Foods to avoid
Condiments: All spices and herbs. Tomato sauce, mayonnaise, American mustard in small quantities due to their high sugar content.	**Condiments:** Excessive amounts Remember that most tomato sauce, dressings, other sauces contain 25 to 50 per cent sugar.
Fats and oils: Only lean and unprocessed meats, lean fish, poultry without skin, low-fat and part-skimmed cheese.	**Fats and oils:** Fried foods and snacks dipped in oil for crispening. All oily foods. Excessive use of butter and margarine.

'I'll often supplement this diet with vitamins and minerals,' the doctor says. 'Since most problem children aren't eating well, they need vitamin and mineral supplements to get proper nutrition. For instance, vitamins contribute to the physiological use of protein, in which these kids are frequently deficient. So I give a general supplement. But since these kids are under a lot of stress, I'll also give them a big dose of C and B complex.'

If you've ever tried sticking to a diet yourself, you might wonder whether it isn't especially hard for kids. Dr Powers is the first to admit that it is.

Winning the child's cooperation is essential. 'If you can't sell it to the child, he's not going to stick to his diet. We need the child's active cooperation. He has to want to take responsibility for getting better.'

One reminder: therapeutic doses of vitamins should be given to children only under a doctor's guidance.

• Hypochondria

A hypochondriac is defined as a person who has an anxious preoccupation with his or her body or a portion of the body that he or she believes is either diseased or not functioning properly. When someone actually proves to be a hypochondriac, doctors and psychologists may work together to help the patient overcome whatever problems he or she faces.

Perhaps the real medical challenge lies in the preliminaries. The doctors have to figure out what they're dealing with. Someone wandering from one doctor to another complaining of vague, shifting and multiple complaints may very well be a hypochondriac. Or he or she may be someone with an elusive physical ailment that's in need of discovery and the proper diagnosis.

Take the case of Cherry Parker, for example. A professional nurse and homemaker in North Carolina, she had always been a very healthy and energetic person. Then one day she woke with a severe headache, dizziness and a runny nose. As the days went by, her symptoms became more and more 'bizarre'. She started having severe chest pains. Her muscles and limbs became sore, tender, weak and numb. She went to a cardiologist, who said her chest symptoms suggested the possiblity of angina. She agreed.

'He also referred me to a teaching hospital for evaluation of the headaches. He wanted to rule out the possibility of brain tumour,' recalls Mrs Parker, whose father and brother-in-law had both died of brain cancer.

She went to the teaching hospital and 'had a complete neurology checkup and X-rays of all kinds. I just had everything done,' she says. 'They came to very few conclusions, and I went home not knowing any more than when I went in.'

The doctors had found a few minor problems, but nothing seemed to explain the symptoms she was experiencing. Even though the headaches and chest pains persisted, a brain tumour and angina were ruled out.

'They sent me home, and I got worse,' she says.

She began labelling herself a 'terminal hypochondriac'. 'I thought, 'Well, there's really nothing wrong with me because they found nothing wrong.' But deep inside, I *knew* there was something wrong. I was too weak to do my housework and had pains everywhere. There were all of those weird symptoms that kept getting worse,' she continues. 'I wanted to find out what was wrong so it could be treated. But when the best doctors in the country can't find it, you begin to wonder if maybe you are a hypochondriac.'

While Mrs Parker emphasizes that most of her doctors gave her very good care and support, some of her experiences at the teaching hospital were exasperating. A few of the younger junior doctors and residents especially seemed to want to chalk up her complaints to hypochondria. 'I felt I wasn't being heard by some of them,' says Mrs Parker. 'When they couldn't find anything, they probably thought, 'This lady is well and just a middle-aged wacky nurse.'

It was enough to make Mrs Parker wonder, but her husband knew better. 'He went to the chief neurologist and said, 'I want to tell you that I've been married to this woman for 25 years, and she complains very rarely. So when she says something is bothering her, please listen.'

Her doctors could have sent her along to a psychiatrist, but they didn't, she adds. They seemed to believe her complaints. They just didn't seem to know what was causing them. It wasn't until Mrs Parker visited another doctor, her daughter's father-in-law, that she discovered what the underlying causes were – food allergies.

At his office, she underwent a 'very comprehensive interview' and proved to be allergic to some degree to practically everything but rice, bottled spring water and their own well water. She was placed on a food elimination diet, and her headaches quickly disappeared. She remains relatively symptom-free as long as she watches her diet pretty carefully.

Although she is uncertain why the food allergies did not erupt earlier, Mrs Parker says she had a few bad allergies as a child. Most of the foods to which she became highly allergic in adulthood were foods she had really enjoyed and had eaten quite often.

'Some doctors think that when you are addicted to certain foods and really crave them, you may eat them and feel better for a long time. But eventually your system breaks down and reacts negatively to those foods,' she says. 'I had had a very busy year, and the allergies may just have hit me at a very weak point in my life.'

Whatever the case, she finds that she rarely pins the 'hypochondria' label on others anymore. 'The worst thing is being sick and not knowing what is making you sick,' she explains. 'Knowing something is wrong but being unable to find it is very distressing. I never would have believed that food could have caused all of those symptoms in me before.'

The unsuspected effects of diet on behaviour have also been substantiated in the medical literature. One report describes patients who were displaying psychoses resembling 'hallucinogenic drug-induced states'. Among other things, the patients complained of perceptual distortions of surroundings, colour and time and of other types of abnormal sensory perception (*Lancet*, 1 March 1980).

Researchers working with the patients suspected that the patients' psychoses could be related to problems in metabolizing *serine* and *glycine*, two amino acids. Since the patients were suspected of having a metabolic disorder, they were placed on a special diet known to be of therapeutic value. They ate foods rich in carbohydrates, moderately low in protein and very low in fat. The researchers discovered that all of the patients recovered from their psychoses within two to five days of following the diet.

Misdiagnosis

If a patient's symptoms persist, other factors besides hypochondria probably should be taken into account, including the original diagnosis. Despite the best training and expertise, doctors occasionally can be fooled by the symptoms before them.

In her book, *The Unkindest Cut*, Dr Marcia Millman tells of a 34-year-old insurance salesman who had complained of abdominal pain and black stool. He was diagnosed as having a gastric ulcer and was placed on tranquillizers and an ulcer diet. When he continued to register various other complaints, they were diagnosed as being consistent with 'an ulcer and a neurotic personality'. Ten months later, he died of cancer that had spread throughout his abdomen.

The young man had seen a dozen doctors. Each one of them had depended too much on the erroneous assumptions of the preceding one. Mistakes in diagnosis were made repeatedly, and important information was disregarded in the case time and again.

'The doctors overlooked clear symptoms of organic disorder . . . because they were so convinced that the patient was neurotic and that his complaints and symptoms could be explained psychologically,' wrote Dr Millman.

> In other cases where physical findings are overlooked, or erroneously discounted, the physician will often excuse his embarrassing error by blaming the patient. If the patient can be 'discredited' as crazy, alcoholic, obnoxious, uncooperative or otherwise difficult or undeserving, then the responsibility for the medical error can be shifted away from the doctor to the patient.

Some doctors are punitive towards patients who ask a lot of questions or who challenge the doctor in any way, Dr Millman says. 'If you are a "management problem' or are "difficult', it's easier for the doctor to ignore your complaints. This is especially true of poor people and of women.' Some doctors prefer their patients to be docile and passive. When they are not, they may be dismissed as hypochondriacs.

Even when a patient is a hypochondriac, help is still needed.

A hypochondriac's health problem is just as painfully real and in need of treatment as any other malady. Unfortunately, some doctors may turn their backs on the hypochondriac's dilemma because they have not been trained to deal with it effectively.

The crux of the problem is that hypochondriacs usually are healthy in body but not in mind. When they do have a physical disability, their hypochondria tends to accentuate it. Hypochondriasis is a psychological disorder that requires a special kind of medical attention and treatment.

'A hypochondriac already believes he is sick,' says Elliott Seligman, a psychologist practising in New York City. 'He keeps going to doctors and gets temporary reassurances that he is well, but he is never convinced of it. He is like someone who gets up for the 20th time to make sure the gas is turned off, just because he's afraid he overlooked something the first 19 times.'

Searching for the cause

While a lot about hypochondria remains anyone's guess, the condition can be a symptom of another disorder, or it can be the illness itself. If hypochondria is a symptom, it means there is an underlying problem that is causing it, says James J. Strain, a psychiatrist at the Mount Sinai School of Medicine in New York.

The doctor has to find out what the underlying disorder or primary disease is. 'If depression is causing the hypochondria, then you must treat the depression,' says Dr Strain. 'If it's caused by schizophrenia, you must treat the schizophrenia.'

When hypochondria is the illness, it should be treated by one primary-care doctor within a medical setting, he continues. The medical setting is preferred, since the hypochondriac believes he is physically, not mentally, ill. By staying with one doctor, unnecessary medical procedures are prevented. Over time, the doctor may establish a good relationship with the patient, and the patient's true problems may be unveiled.

The patient may begin talking about feelings of unhappiness or stress, and the doctor has an opportunity to provide counsel on those problems, says Dr Strain. Hypochondriacs eventually may learn to deal with their troubles and elect to stop the visits to the surgery. Or they may stay on a maintenance programme with their doctor for regular consultation.

It was thought that the elderly tended more towards hypochondria, but that is not true, according to Paul T. Costa, Jr and Robert R. McCrae of the (US) National Institute on Aging. They conducted a study of health assessments of men aged 17 to 97 and found that people's complaints did not increase as they got older. What they found instead was that, in every age group, the more neurotic a person was, the more health complaints he had. That's a pretty fair indication 'that doctors should take the health complaints of the elderly seriously,' Dr Costa told us.

One problem with the 'hypochondria' label is that, once it's attached, some doctors automatically assume the patient is 'overly presenting his symptoms and a bit of a nuisance', says Barr Taylor, assistant professor of psychiatry at Stanford University. The danger lies in the fact that the hypochondriac really could become ill. It's much like the boy who cried 'Wolf!' If the doctor stops listening to the hypochondriac's complaints, a serious physical illness could be ignored.

'I think that we have to believe the patient,' says Dr Taylor. 'It is rare that someone lies about pain. Just because you can't find a reason for it, doesn't mean that it doesn't exist. If the patient says he feels sick, it is true.'

• Hypogeusia (loss of taste)

According to Robert I. Henkin, of the Center for Molecular Nutrition and Sensory Disorders at Georgetown University Medical Center in Washington, D.C, about one-quarter of these cases of loss of taste, or hypogeusia, are caused by zinc deficiencies.

Actually, hypogeusia is not itself a disease. 'Hypogeusia is a symptom that occurs in a whole slew of diseases,' says Dr Henkin. 'A lot of people who have a lot of different diseases have hypogeusia. Zinc deficiency is one cause of hypogeusia, but there are many different causes.'

For example, we all know that taste loss can accompany a bad cold. Nutritional factors may also be involved in hypogeusia. 'Copper deficiency can influence it, vitamin A deficiency can influence it, as well as vitamin B_{12} deficiency and vitamin B_6 deficiency,' Dr Henkin says. 'It's a very active system, and many vitamins and minerals impinge upon it in different ways.

'In terms of taste and zinc, there has been real confusion in the past. The confusion relates to the fact that, by analogy, although a horse is a four-legged animal, all four-legged animals aren't horses. People who are zinc deficient almost uniformly have taste problems, but there are a lot of people who have taste loss who don't have any problem with zinc. Our data suggest that one-third of the people who have taste loss are zinc deficient.

How zinc works

Dr Henkin and Allan Shatzman, a biochemist, set out to demonstrate conclusively the effects of zinc therapy on taste loss and the way zinc was working by intensively studying one patient. 'This was a lot of work,' Dr Henkin says. 'Looking at just one patient requires a lot of effort, which is why we reported only one case, but he is representative of a number of cases we've handled.'

Each day of the study, samples of the patient's saliva were collected from the parotid gland (which secretes the majority of the protein found in saliva) and analysed for their content of zinc and *gustin*. 'Gustin is a salivary protein,' Dr Henkin explains, 'the major zinc-containing protein in saliva. Seventy-five to 80 per cent of the zinc in saliva is bound to this protein.'

The patient's saliva was compared with saliva from normal, healthy people. Both the healthy saliva and the saliva taken from the patient with taste loss were first broken down into separate components – or fractions, as the scientists call them – of the whole saliva from the parotid gland. 'In normal people, and with patients with hypogeusia, all these fractions are about the same, except for fraction II,' Dr Shatzman told us. 'Fraction II is the fraction of saliva which contains gustin, the zinc-containing protein. We could clearly see that something was going on in fraction II of the saliva.'

While the zinc content of all the saliva of patients with taste loss may be about half the normal amount, the deficiency is particularly acute in fraction II of the saliva. There the levels of gustin and zinc are as low as one-fifth of normal. All signs point to gustin, and the zinc it contains, as crucial factors in normal taste.

That suspicion was confirmed when the test patient was given zinc supplements. As the treatment with zinc went on, the levels of zinc and gustin in the patient's saliva increased, and his ability to taste improved dramatically. By the ninth day of treatment, the zinc and gustin levels had reached a peak, and taste returned to normal several days later.

'The patient reached a maximum ability to taste on day 12,' Dr Shatzman told us. 'The return to normal taste followed, by three days, the return to normal biochemistry in the saliva. That makes sense if you believe gustin has something to do with maintaining normal taste buds, because you have to have a return to normal taste bud anatomy and biochemistry before you can have normal taste. It makes sense that there's a lag period.'

Dr Henkin believes that, while this evidence indicates that zinc works to maintain the sense of taste directly in the mouth, zinc may also affect taste centres in the brain where information from taste buds is received and processed. However, he says, 'the majority of patients we see who have taste problems have biochemical problems that are influenced by changes in saliva or the taste buds directly, not in the brain.'

Though a change in diet helps correct the taste problems of many of Dr Henkin's patients, he believes that the original cause of their problems is not an inadequate diet but the way they absorb the food they eat. 'These people are probably taking in the same amount of zinc as you or I, but they don't absorb it properly,' he told us. Unpredictable idiosyncracies in the way their bodies work means that they should take in more zinc than others.

Even considered in terms of the US Government's Recommended Dietary Allowances (RDAs), which set the adult zinc requirement at 15 mg a day (there is no UK RDA for zinc), great portions of the population are not getting enough zinc to meet their needs. The typical person is believed to consume between 10 and 15 mg of zinc a day, which means that he or she is marginally zinc deficient, even by the US government's low standards. Among older people, zinc intake is often less then two-thirds of the US RDA. Older people, not surprisingly, also commonly suffer taste loss.

Dull taste means bad diet?

What this wholesale deadening of taste buds does to our cuisine is anyone's guess. Would it be harder for people to wolf down fast food if they could actually taste what they were eating? Are some people's palates so dull that they can't do anything more subtle than distinguish between crisps and candy floss? Is that why blatant seasonings such as salt and sugar dominate our preparation of food?

This could be the case. Zinc has been tested on ordinary, 'healthy' people who show no overt signs of zinc deficiency, with some interesting results. A study of young women reviewed their zinc status by analysing their blood, saliva, hair and diet. Their zinc status was judged to be normal, and they were given different concentrations of zinc supplements. There was no change in the women's ability to detect three of the four basic tastes – sourness, bitterness and saltiness. However, for women receiving 50 mg of zinc a day, there was a significant increase in their ability to taste sweetness (*Federation Proceedings*, 1 March 1980).

Another study recorded an improvement in older people's ability to taste sweetness with zinc supplementation, plus an improvement in the ability to taste salt. But the improvements were not statistically significant – perhaps, the authors of the study speculated, because the people were receiving only 15 mg of zinc supplements a day (*American Journal of Clinical Nutrition*).

In any case, the interesting thing about those two studies is the improvement in the ability to taste sweetness recorded in both. The more sensitive you are to this, the less sugar you need to eat to achieve the same taste. Getting adequate zinc might be one way to cut back our intake of sugar.

That means eating foods like beef, lamb, liver, cheese, oatmeal, nuts and whole-grain products – all good sources of zinc. It means taking zinc supplements, if necessary. Eating, after all, was meant to be one of the true pleasures of life, not just something you do after the evening news and before prime-time TV. Without sharp taste, good, healthy, enjoyable eating is impossible.

• Hypoglycaemia

The toast pops up, but to her it sounds like a shotgun firing. She spends two minutes deciding whether to use butter or jam. And when she's finished eating, the dirty plate makes her cry. Neurotic? Her husband and doctor think so. And they're both wrong.

Her symptoms – sensitivity to slight noise, inability to make decisions, unjustified weeping – are only three in a long list that all doctors should tack up next to their diplomas and all psychiatrists should post over their couches.

That way, millions of people goaded to a doctor's office by anxiety or depression might get nutritional counselling instead of a knee-jerk prescription for Valium. That way, psychiatric patients might get their diet analysed along with their psyche. That way, millions of tense, troubled and tired people (an estimated 50 million in the US alone) might find out what's wrong with them – low blood sugar.

Doctors call it *hypoglycaemia* – when they condescend to talk about it. Many doctors believe that low blood sugar is a medical fad, a popular catch-all that has been foisted off on an innocent public by books and magazine articles, and by doctors (like the 2000 or so renegade MDs affiliated with the Hypoglycaemia

Foundation in the United States) who have jumped on the low-blood-sugar bandwagon.

One doctor who humbugs low blood sugar told an American medical convention that there *is* an 'epidemic' of hypoglycaemia in the United States – because doctors are treating it when it isn't there. He suggested that patients with fatigue and nervousness take tranquillizers instead (*Ob. Gyn. News*).

And the American Medical Association issued its holy writ on low blood sugar in an issue of the *Journal of the American Medical Association*:

> There is no good evidence that hypoglycaemia causes depression, chronic fatigue, allergies, nervous breakdowns, alcoholism, juvenile delinquency, childhood behaviour problems, drug addiction or inadequate sexual performance.

Quite a list. You have to wonder why so many heretical researchers are up to 'no good' gathering evidence about hypoglycaemia. And what exactly is this condition that causes so much hot air – and cold sweats and ulcers and dizziness and muscle pain and . . .

What hypoglycaemia can do

Blood sugar is glucose, the fuel your body runs on. When it runs low, every part of you can start to sputter and slow down. Muscles can ache. Vision can blur. Digestion can clog. But these are *physical* problems. Why should a near-empty fuel tank befuddle the mind?

The mind is powered by the brain, and the brain, too, is part of the body. And the brain – more than the muscles, more than any other organ – *demands* glucose.

Some parts of the body store glucose and burn reserves if the supply drops below normal, or, in a pinch, use substances other than glucose for fuel. But the brain is a glucose addict. It has to have glucose, and it has to have it *now* – a steady, second-to-second flow. You could say the brain breathes glucose and chokes without it. That's why low blood sugar can cause *any* mental problem. Nervousness, anxiety, irritability, depression, forgetfulness, confusion, indecisiveness, poor concentration, nightmares, suicidal tendencies – all these and more have been linked to low blood sugar.

But if a person about to do himself in simply needs more sugar in his blood, shouldn't he stuff himself with sweets instead of sleeping pills? No. Strangely enough, eating too much sugar is what *starts* the problem.

Normally, less than two teaspoons of sugar circulate in the blood. To keep it that way, extra sugar is stored in the liver and muscles after being converted into glycogen by insulin, a hormone secreted by the pancreas. However, we often upset this delicate balance by gorging on sugar. Sugar in soft drinks. Sugar in ice cream. Sugar in sweets and cake. And sugar in tomato sauce, peanut butter and tinned sweetcorn – the hidden sugar that laces most processed food. The British consume on average, over 90 lb of sugar per person a year, about 35 teaspoons a day. To top it all off, we also gorge on refined carbohydrates such as white flour, and on starchy foods – all of which the body converts into blood sugar. Faced with this flood of glucose, the pancreas pumps out extra insulin – so much that even some of the glucose that should circulate is swept out of the bloodstream. The result: low blood sugar – and low spirits.

The literally stupefying effect of a sugary diet is documented in the book *Body, Mind and Sugar* by E. M. Abrahamson. Dr Abrahamson describes two studies which show that many may have been labelled 'neurotics' because their doctors had made the wrong diagnosis.

In the first study, Dr Abrahamson gave a gluocose tolerance test (GTT), a blood test that will show if a person has hypoglycaemia, to 220 so-called 'neurotic' patients with obvious physical symptoms of low blood sugar, such as daylong fatigue. *The test showed that 205 had hypoglycaemia.* When these 205 depressed, anxious, and fear-ridden people were put on a corrective diet, their physical *and* psychological problems began to clear up.

A man who for six years had blasted at his family with daily temper tantrums was even-tempered and reasonable after a few weeks. A claustrophobic woman who for 20 years had refused to enter a lift, car or tube train was confidently travelling on her own after six months. A woman obsessed by thoughts of suicide was free of them in a week.

Not surprisingly, Dr Abrahamson was intrigued. So intrigued that he gave the GTT to 700 mildly neurotic people who had *no* physical symptoms of low blood sugar. This time, the test showed that 600 had hypoglycaemia. When put on a corrective diet, they regained mental health.

A psychiatrist's office isn't the only place where you're likely to find a hypoglycaemic. A head master's office is another.

Studies in the United States have shown that millions of children have a 'learning disability', a problem that can include wild, erratic behaviour, short attention span, emotional instability and poor memory. Paul J. Dunn, a paediatrician in Illiniois, gave the GTT to 144 children with learning disability and found that 78 per cent had hypoglycaemia (*New Dynamics of Preventive Medicine*).

In a similar study, Sydney Walker III, a neuropsychiatrist in California, found that 44 of 48 children with learning disability, depression, temper tantrums or poor concentration had, among other problems, a blood-sugar disorder. Dr Walker told us that, once these children were put on a sugar-free diet rich in vegetables, fruit and high-protein foods, almost all of them had improved behaviour.

Ten-year-old hypoglycaemic children who binge on sweets and ice cream aren't holding up corner shops and making off with cartons of Mars bars. They get most of their sweets – and their sugar-eating habits – from their parents. In fact, it's not inconceivable that Mum and Dad also have hypoglycaemia. And that their marriage is on the rocks.

Robert J. Rogers, a Florida doctor who has been treating hypoglycaemia for over ten years, says that America's high divorce rate is caused, in part, by hypoglycaemia. 'A husband and wife, both with low blood sugar, who are irritable, moody, anxious and depressed, can't expect to have a happy marriage.'

Dr Rogers believes that many broken marriages – and broken lives – could be prevented if only more doctors realized that hypoglycaemia is a widespread problem. 'Often I see an anxious, depressed patient who has been to half a dozen psychiatrists and other doctors and never had any of them tell him that he has a problem with blood sugar. When I put the patient on a sugar-free diet and he begins to improve, he says to me, 'Why didn't someone tell me about this sooner?''

An anti-hypoglycaemic diet

For a hypoglycaemic under Dr Rogers's care, sugar is not the only no-no. He also restricts refined carbohydrates – be they crisps, biscuits or Pot Noodles. And in severe cases, he limits foods rich in natural sugar such as fruit and honey.

What's left? Plenty. Dr Rogers advises his patients to eat good amounts of protein foods such as meat, dairy products and nuts, and a moderate amount of fat and unrefined carbohydrates such as vegetables and whole grains. He also counsels patients to eat frequent, small meals – as many as six a day – to prevent blood sugar from plummeting.

Nutritional supplements also help keep blood sugar on the up and up. 'Insulin is dependent on zinc, chromium and manganese for its normal functioning,' says Dr Rogers, 'so I give hypoglycaemics supplements of these and brewer's yeast.' The yeast contains GTF (glucose tolerance factor), a compound of chromium, and a specific combination of niacin (nicotinic acid) and amino acids. In this form, chromium becomes more active and available to the body.

According to Robert Herman, chief of the department of medicine at the Letterman Army Institute of Research, San Francisco, a folic-acid deficiency that co-exists with a mild deficiency of FDPase – an enzyme essential for sugar metabolism – can aggravate hypoglycaemia, especially in children.

Dr Herman was able to use some of the properties of folic acid to treat two such cases – a mother and her daughter. The 28-year-old mother complained of fatigue, headaches, shakiness, palpitations, nervousness and hunger. She had been so tired that, during the course of light household chores, she'd have to stop at frequent intervals to rest. In addition, she had inexplicable crying episodes, which mysteriously came over her two to four hours after eating. Her 19-month-old daughter's symptoms were even more perplexing. For two terrifying hours one day, the child slipped into a sort of stupor in which she neither recognized her parents nor responded to verbal stimuli.

Tests showed both mother and daughter had 'reactive hypoglycaemia', which means that their low blood sugar levels occurred as a reaction to eating. No cause could be found (*Biochemical Medicine*).

In an interview, Dr Herman explained how he came up with the theory linking folic acid to aggravation of their problems. 'First of all, I knew that one important, though less common, cause of hypoglycaemia is a deficiency of the FDPase enzyme,' he said. 'Second, I knew from previous studies which we've been doing that folic acid can increase enzyme activity.'

Dr Herman investigated further. He found both mother and daughter to be deficient in the critical enzyme. In addition, both were mildly deficient in folic acid. His theory was right on target. With folic-acid therapy, both patients got well.

In addition, 'vitamin C should be given to hypoglycaemics,' says W. D. Currier, a California doctor. 'People with low blood sugar almost always have weak adrenal glands, and vitamin C helps compensate for this problem.'

How are the adrenal glands weakened by low blood sugar? When blood sugar drops, the brain sends out an SOS. The adrenal glands come to the rescue, pumping hormones into the blood that release the glucose stored in the liver and muscles. However, even a white knight needs a day off and when the adrenal glands are called on time after time, they slow down.

The adrenal glands, however, can play the villain as well as the hero. 'Caffeine, nicotine and alcohol stimulate the adrenal glands, which push blood sugar out of the liver and muscles and into the bloodstream,' explains Dr Rogers. 'This sudden burst of blood sugar triggers the pancreas to release too much insulin, and blood sugar drops. The quick rise in blood sugar is where the kick of coffee and cigarettes and the euphoria of liquor come from. But the lift is temporary. When blood sugar plummets, the only way most people can get on top of things again is to smoke another cigarette, have another cup of coffee or swig another drink.'

In fact, says Dr Rogers, many researchers believe that alcoholism can be caused by hypoglycaemia. (*See also* ALCOHOLISM.) And so can wife-beating, child abuse and suicide, according to Mary Jane Hungerford, director of the Santa Barbara, California, branch of the American Institute of Family Relations. Dr Hungerford told us that a sharp and sudden drop in blood sugar triggers violent impulses and suicidal depression.

Of the people she sees in her clinic, 80 per cent have hypoglycaemia, and when they change their diet, the results are 'fantastic': depression, anxiety and uncontrollable tempers fade in a matter of weeks.

'Low blood sugar *is* epidemic in America,' she says. 'Most doctors don't diagnose it because they're trained to recognize only *one* out of *five* possible hypoglycaemic responses to the glucose tolerance test.'

Has the epidemic hit you yet?

Hypoglycaemia doesn't usually happen overnight. The body was built to last, and it may take years before the pancreas and adrenal glands can't cope with sugar, coffee, cigarettes or alcohol. Then the symptoms start. Early morning headaches. A wave of fatigue at mid-morning or mid-afternoon. A craving for sweets, or constant hunger. Sound familiar?

If so don't worry. As you've seen, it's never too late – or too early – to deal with low blood sugar. After all, life is much sweeter without it.

• Immune system problems

In part, the immune system is chemical warfare: specialized cells secrete substances called *antibodies*, each custom-built to disable one of the myriad organisms that threaten health. These cells have a kind of memory so that, when the same invader comes again, the right weapon will be ready. (This is why you don't get the measles twice – after one bout, your body has the right antibodies to repel any future attacks.) Other chemicals circulate in the blood, ready to attack any organism that has been slated for destruction.

The immune system also sends out special cells that attack invaders directly. Some, like the white blood cells called *lymphocytes*, secrete substances that destroy hostile viruses and fungi. Others, like the bigger, sluggish *macrophages*, swallow bacteria whole.

They all work as a team. Lymphocytes bring macrophages to the place where they are needed; antibodies make it easier for lymphocytes to destroy their prey; lymphocytes aid in the production of antibodies; and the whole system lies under the control of hormones secreted by such glands as the adrenals and thymus.

Although there are many things about the immune system that we don't understand, this we do know: if the team works well, the infection is quashed, the virus is destroyed; if it works poorly, there will be trouble.

Research into the immune system has been intense during recent decades, and no wonder. Although bacterial diseases pose little threat today, disorders like cancer – and especially AIDS – still do. While very little is yet known about AIDS, many scientists now believe that the body's natural immunity may prevent cancer from appearing, keep it from spreading and even provide remissions from the disease. According to one theory, the strength of your immune system determines how long you will live.

Cells too small to see with the naked eye, substances secreted in minute amounts that can be detected only by the most sophisticated of laboratory equipment – it is to them that we owe our lives and health. We owe it to ourselves to keep this interlocking array of defenders as strong as possible. But how? As military commanders from Hannibal on have discovered, armies can only perform at their peak if they are well fed.

We have known for a long time that very poor nutrition has a devastating effect on the immune system. Malnourished children suffer a host of infections. The Black Death in the Middle Ages apparently began its rampage in famine-struck areas of the Far East. More recently, research has established that deficiencies of individual vitamins and minerals can seriously damage the body's ability to defend itself.

Vitamin C

The vital necessity of good nutrition for strong resistance to disease comes as no surprise to those of us who take extra doses of vitamin C to stay healthy. Studies have supported the belief that this vitamin can protect against colds, as well as such serious illnesses as hepatitis and cancer. Apparently, vitamin C keeps disease away by strengthening natural defences on a number of fronts at once.

An experiment conducted at the University of Witwatersrand, South Africa, suggests that, for one thing, vitamin C can increase the amount of antibodies available to fight disease. Researchers gave a group of health students an ascorbic acid (vitamin C) supplement – 1 g daily for 77 days. They compared levels of immunoglobulins (proteins which carry antibodies) in their blood to levels in the blood of a control group who had not received extra vitamin C.

'Our results showed that ascorbic-acid supplementation caused a statistically significant increase' in the antibody-bearing part of the blood, they reported (*International Journal of Vitamin Nutritional Research*).

More proof of vitamin C's effectiveness comes from a case study of a young brother and sister in South Africa. The children had been plagued with frequent bacterial infections. Juvenile acne, pneumonia, recurring sinusitis, ear and upper respiratory-tract infections were just some of the maladies their bodies seemed unable to battle. Both children were also allergic to animal hair, house dust, pollen and certain foods, yet they apparently had no drug allergies.

The children were suffering from an unusual disorder called *chronic granulomatous disease* (CGD) – a severe immune deficiency disease in which part of a person's natural immune system defences are impaired. It is an inherited disease whose victims are young people showing an abnormally high susceptibility to pus-producing infections. These are caused by certain species of bacteria against which the patient's body has no defence.

The brother and sister were treated with drugs that lowered the frequency of infections, but they still had bouts with pneumonia, bronchiolitis (infection of very small airways in the lungs) and sinusitis. Finally, they began taking high doses of vitamin C.

After following a supplementation programme with the nutrient, the two children experienced a 'decrease in the frequency of infection and increased weight and growth rate', researchers noted.

Both children have remained free of infection for a ten-month period, which included the South African winter. In the previous two winters, both children suffered from severe pneumonia and recurrent upper-respiratory-tract infections.

A brother, just over two years old and not included in the study, also had CGD. The boy developed an acute inflammation of the umbilicus shortly after birth. At the age of two weeks, he developed a serious abscess and complications. He was given 1 g of vitamin C daily and the problem cleared up. He has remained free of infection for nine months, the researchers reported.

They concluded that '. . . ascorbic acid [vitamin C] may be an important supplement to prophylactic antibiotics and chemotherapeutic agents in the treatment of CGD' (*South African Medical Journal*, 15 September 1979).

Rounding up invaders

Why did vitamin C apparently help those children ward off infections? One clue that appeared in blood samples of the older brother and sister was an increase in neutrophil activity after taking vitamin C.

'Neutrophils are a type of white blood cell and are the main killer cells that respond to bacteria in the body,' explains Norbert J. Roberts, Jr, assistant professor of medicine and a member of the Infectious Disease Unit at the University of Rochester in New York State. 'Vitamin C appears to be important for the migration of those killer cells. In the absence of vitamin C, the migration of these cells and phagocytosis – the eating – of bacteria can be depressed.'

Dr Roberts and his colleague Dr John P. Manzella have been researching the effects of vitamin C and fever on the immune system. 'There have been numerous speculations on vitamin C's role in immune function,' explained Dr Roberts. 'There also have been a lot of controversy and unknowns about hyperthermia [elevated body temperature]. Is fever good or bad? Should a person take aspirin to reduce fever or not?'

They decided to put both vitamin C and fever to the test, choosing to pit them against an influenza virus. 'An infection with the influenza virus can depress a patient's immune function to other agents,' Dr Roberts told us.

First they took some normal human white cells and stimulated them with a plant substance called PHA. 'Normal cells should respond to PHA. If a person has an immune deficiency, his cell response to PHA will be less,' explained Dr Roberts.

After they observed how the normal cells responded to PHA, they exposed the cells to influenza. When the cells 'came down with the flu', their immunity was lower, as shown by a lower-than-normal response to PHA. When the flu-infected cells were treated with vitamin C, however, they bounced back and exhibited a higher response to PHA. Infected cells that were raised to fever temperature also responded more favourably to PHA.

'Both ascorbic acid and fever appear to enhance the response of the cells and to diminish the adverse effects of the virus, when examined in the test tube,' Dr Roberts said.

It remains open to question whether a person taking vitamin C and avoiding aspirin will find any benefit for the immune system, but our work suggests that he might. Repeated studies we have done show the same thing all over again. However, for certain individuals (a young child or a person with heart disease, for example), it might be important to lower fever. [*Journal of Immunology*, November 1979].

In short, Dr Roberts found that cells infected with a virus seem to have a higher immune response when they have been given vitamin C or have been raised to fever temperature. (*See also* FEVER.)

Boosting the whole system

We asked the eminent Scottish cancer specialist Dr Ewan Cameron how vitamin C can help boost the immune system to fight cancer. His answer:

'It may be true that *all* of the body's natural defences against cancer depend on vitamin C. Originally, my idea was that vitamin C could damp down the invasive capacity of the malignant cells . . . I read a report Dr [Linus] Pauling had made in Chicago about encapsulation of the tumour. It's a very sound suggestion: collagen encapsulates the tumour and prevents it from spreading. Vitamin C is necessary for the synthesis of collagen.

'Furthermore, vitamin C stimulates the immune system of the body. A report came in from German transplant surgeons that, if you make guinea pigs deficient in vitamin C, they can tolerate grafts from unrelated animals. Their immune system becomes quite depressed. But as soon as you give them vitamin C, the immune system comes back and the grafts drop off.

'There was another encouraging report from the [US] National Cancer Institute. They found that if you give healthy people relatively large doses of vitamin C – 5 g – you increase the competence of the immune system very distinctly. And if you give them 10 g you increase it even more. And they've recently found that giving 15 g pushes it still higher. And the effect lasts about two weeks.' (Doses of vitamin C over 1500 mg – 1.5 g should be taken only with your doctor's OK)

Vitamin C is also a natural anti-oxidant – a substance that protects cells from being destroyed by oxidation, which is a sort of slow, internal fire that happens when fat and oxygen mix. And under the right circumstances, oxidative damage may lead to lowered resistance.

The guilty party is believed to be a tiny molecular fragment called a *free radical*. Free radicals are extremely unstable substances that, in the presence of oxygen, combine at random with unsaturated fats to form peroxides. In butter and other highly perishable foods, free-radical reactions lead to spoiling or rancidity, In human beings, these reactions cause irreparable damage to cells and the protective membrane linings that surround them. And this damage accumulates over the years with telltale age spots, wrinkling and worse.

Fortunately, nature has provided us with a way of slowing down such reactions. 'Cells and tissues are protected against oxidizing free radicals by a complexity of anti-oxidant mechanisms,' explained T. L. Dormandy of the department of chemical pathology at London's Whittington Hospital. 'So long as the supply of anti-oxidants lasts, these free radicals are instantly trapped.'

'But one anti-oxidant molecule can scavenge only one free radical,' he warned in the *Lancet*. So a constant 'self-regenerating' supply is needed.

Vitamin E and selenium

Other anti-oxidants also appear to play a key role in fostering immunity. According to Werner A. Baumgartner and co-workers of the nuclear medicine department at the Wadsworth Hospital Center in Los Angeles, body stores of vitamin E and selenium tend to fall sharply when there is a tumour. And this anti-oxidant deficiency may be responsible in part for the depressed immunity so common in cancer patients. They suggest that anti-oxidant supplementation might reverse this often fatal situation (*American Journal of Clinical Nutrition*).

'In fact,' Dr Baumgartner told us, 'there is growing evidence that, even in healthy people, the immune processes require more anti-oxidants than we normally take in with our food. The immune system seems to require *more* anti-oxidants than other cells in the body. So even a slight stress, such as a marginal deficiency of vitamin E, could impair the immune response.'

In still another report, Los Angeles dermatologists Samuel Ayres, Jr, and Richard Mihan have found vitamin E to be of great therapeutic value in many disabling and stubborn skin disorders. And they believe the reason is vitamin E's anti-oxidant properties (*Cutis*).

All the diseases they discuss – including scleroderma, vasculitis and other disfiguring inflammatory disorders – seem to involve a breakdown in which the body's normal defence mechanism goes haywire. Drs Ayres and Mihan theorize that these so-called auto-immune diseases – in which the immune mechanism literally attacks the body's own tissues – are the result of cell rupturing caused by free radicals. Large doses of vitamin E – up to 1600 IU daily – have produced dramatic reversals. (Levels of vitamin E over 600 IU should be taken only under a doctor's supervision.)

Vitamin E's role in immune defence has been recognized for some time, but selenium, too, fits into the picture in a way that has only recently begun to grow clear. Evidently, a special enzyme, *glutathione peroxidase* (GSH-Px, for short), is not only dependent on selenium but may also play a critical role in the immune response – made possible by the presence of selenium. GSH-Px is responsible for normal metabolism of peroxides in cells, protecting tissues from over-oxidation. Julian Spallholz, associate professor of food and nutrition at Texas Tech University, has been studying the relationship between selenium and immunity since he was a post-doctoral fellow, and he speculates that, in the normal course of controlling oxidation, selenium-containing GSH-Px may help cells resist bacteria and viruses.

A diet low in selenium and vitamin E will result in low levels of GSH-Px activity. When GSH-Px activity is low, the health of the white cells suffers, lessening their natural resistance. When selenium is adequate, then, GSH-Px theoretically may increase natural resistance by helping white cells to clear out bacteria, viruses and cancer cells. Vitamin E enhances that effect.

Vitamin A

Unquestionably, there are other nutrients that dramatically bolster the body's natural defences. Dr Benjamin E. Cohen of Houston, has been studying vitamin A over the years and has found that it, too, may boost a person's immune response.

'While I was working at the National Institutes of Health in Bethesda, Maryland, I examined the effects of steroids and vitamin A on mice,' he told us. 'Steroids are chemical agents secreted by the adrenal glands. Among other things, high doses of steroids are known for their suppressive effect on a person's immune response. They are widely used drugs often given to transplant patients so that their immune systems will be less likely to reject the transplanted organ.

'When I gave high doses of steroids to mice, their immune systems were depressed. But when the mice were given vitamin A, the steroids were unable to depress the immune system. Vitamin A blocked the depression.'

Dr Cohen also discovered that vitamin A decreased the animals' susceptibility to a variety of bacterial infections. And when mice were given vitamin A in conjunction with a potent anti-cancer agent, the anti-cancer agent became 100 times more potent.

Dr Cohen came to Britain on a fellowship from Harvard University and began researching the effect of vitamin A on the immune system in humans. 'It has consistently been found that anaesthesia and surgery result in a suppression of the immune response, in patients,' he says. 'Whenever patients are anaesthetized, it generally takes a few weeks for their immune response to recover.'

He theorizes that vitamin A's favourable effects on the immune system might prove to be beneficial in battling certain types of cancers. 'The immune system has been implicated in the control of certain types of tumours,' he told us. 'If that is true, it may be possible to improve the immune system's work with vitamin A supplementation. That may be helpful in arresting or even eradicating the tumour.' Dr Cohen says that vitamin A probably would be given to the patient as additional therapy. 'The nutrient might be used in conjunction with a more traditional approach.'

Zinc

In keeping the lymphocytes that fight micro-organisms strong, other nutrients may be as vital as those already discussed. Studies conducted at New York's Memorial – Sloan Kettering Cancer Center found that zinc, for example, has an essential role.

When a team of researchers tested the blood of three patients with *hypogammaglobulinaemia* – very low levels of the antibody-carrying part of the blood – they found low levels of zinc as well. T-lymphocyte activity was below normal, too: these cells responded poorly to chemicals that normally stimulate them to multiply.

A period of zinc supplementation brought about some improvement in two people, alleviating the diarrhoea that afflicted them. And their T-lymphocytes multiplied more normally when chemically stimulated – the way they would have to when challenged by hostile micro-organisms. A stronger T-lymphocyte reaction suggests an improved ability to fight viruses, fungi and possibly cancer cells, points out a spokesperson for the Sloan Kettering team.

'Zinc seems to be necessary for the T-cells to perform their immunological functions correctly,' this doctor told us. And so zinc deficiency is a danger to which doctors should be alert. 'It can make sick people sicker.'

And he notes that people who are particularly at risk should be tested for zinc deficiency: 'Patients with liver problems, poor appetites, absorption problems or poor dietary habits, for example.'

(This last category could include just about anyone in a hospital. A US Department of Agriculture survey found that the average daily intake of zinc on a hospital diet is less than two-thirds the US Recommended Dietary Allowance. *See also* HOSPITAL MALNUTRITION.)

Other research performed at Sloan Kettering suggests that zinc also strengthens those lymphocytes that produce antibodies. B-lymphocytes from normal blood were cultured and exposed to a sheep's red blood cells (this normally stimulates them to secrete antibodies). Zinc, it was found, increased their response to stimulation – it turned up the immune reaction – and the more zinc added to the cell culture (within a certain range), the better the response.

'This is a test-tube study, a special study,' the Sloan Kettering spokesperson told us. 'But it does suggest that zinc may be able to stimulate B-cells to make antibodies.'

Zinc's support of lymphocyte activity and antibody production may explain, at least in part, the long-observed connection between low zinc levels and susceptibility to infection. One American study found, for example, that men with prostate infections had, on the average, one-tenth as much zinc in their prostatic fluid as healthy men. Similarly, a British doctor reported low zinc levels in 15 of his patients who were afflicted with boils, recurrent infections that had plagued them for three years or more. When eight of these patients were given zinc supplements, their boils disappeared and did not come back.

Iron

When your body's resistance falls, keep iron in mind, too. Iron is essential for healthy blood that can carry plenty of life-giving oxygen, but recent research has demonstrated that the mineral also plays a key role in your body's defences.

Dr William R. Beisel of the US Army Medical Research Institute for Infectious Diseases noted, '. . . most studies suggest that the immune system of man is exquisitely sensitive to iron availability and responds adversely to deficiencies that are too small to lower hemoglobin values' (*Journal of the American Medical Association*, 2 January 1981).

In other words, long before anaemia rears its iron-deficient head, your body could be severely understaffed when it comes to fighting off invading infections.

Vitamin B$_6$

Several of the B vitamins contribute to a healthy immune system, but people over 60 who are prone to infections should pay particular attention to getting adequate amounts of vitamin B$_6$, or pyridoxine. In a study of 473 elderly patients, vitamin B$_6$ was found to be the one *most lacking*. 'That ageing is associated with depressed vitamin B$_6$ levels despite an apparently good diet . . . is confirmed in our study,' wrote the researchers. They added that the B$_6$ deficiency also may play an 'important role in the well-known susceptibility of older persons to severe bacterial and viral infections.' The researchers suggested that the elderly's immune response may decline because of persistent shortages of vitamin B$_6$ (*Journal of the American Geriatrics Society*, October 1979).

Behind the immunological decline produced by vitamin B$_6$ deficiency may be changes in the thymus, a gland closely associated with disease resistance. Without sufficient amounts of B$_6$, researchers at Ohio State University have found, cells within the thymus that should form T-lymphocytes (body defender cells) never do – in a sense they cannot grow up into effective defenders.

Zinc apparently has an essential role to play in the thymus, too. Zinc deficiency causes the gland to shrink. And in the Sloan Kettering study mentioned earlier, zinc supplementation of deficient patients increased levels of a thymus hormone that may be important in keeping lymphocytes active.

Ageing and immunity

Giving your immune system every advantage that good nutrition can provide is especially important as you grow older. Typically, the passing of the years brings about a decline in the size and activity of the thymus, along with a decrease in the ability to produce lymphocytes and antibodies. As a result, perhaps, older people are usually far more prone to certain cancers and infections.

Also, when a spouse dies, immunity drops. Widows and widowers tend to encounter diseases – from heart attacks to cancer – shortly after their spouses' death. These disasters have stimulated much research into the link between catastrophic life changes and disease. They parallel similar observations made by researcher Lawrence Burton, who has reported that patients doing well on immuno-augmentation therapy will often suffer setbacks in the middle of what had been successful treatment if they receive bad news from home.

Before a meeting of the American Psychiatric Association, a psychiatrist disclosed the first clue to the process. He and his associates at the New York Mount Sinai School of Medicine had been observing men whose wives had advanced breast cancer. As early as two weeks after the wives died, the men showed a striking drop in the white cell response to stimulants of the immune system (*Medical World News*, 21 July 1980).

Can you keep up your defences in your later years? Dr Denham Harman believes you can – with the help of vitamin E. The decline in immunity, he theorizes, is due in large part to free radical reactions that impair the cells and chemicals involved. By inhibiting free radical reactions, he suggests, vitamin E can preserve the strength of the immune system.

When Dr Harman gave vitamin E to a group of mice, he found that the loss of immune response that accompanies age was, in fact, slowed down. Their ability to manufacture antibodies did not decline as steeply as that of untreated mice, nor did the loss of lymphocyte activity proceed as quickly (*Journal of the American Geriatrics Society*).

Considering how many nutrients are necessary for immunity (among those we haven't even mentioned are protein, several B vitamins besides B_6, vitamin D and manganese), the conclusion should be obvious: strong resistance must be built on a strong diet.

Build your own diet on a foundation of natural whole foods and nutritional supplements, and you'll be raising high ramparts against the attacks of disease.

• Impotence and sexual dysfunction

When Adam and Eve were told to 'be fruitful and multiply', they didn't think twice about it. It was no trouble for them to get in the mood. At the drop of a fig leaf, desire was there. And why not? What else did they have to do?

Nowadays, it's not always so easy. Even if you've managed to find your own garden of Eden, it probably has a huge mortgage that takes two pay cheques to support. You work under pressure all day, then face household chores all evening. Sure, you can handle it, but something's got to give. And that something often turns out to be desire – sexual desire, to be exact.

If you ask your family doctor about the problem of waning desire, he's apt to shrug his shoulders, lower his eyes and in a half-embarrassed voice suggest you try to relax or read a sex manual. For many doctors, that's about the best (and only) advice they can offer, since they're often not anymore knowledgeable about the subject than you are.

Too bad, too, because there's lots of new information that can help perk up your sex life. First of all, you should know that lack of desire can strike anyone at any time and can be caused by just about anything. The solution, then, is often a matter of changing or eliminating the things that are turning you off, once you identify them. And that's where we can help you out.

Most doctors blame what goes on in your head for what does or does not happen in the bedroom. Actually, there's much more than your head involved, but it's a good place to start.

Loss of desire

'Even people with normal sexual appetites can physiologically turn themselves off with overwhelming problems,' says Wanda Sadoughi, director of the sexual dysfunction clinic at Cook County Hospital in Chicago. 'By the time some patients come to the clinic, they are having major dysfunctional problems – such as impotence or lack of orgasm. But before all that occurred, the first symptom some of these people had was a loss of desire. And desire is crucial to sexuality.'

'Depression, stress and fatigue can damage sexuality profoundly,' adds Helen Singer Kaplan, head of the sex therapy and education programme at Payne Whitney Clinic of the New York Hospital. 'When a patient is severely depressed, sex is the furthest thing from his mind. Even moderately depressed patients lose interest in pursuing sexual activity and are very difficult to seduce and arouse,' says Dr Kaplan, who is also the author of *The New Sex Therapy*.

Good marriages aren't immune either. A survey of 100 happily married couples showed that, when it came to sex, 50 per cent of the men and 77 per cent of the women reported a lack of interest or an inability to relax *(New England Journal of Medicine)*.

Sometimes blind acceptance of cultural myths can dampen desire to the point of extinction. That's especially true of sex and the aged. 'In the geriatric field, one of the last bastions of culturally enforced ignorance persists in the area of sex and sexuality,' wrote William H. Masters, renowned sex therapist and author (with his wife Virginia Johnson).

> The widely accepted cultural dogma that sexual interaction between older persons is not only socially unacceptable, but may be physically harmful, results in thousands of men and women withdrawing from active sexual expression every year. [*Journal of the American Geriatrics Society*, September 1981]

'It's true you can't do at 60 what you did at 20,' adds John P. Wincze, associate professor of psychiatry at Brown University School of Medicine and chief of psychiatry at Providence (Rhode Island) Veterans Administration Medical Center. 'Many of my elderly patients get worried because they don't respond as quickly as they did when they were younger,' Dr Wincze told us. 'They'll see a pretty girl, and it's not the turn-on it used to be. That's a normal part of ageing. Desire may diminish, but just being old doesn't make it disappear. Mostly it's how you perceive yourself,' explains Dr Wincze. 'If you think of yourself as too old for "all that stuff", then you will lose your desires.'

Usually, when people say they're too old for sex, they really mean that they're too anxious about their current level of sexual performance as compared to what they used to be able to do, Dr Masters points out. In fact, anxiety or, more specifically, anxiety about sexual performance is the prime inhibitor of sexual response.

Those fears are particularly evident in people recovering from a heart attack. What's more, heart patients often avoid sex because they are afraid that the stress may bring on another attack. With that thought hanging over them, it's no wonder the desire for sex is lost.

Yet research has demonstrated time and again that the actual amount of physical energy expended by an individual during sexual intercourse is equivalent to such everyday household activities as scrubbing a floor or climbing several flights of stairs, and is well below the energy demands of most jobs. Nevertheless, the myth persists. In one study of 100 heart attack patients, 90 returned to work, but only 40 resumed normal sexual activity *(British Medical Journal)*. Another study showed that of 48 similar patients, 17 had a change in sexual desire or a fear of intercourse, or were depressed *(Annals of Internal Medicine*, April 1980).

'In most instances,' says Dr Sadoughi, 'when a person goes home from the hospital, the danger level has passed.'

'Sex in your familiar home surroundings with your partner of long standing will usually not cause excessive stress,' comments Dr Wincze.

But having an extramarital encounter might. In fact, studies have shown that on the rare occasions when sex did coincide with a heart attack, it was under those circumstances and was usually combined with over-eating and excessive alcohol.

Yet to a patient not properly informed, it may seem logical that any sexual activity would strain the heart beyond its capacity. That's why adequate sex counselling is clearly needed for someone recovering from a heart attack. And it's just as important for his or her spouse to be in on the sessions, too, because she (or he) can be plagued with the same doubts and fears as the patient.

Decreased hormone levels

Nobody really knows for sure why severe emotional states impair our natural desires for sex. Some experts think it's purely in the head. On the other hand, the physiological and hormonal changes that accompany stress and depression may also contribute to a lowered sexual appetite by affecting the central nervous system and by creating a decrease in the body's testosterone supply. (Testosterone, a hormone produced in both men and women, is needed for sexual desire.)

'More specifically,' says Dr Kaplan, 'several recent studies have reported that men who are under stress show a significant and consistent depression of their blood testosterone levels. After the stress has been measured, this level rapidly returns to normal.'

However, it's not just emotional problems that can affect the testosterone levels in the body. If you're a cigarette smoker, you could have a problem.

That's what Dr Sadoughi is investigating. 'We're trying to find out if testosterone is lowered by heavy cigarette smoking,' Dr Sadoughi told us. 'To prove it, we're conducting a study now to see just what the difference in testosterone levels is between smokers and non-smokers.'

'Heavy cigarette smoking involves more than just nicotine,' adds George Schwartz, author of *Food Power* (1979) and associate professor of community, family and emergency medicine at the University of New Mexico Medical Center. 'It leads to the accumulation of large amounts of carbon monoxide in the blood, which impairs an efficient supply of oxygen to the cells. Thus, heavy smoking tends to decrease sexual capabilities.'

The zinc connection

Another way smoking does this is by depleting your body's supply of zinc. 'Heavy smokers in particular might need more zinc,' says Ali A. Abbasi, an endocrinologist in Indiana. 'The cadmium [a toxic heavy metal] in smoke interferes with zinc metabolism and can accumulate in the testicles. Therefore one might suspect there is an increased demand for zinc.' When it comes to a man's sexual functioning, zinc really is the last word. Zinc deficiency will likely impair sexual growth and maturation, because this mineral appears to be essential for the metabolism of testosterone.

According to Carl C. Pfeiffer, head of the Brain Bio Center in Princeton, New Jersey, insufficient zinc can lead to a greatly reduced sperm count, improper development of the penis and testes in young males, and prostate problems. (The prostate supplies the launching fluid for sperm during orgasm.)

Now, however, scientists report that it doesn't require a *severe* zinc deficiency to play havoc with sexual vigour. Even men who are only *slightly* zinc deficient are asking for trouble.

'Sexual dysfunction could be present in the marginal cases because the testes seem to be very sensitive to zinc,' notes Ananda Prasad, professor of medicine and chief of haematology at Wayne State University School of Medicine in Detroit.

To test this hypothesis, Dr Prasad and his colleagues induced mild zinc deficiencies through dietary manipulations in five healthy men aged 51 to 65. By eating controlled meals, the subjects actually lost about 1 mg of zinc a day from their bodies. During a six-month period, sperm counts dropped in four of the men, and testosterone levels dropped in all five. In three men, the sperm counts plummeted below the point of technical sterility, says one of the researchers. And while the results were admittedly 'very subjective', the men complained of diminished sexual desire when fed the zinc-restricted diet, according to Parviz Rabbani, a nutritional biochemist working with Dr Prasad. However, after the volunteers resumed standard meals and were fortified with 30 mg of zinc a day, they returned to normal within 16 to 20 weeks.

A question every man might be asking is: Could I be even moderately zinc deficient? Because smoking, alcohol, infections and medications can winnow away zinc reserves, Dr Rabbani suspects that marginal zinc insufficiencies may be commonplace.

For patients with kidney disease, zinc may be especially important. 'It's a well-known fact,' says Sudesh Mahajan, a kidney specialist at Wayne State University School of Medicine, 'that 70 per cent of renal patients do have some degree of impotence.' The bright side is that zinc supplementation has dramatically reversed these sexual woes in a group of kidney dialysis patients.

One such study was conducted at a Veterans Administration Hospital in Michigan, where Dr Mahajan is chief of nephrology. The 20 subjects, men aged 28 to 65, required machines – artificial replacement for their disabled kidneys – to filter impurities from the blood.

All initially had low sperm counts and testosterone levels. During the double-blind study, no one knew which ten men received the placebo or which ten men got 50 mg of zinc a day.

After a year, every zinc-treated man showed biochemical improvements and reported restored potency. 'In some cases,' Dr Mahajan told us, 'changes occurred in just six weeks. Needless to say, their wives and girlfriends were happy.'

The placebo-fed group, in contrast, could hardly boast of a new boost in their life. Their sex drives never accelerated, and impotency remained a problem. Furthermore, their low sperm counts and testosterone levels never perked up.

Dr Pfeiffer has also found that zinc may contribute to the 'glint in the eye of the more aggressive male' because both the retina (the light-sensitive coating at the back of the eye) and the prostate are exceedingly high in zinc content. He's also discovered large amounts of zinc in the pineal and hippocampus glands in the brain. The pineal gland is directly linked to sex drive, while the hippocampus controls emotions.

'With this knowledge,' he contends, 'we still can't say that anyone's sex life would be better with excess zinc.' Still, he suggests, adequate zinc levels are needed for normal sexual activity and reproduction.

Dr Prasad recommends that once a doctor has ruled out most organic and psychological causes of impotence, plasma zinc levels should be checked. If a zinc deficiency does exist, the doctor can begin treating it with 20 to 30 mg of zinc daily for six months to a year. 'One nice thing about this deficiency,' he says, 'is that it is correctable.'

Sadly, many healthy men report a worsening of sexual function as they grow older. Too often, middle age is middling when it comes to sex. For senior citizens, sex is far too frequently just another pleasant memory. Well, stop remembering old flames and light your fire with zinc!

As we mentioned earlier, zinc is a must for the health of the prostate, the male organ that supplies the fluid that launches the sperm out of the body during orgasm. But that's not all the prostate does. When it's not working right, it can make sex difficult.

Almost every American male over 60 has a prostate problem – swelling (without evidence of cancer) – which doctors call *benign prostatic hyperplasia* (BPH). In addition, many younger men between the ages of 20 and 60 develop *prostatitis*, an inflammation of the prostate. BPH can cause sexual impotence and 'prostatitis can impair sexual function,' according to an article in *Geriatrics*.

A doctor has found that many men with prostate problems have low levels of zinc in their prostates – and that zinc supplements can get their prostates back in shape. Irving M. Bush, professor and chairman of urology at the Chicago Medical School, and a team of researchers tested the zinc levels in the prostates of over 200 patients with prostatitis, many of whom were found to have low levels. Dr Bush gave them from 50 to 150 mg of zinc every day for four months. For more than 70 per cent of these patients – relief.

Dr Bush told us that, in the sexual therapy clinic at Cook County Hospital, there are always patients whose impotency is caused by prostatitis. These men often become potent after taking zinc supplements.

Can zinc treat BPH, too? Dr Bush gave 150 mg of zinc daily to 19 patients with BPH, reducing it to 50 to 100 mg after two months. In 14 of the patients, the swelling seemed to go down.

'It is not specifically known how oral zinc therapy is effective in treating these two diseases,' says Dr Bush, 'but there is no question that it can treat them! It *is* known how zinc treated the impotent men with kidney disease.

'Zinc appears to be essential for the metabolism of testosterone, which is the primary male hormone,' Dr Lucy D. Antoniou, one of the researchers who conducted the study on zinc and impotent kidney patients, told us. Without enough testosterone, sex drive can't get in gear. Without enough zinc, testosterone levels are low.

Improved glucose tolerance

Zinc is not the only nutritional supplement that can help treat impotence. Put brewer's yeast on the list.

This is the richest source of a little-known nutrient, the 'glucose tolerance factor' (GTF). The trace mineral chromium is an important part of that factor, believed responsible for the way your body uses glucose.

Glucose is a simple sugar, the fuel that powers your body. To keep your body's engine from being flooded by glucose – or from running out of fuel – a hormone, insulin, controls the rate at which glucose is stored and/or burned up. And to do its job right, insulin needs GTF.

Without enough GTF, a problem can develop that doctors call *glucose intolerance*: glucose levels bounce up and down like a seesaw. But that doesn't make your body a sexual playground. Just the opposite. Glucose intolerance may be one of the major causes of impotence.

We talked to Stanley Deutsch, the supervising biochemist for the endocrinology laboratory at Queens Hospital Center in New York. Dr Deutsch, who is actively engaged in studying chemical imbalances and impotency, told us that 50 per cent of all males with diabetes – a severe disturbance in glucose metabolism – are impotent.

In one study Dr Deutsch compared the glucose tolerance of a group of men who had become impotent after a history of normal sexual functioning and were patients at a sexual therapy clinic, to a group of men who were potent. The glucose tolerance of the impotent men was 'much more deteriorated' *(Diabetes Outlook)*. However, scientific studies have shown that GTF-rich brewer's yeast can reverse glucose intolerance! Moreover, some researchers have advanced the theory that taking brewer's yeast every day (even just a tablespoonful) could prevent glucose intolerance from developing.

Eating and drinking

'The stress of digesting a big meal can make an evening's sex play out of the question,' says one doctor. His advice is to be moderate at dinner if you want to relish sex later that night. That goes for alcoholic drinks even more than for food.

According to Leon Marder, professor of psychiatry and medicine at the University of Southern California, drinking can undermine sexual desire because it tends to reduce the body's production of sex hormones. Even persons who consume just a drink or two a day can suffer the sexually harmful effects of alcohol, Dr Marder emphasizes.

'In fact, everything we take in has an effect on sex,' Dr Sadoughi told us. 'We're only now beginning to realize how many physiological aspects there are to desire. I believe that the future of sexual research lies in this important area.

'Right now, for example, we know that many drugs, both prescription and over-the-counter, can weaken sexual appetite or destroy it altogether. For example, some birth-control pills may decrease sexual desire.

And the list goes on. You may not realize it, but many tranquillizers, antihistamines, anti-depressants, ulcer medications and drugs to lower blood pressure can have that same detrimental effect. *(See table p 441)*. 'It wouldn't surprise me at all if coffee affects desire, too,' Dr Sadoughi says.

Michael Lesser is already convinced that it does. 'Caffeine addiction creates a thiamin deficiency, leading to depression and associated loss of sexual interest,' says Dr Lesser, who is author of *Nutrition and Vitamin Therapy* (1981).

'The fact of the matter is that sexual activity, one of mankind's most sensitive and easily disturbed bodily functions, is extraordinarily vulnerable to poor eating habits,' add Emanuel Cheraskin and W. Marshal Ringsdorf, Jr, authors of *Psychodietetics*. 'The "I'm too tired" syndrome that sexually disrupts so many marriages can be traced directly to overall nutritional deficiencies, which contribute to an underactive thyroid, which in turn leads to decreased libido [desire] and chronic fatigue.'

Dr Lesser agrees. 'The thyroid is vital to sexuality. An underactive gland results in lethargy, tiredness, overweight and lack of desire and capacity for sex.' That's because the thyroid hormone *thyroxine* controls metabolism. 'If one of my patients has a sluggish sex drive and other signs of a slowed metabolism, I prescribe $150\mu g$ of organic iodine [the essential constituent of thyroxine], along with thiamin, also crucially needed by the thyroid.'

While you're keeping your thyroid healthy, don't neglect the rest of your glands. All of them require proteins (and the amino acids they're made from) for efficient functioning.

'It is logical,' says Dr Schwartz, 'that our sex drive would go down when not enough protein, or protein of the wrong amino acid type, is eaten.'

Now for most of us that's no problem, since we're meat eaters. But what about vegetarians? 'A purely vegetarian diet tends to decrease sexual drive in men, since certain proteins and amino acids are in lesser quantities,' says Dr Schwartz. 'Such a diet may tend to induce a more relaxed state, with

Drugs that may induce impotence

Drug	Comments
Baclofen *Lioresal*	Dosage reduction or withdrawal may be necessary.
Clofibrate *Atromid-S*	Three per cent of 100 patients became impotent within a year of initiating therapy.
Disopyramide *Dirythmin, Rythmodan*	Impotence reported with high serum level, disappeared when dose was reduced.
Fenfluramine hydrocloride *Ponderax*	Impotence and loss of libido have been reported.
Guanethidine sulphate *Ismelin*	Up to 67 per cent of patients may experience disturbance of sexual function.
Methyldopa *Aldomet, Dopamet, Medomet*	Disorders of sexual function are dose-related and common.
Phenelzine sulphate *Nardil*	Impotence in men and difficulty in achieving orgasm in women have been reported.
Prazosin hydrochloride *Hypovase*	Impotence has been reported in 0.7 per cent of 282 patients.
Spironolactone *Aldactone, Diatensec, Laractone, etc.*	The drug causes a reduction in plasma testosterone levels.

SOURCE: *Modern Medicine*, 28 February–15 March 1981.

decreased aggressive drives and a more contemplative attitude.'

However, if it's sex you're contemplating, you may want to be sure your diet contains enough choline, another nutritive substance that may be lacking in vegetarian diets. It's found in highest quantities in egg yolks and meat.

In fact, it's important to take a close look at your diet, whether you're a vegetarian or not. Do you eat a lot of junk food? Do you skip meals, then binge later? Are you getting enough vitamins and minerals?

'The relationship between good nutrition and sex has been known through the ages,' says Dr Lesser. 'Loss of desire and the ability to perform is an early consequence of general malnutrition, as well as a specific symptom of particular vitamin or mineral deficiencies.'

Putting yourself in the mood

If your diet's in good shape and your general physical health is up to par, then maybe you need to reorganize your priorities. How much work do you bring home from the office? How many activities do you chauffeur your kids to? Do you give yourself a chance to unwind before you walk into the bedroom?

'At the end of a work day, there is a natural transition period you need to go through before desire can be sparked,' Dr Sadoughi told us. 'After all, at work you are non-sexual, but at home you are expected to become a sexual being. The front door is like the barrier which symbolizes the changeover from one to the other.'

Except that it doesn't happen quite so fast. You need a transition period to go from one phase to the other. 'Often the man will come home from work and begin his transition period. He gets changed into comfortable clothes, reads the paper and has dinner. He begins to think about sex. The woman, meanwhile, is usually still working. She clears the table, does the dishes and straightens up. He may now be interested in sex, while she hasn't even begun to unwind. It's almost impossible to jump from the kitchen to the bedroom if your mind is still in the kitchen,' Dr Sadoughi emphasizes.

'Some people can learn to put aside or compartmentalize their problems,' says Dr Wincze. 'They can then turn to something else completely and be OK. It's important to learn to divorce yourself from daily stress. I had two patients with the same problems, yet one's sex life was not affected, while the other's was.'

Of course, you can't ignore the fact that the length of a relationship may affect the level of desire, too. 'Aside from a deteriorating physical condition of either or both partners, sexual boredom may be the greatest detriment to the effectiveness of sexual interaction between men and women in any long-standing relationship,' says Dr Masters.

Just look at anyone who's recently fallen in love, and desire will be bursting out all over. Now, we're not suggesting you find a new lover, just that you look at your present partner with new and different eyes.

'Be open to new ways of enjoying sex,' suggests Dr Wincze. 'Throw in an element of risk, too. Dream up a romantic fantasy and take your partner along. Make love in a different location or at a different time of day. Talk about love and desire with your partner, and most of all be knowledgeable, so that myths don't interfere with enjoyment.'

Lower your expectations, too. 'With age, it is less and less likely that, during any given sexual experience, there will be mutually high levels of sexual interest,' says Dr Masters. 'The warm sensual experience of simply holding and being held must not be viewed as a failed sexual experience because orgasm was not achieved.'

Indeed, just removing the pressure to perform can re-establish a healthy level of desire. You may never feel quite the level that Adam and Eve did, but, then do you know how they felt after 35 years of living together?

• Indigestion

Your stomach is a tough customer. Thick muscles clamp down on food and squeeze it for all it's worth. An acid powerful enough to burn your skin bathes the stomach walls. No wonder you and your tummy may get into a tussle every now and then. And those blows above the belt like heartburn and indigestion are enough to make you call for help. Just hope that the 'help' doesn't make you hurt worse.

Many of the treatments recommended by doctors for their patients with stomach problems simply do not work – or actually do more harm than good.

Calcium carbonate, one common antacid ingredient, causes 'acid rebound'. This chemical – which does take the sting out of acid already in your stomach – also triggers the release of a hormone that tells the stomach to pump out more acid. The acid level falls at first but bounces right back – and to a level higher than it was to start with.

However, there are several natural remedies for an upset stomach.

Bran Dr Neil Stamford Painter and his colleagues reported in the *British Medical Journal* that, among 70 patients with diverticular disease of the colon, 11 often felt nausea and stomach upset. But after several weeks of taking an average of two tablespoons of bran daily, seven of these patients reported a complete absence of nausea. Two others said their symptoms were relieved. Many cases of heartburn were also relieved by the bran regimen.

In another study, A. J. M. Brodribb and Daphne M. Humphreys reported that 19 out of 22 patients complaining of nausea were either completely or largely relieved after taking bran *(British Medical Journal)*.

Dr Painter and his colleagues propose a commonsense theory for why bran works: if fibre-rich foods such as bran are necessary for the normal functioning of the lower bowel, then they are probably also needed for the health of the whole digestive tract.

Papaya Another natural aid to digestion is the tropical fruit papaya – a rich source of papain, a powerful protein-digesting enzyme. But if papaya is out of season – or if none of your local shops stocks it – then you can turn to papain supplements. You may find that papain helps relieve not only stomach upset but 'wind' as well.

Fennel In his classic on natural remedies, *Back to Eden*, Jethro Kloss proposed the herb fennel as 'one of the thoroughly tried remedies for gas [wind], acid stomach, gout, cramps, colic and spasms'. Kloss suggested using the herb almost as a spice, sprinkling ground fennel on food to prevent gas in the stomach and bowels. Many herbalists advise making a tea made from the seeds of the plant to be used as a treatment for indigestion.

Catmint Although it may have your cat jumping and wobbling around, catmint may help to set your stomach straight. In their book, *A Guide to the Medicinal Plants of the United States*, Arnold and Connie Krochmal noted that a tea made from catmint is a traditional Appalachian remedy for stomach ailments.

Kloss gave catmint rave reviews, calling it 'very useful in pain of any kind', and excellent in allaying wind and acid. He continued enthusiastically: 'It is a harmless remedy and should take the place of the various soothing syrups on the market, many of which are very harmful. This wonderful remedy should be in every home.'

Anise If your sweet tooth has given you a sour stomach, try chewing on anise seeds. That's the advice of R. Swimburne Clymer in his book, *Nature's Healing Agents*. Dr Clymer noted that parents frequently gave their children cakes covered with anise seeds during the holiday season to soothe the acid stomach that can result from over-eating sweets.

Mint You may never have laid eyes on a peppermint or spearmint plant, but thanks to the popularity of chewing gum, mints and toothpaste, you probably know their distinctive flavours. Well, chewing gum is no remedy for indigestion, but if you've doubled your fun at a dinner party with a big second helping, peppermint and spearmint tea may help you out.

Peppermint, like catmint, has been used in Appalachia to treat indigestion and colic, say the Krochmals. It is also considered a stimulant and is used for all sorts of intestinal ailments. Kloss noted that 'a strong cup of peppermint tea will act more powerfully on the system than any liquor [alcoholic] stimulant, quickly diffusing itself through the system and bringing back to the body its natural warmth. . . .' He points out that it's an excellent remedy for gas in the stomach, nausea, vomiting, diarrhoea and colon troubles.

In contrast to peppermint's enlivening qualities, spearmint is 'very soothing and quieting to the nerves', wrote Kloss. Like peppermint, however, spearmint is a 'highly esteemed' remedy for gas in the stomach, nausea and vomiting.

Sage Sage is valued for counteracting rich and greasy foods such as goose and duck. That's probably why it has a reputation to this day as a digestive aid. In fact, many who take sage for intestinal inflammation testify that the strong, camphorous, slightly bitter tea is quite effective.

Yogurt Another tummy-tamer is yogurt. Yogurt is milk that's been fermented by bacteria like *Lactobacillus acidophilus* and *Lactobacillus bulgaricus*.

Texas osteopath Steven Cordas says, 'I have treated stomach ailments of all kinds with acidophilus. I have also treated oesophagitis, an inflammation of the tube that carries food from the mouth to the stomach, with it. The primary benefit of this bacteria is in the colon, but its secondary benefit is in the entire digestive tract.'

Fellow osteopath Paul Wynn agrees. 'If someone comes into my office with a digestive complaint, I ask them to eat a cup of yogurt a day and come back in a week. Only if their problem persists – and it often doesn't – do I investigate further.'

And a last word about eating itself.

Even though we advise you to exercise whenever you can, don't race through your meals. Make them leisurely and enjoyable. Chew slowly and savour your food. Enjoy conversation – don't argue or complain. When your face turns red with anger, so does the inside of your stomach. Not only the stomach, but the whole digestive tract is very sensitive to your emotions. Wear a smile when you sit down to eat. Indigestion won't dare show its face.

• Infections

To protect against infection, take vitamin C, right? Even people who consider 'good nutrition' to be a 'fortified' sugar-coated cereal have heard the word, it seems, and greet the coming of cold weather with gram-sized supplements to ward off colds and sore throats.

And there's nothing wrong with that. By now, there's more evidence than you can easily keep track of that vitamin C does, indeed, help your body to repel the attacks of cold viruses, sore throat germs and many of the rest of our microscopic foes.

If there's a problem, it's that vitamin C has been *too* dramatically successful – like the basketball superstar who's so glamorous that people start to ignore his less flamboyant but still very effective teammates. In this case, vitamin C's ability to beef up resistance to disease makes people forget about the other nutrients that have a lot to offer in this department – for example zinc and vitamin A – which is unfortunate, since where resistance is involved, you need all the help you can get.

Vitamin E

Another under-appreciated source of help, according to an impressive series of studies conducted at Colorado State University, is vitamin E (*Federation Proceedings*, June 1979). According to Cheryl Nockels and colleagues of the department of animal sciences at Colorado State University, vitamin E – in amounts well beyond the US Recommended Dietary Allowance (RDA) of 8–11 IU (there is no RDA in the UK) – can also play a major role in keeping strong the body's defence against infection.

While many nutritional studies compare the effect of a deficient diet to that of one with an 'adequate' supply of the vitamin involved, Dr Nockels organized things a bit differently. She gave some animals their normal laboratory diet – which supplies the US Recommended Dietary Allowance of everything, including vitamin E. To others she gave the same diet *plus* a supplementary amount of vitamin E. It was like comparing a group of people who ate a 'good' diet with another group who ate a good diet with vitamin E supplements.

'I tried to determine whether supplements of vitamin E, given in excess of what is required for normal growth and reproduction, increased immunity to infection,' she told us.

In one experiment, Dr Nockels reported, researchers gave one group of mice their normal diet and another a diet supplemented with 60 IU of vitamin E per kilogram of food (one kilogram [2.2 lb] is about the amount of food you probably eat in a day). They injected both groups with a sheep's red blood cells. Four days later, the mice were examined.

When mice are injected with sheep red blood cells, their bodies react to them the way they'd react to bacteria – by producing the chemicals called antibodies that take invaders out of action. That vital defensive process was significantly stronger in the mice who had received the vitamin E supplements. For one thing, the weight of their spleens was greater (a sign of increased antibody production), and when the researchers measured the amounts of antibodies in the blood of both groups, the supplemented mice tested considerably higher.

Dr Nockels and her co-workers then tested the effect of vitamin E on immunity in guinea pigs. She gave one group of the small rodents injections of vitamin E in amounts well above the standard dietary level; another group got no injections. Then she vaccinated them with the virus that causes a serious strain of encephalitis (inflammation of the brain and spinal cord). Here, too, the animals that received supplemental vitamin E protected themselves with significantly higher levels of antibodies then those that did not.

Active immunity, the body's ability to manufacture antibodies against invading organisms, provides important protection at any age. However, newborn animals (and this includes human infants) don't have this ability. Until they can establish it on their own, they are dependent on the antibodies transferred to them as they grow in their mothers' wombs, and in their mothers' milk after birth.

According to another of Dr Nockels's experiments, vitamin E can effectively boost the process of 'passive transfer' that keeps defences up at this particularly vital time. She gave one group of hens a diet supplemented with 150 IU of vitamin E per kilogram of food, and the other just the normal feed. After four weeks, she incubated their eggs.

Researchers took blood samples when the chicks were two days and seven days old and measured the antibody levels. The offspring of hens given vitamin E supplements, it was found, had higher levels of antibodies than the controls. The vitamin E their mothers received, it seems, gave them a better start in life.

While laboratory measurements of immune reactions are important, they must be judged with care. Resistance to disease is a complex thing, and a higher level of antibodies does not automatically mean better defence against infection. A small but significant rise in antibodies, for instance, may not make any *practical* difference when real bacteria and viruses are involved. To determine whether vitamin E supplements effectively help to prevent infection, Dr Nockels and colleagues performed a series of experiments with chicks, turkeys and lambs. Using a number of different species, she explained, 'makes generalizations sounder. It strengthens the likelihood that findings will also apply to humans.'

Groups of chicks and turkeys were fed either the normal chick or turkey feed, or normal feed plus vitamin E supplements ranging from 100 to 300 IU per kilogram of food. They were then injected with disease-causing bacteria. Among both the chicks and the turkeys, *vitamin E supplements meant a lower mortality rate*: fewer animals succumbed to the disease.

What's more, there was a significant connection between the size of the supplement and the degree of protection. For example, 25 per cent of the chicks that received no supplements died of the infection, 10 per cent of those who received 150 IU of vitamin E died, and only 5 per cent of those who received 300 IU died.

In another experiment, Dr Nockels and co-workers fed a group of lambs large doses of vitamin E, then inoculated them and an unsupplemented group with *Chlamydia*, a germ that induces pneumonia in sheep. Later examination of the animals showed less damage to the lungs of those that had received vitamin E supplements than to those of the controls. Also, the supplemented animals showed no traces of the bacteria in their bodies, while the pathological organisms could be found in 40 per cent of the controls.

In all three species, Dr Nockels concluded, vitamin E significantly improved resistance to disease.

This particular aspect of vitamin E may be worthy of greater attention, Dr Nockels says. 'I think that further research may show that vitamin E provides positive improvement of immune capability in humans, too.'

Such research may show, among other things, that the US RDA – what is normally considered 'enough' vitamin E – is far too low. 'The RDA does not appear to maintain immunity at full strength,' says Dr Nockels. 'In every case, I found that an amount of vitamin E greater than the RDA for the animal was required to stimulate improved immune response. And with elderly animals, the allowances might have to be even higher.'

Vitamin A

This is another important member of the infection-fighting team. Dr Thomas Moore of Dunn Nutritional Laboratory in Cambridge, commenting on his work with rats in *The Vitamins*, says that the most common causes of death among animals deprived of vitamin A are infections of the lining of the respiratory tract, the intestines, or the urinary tract. Normally protected by mucus, the lining of these body cavities becomes a perfect place for bacteria to take hold when it loses its moist barrier.

According to Leopoldo F. Montes, professor of dermatology, University of Alabama Medical Center, *mucocutaneous candidiasis* (commonly known as 'thrush'), a fungal infection of the skin, mouth, respiratory tract or vagina, seems more likely to attack people who are deficient in vitamin A. Dr Montes tested blood levels of the vitamin in 12 people with the infection and found that seven of them had lower than normal amounts. Vitamin A levels in the other five were in the lower half of the normal range *(Skin and Allergy News)*.

One of the body's gates that is often troubled by persistent infections is the vagina. Mucus secreted inside it normally keeps the inner walls clean and protects against infectious organisms. But the purpose of this natural cleansing mechanism can be defeated if a woman douches or uses feminine deodorant sprays. Even if there is enough vitamin A in the body to keep mucous membranes working properly, washing the mucus away may still leave the lining unprotected long enough to give infections a foothold. Also, drugs such as cortisone which make the body require more vitamin A, and antibiotics, which kill off beneficial bacteria, can make the vagina more liable to become infected. Although some doctors use very high doses of vitamin A for a short period of time to cure such infections, a better idea would be to *prevent* infections by taking *slightly* higher doses of the vitamin to keep the natural defences working as they should. Douches and sprays should also be avoided.

Eli Seifter, associate professor of biochemistry and surgery at Albert Einstein College of Medicine, says that vitamin A increases the body's immune response to pox viruses, a group that once included smallpox (now eradicated). In experiments with mice, animals given extra vitamin A in amounts from five to ten times the US RDA were less affected by injections of viruses. In those animals that did get reactions, fewer 'pox' developed. Vitamin A also extended the disease's incubation period, shortened the duration of illness, and reduced fever *(Infectious Diseases)*.

Speculating as to how vitamin A could have this effect, Dr Seifter explained that the thymus gland, which is vital to the cells' protection against infection, tends to *shrink* when the body is subjected to stress. When this occurs, the body's immune response suffers. Vitamin A, though, *increases* the size of the thymus gland. Whether this explains why vitamin A seems to stimulate the body's defence against disease is not known for sure, but the protective effect is there, and has been confirmed by other reports.

Drs Benjamin E. Cohen and Ronald J. Elin of the Massachusetts General Hospital and the National Institutes of Health Clinical Center in Bethesda, Maryland, respectively, have found that vitamin A can remarkably increase resistance to a wide variety of infectious germs. They purposely challenged two groups of laboratory animals with three different types of infectious organisms. One group also received four consecutive daily injections of 3000 IU of vitamin A.

The vitamin A-treated mice that were infected with what was apparently the most vicious organism were *completely protected*. After 24 hours, *all* the untreated animals were dead from the infection, but the blood of the animals treated with vitamin A was virtually free of infection. In addition vitamin A-treated animals infected with the other organisms fared remarkably better than untreated animals *(Journal of Infectious Diseases)*.

There are many types of infections – from athlete's foot to the flu. Look under each specific ailment for more information.

(*See also* HEALING PROBLEMS, HOSPITAL MALNUTRITION, IMMUNE SYSTEM PROBLEMS.)

• Infertility

More and more couples are showing up at fertility clinics these days, searching for answers, hope and eventual parenthood. In the past, fertility specialists concentrated mainly on the woman when pregnancy failed to occur, but now they're finding that male infertility is increasing in frequency. In fact, the number of sperm that men are producing has dropped by almost half during the last 30 years, according to several studies – from 107 million per measured unit (millilitre: one-thousandth of a litre) to 62 million per unit. Not that 62 million is bad. It'll do the job. But in this case, more is definitely better.

Because the implications of the sperm decline can have far-reaching effects for further generations, scientists are anxious to get to the bottom of it.

Some researchers now think that toxic chemicals should be considered as one of the culprits. They point out that during the same 30 years that sperm counts have been declining, our use of these substances has steadily increased, with thousands entering the environment each year.

One researcher who agrees with that theory is Ralph C. Dougherty, professor of chemistry at Florida State University. 'We are much too casual about the chemicals we introduce into our environment,' says Dr Dougherty. And he should know.

He recently completed a study that found a correlation between lower sperm counts and the presence of polychlorinated biphenyls (PCB) in seminal fluid. The average sperm count of the 132 students tested was found to be 60 million per unit, but 23 per cent of the group had counts of only 20 million per unit or less. This level is often accepted as defining functional sterility. 'More important,' Dr Dougherty told us, 'every seminal fluid sample in the study showed amounts above background level of environmental contaminants such as PCB, hexachlorobenzene [a fungicide] and DDT metabolites. About 25 per cent of the reduced sperm counts correlated with the presence of PCB,' he added. 'PCBs act by inhibiting cell division through DNA damage – the material in genes. It takes eight cell divisions to get to a mature sperm. If cell division is slowed by 10 per cent, it can result in a 60 per cent decrease in the number of sperm produced.'

People become contaminated with these chemicals via the food chain, says Dr Dougherty, where they usually accumulate in fatty tissue, resisting breakdown because of their built-in stability. PCBs above one part per million are in virtually every freshwater fish. And even though they've been banned by the governments of both the United States and the United Kingdom, there are still more than 500,000 tons of PCBs in the US alone, where they are used in industry or discarded into landfills where they can leach out and contaminate the environment.

Occupational damage

In 1977, Dr Donald Whorton, a specialist in occupational medicine at the University of California at Berkeley, was asked to study a group of men who worked with the pesticide *dibromochloropropane* (DBCP) when the male employees began to notice that few of them had recently fathered children. Examination of the semen revealed a low sperm count in 14 of the 25 men tested. Nine of the men had no sperm at all, and two others had counts below one million per unit. Through questioning the men, it became apparent that infertility was associated with the length of time the men had worked with the DBCP. 'The relationship was striking,' wrote Dr Whorton. 'Workers with sperm counts below one million had been exposed for at least three years. None with sperm counts above 40 million had been exposed for more than three months' *(Lancet)*.

'DBCP was the so-called eye-opener to the problem of male infertility due to occupational exposure,' Dr Whorton told us. 'It's an emerging field, which will require years of research. We do know that the damage caused by DBCP is dose dependent. And that goes for its reversibility as well. Where the sperm count has been decreased, it takes three months to a year to return to normal. But where the sperm count has been reduced to zero, it may take up to six years to come back – if ever.'

Occupational exposure to lead, kepone, microwaves, chloroprene – all have had documented effects on male reproduction.

Even something as seemingly innocuous as excessive heat in the workplace can have adverse effects on male fertility. Marc S. Cohen a urologist with the New York Fertility Research Foundation, noticed that men who worked as short-order cooks or pizza bakers were experiencing fertility problems. Dr Cohen thought that their decreased sperm counts might be caused by the high temperatures to which they are routinely exposed. In an effort to help these particular men raise their sperm counts, Dr Cohen recommended cool baths, and has employed the use of a gadget that he refers to as 'very experimental'. During their hot working hours, his patients wear a scrotal pouch (developed by another doctor), which cools the testicles.

Dr Cohen routinely asks his patients with fertility problems about possible occupational hazards. Unfortunately, he's in the minority. According to Dr Kenneth Bridbord, formerly of the (US) National Institute for Occupational Safety and Health, 'Right now, the numbers of doctors are few who actually ask questions. Even those questions that do get asked only touch on a few areas like drugs and medications. The average physician doesn't know enough about occupational medicine to ask the right questions.'

Sperm enemies in everyday life

However, there are more than environmental and occupational hazards that threaten male fertility. Some common medications prescribed by doctors have shown the same disastrous effects as toxic chemicals. Cimetidine (Tagamet), a drug routinely used in the management of peptic ulcers, can cause infertility. So can sulphasalazine (Salazopyrin), a drug used to treat ulcerative colitis.

The list keeps growing. Add coffee, cigarettes, marijuana and alcohol, if you're keeping count.

While a controlled study comparing the amount of alcohol consumed to an actual decrease in sperm count has not been done, Jeanne Manson of the University of Cincinnati says that the evidence strongly suggests a connection between the two. Dr Manson did report, however, that there are studies showing a connection between smoking and sperm. It seems that the percentage of abnormally shaped sperm is directly related to the number of cigarettes smoked daily. And those smoking longer than ten years increased their disadvantage (*Work and the Health of Women*, 1979).

Marijuana smokers have abnormal sperm, too – what's left of them, that is. Experiments showed that young men who smoked marijuana at least four times a week for six months had a decided decrease in sperm numbers in proportion to the amount smoked, falling to almost zero in some very heavy users (*Keep Off the Grass*, 1979).

Although the effect of caffeine on human sperm has not been studied, its effect on animals has. According to Paul S. Weathersbee of the University of California Irvine Medical School, both rats and roosters showed a complete absence of sperm three weeks after being fed caffeine. That could be of some consequence to the man who normally consumes more than 600 mg per day of caffeinated beverages, says Dr Weathersbee – about six to eight cups of coffee a day.

Good nutrition aids reproduction

Are we about to pollute ourselves out of existence? No, not in the immediate future. But the warning signs are there, and they shouldn't be ignored. Nor should the steps you can take to help yourself. Start by eliminating nicotine, caffeine and alcohol from your life.

An overprocessed, nutrient-poor diet appears to play a role in infertility too. Good nutrition is important for all aspects of sexual life – fertility as well as sexual performance (*see* IMPOTENCE AND SEXUAL DYSFUNCTION). But of all the nutrients, vitamin C has shown the greatest promise in restoring fertility.

Vitamin C
Earl B. Dawson of the University of Texas Medical Branch in Galveston measured the effects of a vitamin C preparation (which also contained calcium, magnesium and manganese) on 20 men with *spermagglutination*, a condition

in which sperm stick together in clumps and are unable to swim normally. Seven men were used as controls and received no vitamin C. All 27 men (ages 25 to 38) had been diagnosed as infertile, having decreased motility (the ability of sperm to move in a forward direction) and relatively low sperm counts, the associated factors that make the clumping problem such bad news.

After 60 days, *all 20 men* taking the vitamin C preparation (1 g per day) had impregnated their wives, while none of the men in the control group had. And not only had the vitamin C preparation reversed the spermagglutination, but it had also raised sperm counts by 54 per cent (*Fertility and Sterility*, October 1979).

In a later study of a group of infertile men, only four days of vitamin C supplementation were needed to reverse spermagglutination and raise sperm counts. In that study, Dr Dawson also established that there is a direct relationship between a lack of vitamin C and male infertility (*Journal of the American Medical Association*, 27 May 1983).

Spermagglutination has, by some estimates, been implicated as a cause of male infertility in as many as 10 per cent of all cases. This means that over 150,000 men in the US alone could have a spermagglutination problem affecting their ability to father children.

'Perhaps,' speculates Dr Dawson, 'supplements of vitamin C, calcium, magnesium or manganese can reverse spermagglutination routinely, eliminating the need to use a donor to impregnate the wife.'

However, men aren't the only ones to profit from vitamin C. Vitamin C has been shown to work for women in some cases where fertility drugs can't. Masao Igarashi, a Japanese gynaecologist, tried vitamin C – by itself and in combination with the fertility drug *clomiphene* – on infertile women who had not responded to traditional clomiphene therapy. In two out of five women who habitually failed to produce ova (eggs), vitamin C did the trick by itself. Vitamin C and clomiphene combined corrected that problem in five out of five cases and worked much better than clomiphene alone against several other classes of infertility (*International Journal of Fertility*).

Zinc and vitamin A

Zinc, too, has been used successfully to improve fertility. Ali A. Abbasi an endocrinologist of the Allen Park Veterans Administration Hospital in Michigan, showed that even a mild zinc deficiency caused sperm counts to drop below the point of technical sterility. Supplemental zinc, however, returned sperm counts to normal.

Low semen zinc levels have also been associated with poor sperm motility. Joel L. Marmar, a New Jersey urologist, reported boosting the sperm motility index (per cent and quality of sperm that move) an average of 33 per cent by giving zinc sulphate to men with low semen zinc levels.

A nutrient very closely tied to zinc is vitamin A – and vitamin A is essential for the production of sperm. It has been suggested that the reason so many chronic alcoholics suffer from sterility is that alcohol interferes with the conversion of vitamin A to its active form in the testes *(Science)*.

Vitamins B_6 and B_{12}

One cause of infertility in women is *amenorrhoea,* or the failure to menstruate. Women who do not menstruate obviously are not producing eggs to be fertilized each month.

Scientists at Harvard University treated three women suffering from a malady called *galactorrhoea–amenorrhoea syndrome* with vitamin B_6 supplements. (Galactorrhoea is an excessive, uncontrolled flow of milk from the breasts in non-nursing women.) Within three months, all three women, who were receiving from 200 to 600 mg of vitamin B_6 a day, resumed normal menstruation. When the treatment was stopped, the women suffered a relapse *(Journal of Clinical Endocrinology and Metabolism).*

A second study of vitamin B_6 at the Maury County Hospital in Tennessee involved women with pre-menstrual syndrome (PMS), a collection of symptoms involving headache, backache, breast discomfort, swelling (oedema), weight gain, moodiness, tension, irritability, and/or depression, among other things. Because of reports of the successful use of B_6 in treating menstrual problems, Drs Joel T. Hargrove and Guy E. Abraham decided to try it on 14 women suffering from PMS who, for unknown reasons, were also infertile.

At the end of the trial, 12 of the 14 patients – who had been infertile from 18 months to seven years – were finally able to conceive. The vitamin was given daily in doses ranging from 100 to 800 mg, depending on the dose needed to relieve each patient's PMS symptoms. Of the 13 pregnancies that resulted (one woman conceived twice), 11 occurred within the first six months of therapy, one occurred in the seventh month, and the last occurred in the 11th month of the programme.

Although he is not sure why the women became pregnant, Dr Hargrove says that there was a significant increase in levels of progesterone (a natural hormone that prepares the lining of the uterus to receive a fertilized egg) in five of seven women studied.

Vitamin B_{12} also appears to play a critical role in fertility, for both women and men. Speaking at a conference on nutrition and reproduction held at the National Institutes of Health outside Washington, D.C., Dr Jo Anne Brasel noted that some women who cannot conceive – and for whom no medical reason can be found – may be deficient in vitamin B_{12}. Moreover, documented evidence has shown that conception leading to the birth of a normal infant may occur within a few short months of B_{12} therapy.

Dr Brasel, who is the director of the division of growth and development at the College of Physicians and Surgeons, Columbia University, discovered repeated references to this link while researching the impact of malnutrition on reproduction. These studies – many of which had been published in British medical journals – do not explain why vitamin B_{12} has such an effect on fertility. 'But,' says Dr Brasel, 'it is interesting that the infertility may precede by years overt clinical evidence of pernicious anaemia.' (Pernicious anaemia is an inability to absorb vitamin B_{12} from the intestines.)

And this bit of information is not for women only. 'Furthermore,' she adds, 'semen and sperm abnormalities have been noted in males with pernicious anaemia. There is one spectacular case in which B_{12} therapy led to a return to active participation in sheep shearing by one 73-year-old Australian sheepherder – and pregnancy in his 37-year-old wife.'

Diet and female hormones

Individual nutrients aren't the only food factors that affect infertility. Peter Hill, a researcher with the American Health Foundation in New York, has found a dramatic link between diet and the hormones that control female fertility.

Dr Hill measured hormone levels in Bantu women in Africa who switched from their traditional diet to the standard diet eaten in Western countries. 'All the hormone changes that we observed indicate a decrease in fecundity [fertility] when you switch to a Western diet,' Dr Hill told us.

He stresses that his findings are preliminary and that further research is needed to confirm the possible link between diet and fertility. He says that, at this point, there is no way to tell what it is in the Western diet (or what's lacking) that might limit the ability to conceive children. 'The Bantu's diet is toally different from the Western woman's. The Bantu diet is the vegetable-protein type; they eat a lot of corn [maize] and fruit, and when they changed to the Western diet, they had to change everything.'

Intimately tied to hormones and the special circumstances needed for conception is a woman's percentage of total body fat. Doctors have long recognized the link between extreme obesity and infertility in women, but only recently has it been discovered that underweight women have the same problem. A blanket of excess fat has a profound effect on hormone metabolism, but so can the lack of fat. A woman who is 15 per cent or more below ideal weight risks infertility heralded by disturbances of (or disappearance of) the menstrual cycle. The phenomenon is not uncommon in young women who are lean, lithe runners. To maintain menstruation and, thereby, fertility, it appears that about 22 per cent body fat is necessary (*Medical World News*, 27 April 1981).

So if you're a devoted marathoner but want to be a devoted mother, you may have to slow down a bit in order to conceive.

• Inflammatory bowel diseases

Crohn's disease and ulcerative colitis, which doctors group under the heading of 'inflammatory bowel diseases', affect 8 people in every 10,000 in Western countries, and annually hospitalize over 100,000 people in the United States alone. However, doctors don't know their cause, and other than cutting out the diseased section of the bowel or giving powerful anti-inflammatory drugs, they don't know how to cure them, either. Why? The answer may be simple. Both cause and treatment could involve an area in which most doctors have little expertise – nutrition.

Crohn's disease

Doctors are so mystified by Crohn's disease (also called regional enteritis) that a textbook on digestive disorders states bleakly: 'The physician . . . is powerless to prevent . . . the progression of the disease' (*Clinical Gastroenterology*). That progression goes something like this:

At first, your symptoms are so mild that you ignore them: a bout of diarrhoea every few months and occasional abdominal pain. But as the years pass, the symptoms get worse. You have either diarrhoea or constipation, and your stools are bloody. The fleeting abdominal pain turns into a chronic ache. You lose a lot of weight – 20 to 30 lb – and with it, your energy and ambition. You run a constant fever. But in a way, you're lucky. Most *children* who get Crohn's disease are even worse off. It stunts their growth and delays the start of puberty until they're 20.

Drugs, surgery and the sugar connection

A study in the United States on the three drugs most commonly used to treat Crohn's disease showed that all three were 'useless'. Crohn's disease comes in 'flare-ups' – the symptoms go away for a while but suddenly hit again – and researchers found that the drugs didn't help a patient stay better after a flare-up was over, nor did they prevent flare-ups.

Surgery, too, is of little use. The surgeon can cut out the diseased portion of the bowel, but he can't stop the disease. A study has shown that 89 per cent of those operated on for Crohn's disease have a second operation, perhaps only a few months later. Some doctors even believe that surgery, while often necessary to prevent life-threatening complications, actually encourages the spread of Crohn's disease in the bowel.

Obviously, surgery and drugs don't get to the root of Crohn's disease. Nutrition does.

Crohn's disease was almost *unknown* before the 1930s but now hits millions of people in industrialized countries. The last 50 years have also seen a dramatic increase in the consumption of refined carbohydrates such as sugar and a decrease in the consumption of fibre. Such a diet, say some researchers, damages the bowel and may cause Crohn's disease. Studies help prove their point.

● A German study of patients with Crohn's disease showed that they 'consumed large quantities of refined carbohydrates' (*British Medical Journal*).

● A survey of the breakfast habits of Crohn's patients showed that many regularly ate refined ceareals such as corn flakes (*British Medical Journal*).

● In a survey of sugar intake, researchers found that Crohn's patients ate the equivalent of an average of ten teaspoons a day, while people without Crohn's ate seven (*British Medical Journal*).

● Other researchers found that Crohn's patients added 26 per cent more sugar to tea and coffee and 13 per cent more to cereals than people without Crohn's (*British Medical Journal*).

To test the theory that a cut in sugar intake might help Crohn's sufferers, doctors in West Germany divided 20 people with Crohn's disease into two groups. One group was put on a low-carbohydrate diet (with all refined sugar excluded), while the other group was given a diet high in carbohydrates (and high in refined sugar). Eighty per cent of patients with the most severe cases of Crohn's disease found relief on the diet that restricted refined sugar. And their improvement lasted for the whole length of the study – 18 months. In contrast, 40 per cent of the high-sugar group actually had to be taken off the diet because of increased flare-ups of symptoms (Z. Gastroenterologie, vol. 19, 1981).

Symptoms point to nutritional deficiencies

No one can definitely say that a low-fibre diet inflames and toughens the lining of the bowel, but doctors can be very definitive about the nutritional deficiencies caused by that toughening, which blocks absorption. Crohn's patients, doctors have reported, have deficiencies of protein, iron, calcium, folic acid and vitamin B_{12}. Recently, researchers turned up another deficiency: zinc. That deficiency does the most harm of them all.

Zinc controls sexual maturation and growth: children with Crohn's often have delayed puberty and stunted growth. Zinc controls the sense of taste; numb taste buds mean no appetite, and many Crohn's patients have anorexia, a lack of desire to eat. Zinc is necessary for healthy skin; some Crohn's patients have severe rashes. Normal eyesight needs zinc; some Crohn's patients have night blindness. Zinc is a must for wound healing; low zinc levels may be one of the reasons why Crohn's disease never heals.

To prove some of those connections, researchers measured the blood levels of zinc in patients with Crohn's and in healthy people. Children whose growth had been stunted by Crohn's disease had zinc levels 39 per cent lower than normal-sized children with Crohn's. Adults with Crohn's had zinc levels 15 per cent lower than healthy people, and their sense of taste was 65 per cent duller than the healthy group (Digestion).

But these cases are far from hopeless. A team of doctors at the University of Minnesota headed by Craig McClain (now director of gastro-enterology at the University of Kentucky Medical Center), studied over 50 patients with Crohn's disease who suffered from either delayed sexual maturation or eye problems. He then gave zinc supplements to those deficient in the mineral. In many cases, sexual maturation began to occur and eyesight became normal.

A vitamin C deficiency may also cause some of the symptoms of Crohn's disease. One study showed that a group of Crohn's patients had vitamin C levels 32 per cent lower than a group of healthy people. The researchers who conducted the study advised doctors 'to supplement the diet of all patients with regional enteritis with doses of ascorbic acid [vitamin C]' (Digestion).

Another study showed that low vitamin C levels may be directly responsible for the formation of fistulas – abnormal passageways between two body surfaces – in Crohn's disease. In that study, researchers found that Crohn's patients with fistulas had 54 per cent lower vitamin C levels than patients without fistulas (Gastroenterology).

Other vitamins have been found to be effective in treating Crohn's disease. At a hospital in Linkoping, Sweden, a 31-year-old woman suffering from Crohn's was given large amounts of vitamin A for her psoriasis. The psoriasis began to clear but, surprisingly, so did the chronic diarrhoea caused by the Crohn's disease. 'The most striking effect was a return to normal bowel function,' reported the Swedish doctors. 'Soon after starting the new treatment, the patient found she could eat any food, even plums, without ill effects and with no diarrhoea' (Lancet, 5 April 1980).

This news from Sweden attracted the attention of Ann Dvorak, a research pathologist at Beth Israel Hospital in Boston, Massachusetts. She had taken electron microscope photographs showing intestinal epithelium damaged by Crohn's disease, and these offered a possible explanation for vitamin A's success with the woman in Sweden.

Crohn's patients, Dr Dvorak says, have holes in their intestines. As a result, they might absorb bacteria and food impurities that are normally excreted, and they fail to absorb nutrients, including vitamin A, that they should absorb. When the holes become large enough, the damaged section of the bowel must be removed surgically. She thinks vitamin A might keep tiny holes from becoming big ones by bolstering the epithelium.

'In the past,' Dr Dvorak said, 'we thought that the holes were always large enough to see on an X-ray. Now we're finding out that the large holes start as microscopic defects in the epithelium. I feel very strongly that if Crohn's patients took vitamin A after their first operation, they might not need so many operations later on.' The Swedish doctors seem to agree.

It could be that vitamin A restored some previously impaired intestinal-barrier function. If so, and if, as is suspected, the essential abnormality in Crohn's disease is impaired function of the intestinal barrier, other Crohn's patients might benefit from vitamin A.

Keep an eye out for the results of John Hunter and his colleagues at Cambridge University. They have been very successful so far in treating Crohn's disease with, first, an exclusion diet to rule out any possible allergens; and, then, a high-fibre diet. (*See also* IRRITABLE BOWEL SYNDROME.)

Ulcerative colitis

Like Crohn's disease, no one knows the cause of ulcerative colitis. Of the people it strikes (usually when they're in their teens or 20s), a small percentage have a family history of the disease, which suggests a genetic cause. Some researchers theorize that drugs – antibiotics, anti-hypertensives, anti-coagulants, steroids – can bring on an attack. Other scientists believe it starts with an infection or an emotional upset.

Whatever the cause, something inflames the mucous lining of the colon until it bleeds. Ulcers can pit its surface. Small, worm-like stubs – *pseudopolyps* – grow in scattered clumps. During an attack of this inflammation (which can last for weeks and then not appear again for years), the colon is useless. It can't absorb water, and it can't stop the rush of liquid faeces into the rectum.

The result, of course, is diarrhoea. In mild ulcerative colitis, the diarrhoea is bearable. In severe ulcerative colitis, it's not. You have to run to the lavatory. Immediately after defecating, you feel the urge to defecate again – and again, until the lavatory turns into a prison. You're weak and sickly. You run a high fever. Your painful abdominal cramps never let up. Anaemic from loss of blood, your only desire is to stay in bed (standing up makes your diarrhoea worse).

In a survey of 84 people with ulcerative colitis, 72 said that during a severe attack, social life was impossible because of fear of incontinence, the embarrassment of sudden trips to go to the toilet and tiredness. Many complained of irritability, marital problems and a worsened sex life. Some had to change jobs so they'd be near a lavatory. Others had to get up early in the morning so that their frequent stops to go to the toilet during their journey didn't make them late for work. Half of the women said they did less housework and that shopping was difficult *(Lancet)*.

However, many of those with ulcerative colitis could probably end their misery by making a simple change in their diet.

Food allergy

'I've found that in susceptible people, allergic reaction to commonly eaten foods is the direct cause of ulcerative colitis – and Crohn's disease too,' says Dr Barbara Solomon of Baltimore. She tests all her patients for food allergies, and finds that those with ulcerative colitis are always allergic to milk products and grains that contain gluten (wheat and rye). When she eliminates those foods (and sometimes other foods as well), the disease improves greatly. But not always.

'Food allergy isn't the only cause of ulcerative colitis and Crohn's disease,' she says. 'Sometimes a patient doesn't get well until I take him off tap water and have him drink only distilled water. Tap water is full of chemicals, and any one of them could be causing the problem.'

Robert J. Rogers, a Florida doctor also treats ulcerative colitis as a food allergy. The first patient he cured of the disease was himself. 'I developed ulcerative colitis early in my medical school career,' he says. 'I had bleeding from the bowel, a lot of profuse diarrhoea and terrible cramps. It was very debilitating. I got books out and read about it, and the professors told me about it.

'But the only treatment was drugs. Drugs to slow down the faecal stream, drugs to take the cramps away, drugs to coat the bowel, drugs to tranquillize me. But while I was taking all these drugs, I was feeding the disease with the foods I was allergic to. Eventually I discovered on my own that all forms of dairy products and chocolate and caffeinated beverages were my enemy. If I don't eat those foods, I don't have ulcerative colitis.'

• Insomnia

Lying in bed, unable to fall asleep, is one of life's little tortures. Regrets about the past, tension in the present or anxiety about the future – these common aggravations can sometimes keep us up for hours. And almost all of us know the special frustration of losing sleep over the very task – an impending exam or job interview or long trip – that we need to be rested for.

For years, doctors casually prescribed sleeping pills for temporary insomnia. Many still do, but in the past several years, more and more doctors and psychologists are realizing that these drugs don't work and can be harmful if used frequently. Ironically, sleeping pills have been blamed for actually causing insomnia and fragmented sleep patterns. (*See* DRUG SIDE EFFECTS for more information on sleeping pills.)

Relax yourself to sleep

A far better way to send ourselves quickly to sleep, researchers are finding, is by learning simple skills – like muscle relaxation techniques, deep breathing, imagery, autogenic training and self-hypnosis – that can be applied when needed, without even leaving our beds.

They work because your tossing and turning body is probably in a state of biological turbulence – a state that doesn't share a border with dreamland. 'Many poor sleepers are more aroused than good sleepers,' wrote sleep specialist Richard R. Bootzin of Northwestern University in a recent survey of sleep research. 'Poor sleepers [have] higher rectal temperatures, higher skin resistance, more vasoconstrictions [narrowing of blood vessels] per minute and more body movements per hour than good sleepers.' All of those symptoms mean that the insomniac's autonomic nervous system, which controls involuntary body functions, is preparing him perfectly for dodging rush-hour traffic – but not for sleep. If he can put his autonomic nervous system to sleep, the theory goes, the rest of him should follow (*Progress in Behavior Modification*, vol. 6, 1978).

Progressive relaxation (*see* HEADACHES) is a particular form of muscle relaxation that helps quiet the nervous system, too. Originated in the early 1900s by physiologist Edmund Jacobson, progressive relaxation, or variations of it, are still taught. One of these variations has been evaluated by Thomas D. Borkovec, a psychologist at Pennsylvania State University.

'We have the person start with the muscles of one hand, making a fist, holding it for seven seconds, and then relaxing it,' says Dr Borkovec. 'We ask the individual to learn to identify what both tension and relaxation feel like, so that he will be able to detect tension when trying to fall asleep. After sufficient practice, most people are able to relax themselves deeply within five minutes.'

His students gradually learn to relax 16 of the body's muscle groups, Dr Borkovec says. They also inhale when they tense their muscles, then exhale and relax very slowly (for about 45 seconds). That is good therapy for people whose main problem is falling asleep, and its effect improves with practice.

Proper breathing, just by itself, is another way to reassure the autonomic nervous system that it can tone down for the night. In one experiment in 1976, volunteers were asked to 'focus passively on the physical sensations associated with their breathing and to repeat the mantra [a word or image to fix the mind on] "in" and "out" silently.' Results indicated that this technique is as effective as progressive relaxation.

Imagery

The fine points of breathing have been described by psychologist Beata Jencks in her book, *Your Body: Biofeedback at Its Best*. 'Imagine inhaling through your fingertips,' she wrote,

> up the arms, into the shoulders, and then exhaling down the trunk into the abdomen and legs, and leisurely out at the toes. Repeat, and feel how this slow, deep breathing affects the whole body, the abdomen, the flanks and the chest. Do not move the shoulders.

To inhale deeply, Dr Jencks advises, pretend to inhale the fragrance of the first flower in spring, or imagine that your breathing rises and falls like ocean waves, or that the surface area of your lungs – if laid out flat – would cover a tennis court. That's how much air you can feel yourself breathing in.

Imagery can accompany breathing exercises, and your choice of images doesn't have to be limited to the traditional sheep leaping over a split-rail fence. Any image that you personally associate with feelings of peace or contentment will work well.

One sleep researcher, Quentin Regestein, director of the sleep clinic at Brigham and Women's Hospital in Boston, Massachusetts, told us that one of his patients imagines a huge sculpture of the numeral one, hewn out of marble, with ivy growing over it, surrounded by a pleasant rural landscape. Then she goes on to the numeral two, and adds further embellishment, such as cherubs hovering about the numeral. 'She tells me that she usually falls asleep before she reaches 50,' Dr Regestein says.

'Insomniacs come here from all over the world,' he continues, 'and ask me to prescribe a sleep cure for them. They are sometimes surprised to find that careful scientific investigation substantiates that commonsense remedies really work.'

Heaviness and warmth

Autogenic training is another natural and potent sleep aid. This technique acts on the premise that your mind can compel your body to relax by concentrating on feelings of heaviness and warmth. Through mental suggestion, the 'heavy' muscles actually do relax, and the 'warm' flesh receives better circulation, resulting in 'a state of low physiological arousal', says Dr Bootzin.

In an experiment in 1968, researchers taught 16 college-student insomniacs to focus their attention on warmth and heaviness. At the end of the experiment, the students had cut their average time needed to fall asleep down from 52 to 22 minutes. These results matched the findings of Dr Bootzin in the Chicago area:

Daily practice of either progressive relaxation or autogenic training produced 50 per cent improvement in time to fall asleep by the end of the one-month treatment period.

A rag doll, says Dr Jencks, is one image that can facilitate autogenic training. To feel heavy, she says, 'make yourself comfortable and allow your eyes to close. Then lift one arm a little and let it drop. Let it drop heavily, as if it were the arm of one of those floppy dolls or animals. Choose one in your imagination. Choose a doll, an old, beloved, soft teddy bear.' Once the mind fixes on the doll's image, Dr Jencks says, lifting and dropping the arm in your imagination works as well as really letting it drop.

To invoke feelings of warmth, Dr Jencks adds, 'Imagine that you put your rag doll into the sun. Let it be warmed by the sun. . . . You are the giant rag doll, and you are lying in the sun; all your limbs are nice and warm, but your head is lying in the shade and is comfortably cool.'

Suggestions you give yourself

Self-hypnosis, though it may require some practice in advance, has also been shown to help people fall asleep. Researchers in Britain compared the sleep-inducing ability of four various techniques – sleeping pills, hypnosis, self-hypnosis and a placebo – on 18 volunteer insomniacs. Some of the volunteers learned to put themselves into a trance by picturing themselves in a 'warm, safe place – possibly on a holiday some place pleasant'. When they had put themselves into a trance, the researchers told them, they would be able to give themselves the suggestions 'that this would pass into a deep, refreshing sleep, waking up at the usual time in the morning, feeling wide awake.'

The results showed that the subjects fell asleep faster by hypnotizing themselves than by using either the drug or the placebo. None of the self-hypnotized sleepers needed an hour to fall asleep, while three in the placebo group and four in the drug group did. Twelve in the self-hypnotized group fell asleep in less than 30 minutes, while only seven and ten, respectively, in the other groups did (*Journal of the Royal Society of Medicine*, October 1979).

Rituals also play a role in falling asleep. Dr Regestein told us that when dogs go to sleep, they always sniff around for a warm and comfortable spot, circle it, and finally coil up in their favourite sleeping position. People are a bit like this, he says. They fall asleep most easily when they proceed through a nightly ritual – taking a bath, for example, and then curling into their favourite sleeping position. In support of that theory, researchers in 1930 found that children who assumed a particular posture when going to bed fell asleep faster.

The last but not the least effective route to immediate relaxation is sexual activity. Psychologist Alice K. Schwartz, author of *Somniquest* (1979), a book dealing with sleep disturbances, says that sex 'alleviates tension. It is a powerful soporific. And what is more, it's fun. . . . The road to sleep branches into other byways. Explore all of them.'

Food for thought . . . and sleep

One of the things to consider if you have trouble sleeping at night is the food you ate during the day. We all know about caffeine. You can find it in coffee and cola drinks; it can make you as edgy as a cat in a kennel.

On the other hand, there's alcohol. Will a spot of wine, or maybe a nip of something 'harder', summon the sandman? Perhaps, but one study has shown that even a dose of alcohol as small as that found in a 5 fl.oz glass of table wine, or in a measure of an 80-proof drink, can actually *disturb* your sleep (*Electroencephalography and Clinical Neurophysiology*, June 1980).

So what's a body to do who wants to get to sleep but doesn't want to use a drug of any kind? If current scientific research is any clue, the answer may lie right in our breakfast, lunch or dinner plates. For food may play a much larger role than most of us have thought in whether or not we sleep soundly.

'There is no doubt that certain foods can make us hyperalert or hypoalert,' says Milton Fried, director of the Fried Medical Clinic in Atlanta, Georgia. Dr Fried and his associates have studied the effects of food, as well as vitamins and minerals, on how we sleep. 'I would bet that just about everyone has had the experience of feeling elated and alert after a meal or, on the other hand, terribly drowsy,' he told us. 'Some countries even make a cultural thing of taking a siesta after the noon meal, which allows workers to rest up and return to work refreshed in the late afternoon.'

Dr Fried points out that reactions to food can stem from many causes. 'I've seen patients who either climb the walls or can't keep their eyes open after eating,' he says. 'Sometimes this is the result of an allergy that affects the brain. Another example: brewer's yeast is certainly a food, and because of its high niacin content, we have found it very useful in helping insomniac patients to return to more normal sleeping patterns. It works best on people with low levels of histamine [a natural substance found in the body's cells].'

Part of Dr Schwartz's therapeutic programme involves putting into practice the results of current laboratory research on how what we eat can change what happens inside our brain and, in turn, our sleep.

Dr Schwartz has identified five different types of insomnia, ranging from short sleep to very light sleep, from dream-troubled sleep to waking up and not being able to fall back to sleep. 'But,' she told us, 'by far the most common type of insomnia is what I call *initardia*, which is simply difficulty in falling asleep in the first place. If you suffer from initardia, eating the proper foods can be quite important. Not only that, but you have to eat the right foods at the right time.'

Tryptophan: a natural tranquilliser

What might the right foods be? 'Basically,' says Dr Schwartz, 'there are two different kinds. First, foods that are high in the essential amino acid *tryptophan*. As you know, amino acids are the basic building blocks of protein. Eggs, almost any meat, certain fish such as salmon or bluefish, and dairy products, especially cottage cheese – all of those protein-rich foods have a hefty amount of tryptophan, and tryptophan has been shown in the lab to increase drowsiness and help bring on sleep.

'But,' says Dr Schwartz, 'there is a second type of food you should eat as well. You see, in addition to tryptophan, there are many other amino acids. Once these different amino acids get into the bloodstream, they compete with each other for entry to the brain. For someone who wants to get to sleep, the trick is to give tryptophan a competitive edge.'

And how do you do that? 'It's really quite simple,' she says. 'Animal studies have shown that eating carbohydrate foods – those that are starchy or sweet – liberates tryptophan and gives it greater access to the brain. In fact, the tryptophan in food is hardly used at all by the brain unless a carbohydrate is also eaten, or, interestingly, a food with a carbohydrate–fat combination.

'The implications of this are fascinating,' she explains. 'If you've been eating high-protein, high-tryptophan foods during the day, and you want to fall asleep at night, then it may help to eat some bread, have a banana, drink some grape or apple juice, have some figs or dates – all of those high-carbohydrate foods and many others will help activate tryptophan.'

Dr Schwartz explains further that it's important to eat your carbohydrate food two to four hours before bedtime so that the food will reach its peak effect when you are ready to retire. On the other hand, if your problem is frequent awakenings during the night – quite a common complaint after the age of 40 – or short sleep periods, or light sleep, you should eat your carbohydrate immediately before 'lights out'. Since falling asleep in the first place is not your problem, you will want your carbohydrates to operate at top efficiency after you have been asleep for a few hours.

'In any case,' concludes Dr Schwartz, 'if you tend to fall asleep during the day or early evening, you must try to eliminate carbohydrates during the day. If you usually eat dessert after your evening meal, you should defer your dessert until the time appropriate to your particular sleep problem.'

But what if you wake up in the middle of the night? Is it too late to eat your muesli bars? 'Indeed, it is,' replied Dr Schwartz. 'There is a small child in all of us, and if that child gets used to waking up every night expecting to be 'rewarded' with something sweet, it will become a habit. If you wake up in the night and cannot get back to sleep in half an hour, I recommend getting out of bed and performing some boring, routine task until you feel sleepy.'

Although it is all very well and good to say that, in practice, getting aboard the tryptophan–carbohydrate train will help transport us to dreamland, it's also nice to know why the train takes us there in the first place. Furthermore, knowing why we sleep can actually help us find out what to do if we do *not* want to sleep.

A new theory of sleep

In the past, scientists had noted that, when the level of tryptophan in the brain went up, so did the level of another substance : *serotonin*, a 'neuro-transmitter' that enables brain cells to 'talk' to each other. In fact, the serotonin in our brains is made from tryptophan. Since drowsiness followed a rise in the level of serotonin, scientists came to the conclusion that serotonin must be a kind of 'sleep juice' that told the brain cells when it was time to hit the sack.

Now, however, a pioneering investigator into how tryptophan works has a better idea. In his lab at the University of Illinois College of Medicine, associate professor of pharmacology Miodrag Radulovacki is using a tryptophan analogue in animal experiments with sleep. The analogue is chemically similar to tryptophan but is manufactured rather than found in nature.

Why use this analogue? Because Dr Radulovacki wanted a chemical that would act in the body much like tryptophan except for raising the level of serotonin in the brain. Indeed, unlike natural tryptophan, the analogue actually lowers the level of serotonin. Nevertheless, the animal subjects not only fall asleep as fast as they do with natural tryptophan, but they actually sleep longer.

So much for the idea that serotonin is a sleep juice. 'Yes,' Dr Radulovacki told us, 'an increase in the serotonin level is irrelevant with respect to how long it takes to fall asleep and how long sleep lasts. What is relevant, however, is that both tryptophan and its analogue decrease the level of another group of neuro-transmitters called *catecholamines*. Why is this important? Because these catecholamines have been implicated in promoting wakefulness. Lower the catecholamine levels and you produce the opposite effect: drowsiness.'

Selected foods for sleep

Group A

If you want to sleep, eat any of these (high in tryptophan, high in tyrosine, low in carbohydrates) with or *before* foods in Group B:	beef	kidneys
	cheese	lamb
	chicken	liver
	cottage cheese	milk
	eggs	salmon

Group B

If you want to sleep, eat any of these foods (high in carbohydrates) with or *after* those in Group A:	apples	marrow
	bananas	oatmeal
	beans (pulses)	parsnips
	carob biscuits,	pears
	cherries	potatoes
	dates	raisins
	fruit juices (apple,	rice pudding
	grape, orange),	sweet potatoes
	grain-based foods	watermelon

SOURCES: *Amino Acid Content of Foods*, USDA, 1968.
Calories and Carbohydrates, Grosset & Dunlap, 1971.

Dr Radulovacki explained how the new analogue performs its feats. 'All the amino acids are competing with each other for entry to the brain. In this case, we are concerned with two of them: tryptophan and tyrosine. If tyrosine gets through, then catecholamine levels will rise; if tryptophan wins the race, catecholamines go down.'

The experiments of Dr Radulovacki and others raise an interesting question – namely: If a high-protein food plus a carbohydrate food equals drooping, sleepy eyelids, is there a formula that leads to wide-open, alert eyelids? The answer seems to be yes, and the arithmetic involves a bit of simple subtraction.

Our wake-time food formula should raise tyrosine levels. How do we do that? By eating protein-rich foods but *not* carbohydrate foods.

In one of a series of experiments, Richard J. Wurtman and John D. Fernstrom fed laboratory animals a single meal composed of 40 per cent protein. The result? Tyrosine went up and so did catecholamines. 'These observations,' wrote Drs Wurtman and Fernstrom, 'suggest that . . . catecholamine-containing brain neurons are normally under specific dietary control' *(American Journal of Clinical Nutrition)*.

The formula is clear. If you want to get to sleep, add protein and carbohydrates. If you want to stay awake, add protein and subtract carbohydrates.

Walk yourself to sleep

One of the best ways to get to sleep is to go to bed tired – not frazzled-with-stress tired, but pleasantly fatigued. Insomnia is sometimes a problem of inactivity. If you are sedentary all day, you build up a nervous charge yet don't use your muscles enough to create physical tiredness.

There is absolutely no question that the best way to prepare yourself for sleep is to take long walks during the day. The rhythmic pacing, one foot leading the other down miles of streets or roads, does more to help you rest later than the softest mattress. Not only does walking tire you, but it rests the mind, which is important if you plan to sleep well. If you check with insomniacs, you'll find that most have such weak legs that they can't walk more than half a mile without having to call a taxi.

Did you know that when you exercise, the quality of the sleep you get changes for the better? It's true. What happens is that the rhythm of your sleep changes so that you spend relatively more time in a phase that sleep researchers call 'slow-wave sleep' (SWS). Slow-wave sleep is a very deep form of sleep that is also the most restorative, especially to the physical body. Samuel Dunkell, a New York psychoanalyst and author of the book, *Sleep Positions*, told us that 'strenuous exercise for half an hour three times a week increases SWS. But this should not be done too close to sleep, because after strenuous exercise, the body is very stimulated. Several hours before bedtime is fine.'

Arthur J. Spielman, a clinical psychologist at Montefiore Hospital, in New York City specializing in sleep disorders added that exercise done in the morning has no effect on slow-wave sleep that night. So it looks like the best time to exercise – at least as far as sleeping goes – would be, for most people, between about 4 P.M. and 8 P.M..

But here is the really interesting thing. The exercise-for-better-sleep routine works much better in people who are physically fit. Research by an Australian scientist revealed that when fit and unfit people were given exercise, the amount of slow-wave sleep increased in the fit people but not in those who weren't fit. Curiously, the fit people had relatively more slow-wave sleep even on days when they weren't exercising. That indicates, perhaps, that their bodies have become conditioned to restoring themselves more effectively.

Don't think that exercise won't do you any good, just because you aren't fit. All it takes is a good solid half an hour of rapid walking after dinner every day for a few weeks, and you'll be getting the benefits of SWS along with all the other benefits that come with regular exercise.

Don't smoke and don't worry

One no-no for insomniacs is smoking. A study at the Sleep Research and Treatment Center at Pennsylvania State University compared 50 non-smokers and 50 smokers who had smoked 20 cigarettes a day for more than three years. After four nights, they determined that the smokers had greater difficulty falling asleep than the non-smokers.

On the other hand, when smokers cease smoking, they start sleeping better. In another study, sleep patterns of habitual smokers were observed for four days, and then on the fifth day the volunteers were asked to abstain completely from smoking. The total time they spent waiting to fall asleep decreased by 45 per cent on the first three nights of abstinence. And those former smokers who continued to abstain for up to 12 nights continued to fall asleep sooner than when they smoked (*Science*, 1 February 1980).

One more thing not to do if you suffer from insomnia is to worry about it. There is no law that says everyone must sleep eight hours every night. Many studies do show that the average amount of sleep is $7^1/_2$–8 hours, but others make the startling discovery that the average amount of sleep is not average.

For instance, Wilse Webb, a psychologist at the University of Florida, found that less than 50 per cent of 4000 first-year students averaged the regulation eight hours per night. Not so remarkable, slightly more than half of the students were not 'average'. In the same study, Dr Webb found that 46 per cent of 250 people between the ages of 20 and 27 averaged eight hours per night, while 5 per cent slept more than nine hours and 20 per cent slept less than seven. Nor did he find that the health of those who got more or less than the average amount of sleep suffered. In fact, another study showed that shorter sleepers were psychologically healthier.

Reviewing these findings, David A. Kaufman, a teacher of anatomy, concluded that each person's sleep requirements is individualized. 'Just as there are tall and short people,' he says, 'there are long and short sleepers.'

The best course to follow is the natural course: Find out how much sleep you need and try to work out a schedule that allows you to get it. Attempting to conform to some abstract standard may only cause sleeping disorders.

Finally, if none of the above techniques seems to work for you, there are several changes in daily habits that can, with practice, help you to fall asleep a lot faster in the future. Here are some hints that many sleep researchers recommend.

- Go to sleep and wake up at regular hours.
- Go to bed only when sleepy.
- Don't nap during the day.
- Use your bed only for sleeping and sex; don't read, eat or watch TV in bed.
- Keep your bedroom fairly cool.
- Try drinking a cup of herb tea at bedtime – peppermint, camomile and valerian are all time-honoured remedies for insomnia.

• Irritable bowel syndrome

Irritable bowel syndrome (IBS) is characterized by periodic abdominal pain, diarrhoea and constipation. The intestines are often in a state of tension or abnormal contraction, which makes it difficult for the body to pump waste materials through the system. Sometimes nausea and vomiting add to the misery of IBS.

Many people who suffer from one or more of the manifestations of irritable bowel syndrome feel they must carefully watch their diet to avoid eating anything bulky, or any kind of roughage (dietary fibre) that might cause 'pressure' as it moves through the large intestine (colon). In fact, many people with irritable bowel syndrome have probably been told by their doctors to stick to a low-residue diet, in which there is very little waste material left after the small intestine has done its job of absorption.

Ironically, according to Arthur D. Schwabe, professor of medicine and chief of gastro-enterology at the UCLA School of Medicine, the low-residue diet is exactly the wrong approach to treating IBS. By following a diet high in fruits and vegetables and including two tablespoons of bran a day, Dr Schwabe said, many people may rid themselves of painful symptoms of the irritable bowel syndrome (*Internal Medicine News*, 1 May 1979). Many doctors point out that you should drink plenty of fluids along with your bran to avoid 'wind'.

If you're concerned about the possiblity of taking too much fibre, that won't happen if you begin modestly, and increase the amount of fibre in your diet a little bit every few days. That way, you'll know just how your body is responding.

Foods that irritate the bowels

Another successful dietary approach to IBS involves testing patients for food allergies.

Researchers at Cambridge University, led by John Hunter, asked 21 patients with IBS to limit their diet for one week to a single meat, a single fruit and distilled or spring water. Those whose symptoms cleared on this regimen were then asked to re-introduce a single food daily to determine whether specific foods provoked their symptoms.

Of the 21 patients tested, 14 discovered that their symptoms cleared on the special diet, and that re-introduction of specific foods did indeed provoke the IBS symptoms to reappear.

Of course, 'the detection of food intolerance is not easy,' say the researchers,

> requiring six to eight weeks of single-minded concentration on a diet which is initially severely limited. Only patients with determination and understanding are able to pursue this successfully. However, the benefits, with 67 per cent of patients being symptom-free, justify the effort required by patient, dietitian and doctor. [*Lancet*, 20 November 1982].

'Gut feelings'

An important adjunct to dietary therapy, for many patients, may be psychotherapy. For while doctors don't really know what causes IBS or even what's happening in the gut when it takes hold, they have found that most of the people with IBS have some kind of emotional problem.

'More than 75 per cent of the patients with IBS have abnormal psychological test scores,' says Harold Tucker, a gastro-enterologist at Johns Hopkins School of Medicine in Baltimore.

And a scientific study reported in the *Medical Journal of Australia* (29 November 1980) showed that, when 52 people with IBS received psychotherapy, they had a big improvement in their symptoms: 89 per cent had less pain; 96 per cent, less diarrhoea; 90 per cent, less constipation; 92 per cent, less nausea; and 81 per cent, less vomiting.

The symptoms of IBS, said the doctor who conducted the study, were regarded as a physical expression of emotions caused by 'recent loss or ongoing stressful life situations'. With that in mind, it would make sense for irritable bowel sufferers to give psychotherapy a try, and otherwise explore avenues of stress release and relaxation therapy.

(*See also* INFLAMMATORY BOWEL DISEASES.)

• Itching

Precisely why you itch is really still a mystery. However, even if doctors don't understand the underlying whys and wherefores of itching physiology, there's no denying that the awful feeling is definitely *not* all in your head, although it can drive you very nearly crazy.

'It's not a very satisfying definition, but itching is an unpleasant persistent sensation that makes you want to scratch,' says B. Allen Flaxman, clinical professor of medicine at Brown University and head of the dermatology section at Miriam Hospital in Providence, Rhode Island.

When no physical disorder can be found to explain generalized itching, diagnosis by exclusion takes place: it must be psychosomatic. Such was the decision reached in the case of a 62-year-old woman, suffering with such itching, whose physical examination and dermatological studies were 'negative'.

On this basis, 'psychogenic itching' was the label for her condition, and a tranquillizer was prescribed. When this did nothing for her, she was *thoroughly* examined by a competent doctor, who found a severe anaemia, prescribed iron and restored well-being – with no itching.

For unknown reasons, patients undergoing haemodialysis (kidney-machine treatment) often develop an intense, generalized itching of the skin. Working with 11 such patients, researchers in Oklahoma have found an excellent treatment: activated charcoal.

In an experiment, each patient first received 'one or more [anti-itch] preparations, including lotions, creams, tranquilizers, sedatives, analgesics and antihistamines, without effect.' Next, the patients were given capsules containing 6 g of activated charcoal daily for eight weeks. All the patients but one had their itching relieved. Furthermore, since they stopped scratching, their skin lesions healed, too.

'The mechanism by which charcoal relieves itching is unclear,' wrote the researchers. However, charcoal attracts and holds various organic and inorganic substances as it passes through the intestines, and that 'seems a possible explanation'. In any case, the patients showed no side-effects, prompting the researchers to conclude that 'oral charcoal is an economical, safe and effective treatment' (*Annals of Internal Medicine*, September 1980).

Dry skin, itchy skin

Taking action to prevent dry skin will curb some problem itching.

'A 20-minute lukewarm bath with some bath oil added to it is still unbeatable for most everybody with dry skin,' Dr Flaxman notes. And a cool compress may be all that's needed to combat a stubborn, isolated dry-skin itch.

Then, too, sometimes seemingly intractable *pruritus* – the doctor's description of the itching malady – will succumb to a good heart-to-heart talk.

'It's a great mystery, but day after day I'm impressed at how closely some cases of itching can be linked to emotional stress,' Dr Flaxman says. 'We often see people who've been dealing with great stress all their lives reach an age where they're simply worn down. Itching can be one consequence, especially if they have a background of allergies.

'Unfortunately, some people are born to be itchy,' Dr Flaxman concedes. Persistent scratching and rubbing can contribute to the skin changes associated with eczema and a number of other similar conditions. There may be an emotional component to these problems, but, he emphasizes, they demand a doctor's attention.

While you're waiting for the dermatologist, however, you might try supplementing your diet with vitamin B complex, vitamins A and E, as well as brewer's yeast and desiccated liver. Such nutritional therapies have helped many people over the years. One course of action you should avoid is succumbing to the easy temptations of over-the-counter medications.

Unlike those who race to the corner shop for 'sure cures', New Orleans dermatologist Nia Terezakis turns to conservative remedies, many of which can be found in the average cupboard. A compress made with skimmed milk or powdered milk may spell soothing relief, she says. And soaking the affected area in a 'colloidal bath' made with ingredients such as 'oatmeal, cornflour or baking soda' can often work wonders. So can bland 'shake lotions' such as calamine and milk of bismuth.

At the same time you're taking care of the problem, keep your mind open to what might have caused it in the first place. Your 'second skin' – your clothes – could literally be driving you out of your skin. 'Use only 100 per cent cotton clothing, as well as cotton sheets and pillow slips', Dr Terezakis advises. 'Wash-and-wear fabrics can be very irritating to sensitive skin. And don't use anything fancy in the laundry, especially fabric softeners.'

If the above suggestions make no discernible difference in the life of your skin, however, you also might consider the possibility of some sort of allergy. (*See also* DERMATITIS.)

• Jaundice

Premature infants whose skins turn yellowish with jaundice during their first days of life are being helped by vitamin E. The problem, caused by a buildup in the blood of the orange bile pigment *bilirubin*, can occur when the babies' red blood cells break down too rapidly or if the liver is too immature to dissolve the pigment so that it can be excreted as bile.

To treat the condition, hospitals rely on phototherapy – placing the newborn under special near-ultraviolet lights that break down excess bilirubin in the skin. However, the light can also destroy riboflavin (vitamin B_2) causing a nutritional deficit, and the eyes of the infants must be carefully protected while under the lights.

A study at the Duke University Medical Center in Durham, North Carolina has shown that injections of vitamin E during the first three days of life significantly lowered bilirubin levels in ten premature infants. By the fifth day, levels of the pigment were an average of 30 per cent lower than in ten other babies who got no vitamin E *(Pediatric Research)*.

One of the investigators, Dr Steven J. Gross (who is now director of newborn medicine at Boston City Hospital in Massachusetts), said that the vitamin also shortened the amount of time the infants had to spend under the lights. According to Dr Gross, vitamin E slows down the accelerated destruction of red blood cells.

• Kidney damage

The kidneys filter blood. Anything that the body has no further need for – such as excess acids or sodium or metabolic wastes – the kidneys remove from the blood and add to the urine. Between them, the two kidneys filter 32 fl. oz of blood every minute and produce about 48 fl. oz of urine every day.

There are several ways to help prevent kidney damage. One is to prevent high blood pressure. Another is to prevent urinary-tract infections.

Two medical researchers at the Cleveland Clinic Foundation in Ohio, Gary L. Wollam and Ray W. Gifford, Jr., studied the link between the kidneys and high blood pressure. They reported that the two illnesses form a vicious circle by making each other worse, but the kidney 'is more frequently the victim than the culprit. Hypertension [high blood pressure] that's gone undetected and uncontrolled for more than five years probably has left its mark on the kidneys,' they noted.

Hypertension apparently hardens the blood vessels that feed blood into the millions of tiny sieves which comprise the kidneys, which in medical language are called *glomeruli*. That disrupts the filtration process. The only recourse is to prevent or halt the hypertension. 'Effective treatment of hypertension prevents renal complications if they are not present initially, and retards their progression if they are present,' they wrote in the medical journal *Geriatrics*.

Among the natural therapies for hypertension are a low-salt and low-sugar diet, along with maintenance of ideal weight and exercise such as cycling, walking or jogging. Relaxation techniques, dietary fibre and garlic also can help.

Urinary-tract infections, if uncontrolled, can spread to the kidneys and cause damage. These infections, which are more common among women than among men, often respond to vitamin C and/or cranberry juice.

If you already use vitamin C, you probably know that some of it exits the body through the urine. But according to Alan Gaby, a biochemist and family doctor in Baltimore, Maryland, those extra vitamins are far from wasted. Vitamin C in the urine apparently kills *Escherichia coli* bacteria, the most common cause of urinary-tract infections.

A vitamin K deficiency acting on the kidneys could cause problems for adults, as they are involved in determining how much calcium is excreted from the body. A vitamin K-dependent protein in the kidneys may have an important role in the retention of calcium in the body. A failure of that protein caused by lack of vitamin K might disrupt the supply of calcium to the entire body.

That, of course, would cause a variety of essential biological systems to go on the blink.

A daily requirement for vitamin K has not yet been established, but diets containing plenty of fresh green vegetables will provide adequate vitamin K. Cabbage, Brussels sprouts, cauliflower and spinach are all good sources of the nutrient.

Many drugs can cause kidney damage. These include commonly used over-the-counter (OTC) medications such as antacids and aspirin. The large dose of calcium carbonate found in many antacids is rough on kidneys. (The amount of calcium carbonate in supplements is not dangerous.) It cuts down their blood flow, clogging delicate filters and tubes. The end result, may be a very sick person: no appetite, cranky, tired, nauseated, perhaps dizzy and confused. In one case, a woman taking antacids – and no more than the label recommended – came down with these symptoms. Tests at the hospital showed that her kidneys were in bad shape, and she was taken off antacids. A week later, she was 'mentally normal', and a checkup four months later showed that her kidneys had healed (*Canadian Medical Association Journal*, 8 September 1979).

It's cases like this that make doctors say, 'In view of these hazards we cannot recommend the use of calcium carbonate for routine antacid therapy' *(New England Journal of Medicine)*. Yet plenty of antacids with this ingredient are still on the market.

In a study of patients with kidney failure, doctors found that 20 per cent of the cases were caused by aspirin (or other painkillers such as paracetamol and phenacetin [withdrawn from the UK market some years ago]). What's more, a few patients whose lives depended on having their blood mechanically cleansed by a kidney machine were able to stop using the machine when they stopped taking the OTC painkiller.

'This condition has been unrecognized and under-diagnosed by physicians,' wrote Drs Martin Goldberg and Thomas G. Murray, *(New England Journal of Medicine)*. And, they noted, '85 percent of the patients are women above the age of 35 who have been taking the analgesics [painkillers] for recurrent headache or backache.'

Finally, if your kidneys do not work normally, some nutrients may build up in your body to dangerous levels. Potassium, phosphorus and magnesium are among those that can cause trouble. Anyone with kidney disease should have all supplements approved by a doctor.

• Kidney stones

Kidney-stone sufferers say that no pain, no torture, no desperation quite matches the jagged agony caused by the presence of a small chip of stone inside a human kidney.

Those whose composure has been rocked by one of those attacks have left few stones unturned in their search for the right diet or drug or medical device that will prevent them from ever going through that kind of misery again.

Prevention of these stones is a must because there is no easy way to remove a stone once it forms and lodges itself in the kidney. Open-kidney surgery is still the treatment of choice in the United States, but people sometimes lose kidneys, or parts of kidneys, as a result.

Difficult as they are to get out, most kidney stones get in by a simple biochemical process that anyone can understand. First, imagine a glass of water and a carton of table salt. Start pouring salt into the water and it will dissolve and disappear. Pour in enough salt, however, and the water becomes saturated – it can't hold any more salt – and you'll start to see crystals of salt falling like snowflakes to the bottom of the glass.

Most kidneys stones start the same way. The fluids that pass through your kidneys contain different kinds of minerals and molecules. One of those minerals is calcium, and one of those molecules is oxalic acid, which combine to form calcium oxalate. Normally, it floats invisibly in the fluid, but when there's too much of it, or too little fluid, it starts to fall out of solution. Here or there a calcium oxalate crystal forms and attracts another and another until there are enough to make a nice little stone snowball, with sharp edges to torment its owner while defying almost every effort to get rid of it. This problem has stumped many people, including the inventive Benjamin Franklin, who tried and failed to shake loose his stone by eating blackberry jam and standing on his head.

Results with magnesium

One modern strategy for preventing kidney stones is to fight mineral with mineral. In other words, fight unwanted calcium crystals with crystals of a similar mineral, such as magnesium. Magnesium supplements seem to inhibit new kidney stones from forming in people who are prone to them. And, while magnesium is one of the oldest cures for kidney stones – its use has been documented as far back as 1697 – it is also one of the newest.

Lately, the Swedes have taken an interest in magnesium. In one recent study, Swedish researchers gave 200 mg of magnesium hydroxide to a group of 41 men and 14 women who individually had averaged about one stone per year and who, as a group, had passed a whopping 460 stones during the ten years before the experiment.

Magnesium's effects were excellent. After two to four years of the therapy, only 8 of the 55 patients reported new stones. And as a group, their average rate of developing new stones fell by 90 per cent, to only 0.08 stones per year, per person. For comparison, the researchers kept an eye on a group of 43 stone sufferers who did not use magnesium. They averaged a much higher formation rate. After four years, 59 per cent of those tested had developed new stones.

Like calcium, magnesium can bind itself to oxalic acid and form a mineral compound. When calcium and magnesium are both present in the urine, they compete with each other to link up with any oxalic acid present. The critical difference is that magnesium oxalate is less likely to form crystals. It usually remains dissolved in the urine and passes out of the body – unstoned (*Journal of the American College of Nutrition*, vol. 1, no. 2, 1982).

A role for vitamin B$_6$

Another way to approach the prevention of kidney stones is to lower the amount of oxalic acid in the urine. You can do that by avoiding foods such as spinach, rhubarb, tea, chocolate, parsley, beetroot, unripe tomatoes and peanuts, all of which are high in oxalic acid. You can also do it by taking more vitamin B$_6$. By a complicated chain of reactions that still isn't entirely understood, B$_6$ lowers the amount of oxalic acid in the urine of people who have a disposition towards kidney stones.

Researchers in India recently found that a supplement of only 10 mg of vitamin B$_6$ per day lowered the oxalic acid content of urine 'significantly' in 12 people, all of whom had developed at least one stone per year for the past few years (*International Journal of Clinical Pharmacology, Therapy and Toxicology*, vol. 20, no. 9, 1982). That was a discovery worth reporting. Why? Because the Indian researchers got results with only 10 mg of vitamin B$_6$ per day, while other scientists had been prescribing as much as 100 mg or more per day. And the Indian scientists studied B$_6$'s effects for six months – longer than anyone else.

In addition, they found that vitamin B$_6$ achieved better, faster effects than thiazides. Thiazides are a family of drugs commonly used to lower blood pressure and prevent kidney stones by increasing the output of urine from the body. However, they also cause lightheadedness, and they can elevate the amount of sugar and uric acid in the blood, which can promote diabetes and gout, respectively. Thiazides can also reduce the amount of potassium in the blood, which translates into muscle weakness and cramps. So the vitamin B$_6$ news is truly good news.

Water: no-cost stone prevention

Another natural kidney-stone preventer is water. In fact, many doctors say that this free commodity everyone has on tap at home is all you'll ever need.

'Water is the best and safest treatment for most patients with kidney stones,' Dr William D. Kaehny of the University of Colorado says flatly. Drink the amount of water necessary to produce 3–5 pints of urine a day, he tells stone patients, and set an alarm clock to wake yourself in the middle of the night so that you can urinate and drink another glass of water. Most people, he says, will not develop a second stone if they put themselves on the water wagon.

It's a little ironic that water, which is so cheap, can prevent stones because more than one researcher has called kidney stones a 'disease of affluence'. That's because, in many cases, the people who get kidney stones are those who have enough money to buy and enjoy red meat, chicken or fish almost every day. The connection is simple: researchers have found an association between increased animal-protein intake and higher oxalic acid and calcium in urine, which means more raw material for stones (*Journal of Urology*, January 1981).

What's more, people who develop kidney stones don't eat their cereal or their vegetables the way they should. That's the verdict from a survey conducted in Ireland, where 8 per cent of the population suffer from stones at some point in their lives. Researchers there studied the diets of 51 kidney-stone patients and compared them to the diets of 51 people of similar weight, age and constitution, but without kidney stones. They found three big differences.

First, the stone group ate less fibre, and fibre has been known to affect urinary calcium and oxalic acid excretion. Second, the stone group got fewer of their calories from carbohydrates such as vegetables, grains and fruit. And, third, the stone group had a higher intake of fats such as those found in red meat (*British Journal of Urology*, vol. 53, no. 5, 1981).

British researchers found that diets high in refined carbohydrates (e.g. sugar, white flour, white rice) may encourage the formation of kidney stones. During a period of one month, the researchers fed a diet of low, normal or high levels of refined carbohydrates to 19 healthy young males. Reporting their finds in the *British Journal of Urology*, the researchers concluded, 'There is the likelihood that a dietary structure which includes significant amounts of sugar or sugar products will increase the risk of calcium stone formation.'

Alcohol consumption may also be a risk factor. In an experiment conducted at the University of Vienna Medical School, the relationship between drinking habits and stone formation was studied in 379 patients. The researchers found that those who prefer alcoholic drinks have significantly higher urinary excretions of calcium, phosphate and uric acid – the substances from which most stones are made. Not surprisingly, say the researchers, the more alcohol you drink, the more of these substances you excrete in your urine, thereby increasing your chances of forming a stone (*Journal of Urology*, January 1981).

The message for kidney-stone sufferers is, in effect, just like the advice that more and more doctors have been giving to anyone who eats the typical Western diet: eat less red meat, less fat and get more energy from whole grains, vegetables and fruit. That recipe is recommended not only for kidney stones, but also to prevent heart disease, diabetes and even cancer.

Surgery – and alternatives

For those people who have existing stones, the most common form of treatment is still surgery. In most cases, surgery involves opening the kidney and removing the stone or stones. The risk is that scar tissue may form in the kidney and later cause the organ to fail. Kidney surgery may also entail a long stay in the hospital and a long convalescence.

One American dentist James Nicolette, dreaded the knife enough to travel to Germany to have his stone removed by a new non-surgical method. He was only the 76th person to experience this drugless technique, which uses focused high-frequency (ultra) sound waves to shatter the stone into tiny pieces.

James Nicolette is now back in the United States, and he and a group of people who call themselves the Kidney-Stone Formers Club have mounted a campaign to alert more people to the causes of kidney stones and to convince the US Food and Drug Administration (FDA) to permit the use of the sound-wave treatment. (In the UK, this method is gaining increasing acceptance.) – using an ultrasound machine called a *lithotripter* – But he isn't standing around waiting for the FDA to act. He's busy preventing his next stone the natural way, and he recommends the same for everybody.

'I've been using magnesium and B$_6$ for about seven months,' Nicolette said. 'I've also eliminated a lot of things from my diet. I used to be a big meat eater, but now I eat very little meat. I eat a lot of bran. And I drink as much water as possible – more than I ever drank before. Since this whole thing started, I've become a firm believer in nutrition.'

• Lead poisoning

The early symptoms of lead poisoning – nausea, headache, loss of appetite, fatigue and irritability – could signal the beginning of any number of common ailments. Only later do the more serious effects occur: anaemia, kidney disease, nervous-system disorders, behaviour problems and impaired intellectual functioning.

Most people associate lead poisoning with children eating paint chips – *pica*, as eating foreign objects is called. However, pica is, unfortunately, only a chip off a much larger block of the lead poisoning problem. A US government survey in the Pittsburgh area found that there was no correlation between the type of paint found in the home – lead base or otherwise – and lead levels in the blood.

The sad fact is that lead is inescapable. Just about everything – air, food, water – is contaminated to a measurable degree with lead. Scientists have been measuring lead concentrations in the polar ice layers to give some indication of the growth of worldwide lead pollution – and the data have not been encouraging: since industrialization began, the lead content of polar ice has multiplied 400 times over natural concentrations.

However, the amount of lead found in polar ice is only a yardstick of lead concentrations building up in more important places – like our bodies. According to the Food and Agriculture Organization World Health Organization, the average weekly intake of lead is already 70 per cent of what it calls the 'provisional tolerable weekly intake'.

Low-level exposure

This amount is based on the assumption that the body can take in a certain amount of lead without harm, but recent work indicates that this safety point is nowhere near as high as assumed, if it exists at all. Levels of lead well below those previously thought to be 'safe' have been shown to be quite unsafe.

Dr Anna Maria Seppäläinen of the Institute of Occupational Health in Helsinki used newly developed measuring devices sensitive enough to detect damage to nerves before it became obvious. She and her colleagues found there was indeed damage to the nerves of the arms of 26 workers who had been steadily exposed to 'safe' levels of lead for periods of 1–17 years. Blood levels of lead in all the workers had never gone above 'safe' levels, either.

Although this nerve damage produced no complaints from the workers other than occasional numbness in the arms, Dr Seppäläinen points out that the effect is still serious, because the nervous system has a poor ability to repair itself once damage like this has been done. She says, 'We think that no damage to the nervous system should be accepted, and that, therefore, present concepts of safe and unsafe lead levels must be reconsidered.'

The insidious effects of lead do not stop with the nervous system. Scottish researchers found that, among men with high blood pressure, there were significantly more with high blood levels of lead than there were among men with normal blood pressure. Also, tap water samples from the homes of the men with high blood pressure had higher levels of lead than did the water taken from the homes of men with normal blood pressure.

Low levels of lead can also slowly poison the body's ability to fight off infections and various harmful substances. Many experiments with animals have demonstrated that doses of lead small enough not to cause any obvious signs of poisoning severely hampered the ability to fight off bacterial and viral infections or to survive the poisons that bacteria produce.

Loren D. Koller, professor at the department of veterinary science, University of Idaho, and a colleague carried out experiments showing that lead hampers the immune response to disease by decreasing the number of cells in the body that produce antibodies. The overall effect is to reduce the number of antibodies prepared to fight off invading organisms, which results, as the researchers said, in 'the increased mortality from bacterial and viral diseases in animals that are chronically exposed to lead.'

Such evidence becomes more than academic when you consider that a number of researchers have stated that some groups of people, particularly those living in cities or near major roads, are already exposed on a day-to-day basis to enough lead to bring about these effects.

'In cities across the United States, there are thousands of bridges and other steel structures coated with lead-based exterior paint,' says Edward L. Baker, Jr, assistant professor of occupational medicine at the Harvard School of Public Health.

> Unlike interior paint, which must now contain no more than 0.06 percent lead by weight, exterior paint may contain as much as 90 percent lead. As such paint ages and cracks, rust may form beneath it, causing chips with a high lead content to flake to the ground, where they may be ingested by children. [*New England Journal of Medicine*, 18 March 1982]

The surface soil directly beneath the Mystic River Bridge in Boston, Massachusetts contained up to 48 times more lead than is usually found in North American soils. And when local children had their blood tested for lead, 49 per cent were found to have increased amounts at levels high enough to concern the Center for Disease Control in Atlanta, Georgia.

Canned foods and lead

The canned foods in your pantry may contain more than their labels suggest. Compared to fresh foods, the canned versions almost always contain much higher levels of lead, according to the World Health Organization. That's because lead solder is used to seal the cans.

It's true that the canned-food industry is making great strides to eliminate or at least reduce this problem. An increasing number of canners are now packing their foods in new, seamless cans or in cans with electrically welded side seams, eliminating lead solder altogether. Still, the conversion is far from complete.

If you're using canned foods, there are precautions you can take to minimize your exposure. The US Food and Drug Administration (FDA) advises against the storage of acidic foods, such as citrus and other juices and tomatoes, in opened cans. Studies have shown that lead levels increased up to seven-fold when juices were stored that way. Also, pickled foods packed in cans were found to have 20 to 50 times more lead than the same products fresh or packed in glass jars.

Nutrients that get the lead out

Good nutrition can help to protect against exposure to lead in the environment. The B vitamin *thiamin*, for instance, 'shows a great deal of promise', says veterinary surgeon Gerald Bratton of Texas A & M University.

Dr Bratton conducted a study using two groups of calves. All the animals were given toxic doses of lead for 20 days, but only one group received thiamin (vitamin B_1) during that time. Throughout the experiment, none of the thiamin-treated animals showed signs of lead poisoning. When tissue from both groups was subsequently examined, that from the calves treated with megadoses of thiamin contained 30 to 92 per cent less lead than tissue from calves dosed only with lead.

'It appears,' says Dr Bratton,

that thiamine, in some way, prevented the deposition of lead in all tissues examined, especially the kidney, liver and brain. The prevention of lead poisoning in experimental calves by thiamine strongly suggests the value of this naturally occurring vitamin for the treatment or prevention of lead intoxication. [*Toxicology and Applied Pharmacology*, 15 June 1981].

Thiamin's value for other species is currently being studied.

Minerals, too, play a big part in how well your system can resist lead exposure. And it doesn't necessarily take a profound mineral deficiency, at least when it comes to iron.

Doctors have known for some time that if iron intake was low enough to cause anaemia, it also promoted the absorption of lead. But what if iron intake was just moderately reduced – less than the ideal intake but not low enough to cause anaemia. Would such a degree of iron deficiency increase lead absorption, too?

To find out, researchers fed a group of rats a diet either just slightly deficient in iron or adequately supplemented. After seven days, all the rats were dosed with lead. The rats on the low-iron diet retained 30 per cent more lead than the iron-supplemented group (*Proceedings of the Nutrition Society*, January 1982).

Other researchers have found that zinc can influence susceptibility to lead poisoning. One study on rats showed that as dietary zinc content increased, tissue lead levels decreased, primarily, say the researchers, because less lead was absorbed.

Calcium

Calcium can have an important effect on lead metabolism. Kathryn R. Mahaffey, a research chemist with the FDA's division of nutrition in Cincinnati, has conducted a number of experiments that show calcium's benefits. In one, she found that rats eating a low-calcium diet and exposed to lead had blood lead concentrations four times higher than rats eating a normal calcium diet, although the quantities of lead consumed were equal.

In another experiment, Dr Mahaffey found that rats that drank water contaminated with 12 parts per million (ppm) lead and eating a low-calcium diet had tissue lead levels similar to those of rats receiving water with 200 ppm lead but a normal calcium diet (*Nutrition Reviews*, October 1981).

There's no doubt about calcium's importance in ushering lead out of your system, but where you get your calcium can be just as important as how much you consume. For that reason, forget milk. Not completely, of course, but just as your main source of calcium if lead exposure is a major concern to you. According to Paul Mushak, associate professor of environmental pathology at the University of North Carolina, there may be several factors in milk that actually work to enhance lead uptake, offsetting the calcium benefits in milk. For instance, the protein found in milk – *casein* –may promote lead uptake. In one experiment, he says, 'We observed that rats orally exposed to high doses of lead exhibited more severe toxic response when a purified diet containing casein was employed versus effects in animals maintained on regular rat chow.'

In another experiment, Dr Mushak explored that observation further. He separated rats into two groups, with diets differing only in the type of protein source – casein or soyabean meal. Both groups were given the same amount of lead. After three weeks, the amount of lead was measured in their blood and tissues. In every tissue measured, the rats maintained on the casein diet had significantly more lead (up to three times as much) than the rats eating the soyabean protein (*Bulletin of Environmental Contamination and Toxicology*, January 1982).

'There are two possible explanations for these results,' Dr Mushak says. 'It could be that casein promotes lead uptake, or it may be that soyabean protein retards absorption. Most likely it's a combination of both. Lactose [milk sugar] is another factor in milk to be considered. It, too, has been shown to enhance the absorption of lead. And while it's true that calcium brings down the lead levels in the body, it just isn't strong enough to override the effects of the casein and lactose.'

Even if you do cut down on milk and milk products, you can still get calcium into your diet. There are always sardines, salmon (with the bones), shrimp, pilchards, tofu (soyabean 'cheese'), watercress, almonds, chickpeas and hard tap water.

If you decide to take calcium supplements, the best choices are probably calcium gluconate and calcium carbonate. Bone meal and dolomite are also good calcium sources, but they have also been shown to contain small traces of lead. Although the FDA says that the amount of lead is well within safe limits for adults, it's not a good idea to give bone meal or dolomite to infants, children, pregnant women or breastfeeding mothers.

• Liver disease and cirrhosis

In the United States, liver disease is now the fifth leading cause of death among men in the 25-to-64 age group, and it is the fourth leading cause of death in women between the ages of 45 and 64. Yet there is still little relationship between the magnitude of the liver health problem and the response of the public and the medical health community in both the United States and Britain. Cancer and heart disease get hundreds of millions of dollars and pounds a year in research, and large numbers of people are beginning to understand what they can do to protect themselves against those serious threats to health, but the liver stays largely in limbo. That's a shame, because our dependence on it as a protector against chemical insults grows rapidly as we advance further into the technological age and expose ourselves to more chemical contaminants.

Many chemicals are metabolized into harmless compounds by just one exposure to the liver's rich array of enzymes and enzyme systems. If there is too much of a chemical in the blood for the liver to filter out in one pass, it will get another crack at it later, when circulating blood brings it around again. Eventually, all will be removed.

Alcohol is the drug that the liver is called upon most frequently to metabolize and flush from the human system. Almost the entire job of dealing with alcohol falls on the liver, because very little of that chemical can be disposed of unchanged, through the lungs or the kidneys.

There are limits to the liver's ability to deal with alcohol, though. First, the purification process happens slowly. Your liver can filter out and metabolize the alcohol in one drink in two hours. If you sipped a cocktail, a bottle of beer or a glass of wine for two hours, you probably wouldn't feel any effect. Most people drink faster than that, of course. The excess alcohol overflows the liver's metabolic capacity, goes into circulating blood, reaches the brain and causes intoxication.

What does the liver do with alcohol? It converts it into a chemical called *acetaldehyde*. That's where trouble starts. Acetaldehyde can itself cause problems. It can interfere with the activation of vitamins by liver cells. The heart and other muscles of the body aren't helped by acetaldehyde either. The conversion of alcohol to acetaldehyde in the liver sets up a vicious circle of chemical side-effects, which, if continued over a period of time, can damage that organ's ability to keep functioning.

For women, who are apparently more vulnerable to alcohol damage to the liver than men, the danger level is extremely low. A French study has shown that women who take one normal-sized alcoholic drink a day are statistically more likely to get cirrhosis (hardening and shrinking of the liver due to excessive destruction of liver cells) than are non-drinkers. For men, the point of hazard was shown to be two drinks a day.

While that doesn't mean that one or two drinks a day automatically will cause harm to the liver, the possibility of that happening is there. A significant number of people who are predisposed to liver trouble because of heredity, other illness or exposure to chemical hazards are being hurt by very small amounts of alcohol.

While your liver is busy processing alcohol out of your system, it can't be handling other environmental toxins or drugs as well as it would normally. That is why some people die when they take a lot of tranquillizers while drinking large amounts of alcohol. The liver can't handle it all, and the drugs and alcohol have an adverse and sometimes fatal impact on the body.

Help for the fatty liver

Good nutrition and exercise help the liver. Consider the condition known as 'fatty liver', which is the first stage of harm to that organ caused by alcohol, and which is reversible if you stop drinking. Your liver can also become fatty from eating too much fat. People who eat little fat probably have more liver health in reserve, so to speak, than others.

Steven C. Goheen, Edward C. Larkin and Ananda Rao, a team of blood specialists in Martinex, California, were looking for a dietary treatment for alcoholics with fatty livers when they found a blend of nutrients that might help anyone who wants to make existing fat leave the liver and prevent new fat from accumulating.

Working with rats, the researchers found that alcohol would promote a fatty liver unless a rat was also fed dihydroxyacetone (a carbohydrate), pyruvate (a key factor in carbohydrate metabolism) and riboflavin (also called vitamin B_2). With those supplements, the levels of triglycerides and other fats all declined in the rats' livers (*Lipids*, January 1981).

The unanswered question is whether the supplements can slim down the fatty livers of non-alcoholics. 'My own gues is that they would work for any kind of fatty liver,' Dr Goheen said, adding that so far there have been no tests on humans.

Exercise is another natural way to prevent a fatty liver. In a one-year study at the University of Mississippi, ten dogs were fed a diet rich in cholesterol and lard. All were confined to small cages, but every day, five of the dogs were given an hour of exercise on a treadmill.

By the end of the study, three of the non-exercised dogs had shown signs of liver disease and died. The two remaining non-exercised dogs had fatty, cirrhotic livers. The exercised dogs, however, had essentially normal livers – despite the high-fat diet. 'Effective exercise,' the researchers noted, 'probably minimizes fat storage in the liver . . . by utilizing it as energy' (*Journal of the American Medical Association*).

One of the most powerful detoxification systems in the liver centres around a substance called *cytochrome P-450*. Scientists who have studied cytochrome P-450 feel that it is involved in alcoholism, cancer and the breakdown of environmental chemicals. One group of researchers at the University of Michigan has looked at the effect of nutrition on the amount of this important detoxifying system in the liver.

V. G. Zannoni of the University of Michigan Medical School, and L. E. Rikans of the University of Oklahoma Health Science Center have reported that supplements of vitamin C increased the amount of P-450 produced by guinea pigs. The test animals given vitamin C also showed increased ability to metabolize drugs and eliminate them from their system. That is a very encouraging report and, if confirmed in similar studies with people, could point the way to yet another use for vitamin C in the prevention of disease.

Alcohol and zinc deficiency

Zinc has also been reported to have value in protecting the liver. In one scientific study of cells, researchers investigating cirrhosis looked at the fact that patients with cirrhosis are usually alcohol addicted *and* zinc deficient. Their question was: which of the two factors harmed the liver most?

The researchers studied four groups of rats. Two groups were fed a normal diet, one supplemented with alcohol and the other without alcohol. Two other groups were fed a zinc-deficient diet, again, one with alcohol and the other without. The results were surprising, because cirrhosis is often blamed entirely on alcohol.

The two groups of rats with adequate zinc levels – even the group given alcohol – were protected from liver damage caused by peroxides, a category of highly reactive and destructive molecules. 'Zinc deficiency may modify [liver] metabolism in a way that could cause potentially harmful effects to [cell] membranes,' the researchers said.

The researchers speculated that a zinc-containing enzyme called *superoxide dismutase* might be the protective factor, since it directly inhibits peroxidation. (We want to caution that this is *not* an endorsement of the superoxide dismutase [SOD] sold in shops which may actually harm the body.) They also suggest that sufficient zinc might protect liver cells from toxins other than alcohol, such as the industrial chemical *carbon tetrachloride*, a solvent used in dry cleaning, and *hydrazine*, an ingredient in the making of jet fuel (*American Journal of Clinical Nutrition*, January 1980).

Vitamin E, selenium and thiamin

Research concerning the toxic effects of paracetamol has also yielded potential ways to protect the liver. Paracetamol is known to cause liver and kidney damage when even mildly excessive amounts are consumed, but the damage is minimized by maintaining adequate levels of selenium and vitamin E.

Francis J. Peterson of the Veterans Administration Medical Center in Minneapolis said that the liver converts paracetamol into a potentially damaging 'reactive metabolite'. But vitamin E and selenium seem to tie up the metabolites and cancel their toxic effects.

Studies have also shown that thiamin (vitamin B_1) deficiency may complicate liver disease. Measuring the thiamin levels of patients with chronic liver disease, doctors found that 58 per cent of them had a deficiency of thiamin. When they supplemented the patients' diet with 200 mg of thiamin a day for one week, the disease improved.

'High doses of thiamin,' the doctors wrote, 'should be included in the routine nutritional management of patients with severe chronic liver disease' *(Scandinavian Journal of Gastroenterology).*

• Lung problems

The lungs are one of the body's main filters. They've been called 'an essential biologic barrier between man and his environment'. In brief, here is what the lungs do:

When you inhale, the hairs of the nostrils and the flypaper-like mucous lining of the nose stop most particles that are larger than 10 to 15 micrometres (millionths of a metre), including common air pollutants such as sulphur dioxide or ammonia. Some particles that escape the nose find themselves swept against the tonsils and adenoids, which both have germ-resistant surfaces.

Only the smallest particles go down the windpipe, and most of them stick to the blanket of mucus that lines every surface in the lung except for the alveoli, the delicate sacs where oxygen passes into the blood and carbon dioxide comes out. This blanket moves in waves, pushed back towards the throat by the hair-like cilia, which beat like oars 1000 to 1500 times a minute. In healthy lungs, the mucus 'conveyor belt' carries all the inhaled debris out of the lungs and into the digestive tract in less than 24 hours. Removing debris from the alveoli, however, can take months.

The older you get, the more difficult normal respiration becomes. The physical changes that take place in ageing lungs reduce the total surface area of lung tissue where the exchange of oxygen and carbon dioxide takes place. In addition, the chest wall becomes stiffer, and the muscles that move the chest wall in breathing become weaker. All that can mean serious trouble as you age. For people advanced in years, even a minor respiratory ailment may be too much for their lungs to take.

That's where nutrition comes in. Getting enough of the right nutrients may not prevent the physical changes that occur in your respiratory system with age, but a good diet can prevent many of those respiratory ailments that are so dangerous to age-weakened lungs. Scientific research has found that a number of essential nutrients help protect your lungs against disease.

The most obvious example is found in vitamin C and its effect on the common cold. Vitamin C may prevent colds, which is reason enough to include it in your health regimen. It almost certainly provides relief from the stress of cold symptoms, and that's just as important if you're operating with a respiratory system already taxed by age.

Vitamin C may protect against other kinds of stress to the respiratory system. Researchers have shown that animals fed vitamin C suffer less damage to their lungs when they are exposed to ozone, a highly poisonous pollutant gas and a major component of smog. Scientists believe that vitamin C in the lungs may protect cells from destructive oxidation reactions touched off by ozone.

Vitamin E, another anti-oxidant vitamin, has also been shown to protect laboratory animals from ozone damage. In one study, researchers found that rats deficient in vitamin E had more chemical evidence of lung damage caused by ozone than rats that were not lacking the vitamin. Physical examination of the rats' lungs confirmed the chemical findings. While all the animals in the experiment suffered lung damage from breathing in ozone, almost all the rats suffering *severe* damage were eating a test diet deficient in vitamin E. By comparison, of the rats receiving vitamin E supplements, nearly all suffered only mild lung damage (*Environmental Research*, December 1979).

Vitamin A: an important anti-pollution nutrient

In the ongoing battle against pollution, we must not overlook one of the lung's most important protectors: vitamin A. Vitamin A is particularly valuable, it seems, in preventing damage caused by nitrogen oxide, or NO_2, a pollutant present in car exhaust as well as in cigarette smoke. At the Delta Regional Primate Research Center of Tulane University, James C. S. Kim exposed three groups of hamsters to NO_2 for five-hour periods, once a week for eight weeks. The conditions, he explained, were 'comparable not only to industrial pollution found in an urban – surburban environment, but also to the exposure of the respiratory tract of a habitual smoker.'

The first group of hamsters received a diet lacking in vitamin A. The second received what Dr Kim called a 'vitamin A-adequate' diet. The third was fed a 'vitamin A-high' diet – twice what the second group received. After eight weeks of exposure and observation, their lung tissues were examined.

Vitamin A-deficient animals, Dr Kim noted, responded poorly to NO_2 exposure: 'Rapid and often labored breathing appeared immediately and continued through the five hours. Recovery was slow.' By the fifth week of the experiment, they had visibly started to decline: 'All exposed animals, without exception, were in poor condition.'

Microscopic examination of their lung tissues revealed severe damage. The epithelial lining, it was found, had degenerated badly. The cilia, so necessary for defence against bacteria, had been impaired, and in some cases destroyed. Cells in the alveoli had hardened and were unable to function properly. In many animals, there were signs of pneumonia.

The hamsters that received a vitamin A-adequate diet fared a good deal better. NO_2 made them breathe rapidly, but they showed no signs of distress, and afterwards their breathing quickly returned to normal. They remained in good condition throughout the eight weeks of the experiment and were 'healthy and alert' at its end.

When the lungs of these animals were examined, there were no signs of pneumonia or the severe inflammation that had afflicted the deficient group. The gas had caused damage, certainly, but normal lung tissue had apparently grown back to repair it. 'There appeared to be an increase in cell regeneration in animals supplemented with vitamin A in contrast with those not supplemented,' Dr Kim noted. The epithelial lining, for the most part, was intact, and there were few abnormal cells.

The animals that received double doses of vitamin A survived their polluted environment equally well. Observation and microscopic examination showed them to be much like the vitamin A-adequate group.

Dr Kim summed up the significant implications of his experiment:

High concentrations of NO_2 destroy lung tissue. With enough (or a little more than enough) vitamin A, regeneration of the lung is rapid and successful. But with a low dose, this protective response is retarded – and the animal suffers.

Too little vitamin A in the face of NO_2 exposure can raise the risk of disease, he explained.

Without vitamin A, ciliated epithelium doesn't form. Instead, you get squamous cells – precancerous-type cells. You get abnormal mucous cells, which mean clogging in the respiratory tract, and danger of infection. If the epithelium doesn't form properly, it can lead to emphysema. [*Environmental Research*]

His findings should be of special interest to commuters, Dr Kim says, because they subject themselves to conditions much like those of his experiment. 'If you commute, you have intermittent exposure to NO_2. You may be exposed to urban pollution for five hours, eight hours, then you come back to your house in the suburbs, where the air is cleaner. The next day you go back to the city. The epithelium in the lung has to repair itself accordingly, after each exposure.'

Vitamin A can help the lungs adapt to this less-than-perfect world, Dr Kim says. 'But a commuter who doesn't get enough vitamin A is going to suffer.'

In general, the effects he observed in his lab led Dr Kim to regard vitamin A highly as 'a preventive measure' for safeguarding lung health. Even the lung problems that we associate with old age may be forestalled with the early, regular use of vitamin A supplements, he speculates.

(*See also* EMPHYSEMA.)

Is your house hurting your lungs?

Air pollution is not simply a matter of dirty haze hanging over the centres of our big cities. *Indoor* air pollution may actually be a bigger health problem than pollution outside the home, and measures commonly taken to save energy, measures to seal a house against the infiltration of outside air, can make the problem worse.

James Berk, a researcher at the Lawrence Berkeley Laboratory in California, has been studying the problem of indoor air pollution for several years now and has found that indoor pollutant levels may increase when infiltration of outside air is reduced.

How fast is air replaced?

'It's energy-conservation measures such as weather stripping that will reduce infiltration,' Dr Berk says. Weather stripping involves the plugging of gaps around windows and doors through which cold air can enter a house. It's an essential part of improving the energy efficiency of a building.

All houses, even those that are thoroughly plugged up, allow some exchange of air from outside through cracks in the frame. In the United States – where houses are generally far better insulated than they are in Britain – houses generally let in outside air at a rate of approximately one air change per hour. That means that, each hour, outside air equal to the volume of the house enters the house. Once an hour, an entire houseful of new air has to be brought up to the desired temperature. If you can cut the rate of air exchange, you use less fuel for heating.

You also have less fresh air for breathing. The Berkeley researchers found substantially higher levels of a number of pollutants in insulated buildings. 'In one study,' Dr Berk told us, 'we tested pollutant levels in a school where we could control the rate of exchange through the mechanical ventilation system. That gave us some way to look at the various ventilation rates possible in a building. In that situation, we found elevated levels of carbon dioxide, which were merely a result of the students' breathing.

The levels of carbon dioxide did not exceed the health standards set by various US government agencies, and carbon dioxide was the only pollutant that increased in concentration. 'That was not surprising,' the scientists reported at an international energy conference, 'since there were no obvious indoor sources of pollution other than the occupants themselves.'

When the occupants get involved in activities other than breathing and thinking, though, other pollutants begin to build up indoors. Using gas cookers can produce higher levels of three major air pollutants – nitrogen dioxide, nitric oxide and carbon monoxide. A monitoring of those pollutants carried out a number of years ago in four houses with gas cookers found consistently higher levels inside the houses than outside. The study, conducted for the US Environmental Protection Agency by a Connecticut research firm, found that indoor levels of nitric oxide and nitrogen dioxide were directly related to use of a gas cooker *(Journal of the Air Pollution Control Association)*.

Other pollutants may build up in energy-efficient homes, the researchers in California discovered, independent of what the people inside them are doing. 'We found elevated levels of formaldehyde,' Dr Berk told us, 'which is emitted from a chemical binding agent used to make building materials like particle board and plywood, and to make some furnishings. Formaldehyde is also released into the air by urea-formaldehyde foam insulation.'

Formaldehyde and radon

Foam insulation was added to many American homes in the 1970s as part of the drive to save energy. In the case of urea-formaldehyde foam, energy saving may set up a double health threat. A sealed house with that foam insulation would lock in pollutants from the insulation itself.

Dr Berk and his colleagues measured levels of formaldehyde in special experimental homes designed for maximum insulation. One of the super-insulated houses averaged one air change every five hours, compared to one change each hour in the normal American home. In that experimental house, the levels of total aliphatic aldehydes (the chemical family to which formaldehyde belongs) measured some eight times higher than the levels outside. The scientists reported.

These results indicate that, in general, indoor air has higher formalde-hyde/aldehyde concentrations than outdoor air. The concentration of aldehydes often exceeds the recommended US and European formal-dehyde standards for indoor air in residential buildings.

Levels that high can play havoc with a sensitive individual's health. The University of Washington published the results of an ongoing survey of inhab-itants of mobile homes (i.e caravans). Formaldehyde-emitting plywood and particle board are used extensively in the construction of mobile homes, and the participants in the survey were people who had complained of symptoms much like the standard symptoms of formaldehyde poisoning: 80 out of 92 people complained of eye irritation; 58 suffered irritation of the respiratory tract; and 51 reported headaches (*University of Washington Environmental Health and Safety News*).

A letter to the researchers from a family in Idaho who had read of their work described a typical syndrome:

> We bought a 1977, 14 x 61-foot mobile home last November, and ever since we moved into this mobile home, we have been awfully sick. It makes our skin sting and burn, eyes burn, [and we have] awful head-aches all the time. Our lungs hurt, and we can hardly breathe, we have dizzy spells and have sore throats.
>
> I just don't think we could make it in this mobile home another winter with everything closed up and the furnace turned on. We have got to have the windows open so we can get plenty of air.

One of the more exotic indoor pollutants that the scientists at Berkeley are concerned about is radon gas. 'This is a radioactive gas which can enter a structure from several sources, the primary source often being the soil beneath the house,' Dr Berk says. Radon gas is also emitted from stone, concrete, brick and other building materials. It produces part of the natural radiation we are exposed to every day.

Natural radioactive radium in the soil breaks down to form radon, which, like all radioactive substances, decays further to form four radioactive 'daughter' elements. These daughter elements often become attached to dust particles in the air so small that they slip past the body's own filtration system and are carried into the lungs. Studies of uranium miners exposed to high levels of the radioactive dust clearly suggest that those particles may increase the risk of lung cancer.

'In the literature, there are numerous examples of radon measurements showing higher indoor than outdoor concentrations,' the Berkeley researchers report in one study. 'Due to the fact that the population spends most of its time indoors, the total exposure of the general public to radon daughters will be largely determined by the elevated indoor concentrations.' A comparison of radon levels in US homes with those measured in Swedish homes, which are typically better insulated than American buildings, indicates that the pollutant builds up just like any other when ventilation is reduced.

Recently, the British government has recognized this problem – chiefly affecting those living in areas of rocky soil such as Cornwall and the Lake District – and is sponsoring studies on the effects of radon. It is likely that some help (advisory and/or financial) will be made available to those affected to modify their homes.

There are other potential sources of pollution that the Berkeley scientists have not yet measured, Dr Berk told us. 'If a household includes a cigarette smoker, that most likely would have a significant effect on indoor pollution. Other activities, such as cleaning with various chemicals, could have harmful effects in a tightly insulated house.'

Although the scientists did many of their tests in specially constructed experimental houses, Dr Berk says the levels of pollutants they measured indicate possible problems for all of us. 'What is happening now is that builders are putting up houses and billing them as the energy-efficient houses of the future. They're saying it's worth the extra money to have good weather stripping and so on, so that you can save money on energy in the long run.

'The first house we studied was a research house with an elaborate control system. It was custom-built for energy saving, and it had an air exchange rate of 0.2 air changes per hour. But another house we studied could have been realistically sold on the open market, and it had a ventilation rate of only 0.4 air changes per hour. If builders incorporate certain energy-saving features, a house with 0.4 or 0.5 air changes per hour would not be too hard to build. The question is whether or not such energy conservation measures can cause air-quality problems.'

How to upgrade air quality in your home

Dr Berk stresses that his work does not indicate that energy conservation should be abandoned. 'Our main thrust is to see what levels of pollution exist in an energy-efficient house. We want to see if problems exist, and we have found some potential areas of concern. But we're not saying the energy-conserving measures shouldn't be implemented. There are cost-effective solutions to the problem, short of abandoning energy conservation.'

For example, the researchers at the Berkeley lab have been evaluating devices called 'air-to-air heat exchangers'. The heat exchanger brings fresh air into the house but warms it with the heat from the outgoing exhaust air, thus sparing the home heating system.

There are other ways to save, Dr Berk says. 'If you are building a new, tight house, you can eliminate building materials that might cause problems later, materials which would generate formaldehyde, for example.

'That solution is out, of course, if the house is already built. But in the case of radon, you may be able to take steps to seal the pollutant out of your house. There are usually cracks in basement floors, often in the wall and floor joints, where radon gas may come up from the soil. Drains in the basement sometimes open directly to the ground, and the gas may enter that way.

'If you have a house that is built on a concrete slab in direct contact with the soil, it may be worse than if the house is built over a ventilated crawl space. My house is built that way, with vents at the sides of the crawl space. The radon gas which emanates from the soil is ventilated out around the house, rather than into it.'

'There are also different types of contaminant control devices which can be effective,' says Dr Berk. 'Most odours can be eliminated by using charcoal filters. Highly efficient particulate filters have been manufactured which remove many pollutant particles in the air. We don't have one filter which removes all the different kinds of pollution, but there are a variety of measures that can be used to combat the problem.'

Put aside such hobbies as woodworking and painting for the winter. Stripping and finishing furniture is out, since the chemical solvents used in most finishes and cleaners are poisonous. Many cause respiratory irritation (and some can cause permanent damage to the nervous system).

Exposure to solvents in spray paint without proper ventilation has been followed by nerve damage. A variety of chemicals commonly sold in arts and crafts shops for various purposes can cause cancer. Such materials should never be used in a sealed house in the middle of January. Read a book instead.

Try to stir up as little dust as possible. Leave your spring cleaning for the spring. The chemicals in household cleansers may be hazardous in a closed house.

And if things get too stuffy, turn down your thermostat, bundle up and open your windows for a couple of hours. Even with the windows closed, if you decide to set the thermostat lower than normal, consider wearing a hat. Much of the body's heat can be lost through an uncovered head.

• Lymphatic system problems (lymphostasis)

Under normal circumstances, you would probably be aware of your lymphatic system only when you come down with a viral or bacterial infection. Then the lymph nodes in your neck might swell up and become tender. Yet, the healthy operation of your lymphatic system may be protecting you from the two major killers of adults – heart disease and cancer – and you can easily give your lymphatic system a 'tune-up' so that it does its vital work more effectively.

'The lymphatic system is not studied very much,' says Gerald M. Lemole, chief of the department of thoracic and cardiovascular surgery at the Deborah Heart and Lung Center in New Jersey. 'Most general medical texts devote only one or two paragraphs to it. But the lymphatics, though little known, have three very important functions.'

'First, the lymphatics return protein to the bloodstream. As much as 50 per cent of our serum protein can leak out of our bloodstream during a 24-hour period, and it is the job of the lymphatics to return this protein to the blood.'

'Second, the lymphatics clear the spaces between our cells and carry away toxins and foreign particles such as bacteria, large proteins, cholesterol and viruses. We were taught that the liver and kidneys clear away toxins, but it is actually the lymphatics that clear away the fluid that bathes each cell of our body.'

'Third, the lymphatics are an integral part of our immune system. The white cells called *lymphocytes* circulate in and out of the lymphatics, and they help destroy foreign particles such as bacteria, viruses and parasites.'

What is the structure of this other circulatory system that no one talks much about? 'We've already mentioned the lymph nodes (sometimes called lymph glands). You'll find these bean-shaped nodes not only in your neck but also in your armpits, behind your knees, in your groin, near your arteries, around your heart – in fact, you have many hundreds of lymph nodes, some buried deeply and some near the surface of your body.

The lymph nodes are connected to each other by an intricate system of thin-walled channels that run throughout your body next to your arteries and veins. The whole system is filled with a fluid called *lymph* – usually colourless and containing proteins, fats, lymphocytes and other substances.

What could go wrong with such a seemingly passive and relatively simple body system? Plenty. 'The trouble begins when the lymphatic system becomes blocked or the flow of lymph slows down appreciably – a condition called *lymphostasis*,' says Dr Lemole. 'It's like the kitchen sink: if the drain is clogged but you leave the water running, the water will eventually run all over the floor.

'Similarly, what happens in your body during lymphostasis is that the fluid that is building up in the spaces between your body cells can't be carried away by the lymphatics. So the fluid and the pressure build up in these inter-cellular spaces. Such fluid buildup has definitely been implicated in congestive heart failure. The lymph channels in the lungs become engorged with fluid and stiffen, and so does the left ventricle of the heart, the part that pumps oxygenated blood to the body's tissues.'

A factor in heart disease and cancer

But that's not all. With his colleague, Paschal M. Spagna, chief of cardiac surgery at Graduate Hospital, University of Pennsylvania, Dr Lemole has been studying the effects of lymphostasis on atherosclerosis (clogging of the arteries). 'We feel quite strongly that lymphostasis is a critical factor in generating atherosclerosis,' Dr Lemole says.

'First,' he continues, 'the cardiac lymphatics are responsible for carrying away cholesterol from the intercellular spaces. If the lymphatics are blocked, the cholesterol can't go anywhere. It stays in the walls of the arteries too long, thus contributing to atherosclerosis.'

'This idea is consistent with the fact that in 90 per cent of the cases of coronary atherosclerosis, post-mortem examinations show scarring, inflammation and blockage of the lymphatics.'

In addition to heart disease, Dr Lemole points out, lymphostasis may be a contributing cause of cancer. 'Because the lymphatics are blocked,' he says, 'toxic molecules cannot be moved away from the body cells. This constant exposure to toxins may be a cause of malignancy. The cells most affected in this way from lymphostasis are the epithelial cells [those that line the internal and external surfaces of the body, such as vessels and small cavities].'

Preventing lymphostasis

Fortunately, there are several things you can do to help prevent lymphostasis, and many of those things relate to the way lymph fluid is moved through the body. The lymphatic system doesn't have a heart of its own. 'The lymph is largely moved along by a "milking" effect in your chest, which is created when you breathe,' says Dr Lemole. 'And backflow of lymph is prevented by a system of valves.'

'When you breathe deeply – when you breathe from your diaphragm – it helps the flow of lymph. That may explain why female secretaries have a higher rate of heart disease than female executives. It's almost impossible to take deep breaths while you're sitting down all day.'

'In addition, there are certain conditions that can slow the flow of lymph. We have noticed that cancer sets in about one year after a person has a deep depression or a severe stress. The reason for that may have to do with a lessened lymphatic flow.'

'Hans Selye has shown that stress causes atrophy of the lymphatis,' Dr Lemole points out. 'Furthermore, stress also causes the body to produce the hormones ACTH, pituitrin and adrenalin – and those, in turn, can cause spasms of the lymphatics, leading to lymphostasis. On the other hand, when you are not feeling stressed, when you are feeling good, your body will produce endorphins, which have the opposite effect of ACTH.'

Does Dr Lemole have a prescription for a healthy lymphatic system? Indeed, he does. 'Many of the things that are good for the blood circulatory system are also good for the lymphatics. In a way, I suppose, that should come as no surprise, since the body is really a dynamic system.'

'First, there's exercise, which will help keep the lymph flowing well. When you exercise, you breathe deeply, and when you run, your body produces endorphins. Yoga is also good for the lymphatics.'

'Second, there's the lessening of stress. Your mental attitude is very important to the health of the lymphatics. Meditation, biofeedback or any stress-reducing method can be a great help in cutting down the amount of ACTH you produce and increasing the amount of endorphins.'

'Third, there is dietary control, especially the area of fatty foods. After a fatty meal, much of the fat ends up in the lymphatics. Also, certain fats can increase the cholesterol in your blood, which places a burden on the lymphatics to clear it.'

'You know,' says Dr Lemole, 'I've seen people running, or doing biofeedback, or putting themselves on low-fat diets for their health, and there is one common denominator I can see at work: They all have a positive mental attitude. Maybe that is the most important thing of all.'

'Those people aren't just sitting around and suffering. They're doing something for themselves, and they feel good about it. I've been trying to find a word for it. *Euphoria*, Greek for "well-being,' is almost right. Then there's the Gaelic word *salus* – a feeling of wellness.'

'Of course,' says Dr Lemole, 'it doesn't matter what you call the feeling. It's the feeling itself that counts. It's the most important feeling of all.'

• Malabsorption problems

The small intestine is perfectly designed for absorption. Its inner surface is folded and convoluted and covered by millions of tiny fringe-like projections called *villi*. Like a jagged coastline with many inlets and promontories, it has an enormous amount of exposed area. In fact, the folds and villi of the small intestine create an inner surface as large as a tennis court.

Through this wide wall of intestinal cells, everything your body must get from its food – for energy, for growth, for the maintenance of all biochemical processes – has to pass. In a very real sense, your food has not even entered your body until it goes through the wall of the small intestine. Nutrients that are not absorbed there just keep on going, out of the body and literally down the drain. This is what happens, to a dangerous degree, to intestinal bypass patients. With much of the small intestine taken out of action, they lose too many essential vitamins and minerals along with unwanted calories.

Few of us have to worry about such a grave failure of absorption. However, if you want to get most out of the food you eat, if you want to make sure that the essential nutrients you take in are actually reaching the cells of your body, you should give some thought to the factors that can influence this vital stage in the process of nutrition, for better or worse.

What can interfere with absorption? Just about anything that impairs the health of the digestive system. An infection like the flu, particularly if it causes diarrhoea, means that nutrients pass through the intestine unabsorbed. Food poisoning can have the same effect. Coeliac disease – an inability to digest the protein (i.e. gluten), of wheat and some other grains properly – severely damages the villi and can lead to deficiencies of nearly all vitamins and minerals.

Strange as it sounds, the very physical process of absorption can be powerfully affected by your state of mind. 'Stress can cause abnormal motility [movement] in the digestive tract,' says Dr Mark Tager, who practises 'wellness-oriented' medicine in Oregon. Normally, he explains, digested food passes through the system with an even, wave-like motion. When tension interferes, the movement can be too fast, too slow or too uneven for proper digestion. And poorly digested foods won't be absorbed well.

The malabsorption problems created by emotional stress may become quite serious, adds John W. Erdman, Jr, of the department of food science at the University of Illinois. 'People who have emotional difficulties, who are "hyper", often suffer from frequent diarrhoea. This can have a significant effect on absorption, leading to the loss of such nutrients as magnesium and potassium. For some individuals, it can be a major factor in nutritional problems.'

Good nutrition improves absorption

One factor necessary for effective absorption is so obvious that it is easy to miss – good nutrition. In order to gain all the nourishment from your food, you must be well nourished. Like all the other cells in your body, those intestinal cells involved in absorption require proper nutrition to function at their best. And the elaborate biochemical processes that digest food and transport nutrients across cell membranes depend on proteins, vitamins, minerals and energy supplied by food.

Serious under-nutrition, of the sort found in developing countries, can create serious absorption problems, it has been found. Investigators at the University of Lagos in Nigeria examined a group of people who looked healthy but were thought to suffer from malabsorption. Not only was absorption impaired in these people, they found, but the lining of the small intestine – vital for absorption – had degenerated, and blood tests showed that three-fourths of these patients had low levels of protein.

Improved nutrition led to swift improvement. After two to three weeks of protein and folic-acid supplementation, absorption patterns returned to normal, and the intestinal tissues had begun to regenerate *(British Medical Journal)*.

Protein deficiency may be rare in the West, but low levels of other nutrients are not, and this, too, can impair absorption. 'People who are short of vitamins and minerals are at risk for absorption problems – we need these nutrients to "open the gates" for proper absorption' is the way Dr Tager puts it.

In the case of minerals, the presence of other nutrients can be particularly critical. These vital substances simply are not absorbed easily. Only about half the calcium you eat in your food is absorbed, some 5 to 15 per cent of the iron and mere fractions of the zinc and chromium. Absorption of minerals, in fact, is often more crucial than intake. And the proportion that is absorbed can be raised – or lowered – by the rest of the diet.

A vital interrelationship, for example, exists between vitamin D and calcium. The vitamin is an essential part of the chemial process that brings the mineral through the wall of the small intestine. Without vitamin D, in other words, you can consume calcium by the teaspoon and never get enough of it. Experiments suggest that vitamin D may have an important role in the absorption of phosphorus, too.

Vitamin C may not be essential for calcium absorption, but indications are strong that it can aid the process. In an Egyptian study, investigators gave an oral dose of calcium phosphate to a group of rats. Some of the animals also received vitamin C, others were given pepper juice and others orange juice. Later, the investigators measured the calcium levels in their blood.

'Our data showed that giving samples of ascorbic acid [vitamin C] together with calcium enhanced the rate of its intestinal absorption,' the researchers reported. Pepper and orange juice (both rich natural sources of vitamin C) also improved absorption, they added *(Zeitschrift für Ernährungswissenschaft)*.

Vitamin C makes an even more dramatic difference where iron is concerned. Iron deficiency is no minor problem – it is the leading deficiency disease in the United States and Britain and is widespread throughout the world. Studies at the University of Washington and elsewhere suggest that a solution may lie less in increasing dietary iron than in improving the absorption of the iron that is already there.

This possibility is especially important for those people who, for health or other reasons, eat little or no meat. The iron in meat – 'haeme iron' – is absorbed far more readily than the 'non-haeme iron' found primarily in plant foods. In fact, usually only 3 to 4 per cent of the iron in vegetable foods is absorbed.

According to studies conducted by James Cook, a professor of medicine at the University of Kansas, and Elaine Monsen, a professor of nutrition at the University of Washington, the addition of 280 mg of vitamin C to a meal can double iron absorption – allowing you to get twice as much out of the iron that you take in, in other words. If that dose were divided and taken with each meal, they add, the rate of absorption would more than triple. 'In countries with a high prevalence of iron-deficiency anemia, food fortification with ascorbic acid may be more effective than iron in improving iron nutrition,' they wrote in the *American Journal of Clinical Nutrition*.

If vitamins enhance the absorption of minerals, it seems only right that minerals should aid in the absorption of vitamins. Because minerals are vitally involved in the enzymes of digestion, this may very well be the case. Researchers at the University of California, found that when healthy volunteers were put on a diet that depleted their reserves of zinc, the absorption of folic acid dropped sharply. Why? The folic acid containing compounds in foods – *polyglutamyl folates* – must be split by an enzyme before the folic acid can be absorbed. And this enzyme, they suggested, requires zinc *(Federation Proceedings)*.

Preventing absorption decline

In general, the older you are, the greater the chance you'll run into absorption problems. A decline in secretions of stomach acid and digestive enzymes means poorer absorption of iron and protein. Less and less of the B vitamins and minerals such as calcium make it out of your digestive tract and into your bloodstream. This is one reason why older people are so often beset with nutritional ills. Poor absorption means poor nutrition, which will impair absorption further – starting a cycle that is difficult to stop. Is this inevitable?

'There are widespread differences in the ability to absorb nutrients,' says Dr Tager. 'At least part is rooted in individual history – how a person has used or abused his digestive tract during his lifetime.' The continual use of stimulants, like caffeine, may take its toll over time. So can years of neglected stomach and bowel problems.

By the same token, attention to those things that promote healthy digestion and absorption will pay a double bonus – now and in the future. Making mealtime (and the hours afterwards) relaxed and pleasant is more than just a civilized idea, for this reason. 'I'd suggest a quiet period surrounding digestion,' says Dr Tager. 'It does little good to eat good food and then damage digestion by stress.'

That's also the feeling expressed by psychologist Howard G. Schutz of the University of California and sociologist Pamela C. Baird. After studying the nutritional habits and health status of 100 women living in the Sacramento (California) area, the researchers discovered that if we sit down and enjoy our food, especially in a relaxed, convivial atmosphere, we're likely to get more nutrition out of it *(Journal of the American Dietetic Association*, March 1980).

Ms Baird put it this way: 'If a person "A" perceives food as something to share with friends, maybe on a picnic or after a tennis match, and if person "B" is depressed and perceives food as something that will give him an emotional uplift for his depression, then person "A" may end up having more of the nutrients in his body than person "B" would.' In other words, she says, 'If you make a meal an occasion, you might be much better off.'

Dr Schutz and Ms Baird knew from the start that some people are just physically better than others at digesting the same food. They also knew that some people choose to eat more nutritiously than others. But they hoped to go beyond physical differences and differences in food choice and to isolate the role of such factors as lifestyle and mental attitude in good nutrition.

In their opinion, these so-called socio-psychological variables do make a difference. Choosing the right foods and digesting them well are obviously important, but *the spirit in which you eat* matters, too.

In their experiment, the researchers discovered four basic types of food consumers. First there was the 'depressed' type, the kind of person who regularly polishes off a packet of biscuits and a pint of milk while chain-watching soap operas on a lonely night. Then there was the 'rational' type, a cosmopolitan, calorie-conscious person who would gladly eat cottage cheese instead of steak. Then came the 'picky' type, who would eat fresh vegetables one day and hot fudge sundaes the next, depending on her mood.

The depressed women, as expected, turned out to be under-nourished. Analyses of the nutrient levels in the blood of the second and third types, however, were surprising. The rational eaters had lower nutrient levels than their sound diet would suggest, and the picky eaters were able to glean fairly healthy nutrient levels from a skimpy diet.

Only the fourth type – the 'nutritional ideal,' according to the researchers – both consumed a lot of wholesome food and enjoyed above-average nutrient levels to go along with it. They also had lower blood pressure, lower cholesterol levels and, believe it or not, less flabby upper arms than the other three groups.

Here's how the researchers described this ideal group: 'Happy and accepting' people, they liked a variety of foods, and they enjoyed sharing food with other people. They were mentally and physically active, well- integrated into their communities, and economically secure. They were self- disciplined, but they also knew how to put their work aside and relax. 'In other words,' Dr Schutz wrote,

> good nutrition may not merely be the absence of symptoms of malnutrition; it may also be an entirely positive quality of living in its physical, mental, emotional, social and economic aspects.

Dr Schutz couldn't confirm that gregarious, self-actualized people have a special biochemical mechanism for absorbing nutrients better. 'That's the jump I can't make,' he said. His study, he told us, merely indicates that people who regard eating as 'a pleasant experience' seem to get more out of their food.

Exercise will give your digestive system the same benefits it gives the rest of your body. 'Individuals who don't exercise, who don't get enough oxygen to the cells, tend to have poor absorption patterns,' Dr Tager says. 'Yoga exercises that aim at using stomach and intestinal muscles can do particular good.'

But where digestion and absorption are concerned, the main thing, appropriately enough, is food. Dr Tager emphasizes the virtues of raw foods, whole grains and vegetables. Many people may want to add vitamin and mineral supplements to sound diets based on whole, natural foods to ensure an adequate supply of all the nutrients necessary for efficient absorption. What it comes down to is this: a high-quality diet will help your body get from your food all the good things that nature put into it.

And *that* logic is hard to question.

• Memory Problems

Claire has just been introduced to her husband's new boss. Two minutes later, she can't remember his name.

Jim's just finished doing the breakfast dishes and is about to settle down to read the Sunday newspaper. He reaches for his glasses only to find that they've 'disappeared'.

Sound familiar?

It should, if you're like most people. Everybody's experienced a memory lapse at one time or another, and most probably didn't give it a second thought. Unless you're getting up in years, a good memory is something you take for granted. 'After the age of 50, almost everybody loses some ability to remember names,' says Sandra Weintraub of the behavioural neurology unit of Beth Israel Hospital in Boston, Massachusetts. 'This is normal. Still, up until the 70s, memory shouldn't deteriorate very much. Between 70 and 80, some people show signs of memory failure, and after the age of 80, almost everybody does.'

However, not all kinds of memories fade. Grandma can relate in minute detail how she met and fell in love with grandpa. But she'll forget tomorrow's dentist appointment or that she left something boiling on the cooker.

What's the difference? One involves long-term memory (and lots of repetition), while the others involve short-term memory (with little reinforcement).

'When we think about who was at a recent party or what we need to buy at the supermarket, we are using our short-term memories,' says Elizabeth Loftus, author of the book *Memory* (1980). Ordinarily, without repetition, a short-term memory lasts about 30 seconds and then is gone. But it won't last even that long if interest and attention are lacking. That's what really determines what gets into short-term memory in the first place. 'Many of the problems that we think of as memory difficulties are probably due to lapses of attention,' says Dr Loftus.

'Concentration plays a big part in memory,' adds Nancy J. Treat, assistant professor of human development at Penn State University. 'If you don't get it in, you can't get it out.'

'It's impossible to remember everything,' says Dr Weintraub. 'As you grow older, your responsibilities increase, and you have progressively more things to remember. Your memory is like an elastic band. It can stretch only so far, and then something's got to give.

'I have a great ability to remember phone numbers,' Dr Weintraub told us. 'But now I have so many other things to remember day to day that I can't hold it all. So I've started writing down the numbers in a little book I carry with me. That leaves more room for the things I need to remember now.'

Still, if you want to learn to rely more on your memory and less on paper and pencil (after all, you can't write down the boss's name while you're being introduced), we have five ways to help you increase your memory capacity.

1 Check your choline intake There's lots of excitement in the scientific community concerning the use of choline (or lecithin, a major dietary source of choline) as a memory enhancer. Although it's still in the research stages, it's worth reporting here.

Doctors became interested in testing choline because it is a precursor, or forerunner, of acetylcholine, a brain compound that is essential for the smooth flow of nerve impulses. Studies have shown that extra choline in the diet increases levels of acetylcholine in the brain and may therefore aid memory.

One study, carried out by the (US) National Institute of Mental Health, indicates that a single 10 g dose of choline can significantly improve memory and recall in normal, healthy people. After taking choline, volunteers were able to memorize a sequence of unrelated words more quickly. Interestingly enough, subjects whose memories were poorest at the start of the study were the ones choline helped the most *(Life Sciences)*.

However, choline may do even more for those suffering from Alzheimer's disease, a form of mental deterioration that includes severe memory loss. 'People who have Alzheimer's disease have a deficiency of the enzyme that produces acetylcholine,' says Harvey S. Levin, associate professor of neurosurgery at the University of Texas medical branch in Galveston. 'We also know that the body can synthesize acetylcholine from lecithin.'

Dr Levin and colleague Bruce H. Peters, professor of neurology, decided to test lecithin in conjunction with another substance to see if the memory of these patients would improve. 'Their memory capacity did increase,' Dr Levin told us. 'Not to normal, but it was a measurable amount. And the effects lasted from 6 to 18 months.' *(See also* ALZHEIMER'S DISEASE.)

Best of all, choline (or lecithin) is completely safe to use. There were no side-effects reported even when 20 to 25 g were taken in one day. While researchers stress that proper clinical trials have only just begun, the results thus far are encouraging.

2 Avoid nicotine, alcohol and drugs These can really affect your memory, and there are studies to back it up. Kicking all of them may do wonders for you.

In one experiment, researchers from UCLA divided 23 habitual smokers into two groups. One group was asked to smoke a non-nicotine cigarette and the other a cigarette containing nicotine. Both groups were then asked to recall a series of 75-item lists containing names, professions, animals, vegetables and minerals. After three trials, the non-nicotine group recalled an average of 24 per cent more of the words than the nicotine group *(American Journal of Psychiatry)*.

In another study, 37 smokers and 37 non-smokers were shown a dozen colour photographs of individuals and given their corresponding names. After 10 minutes, they tried to match the correct names with the faces. Non-smokers placed them correctly significantly more often than the smokers did *(British Medical Journal*, 22–29 December 1979).

If you think that's bad, wait until you hear what alcohol can do to your memory. A study at the University of Oklahoma Health Sciences Center tested the memories of young and middle-aged women before and after drinking alcohol. The results, say the researchers, suggest that moderate drinking may lead to memory impairment that may become greater as a woman ages and as she drinks more alcohol. What's more, these problems may be present even when the social drinker is not drinking (*Journal of Studies on Alcohol*, January 1980).

Although that study was done only with women, other research has shown that men's memories are affected by alcohol, too.

It's also known that some tranquillizers and heart and blood-pressure medications can cause memory problems. 'Many older people, in particular,' says Dr Weintraub, 'often take medications for various ailments without realizing that they may cause memory lapses.' It's a good idea to ask your doctor or chemist to fill you in on any possible side-effects that may accompany a particular medication.

3   Take advantage of the time of day   Have you ever noticed that you can remember certain things better at one time of the day than at another? Well, you're not alone. According to studies, short-term memory gets worse as the day progresses, probably from increasing fatigue. However, surprisingly, the opposite holds true for long-term memory. That's what scientists from Cambridge University discovered recently.

They divided volunteers into three groups and tested their long-term memory capabilities at three different times during the day. All the subjects finished the test in about the same amount of time, but the group tested at 10 A.M. didn't do as well as the group tested at 3 P.M. and the 7 P.M. group did best of all (*New Scientist*, 9 October 1980).

4   Use memory tricks   Mnemonics (ni-MON-iks) are gimmicks that you can use to help you improve your memory. There are lots of different ones, but they're all based on the principle of association. In fact, most memory works through association. That means you remember new ideas by connecting them with something that you already know.

'The advantage [of mnemonics] is that it relieves the burden on short-term memory because recall can be achieved through a single association with an already existing code in long-term memory,' says K. Anders Ericsson of the department of psychology at Carnegie–Mellon University in Pittsburgh.

Dr Ericsson and his colleagues found out just how well mnemonics work when they tested the memory capabilities of one of their students. During the course of 20 months of practice (about 230 hours of testing), the student's span for recalling digits steadily increased from 7 to almost 80. He was able to do this in part because of his mnemonic associations. What he did was to categorize groups of digits as running times for various races, as someone's age or as historical dates (*Science*, 6 June 1980).

You may have already used similar tricks any number of times to help you remember. For example, you can probably draw the outline of Italy because you associate it with the shape of a boot. Or you may have learned the musical notes of the treble clef (E, G, B, D, F) as 'Every Good Boy Does Fine'.

To help you even more, researchers suggest that you create images in your mind when trying to associate one unrelated thing to another. That's because it's easier to remember a picture than a word. 'Some researchers feel that the more bizarre the image, the better,' says Dr Treat. 'And make up your own image. It seems to work better than using somebody else's.

'For example, suppose you have to remember the words "eggs" and "milk". You could imagine the eggs floating in a glass of milk,' You may not have a shopping list with those two items on it, but the same principles can be applied to any list of any length.

What about names? The same thing holds true here, also. Let's say you've just been introduced to Mr Frye, who is a mechanic. If you immediately imagine a spanner in a frying pan (for example), you'll remember his name easily the next time you see him.

Use your imagination as creatively as you can. It's fun, and it definitely works.

5 Put yourself in the right mood Did you know that it's easier to remember happy events if you're in a happy mood and sad ones if you're in a sad mood? And that you do better at remembering experiences that occurred in a particular mood if you can get yourself back in that mood? It's true, according to Gordon H. Bower, a psychologist and professor at Stanford University. He's done experiments to prove it.

'We chose to work initially with happiness and sadness, since they are so dissimilar,' Dr Bower told us. 'To induce the moods, we used imagination guided by hypnotic suggestions. After hypnotizing the subjects, we asked them to get themselves into a happy or sad mood by imagining or remembering a scene from their past. Often, the happy scene was a moment of personal success or of close intimacy with someone. The sad scenes were often of personal failure or the loss of a loved one.'

The subjects were then asked to learn two lists of words – one while happy, the other while sad. Their recall of a given list was tested later when the subject was in the same or the opposite mood. The results showed an obvious mood dependency. People who were sad during recall remembered about 80 per cent of the word list that they had learned while they were sad, compared to only 45 per cent of the words they had learned while they were happy. The converse was true, too, with almost identical percentages (*American Psychologist*, February 1981).

'On a practical level,' says Dr Bower, 'to recall an event, you may want to try to recreate the mood of whatever you are trying to remember. And that goes for more than happy and sad. We have also shown experimentally that fear and anger work the same way at evoking memories that occurred in those states.'

Strong emotions seem to act as natural preservatives for memories. Preserve a few for tomorrow.

• Ménière's Disease

Ménière's Disease combines symptoms of hearing loss, intense dizziness and ringing in the ears, usually accompanied by a sensation of pressure there. The attacks come and go, but the frequency may increase as time goes on, and sufferers may actually be housebound by the disorder. Paradoxically, the symptoms may spontaneously disappear for periods of as long as six years.

Nutritional therapies for Ménière's disease have been scant, and responses erratic. Dr Miles Atkinson, formerly at New York University, reported years ago that high doses of B complex vitamins were helpful to some patients. Another long-ago report of some success with vitamin C and bioflavonoid therapy came from the Mayo Clinic. Another and more recent finding in nutritional treatment of the disorder appears to be promising and is certainly simple – nothing more than a low-carbohydrate diet.

This diet is being recommended on the grounds that Ménière's sufferers have elevated levels of insulin, a hormone that controls blood sugar. Dr Bruce Proctor of Wayne State University found elevated insulin levels in three or four of his Ménière's patients, and he now assumes that every patient with the disorder has abnormally high insulin levels until tests prove otherwise. The high insulin is not the direct cause of the symptoms; rather, it is impaired circulation, 'possibly resulting from abnormal . . . insulin concentrations [which] may be the primary cause of Ménière's disease,' he notes.

Because there are periods in which Ménière's patients improve without treatment, the doctor does not label the low-carbohydrate treatment as a cure, preferring to call the results 'symptomatic' relief, at least until five to ten years of sustained improvement have been observed.

Bad eating habits, extra weight, elevated insulin levels, drinking, smoking and high cholesterol levels are among the factors that interact, in Dr Proctor's opinion, to cause Ménière's disease.

(*See also* TINNITUS.)

• Menopausal problems

The menopause is the cessation of menstrual periods that occurs in most women sometime between the ages of 45 and 53. At that time, the body's reproductive machinery shuts down, though the shutdown is hardly an overnight thing. Some women may experience symptoms ten years before their periods actually cease. In some women, periods stop abruptly, while in others the amount and duration of the menstrual flow tapers off gradually. The most common pattern, however, is irregular – there will be a heavy flow one month, scant flow the next month, several months with no periods at all, then another flow or two before the periods stop altogether.

In much the same way, the body's production of sex hormones slows down. The levels of oestrogen (the main female hormone) and progesterone (the female hormone that plays a major part in menstruation) are reduced in the body. Often the reduction comes by fits and starts. The body's hormonal state is shifting into a new equilibrium, and sometimes the shift is jerky and uneven. The result can be a hormonal imbalance – the 'raging hormone' syndrome.

As with every big change in the body's chemistry, good nutrition is essential for a smooth transition. What you eat can help you deal with some of the unpleasant side-effects of the menopause and protect you against ailments that commonly afflict women after the 'change' is complete. As the body's chemical balance shifts, its nutritional needs alter as well.

Some women suffer no symptoms at all at the menopause, but for the majority (according to a survey of 2000 women in a number of European countries carried out in 1969) the best-known symptom is hot flushes (55 per cent). Night sweats (39 per cent), irritability (29 per cent), depression (30 per cent), dizziness (40 per cent) and fatigue (43 per cent) were also common. In addition, weight gain and osteoporosis (a loss of bone density) are often encountered at the menopause.

Medical science has an answer for those problems, but, as is often the case, the conventional remedy can cause more serious problems than those it is meant to relieve. For about 40 years, doctors have administered oestrogen to women suffering the symptoms of the menopause, including hot flushes and osteoporosis. Its use in the menopause is designed to bring relief by dealing with the major change taking place in the body: the drop in the levels of naturally produced oestrogen.

There is controversy over whether oestrogen therapy really does everything it's claimed to do, but there is no question about its side-effects. Therapy with oestrogen on its own increases the risk of cancer of the endometrium, the inner lining of the uterus. Furthermore, a study published in the *New England Journal of Medicine* found higher rates of breast cancer in women given oestrogen during the menopause. Oestrogen-only therapy has also been associated with an increased risk of gall bladder disease and high blood pressure. However, it should be mentioned that many of these side-effects can now be avoided by prescribing progestogen, a synthetic progesterone that will prevent over-stimulation of the uterus, for 7–10 days each month.

Natural relief from hot flushes

In most cases, you don't have to subject yourself to the possible risks of this therapy to get relief. Take hot flushes, for example. The phenomenon is essentially harmless, but uncomfortable and often embarrassing. Through some mechanism that is not really understood, the hormonal changes of the menopause irritate the nerves controlling the blood vessels of the face and neck. If something sets the nerves off, the blood vessels widen and fill up with blood, causing a hot flush.

The flush lasts from 15 seconds up to a minute and is characterized by a deep red colour and a feeling of heat – like a superblush. Some women report chills after a flush, and a few experience a tingling sensation in their fingers and toes.

Rosetta Reitz, the author of *Menopause: A Positive Approach* (1979), talked to hundreds of women about the menopause in the course of putting her book together. She believes there is a simple, natural solution to hot flushes.

Many women have found relief in two days from taking 800 IU of vitamin E. I have seen flushes disappear completely when the vitamin E is also accompanied by 2000 to 3000 mg of vitamin C (taken at intervals throughout the day) and with 1000 mg (also at intervals) of calcium. When the flushes have subsided, usually after a week, the women reduce the vitamin E intake to 400 IU.

Nutrients that chase the blues

Anxiety, irritability and depression are other symptoms of the menopause for which the doctors have an easy fix. Tranquillizers such as Valium and Librium are prescribed to many women to help them deal with the mood swings that often accompany the menopause. However, these emotional problems should be dealt with. Suicide and mental illness in general are prevalent during the menopausal years, but a woman doesn't have to become a member of the drug culture to deal with those problems.

Studies have shown that the essential amino acid *tryptophan* can be effective against depression. There may be a direct link between the depression some women suffer at the menopause and a deficiency of tryptophan in the body. For example, one study found low levels of chemically free tryptophan in the blood of depressed women who had just gone through the menopause. The researchers found a correlation between the low tryptophan levels and the low levels of oestrogen in the women's blood *(British Medical Journal)*.

Calcium and magnesium may also help cure the blues. Those two minerals are closely related to lithium, a substance that has been used to treat depression, and there is evidence that all three elements are involved in the maintenance of mental health.

Lithium treatment has been shown to produce changes in the levels of calcium and magnesium in the blood, and British scientists reported a dramatic drop in the calcium excreted in the urine of patients being treated with it *(Lancet)*. The exact connections are still unclear, and lithium itself is a drug with toxic side-effects.

'The possibility that some mental illnesses may be brought on in a metabolic setting of calcium loss or deficiency is intriguing,' the author of the calcium study concluded. 'Post-menopausal women, and the elderly generally, are more prone to calcium deficiencies . . . and so they are to depression.'

Bone loss and the menopause

Calcium deficiency may or may not be the cause of the depression women can experience at the menopause, but it is clearly involved in the loss of bone mass that occurs in osteoporosis. Twenty-five per cent of all post-menopausal women suffer from this; fractures of the hip that can result from it are a major cause of death in elderly women; and these fractures alone cost the National Health Service at least £100 million a year. All this could be prevented if osteoporosis were eliminated. Calcium has been shown to be an effective weapon against the disease.

Bones are not static organs. In all of us, they are constantly being formed and broken down. At the menopause, the rate at which women's bones lose substance increases dramatically. At the same time, as scientists at the Creighton University School of Medicine in Nebraska have shown, a dramatic shift in the body's calcium balance takes place. The body loses more calcium than it takes in, partly because less calcium is absorbed in the intestines and partly because more calcium is excreted in the urine.

'Both changes are quite small,' Dr Robert P. Heaney and his associates report,

> but are nevertheless sufficient to explain both the balance shift and the rate of bone loss known to be occurring in post-menopausal women. The relation between calcium balance and calcium intake observed in these women is such as to suggest that the change in balance performance can be offset by an increase in the dietary calcium intake. [*Journal of Laboratory and Clinical Medicine*].

Dr Heaney reports that, even in the women he examined who were still menstruating, the calcium requirements were about 25 per cent higher than the US government's Recommended Dietary Allowance of 800 mg. The women who had gone through the menopause needed from 50 to 100 per cent more calcium than the US RDA.

Heart attack

The other big health threat that overtakes women at the menopause is heart disease. A number of studies have reported an increase in the risk of heart disease in women after the menopause. One of the most striking reports was a 1978 update of the Framingham Study. That study of the residents of Framingham, Massachusetts began in 1948, when women were enrolled, given a thorough heart examination, and invited to return every two years for new evaluations.

By 1978, virtually all of the women in the study had ceased menstruating, and it was possible to look into the connections between heart disease and the menopause. The results were striking. Not one of the 2873 women in the study had had a heart attack or died of heart disease before the menopause, but after it, heart disease became a common occurrence. For women aged between 45 to 54, the incidence of heart disease during or after the menopause was double the rate before the menopause (*Annals of Internal Medicine*).

There is a big jump in cholesterol in the blood at the menopause, mostly due to a rise in the low-density lipoprotein (LDL) cholesterol, the kind of cholesterol particularly associated with heart disease (*see* HEART DISEASE). Japanese scientists have also found higher levels of triglycerides, another fat implicated in heart disease, in the blood of post-menopausal women (*American Journal of Epidemiology*, April 1979).

Good nutrition can help you put the odds of developing heart trouble after the menopause back in your favour. Lecithin, a substance found in soyabeans, eggs and liver, has been effective in lowering triglyceride and LDL cholesterol levels in the blood. Vitamin C has also been used to lower high cholesterol levels. Indeed, Emil Ginter, a noted Czech researcher, believes that the recent drop in deaths from heart disease in the United States might be due in part to an increase in the consumption of vitamin C in that country.

Vitamin E also helps the heart by decreasing blood coagulation. The vitamin apparently works by lowering the tendency of platelets, special particles in the blood, to clump together. The clumping together of platelets can lead to a blood clot in arteries feeding the heart or brain, resulting in a heart attack or a stroke.

Magnesium is another nutrient linked to a healthy heart. There is considerable evidence that low levels of magnesium in the heart muscle may contribute to sudden death after a heart attack. And areas with 'soft' drinking water low in magnesium have been found to have higher death rates from heart disease than areas with magnesium-rich hard water.

Good nutrition is obviously an important part of healthy living during and after the menopause. This is a natural development in the ageing process, a change in women's lives that requires some special nutritional precautions, just as other life stages – for example, pregnancy – require special precautions.

• Menstrual problems

Whether characterized by emotional outbursts, depression, food cravings, cramp or a number of other symptoms, pre-menstrual syndrome (PMS) – also known as pre-menstrual tension (PMT) – affects most menstruating women to some degree. Now, doctors and scientists have come to realize that PMS symptoms are not all in a woman's head, and that's good news. The latest studies indicate that PMS, and many other problems associated with 'that time of the month', may respond to treatment with certain nutrients, including magnesium, vitamins B_6 and E, zinc and iron. In fact, many experts are starting to believe that monthly hormonal changes cause deficiencies in some nutrients, and that these deficiencies may be the cause of many PMS symptoms.

'PMS and magnesium deficiency are involved in a vicious circle relationship' according to Dr Guy E. Abraham of Torrance, California. In a study of 26 PMS sufferers ranging in age from 24 to 44, Dr Abraham and his colleague, Dr Michael M. Lubran noted that these women had 'significantly lower' red blood cell levels of magnesium than did healthy controls. Not only that: they also found that many PMS symptoms are quite similar to the classic symptoms of stress. And like stress, PMS by itself may deplete the body's stores of magnesium. At the same time, they noted that 'many of the PMS symptoms may be explained by a magnesium deficiency' (*American Journal of Clinical Nutrition*, November 1981).

It is quite possible that PMS and magnesium deficiency may be self-perpetuating. 'It's both cause and effect,' and the only way to get off the roundabout, as Dr Abraham sees it, is for a woman to increase her intake of magnesium.

Dr Bernard Horn of El Cerrito, California has seen magnesium help relieve menstrual cramps for many women. 'I usually suggest supplementing either one of two ways. Most healthy women should take 400 mg a day, every day, and this may help prevent them from encountering discomfort during their periods. But if a woman objects to taking the supplements every day, I tell her to do this: Starting five days before her period is due, she should take 600 mg daily and continue taking that amount every day until her period is over.'

Dr Abraham also thinks most women should take magnesium every day, and he likes to see them take it along with vitamin B_6, which, he has found, helps magnesium work better. In a study conducted by Drs Abraham and Lubran and another colleague, tests showed that nine seemingly healthy young women had red blood cell levels of magnesium that were below normal. After the women took 100 mg supplements of vitamin B_6 twice a day for four weeks, however, their average red blood cell levels of magnesium had more than doubled. And in six out of the nine cases, normal levels were achieved (*Annals of Clinical and Laboratory Science*, July–August 1981).

Vitamin B_6 does a lot more for women than just give their magnesium a boost. It has also proved successful in relieving many of the symptoms of PMS, including such diverse problems as acne, depression and water retention. In another study conducted by Dr Abraham, working with Dr Joel T. Hargrove, 21 out of 25 PMS sufferers were helped by taking 500 mg of vitamin B_6 for three consecutive menstrual cycles.

The women were divided into two groups. One group took vitamin B_6 for three cycles, while the other group took a do-nothing placebo tablet. Then the groups were switched. Most of the women reported that their symptoms were diminished while they were taking the vitamin, but none responded to the placebo (*Infertility*, April 1980).

Vitamin E and iron

Cramp during menstruation is caused by the body's production of prostaglandins – hormone-like substances that make the muscles of the uterus contract in painful spasms. Two substances that inhibit prostaglandins are aspirin – which has negative side-effects – and vitamin E.

Vitamin E is not only safer than aspirin for treating period pain, but it also has another factor in its favour. By increasing circulation, it increases the amount of blood carrying oxygen to the uterus, so that, when the uterus contracts, more blood and oxygen will be able to pass through. According to a Canadian specialist Dr G. Edward Desaulniers of the Shute Institute in London, Ontario, the cut-off of blood and oxygen to the uterus during contraction is partially responsible for cramp. He believes that vitamin E helps reduce the pain that results.

Even women who never suffer from period pains, acne or any of the other symptoms of PMS may be losing enough iron during their periods to make them likely candidates for anaemia. 'Iron-deficiency anaemia occurs in 67 per cent of women whose menstrual loss exceeds 80 ml [just over 5 tablespoons]' according to a researcher in Manchester (*British Medical Journal*, 17 April 1982). While 80 ml is considered a somewhat heavy menstrual flow, it isn't too far from average.

Paul A. Seligman, assistant professor of haematology at the University of Colorado School of Medicine in Denver, notes that most women lose between 60 and 500 ml. He also believes that women with heavy blood loss during menstrual periods are 'at high risk' of developing anaemia.

Vitamin A for heavy menstrual bleeding

Hysterectomy is often recommended in cases of *menorrhagia* – the medical term for either excessive daily bleeding during menstruation or prolonged menstrual flow, or both. However, with complications of its own, surgery is a high price to pay for recovery – particularly when relief can sometimes be had for the cost of a bottle of vitamin A supplements.

According to a study published in the *South African Medical Journal*, menorrhagia may be caused by a vitamin A deficiency. Women who experience heavy menstruation and have lower than normal vitamin A levels in their blood can enjoy alleviation of their symptoms with moderately high doses of the vitamin, the investigators reported.

The effect of a vitamin A deficiency on the reproductive system of women has never been clearly documented, but it stands to reason that such a deficiency could alter the menstrual cycle. After all, vitamin A is crucial to the development of the ovaries in animals. In animal tests, a laboratory-induced deficiency of this vitamin can decrease hormone production and suspend the menstrual cycle.

Earlier studies put that theory into human terms when researchers demonstrated that vitamin A levels in women fluctuate in a cyclic pattern during the menstrual cycle. They suggest a strong correlation between vitamin A levels and female hormones.

Keeping these findings in mind, Drs D. M. Lithgow and W. M. Politzer of the Johannesburg General Hospital decided to find out whether vitamin A deficiency causes menorrhagia and whether giving vitamin A would cure the condition. To do this, they tested the vitamin A levels in 71 patients suffering from menorrhagia. These figures were then compared to those obtained from blood tests of 191 healthy women between the ages of 13 and 55.

The results clearly indicated that women with this particular menstrual dysfunction have relatively low levels of vitamin A in their bloodstream. In fact, the women tested had on the average only 67 IU of the vitamin per 100 ml of blood. In contrast, the women with normal menstrual periods had about 166 IU per 100 ml – almost $2^1/_2$ times the amount measured in the first group.

To define more precisely the role of a vitamin A deficiency in menstrual dysfunction, the records of 103 patients who presented a wider spectrum of the causes of menorrhagia were combined with those of the original group. A vitamin A deficiency was still found to be the primary cause of the menorrhagia in almost 44 per cent of the total 174 cases studied. In addition, almost 68 per cent of this combined group had lower than average levels of vitamin A in their blood, indicating that a shortage of this vitamin might be a contributing cause of the abnormal bleeding.

Now that the researchers were assured of the cause of the problem, they followed through with treatment using vitamin A supplements. Fifty-two menorrhagia patients were instructed to take 60,000 IU of vitamin A daily for 35 days. (*NB*: It is important that no woman take this high a level of vitamin A except under a doctor's supervision.)

Although a few of these women were lost to follow-up treatment, of the 40 who returned for evaluation one month later, 23 were completely cured, and 14 noted a substantially diminished menstrual flow or a reduction in the duration of their period. The researchers claimed that, all told, close to 93 per cent were either cured or helped with vitamin A therapy.

Heavy menstrual bleeding sometimes afflicts women who go off the Pill, and for some time now, researchers have suspected that the hormones found in oral contraceptives alter the vitamin A levels in the blood. To test this theory, vitamin A levels in two groups of healthy college women were measured. The first group consisted of 11 women with regular menstrual cycles who had never taken the Pill. The other group comprised seven women who had been on the Pill for various lengths of time ranging from two months to slightly over two years (*American Journal of Clinical Nutrition*).

Invariably, the women taking the oral contraceptives had higher levels of vitamin A in their blood than non-users. This may be due to a stepped-up mobilization of the vitamin stored in the liver. The theory is confirmed by animal experimentation: rats given oral contraceptives experience a faster liver vitamin A depletion, indicating a higher vitamin A requirement.

This may explain post-Pill menorrhagia. While women are taking the Pill, their bloodstream is pumped full of vitamin A, which assures them a short and uneventful artificial period. However, should they stop taking the Pill, the vitamin A supply in their blood is cut short. The liver reserve that would be called on under normal conditions has become sharply depleted.

If you've been losing a lot of blood during your menses, you might want to increase your intake of vitamin A. Keep in mind that vitamin E helps improve vitamin A storage and utilization, and that zinc is required to move vitamin A from the large liver reserve to the bloodstream.

More natural approaches to menstrual problems

In many women's health centres in the United States, natural remedies are frequently preferred to ease menstrual disturbances. Health consultants at the Feminist Health Works in New York City have suggested reduced salt intake, exercise, vitamin B complex, iron and calcium supplements and, just prior to periods, a diet free of red meat to avoid excess steroids and hormones.

A booklet produced by the health centre called *Herbal Remedies for Women* serves up a fascinating brew of herbal teas, tonics and tinctures to flush away pre-menstrual syndrome, period pain, water retention, diarrhoea and constipation.

For instance, eating Gruyère cheese, brown rice, barley or bananas or drinking a tea made from mallow root or wild thyme is recommended to help curtail diarrhoea. And to soothe pre-menstrual syndrome, the booklet suggests a variety of herbal tea blends, such as catmint, celery seeds, skullcap, spearmint and a variety of others.

More than 3000 miles away, a health clinic in Oregon offers some commonsense prescriptions of its own. Stimulants such as caffeine and nicotine should be avoided as unnecessary body irritants, says an administrator at the Portland Woman's Health Center. To wake up the circulation, the centre advocates any kind of exercise – whether it be walking a mile a day, jogging, cycling or doing calisthenics. Natural diuretics such as cranberry juice, watercress, parsley and kelp may serve to purge you of excess water.

In general, it helps to pamper yourself with any type of warmth, whether it comes from sipping hot drinks or soaking in a hot tub. Heat promotes blood flow and may ease painful periods. A gentle massage and that old standby – the heating pad – may serve the same purpose.

• Mental retardation

Out of sight for the slow of mind has been standard operating procedure in the treatment of the mentally retarded for most of medical history. And while admirable strides are being made to return some to the mainstream of society, for many the shadow-life of the institution is all too real.

Conventional wisdom holds that there is only so much that can be done with limited abilities . . . unless it were somehow possible to do the unthinkable and treat the retarded mind as an undeveloped flower in desperate need of richer soil. What if proper nourishment could enable it to grow and blossom?

Farfetched?

Maybe not, according to a study conducted by Ruth F. Harrell, research professor at Old Dominion University in Norfolk, Virginia. She and her colleagues examined the intriguing possibility that retardation might be the result of nutritional deficiencies and therefore could be 'amenable to treatment' with supplementary vitamins and minerals.

Nutritional deficiencies?

The scientists' report, published in the *Proceedings of the National Academy of Sciences* (January 1981), is cautiously optimistic.

In her introduction, Dr Harrell related the case of GS, a severely retarded seven-year-old, who, before being treated, was in nappies, could not speak and had an estimated IQ of 25 to 30.

After the boy's tissue and blood were analysed, an appropriate nutritional supplement was devised. It took several weeks of trial and error to get the ingredients just right, but once Dr Harrell had the correct dosage of vitamins and minerals, the boy's progress was remarkable.

In a few days, he was talking a little. In a few weeks, he was learning to read and write, and he began to act like a normal child. When GS was nine years old, he read and wrote on the elementary school level, was moderately advanced in arithmetic and, according to his teacher, was mischievous and active. He rode a bicycle and a skateboard, played ball, played a flute and had an IQ of about 90.

With that heartening result in mind, Dr Harrell enlisted the help of a team of biochemists and psychologists and recruited a group of 16 retarded children (including four with Down's syndrome) whose IQs ranged from 17 to 70, to participate in an eight-month study.

For the first four months, 11 children took an inactive placebo, while five received a six-tablet-daily regimen of 11 vitamins and 8 minerals. The supplements included the B complex vitamins (including folic acid and pantothenic acid) and vitamins A, C, D and E, along with calcium, zinc, manganese, copper, iron and other minerals.

In determining the dosage of most of the nutrients, 'we went far beyond the [US] Recommended Dietary Allowance [RDA],' Dr Harrell told us, 'It was "mega" in size and went up and up and up until we got a mental response.'

To give you an idea of just how 'mega' the dosage was, the 15,000 IU of vitamin A represented approximately four times the RDA, the B complex supplements were over 100 times the RDA, while there was in excess of 25 times what is thought to be the body's normal requirement of vitamins C and E. Most of the minerals, however, were closer to RDA levels.

Following the initial segment of the study, *all* of the children took the supplements for an additional four months. When all the data were collected and analysed and the progress of the children could be examined, 'the results were such that I was afraid to believe them,' Dr Harrell admitted.

During the first four-month period . . . the 5 children who received supplements increased their average IQ by from 5.0 to 9.6 points, depending on the investigator, whereas the 11 subjects given placebos showed negligible change. The difference between these groups is statistically significant. During the second period, the subjects who had been given placebos in the first study received supplements; they showed an average IQ increase of at least 10.2, a highly significant gain.

Several children improved greatly in school achievement. For example, JB (age six), who said only single words such as 'Mama' or 'bye-bye' initially, could recite without prompting the Pledge of Allegiance after eight months of supplementation and could read the first-grade primer. Two (TC and RS) have been transferred from programs for the mentally retarded to regular schools and grade levels, on the teacher's recommendations.

They're not blockbusters – not superior, mind you – but I hope they can fend for themselves in an average sort of way.

All of our subjects who cooperated in taking the supplements showed improvement, sometimes dramatic and surprising to the teachers and other professionals who dealt with them. If our findings are confirmed by more extensive experiments, they bring new hope for improving the quality of life for the mentally retarded 3.2 percent of our population.

In essence, nutritional supplements were instrumental in reducing the mentally retarded portion of the study group by one-quarter. Translate that into the millions of members of the human family considered 'slow' – i.e. with IQs below 75 – and the billions of pounds going into their special, and often custodial, care, and it's easy to see the far-reaching implications of Dr Harrell's study.

If supplements are the key to unlocking the retarded mind – if they enable many of those so afflicted 'to make their own way, to become hewers of wood and drawers of water' – we're clearly on to something major.

What is perhaps startling is that 'everyone posted some kind of gain' across the entire spectrum of retardation, even those with Down's syndrome.

Help for Down's syndrome

This condition – sometimes wrongly called 'mongolism' because the facial features take on a distinctly Oriental appearance – is the result of too much of a necessary thing: an extra 21st chromosome. This 'trisomy 21' – its official medical designation – manifests itself in a number of unpleasant ways, the worst of them being severe retardation.

It has been thought that very little can be done for Down's syndrome children, and they often wind up in institutions. However, unexpectedly, the supplements helped. Three of the four children with the condition 'tended to lose the accumulated fluid in their faces and extremities. The largest IQ gain observed (25 units) occurred in LA after eight months of supplementation.'

Sushma Palmer, a biochemist–nutritionist at the National Academy of Sciences in Washington, D.C., and an expert on Down's syndrome calls the results 'suggestive' and gives at least one possible reason for the dramatic effects.

'Children with Down's are characterized by a number of nutritionally related problems that may stem from a delay in feeding skills,' she says. 'It's frequently difficult for them to eat food. They may eat an insufficient variety and amount, and the outcome can be an unbalanced diet. If the nutritional status of the kids is inadequate, that will likely affect mental performance. The younger the child, the more severe the impact, because that's when the brain is developing fastest.'

If nutritional deficiencies play havoc with the mental development of these children, can supplements *reverse* the damage? Dr Harrell's work suggests that they can. And interestingly enough, more than five decades ago, she had inadvertently done something similar to her most recent experiment by 'curing' another group of retarded boys.

The 'poverty poor' diet of her first Southern students prompted her to undertake personally a voluntary starvation regimen of nothing more than white bread and water. In short order, 'I found I couldn't learn anything new.'

Putting diet and dullness together, she came up with a plan for her teenage pupils. If she could teach them something basic, like cooking, they might become employable, at least on a part-time basis. Her vocational education request for food to prepare was accepted by an incredulous school board, and before long, she was training budding chefs. At the same time, she was encouraging them to eat the healthy meals they'd created.

'Remember, there was no free hot lunch back then,' she explains. But this one good meal a day was enough of a nutritional boost to make an enormous difference in the boys' intellectual lives. 'My 20 boys made greater gains than any others in the school system. The following year, I lost 18 to normalcy!'

She's built on her work since then, with special emphasis on healthier minds through healthier mothers, and more complete recovery from brain surgery with nutritional supplements.

'You can't imagine what a cold shoulder I got,' she relates. The prevailing attitude towards the retarded was a strong 'If God hadn't wanted kids to be idiots, He wouldn't have made 'em that way.' Her steadfast refusal to accept that has led to her breakthrough research.

The immediate question, of course, is 'How does it work?'

Born with special needs

The road to any answer remains as trackless as Stanley's path to Livingstone, but there is an intriguing possibility that retardation is, in part, a 'genetotrophic disease'. Roger J. Williams, a University of Texas biochemist, conceived this concept more than 30 years ago, when he suggested that 'biochemical individuality' could cause problems.

'We're not born with the same genetics,' he told us, 'and we don't have the same nutritional needs.' If we don't get what we require, 'metabolism can't go in the right direction, and one result could be mental retardation.'

Those afflicted with a genetotrophic disease can't rely solely on the established RDAs of the various vitamins and minerals, either, for the very nature of this inborn error of metabolism demands an augmented supply of one or more specific nutrients.

As an example, a metabolic disorder called *homocystinuria* is known to cause retardation because of an excess of the toxic substance *homocysteine*. Under normal circumstances, homocysteine is degraded into a non-toxic substance when vitamin B_6 is present. Because of a failure – a mutation – in the genes directing the entire operation, that doesn't happen and the results are tragic, and often unnecessary.

'About half the patients with this condition are helped by large levels of B_6,' explains William Shive of the Clayton Foundation Biochemical Institute at the University of Texas. Providing considerably more than the RDA is essential to ensure that there'll be enough vitamin B_6 floating around to keep homocysteine harmless.

By contrast with that 'one-vitamin', genetotrophic disorder, treating the many different metabolic causes of retardation with nutrients demands a 'shotgun approach'. 'The real front in nutrition is to develop a diagnostic tool that enables us to identify individual needs,' Dr Shive maintains. But he admits that, for now, researchers must simply try a broad array of nutrients and hope for the best.

Yet there's the exciting possibility that they may prevent retardation from occurring in the first place. 'Everybody needs to care for his or her own internal environment,' Dr Williams asserts. 'And that's doubly true for the internal environment of unborn children. If all mothers were given appropriate supplements, there'd be a tremendous decrease in mental retardation.'

• Motion sickness

Motion sickness has happened to nearly everyone at one time or another. Even astronauts in space aren't immune to it. The standard remedy for this common ailment has been an anti-histamine drug, Dramamine, but a carefully controlled experiment has shown that powdered root of ginger (*Zingiber officinale*) is more effective. The subjects were volunteers of both sexes who reported themselves to be unusually prone to motion sickness. Tested with a motor-driven revolving chair, half the subjects on ginger went the full six minutes; none of those on the drug or a placebo endured that long (*Lancet*, 20 March 1982).

And here's a tip to help you prevent motion sickness in children: An observant pediatrician noted that a small child's view in a car is that of fast moving scenery, via a side window, and of bobbing and vibrating objects. If the child's position is raised – with a car seat – his eyes can focus on relatively still objects, which may avoid or at least lessen motion sickness (*New England Journal of Medicine*, 8 November 1979).

• Multiple sclerosis

The medical profession doesn't offer much encouragement to victims of multiple sclerosis (MS). In fact, for the young adult suddenly crippled by this affliction of the nervous system, the outlook is often hopelessly bleak: an abbreviated lifespan of progressive muscular and sensory deterioration spent largely in a wheelchair. Given enough money and enough time, the MS patient is told, researchers may ultimately accomplish a breakthrough – a miracle drug or inoculation, perhaps – but for now there is nothing.

Multiple sclerosis is characterized by the destruction of myelin, the fat-like substance that surrounds and protects nerve fibres. To the victim of MS, the clinical signs of this breakdown are only too apparent. Tiny, scattered destructive changes in the brain and spinal cord, at first imperceptible, lead to symptoms that include loss of vision, dizziness, impaired sense of touch, clumsiness and loss of equilibrium. There are also periods of overwhelming, extreme fatigue.

In the early stages, MS patients often experience welcome periods of remission when the symptoms disappear (a phenomenon that makes various treatments difficult to evaluate on a short-term basis). But as time goes on, remissions become fewer and further apart. Within 10 to 12 years after the onset of the disease, the patient usually loses the ability to walk.

Roy L. Swank, professor emeritus of the department of neurology, Oregon Health Sciences University in Portland, remarks, 'The nature of multiple sclerosis brings its own built-in periods of depression, extreme fatigue and the awareness of sudden alarming changes in vision, mobility and sensations. Coping with these sometimes daily fluctuations in feelings of well-being becomes a challenge which can test the strongest of individuals.'

Treating MS with a low-fat diet

It was into this arena of gloom that Dr Swank, then with the Montreal Neurological Institute, stepped in 1948 with his low-fat-diet approach to MS. And now, more than 1500 patients later, the results speak for themselves.

Dr Swank points out in his book, *The Multiple Sclerosis Diet Book*:

It is our belief that early diagnosis and treatment with a low-fat diet will arrest the disease in a high proportion of cases. Our aim is the prevention of disability with prolongation of the active productive period of life, a goal which has been successfully achieved by many of our patients . . .

Basically, Dr Swank insists that patients limit their intake of animal fat to 15 g (approximately $1/2$ oz) or less per day, while boosting intake of unsaturated oils to 20 to 50 g daily. To help meet the latter quota, they are advised to take one teaspoon of cod-liver oil every day. In addition, patients must avoid physical and mental strain and get plenty of rest. Mild sedation is also administered for the first few months to help manage potentially debilitating emotional tensions.

Among a group of 146 patients followed for 16 years on the diet, the frequency of exacerbations or relapses dropped sharply, resulting in a 95 per cent reduction. And the remaining attacks were very mild and short.

The treatment also helped keep people walking and working. Dr Swank compares his results with those of a large group of MS patients at the Mayo Clinic who didn't have the benefit of a low-fat diet: 50 per cent of those people were completely disabled after ten years. But after a similar ten year span, only 25 per cent of the patients on the Swank diet were unable to work or walk. Even after 16 years, only 33 per cent had become totally disabled.

More remarkable still was the increase in life expectancy. Normally, only about 70 or 80 per cent of MS victims are still alive 15 years after the onset of the disease. After 35 years, only 30 per cent survive. But among patients on the low-fat, high-oil diet, 94 per cent were still alive after 15 years, and 79 per cent survived 35 years or more!

'It was also observed,' Dr Swank says, 'that when treatment was started in the early stages of the disease with little or no evident disability, 90 to 95 per cent of the cases remained unchanged or actually improved during the following 20 years.'

Most important of all, perhaps, is the change in the patients' attitudes towards themselves and their disease. 'When the patients are first seen,' Dr Swank noted,

they can best be described as 'fragile'. Minor problems, a bit of effort, a hot bath, bad news, and operations or childbirth prove to be major stumbling blocks causing increased fatigue and aggravation of symptoms . . .

When the low-fat diet has been in effect for some months and the patient has weathered the first mild exacerbation with remission and knows that there will be longer remissions in the future, his self-confidence grows. The effort is worthwhile . . .

During the third year, the patients frequently will note a marked increase in their energy and will often remark, 'I am beginning to feel like myself, I am much less fatigued.'

How does the diet help? Dr Swank isn't sure of the exact mechanism involved, but he says that excessive saturated fat in the diet triggers clumping of tiny blood components called platelets. These clumps or tiny clots may be carried along the bloodstream to lodge in the small vessels of the brain, where they cause the nerve-fibre damage that occurs in MS. Unsaturated oils like cod-liver, safflower and sunflower oil, on the other hand, tend to inhibit the platelet-clumping effect.

The idea of dietary modification came to Dr Swank after an analysis of the geographical distribution of multiple sclerosis. Statistics show that, in areas of the world where consumption of beef, butter, milk and other animal-fat foods is high – the United States, Canada, Britain, etc – the incidence of MS is relatively high. In low-fat areas – such as India, the Far East, Latin America – the disease claims far fewer victims.

This difference is especially striking in Europe. In Scandinavia, Germany and other northern European countries with a so-called 'beer–butter' dietary tradition, MS is common. But in southern Europe–Spain, Italy, Greece and other Mediterranean areas known for their 'wine–oil' cultures – there's very little MS. Switzerland, which sits astride the dividing line of the two cultures, is predictably split. The northern Swiss, who follow Germanic eating patterns, have one of the highest rates of MS in the world. Their counterparts in the south, who speak Italian and favour Italian dishes, very seldom get the disease.

Several areas in the northern United States have the highest incidence of MS in the world – a fact that Dr Swank links to changing eating habits. 'Until about 200 years ago,' he points out, 'the fat intake of our Western ancestors was probably around 60 g [2 oz] daily, and much of this fat was contained in vegetable and fish oils.' But with improvements in dairy herds, fattening of beef cattle and the introduction of highly processed, hydrogenated oils, Americans began eating much more saturated fat. By 1909, the average American was eating about 125 g (4 oz) of fat daily. Today that figure has climbed still further, to 150 g.

Prior to those dietary changes, which were occurring simultaneously in much of the civilized world, MS was virtually unknown. 'One wonders if multiple sclerosis is actually, or only apparently, a disease of very recent times,' Dr Swank speculates. 'It is difficult to believe that intelligent observers would fail to recognize a condition so striking in its clinical manifestations if it occurred in anything like its present form and high incidence.'

In their book, Dr Swank and Ms Pullen offer a number of suggestions for converting from a high-fat to a high-oil diet. Patients are strictly forbidden to eat such high-fat foods as whole milk, cream, butter, soured cream, ice cream, chocolate and sausages. Packaged cake mixes, cheeses, commercially prepared sauces, pies, sweet biscuits, crisps and other processed items are also forbidden because they contain hidden or unknown amounts of saturated fat. Margarine, although derived from vegetable sources, is counted as an animal fat – and hence forbidden – because the hydrogenation, or solidifying process, increases saturation.

Conversion tables are provided to help MS patients make meat and poultry selections that will respect their daily limit of 15 g of saturated fat. For example, a 4 oz serving of lean beef would be permissible, but the same amount of bacon would put dieters over their daily fat limit in one fell swoop.

On the other hand, patients are encouraged to eat generous quantities of commercial vegetable oils, mayonnaise, fish, sunflower and pumpkin seeds and other foods rich in essential fatty acids. Old-fashioned, non-hydrogenated peanut butter – the kind in which the oil separates and rises to the top – is also recommended.

Dr Swank also advises patients to eat whole-grain bread and cereals whenever possible, and to take a daily high-potency multi-vitamin capsule with minerals. Wheat germ or wheatgerm oil is also suggested as an additional source of vitamin E, necessary to keep the unsaturated oils from being oxidized once inside the body.

One nice thing about Dr Swank's diet programme is that it's potentially good for almost everyone, not just victims of MS. The low fat content of 15 to 20 per cent is 'a level which approaches that consumed by many Orientals, and which is associated with minimal to insignificant atherosclerosis and a very low death rate from heart disease,' Dr Swank adds.

Could calcium deficiency set the stage for MS?

Paul Goldberg, a research scientist with the Polaroid Corporation, has found an intriguing correlation between the incidence of multiple sclerosis in different parts of the world and the amount of sunlight that falls on those regions *(International Journal of Environmental Studies)*. Vitamin D is necessary for the proper absorption of calcium in the small intestine, and one of the best ways of getting enough vitamin D is by exposure to sunlight. Dr Goldberg applied statistical analysis to a number of previous studies and found that the more sunlight an area received, the lower was its rate of multiple sclerosis. The risk of developing multiple sclerosis is highest in the northern latitudes of Europe and North America and decreases to a low rate as you approach the equator.

Dr Goldberg found that the discrepancies in this general pattern were as interesting as the pattern itself. In Switzerland, Dr Goldberg points out, the rate of multiple sclerosis in various regions differs according to altitude rather than latitude. But, as the rate of MS varies with the altitude, so does the amount of shorter wave-length radiation that reaches the ground through the atmosphere. It's this type of radiation that causes the formation of vitamin D in the skin. So, Dr Goldberg believes, the higher you live on the mountainside, the more shortwave radiation you receive, the more vitamin D your skin forms, the more calcium your intestines absorb and the lower your risk of multiple sclerosis.

William Craelius of the Newark (New Jersey) Beth Israel Medical Center discovered further evidence of a connection between calcium deficiency and multiple sclerosis when he compared the rates of tooth decay and MS in different populations *(Journal of Epidemiology and Community Health)*. When he looked at statistics for Australia and the United States, the pattern was clear – the higher the rate of tooth decay in a particular area, the higher the number of deaths from multiple sclerosis.

Tooth decay is lower among poor Americans than among the rich, lower among Chinese immigrants to Britain than among the natives, lower for blacks than for whites, lower for men than for women. The rate of tooth decay is higher during pregnancy. In all these groups, the incidence of multiple sclerosis seems to follow the incidence of tooth decay. Wherever one is high, so is the other. It's as if the same thing that makes for healthy teeth also protects the body against multiple sclerosis.

Drs Craelius and Goldberg both believe the 'X factor' here is calcium. Calcium is known to speed the production of one of the key constituents of myelin. This fact, plus the general importance of calcium in holding cells together, led Dr Goldberg to conclude that a lack of calcium in a child's critical growth years could irreparably weaken the myelin structure and increase the risk of multiple sclerosis later in life.

Dr Craelius has done work that supports that hypothesis *(Neuroscience Abstracts)*. 'We removed the spinal cord from a chicken embryo,' he says, 'and placed it in a medium where it would continue to grow and we could observe its development. We grew the myelin for several weeks in a medium that was only slightly deficient in calcium. When we looked at the myelin under an electron microscope, we thought that it was not as complete, not as mature as it would be normally.'

Inositol may help MS victims

A Danish researcher believes that multiple sclerosis may be caused by an intermittent deficiency of B vitamin-like *inositol*. Dr Viggo Holm wrote in *Archivos de Neurobiologica* that, in people with multiple sclerosis, the body's metabolism of inositol may be abnormally rapid. This would result in a deficiency of inositol, which could lead to the destruction of the myelin sheaths.

Dr Holm tested the metabolism of 86 normal people and 12 people with multiple sclerosis and found that none of the normal people metabolized inositol abnormally. However, 27 per cent of the MS patients did metabolize inositol 'in an abnormally pronounced way'.

Dr Holm is repeating his test in order to verify the results. 'If this result can be verified,' he wrote, 'the next step should be direct blood inositol determinations in acute cases after intravenous inositol loading, as well as attempts to treat MS with large doses of inositol.'

• Muscle problems

Weakness or stiffness of muscles is a problem that can make anyone feel his age. 'Too much tension and too little exercise greatly increase the natural loss of muscular fitness with age,' wrote Hans Kraus, former associate professor at the Institute of Rehabilitation Medicine, New York University. To help older people with back pain and other muscle problems, Dr Kraus developed a YMCA exercise programme emphasizing relaxation, stretching of tight muscles and strengthening of weak ones. This programme is now offered in nearly 1000 YMCAs around the United States and has an 80 per cent rate of success (*see* BACK PROBLEMS).

'Reconditioning these patients,' wrote Dr Kraus, 'simply means reclaiming abilities that never should have been lost' (*Geriatrics*).

Many scientists besides Dr Kraus believe that ageing muscles, or muscles deprived of exercise, go through a progressive shortening. It's not simply a matter of unstretched muscles staying too short. The muscles actually grow *shorter* the longer they are neglected. *As the muscles grow shorter, they put more and more pressure on the nerves running through the muscle sheaths*. That, some scientists think, may be behind the mysterious muscle aches and pains that commonly afflict older people.

The splinting reflex

It becomes a vicious cycle. Whenever muscle pain occurs, it sets off a 'splinting reflex' in the muscle. This causes the muscle to stiffen for protection. The muscle forms a rigid, natural splint, for the same reasons a doctor uses a splint on a broken leg.

When shortened muscles set off the splinting reflex, however, the contraction of the muscles tightens pinched nerves even more, and the pain increases. The contraction of the muscles increases until they are knotted up in an uncontrollable spasm, exactly the kind of spasm people experience with lower back pain.

Herbert A. deVries, director of the exercise physiology laboratory at the Andrus Gerontology Center in California, describes tests he made of this phenomenon in his book, *Vigor Regained*. Dr deVries and his colleagues measured the electrical activity present in the muscles of injured athletes. A normal muscle, completely relaxed, shows no electrical activity, while a muscle in spasm, or tensed with pain, does.

Dr deVries put his injured athletes through a programme of special stretching exercises. In almost all cases, the stretching produced a sharp drop in the electrical activity of the muscle and partial-to-complete relief of the muscle pain. Stretching seemed to break the cycle of pain – muscle contraction – still more pain.

Stretching for muscle flexibility, Dr deVries believes, is invaluable for older people.

It appears to me that the best insurance (probably the only insurance) against the aches and pains that so often accompany the aging process . . . is that of maintaining an optimum level of physical fitness with appropriate emphasis on [flexibility].

Stretching is also important for people suffering from arthritis. Stretching muscles at arthritic joints several times a day has been shown to be very helpful in preventing permanent stiffness.

How to stretch

Many people think that they're stretching their muscles when they go through bouncy calisthenic exercises like touching the toes. You bounce down quickly to touch your toes, then pop back up into a standing position. But that bounce is what causes problems. Whenever a muscle is stretched too quickly or with too much force, the splinting reflex is set off.

You meet the same kind of resistance when you stretch in a standing position. Muscles in your legs hold your body up by contracting. Stretching leg muscles in a standing position is not as effective as stretching while lying down or sitting, because you're again working against contracted muscles.

Ben E Benjamin, author of the book *Sports Without Pain* (1979), emphasizes that the best way to stretch is to ease yourself into the stretch position. Stretching is a gentle, conditioning exercise. Relaxation is very important. Once you have extended your muscles as far as they want to go, *don't force them any further*. Just keep breathing normally and hold the position for 10 to 15 seconds. Next time you might stretch farther and hold the position longer.

'You must be able to tell where the action is happening,' according to Dr Benjamin. 'Pay attention to precisely where the pulling sensation is. You should feel the pull in the meaty part of the muscle. If the sensation is felt near a joint only, you are stretching the ligament or tendon. Always try to do the exercise so that you feel it throughout the bulk of the muscle.'

Dr Benjamin says that the best time to stretch is after a warm-up. Warm muscles, surging with blood, are more pliable than cold muscles. A common mistake, he says, is that 'people confuse warming up with stretching. They do stretching exercises to warm up when they should be doing it the other way around. Stretching is not really a good way to warm up. It's good for cooling down after exercise.' Both Dr Benjamin and Dr deVries recommend that stretching be done at the end of an exercise routine.

The muscles that probably need the most stretching are those in the lower part of the body. Muscles in the legs and lower back are almost constantly in use during the day, holding us erect. Because of that constant contraction, they are more susceptible to shortening and tightness. The following exercises generally stretch those lower-body muscles, and they can be done with relative ease, even in your office after a mid-day workout.

Calf stretch Sitting on the floor, with your feet about a foot apart, place a towel around the ball of one foot. Without locking your knee, but holding it straight and steady, pull the towel towards you by leaning back. When you feel the stretch in the calf muscle, hold it for about 15 seconds. If it hurts, let up, or don't hold it as long. Alternate feet for two to four stretches. Gradually work up to 30-second stretches.

Wall lean Move on to the wall lean for further stretching of the calves after you have mastered the towel stretch. With your feet two to three inches apart, stand three to five feet from the wall. Put your hands on the wall directly in front of you and bend your elbows until your forearms are resting against the wall. Your feet should be positioned as far as possible from the wall, with your heels on the floor and your legs straight. After holding the position for 10 to

15 seconds, walk towards the wall and relax. The wall lean is fairly tough, so repeat it only three or four times. Over time, you may build up to stretches as long as a minute.

Side stretch Sit in a chair with your feet about a foot apart, and bend your body to the right, imagining as you do so that you are lifting upward against the bend. Don't hold this stretch, just repeat on the left side, then go back to the right. Bend five times on each side. As the stretch becomes easier, add more weight to it by holding your hands behind your head as you bend. For even more weight later on, hold your hands up above your head as you bend.

Back Stretch Sit in the same position in an armless chair. Bend forward, bringing your arms and shoulders between your knees. Lean forward as if you were going to put your elbows on the floor. Repeat the stretch several times, and gradually build up your holding time.

Bath stretch One relaxing way to stretch tired legs is in a bath full of warm water. Sitting in the bath with your legs straight, bend forward slowly until you feel the stretch in the muscles at the back of your legs. Relax, keep breathing normally, and hold the stretch for at least 50 to 60 seconds.

Inner-thigh stretch For this stretch, you need an empty wall about six feet wide. Lie on your back with your legs stretched against the wall, at a 90° angle to your body. Your buttocks and heels should be touching the wall. With your knees slightly bent, open your legs as far as they will go. Let gravity do most of the work of pulling your legs down. Hold that position as long as you feel comfortable, up to five minutes at a time.

Neck Stretch While either sitting or standing, clasp your hands behind your neck and let your head fall forward. Hold that position for 10 or 15 seconds, then raise your head and rest. Repeat the stretch, only this time, hold your hands an inch higher at the base of your skull. That is the maximum stretch and should be done only if it is comfortable.

Firming up weak stomach muscles

Weakened, protruding abdominal muscles are an embarrassment. But worse than that, they are hazardous to your health – particularly to your spine.

'Weakened abdominal muscles can't control the spine,' says Lawrence W Friedmann, head of physical medicine and rehabilitation at Nassau County Medical Center, New York, 'and the result is stress and backache.'

Dr Friedmann's statements are backed up by a study of over 3000 people with back pain. Of those who participated in the study, more than 83 per cent had back pain due to *muscle* problems rather than a specific back ailment (such as a 'slipped' disc or arthritis).

To strengthen your abdomen and to relieve the stress on your spine, says Dr Friedmann, get out of that easy chair and get moving: 'Stress on the spine is greater when you're sitting than when you're standing.' Dr Friedmann points out that the muscles automatically exert hundreds of pounds of force when you're standing up – but even more when you're sitting down. And much of that force is directed right at the spine, especially if you have the common (but bad) habit of leaning forward while you sit.

However, just because your muscles are wrecking your spine doesn't mean they're getting a workout. 'While you're sitting, most of the muscles are in-active,' Dr Friedmann says. And, he explains, inactive muscles weaken over time. 'It is the abdominal muscles more than the back muscles that support the spine, and sitting hits them the hardest.'

Arthur Weltman, director of research and exercise physiology at St Francis Medical Center in Peoria, Illinois, has convincing advice for sedentary people to get up and go. 'Active people – people who walk, cycle, jog, swim or engage in a similar exercise for at least 30 minutes every other day – have lower risk profiles for most diseases than sedentary people. And they also enjoy immediate benefits: firmer muscles, alertness and energy instead of listlessness and fatigue; better and more restful sleep; and fun, recreation and release.'

Obviously, your body doesn't take a sedentary lifestyle sitting down. So, are you ready to get up – and go? Then look for opportunities to *use* your body.

Ways to start moving

Don't drive – walk. Park a few streets away from work and let your feet take you the rest of the way. Ignore the lift and use the stairs instead (if you live or work in a tall building, start with one flight and gradually increase the distance). Most important, start an exercise programme.

'Regardless of age, sedentary people improve as soon as they undertake an exercise programme,' says Dr Weltman. 'If they are very poorly conditioned, just moving around will produce great improvements. But to improve further, they must exert themselves further – not necessarily more strenuously, but vigorously and over a sustained period.'

Yet, as Dr Weltman points out, *every* little bit helps. Even the exercise you do while you're *in* your chair.

Some sitting is unavoidable, of course. But sitting down doesn't have to get you down. Exercise *while* you sit. For instance: Sitting up straight in your chair, lift one knee towards your chest. At the same time, move your head down, easily trying to touch your forehead to your knee. Repeat the exercise with the other leg. Breathe out as you lift a leg up and breathe in as you put it down. Do as many 'lifts' as is comfortable. This exercise helps firm up your stomach muscles.

Even easier: Sit up straight in your chair, hands resting on your knees, and take a deep breath. When you've exhaled completely, keep pulling your stomach muscles in for a few seconds, then relax and breathe easily for a few seconds. Repeat this exercise as often as you like.

For information on muscle cramping, see CRAMP.

• Neck problems

'Appearances are deceptive. I knew a man who acquired a reputation for dignity because he had muscular rheumatism in the neck and back,' wrote J. Chalmers Da Costa in *The Trials and Triumphs of the Surgeon*.

Craning to see distant traffic, hunching to grasp a telephone and rotating for side vision are all in a day's work for your neck. No wonder it sometimes protests with stiffness and pain.

In their home medical manual *Take Care of Yourself*, Drs Donald M Vickery and James F Fries suggest that a doctor be seen immediately for neck pain if it travels down one arm, if an arm is numb or tingly, if pain is associated with fever and headache or if the neck is so stiff that the chin can't be touched to the chest. But quite a few neck aches, pain and stiffness are a result of simple muscle strain and/or tension.

'A friend of mine even strained his neck muscles when he twisted his head quickly to look at a pretty girl,' chortled one physcial education specialist.

John Friedrich, chairman of the department of health, physical education and recreation at Duke University in North Carolina, told us that neck injuries occur easily in daily activities as well as in sports. He had recently injured his own neck by twisting and leaning back on an overhead shot in tennis.

'Neck pain is often related to improper movement – going too far in the wrong direction or just not moving in a sound way. You can injure your neck leaning over to pick up a pencil or lounging in a chair – although some people are never bothered. And I recently heard of a case where the members of a construction crew all ended up with sore necks from constantly having to look up on a job.'

Besides the garden-variety aches and cricks, neck troubles can bring on a host of other symptoms, including headaches, pains in the scalp, face or ears, dizziness, pressure behind the eyes, fainting, and pain or soreness in the shoulder or arm.

Are your muscles shrinking?

Try putting your hands on the back of your neck at the base of the skull. Find the place where the muscles meet, and press on it. Did you jump? If so, you're in the company of 90 per cent of equally stiff adults, according to Los Angeles physical therapist Hyman Jampol. Jampol, who directs the Beverly Palms Rehabilitation Hospital, described a cycle of neck tension to us: 'As neck muscles tense, they shorten. That inhibits the head's full range of motion. And as you move your head less, the muscles get shorter and shorter. Motion is inhibited even more.' And because the neck and the rest of the back are so closely related structurally, a person who suffers with problems in one area could possibly eventually suffer with problems in the other.

Physical therapist, John Reibel, also with Duke's physical education department, told us why: 'A neck muscle strain often results from or is concomitant with an exaggerated curve in the lower back. There's a natural slight S curve in the spine column, but if people get weak abdominal muscles and let their pelvises drop forward, the lower back also goes forward and exaggerates this curve. To compensate, the upper back drops backward and the neck goes way forward. Pain results.'

How do abdominal muscles become weak? Add them to the list of woes brought on by obesity. Your fat, unfortunately, can make your neck ache. Pregnancy and lack of exercise can, too. Good posture helps, according to

Riebel, but the stiff military stance – shoulders back and chin up – that well-intentioned parents urge on their children can actually create problems.

'Even West Point [the US military academy] is getting away from that. Throwing your shoulders back without tightening abdominal muscles exaggerates that spinal curve and leads to trouble,' Riebel advised. Instead of throwing your shoulders back, he added, just hold your belly in.

But what if your neck still aches? Perhaps one of your feet turns or drops, throwing your leg, and in turn your whole spinal curve, out of line. Correcting your gait might help. Maybe you tilt your chin to look at close work while wearing bifocals. A pair of reading glasses might solve the problem. Or, you may have a stronger ear or eye on one side that causes you constantly to tilt your head to listen or see. A hearing aid or glasses might relieve the pain in your neck.

Some simple therapies

Heat may bring relief, whether it comes from a sauna, whirlpool or tub bath, shower, hot moist compress or heating pad. Gentle massage is also comforting. Throwing away your high pillows might be all that's needed. Using traction, a neck collar or a sling might help, but you need expert instruction in their use. Because responses vary so much from person to person, you might have to try several treatments before you find relief.

All of the experts we spoke to agreed that exercise is an ideal way both to treat and to prevent neck problems. Go easy, though, if your neck is already troubling you.

Riebel suggests standing under a hot shower and moving the neck back and forth. If it hurts a little, you're probably doing more good than harm. But get to the doctor, he warns, if you feel tingling in your arm. He also suggests that anyone – and weekend athletes, in particular – would benefit from a simple exercise of circling the neck. Put your chin on your chest and then rotate your head in a complete circle, five or six times a day in both a clockwise and anti-clockwise direction. Arm circles will also help the neck muscles, and sit-ups done correctly are important because they keep the abdomen strong, he added.

'Very simple' is the way Jampol describes the regimen of stretches he advises patients to do daily. 'All of us are under some kind of stress. You can't eliminate tension, but you can control it. It's important to be able to turn the head so far to the side that the nose is in line with the shoulder. Looking straight ahead, begin turning your head until your nose lines up with your shoulder on the right, then on the left. Do this three or more times a day – whenever you feel your neck tensing up – and you'll stop hurting. The human body is a marvellous machine with safety and corrective mechanisms built into it. With a little instruction, you should be able to maintain a pain-free neck and back all your life.'

Save your neck!

Sometimes neck problems are the root of pain in another area of the body.

Prevention magazine editor, Robert Rodale, shares his experience with neck problems.

'You ought to write something about woodcutters' injuries.' My friend Tom Dickson, a local orthopaedic surgeon, said that to me one winter. The American wood-burning season was in full swing, and a parade of walking wounded was passing through his office. 'I'm seeing some pretty bad cases,' he continued. 'One man had a piece of steel from a broken splitting wedge in his leg. It was the size of .38 slug. A woman broke two fingers trying to hold on to an axe that twisted when it hit a tree. It's an epidemic.'

I was thinking of those unfortunate people a few days later when I went out into my small woodlot to cut down 25 pine trees that were crowding each other. No splitting wedges for me, though. And no axes to twist in my hands, either. Just a Scandinavian bow saw, which I thought was as safe as safe could be.

What wasn't safe, though, was the large number of trees. After felling about ten, I realized that maybe I was tackling too much and quit. But the damage had been done. That night I experienced a type of pain that was entirely new to me. When I turned on my side, after having slept flat on my back for several hours, a sharp pain flashed under my right shoulder blade, not far from the centre of my back. That was it – just the one burst. The rest of the night, I felt OK, but the next day, the pain came back.

'It will go away,' I said to myself. All other pains I ever got from working too hard had passed. This one would, too. But it didn't. In fact, it progressively got worse. After about six weeks of trying to wait it out, my right arm hurt so much, all day long, that I was trying not to use it for any work heavier than turning the pages of a book.

There was nothing to do but see Dr Dickson and tell him that, even before I had time to warn our readers, I had acquired my own personal woodcutter's injury.

'You may have bursitis,' he said first off. But then he felt around my shoulder and could find no tender spots. 'There's a possibility the problem is in your neck. I'll need an X-ray to find out for sure.'

Now Tom knows that I like X-rays as much as I would enjoy living next to a nuclear power plant. So he promised that only one exposure would be needed to see whether something happening in my neck could be causing the persistent shoulder and arm pain. I finally said OK, reasoning that in cases where there was a need to know facts about a specific injury, use of X-rays in moderation made sense.

'Here could be your trouble,' he said a few minutes later, pointing to the X-ray of my neck. 'There should be space between the vertebrae, but these two right here are too close.' Dr Dickson was showing me a classic case of a compressed cervical disc. The word *cervical* refers to the neck area. Discs are soft-tissue bodies that provide padding between the vertebrae. When healthy and full-sized, they space out those bones properly, cushioning the nerves, blood vessels and muscle tissue that serve the needs of the body's vital spinal area. When there is too much spinal stress or pressure, one or more discs can become compressed. That puts pressure on the nerves extending from the spinal cord to various other parts of the body. Pain can result in the area to which those pinched nerves extend.

'How did that happen,' I asked. What puzzled me was the possibility of a connection between the squeezed disc in my neck and what I thought was a sore shoulder caused by sawing too much wood too fast. Maybe the two weren't related at all. 'A compressed disc in the neck can be caused by many different kinds of injuries or blows to the head or neck,' Tom said. 'Whiplash from a car accident can do it. I see it in rugby players, who push each other with their heads. Maybe it comes from sleeping with too thick a pillow, or sleeping on your stomach. Both are bad.'

The X-ray picture of my neck showed that the compressed disc area was in the front of the cervical spine. Bending the head forward naturally puts more pressure on that area of the disc, which is the part usually squeezed. Since finding out about my own problem, I've been reading up on squeezed neck discs in the medical literature, and I also studied a sheet of do-and-don't postural and exercise instructions Dr Dickson gave me. I found that posture which causes the head to hang forward for long periods may put too much pressure on those discs. One doctor has said that secretaries often get cervical disc problems, because they work all day long looking down at their typewriters. A fall forward, stopped by your hands, causes your head to snap to the front. That could do it, some doctors believe. I have a large head, which could make me more vulnerable to disc strain than someone with a small hat size.

'Seeing a compressed disc like this on an X-ray isn't proof that it's causing a problem,' Tom explained to me. 'Sometimes we X-ray the neck of a person who has been in a car accident and find several old degenerated discs. Yet they say they never had any pain before the accident.'

All the time that these facts about discs were being explained to me, I was doing some low-key worrying about what kind of treatment would be suggested.

'I used to operate on cases like yours,' Tom told me. Those words 'used to' were comforting. 'Then I found out about what could be done with home traction. In fact, in the seven years I've been prescribing traction at home, I haven't done a single cervical disc operation.'

Home traction
The home-traction apparatus Dr Dickson prescribed was simple to use. It consisted of a pulley arrangement that fits over a door, a length of rope, a plastic bag, and a harness that fits under the chin and around the back of the head. When everything is put together and water placed in the bag, enough upward pull is exerted on the head so that the cervical spine is stretched, relieving the pressure on the disc.

'Put 10 to 15 pounds of water in the bag at first,' Tom told me. 'Give yourself 20 minutes of traction twice a day – morning and evening. You can read to make the time go faster. And every week add two more pounds of weight, until you feel it's enough.'

'How much do you think will be enough?' I asked. I had visions of turning into something like one of those native African ladies with a neck a foot long.

'One patient of mine, a rugby player, went up to 35 pounds,' Tom said.

As it turned out, 25 pounds was enough to do the job for me. Since I started at 10, and added 15 more, the course of treatment lasted seven weeks. I found traction to be not exactly fun, but not unpleasant either. The harness does irritate your chin somewhat, until you get it adjusted or get used to it. And the pulling sensation is vaguely unpleasant. I had time to reflect on all those years when my heavy head was bearing down on those cushiony neck discs, and how the traction was giving needed relief.

Two conditions other than the pain under my shoulder blade and down my arm also cleared up as the weeks of traction passed. For several years, I had not been able to turn my head to the right as far as I could turn it to the left. There was no pain, but I had noticed when sitting by a window on the right side of an aeroplane that I had difficulty when turning to look out. After a couple of weeks of traction, I could turn my head easily in both directions.

Neck stiffness like that is a clear sign of a possible cervical disc problem. You can give yourself a simple diagnostic test. Try to turn your neck left and right slowly and see whether you have a full, unrestricted range of motion in both directions. People with a cervical disc problem might feel a pulling in the shoulder area, some pain and even swelling and tenderness. Another sign is tingling in the fingers. I read about that symptom in the medical literature and recalled that for a year or two I did have an occasional sensation of something tingling in my right hand. Like the neck stiffness, that cleared up, too, after several weeks of traction.

Getting to the root of the pain

This experience has demonstrated to me how important it is when dealing with pain to get to the root of the problem. An event you think is the cause of pain – in my case the sawing of too much wood – may be only a contributing factor. Furthermore, the place where you feel pain may not be the part of the body where the lesion (injury) or nerve pressure causing the hurt is actually located. Treatment directed at the site of the pain is therefore often a waste of time, and possibly even counterproductive.

The whole spinal area, from our neck down to the base of our spine, is where much of this 'referred' pain starts. Visualize, if you will, all those dozens of different nerves leading from your spinal cord off into your arms and legs and points between. Then think also of the vertebrae that are placed there to protect that vital nerve conduit, and the potential for pinching nerves that exists when those bony parts get too close together, slip out of place or are injured in other ways. If it weren't for the soft and cushiony discs between vertebrae, the system simply wouldn't work. Nerves would be pinched every time we moved, and messages of referred pain sent constantly to our limbs and even to our head.

Think for a moment about how much you move your neck. All day long you turn to look from side to side, or up and down. At night, you put a pillow under your head and keep your neck twisted for hours at a time. Consider also that your neck is the bridge between your body and your head. Sudden motion of one or the other can impart 'whiplash' stress. Maybe you can now begin to see why it's important to understand the structures inside your neck and what sensations you can receive if they begin to weaken.

There is a good possibility that pressure on cervical discs can also be a cause of headache, particularly the persistent kind. That theory is put forth by Dr Murray M. Braaf of New York City. He and Dr Samuel Rosner wrote in the *Journal of Trauma* about their work with over 6000 cases of chronic headache, a large proportion of which they could trace to cervical spine injury.

Dr Braaf, in a phone conversation, told us that people with strong necks have less of a problem with headache from that cause. Some minor injuries to the neck can cause headaches that go away in seven to ten days. But there can be a wide variety of other injuries that lead to persistent headache problems. Sometimes trauma to the neck occurs many years before the headache problem starts. Drs Braaf and Rosner also say in their articles that 'Repeated strain or minor injury to the neck may be all that is necessary to precipitate the headache.'

There is a possibility that headaches which originate in neck strain are caused by a more complex series of events than simply a pinched nerve. Drs Braaf and Rosner point out that compression of the vertebral artery, 'even on an intermittent basis', can cause partial restriction of blood flow to the head. That can cause pain and other symptoms, especially dizziness. Another possibility is that pinching of the neck nerves in some way affects the nerves serving the head. My own feeling is that a great deal remains to be discovered about what goes on in the body when the vertebral structures in the neck get out of whack, but it is easy to see that there is a large possibility for pain of different kinds to result.

Also quite clear is the usefulness of traction in relieving these various problems. Except in very serious cases, the neck nerves are not actually damaged. They are merely pressed. Pulling on the head in a regular and systematic way gradually separates the vertebrae slightly, relieving the pressure. Traction treatment is not a permanent cure of the problem for most people, though, Dr Dickson told me, 'Don't forget where you put your apparatus after you're finished with it. You may need it again in a year or two.' Apparently, a compressed disc doesn't return to its original shape and strength.

There is some controversy about which method of applying traction is best. Dr Braaf says cervical traction, to be effective, must be carried out with the patient lying down on his or her back. He feels that traction applied when a person is sitting up 'doesn't pull in the right direction'. The sitting-up position is less comfortable, he says, and the patient can't tolerate the necessary pull for any length of time. Dr Braaf recommends 5 to 15 pounds of pull, which is quite moderate.

People who want to take their traction lying down can do that at home, but the upright, over-the-door method I used is cheaper and easier to set up. As I said before, the discomfort was tolerable, especially considering the relief from pain that traction provided for me.

Preventing neck strain
What about preventing the kind of neck problems I have been describing? There are two aspects to that question. The first is whether there is a preventive approach to neck strain itself that can keep you from having to put your head in any kind of sling. Being so prevention oriented, I asked that question of Dr Dickson.

'There is no way to prevent this that I know about,' he said. But at the same time, he gave me an instruction sheet listing exercises that are useful in cervical strain, as well as 'helpful hints for a healthy neck'. They include instructions to sit straight in your chair instead of slouching, not sleeping on your stomach, and using a thin pillow placed under your neck instead of your head. Special pillows are sold that support the neck instead of the head, but Dr Dickson was less than enthusiastic about them.

One doctor who feels that it is possible to prevent and greatly reduce cervical disc problems is James Greenwood, Jr, chief of neurosurgery at Methodist Hospital in Houston, Texas. He has a three-step programme. First is mild exercise that builds neck strength, such as swimming. Dr Greenwood also believes that such gentle exercise helps to get needed vitamin C and other nutrients to the joints and discs. Without that help, they can degenerate and will have difficulty repairing themselves, he says. Supplementary amounts of vitamin C in the range of 2–3 g are a part of his programme. Finally, he recommends weight control, which is certainly a good idea for more reasons than an attempt to protect your neck from strain.

I mentioned that there are two aspects of prevention in this situation. The second concerns the prevention of false diagnosis of the cause of upper-body pain. Many people have the kind of pain I experienced but are not fortunate enough to identify the neck quickly as the source of the problem. Because we live in such a drug-oriented culture, the first therapeutic thought often is to ask for a prescription for a pain-killing drug or even a tranquillizer. I am trying to help change that situation by writing about my experience. While I don't want you to worry about your neck unnecessarily, I feel more people need to know that an old-fashioned therapy like merely stretching a part of the body that can become compressed has many advantages over the use of chemical treatments.

There needs to be wider understanding of the vulnerability of the neck and what the signs of trouble are. If you have no pain in your arms and shoulders, and can move your neck freely an equal distance from left to right, then just file what I have said about the cervical strain for future reference. But just to be on the safe side, stop sleeping on your stomach, and use a thin pillow under your neck instead of a big bolster at the back of your head. And make sure that the headrest on your car is adjusted properly so that it will support your head in case someone hits you from behind.

• Night blindness

You're driving along a country road at night. There's very little traffic, and nothing breaks the dark monotony except the play of your own car's head-lamps and the winking of the cats'-eyes on the road ahead.

Suddenly, from around the next curve speeds another vehicle – the high beams of its headlamps exploding like a piercing slow-motion flash across your field of vision. Instinctively, you begin braking, while squinting off to the left side of the road, away from the glare.

After the other car passes, you breathe a sigh of relief and begin to accelerate again, only to discover that you can barely see. All is darkness. There are no reassuring cats'-eyes, reflective signs or even dimly perceived shoulders. Shaken, you somehow manage to pull over to the side to wait for the internal darkness to subside.

You are the victim of unexpected night blindness.

For years, night blindness or the loss of visual dark adaptation, has been recognized as an early and classic sign of vitamin A deficiency. (It is also seen in some people with a malfunctioning thyroid gland). When we go from bright sunlight into the darkened confines of a cinema, for instance, it's natural that for a few moments, at least, we will be able to see next to nothing. But our eyes adapt. The person with impaired dark adaptation, on the other hand, may still be struggling to find an empty seat, and bumping shins and spilling popcorn in the process, many minutes after entering the cinema.

Vitamin A is not enough

Traditionally, victims of such episodes of night blindness have been urged to consume more vitamin A. (Remember all the old jokes about eating a lot of carrots?) And, as we'll see a bit later, adequate levels of vitamin A are absolutely essential for healthy eyes.

However, it now turns out that a person may be getting all the vitamin A that a balanced diet and even supplementation can supply, and still suffer from night blindness. At that point, a small amount of the essential dietary mineral zinc may work more wonders than all the carrots in the world.

As Dr Stanley Morrison told the 17th annual meeting of the American Society for Clinical Nutrition in Washington, DC, patients suffering from liver disease often have a poor dark-adaptation response, but among these people – often alcoholics with liver cirrhosis – extra vitamin A brings very disappointing results.

Dr Morrison, a gastro-enterologist, described a clinical study carried out by him and three co-workers at the Veterans Administration Hospital and University of Maryland School of Medicine in Baltimore. Six people with poor night vision who had been heavy drinkers for at least 15 years were selected for the trial.

Two of the patients were given supplements of 10,000 IU of vitamin A daily, but after two weeks, dark adaptation was unchanged in one, and improved but still abnormal in the other. (In the tests, subjects were first exposed to a temporarily blinding bright light, then exposed to a series of flashing lights of various intensities until a threshold of discernment was regained). However, when 90 mg of zinc was given to the same two people daily, dark adaptation improved dramatically in the one and returned to normal in the other.

Three other patients were treated right from the start with zinc, and their dark adaptation improved within eight days. The sixth subject was given both zinc and vitamin A from the first day, and night vision was restored to normal within a week. 'Correction of zinc deficiency in some cirrhotics is effective treatment for night blindness,' Dr Morrison concluded.

Why zinc is needed

How was zinc able to succeed where supplementary vitamin A had failed? Dr Morrison believes that, although many people have all the vitamin A they require stored in their livers, it isn't being mobilized. Zinc, however, apparently steps up the formation of a critical binding protein that latches on to vitamin A in the liver and gets it flowing through the bloodstream to those sites where it's needed. Also, he says, zinc appears to be instrumental in enhancing a vital enzyme's activity in the retina of the eye, necessary for normal visual function.

Dr Morrison noted that the problem of night blindness related to zinc deficiency has also surfaced in West Germany, where a surprisingly high number of applicants for driver's licences have failed night-vision tests. German authorities apparently don't relish the prospect of thousands of visually impaired drivers hurtling down dark autobahns behind the wheels of swift Porsches and Mercedes-Benzes. Many of the Germans who failed the screening tests, Dr Morrison said, had chronic liver disorders.

Similar unsuspected cases of night blindness may be wide-spread in the United States, Dr Morrison told us. 'Most Americans eat pretty well,' he said, 'so they're getting vitamin A in their diet, but they're getting only marginal amounts of zinc, at best. Then you must superimpose on this the renal clearance problem – the fact that exorbitant amounts of zinc are excreted by the kidneys of people with cirrhosis.'

Just how widespread may the problem be? Leaving out for the moment those sober individuals whose diets may simply be deficient in zinc, Dr Morrison noted that 'In the US, we're probably talking about 20 or 30 million people who drink heavily. And a substantial number of them probably have marginal zinc reserves.'

Drinking drains your zinc

Actually, the knowledge that alcohol tends to flush vital zinc right out of the body is not new. 'Zinc deficiency has been indicated as a concomitant of both alcoholism and cirrhosis for the last quarter of a century,' Jack Wang and Dr Richard N Pierson, Jr reported at a meeting of the Federation of American Societies for Experimental Biology.

The pair, associated with St Luke's Hospital Center in New York City, reported that alchoholic rats showed a very sharp drop in liver stores of zinc within two weeks of beginning their alcohol diet. Levels of the mineral in muscle and blood also fell, but more gradually. 'The fact that liver fractions lose zinc rapidly when compared with muscle and [blood] plasma, suggests that the organ most susceptible to alcohol toxicity is the liver,' they said.

However, as we are now finding out, zinc deficiency ultimately shows itself in the eyes also, through its inhibiting effect on vitamin A. To better grasp the link, let's see how our night vision works.

In the light-sensitive layer across the back of the eye – the *retina* – are hundreds of thousands of tiny nerve endings. Some are cone-shaped and some are cylindrically shaped, like rods. Light energy that strikes and stimulates the cones and rods is transformed into nerve impulses, which register in the brain as vision.

Now it happens that night vision, or 'twilight seeing', depends almost entirely on the rods, which are more sensitive to faint light than the cones. The ability of the eye to adapt to changes in light depends on the presence of light-sensitive pigment in the rods called 'visual purple'. When light hits the retina (those high beams on the car approaching you), visual purple is split into its component parts. Back in the dark again (the other vehicle has passed), normal vision is not regained until adequate levels of visual purple have been regenerated.

Without vitamin A on hand, visual purple can't be formed. And Dr Morrison's team and other researchers have now shown that without adequate zinc, the vitamin A to build visual purple just won't be available.

So if you have to venture out after the sun's gone down, whether on the road or simply to take out the rubbish, the message seems clear. Get enough vitamin A, but also be sure to get enough zinc. You'll probably never be able to see as well at night as the wise old owl, but hopefully, you'll never wind up lost in the dark, either.

• Oedema

Oedema is a general term used to describe swelling caused by retention of fluid in the tissues. It is a common problem in pregnancy, and for millions of women before their monthly periods. In his book, *Vitamin B₆, The Doctor's Report*, John M. Ellis recounts how high-level vitamin B_6 (pyridoxine) supplements eliminated the oedema that is so characteristic of women with the high oestrogen levels typical of these conditions.

Dr Ellis related the case of a 37-year-old woman, eight months pregnant, who was suffering from severe oedema. 'The tops of her feet were swollen so tightly that her skin had a light sheen to it,' he recalled. 'It was noticeable from across the room. When I pressed the top of her foot with my finger, the outline of my finger remained several seconds in the swollen flesh of her foot.' Dr Ellis started giving her 50 mg injections of vitamin B_6 every two days. After four days, the puffiness and bloating were almost gone.

Vitamin B_6 can also reduce pre-menstrual water retention. One evening, after finishing his hospital rounds, Dr Ellis noticed a nurse with puffy hands and fingers. Intrigued, since he had recently been relieving the oedema of pregnancy with vitamin B_6, he asked the nurse if her hands tingled or went to sleep – oedema's most common symptoms.

'Dr Ellis,' the nurse replied, 'there is something about this that has to do with my menstrual cycle. About midway between my periods is when I notice that the swelling and soreness begin. It lasts from seven to ten days and goes away when I menstruate.'

Dr Ellis's diagnosis: 'premenstrual oedema'.

He knew that, for years, gynaecologists had been giving diuretics – drugs that make the kidneys excrete the excess liquid causing the puffiness

– in an attempt to control it. But, given his success in treating the oedema of pregnancy wih vitamin B_6, Dr Ellis decided to pit the vitamin against the problem.

When the nurse came into his office the next day, Dr Ellis prescribed two 50 mg tablets of vitamin B_6 daily for five days and asked her to return on the sixth day. She had this to report when she returned: 'After taking the B_6 for two days, my hands were better – in fact, seemed well. By the third day, I was able to wear my rings, use the typewriter and sleep much better.'

For the next 12 months, she took one 50 mg tablet daily and had no pain or swelling. After a year, she decided on her own to take the tablets only on the 10 days preceding menstruation. Then, to make sure that the vitamin B_6 was doing what he thought it was, Dr Ellis asked her to discontinue taking the tablets altogether. It was 1 October. Her next menstrual period was due on 15 October.

Menstruation began, as expected, on 15 October – without difficulties. She continued not taking the vitamin.

On 13 November, she developed a muscular soreness in the back of her neck. During the night, she woke up with pain in her fingers. During the next day she developed severe pains in the joints of her left hand. There was no mistaking it – her face, hands and fingers were swollen. Her fingers were so painful that she could hardly bear to lift a hospital chart. On 15 November, she began menstruating.

Needless to say, the nurse eagerly returned to her daily vitamin B_6 supplement. Her next period was totally without problems.

Over the years, Dr Ellis saw more and more patients with the same problem. In one group of women he treated for this disorder, 4 out of 11 had previously taken diuretics to control their puffiness, but with little success. However, when they took 50 to 100 mg of pyridoxine daily, all their signs and symptoms were relieved by the next cycle of menstruation.

Vitamin therapy, as any drug therapy, is not without its problems. If 200 mg or more of pyridoxine is taken daily, there may be some gastric acidity or nausea. In addition, researchers in Britain have discovered that some women on long-term vitamin B_6 therapy develop nerve damage (e.g. 'pins-and-needles', numbness, etc.) Therefore it is best to take only 40 mg of pyridoxine twice a day, rising to 75 mg if necessary, and to take this for only three days before a period. If any adverse effects occur, see your doctor.

• Overweight

The 'battle of the bulge' is an ongoing struggle for as many as half of us. In a society that glorifies slimness, the desire to lose weight ranks as a national obsession. For good reason. Obesity, while not generally considered to be a disease, is a risk factor for such serious disorders as high blood pressure, heart disease and diabetes. Generally speaking, overweight people live shorter lives, have more frequent illnesses and are subjected to social discrimination, ridicule and stress because of their obesity. Being fat is no fun.

People become overweight in the first place because they consume more food energy – measured in calories – than they expend in physical activity. The body, in its age-old wisdom, stores the excess food energy as fat, just in case the next meal is a few days off – a situation that occurred fairly often in earlier times. In our times, however, the next meal is never more than a few hours off, so the calories keep piling up. What's more, modern life with all its conveniences – cars, lifts, escalators, 'work' that demands nothing more strenuous than pushing a few buttons, the passive entertainment of television – requires far less expenditure of physical energy than did the lives of our ancestors. So, we're burning fewer calories all the while we're consuming more of them. The result is obesity, pure and simple.

The solution *sounds* equally simple: consume fewer calories – eat less – and burn more calories – exercise more. Those, in fact, are the principles of every sensible weight-loss programme. Unfortunately, most fad diets emphasize the first principle – cutting calories – without mentioning the need for exercise. Also, many diets undermine the body's nutritional needs by cutting out essential nutrients along with the calories. Extremely low-calorie diets in themselves can be harmful. (The US Food and Drug Administration [FDA] has warned that diets supplying fewer than 800 calories a day should be used only under a doctor's supervision.) But there are other factors to be considered as well if we are to understand why weight control is really a tricky and difficult problem for many people.

Why Diets Often Fail

Psychological, as well as physical, factors play a big role in weight problems. 'It's no big deal getting people to lose weight. Americans lose millions of pounds every year. But only 2 to 5 per cent actually keep it off,' says Jeanne Segal, a California psychotherapist and author of *Feeling Great!* (1981).

Rapid weight loss tends to be temporary, Dr Segal says, because people merely shed pounds without taking the time to understand why they overeat. 'If you've been doing something for the past 20 or 30 years, there are good reasons for it,' she says. 'You may be bored or lonely, you may be trying to hide your sexual attractiveness, you may simply be trying to numb yourself. But people jump into weight-loss programmes without understanding these underlying reasons . . . and when they do lose weight, they get in touch with what they've been trying to avoid all along. And the weight comes back. What you have to do is eliminate the original reason for overeating.'

Changing a lifelong behaviour pattern like overeating is more permanent if it progresses slowly, Dr Segal says. 'Lots of people are not prepared for how different they feel when they actually lose the weight. They're used to their feeling of 'self', and when that changes at a deep level, people get scared, they feel out of control – and being out of control is frightening to an adult. If you go slowly during this interim period, you feel only a little out of control rather than totally out of control. It gives you time to adjust to that new sense of self.'

Then there's something else: your mind adjusts to weight loss much more slowly than your body does. Months, or even years, after you've slimmed down to your ideal weight, your mind may still be carrying around a pocket-sized self-portrait of a fat person.

In order to help people 'create new memories of themselves' – that is, make their newly won thinness a part of their inner self-image – Dr Segal uses imagery techniques. In a deeply relaxed state, the newly thin are taught to 'visualize themselves as they are now,' so that the mental image of self comes to match the physical one.

Yet even by accelerating the process of self-acceptance with these techniques, getting used to being 10, 20 or 30 lbs lighter is something that just takes time. In the long run, though, making the change slowly is worth it, Dr Segal says, because all that unnecessary flab is more likely to take a permanent vacation.

So get your mind ready for a change before you diet. And while you're at it, consider, too, how others around you feel about your weight. That may be just as important, say some health professionals.

The Jack Sprat and wife-syndrome

The spouses of overweight people are frequently not all that enthusiastic about seeing their mates go on a reducing regimen. Often, though, they come to realize that the reducing programme is *not* a disguised attempt to break away from the relationship, and they learn to accept their new, more slender mates with open arms (even if not *quite* so open as before).

But when you get into the big leagues of overweight, and the surgical approach to weight loss rather than the natural approach, this phenomenon is even more true. And unfortunately, happy endings are not very common.

That's the gist of a study published by three doctors in the *Journal of the American Medical Association*. John R Neill, of the University of Kentucky College of Medicine, and two colleagues describe changes in marriage relationships that occurred after 14 women, all of them weighing well over 14 stone – many of them over 21 stone – underwent intestinal bypass surgery. In that procedure, a portion of the small intestine is rerouted in such a way that food is much less completely digested, resulting in rapid weight loss.

The first curious thing about this study was that half of the men married to these women were actually very thin themselves. Some years ago, one doctor dubbed this the 'Jack Sprat and wife syndrome'.

You might think that these men would be happy to see their wives slim down, but that's not so. Only three were supportive of their wives' decision to have the operation, while an equal number were actively opposed. The rest didn't seem to care one way or the other.

After the surgery, when considerable weight loss had taken place, the doctors found a veritable epidemic of dissatisfaction in these marriages. Two of the women said they had been divorced from their husbands and seven others said their marriages deteriorated, while five said there had been no noticeable change. In not one instance did the marriage relationship improve.

What's more – at least according to the wives – three of their husbands became openly homosexual, while three others became impotent. The men in the latter category fixed the blame for their condition on the 'increased sexual demands' made by their newly slender wives.

The moral of this story seems to be that in marriages such as these, the pathology or weakness of one partner uses the shortcoming of the other partner as a crutch. When one partner suddenly throws away her crutch, the other partner feels lost.

Perhaps, in these days of self-discovery and self-improvement, that kind of change is causing more than a few marriages to become unstable. The trick is for both partners to throw away their crutches together.

If you really want to help your spouse lose weight, the best strategy may be to let a friend help instead. Researchers at the University of Rochester in New York State put 70 people on five different diet plans: behavioural therapy; behavioural therapy plus encouragement from a spouse; behavioural therapy plus encouragement from a friend; behavioural therapy plus encouragement from a spouse *and* a friend; and no therapy at all.

The people receiving therapy plus help from a friend lost the most weight – an average of 14.5 lb. Those receiving only therapy placed second, with average losses of 10.5 lb. Next was the therapy plus friend and spouse group, at 9.6 lb. And, of course, those in the no therapy at all group finished last with weight *gains* of about 1/2 lb each.

And where did the spouse-aided group fit in?

A quarrelsome fourth: 8.8 lb was their average loss. And it's interesting to note that the spouse/friend group lost *less* than the group assisted by friends only. The additional 'support' of the spouse, in other words, had proved to be anything but.

Say goodbye to the binge

Other experts believe that psychological factors can be dealt with by changing how we *act* – a method known as behavioural therapy. 'Overweight is simply a matter of food abuse,' says Laura Jane Walker, a weight-control specialist in Los Angeles. 'People like to blame it on boredom, but that's just an excuse. Overweight people in general have a pattern of anger, eat, anger, eat.' It's a malady known as a 'binge'.

'Many people grab a piece of pizza, look at it as fattening, say 'I blew the diet' and continue stuffing themselves with pizza,' says Dr Walker. 'What's needed here is a behaviour change.'

She believes that such a person could be thoroughly satisfied with just one slice of the pizza by taking smaller bites and eating it slowly, 'In my classes, I make people take a piece of food and really chew it for as long as possible,' she says. 'I tell them to chew it slowly, to roll it around the mouth and savour the flavour. For the first time, some of them actually taste the food. People who wolf down food never taste it. Getting pleasure out of tasting will satisfy you with less.'

Dr Walker also recommends stretching a meal out as long as possible, at least for 20 minutes – the amount of time it takes the brain to tell the stomach the hunger is gone. 'Eating slowly improves assimilation of nutrients,' she says. 'Digestion is improved many times over.'

Eating most of your calories early in the day is another way to promote weight loss. In one study, seven volunteers ate 2000 calories a day at breakfast, and all seven lost weight. But when they ate the same 2000 calories as an evening meal, they lost less weight, or even gained weight. Dieters, say the scientists who conducted the study, should consider 'the importance of timing apart from the amount of caloric intake' (*Chronobiologia*).

One reason for this is that digestion doesn't peak until about seven hours after the last swallow. If most of the calories were eaten at the evening meal, digestion time comes around while you're sleeping, the time when your metabolism is at its lowest ebb. 'People on a normal 9-to-5 schedule should take all their meals before 7 P.M.,' says Dr Walker, who has lost and successfully kept off 30 lb through behaviour modification.

She also recommends eating most of your protein at lunch rather than dinner. 'That way you'll be burning the protein when you're the most active.'

Eating smaller, frequent meals rather than a few large meals is another good habit to adopt. For one thing, 'skipping meals makes you famished, and you'll want to attack the food when the next meal rolls around,' says Dr Walker.

A way to beat hunger pangs is practised widely in Beverly Hills by the patients of Dr Arnold Fox. He recommends carrying around a bag of vegetables for constant munching through the day. 'Eating vegetables makes you feel satisfied and full. Not only that, but you're not as hungry when mealtime rolls around,' he says. 'If you're going to a party or out to dinner, eat an apple or a few carrots before you leave the house. You'll be surprised at how many calories you can save that way.'

Here are some more practical tips and tricks passed on by weight-loss experts:

● Drink plenty of water – up to eight glasses a day. It fills you up, and there are no calories. Just remember that most foods are more than 50 per cent water. So, when you feel hungry, ask yourself: 'Could it be a glass of water that I want?'

● Take up a project, one that keeps your hands busy or even dirty, so you'll find it impossible to reach for food when monotony hits. Yale University psychologist Judith Rodin, says she's found that this helps food lovers keep their minds off snacking. 'Make sure you're busy at the time of the day you're most tempted by food,' she suggests. 'If you get caught up in the project, you won't even think about food.'

● Put your meals on smaller plates. It gives you the illusion of eating more when you're really not.

● Always sit at the table, and never read or watch television while eating. It only distracts you and can make you eat more than you really want or need.

● Eat vegetarian meals at least one day a week. You'll almost always eat fewer calories and take in less fat. You'll load up on nutrients, too.

● Put down your knife and fork or sandwich between bites. You'll be surprised how much longer your meal will last.

● Cut down on salad dressing by mixing the salad and dressing in a large bowl first rather than putting a dollop on top of the greens at the dinner table. Remember that one tablespoon of salad dressing contains about 80 calories. A little can go a long way if it is mixed correctly.

● Always remove the skin from chicken before cooking, if possible. This is high in fat and adds calories you can easily do without. Ditto with fat on steaks and chops.

- Break the fried-food habit. Always choose a baked potato instead of chips, or boiled fish rather than deep fried.
- Don't pour gravy all over your food. Instead, put in on the side and dip a corner of the food into it. You'll consume a lot less for the same flavour.
- Gradually cut down your consumption of red meat, and eat more fish and fowl. You'll save calories, help lower your cholesterol and improve your overall health.
- Never eat when you're not hungry. This ties in with the next tip:
- Learn to sidetrack your eating momentum. A considerable amount of overeating that takes place at dinner-time is the result of an almost mindless momentum that builds up rapidly and doesn't grind to a halt until you've eaten much more than you need and, occasionally, just enough to make you feel as if every cell in your body has been stuffed full of food. Many of us astonish ourselves with our ability to eat large bowls of soup, heaping plates of salad, and big chunks of meat without putting the brakes on that momentum. Often, that eating drive doesn't sputter to a halt until we sneak pieces of food from serving dishes even as we carry them to the refrigerator to be stored.

Yet, 15 minutes later, we feel so overfed that we realize it wasn't true hunger that made us eat all that extra food. It was nothing but sheer eating momentum.

A psychiatrist's method of appetite control

Mehl McDowell is a psychiatrist in Santa Monica, California, whose practice emphasizes natural methods of cure. In an article in Obesity/Bariatric Medicine *(September – October, 1980), Dr McDowell outlined his 'therapeutic breakthrough' in teaching his patients to control their appetites – the key to losing weight. The article is adapted here with his permission.*

Overweight patients have been coming to me for years seeking one of two types of therapy. They all wanted to gain control of the irresistible forces that made them overeat and become fat. One group sought psychotherapy to uncover and resolve subconscious, psychological insecurities that they believed must be giving rise to their uncontrollable appetites. The other group sought the aid of therapy with hypnosis to 'jack up' their weak willpower and put down their appetites.

My success rate with both groups was disappointing.

Psychological and emotional problems could be found in most of the first group and often alleviated, but the food cravings were rarely reduced. Hypnotic therapy was more successful, but, unfortunately, it rarely lasted beyond several weeks of a crash diet programme. Then the patient would gradually return to his former favourite foods, and soon the irresistible cravings would start up again.

The therapeutic breakthrough came when I was searching for a clear-cut, easily definable dietary rule that would simplify weight control. I needed a rule that would be healthy, easy to live by and readily taught by behaviour therapy techniques.

The rule I selected to try was the complete avoidance of all foods containing refined sugar or white flour. Using the habit-retraining techniques with which

I was familiar, I programmed my willing weight-control patients to dislike the sugar – white flour foods and completely eliminate them from their eating style.

Now, the great surprise – the breakthrough – surfaced when patient after patient came to me following several days of eating a diet free of all sugar and white flour and joyfully reported that the irresistible cravings had disappeared. That was a most welcome development, but unexpected and puzzling.

Food addiction

It finally struck me, however, that I was using the same techniques I used to relieve the addictive cravings of smokers, alcoholics and drug addicts. It was a logical consequence to consider the possibility that, with my no sugar – white flour rule, I had unwittingly eliminated foods to which these people had been addicted.

Their irresistible cravings could now be understood as the typical cravings of addicts. The mysterious urges stemmed from the cyclic, biochemical processes of addiction.

I then turned to the medical literature. A few researchers had reported findings to support the theory that an addiction to foods can occur. They also noted that the cravings of their patients had disappeared in several days after totally avoiding the foods to which they were addicted. I was sold. The food addiction hypothesis explained this surprising development better than any other.

Occasionally, a patient will report irresistible cravings for some other food not in the sugar – white flour group, such as shelled nuts, peeled potatoes, polished rice, cheese, dried fruit and more rarely, fresh fruit. When discovered, these foods are then added to our list of 'enemy foods', and the same techniques are used to produce total abstinence.

Sometimes we find a fattening alcoholic habit. Usually this is a wine habit in a woman or a beer habit in a man. In such instances, these beverages are added to the enemy list, and the patients are trained for total abstinence from them.

However, the establishment of total abstinence from the foods identified as the culprits is only the first phase in eliminating the addictive-like, irresistible cravings for those foods. The second phase is extinguishing the conditioned response cravings for those foods.

Totally abstaining addicts – of any kind – soon find that almost any reminder of their former substances of abuse will produce an instant craving. (This is the well-known 'conditioned-reflex' response so well demonstrated and popularized by Pavlov's salivating dogs many years ago.) A good example is the common picture of the ex – cigarette smoker who spends years feeling frustrated and deprived as he watches his smoking friends and longs for a cigarette every time he has a cup of coffee or a cocktail, or whenever he answers the telephone or relaxes after meals. His tobacco intake has been halted successfully by total abstinence, but the conditioned-response cravings have not been adequately removed.

How do I eliminate these conditioned-response cravings in the case of sugar – white flour addicts? I use the term 'glue' and 'glue foods' to mean all foods containing any highly refined sugar or flour.

If a patient has a desire for a dish of chocolate ice cream, for instance, I instruct him to immediately picture that ice cream 'glued' into disgusting fat deposits on his abdomen. This picturing takes place while the patient is in an altered state of consciousness, such as that of deep relaxation, meditation or hypnosis. With sufficient repetition of such imaginary scenes, this 'disgust' feeling becomes associated with that type of food in real-life encounters.

The patient is further instructed to react, deliberately and instantly, throughout his waking life, to every real-life reminder of his enemy foods with this strong, vivid disgust response. He then immediately rewards himself with a sense of being in control, 'captain of my ship', and anticipating his trim self-image.

This use of an interference response coupled with disgust, and then immediately followed by a reward for deliberately feeling negatively towards the enemy foods, has proven of great value in preventing relapse. We call that our 'instant yuk' technique. It only takes a couple of seconds, and it can be repeated for years.

In control

Once the addiction is under control, it becomes much easier to restrain such fattening habits as eating too fast, eating until too full and frequent snacking. It appears that these habits are fuelled by the presence of addictive cravings. They fall away readily after the fire of cravings is extinguished.

Also, many patients find that they no longer have the habit of eating when under psychological and emotional stress. The cravings of an addicted person, regardless of the substance of his or her addiction, are regularly mobilized when the individual is in an excited state – when he or she is 'turned on' by any challenging stress, joy, anger, anxiety, etc. Most patients who have successfully extinguished their addictive states, including their conditioned cravings, do not have a flare-up of their cravings under such psychological and emotional stress conditions.

These successful ex-addicts are frequently surprised and pleased to find that they are not as weak, insecure and neurotically self-destructive as they believed they were during their addictive period.

Since this therapeutic approach eliminates major sources of former eating pleasure, the treatment must stress that a successful outcome is a gain and not a deprivation. The patient needs to learn a new eating style that eliminates his or her enemy foods but is rich in variety and gourmet experiences.

Health magazines and health-food cookbooks are easily accessible sources for developing this type of eating style. One can learn to prepare all types of 'glue-free' dishes from breakfast pancakes to dinner desserts.

Finally, I would like to say that my approach of abstaining from all foods containing any refined sugar or white flour is an economical, health-promoting foundation for anyone's eating style – whether or not he or she is subject to food addiction.

How to overcome sugar addiction

How can you tell if your weight problem may be due to a sugar addiction?

Try this simple test: Double chocolate fudge gateau with ice cream. A thick, creamy strawberry milk shake. Delectable chocolate-covered cream buns. Enticing, chewy Mars bars.

If the mere mention of a sweet snack brings a lip-smacking smile to your mouth, chances are there's a sweet tooth anchored somewhere in that grin. And it's a good bet that it's got you hooked on sugar.

'Any food has the potential for being addictive,' says Dr Lendon Smith, author of *Feed Yourself Right* (1983). 'Sugar is high on the list.'

Of course, no one knows better than the true-blue sugar hounds just how troublesome this problem can be. They're reminded once every day when the nagging craving forces them to rush for that packet of biscuits – or anything else that is gooey, sugary and sweet. And the sugar addicts probably don't need to be told how bad the stuff is for them, either. They know it causes tooth decay. And they know it aggravates a weight problem, diabetes and gout. Yet, they go after it anyway. Like the junkie hooked on heroin, they have to get their daily fix.

Ah, but there is hope. You can kick the sweet habit. Authorities in the field say that it is possible to adjust your palate to desire less sugar, even no sugar at all! To find out how to go about it, we sought out the trade secrets of the medical people who deal with the problem every day. The nicest thing we found is that yanking a sweet tooth requires little pain. Here's a baker's dozen worth of steps leading to a new life without sweets.

1 Keep a sugar diary 'Kicking the sugar habit requires first and foremost a lot of consciousness raising,' says Dr Allen McDaniels, of San Pedro, California. You have to want to get off the stuff. The surest way to convince yourself that you're overloading on sugar is to keep a diary of everything you eat and drink for a week. Check off all the items containing sugar, added either by the processor or by yourself. The second week, start eliminating. Cold turkey is the best way to go about it. If you find this absolutely impossible, start by gradually cutting down.

Just keep in mind that you don't have to breakfast on cola and cake (yes, such people do exist) to be tagged a sugar junkie. Even a teaspoon of sugar in the morning coffee is a sign that you're hooked. The plain truth of the matter is that far too many people eat too much sugar. The latest statistics show that, in Britain, sugar added to food contributes about 18 per cent of the adult calorie intake, and for teenagers, the per centage is much higher. The researchers at Georgetown University, in Washington, D.C. say that such figures indicate 'a potential widespread health problem'. So, just being average puts you at risk. Where do you fall in these statistics? Your weekly sugar diary can give you a clue.

2 Banish all sugars and sweets from the house This may sound like the cure-all for the problem, but unfortunately for sugar lovers, out of sight doesn't also mean out of mind. However, it is a start. 'Keep no sugar in the house – including white and brown sugar, golden syrup and treacle,' advises Dr Smith, 'though one small jar of pure raw honey is OK to keep around.'

Feeding a sugar craving simply is a lot more difficult to do when the goodies are out of reach. And it's not just white sugar you must avoid. Even though white sugar consumption is down, we in Britain still eat far too much of it.

The latest statistics show that we each eat an average of about 90 lb of refined sugar a year, and the story changes dramatically when you add together all things sweet. Take the United States as an example: in 1980, the use of all sugars and sweeteners was at a record high, up about 50 per cent, from 91 lb a year per person at the turn of the century to 143 lb a year. The popularity of corn syrup alone skyrocketed from 2 lb per person in 1972 to 26 lb per person in 1980.

3 Take time out to nibble Sugar craving is a vicious cycle. A quick dose of sugar causes blood sugar to rise rapidly. To compensate for the overdose, the body rapidly releases insulin, forcing the blood sugar level to plummet. The end result? Another sugar attack. Some people suffer such common side-effects as nervousness, crankiness, headaches and bad dreams. 'The trick to avoiding sugar pangs is to keep the blood sugar fairly even,' Dr Smith says. 'Nibbling on good food in between your regular meals is a way to achieve this.' Nuts, seeds, raw vegetables, fruit, cheese and hard-boiled eggs are all good anti-sugar snack foods. 'If you nibble every two to three hours, you'll find out you crave less. You'll eat less at regular meals and be more cheerful in the morning,' he says.

Former cravers told us that nuts are particularly helpful in fending off a sugar urge. 'I can remember staring at this chocolate bar in a shop and really wanting it,' one woman told us. 'It was one of those gooey ones with lots of nuts and caramel. But I resisted, and when I got back to the office, I bought a bag of nuts. They tasted great, and it occurred to me that that's probably what I was really craving all along.' Now she nibbles on nuts when the urge gets strong.

4 Increase your intake of complex carbohydrates We all know that whole grains and fresh vegetables are packed with nutrition. But unfortunately, these same foods are most likely to be at the bottom of the sugar addict's list of favourite foods. 'Overloading on sweets is a bad diet, and a bad diet leads to vitamin deficiency,' says Dr McDaniels. 'The result is craving more sweets. It's a vicious cycle. The straight nutritional approach is the easiest way to get around a sweet tooth. You'll find that eating a good, well-balanced diet helps eliminate the sugar craving.'

Dr Ray C Wunderlich of St Petersburg, Florida adds another bit of advice: 'Make sure you have adequate protein in your diet every day. I don't mean excessive protein, just adequate.' He also touts nuts and seeds as a great substitute for sugar. 'They can take the edge off a sweet craving,' he says, 'but don't just eat peanuts. Try almonds, sesame seeds and sunflower seeds. Be versatile.'

5 Beat binges with exercises Putting the body in high gear, even for just a few minutes, is a great sugar stabilizer, says Dr Wunderlich. 'If the blood sugar is high, exercise will bring it down. If it's low, it will bring it up.' In his own practice, Dr Wunderlich has found that a few minutes spent bouncing on a mini-trampoline can do wonders for a sugar urge. But any kind of exercise will do – calisthenics, jumping jacks, a brisk walk and, of course, jogging. 'If you want sugar, get down on the floor and do a couple of push-ups. It'll put you in a whole new frame of mind,' he says.

But don't just exercise when you get the sugar urge. Regular day-after-day exercise enables your body to handle glucose more efficiently. When you exercise daily, less insulin is needed to control sugar swings.

6 Get a daily dose of B vitamins When it comes to sugar-fighting vitamins, B complex gets an A. The B vitamins are all-important to sugar addicts because of their ability to keep blood sugar working at an optimum level, says Dr Smith. In his own practice, he's found that B vitamins, particulary nicotinic acid (niacin) help assuage the sugar hunger in hypoglycaemic patients – those whose sugar allergy causes sickness and even psychological problems. And, the Bs help sour a sweet tooth, too. What foods contain B vitamins? You guessed it – complex carbohydrates. Whole grains, fresh vegetables, wheat germ – all the goods you've already been encouraged to eat.

7 Get your fair share of chromium, manganese and zinc Like the B vitamins, this trio of trace minerals is important in keeping the blood sugar on an even keel. And, according to Dr Wunderlich, they are the minerals most commonly found to be in short supply in sugar lovers. Chromium helps insulin do its job efficiently. Zinc and manganese help stabilize blood sugar, particularly when it is at an ebb. However, the major role of zinc in nutrition is to enhance taste acuity, and most recently, it has been found actually to help control the sweet tooth. This was discovered when ten healthy people were fed zinc supplements for 15 weeks to see how it would affect their sense of sweet, sour, salty and bitter. Most dramatic was their sensitivity to the taste of sweet. They found they could get by on less sugar *(Biological Trace Element Research*, June/September 1982).

8 Avoid red meats This is strictly anecdotal, but there are people who claim it helps. One such person is William Dufty, whose successful personal war in fighting sugar addiction resulted in the book *Sugar Blues*. He gives the following advice:

> Kick red meat. Just switching from red meat to fish or fowl reduces your
> desire for a sweet concoction at the end of a meal. It makes it easier
> to settle for something natural, like fruit, or even no dessert at all.

Dr Smith says he also has heard similar positive reports from his own patients. 'There's definitely something to it,' he says, 'especially for those who have an allergy to beef. When vegetable protein is used in place of animal protein, it's somehow easier for a person to pass up sweets.'

9 Read package labels very carefully Sugar can end up in the most unlikely items – even some toothpastes contain it – which is why it's important to follow this tip. If some kind of sugar – e.g. corn syrup, fructose, dextrose or honey – is listed as one of the first two or three ingredients, then you can bet the product contains a lot of sugar, and you'd be best off avoiding it. Some things you'd never think of adding sugar to at home – such as soups – often list it as an ingredient when you find them on the supermarket shelf. So get in the habit – read all labels!

10 Avoid artifical sweeteners Trying to trick your taste buds into thinking you're eating sugar when you're not just isn't going to do you any good. 'Saccharin and cyclamates taste sweet, but they are chemicals, and the liver has to detoxify them,' says Dr Smith. 'Besides, anything that tastes sweet promotes the idea that everything must taste sweet.' The bottom line is forget sweeteners. You can live without them.

11 Ward off vending machines A real downfall to many sugar addicts is the vending machine, that handy little fixture that can send you to sugarland at the drop of a coin and a flick of the wrist.

Just how bad an influence a vending machine can be was demonstrated on the campus of the University of Illinois, where the snacking habits of the students were monitored. Thirty-five per cent of the students skipped at least one meal a day, opting instead for sustenance from the vendor. And it was the soft-drink lever that got the biggest workout. Sweets and chewing gum came in second and third. Next came coffee, popcorn, crisps, pretzels, pies, yogurt, fresh fruit, hot chocolate, crackers and milk (*Illinois Research*, Autumn 1979).

One way to snub the vending machine is to carry your own nourishing snacks to work, says Dr Smith, but he has an even better idea. Ask your employer to have the machines removed. Sugar overloading can lead to job dissatisfaction, he says, even in offices that are relatively stress free. 'If the boss wants the best from the workers, he or she would do well to ban the junk machines.'

12 Reach for fruit, the natural sweet Keep an assortment of fresh fruit in the house at all times. It's a great thing to grab during a sugar attack. Take it with you in the car too, if you have the habit of sucking boiled sweets or munching other sugary titbits when you're driving. Not only is fruit high in vitamins, but it also makes you feel full and satisfied much longer. It's also a natural thirst quencher, helping to fight the urge to feed coins into the soft drinks machine.

And, yes, we can't forget those with a six-pack-a-day habit – six-pack of soft drinks, that is. What's a poor addict to do? The answer's simple: Give it up altogether. And it really is simple to do. 'Switch to fruit juices – only the unsweetened varieties,' says Dr Wunderlich. 'Before long, you'll wonder how you could stand drinking all those sweet drinks all day long.' And if it's the feeling of the bubbly carbonation sliding down your throat that you really long for, switch to soda or mineral water with a wedge of lemon or lime.

13 The final reward This one's optional, and you can try it only if you've given the other 12 your best. Take a day every month or so and have a sugar splurge. 'Total deprivation just doesn't work,' says Dr McDaniels, 'You have to be good to yourself. A day of overdosing on sugar isn't harmful, if your problem is a psychological one. For the hypoglycaemic person, it's a different story. But I've found it's fun and a nice reward for living a healthy life to set aside a day on a rare occasion to have a sugar-loading or junk-food day.'

A diet you can live with

Julian Whitaker, director of the National Heart and Diabetes Treatment Institute in Huntington Beach, California, believes that true weight control begins with a lifelong commitment to sensible eating. 'Weight control, like good nutrition, should become an everyday responsibility for the rest of your life,' says Dr Whitaker.

'That means you'll need a diet that you can live with, day in and day out, so it should be appetizing and nutritionally sound. Of course, that eliminates most fad diets right off the bat. The grapefruit diet, the apple, egg and wine diet, the ice cream and bananas diet, and the drinking man's diet can be classified under one common heading: Baloney.

'But those qualifications also eliminate the all-too-popular high-protein, low-carbohydrate diet. This diet is not only less palatable to most people than a well-balanced diet but also presents significant health risks as well.'

The truth about the high-protein, low-carbohydrate diet

'Even in normal people, carbohydrate restriction induces an impairment of glucose tolerance, the body's ability to maintain glucose [blood sugar] at a healthy level,' says Dr Whitaker. 'This phenomenon is called 'dietary diabetes' and is the result of a 40 to 50 per cent decline in insulin, the hormone that regulates blood sugar. Also, the high fat intake of these programmes makes the insulin that is produced by the body insensitive. The fat seems to clog up the works, as far as carbohydrate metabolism is concerned. The combination of these two conditions will almost always create a severe diabetes-like response to glucose tolerance test [a medical test that measures whether glucose levels are stable], much to the shock and concern of both doctor and patient.

'A high protein intake, especially from foods that are high in phosphorus, such as meat and eggs, increases calcium losses in the urine. Secondly, the excess nitrogen and sulphur in the blood from a high-protein diet create an acid condition that literally leaches the calcium out of the bone. The combined effect is a large negative calcium balance [the body loses more calcium than it takes in], so taking calcium supplements may not help when you're eating too much protein. Osteoporosis, the gradual deterioration of the bones, is so common that we consider it normal. Interestingly, severe calcium deficiencies and osteoporosis are rare in countries where the diet is *low* in protein – even when calcium intake is low by our standards.'

'High-protein diets are generally high-fat diets as well, which elevate the cholesterol and fats in the blood. These are the major contributors to the process of atherosclerosis, which is the cause of heart disease, as well as breast cancer, cancer of the colon and other degenerative diseases.

'For these and other reasons, a high-protein, low-carbohydrate diet is dangerous to your health. But people seem to lose weight, don't they? Well, let's examine why, as well as other claims of this faulty nutrition.'

Faster weight loss 'You do experience a rapid "weight loss" on a high-protein diet, but initially you lose water, not fat. Protein uses seven times as much water for its metabolism as carbohydrates use. The weight loss is simply dehydration. Another reason for the dehydration is the rapid depletion of the body's glycogen stores [glycogen is carbohydrate stored in the liver and muscles and used for muscular activity]. When the diet is deficient in carbohydrates, glycogen is rapidly depleted over a 24- to 48-hour period, and it releases twice its weight in water, which is also lost by the body. I've seen people shrivel up like prunes on high-protein diets, only to swell again when they come off the diet. In the meantime, the lack of glycogen markedly reduces their muscular endurance, since glycogen is the primary fuel for muscles.

'Then there's the popular notion that weight loss is accelerated by urinary excretion of calorie-bearing ketones [products of incomplete fat and protein metabolism] during severe carbohydrate restriction. Ketones rise in people who are starving and in diabetic patients who are out of control. Studies show that only a handful of calories are lost through ketones, and their presence in the urine indicates danger and severe stress in the body. Incredibly, several authors of fad protein diets even encourage their readers to spill ketones!'

Protein sparing 'The offspring of the high-protein, low-carbohydrate diet is the protein-sparing modified fast. The theory is that small amounts of protein on a low-calorie diet will spare the body's protein during weight loss. That is a treacherous programme, which for many people proved fatal. Autopsies on young women who died as a result of the protein-sparing fast showed degeneration of heart, liver and other tissues consistent with starvation. [*New England Journal of Medicine*]. The protein-sparing modified fast has no place whatsoever in weight control. Even under a doctor's care, deaths have occurred, and you must wonder about the irreparable damage that has been done to those who did not die on the protein-sparing modified fast. Avoid this programme like the plague – it's worse.

'Dietary protein alone will not maintain the protein tissues of your body. As it turns out, without carbohydrates, the body cannot use the proteins that are ingested. In other words, it is carbohydrates that spare protein and increase protein utilization, not low quantities of protein.'

Improved satiety That is one claim of the protein fad that has some truth. Dieters often report feeling less hungry on a high-protein diet than on other weight-control diets. However, the high-protein diet is not unique in this respect. In my experience with a moderate-protein, very high complex-carbohydrate diet, patients continually protest that they can't eat all the food, yet they continue to lose weight at the same time.

'Since protein is not the good guy and fat should always be avoided, then weight control must be contained with complex carbohydrates or starches.

'For years, the hue and cry was that complex carbohydrates were fattening. Not true. It is the potatoes, rice and bread that are the solutions to obesity, not the cause of it.

'Look, for instance, at Japan, a modern, industrialized nation where obesity is rare. Their diet consists primarily of white rice, vegetables and fish. Intake of fat, protein and refined sugars is below ours, with complex carbohydrates filling the calorie void. The high complex-carbohydrate diet keeps them not only thin, but also healthy. The Japanese outlive us by several years. In fact, the longest-lived peoples of the world eat a diet consisting mostly of complex-carbohydrate foods, with about one-third the fat and one-half the protein of the American diet.'

A professor's 'caveman diet'

'This diet plan,' continues Dr Whitaker, 'is simply our natural diet, what we evolved on. Vaughn Bryant, head of the department of anthropology at Texas A & M University, discovered the caveman's diet – primarily fruits and vegetables (with a few assorted snakes and grasshoppers) – very low in fat and high in carbohydrates and fibre. At the age of 39, and 30 lb overweight, Dr Bryant went on a modified caveman diet by eliminating eggs, butter, oil and simple sugars, and by eating whole-grain pitta bread, fruit, potatoes, rice, lean meat and fish. He lost 30 lb, kept it off, and noted a marked increase in his energy and well-being.'

'It all started about five years ago,' says Dr Bryant. 'Like many people who spend a lot of time behind a desk, I was going to pot. I'm 5 foot 10 inches, and I was over 14 stone. When I went to the beach I would wear a T-shirt to hide my belly. I frantically tried a whole series of diets, but nothing seemed to work. I would drop down to 189 and go back up to 196.

'That summer, my students and I spent a good deal of time doing field work at an archaeological dig in southwest Texas, near the Mexican border. The foods the prehistoric people ate – the cactus, the agave, the wild onions, nuts and berries – are still abundant in the area, and we decided to try living the way they did. We put ourselves on the caveman diet.

'This wasn't for health or weight loss or anything like that. It was just an experiment, something to report in a scientific publication. We just wanted to see if we could survive on this kind of diet – and we did, very nicely.

'In fact, with the combination of this diet and a lot of exercise, (we were walking eight or ten miles a day), I lost nearly 10 lb in several weeks. I was still overweight, though, and as soon as I was back behind my desk, I started thinking about how I'd better go back on the caveman diet – permanently.'

Instead of foraging in the wilds, Dr Bryant started foraging his way through the supermarket. Just like a prehistoric man, he had to learn how to pick out the wholesome foods from all the overprocessed things.

'First, I started reading labels – and that was a revelation! Canned sweet corn or peas, for example, who would expect the third ingredient to be sugar? I started switching to fresh fruits and vegetables. I got away from canned stuff, from processed foods, with their preservatives, additives and oils, from fats like margarine and butter. I cut back on cheese and milk and just wiped eggs out of my diet. Instead of white bread, I got into pitta bread and whole-wheat crackers.

'At the same time, I started taking all the nutritional information I'd been gathering for my caveman studies and applied it to my own diet. Modern science and primitive practice fit together, I found. I substituted fish, poultry and lean meats for fatty meat because of my nutritional readings *and* because this was how the caveman ate (the wild creatures he caught were sure to be very, very lean). The caveman ate vegetables raw or steamed (not boiled), and modern nutritionists agree that this preserves more of the nutrients. So I began to eat my vegetables raw or steamed.

'I also started to change the *way* I eat. Instead of having three big meals a day, I went to snacking. To judge by primitive people like African bushmen and Australian aborigines, humans were originally snackers. The caveman foraged for food throughout the day. He just ate as he went along.'

Carrots for breakfast

'So that's what I started to do,' says Dr Bryant. 'Now I'll get up and have some oatmeal or a piece of fresh fruit or a couple of carrots. Carrots for breakfast? My kids thought I was crazy. When you think about it, though, there's nothing more odd about having carrots in the morning than a big breakfast of bacon, eggs and two cups of coffee.

'I won't have a regular dinner in the evening, either. We're pretty active in my family – kids coming and going all the time – so we rarely have organized meals. Instead, we forage. My wife will broil half a dozen chicken breasts and leave them to stay warm in the oven. Or there might be a stew or homemade soup left on the stove to simmer.

'One thing I do that the caveman didn't is take supplements – some vitamin C, some bone meal or dolomite and a multi-vitamin. Since I don't eat the exact foods that the caveman ate, I can't be sure I'm getting all the nutrients he did. My fruits and vegetables don't come from the wild; even the 'fresh' produce I get at the supermarket has been sitting around losing vitamins. So the supplements are to make sure I'm getting everthing I need.

'I switched my diet rather quickly – over the course of a week or two. Actually, the whole idea excited me. And after a couple of weeks, I added more exercise to my routine. I started riding my bike to work, climbing stairs instead of taking the lift, walking across the campus instead of driving.

'My original motivation was weight loss. And in three months or so, the weight just disappeared: I lost 30 lb. I did this without counting calories and without having to go hungry; it was effortless, really. Those fruits and vegetables are so low in calories that I knew I could eat all I wanted. I think snacking helped, too. It seems when you snack all day, you eat less than if you sit down and gorge yourself at three meals.

'I've been 'eating like a caveman' ever since. For one thing, the hard part is over – learning what to eat, re-educating my taste buds so they'll say that a banana is good for breakfast, instead of bacon and eggs, or that a Jerusalem artichoke is better than a bar of chocolate.'

The naturally thinning foods

Dr Whitaker is enthusiastic about Dr Bryant's caveman diet: 'You see, complex carbohydrates are *naturally* thinning foods. For one thing, they provide large amounts of fibre or bulk, which keeps the stomach pleasantly full and also carries out small amounts of fat and calories via the intestines. Fibre also spreads out the release of the food energy, which prevents large fluctuations in the blood-sugar level and perhaps weight gain. Refined carbohydrates [which are stripped down carbohydrates such as white rice, white sugar and instant potatoes] have a distinctly negative effect on the blood-sugar pattern and should be avoided.

'The complex-carbohydrate foods have fewer calories than the high-fat foods: 1 g of carbohydrate has 4 calories; 1 g of fat has 9 calories. For instance, a large baked potato has 145 calories, while the same baked potato with one tablespoon of soured cream and butter has 272 calories. A pound of apples has only 163 calories, while a pound of Gruyère cheese has 1610 calories. You can easily see how munching on greasy, high-fat snacks during the late film on TV brings on the bulges.

'A diet which emphasizes the complex carbohydrates will not only help you lose weight, but also offers numerous other benefits. It lowers serum cholesterol, eliminates constipation, improves diabetes and protects against colon cancer. It's the perfect weight-loss plan, as it is nutritionally sound, appetizing and healthy. A high complex-carbohydrate diet may take a little

A low-calorie diet you can live with.

Here's a week's worth of sample menus from Dr Whitaker's diet plan.

MONDAY

Breakfast: Oatmeal cooked with ripe banana for sweetener. Non-fat milk. High-fibre, low-fat, whole-grain toast. Herbal tea.

Lunch: Diversified salad – bean sprouts, tomatoes, parsley (loaded with vitamins and minerals), lettuce, cabbage, carrots, garbanzo beans (loaded with protein), etc. Avoid avocado pears. Use lemon, vinaigrette dressing or any salad dressing made without oil.

Dinner: *Mama Mia* – whole-grain spaghetti or noodles (without egg), marinara sauce made with tomatoes, tomato paste (a few brands have no salt!), onion, garlic, mushrooms (adds both flavour and texture), green peppers, spices; simmer for one hour without oil. Diversified salad. Fresh fruit dessert.

TUESDAY

Breakfast: Buckwheat pancakes (use egg whites only for eggs in batter, no butter or margarine); coat skillet lightly with liquid lecithin. Unsweetened fruit spread for topping. Herbal tea.

Lunch: Lentil soup (fresh lentils, soaked and cooked with onions, carrots, herbs and seasonings to taste – no salt or oil). Use a thermos to carry to work. Diversified salad.

Dinner: *The Bellweather* – cooked green peppers stuffed with steamed brown rice, tomatoes, fresh sweet corn, pimento; season with hot spices or a little stone-ground fresh mustard. Diversified salad. Fresh raw fruit dessert.

WEDNESDAY

Breakfast: Seven-grain hot cereal cooked with banana, apricot or small amount of raisins for sweetener. Non-fat milk. Herbal tea.

Lunch: *Pitta Surprise* – whole-grain pitta bread, stuffed with bean sprouts, onions, tomatoes, parsley, cucumbers, seasoned with mustard. (A little mustard goes a long way!).

Dinner: Baked yams. Steamed vegetables (corn on the cob and fresh green beans). Steamed brown rice (no salt or oil) seasoned with herbs and spices. Salad. Fresh fruit dessert.

THURSDAY

Breakfast: Belgian waffles – 3 oz whole-wheat flour, 8 fl oz skimmed milk, 3 beaten egg whites (no yolks). Top with unsweetened apple, apricot or strawberry spread. Herbal tea.

Lunch: Vegetable soup (soup vegetables simmered with spices and herbs, no salt or oil). Salad with lemon, vinaigrette dressing or any salad dressing made without oil.

Dinner: *Irish Uprising* – whole baked potato topped with home-made non-fat yogurt and chives. For this meal, the potato moves to main course. Sweet corn. Fresh salad. Fresh fruit dessert.

FRIDAY

Breakfast: Puffed wheat or rice cereal with no preservatives. Fresh strawberries. Non-fat milk. Herbal tea.

Lunch: *Garbanzo Inroad* – cooked garbanzo beans (kidney beans are a good substitute) with onions and green peppers, mashed until smooth and stuffed into pitta bread with lettuce and tomato.

Dinner: *Chinese Revelation* – steamed brown rice with Chinese vegetables (beans, bean sprouts, water chestnuts), seasoned with tamari sauce diluted half and half with water. (Use very sparingly! This is your highest intake of salt, so easy does it.) Fresh salad. Fresh fruit dessert.

SATURDAY

Breakfast: $1/2$ yellow melon. Cracked whole-wheat hot cereal cooked with banana. Non-fat milk. Herbal tea.

Lunch: Home-made tomato soup (any cookbook recipe will do, only no oil or salt), seasoned with herbs and spices. Salad and matzo bread.

Dinner: *Steamed Garden Diversified* – steamed vegetables (carrots, sweet corn, cucumbers, green peppers and mushrooms), seasoned with herbs and spices. Pitta bread. Fresh fruit dessert.

SUNDAY

Breakfast: Scotch oat cereal, cooked with banana for sweetener. Skimmed milk. Small dish of unsweetened apple-sauce. Herbal tea.

Lunch: Black bean soup (use any recipe and eliminate oil and salt; season with lemon juice). Glass of tomato juice.

Dinner: *Sunday Down South* (my favourite meal) – succotash (broad beans and fresh sweet corn cooked with onions and spices). Black-eyed peas flavoured with onion. Salad. Pitta bread. Fresh fruit dessert. (The combination of sweet corn and beans has a protein efficiency score equal to egg whites!).

getting used to, because the grease- and sugar-crazy food industry has left a real void in the area of nutritious, easily prepared carbohydrate foods. But once you've mastered the art of healthy eating, you can say good-bye to a lot of your health problems, most particularly obesity.'

The best foods for safe, effective, weight loss

As a general rule, natural, unprocessed foods are not only less fattening but also more nutritious than processed foods. On the other hand, when humans start tampering with a food, they tend to do four things: remove fibre, remove nutrients, add fats and add sweeteners. The result? You get fewer and fewer nutrients for each calorie you consume.

What foods do the opposite, keeping you healthy while they keep you trim?

Soup Adding soup to your diet can lower your calorie intake, according to a study conducted by a team of researchers including Jack Smith, director of medical nutrition education at the University of Nebraska Medical Center and the Swanson Center for Nutrition. They analysed the dietary records of 28,000 individuals and found that those who ate soup consumed roughly 5 per cent fewer calories than those who didn't. 'And that counts for all age groups,' Dr Smith says.

He sees several reasons why soup can be beneficial as a reducing aid. 'One thing is that soup contains a lot of water, so it's not calorically dense. Also, soup is generally made out of vegetables, so there are not many calories there, either. It's hot, so you eat it more slowly, making it easier to stretch the meal out to 20 minutes.'

Broccoli When it comes to nutrients per calorie, you can't do much better than broccoli, (preferably quickly steamed, so it's crisp and bright green): 4 oz, containing 40 calories, brings a hefty 3880 IU of vitamin A, plenty of vitamin C and B vitamins, as well as calcium and iron.

Pasta Surprised? Well, you get a good nutritional bonus for every calorie in pasta served with meatballs, tomato sauce and Parmesan cheese. While 8 oz (cooked) contains 332 calories, it also contains 19 g of protein, 124 ml of calcium, plus iron, vitamins A and C, and B vitamins. Be sure to eat the whole-wheat variety for extra fibre.

Kale Here's another vegetable that's super-nutritious and very low in calories. Along with extraordinary amounts of vitamins A and C, kale contains a load of calcium, which is more available to the body than the calcium in spinach – with only 43 calories per 10 oz cooked.

Beef liver Liver is quite simply one of the most nutritious foods you can eat. It's especially good for chronic dieters short on B vitamins and iron, because it's loaded with both. Six ounces of cooked liver packs about 390 calories, but you get 45 gs of protein for that (you need roughly 50 to 60 g daily), plus outstanding amounts of vitamins A and C, and trace minerals.

Lentils Like all pulses (peas, beans, etc), lentils are a good source of protein, iron, B vitamins and fibre. By eating them with grain products, you can increase their protein value. 8 fl. oz of cooked lentils contains 212 calories, or roughly the equivalent of 10 chips – but they pack a nutritional wallop.

Tofu Made of soyabean curd, tofu is an excellent non-meat source of protein and also happens to be stingy on calories. One piece roughly $2^{1}/_{2}$ inches square yields only 86 calories, along with 9.4 of protein and good amounts of calcium and iron.

Chilli con carne For the caloric equivalent of two doughnuts (approximately 340 calories), 8 fl oz of chilli (kidney beans, tomatoes, onions and rice) gives you 19 g of protein, plus calcium, iron, vitamin A and B vitamins. That's a pretty good payoff for something you may still think of as 'junk food.'

Plain Yogurt Eight fluid ounces of plain yogurt has about 139 calories. Flavoured yogurt, due to added sugar, may have up to 280 calories. Yogurt is rich in calcium and riboflavin, with almost a gram of protein to the ounce. Try adding fresh fruit or wheat germ instead of honey.

Hard-boiled eggs An egg is one of the few foods that can be boiled without losing nutrients. Protein costs only about 13 calories per gram, compared with 16.1 for Cheddar cheese, 18.5 for milk and 31.6 for white bread. Eggs are also good sources of vitamins A and B_6 and nicotinic acid (niacin).

Brewer's Yeast Brewer's yeast is a high-powered food of special interest to the weight conscious because it contains chromium, which improves metabolism of sugar, tends to lower high levels of insulin (common in heavy people) and may also decrease appetite. It's loaded with other good things, too: for the 23 calories in a tablespoon, you get a good dose of B vitamins, plus iron, calcium and some protein.

Green and red peppers Calorie for calorie, one of the most nutritious of all foods. Rich in vitamins A and C, a large green pepper contains only 36 calories. The vitamin A value of red peppers is much higher, while calories increase by only 15.

Sunflower seeds If you reach for a handful of raw, unsalted sunflower seeds instead of a sweet or salty snack, you'll be filling up with calcium, iron, potassium, the B vitamins, vitamin E and linoleic acid (an essential fatty acid).

But watch out – like many other highly concentrated natural foods such as nuts and dried fruit, sunflower seeds pack a caloric punch: 406 calories in 8 fl oz. Try not to eat them directly out of the box or bag, because they're working for your waistline only if you partake in moderation.

Potatoes Potatoes are practically fat-free and are a good source of vitamins, minerals and (when the skin is eaten) fibre. It's the butter and soured cream that lead you astray. One large jacket potato contains 145 calories, plus plenty of B vitamins and potassium.

Chicken Chicken (minus its fatty skin) is as economical a source of protein as very lean steak: about six calories per gram. Dark meat furnishes about 18 per cent more calories than white, but however you fix it, chicken makes for good nutrition at a low caloric cost. It is high in B vitamins, iron and calcium.

Aubergine In terms of caloric cost, this is another inexpensive vegetable. A diced 8 fl oz costs you only 38 calories but provides 2 g of protein, plus calcium and other nutrients.

Remember, foods that provide the greatest nutrient density per calorie – not simply the fewest calories – are the best ones for safe, healthy and permanent weight loss.

The importance of exercise

Diets, in the words of Dr Gabe Mirkin, are 'anti-nature'. 'Studies have shown that the success rate of anyone going on a diet and keeping the weight off one year later is 1 in 10. After five years, it's 1 in 20,' says the author of *Getting Thin* (1983).

When it comes to dieting, the body's defences often outweigh the mind's determination. 'When caloric intake is reduced, the body does everything in its power to conserve energy,' Dr Mirkin says.

He explains that the body has an adaptive hormone called *reverse T_3* which goes into action when calories are reduced. 'This hormone slows down the metabolism. An average 150 lb [10 stone 10] person burns about 70 calories an hour while sleeping. When he's dieting, it's reduced to about 40 calories an hour, and the process is slowed down all day long. It's the body's defence against starvation.'

Second, there's the notion that just looking at food can make some people gain weight. That may sound ludicrous, but it's closer to the truth than you may think.

This was demonstrated by Dr Rodin, who measured the reactions in a group of former fat people to a thick, juicy steak sizzling on a grill in front of them. It was to be their reward after an 18-hour fast. Dr Rodin took blood samples as they watched the steak cooking.

'Those who were highly responsive to the steak cooking before them also had high levels of insulin release,' Dr Rodin says. 'Being turned on just by the sight of food set their metabolic process in motion. Insulin accelerates the intake of fat into the cells, so the more insulin that is secreted, the faster the fat will be stored.' In short, those who drooled over the steak turned more of it into fat than those who didn't.

'We think 60 to 70 per cent of the people who are moderately overweight are like this,' says Dr Rodin.

Ever wonder why you keep returning to your original weight, time and time again, no matter how you struggle? That's where another diet blocker comes in. It's known as the 'set-point theory'.

The body has a control system – sort of an inner thermostat for body fat – that seeks a constant set amount of fat in the body. It's the weight you're unthinkingly drawn to, give or take a few pounds, say Dr William Bennett and Joel Gurin in their book *The Dieter's Dilemma* (1982).

Now you'll be better able to understand why exercise is so important. Just a moderate amount of exercise can help speed up your metabolism, lower your set-point and even reduce your craving for food. As little as a 30-minute walk is good for 100 to 150 calories. Walk twice a day and you'll be well on your way to the 500-calorie-a-day mark. Routine exercise can boost a dieter's sluggish 40-calorie-an-hour metabolic rate to 70 or 80 calories an hour, says Dr Mirkin. 'Just a half an hour a day will keep you burning calories at a faster rate all day long.

'Many people are discouraged from exercising when they find out that in order to lose a single pound they must run 4 hours, ice-skate 9 hours, play volleyball 10 hours, or walk 17 hours,' he says. 'But you don't need to do all that exercise at one time. If you spread those hours over a week or two, you'll have lost a substantial amount of weight by the end of the year.'

The exercise doesn't have to be brutal, either. This was proved several years back by a group of obese women in California who lost an average of 22 lb each in one year simply by adding a walk to their daily routine. All 11 women in the experiment were chronic dieters who were never successful at keeping off any of the weight they had lost on repeated calorie-cutting regimens. This time there were no dietary restrictions, but a daily walk was a must. Weight loss didn't start until walks routinely exceeded 30 minutes a day. When weight stabilized, walking time was increased and weight loss resumed.

The importance of walking was demonstrated even more clearly by two women in the group who started to regain weight after they became ill and stopped exercising. Once walking resumed, weight loss started all over again *(Archives of Internal Medicine)*.

You may be worrying that exercise will make you want to eat more. Not so, say the experts. Scientists found this out by counting the calories eaten by a group of obese women who were allowed to eat all they wanted during a two-month experiment. Each underwent three 19-day treatments – one sedentary period, a period of mild daily treadmill exercise and a period of moderate treadmill exercise. Although they gradually became more active, their caloric intake did not increase *(American Journal of Clinical Nutrition,* September 1982).

Climbing up to slim down

People who want to lose weight will find that stair climbing is a potent way to peel off a few pounds without really setting aside time for exercise. If you walked up and down a mere two flights of stairs a day instead of taking lifts or escalators, you would lose an additional 6 lb or more over the course of a year, according to Kelly D Brownell, a University of Pennsylvania psychologist who helps people lose weight.

The number of calories that you expend climbing stairs varies, depending on how much you weigh, how fast you climb and if you're carrying a load. But Lenore Zohman, director of cardiac rehabilitation at Montefiore Hospital and Medical Center in New York City, estimates that a 100 lb [7 stone 2] woman climbing stairs at a comfortable pace would spend about five calories a minute, and a 175 lb [$12^1/_2$ stone] man would spend about eight calories a minute. Those figures would roughly double if you took two steps at a time.

Compared to other forms of exercise, stair climbing, minute for minute, stacks up pretty well. 'Using stairs produces a surprisingly large expenditure of energy,' says Dr Brownell, 'even larger than that for such strenuous activities as jogging, swimming, cycling and calisthenics' *(American Journal of Psychiatry,* December 1980).

A study conducted in Finland agreed that regular stair climbing can help you lose weight. Tests conducted by an insurance company there showed that men who climbed about 25 flights of stairs during the course of a day lost a 'significant' amount of weight after only 12 weeks. And climbing those stairs took surprisingly little time. The average, comfortable climbing rate of those men – who were between the ages of 17 and 64 – was 100 steps a minute. At that speed, climbing a flight of stairs (at 10 steps to a flight) would take only six seconds.

One word of caution: Even normal stair climbing can be surprisingly taxing, and fitness experts advise working up to it slowly. If you work on the fifth floor of an office building, for instance, you might start by taking the lift to the fourth floor and walking up the last flight. Do that for a week, then walk up from the third floor, and so on. Of course, if you have a large number of steps to ascend, you may wish to walk around on one level for a while between flights.

Gardening for a slender body

In the days when our ancestors lived in caves and talked with grunts and sign language, tracking down enough calories to keep the body's furnace stoked was, at most times of the year, more than a full-time job. As we have seen from Dr Bryant's research, roots and wild vegetables were the staples of their diet, with an occasional rabbit or fish or grasshopper thrown in. At certain times of the year, richer fare appeared: fruit, berries, nuts, seeds and eggs. Mother Nature gave people the instinct to gorge themselves silly at such times, to hoard calories in the fat 'silos' of the body for the hungry times ahead.

But Mother Nature had no way of foreseeing this age of supermarket shelves and kitchen cupboards brimming seductively with all manner of sweets, biscuits, cakes, crisps and a host of other calorie-packed concoctions. So we're still left with the instinct to eat as much as we can of whatever's available.

The solution is to get back to the garden (if you have one) – not to grow more food so we can stay fat, but to turn our instincts back towards the natural order of things. If fighting fat is to be a lifelong endeavour, we'd better listen to what Mother Nature has to say: *We were meant to use our muscles to hunt, dig up, gather or otherwise produce the food for our own mouths.* In nature, the rule is that, if you live a fat life, you'll have a fat body.

The wisdom of gardening for a slender body is greater than it may seem. To begin with, an aggressive session with the fork or spade can serve as a healthy outlet for the boredom, anger and frustration that commonly lead to over-eating and drinking. Your garden will love you when you whack it with a spade.

Looking at things in a more positive light, doing manual labour to produce something as basic as your own food imparts a sense of inner strength, tranquillity and pride that's very helpful when you're trying to lose weight. And it's obvious that the food you produce in your garden is bound to be far less fattening and far more healthy than typical supermarket or restaurant fare. You can't grow fruit-flavoured Polos on trees, or crisps in even the most fertile earth.

If you were to slap a cheeseburger between two slices of bread, garnish it with tomato sauce and wash it down with a fruit-flavoured soft drink, you'd be adding about 670 calories to your personal 'silo'. But if you were to take a walk in your garden, instead, and harvest two stalks of celery, two tomatoes, two carrots, five radishes, a head of lettuce, half a dozen spring onions and a large green pepper, you'd have a salad that two people would have a hard time finishing. Yet the total number of calories for each person would be only 140!

Here's how some other garden favourites compare with . . . well, with foods that come from some place else: 8 oz of cabbage (cooked) will provide only about 30 calories; 9 oz of aubergine, 38; $7^1/_2$ oz of broccoli, 40. On the other hand, 1 oz of corn flakes provides 97 calories before you pour on milk; two medium-size digestive biscuits provide 55; a hot dog before the bun, 150; a 16 fl oz serving of spaghetti with meat sauce, 516; a slice of chocolate cake with fudge icing, 420; a doughnut, 135; a piece of cherry pie, 340. It's easy to see how the more you eat out of your garden, the less room you're going to have for those foods that put on the pounds.

Of course, don't be garden-wise and kitchen-foolish. Remember, there's probably nothing you can do to the food you take out of your garden to make it more healthy and less fattening than it is at the moment you pick it. Preferably, you should pick it, wash it and eat it – as soon as possible. If and when you cook it, don't add too many calories by using oil and dressing so that the food loses whatever value it may have had for your weight-loss programme.

Steamed aubergine does everything fried aubergine does – except take along with it hundreds of calories of oil into your system.

To reap all the weight-control benefits of gardening, you must think of your garden as a spa. Go there with the intention of getting some huff-and-puff exercise, working up a little sweat, calling upon resources of strength, burning up some calories. Since many gardening activities, as commonly performed, are less strenuous than a brisk walk around the neighbourhood, you'll have to speed up the action a little. After allowing yourself a few minutes to 'warm up the engine', keep up a good head of steam for at least 15 minutes without interruption, then 'cool down' by tapering off slowly to a walk round the flower bed or a swing in the hammock. Never push yourself to the point of being out of breath. If you can't whistle while you work, like Snow White's seven dwarfs, you may be overtaxing your heart and lungs.

How many calories will you burn up for your efforts? That depends not only on what you're doing and how fast you're doing it, but on how big you are. So we can't tell you exactly how many calories, but here are some guidelines. A 170-pounder (12 stone 2) working at an average pace will burn about 240 calories just puttering around the garden pruning, clipping, watering the plants; 400 calories at activities like hoeing, planting and weeding; and 500 calories at digging or sawing and chopping wood. Figuring that you'll expend an average of about 400 calories per day in your garden, that will amount to a weight loss of about 1 lb a week, or close to 15 lb between June and September. And remember: That's just one way exercise helps you lose weight.

Obviously, the idea here is not to be super-efficient with your body's energy stores. If you can bring yourself to waste a little of that energy, the results will show a lot faster in the mirror. So use your spade, fork and wheelbarrow, and above all your muscles. Spread your garden out, and maybe even dig up more ground than you'll use. The weeds will crop up bountifully, supplying you with quite a few calorie-burning, emotionally therapeutic sessions of yanking them out or whacking them with your spade. Hide your hose and get out the old watering can: you'll save water and get more exercise. And instead of bombing your vegetables with pesticides, plant marigolds, nasturtiums, garlic or onions among them: their odours help keep the bugs away. The defiant bug invaders can be eliminated by the time-honoured method of hand-plucking, best done at the crack of dawn. (Don't forget to check the *undersides* of leaves.) These suggestions may seem terribly impractical, but think of all the people who get their exercise jogging in endless circles in the park.

When you get back in, just don't undo all your good work in 30 seconds with a beer or soft drink. To quench that thirst, rather than down 300 liquid calories when all you really want is water, *simply drink some good, pure water*.

Then take a nice, long bath – you deserve it. And when you climb out, take a long look at that tough, tan, leaner body of yours in the mirror. Mother Nature would be so proud.

Q & A on health and weight

We asked weight-loss experts and consulted the medical literature to answer some tough questions pertaining to weight loss and being overweight.

Q. Is fasting a good way to lose weight?
A. Fasting is sometimes used under a doctor's care for the treatment of massive obesity – a dangerous condition that can lead to diabetes or heart attack.

During a modified fast, a patient may eat nothing each day but a protein and carbohydrate supplement, a multi-vitamin tablet and a potassium supplement. In one such programme, more than 500 patients were placed on a modified fast for about 30 weeks, and 78 per cent of them lost more than 40 lb.

Some people go on one-day fasts, making certain that they drink at least 3 pints of water during the day. Others simply substitute fresh fruit and vegetable juices for solid food. They feel that fasting for a day gives the body the opportunity to detoxify itself – to rid itself of the pollutants that it has unavoidably accumulated from food, tap water and even air.

Other claims made for fasting are that it may help you live longer, help you heal yourself faster when you're sick, help relieve your arthritis and make you more alert.

However, fasting is not just a bowl of cherries. It can be dangerous for people with such medical conditions as diabetes, kidney or heart disease. Children shouldn't fast, nor should pregnant women. Fasting can also have unwelcome side-effects. Nausea, hair loss, dry skin, muscle cramps, fatigue, depression, bad breath, liver problems and loss of interest in sex are a few. Some researchers even think that, under certain circumstances, fasting can increase your risk of getting stomach cancer.

The point is that fasting is not something to be taken lightly. If you decide to try it, check with your doctor first.

Q. What is palsy? And what does it have to do with dieting?
A. According to doctors David G. Sherman and J. Donald Easton of the University of Missouri Medical Center, the casual – and seemingly harmless – practice of dieting can actually result in a type of nerve palsy, or numbness. But don't get too alarmed. The two neurologists say that simple dietary changes can completely alleviate the condition.

For a time, 'peroneal nerve palsy' was linked to sedentary persons who frequently crossed their legs, compressing the peroneal nerve, which runs along the outer side of the leg and controls the muscles of the foot. However, in an issue of the *Journal of the American Medical Association*, Drs Sherman and Easton cited seven examples of 'active and generally healthy' men and women from all walks of life who suffered foot-drop and numbness in one foot. None was prone to prolonged leg-crossing.

In fact, the only common thread that ran through the case histories was weight loss. Each patient reported having lost between 30 and 60 lb while on a weight-reduction diet prior to developing the symptoms of nerve palsy. Once they gave up their strict dietary regimen, the symptoms subsided.

The report didn't zero in on any one dietary factor that might cause this neurologic complication, but the doctors suggested that weight-reducing diets are probably deficient in those vitamins or other nutrients necessary for maintaining normal nerve function – and we know that when it comes to the health of the nervous system, the Bs have it. So, next time you cut out carbohydrates or reduce your regular intake of lean meat, protect your nerves with added doses of the B vitamins. Remember, there are relatively few calories in brewer's yeast or dessicated liver compared to the concentrated boost of B vitamins and other essential nutrients they deliver. So heap a teaspoon high with brewer's yeast and stir it in your morning orange juice. Or toss some in your green salad for lunch. Be liberal about it – it's common sense for healthy dieting.

Q. Is being overweight linked to infertility?

A. Extremes of body fat in women – either too much or too little – can lead to infertility. The direct evidence is loss of ovulation. If the egg is not released, pregnancy is obviously impossible.

The relationship between too little or too much body fat and infertility is supposed to be hormone related, but it isn't well understood. At any rate, normal body weight is a goal for those who wish to conceive.

Q. What exactly is the link between obesity and breast cancer?

A. Researchers have found that a diet high in fat makes a woman more susceptible to breast cancer. In other words, the fatter she is, the more likely she is to develop the disease. The fatty nature of breast tissues combined with circulating hormones makes the breasts more vulnerable to the harmful influence of cancer-causing substances (*carcinogens*) that enter and circulate throughout the body.

Fat-soluble carcinogens are easily stored and recycled not only by breast fat but by total body fat in general. Consequently, it's to a woman's advantage to reduce her fat intake and to keep her weight down.

Q. Is it possible that overweight people are accident-prone – or does it just seem that way?

A. 'Significantly overweight people – those who are more than 30 per cent above their ideal weight – have an increase in accident-proneness,' says Willard Krehl, professor emeritus of Jefferson Medical College in Philadelphia. And, Dr Krehl told us, 'The tendency toward accidents increases as the person gets heavier.'

Q. It seems that everyone is calorie conscious these days. But obesity is still a problem. Why?

A. In the United States, at least, people *are* consuming fewer calories, according to preliminary findings of a survey conducted by the US Department of Agriculture's Human Nutrition Center. But although their calorie intake is less, other studies indicate that Americans are getting fatter – possibly because the're leading more sedentary lifestyles.

Also, because of the decline in calorie intake, it is becoming more difficult for some people to consume the Recommended Dietary Allowance of certain nutrients, says D. Mark Hegsted, administrator of the centre. 'Indeed a "well-balanced diet" by most definitions may not meet the Recommended Dietary Allowance for several nutrients at certain calorie levels,' he says.

Dr Hegsted says there has been some public response to nutritionists' recommendations to reduce fat, sugar and salt in their diets, while increasing their consumption of fruits, vegetables and grain products. But he added that the increase in obesity, higher alcohol consumption and greater use of sweeteners were discouraging trends.

• Paget's disease

There is new hope today for victims of Paget's disease, a painful degeneration of the bones. Doctors don't know what causes Paget's disease, although it sometimes runs in families. Any bone in the body may be affected, but the most common sites are the long bones of the legs, the lower spine, the pelvis and the skull. In the early stages of the disease, calcium is removed from the bones, softening them. In later stages, the bones begin to grow again. But, somehow, the new growth is distorted. The bones remain soft and become abnormally thick.

Deep, dull, aching bone pain is one of the symptoms. If the deformity is in the skull, headache may occur. Deafness and blindness can also result if a deformed bone in the skull presses on a nerve. When leg bones are affected, the legs become bowed under the weight of the body.

Until a few years ago, there was no effective treatment for Paget's disease, although doctors tried several drugs and therapies. Then it was discovered that *calcitonin*, a hormone secreted by the thryoid gland, relieved pain when given by injection. Unfortunately, the treatment is extremely expensive, and the drug also produces nausea in many people and may be the cause of allergic reactions.

However, now a safe, effective, low-cost treatment for Paget's disease has been developed by an Australian physician. Dr R. A. Evans, of the Repatriation General Hospital in New South Wales has successfully used calcium supplements and a combination of medications designed to keep blood levels of calicum high in nine sufferers of Paget's disease.

Searching for an alternative to expensive, hazardous drug treatment, Dr Evans decided to try to raise the blood level of calcium in people with the disease. To do this, he gave them from 500 to 1000 mg of calcium three times a day between meals, an antacid tablet with meals to keep phosphorus from interfering with calcium absorption, and a drug to keep calcium from being excreted in the urine. The treatment went on for 200 days.

In Dr Evans's words,

> Bone pain subsided or was considerably reduced in eight of the nine patients after a period of 20 to 70 days . . . Two female patients who were invalids prior to commencing therapy were able to return to light household duties. There were no serious side-effects.

Dr Evans believes that the treatment works by stimulating the body's natural secretion of calcitonin, which the thyroid gland secretes when blood levels of calcium rise. Biochemical tests performed by Dr Evans confirmed that his patients were not merely experiencing a 'placebo response' to the treatment.

He went on to say that:

> The regimen described here costs approximately 2 per cent [of the usual drug treatment] and can be made still cheaper by the use of simpler forms of the drugs . . . In view of the extremely low cost of this drug combination and its lack of side-effects, it is suggested it be considered as a treatment of Paget's disease of bone. [*Australian and New Zealand Journal of Medicine*].

• Pain

Pain – dull pain, sharp pain, vague pain, acute pain, occasional pain, chronic pain. Even the healthiest of us experience pain once in a while.

What we're going to discuss here concerns natural ways of coping with the sort of pain that lasts some time – from a few days to years. That's the kind of pain that can really interfere with your life, making it hard to work, socialize, exercise, that can make you resort to drugs for relief. We'll tell you how therapists are using new and traditional techniques to relieve pain, and about ways to muster your own internal defences against pain.

Nutritional treatments for pain

If anyone tells you that eating 'toe of toad' and 'wart of hog' will cure your pain problems, and if you want to *believe* that – well, it's up to you. After all, people in pain are desperate. But you needn't resort to exotic substances, for relief may be a mere nutrient supplement away. Tryptophan (an amino acid) and magnesium have both been identified as pain relievers.

Tryptophan

A medical research team at the Temple University School of Dentistry in Philadelphia have reported a definite connection between the amino acid *tryptophan* and pain tolerance. People who received tryptophan supplements were able to tolerate greater amounts of pain than were people who received non-therapeutic placebos (*Pain* vol 11, no 2, 1981).

According to Samuel Seltzer, professor of dentistry and leader of the research team, subsequent studies have shown 'very significant' increases in pain tolerance thresholds in patients with chronic pain who are placed on 3 g daily tryptophan supplements. 'Most of these patients had suffered from dental, facial and headache pain for years,' Dr Seltzer says. 'They had made the rounds, but nobody was able to help them.'

Dr Seltzer reports a 75 per cent success rate when patients are given tryptophan for one month. 'If we break the cycle, the pain doesn't come back,' he notes. 'We don't know precisely why, but we are working on it.'

Tryptophan, which works by altering pain receptors in the brain, is best utilized when it doesn't have to compete with other amino acids (protein 'building blocks') for space in the brain. For that reason, patients are also advised to decrease their total protein consumption.

'In general, most people are overeating protein,' says Robert L. Pollack, chairman of the department of biochemistry and nutrition and director of the Nutrition Health Center at the school. He has been working with Dr Seltzer on the project. The US Recommended Dietary Allowance of protein is between 44 and 56 g per day, but Dr Pollack says that most people who eat protein at every meal are getting more than they need. 'We counsel people to adjust their protein consumption to the recommended 'normal' level, which they can get from a single 6 oz serving of chicken. 'We don't want anybody to eat less than the recommended amount,' he cautions. 'We just want to lower the competition between tryptophan and the other amino acids.'

Dr Pollack says good dietary sources of tryptophan include soyabeans, wheat germ and sesame seeds. Dr Seltzer also suggests avoiding sweet corn because it is high in the amino acid *leucine*, which is tryptophan's greatest competitor.

Magnesium

We've often heard that our bodies know what is best for us, and perhaps that is more true than ever in the case of magnesium. If we are low in magnesium and then take some, our bodies drink it in as a thirsty man lost in the desert would drink water. You'd almost think our bodies were trying to tell us that magnesium is all-important – and you'd be right.

'Magnesium is truly an essential element in human health and disease,' says Dr Bernard Horn. 'For 13 years, I have administered it to my patients – even my own daughter – with excellent results.' Before retiring, Dr Horn, a Fellow of the American College of Nutrition, was a physician and anaesthetist in California, and during his long career, he attended the operations of between 7000 and 8000 patients.

We asked Dr Horn if he had ever recommended magnesium for the relief of period pain. 'Certainly,' he said. 'My own daughter suffered from such severe cramping that she would have to go to bed for several days. Conventional painkillers didn't help her much. Then I put her on magnesium, and the result was amazing. Her cramps completely disappeared. 'Such treatment may not work for everyone, but it certainly worked splendidly for her. Magnesium also helps reduce water retention during menstruation, since it is a natural diuretic.'

How much magnesium would Dr Horn recommend a woman take for period pain? 'There are two ways of approaching it,' he says. 'You can either take 400 mg per day, every day, or you can take 600 to 800 mg per day beginning four to five days before the period.'

Other forms of pain and cramp seem to be associated with magnesium in ways we do not yet understand. For example, magnesium levels fall in people who have had serious heart attacks, and in a recent study of surgical patients and those with acute medical conditions, an interesting facet of magnesium was revealed.

The results of the study showed that in 32 of the acutely ill medical patients who did not have pain, magnesium levels were normal, but in 28 patients with 'pain as a major symptom', magnesium levels were well below normal. Similarly, in surgical patients undergoing elective surgery, magnesium levels were normal; however, in those undergoing emergency surgery where pain was involved, magnesium levels were 'significantly lower than normal' both before and after surgery. 'Our findings,' wrote the researchers,

> show a definite and acute fall in serum magnesium levels only when acute illness (be it medical or surgical) is associated with pain, with no correlation with the severity or type of illness . . . It does seem that the acute fall in serum magnesium in those widely differing situations may be due to the common denominator of pain. [*Biochemical Medicine*, August 1980].

In addition to magnesium supplements, there are many good food sources of magnesium. They include wholemeal bread, shrimps, bananas, black treacle, nuts, peas, and soyabeans.

The painkiller in your mind

John, a 52-year-old cardiologist, lived with constant, agonizing low-back pain following treatment for rectal cancer. The pain, he said, was 'unbearable' and had reduced his options to three: successful treatment, somewhere; voluntary commitment to a mental institution; or suicide. He could not go on living without relief. In desperation, he sought the help of a psychologist at the pain-control unit of a local hospital.

In reviewing John's records, the psychologist noticed that, during an earlier psychiatric workup, John had described his pain with terrible vividness: It was like 'a dog chewing on my spine,' he had said. Believing that this image was more than merely picturesque – that it was, in fact, a sort of nightmarish picture postcard from the source of his pain – the psychologist tried to convince John to make contact with the dog, to talk to it, to find out why it was chewing his spine and, somehow, to make it stop.

With his training in orthodox medicine, John at first considered the idea absurd, but his pain was so intense that he decided to give it a try. Over a series of sessions, the psychologist taught John to relax physically and mentally and to open his mind to the image of the dog. Then John started talking to it – and the dog talked back.

The dog said that John had never really wanted to be a doctor in the first place; he'd wanted to be an architect, but his mother had pressured him into medical school. As a result, his glowering resentment was directed at his mother, his colleagues and his patients. It was also directed inward, the dog said, and had contributed to the development of his cancer and his low-back pain, too.

The dog told John that he was a good doctor. 'It may not be the career you wanted, but it's time you recognized how good you are at what you do. When you stop being so resentful and start accepting yourself, I'll stop chewing on your spine.' These insights were accompanied by an immediate easing of pain, and during the following weeks, it slowly subsided.

The 'land of imagery'

This may sound like an unorthodox – not to say just plain nutty – approach to the problem of chronic pain. 'After all, what would be your initial reaction to a doctor who encouraged you to talk to little animals in your head?' asks David E. Bresler, director of the Breslor Center for Allied Therapeutics in Los Angeles, and author of *Free Yourself from Pain* (1979).

But Dr Bresler, who described in his book how he helped John by using pain-control imagery techniques, says the method is 'basically just a way of talking to ourselves, which is hardly a new concept.' Yet for the many who suffer from chronic pain – pain that persists after the solutions offered by orthodox medicine and psychiatry have been exhausted – it could provide blessed relief.

'The divorce rate among chronic-pain sufferers is horrendous,' says Neal H. Olshan, director of The Center, a pain-control unit at Mesa Lutheran Hospital in Arizona and author of *Power over Your Pain without Drugs* (1980). 'Typically, they've been on a kind of merry-go-round of drugs and surgery, seeing specialist after specialist, with only limited relief. In my experience, pain-control imagery is really the key.'

How does it work? By triggering the release of the body's natural painkillers. Called *endorphins* – literally, 'morphine within' – these complex substances affect the body very much like a narcotic. By 'talking' to our bodies, we can learn to control endorphin release, easing pain without the side-effects of powerful synthetic drugs. Dr Bresler explains that this inner dialogue also contacts the autonomic nervous system, which controls such involuntary functions as heart rate and digestion and plays a critical role in the relief of chronic pain.

Because the autonomic nervous system is linked to the unconscious part of our minds – the part that processes information in an abstract, symbolic way – the only language it understands is that of symbolism and imagery. We can reach parts of our bodies controlled by the conscious mind with verbal commands: 'Arm, reach for the sky!' or 'Tongue, stick out!' But to the unconscious mind, these commands are a foreign language. To talk to it, Dr Bresler says, we need a new language, though 'the land of imagery is largely neglected, and its language is often as unfamiliar as one spoken in a faraway country.'

For example, try telling your mouth to 'produce and secrete saliva' (an involuntary function). Any luck? Then try imagining – as clearly and vividly as possible – a fresh, juicy, yellow lemon . . . imagine the spray of bright, tart juice as you slice it open with a knife . . . then take a wet slice and slip it in your mouth, tasting its incredible sourness, its sharpness, its wetness. Did that work any better?

With practice and guidance, the power of this kind of mental image-making can often be harnessed to ease pain caused by everything from arthritis to angina. And in pain-control centres in the United States and Britain, the use of imagery techniques has become increasingly common.

Dr Olshan warns, however, that imagery's effectiveness could be dangerous if improperly used: 'Pain is the body's warning signal,' he told us. 'It wouldn't be appropriate to use these techniques for an undiagnosed pain, because they could mask the symptoms. You should see a doctor first.'

In essence, imagery techniques are a way of re-establishing contact between mind and body. How Western medicine ever got them separated in the first place is a long story, but what is now becoming abundantly clear is that they've had a marvellously complex and intimate affair going all along, like two lovers conversing with winks and signals across a crowded room. Each one, it's now known, has an astonishing degree of control over the other.

The so-called 'placebo effect' for example, has been described as 'one of the most remarkable of all medical phenomena', yet it's so common that it's a factor in every medical experiment. Give a group of people some utterly worthless treatment, such as a sugar pill or a saltwater injection, tell them it's powerful medicine, and a certain percentage of them (usually about one-third) will actually get better. What's important, apparently, is not the treatment itself but the persons belief that it will work – an image of healing that becomes real (that is, physical) through a mysterious transformation that we are only beginning to understand.

The mind's ability to trigger the body's self-cure, given the proper suggestion, is so powerful that, in some cases, it has been known to *reverse* the effects of strong drugs. In one case, a pregnant woman complaining of nausea was given ipecacuanha – one of the most widely used emetics (vomiting-inducing agents) known – and was told it would soothe her discomfort. Within minutes, her nausea disappeared! It's a phenomenon that led Dr Irving Oyle to declare in his book *The Healing Mind* (1979), 'Whatever you put your trust in can be the precipitating agent for your cure.'

Of course, most of us can't just 'take' the placebo effect any time we want, like a pill – if we could, there wouldn't be any doctors, drugs or hospitals. We'd just cure ourselves at will. But the power is still there, whether we know how to use it or not; refining the technique of calling it up when it's needed is what the new pain-control therapies are all about.

With new research into the actual mechanism behind the placebo effect, it now appears that endorphins play a key role. In one study at the University of California, 23 dental patients who had had teeth pulled a few hours earlier were injected with a placebo. Over one-third reported that their pain eased up as a result, but when they were injected with a second substance that blocks the action of endorphins, pain returned to all of them. Apparently, their belief that the placebo was working triggered the release of those natural painkillers, which really do provide 'fast, safe relief'.

Are pain-control imagery techniques really effective in doing the same thing? Dr C. Norman Shealy, founder of the Pain and Health Rehabilitation Center in Wisconsin, says that he has found relaxation and visualization techniques to be 'the single most important therapy which we can offer to chronically ill individuals with a wide variety of problems.'

Dr Bresler says drugs and surgery are often the least effective methods of dealing with chronic pain. And Dr Olshan reports that his rate of success – that is, the number of people who learn to reduce and control their pain to the point that they're able to resume a production lifestyle – is roughly 60 per cent, with many more achieving 'at least significant relief'. Do any of them relieve their pain completely? 'Those people are in the minority, although there are some who do,' he told us. 'But most people, by their own subjective rating, learn to reduce their pain by 60 to 80 per cent.'

A real 'pain in the neck'

Deep relaxation is the foundation of all the pain imagery techniques, Dr Olshan explains. The reason is that, when the mind and the body are relaxed, many physiological changes occur, including an increase in the body's ability to produce endorphins. 'You're putting your body in the best posture to work towards healing itself,' he says. 'I like to look at the body as a self-righting sailboat: if you just relax and leave it alone, it will right itself.'

Then, in a state of deep relaxation, the patient is guided through various exercises designed to focus relief on the source of the pain. All these exercises are actually a form of self-hypnosis, Dr Olshan explains – a way of putting the conscious mind 'to sleep' so that all messages will be funnelled to the subconscious mind and the involuntary nervous system.

Dr Bresler uses one exercise called 'glove anaesthesia', in which the patient is first taught to make his hand numb, then is told to transfer that numbness to the body part that's in pain. In another, patients are instructed to seek an 'inner adviser', usually an animal (like John's dog), who can provide advice on how to reduce stress and pain and also help the sufferer discover 'the message behind the pain'. Sometimes the message is one of repressed anger and frustration, as in John's case. Other times, the pain may have its source in an anxiety-producing lifestyle or an unpleasant relationship.

In fact, there may be people in your life who are quite literally 'a real pain in the neck', 'a constant headache' or just 'too much to stomach', according to René Cailliet, professor of rehabilitation medicine at the University of Southern California and author of nine textbooks on pain syndromes. Dr Cailliet told us that Americans may be spending billions of dollars and subjecting themselves to unnecessary surgery for chronic pain caused by relationships that hurt – and show up as low-back pain, migraines, peptic ulcers or even heart attacks.

'Most people aren't aware that the cause is emotional,' Dr Cailliet says. 'But with back pain now one of the most common of all patient complaints in the nation, back surgery isn't being done as often without a psychological evaluation first.'

Other times, Dr Olshan says, the 'message behind the pain' turns out to be a sort of 'pain payoff'. Whether consciously or not, some people discover that their pain has its rewards. Usually, it's one of two things: the attention they crave; or an excuse for avoiding something they don't want to do. Getting these people to face the real reason for their pain can sometimes be extremely difficult, Dr Cailliet says.

However, according to Dr Olshan, for those who are willing to 'take responsibility for their own health, instead of waiting for a doctor to do something to them, and who can make a lifetime commitment to controlling their pain, the gains can be tremendous.'

Boost your 'serum fun levels'

Improbable as it may sound, pain may succumb to what might be called 'The Laurel and Hardy School of Medicine.'

When's the last time you had a good hearty belly laugh? You know – the kind in which your whole body gets involved. You find yourself thrown against the back of your chair one minute and then doubled over the next. Great loud noises burst from your upturned and opened mouth. Tears flow from the corners of your eyes, and you grasp your sides in mock agony. At the same time, tense muscles go limp – so much so that, at the height of your enjoyment, you may not even have the strength to make a fist.

If you find yourself in this predicament often, consider yourself lucky. It's no joke – laughter is serious medicine. *How* serious is only just becoming apparent, even though doctors have long speculated that laughter is good medicine for the body as well as the mind. Back in 1942, for example, Dr E. Forrest Boyd wrote that laughter aids the circulation, massages the abdominal muscles, stimulates digestion, lowers blood pressure, 'begets optimism and self-confidence and relegates fear and pessimism to the background' *(Southwestern Medicine)*.

But it's only since Normal Cousins, the long-time editor of the American journal *Saturday Review*, cured himself of a potentially fatal disease with laughter and vitamin C that interest in the healing power of laughter has soared. Cousins attributes his recovery to Marx Brothers' movies, not modern medicine.

A natural anaesthetic for aches and pains

Some aches and pains can be made worse just by paying attention to them, explains Dr Raymond A. Moody, Jr, author of *Laugh after Laugh: The Healing Power of Humor*. But when you laugh, you can forget your troubles. Perhaps humour sometimes works simply by withdrawing attention from pain. On the other hand, it's possible that the anaesthetic benefits of laughter could be related to the decrease in muscle tone that occurs with genuine body-shaking laughter.

Normal Cousins speculates that laughter may increase the production of endorphins. That may be why he found that ten minutes of genuine belly laughter would give him at least two hours of pain-free sleep while he was battling his severe illness.

However, laughter's benefits are not restricted to the seriously ill. People suffering from chronic pain (no matter what the reason) should use humour to relieve it, says Dr Bresler. He routinely enquires about his patients' 'serum fun levels'.

'To me, serum fun levels are a logical extension of conventional medical measurements like serum cholesterol levels – an important indicator of your well-being. They concentrate on the amount of pleasure in a person's life.

'People with chronic pain often don't do things they would normally enjoy. They feel they can't because of the pain. But it's often the other way around,' claims Dr Bresler. 'Their pain actually persists longer because they don't have any fun.'

Sounds like the easiest medicine in the world to swallow, doesn't it? But what if you just don't feel full of fun and laughter?

'Pretend.' That's the suggestion of June Biermann and Barbara Toohey, authors of *The Diabetic's Total Health Book* (1980), but their advice can be applied to everyone, not just diabetics. 'You have to start somewhere,' says psychologist Harry A. Olson, 'even if it means going through the motions at first. Because if you decide to be healthy, hopeful and fun-loving, *that's* what you'll be.'

Besides, everyone has the potential for a sense of humour, and we're all born with the capacity to laugh. It's just that some people were brought up without positive reinforcement of their funny bone, while others can find humour even in the most serious of situations.

'Eliminate the negative people,' suggest Biermann and Toohey, 'and surround yourself with the positive ones – people who fill you with joy and laughter, rather than gloom and doom.'

'I find it draining to be around serious-minded people all the time,' adds Dr Bresler. 'Uplifting people uplift others.'

Dr Olson calls that 'modelling', and it's one of the fastest ways to develop a positive sense of humour. 'Humour cannot be taught systematically' says Dr Olson, 'but must be observed and personally experienced to be mastered.'

And while you're at it, make it a point to be good to yourself. According to Biermann and Toohey that means doing something you especially enjoy and never have time for, even if it's just doing nothing. Don't keep putting off fun until you have more time, finish this or that project, feel better or whatever other excuse you can come up with.

The positive relationship between good humour and good health can't be denied. Neither can the association between laughter and longevity. A doctor whose speciality is geriatric medicine has concluded that one thing which almost all his very healthy elderly patients seem to have in common is a good sense of humour.

Or as another doctor aptly put it, 'He who laughs, lasts.'

Acupuncture

Acupuncture, the mysterious Chinese needle therapy, became widely known in the West only in the early 1970s, but, already, research has shown that its pain-relieving abilities may work by stimulating the brain to release endorphins.

Bruce Pomeranz, professor of neurobiology at the University of Toronto, began his investigation by recording the electrical impulses carrying pain signals from the spinal cord to the brain of experimental animals. When the skin was merely touched, cells in the spinal cord produced Morse code-like signals that were sent to the brain. When the skin was stimulated strongly enough to be painful, the signals pulsed ten times faster, telling the brain to register 'pain'.

Dr Pomeranz and his assistants then administered acupuncture needles and measured the pain signals. At first, there was no change, but 25 minutes later they noticed that the pain pulses had slowed down considerably. The non-painful 'touch' signals were not affected, however. And even after the needles were removed, the pain-dulling effect persisted for an hour.

This 'time delay' effect of acupuncture led the researchers to wonder whether or not some chemical was involved in the pain-killing effect of acupuncture. Presumably, it would take longer to kill pain if the needles were actually stimulating the release of a chemical some distance away from the site of the pain.

While Dr Pomeranz and his colleagues were working, other researchers completed experiments demonstrating that a pain-killing chemical *was* present in the brain. Chinese doctors transferred cerebrospinal fluid from an animal undergoing acupuncture to another animal and found that the second animal also experienced a dulling of pain. Other research teams in Scotland, the United States and Sweden found that the chemicals in the brain are – once again – the endorphins.

Dr Pomeranz then sought to test his hunch that acupuncture stimulated the release of endorphins by the brain, which in turn dulled the sensation of pain. He injected animals undergoing acupuncture with a substance that blocks the action of both morphine and endorphins. As he suspected, the acupuncture failed to kill pain.

On the basis of his own work and the reports from other laboratories that this effect also occurs in humans undergoing acupuncture, Dr Pomeranz offers a probable explanation for the way acupuncture kills pain:

> Perhaps endorphins control the manner in which one nerve cell 'talks' to another, and may relieve pain by blockage of messages in nerve cells in the pain pathways. Needling may activate deep sensory nerves which cause the brain to release endorphins. These endorphins block signals from getting through the nerve chains in the pain pathway carrying messages from spinal cord to the brain. [*New Scientist*].

Dr Pomeranz also said that the release of a brain chemical to kill pain is preferable to injecting drugs, because injections are addictive, but acupuncture is not.

Exercise can mimic acupuncture effects

According to research done at the University of Sydney, exertion in the form of exercise may activate the same natural painkillers that acupuncture does – minus needles.

The scientists rigged a man's arm with an inflatable cuff, much like the ones used to measure blood pressure, which could be tightened progressively to produce pain. He was asked to indicate when he first felt pain and when the pain became severe. The times to both responses were recorded both before and after the man went on a 40-minute, three-mile run.

Over a six-month period, 15 such trials were conducted. The results were overwhelming: in 13 of 15 post-run measurements, he reported pain onset later than before the run; in 14 of those post-run tests, he waited longer before reporting 'marked discomfort' (*Medical Journal of Australia*, 2 June, 1979).

Acupressure (shiatsu)

Another Oriental technique that follows the same general principles as acupuncture – *shiatsu* – uses finger pressure rather than needles, many therapists have become adept at relieving pain using this.

The toughest audience Jerry Teplitz, an American shiatsu practitioner, ever had to work with was inside a prison. 'The prisoners didn't know who I was or why I was there or what on earth I was going to do,' recalls Jerry. 'They were basically told they could either work or see my programme, so they obviously chose me over work.'

There were moments on stage when Jerry wished they hadn't. Usually, five minutes into his programme, he would have nearly 100 per cent audience participation as he instructed people how to use various techniques to relax or to energize their bodies. But the prison audience was different – restless, talkative, smoking and shuffling around.

To make matters worse, in order to demonstrate shiatsu, Jerry usually picks someone from the audience who has a headache. Unknowingly, he picked a prison ringleader from the fidgety crowd. 'He sat down on stage, and I demonstrated the headache technique on him. When I got done, he said his headache was *worse*,' laughs Jerry, who still remembers the misery of the moment. 'I talked to him a little more and discovered he was having a *migraine* headache which he got all the time. So I did the shiatsu treatment for migraine on him, and his pain completely disappeared.'

When Jerry arrived at the meditation part of his programme, he led the prisoners through a meditation exercise and lectured on the merits of meditating twice a day. 'I told them they needed to get up 20 minutes earlier in the morning to meditate. Then all of a sudden I began wondering – do they get woken up by the bell? Are they allowed alarm clocks? Do they *have* 20 minutes?

Before the prison performance, Jerry had always been astonished by the success of his programme. Whether he faced a crowd of college students, business executives or older adults, it seemed to have something for everyone. Maybe an audience full of convicts was stretching his luck a little too far. And then the prisoners' performance evaluation forms were turned over to him. To his surprise, the prisoners had written that they believed shiatsu and meditation would help them in their lives.

Subsequent feedback from prison staff members further boosted Jerry's spirits. 'The monetary system of the prisoners is cigarettes,' relates Jerry. 'A staff member told me that one prisoner earned two packs of cigarettes by doing shiatsu for another one's headache. And the toughest guy in the prison is a Muslim who carries a file folder with all of his prayers in it. Tucked within that folder is the shiatsu headache diagram I left with them.' Jerry says, 'It was the toughest audience I ever went through, but there, too, it worked.'

In his programme, audiences learn by doing different finger-pressure techniques used to relieve headaches, migraine, sore throats, sinus colds, eye-strain and neck fatigue. 'It's a seed-planting profession,' says Jerry. 'I'm planting the seed for people so that they can heal themselves in a whole variety of ways. They've got more power and potential than they probably ever thought they had.'

Jerry admits he faces a roomful of sceptics at the beginning of every performance. He promises to pay $4 to anybody who does not leave feeling more relaxed. 'I've done the programme now for about 100,000 people, and I've had only three people ask me for the $4,' he adds.

Actually, Jerry admits he isn't one to quibble over scepticism, since he was the biggest sceptic of all when first introduced to what he does now. A graduate of Northwestern University Law School, Jerry was a lawyer with the US Environmental Protection Agency before he abandoned law for a more unorthodox lifestyle.

'If you had asked me in law school if I could see myself doing this five years after I graduated, I would have thought you were crazy,' he quips. 'As a lawyer, you are trained in scepticism and to tear things apart. I tried to tear these things apart. They wouldn't tear. The more I tried, the more I experienced, and the more excited I got.' He began attending the Temple of Kriya Yoga in Chicago and became a master teacher of hatha yoga. Eventually, he quit the law profession. 'It was like taking a deep breath and, in a sense, going off the deep end – but knowing there wasn't a deep end there.'

Jerry has written a book with Shelly Kellman entitled *How to Relax and Enjoy*, which describes some shiatsu methods, hatha yoga exercises and general relaxation and meditation techniques, and discusses proper nutrition. He claims that, in as little as two hours, he can teach people relaxation and energizing techniques they will be able to use for the rest of their lives.

'You can use shiatsu on yourself as well as on other people,' explains Jerry. 'My goal is to make people self-sufficient. My real purpose in doing a lot of this actually is to put me out of business. That will mean everybody is running around healthy because they know how to do these things. They will be practising shiatsu, meditation and good nutrition, and will be feeling a lot better as a result.'

When shiatsu works

Shiatsu practitioners who want to relieve a headache use the fleshy part of their thumbs to bear down on a series of pressure points along the skull and the back of the neck. Jerry reports that headaches and hangovers can be relieved in as little as a minute and a half. In some cases, a second or third treatment is necessary to alleviate all pain. 'Of course, if anyone has an ongoing problem, I recommend seeing a doctor,' he adds. 'The individual should also look at what is going on in his or her environment. Something is really pretty intense either physiologically or externally that needs treating.'

However, for ordinary ailments, shiatsu is quite effective, says Jerry, although no one really knows why. 'There are several theories,' he continues. The hard pressure exerted by the thumbs may cause extra blood to circulate through the painful area. The blood acts as the natural cleanser of the body, bringing antibodies and oxygen to the area and removing waste products and carbon dioxide, he says. A second possibility is that shiatsu may act like acupuncture, stimulating certain nerve meridians and motivating the body to heal itself. Others suggest that, when pressure is put on the head, endorphins are released in the brain. Another theory is based on the physics concept that every action has an equal and opposite reaction. 'With a hangover, a person has constricted blood vessels,' says Jerry. 'The shiatsu pressure may cause the blood vessels to expand and relieve the pain.'

Whatever the scientific explanation may be, Jerry says, shiatsu often works as long as people follow the directions. 'When people work on the neck area, we tell them they must *not* press directly on the spine. Instead, the pressure is placed on both sides of the spinal column. Also, the practitioner instructs the person to say 'ouch' whenever pain is felt during a treatment. At that point, the practitioner leaves that area and continues with the treatment,' Jerry explains. When the practitioner returns to the pain point, he presses gently first and then gradually presses harder. 'Either you'll be able to get more pressure on before they say 'ouch' again, or, in many cases, the pain has just disappeared completely.'

Shiatsu practitioners are told to press no more than three seconds when working in areas of the neck and above. They press no more than seven seconds on each area below the neck, says Jerry.

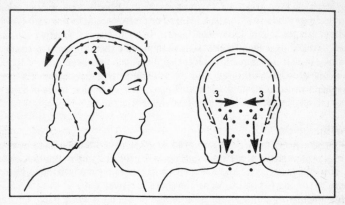

To relieve headache: Draw an imaginary line from centre of forehead to base of skull (left) and apply pressure to each point. Then press points from brow of head to temples, as shown by arrow. Press points on each side of head simultaneously. (Points are about 1 inch apart).
Then find middle rear of ear lobe (right) and press on points in direction of arrows. First point is 2 inches from lobe, next is half the distance to centre, third is centre or medulla. Then follow spinal column to shoulders, pressing next to spine (not on it).

Another type of therapy for pain

'It's nice to know that you are the master of your fate – that you need never suffer muscular pain again.' So says exercise therapist Bonnie Prudden. That may sound like a pie-in-the-sky promise. It isn't. That is the nice sense of assurance you enjoy when you master the art of trigger-point pressure with exercise therapy, a natural do-it-yourself technique that Bonnie has devised and demonstrates at her seminars, at her pain clinics and at the Institute of Physical Fitness, which she heads, in Stockbridge, Massachusetts.

If you've ever had excruciating low-back pain, bursitis, tennis elbow or some other form of muscular torture, you know that the usual medical treatment involves drugs, muscle relaxants, injections of cortisone, or just a sharp needle. Bonnie uses none of these. Only fingers, knuckles and elbows, exercise to stretch the muscles, and a spritz of coolant spray. The amazing thing is that it works. This natural method that anyone can learn does bring release from pain, sometimes pain of long-standing duration and sometimes pain incurred by a recent injury.

How does it work?

Most muscular pains have a trigger point, an irritable spot, which can cause the muscle or muscles in that area to go into spasm.

However, it may not be the area in which you are feeling the pain, for the muscle sends referral messages along its circuit. Bonnie probes for the main culprit, the trigger point, then applies pressure for ten seconds. 'We don't know exactly why it works,' Bonnie told us, 'but we believe the pressure shuts off the oxygen supply to the trigger point. Denied oxygen, the trigger point seems to stop firing, and the muscle no longer holds the spasm; it relaxes, the muscle unwinds, and the pain lessens or disappears. There may be a whole series of trigger points to be worked out.' Bonnie checks all along the edges of the muscles at 1 inch intervals. She then exercises the muscle to stretch the kink out of it and applies a coolant spray, which helps the muscle to relax. You could use the edge of an ice cube for the same purpose but it's messy. With children, usually one treatment is enough. With adults, three or four may be necessary, especially for long-standing problems.

Banishing pain

Everybody, it seems, has some area of pain. Just mention your low-back syndrome at a party, at a PTA meeting, at a yoga class or at the office coffee pot. You'll hear an excited babble about a gaggle of agonies that involve every muscle in the human body – of which there are over 600.

This ubiquity of pain was apparent at one of Bonnie's workshops. One after another, children and oldsters climbed on the table to have their aches and pains kneaded out as Bonnie worked on their offending trigger points. Don't think it doesn't hurt. It does. But everyone agreed the results are worth the brief moaning, groaning or silent wincing.

'I can't believe it,' one woman said, lifting her arm over her head. 'I haven't been able to raise that arm more than an inch for years.' Other comments were: 'My leg feels lighter,' 'My leg feels longer' and 'My arm feels warmer.' All of these reactions indicate unkinked muscles and better circulation, as the body relaxes and becomes balanced. No one muscle is now being taxed with a disproportionate tugging at its mooring.

Many of the aches and pains we suffer may be rooted in long-forgotten mishaps – a flop on the ice, a fall from a tree, a blow sustained on the playground or athletic field. The bruises heal and we forget them, but the injury lingers on in the form of a sleeping trigger point, a tender spot that may flare up at the first invasion of tension.

That was the case with 15-year-old Craig, who, as a result of a severe blow to his head when he was four, suffered blinding headaches ever since. Doctors were unable to find a cure. All the medical tests ruled out disease or injury. After Bonnie worked on trigger points in his neck and head, Craig said his head felt much lighter and the pain was lessened.

He visited the Institute for more treatment three times at one-month intervals. In between visits, his mother, who had witnessed the technique at one of Bonnie's workshops and got further training at the Institute, worked on trigger points that Bonnie had located. Today, Craig is free of pain and is skiing and participating in sports he couldn't enjoy before. There is no guarantee that his pain will not recur, Bonnie warns, but at least now Craig and his family know how to erase it.

You never know – until you try – what kind of pain this technique will alleviate. Would you believe a toothache? Granted – not all toothaches. Don't divorce your dentist. But Lori J., who attended Bonnie's workshop, had an excruciating pain in a molar that her dentist had given up on. 'There's nothing more I can do,' he told her, 'except pull the tooth or do a root-canal job.' The tooth had been filled in England three months earlier, and ever since, Lori had been in such agony that she sometimes took 12 aspirin in a single day.

On a hunch, one of Bonnie's associates worked out some trigger points in Lori's head, and, believe it or not, the pain that had plagued her for three months folded its fangs and went away.

Tennis elbow is a common affliction. Mrs J. was suffering from this particular annoyance, which she had incurred in the course of taking hour-long golfing lessons. Starting from the point that hurt the most and working other points down into the wrist, Bonnie brought her relief.

Back at the Institute of Physical Fitness, Bonnie and her staff work out trigger points on patients referred to them by local doctors. 'We've never yet had a headache we couldn't get rid of, unless the patient, for some psychological reason, wanted to keep his headache. Very infrequent, but it does happen.' One patient, a football coach who was in a coma for seven months as a result of a car accident, is now walking and conversing and no longer has pain.

Musicians are prime candidates for muscular pain, and members of the Boston Symphony Orchestra keep the staff at the Institute hopping from shoulders to arms to hips. Every instrument in an orchestra has its own particular potential for causing tension pain. The violinist gets it in the neck and shoulder, the flautist in the fingers and arms, the drummer in the hips.

How was Bonnie's method discovered? By serendipity. For many years, she was associated with a well-known doctor who used injections to erase muscle pain. Bonnie would locate trigger points, and the doctor would inject them. One time, as she was probing for trigger points, Bonnie discovered that a little angled pressure sometimes brought relief without the needling.

One day, a woman headed for Chicago came in with a disabling pain in her hip. 'I knew I didn't have enough hand strength to work that one out, so I suggested she see a doctor for an injection. 'I don't have time to go there,' she said. 'Can't you use your elbow?' So I did and bingo it worked.' Ever since, it's elbows, fingers and knuckles – whichever works best.

The really great part of this therapy is that anybody can do it – even children. Bonnie taught an 11-year-old girl how to ease the painful muscle spasms that her mother, a victim of multiple sclerosis, had been suffering. The child works out trigger points every evening, making it possible for her mother to turn herself, change positions without pain and get a restful sleep.

Helen Martell, who teaches six-year-olds at St Thomas School in Sanford, Maine, taught the technique to her class. 'They use it very effectively on each other and on their parents,' Ms Martell told us.

Simplified 'releases' for stiff neck and headache

Stiff neck

Suppose you wake up with a stiff neck or you have acquired a stiff or painful neck at the end of a trying day. Here's what you do:

Grab the back of your neck with your open hand. Place four fingers on one side of your neck and your thumb on the other side. Your spine is in the middle.

Draw your fingers and thumb towards each other to within 1 inch on each side of the spine. Now you have the trapezius muscle under your thumb and fingers.

Work your fingers and thumb alternately up the neck along the trapezius muscle in a gentle movement as if you were fluting the edge of a pie-crust. First, go up one side of the neck using the fingers. Then go up the other side using the thumb. Go all the way up to about 2 inches into the hairline.

When you find a sensitive spot, get someone to press that spot as hard as you can stand it, and hold it compressed for ten seconds. You can do it yourself if you can stand the pain.

Release the pressure slowly.

Stretch the muscle by bending your head forward and then sideways; bring your right ear towards your right shoulder and then your left ear towards your left shoulder.

When one little girl had her leg confined in plaster for six weeks because of a fractured ankle, the children took turns giving her foot resistance exercises to keep her leg and foot muscles strong and blood circulating. When the plaster cast was removed, the children went on a hunt for trigger points and then took turns massaging the little girl's leg.

One of the nice features of this do-it-yourself therapy is that you can't do any harm. Of course, you don't work on broken bones – and breaks should always be ruled out by a doctor's examination and X-ray where indicated.

Recently the head master of a school came to the Institute suffering agonizing pain in his hip, thigh and shoulder. He had been in pain for 12 years and had been treated by orthopaedic physicians and neurologists. After $1^1/_2$ hours of work on the deep-lying muscles in his trunk, he felt as if an angel had swooped down and lifted his burden of pain. 'What am I going to do now to help other people like you have helped me?' he asked. 'Put an anatomy course in the curriculum in your school,' Bonnie told him. That is exactly what he is planning to do.

'We have to teach people that they can take care of themselves,' says Bonnie. 'Everybody should know more about his own body. Go to an art-supply store and get a book on anatomy. Study the muscles, where they begin and where they end. When you have a pain, locate the offending muscle and hunt for trigger points.'

Repeat this whole process, looking for other sensitive areas along the base of the skull from ear to ear, There are usually several sensitive areas.

Now, place your right hand on your right cheek and turn your head to the right, giving a little resistance with your hand so the muscles must work. Do the same to the left. Repeat this resistance exercise.

Every two hours, until the muscles have relaxed, repeat the whole procedure, starting from the trigger-point hunt.

Tension headache

Close your eyes.

With the three middle fingers of each hand, press on the temple area in front of and above the ears.

Put pressure on one finger at a time, and move your fingers around looking for sensitive spots. When you find one, hold the pressure for ten seconds. Release slowly.

Repeat the same procedure in the area around the eyes. Then loosen the scalp with rhythmic massage.

Without opening your eyes, raise your eyebrows. Screw up your eyes and then relax. Repeat the eyebrow exercises three times.

Wait a few minutes to see where the pain has moved. Then repeat the whole process.

After a few cycles, rub the tip of an ice cube across the forehead with swipes $1/2$ inch apart, always going in the same direction.

Physical therapy

Physical therapy, or physiotherapy, is a growing professional field whose usefulness is gaining recognition from doctors and lay people. No longer just a strengthening programme for after surgery, many people are bypassing surgery for musculo-skeletal problems and have found relief from debilitating pain through safe, natural physical therapy.

Working in cooperation with orthopaedists, physical therapists spare thousands the trauma of surgery or the blank euphoria of drug dependence. The new role of physical therapists, according to Sandy Burkart, associate professor of anatomy at West Virginia University and a practising physical therapist, is 'extremely active'.

'We're no longer just technicians who carry out the surgeon's orders,' Dr Burkart told us. 'We're taking an extremely active role in the diagnosis and evaluation as well as the treatment. Physical therapy is really a holistic therapy. In order to treat low-back pain, for instance, we've often got to be able to treat the whole individual, psychologically and physically. We've got to be able to change his or her attitude toward exercise and posture.'

Physical therapists are highly trained professionals who must meet rigid requirements before they can practise. Prospective therapists learn evaluation and treatment. They study human anatomy and physiology, with special emphasis on the structure and function of the muscular, skeletal and nervous systems. They acquire a working knowledge of various fields of medicine such as orthopaedics, paediatrics and rheumatology, and devote much time to learning the various treatments they will use in their practice. Qualified physical therapists know how to use heat, cold, massage, traction, braces, electricity, ultrasound, diathermy and, of course, exercise and manipulation.

When physical therapists talk about their work, back problems are sure to be discussed. And with good reason: low-back pain, disc problems and associated joint and nerve difficulties are practically par for the course in our society. Whether it is temporary stiffness or a crippling herniated disc, nearly everyone has back trouble at some time or other.

Why are backs so troublesome? Aside from the rare inherited abnormality or damage done by accidental injury, the fault lies with human anatomy and posture, and habits that aggravate the weaknesses of both. The spine, though a masterpiece of structural engineering, has weak spots.

'Human beings just aren't made to stand upright,' says Jerry Adkins, director of physical therapy at Cabell Huntington (West Virginia) Hospital. 'We'd do fine on all fours, but standing improperly puts the stress in the wrong place.'

The wrong place usually turns out to be the lower back, or more specifically, the lumbosacral area, where the spinal 'S' terminates in five fused vertebrae. It is a sturdy foundation that can support the entire weight of the body.

However, humans weren't meant to stand for hours on end, nor to sit all day, nor to lounge around letting their muscles deteriorate. No matter how straight you hold your back, sitting puts enormous stress on the lumbar (lower) region. The soft, shock-absorbing discs between the vertebrae are compressed and the muscles weakened. Sedentary lifestyles and poor work habits – lifting with the back and not the legs, twisting and lifting at the same time – can put a stiff, weakened lower back 'out', painfully. Typically, no unusual activity is involved.

Anita Ball found that out the hard way.

A near-miss that hurt

'I hit the brakes hard,' she remembers. 'I was turned, looking out for traffic, when this car came screeching up to me. I jammed on the brakes, and we came within inches of hitting each other.'

Not an unusual occurrence, surely, and Mrs Ball thought nothing more of it. But within a few days, she had pain, a curious 'running' pain, 'like electricity or hot water that ran across my back and down my leg whenever I sat or stood. I could move around and walk all right, but whenever I sat down or stood up, I had pain. I had no idea what was causing it.'

Her family doctor sent her to a local orthopaedic surgeon, who ordered bedrest. That helped, but when she went on a lengthy car journey, the pain returned, and she sought relief from painkillers. When she returned, about one month after the original incident, she put herself on bedrest. 'But this time it didn't help. I got worse.'

The surgeon diagnosed a ruptured lumbar disc and pinched sciatic nerve, and ordered her into hospital, where she was put in traction under heavy medication.

'They told me traction was 'the next step' she recalls. 'I had been telling them from the beginning not to talk about surgery. I'm just glad I had a conservative orthopaedist.'

Her medication was codeine, to relieve the excruciating pain, and Valium, to relax the spasmed muscles around the injured disc and allow the traction apparatus to spread the vertebrae to relieve pressure on it. In a few weeks, she was out of the hospital, in a back brace, having been instructed in a few basic exercises to be done daily. She thought she was improving.

Then a careless step landed her back in traction and back on heavy medication to control the agonizing pain. She remained in the hospital for five days, then was released with instructions to continue using the back brace and the drugs.

Four months had now passed since the original incident. Her orthopaedist told her that, if the drugs and back brace did not bring improvement within three weeks, he would recommend surgery. Mrs Ball remained reluctant to undergo an operation, and contacted Dr Burkart. He reviewed her history and received permission from her surgeon for a three-week 'trial' of physical therapy

'The first thing Sandy did was help me break the emotional barriers to movement I had built up. I was walking like a zombie, so tight with fear of surgery and pain. When I moved my head, it hurt; when I lifted my hands, my back hurt all the way down. It was frightening. You don't know how much you can move or what you can do.' So she did nothing, awaiting surgery.

Dr Burkart explained her problem in detail and showed her that she could move and exercise in ways that helped rather than worsened the problem. He showed her simple exercises, mostly stretching and mild strengthening poses, and encouraged her to do them.

'He put my mind at ease about pain,' she told us 'by showing me how it indicated improvement in my range of motion.'

In fact, Dr Burkart had her keep a 'pain journal', to record what activities hurt, how much and how often. (Today, she still keeps the journal, but calls it instead her 'exercise journal'.) Most important from her point of view, he weaned her away from Valium, on which, she says, she had become dependent.

After three weeks, she returned to her orthopaedist. 'I was walking, I was off drugs, I was beginning to see people and have some social life. You see, I had developed an invalid complex. I was just going down into a pit.'

Surgery wasn't discussed, but she knew she had a long way to go. As she improved, Dr Burkart urged her to walk every day and to perform 'spinal decompression' exercises – a two-hour rest period during which she lie still, allowing the spine to recover from the stress of gravity. She structured her days around this lunch-time break.

After three months of physical therapy, she was walking briskly and doing most household chores by herself. By July, she was free of pain and walking two or three miles each day. By September, she was looking forward to tennis the following spring. A year of pain and hard work was over, and a near-miracle of natural healing had occurred.

Central to Dr Burkart's plan for Mrs Ball was regular home visits to show concern, advise her family of what she could and couldn't do, and teach her how to work within her limitation while monitoring her improvement. By forcing her to take responsibility for her own healing, he kept her from becoming a 'back derelict', an emotional as well as physical cripple. Most important, it was accomplished without drugs.

Valium is widely prescribed for back problems because it is a swift and sure muscle relaxant, and relatively safe. But Dr Burkart and other physical therapists feel it is overprescribed and can hinder therapy in some cases. Mrs Ball says Valium 'robbed me of my will and my ability to fight back against pain.'

Therapists call Mrs Ball's exercises 'active' – she did them herself, gradually pushing back the barrier of pain as she stretched and strengthened injured tissues and relieved pressure from the disc.

Manipulation

Manipulation, as osteopathy and chiropractic are collectively called, has been looked down upon by conventional medicine, but it is enjoying a revival. In this section, Prevention *magazine editor Robert Rodale explores the uses and benefits of the various manipulative therapies.*

Sometimes, the natural healing process needs a boost. Some injuries and strains to the body's framework are too serious to be left just to time. There is need for a healing force applied from outside, or at the very least informed guidance on the best ways to help speed the natural healing process. I believe therapy for physical injuries and displacements is especially needed as we get older. With advancing age, your body heals more slowly. If you try to stay active or athletic into late middle age, you can find yourself spending much more time waiting out the healing of injuries than makes sense. A bad back, especially, turns a life that should be full of vigour and activity into a scenario of continual pain.

Manipulation is one excellent answer to many of these painful problems. A medical book on manipulation calls that therapy 'passive movement with therapeutic purpose using the hands'. That definition refers mainly to the kind of manipulation of the spine and joints done by chiropractors, osteopaths and those few doctors and physical therapists who have been trained in pressing and pulling the body back into shape to speed healing and reduce pain. I would go further, and include any kind of pressure and reconstructive force as manipulation, including such things as traction (pulling), certain kinds of bandaging, the use of braces and arch supports, deep friction massage and even the application of heat and cold. The prescribing of pain-killing drugs and muscle relaxants is an approach entirely opposite to manipulation. A major purpose of the hands-on technique against pain is to avoid drugs, which can have serious side-effects. Also, drugs seldom get to the root of the problem. The whole idea of manipulation is to find the spot where a part of the body has become misaligned (or cramped up), reach it physically in therapeutic ways and thereby help put everything to rights so that normal activity can be resumed as quickly as possible.

The spine is the most frequently manipulated part of the body, and for good reason. Our backbone is central, and made up of many little parts that can move out of proper position. It also has numerous discs between the bones (vertebrae), which can become compressed or even herniated (i.e. it may burst out of its normal position and press on nerve fibres). Whenever heavy work is done, the spine bears much of the stress and pressure. The many large muscles of the back that connect to the spinal area are also an important part of the picture, as are nerves, ligaments and other kinds of connective tissue.

Hippocrates wrote about manipulation roughly 2300 years ago. For treatment of back trouble, he advised that the patient lie face down on a board with bands fastened to the head, pelvis, knees and ankles. Two assistants were told to pull on the bands, thereby applying traction, while the doctor pressed sharply on the troubled area. That's not a dangerous manoeuvre, we are told by Hippocrates. Nor is it dangerous for the doctor to sit on the patient's back during traction, Hippocrates even suggested, bouncing up and down a little. An alternative method was to stick a heavy board into a hole in a wall, next to the strapped-down patient, and use it as a lever to press down even harder on the back. Put a soft wad of cloth or a leather pad between board and back, though, he advised.

Doctors of the Middle Ages used and wrote about similar methods for manipulation of dislocated vertebrae. It was good medicine. Pulling on the spine exerts centripetal force. (I'm sure you know what *centrifugal* force is. It moves objects outward from a centre. Well, centripetal force is the opposite. It pushes or exerts force towards a centre.) Traction may help to move dislocated spinal parts back together, and also spaces them out so pressure by the doctor's hand can move them into place. Modern manipulators do roughly the same thing for some spinal injuries.

There are plenty of references to an even simpler and, you might say, cruder type of manipulation in the history of folk medicine. In many different cultures, people practised what they described (accurately) as 'trampling'; sometimes it was also called 'stamping'. The person with pain lay face down on the ground, and a woman was called in to walk on his or her back. A virgin was preferred, or a mother who had given birth to twins. Rough treatment, you might say, but it worked! Dr Eiler H. Schiötz, who co-authored the book *Manipulation Past and Present* with Dr James Cyriax, still uses that technique.

'I may say that I have used trampling when I got lumbago myself,' says Schiötz, 'with good result. I employed my little daughter as the stamper, since my wife . . . was not suitable, being neither a mother of twins nor a virgin. I have also used the method with good results in patients with a flattened lumbar curve presumably caused by a disc protrusion.'

Preventive use of stamping has been reported in folk stories coming from countries as diverse as India, Egypt, the Aegean Islands. Bohemia and China, according to the Schiötz and Cyriax book.

Farm workers got their children to walk on their backs after a hard day's work stooping. The same applied to the Cossacks in Russia when they came home after a day on horseback.

Another simple type of manipulation, sometimes practised by European peasants, is called 'weighing salt'. It's a two-person operation. A pair stands back to back, joining arms at the elbows. Then, they alternatively lift each other off the ground. That simple manoeuvre both exerts traction and has a pressing effect on the spine.

And no history of manipulation, no matter how brief, would be complete without mention of the 'bonesetters' who practised in Europe during the 18th and 19th centuries. Their special skill was the ability to apply pressure at exactly the right place to stiff or displaced joints. Some charged very high fees and could put right in a few seconds a hand, knee or foot that hadn't been used normally for years. Often they kept their art a secret, passing it from one generation to another.

Mobilizing forces within the body

The modern era of manipulation starts with the ideas of Andrew T. Still, who lived from 1828 to 1917 and founded the discipline of osteopathy.

Still's concept was that all disease could be fought by mobilizing forces within the body. Furthermore, he believed that disease started when bones became dislocated, when ligaments were abnormal, or if muscles contracted the wrong way. These problems, he said, created pressure on blood vessels and nerves, causing a lack of circulation and obstructing the 'life forces' that passed along the nerves to all parts of the body.

Many osteopathic doctors became good manipulators. Over the years, they have helped many people recover from back and other problems related to joint displacement.

Chiropractic is a newer discipline. The fathers of that concept were D.D. Palmer and his son, B.J. Palmer. They also focus on dislocation of the spine, and also have a great interest in more subtle misalignments called *subluxations*. Here is an official description of chiropractic activity from a publication of the American Chiropractic Association:

The most characteristic aspect of chiropractic practice is the correction (reduction) of a subluxated, vertebral or pelvic segment(s) by means of making a specific, predetermined adjustment. The purpose of this correction and its determination is to normalize the relationships of segments within their articular [joint] surfaces and relieve the attendant neurological, muscular and vascular disturbances.

Chiropractors manipulate more than any other group of health professionals, but they get into other fields as well – nutrition, personal hygiene, lifestyle and so forth. They are a controversial group of professionals in the minds of some people (especially orthodox medical doctors), but they have achieved progress towards acceptance in recent years.

[You do not need to be medically qualified to be either an osteopath or a chiropractor, although they do train for a long time. Because manipulation (particularly of the spine) can be dangerous in unskilled hands, it is important to consult only those practitioners who belong to a recognized association: the British Chiropractors Association, the British College of Naturopathy and Osteopathy, the British Osteopathic Association (for medically qualified osteopaths), the General Council and Register of Osteopaths.]

Manipulation and you

The number of medical doctors who manipulate the back and other parts of the body is indeed tiny, but there are some. Foremost among them [in the United States] is James Cyriax, co-author of the history of manipulation I mentioned earlier. Dr Cyriax has also written a textbook of orthopaedic medicine, which describes in detail many manipulative techniques. And he has worked for years in both England and the United States to teach manipulation to both medical doctors and physical therapists.

Medical manipulation is somewhat different from that done by chiropractors and osteopaths. While the chiropractor usually manipulates to align the vertebrae properly, the orthopaedic manipulator tries to stretch the supporting tissue of the joints, and uses traction during manipulation much more. (They are actually closer to the Hippocratic method than are chiropractors and osteopaths.) Sometimes the pull exerted, such as during neck manipulations, is well over 200 lb. We are assured by Dr Cyriax in his book that that is a safe procedure. He does not recommend that the patient be put under anaesthesia for such manipulation, although some doctors do that.

Dr Cyriax doesn't believe that chiropractic manipulation is based on sound scientific theory, but he admires the results that they get. And since he recognizes that the number of medical doctors who manipulate is very small, many people needing that treatment go to a chiropractor. Here are his own words on the subject:

> Even today, most people have to go outside the medical and physiotherapy professions to various shades of lay manipulators for rational therapy for spinal articular displacements. A curious paradox results. It has now become obvious that these men, biased and untutored as they may be, have for all these years been giving what logic now shows to be the correct treatment for many spinal troubles, whereas under the best medical auspices, the rational treatment – namely, manipulation – has been withheld.

Research into chiropractic treatment by doctors other than Dr Cyriax has produced evidence that supports his statement. A fascinating study of the results of both chiropractic and medical treatment for back and spinal problems was published in an issue of *Lancet*. Authors of the report were five members of the department of family and community medicine of the University of Utah College of Medicine. 'Although the theoretical basis of chiropractic is still unsubstantiated by traditional scientific evidence,' the researchers concluded, 'none the less the intervention of a chiropractor in problems around neck and spine injuries was at least as effective as that of a physician, in terms of restoring the patient's function and satisfying the patient.'

The University of Utah study had investigated the cases of 122 people with back problems who went to chiropractors and compared them with 110 who went to regular doctors. They found that chiropractors required almost twice as many patient visits to treat a case as did the doctors, but the whole course of chiropractic treatment was shorter. The great majority of people in both groups was satisfied with their treatment, and they were able to return to normal functioning. However, the people who went to chiropractors said that they got more sympathy and that they were told more clearly what was wrong with them. They said the chiropractor did not take a superior attitude or treat them like a subordinate.

Still another study of chiropractic was completed by a New Zealand Commission of Inquiry. Its report, published in 1979, concluded that modern chiropractic is safe, is effective in relieving musculo-skeletal symptoms and is far from being an unscientific cult. 'Chiropractors should, in the public interest, be accepted as partners in the general health-care system,' the New Zealand Commission advised.

Walter I. Wardwell of the University of Connecticut, generally endorsed the New Zealand findings in an article he wrote in the 20 March 1980 issue of the *New England Journal of Medicine.* He outlined the tremendous and deep-seated antagonism between chiropractors and medical doctors, and attempted to suggest a way they could end their fighting and work together.

His idea is that chiropractors would do well to accept a more limited role, concentrating just on manipulation and related functions, in exchange for their being given a place in the regular medical community. Presumably, medical doctors would then refer patients needing manipulation to chiropractors.

My guess is that a truce between doctors and chiropractors will not occur for many years. Chiropractors are not like foot doctors or optometrists or dentists, who handle the problems of only a part of the human body and who are either non-controversial or have differences with standard medical theory that can somehow be resolved. I believe that many chiropractors claim to address almost all illness problems and use a theory that is far removed from orthodox medical thinking. Those two factors make compromise extremely difficult.

That is unfortunate. We are going to have much greater need for manipulation in the future, and it would be nice to have a coordinated and cooperative body of practitioners to take our problems to. There are several big reasons why our need for manipulation is going to increase. First [in the United States] we are getting older, and more numerous as well. That great number of older, less flexible people will be having more back and other problems that need putting right.

Conservation of energy will also be a big factor. We are going to have to walk more and do more riding of bicycles. There will be more digging in gardens, and I believe that we will quickly see a return to many types of hard, physical work that we thought were gone for ever. That will put new stress on backs, shoulders, legs and necks. Without wide availability of the most effective kind of manipulation, our ability to work effectively and enjoy a pain-free life will be reduced.

You and I should not leave the controversy between professions to the chiropractors and the doctors to fight out among themselves. For one thing, while the back-biting is going on, the art of manipulation itself is suffering. Too many people who could use the therapy are told by their doctors that it doesn't work, when in fact it can. And because the access of chiropractors to high-quality research facilities is limited, the art of manipulation is not improving as fast as it might.

One improvement I think needed badly is an approach to manipulation that relies less on X-rays. Doctors, osteopaths and chiropractors use X-rays too much. The reasons why they do are too complex to go into here, but you and I end up getting the radiation and (from the latter two) the bills, both of which can be harmful. Undoubtedly, there will always be need for some X-ray analysis of possible dislocations, but if we all express strong resistance to irradiation, you can bet that ways will be found to get good results with far less use of that technique.

(*See also* BACK PROBLEMS.)

• Phobias

There are lots of bright, capable and essentially normal people out there who suffer from apparently silly, irrational fears that in many cases restrict their lives for decades. When fears reach that stage, they're called *phobias*.

The study of phobias is fairly new. In mid-1981, a Phobia Society of America was founded by experts in the field. Only since the late 1970s have American doctors, universities and even the (US) National Institutes of Health opened clinics for phobias and other anxiety disorders.

For some phobics – as phobia sufferers are often called – the clinics have meant relief. We talked to men and women who said that a clinic programme enabled them to control the anxiety that had controlled them for years. For those men and women, a combination of group therapy, relaxation techniques, diet changes, family support and gradual exposure to the causes of their phobias has been very good medicine.

One of those people was 48-year old, Wanda Falci. She told us that she had been frightened by churches since childhood and by restaurants since her 20s. 'When we went to church,' she recalls, 'I always picked an aisle seat as close to the door as possible so that I could escape if I had to. Usually I would just sweat and 'white-knuckle' it. I always left the church mentally and physically drained. It ruined every Sunday.

'Restaurants were the same way. When we went out, I always made a lot of trips to the toilet because I thought I might get sick or pass out, which I never did. Passing out is what a lot of phobics are afraid of, but it never happens,' she says.

Since Mrs Falci had the usual frightening symptoms of phobia – dizziness and light-headedness, rubbery legs, difficulty breathing and fears of impending death or insanity – she assumed that she had a serious ailment. So, like many phobics, she had her head examined two ways – with a test for a brain tumour and ten months of psychotherapy. But there was no tumour and psychiatry didn't seem to help.

Dealing with a phobia

Then Mrs Falci enrolled in the Phobia Program of Washington, a clinic that was opened in 1978 by Dr Robert L. DuPont. The 16-week programme includes three steps.

The first step is an interview with a psychiatrist. The second step consists of weekly 90-minute meetings with six to ten other phobics, a therapist and perhaps a family member. The third step is a weekly one-hour expedition into the real world, where a phobic and a therapist try to face the feared object in a process called 'supported exposure'. Since Mrs Falci was working on her restaurant phobia, that meant starting with a quick visit to a fast-food hamburger restaurant and working up to a comfortable meal at a formal, expensive one.

Mrs Falci's therapist at the Phobia Program, psychologist Jerilyn Ross, explained to us how a phobia differs from a normal fear. 'It is unlike any feeling you've ever experienced if you've never had a phobia.' she says. 'It's irrational, involuntary and inappropriate to the situation. To explain it would be like trying to describe colour to a blind person. These people react with the intensity that a two-year-old feels when he loses his mother in a department store.'

Ms Ross taught Mrs Falci several antidotes for her fears. One was relaxation. Mrs Falci practised relaxation techniques for 20 minutes a day until she became so adept at them that she could compose herself at the first sign of a panic attack. She also learned the concept of 'paradoxical intent'. Whenever she felt impending anxiety, she said to herself, 'OK, phobia, come and get me,' and the panic would pass. 'It's when you say, "Don't come" that the panic takes over,' she told us.

Ms Ross described a few of the other phobics she has treated. In one case, a professional auctioneer in his late 30s was terrified by bridges – a fear that is technically called *gephyrophobia*. Because of his work, however, he often had to cross the five-mile-long, 185-foot-high Chesapeake Bay Bridge between the eastern and western shores of Maryland. To avoid the bridge meant adding 40 to 50 miles to the trip.

As a solution, he first had his wife drive him across the bridge. But he was still afraid he might panic and jump out of the car, so he handcuffed himself to the steering wheel while she drove. That didn't work either, and before he finally sought effective help, he resorted to having his wife lock him in the boot of the car.

(The Toll Facility Police who look after that bridge have, for more than 25 years, accommodated other gephyrophobes by driving them across. During the busy months of July, August and September of one year, the police made 407 trips for phobics.)

In another case, a woman was so terrified at the thought of cockroaches in her house that she would not keep food there. Fearing that food would attract the insects, she ate all her meals out and wouldn't entertain guests for fear they might be carrying stray crumbs from their last meal. Her treatment involved gradually bringing food home with the ultimate goal of giving a dinner party.

Washington lawyer Burt Rubin was another patient at the Phobia Program. He'd had a fear of public speaking since he muffed his lines in a school play at the age of eight. His programme of supported exposure started when, accompanied by Ms Ross, he began reading to a blind woman. He has since become active in Toastmasters International, a service group devoted to the art of public speaking.

Ms Ross herself was once phobic about heights. She avoided going up more than ten floors in any building. Unfortunately, she lived in New York City, the home of skyscrapers. The phobia struck for no apparent reason when she was 25, and she was afraid to tell anyone about it for two years. 'The phobia literally ran my life,' she told us. Like many former phobics, she became a phobia therapist.

Therapies that don't work

Supported exposure is only one of many treatments for phobias, but some have a better track record than others. Most of the people we talked to said that couch-style psychoanalysis didn't work for them. At the Phobia Program, Ms Ross says, her patients had made an average of 220 visits to psychiatrists and other mental health professionals and had spent thousands of dollars before coming to the clinic.

For some phobics, it's consoling to learn the root causes of their phobia, but the knowledge of its source doesn't necessarily put an end to their panic attacks. A survey of more than 100 phobics at Massachusetts General Hospital in Boston showed that they had averaged 3.8 years of psychiatric care but were still 'severely disabled' by their symptoms.

Tranquillizers apparently aren't effective either. Of the patients in the Boston survey, 98 per cent found no relief from them. Fifty-seven patients had consumed about 660,000 minor tranquillizer tablets, but they all continued to have panic attacks. The study also found that

> no reliable evidence supports the use of antipsychotic drugs (so-called major tranquilizers) although they are prescribed for nearly half of all persons afflicted with agoraphobia [the most general and common phobia, characterized by a fear of public places].(*Harvard Medical School Health Letter*, August 1979)

Also, members of a phobia self-help group in Britain surveyed themselves and found that

> their previously unsuccessful treatment had included psychoanalysis, narcoanalysis [using barbiturates to release repressed thoughts], hypnosis, behaviour therapy, psychotherapy, modified leukotomy [prefrontal lobotomy], LSD, group therapy, occupational therapy, insulin therapy and, in the words of many, 'drugs and more drugs'.

So much for therapy that involves doctors and drugs and costs a lot of money.

Self-help

What then, besides seeking the help of a phobia therapist, can fearful or phobic people do for themselves? Change their diet, for one thing, get some support from spouses and children, and learn a few simple behaviour modification techniques.

Phobia experts and former phobics told us that the symptoms of a panic attack, coincidentally or not, are very similar to those of hypoglycaemia (low blood sugar). In both cases, blood rushes from the victim's brain to his limbs, causing light-headedness.

'The typical diet of someone who comes to see us includes eight to ten cups of coffee a day, lots of sweets and very few slow-release, high-protein foods [which help control hypoglycaemia],' says Alan Goldstein, director of the Agoraphobia and Anxiety Center at the Temple University Medical School in Philadephia. 'They might have coffee and a doughnut for breakfast, more coffee at mid-morning, a white-bread sandwich at lunch and maybe a good supper. Then something sweet before they go to bed. If I ate like that, I'd be anxious too,' he told us.

In some but not all cases, a change of diet has worked. One woman in Dr Goldstein's clinic stopped drinking coffee and ate many small meals rather than three large ones, and her anxiety levels dropped by half.

Philip Bate, psychologist and director of the Maitland Psychological Clinic in Florida, also links hypoglycaemia and phobias. He told us that phobics often mistake a hypoglycaemia attack for a phobia attack. What they should do, he says, is carry a bag of nuts, seeds and raisins and munch on them to bring up their blood sugar levels. Treating the hypoglycaemia will often stop the anxiety, he believes.

Dr Bate thinks he knows why many phobics say they're afraid to leave the safety of their own homes. They stay home, he says, because going out would separate them from their refrigerators and the sweets they're addicted to. 'The most important thing is to get them away from sugar and white flour,' he says.

Another home remedy for phobias comes from therapist Claire Weekes, of the Rachel Foster Hospital in Sydney. Her suggested treatment for agoraphobia has four parts: *facing, accepting, floating, and letting time pass*. She believes that many phobics try to withdraw from their fears and turn to any handy activity that will distract them. 'This is running away, not facing,' she wrote (*The Female Patient*, April 1979). Phobics also cope with panic attacks by tensing themselves – clutching something so hard that their knuckles turn white and digging their fingernails into their palms. 'This is fighting . . . fighting brings more tension, more sensitization and further illness,' Dr Weekes said.

Floating is the next step.

> The simple words, 'float, don't fight,' have cured some people. If, instead of trying to fight her way forward as she instinctively does, the patient were to imagine she was floating, she would release enough tension to encourage movement.

The last step involves patience.

> Since impatience creates further stress, it is important to be willing to let more time pass. [A phobic in a frightening situation] should take a deep breath, let it out slowly, let her body slump in her chair, and accept the flash of panic as willingly as she can. If she faces panic this way, it will not mount.

Dr Weekes and other therapists seem to agree that a phobia binds its victims with not one but two fears. First comes the fear of restaurants and bridges or cockroaches. Then comes the second fear, 'the fear of the first fear', the fear that the phobic will lose control and do something embarrassing or dangerous in public. Dividing these fears and conquering each one separately might be the best way to cure a phobia.

Another factor is family. Ms Ross states plainly that 'the amount of progress phobics make during treatment is often dependent on the degree of support they receive from their spouses or other family members' (*Learning Theory Approach to Psychiatry*, 1982).

We asked two former phobics what single best piece of advice they would have for other phobics. Both recommend turning candidly to friends and family rather than hiding the problem. Mrs Falci says, 'Let people know about it. Don't be embarrassed to tell someone. I told my husband, "As long as I know you won't get upset with me, I'll go out with you in spite of my fears." ' Linda Spivak, who used to fear aeroplanes, says 'Having a phobia is a very lonely feeling. You must believe that there is hope and that you are not alone.'

How phobias start

There are lots of theories about what causes phobias. Phobics themselves usually know what triggered their problem – a physical illness, domestic stress, loss of a loved one, stress at work or a domineering parent. The phobia often starts with an inexplicable panic attack. If the attack occurs in a crowded shop, shops might become fearful reminders of it. From that point, as one psychologist put it, 'The phobia takes on a life of its own.'

The National Institute of Mental Health, outside Washington, DC, has focused some attention on the source of phobias. Thomas Uhde, director of anxiety research at NIMH, told us that he's investigating biological factors in phobia. Preliminary evidence also suggests that some people with agoraphobia are very sensitive to issues of separation and loss.

Also, there appears to be a high incidence of alcoholism in the families of patients wtih agoraphobia, particulary those who also have panic attacks.

Women in their late teens or 20s are the most likely candidates for agoraphobia. Anxiety about leaving the family and the stress of an unhappy marriage are among the causes that can initiate the disorder. Perfectionists and people who have an 'all or nothing' attitude towards life are also at risk.

Phobia therapists tend not to speak in terms of a 'cure' for their patients. 'A cure does not necessarily mean the elimination of anxiety,' says Ms Ross. And her colleague Dr DuPont states, 'We emphasize to the patients that they need to learn techniques to live with anxiety and that as they learn to fear their fears less, the fears will diminish – although probably not disappear,'

Practice is an essential part of recovery. 'The most obvious lesson clinically is that those people who are best able to practise dealing with their fears on a daily basis are the ones who do the best,' Dr DuPont adds. Graduates of his programme can stay in mental shape by attending informal monthly self-help sessions.

Sometimes, oddly, it's helpful for a phobic to look forward to her next panic attack. Dr Weekes says that this is the only route to permanent relief. The phobic, she writes, 'should try to view [a panic attack] as an opportunity to practise going through the fearful episode the right way until it no longer upsets her.'

'A more realistic goal,' concludes Ms Ross 'is to teach phobics how to lead a normal life by confronting, rather than avoiding, feared objects or situations by developing a positive and challenging attitude towards the fear.'

• Pregnancy problems

We're not suggesting that pregnancy is a disease, of course, but it is an extraordinary time in a woman's life. During pregnancy, the needs of two people must be met and a vulnerable life must be protected and nurtured.

What follows is not a comprehensive health plan for pregnancy – that would take an entire book – but a rundown of very important things to do, and avoid, to help make pregnancy as easy and healthy as possible.

At the outset we have to emphasize that the best thing a woman can do for herself and her unborn baby is to get good ante-natal care as soon as she knows she is pregnant and have regular checkups throughout her pregnancy.

In this chapter, we'll tell you about some of the most common problems women have during pregnancy, and some safe, natural ways to deal with them.

Morning sickness

If you are pregnant now or are planning to have a baby in the future, there's one thing you can predict with about 80 per cent accuracy – morning sickness. So common is this problem that it's not a matter of *if* you'll have it but *when* and *how long*.

However, just because it's as much a part of pregnancy as pickles and ice cream, that doesn't mean it should be dismissed as unimportant or inconsequential. Indeed, doctors and scientists have begun to look at the problem and its possible effects on the mother and foetus.

And it's about time. Not too long ago, the popular theory among (male) doctors was that morning sickness was all in the woman's head. Today, we know better. Morning sickness (a misnomer, since nausea is rarely isolated to a particular time of day) has a definite physiological basis, though the exact cause remains unclear. Most theories point to the drastic alterations in hormone production as a possible cause. Some think it's an increase in the progesterone level (it's very high during the first trimester of pregnancy). Others lean towards oestrogen as the culprit. And in fact, anyone who's become nauseated from oestrogen-containing birth control pills would probably nod her head in agreement.

Nutritional elements are a possible factor, too, according to George E. Verrilli, chief of obstetrics and gynaecology at Northern Dutchess Hospital in Rhinebeck, New York. 'Too little vitamin B_6, too little glycogen (the natural sugar stored in your liver) or an overly acidic stomach can all cause that queasy feeling.'

Problems arise when being nauseated turns into prolonged and continuous vomiting. 'Four to seven days without food or liquids can compromise both the mother and her baby,' says Dr Verrilli, who is also the coauthor, with Anne Marie Mueser, of *While Waiting: A Prenatal Guidebook* (1982). 'Dehydration and malnutrition must be corrected immediately. And sometimes that means hospitalization with intravenous fluids and nutrients.'

Fortunately, only about 2 per cent of pregnant women have it that bad. Nevertheless, severe nausea, even without vomiting, can be extremely debilitating, especially if you have other children to care for or are trying to hold down a full-time job – along with your meals. Here are some non-drug approaches to try:

• Take extra vitamin B_6. Dr Verrilli recommends about 30 to 40 mg per day.

• Keep food in your stomach. You heard right. Nausea is especially bothersome on an empty stomach (that's why it often strikes in the morning and in the late afternoon). Try a high-protein snack at bedtime or at any time when there will be long stretches between meals. (Protein takes longer to digest.)

• Drink your fluids between, rather than with, meals.

• Avoid greasy foods.

• Keep biscuits, cream crackers or dry cereal on your bedside table. If you wake up feeling queasy, nibble on those even before you get out of bed.

• Apply pressure to 'neikuans'. These are points located on the inside of the wrist, about three finger-widths up from the crease at the wrist, towards the elbow. This acupressure technique works even after the nauseated feeling strikes, according to one cancer specialist who also uses it for the nausea that accompanies chemotherapy.

Breech position

At some point in your pregnancy, your doctor may find that your baby is facing the wrong way for its entrance into the world.

A simple, effortless posture practised for ten minutes, twice a day, can often save a pregnant woman from the complications of a breech delivery – a buttocks-first presentation of the foetus in labour. Dr Juliet DeSa Souza, retired professor of obstetrics and gynaecology at Grant Medical College in Bombay, told the World Congress of Gynecology and Obstetrics that this posture corrected the breech presentation to a head-first presentation in 89 percent of 744 patients studied. She also reported that, in her private hospital, 70 of 73 cases were corrected *(Ob. Gyn. News)*.

The posture involves lying for ten minutes on a hard surface with the pelvis raised by pillows to a level 9 to 12 inches above the head. This position should be practised twice a day on an empty stomach. To be effective, you should start at the 30th week of pregnancy and continued for at least four to six weeks.

Food cravings

According to long-standing tradition, sometime during pregnancy, usually at an inopportune time, expectant mothers develop a craving for some sort of bizarre food.

'It's clear that these cravings are very real and are not the result of emotion,' Judith Brown told us. Dr Brown is director of the Program in Public Health Nutrition at the University of Minnesota. According to her research,

the vast majority of pregnant women reported increased preference for sweet and salty foods, and 86 percent reported changes in the taste of foods (mainly sweets, beef and salty snacks) and 55 percent in the odor of foods (mainly coffee, beef and beer). Taste and odor changes were noticed within six weeks after conception. Seventy-seven percent reported cravings for specific foods during pregnancy. It appears that changes in taste perceptions may be related to changes in food intake during pregnancy. [*Federation Proceedings*, March 1981]

Fluctuations in hormone levels or altered taste sensitivity probably explain the cravings, she noted.

However, could the desire for pickles be the body's way of saying 'more salt', and might the cry for ice cream represent a subconscious cry for more energy and calcium? 'Pregnant women are more vulnerable to dietary deficiencies,' Dr Brown says, but a cause-and-effect link with cravings has not been proved.

On the other hand, Mary M. Hastings, a researcher for the Proctor & Gamble Company, has reported that 'zinc-deficient rats develop an appetite for salt' (*Federation Proceedings*, March 1980). Could salt-craving mothers-to-be have the same deficiency?

'One of the features of pregnancy is a significant redistribution of body zinc. In effect, it becomes less available to the mother. There's a functional zinc deficiency,' Robert I. Henkin told us. Dr Henkin is director of the Center for Molecular Nutrition and Sensory Disorders at Georgetown University Medical Center in Washington, D.C. and an expert in the role minerals play in appetite – normal or bizarre.

Zinc's importance to proper growth is well known. So it's not terribly surprising that zinc deficiencies in pregnant women can cause problems for both mother and child, as two studies have shown'.

Actually, a drop in zinc levels around the second trimester is normal, but a group of British doctors at St Thomas' Hospital and Medical School in London found that women whose zinc levels drop *unusually* low during this period frequently give birth to smaller than normal babies. Although they were unable to determine the reason for this dangerous dip in some of the women they studied, they suggested that it 'is likely to be dietary'. Since zinc is mainly present in dietary protein, they added, zinc depletion and protein deficiency tend to go hand in hand.

'This study demonstrates that maternal leucocyte [white blood cell] zinc depletion is associated with impaired foetal growth,' they concluded. The doctors admitted that it's unclear whether zinc depletion actually *causes* this low birth weight or if low zinc levels are merely 'a marker of foetal growth abnormality' (*Lancet*, 21 November 1981).

In another study, at Charity Hospital in New Orleans, zinc deficiencies apparently increased the risks to both teenage mothers and their babies. Among 272 adolescent mothers, researchers found 'one of the lowest mean plasma zinc levels yet reported in pregnancy', probably because of bad eating habits on top of increased zinc needs due to pregnancy and the teenagers' own growth.

As a group, the young women were found to have about three times the normal rate of a high blood pressure condition associated with toxaemia of pregnancy. Those who suffered from it had 'a significantly lower plasma zinc level' than those who didn't. And among the infants born with defects, those with undescended testes or foot deformities were delivered by mothers whose zinc levels were 'well below the mean for the group' (*American Journal of Clinical Nutrition*, November 1981). The best source of zinc are animal foods such as liver, lean meat and poultry.

Eating 'funny things'

Dr David Z. Kitay of Pensacola, Florida feels that iron deficiency may be at the root of some maternal appetite changes.

Dr Kitay, a Fellow of the American College of Obstetricians and Gynecologists, offers a long list of 'funny things' eaten by some of his patients (not all of whom were pregnant) over the years: 'Laundry starch, white clay, white dirt, flour, ice, powdered milk, snuff, baking soda, kaolin – but it's not funny, because these women were ingesting only slightly nutritious or non-nutritious items to the exclusion of more nutritious things,' he explains.

The medical term for this behaviour is *pica*. It occurs in all sorts of people and often has them eating bewildering, even harmful, 'foods'.

'Remember that iron deficiency is a cause rather than an effect of pica,' Dr Kitay told us. He's found that an iron supplement to rebuild drained supplies works wonders and often eliminates pica in as little as a week.

Nutrients for pregnancy

Other nutrients you and your baby need during pregnancy might not send out such strong signals. But the old saying – that you're eating for two – is true in terms of quality (*not* quantity), and a good diet for you is the best present you can give your baby before it's born.

'Generally, obstetricians view the expectant mother in terms of a uterus and a placenta,' says Tom Brewer, eminent obstetrician and gynaecologist and founder of the Society for the Protection of the Unborn through Nutrition (SPUN). 'They fail to realize that she's got a mouth, a GI tract and a liver.' What goes into her digestive system during pregnancy has a direct bearing on what emerges from her reproductive system nine months later.

Unfortunately, many doctors still believe that the foetus acts as a sort of all-powerful parasite, sapping whatever nourishment it needs from the mother regardless of what food she may or may not be eating. When it comes to diet, their only concern is in calories and pounds. They may prescribe restricted low-calorie, low-salt diets plus diuretics (drugs that increase urination) to reduce water retention and badger their patients who gain more than 2 lb per week. Keeping a mother-to-be's weight down is still thought by many (especially American) doctors to reduce complications in pregnancy and facilitate easy delivery.

You don't have to look very far to find that it just isn't so. The Committee on Maternal Nutrition of the Food and Nutrition Board of the (US) National Research Council published the book *Maternal Nutrition in the Course of Pregnancy*, in which it states:

> Caloric restriction to limit gain in weight during pregnancy became widely advocated as a means for preventing toxemia and other complications. The idea found its way into textbooks of obstetrics and was widely accepted by the medical profession. Seldom has a medical idea with such a basis (hearsay evidence) been applied so widely and backed by so little scientific study.

Nevertheless, more than 30 million human pregnancies, Dr Brewer estimates, have been treated by this food-restricted medicated regimen since 1958, when diuretics were first introduced on to the medical scene. And yet, as the New York obstetrician reports, a (US) National Institutes of Health survey of 55,000 deliveries in 14 leading American hospitals showed a direct relationship between maternal weight gain and birth weight, length and brain damage in infants. Women with the severest dietary restrictions (weight gain of 0 – 5 lb) had over twice as many brain-damaged infants as had those with a weight gain of 36 lb or more.

Of course, that doesn't mean you've got to gain 40 lb in order to ensure yourself a healthy bundle of joy. But, on the other hand, if you do, don't panic. It's not really how much you eat that counts – it's *what* you eat that makes the difference.

'Gaining 50 lb on a junk-food diet may *increase* your chances of developing toxaemia and other complications of pregnancy,' says James Webb, an obstetrician in Tennessee. 'A good, balanced diet with plenty of protein is your best insurance, no matter what your weight gain. . . . Unfortunately, we went off the deep end years ago with those restricted diets. If you're gaining more weight eating the right kinds of food, you're definately on the plus side.'

So throw away your scales. 'A preoccupation with pounds precludes a preoccupation with nutrition,' Dr Brewer told us. 'Obstetricians who emphasize the importance of the weekly weigh-in almost invariably suffer from "nutritional nonchalance."'

Dr Brewer knows firsthand the devastating effects of 'nutritional nonchalance'. In 1950, when he was in his third year as an obstetric student at the Charity Hospital in New Orleans, he observed many women suffering from metabolic toxaemia of late pregnancy (MTLP). Women with MTLP experience a sudden rapid weight gain, extreme swelling, high blood pressure and a lack of protein (albumin) in their blood. In the severest type of toxaemia, eclampsia, expectant mothers suffer convulsions, or 'fits', coma, heart failure, fat in their livers and bleeding into their livers. Death for both mother and baby sometimes results. Brain damage, cerebral palsy, epilepsy and other nervous-system disorders are all possible consequences.

Yet, despite the threat posed by toxaemia, no one seemed to know – or even care – what caused it. So Dr Brewer took it upon himself to uncover a pattern in these afflicted women that might reveal the nature of the illness. He found a link in eating habits.

Rx for toxaemia: protein

Most of the women in the clinic were from low-income families and could not afford good food. Their diets were miserably lacking in high-quality protein and other nutritious foods. They survived largely on diets of salt pork (which is almost all fat), field peas, okra (ladies' fingers), soda and starch, supplemented by crisps and chocolate bars.

Dr Brewer's findings, however, were not new or unique. In 1935, Maurice B. Strauss, a doctor trained at Harvard, had already recognized that pregnant women got sick if they didn't have enough protein in their diets. He studied pregnant women at Boston City Hospital in Massachusetts during the Depression, when meat was scarce and nutritious high-protein foods were at a premium. He found that, when toxaemic women were fed a diet consisting of 2200 calories with 260 g of protein (more than twice the usual amount) and were given injections of B vitamins, their conditions improved markedly.

In 1942, another Harvard figure, nutritionist Bertha S. Burke, made a study of the role of nutrition in pregnancy. She found that of women who ate a good diet consisting of 75 g or more of protein per day, none developed toxaemia. However, of women whose diet was restricted to less than 55 g of protein, 44 per cent had evidence of toxaemia. The difference between a poor and a good diet for pregnancy – as far as protein goes – can be easily made up by adding a hard-cooked egg, a slice of Cheddar cheese, five dried apricots and two handfuls of almonds to your already-good daily diet. Or add just 6 oz of cottage cheese to your lunch menu.

There are numerous theories as to why good nutrition plays such a key role in the prevention of toxaemia. Dr Brewer feels that it is related to liver function.

When an expectant mother isn't eating right, her liver cannot produce enough albumin. Albumin is a type of protein that is responsible for holding water in the bloodstream. The more water in the blood, the greater the overall blood volume. And since blood volume should increase 40 to 70 per cent during a normal pregnancy, good nutrition and a healthy liver are essential.

Otherwise, the water leaks out of the bloodstream and into surrounding tissues, causing the excessive swelling and the sudden weight gain associated with toxaemia. 'That's why toxaemic women who begin eating more of the right kinds of food lose weight initially,' Dr Brewer explains. 'They're not losing protein weight, only water weight.'

'Some degree of swelling is normal during pregnancy,' says Dr Brewer. 'Restricting the salt intake often causes the kidney apparatus to go awry and sets off high blood pressure, another symptom of toxaemia . . . No veterinarian would think of depriving a pregnant cow of salt. Pregnancy increases an animal's demand for salt.'

Don't shun salt

So, why not a human's? 'Research strongly suggests that pregnant women probably do need more salt,' Joan Gussow, chairperson of the nutrition education department of Columbia University, admitted to us. 'Of course, we need additional research on the subject, but based on the animal studies at hand, I would say salt restriction during pregnancy is not a good idea.'

Phyllis S. Williams, nutrition consultant and health education coordinator for the Maternal and Child Health Council in Maine, agrees. 'Salt is a necessary nutrient in pregnancy,' she assured us. 'An adequate salt supply helps to maintain the expanded blood volume of pregnancy.'

Quite by accident, one doctor found that when 50 pregnant women suffering from leg cramps were prescribed salt tablets, none developed toxaemia. Prompted by that discovery, British doctors gave salt to 1019 women and compared their progress to 1000 other women who were on low-salt diets. Of those *not* receiving salt, 97 developed toxaemia, while only 38 of the women taking salt showed symptoms of this. Moreover, *none* of the latter developed eclampsia, the severest form of toxaemia. In addition, foetal and newborn deaths occurred twice as often in the low-salt group. Haemorrhaging and caesarean sections were also more common in the women deprived of salt.

What about the practice of prescribing diuretics (water pills) during pregnancy? 'It's a wholesale approach to murder,' Dr Brewer says passionately. 'Their use in human pregnancy is much worse than thalidomide.'

Dr Brewer sees evidence of diuretic damage everywhere he looks. 'Just listen to this,' he said during an interview at his New York home. 'Here's an article from the newsletter published by the President's Council on Mental Retardation, which states that 'the number of young people with disabilities in the Boy Scouts has increased 100 per cent since 1970, according to Arch Monson, Jr, national president.' Boy Scouts are 11 or 12 years old, which means, of course, that the time of their conception coincides precisely with the 1958 introduction of potent oral diuretics.

Dr Brewer does not stand alone in his fight against diuretics. Dr Ernest W. Page, formerly of the University of California Medical School, suggested at a meeting of the American College of Obstetricians and Gynecologists that 'the use of diuretic drugs during pregnancy should be considered potentially hazardous.' In his study comparing 4035 women taking diuretics with 13103 who were not, Dr Page reported that the incidence of stillbirths and newborn deaths was higher in the diuretic group. In fact, the death rate among full-term births was 16 per cent higher in women prescribed diuretics.

The time has come to re-evaluate a 20-year, primarily American tradition of putting pregnant women on low-calorie, low-salt diets and routinely prescribing diuretics. 'The pendulum is swinging back,' says Dr Brewer.

That means you've got to step up your caloric intake. Even if you're overweight at the start of your pregnancy, this is not the time to begin to think of reducing. From start to finish of pregnancy, you must consider your child's nutritional needs. There is recent evidence that your baby's brain is growing at its most rapid rate during the last two months of pregnancy, so don't slow down towards the end, even if your appetite has trouble keeping up with you.

Choose your calories wisely. Don't waste your money or strength eating processed cereals, white bread, crisps, soft drinks, sweets, chips, commercial cakes and biscuits. Put high-protein foods on your shopping list.

Dr Brewer suggests that, to meet your own needs and those of your developing baby, you should include the following every day: 32 fl oz of milk; two eggs; two servings of fish, chicken, turkey, lean beef, veal, lamb, pork, liver or kidney; two servings of fresh, green leafy vegetables; five servings of whole-grain breads, cereals or pancakes; and two choices from a jacket potato, green pepper, grapefruit or tomato. Also include a yellow or orange-coloured vegetable or fruit five times a week and liver once a week. And three pats of vitamin A-enriched butter. Salt to taste. And avoid any type of drug unless it's absolutely necessary.

Supplements during pregnancy

A woman's needs for many vitamins and minerals are increased during pregnancy, and most doctors recommend taking a balanced multi-vitamin and mineral supplement – just to be sure.

Vitamin supplementation before and during pregnancy contributes to a sharp decline in a certain type of recurring birth defect. That was the preliminary finding of a British study of women planning another pregnancy who had previously borne one or more offspring with a neural-tube defect (NTD). These congenital aberrations include spina bifida (defective closure of the spinal cord), hydrocephaly (abnormal fluid accumulation in the brain) and anencephaly (having almost no brain).

The women were recruited from genetic counselling clinics and by doctors into a trial of multi-vitamin supplementation. Study mothers took one vitamin tablet three times daily for more than a month prior to conception. They continued this regimen at least through the second missed menstrual period – well after the time of neural-tube closure. The control group similarly comprised women who had previously borne one or more NTD babies; however, these women were either already pregnant again or declined to participate in the supplementation trial.

Among the full supplemented group, only one of the 178 live births or spontaneous abortions (miscarriages) had an NTD. This compared with 13 of 260 infants or foetuses affected with an NTD born to the unsupplemented mothers. According to researchers, the control group's recurrence rates of congenitally damaged infants were 'consistent' with those previously reported; in contrast, the supplemented mothers had a 'significantly lower' recurrence rate of NTD children (*Lancet*, 16 February 1980). [Since that study it has been ascertained that the nutrient that seemed to prevent NTDs was the B vitamin, folic acid. This is now routinely given to pregnant women, usually in combination with iron.]

Vitamin B_6 – for both mother and baby

Many doctors still recommend daily doses of about 4 mg of B_6 during pregnancy, but evidence seems to suggest that that's woefully inadequate, especially if you were using oral contraceptives prior to conceiving.

'After some time on the Pill, B_6 reserves may be greatly reduced,' says Avanelle Kirksey, professor of food and nutrition at Purdue University in Indiana.

If the intake of B_6 is not adequate to meet the needs of pregnancy and to overcome the possible depletion by previous use of oral contraceptives, both the mother and the foetus could suffer.

It might be a good idea to check the mother's B_6 level during the fifth month of pregnancy because an inadequate supply at that time could affect the development of the baby's central nervous system, which crucially depends on vitamin B_6. [*American Journal of Clinical Nutrition*, November 1979].

Dr Kirksey and her colleague, Judith L.B. Roepke, found that mothers whose infants had low Apgar scores (a numerical indicator of the newborn infant's physical status) had significantly lower intakes of B_6 than mothers whose infants had satisfactory scores.

'The 15 women whose infants had low Apgar scores were actually taking B_6 well *above* that recommended for pregnant women,' Dr Kirksey told us. 'Apparently, some women may need a good deal more B_6 on a regular basis during pregnancy than has previously been thought.'

Pregnant or lactating women should be advised, however, that infants sometimes develop a dependency on vitamin B_6 (and later demonstrate withdrawal symptoms) when their mothers' daily doses of the vitamin exceed 50 mg. Prescribing vitamin supplements is complex. The correct dosage for one woman may be too high or too low for another woman. Women considering adding a vitamin supplement to their diets should check with their doctors first.

Folic acid counts

The US Recommended Dietary Allowance (RDA) for pregnant women for folic acid is 800 μg a day, but in Scandinavia, a survey of pregnant women revealed they were getting an average of only 82 μg a day. As many as 30 per cent of all pregnant women are estimated to suffer from folic-acid deficiency anaemia, a condition that raises the risk of premature delivery or birth defects.

Also, during pregnancy, many women suffer from inflamed gums – estimates range from as low as 30 per cent to as high as 100 per cent. However, a study of 30 women during their fourth and eighth months of pregnancy showed that those who rinsed their mouths twice daily for one minute with a folic-acid mouthwash experienced a 'highly significant improvement' in the health of their gums during the eighth month (*Journal of Clinical Periodontology*, October 1980).

Riboflavin aids folic acid and iron

A researcher at the University of Ghana in West Africa – where diets are commonly low in riboflavin (vitamin B_2) – found a special relationship between this and folic acid. Knowing that folic acid is responsible for the production of red blood cells, the professor found that it works much better if it is reinforced by a dose of riboflavin. 'Riboflavin may be exerting its effect through its involvement in folate [folic acid] metabolism', he noted (*International Journal for Vitamin and Nutrition Research*, vol. 50, no. 3, 1980).

The researcher also found, by a separate process, that 'riboflavin is involved in the absorption and utilization of dietary iron' in the blood. He suggested that riboflavin supplements should accompany iron therapy, adding that 'in pregnancy, iron and folate deficiencies are common, and the addition of riboflavin to iron and folate used in treatment may be advisable.'

Vitamin C and abruptio placentae

Vitamin C may also be needed to ensure a healthy pregnancy, research suggests. A study conducted at the Methodist Hospital in New York by Dr C. Alan B. Clemetson, discovered that, when the levels of vitamin C in the blood fall below a certain level, blood levels of the toxic substance histamine rise significantly. Evidence going back as far as 1926 indicates that histamine might be responsible for a potentially fatal complication of pregnancy called *abruptio placentae*, in which the placenta separates from the womb prematurely.

Studies of women with that condition have found that they usually have abnormally low levels of vitamin C in their blood. Histamine injected into guinea pigs and cats has been shown to cause *abruptio placentae*. And Dr Clemetson found that histamine begins to build up in the blood long before vitamin C levels fall to the point where scurvy, the classic vitamin C-deficiency disease, begins to develop (*Journal of Nutrition*, April 1980).

So Dr Clemetson believes that it might be a good idea for pregnant women to supplement their diet with vitamin C. He does not have the final, unshakable proof that this nutrient prevents *abruptio placentae*, but he thinks that taking vitamin C might be a good idea all the same.

Things to avoid during pregnancy

As we said in the beginning of this entry, there are things to avoid during pregnancy. Chief among them are drugs of any kind.

Aspirin This is the drug most frequently used during pregnancy – a study of pregnant women showed that 64 per cent used aspirin, and many took it regularly for as long as six weeks. The result of regular use may be a higly irregular pregnancy – a longer pregnancy, with longer labour and more bleeding before and after delivery. Babies born to mothers who use aspirin during pregnancy also have a tough time of it – they weigh less and are more often stillborn or die shortly after birth. Perhaps worst of all, mothers who use aspirin during pregnancy may have a four times greater risk of having a baby with a certain type of birth defect.

Taking aspirin during late pregnancy may particularly threaten the baby. Besides harm to foetal lungs and interference with blood clotting, the dangers of aspirin could include haemorhage of the brain in premature infants when the drug has been taken within a week of delivery. Warnings against its use now extend to the final three months of pregnancy.

Tranquillizers At the University of Pennsylvania and Children's Hospital in Philadelphia, Dr Sumner Yaffee and associate Chhanda Gupta found that phenobarbitone, a widely prescribed sedative, may affect the unborn in subtle ways. Gross anatomical deformities in animals, usually the criterion of adverse effects on the foetus, didn't appear when the drug was administered to rats late in pregnancy, but the young were smaller than the control pups, and the females suffered delayed puberty and disturbances of the reproductive processes, resulting in 60 per cent infertility.

The scientists didn't leap from rat to woman in their conclusions, but Dr Yaffee told us that careful scrutiny is needed to determine whether these agents are safe during human pregnancy.

This reminds us to remind you: A pregnant woman should never take *anything* that she wouldn't be willing to give directly to her newborn baby. The only exception is medication needed in life-and-death situations, which leaves out barbiturate sedatives. It also leaves out Valium, for experiments have shown that animals administered this tranquillizer in pregnancy give birth to young with behavioural changes suggesting alteration of cellular development – particularly in the nervous system.

A study of 168 women funded by the US Food and Drug Administration (FDA) and published in the *Journal of the American Medical Association* showed that all the women took at least two 'drugs' in pregnancy. (The quotation marks indicate that iron supplements were considered drugs in this study.) The average number of medications taken by these pregnant women was 11, the most hazardous being appetite suppressants. The study concluded that:

> The need for minimized drug prescribing during pregnancy cannot be overemphasized . . . pregnant women receive a vast array of prescription and nonprescription drugs, many of whose safety in pregnancy has not clearly been demonstrated.

Alcohol   If you wouldn't think of giving babies spirits after they are born, should you be giving them some *before* they are born?

Analysing data from 32,019 women early in their pregnancies, researchers at the National Institute of Child Health and Human Development in California discovered that women who drank alcohol daily had a higher rate of spontaneous abortion (miscarriage) than non-drinkers – regardless of smoking habits, age, previous childbirth or abortion. Those who took more than three drinks daily were more than $3^1/_2$ times more likely to have a miscarriage during the second trimester (15 to 27 weeks) of their pregnancy than non-drinkers. Women who drank once or twice daily still faced almost twice the risk of abstainers. No problem was found for women who drank less than once a day.

The researchers concluded that 'Alcohol may harm human foetuses not only when it is abused but also when it is taken in moderation, once or twice daily' (*Lancet*, 26 July 1980).

An official in the US Department of Health and Human Services concurs with warning pregnant women or women contemplating pregnancy to avoid drinking even small amounts of alcohol. Dr Edward N. Brandt said that as little as 2 fl oz of alcohol a week greatly increases the chance of miscarriage, and 1 oz a day can mean a low-birth-weight, high-risk baby. He asked doctors to inform their patients about these hazards.

Caffeine   Of a group of pregnant women drinking at least eight cups of coffee a day, only one avoided severe complications. According to a study that appeared in *Postgraduate Medicine*, only one woman out of 16 who had a high intake of caffeine had an uncomplicated delivery. The other 15 pregnancies ended in spontaneous abortion, stillbirth or premature birth. A cause-and-effect relationship wasn't proven in this study, but moderation will surely be invited if the mother asks herself a simple question: 'If my baby were already born, would I give him or her caffeine?'

Cigarettes   Still another hazard has been uncovered for infants whose mothers smoked heavily during pregnancy. In addition to lower birth weights and increased mortality, a study from Scotland indicated that offspring of heavy puffers experience more behavioural problems, in part related to impaired hearing.

The report, from Ninewells Hospital in Dundee, compared the behaviour-assessment scores of 17 newborns of non-smoking mothers with 15 babies whose mothers smoked more than 15 cigarettes a day throughout their pregnancy. According to the report,

> it became clear that a difference in behaviour and responsiveness did exist. In general, the [babies of the smokers] group tended towards irritability, decreased ability for self-control and a general lack of interest, whereas the [babies of the non-smokers] group tended to be less irritable and better orientated. [*Early Human Development*]

Infants of the smokers group also showed less response to bells and other sounds than the control babies, suggesting some loss of normal hearing.

One possible explanation cited: elevated levels of carboxyhaemoglobin (carbon monoxide combined with haemoglobin) in the blood of mothers who smoke are transferred and further concentrated in foetal blood. And carboxyhaemoglobin may have a toxic effect on the cochlea (part of the inner ear) reducing the oxygen supply to that organ.

Marijuana Marijuana causes profound changes in the hormone chemistry of women, and its toxic materials *do* cross the placenta and pose a threat of permanent glandular and behavioural changes in the baby (*Journal of the American Medical Association*, 21 September 1979).

X-rays The FDA is proposing ways in which doctors, X-ray technicians and patients can protect unborn babies from radiation by limiting the exposure of pregnant women to medical X-rays. Exposure of foetuses to X-rays may cause a slightly increased risk of the child's getting leukaemia or other childhood cancers. The proposed recommendation would apply to any unnecessary X-rays of the hips, pelvis and lower-abdomen and lower-back regions of pregnant women.

Surveys have shown that, each year, 300,000 pregnant women in the United States receive abdominal X-rays that directly expose the foetus to radiation, says Austin Hayes, Acting Deputy Director for the National Center for Devices and Radiological Help, a branch of the FDA.

Hot tubs and saunas During a prolonged session in a hot tub, vaginal temperature can rise to 102°F (38.9°C). That is possibly high enough to threaten the central nervous system of a developing foetus. According to a recent report, the critical temperature may be reached in as little as 15 minutes in a tub at 102°, or 10 minutes at 106°. 'Social' hot-tubbing is usually done at 102°; and 106° is *hot*. Few cases of malformation of babies have been linked to the use of hot tubs by their mothers, but reasonable caution should be observed. Don't stay in too long, and refrain from hopping in and out. 'Core temperature' may be elevated, even though you feel cool (*Science News*, 24 January 1981).

Several studies suggest that defects in the central nervous systems of babies may follow excessive stays in saunas by pregnant women. However, since Finland doesn't seem to suffer such penalties in its newborns from its national habit, it is suggested that limiting the use of the sauna to 10 minutes or less should present no hazard. (The Finns' sauna-bathing averages 6 to 12 minutes, but women in Finland normally tend to shorten their time in the sauna during pregnancy.) It is also possible that the adverse effect endangers only those babies whose mothers experience a significant rise in body temperature when sauna bathing. Some mothers don't, some do (*Canadian Medical Association Journal*, 1 July 1981).

Keeping fit during pregnancy

Experts agree that a moderate fitness programme during pregnancy is safe, effective and recommended. Here are answers to some of the most common questions about exercise during pregnancy.

Q. Is it safe for a pregnant woman to continue a jogging regimen that includes five to seven miles per day?
A. Women who have been regularly involved in this kind of activity well before pregnancy may continue, providing they don't run themselves to the point of exhaustion. Although there is a great deal of controversy about what 'exhaustion' really means, most authorities agree that overdoing it can be determined by the talk test. Simply stated, that means you never exercise so vigorously that you are unable to carry on a conversation or you are gasping for breath. Since it is known that exercise diverts blood flow from the uterus into muscles and fat, running interspersed with walking is recommended during the first trimester. Tapering regular exercise by 30 per cent is advised in advanced pregnancy.

Q. Does vigorous exercise place certain women at greater risk during pregnancy?
A. Definitely. In fact, high-risk women should eliminate *anything* that could jeopardize their pregnancy, and that includes strenuous exercise. Women should consider themselves in this category if they have a history of premature labour or might be bearing twins. Of course that also goes for those with lung disease, high blood pressure, heart disease or diabetes.

Q. Are there any activities or exercises that pregnant women should avoid or at least be cautioned about?
A. Activities that cause undue strain or stress, particularly in the lower back or abdominal muscles, are better avoided during pregnancy. Back strain during pregnancy can contribute to back problems later. The key word here is *moderation*. Recreational bowls, for example, can be continued if the woman is aware of and adapts to the postural changes that have occurred in her body.

Other more strenuous sports such as skiing are ill-advised during pregnancy because of the obvious physical risks involved. An activity like deep-sea diving is also not recommended because the changes in pressure can harm the foetus.

Q. Women not involved in regular exercise programmes often become worried about what is happening as their body stretches out of shape. They ask, 'What shall I do now?'
A. Walking is the very best thing to do, if you have not maintained any other regular kind of exercise programme *before* your pregnancy. As you gain stamina, you may increase your regimen to 20 or 30 minutes per day.

Q. What about risks of elevated temperature with exercise?
A. There is some concern that elevated temperature after extreme exercise in the heat may cause physical defects in the developing foetus. Studies have shown that women who had raised body temperatures during pregnancy gave birth to babies with defects. Pregnant women are advised not to exercise in hot weather and to restrict the time they spend in hot tubs and saunas (*see above*).

Q. How safe are tennis and aerobic dancing?
A. Recent studies suggest that the foetus tolerates exercise pretty well if the mother is in good condition. If aerobic dancing and tennis are not taken to extremes, they most certainly may be continued. Tennis is a stop-and-start game that would probably be best tolerated as doubles. Aerobic dancing is fine as long as you don't exercise so hard that you don't pass the talk test. It is only when you become anaerobic (lacking in oxygen) that you deprive the foetus of oxygen, perhaps causing a potential problem.

Q. What about sports such as cycling and swimming?
A. Both cycling and swimming are non-weight-bearing exercise and, therefore, are excellent ways to maintain fitness. The amount you should do depends, of course, upon how much you did before pregnancy.

Q. I've been told that women who keep fit during pregnancy have easier deliveries. Is that true, and, if so, what types of exercises will specifically help prepare me for labour and delivery?
A. Women who are physically fit do not necessarily experience earlier or easier deliveries. Some do seem to have an easier time, however, in the second stage of delivery (when the baby is actually born). Again, the best and safest exercise is walking.

Q. When is it safe to resume an exercise programme after delivery?
A. Doctors disagree on this question. Some say that women may resume exercise whenever they feel up to it, and then they should begin it slowly. Others feel women should wait until after the first post-partum visit (from four to six weeks after delivery). All agree that nursing mothers should avoid dehydration at this time.

Q. What type of exercise is recommended for post-partum fitness?
A. After delivery, your stomach is apt to be closer to the size it was when you were five months pregnant, but now you don't have that taut look. Although nursing is the best toner for abdominal muscles, many women find

that an exercise programme of bent-knee sit-ups is a good way of ensuring that those muscles are tightened. And you can do it at your convenience.

Again, start gradually. Don't jump into anything very vigorous at first. Follow your body signals when you exercise, and ease up if you need to. You might also want to check with your obstetrician before beginning this, or any other, exercise programme.

• Prostate problems

Among men 40 years of age and over, some kind of prostate problem is nearly epidemic – an estimated 12 million men in the United States alone can attest to that personally. Among men over 60, the likelihood of suffering from an enlarged prostate gland is even greater, increasing to nearly 95 per cent by age 85. And perhaps most disturbing is the increasing rise in deaths from prostate cancer – for example, over 18000 American men each year.

What is this troublesome gland, and why is it such a problem?

The prostate gland is an accessory organ of the male reproductive system, whose only known function is to produce the lubricating fluid which transports sperm cells out of the body. (That's why the prostate has been proverbially associated with sex.) The gland rests just below the bladder and completely surrounds the top of the urethra, the tube that moves liquid waste from the bladder to the outside of the body. Healthy, the prostate is about the size of a walnut. Diseased, it grows and can reach the size of an orange.

That's the essential problem in the most common kind of prostate trouble – benign prostate hypertrophy (BPH for short), which means simply a non-cancerous enlargement of the prostate. Picture the urethra as a garden hose. The enlarged prostate can pinch off the urethra, interfering with urination. The symptoms are increased need to urinate, a burning pain, false starts, dribbling and inability to void the bladder.

The other two major kinds of prostate trouble – prostatitis (inflammation of the prostate) and prostate cancer – usually show the same symptoms.

All these kinds of prostate trouble can be treated. Antibiotic therapy for bacterial prostatitis and surgical removal of all or part of the prostate for both BPH and prostate cancer (as well as treatment with female hormones for the latter) are the commonest treatments. These are still the only reliably tested treatments for the major prostate diseases. Yet each has difficulties, risks and failures. So it's worth considering what can be done to *prevent* prostate trouble before it starts. Fortunately, there are several promising leads.

Too much fat

The prostate wasn't always so troublesome. According to one prostate researcher, Dr Erik Ask-Upmark of the department of medicine at Sweden's University of Upsala, prostate disease 'represents a relatively new pathologic entity. When I was studying medicine, one heard of its existence, but chiefly as a . . . curiosity' *(Grana Palynologica)*. Apparently, in our century some basic change has come about that has made alarmingly common what was once a rare disease. There is evidence to indicate that this basic change has to do with the way we Westerners now eat.

For one, high-fat diets may be to blame for BPH. That's been indicated in studies by Carl P. Schaffner, professor of microbial chemistry at Rutgers University in New Jersey. Man's best friend shares man's prostate problems, and Dr Schaffner discovered that by reducing cholesterol levels in aged dogs, he was also able to reduce the size of the animals' enlarged prostates *(Proceedings of the National Academy of Sciences)*.

Another study, reported to the Amercian Urological Association, using autopsied *human* prostates, corroborates the possibly harmful effect of high choloesterol levels on prostate disease. Camille Mallouh, chief of urology at Metropolitan Hospital in New York, examined 100 prostates from men of all ages and found an 80 per cent increase in cholesterol content of prostates with BPH.

There may also be a link between BPH and prostate cancer. In a study involving almost 1200 case histories, researchers from the department of epidemiology at Johns Hopkins University and the department of biostatistics at Roswell Park Memorial Institute discovered an almost four times greater risk for prostate cancer among cases of BPH. They estimate that, in countries where males have long life expectancies, 43 per cent of the cases of prostate cancer could be attributed to BPH *(Lancet)*.

The link between BPH and prostate cancer may involve high fat levels in our food. Observing that rural black South Africans – who eat a low-fat, whole-food diet – are a low-risk group for prostate cancer, Peter Hill, from the Netherlands, conducted a study at the American Health Foundation in New York City to test whether diet was responsible for their relative immunity.

Dr Hill and his associates placed a group of black South African volunteers on a typical Western diet with lots of fats and meats. At the same time, a group of North American volunteers, blacks and whites, were put on a low-fat diet. To determine the potential effect of these diets on inducing prostate cancer, Dr Hill tested for diet-induced hormonal changes that are associated with the development of prostatic cancer. 'By changing diet, you can change hormonal metabolism,' explains Dr Hill, 'and prostatic cancer seems to be a hormonally associated disease.'

After three weeks, Dr Hill found that the South Africans eating the Western diet were excreting more hormones, while the reverse occurred with the North Americans eating the low-fat diet. The metabolic profile of the North Americans now resembled that of the low-risk group *(Cancer Research,* December 1979).

'This study is a preliminary indication that a low-fat diet is one of the factors which can lower the risk of prostatic cancer,' Dr Hill told us. 'By reducing total calorie intake and substituting fruit and vegetable calories for animal calories, a high-risk prostatic cancer group was switched to a low-risk one.'

Too little zinc

If those who suffer from prostate diseases have too much fat in their diets, one nutrient they apparently have too little of is zinc.

That zinc is somehow essential to the health of the prostate gland has been known for about 50 years. Normally, there is an extraordinary concentration of zinc in healthy human prostatic fluid – 7 mg per gram of fluid – but zinc is also one of the nutrients hardest hit by food processing.

A cooperative study by the Chicago Medical School, Cook County Hospital, Hektoen Institute for Medical Research and Mt Sinai Medical Center in Chicago checked prostate zinc levels in 265 healthy men of various ages. Researchers found that 7 per cent of the men had low prostate and semen zinc levels and that 30 per cent more were borderline cases. In other words, more than one out of every three men didn't have an adequate amount of zinc in the prostate.

An extensive study led by Dr Irving M. Bush of Chicago's Cook County Hospital has dramatically shown the healthy prostate's reliance on zinc. Dr Bush and his associates discovered that zinc levels drop when disease strikes the gland. They found that patients with chronic prostatitis generally suffer from low levels of zinc in both prostate and semen. And they found that patients with prostate cancer also have similar low zinc levels.

Encouraged by these findings, Dr Bush started treating 755 patients suffering from various prostate complaints with zinc supplements. He reported his reports at a national convention of the American Medical Association.

Nineteen of his patients with BPH received 34 mg of oral zinc a day for two months and were then placed on a long-term programme of 11 to 23 mg daily. Lab tests revealed gains in semen levels of the mineral, but more important, all 19 patients reported an easing of their painful symptoms, and on examination, all but five of them showed a decrease in prostate size.

The effect of zinc therapy on patients suffering from infectious prostatitis is even more impressive. Two hundred patients were given between 11 and 34 mg of zinc per day for up to 16 weeks. They all registered higher semen levels of zinc. And 70 per cent reported relief of their symptoms.

Although, according to Dr Bush, zinc therapy isn't ready to replace the conventional treatments of most prostate disorders, such evidence does help explain why so many who have taken zinc have seemingly been helped.

• Psoriasis

American television commericals used to refer to 'the heartbreak of psoriasis'. That may sound like typical advertising hyperbole, but it's an accurate description to a psoriasis sufferer.

The red patches of skin covered with silvery scales that characterize psoriasis are unsightly and uncomfortable, especially when they appear on such vulnerable places as the hands or the soles of the feet. Psoriasis victims are frequently very self-conscious because of their skin problem, and frustrated by fruitless attempts to control it.

The traditional therapy for psoriasis involves applying coal tar to the scaly patches, which are then exposed to ultraviolet light. This is messy and time-consuming but reasonably effective in the short run. (In the long run, psoriasis almost always comes back.) In the early 1970s, researchers developed a psoralen drug, which makes the skin more sensitive to light. Patients are given the drug orally then are put under high-intensity ultraviolet light. This treatment works, too. However, with both treatments, psoriasis victims run the risk of developing skin cancer.

Searching for a safer type of treatment, doctors at Stanford University's dermatology department turned to heat therapy. They have utilized hyperthermia on psoriasis with great success.

'It's especially good for small specific areas of psoriasis, like elbows and knees,' says Elaine Orenberg, who conducted the study. 'In our experiment, we treated 22 different areas of psoriasis on nine separate people. By using a special ultrasound device, we heated the psoriasis plaques to 110°F [43.3°C] for 30-minute periods, three times weekly for a total of four to ten treatments. In that time, 68 per cent of the psoriasis areas cleared completely and another 23 per cent responded partially.

'This method of treatment has a distinct advantage,' Dr Orenberg told us. 'There are no adverse side-effects as there often are with drug therapies.'

The main problem with hyperthermia is that it can't be done at home. A heating pad, for example, would not do the job, says Dr Orenberg, because it doesn't get hot enough. You'd have to sit with it on for about six hours every day to match the effect of the treatment device they use.

More promising treatments

Doctors are also investigating the effectiveness of etretinate (Tigason), a vitamin A-derived drug, in the treatment of severe psoriasis, and the results have been very encouraging. Etretinate has been described by Dr Eugene M. Farber of Stanford Unviersity and president of the International Psoriasis Research Foundation as 'one of the most exciting drugs in the history of dermatology'. Unfortunately, there are side-effects, including possible birth defects, so etretinate should not be used during pregnancy or for 12 months before conception. In the UK, it can only be prescribed by a hospital consultant.

Some results have been reported using a form of nicotinic acid – a B vitamin – taken by mouth to treat psoriasis. One study combined a topical aminonicotinamide drug with niacinamide for a 'significant' recovery in 85 of 99 psoriasis patients *(Archives of Dermatology)*.

Don't rule out food allergies, either. While psoriasis has not been proved to be caused by allergies, the theory has not been disproven. Putting psoriasis patients on a gluten-free diet (i.e., no wheat, rye, barley or oats) resulted in 'remarkable improvements in these patients'. One doctor reported that his wife's psoriasis cleared up when she stopped eating fruit (especially citrus), nuts, maize and milk. Other patients under the same doctor's care improved on similar programmes *(Western Journal of Medicine*, November 1980).

• Raynaud's disease

For his patients with the uncomfortable and sometimes disabling circulatory disorder called Raynaud's phenomenon, a Vermont doctor has come up with an unusual natural therapy. Patients are advised to swing their arms like windmills or propeller blades. No one has actually left the ground yet, but some have experienced dramatic and rapid relief!

Raynaud's phenomenon is characterized by episodes of small artery tightening or constriction in the extremities. Fingers turn deathly pale, only to blush bright red later. Drugs and even surgery are common treatments.

However, the Vermont doctor Donald R. McIntyre has another idea. Observing the success of local skiers in warming up cold hands by whirling their arms, he devised the following manoeuvre (reported in the *Journal of the American Medical Association*): The patient swings the affected arm briskly at about 80 revolutions per minute in the direction that a rounders player would move his arm – i.e. downward behind the body and then upward in front. This continuous motion puts both gravity and centrifugal force to work pushing blood into the outstretched fingers.

A 40-year-old man whose attacks were triggered by cold exposure after typing, complained of whiteness in his fingers for an hour. Using the whirling technique, he reversed attacks in just 90 seconds. A woman, troubled by Raynaud's phenomenon since her teens, experienced relief after whirling her arm only six to eight times.

Dr McIntyre considers his remedy simple, fast and effective. 'The manoeuvre's only complications and adverse side-effects thus far . . .,' he notes, 'have been glancing blows to fingers striking unnoticed ceiling fixtures and also a degree of embarrassment that befalls one in public while waving the arms about.'

Vitamin E is another natural remedy. One man suffering from Raynaud's had six ulcerated fingers; gangrene was actually present in three of them. Yet doctors report that he 'virtually healed eight weeks after using vitamin E' both by mouth and directly on his fingers, and he was still well at a one-year follow-up, as he continued to take the vitamin. The doctors say that several other patients with this condition were given vitamin E, and although their cases were not so dramatic, the majority did show favourable response *(Cutis)*.

• Restless-legs syndrome

This is a condition characterized by a disagreeable sensation deep inside both legs, especially at night. Pregnant women seem especially prone to the problem, but it may be more a result of low stores of folic acid (a B vitamin) than a side-effect of pregnancy.

In a Canadian study, 21 pregnant women were given regular follow-ups during their pregnancies and six weeks after delivery. At each visit, they were rated for severity – or lack – of restless-legs syndrome. Eleven of the women received folic acid while the other ten received a multi-vitamin that did not contain folic acid.

The results? Of the nine women who had restless legs syndrome, only one had taken folic acid. However, of the 12 women who had no symptoms of restless legs, ten had taken folic acid supplements. Said the researchers: 'Our preliminary data suggest that restless-legs syndrome in pregnancy could represent a sign of low serum folate [folic acid] concentration' *(Nutrition Reports International)*.

Pregnant women aren't the only ones to suffer from restless-legs syndrome. Some doctors suggest that the condition is caused by excessive consumption of drinks containing caffeine – such as coffee, tea and cola. And two Los Angeles dermatologists, Richard Mihan and his associate Samuel Ayres, Jr, have used from 400 to 1,600 IU daily of vitamin E to control successfully the disorder in several of their patients.

• Reye's syndrome

Studies done in Ohio and Michigan were the first to implicate aspirin as a possible contributing factor in Reye's syndrome in children, a complication of viral diseases such as chicken pox and influenza. Patients with Reye's syndrome suffer severe vomiting followed by lethargy, personality changes, convulsions and, in some cases, death.

As a result of these and other studies, the US and, in the autumn of 1986, the UK governments requested chemists to withdraw all their stocks of aspirin preparations for children (e.g. Junior Disprin). It is now recommended that all children under the age of 12 (and, ideally, those under 18) should avoid aspirin. Paracetamol products can be taken instead, although because excessive dosages of these can cause serious liver damage, parents and children should take care not to exceed specified dosages.

• Schizophrenia

Peter: 'In the hospital they serve me meat from the morgue and poisoned food. My medicine is really LSD. If I smoke a cigarette, a friend will die.'
Martha: 'God told me I was going to have Christ's baby. He told me to walk with a cane. Then He told me to swim in the ocean; I fought with monsters for eight hours.'
Mitch: 'They say my grandfather died two years ago, but I know better. I talk to him every night. He comes into my room and floats above the bed. Someone turned him into a purple ball.'

Three schizophrenics. Three out of millions.

In the United States alone, around 25 per cent of all people hospitalized are hospitalized for schizophrenia. A hospital is where they belong. In schizophrenia, *thought* and *perception* are diseased.

You hallucinate, seeing what isn't there and hearing voices when no one speaks. In a moderate case, you know you're hallucinating, but when it's worse, you can't tell the difference between what's real and what's not. Your thoughts are bizarre and illogical, perhaps paranoid, and you act on them. You might think there's a plot against you. You might think you're God. You could talk of suicide, and very possibly, commit it. Schizophrenics have a suicide rate about 20 times higher than the rest of the population.

A psychiatrist tries to keep a schizophrenic out of a coffin by putting him on a couch. He wants the schizophrenic to talk things over – and over, and over. Only in this way, he says, will the schizophrenic recognize and root out the cause of his disease: emotional trauma during childhood. However, mummy and daddy aren't always the villains the psychiatrist thinks. Studies have shown that psychoanalysis almost never cures a schizophrenic.

Instead, some are helped by having their brains stunned by electro-convulsive therapy (ECT) – commonly known as 'shock therapy'. Many others live somewhat normal lives by taking powerful drugs. Those treatments have drawbacks, of course. But they work because they affect a schizophrenic's body. They work because schizophrenia is more than a mental illness.

Healing with nutrition

The weird thoughts and strange perceptions of schizophrenia are often the symptoms of *physical* disorders. Disorders that can be healed with nutrition. Unlike the psychiatric approach, that's not a theory. Thousands of schizophrenics have already been cured with a nutrient – nicotinic acid (niacin).

Nicotinic acid is one of the B complex vitamins – and one of the most important. A lack of it can cause severe skin rashes and digestive problems. It can also cause madness. Soon after American processors of white flour began fortifying it with nicotinic acid, 10 per cent of all patients in hospitals run by southern states were 'cured'. They had been diagnosed as schizophrenics, but they actually had pellagra, the nicotinic-acid-deficiency disease. Some of the mental symptoms of pellagra – hallucinations and paranoia – perfectly mimic schizophrenia.

'If all the nicotinic acid were removed from our food, everyone would be psychotic in one year,' says Abram Hoffer, a psychiatrist in British Columbia.

Dr Hoffer was a pioneer in the nutritional treatment of schizophrenia. In 1952, he and a colleague gave nicotinic acid to eight schizophrenic patients. They immediately improved. Continuing the study, the doctors checked their patients' progress for the next 15 years. All were well 15 years later – and all were still taking nicotinic acid *(Orthomolecular Psychiatry)*.

Schizophrenia can last a lifetime, or a few weeks. Many patients walk out of hospitals, only to return. To see if nicotinic acid could keep schizophrenics permanently out of hospitals, Dr Hoffer gave 73 hospitalized schizophrenics the vitamin and compared them to 98 who did not take it. During the next three years, only seven of the nicotinic-acid patients had to be readmitted, while 47 of those not prescribed the nutrient were readmitted *(Lancet)*.

The patients that Dr Hoffer treated did *not* have pellagra. They had what he calls a 'vitamin dependency'. A vitamin dependency, he explained to us, is the need for a larger amount of a vitamin than most people require. If you don't get that amount, you can suffer from a variety of physical and mental ills. Schizophrenia is one of them.

The dependency could be inherited, or if you were deprived of the nutrient over a long period of time, you might need more of it to function normally. Many of the mental patients with pellagra, for instance, had to take 600 mg of nicotinic acid every day for the rest of their lives. Most people need only 5 mg.

Nicotinic acid isn't the only nutrient involved, however. Vitamin C is another.

When a normal person is given 5 g of vitamin C, his tissues are saturated – he can't absorb any more. But studies have shown that it takes *20 to 40 g* of vitamin C to saturate the tissues of schizophrenics. They don't need that much to get better, though. A doctor gave 1 g of vitamin C a day to 40 schizophrenics, all of whom had had the disease for years. Many of them showed significant improvement.

Why vitamin C and nicotinic acid?

'Nobody knows for sure,' Dr Hoffer told us. 'The scientific community is only beginning to look at the relationship of these substances to mental functioning. But even if the role of nutrients in schizophrenia isn't completely understood, there's no doubt in my mind that the disease is caused by a biochemical imbalance in the body that can be corrected with proper nutrition. I've treated 4000 cases of schizophrenia, and I haven't ever seen one caused by psychological factors.'

Biochemical imbalances
Another doctor who believes that schizophrenia is caused by a biochemical imbalance in the body is Carl C. Pfeiffer, the director of the Brain Bio Center in Princeton, New Jersey. Dr Pfeiffer calls schizophrenia a 'biochemical wastebasket'. Into that wastebasket, he says, have been thrown ten diseases, all of which were once thought to be schizophrenia (because their symptoms are identical to those of schizophrenia), but which are now classified as separate diseases with separate causes. Among them are brain syphilis, a thyroid disorder and a type of epilepsy.

Dr Pfeiffer has turned that wastebasket into a filing cabinet. He believes that he has isolated the remaining biochemical abnormalities that cause schizophrenia. There are five, and nutrition can treat them all.

One of them is *pyroluria*. In this disease, a person eliminates abnormally large amounts of the chemical *kryptopyrrole*. Unfortunately, on its way out, kryptopyrrole grabs on to zinc and vitamin B_6, both of which are crucial to normal brain functioning. The result is very low body levels of those nutrients – and schizophrenia. The treatment, however, is simple: replace the vitamin B_6 and zinc. And the cure is almost automatic – 95 per cent recover. Unless they're taken off the nutrients – then schizophrenia returns in two days.

Thirty per cent of all schizophrenics have pyroluria, says Dr Pfeiffer. And most of them are under 20. 'Stress increases the amount of kryptopyrrole that is excreted,' he explained, 'and people from the ages of 15 to 20 face the greatest level of stress.'

Another 60 per cent of schizophrenics suffer from a histamine disorder, according to Dr Pfeiffer. Histamine, as any hayfever victim who takes antihistamines can tell you, is involved in allergic reactions. But that's not all it's involved in. 'It would take a half hour to explain all of histamine's functions in the body,' says Dr Pfeiffer. One of those functions is as a neuro-transmitter, a chemical that relays information in the brain, but when histamine levels rise too high or dip too low, the brain can relay the wrong information: your deceased uncle is standing in the corner; there's a plot against you; you're the saviour of the world. In short, schizophrenia.

For schizophrenics with high histamine, Dr Pfeiffer prescribes calcium, which lowers histamine levels and relieves the constant or frequent headaches that accompany the disorder. Along with calcium, he gives the minerals zinc and manganese. The treatment also includes the amino acid *methionine*. 'This helps to lower blood histamine by a process known as *methylation*,' says Dr Pfeiffer.

'For patients with low histamine, large doses of nicotinic acid and vitamin C are usually effective,' he explains. He also gives them zinc to lower their copper levels.

Studies have also shown that schizophrenics often have high levels of copper in their blood and tissues. 'Copper and zinc are biological antagonists. When one comes in, the other goes out,' says Dr Pfeiffer.

'In our present environment we are saturated with copper,' he continues. 'The main source is drinking water. Almost all water pipes are lined with copper, and it leaches into the water. If the water is very acid, such as well water, the copper levels will be very high. This copper in the water burdens the body in many ways. Schizophrenia is not the only problem associated with it. I believe it may also be a cause in miscarriage, birth defects, high blood pressure and depression.'

To prove his point, Dr Pfeiffer cites a survey of drinking water in homes across the United States. Every home that had a level of copper in its water higher than the US Public Health Service considers safe also had at least one family member with psychiatric problems *(Journal of Applied Nutrition)*.

He also points out that dialysis, a procedure to cleanse a kidney patient's blood, concentrates copper in the water used for cleansing. A problem associated with dialysis is madness and depression, a disease called 'dialysis dementia'. Although opinions differ on its cause, a widely accepted theory says the problem is caused by copper overload.

Food allergies and low blood sugar

The remaining 10 per cent of schizophrenics, says Dr Pfeiffer, have a cerebral allergy. In cerebral allergy, a person has an allergic reaction to a commonly eaten food. But the reaction occurs in the brain – 'hives [nettle rash] of the brain' as one researcher put it.

Dr Pfeiffer isn't the first scientist to recognize food allergy as a cause of schizophrenia. Gluten, a substance in wheat and some other grains, has long been thought either to cause or complicate schizophrenia. During World War II, when wheat and other cereals were rare in Greece, psychiatrists noted an improvement in the symptoms of schizophrenic patients *(Lancet)*. In another study, a researcher took the gluten out of the diet of 14 schizophrenics, who began to improve. After a month, he put it back in – and they got worse.

When, a month later, he took them off gluten again, their recovery continued (*Science*).

Hypoglycaemia often complicates a schizophrenic disorder, says Dr Pfeiffer. In hypoglycaemia, brain levels of blood sugar plummet, causing mental problems that can include anxiety, depression, suicidal tendencies and paranoia. Many doctors believe that eating too much sugar and other refined carbohydrates can cause hypoglycaemia. Could eating less sugar help cure schizophrenia?

'I have seen a large number of patients who had been much improved by other treatment, but who did not become well until they went onto a sugar-free diet,' says Dr Hoffer.

Proper nutrition seems to be the best way to treat schizophrenia. Yet the American Psychiatric Association and the US government's National Institute of Mental Health have been 'powerful opponents' of treating schizophrenia with nutrition. Why?

'Resistance is the typical medical reaction to all ideas that strike out on new therapeutic ground,' says Dr Hoffer. 'The attack on nutritional treatment is illogical, unjustified, extreme, emotional and not backed up by scientific evidence.'

It's also deadly. Doctors estimate that the failure to treat schizophrenia properly causes more than 200 suicides a year, lives that could have been saved if they had received the correct nutrients.

Other treatments

Injections of endorphins – the body's natural painkillers – have also been given to schizophrenics. Some scientists have theorized that a lack of endorphins in the brain might cause their bizarre behaviour.

Nathan Kline, a New York psychiatrist, used endorphins to treat 15 patients – not only schizophrenics, but several depressed patients and a woman suffering from agoraphobia, a condition of intense, irrational fear in which she was afraid to walk to her car alone. The results were astonishing: seven of the patients reported an improvement of mood that lasted several hours. Over the next few days, hallucinations faded and normal behaviour returned in some (*Archives of General Psychiatry*).

Another doctor is using running as a therapy for one schizophrenic patient. Dr Thaddeus Kostrubala says that exercise has meant the difference between mental health and mental illness for this patient. 'As long as he keeps up his running, there's no trace of his disease visible in any kind of examination. But his symptoms come back very clearly if he stops running,' says Dr Kostrubala. 'He has a complete choice available to him. He can choose to be schizophrenic or well.'

Although the Chinese use anti-psychotic drugs, they report that acupuncture is more helpful than medication in treating schizophrenia. Behavioural scientists at the Albert Einstein College of Medicine and South Beach Psychiatric Center in New York have also favourably used acupuncture as a treatment for schizophrenia. They tested three medication-free groups: (1) those given acupuncture at the precise meridian points adopted by the Chinese; (2) those given pseudo-acupuncture – with the needles located at places other than the known meridians; (3) those given no acupuncture, but who had contact with a psychiatrist.

Improvement was found during and just after the treatment of the first group, but no improvement occurred in groups two and three. The experimenters believe that acupuncture alters activation of the cortical (thinking) brain.

• Seborrhoea

One of the most common conditions that brings patients to dermatologists is seborrhoea, particularly of the scalp. The condition, marked by scaliness of the nose and lip area, heavy dandruff (sometimes with hair loss), inflammation of the eyes, and 'cradle cap' in the newborn, is resistant to many types of treatment.

Most of the therapies in the past have been local – application of one medication or another directly on to the affected area. Drs Wolfgang A. Casper and Orlando Manfredi reported that patients with seborrhoea showed a remarkable response to intramuscular injections of vitamin B_{12} *(Cutis)*. Those responses invited an investigation of malabsorption of the vitamin, since dietary deficiency in B_{12} – except in purely vegetarian diets – is extremely unlikely. Any diet adequate in animal protein is almost certainly a good source of the vitamin.

These researchers discovered that the deficiency originates with malabsorption of the vitamin, probably in the section of the small intestine known as the ileum. Further, many of the patients with seborrhoea were found to be victims of easily disturbed carbohydrate metabolism, some of them showing a hidden (chemical) diabetes, with a higher-than-average carbohydrate intake. This is significant because it is known that diabetics have a diminished reabsorption of vitamin B_{12} from the intestine.

According to the researchers, doses of B_{12} by mouth may not produce similar satisfactory results, since absorption of the vitamin is limited.

• Senility

The teacher, in his mid-60s, went to the hospital with chest pain. Put under observation, he was given a drug for angina and high blood pressure. He woke up the next morning a changed man – but not changed for the better.

He hardly seemed to know he was in a hospital and denied he was sick. He babbled about things that had happened 20 years before. And after the brain specialists were through with him – finding his memory bad, his speech garbled and his intellect so muddled he could barely add two and two – they diagnosed him as senile.

A story like this usually has a sad ending – the nursing home – but in this case, the family didn't accept the diagnosis. They insisted he wasn't senile and convinced the doctors to take him off the drug he had received in the hospital. By the next day, he was thinking more clearly, and in two weeks, his 'senility' had disappeared.

This case isn't a rarity. Perhaps 30 per cent of the people diagnosed as senile are, in fact, suffering from some other problem – a drug side-effect, an infection, a hormone imbalance, a vitamin deficiency. 'There are more than a hundred possible different conditions whose causes lead to symptoms that we mistakenly, tragically picture as senility,' wrote dental surgeon Arthur Freese in his book *The End of Senility*.

Why is it that doctors so often miss diagnosing those conditions and instead label someone 'senile'? 'The most potent reason,' says geriatrician Richard W. Besdine, 'is ageism – prejudice against old people.

'It has been proven that old people receive less careful medical attention,' Dr Besdine, affiliated with the Hebrew Rehabilitation Center for the Aged and the Harvard Medical School in Boston, Massachusetts, told us. 'And when an old person is demented, the medical care he receives is even less attentive.

'Many doctors accept the false belief that the natural state of old people is to get senile, and that senility by its very existence is irreversible,' Dr Besdine continued. 'So when an old person comes into their surgery with symptoms such as forgetfulness or confusion – which they would thoroughly investigate in a young person to discover the underlying cause – they simply pigeonhole the person as senile.'

However, as gerontologist Alex Comfort points out, 'Old people do not, in fact, become weak, frail, immobile or demented through any . . . near-universal change coupled to chronological age.' In short, he says, senility is a myth (*Postgraduate Medicine*, March 1979).

What is a *fact*, according to an article in the *Journal of the American Medical Association* (18 July 1980) entitled 'Senility Reconsidered', is that 'the aged brain is extremely sensitive,' and that almost *any* change for the worse in the body or mind of an older person can cause the symptoms that some doctors pass off as senility. And the two major causes of *reversible* senility – 'the double Ds of dementia' as Dr Besdine calls them – are drugs and depression.

Drug side-effects

The typical elderly American or Briton takes from between four and seven drugs every day, and perhaps as many as 13 different drugs a year. To complicate matters, the ageing kidney is less able to rid the body of those drugs, and they can build up in the system. The end result can be a side-effect (e.g. the elderly make up 11 per cent of the US population, but suffer more than 50 per cent of all drug side-effects). And some side-effects – confusion, irritability, anxiety, slurred speech – mimic senility.

Which drugs cause the problem?

'Any drug can do it,' says Lissy Jarvik, a professor of psychiatry at UCLA. And one drug often singled out by experts as a cause of reversible senility is digoxin, a drug prescribed for heart patients. 'The danger of giving digitalis [digoxin] to the elderly has received much attention in the past 20 years,' says a report in the *Journal of Clinical Pharmacology* (November – December

1979). The article goes on to describe four elderly people who suffered from 'digitalis intoxication'.

One woman, who 'before admission lived independently without mental impairment or depression, appeared depressed and lost her capacity for self-care' after one week on digoxin. After three weeks on the drug, 'she was severely depressed, unmotivated and at times lethargic. She stated, "I have given up."'

Another woman was 'alert and cooperative' but became 'anxious and restless' after two weeks on digoxin. After doctors took her off the drug, however, 'she appeared relaxed and was resting comfortably.' In the next two days her 'mental status' returned to normal.

However, digoxin isn't the worst offender. Psychoactive drugs are. These include sedatives, tranquillizers, sleeping pills and the like. 'It's very easy to understand why psychoactive drugs can make you demented with chronic use,' says Dr Besdine. 'They interfere with neuro-transmitters, the chemicals that regulate brain function. And they weaken coordination between the parts of the brain. These drugs have the potential to cause intellectual impairment in a person of any age, and the elderly are the most vulnerable. Old brains are more sensitive to the confusion-inducing side-effects of psychoactive drugs.'

In a study that bears out Dr Besdine's statement, 38 out of 236 patients over 65 who were hospitalized for 'behavioural disturbances' were later found to be suffering from the side-effects of psychoactive drugs (*Journal of the American Medical Association*, 20 June 1980).

What's worse, older people with drug-caused reversible senility probably receive *more* psychoactive drugs to 'cure' their condition. A professor of psychiatry at the Washington (State) University School of Medicine points out that a drug given to control drug-caused behavioural symptoms could worsen the symptoms – and lead to an increase in the amount of drugs (and, perhaps, a further worsening of the symptoms). That cycle isn't vicious. It's tragic.

And an older person can overdose himself into senility on what is considered a normal and safe dosage of a psychoactive drug. As Dr Freese warns, if Valium (a so-called 'minor' tranquillizer) is given to a man of 70 at the same dosage that is appropriate for a man of 30, it can 'easily accumulate to an excessive degree, with serious mental side-effects'.

'There are no minor tranquillizers for the elderly,' says Dr Comfort. And he cautions doctors against prescribing sleeping pills for 'the common later-life pattern of light sleep and frequent waking'.

Older people are also more likely to be drowsy after taking a psychoactive drug – a side-effect that could be easily mistaken for senility. One doctor called drowsiness a 'major problem' among old people who take tranquillizers. And if you've had two different psychoactive drugs prescribed for you, or if you drink alcohol before the drug is out of your system, or even if you use some kinds of over-the-counter cough medicine while you're on the drug, the drowsiness will be worse.

Deceptive depression

However, perhaps the most dangerous side-effect of psychoactive drugs is a mental disorder that, in the elderly, is *very* often misdiagnosed as senility: depression.

> Drugs, either prescribed by a physician or taken independently, often are responsible for the development of depression, the aggravation of a preexisting depression or the production of depression-like symptoms such as sedation, apathy and lethargy

says an article in the *Journal of the American Geriatrics Society*. And, the report continues, the elderly are 'particularly likely' to develop 'depressive side-effects'.

Whatever causes depression in an older person (and depression is the most common mental illness among the elderly), many doctors overlook it and instead diagnose a person as senile.

'Many symptoms of depression are similar to those of people with senility,' Robert Kahn, an associate professor of psychiatry and behavioural science at the University of Chicago, told us. 'Those symptoms also occur in the young. But when they occur in the old, the immediate assumption of most doctors is that the person is senile. After all, he *must* be senile – he's old.'

'It can be difficult to distinguish irreversible senile dementia from depression,' says Dr Besdine. 'If an older patient can't or won't answer a doctor's questions, there is a tendency among doctors to label that person senile. But a depressed person may not answer questions because he's too depressed to care about them. Depression that mimics dementia is such a common phenomenon that there is a scientific term for it – *pseudo-ementia*.'

In one study on pseudo-dementia, 12 of 22 elderly patients whom doctors thought were demented were ultimately found to be depressed. 'This error is made more frequently in general practice than is realized,' says a report in the *Canadian Medical Association Journal* 3 November 1979).

Drugs are far from the only cause of depression in the elderly. 'The early stage of a systemic disease such as cancer or heart disease can produce depression in an older person,' says Dr Besdine.

'There are a number of physical illnesses that appear to generate depressive symptoms in the elderly,' wrote Dr Monica D. Blumenthal. 'When recognized, [depression in the elderly] is amenable to treatment; misdiagnosed, it can lead to invalidism and death' (*Geriatrics*, April 1980).

And, misdiagnosed, *stress*-caused senility can lead to the same thing. 'Any stress can induce senility that is reversible,' says Dr Kahn. 'Many older people have some changes in their brain tissue but still function normally,' he explains. 'But subject them to some kind of stress and they will manifest behaviour that resembles senility.

'We studied older people who were coming into the hospital to have cataracts removed. During this type of operation, older people often develop disturbed senile-like behaviour, but we didn't understand why. In an attempt to isolate and eliminate the cause of the problem, we put people to bed and bandaged their eyes *before* the operation – and most of them exhibited senile-like behaviour. Just the stress of bandaging the eyes and putting people to bed produced behaviour that looked like senility but was reversible.'

Dr Kahn also points out that people who are misdiagnosed as senile and put in nursing homes and hospitals may become more 'senile' because of the stress of institutionalization. 'Nursing homes and hospitals are filled with older people who are depressed but misdiagnosed as senile or have an acute disease with symptoms of senility. In those institutions, they are under stress – they are in precisely the kind of environment that maximizes senile-like behaviour in the elderly.'

The importance of nutrients

A nutritional deficiency can also cause reversible senility. 'A deficiency of vitamin B_{12}, folic acid, iron, protein or calories can affect the brain and make people demented,' says Dr Besdine.

In one study, ten elderly patients who were in a confused mental state were tested for blood levels of folic acid. All ten had a deficiency *(British Medical Journal)*.

Other experts mention deficiencies in nutrients such as vitamin B_6 as a potential cause of reversible senility. Laboratory animals fed a diet deficient in B_6 developed changes in their brain cells that resembled those found in senile human beings. The researchers concluded: 'Our findings show the importance of nutrition, particularly B_6 . . . in relation to human senility' *(Federation Proceedings,* 1 March 1980).

Thiamin (vitamin B_1) also has a profound effect on the brain and nervous system. Even a *slight* deficiency of thiamin wounds the brain. Poor memory, irritability, depression, lack of initiative, insomnia, inability to concentrate: these are the symptoms of a *mild* thiamin deficiency, symptoms too often diagnosed as senility or neurosis.

Researchers compared the thiamin levels of 18 women with senility to those of ten healthy people. Fifteen of the 18 women had 'suboptimal blood levels' of thiamin, while all ten of the healthy people had normal levels *(International Journal of Vitamin and Nutrition Research)*.

And there are other causes of 'senility'. An elderly person who falls and bruises his head may develop senile-like symptoms as the bruise swells and puts pressure on his brain. Infections can also be a cause. So can a heart condition. A diseased thyroid. A weak kidney. Given that 80 per cent of people over 65 suffer from one or more chronic health conditions (and that many of them take drugs for those conditions), the possibility of an older person developing reversible senility isn't that farfetched.

Dr Abram Hoffer startled a Huxley Institute audience when he reported unpublished research that indicates a *water* deficiency can be an important cause of senile behaviour. The problem begins when the thirst mechanism, like the senses of taste and smell, declines with increasing age. With inadequate water intake, the blood itself becomes dehydrated – thicker, with reduced circulation, making the brain an early and very susceptible target. Coupled with other physiological responses to dehydration, the process can cause symptoms of senility.

It pays to be sceptical

What can you do if a doctor diagnoses a parent, spouse, relative or friend as senile? For starters, don't believe it.

'If there is any diagnosis of senile dementia, demand a comprehensive evaluation,' says Dr Besdine. 'No one should be allowed to go into a nursing home without such an evaluation. And the more sophisticated and thorough the evaluation, the more likely that reversible dementia is going to be found.'

'A person should have an intensive workup before he's labelled senile,' says Dr Jacob Brody at the National Institute on Aging in Bethesda, Maryland. 'When cancer is suspected, for instance, a very intensive investigation is conducted before a final diagnosis is made. The same serious investigation should precede the diagnosis of senile dementia. And even if the person is diagnosed as having senile dementia, you should get a second opinion from someone who specializes in the medical care of older people – a geriatrician.'

Dr Jarvik agrees. 'Don't take one doctor's word for it that nothing can be done because the person is senile,' she told us. 'See someone who is a specialist in geriatric psychiatry or, if none is available, a specialist in geriatric medicine.'

And, if the person is taking drugs, the drugs should be stopped under the supervision of a competent doctor. 'In drug toxicity,' says Dr Besdine, 'one of the first symptoms is the onset of confusion or dementia. If a person shows these symptoms, the first thing I do is to stop every drug he is taking and add them back only as the person shows a definite need for them.'

Dr Besdine points out that this isn't necessarily a dangerous procedure: 'In a study in Britain, 200 people over 70 who were taking digitalis [digoxin] went off the drug cold turkey. Less than half showed a need for the resumption of the drug.'

If the problem is diagnosed as depression, don't let a doctor convince you that depression – like senility – is incurable in the elderly. 'Depression isn't hopeless in the elderly,' says Dr Jarvik. 'We are treating patients in their 70s and 80s, and they are doing very well.'

And all the professionals we talked to agreed that the most important point to remember – for doctors and lay people alike – is that the natural state of an older person is *not* senility.

'Senility should always be considered a disease – not the natural consequence of growing old,' says Dr Brody. 'If a doctor sees a person with senile-like symptoms, he can't just sit back and say, "It's ageing." It's not. Senility is a myth.'

(*See also* ALZHEIMER'S DISEASE and MEMORY PROBLEMS.)

• Shingles

Remember when you had chicken pox as a child? You were pretty miserable (not to mention unsightly) for about two or three weeks. But finally, the last scab fell off, and you went skipping back to school feeling incredibly happy to be rid of the disease once and for all.

Or so you thought. Fact is, the same nasty little bug that gave you chicken pox as a child can come back – only worse – to haunt you decades later as an ageing adult. The bug is herpes, the disease – shingles.

It's true. The pox may be gone, but the germs linger on. After a bout with chicken pox, *herpes zoster* (the official name of this virus) sometimes takes up residence in the spinal nerves, where it promptly goes into hibernation. You think it's gone for ever, but it can wake up at any time and start multiplying.

When that happens, the affected nerve becomes inflamed, and pain radiates all along its path. The herpes virus then passes down the nerve and multiplies again in the skin, causing clusters of sores to erupt.

For four to five days before the expected rash, however, you may feel anything from numbness and superficial tingling, itching or burning sensations to severe, deep pain. Discomfort may be intermittent or constant. At its worst, the pain may even be mistaken for appendicitis, a gall bladder attack or pleurisy. As if that's not enough, you may also run a fever for days and feel generally out of sorts, too. All this before eruption!

When the rash does make its appearance, it starts out as small reddened areas that quickly puff up with fluid to the size of a 5-pence piece or, in some cases, larger. The skin over the blisters becomes increasingly rigid until finally, by about the fifth day after eruption, the blisters burst. During the next week or two, crusts develop, but a total of two to four weeks may elapse before you see the last scab fall off.

The sores are not randomly distributed on the body as with chicken pox. The affected areas are always along the course of one or more of the spinal nerves beneath the skin. Most typically, the rash progresses in a band around one side of the chest (55 per cent of the cases), the neck (20 per cent), lower back (15 per cent) or the forehead and eyes (15 per cent), and all the while you may be feeling extreme discomfort. The distribution and appearance of the sores is so characteristic of *herpes zoster* that no testing is necessary to confirm diagnosis.

Who gets shingles?

True, its appearance is similar to chicken pox, but shingles is not a youngster's disease. On the contrary, it's those over the age of 50 who are most susceptible. In fact, it's been estimated that half the people reaching 85 years of age have suffered from at least one attack of *herpes zoster*.

These are not necessarily sickly folks, either. Believe it or not, shingles often occurs in otherwise healthy older people. Sometimes it's a physical injury that precipitates a bout of shingle. At least that's what several researchers discovered some years ago. They found that 38 per cent of their *herpes zoster* patients had an injury to the shingles-infected area two weeks before the appearance of sores *(British Medical Journal)*.

That finding, coupled with the decreased natural immunity that often accompanies old age, may help explain the prevalence of shingles in older people. Of course, anything that lowers your resistance may also trigger an outbreak of shingles. That means you may be more susceptible in times of physical or emotional stress or when your natural immunity has been compromised by another illness.

One thing's for sure, though: you can't catch shingles the way you do chicken pox. Most patients with *herpes zoster* have had no recent exposure to others infected with it or with chicken pox. That's why the incidence of shingles does not increase during seasonal chicken-pox epidemics. On the other hand, a person susceptible to chicken pox can catch it from someone suffering from shingles. What's more, shingles is not a once-and-for-all disease like chicken pox. That means you can come down with a second or third outbreak, and it can affect the same nerve as it did the first time or a different one completely.

However, no matter how or why the eruptions occur, each person is affected to a different degree. As with most diseases, some people get off with only a mild sentence, while others wonder if they'll ever be set free.

Let us reassure you right now. Complications can be severe and quite serious, but they are rarely fatal or even permanent. Still, you should know that *herpes zoster* is occasionally associated with paralysis of the arms, legs and chest muscles. Even when that occurs, however, adequate functioning returns in over 75 per cent of cases. Eye involvement, on the other hand, may result in pemanent visual impairment due to scarring of the cornea. Skin, too, may be permanently scarred if the sores are very deep.

The most common and troublesome part of shingles is pain that lingers long after the obvious infection has gone. Doctors call this *post-herpetic neuralgia* and believe it is caused by scarring of the damaged nerves. It doesn't afflict everyone, fortunately, but once again it's older people who suffer the most. As many as 70 per cent of those over 60 years of age can expect moderate to severe pain for more than two months or, in some cases, for years.

Relief measures

While there doesn't appear to be any definitive way to ward off an attack of shingles (except to boost your own natural immunities with good health habits), there are numerous ways to help relieve the discomforts of shingles, if it should strike.

First of all, while the sores are erupting, wear loose-fitting clothes. 'And, especially, stay away from fuzzy garments,' says Richard Mihan of the University of Southern California School of Medicine. As a dermatologist practising with Samuel Ayres, Jr, Dr Mihan has treated numerous cases of *herpes zoster* and the often-accompanying post-herpetic neuralgia. 'The pain may be severe at times, requiring sedation and causing almost unbearable discomfort and loss of sleep,' says Dr Mihan.

Vitamin E
Rather than resorting to drastic measures like cutting out the root of the affected nerve or repeatedly injecting local anaesthetics into the area (which causes other negative side-effects), Drs Ayres and Mihan have found a better, safer way to relieve the prolonged suffering – vitamin E.

Over a period of four years, they treated 13 patients with chronic post-*herpes zoster* neuralgia with vitamin E, administered both orally (400 to 1600

IU daily) and directly on to the sores. (Levels of vitamin E of over 600 IU daily should be taken only under a doctor's supervision.)

Eleven of the patients had had moderate to severe pain for over six months. Seven of those had suffered for over one year; one for 13 years and one for 19 years! Yet after taking vitamin E, nine patients reported complete or almost complete control of pain. The two patients who had had post-herpetic neuralgia longest were in this group. Of the remaining four patients, two were moderately improved and two were slightly improved *(Archives of Dermatology)*.

'The mechanism by which vitamin E relieves the persistent pain of post-*herpes zoster* neuralgia is not known,' concluded Drs Mihan and Ayres, 'but in view of its long duration in many of our cases, we do not believe it is coincidence.'

'Vitamin E may not be 100 per cent effective,' Dr Mihan says, 'but many of my patients get relief from persistent pain.'

Vitamin E does more than relieve pain. It also helps stop the rash from spreading. One woman told us, 'A few months ago, I noticed a sore about the size of a silver dollar [i.e. about 1 inch across] on my back. When I touched the spot, it burst as if it were a blister. I thought nothing of it until late that same evening, when I felt a rash very rapidly spreading all over my back. It was annoying and felt as though ants were crawling on my skin.

'Not knowing how to stop it from spreading, I wondered if vitamin E might help. I cut the tips of three vitamin E capsules (each 400 IU) with scissors, let the oil drip into a saucer and applied it to the reddish, tender sores. Vitamin E stopped the rash from spreading instantly and gave me so much relief that I was able to sleep well that night. By morning, my husband was amazed to notice how the sores had begun to heal and were already forming scabs.

'I paid a visit to our family doctor that afternoon, and he confirmed my own suspicions: it was shingles. Healing progressed quickly and completely as I continued applying vitamin E oil to the infected area, and during that time, I was never laid up and was able to do all of my housework. It's no wonder that vitamin E is called the "miracle vitamin".'

Vitamin C

Still, vitamin E doesn't work for everyone. But don't despair. Vitamin C may help do the job for you.

According to Irwin Stone, author of *The Healing Factor: Vitamin C Against Disease*, this vitamin has been shown to stop the pain, dry the blisters and clear the lesions within three days of being administered through injection.

More recently, Dr Juan N. Dizon of New York treated *herpes zoster* with oral vitamin C and got excellent results: 'I have treated three cases of shingles with 10 g [10000 mg] of vitamin C daily (1 g every hour) until the lesions dry up,' says Dr Dizon. 'In each case, the lesions dried up within two to five days.' (That amount of vitamin C should be taken only under a doctor's supervision.) I told another physician of these findings. When he tried the same on his patients, he had similar results.

'I am aware that this is all anecdotal and non-scientific, but considering that there is no good scientific tretment for herpes and that vitamin C is virtually harmless, I would hope that others will try this method on their patients and report their results. After enough anecdotal cases have been submitted, maybe somebody will do double-blind controlled studies.'

If vitamin C works for you, says Irwin Stone, it may be because ascorbic acid enhances the body's production of interferon, a natural protein made by white blood cells in response to a viral attack, such as *herpes zoster*.

Interferon has been shown to be effective in stopping the spread of shingles, according to a recent experiment done at the Stanford University School of Medicine in San Francisco, but this natural protein cannot be bought for home use. Besides being prohibitively expensive, it's not even available in sufficient quantities to make a dent in the millions of shingles patients. That's why it's better to produce your own, if you can, by taking vitamin C.

Acupuncture

While vitamins E and C have been beneficial to many, still others have found relief in acupuncture.

Dr Nolan R Cordon of California treated 11 patients with acute *herpes zoster* by using various acupuncture techniques. In ten of the 11 patients, the intense and severe pain was controlled, said Dr Cordon. What's more, once treatment was initiated, there was no further spread of the disease and the healing of existing sores was accelerated *(American Journal of Acupuncture)*.

Since shingles is one of those diseases that have no known cure, you'll want to try everything you can that may possibly bring relief from your suffering. An outbreak of shingles is not the end of the world, but it can certainly change your outlook on it for a while. Keep yours bright with vitamins E and C, and hopefully, shingles will be just a short lapse in an otherwise healthy life.

• Sickle-cell anaemia

People with sickle-cell anaemia, an inherited disease, suffer from an abnormality of haemoglobin that affects their circulating red blood cells with sometimes disastrous results. Haemoglobin is the iron-rich reddish pigment inside the cells that carries vital oxygen to all the tissues of the body.

Unfortunately, sickle-cell victims have an unusual molecular form of haemoglobin that can actually cause the red blood cell to bend into a distorted crescent-moon or sickle shape. This shape makes it impossible for the red cells to squeeze through the tiniest of blood vessels, or capillaries. Those vessels are so small in diameter that even normal blood cells have to march through in single file. Sickled cells, which can elongate to three or four times the length of normal cells, get caught and hopelessly jammed. Sickle-cell victims suffer from recurring attacks of fever and pain in the arms, legs and abdomen as sickled cells back up in blood vessels, causing painful 'sickling' crises.

[Sickle-cell aenaemia is the result of an adaptation by the red blood cells as a resistance to malaria. Thus, those carrying this genetic adaptation either come from those areas of the world where malaria is prevalent – e.g. central Africa, parts of the Middle East, South-east Asia – or their ancestors did (i.e. black populations of the UK, the US and elsewhere).

Dr Danny Chiu, a researcher at the Children's Hospital Medical Center in Oakland, California, and a colleague, Dr Bertram Lubin, have now discovered that patients with sickle-cell anaemia also have a vitamin E deficiency. As Dr Chiu suggested at an annual meeting of the Federation of American Societies for Experimental Biology, inadequate levels of the vitamin in sickle-cell patients' blood plasma and red blood cells may contribute to the sickling process.

For one thing, the scientists found that the extreme susceptibility of red blood cells from sickle-cell patients to lipid peroxidation (a chemical reaction between oxygen and fat that damages the thin, protective membrane around the cell) can be prevented – at least in the test tube – by vitamin E. Dr Chiu speculates that vitamin E's action as an anti-oxidant may alter the red cell membrane's stability, making it less vulnerable to bending and distortion.

Irreversible sickling

'Normally, most cells of sickle-cell patients sickle only under certain circumstances,' Dr Chiu explains. 'Otherwise, the molecular defect isn't expressed clinically. But some cells, which we call ISC, or irreversibly sickled cells, always sickle. The amount of these cells varies from one patient to another, from 5 to 30 per cent.'

According to other scientists, supplemental vitamin E can reduce the percentage of ISC by more than half. Researchers from Hoffmann – La Roche and Columbia University told the same conference that when 13 sickle cell patients took 450 IU of vitamin E a day, the proportion of irreversibly sickled cells dropped from 25 to 11 per cent.

Since life expectancy of such patients is only about 20 years, most of the patients seen are children. And because there is no cure, doctors concentrate mainly on relieving the patients' pain, extending their lifespan and helping them live more comfortably.

As Dr Chiu mentioned, in sickle-cell patients, not all the blood cells are always in the sickled or otherwise irregular shapes. Most may be somewhat oval or round, but under conditions of physical or mental stress, a large proportion of cells will become sickled and clog up the circulation in the capillaries. All that causes pain so excruciating that the child often will black out. During such a sickling crisis, the fragile cells are broken up – their precious contents lost – so there are never enough blood cells. That causes anaemia, owing to loss of valuable nutrients such as calcium, iron and, especially, zinc.

Replacing lost zinc

Nydia Meyers, a researcher in the department of human genetics at the University of Michigan Medical School, is part of a team that has been exploring the relationship of zinc and calcium in the red blood cells of patients afflicted with sickle-cell anaemia.

The research team began to use zinc as a therapeutic agent in sickle-cell anaemia because many of the children were poorly nourished, appeared dwarfed and suffered from delayed development. They resembled people in the Middle East who had been helped by zinc supplements.

When a group of sickle-cell children ate nourishing food with zinc supplements, they grew 1–3 inches within two years. It was noticed that their general health improved, and there were fewer trips to hospital because of sickle-cell crises. That prompted the research team to examine more closely the role of zinc.

They found that added zinc enabled the cells to squeeze through the capillaries' tiny passageways. And they also discovered that zinc may have an additional benefit for those with the condition: it could protect them against lead toxicity in their environment. Sickle-cell patients who live in urban areas where the air contains a high number of lead particles tend to inhale lead, which is quickly absorbed by their already weakened bodies. Zinc seems to counter lead's effects.

• Sinusitis

'No one really knows the purpose of the sinuses,' says Dr Stanley N. Farb, but millions of people can tell you what sinuses are for: making life miserable.

Your nose is swollen and you have pains in your chest. Your ears are ringing, your head aches, you can't breathe and it's difficult to speak. There are tears in your eyes and dark circles under them. A sinus attack can leave you looking as if you accidentally stepped into the ring with Muhammad Ali, and it can leave you feeling worse. There is no referee to call time-out, no trainer to hold your belligerent sinuses at bay.

However, there is hope. Vitamin A, a more humid environment and some changes in your diet may give you a fighting chance.

Eight sinus cavities, symmetrically arranged in four groups of two, are located in the vicinity of your eyes and nose. Any one of them is liable to become inflamed, resulting in a condition called 'sinusitis'. To those of us bullied by it, sinus trouble is more common than the common cold. In fact, many of the symptoms are so similar that sinus trouble is often mistaken for a nagging cold. However, although the latter may instigate an attack of sinusitis, most people approach treatment the wrong way.

'The worst thing you can do is take "cold remedies" – nose drops and antihistamines – when you have sinusitis,' says Dr Farb, who is chief of the oto-rhino-laryngology (ear, nose and throat) departments of Montgomery Hospital and Sacred Heart Hospital in Pennsylvania, and on the staff of Thomas Jefferson University Hospital in Philadelphia.

'Nose drops may provide relief for a few days, then they cause something called the "rebound phenomenon", which is somewhat like an addiction,' Dr Farb told us. 'The stuffiness actually becomes worse as a result, and you end up needing more nose drops, more often. We've all known people who start taking nose drops, and then six months later, they're still taking them. It's a very common problem.'

Mucus must flow freely

In his book, *The Ear, Nose and Throat Book: A Doctor's Guide to Better Health*

(1980), Dr Farb explains that anti-histamines may actually block the sinuses by thickening the mucus that lines the nasal passages and sinus cavities.

Normally, mucus flows freely between nose and sinus via a tiny duct – it's about the diameter of a pencil lead – that is the only way in or out of the sinus. 'Think of a room with only one door,' Dr Farb explains. Thick mucus will block the door, turning the affected sinus into a veritable chamber of horrors.

'It's a dark, damp place, and when it's blocked off and there is no air to clean it out, it can be a breeding ground for bacteria,' warns Dr Farb. He adds that 'normally, a sinus does not contain bacteria.'

Harmful bacteria, dust and pollutants in the air are usually trapped by tiny, hair-like cilia and drowned in the mucus that lines the nose, before ever reaching the sinuses. Mucus lines and protects the sinuses, too; in fact, all our body orifices are protected by mucus. Although mucus is widely misunderstood and blamed for such nasty experiences as 'post-nasal drip' (catarrh), it becomes a problem only when it is thick. Then, it clogs not only the sinus ducts but also the canal – formed by nose, throat and windpipe – connecting the respiratory system with the ear. That's one reason sinus sufferers often report problems with their ears and hearing.

It's heavy mucus that you feel running down the back of your throat when you have catarrh. 'That mucus is always circulating through there, at a rate of about a quart [32 fl. oz] a day,' notes Dr Farb. 'It's only when it's thick and sluggish that it becomes uncomfortable.'

The trick, then, is to thin out your mucus and keep it flowing. 'One of the oldest methods also happens to be one of the best,' says Dr Farb. 'A humidifier. Especially during winter, when the air inside is so dried out by central heating, a bedside humidifier is an excellent idea.'

So is taking vitamin A.

Although vitamin A is usually thought of in terms of its beneficial effects on the skin and eyesight, a deficiency can also have profound effects on the respiratory tract, including the sinuses.

Vitamin A not only thins mucus, but it is also directly responsible for the growth of healthy mucus-producing cells. A deficiency hardens the membranes and kills the cilia, which normally keep the mucus moving by literally sweeping it along its way. Vitamin A is also important to the body's immune system. In general, 'susceptibility to infections, such as sinus trouble . . . is a common finding when vitamin A is lacking in the diet' *(Nutritional Support of Medical Practice)*.

A very good way to put more vitamin A into your diet is by eating liver. An average serving of calf's or beef liver provides six times the US Recommended Dietary Allowance (RDA), while an equal amount of chicken liver supplies twice the RDA. Other good sources are spinach, turnip greens, string beans, broccoli, apricots, sweet potatoes and, of course, carrots.

'Heat, applied locally and in a warm, well-humidified room, promotes relief of pain and thinning of secretions,' advises a team of doctors writing in the *Nebraska Medical Journal*. Another doctor, Byron Bailey from Galveston, Texas, recommends applying that heat with hot towels – for one to two hours four times a day.

Drinking plenty of liquids – a time-honoured remedy – also helps clear congestion. Double the amount you normally drink, using water, fruit juice and herbal teas. (Fenugreek, anise and sage teas are traditional herbal remedies for ridding yourself of mucus.)

Allergies

While it is important to make sure you are eating the right things, your sinuses may be reacting to your having eaten the *wrong* things: foods to which you may be allergic.

'It's very common for people to think they are catching "colds" when what they are having is a respiratory flare-up caused by something else entirely,' says Dr Meyer B. Marks. 'These people get "colds" eight, 10, 12 times a year, but I'd say that anybody who has more than three to four "colds" a year is an allergic individual.'

Dr Marks is clinical professor of paediatrics and head of the allergy division at the University of Miami School of Medicine and also director of the Pediatric Allergy and Immunology Clinic at Jackson Memorial Hospital in Miami. Some 35 years of practice have convinced him that allergies are often the cause of chronic sinusitis. 'Sinusitis is usually caused by an allergy plus an infection,' he told us.

'Many allergies are food allergies,' adds Kansas doctor Michael E. Aronoff. 'The most common ones are milk, wheat, corn [maize] and yeast, in that order.' Other common allergens, he adds, are things you shouldn't be eating anyway: 'coffee, chocolate, soft drinks and all sorts of chemical food additives, artificial colourings, sweeteners, preservatives and sugar.'

Dr Aronoff recommends starting a 'diet diary' to pinpoint your allergies. 'Take one food group at a time,' he advises his patients, 'such as milk and milk products. Eliminate that one group entirely for four days. Make a chart as to how you feel on days one, two, three, four; and on day five reintroduce that food in the usual amounts. Be sure to note whether there is a change in the way you feel. If you have a reaction when the food is reintroduced, it means you are allergic to that food and it is not a safe food.'

A natural anti-histamine

The symptoms of nasal allergy – runny nose, inflamed and swollen mucosa – are caused by histamine, a chemical in the body. Vitamin C, studies have shown, is a natural *anti*-histamine.

Researchers had 17 healthy volunteers inhale histamine and measured their levels of 'airway constriction'. The next day, the volunteers again received histamine – but this time they got 500 mg of vitamin C first. With vitamin C, the degree of airway constriction was 'significantly smaller' (*Journal of Allergy and Clinical Immunology*).

Since vitamin C could prevent the histamine-caused inflammation of the mucosa in nasal allergies, it could prevent and help treat sinusitis. In his allergy practice, Dr Aronoff advises his patients to take vitamins A, B complex and C, and also a zinc supplement to boost their resistance, which is often very low in allergy sufferers.

Deviated septum

Dr Aronoff has also found that his allergy patients often share another common trait as well: a deviated septum.

'Of my patients, I'd say about one in three has a physical deformity of the nose,' he claims, and Dr Marks concurs with that figure. 'It's an interesting coincidence,' says the Florida physician, 'but one-third of all people with this sort of allergic sinusitis somehow develop a deviated nasal septum, but I can't say which is cause or effect, or even whether there is such a relationship.'

A deviated septum means that the septum – the ridge down the centre of your nose – is off to one side. This obstructs breathing through one nostril and in extreme cases may close off the duct leading to one of the sinuses, resulting in chronic sinusitis. Nasal polyps – small benign growths about the size of a pea – also may interfere with breathing and clog sinuses.

The odds are in your favour, though, that your sinus problem can be controlled with good nutrition, a change in your environment and elimination of foods that might give you an allergic reaction. So breathe easier.

(*See also* ALLERGY, COLDS, COUGHING.)

• Sore throat

A sore throat is often the first symptom of a winter-time assault on your health like a cold or the flu. It can also be from overuse – like cheering yourself hoarse at an exciting football match.

At least with that kind of sore throat, you know what caused it. But if you come down with one during the colds-and-flu season, and it becomes severe, you may have a serious bacterial infection called 'strep throat' – i.e. an infection caused by streptococci bacteria.

While strep throat is nowhere nearly as common as it was many years ago, enough cases do turn up to make *what kind* of sore throat you have important to determine. If it *is* a strep throat, you'll want to be treated by a doctor as, left untreated, it can lead to rheumatic fever. While only about 3 per cent of untreated strep throat cases develop into this, those that do can leave their victims with a damaged heart and kidney disease.

A strep throat is *very* painful. It will be accompanied by chills and high fever (over 102°F [38.9°C]). The appearance of a strep throat is somewhat different, too. You should use (or have someone use) a flashlight and a tongue depressor (a spoon will do) to examine your throat. If it's fiery red and has white patches here and there on the back of the throat and tonsils, it could be strep throat. Call the doctor. He or she will more than likely do two things after examining you: give you an injection of an antibiotic and take a swabbed sample of the fluid in your throat. This will be tested at a laboratory to determine what the infecting organism is. But the doctor will treat you as if it were strep throat because the lab report takes a few days.

If your sore throat doesn't have the telltale signs of strep throat, your worries aren't exactly over. It could be the flu, or it could be just another cold. The problem here is that both the common cold and the flu are caused by viruses. So what seems like a cold at first may develop into a full-fledged attack of flu. And while the cold may allow you to function more or less normally, the flu can make you feel as if you've been marched over by a division of soldiers. And it gets even more complicated, because the flu sometimes sneaks up on you and doesn't produce *any* symptoms at first. But if you don't take care of yourself, you could end up with viral pneumonia. (*See also* COLDS, FLU.)

Herbal remedies for a sore throat may do you more good than commercial gargles. The latter contain alcohol and a host of other chemicals you can be sure didn't grow on the end of a branch or a stalk. The herbs most valued for use as a gargle or tea to ease the pain of a sore throat are sage (especially red sage), eucalyptus, horehound, fenugreek, and marshmallow. Don't skimp on the honey when drinking these teas for a sore throat.

• Stammering

'The ability to communicate through language defines us as human beings in a human society,' wrote Gerald Jonas in his book *Stuttering: The Disorder of Many Theories*. 'When men learned to speak, they set themselves off from all other creatures. Stuttering strikes at the very heart of this distinction.'

In Western countries, no matter what language or local dialect is spoken, about 1 per cent of the population suffers from the 'speech disfluencies' we know as stammering, or stuttering. Usually, that means a rapid-fire repetition of sounds, especially at the beginning of words; unnaturally prolonged sounds in the middle of words; and complete verbal blocks. The blocks, Jonas wrote, are the worst.

> In the struggle to terminate a block, some stutterers become so agitated that they resemble an epileptic having an attack: cold sweat appears on their foreheads, they gasp for breath, their eyes bulge, their lips quiver . . . they seem to be literally trying to shake the words loose from their tongue.

How can it be that such a disabling problem can be so widespread? And if it is, why hasn't a cure been found? The trouble with stammering is that it's a bundle of clues, all seeming to point off in different directions. Many stammerers, for instance, are fluent if they sing, whisper, put on an accent, address an animal or even their own image in a mirror. But when addressing a figure of authority or uttering their own name, their stammer often worsens dramatically. Surely the problem has its roots in some psychological or emotional disturbance.

Yet worldwide, males are three or four times more likely to stammer than females; and if one identical twin stammers, the other almost invariably does too. Among fraternal twins (who develop from different eggs and thus have a different genetic makeup), it's far more likely that one will stammer and the other will not. So surely it's some organic defect, genetically passed down the family tree. Or could it be learned behaviour? Or all three? Over the years, stammering has been blamed on each of those likely sounding explanations, alone or in combination, as well as on a host of other more doubtful possibilities (one Greek suggested an excess of 'black bile' might be at fault). As the great speech therapist (and stammerer) Dr Charles Van Riper has observed,

> Many explorers have attempted to trace the course of the river of stuttering to what they thought were the lakes of its origin. It should not surprise us to learn that different explorers found different lakes.

From fresh air to Freud

If the theories used to explain stuttering were strange and varied, so were the treatments used to 'cure' it. The stumble-tongued Demosthenes learned to speak clearly by outshouting the surf through a mouthful of pebbles. Aristotle and generations of medical minds that followed him tended to think of stammering as a defect of the speech organs, mainly the tongue: it was too thick or stiff or hard, too weak, too cold, too wet. 'Cures' for these shortcomings ranged from draughts of hot wine to actually snipping off pieces of the offending organ (an operation performed by a Prussian surgeon with – so he said – great success).

In the mid-19th century, schools of public speaking, like the Vocal and Polyglott Gymnasium in Philadelphia, designed elaborate programmes for the treatment of stammering through proper breathing, diligent practice of proper phrasing and a general 're-education' of tongues simply believed to have picked up sloppy habits along the way. Others thought stammering was contagious, or that plain old fresh air would do the trick.

By the beginning of the 20th century, investigators were exploring the possibility that stammering might be caused by brain damage, or – using the new language of Freud – were searching out its roots in one neurosis or another. (Freud himself failed to cure an early patient of a bad stammer.)

Today, all these years later, it would still be safe to say that nobody really knows why people stammer. Yet speech therapists and psychologists are treating the problem using an amazing number of different approaches – many of which have produced significant improvements. As one researcher says, 'We know enough about the physical processes to be able to work without any underlying assumptions about its cause.'

Rebuilding a stammerer's speech

At one end of the modern spectrum of stammering therapy is the 'Precision Fluency Shaping Program' developed by Ronald Webster, a research psychologist and director of the Hollins Communications Research Institute at Hollins College in Virginia. Dr Webster's approach centres on the painstaking 'rebuilding' of a stammerer's speech, first by drastically slowing it down and then by practising the proper muscle movements of respiration and the voicing and articulation of individual parts of speech.

'Speech is very complex, so we break it down into many small, well-defined movements and teach these one at a time, then integrate them into the speech flow,' he says.

Students are also taught to master one skill that Dr Webster considers critical: making the voice gentler at the beginning of each syllable rather than 'attacking' them abruptly and with too much force – which makes the vocal cords (which create sound in the voice box) snap shut. Dr Webster says that every stammerer he has ever seen has had this problem.

Computer 'voice monitors' are used to help stammerers measure the quality of their performance and guide their learning as they master this whole new system of speech movements. Effective vocal control, Dr Webster says, is crucial to the success of his programme. Then the students' speech is slowly cranked back up to normal speed, and they are sent out to practise their new skills in the real world – ordering a pizza by phone, asking directions.

The programme, whose most famous graduate is former astronaut John Glenn's wife Annie, includes about 100 to 120 hours of therapy (about three weeks). Dr Webster indicates that over 80 per cent of his clients have established and retained normal levels of fluency. 'None of our clients would claim to be cured,' he says, 'but they do have a decent set of compensatory skills and can function as normally fluent speakers.'

Although he doesn't claim to know what causes stammering, Dr Webster says he suspects it may be a defect in the body's feedback system, or the way a person processes the sound of his or her own voice. There is some evidence for this view. A special tape recorder that delays the hearing of one's own voice for a fraction of a second causes many normal speakers to begin stammering; yet many stammerers, using the same device, become fluent. This seems to suggest that there is something wrong with the way the latter hear themselves. And, in fact, some success in therapy has been reported using devices like the 'Edinburgh Masker', which simply prevents stammerers from hearing their own voice.

The 'airflow' technique

What role, if any, does psychology play in stammering? Martin F. Schwartz, a medical research professor at New York University Medical Center, has developed a therapeutic approach that treats it as both a psychological and a physical problem.

In Dr Schwartz's view, stammerers are people who have inherited a physical tendency to dilate their throat, larynx and vocal cords – making them momentarily speechless – when they feel a blockage in their airway. Since all speech requires an obstruction in the airway (tongue, vocal cords, etc), normal infants learn to inhibit this response, which Dr Schwartz calls the 'airway dilation reflex'.

But stammerers don't. Instead, they learn to panic at their speechlessness, tensing their vocal cords so hard in an effort to produce sound that they lock up in what he calls a 'laryngo-spasm'. Though the original physical cause – a disturbance in the airway dilation reflex – may have disappeared by adulthood, by then stammering has become 'pure habit', Dr Schwartz says, and the stammerer's vocal cords continue to lock up in response to psychological stress.

Dr Schwartz's treatment is fairly simple: he teaches patients to release a gentle, silent exhalation of air just before getting ready to speak, to set the vocal cords vibrating and avoid a speechless 'spasm'. Winston Churchill, Dr Schwartz points out in his book, *Stuttering Solved*, was using the 'airflow' technique when he used a long humming '*mmmm*' before starting to speak. His socially acceptable way of breaking a verbal block – '*Mmmmm* We shall never surrender' – became part of his famous style.

Joseph Sheehan, a psychology professor at UCLA and a self-cured stammerer, takes a more psychological bent. To him, stammering is 'a conflict between expressing yourself and holding back.' Or, 'stuttering is what you do when you try not to stutter.'

What comes first in Dr Sheehan's programme is not speech training but an attempt to get stammerers to 'accept their role as stutterers', to face honestly their fears and anxieties about it and to avoid struggling against it when they begin to stammer.

'If you can learn to stutter smoothly, you don't have to fear it any more,' Dr Sheehan says. 'So if you're going to stutter, go ahead, don't fight it, don't fear it. The struggle is half the problem.'

How successful has his method been? Well, that really depends on how you measure success, he says. 'Success rates vary according to how careful the researcher is and how stringent the standards are. My goal is to help people speak as effectively as they can, not to become 100 per cent fluent. After all, even normal speech involves some stumbling.'

Dr Sheehan's critics have claimed that he is merely turning out 'happy stammerers'. But he protests. 'There is a real sense of freedom in stutterers who have learned to accept themselves – to say, like Popeye, "I am what I am" – that I don't see in those who have merely increased their level of fluency.'

Although the therapists may argue over which method is the most effective or long lasting, help for stammerers has begun to come from an unexpected quarter in recent years: other stammerers. The Washington, D.C.-based National Council of Stutterers, for example, was formed primarily to bring stammerers together for mutual sharing and support.

'For most of us, stuttering has been this awful, untalked-about thing you do – lots of us never even talked about it with our own parents,' says Michael Hartford, the group's current co-chairman. 'But by getting together and talking with other people who stutter, many of us get the first real gut feeling of how we come across to other people. And once you realize it's not really that bad – that you're more tuned in to your stuttering than anyone – it's a real breakthrough!'

Adds executive secretary Sandra Wagner: 'There's nothing like talking to somebody else who's been through what you have, who understands.'

[In the UK, the relevant organization is the Association for Stammerers (c/o The Finsbury Centre, Pine Street, London EC1R 0JH). With self-help groups nationwide, they can provide information about stammering and its alleviation and a national link-up with speech therapists.]

Although stammering's cause – or causes – may elude the experts for years to come, it no longer has to mean despair and isolation. Says Dr Sheehan:

'We really know enough that the adult stutterer with courage really can find hope – and help.'

• Stress

Assuming you'll always have occasional periods of heavy-duty stress in your life, you should learn how to deal with what life dishes out – how to minimize the effects of stress. Not after three months of psychotherapy or eight weeks of weight training, but right now, while the stress is beating down on you.

To help, we've compiled a list of ten quick stress dischargers that you can use today, if you need them, or anytime. Find what works best for you, then keep this handy and pull it out when you need to put stressful events into proper perspective.

1 Have a good cry Don't hold back tears of frustration, anger or pain. Those emotional tears may be carrying off far more than grief. According to William H. Frey, a biochemist at the St Paul – Ramsey Medical Center, tears may help relieve stress by ridding the body of potentially harmful chemicals produced in times of stress.

To support this theory, Dr Frey and his colleagues compared emotionally induced tears to tears that were produced in response to eye irritation, such as those caused by peeling onions.

'So far, we know that the two types of tears have different chemical compositions,' Dr Frey told us, 'but we haven't as yet identified the specific chemicals related to emotional stress. We *do* know, however, that people feel better after crying. In one survey, 85 per cent of women and 73 per cent of men reported that they generally felt better.'

On the other hand, those who hold back tears may be at greater risk for stress-related disorders, such as ulcers and colitis.

In a recent experiment done at the Marquette University College of Nursing in Wisconsin, researchers studied 100 men and women with those stress-related disorders. They were then compared to 50 healthy volunteers. The doctors found that those with ulcers and colitis were more likely to regard crying as a sign of weakness or loss of control than the healthy group of people.

'It seems to me,' says Dr Frey, 'that people should cry if they want to. Sayings like "big boys don't cry" or "now, now, don't cry" may be a mistake. Emotional tears are a uniquely human occurrence, and I doubt that they can be passed off as incidental or purposeless. Evolution simply does not favour unnecessary developments.'

2 Learn to pray 'Don't rely only on prayers that you know by heart,' says Louis Savary, co-author with Patricia Berne, of *Prayerways* (1980). 'A lot of praying is simply a recitation of words. But it won't help at all to reduce stress unless you are conscious of the meaning of the words.

'Better yet,' Dr Savary told us, 'construct your own prayers when under stress. There are no rules governing a "proper" prayer. I find that the most effective prayers involve the body and the mind as well as the spirit working together. Don't just talk to God; write a letter to God instead. If you're angry at someone, tell God you're angry by putting the person's picture on the floor and dancing around it. The effects of stress show up as physical symptoms, so you need a physical outlet as well as the spiritual aspect to reduce the stress.

'If you play the piano, guitar or other musical instrument, make a prayer song, then play and sing it to God. It's a great stress discharger.

'Using your hands to create something is a form of praying, too. Recently, I counselled a man who was under a great deal of stress over a relationship with a dear friend. He wanted to pray about it but didn't know how. I gave him two pieces of clay and asked him to mould one piece to represent himself and the other to represent his friend. "Let your work with the clay be your prayer," I said, "and offer the finished product to God."

'When he had completed the project, he noticed that he had made his own shape much smaller than the one that represented his friend. He suddenly realized that his own self-image was poor, and it was causing conflicts in his feelings for his friend.

'Working with clay had given him insights into the sources of his stress, and he was then able to deal with it on a practical level,' Dr Savary told us. 'His prayer worked. He found an answer to his problem.'

3 Talk it out Don't bottle up what's troubling you until you blow your top. If you find yourself always getting angry when unfairly confronted by a boss or parents or any authority figure, you could be heading for high blood pressure.

Staying cool, on the other hand, has been shown to be related to lower blood pressure. According to Ernest Harburg of the University of Michigan School of Public Health, 'confronted with hostility, people usually explode in anger, bottle it up or take steps to resolve the conflict. We found that people who refused to get angry when confronted with conflict had lower than expected blood pressures. A typical beneficial response for an employee attacked by his boss was, "Let's be cool, let's deal with the problem." '

Researchers refer to this method as the 'discuss approach'. 'It's a way in which you explore the problem in a detached manner,' says Dr Harburg. 'You acknowledge your anger, but you are not openly hostile, verbally or physically. Discussion involves detachment, reflection, conversation and a willingness to solve the problem.'

4 Have some fun It's so simple that it's easy to overlook this most obvious of solutions. 'Recreation allows you to transfer your stressed mental state into other areas away from the self,' says Daniel Garfinkel, associate director of the Family Practice Center at Moses H. Cone Memorial Hospital in North Carolina. 'Movies, television, books, painting, needlepoint, even spectator sports can provide relief from day-to-day stress. It's also important to learn when you're most susceptible to stress. Recreation should come just after that period to be most effective. In fact, it can be as effective as drugs in treating certain stress-related illnesses, but without the dangerous side-effects.'

5 Take a walk Or do other forms of moderate exercise. Actually, this could be considered a form of recreation, but we thought it deserved a separate heading – it's *that* worthwhile.

Best of all, you don't have to walk for long periods of time or make your walk particularly strenuous. In fact, it's better if you don't, says Herbert A. de Vries, director of the physiology-of-exercise laboratory at the Andrus Gerontology Center, University of Southern California, in Los Angeles.

That's what Dr deVries and his colleagues discovered when they tested ten elderly people suffering from neuro-muscular tension brought on by stress. In their experiment, the researchers measured electrical activity in the muscles to evaluate the tranquillizing effect of exercise at a heart rate of 100 beats per minute, exercise at 120 beats per minute, meprobamate (Equanil; a tranquillizing drug) and a placebo (a harmless blank pill).

'We found that exercise at the lower heart rate decreased electrical activity significantly for at least 90 minutes, the longest period of measurement,' Dr deVries told us. 'Exercise at the higher heart rate had an insignificant tranquillizer effect. And the meprobamate and the placebo had no effect at all on electrical activity.

'Twenty minutes of walking would do the job nicely to reduce stress. With heavy exercise (more than 40 to 50 per cent of capacity) you start to get a release of adrenalin,' explains Dr deVries. 'And that just acts to stimulate you more.'

6 Try a massage You know how good it feels to have your back rubbed? No wonder cats purr. Well, you'll be purring, too, after a full-body rubdown.

'With the physical method of massage, the muscles, tendons, joints, skin and fat tissues are manipulated,' explain Donald Roy Morse and M. Lawrence Furst, co-authors of *Women under Stress* (1982). 'The primary purpose is to relieve partial muscle contractions (knots) and subsequently induce relaxation.'

Enlist the aid of your partner or a close friend. And if you're not sure how to do it, buy one of the many books on the subject. If you can't find a helpmate when you need one, try a shower massage, say Drs Morse and Furst. There are specially fitted shower heads that force water out in soothing, rapid-fire pulsations.

7 Take a hot bath But not too hot, because extreme prolonged heat is a stresser in itself. On the other hand, bath water at about 98°F (36.7°C; body temperature) is just right for a short, relaxing soak.

If you're lucky enough to have access to a hot tub, use it, but don't despair if you don't. Your own bathtub can serve as a highly acceptable second choice when stress is overtaking you.

And don't worry about washing off. This type of bath is meant to clean the worries from your mind, and not the grime from your body. Just step in, sink down, put a rolled-up towel behind your head and close your eyes. In a few minutes, you'll feel like a new person.

8 Breathe more slowly Next time you're overwrought, notice how you're breathing. Chances are, if your juices are really flowing, then your breathing is probably rapid and shallow, too. Slowing down your breathing is one of the quickest ways to reverse the effects of overstress, according to Jenny Steinmetz, a psychologist at the Kaiser – Permanente Medical Center in California.

'I tell my clients to slow their breathing to a seven-second inhale and an eight-second exhale,' says Dr Steinmetz, who is co-author of *Managing Stress*

Before It Manages You (1980). 'Do four of those per minute for a total of two minutes, and that discharges the stress immediately.'

Using the second hand of a watch or clock is the easiest way to count the seconds, but if you don't have one nearby, Dr Steinmetz has devised a clever alternative.

'All you have to do is say a number and then a three-syllable word to equal one second. For example, *one-el-e-phant, two-el-e-phant,* etc. I'll have people tell me that they've just had a 'ten-elephant' phone call or a 'six-elephant' lecture.

'The best thing about this method is that it can be done anywhere, anytime, and you don't have to stop any other activity to do it. With enough practice, it can actually become an "automatic" type of response to stressful situations.'

9 Learn to relax Each of us possesses a natural and innate protective mechanism against overstress, which allows us to counter the harmful effects of the fight-or-flight response, says Herbert Benson, associate professor of medicine at Harvard Medical School and author of *The Relaxation Response.*

This response against overstress brings on bodily changes that decrease heart rate, slow down breathing and calm that jittery feeling. To learn the relaxation response, all you need is a quiet environment, an object to dwell on (like a word or sound repetition), a passive attitude, which means emptying all thoughts and distractions from your mind, and a comfortable position.

Start by sitting quietly and comfortably with your eyes closed, says Dr Benson. Relax all your muscles, breathe slowly and repeat the word you've chosen (like 'one' or 'love') with each exhale. And, most important, let your mind go blank. Continue this for 10 to 12 minutes.

That's all there is to it. Most people say they feel a sense of calm and relaxation. Others have reported feelings of pleasure, refreshment and well-being. (*See also* relaxation techniques suggested under ASTHMA, BACK PROBLEMS, HEADACHES.)

10 Turn to your friends 'Having one or two close friends that you feel free to say anything to is invaluable,' says Dr Steinmetz. 'Often when you are overwhelmed, you don't trust your own judgment enough to realize that you're really OK. But an objective view from a friend helps validate your opinion.'

This kind of social support can be expanded to the workplace, too, adds C. David Jenkins, professor of preventive medicine and community health at the University of Texas medical branch in Galveston. To illustrate this point, he recalled a hospital that provided the opportunity for its intensive-care nurses to hold weekly group sessions with a very warm and nurturing psychiatrist. The nurses gained support from each other and from the psychiatrist and were able to surmount their crises with less emotional drain.

James S. House knows how important social support is, too. He's the author of *Work Stress and Social Support* (1981) and is an associate research scientist at the Institute for Social Research, University of Michigan. Social support may buffer or alleviate the impact of stress on health, says Dr House. It's true that there's a certain amount of irreducible stress associated with any work organization – deadlines, production pressures. Social support apparently helps to buffer these stresses and makes them more tolerable.

• Stroke

A stroke – known medically as a 'cerebral vascular accident' – is most commonly caused by a clot in a blood vessel in the brain. And strong evidence links *platelet* problems with stroke.

Normally, the tiny blood cells called platelets are your body's way of keeping bloodshed to a minimum. After any injury, they pile on top of one another to form a living wall, the nucleus of a clot that brings bleeding under control. Were platelets not on the job, any minor mishap could turn into a major catastrophe. Properly functioning, they are life-saving.

Functioning improperly, however, they can be life-threatening. Time and again, when researchers investigate trouble in the heart and circulatory system, they find platelets in the midst of it.

The big question, obviously, is this: How can we keep platelets on the job but out of trouble?

Before we can attempt an answer, we need a better understanding of the problem. Which means asking another question: What are platelets supposed to do – and what makes them go wrong?

Ordinarily, platelets float peacefully and independently in the bloodstream, right alongside the red blood cells, which carry oxygen, and the white cells, which defend the body against invaders. A slip of the paring knife or a fall from your bike, however, lets blood out of the bloodstream – and sends platelets into action.

Instead of flowing freely out the wound, platelets begin sticking to the injured blood vessel and to each other. This is called 'platelet aggregation', and it resembles the way logs and twigs swept down a river may start to pile up at a snag.

What happens next is very important, and a bit more complicated. The platelets don't just lie there like a growing pile of logs; when they aggregate, they release a host of chemicals, including highly active enzymes and hormone-like substances called *prostaglandins*. Some of these chemicals make that loose bunch of platelets cling together much more firmly, and that jumble of logs and twigs tightens up into a real dam. Soon, other clotting materials are deposited by the blood, a safe, solid clot puts a stop to bleeding, and all is well.

All is not well, however, when platelets get carried away in the performance of their duties – when, without waiting for the proper occasion, they start to clump together on their own or congregate on the walls of veins and arteries.

Why does this happen? No one can say for sure, but a lot of recent attention has focused on the chemistry of the process. Some of the chemicals released by aggregating platelets, it seems, can go either of two ways. They can be converted into substances that promote clotting or into substances that prevent it.

When a platelet collides with the wall of an artery, for example, it releases its chemicals, and an enzyme in the artery wall turns them into *prostacyclin*, which prevents platelets from clumping together – a natural protection against blood clots inside the vessels.

Normally, there's a balance between clot-promoting and clot-preventing chemicals, scientists speculate. It's an imbalance that causes dangerous, unnecessary clots.

The exact mechanism may be unclear, but there's nothing indefinite about the results when platelets clump together too easily. Often, this happens after surgery. Immobilized in bed, a patient may develop a blood clot in a vein of his leg. This is painful enough, but if the clot breaks off and travels up to his heart, lung or brain, it may threaten his life.

There's a connection between 'sticky' platelets and strokes, according to a Kansas University Medical Center research team that tested the blood of 59 stroke victims and 15 healthy controls. They further divided the subjects into two groups – young (60 years of age and under) and old (61 years of age and older). They found that in the younger group, platelets of stroke victims had a heightened tendency to aggregate.

'This leads us to suggest that the treatment of platelet hyperaggregability [the increased tendency to clump together] is a reasonable thing in the prevention of stroke,' said researcher James R. Couch.

Another study offers an especially ominous finding: 20 per cent of people killed instantaneously in car accidents (whose death, that is, was not caused by bad health) had tiny clots forming in the veins of their legs. These 'silent thrombi' ('thrombi' are blood clots; these are called 'silent' because they give no sign of their presence) suggest that platelet problems are far from rare.

Obviously, there's a lot to be said for keeping platelets in line. But is it possible?

Doctors and scientists have long been intrigued by the question. For years, they have used anti-coagulant drugs (drugs that keep the blood from clotting) to prevent strokes. Right now, two major studies are investigating whether aspirin, which inhibits platelet aggregation, can decrease the risk of heart attack and stroke.

But there are problems. Because they are so effective in preventing clotting, anti-coagulants can cause dangerous bleeding. Aspirin often causes stomach bleeding, too. And, it has been suggested, as aspirin slows down platelet function, it also interferes with other aspects of body chemistry.

The role of nutrition

A long history of experimentation, however, suggests that it is possible to keep platelet activity under control without powerful drugs and their dangerous side-effects – by natural, nutritional means. These can restore the chemical balance necessary for normal platelet activity and enhance the body's *own* protective mechanisms. Among those nutritional helpers are the bioflavonoids, a group of vitamin-like compounds.

In a paper delivered to the 20th International Congress of Physiology in Brussels, Dr Boris Sokoloff and his colleagues detailed the case histories of 13 patients who had suffered 'little strokes' – recurring, relatively minor episodes of bleeding in the brain that over the course of time can produce paralysis, palsy, failing intellectual power and personality changes. The problem occurs mostly in older people. The scientists administered 600 mg of bioflavonoids daily to the 13 patients. One patient died of a stroke two weeks after his treatment began, and two others moved to another city and left the study after a short period of time. The condition of the remaining ten patients, observed for periods ranging from 12 to 32 months, either improved or remained satisfactory. None of them suffered further strokes.

Ralph Robbins of the University of Florida has done extensive work on bioflavonoids and believes they may regulate the tendency of blood cells to clump together. He established that the bioflavonoids have a direct effect on blood-cell aggregation, the clumping together of blood cells that often occurs in states of illness:

> Decreased blood-cell aggregation may explain the reported beneficial effects of flavonoids on abnormal capillary permeability and fragility, the decreased symptoms in many diseases, and the protective effect against various traumas and stresses.
>
> An effect of aggregation is decreased capillary blood flow . . . Decreased blood flow may be reflected in changes in capillary permeability and resistance to rupture. [*Clinical Chemistry*]

Dr Robbins reported that research has demonstrated a close relationship between blood flow and capillary permeability. When blood flow through the capillaries is blocked, the capillaries become more permeable and components of the blood are lost; when the blood flow is restored, the capillaries return to normal. What happens, then, is that bioflavonoids decrease blood cell clumping, which increases blood flow and results in less permeable, healthier capillaries.

Vitamin E

If you know your vitamins, it won't surprise you to hear vitamin E mentioned as a protector against blood clots and strokes. More than a quarter of a century ago, Alton Ochsner, famed surgeon and teacher at the Tulane University School of Medicine in New Orleans, started giving his patients large daily doses of vitamin E. The result: blood clots, always a danger after surgery, became rare on his wards.

Since then, a lengthening series of experiments has zeroed in on vitamin E's ability to cut down on blood clots. It works, say researchers, by discouraging platelets from clumping together.

In two young patients, a recent study found, a deficiency of vitamin E produced an abnormal tendency towards platelet.aggregation. High doses of the vitamin brought platelet activity back to normal. In another study, researchers gave healthy volunteers daily doses of vitamin E. Here, too, the supplements kept platelet clumping to a minimum.

How does vitamin E keep platelets in their place? The process is not fully understood, but Manfred Steiner, a professor of medicine at Brown University in Providence, Rhode Island, suggests it interrupts the chain of clotting events at the crucial point of the 'release reaction' – the point at which the loose bunch of platelets hardens into a solid mass. Vitamin E 'has a definite inhibitory action on the platelet-release reaction,' says Dr Steiner. It steps in to prevent the formation of those potent chemicals that bond platelets to each other.

Vitamin C

Another nutrient with the ability to prevent blood clots and protect against stroke is vitamin C. And here, too, it seems that at least part of its power lies in its ability to regulate the reactions of platelets.

In England, Dr Constance Leslie gave 1 g daily of vitamin C to 30 patients who had had operations that left them particularly vulnerable to clots. A similar group received no vitamin C. Patients in the vitamin C group, she reported, suffered only half as many incidents of deep-vein thrombosis as the unprotected patients. And when clots did form, they were less severe.

Elsewhere in her hospital, years of experience demonstrated that 'vitamin C has a powerful protective action against thrombosis,' Dr Leslie added. The burn unit of the hospital had, as a routine practice, given all patients 1 g daily of vitamin C since opening seven years earlier. 'Only one death from pulmonary embolism [blood clot in the lung] has been recorded, and no cases of clinical deep-vein thrombosis have occurred for at least $5^1/_2$ years,' wrote Dr Leslie *(Lancet)*.

While she could offer no explanation of vitamin C's 'powerful protective action against thrombosis', two recent experiments suggest that, as with vitamin E, control of platelets is the heart of the matter.

When a team of researchers led by Kay E. Sarji and John A. Colwell at the Veterans Administration Hospital at Charleston, South Carolina tested the platelets of diabetics, they found two things. The platelets were abnormally sensitive to aggregating agents – they clumped together too easily – and they had low levels of vitamin C. This excessive 'stickiness', Dr Sarji told us, may contribute to the development of the complications of diabetes. 'When platelets are more adhesive than normal, you may be more likely to develop thrombosis,' she said, 'and many of these complications are related to thrombosis.'

When Dr Sarji and her colleagues took plasma samples from normal subjects and added ascorbic acid (vitamin C) to them, a striking change took place: the tendency of the platelets to clump together was much reduced. To investigate further the effect of vitamin C on platelet clumping, Dr Sarji gave oral doses to eight healthy non-smoking men – 2 g daily for a week. Here, too, their platelets became significantly less 'sticky' – less prone to clump together.

At the Louisiana State University School of Medicine in New Orleans, another study had similar results. A research team led by Alfredo Lopez added vitamin C to blood samples and gave oral doses of vitamin C to 12 healthy students. In both cases, Dr Lopez reported, there was a consistent increase in the 'lag time' of platelet aggregation induced by collagen – a substance that normally makes platelets clump. 'The adherence of the platelets to the collagen is impaired,' he explained to us. 'It takes longer for them to stick.'

This could have very important implications. According to one theory, platelets clumping on artery walls can be the first step in the formation of the dangerous blood clots that accompany stroke. The deterioration of the artery wall exposes collagen, which is in the connective tissue below the wall layer. When platelets adhere to the collagen, the process that leads to thrombosis is set in motion. Dr Lopez's study indicates that vitamin C inhibits platelets' adherence to collagen. 'If that theory is correct, this inhibition could be highly significant,' Dr Lopez says.

How does vitamin C discourage platelets from aggregating too easily? One explanation, which Dr Sarji cautions is 'highly speculative', involves the prostaglandins, those very potent chemicals that have a strong influence on platelet behaviour.

'Platelets produce chemicals that can be turned into thromboxane, which *causes* aggregation, or prostacyclin, which *inhibits* aggregation. Possibly, vitamin C shifts the pathway, to favour the production of prostacyclin,' she says. In other words, vitamin C may help your body produce its natural protective substances.

Dietary fat

Their work on platelets and vitamin C is suggestive but not conclusive, Drs Sarji and Lopez are quick to warn, but there seems little question about the effect – good or bad – that dietary fats can have on your circulatory health. Saturated fats are widely associated with increased risk of heart disease and polyunsaturated fats with decreased risk. Although most attention has been paid to the connection between fats, cholesterol and the fatty deposits of atherosclerosis, it seems that platelets are involved here, too.

In Finland, a research team studied two groups of men. One was given the normal Finnish diet, which is high in fats, most of which are saturated. The other group was put on a diet in which most of the saturated fats were replaced by polyunsaturated fats. When the researchers took blood samples from both groups, they found that the platelets of those on the polyunsaturated fat diet were significantly less prone to aggregate than those of the men who ate 'normally' *(Lancet)*.

In another study, the fat in the diet of 19 apparently healthy men was largely replaced by sunflower seed oil, which is 65 per cent polyunsaturated linoleic acid. Three, four and five weeks after the experiment began, their blood samples were subjected to tests.

'Most tests changed in a direction opposite to that found in vascular disease, thus suggesting decreased platelet activity,' the researchers reported. 'Clearly, if ingestion of an unsaturated fat diet is beneficial, these effects on platelets may be, at least in part, responsible' *(Lancet)*.

Dr Antoine J. Vergroesen, one of the authors of that study, summed up the implications of research on dietary fats and platelets:

> It might be worthwhile to note that relatively simple dietary change can significantly decrease platelet aggregation and adhesion without the risk of an increased bleeding tendency.

This 'relatively simple dietary change' – from saturated to unsaturated fats – regulated platelet activity, quite possibly, through its effect on blood chemistry. Linoleic acid (the most common of the polyunsaturated fats) is the substance from which the body manufactures some of its own anti-clotting chemicals. By taking in more of these fats, then, you very likely increase your supply of these protective substances. (Lecithin, as well as sunflower oil, is a good source.)

What if you are unabashedly addicted to ham, eggs and other saturated fat bonanzas? Unlikely as it sounds, a garnish of onions may be just the thing to keep your platelets from acting out the consequences.

At Queen Elizabeth College in London, investigators gave nine healthy volunteers three different test breakfasts. One was a low-calorie, low-fat meal, which included grapefruit, corn flakes, skimmed milk, bread and marmalade. Another was a hearty breakfast, high in calories and in saturated fats – cream, bacon, sausage, bread, butter and fruit. For the third test meal, the experimenters added about 2½ oz of fried onions to the heavy repast.

'The rate of platelet aggregation was significantly greater after the fat meal, compared with the control,' they reported. 'But when onion was included in the fat meal, the results were not significantly different from the control values.' In other words, a high-fat meal increased the aggregation of platelets – but the onions neutralized the effect (Lancet).

Vitamin A-rich foods lower stroke risk

A major study has concluded that the amount of vitamin A in our diet may have a profound effect on whether or not we fall prey to stroke and other cardiovascular diseases.

The study, conducted in Israel by Aviva Palgi, analyzed 28 years' worth of data in order to determine the cumulative effect of dietary changes on specific disease mortality rates.

Dr Palgi, who has conducted research in nutrition at Harvard Medical School and is now at the American Health Foundation in New York City, found that between 1949 and 1977, the death rate from heart disease more than doubled, while the death rates from stroke, high blood pressure and peptic ulcer also increased significantly. Meanwhile, during that same timespan, the Israelis had changed their eating habits. By the 1970s, they were consuming 52 per cent more fat than in previous years. What's more, they had decreased the amount of calories coming from complex carbohydrates (such as grains), while almost doubling their intake of simple carbohydrates (refined sugars).

But what makes this study special is that Dr Palgi not only looked at such obvious dietary factors as fats and carbohydrates, but she also examined how specific vitamins and minerals can directly affect those same diseases – and that's where the exciting news about vitamin A comes in.

'Vitamin A,' says Dr Palgi, 'consistently had a significant negative association with mortality rates.' This means that the more vitamin A individuals in the study consumed, the less likely they were to suffer from stroke, heart disease, high blood pressure and peptic ulcer.

Apparently, while some Israelis were eating more fats, others were enjoying lots of fruits, vegetables and other foods high in vitamin A. And those who ate those foods stayed healthier than those who didn't. In fact, Dr Palgi's study concludes by suggesting that reduced total fat intake and increased vitamin A consumption (through fruits and vegetables) may prove beneficial in reducing death rates due to stroke, heart disease, high blood pressure and peptic ulcer (*American Journal of Clinical Nutrition*, August 1981).

'We are just beginning to see the benefits of vitamin A in the diet,' Dr Palgi told us, 'and it's very exciting. My study merely emphasizes how much research still needs to be done, especially clinical experiments with human volunteers.

'Right now we know that 5000 IU of vitamin A daily is an absolute requirement for health. But for people in a pre-disease state, more may be needed. I know that, in view of the results of my study, I am more conscious of my diet, and I try to eat plenty of vitamin A-rich foods while also keeping my total fat intake as low as possible.'

Alcohol and strokes

Young people shouldn't consider themselves completely immune from strokes. For one thing, the 'little strokes' mentioned earlier often happen to people even in their 30s. Another stroke risk is over-indulgence in alcohol.

A study of the case histories of 76 patients at the University of Helsinki found that even occasional intoxication seems to increase the risk of strokes in young adults (*Lancet*). Scientists in the university's department of neurology had noticed that strokes in young patients were often preceded by drinking bouts. They decided to take a look at the medical records on file for all stroke patients under the age of 40.

They found that drunkenness preceding strokes was two to three times as common in men, and three to four times as common in women, as the general rate of intoxication in Finns of the same ages and sex. Fifteen of the 76 patients were stricken within 24 hours of a drinking spree, and two suffered strokes while they were still drunk. Over half of the cases were reported on a weekend, when drinking in Finland is at its heaviest.

If strokes 'run in the family', the information above may serve you well. In addition, you should take measures to prevent hypertension – or lower your blood pressure if it is already high – because hypertension is an important risk factor for stroke. (*See* HIGH BLOOD PRESSURE.)

• Subclinical malnutrition

Your body may have a 'hidden hunger' for the proper levels of minerals, vitamins and protein. Technically, such hidden hunger is called subclinical, or marginal, malnutrition. 'If a person has a subclinical nutritional deficiency, he or she might appear perfectly normal,' says Frank Beaudet, an instructor at the Leonard Davis School of Gerontology, University of Southern California. 'There will be no obvious symptoms that anything is wrong nutritionally. But when the person is under physical or emotional stress, then we will see the full impact of marginal levels of nutrition.

'Subclinical malnutrition can lead to, among other things, an increased susceptibility to disease and a longer recovery time from surgery. It could even lead to an adverse reaction to a flu vaccination due to lowered immune response.'

Is subclinical malnutrition someting new? 'Not really,' says Beaudet, 'but it has only been recognized within the past five years. Our knowledge of, and ability to recognize, subclinical malnutrition have developed along with the renaissance in nutrition in general and geriatric nutrition in particular.'

Is the problem very widespread? 'Malnutrition itself is not an epidemic among older adults,' Beaudet says. 'But countless numbers suffer from subclinical malnutrition – and may not even be aware of it.'

Arnold Schaefer agrees. Dr Schaefer is executive director of the Swanson Center for Nutrition in Omaha, Nebraska, and professor of biochemistry and internal medicine at the University of Nebraska Medical Center. 'Subclinical nutrition deficiencies ("hidden hunger") do exist, often in alarming numbers,' says Dr Schaefer.

In the area of minerals, for example, Dr Schaefer points out that iron deficiency may be a problem in older people. 'Iron-deficiency anaemia may result from dietary insufficiency, impaired absorption of iron or excess blood loss,' he says. 'Mild iron deficiency results in 'lack of energy,' fatigue, anxiety and sleeplessness.. . .

'The inclusion of meat, fish, poultry and foods containing vitamin C enhances iron absorption,' says Dr Schaefer. 'Good food sources of iron are lean meat, liver, dried fruits, whole-grain . . . bread and cereal products, and dark green, leafy vegetables' (*Nutrition News*, October 1980). (*See also* ANAEMIA.)

You can be subclinically deficient in other minerals, as well – for example, calcium. Anthony Albanese of the Burke Rehabilitation Center, White Plains, New York points out that poor absorption of calcium is common in older people and reduces 'calcium bioavailability despite adequate intake'. According to Dr Albanese, 'There is abundant evidence that long-continued intake of calcium in amounts below individual requirements may lead to osteoporosis' – a decrease in the total amount of bone mass. Sometimes severe bone loss can occur 'long before symptoms or outward physical changes appear . . .

'Support is growing for the view that liberal calcium intake (1000 mg per day or more) may be beneficial in elderly women,' he says. The results of a study conducted by Dr Albanese 'suggest that when calcium intake in elderly women is low due to inadequate consumption of dairy products, calcium supplementation may slow or reverse bone loss' (*Postgraduate Medicine*). (*See also* OSTEOPOROSIS).

Your body may also have a hidden hunger for one or more vitamins. 'In the United States today, we rarely see cases of classical vitamin deficiency, such as scurvy and pellagra,' says Dr Richard Rivlin of the Memorial Sloan – Kettering Cancer Center and New York Hospital – Cornell Medical Center, New York City. 'But we are now beginning to recognize a vast new series of marginal deficiencies related to disease and therapy.. . . Marginal deficiency, it now appears, may be a surprisingly common phenomenon.' (*See* SCHIZOPHRENIA.)

In a paper presented to the Vitamin Nutrition Issues Symposium in Boca Raton, Florida, Dr Rivlin used riboflavin (vitamin B_2) to illustrate his point. He noted that animal studies have shown that, when your body is low in riboflavin, the production of an enzyme that the body needs to use the riboflavin in the first place is inhibited. 'The less [riboflavin] you have,' said Dr Rivlin,

the less you are able to utilize; once the body gets sick, it gets sicker, because it lacks the enzyme and therefore cannot utilize what little vitamin there is in the diet. . . . The important concept is that deficiency itself produces changes in the ability to utilize that same vitamin.

Riboflavin is important in blood formation, in the brain, in the fat metabolism, in degrading drugs and foreign substances and in maintaining the skin. And because one vitamin is involved in the metabolism of another, the effects of one deficiency are compounded by the effects upon others.

The causes of subclinical malnutrition

Vitamin antagonists, as they are officially known, are the villains of the nutritional world. In one way or another, they either destroy vitamins directly or alter them in a way that makes them useless to your health.

An antagonist may interfere with the conversion of a vitamin to its active, or co-enzyme, form – often because the antagonist is so closely related to the vitamin itself. The antagonist may enhance the development of enzymes that destroy certain vitamins. It may cause excessive elimination of nutrients, or impair your body's ability to absorb them. In fact, there are so many different ways your body can be burglarized that it's foolish to think you're actually making use of everything those tidy little nutritional charts promise.

'If we grew all our own vegetables like people did in grandpa's day, we might not have as many problems using all the vitamins we get,' says H. Curtis Wood, Jr, a nutrition-oriented Philadelphia doctor who is the author of *Overfed but Undernourished*. 'But today, there are more than 3000 chemicals used in the commercial foods we eat. And in one way or another, many of them can be antagonists.'

Insecticide residues and pollutants in the air and water also can raid our vitamin stores, Dr Wood told us. Even vitamins can sometimes act as antagonists to other vitamins. Large amounts of a single B vitamin actually may increase your need for others in the B complex, Dr Wood says, so it's best to take all the Bs together. Life's circumstances also can become antagonists – stress, advanced age, disease, pregnancy, increased physical activity and even lack of sleep all can destroy vitamins at a stepped-up pace.

'Everyone has individualized nutritional needs,' Dr Wood points out, 'but a single person may also vary rather widely in his or her requirements from day to day, depending on stress, exercise, diet and so on. There are so many things that can act as antagonists, it's just unrealistic to think the RDAs [Recommended Dietary Allowances] will give you all the nutrients you need.'

Among the most widespread bandits, he says, are drugs. That powerful ones often cause powerful side-effects, altering our metabolism of nutrients in complicated ways, isn't really too surprising. But even 'harmless' drugs can take their toll.

'Among the drugs shown to cause tissue depletion of ascorbic acid [vitamin C], aspirin is the most important,' wrote Daphne A. Roe in her book, *Drug-Induced Nutritional Deficiencies*. Dr Roe went on to point out that diuretics can cause a loss of calcium, magnesium and zinc, and that mineral oil, sometimes used as a laxative, may cause deficiencies of vitamins A, D and K.

Some drugs act as antagonists by interfering with the absorption of nutrients through the digestive system. They may actually change the microscopic structure of the villi – the tiny, finger-shaped ridges that line the small intestine. That in turn may destroy the enzymes the villi normally produce to break down and absorb nutrients.

The antibiotic *neomycin*, for example, was shown to cause structural changes in the intestinal villi of people within six hours after it was administered. Neomycin, as a result, interferes with absorption of potassium, calcium, vitamin B_{12}, iron and other substances.

Other drugs, such as certain laxatives and cathartics, greatly speed up the intestinal transit time, causing nutrients to pass through the intestines too rapidly to be absorbed fully.

And some drugs rob your body by binding with nutrients to form a new substance that the body cannot use. For example, a common antacid, aluminium hydroxide, binds with phosphates in the intestines, causing the phosphates to be passed – unused – out of the body. Phosphate depletion, linked with long-term use of these antacids, can be dangerous because it interferes with proper bone formation.

Oral contraceptives are among the most nutritionally disruptive drugs. In a review of the medical literature, James L. Webb reported that contraceptive steroids have been shown to lower the level of six nutrients in the body: vitamins B_6, B_{12} and C, riboflavin, folic acid and zinc (*Journal of Reproductive Medicine*, October 1980). Dr Webb concluded that 'females consuming oral contraceptive agents should pay particular attention to vitamin and mineral intake and, if warranted, consume . . . supplements of needed nutrients.'

Smoking and drinking

You may be careful about avoiding unnecessary drugs, but if you smoke or drink, you are flirting with two of the best-known vitamin antagonists around. In fact, after a two-year study of alcoholic prisoners in California, Dr Jerzy Meduski summed up alcoholism in three scary little words: 'basic nutritional disaster'.

The trouble with alcohol (besides the obvious) is that it provides only 'naked' calories, completely bare of nutritional value. And though it's not a nutrient, alcohol is metabolized or processed in the body the same way nutrients are and can interfere with the body's absorption of food.

For example, it has been known for the past 20 years that alcoholism and its offshoot, cirrhosis of the liver, usually are accompanied by zinc deficiencies, though exactly how booze flushes zinc out of the system is not understood. ('Zinc before you drink' is the warning in some circles). However, zinc isn't the only nutrient drinking destroys. Alcoholics also often show deficiencies of thiamin, folic acid, vitamins B_6, B_{12}, C, A and D, and calcium, iron and magnesium.

There may even be vitamin destroyers awaiting those who are not long-term heavy drinkers. A researcher at Ohio State University reports that six or seven drinks a day for as little as two weeks can throw the digestive system into reverse, causing the small intestine to begin secreting fluids that flush food from the body before it's used. Dr Hagop S. Mekhjian found that folic-acid supplements could partly correct these alcohol-induced changes – and quitting drinking stopped them completely (*Science News*, 10 March 1979).

To add insult to injury, it appears that heavy drinkers are very often heavy smokers, with one researcher even suggesting that 'heavy cigarette smoking constitutes part of the syndrome of alcohol addiction.' In addition to the nutritional devastation of alcohol, some researchers warn that smoking drains your body of vitamin C – to the tune of 25 mg per cigarette, according to some estimates.

There are hopeful signs, however. Over the past several years, a group of Pennsylvanian researchers have been examining natural substances that can block a toxic chemical called *acetaldehyde*, which occurs in cigarette smoke and is produced in the body when alcohol is consumed. Herbert Sprince, chief of research biochemistry at the Veterans Administration Medical Center in Coatesville, Pennsylvania, and his associates described how they gave rats lethal doses of acetaldehyde after first administering large doses of certain nutrients.

The results? A combination of vitamin C, thiamin and an amino acid called cysteine (plentiful in nuts, eggs, soyabeans and brewer's yeast) 'gave virtually complete protection' *(Agents and Action)*.

The researchers point out that these were animal and not human studies, but they go on to add that

> our findings point the way to a possible buildup of natural protection against the chronic body insult of acetaldehyde arising from heavy drinking of alcohol and heavy smoking of cigarettes.

Protein defiency

Although we keep hearing that we eat too much protein, nevertheless too little protein can be a problem in subclinical malnutrition. 'Protein-calorie malnutrition, or PCM, is the most undiagnosed nutritional disorder in the world today and affects all age groups and social classes,' says Steven R. Gambert, chief of the division of gerontology and geriatric medicine at New York Medical College. 'Very few people have pure PCM, but milder varieties often go unnoticed.

'PCM can lead to a lowering of your defences against disease, muscle wasting, body-fluid buildup, and can lengthen the time it takes you to recover from surgery,' Dr Gambert says. 'One group especially at risk is medical and surgical patients. PCM may affect from 25 to 50 per cent of all patients whose hospital stay lasts for two weeks or longer.' (For more information, *see* HOSPITAL MALNUTRITION.)

'Also at risk is the 'tea-and-toast' group – those older people whose diets are pretty heavy in starches and low in protein,' he says. 'And then there are those who simply have problems with food absorption, utilization, storage or digestion.

'Finally,' says Dr Gambert, 'people on quick weight-loss diets are also at risk. Say, for example, that you weighed 300 lb [21 stone 6] and quickly lost 50 lb. Most of that weight loss would be in the form of muscle – much of it is your own body protein – and, to a lesser extent, fat. In an older person, that can be doubly dangerous, since, as we grow older, the proportion of fat we have in our bodies increases and the amount of lean muscle decreases. In this way, an overweight older person on a quick weight-loss diet may have a severe protein-calorie malnutrition, even though that person is still very overweight.

'The point,' says Dr Gambert, 'is that for older people – or anyone, for that matter – weight should be taken off slowly, and you should exercise while you are losing weight, as well.'

Guarding against hidden hunger

Subclinical malnutrition is a complex problem, and one whose seriousness is only now being fully recognized. Although the answers aren't all in, health professionals do recommend various steps you can take to make sure you don't have hidden hunger.

• Dr Schaefer says that drug-induced vitamin and mineral deficiencies can be avoided if you take high-potency nutritional supplements.

• Dr Gambert notes that, although it appears that protein requirements don't increase with age, we still have to make sure we are eating enough protein. That means 0.8 g of high-quality protein per kilogram of body weight, or at least 2 oz of pure protein per day for a 150 lb [10 stone 10] person. (For example, if during the course of the day you ate 8 fl oz of yogurt, two slices of whole-wheat bread, 6 oz of cottage cheese and 3 oz of either lean beef, chicken, fish or liver, you would easily meet your protein requirements.)

• Frank Beaudet points out that, since taste perception decreases with age, many older people do not eat properly because their food seems relatively tasteless. 'We should increase the amount of seasoning in our food as we grow older,' says Beaudet. 'That means using more of such green herbs as basil and tarragon and using more garlic or onion for a more flavourful diet. (*See also* HYPOGEUSIA.)

'The best recommendation I can make for older people,' says Beaudet, 'is to try to eat a diet with foods as high in nutrient density as possible. That means foods with high nutrition per calorie. Foods with low nutrient density, like pastry, should be avoided. Also, although it's not, strictly speaking, a nutrient, fibre can also be marginally low in the diet, causing intestinal problems. For fibre, I recommend eating whole-wheat bread, bran cereals and fresh fruits and vegetables.

'Older people are regularly under emotional and physical stresses, and proper nutrition can cushion the effects of those stresses. No older person should have to suffer from the effects of subclinical malnutrition.'

• Sudden infant death syndrome

Every year about 2000 infants in the UK go to sleep and, for reasons unknown to medical science, never wake up. Researchers chip away at the mystery of sudden infant death syndrome (SIDS) – commonly known as 'cot death' – but all that most of them have come up with as treatments is an assortment of drugs, an alarm that goes off when the infant stops breathing and a chorus of controversies over *which* factor is *the* factor.

Derrick Lonsdale, a paediatrician in Cleveland, Ohio, knows about all the controversy and the drugs. And he happens to make a point of using the electronic alarm, too. But in his chipping away at the mystery of SIDS, he has found something else: thiamin, the first member of the B complex. And while Dr Lonsdale acknowledges that thiamin isn't the answer to preventing SIDS, the fact is that out of the 15 'at risk' infants he has treated with thiamin, all 15 have survived.

A medical detective story

Dr Lonsdale didn't at first set out to find a treatment for SIDS. He examined children with inborn errors of metabolism, inherited malfunctions of their body chemistry. One of these was something called 'intermittent maple syrup urine disease' (named after a characteristic odour of the urine), a malfunction in biochemistry that usually produces symptoms of mental retardation.

There was a child in the clinic at the time who seemed to have the symptoms of intermittent maple syrup disease, the primary one being ataxia, or lack of muscular coordination. The doctors researched this child for two years and finally found that he actually suffered from a major defect in energy metabolism. He had a deficiency in a certain crucial enzyme. Among the co-factors is the B vitamin *thiamin*, or B_1. The child seemed to be imitating the symptoms of thiamin deficiency, or what is called beriberi. But it wasn't a dietary deficiency.

Dr Lonsdale put him on thiamin, and his biochemical abnormalities disappeared. Surprisingly, he stopped having his attacks of ataxia. He's now been on thiamin for about nine years, and he's a normal, healthy boy.

The next piece of the puzzle to arrive showed up in the form of a baby referred to Dr Lonsdale with what his doctor diagnosed as a fistula, or abnormal passageway, between the trachea (windpipe) and the oesophagus. The baby came into the hospital and had 11 cardio-respiratory arrests. A baby with a fistula of this sort usually chokes to death, because fluid gets into the windpipe and into the lungs. But the doctors couldn't find any fistula! He was behaving as if there was one, yet there wasn't.

Dr Lonsdale suspected that this child might be imitating the symptoms of infantile beriberi. Infantile beriberi, childhood beriberi and adult beriberi are three different things. Around this time, Dr Lonsdale read reports in the medical literature of a urine test that could reveal a substance that inhibited thiamin metabolism and adversely affected energy and nerve impulses. The test was done on this baby's urine, and it was found that the inhibitor was present. Both the parents had the substance, too.

Knowing that, Dr Lonsdale felt it was reasonable to try thiamin on the baby. Within 48 hours, the symptoms disappeared entirely, and the baby has been well every since. And every time the doctor tries to take this child off thiamin, he relapses into choking, fluid in the lungs and the other symptoms.

All of this really started to come together when Dr Lonsdale saw a 13-year-old girl with a curious condition known as 'Ondine's curse'. Ondine was a water sprite in Greek mythology who fell in love with a mortal, who jilted her. So she cursed him with the loss of automatic functions: he had to remember to breathe, move his eyes, his heart, his organs – all the things our bodies normally do automatically. In this girl's case, she had had a pulmonary infection and lost respiratory function. She had to breathe voluntarily, but she couldn't relax and let her breathing continue automatically. Her symptoms and a family history of sudden death reminded the doctor of the mechanism involved in SIDS babies.

An article in the *British Medical Journal* was the next clue to fall into place for Dr Lonsdale. Before the Japanese invasion and occupation of Hong Kong during World War II, the infant mortality rate among the Chinese from all causes was 350 per 1000 live births. There was, however, a hard core of infant deaths that occurred almost invariably in the best-nourished male infants of the family. The peak incidence of these deaths was between the ages of three and four months. The deaths were nocturnal, and nothing abnormal showed up at autopsy. Exactly the same epidemiological profile as SIDS.

However, when the Japanese invaded the colony, the infant death syndrome disappeared overnight. Although there was serious, chronic malnutrition in breastfeeding mothers because they cut back the rice ration drastically, the SIDS deaths disappeared. When the Japanese left the colony the rice ration was restored and the SIDS came back, too. To Dr Lonsdale this meant that there must be a relationship between the amount of calories taken in and the combustion of those calories. The body has to be able to burn all those calories and release energy from the process. If too many calories are taken in and there's not enough spark to burn them, the body becomes like a choked engine in a car. It stalls.

That's what was happening to the babies in Hong Kong. Their mothers were eating high-calorie rice, which was deficient in thiamin, and transferring the deficiency to them through the breastmilk. Evidently, the B_1 deficiency was more dangerous with a high-calorie intake than a low-calorie intake.

At a conference in 1958, experts from all over the world gathered to discuss thiamin deficiency. Five different investigators made separate statements that, wherever you find a population where there is infancy death between one and five months with a peak between three and four months, this is characteristic of infantile beriberi in that population.

With this evidence, it seemed reasonable to Dr Lonsdale to give thiamin therapy to babies who came in with the symptoms of SIDS and see if he could reverse them. He never diagnoses a baby as being at risk for SIDS unless it has had repeated episodes of apnoea (i.e. stopped breathing) which have been observed. Other symptoms may show up before the apnoea. Automatic functions show irregularities: changes in heart rate, respiratory rate. The brain attempts to signal that it's in trouble because it's not getting enough oxygen. Sometimes there are respiratory changes whch suggest a mild cold. Dr Lonsdale had one baby who would go through the motions of crying, but there were no sounds. With another one, just the simple act of swallowing food would raise the heart rate to 200. The swallowing reflex was malfunctioning.

Besides thiamin, Dr Lonsdale also uses an electronic alarm system that goes off if the baby stops breathing. It allows the mother and father to get some sleep. If they didn't have it, they'd sit up with the child all night. Usually, they can easily start the breathing again just by tickling or poking the baby's foot.

Dr Lonsdale has treated about 15 babies so far. All of them have benefited, even if their symptoms have not been completely abolished. 'Of course, I can't prove beyond a shadow of a doubt that the thiamin is what's doing it, especially since the symptoms go away by themselves as the infant matures. But I don't think I've done nothing. The changes I've observed are facts. To prove it scientifically, we'd need a controlled study with thousands of infants. But I also have an obligation to the families who come to me. I have reasonable, factual knowledge that thiamin is beneficial and completely harmless.'

Biotin a factor in SIDS?

Sudden infant death syndrome may also be linked to marginal deficiencies of the B vitamin *biotin*, say researchers in Australia and Britain. Apparently, SIDS closely resembles a disorder in which marginally biotin- deficient chickens die when subjected to even mild stress. None of the classic signs of biotin deficiency is present in the chickens, but there are low levels of biotin in their livers, and supplementation with biotin eliminates the problem.

The Australian and British scientists examined the livers of infants who had died of various causes and found that those with SIDS had significantly lower levels of biotin, just like the chickens. All of the SIDS victims but one had suffered some mild disease at their death, but nothing severe enough to explain why they died. The stress of that mild disease – coupled with a biotin deficiency – may have been sufficient to kill them, the researchers suggest. They recommend that infant formulas be supplemented with biotin as a precaution (*Nature*, 15 May 1980).

Warning: no infant or small child should receive nutritional supplements except under the supervision of a doctor.

• Tardive dyskinesia

Tardive dyskinesia (TD) is an embarrassing and disfiguring condition in which the person suffers from a host of uncontrollable twitches of the facial muscles. The tongue rolls or protrudes, lips smack and pucker, and eyes blink rapidly. Ironically, tardive dyskinesia is not really a disease but rather a side-effect of certain tranquillizers and other anti-psychotic drugs routinely prescribed for the mentally disturbed. It's been estimated that as many as half the patients in state mental hospitals in the United States have TD. And the symptoms often go on indefinitely, long after the drugs that triggered the problem have been discontinued.

Psychiatrists have suspected that TD is actually the result of an acetylcholine deficiency created by the anti-psychotic drugs. Acetylcholine is a neuro-transmitter that makes it possible for messages to travel from nerve cell to nerve cell. Without acetylcholine, thinking, muscle coordination and other routine functions of the nervous system are disrupted.

Dr Richard J. Wurtman of the Massachusetts Institute of Technology and several associates treated a group of 20 patients with oral doses of choline, a nutrient that is a precursor of acetylcholine. Dr Wurtman, who is associated with MIT's nutrition and food science department, had already discovered that feeding supplementary choline to animals boosted levels of acetylcholine in the brain. And he'd found that feeding extra choline to people had raised levels of choline in the cerebrospinal fluid. So expectations were high.

The people selected were all patients in a state hospital, and many were elderly women who had been taking mind-altering drugs for many years. Half of the group took supplementary choline (approximately 9–12 g daily) for two weeks, while the others took an inactive but identical-appearing placebo. Then after a ten-day 'breather', the regimens for the two groups were reversed and continued for another two weeks. Neither patients nor staff knew who was receiving choline until the trials were complete.

Results were impressive. Involuntary and irregular movements decreased in nine patients, worsened in one and were unchanged in ten while taking choline *(New England Journal of Medicine)*.

One 36-year-old woman, a schizophrenic, 'had rapid, tremulous tongue movements, which virtually ceased during choline therapy.' Two other women 'had slower, rolling tongue movements within the mouth; these movements, too, were greatly suppressed during choline treatment . . .'

Another patient, aged 75, exhibited a condition known as 'serpent's tongue'. Her tongue would protrude rapidly – 20 times in a 30-second period. But while taking choline, the rate decreased dramatically, only to return to former levels when the choline was discontinued.

Still another patient had no facial twitching but 'was unable to sit still, and moved her feet 30 times every 30 seconds. These movements were not altered during placebo ingestion but nearly ceased during choline administration.'

Best of all, the authors point out, 'No serious side-effects were encountered in any subject during the course of the study.'

As promising as those results with choline were, Dr Wurtman and his co-workers found that lecithin, a source of choline, might be an even better way to overcome a lack of acetylcholine in the brain.

When healthy volunteers were given a meal supplemented with lecithin granules, levels of choline in their blood increased by 265 per cent. However, when they consumed an equivalent amount of choline alone levels were raised by only 86 per cent. What's more, choline levels returned to normal within four hours of the latter meal, but lecithin users still displayed higher elevated choline levels 12 hours after their meal *(Lancet)*. So presumably, more choline was available for the brain to render into acetylcholine.

'Lecithin might thus be a more effective therapeutic agent . . .' the authors concluded, adding that dietary choline is normally ingested as lecithin anyway. (Even individuals not taking supplements consume a small and variable quantity of lecithin daily, in egg yolks, liver, soyabeans and other foods.)

Since then, Dr Wurtman and others have given supplementary lecithin to tardive dyskinesia patients with good results. In one study involving three people, jaw tremors, facial grimacing and tongue-twitching movements decreased after taking lecithin *(New England Journal of Medicine)*. And as they pointed out, 'Lecithin may be more acceptable to patients since it does not have the bitter taste of fishy body odor associated with choline ingestion.'

Preventing TD with vitamins

In a paper presented at the Tenth Anniversary Symposium of the Academy of Orthomolecular Psychiatry, two American psychiatrists suggested that a nutritional programme they developed may 'point the way towards a safe and effective preventive for this puzzling disease.'

David R. Hawkins and Charles Tkacz, directors of the North Nassau Mental Health Center in New York, have been employing nutritional therapy in combination with more traditional psychiatric methods for over 15 years. Along with anti-psychotic drugs, they have been using vitamins C, E and B_6 and nicotinic acid (niacin) or niacinamide to treat schizophrenia and other disorders.

During the summer of 1978, they noticed that although reports of TD were appearing with 'alarming frequency', they themselves were seeing the disease only in patients who were being referred to them from other hospitals and doctors. In fact, they wrote,

> we found to our astonishment that among our patient population (10,000 outpatients during a ten-year period; 1000 inpatients at our hospital during a ten-year period) not one case of tardive dyskinesia developed.

Dr Tkacz says that among those referral patients who already had TD when they arrived, 'our impression was that it [the vitamin programme] improved their condition.'

Although the doctors admit they cannot be sure which vitamin or combination of vitamins may be responsible for preventing TD, 'there were simply no common denominators other than vitamins to explain our results.'

• Temporo-mandibular joint (TMJ) syndrome

Many, if not most, headaches stem from muscular tension, and much of that tension has been found to originate in the mouth. The lower jaw, or mandible, is located and controlled by several sets of muscles that allow it to perform its varied movements. The mandible joins the skull just in front of the ears, forming a pair of joints called the temporo-mandibular joints, or TMJs for short.

In many people, one or both TMJs have been forced out of place, according to Harold Gelb, a New York dentist who has spent most of his career studying this joint and its effects on muscles, bones, nerves and blood vessels of the face, head, neck and shoulders. Irregularities of the TMJ often result in the 'TMJ syndrome', of which headache is a common symptom. Gelb says that '90 per cent of all headaches are muscle contraction headaches, and a good portion of those are TMJ related.'

Gelb lists the common indicators of the TMJ syndrome as: pain in or about the TMJ; pain behind the eyes, in the sinuses and in the ears (without infection); chronic neck and shoulder pain; loss of hearing, stuffy sensation and noise or ringing in the ears; dizziness without associated eye movement problems; a burning sensation in the throat, tongue and side of the nose; dry mouth; and a 'locked' jaw muscle. A most common symptom of the TMJ syndrome is chronic head, ear and facial pain. Other indicators are persistent jaw clenching, a 'clicking' jaw and chronic bruxism (grinding or shuffling the teeth; *see* BRUXISM). Such dental problems as frequent cheek or lip biting, inexplicable fracturing of teeth and fillings, and worn teeth can also result.

Improper bite

There are various causes for TMJ problems – whiplash from car accidents, joint diseases, skeletal or postural abnormalities due to injury or genetic heritage – but Gelb asserts that 'a much more common cause is malocclusion,' or improperly meshing teeth.

A set of teeth has hundreds of surfaces that fit together more or less well when the mouth is closed. If two teeth come together perfectly, all is well. If, however, they strike each other imperfectly, stress occurs, and the jawbone automatically (that is, without conscious direction) moves to alleviate the stress. A subtle shift occurs as the teeth find a more comfortable fit. If there is more than one area of stress, the jawbone compromises, picking the path of least resistance, as it were.

Many people with ill-fitting teeth live their whole lives without complications, but problems most commonly occur in the vulnerable TMJ area. Carl Rieder, a professor at the University of Southern California School of Dentistry, is a leading authority on treatment of TMJ problems. He describes the situation as being 'like forcing a six-foot-tall man to stand up in a room five-foot ten inches high. He can stand up for a while, but if he's forced to stay in that room for extended periods, it's torture.

'If you're never able to let your jaw go back to its proper skeletal position, a muscular brace develops. The muscles must support it continuously.'

The muscles of the head and neck, then, try to do their job of locating the jawbone relative to the TMJ but are thwarted by teeth that don't fit together. Since teeth are harder than muscle tissue, they prevail, forcing the TMJs, however minutely, out of place, causing constant tension. Many people can and do live with such a condition all their lives without pain, learning to adapt to stress that doesn't quite manifest itself as pain. They may be totally unaware of the condition, or only casually aware of some minor symptoms, until some change in the balance adds enough stress to cause spasm. According to Gelb,

This added stress [from accident, emotional crisis, tooth extraction, etc.] makes the already tense muscles in head, neck and shoulders go into spasm. Circulation in these muscles will be limited because of their tautness, and where circulation is poorest, metabolic wastes will build up and form trigger points within the tissue. Trigger points can refer pain anywhere in the body.

Because most of the stress caused by the jaw imbalance centers around the tissue of the head, neck and shoulders, most of the symptoms occur in that region. [*Behavioral Medicine*]

'Referred pain' disguises TMJ problems

The phenomena of 'trigger points' and 'referred pain' are widely recognized, though imperfectly understood. Harold Arlen, an ear-nose-throat specialist, has seen how TMJ problems show up in other areas.

'We can often predict where pain refers,' Dr Arlen says. 'For instance, one of the referral points for spasm of the temporalis muscle [the large muscle connecting the side of the head and the jawbone, a primary muscle of chewing] is below the eye. People say that they have "sinus trouble".'

Another muscle, the tensor tympani, pulls the eardrum when it contracts, according to Dr Arlen, resulting in diminished hearing and a feeling of fullness in the ears. Spasms of another muscle associated with TMJ problems, the sternocleidomastoid muscle at the side of the neck, result in a 'sore throat' or a 'lump in the throat', although no infection is present. Other muscle spasms refer pain to the shoulders, neck or back.

Yet many medical doctors remain ignorant of the TMJ syndrome and consequently misdiagnose such symptoms. Take the case of Robert Wergin, for instance. Wergin, of Houston, Texas, spent his whole adult life troubled by headaches so painful that he became 'an aspirin addict'. He says he saw 'five or six' doctors, including specialists, and 'went through all the tests. I went to specialists, to hospitals all over the place. Nobody ever mentioned my jaw.'

Wergin got lots of pain pills and muscle relaxants, but never a firm diagnosis of his problem. Doctors spoke of 'tension headaches', with a subtle or not-so-subtle implication that emotional factors were to blame.

Fortunately, Wergin's occupation – he is a dental-practice management consultant – brings him into frequent contact with dentists. He eventually met dentist Roy W. Bell, who diagnosed his problem as TMJ-related muscular spasms associated with poor occlusion, treated him, and freed him from headache pain for the first time in 15 years.

'It was amazing, the most amazing thing that ever happened to me,' Wergin exclaims. 'All of a sudden, it felt like I had a whole lot of new teeth in my mouth. And best of all, no headaches.' (Wergin, it should be noted, had had extensive orthodontic treatment as a teenager.)

Sharyn Wehmueller of Independence, Missouri, had swollen neck glands for a decade. 'I'd feel physically ill because they hurt me so much,' she remembers. 'They were hard and sore to the touch, and hurt in the morning. I felt really tired, too, I guess because I wasn't sleeping well.'

Various doctors were 'baffled by it', she recalls. 'They thought it was a virus, gave me penicillin and antibiotics. An internist ran me through all kinds of tests and didn't find anything. He said that I probably "just get swollen glands the way other people get colds".'

Wehmueller often gritted her teeth and had headaches and stiff necks, but the doctors she consulted over the years 'had no idea it was my teeth'. Finally unable to sleep without muscle relaxants and a specially rigged pillow to prop her neck on, she was referred by a friend to Jack Haden, a Kansas dentist who first relieved the chronic muscle spasms, then rearticulated her jaw and fixed her occlusion. The result was immediate and total relief.

A precise yet simple treatment

What dentists Bell and Haden performed on their patients was a series of dental adjustments collectively called 'occlusal equilibration', or the equalization of stress within the jaw by modifying the biting surfaces of the teeth. In those three cases and in thousands more like them, a precise yet simple procedure solved problems that years of medical treatment could not.

The first step in treating TMJ-related pain is determined by the patient's condition. Often, especially in cases where bruxism, or tooth grinding, is present, the dentist will fashion a 'bite plate' (also called an 'occlusal splint') to fit over the patient's upper or lower teeth. This plastic device prevents the teeth from coming together improperly, thus relieving strain on the jaw muscles. Many patients with severe symptoms report immediate improvement simply from wearing the splint during their sleeping hours, which tells the dentist he or she is on the right track.

Once the jaw muscles are relaxed, the dentist feels (palpates) them to determine the extent of the correction and to discover which teeth may need treatment.

In the equilibration treatment, the dentist guides the TMJ into proper alignment by gently directing the upper and lower jaws to the position of maximum closure, then requests the patient to close the jaws very slowly, being alert for the first contact between the teeth. Sometimes this has to be repeated until the patient becomes aware of any abnormal contact, called a 'prematurity', but there usually is one and the patient can usually feel it.

The next step is to construct a working model of the patient's mouth and jaw. The dentist takes precise measurements of the patient's head, mouth and jaw, and uses that information to adjust a machine called an articulator, which is in essence a mechanical skull and jawbone.

The dentist makes a cast of the patient's teeth and inserts it into the articulator, making it an accurate, life-sized, mechanical model of the patient's head and mouth, with all the idiosyncrasies intact. The dentist can then precisely mimic a patient's chewing motion to see just how biting stress is distributed among the various teeth. From his observations, he formulates a plan for modifying the teeth to achieve proper occlusion.

This time-consuming and laborious process takes place before the dentist even considers grinding or building up a tooth. Anyone who has ever tried to level a wobbly table by cutting one leg or the other can appreciate the difficulty in trying to equalize pressures among *hundreds* of surfaces. It simply can't be done without precise measurements.

Once the measuring and observation is complete, treatment is relatively simple: the offending teeth are either ground and filed (*equilibration*), or built up and capped (*restoration*), as needed. In some cases of severe dental deterioration, orthodontics – the forced moving of teeth to one side or the other, or front or back – may be required, and in a few cases major surgery to reconstruct the jawbone may ensue. For an estimated 30 per cent of TMJ patients, however, equilibration is sufficient. Another 30 per cent need only equilibration and restorative dentistry.

Follow-up 'fine tuning' of the bite is sometimes necessary as the muscles adjust to the new dental surfaces, and as the symptoms of TMJ distress disappear. The result: 'Instead of the teeth dictating an improper jaw position, the teeth come together harmoniously, when the jaw is in the proper place,' explains Carl Rieder. Many patients are astounded at the change.

Dentists are quick to caution that facial and cranial pain has many different

---

Two self-tests for TMJ distress

So many of the symptoms of TMJ distress can be attributed to other causes, and so many disarticulated TMJs are not diagnosed until severe pain occurs, that many potentially simple cases are neglected until they become complex cases. According to Harold Gelb, two simple tests can indicate TMJ dysfunction.

(1) Gently insert the ends of your little fingers into your ears and press forward, towards the front of the ear, while opening and closing your mouth several times. If your TMJ is normal, you will feel nothing unusual. If your jaw is unbalanced, however, you will feel the condyle, or head, of the jawbone pushing against your finger. This will be quite noticeable on the side that is most severely out of place. Any pain you may feel is further indication of trouble.

(2) Place the index fingers on the cheek just in front of the centre of the ear, press in gently, and open and close your mouth several times. Any grinding, cracking, popping or similar noise is indicative of TMJ problems, though probably not as severe as when Test 1 is positive. Again, pain indicates problems.

. . . And five questions your dentist should ask you

Niles Guichet, an acknowledged authority on occlusal problems, suggests that dentists ask their patients the following questions about possible TMJ distress.

1 Are you aware or have you been made aware of clenching your teeth?
2 Do you ever wake up in the morning with an awareness in your teeth or jaws that you have had them clenched in your sleep?
3 Do you have or have you had pain in your jaw joints or on the side of your face about your ears?
4 Do you have chronic headache?
5 Do you have chronic neck or shoulder pain?

causes, and it may be necessary for sufferers to seek medical diagnosis and treatment. But if the best medical science can do is to mask the pain, the dentist may be able to help.

Why then aren't more dentists performing routine articulation measurements and asking their patients about headaches, earaches and the like? And why don't medical doctors routinely refer their 'incurable' headache patients to a dentist? The answer is in the training each doctor and dentist receives and the habits they develop over years of practising. Occlusal treatment, while known for over 40 years, has not been stressed in many dental schools. It has been only within the past two decades that a relationship between the TMJ and referred pain has been seriously studied and researched.

'Part of the problem is the "one-tooth dentist",' says Rieder, 'the dentist who treats one tooth at a time. Another greater problem is the patient who resists any effort to improve his occlusion because he can't feel the problem. It doesn't hurt him at the moment. He may have a missing back tooth, for instance, and over the years the stress increases, but so does his tolerance of it. When he has a dental problem, he tells the dentist to "just patch it up".'

'I've had patients come to me who have had brain scans, X-rays, every test known to man – but very few doctors have actually touched them,' adds Harold Gelb. 'Nobody palpates the muscles or joints, checks their ears – nothing!'

'We have to treat the whole person, the whole masticatory system,' Rieder concludes. 'Treating one tooth is no longer satisfactory.'

• Tics and Tremors

Many diseases and conditions can send muscles a garbled message about how to perform. The result may be involuntary quivering, shaking or jerking of muscles – tics, tremors, twitches. One very common cause of these muscular mistakes is nutritional – a deficiency of potassium or magnesium.

These minerals perform a very important function at the neuro-muscular junction, the meeting place between the nervous system and a muscle. At that junction, electrical impulses pass from the nerves into a muscle and control its movement. The impulses are conducted by minerals, but if those minerals are out of balance – if there's too little potassium, for instance – then too much electricity gets through. Your muscle is zapped.

'Potassium lack is a common nutritional deficiency,' says Richard Kunin, a psychiatrist from San Francisco and author of *Mega-Nutrition* (1980).

And, says George Mitchell, a doctor from Washington, D.C., 'Giving potassium is one part of a nutritional approach to solve a muscular disorder such as a tic or twitch. Potassium deficiency is a particularly big problem among people who regularly drink cola, tea or coffee. Those liquids work like a diuretic and wash potassium out of the body.'

Dr Kunin believes that a potassium deficiency can also be caused by a sugary diet. 'When you ingest too much sugar, the body has to convert it into a chemical called glycogen and store it, and this process uses up a great deal of potassium,' he says. 'The end result may be a twitch or tic.'

If you have a potassium deficiency, you're probably low on magnesium, too. 'People are commonly deficient in both potassium and magnesium,' says Dr Kunin. 'I find that a tremor in the tongue or the arms or legs often clears up when I give a person magnesium.'

'Magnesium deficiency is a cause of a lot of muscular problems because one of its functions is to relax muscles,' says Dr Mitchell.

'Muscle jerks are often very easily helped with something as simple as dolomite,' says Tennesee doctor Donald Thompson. 'Our society tends towards a deficiency in magnesium – it's the magnesium in dolomite that makes it such a valuable substance.'

Another doctor who feels the same way is Arnold Brenner: 'I've treated several patients who had tics or tremors with dolomite, and their symptoms cleared up. In each case, I used one to two teaspoons a day. Analysis of their hair showed low magnesium levels, so it is apparently the magnesium portion of the dolomite that was effective in these individuals.'

B complex vitamins for the nerves

'Tremors sometimes respond to magnesium and high levels of B complex vitamins,' says Dr Warren M. Levin of New York City. Dr Levin and many other physicians use B complex vitamins because some tremors are caused by a disorder in the central nervous system. For the health of the central nervous system, B complex vitamins are a must.

'The B complex vitamins work on the central nervous system,' says Dr Kunin. 'B_6, for example, is a natural tranquillizer. Niacin [nicotinic acid] inhibits chemical activity in the brain that may cause tremors.'

'I get some results clearing up tremors using vitamin B_{12},' says Dr John Siegel from Minnesota.

Dr Mitchell also treats tremors with B complex. 'B_6 is especially important,' he says, 'because it plays a role in the body's utilization of magnesium.' But, he points out, 'a person with a tremor is usually deficient in several of the B vitamins.'

A tremor isn't always caused by what's lacking. It can also be caused by an excess – of lead. 'A number of patients with tremors have higher-than-average lead levels – levels close to the toxic range,' says Dr Howard Lutz of the Institute of Preventive Medicine in Washington, D.C. 'But if we give those people calcium or zinc, the minerals force much of the lead out of the body, and the tremor is cleared up.'

Dr Lutz also believes that many tremors are caused by food or chemicals to which a person is allergic. 'If we relieve the allergic stress, tremors will go away in 50 per cent of the cases,' he says. 'The other 50 per cent will have a less marked tremor or a tremor that occurs less frequently.'

Drugs that can cause tremors

To avoid chemical stress that may cause a tic, tremor or twitch, stay away from unnecessary drugs.

'When I see an elderly person who has a tremor, the first thing I do is check his or her medication,' says Dr Frederick Klenner. 'Many tranquillizers can cause tremors. If the medication is discontinued, the tremor clears up. And very few of these people really need tranquillizers anyway.'

A tranquillizer-like ingredient in anti-histamines may also cause a tic, tremor or twitch. An article in the *New England Journal of Medicine* described a woman who used anti-histamines regularly and developed twitches and tremors in her face. When she stopped using the medication, her condition improved.

And the *Journal of the American Medical Association* reported a case of 20 hyperactive children who developed tics from their medication.

However, tics, tremors and twitches can have many causes – not all of them treatable by nutritional supplements and a more natural lifestyle. 'If you don't get rid of the problem with your own treatment, then consult a doctor and have him or her check you out for further disturbances,' says Dr Kunin.

• Tinnitus

Tinnitus – ringing, hissing, buzzing or roaring in the ears – affects millions of people in one form or another. You don't have to be deaf to have it; most tinnitus sufferers aren't. In fact, everybody has probably suffered from a temporary form of tinnitus – when, for example, you've stood too close to a car backfiring, or banged your head – and usually it's no big deal. But for those who suffer from tinnitus for prolonged periods, it can be anything from a persistent annoyance to an unbearable affliction.

The fact that the majority of tinnitus sufferers are told by their doctors only to try to live with their problem doesn't help. Although ear specialists have tried various treatments for tinnitus, including surgery and drugs, they have had few successes. Even 'tinnitus maskers', hearing aid-like devices that drown out the noise with other sounds, only cover up the symptom without helping the underlying problem. And tinnitus is always a symptom of an underlying hearing disorder, which often leads to some form of hearing loss.

Noise from a starving ear

An approach by Paul Yanick, Jr, a clinical audiologist and adjunct assistant professor at Monmouth College in New Jersey, offers hope to tinnitus sufferers. Dr Yanick believes that tinnitus as well as many other hearing problems can be traced to metabolic disturbances, and in partnership with several doctors, he has developed a theory into a successful clinical therapy.

Dr Yanick started to develop his theory that tinnitus and other hearing problems are caused by metabolic imbalances in 1974, when he and Dr E.J. Gosselin studied the metabolism of 90 patients with hearing loss. They found an extremely high correlation between metabolic disorders and hearing disorders *(Journal of the American Audiology Society)*.

Hypoglycaemia (low blood sugar), Dr Yanick is convinced, is the most commonly under-rated cause of tinnitus and other hearing problems, including progressive deafness. 'A diet high in refined carbohydrates raises the blood sugar level too high and too fast,' he explains. 'The pancreas over-reacts to these dangerously high sugar levels by producing too much insulin. Then the insulin *drops* the sugar level down too low and too fast. Since the inner ear has the highest energy requirement of any organ in the body, the drop in blood sugar puts a lot of stress on it. Finally, the body's stress reaction floods the system with adrenalin, which constricts the highly sensitive vascular network in the ears – this is often what causes the ringing of tinnitus. As a result, the ear is starved of energy and oxygen, and can't get the nutrients it needs to function.

'Hearing improvements with vitamin A are well documented,' Dr Yanick says. 'A recent animal study found ten times more vitamin A in the inner ear than in other tissues of the body. Probably all sensory receptor cells, such as those in the inner ear, are functionally dependent on vitamin A. The B vitamins, too, are important for nerve functions. And they also play a major part in glucose metabolism.'

One of Dr Yanick's patients was a 33-year-old contractor who consulted him about fluctuating tinnitus, a variety that seems to come and go. The ringing was worst in the quiet of the night, and soon it made it difficult for the man to sleep. He resorted to drugs – aspirin at first and then Valium – but the tinnitus remained.

Dr Yanick's hearing tests revealed that the contractor was already suffering from a slight, undetected hearing loss. Observation and questioning further revealed that the hearing loss, which was not evident to the patient, put great strain on him in social situations. 'The person with a hearing problem,' Dr Yanick explains, 'is under great stress. He's concentrating, trying to grasp every word.'

Dr Yanick further discovered that in the course of his patient's work as a contractor, he was sometimes exposed to loud noises. Metabolic and bio-chemical tests revealed that the contractor was hypoglycaemic and deficient in magnesium, chromium and, especially, zinc.

The first thing Dr Yanick did was to prescribe a pair of earplugs. 'Exposure to loud noise is dangerous,' he explains. 'It constricts the blood vessels in the inner ear and deprives it of oxygen and essential nutrients.' Then he equipped his patient with a carefully fitted hearing aid. By correcting his slight hearing loss, this immediately relieved much of the stress he felt in social situations. 'And,' Dr Yanick points out, 'better hearing can itself drown out moderate tinnitus.'

The patient's nutritional problems were also tackled. Dietary reforms were suggested, as well as a programme of fast walking. Proper exercise makes the heart and blood vessels more efficient, helping to provide enough nourishment for the ear.

After two months of treatment, the contractor showed a 20 per cent improvement of hearing and no more tinnitus. He was now also able to get on happily without tranquillizers and sleeping pills.

Hypoglycaemia isn't the only metabolic abnormality related to hearing problems; too much fat in the blood is, too. 'High blood levels of fats,' Dr Yanick explains, 'causes red blood cells to stick together, reducing the flow of oxygen to the inner ear. When tests reveal that a patient has this problem, we recommend supplements of lecithin, iron and potassium, along with a diet high in grains, fruits and vegetables. That regimen has been very helpful in lowering fat levels and increasing the supply of oxygen.'

Another biochemical disorder that can cause hearing problems is electrolyte imbalance. Electrolytes are substances in the fluids of the inner ear. 'Low blood levels of potassium,' Dr Yanick says, 'cause electrolyte imbalance and consequent hearing problems. Supplements of potassium and B vitamins, along with an individualized dietary and stress-reduction programme, can often restore the proper balance and improve hearing.'

Other ear specialists advocate the use of vitamins A, C and B_{12} and nicotinic acid (niacin).

Self-help

If your tinnitus persists, try giving up aspirin. Sometimes that's all it takes to stop the ringing. That's because aspirin, in chronic standard doses, such as those used in treating arthritis, can cause tinnitus. In fact, it can do much worse – it can cause deafness. So can certain prescription drugs, including some commonly used antibiotics.

Consider, too, that stress can play a part. Stress-reducing techniques, as well as a hearing aid that is scientifically tuned to deliver maximum clarity and comfort, are also important in Dr Yanick's holistic programme.

'For some people, tinnitus gets louder just by worrying about it,' he says. 'Stress is a cause as well as a result of metabolic disturbances and plays a major part in hearing problems, especially tinnitus. I've found that, with my patients, fast walking or jogging usually helps to relieve ordinary stress.'

Diet, nutrition, exercise, relaxation. 'It's obvious that the ear is part of the body,' Dr Yanick concludes, 'and it makes no sense to treat hearing problems in isolation from the body's general well-being.'

• Tooth decay

Scientists have nailed refined sugar to the wall as a major cause of tooth decay (dental caries). In probably the most conclusive study yet, researchers re-examined data collected in the US government's Ten-State Nutrition Survey. The figures show a crystal-clear relationship between how much sugar you eat and how many fillings you get. Of 2514 adolescents surveyed, those reporting high numbers of decayed, missing or filled teeth ate *ten times* as much sugar as those with few fillings. Kids with high sugar intake had twice as many fillings as those with low intakes (*Ecology of Food and Nutrition*, vol. 9, 1980).

'There are very large and systematic differences in sugar-food intake according to the level of caries observed,' the researchers reported. The correlation is so strong that 'any given increase in sugar-food consumption is associated with a comparable increase in dental caries.'

Sugar's main henchman in cavity formation is a bacterium named *Streptococcus mutans*. These mouth-dwelling microbes love sugar and use it not only as an energy source but as the building block of a bacterial 'armour plate' called *plaque*.

Plaque sticks to teeth and forms a nice protective roof over *S mutans* colonies so they can do their dirty work out of harm's way. Saliva can't wash the bacteria downriver, and their 'digestive juices' – lactic acid – can progressively eat away at a tooth's surface.

However, even though sugar is the main problem, a lack of certain vitamins and minerals can also hurt teeth. 'Strong epidemiological evidence suggests that there is a developmental nutrition component to dental caries,' wrote Michael C. Alfano of the Oral Health Research Center at Fairleigh Dickinson University in New Jersey (*Journal of Dental Research*, December 1980).

For example, he noted that vitamin C-deficient diets resulted in 'irreversible defects in jaw growth' in pigs, that protein deficiency in unborn rats caused 'biochemical and functional alterations in the salivary glands' and that ante-natal 'iron and zinc deficiencies can also enhance subsequent caries susceptibility.'

Other researchers have focused on the nutrient – tooth decay link. At the University of Alabama's Institute of Dental Research, for instance, two researchers, Juan Navia and Susan S. Harris, have been investigating the role of vitamin A in the formation of teeth. They've found that infant teeth are prone to decay if they lack vitamin A while they are forming within the gum.

In the normal construction of teeth, vitamin A is essential for the formation of a scaffolding made up partly of carbohydrates called *mucopolysaccharides*. If that framework is properly built, calcium and phosphorus lock into place, and the result is a healthy tooth. Without enough vitamin A, however, there will be chinks in the new tooth, and bacteria will seep in like rain through a leaky roof.

'Caries initiated at the enamel surface,' Drs Navia and Harris reported, 'would meet a less effective barrier at the enamel – dentine [the two outermost layers of the tooth] junction, leading to development of severe, deeply penetrating lesions' (*Archives of Oral Biology*, vol. 25, no. 6, 1980).

Anti-decay foods

'There's an increasing amount of research interest in the cariostatic [caries-preventing] abilities of certain foods,' explains William H. Bowen, director of the caries-prevention branch of the National Institute of Dental Research (NIDR).

Certain cheeses actually prevent decay, according to a dental research team led by Charles Schachtele, professor of dentistry and microbiology at the University of Minnesota. Cheeses that work best in this regard are aged Cheddar, the American cheese Monterey Jack and Gruyère. These work by blocking other foods, especially sugar, from forming an acid layer on the teeth. Typically, contact with sugar will cause a 1000-fold increase in tooth acid. However, when volunteers at the University of Minnesota chewed on pieces of cheese and then swished their mouths with sugar water, the acid balance returned to its healthy, normal level within minutes.

'We aren't sure just what it is in cheese that has this beneficial effect, but we're working to find out,' Dr Schachtele says. 'It appears to be either a protein or a lipid [fat]. Once we are able to isolate it, we may be able to add it to other foods and give people even broader protection from cavities.'

Besides Cheddar, Monterey Jack and Gruyère, other tooth-saving cheeses are Gouda, Brie, mozzarella and varieties of blue cheese. The carbohydrates in these won't turn to acid on your teeth, although they lack that mysterious agent that protects teeth from foods that do. Other foods that are good for the teeth include certain fish, as well as whole raw peanuts.

Paul Keyes, a former clinical investigator at the NIDR, has examined the anti-bacterial action of citrus fruits, and has concluded that 'citric acid makes plaque looser.' He explains that calcium is part of the 'mortar' holding plaque together. When citric acid washes over the teeth, it chelates this mineral: it literally causes plaque to come unglued. If you've ever watched a high tide sweep over a sand castle, you know the end result.

Another scientist thinks that seed and grains might help protect teeth. 'Researchers should look for anti-cariogenic, food-grade and naturally occurring seed coverings that can be incorporated directly into snack foods,' wrote Kenneth O. Madsen, professor of nutritional biochemistry at the University of Texas Health Science Center in Houston, in *Cereal Foods World* (January 1981).

Dr Madsen has already uncovered a number of candidates, all of which inhibited caries in laboratory rodents, which, because they're dedicated nibblers, are very susceptible to tooth decay. (The more often you eat, the more grist for the cavity mill you provide those hard-toiling bacteria.) He found that adding oat and sunflower hulls, rice, maize and oat bran, along with whole wheat and other seed hulls, to 'snack' foods, could turn the tables on the evils caused by indulging.

Why those substances work is unknown, he says, but the anti-decay effects are very significant, with caries decreases as high as 78 per cent in some laboratory tests. 'There's a real potential for believing it would work in humans,' he enthusiastically predicts. And in addition to their anti-bacterial action, these less refined, whole grains would have other benefits.

'They're less retentive,' which gives *Streptococcus mutans* less time to work its mischief. 'Raw, fibrous foods mean more mastication, and the more you chew, the more salivation. This is protective in and of itself.'

More checkups, more fillings?

Evidence presented by Dr Aubrey Sheiham, of the department of community dental health, London Hospital Medical College Dental School, suggests that routine six-month dental checkups may actually benefit the dentist more than the patient – by inviting unnecessary over-treatment. Regular professional care at *more reasonable intervals*, combined with a sensible diet and conscientious brushing and flossing at home, may be the best way to a healthy mouth.

Writing in the *Lancet*, Dr Sheiham explains the rationale for his study:

A review of the value of screening for a number of medical conditions such as diseases of the lung, cardiovascular diseases and cancer has shown that much more research is necessary before such screening procedures can be generally recommended. Since a dental examination is the most common screening test, it too needs evaluation.

Dr Sheiham didn't need to look far for data to evaluate. Under the National Health Service, all adults are entitled to a free dental exam every six months, and approximately half take advantage of it.

The first thing he compared was the incidence of dental caries, or decay, the most common oral affliction not only in Britain but in most other Western countries as well. 'The most striking and important finding,' he reported, 'is the long interval (three to four years) between the initial enamel lesion [decay] and its extension to dentine. Fifty per cent of the initial lesions did not progress at all over a four-year period.'

The enamel is the armour-like covering on the crown of the tooth – the hardest tissue in the human body. The dentine, which underlies the enamel, being somewhat softer, is thus more vulnerable to the spread of decay.

Among one group of adults aged 21 to 24, Dr Sheiham wrote, it took an average of 32.3 months for decay to progress through the enamel to the dentine. Less than 20 per cent of all initial decay reached the dentine within 24 months of first being diagnosed. So those who failed to see their dentists on a six-month basis were hardly at a disadvantage.

On the other hand, those who faithfully saw their dentists twice a year were facing a different sort of risk. As Dr Sheiham put it:

Prolonging the interval between examinations has its advantages. Less unnecessary treatment is carried out. There is abundant evidence to support this view. One would expect regular attenders to have the same or even less dental decay than irregular attenders. Yet we find that regular attenders have fewer healthy teeth. They have had more teeth filled than irregular attenders have had decayed, and this can only be a result of a tendency to over-reat.

A further advantage of prolonging the interval between examinations is that initial lesions may remineralize, making treatment unnecessary. Remineralization occurs quite often. In one study, more than half the early lesions were diagnosed as sound at later examinations.

For adolescents in the 12- to 16-year range, Dr Sheiham suggested an interval of 12 months between dental visits. For people over 16, he believes this could be stretched to 18 months. A word of caution: remember that Dr Sheiham's recommendations are based on *averages*. Some people's teeth may be more susceptible to rapid decay than the majority, thus requiring more frequent checkups. Also, because of a lack of data on the rate of decay of primary teeth, Dr Sheiham is not proposing that children under the age of 12 abandon the practice of checkups every six months.

A personal prevention programme

This report should not be taken as a licence to forsake regular dental checks. After all, there is no substitute for a dentist's professional competence in detecting serious dental problems and applying appropriate treatment. However, Dr Sheiham's findings underline for us the importance of personal responsibility in matters of oral health. Taking good care of your own teeth on a daily basis is the best way to keep follow-up dental visits to a minimum.

Learning how to clean the teeth properly is important for their survival. However, in a report written for the Health Education Council by P. J. Holloway, professor of child dental health at the University Dental Hospital of Manchester, and two colleagues at the University of Edinburgh,

> It is commonly assumed that dental decay can be reduced by removing the dental plaque and it would be expected that regular toothbrushing, by removing plaque, would reduce dental caries. However, there is little evidence to show that this is the case. It is probable that most decay occurs on areas of the tooth surface not accessible to a toothbrush.

However, Professor Holloway and his co-authors continued, 'Regular oral hygiene is important in the health of the gums.'

Since the trick is to keep bacterial plaque from forming on our teeth, you may think a simple brushing three times a day would be best. But brushing only *once* a day is enough if we do it correctly. 'Bacteria require from 24 to 36 hours to become plaque or a waterproof colony on the teeth. Once it's waterproof, saliva can't get in to neutralize acids and enzymes that can cause cavities and gum disease,' says W.K. Hettenhausen, executive director of the 'Your Teeth for a Lifetime' Preventive Dentistry Foundation, Ontario.

Dr Hettenhausen recommends using two brushes and dental floss in a cleaning routine that may take as long as 15 minutes. 'The average person spends 45 seconds on his teeth three times a day. If he misses a spot, that's where the bacteria are going to organize. Our patients learn that they can brush their teeth while reading the morning paper, watching TV, listening to their stereos or just relaxing.'

The first brush is a two-row *sulcular* soft brush with rounded bristles designed to clean the *sulcus*, or crevice where the tooth meets the gum. The birstles are gently vibrated at a 45-degree angle into the sulcus to disorganize the plaque. Using this brush, patients gently jab and jiggle the area where the tooth meets the gum, then they direct the brush away from the gum line. Both the inner and outer surfaces of the teeth are cleaned in a systematic brushing pattern.

After cleaning the sulcus, patients use dental floss. 'Brushing and flossing are the best insurance people can have to help keep their teeth for a lifetime,' says Dr Hettenhausen. 'When we brush our teeth, we are cleaning only 65 per cent of the tooth. Flossing is absolutely vital to the oral hygiene programme, since most dental problems begin *between* the teeth. You wouldn't think of going a whole day without cleaning between the tines of your fork.'

Dr Hettenhausen feels that beginners should use waxed dental floss at first, then switch to unwaxed after they are more accustomed to the flossing procedure. He also suggests that beginners rinse their mouth after flossing. 'When people first start using dental floss, they can get sore throats and infections if the loose plaque and bacteria aren't rinsed from their mouth. The bacteria in between their teeth have been there a long time and have built up considerably.'

After flossing, Dr Hettenhausen suggests that a three- or four-row soft brush be used for general cleaning and gum massage. The bristles should be rounded and should gently massage the gums. Patients are instructed to roll the brush in such a way as to stimulate blood flow to supporting structures and the roots of the teeth and to clean from the level of the gum to the biting surface of the tooth. The brush is moved in a vertical direction, since horizontal brushing 'goes against the grain of the teeth and can cause toothbrush abrasion,' says Dr Hettenhausen. The palate, the top surfaces of the teeth and the tongue should also be brushed.

'It's not so important what you use on your brush but how you use it,' adds Dr Hettenhausen. 'Synthetic brushes are good because the bristles maintain their original shape unless you are brushing too hard. If the bristles splay out, you are brushing too aggressively. The problem with natural bristles is that they may become soggy after a little bit of use.'

• Toothaches

Anyone who's ever experienced the misery of a toothache, from a filling, an abscess or some other cause, knows that a good pain reliever is hard to find. Dentists usually prescribe aspirin or stronger drugs to deaden the ache until the tooth can be treated. However, some Canadian researchers have found a new, drug-free way of treating dental pain that involves a combination of ice massage and acupuncture. With it, they've successfully taught a number of dental clinic patients to lessen the discomfort of toothache.

To show just how effective the technique is, researchers conducted an experiment involving 40 patients at the outpatient dental clinic of Montreal General Hospital. Some of the patients were taught to massage gently with a piece of ice a particular acupuncture point of the hand on the same side as the pain. The point lies in the fleshy web between the thumb and index finger. It was already known that acupuncture applied to this point could relieve dental pain. As a control, other patients massaged the point, but with a wooden ball instead of ice. A pain questionnaire was administered to both groups to measure the degree of pain relief.

Even though both groups showed similar levels of pain before the experiment, pain reduction was significantly greater among the patients who massaged with ice. Ice massage decreased the intensity of pain by 50 per cent or more in the majority of patients treated (*Canadian Medical Association Journal*, 26 January 1980).

Aloe to soothe a painful tooth

Rick Chavez, a dentist in Seattle, Washington, has found that a traditional remedy works well for at least one type of toothache.

'Baby teeth sometimes become infected when they are ready to come out,' he explains. 'That can give a child a very bad toothache.' In addition to prescribing antibiotics, dabbing the offending tooth with aloe vera 'will relieve the pain completely in about 15 minutes. It's only temporary relief, though, because the problem is that saliva will wash it away. But I had one eight-year-old boy I treated in this way who was able to make it through the night pain-free, until I could arrange to pull the tooth the next day. His mother brought him into my office with severe pain, but the swelling and pain were gone when he came in the next day. And in that case, aloe vera worked when his mother told me aspirin was no help.'

Sensitive teeth? it could be sugar

Like a thin layer of insulation between tooth and bone, the cementum outlines the entire root of the tooth below the gum line. The cementum, although hard, bristles with nerve endings – sensitive nerve endings. As years pass, however, and the gum line slowly and naturally recedes, the body works gradually to desensitize the cementum. That way, when the very tip of it is exposed – an inevitable result of growing older – there won't be any pain.

At least that's the way it *should* happen.

However, if a person eats about 90 lb of refined sugar a year – the amount eaten by the average Briton – many times the gum doesn't recede slowly. It recedes quickly. So quickly that the cementum is exposed before the body has a chance to desensitize it. And sugar on those living nerves is like salt on an open wound. Painful.

'You can't consume that much refined sugar a year without something falling apart. And the teeth go first,' says Bruce Pacetti, a dentist and director of the Page Clinic in Florida. He has treated hundreds of people with this problem. A problem, he says, that's becoming more common.

'At the turn of the century,' he says, 'people ate 5 to 8 lb of refined sugar a year. Now people may eat as much as 270 lb. The human body was never built to be subjected to so much sugar. Tooth decay is the inevitable result. And once you get to a certain point of decay, the cementum is sensitive not only to refined sugar, but to natural sugars as well.'

These sugars, says Pacetti, are found in milk, fruit and sweeteners such as honey, treacle and maple syrup. 'Where a chocolate bar might knock you off your feet, an apple will just give a little twinge.'

To cure the problem, Pacetti has his patients eliminate all sugars – natural and refined – for six months to a year. 'The cementum gradually becomes desensitized when there is no sugar in the diet,' he explains. 'After six months to a year, a person can return to the moderate use of natural sugars – and he probably won't feel any pain.'

During this transition period, Pacetti advises his patients to eat a natural and varied diet. 'Meat, grains, vegetables, seeds, nuts, cheeses – these and other natural foods are enough to give anyone an interesting and nutritious diet.'

Why isn't someone with an exposed cementum sensitive to all foods? Why only sugar? 'Because bacteria break down sugars into acids which can penetrate the cementum,' explains Howard Marshall, a periodontist practising in New York City. 'Immediately beneath the cementum is the dentine, which has many tubules [fine openings] running down towards the nerve. The change in the fluid within the tubule caused by the acids stimulates the nerve, and the response is felt as pain.'

Sugar isn't the only irritant that both causes and aggravates the problem. 'Brushing teeth with a vengeance can literally saw the gums away, exposing the cementum,' says Michael Lerner, a dentist in Kentucky. 'A person with an exposed cementum should use a soft-bristle brush, be less forceful when brushing and brush only once a day. They should also use toothpaste just on the biting surface, not on the gums.'

Lerner also believes that the pain of an exposed cementum is, in a way, beneficial. 'Sensitivity is a signal,' he says. 'It tells us that something is happening that shouldn't be happening. It's the body's way of giving us a warning to stop an activity – in this case, eating sugar or overbrushing – that can make us sick.'

And Bruce Pacetti adds that an exposed cementum isn't the only cause of sensitivity. 'People who eat a lot of sugar have open cavities – the dentine below the enamel is exposed. With an open cavity, any food, including sweets, will cause discomfort.'

The way to really deal with the problem, then, is to stop eating sugar or overbrushing before the cementum is exposed. Otherwise, if you bite into a chocolate bar, your sweet tooth may bite you back.

• Trauma

Trauma – 'the forgotten disease' – is a general term for all those wounds and injuries that flesh is heir to. Trauma is a common cause of death – the fourth most common in the United States alone, after heart disease, cancer and stroke. Tragically, trauma's most common victim is a young man in his 20s.

Yet the care and nutrition of trauma patients has been largely overlooked by medicine, according to Augusta Askari, assistant professor in the department of surgery at the Medical College of Ohio in Toledo. To help fill in the gaps in knowledge about trauma, Dr Askari and her colleagues have been studying zinc and nitrogen metabolism in injured rats. And they've discovered that trauma accelerates losses of both these minerals, at a time when the need for them is especially high.

'Zinc is an essential trace element, vital to life,' Dr Askari told us. 'It's part of RNA and DNA – it's in every single cell in the body. In trauma, it appears to be particularly important because of its role in wound healing and the formation of new protein.'

In their study, Dr Askari's group looked at zinc and nitrogen loss in 33 laboratory rats being fed intravenously. They chose to study animals being fed in this way because it's common among trauma patients and because intravenous feeding can itself increase urinary zinc loss. Sixteen of the 33 rats had broken hind legs, and for the next seven days both injured and uninjured rats were monitored for weight as well as zinc and nitrogen loss.

The researchers found that the injured rats lost far more zinc and nitrogen than the uninjured ones. They concluded that these losses must have been caused by the injury alone, because the feeding solution was identical for both groups of animals.

The problem, in short, is a double one: trauma deprives the body of these substances just when they're needed most to form new proteins, heal wounds and speed recovery.

(*See also* HOSPITAL MALNUTRITION.)

• Traveller's diarrhoea

A severe type of gastro-enteritis – variously called *turista*, 'Montezuma's revenge' and 'holiday tummy' – afflicts many who travel to tropical and subtropical regions. It probably has many causes but most often seems to be due to bacteria called *Escherichia coli*. A few commonsense precautions will decrease your chances of falling ill with traveller's diarrhoea or at least reduce its severity.

Always wash your hands before eating. Drink bottled water (make sure that the seal on the bottle is broken in your presence). Use bottled water for brushing teeth. Eat well-cooked dishes. Pass up raw vegetables, fruits not peeled in your presence, ice in your drinks, and cold meat, custards, mayonnaise and shellfish in areas where refrigeration is questionable. Avoid *like poison* those luscious outdoor buffet dinners featured at tropical resort hotels. Often, the food is kept out for long periods, and the flies get to it before you do.

Questionable water can be sterilized by boiling for ten minutes or using iodine compounds available for the purpose. Hot water from the tap or from water filters is *not* reliable.

Antacids may also set you up for traveller's diarrhoea. Two people travelling abroad developed brucellosis (a type of infection) after eating dairy products – and they were the only two people among their fellow travellers who were taking antacids. The doctor who reported the cases said that brucellosis bacteria are usually tamed by stomach acid, but in this instance there probably wasn't enough acid to do the trick. And, he pointed out, the low levels of stomach acid produced by antacids may also target a person for traveller's diarrhoea and other diarrhoea-causing bacterial infections that tourists sometimes pick up, such as amoebic dysentery and cholera (*Lancet*).

If you're looking for a safe, sanitary place to eat and sleep, ask the airline crew where they are staying. Many airlines exercise some control over the facilities used by their people, and they are careful. Having an aircraft grounded in a remote part of the world by the crew's diarrhoea would be an embarrasement to the crew and an expense to the airline.

What if, despite your precautions, you do fall ill? You can generally secure competent medical or dental care while travelling by asking the nearest medical or dental school for the name of a doctor or dentist, or you could contact the nearest British embassy or consulate.

Since activated charcoal stifles bacteria in the intestines, some doctors recommend it for traveller's diarrhoea. 'Charcoal is an excellent remedy for traveller's diarrhoea,' says Marjorie Baldwin, a doctor at the Wildwood Sanitarium and Hospital in Georgia.

One last pointer: The most important time to protect your health may be after you have returned your luggage to the wardrobe and the quaint villages have become a happy memory. If you get sick after returning home, be sure to mention your trip to your doctor. Travellers back from the tropics may, six months or more later, develop unusual illnesses that most doctors have never seen.

(*See also* DIARRHOEA)

• Ulcers

At 2 A.M. the pain suddenly wakes you up. It feels as if a small animal is gnawing its way through your gut. Woozy with nausea, you sleepwalk to the kitchen for an antacid or something to eat. Gradually the pain subsides, and you can go back to bed.

You've just had a typical peptic ulcer attack.

What is a peptic ulcer? It's a penny-sized, crater-like sore on the inner wall of your stomach or duodenum (the first section of your intestines), and its cause is excess stomach acid, a malfunction of the protective mucous lining or both. Many ulcers heal by themselves, but a few lead to internal bleeding and death. It's estimated that one man in 10 and one woman in 20 will experience a peptic ulcer during their lifetimes.

Misconceptions about ulcers have confused doctors and their patients for decades. Somehow, the idea has stuck that only harried executives get ulcers, or that ulcers are strictly a male disorder, or that bland foods and milk make up the best ulcer diet, or that ulcer patients should be fed six times a day. These are myths, however, and the following might debunk them, as well as offer new information on natural therapies for ulcers.

Myth 1:   only executives and others with high-stress jobs get ulcers

Traditionally, ulcers have been considered the 'purple hearts' of the business world, a red badge of courage that the executive earns for working hard. It's true that executives and professionals are among those who get ulcers, but there's little evidence that just because you have a high-stress job, you're going to get an ulcer. It's not the stress itself but how you react to it that counts.

For example, being a doctor might be considered a high-stress occupation, but a study of doctors in Massachusetts failed to show an unusually high rate of ulcers. Another study, by the US Federal Aviation Administration, showed that male air-traffic controllers – men who are symbols of stress – had an insignificantly higher ulcer rate: 2.4 new cases per year per 1000 workers, compared to 2.1 for the general population.

On the other hand, if you are easily burdened by stress, you may be a candidate for an ulcer. 'The ulcer patients I have seen tended to be anxious and stressed. We see it in fairly high-strung individuals,' one doctor told us. In two case histories described by another doctor, an ulcer flare-up coincided with marital stress for one patient, and with a deadline for a grant application for another. Dr Sandor Szabo of the Harvard Medical School says that, typically, 'potential ulcer patients are exposed to long-standing anxiety and/or emotional tension.'

Myth 2:   only men get ulcers   This was almost fact 30 years ago, when the ratio of male to female ulcer sufferers was 20 to 1. But today the ratio is only 2 to 1. 'This is one instance in which equal rights for women is becoming a reality,' one doctor quips. A falling ulcer rate among men accounts for part of the change, but not all of it. Also, it was once thought that female hormones offered protection from ulcers, but the rising rate of ulcers among women has disproved that.

Increased cigarette smoking among women in recent years may be the cause. Smoking promotes ulcers of the duodenum – the section of the small intestine just below the stomach and the site of most ulcers – and delays their healing. Apparently, smoking inhibits the release of bicarbonate, a natural antacid, from the pancreas to the duodenum. Smoking may also cause the liquid parts of a meal to move out of the stomach and into the duodenum sooner than the solid parts of the same meal. Without the solid food to 'buffer' the liquid food – that is, to neutralize its acidity – it is more likely to burn the duodenum and cause an ulcer.

Children and adolescents may be just as susceptible to ulcers as adults, if they are under enough stress. 'The real or threatened loss of a loved one' can contribute to such ulcers, according to researchers at the Albert Einstein College of Medicine in New York City. Among 24 teenage and pre-teen ulcer patients, they found that 10 of them, or 42 per cent, had lost a close family member or personal friend through death, illness or separation within the year before their ulcer diagnosis (*Psychosomatic Medicine*, August 1981).

Myth 3:   milk and a bland diet are good for an ulcer   This practice has been attributed to one Bertram Sippy, who in 1911 pioneered the feeding of milk and antacids to ulcer patients every hour. Even today, some medical textbooks recommend that regimen, but many doctors now agree that bland diets have only 'demoralized patients and deprived them of one of the earthy pleasures of life – good food' (*Journal of the American Dietetic Association*, October 1979).

Milk, surprisingly, may not be good at all for ulcers. It neutralizes stomach acid at first, but then it backfires. Its calcium content promotes the secretion of gastrin – a hormone that triggers the release of more acid *(Family Practice News)*.

Bland diets may be no more effective than milk. One American doctor surveyed 326 hospitals in all 50 states and found that 77 per cent of them still place their ulcer patients on bland diets – diets without hot spices, fried foods or processed meats, for example – even though, he argued

at least five studies since 1942 have demonstrated that slightly modified or regular diets produce . . . healing or relief of symptoms at a similar rate in patients with duodenal or gastric ulcers as strict or bland 'peptic ulcer diets . . . .' An individualized diet with few restrictions . . . seems to be the most rational approach. *(Gastroenterology)*

Foods that increase acidity in the stomach or duodenum should be avoided though. These include coffee, refined sugar and refined flour. Coffee has long been known to be a direct stimulator of stomach-acid secretion, but sugar and white flour may work indirectly.

In the case of white sugar, a British doctor found out by accident that it promotes ulcers. When he put his obese patients on a low-carbohydrate (low in refined sugar and starch) weight-loss diet, their digestive problems cleared up.

To test this discovery, he gathered together 41 people with chronic stomach problems, with or without ulcers. For three months they ate a low-carbohydrate diet, and for three months a high-carbohydrate diet. At the end of the experiment, 28 of the 41 patients said their stomachs felt better with the low-carbohydrate diet. Eleven felt no change and only two said they felt better on the high-carbohydrate diet. After further experiments, the doctor showed that sugar, not starch, was the chief culprit and that a high-sugar diet maintained for only two weeks could drive the stomach-acid levels of healthy volunteers up to 20 per cent (*British Medical Journal*, 16 February 1980).

White bread seems to harm the duodenum the way cigarettes do. Researchers at the University of Manchester found that when volunteers ate a meal of water and lightly buttered bread made with white flour and white sugar, the liquid portion of the meal moved from the stomach to the duodenum faster than it did when they ate a meal of water and lightly buttered bread made with whole-grain flour and dark-brown sugar. As with cigarettes, the liquid part of the white-bread meal was less buffered and more acidic. Said the researchers, 'the substitution of whole-meal bread for white bread might be of benefit to patients with duodenal ulcers and non-ulcer dyspepsia' *(Gut)*.

Whole-meal bread is rich in fibre – and that may explain some of its benefits. Norwegian scientists have found that fibre can prevent or delay recurring stomach ulcer attacks. In one experiment, 73 people who had had ulcers but were now healed were asked to change their diet for six months. Of the 73, 38 were told to eat lots of whole-grain bread, porridge made from wheat, barley, rye or oats, and lots of vegetables. The remaining 35 were told to avoid these foods.

After six months on the experimental diet, 28 (or 80 per cent) of the low-fibre group had suffered a relapse, compared to only 17 (or 45 per cent) of the high-fibre group. Significantly, of the 15 people who ate the least amount of fibre in the study, 14 developed new ulcers (*Lancet*, 2 October 1982).

Myth 4: antacids help stomach ulcers In a study of patients with a gastric (stomach) ulcer – 15 of whom took an antacid and 13 a placebo – doctors found that 'the rate of healing of the ulcer and the relief of pain is not influenced by treatment with a standard antacid preparation.' In short, the study showed that antacids don't work. But doctors *think* they do. 'All [physicians] prescribe antacids' for stomach ulcers, wrote the doctors who conducted the study *(Digestive Diseases)*. Every last one of them is probably wrong – and they make the same mistake when they prescribe antacids for a duodenal ulcer (an ulcer in the first part of the intestines).

'Antacids are generally accepted as effective in the relief of pain arising from duodenal ulcer,' wrote a team of doctors who conducted a study to see if there was anything to this belief. There wasn't. Of the 30 patients with duodenal ulcer who took either an antacid or a placebo to relieve pain, four had more relief from the antacid and three from the placebo, while 23 thought neither was better *(Gastroenterology)*. Once again, antacids didn't work.

Myth 5: an ulcer patient should eat six times a day This doctrine, which is still followed in many hospitals, might be the worst thing for the stomach, because the stomach releases digestive acids whenever it is fed. 'Frequent feedings repeatedly stimulate gastric-acid secretion, and there are no data to support the assumption that they are more beneficial in healing ulcers than three meals a day,' said the same researcher who investigated bland diets.

'There's definitely a vicious cycle,' adds Dr Vincent Speeg, Jr of the National Veterans Administration Hospital in Nashville, Tennessee. 'It's true that food buffers stomach acid somewhat, but it also causes the stomach to secrete acid. Eating only three meals a day with no snacks in between is the best way to go.'

Finally, it's not only a matter of what you eat, but *how* you eat it when battling peptic ulcers, says Dr Jon I. Isenberg of Wadsworth Veterans Administration Hospital Center in Los Angeles. Animal research findings indicate that food which is not chewed thoroughly does not have the chance to mix properly with a substance called *urogastrone* from the salivary glands. This protects the intestinal lining from erosion in experimental animals, so chewing food thoroughly may be the best safeguard against peptic ulcer.

Effective treatments

So much for the myths. Now let's look at some neglected facts, like the use of nutrients to treat ulcers. It's seldom talked about, but when it is, zinc comes up. 'Zinc,' says longtime ulcer researcher Carl J. Pfeiffer, 'has very consistently been shown to be effective in preventing or reducing the severity of experimentally induced gastric ulcers in animals.'

In an experiment at Memorial University in St John's, Newfoundland, Dr Pfeiffer and colleagues found that zinc supplements protected the stomach cells of rats who had been given reserpine, a tranquillizer that can induce ulcers in humans and rats. The reserpine apparently broke open the lysosomes – tiny sacks of enzymes in the cells of the stomach lining – thereby releasing the enzymes that, in turn, damaged the cells.

The zinc supplements, however, seemed to strengthen the lysosomes and kept them intact. Importantly, the zinc was effective in doses that didn't harm the rats, and Dr Pfeiffer called these 'promising findings' *(European Journal of Pharmacology*, 22 February 1980).

Zinc supplements may also block a chemical chain reaction that can lead to an ulcer. Chi H. Cho, a colleague of Dr Pfeiffer's, found that when he gave rats the drug *methacholine*, their stomach cells released histamine. The histamine triggered acid secretion, which caused ulcers. Zinc, however, stopped the domino effect by preventing the release of histamine *(Pharmacology)*. For the best absorption, take zinc supplements with meals.

Vitamin A may also fight ulcers. One survey in Israel showed that the rate of deaths caused by peptic ulcers in that country rose 81 per cent between 1949 and 1977. The researchers making the survey blamed the increase on the consumption of dietary fats, which rose 52 per cent over those years. However, the death rate would have been even higher, they believed, had the average Israeli's daily consumption of vitamin A not gone up 34 per cent in that period, from 3195 to 4291 IU.

> This increase in vitamin A consumption probably dampened some of the effect of the simultaneous increase in fat consumption. Peptic ulcer mortality was correlated directly and significantly with total fat and inversely with total protein and with vitamin A.. . . Reduced total fat intake and increased vitamin A consumption via fruits and vegetables may prove beneficial in reducing mortality rates of the Israeli population due to heart disease, diabetes and peptic ulcer. [*American Journal of Clinical Nutrition*, August 1981]

Juice from the humble cabbage may also be an anti-ulcer weapon. In the late 1940s and early 1950s, a San Francisco doctor, Garnet Cheney, treated ulcer patients with raw cabbage juice. He felt that ulcers were caused by 'disordered nutrition' and that an unknown factor, which he called 'vitamin U' (for ulcer), in the cabbage juice corrected the problem. Comparing his one-litre-a-day cabbage-juice therapy to the standard ulcer therapy of bland diet and antacids, Dr Cheney found that his patients healed in an average of 13.4 days of treatment, compared to 50 days for those on the standard therapy. Vitamin U, said Dr Cheney,

> increases the resistance of the mucosal lining of the oesophagus, stomach and intestine to the erosive and ulcerating action of gastric juice, which is high in acid content and rich in pepsin [an enzyme necessary for digestion]. [*American Journal of Gastroenterology*]

The most frustrating aspect of coping with a peptic ulcer is probably its tendency to recur or relapse. Not even the newest ulcer drugs can prevent a recurrence once a patient stops taking the drug.

The best mode of treatment and prevention may be to eliminate as much stress, white sugar, white flour, fats, coffee and aspirin from your life as possible, and to supply yourself with natural ulcer fighters: vitamin A, zinc, fresh vegetables and whole-grain breads.

• Urinary problems

Urine is a body fluid, just like blood or spinal fluid, and bacteria can grow in it and cause infections of the bladder or kidneys. Also, some cancer-causing chemicals we're exposed to pass out of the body through the urine. Since those chemicals come in contact with the bladder, they probably increase the risk of bladder cancer. However, there is at least one nutrient that may protect you against those problems.

Vitamin C can actually kill some bacteria, including *Escherichia coli*, the most common cause of urinary-tract infections. That killing power is especially strong at the uniquely high vitamin C levels that are possible in the concentrated fluid of urine. Doctors have used vitamin C for years to prevent urinary infections in people likely to develop them. Although it has been generally assumed that the vitamin works by producing an acid urine that inhibits the growth of bacteria, in fact, vitamin C does a poor job of acidifying the urine. The effectiveness of the vitamin is more likely related to a direct bactericidal (bacteria-killing) action, according to the *Journal of the American Geriatrics Society* (January 1979).

As we said, the kidneys rid the body of various waste products and environmental poisons, and urine contains a wide range of toxic chemicals, some of which have the potential to cause cancer. However, a few of those chemicals don't become cancer-causers until they undergo a chemical reaction called oxidation. A nutrient that could prevent oxidation – an anti-oxidant – should lessen the number of cancer-causing chemicals the bladder is exposed to. Vitamin C is an anti-oxidant. It's been shown to prevent the development of bladder cancer in animals exposed to a cancer-causing compound that's often found in human urine *(Proceedings of the Society of Experimental Biology and Medicine)*. And Jorgen Schlegel, former chief of staff at Tulane University Medical Center in New Orleans, believes that vitamin C may be effective in preventing human cancer, too *(Annals of the New York Academy of Sciences)*.

However, you have to take enough vitamin C to make sure some of it spills over into the urine. For most people, 300 mg a day would do the trick, but those with an increased need for vitamin C – smokers, diabetics, the elderly, the stressed, the allergic and persons taking certain drugs – need more. Other nutrients such as vitamin E, zinc and selenium are also anti-oxidants and might help prevent bladder cancer.

Cranberry juice

'One of the most common complaints encountered in general practice is recurrent dysuria [painful urination], frequency and urgency of urination in the female patient,' Dr D. V. Moen reported in the *Wisconsin Medical Journal*, outlining the common symptoms of cystitis (*See* BLADDER INFECTION).

Many also suffer with chronic urinary infection and inflammation. According to Dr Moen, 'They do not respond satisfactorily to sulfas, antibiotics, bladder sedatives, urethral dilations or bladder irrigations.' And even if there is a response, the symptoms keep coming back. 'This particular group has been most gratifyingly relieved of all urinary symptoms as long as they continue to take 6 oz glassfuls of cranberry juice daily.'

Dr Moen also gave this cranberry regimen to a 66-year-old woman with chronic pyelonephritis (kidney inflammation). She had been ill for five years, and drugs had failed to help her.

> After eight weeks of the juice therapy, the urine gradually began to clear. At the end of nine months, there were only occasional pus cells. . . . The urine is still negative, and the patient refuses to stop the cranberry juice because she feels so much better and knows no other medication has helped her before.

Don't reach for a soft drink when you've worked up a thirst. Carbonated soft drinks when consumed in large quantities, have been known to cause blood in the urine. For more information, see HAEMATURIA.

• Vaginal infections

Whether you get vaginal infections once a month or once a decade, you *know*. At best, they're thoroughly annoying – and you'd do anything to get far from the maddening itch. At worst, they can seriously affect your health.

Is it possible to treat, and clear up, vaginal infections yourself? The answer is: sometimes, especially if you catch them early enough. But often, they require prompt medical attention.

However, the good news is that you can *prevent* most vaginal infections, most of the time.

The key to prevention – and sometimes treatment – is understanding the vaginal 'ecosystem'. We call it an ecosystem because, in spite of the occasional annoyances, the vagina is usually a wonderfully efficient, and astonishingly complex, self-maintaining system. It washes itself out; it harbours good micro-organisms that keep it healthy, and shuts off bad ones.

So usually, the best kind of health maintenance you can do – especially for the internal areas – is nothing. The more you interfere with the vagina's natural systems – for example, with vigorous douching – the more likely you are to upset the balance. Understanding how that marvellous balance works is the first step to staying healthy.

Your natural defence system

The vagina keeps itself healthy and clean with some ingenious protective systems.

Perhaps the most common is the acid balance. A healthy vagina is usually slightly acidic (it registers about 4.0 to 5.0 on the pH scale that runs from 1.0, most acidic, to 14.0, most alkaline). Acidity prevents many different kinds of bothersome bacteria and other micro-organisms from flourishing. Interestingly, a kind of friendly bacteria keeps the vagina acidic. The 'good guy' bacteria are called *lactobacilli*, or Doderlain's bacilli.

If it weren't for the lactobacilli, the vagina might always be a sugary, alkaline breeding ground for infections. That's because the cells of the vaginal wall store sugar, in the form of glucose; secretions in the vagina slough off the cells, releasing the glucose. Bacteria, fungi and protozoa love to feed off that sugar. The lactobacilli thrive on sugar, too, but unlike the other organisms, the lactobacilli turn the sugar into weak lactic acid. The acidity kills off many of the bad organisms.

Another important protective system is the vaginal mucus. Some women think of the mucus as 'unclean', but, in fact, the opposite is true. Unless the discharge is an unusual colour or has a very strong odour, it's a sign that the cleanup process is working fine.

Mucus cleans out the vagina with the help of gravity. The mucus comes from the cervix, and the amount, colour and thickness depend on where you are in your monthly cycle. As it moves down the vagina, the mucus picks up some additional moisture from the vaginal walls. And it also picks up dead cells that line the vaginal walls, cleaning them right out. (The cells contribute to the whitish colour.) The mucus also moistens and protects the vaginal walls. And it 'plugs' the cervical opening, to defend the sterile uterus from micro-organism invasion.

Things that go itch in the night

You're going 'itch' in the night – or day. Something's wrong. Your discharge has taken on a yellowish or greyish colour. There's been a coup: some micro-organism is holding your vaginal ecosystem hostage.

What have you got? It could be a lot of things. The general term for vaginal infections is 'vaginitis', but that covers a lot of territory. There are five major kinds of vaginal infections:

Fungal, or yeast, infections – the most common is *candidiasis* (also called *moniliasis* and, more commonly, 'thrush') – are caused by microscopic, plant-like organisms called *Candida albicans*. A few are normally present in the vagina – and in the bowels, whence they can be brought over to the vagina. They can also be sexually transmitted, and they flourish in a sugary alkaline environment.

Protozoan infections are caused by small, one-celled animals. The best known is *trichomonas vaginalis* (sometimes referred to as 'trich'). Like fungal infections, protozoa thrive in alkalinity. Sexual contacts, wet washcloths – there are a variety of ways to pick up trich. One estimate is that half of all women normally have a few trich swimming around in their vagina; only 15 per cent will get a full-fledged outbreak.

Intermediate organism infections are caused by micro-organisms that are a sort of cross between a bacterium and a virus. *Chlamydia* is the most common; it's virtually always sexually transmitted.

Bacterial infections can be triggered by various kinds of bacteria. Most common is *Haemophilus vaginalus* (or HV). Bacteria can be imported from the bowels, or transmitted sexually; like fungi, they thrive in alkalinity. If your vaginal acidity is high, you'll probably resist the invasion; if not, the bacteria will flourish. However, this is far more common in the United States; it is rarely found in Britain, perhaps because douching is very infrequently done here.

Both gonorrhoea and syphilis are caused by bacteria. 'Toxic shock syndrome' is also considered a bacterial infection; it's caused by the bacteria *Staphylococci aureus*, which can thrive in the vagina when super-absorbent synthetic tampons are used.

Viral infections are among the hardest to treat. Herpes is the most notorious; the kind of herpes associated with genital lesions is *herpes simplex* Virus-2 (HSV-2). It's virtually always transmitted through sexual contact.

Miscellaneous irritations you can also get a variety of rashes and inflammations, usually from allergies or bad reactions to something being used in, or near, the vagina. For example, a diaphragm left in too long can trigger an inflammation, or you can be allergic to deodorant sanitary towels. These usually clear up when the sources are removed.

Most vaginal infections are not life-threatening, but they should be treated promptly. Left untreated, some can cause complications such as *cervicitis*, an inflammation of the cervix. For the infections that are sexually transmissible, your partner should be treated, too – even if he has no symptoms, he can re-infect you. And it is, unfortunately, possible to get more than one kind of infection at a time. If your doctor tells you you have nonspecific vaginitis – don't accept that as an answer. You need to know which it is to receive proper medication.

Why you got it

Once you figure out *what* you've got, you probably start wondering *why* you got it.

One possible cause is the arrival of a new organism in the vagina. What brings in these unwelcome visitors? An obvious vehicle is sexual intercourse, which can give you anything from an annoying yeast infection to a serious case of gonorrhoea.

But sex is hardly the only source of trouble. Some problem-causing organisms inhabit the lower intestine. Wiping yourself the wrong way – from back to front – after a bowel movement can deliver bacteria or fungi that normally dwell peacefully in the bowel over to the vagina. A shifting sanitary towel can also provide transportation. Careful front-to-back wiping, daily washing of the vulva (the outer vaginal area), daily changes of underwear and frequent changes of sanitary towels – all those standard sorts of hygiene measures – will go a long way towards preventing this problem.

Wet toilet seats and damp towels can also harbour and spread certain micro-organisms. Your own diaphragm, if not properly washed between uses, can bring back an infection you thought you'd cleared up.

However, in many cases, even the arrival of a new micro-organism isn't enough to start an infection. After all, many women who never get vaginitis have some of the problem-causing micro-organisms swimming around inside them.

It's the ecological balance of the vagina, especially the acid balance, that determines whether the spark will blaze on or fizzle. And there are all kinds of conditions that can make your vagina more – or less – inflammable.

Stress, anxiety and lack of sleep can lower immunity, and may even lower vaginal acidity, opening you up to all kinds of infections. Your monthly cycle also affects susceptibility to infection. Cervical mucus is slightly more alkaline when you're most fertile. And during menstruation, your vagina is at its most alkaline – because the blood that floods the vagina is a sweet alkaline medium. That's one reason many women find that their yeast or trich symptoms escalate during or after their periods.

Pregnancy is also a time when women may suffer more from vaginitis. Hormonal changes are causing more sugar to be stored in the vaginal cells, increasing alkalinity. The Pill can have the same effect.

Antibiotics can make you more prone to vaginitis. The problem is that antibiotics kill off the good bacteria – the lactobacilli – which keep the vagina acidic. They'll also kill off the bad bacteria, but antibiotics *don't* kill fungi, and fungi love alkalinity so they spread like wildfire. Many women find themselves with yeast infections whenever they have to take to antibiotics.

Anything that scratches the vaginal walls can cause trouble. A wound can provide bacteria or viruses with safe harbour and feeding ground. You can scratch yourself with anything from a douche nozzle to a tampon applicator.

One particular kind of internal abrasion may be linked to toxic shock syndrome. Scientists have found that super-absorbent tampons are far more likely to cause 'micro-ulcerations', tiny wounds, in the vaginal walls. They speculate that toxic shock syndrome may be triggered by the combination of trapped blood and mucus in the tampon – a perfect breeding ground for germs – plus the scratches.

No tampon should be left in too long, because it can breed bacteria. Change tampons at least twice a day (on the other hand, changing them too often may cause irritation). And don't wear a tampon when you're not menstruating, or on 'light' days. Not only is there a greater friction and irritation; but the tampon also absorbs the mucus, robbing the vaginal walls of the protective moisture they need and interfering with the 'washdown' process. It's also a good idea to alternate between towels and tampons during your menstrual period. Don't leave a diaphragm or cervical cap in too long, either – bacteria can breed there.

IUDs can also cause infections. The dangling string from the uterus is a bridge that nature didn't build. It can bring problem-causing micro-organisms from the vagina to the uterus.

The myth of 'feminine hygiene'

Feminine hygiene products can throw your vaginal system completely out of kilter. They're not only unnecessary, and ineffective, but they can be down-right harmful.

Feminine hygiene sprays are the worst villains. They can cause irritation and inflammation of the delicate tissue in the vulva and vagina. Deodorant tampons and sanitary towels can do the same thing. Deodorant tampons are a particularly worthless idea, since menstrual blood has no odour until it's been outside, in the air. You don't need extra chemicals inside you. The best way to prevent odours is to change underwear and wash the vulva daily, and to change tampons and towels at least two or three times a day.

Coloured toilet papers, bubble baths, scented powders and soaps can also cause allergic reactions and inflammations. Anti-bacterial deodorant soaps can kill off some healthy bacteria and trigger vaginitis. Even anti-bacterial products for cleaning the bathtub may have the same effect.

Another thing that can upset the vaginal ecology is douching. Far more common in the United States, American women have been programmed by generations of vigorous douchers: their mothers did it, and so did their grandmothers.

Douching is virtually always completely unnecessary. As we've mentioned, unpleasant odours form on the outside, not the inside, so it's a better idea to concentrate on keeping the outside clean. The normal flow of mucus does a good job of cleaning you out. All you have to do is keep the outside clean.

You can have a bad reaction to the chemicals that go into perfumed, commercially prepared douches. Douching also dries out the protective mucus and can irritate or damage the vaginal walls and upset the acid balance, setting you up for infections. Worse, improper douching can propel micro-organisms from the vagina into the uterus, and even beyond, if it's done at too high a pressure. It can erode the mucus plug that acts as a protective barrier to the uterus. It's a particularly bad idea to douche during your period; then the cervix is open, and the upward flow can bring infected material to the uterus.

What about the vinegar-and-water douche that many women's self-help advocates recommend to restore acid balance and possibly clear up infections? If you really want to, says Janet Wilson, a staff doctor with the Elizabeth Blackwell Women's Health Center in Philadelphia, go carefully, and certainly don't do it frequently. An alternative to douching – though possibly not quite as penetrating – is a sitz bath (*see below*).

How you can help yourself

It's a good idea to consult a doctor as promptly as possible for most vaginal infections.

However, there are things you can do for yourself to prevent – and even treat – certain kinds of vaginitis flare-ups. Here are some of the best self-treatments.

Sitz baths These are a milder, safer alternative to douching. One of the most effective kinds of sitz baths for thrush is a saltwater bath, says Gideon G. Panter, a prominent New York City gynaecologist and faculty member at New York University – Cornell Medical Center. If you're not sure what kind of vaginitis you've got, try the sitz bath; if it's thrush, it may well clear up the problem.

How do you take a sitz bath? Add a half-cup of table salt to a shallow tub of water. Sit in the tub with your legs spread apart – it's a good idea to rest your legs on either side of the tub. Inserting a finger helps get the solution inside.

This saltwater solution isn't acidic – but it is a good approximation of saline, normal body fluid, similar to the tears that are constantly bathing and cleaning your eyes. 'The saline bath will reduce the population of any invading or excessive organisms and enable your own body defence mechanisms to do a better job in fighting infections,' says Dr Panter. 'Nine times out of ten, these baths at bedtime will clear up the infection and save a trip to the doctor's.'

A vinegar-and-water sitz bath can help restore the acid balance, and possibly head off or clear up outbreaks of organisms that flourish in an alkaline environment. Add 4 fl oz of white vinegar to your shallow, warm bath water.

Yogurt Many women have reported success in treating yeast infections with yogurt. You need plain, *lactobacillus acido-philus* yogurt – that's the kind that contain live lactobacilli, the same bacteria that make the vagina acid. Many commercial yogurts don't contain this strain of bacteria, so for extra insurance, it's a good idea to buy some acidophilus tablets or powder in your health food shop or chemist. Add about two tablespoons of the powder (crushing the tablet, or opening the capsule) to 4 fl oz of plain yogurt. Mix well. Then, with a vaginal medication applicator, contraceptive foam applicator or small spoon, insert about two teaspoons of the mixture into the vagina. (A sanitary towel will help reduce the mess.) Or you can try simply inserting one or two lactobacillus tablets in the vagina.

If you're particularly prone to yeast outbreaks when you take antibiotics, insert yogurt while you're on the drug. It's not a bad idea, either, to eat yogurt and swallow lactobacillus tablets, whether you're on antibiotics or not. They'll help eradicate the bad bacteria and fungi from the intestine, meaning there's less chance they will find their way from the anal area to the vagina.

[However, it should be noted that recent reports have blamed the insertion of natural yogurt into the vagina for *causing* infection in a few women, perhaps for the same reasons that douching should be avoided.]

Garlic This has often been recommended for *trichomonas vaginalis*, but don't insert it directly in the vagina; according to herbalist Nan Koehler, women who do can get 'burns' on the sensitive tissue. Instead, try crushing a clove of garlic and adding it to your bathwater for a sitz bath.

Boric acid This is non-toxic and can also help acidify the vagina to clear up fungus. Dr Richard Lumiere recommends, in *Healthy Sex* (1983), making up 600 mg gelatine capsules of boric acid, and inserting them.

Diet The foods you eat affect the vaginal ecology. Refined carbohydrates and sugars – pastries, ice cream, even wine and cocktails – can make you more prone to vaginal infections, particularly yeast infections.

Although the link has never been scientifically proven, plenty of women and women's health care practitioners agree that cutting out sugar cuts down infections. The connection makes sense. Remember, cells in the vaginal wall contain sugar, which is released as they're sloughed off. It's possible to have an overload of sugar; that's why diabetes, pregnancy and the Pill can trigger frequent attacks of thrush. They all increase the amount of sugar that's stored.

Another problem with a sugary diet is that it may reduce your immunity generally. Proper nutrition is important to keeping resistance high. Vitamin supplements can help ensure a strong immune system. Nutrients particularly important to build immunity include vitamins A, B_6, C and E, and iron and zinc. (*See also* IMMUNE SYSTEM PROBLEMS.)

There's yet another dietary link to vaginitis: some doctors believe that fungus-related foods may encourage candida, the fungus that causes thrush. Candida is biologically related to moulds in cheese and yeast in beer, wine, vinegar and breads. Eating these foods may overload the system with moulds or yeasts, which can cause a yeast infection to flare.

So if you're really at your wit's end with thrush, here are some of the foods to avoid: processed meats and fish; meats and fish breaded in batter; milk fortified with vitamins; buttermilk; malt-flavoured milk; cereals containing malt or fortified with vitamins; farina; breads made with wheat or rye flour; crackers; pasta; soups thickened with wheat flour; mushrooms; chilli peppers; dried fruit; frozen or canned citrus juice (only fresh- squeezed is yeast free); root beer; dry ginger; alcoholic beverages; vinegar; brewer's yeast; baker's yeast; B vitamins made from yeast, or multi-vitamin supplements containing B vitamins made from yeast (check with the manufacturer); selenium and chromium supplements derived from yeast.

Incidentally, some livestock are fed antibiotics – which, of course, can trigger yeast infections. You might want to try a meat-free diet, or stick with additive-free meat if a yeast infection is persisting.

Diet can also have a big impact on herpes recurrences. Many people have reported success by adding more lysine, an amino acid, to their diets. Foods high in lysine include brewer's yeast, dairy products, meat and eggs, or you can take lysine supplements. Lysine therapy also means avoiding arginine, another amino acid that 'opposes' lysine. Foods to avoid, because of their arginine content, include peanuts, cashews, pecans, seeds, almonds and chocolate.

Vitamins may also help herpes sufferers. Particularly recommended are vitamins A and B, pantothenic acid, zinc and calcium. Vitamin C is controversial; some herpes sufferers swear by it; others say it makes their outbreak worse.

Clothes The right clothes can mean the difference between an organism waxing or waning. A hot, moist environment encourages infections – yeast infections are far more common in the summer-time, for example – so the idea is to keep yourself as cool and dry as possible.

Always wear cotton pants, or pants with a cotton crutch, and make sure your trousers are loose enough to permit the vaginal area to breathe. Avoid tight jeans and synthetic fibres. Tights are out, unless they have a sewn-in crutch. When you're recovering from vaginitis, wear airy loose caftans at home, skip pyjamas and underwear; a cotton nightgown will do. If you can avoid it, don't sit around in a wet bathing costume; make a quick change to a dressing gown or skirt. Powdered natural clay can also keep the vaginal area dry – but never use talc.

• Varicose veins

The patient, a robust woman in her 50s, couldn't quite fathom what went wrong in paradise. Wearing a new shell necklace and a flawless tan, she'd just flown into New York after three weeks in Hawaii. Of course, everything had been fabulous, from the Polynesian repasts at the Kahala Hilton to the languid sunbathing at the pool. What, then, could possibly account for the painfully inflamed veins she developed her first day home? 'I can't understand it,' she complained to her doctor. 'It was such a wonderful trip.'

No doubt it was, agreed her doctor, Howard C. Baron, an attending vascular surgeon at the Cabrini Medical Centre in New York City. The culprit, however, wasn't the vacation itself but the tedious, uncomfortable eight-hour jet ride home. Perhaps if the woman had suspected a predisposition to varicose veins, she'd have occasionally flexed her calf muscles and left her cramped seat every hour to stroll up and down the aisle.

Obviously, the patient didn't know that 'movers and shakers', as Dr Baron dubs fitness enthusiasts, are the best candidates for healthy legs. For that reason, he singles out exercise and diet in his book *Varicose Veins: A Commonsense Approach to Their Management* (1979) as the key preventives against symptoms and complications of those bulging bluish cords down the leg.

It's no secret that those gnarled and swollen leg veins afflicting one in four women and one in ten men aren't very pretty. They're malformed, defective blood vessels that are no longer elastic. Stretched out of shape, they appear enlarged, twisted and discoloured. That all stems from problems with the delicate valves within the leg veins that provide a pathway for used blood to be carried back to the heart from everywhere in the body. To ease the arduous task of forcing blood up the leg against the gravitational pull, the tiny, one-way valves close between heartbeats to prevent a back flow of the pumped blood.

Normally, that action occurs millions of times throughout life without a hitch, but in the leg veins, the process may be disrupted. Pressure on the leg veins may interfere with the circulatory system and prevent the valves from shutting properly. When this happens, or if vein valves are inadequate, defective or malfunctioning, blood seeps back and pools in the legs, further dilating the veins. After a few years, the vessels begin to lose their flexibility. They sag and push towards the surface, shifting the entire burden to the larger, deeper veins.

Many people dismiss the early warning signals of varicose veins – the slight tingle of impaired blood flow followed by the eruption of small bluish veins near the skin's surface – unless they pose a cosmetic problem. Some doctors, however, like Dr Baron, believe that early detection and treatment can prevent more serious symptoms and complications from occurring.

Unfortunately, millions do suffer, typically exiencing a dull aching heaviness and fatigue in the legs. Ankles may swell, particularly in warm weather, painful calf cramps may develop at night and legs may itch or burn. More serious complications such as leg ulcers, phlebitis (inflamed veins, a condition that plagued former President Nixon), blood clots and haemorrhage may occur. Disfigurement, emphasizes Dr Baron, is the most blatant sign of the disorder. He describes the appearance of the troublesome vein as 'bunched, twisted, lumped and contorted into an angry blue rope with grape-like bulges.'

The causes of varicose veins

Although many people die annually from a related complication – blood clots in the lung – doctors are still divided on the precise cause of varicose veins. Many experts, like James A. DeWeese, blame one's ancestors for the affliction. 'It's a degenerative process that runs in families, and when the cause is due to heredity it can't be prevented,' maintains Dr DeWeese, a renowned vascular surgeon at the University of Rochester (NY) Medical School.

Robert A Nabatoff, a clinical professor of vascular surgery, also indicates genetics as the major contributing factor to varicose veins. 'The vast majority of patients have inherited their condition, and the veins usually first appear in the late teens or early 20s,' says Dr Nabatoff, who teaches at Mount Sinai School of Medicine in New York City.

None the less, the notion of varicosities as an environmentally induced disorder is gaining credence and increased respectability among a number of doctors. Among them is Denis P. Burkitt, who believes highly developed and industrialized cultures pay a severe price for progress with heart disease, ulcers, obesity and varicose veins. This prominent British surgeon contends that inflamed vessels are rare among primitive people living on fibre-rich diets, but are common in Western nations where meals are low in roughage. A fibre-depleted diet, he explains, necessitates abdominal straining to evacuate small, hard stools, putting enormous pressure on leg veins. Prolonged toilet sitting, he says, further aggravates the dilemma by cutting off circulation along the back of the legs.

Other forms of inactivity such as standing or sitting too long in one place may also exacerbate varicosities. Because the malady results from impaired circulation, authorities speculate that chair sitting may especially wreak havoc on one's legs. In fact, it all started with the Egyptians, and they, too, had varicose veins. 'The chair,' states Dr Baron, 'is a terrible invention of civilization. While it makes sitting comfortable, it increases the pressure on the leg veins, and it also leads to a damaging habit – crossing your legs.'

Although the problem is far more prevalent in women, a popular misconception, notes Dr Baron, is that pregnancy causes varicose veins. Instead, it's generally thought today that female hormones, especially those released during pregnancy, play a role in producing varicose veins in susceptible women. Frequently, inflamed veins may be the first sign of pregnancy, even before a missed menstrual period, but they often recede after childbirth. Because the unsightly blue cords pop out before the veins come under increased pressure, this suggests that the weight of the foetus may be less a factor than hormones.

Diminishing varicose veins

If you already have varicose veins, there's no need to despair. Dr Baron believes that minor adjustments in daily routines may help diminish the number and even the size of the snake-like embarrassments. Some tips for preventing and 'pampering' varicose veins, as well as precluding future complications, include the following:

• Avoid whenever possible long periods of sitting or standing. If you must do so, make a conscious effort to flex your leg muscles. Wiggle your toes frequently, and slowly raise and lower yourself on the balls of your feet. Don't cross your legs. Break up lengthy car trips by stopping and walking several minutes every hour or two. On long plane or train rides, pace up and down the aisle at least once an hour.

• Get sufficient exercise through walking, jogging, running, cycling or swimming. Walking, note Drs Eric P. and Karl A. Lofgren, both of the Mayo Clinic in Rochester, Minnesota, lowers the venous pressure to about a third of the standing pressure under normal conditions *(Geriatrics)*. Dr Robert May, a specialist in surgery and circulatory problems at the University of Innsbruck in Austria, advises brisk walks for 15 minutes four times a day. He also advocates going barefoot at home to help exercise the foot muscles and improve venous blood flow *(Medical Tribune*, 27 February 1980).

• Adopt a high-fibre diet. A lack of roughage hardens stools and puts pressure on the pelvic veins. Dr May recommends that patients eat salad daily, along with vegetables and jacket potatoes, and take two to three tablespoons of wheat germ. Whole grains, bran and fresh fruits are other good sources of fibre.

Robert I. Lowenberg, a vascular surgeon in Atlanta, Georgia, suggests increasing the daily intake of dietary fibre fivefold.

• Shun tight garments such as calf-length boots, tights too snug at the groin, girdles, corsets and binding belts. Any clothing that tends to constrict the venous blood flow just beneath the skin can be hazardous to your health.

• Elevate your feet, whenever possible. Lean back, kick off your shoes and put your feet up on your desk. Placing the legs 12 to 24 inches above heart level reduces pressure in the veins to nearly zero.

• Don't read on the toilet. The shape of the hard wood or plastic seat puts undue pressure on the abdominal veins, which, in turn, puts pressure on leg veins, notes Dr Baron.

• Avoid bathing in a tubful of hot water, warns Dr May, who recommends showers in the morning and at night. He also suggests a final spray of cold water on the legs.

• Wear elastic support stockings throughout pregnancy and support hose at other times if you must stand a lot.

Untreated, varicosities can become disfiguring and disabling. 'Although no absolute cure has been discovered,' wrote Dr Karl Lofgren, 'much can be done to control this chronic venous disorder, to provide relief of symptoms and to prevent complications.'

For uncomplicated varicose veins, either bandages or well-fitted elastic stockings can be used to relieve symptoms by acting like muscles to facilitate blood flow. Because the fit is so critical, however, Dr Baron cautions about the stockings' main drawback: they stretch out gradually and support may disappear. They must also be put on before you get out of bed in the morning, when any swelling will be at its least.

Should those fail to provide sufficient relief, a treatment popular in Britain involves injecting a chemical into the veins to close them off. Called *sclerotherapy*, it is now seldom used by American specialists because of its high failure rate, permanent brown pigment stains left in the skin and serious side-effects.

Experts agree that complete surgical removal of the malfunctioning veins has proved to be the best approach for correcting significant varicosities. The most common method involves tying off and removing the troublesome veins – also known as 'stripping' them. Once the defective vessels are removed, other healthy ones assume their function without harming normal circulation.

Even though the procedure is deemed safe and often yields permanent results, the treatment and cure of varicose veins in a sense are always failures – of prevention.

• Vision problems

According to the Popeye school of nutrition, it's all very simple. You eat spinach for strong muscles. You drink milk for white and shiny teeth. You eat carrots for sharp, clear vision.

We know good nutrition is more involved than that, that the best diet is one that serves our total needs. Sometimes, though, in spite of ourselves, we end up relying on one specific food targeted to knock out one specific ailment.

Good eyesight, for example, has traditionally been associated with vitamin A alone. However, now a growing body of research indicates that a host of nutrients other than vitamin A may be required for the maintenance of healthy eyes, and some researchers are suggesting that poor nutrition might even be involved in ordinary short-sightedness.

Ben C. Lane, a New Jersey optometrist, found significant differences in the way his more short-sighted patients were eating. The eye, he believes, is particularly sensitive to the body's nutritional state.

'We may say a healthy person can be short-sighted,' Dr Lane told us, 'that with myopia you can have good health. But I think myopic people's resistance to environmental stresses is reduced in ways that do not show up in an ordinary doctor's examination. It's a subtle difference, and optometrists and ophthalmologists are in a better position to notice the difference. The eye is a magnificent place to observe these things. It's very sensitive to nutritional problems.' The eye is certainly a complex organ, and the different parts require a variety of nutrients to function properly. Vitamins A, E, C, B complex and zinc are all essential.

The eye's structure

A number of different kinds of tissue in the eye are necessary for sight. The eye is a ball filled with jelly-like fluid. the tissue surrounding this fluid is called the *sclera*, which is visible as the whites of our eyes in front, but extends back around the eye as well. The very front of the eye is covered by transparent tissue called the *cornea*.

Light enters the eye here, passes through the lens directly behind the cornea and is focused on light-sensitive cells lining the inner wall at the back of the eyeball. When everything is working properly, the cornea and lens bend the light as it enters the eye and focus it on the back wall of the eye (called the *retina*), which activates the optic nerve. The optic nerve sends a message to the part of the brain that registers sight, and we see the focused image.

Vitamin A

The best-known connection between diet and sight involves vitamin A. The retina is made up of light-sensitive cells called cones and rods. The cones are sensitive to colour, while the rods are only able to detect different shadings of light. The rods contain a pigment called *rhodopsin*, which is a chemical cousin of vitamin A. When light strikes a rod, its rhodopsin is chemically broken down and can be restored to working order only if vitamin A is present.

In this case, a vitamin is the very stuff from which vision is 'made'. If the body is lacking in vitamin A, the natural restoration of rhodopsin to working order does not take place, and the rods quit working. The first sign of the breakdown is a loss of night vision, in dim light when the eye can no longer distinguish colours and must rely totally on its black-and-white vision. Proper night vision is totally dependent on the rods, and vitamin A. In severe cases of vitamin A deficiency, there is extensive damage to the cornea as well, but the centre of vitamin A's action seems to be in the retina. (*See also* NIGHT BLINDNESS.)

Vitamin E

Other nutrients have been shown to aid vitamin A. Scientists working at the US government's National Institutes of Health laboratories demonstrated the close interaction of vitamin E with vitamin A in the retina (*Investigative Ophthalmology and Visual Science*, July 1979).

Tests with rats showed that vitamin E had an important effect on how much vitamin A was available for use in the eyes, but it was also shown to have a direct effect on the retina. Rats fed diets containing no vitamin E, but adequate vitamin A, devleoped significant retinal damage.

When the diets were deficient in vitamin A as well, the same damage occurred, plus an additional loss of light-sensitive rods and cones in the retina. 'Rods and cones were involved equally,' the scientists reported, 'and their pattern of loss was not like that found in vitamin A deficiency.' The lack of vitamin E seemed to compound the damage usually done by a lack of vitamin A.

A number of other studies have explored the effects of vitamin E, or the lack of it, on the health of the eye. W. Gerald Robison, Jr, chief of the experimental anatomy section, Laboratory of Vision Research of the National Eye Institute in the United States, has been examining the effects on animal retinas of diets deficient in vitamins E and A. Results? 'A highly E-deficient animal will go blind in time,' he said.

Although he cautions that his work so far has been with animals only, and that it's unlikely a human would develop vitamin E deficiencies as extreme as those he's produced in the lab, Dr Robison's studies have produced some intriguing clues into the nourishment of the eye.

The retina changes light (via chemistry) into electrical impulses, the language of the nervous system. The cells it's made of, Dr Robison explains, especially the light-sensitive or photo-receptor nerve cells – the things we 'see' with – contain large amounts of unsaturated fatty acids. Because these fatty acids are readily oxidized (broken down by oxygen, or 'rusted out'), 'we can suspect that the retina is quite susceptible to oxidation, unless it's protected by an anti-oxidant,' he says.

Because vitamin E is a potent anti-oxidant, or protective agent against organic 'rust', Dr Robinson decided to test the effect of a grossly E-deficient diet on the retinas of rats. He also tested the effects of diets that were deficient in *both* vitamin E and vitamin A.

After five months, he told us, a diet low in vitamin E but adequate in A 'produced a significant degeneration of photo-receptor cells, and an accumulation of aging pigments [highly oxidized, insoluble fatty acids] that was five times greater than normal.' Because the visual cells were damaged but not killed, he says, 'the damage *may* be reversible.' A diet deficient in *both* A and E, on the other hand, resulted in the permanent destruction of nearly *half* the visual cells in eight months. 'Vitamin A,' he concluded, 'appears to protect against this cell loss.'

In another study at Cornell University, dogs fed diets deficient only in vitamin E were also found to develop retinopathy, or damaged retinas. The damage first showed up on the retina after as little as three months. Next came night blindness and finally 'severe day visual impairment' (*American Journal of Veterinary Research*, January 1981).

Other nutrients

Zinc is also closely tied to vitamin A in maintaining good vision. One of the highest concentrations of zinc in the body occurs in the retina of the eye. Zinc is necessary to keep blood levels of vitamin A at the proper level and to mobilize it for use from its storage place in the liver. Animal studies conducted at Harvard University have shown that 'zinc deficiency can interfere with the metabolism of vitamin A, especially in the retina' (*Journal of Nutrition*).

Revealing studies of zinc and vision were carried out by scientists at the University of Maryland. The researchers treated six patients suffering from cirrhosis of the liver and night blindness, a common complication of that disease and, as we have seen, of vitamin A deficiency. One patient, given both vitamin A and zinc from the start of the study, regained normal night vision within a week. Three patients treated with zinc alone also returned to normal.

However, two patients fed vitamin A alone for a period of two weeks did not do as well. Although one improved, the other showed no response at all. Only when zinc was added to their treatment did their sight return to normal (*American Journal of Clinical Nutrition*).

Other nutrients are involved in good vision, in ways that have no apparent connection with the action of vitamin A on the retina. A study of some 900 schoolchildren in India revealed some interesting connections between the B vitamins and general good vision. The children were screened for signs of possible B vitamin deficiency and had their vision tested. One month later, the tests were repeated.

Of the 715 children with evidence of vitamin B complex deficiency, 126 (17 per cent) had altered acuity of vision, whereas of 247 children without signs of vitamin B complex deficiency, only 6 (2 per cent) had altered visual acuity. There was a significant association between different vitamin B complex deficiency signs on the one hand and visual defects on the other. [*British Journal of Nutrition*]

The clincher, however, came when the researchers tested the effects of B vitamin supplementation on the children's vision. When supplemented children were examined after one month, B vitamin intake was found to be closely associated with improvement in vision. 'While 56 of 70 supplemented children had shown improvement, only 4 of 26 of the unsupplemented children had improved.'

Thiamin (vitamin B₁) has been used in other studies to correct disorders of the optic nerve interfering with normal vision. Here the problem was not with the sensitive cells receiving the image but with the nerves that carry the image to the brain. Studies have shown that thiamin-deficient diets cause degeneration of the optic nerve in rats *(Medical Journal of Australia)*. In other research, two ophthalmologists examined people on special diets who did not seem to be getting enough thiamin. In all four cases, the patients suffered similar losses of vision near the centre of their visual field. And in all four cases, the problem was corrected when the patients were given thiamin supplements *(British Journal of Ophthalmology)*.

At John Hopkins Hospital in Baltimore, David L. Knox, associate professor of ophthalmology, has been exploring the effect of folic acid, vitamin B_{12} and other nutrients on an unusual eye problem called 'nutritional amblyopia'. Although his results are still unpublished, he says, 'I've been studying the possibility that folic acid or some other unknown vitamin from green and yellow vegetables may be essential to the maintenance of normal vision and optic-nerve function.' It is, he says, 'extremely important for people to eat enough green and yellow vegetables to maintain normal vision.'

MSG affects the eye

Some food additives, particularly monosodium glutamate (MSG), may have a less-than-wholesome effect on the eye according to John Olney, professor of psychiatry and neuropathology at Washington University in St Louis, Missouri. Glutamate is a naturally occurring substance that is harmless when it's part of a protein molecule. However, when it's added to commercial foods in large amounts (as a flavour enhancer), it may damage nerves in the retina and parts of the brain by 'exciting them to death'.

Although Dr Olney's animal studies have involved the ingestion of massive doses of MSG, well beyond the amounts the average adult would ingest, he said that 'I would definitely go out of my way to avoid feeding MSG to children.' While adults have well-developed barriers to the toxic effects of glutamate, he explained, a child's system is less fully developed and thus more vulnerable to visual and brain-cell damage.

Preventing cataracts with good nutrition

Riboflavin (vitamin B_2) has been linked to the prevention of cataracts, another of the many disorders that can rob us of our vision. Cataracts are a clouding of the lens that focuses the image on the back of the eye. Scientists have produced this clouding in several kinds of fish by feeding them diets lacking riboflavin. When researchers at the University of Alabama tested cataract patients for riboflavin deficiency, they found that 8 out of 22 were not getting enough riboflavin.

> Our data suggest that riboflavin deficiency may play a role in cataract development in man. Exploration of this possibility is particularly attractive because . . . the administration of riboflavin [is] easily accomplished and might lead to either the prevention or regression of cataract formation. [*Lancet*]

Vitamin C might also be involved in preventing cataracts. Scientists at the University of Maryland have found that vitamin C protects the lens against chemicals normally produced by the action of light. That finding was particularly interesting, given the high concentration of vitamin C naturally found in the lens of the eye and in the fluid directly in front of it, between the lens and the cornea. In fact, the concentration of vitamin C in that fluid, called the aqueous humour, is among the highest of any of the various fluids in the body.

'These findings,' the University of Maryland scientists said, 'further emphasize the concept of the importance of essential nutrients in prevention of certain forms of cataracts' (*Proceedings of the National Academy of Sciences, USA*, July 1979).

A special form of cataracts triggered by high levels of sugar in the body can occur in diabetics, and, again, essential nutrients are important in preventing their formation. The bioflavonoids, a class of nutrients that complement the action of vitamin C, have been shown to inhibit the action of the enzyme that may set off the formation of diabetic cataracts.

The importance of lighting

To do their best, older eyes need proper nutrition, exercise, rest and, above all, sufficient and proper lighting. Strangely, many people who are conscientious about the first three factors ignore the last. They fail to realize that older eyes need more and better light.

We can't always control the amount and quality of light in our environment, but even when we can, we often don't do as well as we might. A study at London's St Bartholomew's Hospital measured the visual acuity of 56 older Britons (average age 76) in their homes and in a controlled clinical setting. They concluded that 'general levels of lighting are often so poor in the homes of elderly people that the number of people functioning as 'blind' is twice what it need be.' *Just turning up the wattage of existing lighting, they discovered, improved vision in 82 per cent of the subjects* (*Lancet,* 24 March 1979).

Commenting on these and other experiments, ophthalmologist M.J. Gilkes criticizes health-care workers for assuming that people who complain of vision problems automatically need stronger glasses: 'The only reasonable initial response to the cry "I can't see" is "Are you sure you have got an adequate light?"' (*British Medical Journal,* 23 June 1979). Clearly the answer to that question is often 'no'.

Although vision loss is a lifelong process, it manifests itself most noticeably in middle age. Numerous clinical studies have detailed the plight of the ageing eye. Dr Philip C. Hughes, a lighting expert, and Dr Robert M. Neer of Harvard Medical School have summarized the research for an issue of the journal *Human Factors*. They paint a gloomy picture: as the eye ages, the lens becomes clouded and less pliable, and the pupil decreases in size. Less light reaches the retina, and near-focusing ability declines.

The loss of near-focusing ability, called *presbyopia* (i.e. long-sightedness), is easily corrected by prescription lenses, but the reduction of light entering the eye is another story entirely. Drs Hughes and Neer cite research that pegs the reduction of light reaching the retina at 50 per cent by age 50 and 66 per cent by age 60. In some people, the opacity or cloudiness of the lens drastically reduces the light usable for vision. We say they have 'cataracts', and eventually they must have the lens removed. For most people, though, the gradual darkening of the lens and decrease in pupil size simply mean that they don't see as well, and there is no treatment for that. As if that weren't enough, the older eye also reacts much more slowly to changes in light levels and – again due to the growing cloudiness of the lens – tends to scatter some of the light that does enter the eye.

The remedy is more and better light. Dr Gilkes explained:

> Added illumination on the object being looked at increases the amount of light available to, as it were, push its way past any impediments in the visual media such as early cataract . . . or even to give added stimulation to an aging retina. . . . The vast majority of older people who experience any kind of visual difficulty . . . should use some form of lighting system that delivers an adequate amount of light, that does not shine into their eyes and that can be deployed at a satisfactorily close range.

Older, less efficient eyes, then, need more and better light to function. But they seldom get it.

> The problem is that visual deterioration is so gradual that a person does not always realize that his eyes have changed, and we tend to take light for granted because it's all around us all the time. We humans feel we can adapt to anything in time, and it's true: we can adapt. But the error with respect to eyesight is that we adapt but our sensitivity and production are not the same.

So we squint, or wrinkle our brows, or push our faces into the book we're reading, or pretend we've lost interest in the task we're attempting. We glumly accept a dimmer view of the world than we need to, without thinking about what we can do to improve our eyesight. Our eyes will serve us better if we give them the light they need.

Office workers need high-quality light

Much of the research in this area has concentrated on the workplace rather than the home and is particularly relevant to millions of office workers aged 45 and above. These administrative, clerical and sales workers are doubly at risk: their eyesight is deteriorating, and they are required to concentrate on detailed visual tasks in artificially lighted environments. For them, proper illumination is of the utmost concern.

Several studies have shown that middle-aged workers need more light than their younger co-workers. And the contrast between their immediate work site and the background must be high. An Ohio State University study found that 30- to 40-year-olds need 17 per cent more contrast to see an object as clearly as 20- to 30-year-olds, and that those in the 60 to 70 age bracket need $2^1/_2$ times as much contrast to see as well as the younger group (*Journal of the Illuminating Engineering Society*).

The quality of available light is just as important as the quantity, according to Dr Hughes. High-quality light, he says, must be sufficient to illuminate the area or task in question and should not emanate from the 'offending glare zone', which is 'that area in the ceiling where a light source will produce "veiling reflections."'

'If a light is directly above and in front of an office worker, for example, it will hit the work surface and bounce right up into his or her eyes,' Dr Hughes explains. 'It produces a haze or veil of glare over the work.'

Since older workers are particularly vulnerable to glare, veiling reflections cause them more problems. Fatigue and low productivity can result, even though the worker may not be consciously aware of the glare.

Windows can cause direct glare or play havoc with an older person's ability to adapt to varying light levels. An expanse of glass invites a desk-bound worker to gaze at the out-of-doors, Dr Hughes explains, but

> if the ratio of brightness between the window and the desk or work area is too high, the light causes their pupils to constrict. Then, when they look back down, there's less light and their eyes dilate.

This back-and-forth adaptation, particularly for older persons, whose eyes are slower to react, can cause fatigue. And modern offices make liberal use of glass. 'I've been in offices where people face glass windows all day,' he says. 'The brightness can be overwhelming, or at the very least, highly fatiguing, particularly over an eight-hour day.'

Dr Hughes recommends a simple test to determine if a light source is in the 'offending zone'. Place a mirror on the table or desk at which you work. If you can see a light source in that mirror when you are seated normally, the light source is in the offending zone. To avoid glare and veiling reflection, move the work surface.

Lighting in the home

What about lighting in your own home? 'It's often quite difficult to evaluate the home environment,' Dr Hughes continues. 'One thing to look for are bright areas which cause you to blink, squint or turn away. That probably means there's a bright window or a surface that's too highly reflective. Also, most glare in the home comes from a light bulb that's not properly shaded.'

A classic and dangerous example of harmful high-contrast transition is a dark stairwell at the end of a well-lighted hall found in many homes. Overhead fixtures in the offending glare zone can make kitchens particularly bad.

'I would say, though, that there is usually *not enough* light in the home,' Dr Hughes hastens to add. 'One way to correct that is to paint walls in lighter shades to reflect more light.'

Another aspect of lighting quality is spectral power distribution, which is fancy talk for the nature of the light itself. Sunlight contains the full spectrum of light from infrared to ultraviolet, in a definite ratio. Most artificial light is different and hence produces a different effect in our eyes. Cool white fluorescent light, which is high in yellow-green light, tends to wash out colours and reduce perceived visual clarity. The new full-spectrum fluorescents nearly duplicate sunlight and render colours faithfully.

Understanding and accepting the fact that your eyes may change with age can be painful, but you can apply that understanding to making the most of what you have got. Begin by taking a closer look at your home. Do you have enough light, and is it placed effectively?

Dr Gilkes cites the 'inverse square law' of illumination, which states that the amount of light falling on a surface varies both with the power of the light source and the distance the light must travel. In other words, moving a 25-watt bulb from eight feet away to four feet is the equivalent of replacing it with a 100-watt light bulb. 'Whenever inadequate or deficient lighting is suspected of forming part of an individual incapacity,' he wrote, 'the simple measure of bringing the light nearer . . . will in many cases produce an increase in vision totally out of proportion to the simplicity of the solution.' So if you have trouble reading, move the light closer. And keep it behind and to the left of you, to avoid veiling reflections.

Don't think that you can't afford good light. A typical household fixture fitted with a 100-watt bulb costs only a tiny amount more to operate for an entire year than the same fixture with a 60-watt bulb. Save energy when you can, but don't shortchange your eyes. Light placement is crucial, so beware of poorly placed fixtures. Is there a dangerously dark spot at the top of your stairs?

Take a look at your windows, too. Do they cause you to squint or turn your head? Perhaps you need new curtains or shades. Are the appliances and working surfaces in your kitchen blinding you with reflected light? Maybe you should change the light source or reduce the reflectivity of the surfaces.

Remember that your eyes run on light, just as your car runs on petrol. If you're having any problems seeing, see to your environment as well as your eyes. For more information, see entries on specific eye ailments.

• INDEX

in colic, 139
of cortisone, 327, 400
of decongestants, 137
depression in, 158-9
    from birth control pills, 152
of digoxin, 609-10, 613
of diuretics, 590, 640
healing problems in, 327, 400
heavy menstrual bleeding in, 504-5
in hyperactivity, 405, 412
in hypertension, 381
infertility in, 450
kidney disorders in, 470
liver disease in, 480
memory problems in, 496
nutritional deficiencies in, 639-40
of paracetamol, 470, 480
in pregnancy, 590, 593-4
senility in, 609-11, 613
sexual functioning in, 441
of sleeping pills, 457
tardive dyskinesia in, 645-7
tics and tremors in, 653-4
vaginal infections in, 673-4
vitamin C blocking, 647
vitamin E blocking, 480, 647
Dumping syndrome, 179
Duodenum, ulcers of, 665-9
Dust, household, and asthma, 57
Dyes in food. *See* Additives in food
Dyskinesia, tardive, 645-7
Dyslexia, 406, 407
Dysplasia, of uterine cervix, 123, 130-1, 209
Dysuria, 670

E
Ear problems
    dizziness in, 184
    hearing impairment in, 149-52. *See also*
        Hearing problems
    noise-induced, 149-51, 655
        prevention of, 150
    tinnitus in, 654-6
    wax accumulation in, 152
Eclampsia of pregnancy, 588, 590
Eczema, housewives', 166-7
Elderflower lotion, for heat rash, 343
Emotional problems, 212-56
    in alcoholism, 25-6
    in bedwetting, 85
    in depression, 152-66. *See also* Depression
    in family relationships, 244-56
    in food allergy, 35-7
    irritable bowel syndrome in, 465-8
    itching in, 467, 468
    malabsorption in, 492-3
    in menopause, 499, 500
    in overweight, 530-2
    in phobias, 579-84
    in schizophrenia, 603-8. *See also* Schizophrenia
    in stammering, 625-6
Emphysema, 256-8, 483
Empty-nest stage in families, 254-6
Endorphins, 165
    in pain relief, 559, 560, 561, 562, 563, 564
    as therapy in schizophrenia, 607
Enuresis, 85
Epilepsy, 258-63
Etretinate, for psoriasis, 601
Eucalyptus, in nasal congestion, 200

Exercise-induced problems
    asthma, 57, 59
    back pain, 65, 74
    fever, 273
    of foot, 288-90
    infertility, 453
Exercise programmes
    in ageing, 18-23
    in arthritis, 55, 515
    in asthma, 59-60
    in atherosclerosis prevention, 352
    in back problems. *See* Back problems, exercise
        therapy for
    in bone disease, 91-2, 98
    in constipation prevention, 140
    in cystic fibrosis, 148
    in depression, 160-1, 163, 164
    in diabetes, 177-8
    in emphysema, 257
    in fatigue, chronic, 270
    in fatty liver, 479
    in foot problems, 288, 289, 290
    in gallstone prevention, 293
    in headaches, 316-7
    in heart disease, 46-7, 365-70,
        risks of, 369-70
    in hypertension, 393
    in insomnia, 463-4
    in lymphostasis prevention, 489
    in malabsorption 493
    in menstrual problems, 506
    in muscle problems, 514, 515-18
    in neck problems, 517, 520, 525
    in pregnancy, 596-98
        for breech position, 585
    in schizophrenia, 607
    in stress relief, 628-9
    in tinnitus, 656
    in varicose vein prevention, 679, 680
    in weight problems, 538-9, 548-52
Eyes, 680-6. *See also* Vision problems

F
Facial expression, in non-verbal communication, 216
Facial muscles, in tardive dyskinesia, 645-7
Families, 244-56. *See also* Marital relationships
    communication in, 245
        non-verbal, 216
    importance of touching in, 227-9
Fasting, for weight loss, 553
Fat
    applications of, in athlete's foot, 62
    blood levels of, and tinnitus, 655-6
    dietary
        and acne, 6-7, 8
        and arthritis, 52-3
        and blood pressure, 389-90
        and breast problems, 100
        calcium affecting absorption of, 359-61
        and cancer risk, 103-5
        in cystic fibrosis, 147-8
        in diabetes, 172-3
        and dizziness, 185
        in epilepsy therapy, 260-1
        food sources of, invisible, 331-2
        in gallstones, 291
        and hearing impairment, 151-2
        and heart disease, 331-2, 335
        and multiple sclerosis, 511-3
        and prostate disorders, 103-5, 598-9
        saturated and polyunsaturated, 331-2
        and stroke, 635-7

and body odours, 89
in breast discomfort, 101
in cancer prevention, 123
and carpal tunnel syndrome, 129
in depression, 154, 155
in diabetes, 175-6
in epilepsy, 259
in fatigue, 264-5
in food addiction, 36
in healing process, 400-1
in heart disease prevention, 358-9
in homocystinuria, 509
in hospitalized patients, 397, 400-1
in hyperactivity, 410
and immune response, 433
in infertility, 452-3
in kidney stone prevention, 472, 474
in menstrual problems, 452, 502
in oedema, 528-9
in oral contraceptive use, 208, 591
and platelet aggregation, 358-9
in pregnancy, 176, 591-2
and infant dependency on, 592
in schizophrenia, 605
in senility, 612
in tardive dyskinesia prevention, 647
in tics and tremors, 653
in violent behaviour, 146
Pyrogens, endogenous, in fever, 271-3
Pyroluria, in schizophrenia, 605

R
Radiation exposure, for X-ray analysis. *See*
X-ray analysis
Radiation therapy, in cancer, 112-3
Rash
in heat, 372-3
nappy, 201
in shingles, 614
Raspberry leaf lotion, for heat rash, 373
Raynaud's disease and phenomenon, 275, 602
Rectal cancer, prevention of
vitamin C in, 116
vitamin E in, 119
Red blood cells
in ageing, 13, 15-16
in cystic fibrosis, 148
in sickle-cell anaemia, 617
vitamin E affecting, 15-16, 147-8
Reflux, gastro-oesophageal, 378, 379
Relaxation techniques, 630
in angina pectoris, 48
in arthritis, 56-7
in asthma, 58-9
in back problems, 67
groaning therapy in, 218-20
in hypertension, 393
in insomnia, 458
in irritable bowel syndrome, 467
massage in, 230
in pain, 560, 561
in phobias, 580
in tension headaches, 311-5
in workaholism, 241
Restless legs syndrome, 602-3
Retardation, mental, 506-9
Retinoic (vitamin A) acid therapy
in acne, 5, 7
in skin cancer, 113
Reye's syndrome, 603
Rheumatoid arthritis, 50
conventional therapies for, 54

diet in, 52-3
juvenile, 51, 56
sleeping bag treatment for, 51
stress affecting, 56
vitamin C deficiency in, 55
zinc therapy in, 53-4
Rhinitis, allergic, 309
Riboflavin (vitamin B₂)
in ageing, 8, 10
in blood formation, 44
and cataracts, 684
deficiency of
subclinical, 640
food sources of, 44
in healing process, 400
in pregnancy, 592
Rickets, 97
adult, 95
Ringworm, and athlete's foot, 61-2

S
Sage, for indigestion, 444
Salicylates. *See also* Aspirin
foods containing, and hyperactivity, 403-4
Saliva, in healing process, 330
Salt
and acne, 6, 8
alternative seasonings to, 384-5
and breast problems, 101
dangers of, in dehydration from diarrhoea, 178
for gum disease, application of, 300
headaches from, 322
in hot weather, 374
in hypertension, 382-5
in pregnancy, 589-90
in sitz bath, 675
Schizophrenia, 603-8
drug therapy for, tardive dyskinesia from, 646
Sclerosis, multiple, 510-14
Scurvy
arterial disorders in, 350
healing problems in, 326, 401
Seborrhoea, 608
Sebum, in acne, 4
Sedatives, senility from, 610
Seizures
in epilepsy, 258-63
in pregnancy, 588
Selenium
in cancer prevention, 119-21
deficiency of, 355-8
in epilepsy prevention, post-traumatic, 260
and immune response, 430-1
reducing toxic effects of paracetamol, 480
Self-communication techniques, 240
Self-hypnosis
in chronic pain, 561
in insomnia, 460
Senility,
in Alzheimer's disease, 37-9
drug-induced, 202-3
in vitamin deficiencies, 11-3
Serotonin
in depression, 226
in hyperactivity, 410
and sleeping patterns, 462
Sexual functioning, 434-42
in arthritis, 55-6
and cystitis, 87
drugs affecting, 207-8
in heart disease, 367
and infertility, 448-453

Sexually transmitted diseases, 672
Shiatsu. *See* Acupressure
Shingles, 613-7
Shock, post-operative, 399
Shoes, 287-90
Short-sightedness, 681
Shoulder
  frozen, 69
  pain in, 68-71
Sickle-cell anaemia, 617-9
SIDS (sudden infant death syndrome), 643-5
Sinusitis, 619-22
Sitz baths, for vaginal infections, 675
Skin
  acne of, 4-8
  in ageing, 17, 96
  of breast, stretch marks in, 99
  cancer of
    and sunlight exposure, 126-7
    vegetables in prevention of, 109
    vitamin A acid therapy in, 113-4
  in cortisone therapy, 194-6
  dermatitis of, 166-8
  of foot, fungal infections of, 61-2
  in heat rash, 372-3
  itching of, 467-8. *See also* Itching
  medications for, side-effects of, 201
  in nappy rash, 201
  psoriasis of, 55, 600-1
  in shingles, 613-7
  vitamin D synthesis in, 95-6
Sleep
  back problems from habits in, 65, 74-6
  bedwetting in, 85
  bruxism in, 102, 323
  deprivation of, as therapy in depression, 162
  hours for, 269
  and insomnia, 457-65
    from sleeping pills, 204
  under covers, headaches from, 323-4
Sleeping pills, side-effects of, 203-5
Smoking
  addiction to, 34
  in alcoholism, 26
  and arthritis, 51
  benefits of quitting, 125-6
  and bone disease, 98
  and bronchitis, 102
  and cancer, 125-6
  carbon monoxide effects in, 364-5
  and emphysema, 256-7
  in hay fever, 309
  and headaches, 316, 317
  and heart disease, 48, 364-5
  and hypertension, 392-3
  and infertility, 450
  and insomnia, 464
  and malnutrition, subclinical, 640-1
  and memory, 498-9
  in pregnancy, 594-5
  and sexual dysfunction, 436-7
  and ulcers, 666
  vitamin C deficiency in, 126, 640
Sodium, 382-5. *See also* Salt
Soft drinks
  and bloody urine, 305, 671
  caffeine content of, 158-9
  and hyperactivity, 411
Sore throat, 622-3
  herbal remedies for, 140-1
Soyabeans
  in cancer prevention, 108
  in gallstones, 291-3
Spastics. *See* Cerebral palsy
Spearmint, for indigestion, 443
Speech. *See also* Communication
  stammering in, 623-7
Spina bifida, 591
Stammering, 623-7
Steroid therapy, side-effects of, 194-6, 210
Stomach, 442-4
  aspirin affecting, 186-7
  cancer of
    in iron deficiency, 124
    in magnesium deficiency, 124
    and vitamin C, 115-6
  in hiatus hernia, 378-80
  pains in, in infants, 139
  ulcers of, 665-9
Stress and anxiety, 627-30
  accident-proneness in, 1-2, 3-4
  acne in, 7
  and arthritis, 56
  back problems in, 64, 66
  bruxism in, 323
  cold sores in, 131
  in family money worries, 251-4
  groaning therapy in, 218-20
  hair problems in, 300, 303
  headaches in, 310-15
  in hypoglycaemia, 422-6
  insomnia in, 458-9
  irritable bowel syndrome in, 466-7
  in loneliness, 236-7
  malabsorption in, 490
  mouth ulcers in, 133
  phobias in, 582
  senility from, 611
  sexual functioning in, 435, 436, 441-2
  tranquillizers for, side-effects of, 205
  and ulcers, 665-6
  vitamin B complex in, 303
Stroke, 631-7
  prevention of
    vitamin E in, 353
Stuttering. *See* Stammering
Sudden infant death syndrome, 643-5
Sugar
  addiction to, 27-9, 535-40
  and alcoholism, 26, 27-9
  in cough medicines, 198
  and criminal behaviour, 145
  and Crohn's disease, 454
  and diabetes, 171-4
  diarrhoea from, 178
  and heart disease, 334-5
  and hyperactivity, 408-9, 414
  and hypertension, 391-2
  and hypoglycaemia, 423-5. *See also* Hypoglycaemia
  and tooth problems, 656, 662-3
  and vaginal infections, 676
Suicidal behaviour
  barbiturates used in, 205
  in hypoglycaemia, 423
  warning signs of, 213-4
Sunlight exposure
  headaches from, 324
  recommended amount of, 97
  and skin cancer, 126-7
  and vitamin D synthesis
    seasonal variations in, 94-6
Sunstroke, 324
Sweat, odour of, 89
Sweeteners, artificial, 539-40